Computer Science
and
Artificial Intelligence

Proceedings of the International Conference on
Computer Science and Artificial Intelligence (CSAI2016)

Computer Science
and
Artificial Intelligence

Proceedings of the International Conference on
Computer Science and Artificial Intelligence (CSAI2016)

Guilin, China, 13 – 14 August 2016

Editor

Wen-Jer Chang

National Taiwan Ocean University, Taiwan

World Scientific

NEW JERSEY • LONDON • SINGAPORE • BEIJING • SHANGHAI • HONG KONG • TAIPEI • CHENNAI • TOKYO

Published by

World Scientific Publishing Co. Pte. Ltd.
5 Toh Tuck Link, Singapore 596224
USA office: 27 Warren Street, Suite 401-402, Hackensack, NJ 07601
UK office: 57 Shelton Street, Covent Garden, London WC2H 9HE

British Library Cataloguing-in-Publication Data
A catalogue record for this book is available from the British Library.

COMPUTER SCIENCE AND ARTIFICIAL INTELLIGENCE
Proceedings of the International Conference on Computer Science and Artificial Intelligence (CSAI2016)

ISBN 978-981-3220-28-7

Printed in Singapore

Preface

Held in Guilin, Guangxi, China from August 13-14, 2016, CSAI2016 [The 2016 International Conference on Computer Science and Artificial Intelligence] hopes to provide an excellent international platform for all the invited speakers, authors, and participants. The conference enjoys a wide spread participation, and we sincerely wish that it would not only serve as an academic forum, but also a good opportunity to establish business cooperation. Any paper and topic around computer science and artificial intelligence would be warmly welcomed.

CSAI2016 proceeding tends to collect the most up-to-date, comprehensive, and worldwide state-of-art knowledge on computer science and artificial intelligence. All the accepted papers have been submitted to strict peer-review by 2-4 expert referees, and selected based on originality, significance and clarity for the purpose of the conference. The conference program is extremely rich, profound and featuring high-impact presentations of selected papers and additional late-breaking contributions. We sincerely hope that the conference would not only show the participants a broad overview of the latest research results on related fields, but also provide them with a significant platform for academic connection and exchange.

The Technical Program Committee members have been working very hard to meet the deadline of review. The final conference program consists of 116 papers divided into 3 sessions. The proceedings would be published in a volume by World Scientific Publishing Company.

We would like to express our sincere gratitude to all the TPC members and organizers for their hard work, precious time and endeavor preparing for the conference. Our deepest thanks also go to the volunteers and staffs for their long-hours work and generosity they've given to the conference. The last but not least, we would like to thank each and every of the authors, speakers and participants for their great contributions to the success of CSAI2016.

CSAI2016 Organizing Committee

Editor I

Prof. Wen-Jer Chang

Department of Marine Engineering

National Taiwan Ocean University

Biography

Wen-Jer Chang received the B.S. degree from National Taiwan Ocean University, Taiwan, R.O.C., in 1986. The Marine Engineering is his major course and the Electronic Engineering is his minor one. He received the M.S. degree in the Institute of Computer Science and Electronic Engineering from the National Central University in 1990, and the Ph. D. degree from the Institute of Electrical Engineering of the National Central University in 1995. Since 1995, he has been with National Taiwan Ocean University, Keelung, Taiwan, R.O.C. He is currently the Vice Dean of Academic Affairs, Director of General Education Center, Director of Center for Teaching and Learning and a full Professor of the Department of Marine Engineering of National Taiwan Ocean University. He is now a life member of the IEEE, CIEE, CACS, CSFAT and SNAME. Since 2003, Dr. Chang was listed in the Marquis Who's Who in Science and Engineering. In 2003, he also won the outstanding young control engineers award granted by the Chinese Automation Control Society (CACS). In 2004, he won the universal award of accomplishment granted by ABI of USA. In 2005 and 2013, he was selected as an excellent teacher of the National Taiwan Ocean University. Dr. Chang has authored more than 110 published journal papers and 100 refereed conference papers. His recent research interests are fuzzy control, robust control, performance constrained control.

Education

Ph.D.: Electrical Engineering, National Central University, 1995.

M.A.: Computer Science and Electronic Engineering, National Central University, 1990.

B.A.: Marine Engineering (major course) and Electronic Engineering (minor one), National Taiwan Ocean University, 1986.

Experience

Associate Professor Department of Marine Engineering, National Taiwan Ocean University, 1995.8 - 2001.7
Head Teaching Support Section of Computer Center, National Taiwan Ocean University, 2000.8 - 2002.7
Chairman Department of Marine Engineering, National Taiwan Ocean University, 2002.8 - 2004.7
Professor Department of Marine Engineering, National Taiwan Ocean University, 2001.8 - present
Director Center for Teaching and Learning, National Taiwan Ocean University, 2005.8 - present
Vice Dean Academic Affairs, National Taiwan Ocean University, 2008.8 - present
Director General General Education Center, National Taiwan Ocean University, 2014.8 – present

Professional honors and awards

1. 1997, 1998, 1999, 2001 Grade "A" Research Awards, National Science Council, Taiwan, R.O.C.
2. 2003-present Listed in *Marquis Who's Who in Science and Engineering*
3. 2003 Outstanding Young Control Engineers Award, Chinese Automatic Control Society, Taiwan, R.O.C.
4. 2003 Outstanding Paper Award, Taiwan Society of Naval Architects and Marine Engineers, Taiwan, R.O.C.
5. 2003 Outstanding Student Paper Award, CACS Automatic Control Conference (Adviser), Taiwan, R.O.C.
6. 2003 Best Thesis Award for Outstanding M.S. Thesis Supervision, Chinese Fuzzy Systems Association (Adviser), Taiwan, R.O.C.
7. 2004 Winner of International Scientist of the Year 2004, International Biographical Centre.
8. 2004 Winner of 2004 Universal Award of Accomplishment, American Biographical Institute.
9. 2005 Outstanding Teaching Award, National Taiwan Ocean University, Taiwan, R.O.C.

Editor II

Prof. João Manuel Ribeiro da Silva Tavares

Departamento de Engenharia Mecânica
Faculdade de Engenharia da Universidade do Porto

Education

Habilitation: Mechanical Engineering, University of Porto – Portugal, 2015.
PhD: Electrical and Computer Engineering, University of Porto – Portugal, 2001 (Computational Vision).
MSc: Electrical and Computer Engineering, University of Porto – Portugal, 1995 (Industrial informatics).
BSc (5 years): Mechanical Engineering, University of Porto – Portugal, 1993.

Actual position

Associate Professor (with Habilitation) at the Faculty of Engineering of the University of Porto, Department of Mechanical Engineering, since December 2011. (www.fe.up.pt).

Areas of Research:

- Computational Vision, Image processing and analysis, Medical imaging;
- Computer Graphics, Scientific Visualization;
- Biomedical Engineering;
- Modelling and Simulation;
- Product development.

Awards

1. Paper more downloaded in 2014 of the journal Computer Methods in Biomechanics and Biomedical Engineering: Medical image registration: a review, Francisco P.M. Oliveira, João Manuel R.S. Tavares.

2. Award of Scientific Excellence Award 2015 from the Faculdade de Engenharia da Universidade do Porto, Portugal, in January 2015.
3. Award of Incentive to Research - Publications from the Faculty of Engineering of University of Porto, Portugal, in January 2015.
4. Award of Incentive to Research - Publications from the Faculty of Engineering of University of Porto, Portugal, in January 2014.
5. Best paper published in 2012 in the journal Pattern Recognition award: Efficient Supervised Optimum-Path Forest Classification for Large Datasets, João P. Papa, Alexandre X. Falcão, Victor Hugo C. de Albuquerque, João Manuel R. S. Tavares, Pattern Recognition, Elsevier, ISSN: 0031-3203, DOI: 10.1016/j.patcog.2011.07.013, Volume 45, Issue 1, pp. 512-520, January 2012.
6. Award of Incentive to Research - Publications from the Faculty of Engineering of University of Porto, Portugal, in January 2013.
7. Award of Incentive to Research - Publications from the Faculty of Engineering of University of Porto, Portugal, in January 2012.
8. Award of Incentive to Research - Publications from the Faculty of Engineering of University of Porto, Portugal, in November 2010.
9. Award of Incentive to Research - Patents from the Faculty of Engineering of University of Porto, Portugal, in November 2009.
10. Award of Incentive to Research - Publications from the Faculty of Engineering of University of Porto, Portugal, in November 2009.
11. Best paper award: Magnetic resonance imaging of the vocal tract: techniques and applications, Sandra M. Rua Ventura, Diamantino Rui S. Freitas, João Manuel R. S. Tavares, 1st International Conference on Imaging Theory and Applications (IMAGAPP), ISBN: 978-989-8111-68-5, INSTICC Press, pp. 105-110, 5-8 February 2009, Lisboa, Portugal.
12. Award of Incentive to Research – Patents from Faculty of Engineering of University of Porto, Portugal, November 2008. João Manuel R. S. Tavares Curriculum Vitae 151.
13. Project awarded for 2003/2004 of the Scientific Research in Pre-Graduation Program in the field of Engineering, Title: "ANDAR – System of Acquisition for Analysis of Data of the Gait of People with Prosthesis Devices in the Inferior Limbs", participant Institutions: FEUP – Faculty of Engineering of University of Porto, INEB – Institute of Biomedical Engineering, Responsible Research: Miguel V. Correia from the Department of Electrical and Computer Engineering of FEUP, 2004/2005.

Keynote I

How to deal with high complexity?

Prof. Bernd Steinbach

Department of Computer Science,
Freiberg University of Mining and Technology

Abstract

Many problems of the real life can be modeled as Boolean problem and belong to the most complex class defined by the complexity theory. The combinational explosion limits their solution. We explore convenient models and tools for their solution, and identify limits in time and space. As general method to break these limits we found the combination of a deep analysis of hidden properties of the problem to be solved by human beings with the utilization of optimized algorithms and powerful computers.

Speaker's Bio

Bernd Steinbach studied Information Technology at the University of Technology in Chemnitz (Germany) and graduated with an M.Sc. in 1973. He graduated with a Ph.D. and with a Dr. sc. techn. (Doctor scientiae technicarum) for his second doctoral thesis from the Faculty of Electrical Engineering of the Chemnitz University of Technology in 1981 and 1984, respectively. In 1991 he obtained the Habilitation (Dr.-Ing. habil.) from the same Faculty. He was working in industry as an Electrician, there he had tested professional controlling systems at the Niles Company. After his studies he taught as Assistant Lecturer at the Department of Information Technology of the Chemnitz University of Technology. In a following period of industrial occupation as a research engineer he developed programs for test pattern generation for computer circuits at the company Robotron. He returned to the Department of Information Technology of the Chemnitz University of Technology as Associate Professor for design automation in logic design. Since

1992 he is a Full Professor of Computer Science/Software Engineering and Programming at the Freiberg University of Mining and Technology, Department of Computer Science. He has served as Head of the Department of Computer Science and Vice-Dean of the Faculty of Mathematics and Computer Science. He published more than 240 chapters in books, complete issues of journals, and papers in journals and proceedings.

Committees

Editor

Wen-Jer Chang, Professor, National Taiwan Ocean University, Taiwan, China
João Manuel R.S. Tavares, Associate Professor, Universidade do Porto, Portugal

Technical Program Committee

Mario Pavone, Assistant Professor, University of Catania, Italy
T.Madhu Principal, Swarnandhra Institute of Engineering & Technology, Seetharampuram, Jawahar lal Nehru Technological University, India
Francesco Masulli, Associate Professor, Univ. Genoa, Italy
Janusz Kacprzyk Academician, Professor, Systems Reserach Institute, Polish Academy of Sciences, Poland
Zeshui Xu, Professor, Sichuan University, China
Dudek-Dyduch Ewa, full professor, AGH - University of Science and Technology, Poland
Vicki H Allan, Associate Professor, Utah State University, USA
Hanmin Jung, Chief Researcher, Korea Institute of Science and Technology Information, Korea
Tae Yoon Kim, Professor, Keimyung University, Korea
Bonifacio Llamazares, Associate Professor, University of Valladolid, Spain
Iveta Zolotová, Professor, Technical University in Košice, Slovakia
Bernard De Baets, Full Professor, Ghent University, Belgium
Fusaomi Nagata, Professor, Tokyo University of Science, Japan
Cungen Cao, Professor, Institute of Computing Technology, Chinese Academy of Sciences, China
Emilio Jiménez, Professor, University of La Rioja, Spain
Jian Li, Professor, Guizhou university, China

Contents

Session I

Computer Science

A Multi-View System Appropriate for 3D Renewal

Jin-Yu Tang

Arts Department, Guangdong Vocational and Technical College
Foshan city of Guangdong province, 528041, China
E-mail: 342756567@qq.com

This paper realizes stereo matching of multiple views from arbitrary visual angles and gives a high-precision stereo matching algorithm under the premise that image correction is not made (the epipolar lines are not parallel), while a complete multi-view stereo matching algorithm from arbitrary visual angles is designed. Experiments have demonstrated that the algorithm in this paper has high precision and strong reflexivity, able to meet the smoothness constraint and obtain the overall optimal effect. The dense depth graph obtained by use of this algorithm can be used in three-dimensional model rebuilding.

Keywords: Multi-view; Matching System; 3D point; With Arbitrary Viewpoints; Corner Detector.

1. Introduction

This paper proposes a complete algorithm that illustrates in detail the whole process of calculating high-precision depth graphs based on multiple views from arbitrary angles. First, feature points are extracted from each view for feature point matching between the views, to calculate the fundamental matrix and the camera matrix of each view [1]. Second, an expansible main framework is built. The camera matrixes of all views are built in the same projection space and use the same coordinate system. Finally, the overall optimal depth graph is obtained by converting the stereo matching problem into the network maximum flow and minimum cut problem that distributes the weight of each side in the network appropriately.

The stereo matching algorithm should meet several constraints as follows: ① For the epipolar line constraint: the matching points must be located on the corresponding epipolar lines in two graphs. In favor of expansion and precision increases, image correction is not made herewith, while such constraint should be converted into the scan line constraint; ② The uniqueness restraint: the matching points in two images should be unique; ③ The smoothness constraint: a depth graph should be subject to certain smoothness, controlled herein by value of the smooth side; ④ The ordering constraint: on the corresponding epipolar lines in two images (which are scan lines in this paper).

2. Related Studies

The earliest feature point extraction and matching algorithm can be traced back to 1981, when Moravec proposed the corner detector. In 1999, Lowe proposed the SIFT [2] algorithm. It conducts calculation on the spatial domain and the scale region, which feature point extraction and matching algorithm is more suitable for large visual angle conversion and large base line matching, and can outstandingly complete feature point matching and object identification even under the situation that huge distortion, rotation and translation exist in images. This paper uses the latter method for feature point extraction and matching.

3. Calculation of the Camera Matrix of the Projection Space

A certain number of matched points should be inferred first to determine the geometrical relations between the views. The traditional least square method will be out of function. Therefore, this paper provides a more powerful and more precise algorithm. Once the multi-view relation is established, it can be used to look for more matches and these matches can further be used to refine the relation between multiple views [3]. First, we select two images to initialize the entire structure. Then the camera parameters of other images can all be determined. Each time an image is added in, the entire structure will be refined and expanded. Once all images are added in, we will use the bundle adjustment to refine the overall 3D structure and the camera matrixes [4].

3.1. *Building relations between images*

3.1.1. *Extraction and matching of feature points*

This paper uses Lowe's SIFT [5] algorithm that computes on the spatial domain and the scale region concurrently. Firstly, apply several continuous Gaussian filters on images to form the first scale group, and then reduce the images to half of the original and apply continuous Gaussian filters to form the second scale group, with the remaining treated alike, until the images are smaller than some given threshold. Later, within each group, take differential treatment on various

Gaussian images to form the Gaussian differential scale group, i.e., the DoG images. Take the partial maximum values of the central points in these DoG images to extract feature points from various scale domains. Further, each point should be matched with its descriptors for matching between two images. The descriptor of each feature point generally has a 128-dimensional length.

The SIFT matching algorithm computes the Euclidean distance between two descriptors, which ratio is calculated by finding two neighboring feature points as the closest and second closest Euclidean distances. If it is smaller than the threshold, it is regarded as a successful match, otherwise matching is failed.

3.1.2. *Calculation of double-view fundamental matrixes*

The fundamental matrix is the basis for follow-up work, which precision will largely affect the camera matrix P. This algorithm uses the RANSAC engine [1] to get the initial fundamental matrix F, and uses nonlinear iteration and guide complementary matching to refine F. It only increases the precision of F, but also uses the inferred F to compute many additional matched points, as indicated in Fig. 2. The algorithm flowchart of automatic calculation of a fundamental matrix is as follows:

(1) Compute the feature points in each image.

(2) Compute the matching between these feature points.

(3) RANSAC robust estimation: repeat sampling N times, and N hereof is determined by the adaptive algorithm.

(4) Nonlinear estimation: Re-estimate F from all matches that are classified into internal points by use of the gold standard algorithm [1].

(5) Guided complementary matching: Use the estimated F to define the searching scope near the epipolar line (the distance from the defined search scope in this paper to the epipolar is less than 1.5 pixels) in favor of further defining of matched feature points.

There are several points as follows needed for attention: ① Distance measurement: A current estimation should be made to F from the RANSAC sample, while using Distance d to measure the degree of closeness for a pair of matched points to meet the epipolar geometry. Regarding d, there are two obvious options: the reprojection errors, i.e., the Euclidean distance between a point and an epipolar line; or the Sampson approximation for the reprojection errors, where this paper chooses the Figure 1; ② Guided complementary matching: the current estimation of F defines the search scope around the epipolar line Fx of x in the Figure 2, able to search for the matching point of Point x within this scope. The realization method in this paper uses guided complementary matching, i.e., the ultimate result is (the result derived from guided matching between the Figure 2 and the Figure 1) ∩ (the result derived from guided matching between the Figure 2 and the Figure 1); ③ The realization details: in common situations, the parameters applied in this paper are as follows. The search window size is 100 pixels; the internal point threshold value is 1.5 pixels; the guided complementary matching searches within 1.5 pixels around the epipolar lines.

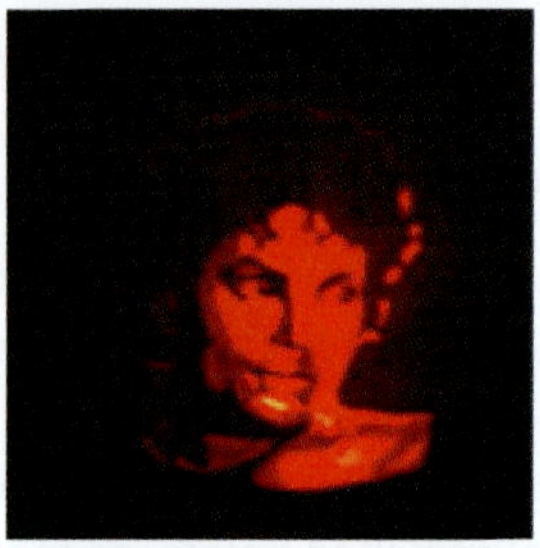

Fig. 1. The 1st example of computing fundamental matrixes

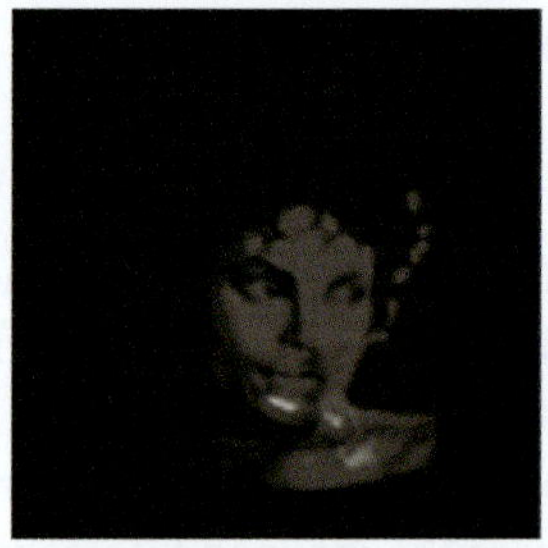

Fig. 2. The 2nd example of computing fundamental matrixes

3.2. *Building relations between images*

In the above content, the establishment of multi-view relations is realized. Such relations will be used to restore the scenic structures and camera parameters. First, we choose two images to initialize the entire structure, and then the camera parameters of other images can be determined. Here we've done an experiment on cameras moving in order.

3.2.1. *Structure and motion initiation*

Two initial images are used to initialize an initial framework. Relations are built between the global coordinate system and the first camera, i.e., the newly built global center coincides with the camera center in the first image. Then through the fundamental matrix F of the previous two images, their camera matrixes can be initialized as:

$$P_1 = [I \mid 0] \tag{1}$$

$$P_2 = [[e]_x F + e a^T \mid e] \tag{2}$$

In the above terms: $e^T F = 0$, whereas $[e]_x$ is an antisymmetric matrix.

$$A = [0,0,0]^T \tag{3}$$

Assume the camera matrixes constructed above are all precise, the following linear triangular method can be used directly to calculate the spatial 3D points. However, the measured points $\vec{x}$ and $\vec{x}'$ both have errors, therefore the reversely projected radials are not collinear, indicating there is no spatial point $\vec{X}$ that precisely satisfies the relation

$$\vec{x} = P\vec{X}, \vec{x}' = P\vec{X}' \tag{4}$$

This paper uses the Sampson [1] approximation to correct the measurement points.

3.2.2. *Renewing structures and motions*

When a view is added in, first the camera matrix should be estimated, followed by the renewal of the 3D structure and finally the new 3D points will be initialized. According to the fundamental 6-point method, as for each correspondence $\vec{X}_i \leftrightarrow \vec{x}_i$, we can infer a relational expression

$$\begin{bmatrix} 0^T & -w_i\vec{x}_i^T & y_i\vec{x}_i^T \\ w_i\vec{x}_i^T & 0^T & -x_i\vec{x}_i^T \end{bmatrix} \begin{bmatrix} \vec{P}^1 \\ \vec{P}^2 \\ \vec{P}^3 \end{bmatrix} = 0 \tag{5}$$

The camera parameters can be calculated by use of multiple close visual angles. First, conduct epipolar geometrical computation on the relation between the current view and the former N views to infer the matched points. According to the relation between these matches and the structures built beforehand, the correspondences between a series of 3D points and 2D points can be calculated. Thus we can use this serial correspondences, through the above fundamental 6-point method, to infer the camera matrix P. The procedures of calculating the camera matrix are:

(1) Take n pairs of 2D points x corresponding to the spatial 3D points X.
(2) Unify the 2D points x and the spatial 3D points X.
(3) Make the RANSAC robust estimation: repeat sampling N times and the recycling times N applies the adaptive method.
(4) Nonlinear estimation: Re-estimate P from all matches of those classified into internal points.
(5) Guided complementary matching: Use the estimated P to define the search scope close to the projected point in favor of further defining the matching of feature points.

3.2.3. *Refinement of structures and motions*

Once a 3D structure is built, it is best to use the bundle adjustment method for an overall adjustment [10,11]. The target is to find a relatively precise camera matrix Pi and 3D point Mj, to minimize the following term

$$\sum_{i=1}^{m}\sum_{j=1}^{n} D(m_{ij},\hat{P}_i(\hat{M}_j))^2 \tag{6}$$

4. Building Expansible Main Framework

The algorithm will make stereo matches for building an expansible main framework of multiple views from arbitrary visual angles. It is an improvement to the traditional double view epipolar line parallel framework. Assume a group of camera matrixes $P_1,P_2,...P_N$, correspond to N views $I_1,I_2,...I_N$ in a scene, in which I1 is the base view, i.e., the depth graph should be calculated for I1. We now introduces the following symbols: the global coordinates of Point $\vec{X}$ should be represented by the homogeneous coordinates (X,Y,Z,1)ʳ; the image point $\vec{x}$ is converted into the form of 3-dimensional homogeneous coordinates; P_i represents a 3×4 homogeneous camera matrix. Then the camera matrix P_i can project a 3D spatial point through the following term onto View I_i.

$$\vec{x} = P_i\vec{X} \tag{7}$$

As the camera matrix of the base view inferred beforehand is

$$P_i = \begin{bmatrix} 1 & 0 & 0 & 0 \\ 0 & 1 & 0 & 0 \\ 0 & 0 & 1 & 0 \end{bmatrix} \tag{8}$$

Each point (x,y) in the base view can be distributed with a disparity value $d(d=1/z$, z is a depth value), to obtain its corresponding spatial 3D point $(x,y,1,d)^T$.

To be able to better treat the situation where the disparity is zero in this coordinate system, Disparity d should be used to calculate the coordinates of the spatial point, without the use of the depth value z. Then we can use the camera matrix of each view $P_2,...P_N$, to project the spatial point $(x,y,1,d)^T$ generated from the base view coordinates (x,y) and the disparity value d onto any view, followed by elimination of the homogeneous factor, to obtain the view plane coordinates.

5. Conversion from Stereo Matching Into the Maximum Flow Problem

First, let us simplify the problem into a one-dimensional situation. For two corresponding scan lines L(x) and R(x), x=1,2,…,N, set the calculated disparity scope as $d\in$ [dmin,dmax]. Take x,d as the horizontal and vertical coordinates to build a 2D network as illustrated. The value of each point (x,y) in the network represents the dissimilarity degree between Point L(x) and Point R($x+d$) (i.e., the smaller its value, the larger the possibility of being matched). We can simplify this cost function as: $cost(x,d)=|L(x)-R(x+d)|$.

To control the smoothness of disparity graphs, the smooth side and the side with disparity should be distinguished, which definition is given in Literature. The cost of the smooth side directly controls the smoothness of the disparity graph, which has complete examples in Literature.

The same as the case that one-dimensional stereo matching can be converted to a 2D network maximum flow problem, two-dimensional stereo matching can also be converted to a 3D network maximum flow problem, i.e., take x,y,d as the coordinates to build a 3D network, in order to find its cut curved surface with the minimum cost sum. This curved surface contains all disparity information of the base view, through which the depth graph of the base view can be inferred.

To sum up, the procedures of converting stereo matching into the maximum flow problem can be summarized as: ① build 3D network; ② calculate the cost value for the smooth side and the side with disparity; ③ find the minimum cut curved surface of this network; ④ use the information about the curved surface to calculate the depth graph.

6. Experiments and Analysis

It can be learned from these experimental data that proper adjustment of the parameters in Table 1 can reduce the overall average pixel errors and increase the camera precision. The larger the number of views, the smaller the difference between visual angles and the larger the number of matches will be; whereas the higher the resolution of disparity, the larger the SSD window in calculating the cost of the side with disparity, the more precise the cost of the side with disparity in the network, and the better the smoothness of the depth graph and its effect will be. However, this means the calculation time will largely increase. Experimental results have demonstrated the effectiveness of this algorithm, and if it is based on these depth graphs followed by histogram filtering, Gaussian filters, median filters and average filters, *etc.*, and then the interpolation calculation, more precise depth graphs will be obtained in favor of three-dimensional model reconstruction.

7. Conclusions

This paper infers the high-precision camera matrix P under the same space coordinate system. An expansible main framework is built for multiple views from arbitrary angles. Based on image coordinates and the disparity scope automatically computed, a 3D network is built, to distribute a proper weight to each side and convert the multi-view stereo matching problem into the network maximum flow problem. This paper analyzes the theoretical grounding of this algorithm and verifies its effectiveness and precision. This algorithm ensures both high precision and smoothness, as experimental results have demonstrated that it is suitable for three-dimensional model reconstruction, the parameters are shown in table 1.

Tab. 1. Parameters and calculation results of network construction

Experiment No.	Disparity Scope	Disparity Resolution	Size of SSD Window in Calculating Cost of the Side with Disparity	Result Photo
Ex1.1	[7,44]	112	5×5	Fig.3(a)
Ex1.2	[6,45]	118	5×5	Fig.3(b)
Ex1.3	[6,45]	157	11×11	Fig.3(c)
Ex2.1	[5,32]	109	3×3	Fig.4(a)
Ex2.2	[-1,31]	129	15×15	Fig.4(b)

In the above table, the result of Ex1.1 is shown in Figure 3(a), the result of Ex1.2 is shown in Figure 3(b), the result of Ex1.3 is shown in Figure 3(c), the result of Ex2.1 is shown in Figure 4(a), the result of Ex2.2 is shown in Figure 4(b).

In addition,the original base view of Ex1 is shown in Figure 3, the original base view of Ex2 is shown in Figure 4.

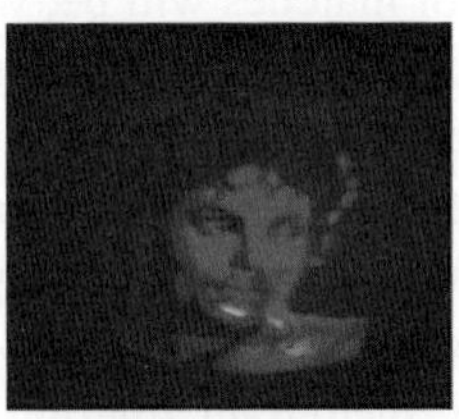

Fig. 3. The original base view of Ex1

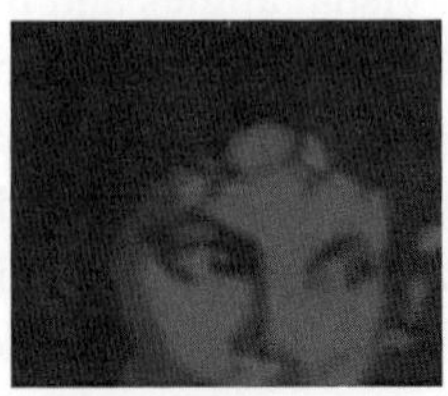

Fig. 3(a). The result of Ex1.1

Fig. 3(b). The result of Ex1.2

Fig. 3(b). The result of Ex1.2

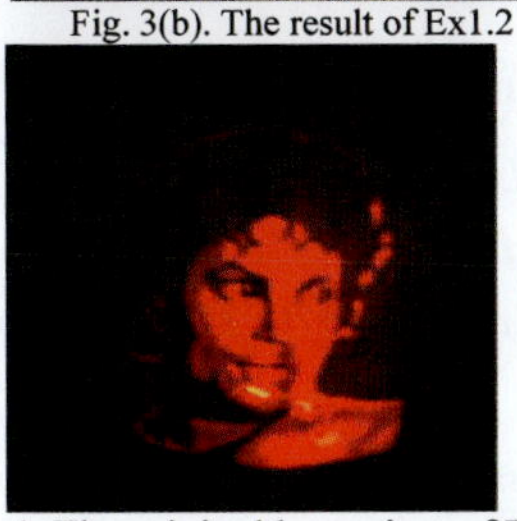

Fig. 4. The original base view of Ex2

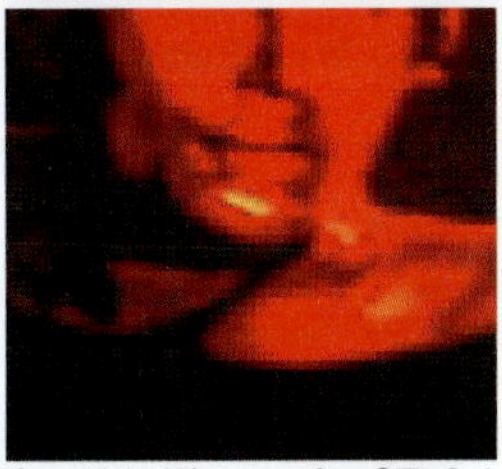

Fig. 4(a). The result of Ex2.1

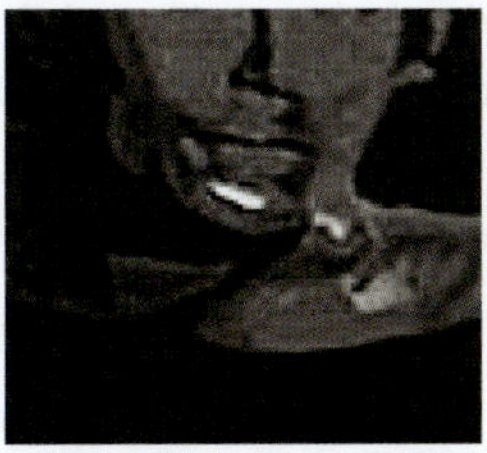

Fig. 4(b). The result of Ex2.2

References

1. Eggert DW, Lorusso A, Fisher R B. Estirnating 3-D Rigid Body Transformations: a Comparison of four Major Algorithms. Machine Vision and Application 2013, **9**: 272-290.
2. Yu Q S, Zhang J. The Data Concurrent Operation of Multi Medial Xtension Technique. Applied Mechanics and Materials. April. 2013, **263**: 316-321.
3. Li C W, Zhang J, Ou H Y. Design and Application of High-power LED Drive and Control Circuits. Applied Mechanics and Materials. April. 2013, **397**: 1822-1827.
4. Zhang Jian, A view-dress based algorithm for rebuilding 3D models [J]. The 13th IEEE Joint International Computer Science and Information Technology Conference, 2011, (01): 344-347.
5. HUANGM in, ZHANGJ Jan. The Dress Recognition Algorithm of Model Posture of Three Dimensions View in Dressing System [J]. JOURNAL OF ONGHUA UNIVERSITY, 2008, **29**(5): 42-46.

An Improved RBF Neural Network Applies to Infrared Gas Sensor

Wen-Juan Cheng[a], Xing-Xing Huang[b] and Shi-Xiang Tang[c]
School of Computer and Information, Hefei University of Technology
HeFei, AnHui, China
E-mail: [a]cheng@ah.edu.cn, [b]xingx_huang@126.com, [c]1157983522@qq.com

Infrared gas sensor detecting gas concentration inaccurately is mainly because infrared gas sensor is susceptible to temperature, wind and other factors. This paper proposes an improved RBF neural network which can substantially overcome the environmental influences. Its idea is to optimize the parameters of RBF neural network by gradient descent method. Experimental results show that compared with RBF neural network the error of the improved RBF neural network is smaller.

Keywords: Gas Concentration; RBF Neural Network; Gradient Descent Method.

1. Introduction

The infrared gas sensor with wide measurement range, quick response, long life has been widely used in coal mine to detect explosive gas [1]. However, the infrared gas sensor is susceptible to environment. So the detected gas concentration is inaccurate. Hardware or software method can solve this problem. Because the hardware is very expensive so many researchers choose the software, such as references [2], [3], [4]. The reference [2] described a classic algorithm, its main thought was to remove the maximum and minimum in n data then averaged the remaining data. It was simple and easy, but when the n was too large its sensitivity would reduce. The reference [3] used the least squares algorithm to calculate the gas concentration. The method not only ensured the continuity of data but also had quick response. But it was inefficient. Reference [4] was based on RBF neural network which was applied to collected gas concentrations; it basically eliminated the influences of temperature and humidity. The width, center value and weight vector of the RBF neural network would badly affect gas concentration if these values were not best.

In this paper, gas concentration deviation is defined as the difference between the detected gas concentration and standard gas concentration, called deviation for short. Deviation is caused by coal mine environment. RBF neural network can not only approximate any nonlinear function and conduct the law which is too difficult to interpret in system but also have good generalization and quick convergence. Nevertheless, the center value c, the width σ of the basis function and the weight vector $\vec{w}$ are keys to RBF neural network. This paper firstly chooses the gradient descent to optimize c,σ, $\vec{w}$; Secondly, establishes RBF neural network model; Lastly, uses the established mathematical model to predict the deviations. The experimental results show that compared with RBF neural network the improved RBF neural network has smaller error.

2. Theory

2.1. *Lambert-beer law*

Infrared gas sensor is based on that the absorption spectrum of molecular vibration and rotation is consistent with the emission spectrum of infrared light [5]. While the infrared light passing through the gas which will be detected, the intensity of infrared light becomes weaker. The gas absorbing infrared light will follow Lambert - Beer Law. As Eq. (1) show.

$$I = I_0 e^{-KLC} \tag{1}$$

Eq. (1): I is the transmitted light intensity; I_0 is the incident light intensity; K is the absorption coefficient; L is the thickness of gas; C is the gas concentration.

2.2. *RBF neural network*

RBF neural network usually solve the uncertain connotative law in limited data [6]. The RBF neural network model structure show in Fig. 1

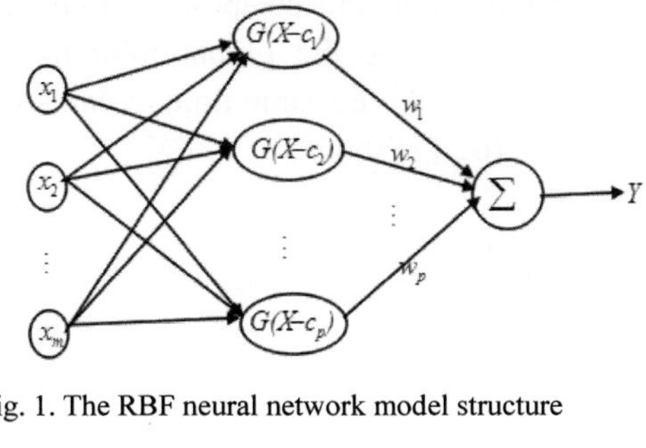

Fig. 1. The RBF neural network model structure

As we can see from Fig. 1. Hidden layer output values shows in Eq. (2).

$$\begin{cases} y_1 = G(\|x_1 - c_1\|) + G(\|x_2 - c_1\|) \cdots + G(\| x_m - c_1 \|) \\ y_2 = G(\|x_1 - c_2\|) + G(\|x_2 - c_2\|) \cdots + G(\| x_m - c_2 \|) \\ \vdots \\ y_p = G(\|x_1 - c_p\|) + G(\|x_2 - c_p\|) \cdots + G(\| x_m - c_p \|) \end{cases} \tag{2}$$

The output value of output layer shows in Eq. (3).

$$Y = \sum_{i=1}^{p} w_i \times \exp(-\frac{X - c_i}{\sigma_i^2}) \tag{3}$$

Eq. (3): w_i is the i-th value in $\vec{w}$; Y is the output value; c_i is the center value; σ_i is the width.

In order to making RBF neural network predictive value to approach the test value. We should set the approximation function. As shown in Eq. (4).

$$f(X) = \frac{1}{2}(\sum_{i=1}^{p} w_i \times \exp(-\frac{X - c_i}{\sigma_i^2}) - d)^2 \tag{4}$$

Eq. (4): *d* is the test value, the smaller value of f(x) is the better the predicted value is.

The center value c, width σ and weight vector $\vec{w}$ would directly impact on predicted value. How to choose the c, σ, $\vec{w}$ is very important. Width and center values of basic functions are generally not easy to find the globally optimal solution.

2.3. *Gradient descent method*

Gradient descent method starts with arbitrary initial values of the parameters. Then with a very small step repeatedly modifies the parameters. Each modification step should along the steepest decline in error surface. Repeat above steps until error value is the global minimum [7]. Gradient descent method can optimize σ, c, *w*. At the same time, it can solve the globally optimal problem. As the Eq. (5), (6), (7) show.

$$\Delta w_j = -\eta \frac{\partial f(X)}{\partial w_j} = \eta \sum_{i=1}^{p} e_i G(\| X_i - c_j \|) \tag{5}$$

$$\Delta c_j = -\eta \frac{\partial f(x)}{\partial c_j} = \eta \frac{w_j}{\delta_j^{\,2}} \sum_{i=1}^{p} e_i G(\| X_i - c_j \|)(X_i - c_j) \tag{6}$$

$$\Delta \delta_j = -\eta \frac{\partial f(X)}{\partial \delta_j} = \eta \frac{w_j}{\delta_j^{\,3}} \sum_{i=1}^{p} e_i G(\| X_i - c_j \|)(X_i - c_j) \tag{7}$$

Eq. (5), (6), (7): η is the constant. It decides the searching gradient of gradient descent method.

3. Building Model

In this paper, data set D contains temperature, wind, CO concentrations. Data set C contains gas concentrations.

$$D = \begin{bmatrix} d_{11} & d_{12} & d_{13} \\ d_{21} & d_{22} & d_{23} \\ \vdots & \vdots & \vdots \\ d_{m1} & d_{m2} & d_{m3} \\ \vdots & \vdots & \vdots \\ d_{n1} & d_{n2} & d_{n3} \end{bmatrix} \quad C = \begin{bmatrix} c_1 \\ c_2 \\ \vdots \\ c_m \\ \vdots \\ c_n \end{bmatrix}$$

Deviations matrix is shown in Eq. (8).

$$\Delta C = \begin{bmatrix} \Delta c_1 \\ \Delta c_2 \\ \vdots \\ \Delta c_m \end{bmatrix} = C - \overline{C} \tag{8}$$

Eq. (8): ΔC is the deviations matrix; C is the gas concentrations matrix; $\overline{c}$ is standard gas concentrations matrix. The software has four steps.

(1) $D_{3\times m}$ and $\Delta C_{1\times m}$ are the input data of RBF neural network. Eq. (5), (6), (7) can be used to optimize the c, σ, $\vec{w}$. The optimized parameters can build the RBF neural network.

(2) It makes the rest of n-m in D as the established RBF neural network input value and can achieve the prediction deviations matrix $\Delta C = [\Delta c_1, \Delta c_2 \cdots \Delta c_{n-m}]^T$.

(3) $[\Delta c_1, \Delta c_2 \cdots \Delta c_{n-m}]^T$ is substituted into the Eq. (8), then can get the processed gas concentration matrix Q.

(4) As Eq. (9) show, use average method to calculate gas concentration.

$$\overline{Q} = \frac{1}{n-m} \sum_{i=1}^{n-m} q_i \tag{9}$$

4. Result

According to the collected temperature, wind, CO concentrations and gas concentrations, use the above steps to build the RBF neural network. Make standard gas concentration 0.55% as example. Choosing three methods which are the direct detection and using RBF neural network and improved RBF neural network to process the data. It can get the comparison figure as Fig. 2 shows.

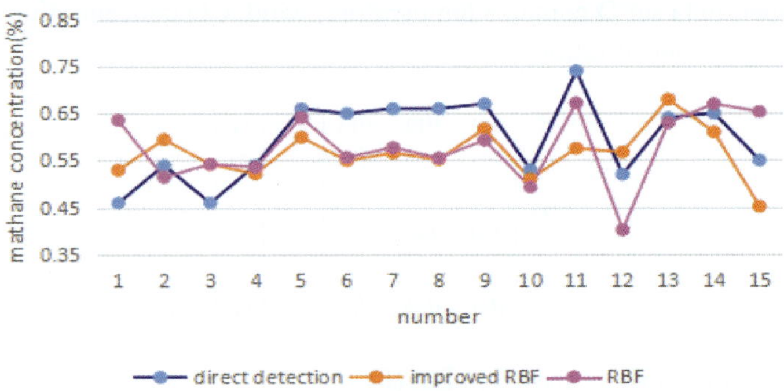

Fig. 2. The comparison of three methods

It can be seen from Fig. 2 that the stability of direct detection is weakest. The improved RBF neural network is best. Thus, the improved RBF neural network is better than other two methods. Through the analysis of experimental results can get Table 1 and Table 2.

Tab. 1. 0.55% error and variance

Schedule	direct detection	RBF	improved RBF
variance	0.1326	0.0915	0.0455
error (%)	8.24%	5.12%	2.64%

Tab. 2. 0.0% error and variance

Schedule	direct detection	RBF	improved RBF
variance	0.085	0.063	0.0235
error (%)	4.4%	3.29%	1.35%

As we can see from table 1 and table 2, compared with the direct detection and RBF neural network both error and variance of the optimized RBF are least.

5. Conclusion

This paper describes some common software methods and analyses them then puts forward a new software method. Using the gradient descent to optimize the RBF neural network parameters can accurately predictive the deviation. Thereby the gas sensor detects higher accuracy gas concentration. The method can substantially eliminate the influence of environmental factors on infrared gas sensor, increase the accuracy.

Acknowledgments

In this paper, the research was sponsored by the National Natural Science Foundation of China (Project No.51274078) and the Fundamental Research Funds for the Central Universities (Project No. JZ2014HGBZ0009).

References

1. Weilin Ye, Chuantao Zheng, Yiding Wang. “Stability Measurement and Temperature Compensation of Mid-infrared Gas Detection Device.” [J]. Acta Optica Sinica, 2014 (3): 265-269. (In Chinese).
2. Guangjie Lv. “Application Research on Gas Measurement Based on Infrared Technology and Spectrum Absorption” [D]. xi’an:Xi’an University of Science and Technology, 2009. (In Chinese).
3. Cong Zhao, Hui Lin, Chuwu Peng. “Design of Gas Density Detector Based on Non-dispersive Infrared Spectrum Absorptive Fundamentals.” [J]. Comp uter Measurement & Control, 2009 (6): 1229-1231. (In Chinese).
4. Li Zhang, Rulin Wang, Ying Wang, Yukai He. “Research of Detection Model of Mine-used Infrared Gas Sensor Based on Neural Network.”{J]. Industry and Mine Automation, 2009 (8): 18-21. (In Chinese).
5. Dafeng Luo, Jianhua Yang, Chonggui Zhong. “Detection Technology of Gas Concentration Based on Infrared Absorption Spectrum.”[J]. Spectroscopy and Spectral Analysis. 2011, 31(2): 384-386. (In Chinese).
6. Hua Fu, Dandan Shu, Xinxin Wang. “A Dynamic Compensation Algorithm Based on Improved IGA-RBF Neural Network for Sensor.” [J]. Computer Measurement & Control, 2013, 4:089. (In Chinese).
7. Tom M. Mitchell. Machine Learning. China Machine Press. 2014:66. (In Chinese).

Fast Basic Shape Feature Computation

Li-Feng He[1,2,a], Xi-Wei Ren[1], Qi-Hang Gao[1], Xiao Zhao[1], Bin Yao[1] and Yu-Yan Chao[3,b]

[1]Artificial Intelligence Institute, College of Electrical and Information Engineering
Shaanxi University of Science and Technology,
Shaanxi 710021, China

[2]Faculty of Inf. Sci. and Tech., Aichi Prefectural University,
Aichi, Japan

[3]Faculty of Environment, Information and Business, Nagoya Sangyo University,
Japan

E-mail: [a]helifeng@ist.aichi-pu.ac.jp, [b]chao@nagoya-su.ac.jp

Basic shape features of objects in a binary image are very important for image analysis and pattern recognition. In conventional algorithms, for basic shape feature computation, a labeled image generated by a connected-component labeling processing is usually necessary. This paper proposes a fast two-scan algorithm for calculating shape features of objects in a binary image without the use of a labeled image. Experiments demonstrated that the proposed algorithm is much more efficient than conventional algorithms for calculating basic shape features of objects in a binary image.

Keywords: Shape Feature; Image Analysis; Pattern Recognition; Labeling.

1. Introduction

Basic shape features of objects, i.e., area, perimeter, circularity, and centroid, are very important for pattern recognition, image analysis, and computer vision [1], [2].

In binary images, the concept of objects is equal to that of connected components. Therefore, by conventional methods, before calculating basic shape features of objects in a binary image, we usually need to perform connected-component labeling to distinguish different objects in the image.

By connected-component labeling, a labeled image will be generated, in which all pixels of each connected component (object) in a binary image will be assigned a unique label corresponding to the object; thus, we can distinguish different objects by their labels.

By scanning the labeled image once, we can calculate the basic shape features of each object according to its label. Thus, if we use the two-scan labeling algorithm proposed in Ref. [3], refered to as the *HCS* algorithm, for calculating basic shape features of objects in a binary image, three scans are necessary. For convenience, we denote this extended algorithm as to the F_{HCS} algorithm. On the other hand, if we use the contour tracing labeling algorithm proposed in Ref. [4], call the *CT* labeling algorithm, where labels assigned to object pixels will never change, we can easily incorporate basic shape feature computation into the CT labeling algorithm. For convenience, we denote this extended CT labeling algorithm as to the F_{CT} algorithm.

This paper proposes an efficient two-scan algorithm for calculating basic shape features of objects in a binary image. Our proposed algorithm summarizes the related data for each equivalent label set to calculate basic shape features of the corresponding object by use of the image generated by the first scan of a two-scan labeling algorithm. Thus, our proposed algorithm can complete basic shape feature computation by two scans. Experimental results demonstrated that our proposed algorithm outperforms conventional algorithms for calculating basic shape features.

2. Preliminaries

For an $N \times M$-sized binary image, we use $p(x, y)$ to denote a pixel as well as its value at (x, y) in the image, where $0 \le x < N$ and $0 \le y < M$. As in almost all related literatures on basic shape feature computaiton [1], [2], we consider cases where no hole is in objects.

2.1. *Definitions of basic shape features of object*

As introduced in [1], for calculating basic shape features of objects in a binary image, we need first to label the image. After labeling, all pixels of each object in the labeled image will be assigned the same label (value), which is unique to any label assigned to other objects. An object with label l, denoted to $O(l)$, is represented by $O(l) = \{ p(x, y) \mid p(x, y) = l\}$.

The *area* of, $A[l]$, is defined as the number of the pixels of $O(l)$ (i.e., the number of pixels with label l in the labeled image), that is,

$$A[l] = |O(l)| = |\{p(x,y) \mid p(x,y) = l\}| \quad (1)$$

The *centroid* of *O(l)*, *(X[l], Y[l])*, is defined to the average location of row and column of the pixels in *O*(*l*), i.e.,

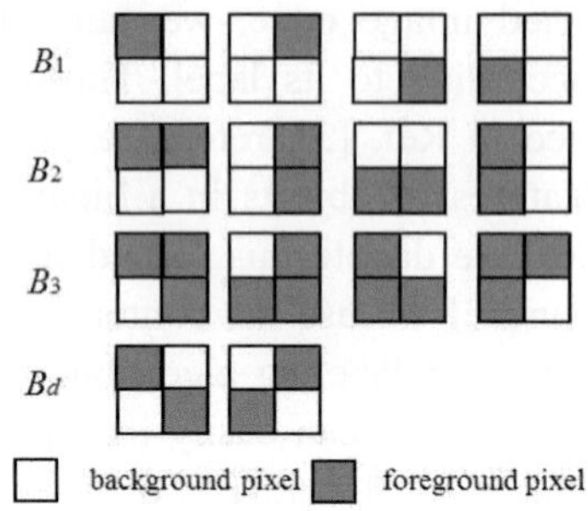

Fig. 1. Patterns for calculating perimeter

$$X[l] = \sum_{p(x,y)=l} x \bigg/ A[l] = \alpha[l] / A[l] \tag{2}$$

$$Y[l] = \sum_{p(x,y)=l} y \bigg/ A[l] = \beta[l] / A[l] \tag{3}$$

On the other hand, the *perimeter* of *O*(*l*), *P*[*l*], can be calculated by the numbers of patterns B_1, B_2, B_3, and B_d shown in Fig. 1 consisting of foreground pixels with label *l*. For covenience, we denote a pattern B_t (t = 1, 2, 3, d) with label *l* as $B_t(l)$. Let $N_t(l)$ be the numbers of $B_t(l)$ in the labeled image, respectively, then, *P*[*l*] can also be calculated as follows [1]:

$$P[l] = N_2(l) + \frac{1}{\sqrt{2}}(N_1(l) + N_3(l) + 2N_d(l)) \tag{4}$$

Lastly, the *circularity* of *O*(*l*), *C*[*l*], is defined as follows.

$$C[l] = 4\pi A[l]/(P[l])^2 \tag{5}$$

3. Proposed Algorithm

After the first scan of the HCS algorithm, all provisional labels assigned to each object will be combined in an equivalent label set. Let *S*(*l*) be such an equivalent label set. Then the representative label of all provisional labels in *S*(*l*) is *l*, and all provisional labels in *S*(*l*) will be replaced by *l* in the second scan, the object corresponding to *S*(*l*) will be *O*(*l*) in the labeled image.

According to the above analysis, we know that each pixel of *O*(*l*) will be assigned a provisional label in *S*(*l*) after the first scan. Therefore, the work for calculating the basic shape features of the object *O*(*l*) based on the pixels with the label l in the labeled image can be exactly done based on the pixels each of which is assigned a provisional label $S(l)$ after the first scan. Thus, we can calculate basic shape features of objects by use of the image generated after the first scan of the HCS labeling algorithm. In the other words, instead of the labeled image generated by the second scan of the HCS algorithm, we can use the image generated by the first scan for basic shape feature computation.

Now we explain our proposed algorithm in detail. After the first scan of the HCS labeling algorithm, we process each pixel $p(x, y)$ of the generated image by the second scan as follows, where all elements of arrays X, Y, A, and P are initialized to 0:

For each current pixel $p(x, y)$ being processing, we check whether the pattern of $\begin{bmatrix} p(x-1,y-1) & p(x,y-1) \\ p(x-1,y) & p(x,y) \end{bmatrix}$ is one of the patterns shown in Fig. 1. If it is, say, B_i (i = 1, 2, 3, or d), then there is at least a foreground pixel in the pattern. Let t be any provisional label assigned to an object pixel in pattern B_i, we do the following calculation, where $D_i = \sqrt{2}/2$, 1, $\sqrt{2}/2$ and $\sqrt{2}$ for i = 1, 2, 3, and d, respectively.

$$\mathrm{P[t]} \leftarrow \mathrm{P[t] + Di}$$

Moreover, if the current pixel is an object pixel assigned a label t, we do the following calculations:

$$\mathrm{X[t]} \leftarrow \mathrm{X[t] + x}$$

$$\mathrm{Y[t]} \leftarrow \mathrm{Y[t] + y}$$

$$\mathrm{A[t]} \leftarrow \mathrm{A[t] + 1}$$

Then after the scan, for each object corresponding an equivalent label set $S(l)$, $O(l)$, the area $A[l]$, the centroid ($X[l]$, $Y[l]$) and the perimeter $P[l]$ of the object can be calcualted as follows.

$$A[l] = \sum_{t \in S(l)} A[t]$$

$$X[l] = \sum_{t \in S(l)} X[t] \Big/ A[l]$$

$$Y[l] = \sum_{t \in S(l)} Y[t] \Big/ A[l]$$

$$P[l] = \sum_{t \in S(l)} P[t]$$

Notice that for each label $t \in S(l)$, we have $R[t] = l$, therefore the above work can be made as follows, where L is the largest provisional label assigned in the first scan of the HCS labeling algorithm.

For t from 1 to l
| **If** $t \neq R[t]$
| | $X[R[t]] \leftarrow X[R[t]] + X[t]$, $Y[R[t]] \leftarrow Y[R[t]] + Y[t]$
| | $A[R[t]] \leftarrow A[R[t]] + A[t]$, $P[R[t]] \leftarrow P[R[t]] + P[t]$
| **EndIf**
EndFor
For t from 1 to l
| **If** $t = R[t]$
| | $X[t] \leftarrow X[t]/A[t]$, $Y[t] \leftarrow Y[t]/A[t]$, $C[t] \leftarrow 4\pi C[t]/(P[t]\times P[t])$
| **EndIf**
EndFor

On the other hand, with $A[l]$ and $P[l]$, $C[l]$ can be calculated by formula (5).

4. Experimental Results

We compare our proposed algorithm with the F_{HCS} algorithm and the F_{CT} algorithm. All algorithms were implemented in the C language on a PC-based workstation (Intel Core 2 6400 2.13GHz, 2MB Memory, CentOS 6.6 OS), and compiled by the GNU C compiler (version 4.4.7) with the option –O3. All experimental results presented in this section were obtained by averaging of the execution time for 5000 runs.

The images shown in Fig. 2 are used for test. The executing times of different algorithms are shown in Table 1, where *ms* is the abbreviation of millisecond. We can find that the F_{HCS} algorithm is a little more efficient that the F_{CT} algorithm, and our proposed algorithm is much faster than the other two algorithms.

5. Concluding Remarks

This paper presented a fast two-scan shape feature computation algorithm. Experimental results demonstrated that our proposed algorithm outperforms conventional algorithms for calculating basic shape features.

(a) (b) (c)

Fig. 2. Images used for test

Tab. 1. Experimental results (ms)

	Fhcs	*Fcr*	Ours
Fig. 2(a)	0.97	0.98	0.57
Fig. 2(b)	0.98	1.05	0.64
Fig. 2(c)	1.02	1.42	0.66

Acknowledgements

This work was supported in part by the Grant-in-Aid for the National Natural Science Foundation of China under Grant No. 61471227, the Scientific Research (C) of the Ministry of Education, Science, Sports and Culture of Japan under Grant No. 26330200, and the Scientific Research of Shaanxi Province of China under Grant No. 2014K11-02-01-13.

References

1. R. C. Gonzalez and R. E. Woods. *Digital Image Processing*, Addison-Wesley, Reading, Massachusetts, 1993.
2. L. Wang, T. N. Tan, W.M. Hu, H. Z. Ning, "Automatic gait recognition based on statistical shape analysis," *IEEE Trans. Image Processing*, 12 (2003), 1120–1131.
3. L. He, Y. Chao, K. Suzuki, K. Wu. "Fast connected-component labeling," *Pattern Recognition*, 42(9) (2009), 1977-1987.
4. F. Chang, C. J. Chen and C. J. Lu, "A linear-time component-labeling algorithm using contour tracing technique," *Comput. Vis. Imag. Underst.* 93, 2004, pp. 206-220.

Summarize of Communication Network MAC Layer Protocol Oriented Network Fire Control

Guo-Hui Zhang, Ang Gao, Jie Cao, Yuan Wang

Armored Force Engineering Institute Faculty of Informatics, Tactical Communications Laboratory, Dujiakan 21th courtyard of Fengtai Zone in Peking
Peking, Fengtai Zone, China
E-mail: 236211566@qq.com

This paper, first briefly introduces the concept of network fire control system, communication network architecture oriented network fire control, and then a detailed analysis for the demand of communication network oriented network fire control for MAC. Then, according to these demands, proposes the innovation point of this MAC protocol design, and summarizes the design of MAC layer protocol. Finally, it analyzes the performance of the MAC protocol superior place and the need to further perfect it.

Keywords: MAC; The Distributed Network; The Real Time; RTS; CTS.

1. Introduction

1.1. *The concept of network fire control system*

Networked fire control system is able to comprehensive utilize the detection information of one or more nodes in combat cluster, comprehensive control the variety of fire nodes in combat cluster to hit the target Collaboratively. Networked fire control system using distributed architecture, sharing the operational information resources between each node within the cluster, the integrated application of fire control, on the physical location, function and control implementation across nodes, distributed target acquisition, tracking, calculating, shoot, make the traditional fire control system from centralized type tightly coupled to the distributed open.

Networked fire control system is a traditional fire control system in the network under the condition of system upgrade and function extension, is the combination of information technology and control technology, has realized the operational mode from one to one simple shock to many-to-many system against, can effectively improve the combat troops from sensors detect target to the implementation of the fire fighting of rapid response, and effectively strengthen the equipment through many weapons platform collaborative mode of operations and capabilities.

2. The Demand of Communication Network Oriented Network Fire Control for MAC

2.1. *Support for a variety of different types of business delivery timeliness*

For fire control communication network faces data business types are varied, the proposed MAC protocol to support a variety of different types of business delivery timeliness, especially to be able to support real-time data, words, video, images, and other business data distribution.

2.2. *With strong portability and scalability*

Networked fire control emphasizes the idea that under the condition of information technology, based on network communication and charges platform, makes every effort to giving full play to the advantages of small units, through flexible, rapid, accurate and closely cooperate with the implementation of small combat force aggregation of power, rather than a massive forces concentrated. It fully mobilizes the various small scattered on the battlefield combat unit speed advantage, through the acceleration of target selection and target as the focal point of motor, in many ways, more direction quickly to meet the enemy, proactive, take the most favorable potential, the attack on the enemy's important target to implement all-round.

2.3. *With a good anti-jamming*

Network oriented facing the complex electromagnetic environment of fire control communication network, in order to prevent eavesdropping and jamming, fire control for network communication network spread spectrum communication technology should be adopted.

3. Design of Mac Protocol Oriented Network Fire Control

This section combined with the second battlefield distributed network MAC layer demand, this paper proposes a high rate, more business, strong electromagnetic fight battlefield environment of distributed network MAC layer design scheme.

According to section 1 of the network control system of fire control definition, hypothesis in the network node number is 32 biggest, node and the communication between the distance of 5 km, the clock error in each node can be calculated by no more than 16.6667 mu s, now take 3.3333 mu s as protection. The rate at which assumes that the network of 500 Mbit/s (0.5 bit/μs). Absolute clock error is not more than 4 s all nodes, and network using jump frequency synchronization, the update cycle for 16 s.

For network communication network MAC layer of fire control communication in MAC protocol frames, figure 1 is a MAC protocol frame structure.

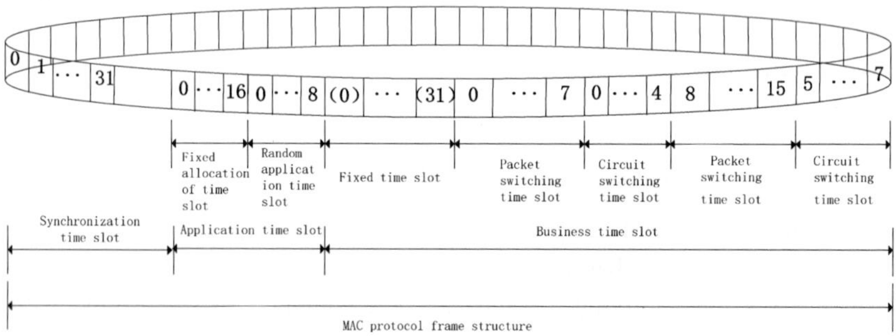

Fig. 1. MAC protocol frame structure

A MAC protocol frame by the time slot synchronization time slot period, application time slot period, business segments, business time slot, and can be divided into fixed time slot and a number of packet switching time slot, circuit switching time slot. Effects of synchronous time slot is the synchronization between nodes, the exchange of nodes in the information, also is not the net node time slot in synchronous to the network segment. Applying for the time slot period (for business channel resources and make an appointment the receiving node; business time slot is the function of data transmission business, MAC protocols for different types of business offers a different time. Each node using fixed fire time slot section to upload their own situation to the center node, center node in the final time slot, the trend of information fusion, generate a unified situation maps to issue to each node. Packet switching time slot and circuit switching time slot is fixed allocation time slot and random application time slot allocation of time slot and on-demand appointment time slot, mainly carries on the transfer of the business of fire control, ensure the real-time performance of different types of business transfer.

3.1. *The time and frequency hopping synchronization*

Each fire inside the node has a precision of 1 mu s 36 bits clock, because each fire node internal clock between the absolute error of less than 4 s(μs),So the node internal clock[35 ~ 22] bit values are less than 1.To enhance the anti-interference ability of the network, this paper designed frequency for 16 s updated once, so this paper set the node within the first [0 ~ 22] bit for clock synchronization, [24 ~ 35] for fh synchronization, When 24th(μs) refresh again after waiting for 4.194303 s can realize the synchronization of time and frequency hopping. Synchronous data frames as shown in the figure 2:

TYPE	Submit ID	Source IP	Relationship between nodes	Clock synchronization nodes IP	The clock version	clock 36bit

Fig. 2. Synchronous data frames

3.2. *Support for a real-time of different types of data business*

Time slot period will be based on the business, the time slot is divided into fixed time slot, packet switching time slot, circuit switching time slot. Fixed time slot period, each node will own situational information transmission to a central node, the center node will fusion, generate a unified issued to each node. Packet switching time slot, circuit switching time slot is used to pass the fire control information, the allocation of time slot and make an appointment in the time slot period completed application. Time slot period is divided into fixed allocation time slot and random application time slot. Time slot in a fixed distribution, assuming that 32 node in the network, address 0 ~ 31, respectively, then the nodes in the case of % 16 time slot, I have the highest priority, in the time slot, at most two node with the highest priority, in the network is in low traffic mode, very little conflict, but when the network at a high volume, the network will be in a high conflict model, then, in the time slot application period, designed the RTS and CTS data frames to avoid conflict, ensure that all types of business delivery timeliness. as shown in the figure 3:

To avoid conflict RTS					
Type	Submit ID	Source IP	Coordinate nodes	Threat level assessment	Application time slot number
To avoid conflict CTS					
Type	Submit ID	Source IP	Destination	To apply for reply	Application time slot number

Fig. 3. The RTS and CTS data frames

When the node and conflict within the scope of a shock, local node to conflicts node sends to avoid RTS data frame, when conflict node received the RTS, if there is no data to be sent, is directly applied to reply in CTS frame into the agreed to apply for, sent to the node, the node receives the CTS, can apply for a certain time slot. If conflict node has data to send, then, to this node threat level assessment and the conflict between nodes in fire control system of threat level assessment of information to be sent, threat level evaluation of high priority to send, if the node's threat level is high, the CTS frame application response into the agreed to request, sent to this node, the node receives the CTS, can apply for a certain time slot. If conflict node threat level is high, the application response into don't agree with the application in CTS, and applying for a time slot in writing to apply for a time slot number, sent to this node, the node after receiving the CTS, according to the node of the network topology relations, compute nodes which is free, and then apply for time slot in random section, competition in the form of CSMA/CA channel resources. If conflict nodes are two jump node of this node, then the conflict between nodes in the form of hidden terminal, need to find a common neighbor node to coordinate as a node, if didn't receive the CTS neighbor node, is to send a CTS, otherwise does not carry on the RTS response. as shown in the figure 4:

Type	Submit ID	sourceIP	Packet switching time slot bitmap16bit	The receiving node bitmap 32bit	Circuit switching time slot application way16bit	Circuit switching Destination node

Time slot for data frames

Type	Submit ID	The serial number	destination	apply for The end

Circuit slot application answer

Fig. 4. Time slot for data frames and Circuit time slot application response

4. Conclusions

This article first time slot in synchronous period adopted the design scheme of frequency hopping clock synchronization, guarantees the network anti-jamming, the second time slot in the business section of set a fixed time slot, ensures that each node real-time data transmission, the formation of unified situation maps and powerfully promoted the effective transmission of information flow in the fire control. Third, in the distribution of fixed time slots, adopts the threat level assessment method, effectively avoid the conflicts and to ensure the real-time high important information transmission. Fourth, in applying random time slot period, in the form of CSMA/CA access, not using the time slot for the competition, some non real-time business are arranged in the random application time slot period, greatly improving the utilization rate of channel. Of course, there are many problems need to further perfect the MAC protocols, such as locating slot, subnet division and integration, etc.

Acknowledgments

In this paper, the research was sponsored by the National Natural Science Foundation of China (Project No.61302110).

References

1. Hui-Gang Xu, Guo Zhi "network fire control system and its construction" journal of nanjing university of science and technology of 2007.04.

2. Ceng Qingquan “battlefield based on WSN is a distributed network technology research, master degree theses of master of xian university of electronic science and technology in 2009.
3. Surianoka, kit, Linda, gao-peng wang studies of networked air defense fire control system architecture of these 2009.09.
4. Chen Yong, ke-min liu, sun happiness “network fire control in some key technologies to be solved,” journal of fire and command control 2011.06.
5. Shen Song, Ji Qian, Shen Bin in 2030 by the American command and control system of unmanned systems integration structure of liaoning university press, 2013.
6. Zhu Yuanwu, zhi-gang lu “army weapons development platform of networked fire control system” fire and command control journal 2013.10.
7. Hao Yusheng, Jia Lirong, Wei Jieying tanks networked fire control system, journal of computer development and application of 2013.12.
8. Chun-Lei Sun the componentization of the networked fire control simulation system design and research on load balancing of master degree theses of master of Beijing institute of technology in 2015.
9. Forest the MAC protocol research and tactical data link simulation master degree theses of master of university of electronic science and technology in 2011.
10. Ceng Xiangbo tactical data link message standard research paper 2015 master's degree in Beijing jiaotong university.
11. Wen-Zheng Wang the tactical data link time slot allocation agreement and simulation research, national university of defense technology Ph.D. Thesis, 2010.
12. Liu Xing, He Zhaoxiong, jing-lun zhou the TDMA tactical data link in fixed time slot allocation algorithm of minimum delay jitter is system engineering of 2012.06.
13. Jia-Yuan Chen the tactical data link time division multiple access time slot allocation algorithm study of master degree theses of master of Beijing jiaotong university in 2015.
14. Xu Sheng “tactical data link network protocol architecture and MAC protocol study of master degree theses of master of national university of defense technology, 2009.

Stock Market Prediction with Improved BP Neural Network

Shuo Zhang[a] and Tian-Sheng Xu[b]

School of Information, Capital University of Economics and Business

Beijing, 100070, P. R. China

E-mail: [a]zhangshuo_cueb@sina.com, [b]xuts@cueb.edu.con

As a product of market economy, the stock market has its characteristics of high stakes and attractive benefits. But the fluctuation of stock price is always affected by many complexity factors. In this paper, China Merchants Bank stock is chosen as an example in utilizing good classification capability of BP neural network to forecast its future trend. In addition, the accuracy and stability of four kinds of neural networks in prediction of stock market trend are analyzed. Simulation experiments show that BP neural network has better performance than other approaches in learning capacity and generalization.

Keywords: Stock Trend Prediction; BP Algorithm; Probabilistic Neural Network; Fuzzy Neural Network; Wavelet Neural Network.

1. Introduction

Since the birth of stock market, it is essentially dynamic, non-linear, non-parametric and chaotic in nature[1]. In addition, the fluctuation of stock market trend is affected by many complexity factors such as economic conditions, investors' expectation, bank rate and national policies[2-4].

According to Efficient Market Hypothesis[5], investors can achieve average trading advantages based on historical and present information. Recently, artificial neural network(ANN) based models are applied to predict stock market trend because of their inherent learning capability[6-8]. However, the ANN especially back propagation (BP) ignores the tremendous noise and non-stationary characteristics in stock market data. Miao pointed out the solutions of BP are likely to fall into minimum optimal[9]. Then, Li Huo[10] and Qi Sun[11] introduced improved BP neural network models respectively. Nowadays, a variety of neural networks such as WNN[12], PNN[13] and FNN[14] are applied to predict stock market trend.

This paper is organized as follows: Section 2 presents the results from BP, PNN, FNN, WNN and analyzes their accuracy and stability in prediction. Finally conclusion is given in Section 3.

2. Stimulation Experiments

In this paper, we aim to predict stock price trend in a short term and analyze the accuracy and stability of BP, PNN, FNN, WNN in prediction.

We design a three-layer BP neural network model and choose opening price, closing price, the highest/lowest price, the adjusted closing price, total volume of stock traded as input nodes and closing price as output nodes.

In addition, we use init function to produce a initial value within the range of [-1,1], tansig, logsig as transfer function, traindx as training function, learngdm as learning function and mse as performance function.

2.1. *Experiments data*

In this paper, we choose China Merchants Bank stock's historical data from March 18th, 2002 to November 12th 2014 as training data, data from November 13th,2014 to February 3rd, 2016 as testing data to forecast its trend in a short term. In predicting process, we choose 3000 data as training data, 300 data as testing data and define learning number as 200,000, learning rate as 0.01, error as 0.001, hidden layer as 9. The regression process is shown in Figure 1.

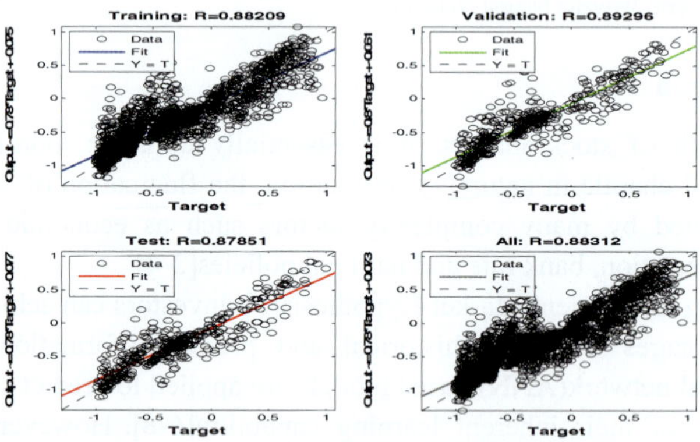

Fig. 1. The regression process of BP neural network(hidden layer nodes=24)

As we can see from the result, it meets the best validation performance at epoch 24. Although it has high speed, it is likely to fall into local optimal. In following section, we will change the number of hidden layer nodes to find a relatively fast and accurate BP neural network model.

2.2. *Optimization of BP neural network model*

In this section, we will change the number of hidden layer nodes to find a relatively fast and accurate BP neural network model.

The different results are shown in Table 1.

Tab. 1. The contrast between different hidden layer nodes

Number	Epoch	Performance	Gradient	Validation Check
9	27	0.0484	0.0126	6
14	35	0.0491	0.00392	6
19	106	0.0410	0.00690	6
24	98	0.0353	0.00157	6
29	71	0.0447	0.00764	6

Table 1 shows that the gradient, error and convergence rate are relatively best when the number of hidden layer nodes is 24. The deviation and fitting curve are shown in Figure 2 and Figure 3:

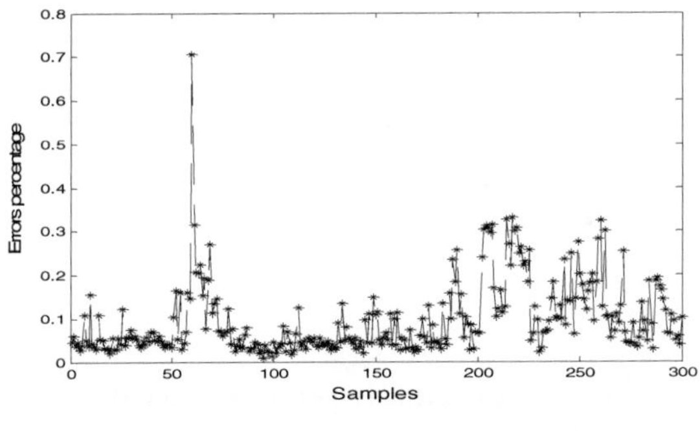

Fig. 2. The deviation curve(hidden layer nodes=24)

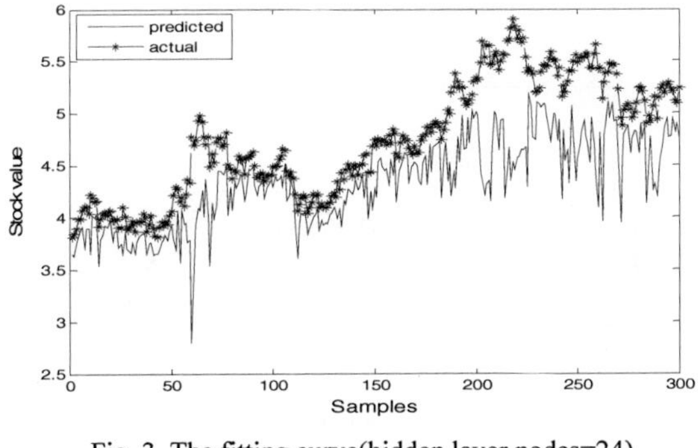

Fig. 3. The fitting curve(hidden layer nodes=24)

2.3. *Comparison of different neural network models*

In this section, we choose the same group of data to compare the prediction results of four kinds of neural networks

(1)The prediction effect of PNN is shown in Figure 4.

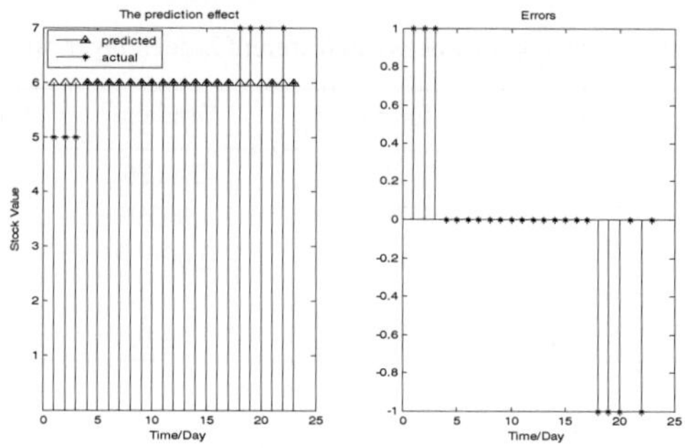

Fig. 4. The prediction effect of PNN network

(2)The prediction effect of FNN is shown in Figure 5.

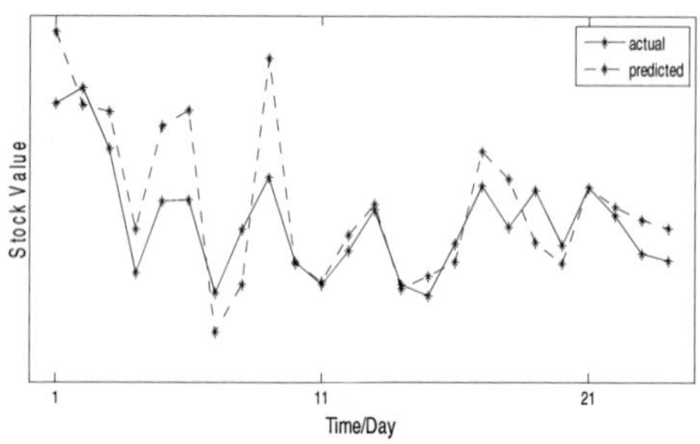

Fig. 5. The prediction effect of FNN network

(3)The prediction effect and deviation curve of WNN are shown in Figure 6 and Figure 7.

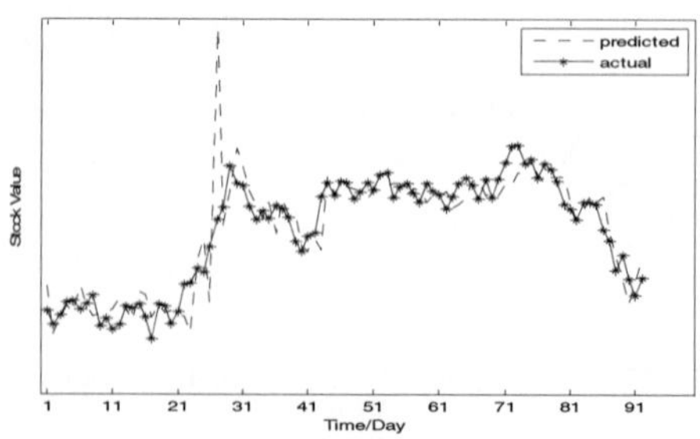

Fig. 6. The prediction effect of WNN network

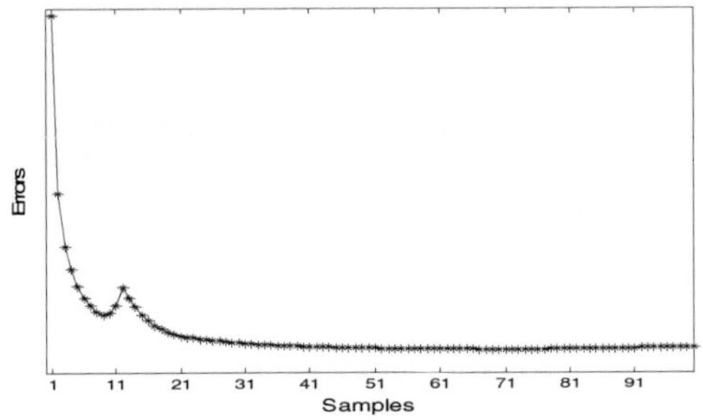

Fig. 7. The deviation curve of WNN network

We record the last 20 day's prediction data of the above neural network models and actual stock value in Table 2. Figure 8 shows the comparison of prediction errors.

Tab. 2. The prediction results of neural network models

Day	Pnn	Fuzzy	Wnn	BP	Closing price
1	5	2.42	5.42	4.68	5.97
2	6	2.37	5.54	4.48	6.08
3	6	1.74	5.55	4.82	6.17
4	6	2.09	5.63	4.05	6.22
5	6	2.41	5.75	4.45	6.28
6	6	1.89	5.96	4.98	6.56
7	6	1.80	5.89	4.39	6.45
8	6	1.93	6.07	4.36	6.63
9	7	2.27	6.03	4.09	6.46
10	7	1.69	6.53	4.48	6.7
11	7	1.67	6.56	4.48	6.71
12	7	1.99	6.22	4.48	6.71
13	7	2.52	6.21	4.69	6.75
14	7	2.22	6.59	4.76	6.97
15	7	2.69	7.04	4.50	7.19
16	7	2.06	7.13	4.50	7.19
17	7	2.49	7.21	4.81	7.29
18	7	2.25	7.08	4.64	7.15
19	7	2.01	7.22	4.85	6.87
20	7	1.90	8.01	4.55	7.25

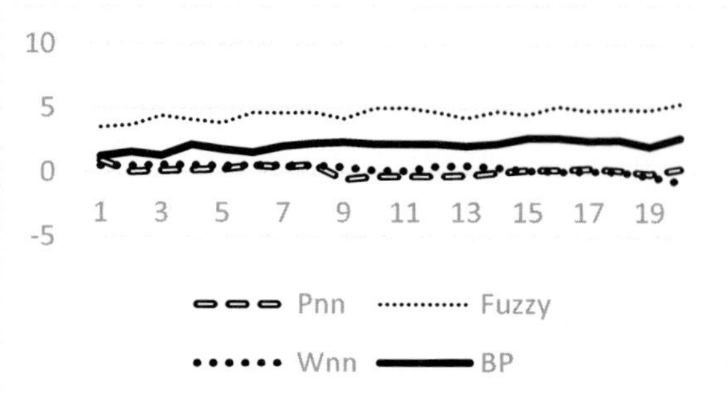

Fig. 8. The comparison of prediction errors

3. Conclusion

In this paper, we propose a optimal three-layer BP neural network model to forecast stock price trend and compare the prediction results of four kinds neural network models.

The probabilistic neural network model is very prominent in prediction accuracy, but it cannot provide investors with a timing of stock trading. Therefore, people usually apply it to the classification problems such as predicting the direction of stock prices' changing. The wavelet neural network has been widely used in various fields recently, it has not only good constringency rate but also high accuracy. The main difference between it and BP neural network model is the neurons in hidden layer. The disadvantage of the wavelet neural network is its poor stability. The fuzzy neural network has also been widely used, but it has the maximum experimental errors during the stimulation experiments. The reason why we do not choose it to predict the stock market trend is because it is more complexity than BP neural network and need more parameters during learning process.

Therefore, we can believe BP neural network has perfect learning capacity and generalization ability among variety approaches and it can be used to predict the stock market trend.

References

1. Tan et al (2005). Brain inspired genetic complimentary learning for stock market prediction. In IEEE congress on evolutionary computation, 2-5th September (Vol. 3, pp.2653-2660).
2. Cheng S, Li Z. The Chinese Stock Market Volume I[M]. Palgrave Macmillan UK, 2015.

3. Zhao J. The Empirical Study on Characteristics of QFII Holdings in China's Stock Market[C]. E-Product E-Service and E-Entertainment (ICEEE), 2010 International Conference on. IEEE, 2010:1 - 4.
4. Long W et al. Characteristics of different Styles and Sectors in China's Stock Market[M]. The Chinese Stock Market Volume Palgrave Macmillan UK, 2015:N1-7.
5. Malkiel B G. Reflections on the Efficient Market Hypothesis: 30 Years Later[J]. Financial Review, 2005, 40(1):1-9.
6. Galloppo G, Aliano M. Alternative Neural Network Approaches for Enhancing Stock Picking Using Earnings Forecasts[M]. Studies in banking and financial institutions. 2013:16.
7. Nenortaite J, Simutis R. Development and Evaluation of decision-Making Model for Stock Markets[J]. Journal of Global Optimization,2006, 36(1):1-19.
8. Cao Q, Parry M E, Leggio K B. The three-factor model and artificial neural networks: predicting stock price movement in China[J]. Annals of Operations Research, 2011, 185(185):25-44.
9. Miao.K, et al(2007). Stock price forecast based on bacterial colony RBF neural network. Journal of QingDao University, 20(2), 50-54.
10. Huo L, et al. A BP Neural Network Predictor Model for Stock Price[M]. Intelligent Computing Methodologies. 2014:362-368.
11. Sun Q, Che W G, Wang H L. Bayesian Regularization BP Neural Network Model for the Stock Price Prediction[M]. Foundations and Applications of Intelligent Systems. Springer Berlin Heidelberg,2014:521-531.
12. Owa K, Sharma S, Sutton R. A Wavelet Neural Network Based Non-linear Model Predictive Controller for a Multi-variable Coupled Tank System[J] International Journal of Automation&Computing, 201512(2).
13. Ramakrishnan S, Emary I M M E. Comparative study between traditional and modified probabilistic neural networks[J].Telecommunication Systems, 2009,40(1-2):67-74.
14. Kuo R J, Tseng Y S, Chen Z Y. Integration of fuzzy neural network and artificial immune system-based back-propagation neural network for sales forecasting using qualitative and quantitative data[J].Journal of Intelligent Manufacturing, 2014:1-17.
15. Zhang Y, Wu L. Stock market prediction of S&P 500 via combination of improved BCO approach and BP neural network[J]. Expert Systems with Applications An International Journal, 2009, 36 (5):8849-8854.

Structure Effects Modeling Method for C4ISR System Based on Information Flow Model

Jin-Feng Zhang[1,2,a], Fang Zhou[1,b] and Ming Lei[1,3,c]

[1]*Information Systems Engineering Laboratory*
Nanjing 210007, China
[2]*Collaborative Innovation Center of Novel Software Technology and Industrialization*
Nanjing 210007, China
[3]*Collaborative Innovation Center of Social Safety Science and Technology*
Nanjing 210007, China
E-mail: [a]zjfl9860506@163.com, [b]zf_lan8677@163.com, [c]storm_sky@126.com

Up against the performance effect of the C4ISR system structure produced by cyber threats, a structure effect modeling method for C4ISR systems based on information flow was proposed. Firstly, the effect concept of C4ISR system structure was elaborated in this paper, and proposed lowering effect and damage two attacks and three attack strategies, and a structure information flow model was established. On this basis, the mathematical model of the damage degree for system structure based on the information flow and mathematical model of fallback effect for system structure based on the information flow delay is proposed.

Keywords: Attack Strategy; Information Flow Model; Damage Effects; Fallback Effect.

1. Introduction

With the rapid development of emerging technologies and rapid changes of combat-style, C4ISR system has become the core of the system capacity, which is the focus of the war dominance contention, and is the primary goal attacked by the two sides [1-2]. C4ISR system is vulnerable to all kinds of Cyber threat of attack especially when the system enters C4ISR network era, so that part of the C4ISR system node failure, paralysis or damage [3] .Once a node is bound to suffer Cyber attacks, it will spread to other system nodes, which influences the ability and quality completing the task of the whole system [4]. How to assess the impact to C4ISR system caused by Cyber attacks is an effective way to measure the merits of C4ISR systems structure, but also is the key to enhance ability of C4ISR systems against the Cyber attacks.

However, the research about impact assessment on Cyber attack has just started; as a result there is a little theoretical appraisal methodology. Therefore, in order to effectively analyze the impact to the network C4ISR system brought by Cyber attacks, we combine a variety of attacks and attack strategies, and propose effects assessment method for C4ISR system structure based on information flow model, providing the analysis method for impact effectiveness of C4ISR systems suffered from Cyber attacks.

2. Connotation of C4ISR System Structure Effects

System structure effect means that the threat of cyberspace acting on communication networks elements, wireless transmission systems elements, data link applications, sensors, combat business processing system and so on in C4ISR systems. It causes elements of the system physical destruction "hard Injury" and sabotage battlefield communications network. Besides that wireless transmission link is interrupted or blocked, and information processing systems or weapons control units were paralyzed, those will cause that C4ISR system structure is destroyed and the operational efficiency of system structure is reduced and other phenomenon [5]. The effect is to show the impact on C4ISR system caused by Cyber threats from the level of system structure, focusing on the extent of the damage to the system structure.

According to the concept of structural effects of C4ISR systems, the structural effect of the system is divided into two forms: the system of structural damage effects, system structure fallback effect.

(1) Damage effects of system structure: analyze the cyberspace threat of injury to the system structure from the angle about cyberspace attacks on system integrity damage the structure.

(2) Fallback effect of system structure: it analyzes the impact to system structure efficiency caused by cyberspace threats from angle about Cyber attacks on the operating efficiency damage of system structure. The operating efficiency of system structure will be measured by the time of completing combat missions. Therefore the impact of cyberspace threats to system structural effects is equivalent to the impact of time completing the system tasks required.

3. Attack Model for C4ISR System Structure

According to the mechanism that Cyber attack wired networks, wireless networks, sensors, combat application system in battlefield C4ISR system, Cyber attack model will be mapped to the system structure attack, and established the Cyber attack model that system structure suffered.

(1) Propose the attack model for system structure

The network structure attack strategy can be divided into random attacks and deliberate attacks for the cyberspace attacker. The random attack is random to remove the network nodes or edges, because the attacker is "ignorant" on the system structure, so that only random attack system nodes or edges. While the deliberate attacks remove the network nodes or edges according to their importance, which means the attacker obtain all the information about the system structure. So the system nodes or edges will be attacked selectively with an important criterion.

However, the attacker can obtain communication network protocol, topology and some other related information through intelligence and reconnaissance, data interception, and other network monitoring and detection means in actual cyberspace confrontation environment. Because of the concealment of C4ISR systems and multiple levels security system, the attacker is difficult to obtain complete network structure information and only get partial information. Thus, the attacker will attack under the conditions of incomplete information, which means it can get part of the system structure information, and some system structure information is unknown [6].

From the perspective of cyberspace attack, the failure mode for network structure is divided into to the point and to the side, namely direct removal of nodes and edges. When the actual system structure suffering Cyber attacks, system nodes or edges are not completely fail, but information processing capacity of the system node decreased or the transmission efficiency of network link decreases, which means the system nodes and edges in the fallback state. For example, when the battlefield wired network node is attacked by low-intensity service, the network transmission link and the node is not completely interrupt or fail, but the network delay increases, which means network transmission descend of efficiency. Therefore, based on the traditional network attacks mode, this paper add the on the fallback attack mode of network nodes and edges.

Combining two aspects of the above analysis, this paper presents a model Cyber attacks incomplete information system structure suffered, including three kinds of attack strategies: random attack, deliberate attack, attack conditions, four kinds of attack: to the point of attack, go side attack, attack node fallback mode, while lowering effect of attacks, as shown in Table 1.

Tab. 1. System architecture attack and attack strategy

Attack mode	Random attack strategy	Deliberate attack strategy	Conditions attack strategy
delete point attack	random delete point attack	•the degree of priority to attack •number of priority referrals to attack	priority to attack random to attack
delete edge attack	random delete edge attack	•number of priority referrals to the side attacks	priority to edge attack random defringe attack
node fallback attack	random node fallback attack	•the degree of preference node fallback attack •medium priority node number fallback attack	priority node fallback attack random node fallback attack
edge fallback attack	random edge fallback attack	•number of priority referrals edge fallback attack	priority edge fallback attack random side fallback attack

Said node fallback attack, edge fallback attack and attack strategy is defined as follows:

Definition 1: node fallback attack: reduce their processing capacity, such as reducing data network routing forwarding capability of node, distribute intelligence service capacity of information processing system.

Definition 2: edge fallback attack: reduce edge's ability of information transmission, such as increasing the signal transmission delay of wireless transmission link.

Definition 3: random node/edge fallback attack strategy: randomly selected nodes or edges, reduce processing and transmission capacity of node/edge.

Definition 4: priority node/edge fallback attack strategy: The node/edge is in descending order of importance, and reduce processing and transmission capacity of node/edge.

4. Model for C4ISR System Structure Effect

4.1. *Information flow model*

C4ISR system is operating system essentially taken information interactions as the core, so you can describe the information effect through parameter characterize of "information flow" to.

Information flow is that information is spread and flow between the various systems entities, specifically the intelligence information, command information, control feedback information flow processes in the system.

In this article, the flow of information is the path of information procession or a link connected star to end by the information relationship. Based on C4ISR system business processes, information flows are divided into the intelligence information flow, command and control information flow and collaboration information flow [7]. To facilitate give the mathematical definitions of three kind information flows, let the information flow and $w = n_0 r_0 \ldots n_i r_i \ldots . n_k$ is a simple path (sequence of vertices in the path of non-repetition) from node n_0 to node n_k, abbreviated as $w(n_0, n_k)$. The following are three types of information flow modeling.

(1) Intelligence information flow

Intelligence information flow is an information processing path achieving security and intelligence shared between the reconnaissance unit and the decision control unit, the all intelligence and sharing relationships between the reconnaissance unit and the decision control unit uses the set ID represents.

Intelligence information flow is generated using Figure $G_{ID} = G[I \cup P \cup D]$ path $w_{ID}(i_i, d_j)$ in Figure G, which $i_i \in I$ was reconnaissance unit, $d_j \in D$ for decision-making control unit.

(2) Collaboration information flow

Collaborative information flow is an information processing path achieving synergy between execution units, the all collaborative information relationships between the execution units were represented by a collection AA. Collaboration information flow is generated using Figure $G_{AA} = G[D \cup A]$ path $w_{AA}(a_i, a_j)$ in Figure G, wherein, $a_i, a_j \in A$ in response to the execution unit.

(3) Command and control information flow

Command and control information flow a information processing path from reconnaissance unit, through information processing unit and decision control unit, and ultimately to respond to the execution unit, achieving the visualization-judge-Decision-Action (OODA). It represents a complete command and control chain. Command and control information is generated using the path $w_{IDA}(i_i, a_j)$, wherein $i_i \in I$ is the reconnaissance unit, $a_j \in A$ in response to the execution unit.

4.2. *Structure fallback effect modeling based on information flow delay*

Based on C4ISR system information flow model, from the transmission speed of system information flow the point of view, we calculates the change of time generating information flow the system around cyber attack (change amount of information flow latency) to characterize the effect of information.

(1)the information flow delay

The information flow delay is the sum of the unit processing delay and propagation delay between systems units that the information flow pass and its calculation model as follows in Eq(1).

$$delay(w) = \sum_{w} (n_i.Delay + r_i.Delay) \tag{1}$$

Where in the information flow $w = n_0 r_0 \ldots n_i r_i \ldots n_k$, suppose $p(v_i, v_j) = (v_i, v_s, \ldots, v_x, v_y, \ldots, v_t, v_j)$ represents a message flow system unit between v_i and v_j, the information flow delay is:

$$\begin{aligned} delay(p(v_i, v_j)) = {} & delay(v_i, v_s) + delay(v_s) + \ldots + delay(v_x) \\ & + delay(v_x, v_y) + \ldots + delay(v_t) + delay(v_t, v_j) \end{aligned} \tag{2}$$

For different kinds of information flow, information flow delay reflects different meanings. The intelligence information flow delay $delay(w_I)$ reflects the timeliness of the process that the information from the process to use. The collaboration information flow delay $delay(w_{AA})$ reflects the collaborating timeliness between the two actors. The command and control information flow delay $delay(w_{IDA})$ reflects the timeliness of OODA process.

(1) Calculated before and after the attack traffic delay

System after suffering network electromagnetic attack, three types of information flow delays will be extended to varying degrees. Therefore, the key of calculating information flow delay after the attack is that quantify attack threat to the computing model to three types of information flow delays. Based on the network electromagnetic attack model system suffered, information flow delays were calculated under four categories, namely delete point attack, delete edge attack, edge node fallback attack and edge fallback attack.

Where the node fallback attack impact on the system information flow delays is reflected in the delay increase that node process information, leading all information flow through the node delays extended.

Edge fallback attack effects on the system information flow delay is reflected in increased delay communication link transmitting information, leading all information flow through the edge delays extended.

(2) The structure fallback effect Model based on the system information flow delay

After system suffering node/link a denial of service and blocking attacks, intelligence information flow delay, command and control information flow delay and collaboration information flow delay will extend differently. Thus, according to the method above-described, three types of information flow delay were calculated after attacked, and establish effect model based on the information flow delay, details as follows:

The fallback effect model of system structure based on the average of intelligence information flow delay:

$$\Delta Delay_{OD} = Delay_{OD}{}' - Delay_{OD} = \frac{1}{N_I}\sum_{i=1}^{N_I} Delay(d_j, I)' - \frac{1}{N_I}\sum_{i=1}^{N_I} Delay(d_j, I) \quad (3)$$

The fallback effect model of system structure based on the average of command and control information flow delay:

$$\Delta Delay_{ODA} = Delay_{ODA}{}' - Delay_{ODA} = \frac{1}{N_D}\sum_{a_k \in A} Delay(a_k, Ia_k^*)' - \frac{1}{N_D}\sum_{a_k \in A} Delay(a_k, Ia_k^*) \quad (4)$$

The fallback effect model of system structure based on the average of collaboration information flow delay:

$$\Delta Delay_{AA} = Delay_{AA}{}' - Delay_{AA} = \frac{1}{N_A}\sum_{(a_i,a_j)\in A} Delay(a_i, a_j)' - \frac{1}{N_A}\sum_{(a_i,a_j)\in A} Delay(a_i, a_j) \quad (5)$$

The fallback effect model of system structure based on the average of all three kinds of information flow delay:

$$\Delta Delay = \varepsilon_1 \times \Delta Delay_{OD} + \varepsilon_2 \times \Delta Delay_{ODA} + \varepsilon_3 \times \Delta Delay_{AA} \quad (6)$$

5. Conclusion

Under the node fallback attack mode, the delay of three types of information flow changed slowly, no matter what strategy. And the delay variation of command and control information flow is relatively large, because the command and control information flow is a complete command and control chain from observer to execution unit through decision maker, and any unit fallback in the system will increase the delay of information flow. At the same time, because the system unit has not been attacked fails completely, backup/successor mechanism the system unit is not enabled made, so the delay of system information flow is shown increasing when the number of attack nodes increase.

References

1. Yushi Lan. Understanding the Network-Centered Command Information System[J].Command Information System and Technology,2010,1(1): 1-4.
2. Shaojie Mao, Kebo Deng, Heng Wang, Kan Yi. Complexity of Net-Centric and Service-Oriented C4ISR System[J]. Command Information System and Technology, 2012, 3(4): 1-6.
3. DOD.Department of defensedictionary of mil itaryand associated terms [M].Washington D.C.: DOD, 2014.
4. United States Army Combined Arms Center. Cyber el ectro magnetic Activities[R].Washington D.C.: Department of Army, 2014.
5. U.S.Army Capabil ities Integration Center.Cyberspace operations concept capabil ity pl an 2016-2028[R].Washington D.C. Department of Army, 2010.
6. Kan Yi, Heng Wang, etc. Information Flow based Survivability Assessment Method for Networked C4ISR System Structure [J]. System Engineering Electronics, 2014, 36(8):1544-1550.
7. Yushi Lan, Kan Yi, Heng Wang, etc., Delay assessment method for networked C~4ISR system architecture [J], System Engineering Electronics, 2013, 35(9):1908-1914.

Research of Software Defect Prediction Technology Based on Complexity

Xue-Jing Ding[a] and Liang-Fen Wei[b]
Department of Computer Science and Technology, Anhui Sanlian University
Anhui Hefei, China
E-mail: [a]330545497@qq.com, [b]649489564@qq.com

Software defect prediction technology is designed to automatically detect whether the program module contains defects, so as to improve the quality of the software system. In view of the current LASSO feature selection method, limitations exist in the complexity metrics attributes selection, so LARS algorithm is added. This makes the complexity metrics attributes selected to be more concise and representative. The optimized metrics attributes are better in both the computation time and the software defect prediction capability.

Keywords: Software Defect Prediction; LASSO; LARS; SVM.

1. Introduction

With the increasing scale of software system and its logic complexity of growing, the defects of potential and not found in software will affect the quality of software. Through the research of software defect prediction technology [1], we can count the number of defects and defect distribution in the system, so that it can help the tester to evaluate the performance of the software.

In this paper, based on the traditional LASSO feature selection method [2], the LARS algorithm is added, which makes the attributes of software complexity metrics selected more concise and more representative. By experiment on the SVM prediction model, the optimized measure attributes is better in both the computation time and the software defect prediction capability.

2. Feature Selection of Software Complexity Metrics Based on Lasso Method

The basic idea of lasso is that under the constraint conditions of absolute value of regression coefficient is less than a constant value, to minimize the sum of squared residuals which can produce some strict regression coefficient is equal to zero, obtained the model that can be explained last.

The core of Feature selection method is to reduce the dimension of the observed variables [3], and exclude observed variables which have the smaller influence factor. Its essence is to add some constraints, to set the regression coefficients of observed variables which have smaller influence factor to 0. The constraint conditions are different, which make up the different feature selection methods.

Firstly, the LASSO feature selection problem is constructed based on software modules and complexity metrics attributes which constitute the date set of software complexity metrics. Secondly, according to the requirement of constraint conditions of the LASSO method on the results, combined with the data attributes of complexity metrics that need to deal with, using LARS algorithm[4] of iterations to obtain a certain number of Lasso problem solution. The Lasso problem solution is the complexity metrics attribute subsets which have the greatest impact on the software defect prediction model construct. Research ideas are shown in Figure 1:

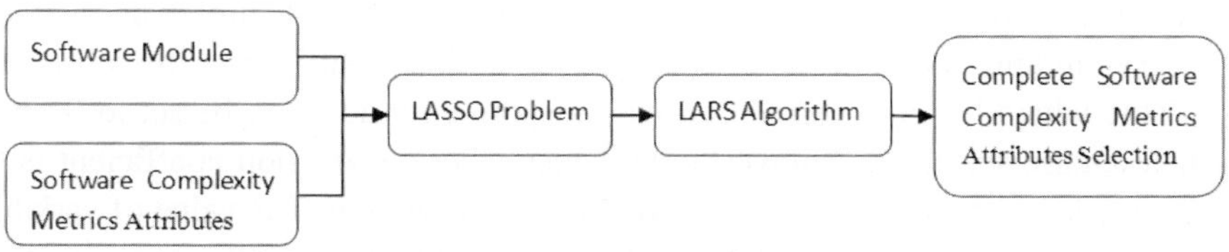

Fig. 1. Research ideas of software feature selection

2.1. *LASSO method*

Use LASSO method first need to center standardized processing on complexity metrics attributes data set, to eliminate the influence of different index dimension, make it meet the following requirements, in Eq.(1).

$$\sum_{i=1}^{n} y_i = 0, \sum_{i=1}^{n} x_{ij} = 0, \sum_{i=1}^{n} x_{ij}^2 = 1, j = 1, \cdots, m \quad (1)$$

Where y_i is attribute variable of 0-1. It is used to reflect the module of data set whether there is a defect module. x_i is complexity metrics attribute value of software module. Variable m is the number of module attributes in complexity metrics data set. Variable n is the number of module for data set.

Define the sum of the squared differences, in Eq. (2):

$$S(\hat{\beta}) = \left\| Y - \hat{\mu} \right\| = \sum_{i=1}^{n} (y_i - \hat{\beta}_0 - \hat{\mu}_i)^2, \hat{\mu} = X \hat{\beta} = x_{ij} \hat{\beta}_j \tag{2}$$

Where yi is called response variable, xi= (xi1, xi2…xin) is called Observed variables, $\hat{\beta}_j$ is regression coefficient of j-th complexity metric attributes. Its significance is that under the fixed condition of other complexity metrics attribute, the impact generated on variable yi as each add a complexity metrics attribute. $\hat{\beta}_0$ is a random variable, it is usually assumed to obey the standard normal distribution.

Assume sum of the $\hat{\beta}$ absolute value following, in Eq. (3):

$$T(\hat{\beta}) = \sum_{j=1}^{m} \left| \hat{\beta}_j \right| \le t \tag{3}$$

LASSO method is under the constraint condition of $T(\hat{\beta}) \le t$, by adjusting the regression coefficient and β_j of each variable, to calculate the least sum of square difference between response variable y_i and regression variable μ, that is to calculate the least value of S (β), this process is the LASSO problems.

By adding the constraints (3) on regression coefficient, the observed variable which has low correlation with response variable can be set to 0.Thus when feature selection, remove the variables whose regression coefficient is 0, and only keep the variables which have strong correlation. The value of variable t is between 0 and ∞. When the value of variable t is small, some variable coefficient which have low relevant is compressed to 0 and then will be removed, to achieve the purpose of feature selection; When the value of variable t is large enough, will no longer have the function of the constraints, at this time all attributes will be selected and formed a variable selection sequence.

2.2. *LARS algorithm*

LARS algorithm is based on the regression residuals to choose a new variable; the process is a process of continuous reduction of the residual, with a high computational efficiency. The basic idea is: first select a observed variable which have the largest correlation with response variable, the corresponding physical meaning is to choose the complexity metrics attributes which have the greatest impact on whether the software have defect. Then walk along this direction for a certain length, until the second observed variables. If the two observed variables have same correlations with the residual, then go continue along with the direction which have same angle with the two variables, and so on, choose the required observed variables.

Algorithm steps as follows:

- All the regression coefficient $\hat{\beta}_j$ which is corresponding with complexity metrics attributes is set to 0, and then find the observed variables called x_{j1} that is most relevant with response variables y_i.
- To maximize the $\hat{\beta}_j$ along the direction of this observation variable, until you find another observation variable called x_{j2} that is most relevant to the current residual $r = y - \mu_i$
- $\hat{\beta}_j$ increased along the direction of (x_{j1},x_{j2}), until the emergence of third observed variable xj3 which is most relevant to the current residual.
- Continued increased along the direction of (x_{j1},x_{j2},x_{j3}),until the emergence of fourth observed variables, and so on.

A feature sequence can be obtained by realizing the algorithm above on software complexity metrics data set. When constraint value t is large enough, path will contain all of the variables, and then will get feature sequence which is ordered, that is the feature analysis of LARS algorithm for software complexity metrics data set.

3. Software Defect Prediction Model Based on Svm

The basic idea of SVM (support vector machine) [5] is to find the kernel function and the two programming problem. Through kernel function, the data can be mapped to high dimensional feature space to solve the nonlinear problem. Radial basis function (RBF) has a wide range of convergence, which is the ideal classification basis function. Its expression is in Eq. (4):

$$K(x_i, x_j) = \exp(-\gamma\|x_i - x_j\|^2, \gamma > 0 \qquad (4)$$

Where x and x_i are feature vectors, γ is the broadband of radial basis function.

In the two classification problems, assuming a given training set in Eq. (5):

$$T = \{(x_1, y_1), \cdots (x_k, y_k)\} \in (R^n \times y)^k \qquad (5)$$

Where xi∈Rn, yi∈Y= {+1,-1},i=1,2,…,k, xi is feature vector, yi is category label. Solving of decision function will be transformed into the solving of two planning problems with constraint conditions using SVM, as shown in Eq. (6).

$$\min_{\alpha} \frac{1}{2}\sum_{i=1}^{k}\sum_{j=1}^{k} y_i y_j K(x_i, x_j)\alpha_i \alpha_j - \sum_{j=1}^{k}\alpha_j \text{ s.t. } \sum_{i=1}^{k} y_i \alpha_j = 0, 0 \le \alpha_i \le C, i = 1,2,\cdots,k \tag{6}$$

Where αi and αj are Lagrange Multiplier, K(xi,xj) is kernel function.

The solution of the equation is:α*=(α1*,…,αk*)T, the value of b* in decision tree is shown in Eq.(7):

$$b^* = y_j - \sum_{i=1}^{k} y_i \alpha_i^* K(x_i, y_j) \tag{7}$$

Decision function as shown in Eq. (8):

$$f(x) = \text{sgn}(\sum_{i=1}^{k} y_i \alpha_i^* K(x_i, x) + b^*) \tag{8}$$

This paper introduces the idea of SVM to implement the software defect prediction. There is a certain mapping relation between the number of defects contained in software module and complexity metrics attributes. Using SVM algorithm to train the software module attribute value which has error prone, make it corresponding to the error rate of software module, and then forming a black box model. Using this model to predict the error prone of the rest of the software module can achieve the purpose of forecasting software defects.

Software defect prediction process:

Obtain software complexity metrics attribute data set;

- Using LASSO-LARS method to reduce dimension, and get a simple subset of attributes;
- Building the framework of the SVM system;
- Using the attribute subset that obtained with the method of using cross validation algorithm combined with LASSO-LARS feature selection to train SVM related parameters.
- The test samples are input to the trained SVM system to carry out the software defect prediction.
- Experiment end, and output the classification results of software defect prediction.

4. Experiment

In this paper, 10-fold cross validation algorithm is used to carry out to optimize the penalty parameter C and kernel function parameter g of SVM. Firstly the training subset were divided into 10 groups, each subset data will be a validation set respectively, and the rest of the nine groups of subset data as the training set to train the SVM classifier, and finally get the accuracy rate average of all classification.

5. Conclusions

The contribution of this paper is introducing a new feature selection method to the software defect prediction. There exist a lot of complexity metric attributes which have little effect on analyzing results in the raw data, to simplify and optimize these attributes, retain only a small part of these attributes which have huge effect on analyzing results. We not only save the computing time, and to a certain extent, it is possible to improve the ability of software defect prediction.

Acknowledgments

It is supported by the Natural Science Key Fund Project of Education Department of Anhui Province (NO: KJ2016A252)

References

1. Challagulla V U B, Bastani F B,I-Ling Yen, Paul R A. Empirical assessment of machine learning based software defect prediction techniques// Proceedings of the 10th IEEE International Workshop on Object-Oriented Real-Time Dependable System. Washington. DC. USA. 2005:263-270.
2. KAYNAR D, LYNCH N, SEGALA R, et al. The theory of timed I/O automata [M]. [S.I.]: Morgan & Claypool Publishers.2005.
3. Shengli Jiang. Research on feature selection and feature extraction of high dimension data [D].Xi'an: Xidian University, 2011.(In Chinese)
4. EFRON B, HASTIE T, JOHNSTONE I, et al. Least angle regression [J]. Journal of the Institute of Mathematical Statistics, 2004, 32(2):407-499.
5. Junxue He. Research on software reliability model based on support vector machine [D].Lanzhou: Lanzhou University of Technology, 2009.(In Chinese)

Improved Dijkstra Algorithm Based on Fibonacci Heap for Solving the Shortest Path Problem with Specified Nodes

Shuai-Lei Guo[1,a], Jin Duan[1,b,*], Yong Zhu[2,c], Xiu-Chang Li[1,d] and Tian-Wei Chen[1,e]

[1]*Institute of space photovoltaic, Changchun University of Science and Technology Changchun, Jilin, China*

[2]*Institute of computer, Changchun University of Science and Technology Changchun, Jilin, China*

E-mail: [a]598189752@qq.com, [b]duanjin@vip.sina.com, [c]zhy991112@sina.com, [d]943051273@qq.com, [e]635226729@qq.com

The classical Dijkstra algorithm of graph theory only applies to solve single-source shortest path problem. Common Dijkstra algorithm will no longer apply if the shortest path must go through a specified set of nodes. This paper presents an interpolation algorithm based on improved Dijkstra algorithm which can solve the problem of obtaining the shortest path visiting a given set of nodes. This algorithm uses the Fibonacci heap to improve ordinary Dijkstra algorithm, and causes the given set of nodes to find the best insertion position sequentially. The nodes are then inserted using optimized Dijkstra algorithm. Finally, the shortest path approach can be generated through the specified set of nodes. Experimental results show that this algorithm can find the path which has smaller weight in a relatively low time complexity.

Keywords: Dijkstra; Shortest Path; Specified Set of Nodes; Fibonacci Heap; Interpolation.

1. Introduction

Dijkstra EW.A put forward famous Dijkstra algorithm in 1959[1]. This is a classic single-source shortest path algorithm for calculating the shortest path from one node to all other nodes. The main idea is using the principle of greed and making the start point as the center layers extend outward, until extend to the end point. The traditional Dijkstra algorithm based on adjacency matrix

---

*Corresponding author.

requires a huge network data storage space, which will lead to the space complexity of the algorithm greatly increased. Even if use the adjacent table network storage structure, it has no slightest improvement for time complexity of the algorithm in essence when improving storage needs and space complexity. The time complexity of the algorithm is the most important factor to measure the efficiency of an algorithm. Although the Dijkstra algorithm based on adjacency table can reduce some operational steps, but the time complexity of the algorithm is still O(n2), where n is the number of nodes[2].

Fanding Duan put forward SPFA algorithm in 1994[3]. The principle is using priority queue as the storage pool of nearest candidate nodes, and using the features that the head of queue always store the most recent node to reduce the time complexity of traditional Dijkstra algorithm when it find the nearest node each time. Verification results show that the time complexity of the algorithm is O((m + n) log m), where n is the number of nodes and m is the number of arcs. Concern the dense graph has larger values of m, time complexity of the algorithm is still high. Feng Lu put forward improved Dijkstra algorithm based on quad heap priority queue in 1999[4]. The principle is using a complete quad-tree realize priority queue, reducing the time complexity of decrease-key operation in priority queue. Verification results show that the time complexity of the algorithm can be reduced to O((m + n) log n).

Michael L. Fredman and Robert E. Tarjan developed Fibonacci heaps in 1984 and published them in a scientific journal in 1987[5]. For the Fibonacci heap, the find-minimum operation takes constant (O(1)) amortized time. The insert and decrease key operations also work in constant amortized time. Deleting an element (most often used in the special case of deleting the minimum element) works in O(log n) amortized time, where n is the size of the heap. In this paper, use Fibonacci heap as a priority queue to improve Dijkstra algorithm. Verification results show that the time complexity can be reduced to O(m + n log n).

Current graph algorithm research for the problem of shortest path visiting specified nodes is less. Shuli Huang gave a way to solve such problems based on Dijkstra algorithm and greedy theory[6]. The algorithm make source node, destination node and specified nodes as three subsets, seeking the partial shortest path communicating three subsets respectively, thereby forming a global candidate shortest path. However, use the greedy principle directly to find the shortest path of subsequent nodes in order easily lead to path be occupied, eventually leading to the situation that no solution or path weight is too large.

This paper presents an improved algorithm. Let the specified nodes try to insert each position which can be inserted using the improved Dijkstra algorithm and calculate the appropriate weights, finally choose the position which has minimum weights to insert. It can avoid the situation that path is occupied ahead and cause no solution. At the same time It can greatly reduce the total weight of the path and make it tends to be the optimal solution.

2. Optimization of Dijkstra Algorithm and Generation of Shortest Path with Specified Nodes

2.1. *Dijkstra algorithm optimized by fibonacci heap*

2.1.1. *Creation of fibonacci heap and manipulation of the heap*

Fibonacci heap is the collection of minimum heap and ordered tree in computer science. It has similar properties with Binomial heap, which can be used to implement the merger of priority queue. The key idea of the Fibonacci heap is that delay to maintain the heap as much as possible. For example, it don't merge the tree, instead, the job is left to be operated by EXTRACT-MIN when inserting a new node to Fibonacci heap or merging two Fibonacci heap.

Every node x in Fibonacci heap has the following contents:

- Node value x,
- Parent p[x],
- Pointer child[x] pointing to any child (children of node x are linked into a ring-shaped and double-linked list, called child table of x),
- Left brother left[x],
- Right brother right[x] (when left[x] = right[x] = x, description x is an only child),
- The number of children degree[x],
- Boolean range mark[x] (mark whether lost a child).

The structure of stack H:

- Number of nodes n[H],
- Pointer *min pointing to minimum node.

The main operations content of the Fibonacci heap include heap creation, insertion and deletion of nodes, getting the lowest node and decreasing the keywords.

The pseudo-code of creating a Fibonacci heap is as follows:

```
Make-Fibonacci-Heap()
  n[H] := 0
  min[H] := NIL
  return H
```

After inserting a node x, initializing each domain of node, assignment, and then construct their own circular doubly linked list, x will join the root table of H . Pseudo-code as follows:

```
Fibonacci-Heap-Insert(H, x)
 degree[x] := 0
 p[x] := NIL
 child[x] := NIL
 left[x] := x
 right[x] := x
 mark[x] := FALSE
 concatenate the root list containing x with root list H
 if min[H] = NIL or key[x]<key[min[H]]
  then min[H] := x
 n[H]:= n[H]+1
```

Figure. 1 shows that a node is inserted into Fibonacci heap whose keyword is 21. The node becomes a minimum heap ordered tree with itself, which is added to the root table, as left brother of the root.

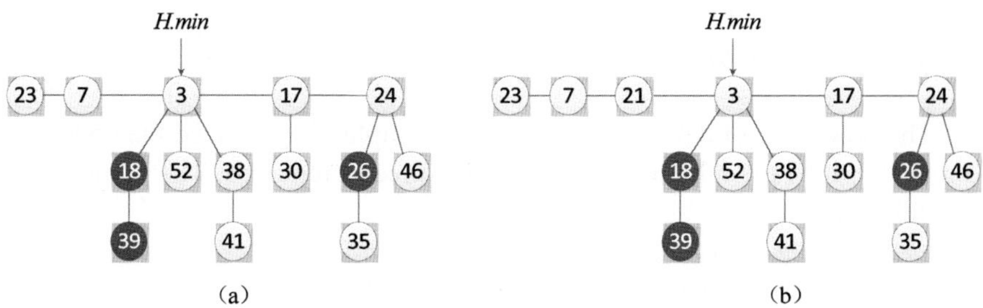

Fig. 1. A node is inserted into Fibonacci heap.

The pseudo-code of obtaining minimum node is as follows:

```
Fibonacci-Heap-Minimum(H)
 return min[H]
```

The basic process of reducing the keywords is as follows: Cut the node if it destroy the character of the minimum heap after being reduced. That is, remove the node from the doubly linked list where it is in and insert it into the doubly linked list which is formed by the minimum root nodes, and then performed cascade prune recursively from parent [x] to the root node. The pseudo-code is as follows:

```
CUT(H,x,y)
 Remove x from the child list of y, decrementing degree[y]
```

```
  Add x to the root list of H
  p[x]:= NIL
  mark[x]:= FALSE
CASCADING-CUT(H,y)
  z:= p[y]
  if z <> NIL
    then if mark[y] = FALSE
      then mark[y]:= TRUE
      else CUT(H, y, z)
        CASCADING-CUT(H, z)
Fibonacci-Heap-Decrease-Key(H,x,k)
  if k > key[x]
    then error "new key is greater than current key"
  key[x] := k
  y := p[x]
  if y <> NIL and key[x]<key[y]
    then CUT(H, x, y)
      CASCADING-CUT(H,y)
  if key[x]<key[min[H]]
    then min[H] := x
```

The procedure of deleting a node is very simple, first reduced the node until to min [H], then the minimum value can be directly removed. The pseudo-code is as follows:

```
Fibonacci-Heap-Delete(H,x)
  Fibonacci-Heap-Decrease-Key(H,x,-infinity)
  Fibonacci-Heap-Extract-Min(H)
```

2.1.2. *Fibonacci heap on optimization of dijkstra algorithm*

Dijkstra algorithm optimized by Fibonacci heap mainly use the feature of Fibonacci heap has O(1) amortized time without deletion of elements operating, optimized algorithm steps is as follows:

(1) The source weight is set to 0, the other nodes weight are set to infinity;
(2) Insert source node into Fibonacci heap, then mark it in the heap and has found the shortest path to it;
(3) Obtain the node who has minimum weight if the heap is not empty and name it minR, mark source node as precursor of minR, and mark minR as the node who has found the shortest path, otherwise end of the process;

(4) Find the nodes adjacent to minR in the adjacency table who did not been marked as having found the shortest path. Calculate that whether the weight between the nodes and minR plus the weight of minR is less than its own weight. If is , update the nodes' weight and mark minR as precursor of the nodes. Reduce the nodes' weight as their keywords if they are already in the heap, otherwise insert the nodes into Fibonacci heap and mark them in the heap;
(5) Remove minR from the heap, skip to step (3).

2.2. *Using interpolation method for solving the shortest path with specified nodes*

The specified nodes take the way of exhaustive searching which position can be inserted and choosing the minimum weight position to insert after comparing the weight when inserted. The insertion position include the position between source and adjacent specified node, the position between two specified nodes, the position between destination and adjacent specified node. So make sure the number and location of specified nodes in the generated path before inserting.

Specific steps of inserting the specified nodes:

(1) Take the first specified node, generate the shortest path from source to it using the improved Dijkstra algorithm and mark the nodes in the path is accessed, then generate the shortest path from the node to destination using the improved Dijkstra algorithm and mark the nodes in the path is accessed;
(2) Find the number of specified nodes in the path and mark the location of each specified node;
(3) See whether next specified node is in the path. If is, skip this node and view next one. Otherwise, traversal insert this node into the position where can be inserted and calculate the weight of the path. Erase the access mark of the original nodes on the path before inserting. Finally, insert this node into the minimum weight position on the path;
(4) Skip to step (2) circulating until all specified nodes are inserted, and ultimately generate a complete shortest path.

Figure. 2 is a process schematic of looking for the best insertion position for the second specified node after inserting the first specified node into the path. Where S is the source node, T is the destination node, A is the first specified node, B is the second specified node who will be inserted after the first specified node.

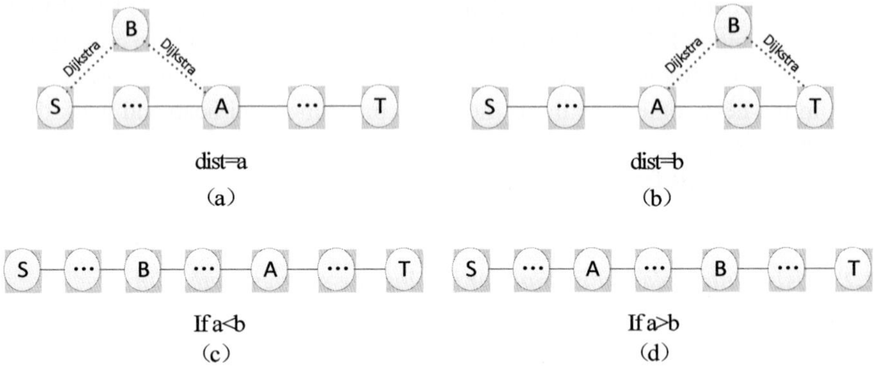

Fig. 2. The process schematic of inserting specified nodes.

3. Analysis of Experiment Results

The experimental environment of this paper is as follows:

- CPU: Intel i3-2350CPU 2.3GHz,
- RAM: 2GB,
- Translater: gcc 4.8.4,
- Operating system: Linux Ubuntu 14.04.3 LTS 64-bit.

3.1. *Comparison and analysis of the experiment results for optimized dijkstra algorithm*

Experiments using three different sizes of network topology data separately validate ordinary Dijkstra algorithm, Dijkstra algorithm optimized by priority queue, Dijkstra algorithm optimized by quad stack and Dijkstra algorithm optimized by Fibonacci heap.

The size of three experimental data is as follows:

- Topology 1: 1000 nodes, 20000 edges,
- Topology 2: 10000 nodes, 200,000 edges,
- Topology 3: 50000 nodes, 1 million edges.

The out degree of each node in the three topology is 20.

Analyze the optimization efficiency by comparing these algorithms. The experimental results are shown in Table. 1.

Tab. 1. Comparison of the efficiency for different methods to optimize the Dijkstra algorithm.

Scale of the data	1000 nodes	10000 nodes	50000 nodes
Method of optimization		Time consuming / ms	
Ordinary	8	321	836
Priority queue	3	75	124
Quad heap	1	32	58
Fibonacci heap	1	25	29

It's evident to analyze the experimental results from Table. 1, there are little different between the time-efficient of these several optimization method in small-scale data. When the data size increases to a certain extent, the superiority of Dijkstra algorithm optimized by Fibonacci heap began to show. It can be concluded that the search for the shortest path of single source in large-scale dense network topology, the Dijkstra algorithm optimized by Fibonacci heap can greatly save search time.

3.2. *Comparison and analysis of the experiment results for interpolation algorithm and combinatorial sorting algorithm of the specified nodes*

Experiments using three different sizes of network topology data which have specified nodes separately validate the method proposed by Shuli Huang that constitute and range the specified nodes to generate the shortest path using Dijkstra algorithm and the method proposed by this paper that find the optimal position to insert the specified nodes using Dijkstra algorithm for generating the shortest path.

The size of three experimental data is as follows:

- Topology 4: 500 nodes, 5 specified nodes, 10000 edges,
- Topology 5: 1000 nodes, 20 specified nodes, 20000 edges,
- Topology 6: 2000 nodes, 100 specified nodes, 40000 edges.

The out degree of each node is 20 and the weight of each edge is range from 1 to 100 in the three topology.

Analyze the efficiency by comparing this two algorithms. The experimental results are shown in Table. 2.

Tab. 2. Comparison of interpolation algorithm and combinatorial sorting algorithm.

Scale of the data	500 nodes	1000 nodes	5000 nodes
Path generation algorithm	Time consuming / ms, weight of path		
Combinatorial sorting	4872, 169	$>10^6$, 644	$>10^9$,----
interpolation	7, 169	3875, 558	13937, 3621

It's evident to analyze the experimental results from Table. 2, there are little different between the weight of paths generated by this two algorithms when the number of specified nodes is few. But the time efficiency of interpolation algorithm is better than combinatorial sorting algorithm evidently. The time complexity of combinatorial sorting algorithm is too large to give a specific path when there are a large number of specified nodes. It can be concluded that interpolation algorithm is better than combinatorial sorting algorithm in time efficiency and the weights of the paths. Interpolation algorithm is a fast and efficient algorithm to find the shortest path with specified nodes.

4. Conclusions

The shortest path problem with specified nodes is a special case of the "Traveling salesman problem", and also is a NP-Hard problem. So far there is no algorithm can accurately obtain a minimum solution in polynomial time, so look for a fast algorithm for the approximate solution is the necessary way to solve such problems.

After verification, the shortest path method based on the Dijkstra algorithm optimized by Fibonacci heap to interpolate the specified nodes proposed by this paper is a simple and efficient algorithm for obtaining the shortest path with specified nodes. Currently, integer linear programming solver is used more on the market. Integer linear programming algorithm is characterized by speed, excellent results, the disadvantage is that it need to build mathematical model for the problem[7]. Although the algorithm proposed by this paper is not as good as integer linear programming on the precision of results, but eliminates the need of modeling for the problem and makes solving step easier.

The algorithm proposed by this paper is suitable for solving small and medium size shortest path problem with specified nodes, it should be improved for solving the large-scale problem. This algorithm needs to be improved continually in time efficiency and accuracy of the result.

References

1. Dijkstra E W. A note on two problems in connexion with graphs[J]. Numerische mathematik, 1959, 1(1): 269-271.
2. Weimin Yan, Weimin Wu, classification, etc. Data structure (C language version)[J]. Computer education, 2012, 12: 017, (In Chinese).
3. Fanding Duan. SPFA fast algorithm for shortest path[J]. Southwest Jiaotong University, 1994, 29 (2): 207-212, (In Chinese).
4. Feng Lu, Dongmei Lu. Improved Dijkstra algorithm based on quad heap priority queues and the reverse adjacency table[J]. Chinese Journal of Image and Graphics: A Series, 1999, 4 (12): 1044-1049, (In Chinese).
5. Fredman M L, Tarjan R E. Fibonacci heaps and their uses in improved network optimization algorithms[J]. Journal of the ACM (JACM), 1987, 34(3): 596-615.
6. Shuli Huang, Dasha Hu, Yuming Jiang. Algorithm for finding shortest path which must go through specified intermediate node set. Computer Engineering and Applications, 2015, 51(11): 41-46, In Chinese.
7. de Andrade R C. Elementary shortest-paths visiting a given set of nodes[J]. Simpósio Brasileiro de Pesquisa Operacional, 16-19.

Boiler Drum Water Level Warning Method Based on D-S Evidence Theory

Xi Ma[1,3,a], Fei Xia[1,2,3,b,*], Hao Zhang[1,2,3], Dao-Gang Peng[1,3], Zhi-Jiang Luo[1,3], Peng Sun[1,3], Yuan Bo[1,3] and Zhi-Cheng Wang[1,3]

[1]*College of Automation Engineering, Shanghai University of Electric Power Shanghai, China*

[2]*School of Electronic and Information, Tongji University Shanghai, China*

[3]*Shanghai Engineering Research Center of Intelligent Management and Control for Power Process, Shanghai, China*

E-mail: [a]maxiyolo1023@163.com, [b]xiafeiblue@163.com

One of the important parameters to ensure the safe operation of boiler is the boiler drum water level in the thermal power plant, which is also a difficult one to measure due to the actual constrained situation. So it has practical significance to improve the accuracy and reliability of the boiler drum water level alarm. Through the study of the boiler drum water level alarm system, this paper proposes a new method based on D-S (Dempster-Shafer) evidence theory combined with fuzzy function and neural network in order to prevent a malfunction leak seized false detection by the single diagnostic method. Firstly, the boiler drum water level has been fuzzed. Then BP (Propagation Back) neural network and RBF (Basis Function Radial) neural network are respectively used to determine the alarm type. Finally, the diagnostic results of two neural networks are combined by the D-S evidence theory to determine the ultimate alarm type. Through the simulation experiment, the accuracy of the boiler drum water level alarm is higher than that of the current method and is also higher than that of a single neural network diagnostic method.

Keywords: Boiler; Drum Water Level; Alarm; D-S Evidence Theory; Neural Network.

---

*Corresponding author.

1. Introduction

Boiler drum water level is the key component of power generation control system in thermal power plant, the well or badly of the control unit of the boiler drum water level will directly affect the safe operation of the thermal power unit. The drum water level is too high to damage the steam turbine blade by the steam water; the drum water level is so low that the boiler water wall is short of water and the heated exchange surface blasts. The accidents caused by the unreliability of the alarm system will cause serious economic losses. A variety of mechanical vibration causes measurement errors in boiler feed water flow and steam flow. In spite of various intelligent technology such as the neural network have been introduced into the boiler drum water level alarm system. Although the BP neural network algorithm with high precision can quickly learn the feedback of multilayer feed forward network. But because its mathematical foundation has the problem of nonlinear optimization, it is possible to fall into the local minimum area [1]. RBF neural network algorithm with the best approximation properties has a quick learning speed, but due to limited training samples the actual alarm is still not accurate [2].

The boiler drum water level alarm system with fusion technology is studied in this paper. Firstly, fuzzy set theory is applied to get the membership function of the boiler drum water level alarm type. It is the neural network that completes local fault diagnosis. Independent evidences are obtained. And the D-S evidence theory is used to decision fusion. It is beneficial to use the advantages of the redundant and complementary information among the various data sources, which can improve the accuracy and robustness of decision system [3]. Thus it will provide an effective way to improve the accuracy of alarm system. The study of the boiler drum water level alarm system verifies the accuracy of the alarm type based on the information fusion, and effectively avoids the misdiagnosis situation [4].

2. Drum Level Alarm Method Based on D-S Evidence Theory

The recognition framework is judged by some unrelated evidence sets. Then two or more basic probability assignment functions are fused by the Dempster combination rule. When determining the alarm type of boiler steam drum water level, the judgment of BP and RBF neural network in the same time are fused to get more accurate alarm results.

Different alarm results which obtained by diagnosis methods structure the basic probability assignment (BPA) functions of the evidences for D-S evidence theory fusion. Structural method [5] is as Ep. (1):

$$m_i(j) = \frac{C_i(j)}{\sum_j C_i(j)} \times R(i). \tag{1}$$

j indicates the boiler drum water level alarm type, i indicates the method i for determining the alarm type. $C_i(j)$ indicates the diagnosis output that applies the method i for determining the alarm type j . $R(i)$ indicates the reliability coefficient of determining the alarm type by method i .

So the Ep. (1). is used to construct the basic probability assignment functions which are composed of two independent sources of evidences, including the results from BP and RBF neural network.

3. The Method of Boiler Drum Water Level Alarm

3.1. *Alarm method based on information fusion*

In the DCS system of the power plant, it is measured by three sets of differential pressure type water level gauge to get the measurements and the corresponding alarm values. This paper presents a method for boiler drum water level alarm type based on information fusion. The main flow of the method is shown in Figure. 1

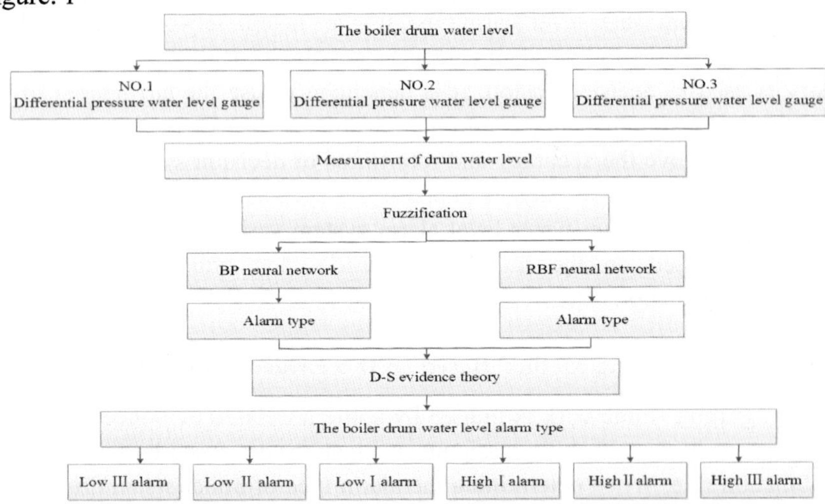

Fig. 1. The boiler drum water level alarm method based on information fusion

In order to describe the information reflected by the water level gauge better, the measurement is fuzzy by the appropriate membership functions and the measurement of the water level gauge corresponds to the degree of different alarm level. The alarm types are divided into high III alarm, high II alarm, high I alarm, low I alarm, low II alarm and low III alarm.

Next, neural network is trained with the fuzzy water level values as the input and the corresponding alarm types as the output. Two networks are respectively used to determine the alarm value. Different judgments are gotten such as the low III, low II, low I and high I, high II and high III alarm. Finally, the D-S combination rule is applied to get more accurate alarm types.

3.2. *Fuzzy method of drum water level*

In this paper, the measurement value of differential pressure gauge is fuzzed by the membership function as shown in Table. 1 based on the existing experiences of the experts [6]. In this paper only the high water level alarm are tested in Table 1 which are high I, high II and high III.

Tab. 1. Membership function of water level meter

Water level meter	Membership function	
High I level alarm	0	x<80
	exp[-((x-150)/25)^2]	80<x<220
	0	x>=220
High II level alarm	0	x<180
	exp[-((x-150)/25)^2]	180<x<320
	0	x>=320
High III level alarm	0	x<320
	1	x>=320

4. Alarm Judgment Example

In order to verify the method proposed in this paper, we performed a case based on the boiler drum water high level. The boiler drum water level has been fuzzed by the membership function in Table. 1 Part results based on BP and RBF neural network are shown in Table. 2

Tab. 2. Neural network alarm results

	BP neural network alarm				RBF neural network				Actual
1	0.9528	0.2512	-0.5456	I	0.0000	0.9999	0.0000	II	II
2	0.0458	1.0040	-0.0050	II	0.0000	1.0000	0.0000	II	II
3	1.0520	0.2850	-0.7220	I	1.0000	0.0000	0.0000	I	I
4	0.0964	-0.020	0.9549	III	0.0000	0.0000	0.9999	III	III
5	0.5598	0.1259	0.1438	I	0.9999	0.0000	0.0000	I	I

As seen from Table. 2, there is a false alarm that high II alarm is mistakenly judged high I alarm by the BP neural network. It may bring more serious consequences for the actual operators to execute action. The output of the neural network is not enough to fully confirm the value of the alarm type (such as the value of 0.95). It means this alarm judgment is uncertain.

The alarm type and the actual type are consistent by the RBF neural network. But on the basis of reliability, since BP neural network method makes a false alarm. Therefore, we can not guarantee that the alarm type which is drawn by RBF neural network must be correct. In this case, we need to use the method of D-S evidence theory to integrate the results by two different methods to make the decision of the final alarm type. The first group and the fifth group alarm data described in Table. 2 will be explained in detail. So there are four evidences for D-S fusion, the BPA functions are shown in Table. 3

Table. 3. The BPA functions of evidences

$m_i(j)$	High I	High II	High III	Uncertain
m_{BP1}	0.3939	0.1039	0.0056	0.4966
m_{BP5}	0.1837	0.0414	0.0472	0.7277
m_{RBF1}	0.0000	0.9999	0.0000	0.0001
m_{RBF5}	0.9999	0.0000	0.0000	0.0001

The data combined by D-S evidence theory is shown in Table. 3 The alarm types are shown in Table. 4

Table. 4. Alarm types based on D-S evidence theory

$m_i(j)$	High I	High II	High III	Uncertain
$m_{BP1} \oplus m_{RBF1}$	0.0000	0.9952	0.0000	0.0048
$m_{BP5} \oplus m_{RBF5}$	0.9960	0.0000	0.0000	0.0040

From Table. 4, alarm type values have been integrated by the D-S evidence theory. In the first group of alarm data, the output of the high II alarm reaches 0.9952, which is far greater than other alarm types. Similarly, in the fifth group of alarm data, the output of high I alarm reaches 0.9960, also far greater than others. According to the above results, it is known that the output is more obviously improved than that given by only one kind of method. Through the above two groups of test data it is obvious that the method of this paper can effectively eliminate the uncertainty of the boiler drum water level alarm and improve the accuracy of the alarm type.

5. Conclusion

This paper presents the method for the comprehensive boiler drum water level alarm results.

- The membership function is gotten by fuzzy set theory.
- The alarm type is preliminary diagnosed through different neural network.
- The diagnosis results are converted into BPA functions. The BPA functions are combined by D-S evidence theory.
- The type of boiler drum water level alarm is determined according to the decision criteria.

This algorithm makes full use of the advantages of fuzzy set theory and D-S evidence theory in dealing with uncertain information. It improves the accuracy and reliability of the boiler drum water level alarm. At the same time, it has the obvious characteristics of simple realization. It provides an accurate and efficient low cost method for the water level alarm of equipment. Through the accurate water level alarm of the equipment, it can achieve the purpose of improving the reliability of equipment operation and reducing the accident rate of equipment.

References

1. Jianqiang Gao, Peng Chen. *Application of Multi-dimensional BP Neural network in Fault Diagnosis of Boilers*, Thermal power generation, Vol 40(2014), pp.77-80, (In Chinese).
2. Yaoyao He, Qifa Xu, Shanlin Yang. *A Power Load Probability Density Forecasting Method Based on RBF Neural Network Quantile Regression,* Proceedings of the CSEE, Vol 33(2015), pp.93-98, (In Chinese).
3. Ping Li, Guoliang Huang, Daogang Peng. *Research of Fault Diagnosis Based on Neural Networks and D-S Evidence for Condenser in Power Plant,* East China Electric Power, Vol 42(2014), pp.1227-1232, (In Chinese).
4. Wei Ma. Fault Diagnosis of the Power Plant Boiler Based on the Evidence theory of Information Fusion, Master's thesis, North China Electric Power University (2010), (In Chinese).
5. Lijuan Zheng, Hongwei Wang. *Sentiment intensity of online reviews based on fuzzy-statistics of sentiment words,* Journal of systems & management, Vol 23(2014), pp.324-330, (In Chinese).
6. W.Y. Liu, J.G. Han, X.N. Lu. *A high speed railway control system based on the fuzzy control method,* Expert Systems With Applications, Vol 40 (2013), pp.6115-6124, (In Chinese).

1-D Barcode Detection Based on the Feature of LBP and HOG

Xin Luo[1,2,a], Hua-Zhu Liu[1,b] and Xue-Fang Chen[1,c]

[1]Dept. of Electronic Engineering, Dongguan University of Technology
Dongguan 523808, China

[2]Dept. of Electronic and Information Engineering, South China University of Technology
Guangzhou 510641, China

E-mail: [a]liuhz@dgut.edu.cn, [b]654650052@qq.com, [c]chenxf@dgut.edu.cn

A new method of one-dimensional barcode detection based on pattern recognition is proposed, which is the rotation invariant LBP features combined with HOG features used in barcode detection. Firstly, a rotation invariant LBP feature image is generated by the rotation invariant LBP operator acting on the original barcode image, and it turns the feature image into a series of sub-blocks which have the same size, to produce a one-class classifier (barcode detection model) aiming at detecting barcode by SVDD training from some small image blocks of barcode samples. When letting the rotation invariant LBP feature sub-image be the input of the classifier, it can get an output on whether this sub-image is a part of barcode. Therefore, when the model acts on all sub-blocks of a picture on detecting, a rough position of barcode on this picture will be known. Finally, using HOG features of each original image's sub-blocks and a relevant search algorithm to obtain a precise position about barcode. Experiment shows that the precision of this method compared with some current popular algorithm about barcode detection is higher.

Keywords: One-dimensional Barcode; Rotation Invariant LBP Feature; HOG; SVDD.

1. Introduction

One-dimensional barcode detection and recognition played an important role in the industrial production and everyday life. It provided the much convenience for the correct classification of goods and their management. For one-dimensional barcode recognition, the first step is to detect the position of barcode in image. Industrial barcodes detection is different from the barcode detection of commodities. Often in addition to the barcode area, there is less text around the barcode in industry, but the complexity of the background still remains high, and in the industrial background, for barcode detection, the accuracy is more important than the speed.

Aiming at the key technology of barcode detection, a large number of scholars put forward appropriate solutions for different situations. There are mainly the method based on scanning lines [1], method based on morphological operation [2-6], method based on transform domain [7-8] and the method based on feature transformation [9-12], and so on. The method based on morphology is simple and efficient, but it is easy to make the barcode area and other area connect together to detect mistakenly or detect incompletely. For the method based on transform domain [8], when other area proportion is higher than the proportion of the barcode in certain image, the detection precision of the algorithm will have fallen sharply. The method based on scanning lines detects the barcode by having the multidirectional scan. On the one hand there are large amount of calculation, on the other hand, it has the poor robustness for barcode missing partly. There are a lot of methods based on feature transformation, some researchers use Hough transform[11] to detect barcode, but when the barcode is very wide and their strip zone is very intensive, the method couldn't detect the correct line, which would cause mistaken detection.

Based on these points, the method that combines barcode characteristic patterns with pattern recognition technology to extract one-dimensional barcode location has some advantages, such as high accuracy and less manual intervention. The LBP feature has a good reflection for the image texture, and one-dimensional barcode consist of a set of parallel bars and spaces. Its HOG feature is single relatively. Therefore this paper proposes a method that utilizes the rotation invariant LBP feature of barcode and SVDD model to obtain the rough barcode area on image, then use HOG feature of barcode to realize the subsequent restoration so that it can obtain an accurate barcode area.

2. Proposed Method

It can get a rough position of barcode on detecting image by combining the local binary pattern of barcode and support vector data description. Then using the histogram of oriented gradients (HOG) of barcode sub-block image to repair the rough result, it can get a precise position. For the two steps, this paper will introduce them respectively.

2.1. *The rotation invariant LBP features extraction*

Before extracting the rotation invariant LBP features, it is necessary to have little preprocessed for the image containing one-dimensional barcode. In order to facilitate image blocking. The first step is adjusting the size of the original image denoted by $I_{original}$ to a suitable size, such as $1024px*512px$. Currently there is a large of image zooming algorithm. This paper adopted the bilinear interpolation method, therefore it can obtain the image denoted by I_{resize}. As shown in figure 1.

Then Iresize will be divide into many blocks, in view of the fact that barcode region zoom out after size modification. This paper use $16px*16px$ as the block size. Therefore, Iresize whose size is $1024px*512px$ will be consisting of 2048 image blocks, they are denoted by $\{B_i, i=1,2,...2048\}$. At the same time, Bi will be set some logic symbol, they are respectively ID number indicating the Bi position on I_{resize}, its value range from 1 to 2048, and the flag indicating whether the block has been processed, which is denoted by flag_proc, and the flag indicating whether the block has been recognized. These flag is initialized to be 0; it means the block is not been processed and recognized.

The image blocks as shown in figure 2.

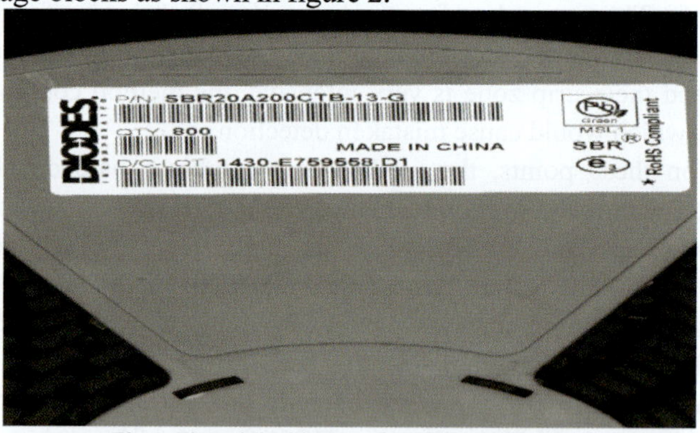

Fig.1. The original image after size modification

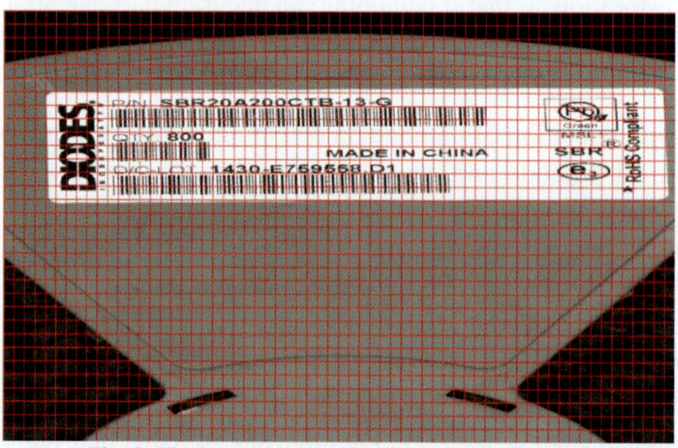

Fig. 2. The image blocks after the image is chunked

In most cases, the barcode labels are stuck to the products in industry. The difference of gray value between the label and the product are big. So the binaryzation can be applied to I_{resize} for extracting the region of interesting which is the tag location including barcode. If so, one hand it can reduce the amount of calculation for subsequent processing, on the other hand it can indirectly enhance the accuracy of the identification on barcode detecting. The paper use OSTU algorithm to have the image binaryzation to I_{resize} so that it can generate the binary image I_{binary}. As shown in figure 3, in order to extracting the region of interesting, the operation getting the maximum bounding rectangle on the target label of I_{binary} is necessary. The corresponding ROI can be obtained by the operation. It should be emphasized that this ROI is constituted by block-level elements. They can be denoted by $I_{roi} = \{B_{i_k}, k = 1,2,\ldots,N\}$, this result is the real ROI but it can be realized by I_{binary}. The ROI based on image blocks is shown as figure 4.

Fig. 3. The binary image obtained by OSTU algorithm

Fig. 4. The ROI image based on image blocks

Then we can extract the LBP feature, Local Binary Pattern (LBP) is a way to express local image texture features operator. With the continuous deepening of its research the LBP feature also produced many variants. The biggest drawback of original LBP operator is that it only covers a small area within a fixed radius, which obviously can not meet the needs of different size and frequency of the texture. If a 3*3 neighborhood is extended to any neighborhood, and square neighborhood is replaced with a circular neighborhood, you can expand LBP description, at this time, if the value of the upper left corner is regarded as the highest bit of binary number, so The original LBP can be expressed by the formula 1,

$$LBP_{C,P} = \sum_{p=0}^{P-1} s(g_c - g_p) * 2^p \tag{1}$$

Among them, g_c is the pixel value of the center, g_p is the pixel value of the neighborhood, P is the number of neighborhood points compared with the center. And $s(x) = \begin{cases} 1 \cdots if x > 0 \\ 0 \cdots else \end{cases}$

If processing the image including barcode directly with the original LBP operator, the feature vector will be affected severely by the rotation of image. In order to solve this problem, the LBP variants called by rotation invariant LBP operator will be used. The operator can be expressed with following formula 2:

$$LBP_{C,P}^{ri} = \min\{ROR(LBP_{C,P}, k) \mid k = 0,1,\ldots,P-1\} \tag{2}$$

Among them, $ROR(x,k)$ denote a binary number obtained by letting x cyclic shift to right k-bit, then the rotation invariant LBP operator can reduce the dimension of target pattern which changes the dimension of the feature vector from 256 to 36. Therefore it can solve the problem of image rotation and shorten the training time of recognizer.

This paper utilizes the rotation invariant LBP operator whose radius is one. By making convolution between I_{roi} and the operator, we can obtain the result denoted by I_{rilbp}. Because I_{roi} was described based on block-level elements, I_{rilbp} was also based on block-level naturally. But its original image block B_{i_k} will turn to be the feature image block denoted by B_{i_k-lbp}. But their logical flags are same. So I_{rilbp} can be expressed as $I_{rilbp} = \{B_{i_k-lbp}, k = 1,2,\ldots,N\}$, But some details must be dealt with. That is when calculating the LBP value of pixels of the image edge, due to its neighborhood pixels may be not existed, the paper solve it by setting the inexistent neighborhood pixels of image edge to zero for reasonable calculation. Moreover, because the original LBP feature image and rotation invariant LBP feature image is not very clear, the paper inverts their color as following figure 5 and figure 6.

Fig. 5. LBP feature image of ROI

Fig. 6. Rotation invariant LBP feature image of ROI

2.2. *SVDD model training and recognition*

After getting the LBP feature vector of barcode, the next step is using support vector data description algorithm (SVDD) [13] to have a classification. As a kind of one-class classifier, its based model is to find a minimum hyper sphere containing most training samples; the paper will only introduce its fundamental.

It is assumed that the training set is $\{x_i, i = 1, 2, ..., N\}$, among them, $x_i \in R^m$, it represents an m-dimensional feature vector, because of one-class classification, the goal of training is to find a reasonable hyper sphere. In order to solve the problem of linear inseparability, the paper uses the SVDD based on kernel function to expand it to a high dimensional separable characterization space. After the solving procedure of SVDD algorithm, if the output is 1, it represents the target; if the output is -1, it represents the background.

For applying the algorithm on this paper, the specific step will be described as following. First starting to train the one-class classifier based on SVDD algorithm. The paper chooses the Radial Basis Function (RBF) as the kernel function which has a good effect on classification about linear inseparable problem. The paper use N (actually, N is 800) barcode image blocks whose size is 16px*16px as the training set. They are denoted by $\{Ibar_i, i = 1, 2, ..N\}$. After extracting their rotation invariant LBP feature, it generates a series of feature histograms having 36 bins. In fact, they are a feature vector group (training set) containing N feature vectors. Their tag will be given to 1; the dimension of each feature vector is 36. Some samples is shown as following figure 7.

Fig. 7. Some training samples

Then, it is important to initialize the SVDD model parameters and the kernel function RBF parameters. The next step is letting these feature vectors from training set as the input of the SVDD model. After training, a barcode classifier model can be obtained. It is obvious that the model will have a not good effect. But it doesn't matter, only the model can get an approximate barcode region (rough result), we think it do work well. Finally, each image block ($B_{i_k-lbp}, k=1,2,...,N$) of I_{rilbp} will be the input of trained SVDD model at the same time we set the flag_proc of B_{i_k-lbp} to 1, which represents the image block has been as the input. By the decision function, the output can be known. If it is 1, it indicates the image block belongs to barcode and its flag_reco will be set to 1 representing it has been recognized to a part of barcode. Otherwise, the flag_reco of the image block is set to 0 which represents that it is still be not recognized to a part of barcode. As shown in figure 8, this is a rough result.

Fig. 8. The rough result not been repaired

2.3. *HOG repairing target*

Histogram of oriented gradient was also called HOG feature, which was a kind of feature descriptor used to detect the target. It often stat the times of oriented gradient of local image region so that it can obtain the histogram of different oriented gradient. Because the one-dimensional barcode always consists of a series of bars and spaces, their oriented gradient appears to be simple. For the problem repairing the incomplete barcode region, finding the similar properties is a necessary measure, so the HOG feature of barcode will be a good choice.

If the image blocks belonging to barcode are denoted by $B_{t_1-lbp}, B_{t_2-lbp}, ..., B_{t_M-lbp}$ in I_{rilbp}, but the SVDD one-class classifier can only recognize a part of complete barcode, they are denoted by $B_{t_1-lbp}, B_{t_2-lbp}, ..., B_{t_P-lbp} (P < M)$, it is necessary to repair the region which consists of $B_{t_k-lbp} (k=1,2,...,P)$. Then the restoration can be based on HOG feature of sub-blocks. This involves a search algorithm about node. The algorithm is to how to find the entire unrecognized barcode image blocks (rest M-P barcode image blocks) from each B_{t_k-lbp} on.

For each B_{t_k-lbp}, its feature vector of HOG can be calculated, and then these feature vectors will be averaged to be $\overline{vec_{t-hog}}$. As for the problem what the minimum area size calculated should be, due to the size of image block is enough small(16px*16px) in this paper, then when extracting the HOG feature, block operation will be more little so that it can reduce the time costs. As shown in figure 9 and figure 10, they are respectively the HOG feature of one barcode image block and the average HOG feature of barcode.

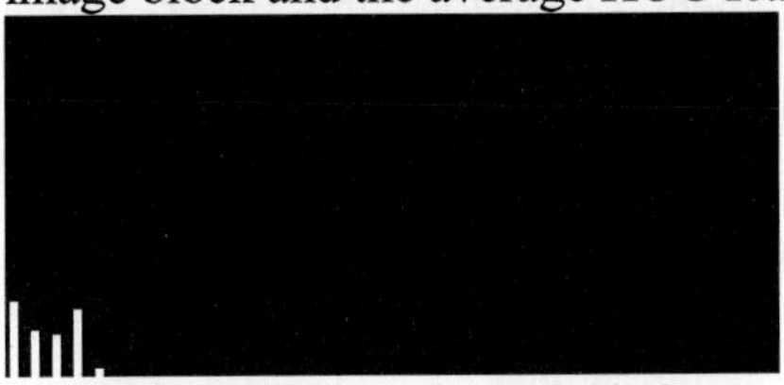

Fig. 9. HOG feature of one sub-block

Fig. 10. The average HOG feature

The next is traversing the barcode image block B_{t_k-lbp}, if the flag_proc is 1 and the flag_reco is 0 for every neighborhood image block of B_{t_k-lbp}, then the HOG feature vector of neighborhood image block will be calculated and be written by vec_{t_j-hog}. If the distance between $\overline{vec_{t-hog}}$ and vec_{t_j-hog} is within a threshold value (T_{hog}) range, it means the distance meets following formula 3.

$$diff(vec_{t_j-hog} - \overline{vec_{t-hog}}) \leq T_{hog} \tag{3}$$

Among them, $diff$ is the function getting the difference, the paper decides the Euclidean distance.

If so, it can be considered that this neighborhood image block belongs to the barcode region and its flg_reco is set to 1. After finishing the restoration of all of neighborhood image blocks around certain barcode image block (B_{t_k-lbp}), the same operation can be applied recursively for the other barcode image blocks (including the new image block identified to belong to barcode). It is noted that the searching operation must be applied to these original barcode image blocks in rough result. Only after that, the searching operation can be applied the new barcode image block. Otherwise the searching operation will end prematurely.

Until the flag_reco of all neighborhood image block of any barcode image block is 0, it represents the end of complete restoration.

Of course, there is a problem about dealing with bad image blocks, it refers to some image blocks were considered to belong to barcode, but actually, and it is not. For this situation, using the HOG feature to repair barcode region is still feasible. The set of error image blocks is denoted by $B_{e_k-lbp}(k=1,2,...,L)$. It is known to that the amount of the neighborhood image blocks of B_{e_k-lbp} which meet the formula 3 is few. According to the continuous distribution of barcode, the number of them will be not more than 3. However the real barcode image block appears to be continuous arrangement. Therefore the paper had a verification of continuity for the above result. When the number of continuous blocks is less than 3, the region will be removed. So much for that, the accurate area of the barcode is extracted completely. As shown in figure 11

Fig. 11. Final result (the accurate area)

3. Experiments

In the process of training barcode classifier, some barcode sub-blocks are used to be the training sample set. Because the SVDD algorithm has not too high requirements for the number of training sample, the paper selected many sub-blocks of different location of different barcodes; there are altogether 500 training samples. Considering the orientation of barcode, the training sample including many rotating barcode sub-blocks. In the process of recognition, the test image is divided into a lot of image blocks. After the feature extraction, they were as the input of the SVDD model trained, then the output will be repaired and it will obtain the final accurate result. Just like the figure 11, many small boxes almost occupy the barcode area.

In order to reflect the accuracy of the proposed method, here the paper compare the proposed method and some other methods, such as the method based on morphological operations, the method based on scanning lines, the method based on transform domain. As shown in table 1, the proposed method ensured the high precision of detection.

Tab. 1. Results for different methods

Barcode detection methods	The number of test samples	Detect successfully	Detection rate
Scanning lines[a]	200	158	79%
Morphological operation[b]	200	163	81.5%
Transform domain[c]	200	169	84.5%
Proposed method	200	181	90.5%

Note: Table Notes
[a]Method for reference [1]
[b]Method for reference [5]
[c]Method for reference [8]

4. Conclusion

For one-dimensional barcode detection, the paper utilized the rotation invariant LBP feature and SVDD model to generate a one-class classifier for barcode, and applied the classifier to these image blocks of ROI of test image to obtain a rough barcode area. Then with the HOG feature comparison for image blocks, the rough result was repaired to get an accurate barcode area. Experiments show that the proposed method has certain robustness for the image rotation and size variation, compared to other conventional barcode detection algorithms, in industrial production, especially in the occasion of relatively high detection accuracy, this method still has good effects.

Acknowledgments

This work was supported by Provincial Science and technology project of Guangdong Province, Grant No is 2016A010101038, 2016A050502066.

Appendix

SVDD principle and the solving procedure:

(1) First of all, the algorithm defines a hypersphere including the training set whose center is a and radius is R(R>0). To reduce the impact of singularity, it introduces the slack variables $\xi_i, \forall i$. Thereupon the SVDD training problem can turn to be solving quadratic programming problem.

$$\min\{R^2 + C\sum_i \xi_i\} \quad s.t. \| \varphi(x_i) - \varphi(a) \| \le R^2 + \xi_i^2, \xi_i \ge 0, \forall i \quad (4)$$

Among them, C is the regularization parameter, $\varphi(\bullet)$ is corresponding kernel function.

(2) According to solving the extremum with Lagrange function, the dual problem of the original problem can be expressed as following formulas 5.

$$L=\sum_i \alpha_i \langle \varphi(x_i)\bullet\varphi(x_i)\rangle - \sum_i \sum_j \alpha_i \alpha_j \langle \varphi(x_i)\bullet\varphi(x_j)\rangle \qquad (5)$$

$$s.t. \sum_i \alpha_i = 1, 0 \le \alpha_i \le C, \forall i$$

By the KKT conditions, it is known that these corresponding points meeting $\alpha_i = 0$ will be in the suprasphere, and these points meeting $0 \le \alpha_i \le C$ will be on the supraphere which represent the support vector, other points are outside.

(3) Introducing the kernel function $\langle \varphi(x_i)\bullet\varphi(x_j)\rangle = K(x_i, x_j)$ into the formula 5, then it can obtain following formula 6.

$$L=\sum_i \alpha_i K(x_i, x_i) - \sum_i \sum_j \alpha_i \alpha_j K(x_i, x_j) \qquad (6)$$

$$s.t. \sum_i \alpha_i = 1, 0 \le \alpha_i \le C, \forall i$$

Therefore, A group of optimal solution about α can be obtained, which is denoted by $\alpha^* = (\alpha_1^*, \alpha_2^*, ...)$;

(4) For realizing the model, a decision function G(z) is also needed. It should meet the following conditions.

$$G(z;a,R) = sign(\| \varphi(x_i) - \varphi(a) \| \le R^2)$$

$$= sign((K(z,z) - 2\sum_i \alpha_i K(z, x_i) + \sum_i \sum_j \alpha_i \alpha_j K(x_i, x_j)) \le R^2) \qquad (7)$$

References

1. R. Adelmann (2006), “Toolkit for bar code recognition and resolving on camera,” in Phones - Jump Starting the Internet of Things. In: Informatik 2006 workshop on Mobile and Embedded Interactive Systems.

2. Bodnar, P., and Nyul, L. G. (2012) Efficient barcode detection with texture analysis, *in Signal Processing, Pattern Recognition, and Applications, Proceedings of the Ninth IASTED International Conference* on, pp. 51–57.
3. Bodnar, P., and Nyul, L. G. (2012). Improving Barcode Detection with Combination of Simple Detectors. *Eighth International Conference on Signal Image Technology and Internet Based Systems* (Vol.42, pp.300-306).
4. Lin, D. T., Lin, M. C., and Huang, K. Y. (2011). Real-time automatic recognition of omnidirectional multiple barcodes and dsp implementation. *Machine Vision and Applications, 22*(2), 409-419.
5. Bodnár, P. and Nyúl, L. G., and Bodnár, P. (2012). Barcode detection with morphological operations and clustering.
6. Juett, X., and Qi, X. (2005). Barcode localization using bottom-hat filter. *Nsf Research Experience for Undergraduates.*
7. Felzenszwalb, P. F., and Huttenlocher, D. P. (2004). Distance transforms of sampled functions. *Theory of Computing, 8*(19), 415-428.
8. Tropf, A., and Chai, D. (2006). Locating 1-D Bar Codes in Dct-Domain. *IEEE International Conference on Acoustics, Speech and Signal Processing* (Vol.2, pp.II-II). IEEE.
9. Muniz, R., Junco, L., and Otero, A. (1999). A robust software barcode reader using the Hough transform. *International Conference on Information Intelligence and Systems*, 1999. *Proceedings* (pp.313-319). IEEE.
10. Wang, M., Li, L. N., and Yang, Z. X. (2010). Gabor filtering-based scale and rotation invariance feature for 2d barcode region detection. *Computer Application and System Modeling (ICCASM), 2010 International Conference on* (Vol.5, pp.V5-34-V5-37). IEEE.
11. Zamberletti, A., Gallo, I., and Albertini, S. (2013). Robust Angle Invariant 1D Barcode Detection. I*apr Asian Conference on Pattern Recognition* (pp.160 - 164). IEEE Computer Society.
12. Gallo, O., and Manduchi, R. (2010). Reading 1d barcodes with mobile phones using deformable templates. *IEEE Transactions on Pattern Analysis and Machine Intelligence*, 33(9), 1834-1843.
13. Kang, D., Park, J., and Principe, J. C. (2010). Binary classification based on SVDD projection and nearest neighbors. *Neural Networks (IJCNN), The 2010 International Joint Conference on* (Vol.54, pp.1-6). IEEE.

A Novel RBF-PID Control Strategy for Main Steam Temperature Based on QPSO Algorithm

Yue-Chao Wang[1,a], Feng-Ping Pan[1], Ling-Ling Shi[1], Zhi-Qiang Pang[1], Juan-Juan Ren[1] and Ying-Nan Wang[2,b]

[1]*Electric Power Research Institute of Guangdong Grid Company, Guangdong Guangzhou, 510080, China*

[2]*North China Electric Power University, Beijing, 102206, China*

E-mail: [a]yuechaoster@me.com, [b]yingnan120@163.com

Against such characteristics as uncertainty of controlled object in the main steam temperature control of thermal power plants, a novel PID control strategy with radial basis function (RBF) network tuning based on quantum-behaved particle swarm optimization (QPSO) algorithm is proposed. The QPSO algorithm is applied to optimize the initial parameters of RBF network, thus achieving dynamic control of the main steam temperature. The proposed controller has a self-learning ability, which can strengthen the system of uncertainties adaptability. Simulation results show that the control system performance is obviously better than the conventional cascade control.

Keywords: Main Steam Temperature; RBF Neural Network; QPSO; PID.

1. Introduction

In thermal power plant, boiler superheated steam outlet temperature (main steam temperature) is one of the important parameters affecting the security and efficiency of unit [1]. Considering the main steam temperature control system is a typical large inertia, large delay, nonlinear and time-varying system, the system has a complex structure and difficult to control [2]. Therefore it is very important to control the main steam temperature accurately.

Many scholars apply various control strategies to main steam temperature control system. Conventional PID cascade control method often fails to obtain satisfactory results. Predicative control strategies, such as Smith method [3], DMC and internal mode control (IMC) are much dependent on precise models of the plants. The PID control strategy with RBFNN tuning is proposed [4], but the selection of the network parameters has great influence on the performance of the controller, the improper selection will cause the loss of approximation accuracy and even the divergence of the RBF network [5].

Found on the above situation, a novel RBFNN-PID controller is proposed, in which the QPSO algorithm has been used in training RBFNN to determine the centers and widths of RBFs. Finally the effectiveness of the control program is simulated by MATLAB.

2. PID control strategy with RBF neural network tuning

2.1. *RBF neural network architecture*

RBF Network is structured by embedding radial basis function in hidden layer and it has three layers feed-forward neural network [6]. The Redial Basis Function neural network model is shown in Fig. 1.

Set the input sample X, the output of the hidden layer can be calculated, as in Eq.(1).

$$h_j(x) = \exp(-\|x - c_j\|^2 / 2b_j^2), j = 1, 2\cdots, m \tag{1}$$

where c_j is the center of basis function, b_j is the basis function radius parameters. Consider w_j is the j th hidden layer to output layer weights. The identifying output of RBF network can be calculated, as in Eq.(2).

$$y_m(k) = w_1 h_1 + w_2 h_1 + \cdots + w_m h_m \tag{2}$$

In RBF neural networks, we need to determine the parameter values: number of hidden layer nodes, weights of the hidden layer to output layer, centers and widths of basis function.

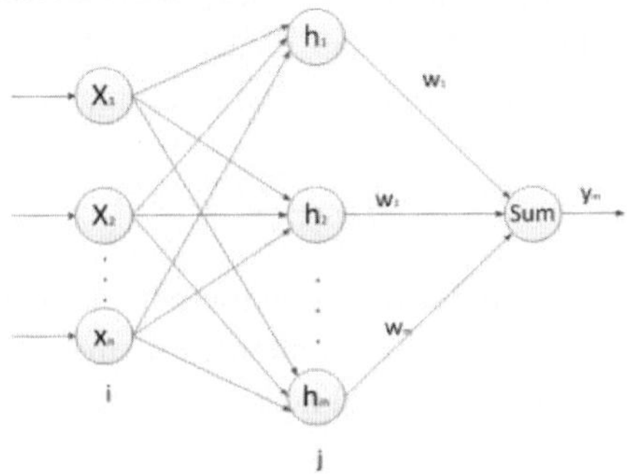

Fig. 1. RBF network architecture

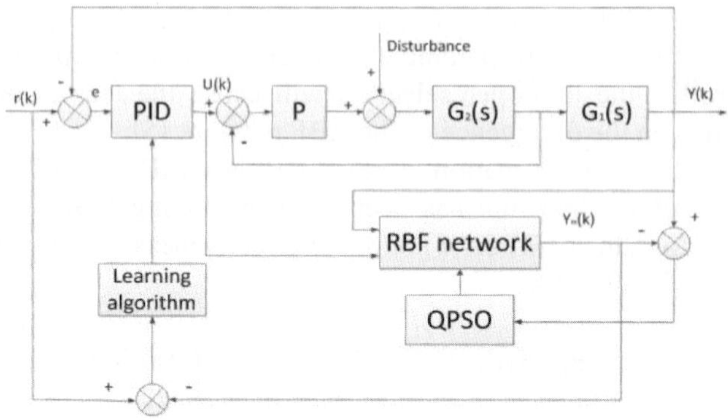

Fig. 2. The novel RBF-PID control system

2.2. *RBF-PID control algorithm design*

Considering the main steam temperature control system is a typical large inertia and large delay system, the cascade control structure is used in this paper.

By RBF neural network identification, the PID controller parameters are adjusted in real time. And the incremental PID controller is used in this paper. The novel control strategy is shown in Fig. 2.

3. Quantum-behaved particle swarm optimization

When a QPSO[7] is used to train the RBFNN, a decision vector represents a particular group of network parameters including c_k, b_k and w_k $(k=1,2,\cdots m)$. It is further denoted as $X_i=(c_1,c_2,\cdots,c_m,b_1,b_2,\cdots,b_m,w_1,w_2,\cdots w_m)$ Initialization of the population involves generating randomly the position vector $X_i(i=1,2,\cdots,M)$ and setting the personal best position $pbest_i=X_i$. Since a component of the position corresponds to a network parameter, a RBF network is structured according the particle's position vector. Training the corresponding network by inputting the training samples, we can obtain an error value computed by the following formula. E denotes the error function (fitness function), in this paper, which can be written as in Eq.(3).

$$E(X_p)=\frac{1}{2M}\sum_{p=1}^{M}\sum_{q=1}^{N}(d_q^p-y_q^p)^2 \tag{3}$$

where d_q^p and y_q^p are the q th desired target output and actual output of p th the input. In a word, the error function is adopted as the objective function to be minimized in QPSO based RBF neural network.

4. Design of control scheme for the main steam temperature system

4.1. *The simulation object and parameter settings*

The paper adopts a typical loads of a 600MW supercritical boiler [8], the system structure is shown in Fig. 2. And the dynamic characteristics model when the main steam subjects to spray-water disturbance is shown in Table 1:

Table 1. The dynamic characteristics model of main steam temperature

Temperature of leading area	Temperature of inert area
$8/(1+15s)^2$	$1.125/(1+25s)^3$

In the RBF-PID control system, the architecture of RBF network is 3-6-1, the input of network identification is $u(k)$ and $y(k)$ and $y(k-1)$, and the output is $y_m(k)$. In this method, the secondary loop uses P controller to quickly eliminate bias of the leader region's steam temperature, which remains same in the simulation and is chosen as: $K_p = 25$. In the main loop, the parameters of PID controller is chosen as: k_p, k_i and k_d and the learning rate $\eta_p = 0.02$, $\eta_i = 0.02$ and $\eta_d = 0.03$. In RBF network, the learning rate η is chosen as 0.25, the momentum factor α is chosen as 0.02. The parameters of the QPSO algorithm are set as Table 2.

Table 2. Execution parameters for QPSO

Parameter	Population size	Iterations	Centers C	Width B	Weight W
Value	20	2000	[-3,3]	[0.1,3]	[-1,1]

After the iteration, the parameter optimization value of the Gaussian basis function in RBF Network are shown in Table 3.

Table 3. Execution parameters of RBF

Parameter		Value
	$c1$	[-0.4009 1.1576 0.8185 0.1097 -1.8579 -0.4880]
Centers vector C	$c2$	[-0.3633 -0.2598 0.2623 0.7462 0.1436 0.0698]
	$c3$	[-0.4255 1.2068 -0.8853 -0.2271 1.0736 0.1047]
Width vector B		[1.1472 1.0579 -0.2699 1.1338 0.3236 1.9754]
Weight vector W		[-0.4137 0.7924 -0.8384 -0.9216 0.2679 0.5135]

4.2. *Test results*

4.2.1. *Step responses to two kinds of cascade control systems*

In this paper, the novel RBF-PID cascade control is compared with PID cascade control by simulation approach. The step responses for the closed-loop system are shown in Fig. 3. From Fig. 3, it can be concluded that the performance of RBF-PID cascade control system is superior to the conventional PID cascade control system, and the former strategy can overcome the contradictions of rapidity and stability.

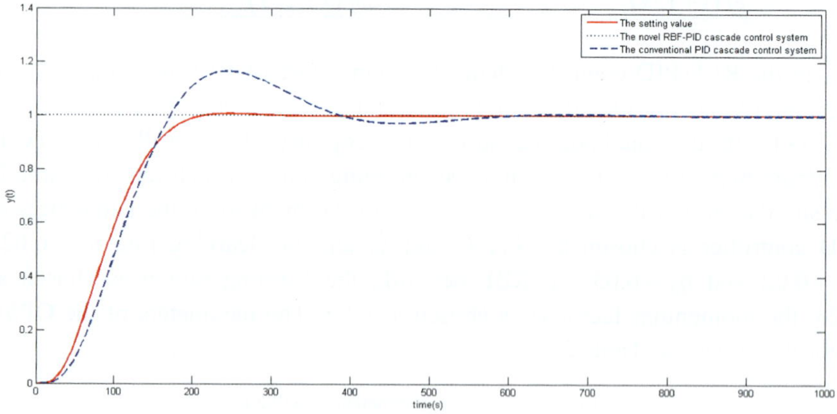

Fig. 3. Comparison between the behaviors of two kinds of cascade control systems responding to a disturbance occasioned by a step change of the setting value

4.2.2. *The robustness of the control system*

There will be an obvious change of the dynamic characteristics of the main steam temperature along with the change of load and working condition, so the design of the control system should have strong robustness. In this paper, the main steam temperature object will change into the following form due to the load change of the system, as shown in Table 4.

Table 4. The changed model of main steam temperature

Temperature of leading area	Temperature of inert area
$9.54/(1+20s)^2$	$1.025/(1+35s)^3$

The algorithm and controller parameters remain the same, the responses to main steam temperature disturbance for the closed-loop system are shown in Fig. 4. It can be seen that the transient time and overshoot of the RBF-PID control strategy is smaller than the conventional one, so the proposed method can achieve better control performance and robustness.

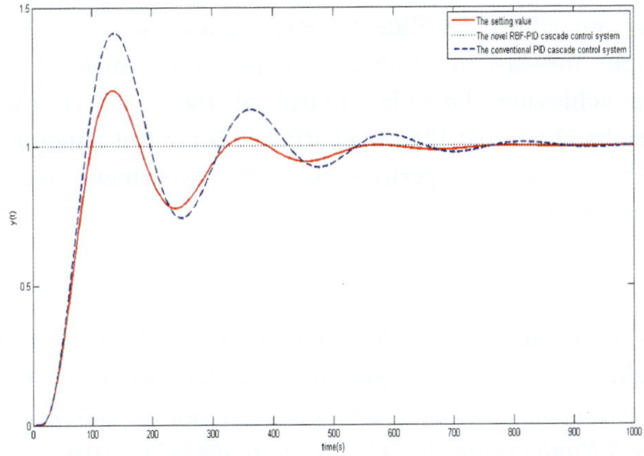

Fig. 4. Comparison of the behavior of the two kinds of control system's in response to main disturbance caused by a 20% load step-change

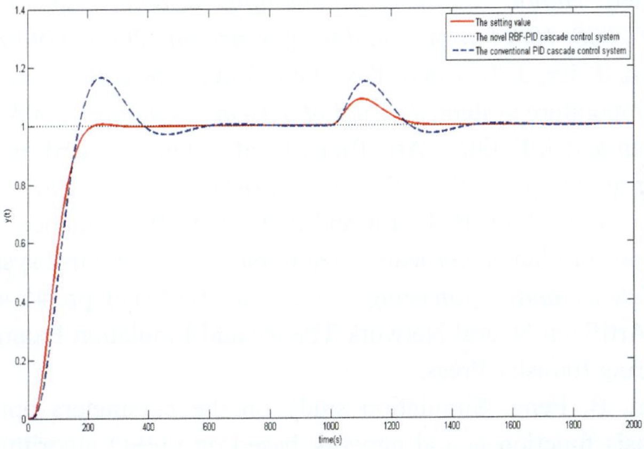

Fig. 5. Comparison of the behavior of two kinds of cascade control system's in response to a steam temperature disturbance

4.2.3. *The capacity of resisting disturbance in the control system*

In the simulation, a 20% load step disturbance occurs at t=1000s, the response curves are shown in Fig.5. Compared with the conventional PID control strategy, the proposed method has a strong capacity of resisting disturbance and achieves good control quality.

5. Conclusion

A novel RBF-PID cascade control scheme was proposed for main steam temperature of a 600MW supercritical boiler was studied. The parameters of PID controller are adjusted online by RBF neural network. And the QPSO algorithm is put forward to optimize the initial parameters of RBF neural network, thus achieving dynamic control of the main steam temperature. Simulation results show that the novel RBF-PID control structure can achieve better disturbance rejection performance and robustness and is worth to implement in practice.

References

1. Y. Z. Yu, Z. B. Zhang, H. C. Xu, D. G. Chen, G. J. Dong, B. Shen, S. Liu. Investigation for 600 MW Supercritical Boiler's Main Steam Temperature Control, *Proceedings of the 2010 International Conference on Electrical and Control Engineering (ICECE 2010)*, p 3848-51, 2010.
2. S. Lee, Y. Shin, E. Jang, Hwi-Beom, Shin. New Smith Predictor Control Using Disturbance Observer for Steam Superheater and Steam Pressure of the Boiler, *Hanoi: Control, Automation, Robotics and Vision, 2008. ICARCV 2008. 10th International Conference on* , 2008. 979-981.
3. Z. Y. Liu, J. Lv, J. L. Chen. RBF neural network control on super-heated steam temperature system. *Journal of System Simulation,* 2004.
4. H. G. Han and J. F. Qiao, An efficient self-organizing RBF neural network for water quality predicting, *Neural Networks*, 2011. 04. 006.
5. Q. Z. Li, Y. G. Niu, B. L. Lu and Z. C. Lan, Performance evaluation of thermal power plant superheated steam temperature control system, *Electric Power Science and Engineering*, vol. 27, no. 7, (2011), pp. 45-49.
6. J. Gao. Artificial Neural Network Theory and Emulation Example. Beijing: Engineering Industry Press.
7. W. Chen, B. Feng. Simulation study on the parameters optimization of radial basis function neural network based on QPSO algorithm. *Computer Application*, 26(8), 1928-1930.
8. D. G. Peng, Fuzzy immune PID control and its application to main steam temperature control system. *Computer Measurement & Control* (2005).

Research on Lag Synchronization Control Based on BP Neural Network for Full Trailer Vehicles

Ning Chen[a], Xiao-Lei Chen[b] and Xin Lu[c]

College of Mechanical and Electronic Engineering, Nanjing Forestry University
Nanjing City, Jiangsu Province, China
E-mail: [a]chenning@njfu.com.cn, [b]wehihh@163.com, [c]975566754@qq.com

In this paper, the model of the full trailer and the fractional order BP network are introduced. The error of the relative yaw rate of the tractor and the trailer as the training error of neural network is put forward and the steering control of the trailer is realized by neural network. In view of the control problem, the angle of trailer is compensated and greatly optimized the path tracking performance of the trailer on the basis of BP network. Finally, the driving path of the tractor and the trailer is completely consistent.

Keywords: Full Trailer; Fractional Order BP Neural Network; Lag Synchronization; Compensation Control.

1. Introduction

Vehicle stability and security has always been a topic of concern; the full trailer is a vehicle of transport. The full trailer is usually composed of a tractor with power and a trailer with non-powered. When the full trailer is driving, the driving stability of the trailer is noteworthy. If the trailer swing around, the traffic accidents are easy to happen. Therefore, the research on how to improve the running stability of the trailer is worth studying. The memory and heredity of the fractional order make the neural network for recurrent neural networks connect with the front and back information in a natural way. In the same way, if fractional order neural network has an infinite memory, the application will be very effective in parameter estimation. The fractional order artificial neural network has become a hot research topic. Lots of researchers have established a fractional order neural network model, and thoroughly studied the limit cycle, chaotic phenomena and chaotic synchronization [1].

The system dynamics simulation model of the vehicle body side deflection caused by towed trailer braking is established by using the Lagrange equation in literature [9]. The whole mathematical model ignores the interaction force at the connection point. Through the simulation experiment, we found the most important parameters that affect the braking of the trailer and the experimental results confirmed the previous hypothesis. We analyzed the braking process of the full trailer on flat road and confirmed the incentive factors of vibration of towed trailer in literature [10]. We applied the Wilson-Θ step-by-step integration method and the MATLAB programming language to the simulation calculation of the trailer braking process. We found the simulation results were in agreement with the experimental results. Literature [11] proposed an anti-lock brake control method which applies to the trailer based on target slip ratio logic threshold control. The simulation results showed the ABS system can effectively prevent the locking of the wheel brake. Through the adjustment of the trailer and tractor brake pressure, we established the time to coordinate the braking strength of the trailer and tractor, so the whole braking process had a certain role of "straightened". The braking stability of trailer is significantly improved, and the occurrence rate of "folding" and other braking instability phenomena is reduced. Literature [12] installed an anti-lock braking system on the tractor and trailer respectively. Also, it set up the related coordination module to make the two systems work in coordination and made the linear braking simulation to the trailer with no installation and installation of ABS system on the road of high adhesion coefficient. By analyzing and comparing the simulation results, it is proved that the coordination module makes the two sets of ABS system work smoothly, and the braking strength of the trailer is coordinated with the tractor, which significantly improves the braking stability of the vehicle.

Some passive steering systems and self steering axles were designed for trailers in low speed path tracking (Path-following Off-tracking, PFOT).However, though these devices can improve the tracking performance of the trailer at low speed, it also reduces the stability of high speed [13].

In terms of the influence of the parameters on the lateral stability, the mathematical model of three degrees of freedom of the all wheel steering trailer is established by literature [14], and the parameters are analyzed in detail. Also, the parameters of ADAMS and MATLAB are simulated by two kinds of software, and the results are satisfactory. The mathematical model of the lateral swing of trailer was established by using the method of quantitative analysis of parameters based on literature [15]. Using MATLAB software to simulate and analyze the influence of the kinematic parameters and the structure parameters on the stability of trailer. The similarity theory and experiment data were used to make the similar model of the whole car, and the improvement, installation, debugging and testing of the existing simulation pavement test system were carried out.

In terms of the lateral stability control, there are two main types of methods: One kind of method is based on the braking control; another kind of method is based on the steering control. Literature [16] made a differential braking control for 3 trailers to suppress unnecessary trailer sway, so the trailer trajectory can track front axle trajectory of tractor and the transverse stability of the trailer is improved. Literature [17] adopts the active steering control; the rotation angle of trailer front axle is proportional to the driver input. Studies have shown that trailer steering can reduce the sideslip angle, lateral force and the derailment phenomenon of the trailer, but the maneuverability became deteriorating. The study also showed that good stability of the vehicle should have smaller "latter magnification (Rearward amplification ratio, RWA ratio)". The "latter magnification" refers to the ratio of the maximum lateral acceleration at the center of mass of the trailer and the maximum lateral acceleration at the center of mass of the tractor when the trailer is changing lanes[13]. Therefore, literature [9] proposed the active steering system (active trailer steering of trailer, ATS), and use the RWA ratio as the controller design criteria. The simulation results show that the system can not only improve the stability of high speed, but also reduce the turning radius of the low speed steering. Literature [4] applied the linear quadratic regulation device (linear quadratic regulator, LQR) technology to design the ATS controller. The results show that the controller reduces the RWA ratio. At the same time, there is no large change in the baseline trajectory (trajectory baseline) of the trailer at low speed. Active steering strategies proposed in literature [18] can significantly reduce the trailer skidding, tail flick and the derailment, the method don't need observer to estimate the state of the vehicle and is suitable for the traction rod trailers and semi trailers.

For conflicting problem of the low speed path tracking and high speed stability control, people proposed for using the passive steering system to effectively reduce the PFOT value at low speed and using ATS system to lock passive steering system at medium and high speed. This method can coordinate the contradiction between the two parties to a certain extent, but the structure is more complex because the trailer both has the passive and active steering system. Literature [19] studied the trailer which has three trailers, and used the steering LQR controller to reduce latter magnification and the path deviation indirectly at the same time. The front wheel steering angle of the trailer is proportional to the angle of the hinge point. In order to solve the problem of the design of towed trailer, researchers putted forward a double circuit design [20].

In the first loop design, according to the name parameters of the trailer, using optimization method to determine the weighting factor for the LQR controller. Then, according to the weighting factor in the second loop, we can get the optimization of design variables and the gain matrix of the LQR value. But the research shows, due to its own defects, its search space and optimization are relatively limited. Therefore, scholars have also put forward the design method of single loop which optimizing the ATS controller and the trailer design variables. This method introduced the driver model, and designed two controllers to improve the handling and stability of the vehicle.

2. BP Algorithm Based on the Caputo Definition of Fractional Order

The BP neural network consists of input layer, hidden layer and output layer, each layer is composed of a number of neurons. The hidden layer can be a layer, and it can also be a multilayer. Although the hidden layer is not connected with the outside world, its state is very important, which directly influences the mapping between input and output. Many scholars have proved that three layer BP network including input layer, hidden layer and output layer has strong approximation ability [2, 3].

This section takes the three layer BP neural network as an example to illustrate the data training process of BP neural network. Which s, t, k, respectively represent a neuron node in the input layer, the hidden layer and the output layer. The number of neurons in each layer is m, p, n. The W_{st} is the value of the node s in the input layer and the node t of the hidden layer, W_{tk} is the value of the node t in the hidden layer and the node k in the output layer. x is the input data that is the sample set, x_s represents the input value of the node s, θ represents the node threshold, θ_t represents the threshold value of the hidden layer node t, θ_k represents the threshold value of the hidden layer node k.

The sample data is input from the input layer to the hidden layer, and the input of the single node t of the hidden layer is

$$net_t = \sum_{s=1}^{m} W_{st} x_s - q_t, t = 1, 2, L, p \tag{1}$$

The output of the hidden layer node t is

$$O_t = f\left(net_t\right), t = 1, 2, \cdots, p \tag{2}$$

Here, f (·) is the node function or the excitation function of the hidden layer. Generally, according to the actual situation of the sample, we can select different functions, such as linear function, hyperbolic tangent function etc. The most commonly used function is the Sigmoid function, it will be described in detail in the following chapters. The data is then input from the hidden layer to the output layer, and the input of the single node k of the output layer is

$$y_{i_k} = \sum_{t=1}^{p} W_{tk} O_t - \theta_k, k = 1, 2, \cdots, n \tag{3}$$

The output of the node k of output layer is

$$y_{o_k} = f\left(y_{i_k}\right), k = 1, 2, \cdots, n \tag{4}$$

$f(\cdot)$ is the node function of the output layer

In the initial stage, there is an error between the actual output value and the expected value of the network. In the actual data training, the error calculation usually uses the square error equation shown as

$$E = \frac{1}{2} \sum_{k=1}^{n} \left(y_k - y_{o_k}\right)^2 \tag{5}$$

Here, y is the desired output value; y_k is the desired output value of the output neuron k. The error E is the sum of the errors in the output layer of all neurons.

In the final steady state of the neural network, the actual output value is the same or infinite close to the expected value. Therefore, in the training of data, we need to correct the connection weights and thresholds of the neural network. The weight of the neural network is used to modify the gradient descent method, the essence of which is a simple steepest descent algorithm.

$$W_{st} = W_{st} - u \cdot \frac{\partial E}{\partial W_{st}} \tag{6}$$

$$W_{tk} = W_{tk} - u \cdot \frac{\partial E}{\partial W_{tk}} \tag{7}$$

In above equations, u is the weight correction factor, which is the learning rate. The learning rate affects the convergence rate of the algorithm. If the learning rate is too small, the convergence rate of the network will be very slow. If the learning rate is too fast, it will cause the network to appear oscillation and could not converge the all network. Therefore, it is generally not used to optimize the learning rate of one-dimensional search, but the use of a certain value between 0 and 1.

According to the Caputo definition of the fractional differential, the fractional order differential of the composite function can be derived from the product of integral order and fractional differential [4]. Assuming function $h(v(t))$, then we can get

$$D_t^z h(v) = \frac{\partial}{\partial v}(h(v)) \cdot D_t^z v \tag{8}$$

According to Eq. (8), the weight correction can be written as follows

$$_c D_{W_{st}}^z E = \frac{\partial E}{\partial net_t} \cdot {}_c D_{W_{st}}^z (net_t) \tag{9}$$

Here,

$$\frac{\partial E}{\partial net_t} = -\sum_{k=1}^{n} \left(y_k - f\left(y_{i_k}\right)\right) f'\left(y_{i_k}\right) W_{tk} \cdot f'(net_t) \tag{10}$$

Eq. (10) is based on the solution of integer order, and another part of the differential is calculated according to the Grümwald-Letnikov definition of fractional order differential, the Eq. (1) is decomposed into the differential part and the constant part of the independent variable. The single W_{st} is the connection weights between the nodes of an input layer and the hidden layer which are regulated by the error, and it is used as an independent variable in the derivative. The constant part is the input quantity after the input part which is related to the weight of the adjustment.

$$net_t = \sum_{s=1}^{m} W_{st} x_s - \theta_t = W_{st} x_s + \sum W_{st} x_s - \theta_t \tag{11}$$

Take Eq. (11) into the item $f(x\text{-}kh)$ in Grümwald-Letnikov fractional calculus definition and give value to it,

$$\left(W_{st}-kh\right)x_s+\sum W_{st}x_s-\theta_t=net_t-khx_s \tag{12}$$

Then we can get

$$_cD^z_{W_{st}}\left(net_t\right)=h^{-z}\sum_{l=0}^{\left|\left(W_{st}-c\right)/h\right|}(-1)^k\binom{z}{l}\left(net_t-lhx_s\right) \tag{13}$$

In Eq. (13), net_t is the input of the hidden layer node t, x_s is the input of the input layer node s.

Similarly, the connection weights of deviation E of the input layer and the hidden layer is

$$_cD^z_{W_{tk}}y_k=h^{-z}\sum_{l=0}^{\left|\left(W_{tk}-c\right)/h\right|}(-1)^l\binom{z}{l}\left(y_{i_k}-lhO_t\right) \tag{14}$$

In Eq. (14), y_{ik} is the input of the output layer node k; O_t is the output of the hidden layer node t.

3. Dynamic Model of Full Trailer

According to the two degree of freedom model, we think the car speed is a fixed value, and the tire side slip characteristic is in the linear range. Ignoring the effect of the steering system and the suspension, the dynamic model of the full trailer is established by considering its lateral translational and transverse motion. The front and rear wheels of the whole trailer are provided with steering angle and the relevant balance equations are listed in turn.

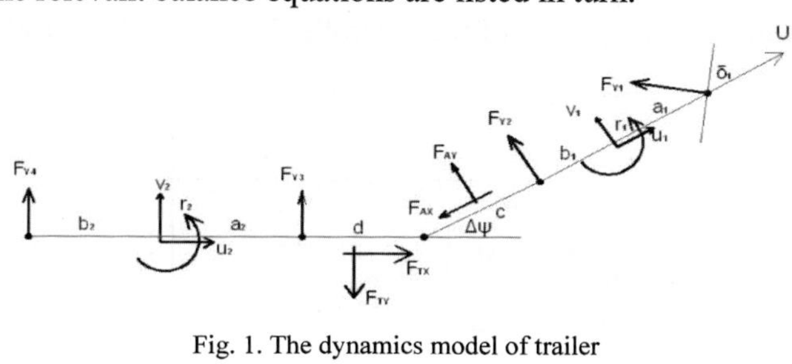

Fig. 1. The dynamics model of trailer

The dynamic model of a full trailer vehicle can be expressed as the state space equation [4].

$$AX' + BX = C_1\delta_1 + C_3\delta_3 + C_4\delta_4 \tag{15}$$

The X is the state space variables $X = [\beta_1 \quad r_1 \quad r_2 \quad \Delta\varphi]^T$

In Eq. (15), δ1 is the front wheel angle of tractor. δ3 and δ4 are the front and rear wheel steering angle of towed trailer. β1 is the sideslip angle of the vehicle. r1 is the yaw angular velocity of the tractor, r2 is the yaw angular velocity of the trailer and Δφ is the relative slip angle.

4. Lag Synchronization Control of Full Trailer

In the process of running, the most stable condition is the track of the tractor and the trailer. In other words, at the same point, the steering angle of the tractor and the trailer are the same. There is a time interval between the tractor and the trailer to arrive at the same point in the same direction. The delay time is calculated by the following equation.

$$\tau = (b_1 + c + d + a_2) / u \tag{16}$$

In the equation, b1 is the longitudinal distance from mass center to rear axle of the tractor, c is the distance from hinge point to the rear axle of the tractor, d is the distance from hinge point to the front axle of the trailer, a2 is the distance from the mass center to front axle of the trailer, and u is the vehicle speed.

The control structure of the whole vehicle model is shown in figure 2. In the equation, r1 is the yaw angular velocity of the tractor, r2 is the yaw angular velocity of the trailer, τ is the lag time, and e is the back propagation error of the neural network. δ is the input of the rotation angle of the trailer wheel. The output β1, r1, r2 and Δφ of the vehicle model is the input of the neural network controller, and the output value of the controller is used as the wheel angle input of the trailer.

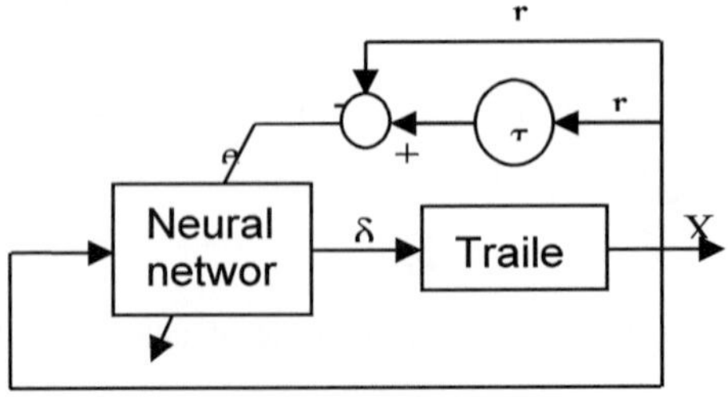

Fig. 2. Neural Network Control of Trailer Model

Usually, the error between the output of the neural network controller and the reference value is used as the back propagation error of the neural network to modify the connection weights of the network. In the control strategy, considering difference in time between the trailer and the tractor at the same point, calculate the error between the yaw rate of the current time of the trailer and the tractor before a certain time, and take back propagation to the neural network to modify the connection weights of the network. Through the constant online adjustment of the network, eventually achieve the tractor and trailer lag synchronous driving.

The error of BP network is defined as the lag deviation of yaw rate of tractor and trailer.

$$e = r_1(t-\tau) - r_2(t) \tag{17}$$

The equation of the trailer sideslip angle β2 is as follows

$$\beta_2 = \beta_1 + \Delta\varphi - r_1 \frac{b_1 + c}{u} - r_2 \frac{a_2 + d}{u} \tag{18}$$

The vehicle trajectories are computated using the yaw rates and sideslip angles of tracter and trailer.

The turning angle of the tractor is the sine signal. The amplitude is 0.02 rad, the frequency is 0.05 rad/sec. Considering there are integrity and negative values on the turning angle of the trailer, the node function of the neural network can use the bipolar Sigmoid function.

$$f(x) = \left(1 - e^{-x}\right) / \left(1 + e^{-x}\right) \tag{19}$$

According to the differential equations of motion with the wheel steering control and the neural network algorithm to write MATLAB program, mad a dynamic analysis through the dynamic driving track, vehicle yaw rate and sideslip angle of the vehicle.

4.1. *Front wheel steering control of the trailer*

The number of neurons in the hidden layer is 6, and the learning rate is 0.5. Program operation results are shown in figure 3.

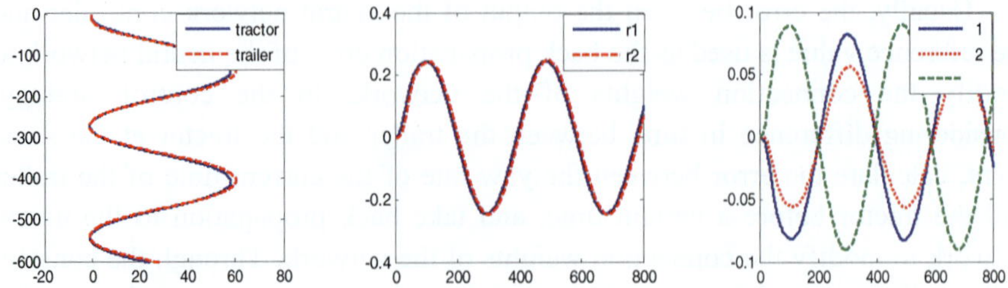

(a) (b) (c)

Fig. 3. The Track of Full Trailer and the Transient Response Curves of Outputs

From the figure 3(a), it can be seen the tractor and trailer driving path is basically the same in the initial stage, the overall path tracking performance is good, and there is a little deviation in the sharp turn of road. Along with the moving of the vehicle, the track deviation of both the tractor and the trailer becomes larger, that is, the path tracking performance becomes worse. Figure 3(b) shows that there is a lag between the yaw rate of the trailer and the tractor. Figure 3(c) shows the sideslip angle of tractor and trailer. Therefore, the lag synchronous control of the yaw rate of the trailer is helpful to improve the tracking performance of the trailer.

4.2. *Compensation control of the rotation angle of the trailer*

It can be seen from the upper section, using the error of yaw rate between the tractor and the trailer to control the rotation angle of the trailer, but the optimal path tracking performance still cannot be achieved. In actual driving, because the path is not a straight line, so the distance between the center of mass and the mass of the trailer is not equal to the value of the equation. Considering the error and the rotation angle of the wheels of the trailer is controlled by the compensation, namely make the compensation of the values between the two relative sideslip angle.

After repeated regulating parameters, the front wheel rotation was compensated γ times of the relative sideslip angle on the basis of the last section.

$$\delta_3 = \delta + \gamma \cdot \Delta\varphi \tag{20}$$

The δ is the output of the BP neural network, the γ is the correction factor associated with the trailer structure parameters and here is $\gamma=0.8$. Trajectory and yaw rate and sideslip angle response as shown in Figure 4. Figure 4(a) shows that the driving path of the tractor and the trailer is exactly the same, which shows the feasibility and superiority of compensation control. Figures 4(b) and 4(c) show that both the same realization of the lag synchronous driving.

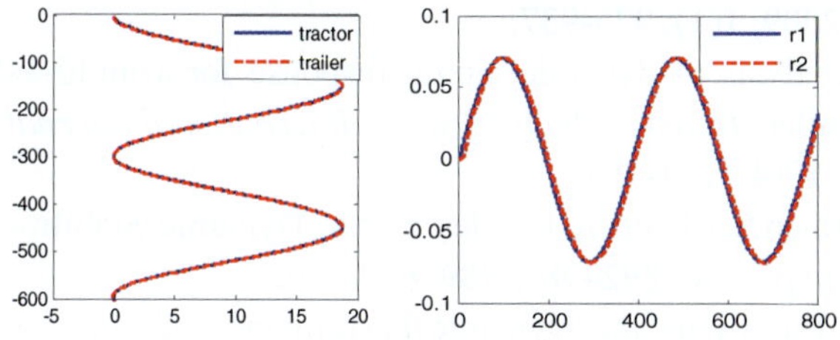

Fig. 4. The Track of Trailer and The Transient Response Curves of Outputs

5. Conclusion

The path tracking performance of the trailer is improved by using the fractional order BP network to control the trailer steering. In view of the problem of the rotation angle compensation control, the trailer and tractor driving path is exactly the same, and achieved a better control.

Acknowledgment

This work was supported by the National Natural Science Foundation of China (Grant No. 11272159).

References

1. Juan Yu,Cheng Hu, Haijun Jiang.α-stability and α-synchronization for fractional-order neural network[J].*Neural Networks*,2012,35:82-87.
2. Cotter N. The stone-weierstrass theorem and its applications to neural network. *IEEE Transaction on Neural Networks*, 1990, 1(4):290-295.
3. Ito Y. Representation of functions by superposition of a step or sigmoidal functions and their application to neural network theory. *Neural Networks*, 1991, 4(3):385-394.
4. Yang, Jie, Chen Ning , A trailer steering model tracking compensation cont rol, *World Congress on Intelligent Control & Automation, Shenyang,China,* 2014:4067-4071.
5. Boroomand Arefeh, B. Menhaj Mohammad. Fractional-Order Hopfield Neura l Network. *Advances in Neuro-Information Processing*, 2009, 5506:883-890.
6. Zimic N, Mraz M. Decomposition of a complex fuzzy controller for the truck-and-trailer reverse parking problem [J]. *Mathematical and Computer Modelling*. 2006, 43(5-6): 632-645.

7. Hac A, Fulk D, Chen. H. Stability and Control Considerations of Vehicle-Trailer Combination. *SAE International Journal of Passenger Cars: Mechanical Systems*. 2009, 1(1): 925-937.
8. Wu D H, Lin J H. Analysis of dynamic lateral response for a multi-axle-steering tractor and trailer. *Heavy Vehicle Systems-International Journal of Vehicle Design*. 2003, 10(4): 281-294.
9. Aurell J E S. The Influence of Steered Axles on the Dynamic Stability of Heavy Vehicles. *SAE paper* No. 892498. 1989: 612-629.
10. Winkler C F P C O. Improving the Dynamic Performance of Multitrailer Vehicles: A Study of Innovative Dollies. *Transportation Research Institute, The University of Michigan, Vol. I, Final Technical Report.* 1986: 235-247.
11. Altafini C, Speranzon A, Wahlberg B. A feedback control scheme for reversing a truck and trailer vehicle. *IEEE Transactions on Robotics and Automation*. 2001, 17(6): 915-922.
12. Kristopher J Seluga R M O I. Articulated vehicle yaw stability during braking-a parametric study. *SAE Thchenical Paper Series*.2004-01-2630. 2004.
13. Fancher P, Winkler C. Directional performance issues in evaluation and design of articulated heavy vehicles. *Vehicle System Dynamics*. 2007, 45(7-8): 607-647.
14. Weiwen D. Parametric study on vehicle-trailer dynamics for stability control. *SAE Technical Paper Series*.2003-01-1321. 2003.
15. Fancher P W C E R. Using Braking to Control the Lateral Motions of Full Trailers. *Vehicle System Dynamics*.1998, 29: 462-478.
16. Rangavajhula K, Tsao H. Effect of multi-axle steering on off-tracking and dynamic lateral response of articulated tractor-trailer combinations. *International Journal of Heavy Vehicle Systems*. 2007, 14(4): 376-401.
17. Rangavajhula K, Tsao H J. Active trailer steering control of an articulated system with a tractor and three full trailers for tractor-track following. *International Journal of Heavy Vehicle Systems*. 2007, 14(3): 271-293.
18. Odhams A M C, Roebuck R L, Cebon D, et al. Dynamic safety of active trailer steering systems. *Proceedings of the Institution of Mechanical Engineers Part K-Journal of Multi-Body Dynamics*. 2008, 222(4): 367-380.
19. He Y I M W T. An Integrated Design Method for Articulated Heavy Vehicles with Active Trailer Steering Systems. *SAE Int. J. Passenger Cars—Mech. Syst*. 2010, 119(6): 158-174.
20. He Y, Islam M M. An Automated Design Method for Active Trailer Steering Systems of Articulated Heavy Vehicles. *Journal of Mechanical Design*. 2012, 134(4):125-140.

Visual Strategies in Excellent Course Construction

Pei Pei

School of Computer Science, Anhui Sanlian University
Anhui 230000, China
Email: elfinpeipei@sina.com

This paper aims to demonstrate the visualization strategies in excellent course resources design, development and management. Firstly, define the meaning of visualization according to the literature, summarize relevant data, information, knowledge of the excellent course resources and the application in the field by visualization. To theoretically discusses in design, development and management through visualization and content of the theoretical basis. Visualization should be throughout the whole process of the construction of the curriculum resources. The visualization of the high-quality goods curriculum resources not only improves the individual learning effect, but also guarantees the quality of the scale of the curriculum resources. Finally, the field of the practice of the fine course "computer culture basis" is based on the function of the visualization of high-quality goods curriculum resources optimization, and from the aspects of universality, collaborative and iterative visual strategy is proposed.

Keywords: Excellent Course Resources; Visualization; Strategies.

1. Introduction

On April 8, 2003, the ministry of education issued "about start high school teaching quality and teaching reform project construction" and clearly put forward excellent courses is a high-quality of the model curriculum which including an elite teachers, first-class teaching content, intellectual teaching methods and top teaching management. It is required that the colleges and universities to establish the high-quality goods curriculum system, to improve the quality of education [1]. So far, the national colleges and universities have developed thousands of excellent courses at national top-quality level, provincial level and school level. In the process of curriculum development and construction, resource turns to be the most important factor. Only develop and built Sharing resources, can truly reflect the fine course model.

Good teaching is not to go looking for better teaching methods for teachers, but better opportunities for students to construct. As so far, the idea of high-quality curriculum is less researching on learners' needs and requirements of social development, less researching on teachers how to effectively guide the students into the curriculum resources, less introducing the concept of "teach them to fish (learning and thinking method)", personalized learning, organizational learning and effective learning into curriculum resources design [3].

These problems are rooted in space and time separation between teachers and students. To solve this problem, it should find the answer from the opposite of question. "Visualization" is an inevitable choice to solve the series problem from separation. At the same time, the development of education technology and management science provides an important theoretical and technical support for this option. The application of the visualization method and technology research will improve overall efficiency, guarantee the quality of resources, improve the effect of learners' learning, complete the course construction and promote the sustainable development.

2. Visualization Overview

2.1. *The meaning of visualization*

Visualization is such as "visible, clear present, graphic". Card and other scholars believed that visualization is using the visual interactive of computer and abstract data into intuitive method of graphic, in order to enhance people's cognition to the data [4]. While knowledge visualization refers to all can be used to construct and communicate complex knowledge means of illustration, the purpose is to transfer ideas, experience, attitude, values, expectations, views, opinions, and prediction and so on, and to help others in this way correctly refactoring, memory, and apply the knowledge[5]. Burkhard & Eppler (2004) argues that knowledge visualization is an emerging research area based on scientific computing visualization, data visualization, information visualization. Visualization can be applied to excellent course related in the field of data, information, knowledge and learning management.

2.2. *The application of visualization in excellent courses*

During the construction of excellent courses, more research scholars in visual design and development of resources discuss knowledge representation absolutely from the perspective of learning resources and learning process, lack of comprehensive research in design, development and management. At present, journal, can be able to be found that Gao Hengyu, thinks knowledge visualization can be used as a tool to solve the problem of distance education, based on the existing research results and the sorting of literature and the analysis of the actual situation, it demonstrates the knowledge visualization application feasibility of long-distance education theory and reality. Ma Xiulin thinks in online learning conditions, network curriculum design, construction, learning management visualization technology are very important, and from the perspective of open learning management system to study resources construction and progress management. Moreover, Zheng Yongbai puts forward the concept of "comprehensive education and technology". He thinks that it is necessary to study the education media and learning resources combined problems in the big background. It should be from the design, development, utilization, evaluation and management of five aspects to research learning resources and learning process, to realize optimization of education information transmission. This concept provides the research idea and analysis framework to visual strategies in excellent courses construction.

3. The Visualize Content Selection and Theory Foundation of Excellent Course Resources

3.1. *Learning resource visualization*

"Any kind of new technology invention and application of the (extension of feeling) are changing our way of thinking and behavior, that is the way we perceive the world"[5]. "Tell me I will forget, show me I will remember, let me to participate in I will understand"(Aristotle). These show the importance of "see". Supported by information technology, Curriculum designer present the knowledge content in such intuitive way like chart, mind maps, knowledge map form and combined with the subject of teaching design. This visual processing can fully mobilize the visual and auditory sensory channel to receive information, expand information capacity. Visualization focus on the before and after the logic relation, meaning, concept, composition principles, processes procedures, technology, method and experience of knowledge itself exists in expression. One experimental results show that 83% of the total receiving information is through the visual channel. Palvio's dual coding theory is put forward: knowledge visualization has made very good auxiliary and complement in knowledge representation. It reducing the cognitive load of language channel and promote the training of thinking.

3.2. *Evaluative resource visualization*

Evaluation resources visualization is to give learners visualize evaluation information in order to facilitate them to establish a reasonable learning motivation and to make rational decisions. Under the web open education condition of high quality courses, communication between students and teachers increase the test of time and space, sometimes during studying due to the lack of face to face communication with teacher in the first time, it will cause separation. Present visual information in the curriculum resources will help learning problem diagnosis. Evaluative resource visualization main content is about the course of learning convenience, learning outcomes of information, to guide the learners in autonomous learning, to achieve the correct choice way of curriculum resources, content, optimize curriculums and enhance learning effect. This visualization includes: learning guidance visualization which is obtained by reviews, learning process and method visualization. Evaluation of resources visualization is an important driving force to enhance the utilization and ratio of application of the resources. It is convenient for learners to understand learning situation and generate targeted, continuous learning behavior.

3.3. *Course process visualization*

Course process visualization is based on learning content, logic framework, knowledge level relationship visual design and rendering. It makes the learning process information such as each learning knowledge node of the learners participate in, homework completion, interactive situation, learning effect visualize present. So that learners can control autonomous learning process, manage their own learning resources, improve learning efficiency and effectiveness. Relevant education researchers survey the problem of the high drop out of current popular hybrid teaching MOOC, it is concluded that: in the process of video course because of a lack of clear learning objectives, reasonable expectations and standardization of learning content, learning process and learning result lack of standard design. During this kind of informal learning, it is hard to keep self-control study pace. When learners faced with huge amounts of information and complicated network environment, they must be fall into shallow level of learning, lack of depth and innovation, fewer personal satisfaction and pleasure. Sequentially, it is hard to continue studying. Therefore, standardized, orderly and simple visual video course resources not only can make learners to continue learning, also can cause the resource providers, builders continue to provide quality support services, formed mature, high-quality resources construction of the system.

4. Visual Strategies in Excellent Courses Construction

The author summarized the resources construction in design, develop and update of curriculum resources combined with "the concept of comprehensive education technology". Based on the analysis of the above research, the author presided and develop a school level top course "computer culture basis" explore curriculum construction practice, and the author thinks that excellent construction has three visual strategies as blow:

4.1. *General strategy*

From the perspective of management, the visualization of High-quality curriculum resource development, design and management involves the reasonable allocation of various resources and use. The corresponding strategy is to consider the current problems existing in the construction of curriculum resources, and put forward countermeasures to solve. The problems existing in the main are: focus on the use of advanced technology, while nor from the perspective of the learner's; need for the assessment, research, while cannot provide more social education services; just teachers' teaching design ability to play, without considering the learners' learning needs. The national fine course construction, which as a result of education technology specious technologism has two skin problems in common curriculum resources and curriculum (did not reflect the nature of curriculum resources problem). These exquisite courses learning resources are being used by schools or teaching workers less and most are decomposed into bits and pieces of material resources [9]. This shows the existing curriculum resources lack of recognition accept group. Therefore, to form the first examine applicability for the resource development and construction, and taking visual resources development strategy: (1) Establish a visual teaching resources construction system, make resource standard and guarantee the applicability and rationality .Make sure the quality of resources, provide the basis for curriculum promote and accept. For this purpose, at the beginning of the course resources construction, designers should increase analysis of the audience's demand mining pain points, strengthening theory research on design meet the need of curriculum construction and resources development and other related construction, explore the standards and specifications, and to constantly improve. (2) Take learners' demand as guidance, build visualization resources in blended learning, autonomous learning as urgent need. The key is to determine the visual type of curriculum resources and the development direction. Based on the audience demand, summarizing cases of the learners puzzling when they are studying the curriculum. Sometimes because of the limitation of the resources, it is becoming a barrier of their further study. Thus, the author introduces visualize thinking.

In the process of learning, learners have access to the knowledge includes the designer's goals and purpose. However, the feedback from the reality is often shows like teaching goal orientation is very narrow, limited or lag, which does not favorable for learners to fully understand the problem, and has caused certain obstacles on the learners to problem solving. Such problems can be designed with the help of a visual representation, by analogy, metaphor or assumption, to encourage problem solving ability enhancement on the construction of the mental model as the basis. By allowing learners outside of knowledge structure and mental model characterize of manifestation, will produce more tactic knowledge. To some extent, this will broaden the degree of freedom when design, at the same time can have a thorough understanding of goals and purpose by comprehensive thinking. The more fully and timely feedback from reality, the more promotion in learners knowledge externalization. Jonathan thinks, when the designer requires learners through the original knowledge network (experience, emotions, etc.) to solve the problem, it must through the provision of relevant cases to support these experiences. The related cases by offering them the characterization of without experience to support the construction of meaning. Compared with description of pure text analysis learning, learners more easily use the case analysis of visual design to get more intuitive understanding; meanwhile a profound perceptual knowledge can promote the formation of the preliminary mental model. Not only similar analysis of visualization cases can increase learners' indirect experience of problem solving, but to prop up their memories and to provide reference, make the conversion between explicit knowledge and tacit knowledge, promote the recessive knowledge into explicit knowledge.

4.2. *Collaborative strategy visualization*

When a learner gives personal views and understanding in the group study, it makes originally only oneself-known tacit knowledge into visible reference for other members. If he shows this implicit knowledge without visualization, the other members are unable to learn the ins and outs of this knowledge which is unable to truly grasp the connotation of the knowledge. By using concept mapping tools or software for knowledge modeling, based on the concept of deconstruction and construction, it makes sense of all kinds of knowledge transfer from pure abstract meaning into visual graphic. This will achieve concept test in high-quality class learning; through a variety of visualization tool software and communication platform, cognition of the original model, the knowledge transfers. In the process of the blended learning model, a lot of knowledge change into the "silence for massive different types of knowledge are different and varieties pattern. To activate this knowledge, one first needs to establish the cognitive structure of knowledge. Course designers should set the function of collaboration. This will encourage every learner to participate in, to share without reservation and to establish full communication and knowledge sharing culture, make learning group become a learning organization.

4.3. *Iterative strategy visualization*

Due to accelerate upgrading of technology, with the deepening of knowledge updating and application, the high-quality goods curriculum resources not only needs to update, but also needs constantly development in the process of construction technology. In a long time, the audiences generally reflect the low visual learning resources, lag update. These existent problems affect the learners' learning interests and learning motivation, reduce absorption rate greatly. It generates an obstacle to knowledge-internalization and the form of tacit knowledge. Therefore, establish a dynamic curriculum resources iteration model is a kind of inevitable choice. "Knowledge visualization cannot merely make for the static objects of knowledge transfer, but need to build an iterative, collaborative, dynamic process [10]. The past curriculum resources development is mainly based on the knowledge and technical conditions at that time, take the waterfall model, use a one-off design concept and idea, which lack of iterative design. It is take a long time in interpretation, but lack of knowledge in visual graphics, and the multimedia technology is not enough to develop a system design. Therefore, the excellent curriculum resources should avoid these problems. When get in iterative design process, choose visual resources according to the learners' feedback of use and expert evaluation, make the modification and update throughout the process, using the product development life cycle as the comprehensive construction guidance. General speaking, there are three aspects embodied in it: The first level, visual demand level. Take visual analysis on the curriculum goals and learners, make sure the subsequent course construction based on knowledge and learners' individual needs. For example, using 5w2h method, clear present the object, the curriculum nature, start time, educated people, what impact and the value of these effects. The second level is resources visualization level. Design visual learning resources on the basis of the learner centered, meanwhile create visual interactive situation in the process of resource building. Teachers can convenient input knowledge points in the process, and indicate the links between knowledge. Through the programming language to generate diagrams and knowledge map, the dynamic update of curriculum resources and intervention strategies by the students and teachers incentives to promote learners' participation. The third level is visual evaluation level; the curriculum resources platform should be started with the perspective of the overall system of visual design, implement dynamic process records of individual learning and overall connection. Provide technical support, teachers can convenient input knowledge points in the system, and indicate the relationship between the knowledge points, thus generating knowledge map, which promote renewal of curriculum resources. Given learners study diagnosis and case analysis during real time recording. The main process is summarized as follows: input the knowledge and the correlation into the management platform, provide additional learning resources, generate knowledge map according to the knowledge node table and the associated table and additional resources to, dynamic record learners' mastery of knowledge points according to the lesson plan, and form the visual learning diagnosis.

5. Conclusion

Visual knowledge design, development and management are a new kind of thought. The development history of network learning in our country is short, too. This article proposes an integrated research of these two. So far, there is no system of studying. Some research is still in stage of pioneer. In this paper, take excellent course resources as object, with network learning as the backing, take visual knowledge construct as key research point. Put forward some innovative ideas:(1) Research on visualization in knowledge building and network learning process nature and characteristics, analysis of the current problems of online learning and proposed the possible solutions.(2) Take the theory of knowledge management, knowledge visualization theory and constructivist instructional design theory as the instruction, construct visual strategies based on visualization network learning, and try to make some integration of groundbreaking research.

Acknowledgements

This paper is one of the result in College Quality project of Anhui Sanlian University (project No14zlgc008) and also one of the achievement of the Network Engineering Talents Cultivation Pattern Exploration and Practice Research base on school-enterprise cooperation (project No 2014zdjy144)

References

1. Li Yiyuan. *The Research of College excellent courses network resources development demanding and status*. Vol 13(E-Education Research.2009), pp.45.
2. Huo Hongtian. *Thinking of the high-quality courses design and development*. Education Research and Experiment. Vol 2(2009).pp.16.
3. Novak J.D. & A.J. Canas. The Theory Underlying Concept Maps and How to Construct Them http://emap.ihmc.us/Publications/, 2012-11-12.
4. Guoqing, zhao, Ronghuai, huang, Zhijian, Lu. *The theory and the method of knowledge visualization*. Open education research. (2005)No 11 (1) .pp.23.
5. Chao-yun wang. *The theory and application of knowledge visualization*. Journal of modern education technology.2007, (6). pp.18.
6. Fan Wenqiang. *Open courses (MOOC) and its learning support based on the mass of associated network*. Journal of distance education. (2012)No 3.pp.31.
7. Huang Anxin. *Visual strategies of learning resources design, development and operation*. Journal of distance education and network education. (2015)No 7.pp.66.

Erbium Doped Fiber Attenuation Influenced by the Irradiation Dose

Zong-Feng Ma[1,a], Dong-Xing Li[2,b] and Yun-Yang Li[2,c]

[1]*Shandong Aerospace Electro-technology Institute*

Yantai, China

[2]*School of Mechanical Engineering, Shandong University of Technology*

Zibo, China

E-mail: [a]*mzf706@163.com,* [b]*lidongxing_1@163.com,* [c]*liyunyang_1@163.com*

Space radiation contains various types of radiation, such as electrons, protons, gamma rays, and so on. In order to evaluate the adaptability of erbium (Er) doped fiber in the space radiation environment, a radiation source (Co^{60} gamma ray source) is used to generate the dose rate and the total amount of radiation which is approximately equivalent to the ones via the space environment. By measuring the attenuation of the optical fiber for unit length in 1550 nm, the attenuation of the optical signal through the erbium doped fiber is measured. The radiation effect principle of the optical fiber is analyzed by the energy band theory and the energy level transition theory. The theoretical analysis and experimental results show that the attenuation of Er doped fiber is increased with the increasing of irradiation dose and tends to saturation.

Keywords: Radiation Effect; Erbium Doped Fiber; Irradiation Dose.

1. Introduction

Space Doppler wind lidar is the only direct measurement of global wind profile instrument. With the development of space technology, the erbium doped fiber (EDF) applications in spacecraft attract more and more attention, including EDFA (erbium doped fiber amplifier); Erbium doped fiber broadband super radiance light source, etc. In space, optical fibers are likely to be exposed to high doses of electrons and protons. The typical dose rate is 0.1rad/h-1rad/h, and the total dose of is estimated to have a total dose of 20 krad per year in spacecraft [1]. Due to the space radiation environment is very complicated, the performance of fiber optic devices under irradiation conditions is the deterioration of the performance of different degrees. For example, the fiber loss increases and the fiber amplifier will produce color centers to bring down the gain. So it is necessary to study the radiation adaptability of the optical fiber devices [2, 3]. EDFA can greatly improve the signal transmission power and distance, and improve the detection effect of the system. Therefore, the working process of EDFA is analyzed, and the radiation effect theory of optical materials is studied. The radiation effect experiment of EDF was designed.

2. The Working Principle of EDFA

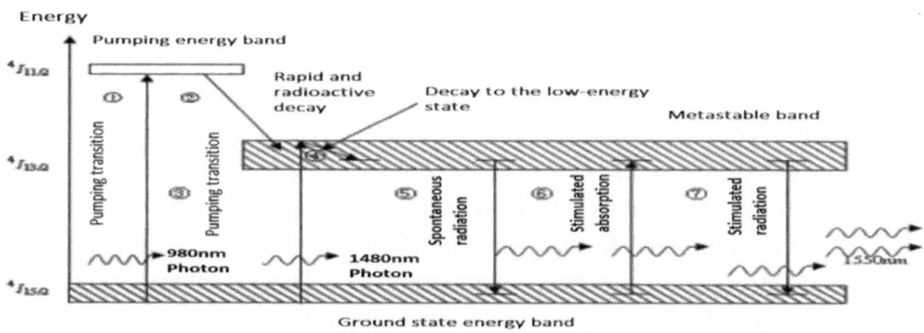

Fig. 1. Various transition processes of ion in Er doped fiber

As shown in figure 1, in the role of the pump light, most of the Er3+ ions jump from the ground state to the upper state leap, then through non-radiative transitions, it jumps into between energy states and the ground state, and the long-lived metastable particles, it is easy to form a population inversion between the steady state and the ground state. When the signal light passes through the erbium doped fiber, it interacts with in Er3+ which is in metastable and it stimulates to occur radiation effect, resulting in a large number of photons which are identical with their own, thus greatly increase the number of photons. To achieve the amplification of light, it makes the signal light in the optical fiber into a strong input light signal [4].

EDF is the most important element in EDFA, and it acts as the role of the amplification medium. EDF radiation adaptability is good or bad, which will directly affect the application of EDFA in space. Gauss distribution of approximate field in optical fiber signal light and pump light in the fiber core, on the axis of the strongest intensity. Doping, as far as possible to make the impurity particles concentrated in the near axis region, so as to improve the energy conversion efficiency.

3. Theory of Radiation Effects on Optical Materials

The optical radiation effect can be divided into the primary stage, the secondary stage and the defect formation stage. Gamma rays interact directly with optical fiber through the photoelectric effect. Compton scattering and electron pair effect, which lead to the ionization of the electron hole pair in the optical fiber. Secondly, under the irradiation of space, the optical materials are subjected to high energy radiation, and the defect structure can be changed into other types of point defect structure after capturing electrons or holes. The formation of new materials in optical absorption center, which are the color center. New absorption bands are introduced in the optical fiber. The captured electrons may jump to the conduction band by thermal excitation or light excitation, causing degradation of color centers [5].

It is divided into stable and unstable color center in the fiber. Stable color centers are formed and not receded at once and it can be stably present in the fiber after irradiation, and forms a stable light absorption. Unstable color center is apt to deteriorate by the heat degradation [6]. Therefore, the optical fiber attenuation is not stable, and there is the annealing effect.

The fiber center attenuation is also affected by optical fiber transmission. In the process of radiation, light will transfer from "weak light" for the success rate of larger "light". It will be degraded that there are the number of fiber color centers [7].

The defect level is close to the conduction band; the color center is more easily degraded. Electrons which jump to the conduction band jump back to the valence band by deexcitation. From the above analysis, the fiber attenuation is the main color of fiber optical absorption results. Radiation induced attenuation of the optical fiber is mainly the result of the fiber optical absorption of color centers, and a variety of factors influence color centers production, color centers degradation so they affect the reduction of radiation attenuation.

4. Erbium Doped Fiber Radiation Absorption Model

Optical fiber attenuation depends on the unit length of the fiber color center, and color center absorption ability of the light signal. We can analysis the relation of the density of color centers and radiation dose. The theory is that color centers can jump to the conduction band due to the excitation leaving the degradation of color centers in the corresponding defect levels. Unstable centers have their own life ti [8]. Color change in the number of level a fiber defect rate during radiation can be said:

$$\frac{dn_i(t)}{dt} = k_i D - \frac{n_i(t)}{\tau_i} \tag{1}$$

Where n_i is the number of the I energy center, D for irradiation dose rate, k_iD for the rate of the center, k_i for the color heart to produce factors number relative to the irradiation dose rate.

In certain cases, some centers can exist and this solution type should be considered, this equation is,

$$A_j(t) = b_j D(t) \tag{2}$$

b_j is a coefficient and color center generation, color center absorption coefficient of light, irradiation dose rate, the amount of life center.

Therefore, there is multi component saturation index model [9],

$$A(D) = \sum^{n_1} a_i \left[1 - \exp\left(-\frac{D}{D_{si}}\right)\right] + \sum^{n_2} b_j D \tag{3}$$

Type a_i as experimental constant, D_{si} Center for the i defect level saturation dose, both color center generation and degradation of radiation dose to achieve balance.

5. Radiation Effect Experiment of Erbium Doped Fiber

The experimental apparatus is shown in figure 2.

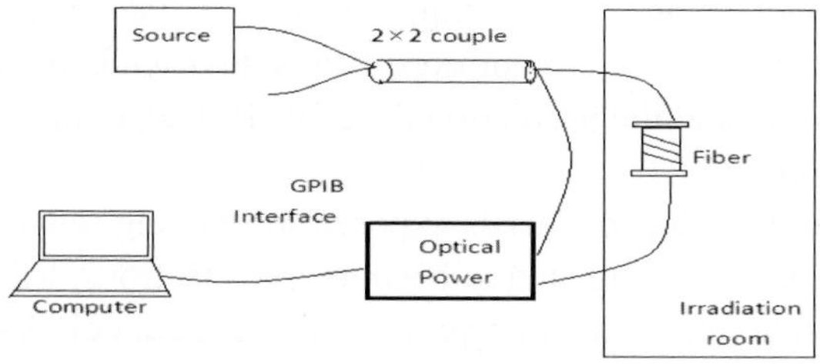

Fig. 2. Fiber optic radiation attenuation measurement device

In the experiment, the radiation effect of the optical fiber is studied by using the radiation environment of the Co^{60} gamma ray source. The emergent light from the light source through 2×2 coupler is separated into two beams, a bunch of light as test optical signal is inputted to the fiber under test by an optical fiber jumper wire, another as a reference signal compensate power fluctuation of the light source on the measurement of the influence. The output signal from the optical transmission fiber jumpers out of the irradiation chamber and it uses the optical power meter to measure. In order to avoid the effect of the energy level transition on the test, the Er doped fiber has been tested by 1550 nm light.

In practice, the relationship of $y=a\ (1-e^{-bx})$ to Eq. (3) -type multi-component saturation index model is simplified. Where y represents the optical fiber loss, x represents the irradiation dose, for a given optical fiber a is constant, b is an electronic defect trapping (electron trapping centers) or holes (hole trapping centers) section of the formation of color centers. A group of a=0.398, b=0.104 and two groups of a=0.121, b=0.179 were obtained respectively.

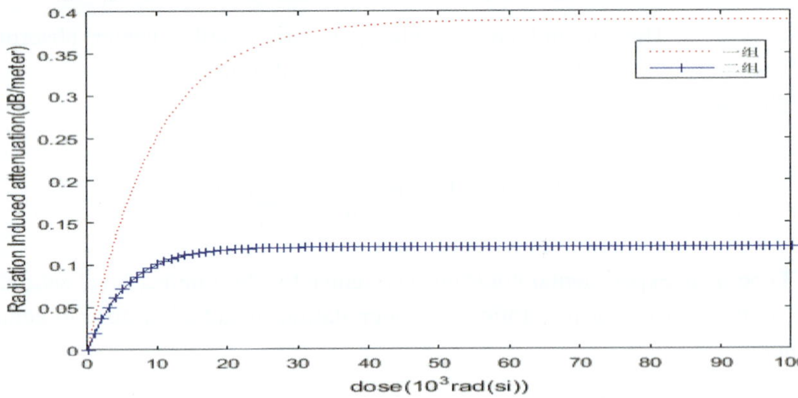

Fig. 3. Erbium-doped fiber loss with the change of dose

From Figure 3, erbium doped fiber loss and irradiation dose is monotonically increasing relationship, when a=0.398, b=0.104 and at the irradiation dose 50×10^3*rad*, erbium doped fiber loss tends to saturation. When a=0.121, b=0.179 and at the irradiation dose 20×10^3*rad*, erbium doped fiber loss tends to saturation.

When the erbium-doped fiber is exposed to ionizing radiation, the electron in the valence band are stimulated to become free electrons, leaving holes in the valence band, free electrons transport in the conduction band, when it is captured by the sun vacancy and form color hearts. At this time, the material continued to be irradiated. Since the material does not exist in the sun room, it does not colored heart anymore, and saturation phenomenon appeared.

6. Conclusions

In order to solve the problem of the radiation protection of the space device, the experiment of the radiation effect of the erbium doped fiber is carried out. In the radiation induced attenuation experiment, the radiation effect of the optical fiber is studied by using the space ionization radiation environment which is simulated by Co60 gamma ray. Radiation induced attenuation of the optical fiber is mainly the result of the fiber optical absorption of color centers, and a variety of factors influence color centers production, color centers degradation so they affect the reduction of radiation attenuation. Experimental results show that the erbium doped fiber loss tends to saturation with the increase of irradiation dose.

Acknowledgement

In this paper, the research work was supported by National Natural Science Foundation of China under Grant (Project No. 61302162) and National High Technology Research and Development Program 863 under Grant (Project No. 2012AA120605).

References

1. J. N. Sandoe, P. H. Parkies, S. Parke. Variation of Er3+ cross section for stimulated emission with glass composion [J]. J. Phys. D: Appl. Phys., 1972.
2. Winker D M, Couch R H. An overview of LITE: NASA's Lidar In-space Technology Experiment[C]. Proceeding of IEEE, 84(2), 1996.
3. F. Berghmans. An introduction to radiation effects on optical components and fiber optic sensor[C]. Optical Waveguide Sensing and Imaging, 2008.
4. Wang Jian, Yang Shcngsheng, Wang Yunfei, et al. Analysis of Space radiation effects on EDFA [J]. Vacuum & Cryogenics, 13(4), 2007.
5. Elisc Regnier, Ivo Flammer. Low-dose radiation induced attenuation at infra-red wavelengths for P-doped, Ge-doped and pure silica-core optical fibers [J]. IEEE Transactions on Nuclear Science, 54(4), 2007.
6. B. Brichard, P. Borgermans. Dedicated optical fibers for dosimetry based on radiation-induced attenuation, experimental results[C]. SPIE, 3872(1999).
7. E. J. Friebele, M. E. Gingerich, D. L. Griscom. Survivability of optical fibers in space[C]. SPIE, 1992.
8. Borgermans P, Brichard B. Kinetic models and spectral dependencies of the radiation-induced attenuation in pure silica fibers[J]. IEEE Transactions on Nuclear Science, 49(3), 2002, pp. 1439-1445.
9. O. Gilard, M. Caussanel, H. Duval. New model for assessing dose, dose rate, and temperature sensitivity of radiation induced absorption in glasses [J]. Journal of Applied Physics, 108(093115), 2010.

Research on Diffraction Efficiency and Light Intensity for AOM

Zong-Feng Ma[1,a], Dong-Xing Li[2,b] and Li Ying[2,c]

[1]Shandong Aerospace Electro-technology Institute
Yantai, China
[2]School of Mechanical Engineering, Shandong University of Technology
Zibo, China
E-mail: [a]mzf706@163.com, [b]lidongxing_1@163.com, [c]liying_1@163.com

Acousto-optic modulator (AOM) is one of the key technologies of coherent wind lidar system. By the theoretical analysis and the simulations, the mathematical model of the diffraction intensity and the diffraction efficiency of the AOM are obtained. The intensity of 0 - stage and 1 – stage diffraction beam change periodically with the increase of the ultrasonic power. When the wavelength of incident beam is 1550nm, the diffraction efficiency can reach about 84%, which is consistent with eye-safe.

Keywords: AOM; Bragg Diffraction; Diffraction Intensity; Diffraction Efficiency.

1. Introduction

Doppler wind lidar system is widely used in meteorological fields, and it's working principle is to determine the radial velocity of the target by the frequency shift of the scattered signal which is irradiated to the target. Doppler wind lidar is one of the most effective means to measure the wind field data in large area[1~3]. AOM was applied to Doppler velocimetry[4]. The AOM of all-fiber-coupled input and output avoid the trouble of optical modulation between optical devices and it has high integration. The diffraction efficiency can reach 84%[5]. It has broad application prospect as the core device to realize the frequency shift in Doppler lidar system.

2. Working Principle of AOM

The radio frequency signal output by the driving light source is applied to the piezoelectric transducer of the acousto-optical crystal through an impedance matching network, and the transducer converts the electric signal into an ultrasonic wave and transmits it to an acousto-optic medium. The elastic deformation of medium leads to the change of the refractive index of the medium. The propagation direction will be changed when the laser passes through the medium. That is, the diffraction phenomenon occurs[6]. The intensity, frequency and direction of the diffraction beam are changed with the change of the ultrasonic field. Acousto-optic frequency shift is the process which the frequency shift signal is added to the carrier via AOM.

3. Bragg Diffraction

3.1. *Principles*

When the incident beam meets some certain conditions, diffraction beam at all levels in medium will interfere with each other. Advanced diffraction beam will cancel each other out, with only 0 - stage and 1– stage diffraction beam, which is Bragg diffraction. When the incident angle is Bragg angle, and the wavelength of the ultrasonic wave and the length of acousto-optic effect in medium satisfy

$$U = 2\pi L\lambda/\Lambda >> 4\pi \tag{1}$$

In Eq. (1), L is the length of the acousto-optic effect, λ and Λ are the wavelength of beam and the ultrasonic wave in medium.

3.2. *Diffraction intensity*

When the acousto-optic interaction is normal, if the incident beam pass through the acousto-optic medium at angle θ:

$$\frac{dE_m(x)}{dx} - j\Delta k_m E_m(x) = -\frac{\pi \cdot \Delta n}{\lambda_0 \cos\theta}\left[E_{m-1}(x) - E_{m+1}(x)\right] \tag{2}$$

$$\Delta k_m = \frac{mk_s}{\cos\theta}\left(m\frac{k_s}{2k} - \sin\theta\right) \tag{3}$$

In Eq. (2) and (3), E_m is the energy of diffraction beam, Δn is the change of the refractive index, λ_0 is the wavelength of the beam in the vacuum, κ_m is the wave vector of the m-stage diffraction beam, κ_s is the ultrasonic wave vector.

When 1-stage diffraction beam satisfy momentum matching condition $\Delta\kappa_1=0$, the incident angle of beam meet

$$\sin\theta_B = k_s/2k = \lambda/\lambda_s \tag{4}$$

In Eq. (4), λ is the wavelength of the beam in medium, θ_B is the Bragg angle. 0-stage and 1-stage diffraction beam satisfy momentum matching condition, so the light intensity is large due to in-phase superposition, the other levels of beam does not satisfy the momentum matching condition so the light intensity is small[6]. Then, the output beam is mainly 0-stage and 1-stage beam, and the maximum value of diffraction efficiency of the 1-stage beam can be achieved.

The intensity of 0-stage and 1-stage diffraction beam can be obtained by the theory of acousto-optic interaction.

$$\begin{cases} I_0 = I_i \cos^2(v/2) \\ I_1 = I_i \sin^2(v/2) \end{cases} \tag{5}$$

In Eq. (5), Ii is the intensity of incident beam, v is the additional phase delay when beam pass through the ultrasonic field, it can be represented by the change of sound-induced refractive index Δn.

$$v = \frac{2\pi}{\lambda_0} \cdot \Delta n L = 2\frac{\pi}{\sqrt{2}\lambda_0}\sqrt{\frac{L}{H} M P_s} \tag{6}$$

3.3. *Diffraction efficiency*

Introducing parameters

$$\xi = -\frac{2\pi}{\lambda_0 \cos\theta} \cdot \Delta n L \approx -\frac{2\pi}{\lambda_0} \cdot \Delta n L \tag{7}$$

$$Q = k_s^2 L / k \cos\theta \approx k_s^2 L / k \tag{8}$$

$$\alpha = k \sin\theta / k_s \approx \sin\theta / 2\sin\theta_B \tag{9}$$

Taking Eq. (7), (8) and (9) into Eq. (2) and (3), we get

$$\frac{dE_m(x)}{dx} - j\Delta k_m E_m(x) = \frac{\xi}{2L}[E_{m-1}(x) - E_{m+1}(x)] \tag{10}$$

$$\Delta k_m = mQ(m - 2\alpha)/2L \tag{11}$$

When the incident angle is Bragg angle θ_B, the other levels of beam can be neglected and only the $E_0(x)$ and $E_1(x)$ are considered. Then, ordering Eq. (10) m=0 and m=1, and taking the critical conditions of $E_0(x)$=E_0 and $E_1(x)$=0 into Eq. (10), we can get

$$E_0(x) = E_0 e^{-j\varsigma x/L}\left(\cos\frac{\sigma x}{L} + j\frac{\varsigma}{\sigma}\sin\frac{\sigma x}{L}\right) \tag{12}$$

$$E_1(x) = E_0 e^{-j\varsigma x/L}\frac{\xi}{2\sigma}\sin\frac{\sigma x}{L} \tag{13}$$

Among them

$$\varsigma = -\Delta k_1 L/2 = Q(2\alpha - 1)/4 \tag{14}$$

Introducing

$$\sigma^2 = \varsigma^2 + (\xi/2)^2 \tag{15}$$

The diffraction efficiency of the 1-stage diffraction beam is

$$\eta = \frac{I_1}{I_i} = \frac{|E_1(L)|^2}{|E_0(0)|^2} = \left(\frac{\varsigma}{2}\right)^2\left(\frac{\sin\sigma}{\sigma}\right)^2 \tag{16}$$

In Eq. (16), I_1 and I_i are the intensity of 1-stage diffraction beam and incident beam. When ξ=0, from Eq. (13) we can get

$$\eta = \sin^2(\varsigma/2) \tag{17}$$

We can make full use of the energy of incident beam when $\xi=\pi, \eta=100\%$. Therefore, AOM is used in Bragg diffraction and often working at Bragg angle in practical application. Taking Eq. (7) into Eq. (17), we obtain

$$\eta = \sin^2(\pi\Delta n L/\lambda_0) \tag{18}$$

4. Simulations

Under the ideal condition to meet the Bragg diffraction, when the energy of incident beam I_i=0.5*mJ*, the quality factor of the acousto-optic medium M=150×10^{-15} m^2/W, the length of the transducer L=15*mm*, the width H=5*mm*:

(1)When the wavelength of incident beam λ=1550*nm*, the variation of diffraction intensity with the ultrasonic power P_s is shown in Figure. 1. As can be seen from the figure, the intensity of the 0-stage and the 1-stage diffraction beam are changed as a sine low with the increase of ultrasonic power. When the ultrasonic power makes $(\sqrt{2}/\lambda_0)\sqrt{(L/H)MP_s}$ reach 1, the intensity of 1-stage diffraction beam reaches the maximum and the intensity of 0-stage diffraction beam is the smallest.

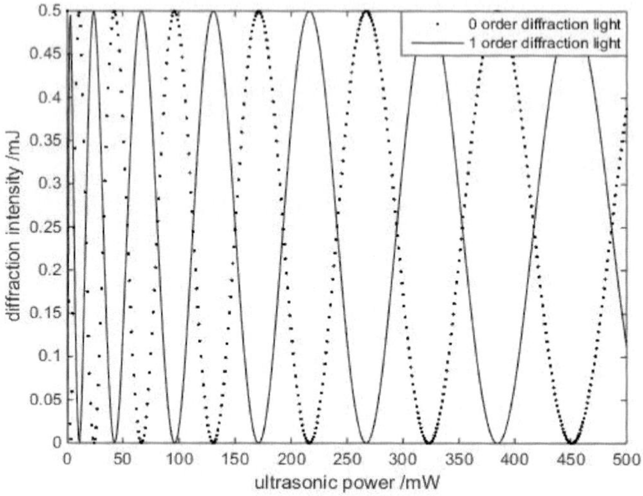

Fig. 1. Relationship of diffraction intensity and ultrasonic power

(2)When ultrasonic power P_s=1.5W, the variation of diffraction efficiency with the wavelength of incident beam is shown in Figure. 2. From Fig. (2), when the wavelength of incident beam is near 1160*nm*, the diffraction efficiency is the highest and it decreases monotonically with the increase of the wavelength. When λ=1550*nm*, diffraction efficiency is about 84%.

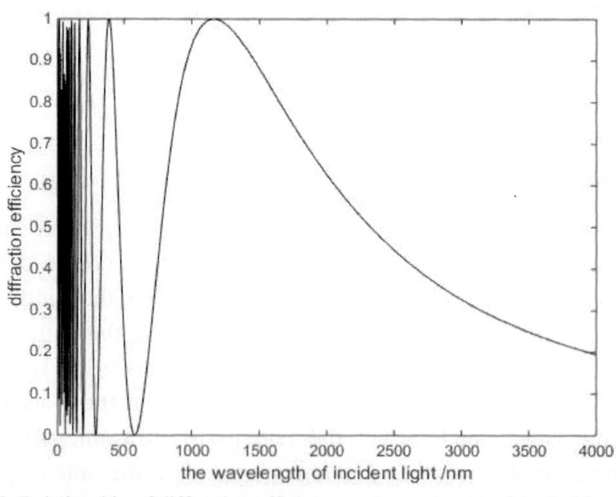

Fig. 2. Relationship of diffraction efficiency and wavelength of the incident beam

5. Conclusions

In this paper, the principle of the fiber AOM and the Bragg diffraction when the laser passes through the AOM are analyzed by the theoretical analysis and the simulations. The results show that the intensity of the 0 - stage and 1 – stage beam is changed as a sine low with the increase of ultrasonic power. The diffraction efficiency is the highest when the wavelength of incident beam is near 1160 *nm*, and it decreases monotonically with the increase of the wavelength. When Bragg diffraction condition is satisfied, the diffraction efficiency can be increased to the maximum extent, and the energy of incident beam can be fully utilized.

Acknowledgement

In this paper, the research work was supported by National Natural Science Foundation of China under Grant (Project No. 61302162) and National High Technology Research and Development Program 863 under Grant (Project No. 2012AA120605).

References

1. J. Hildebrand1, G. Baumgarten1, J. Fiedler1, et al.. Combined wind measurements by two different lidar instruments in the Arctic middle atmosphere[J]. Atmospheric Measurement Techniques, 2015(5): 2433-2445.
2. David Schlipf, Po Wen Cheng, Jakob Mann, et al.. Model of the Correlation between Lidar Systems and Wind Turbines for Lidar-Assisted Control[J]. Journal of Atmospheric and Oceanic Technology, 2013, 2233-2240
3. "Novel Hemisphere Scanner for a Coherent Fiber LIDAR System", The NASA SBIR Phase II final report, Sibell Optics, 2014.
4. C. F. Abari, A. T. Pedersen, E. Dellwik, et al.. Performance evaluation of an all-fiber image-reject homodyne coherent Doppler wind lidar[J]. Atmospheric Measurement Techniques, 2015(8): 5145-5153.
5. Wu Wei. Study on a Fiber Acousto-optic Shifter for Doppler Laser Radar System[J]. Piezoelectrics & Acoustooptics, 2013, 35(3): 339-341.
6. Yu Weijuan. Experimental Research on 1.55 um All-Fiber Acousto-Optic Frequency Shifter Diffraction Efficiency and Laser Heterodyne [D]. 2008

A New Method on Parameters Estimation of Accelerated Degradation Test Model Based on Wiener Process

Yun-Di Bai[a], Jiu-Long Xiong[b], Xiao-Ming Wang[c] and Qi Zhang[d]

Department of Instrument Science and Technology,
National University of Defense Technology
Changsha, Hunan, China
E-mail: [a]785262328@qq.com, [b]13787 202019@139.com, [c]359654305@qq.com,
[d]zhang_qi_7223@hotmail.com

With the popularization of accelerated test, how to get reliability and lifetime information accurately with limited samples has been more and more important. In this paper, a cyclic iterative algorithm of data and parameters to get more accurate parameters of accelerated degradation test (ADT) with a few samples is proposed. The method uses the parameters of acceleration model which is estimated by raw data to transform the data of stress at higher level to the data of stress at this level to increase the number of data in this level. Then, using the new data to estimate the new parameters until the parameters are not changed or changed negligibly. The maximum likelihood estimation (MLE) method is used to get more accurate parameters in each step of the cycle. Particle Swarm Optimization (PSO) algorithm is used to hunt for the optimum solution of the maximum likelihood function. In order to verify the validity of the method, a simulation model is built with MATLAB and an experiment of electric energy meter has been done. The proposed method is compared with the conventional methods in terms of their accuracy of parameters, which can fully demonstrate the effectiveness of the proposed method.

Keywords: Wiener Process; Parameters Estimation; PSO; Cyclic Iterative Algorithm; Reliability Prognostics.

1. Introduction

With the development of manufacturing process, the reliability and the lifetime of products have been increased significantly. Therefore, it becomes more and more difficult to predict the reliability and lifetime of products by using the conventional method. In this context, a new method called accelerated test has been proposed. The accelerated degradation test (ADT) is a kind of accelerated test, which can accelerate the degradation process by subjecting products to severe working conditions. After the acceleration data is obtained by ADT, the reliability of product in normal operating conditions can be predicted by using the acceleration models. However, how to use the acceleration data to estimate the parameters of the acceleration model accurately has been a difficult problem. It is well known that increasing the number of samples can effectively improve the accuracy of the data. However, actually, increasing a large number of samples is not realistic. In this paper, we present a new method with increasing the pseudo sample data by using cyclic iterative method of data and parameters to predict the reliability more accurate.

Usually, the Wiener process is used in ADT to describe the degradation processes of the products. At present, describing the degradation process by Wiener process has been widely used. Liu Rui and Wang Lixin used the nonlinear Wiener process to study the storage life of accelerometer in [1]. Chao Daihong and Wang Tao used the one-dimensional Wiener process to study the degradation of SLD in [2]. Tseng and Peng used the nonlinear Wiener process to model the constant stress ADT (CSADT) in [3]. However, in these studies, the way to improve the accuracy of the model parameters has not been considered.

A classic work about estimating the unknown modeling parameters by the MLE method is presented by [4]. The nonlinear Wiener process has further been applied in [5], and [6, 7, 8] has took the measurement errors into account. However, for complex maximum likelihood equations and multiple unknown parameters, simple and direct calculation can't meet the accuracy requirements. According to this situation, we use the particle swarm optimization (PSO) algorithm to estimate the model parameters. In this part, we have also presented a cyclic iterative method of data and parameters, which can increase the number of pseudo samples at a stress level by circulating the data and parameters.

2. Degradation Modeling and Acceleration Modeling

2.1. *Degradation modeling*

The most commonly using of Wiener process in accelerated degradation modeling is time-transformed Wiener process [9, 10, 11]. So, in this paper, the time-transformed Wiener process has also been used to model the degradation process of ADT.

The standard form of the time-transformed Wiener process has been shown as follows:

$$y_t = \lambda\Lambda(t) + \sigma B(\Lambda(t)) + y_0 \quad (1)$$

where y_t denotes the degradation value at time t, λ is the drift parameter, $\Lambda(t)$ is the calculation time in the Wiener process model and σ is the diffusion parameter, and $B(t)$ is the standard Brownian motion. When the $\Lambda(t) = t$, (1) becomes the traditional linear drift-based Wiener process. In order to simplify the calculation, we define Δy as the increment between y_{t_2} and y_{t_1}.

$$\Delta y = y_{t_2} - y_{t_1} \quad (2)$$

Substitute (2) into (1) , we can obtain

$$\Delta y = \lambda(\Lambda(t_2) - \Lambda(t_1)) + \sigma B\left((\Lambda(t_2) - \Lambda(t_1)\right) \quad (3)$$

We suppose that $\Delta\Lambda(t) = \Lambda(t_2) - \Lambda(t_1)$

$$\Delta y = \lambda\Delta\Lambda(t) + \sigma B\left(\Delta\Lambda(t)\right) \quad (4)$$

Because the Wiener process has infinite divisibility property, and $B(\Delta\Lambda(t)) \sim \mathrm{N}(0, \Delta\Lambda(t))$, we can obtain $\Delta y \sim \mathrm{N}(\lambda\Delta\Lambda(t), \sigma^2\Delta\Lambda(t))$. So we can find that every product has different degradation increment process. The product-to-product variability among the degradation processes can be considered.

Obviously, this degradation model can indicate the different degradation processes of different individuals. The drift parameter λ is determined by working conditions. And for σ, most papers assumed that it is remains unchanged to simplify the calculation. But, in fact, the working conditions have a great influence on diffusion parameter. In this paper, we assumed that λ and σ both change with the working condition.

2.2. *Acceleration modeling*

Acceleration model presents the transformation relationship between the degradation characteristics under accelerated conditions and the degradation characteristics under normal operating conditions. The conventional acceleration model includes the Arrhenius model, Eyring model, Peck model and so on. Peck model is generally used for materials affected by temperature and humidity. For more details of the acceleration model, see [12]. In this paper, we chose the Peck model for an example.

For the nonlinear degradation process given in Eq. (1), the conventional Peck model can be expressed as

$$\lambda(S) = a_1(RH)^{-b_1} e^{-c_1/(kT)} \tag{5}$$

$$\sigma(S) = a_2(RH)^{-b_2} e^{-c_2/(kT)} \tag{6}$$

where S denotes a stress variable, RH represents a humidity variable, T is temperature. We suppose $y_{k,t}$, $y_{0,t}$ denote the degradation values at time t under the stresses of S_k , S_0 . And we suppose that AF denotes the acceleration factor, which can be defined as

$$AF_{k,0} = y_{k,t} / y_{0,t} \tag{7}$$

Zhou pointed out that $AF_{k,0}$ should be a constant, which does not change with time t, and depends only on S_k , S_0 , otherwise, the acceleration factor cannot be applied to engineering application. In paper [13], it concluded that a relational formula which can be denoted as

$$AF_{k,h} = \lambda_k / \lambda_h = \sigma^2{}_k / \sigma^2{}_h \tag{8}$$

where $AF_{k,h}$ denotes the acceleration factor between S_k and S_h , λ_k and λ_h means the drift parameter of S_k and S_h , $\sigma^2{}_k$ and $\sigma^2{}_h$ denotes the diffusion parameter of S_k and S_h . For more details of the AF constant principle, see [14]. So we can get that

$$b_1 = b_2, c_1 = c_2 \tag{9}$$

Substitute Eq. (9) into Eq. (5), Eq. (6) and specify b_1=b_2=b, c_1=c_2=c, we can obtain

$$\lambda(S) = a_1(RH)^{-b} e^{-c/(kT)} \tag{10}$$

$$\sigma^2(S) = a_2(RH)^{-b} e^{-c/(kT)} \tag{11}$$

In this following, we develop a parameters estimation method to estimate the parameters in the proposed models.

3. Parameters Estimation

MLE method is a basic method of parameter estimation. In [15], a two-step MLE method has been proposed to estimate the unknown parameters. Without loss of generality, in this paper, we set $\Delta\Lambda(t) = t^{\theta}$. The process is similar for other types of $\Delta\Lambda(t)$.

For CSADT, it is assumed that there are m stresses in all. For each stress, there are n_i tested products under stress S_i. The tested time is from t_1 to t_L for all stresses. Thus, there are N products in all. Suppose z_{ijk} denote the increment value for the jth product at time t_k under stress S_i. Then we have

$$z_{ijk} = \lambda_i(\Lambda(t_k) - \Lambda(t_{k-1})) + \sigma_i B(\Lambda(t_k) - \Lambda(t_{k-1}))$$

$$= a_1(RH_i)^{-b} e^{-c/(kT_i)}(\Lambda(t_k) - \Lambda(t_{k-1})) + \sigma_i B(\Lambda(t_k) - \Lambda(t_{k-1}))$$

where i=1,2,...,m, k=1,2,...,L;

$$\text{Under Si}, \ \sum_{i=1}^{i-1} n_i < j \le \sum_{i=1}^{i} n_i \tag{12}$$

From $\Delta y \sim \mathrm{N}(\lambda\Delta\Lambda(t), \sigma^2\Delta\Lambda(t))$, the z_{ijk} obey the normal distribution as follows

$$z_{ijk} \sim N(\lambda_i(\Lambda(t_k) - \Lambda(t_{k-1})), \sigma_i^2(\Lambda(t_k) - \Lambda(t_{k-1}))) \tag{13}$$

Let $\Theta = \{a_1, b, c, a_2, \theta\}$; then the likelihood function can expressed as

$$\mathrm{L}(\Theta \mid \mathrm{Z}) = \prod_{i=1}^{m} \prod_{j=n_{i-1}+1}^{n_i} \prod_{k=1}^{L} \left(\frac{1}{\sqrt{2\pi\sigma_i^2(t_k^{\theta} - t_{k-1}^{\theta})}} \cdot \exp\left(-\frac{\left[z_{ijk} - \lambda_i(t_k^{\theta} - t_{k-1}^{\theta})\right]^2}{2\sigma_i^2(t_k^{\theta} - t_{k-1}^{\theta})}\right)\right) \tag{14}$$

The log-likelihood function can be expressed as

$$\ln\mathrm{L}(\Theta \mid \mathrm{Z}) = -\frac{1}{2}\sum_{i=1}^{m} \sum_{j=n_{i-1}+1}^{n_i} \sum_{k=1}^{L} \left(\ln 2\pi + \ln(\sigma_i^2(t_k^{\theta} - t_{k-1}^{\theta})) + \frac{\left[z_{ijk} - \lambda_i(t_k^{\theta} - t_{k-1}^{\theta})\right]^2}{\sigma_i^2\left(t_k^{\theta} - t_{k-1}^{\theta}\right)}\right) \tag{15}$$

Let $G_i = (RH_i)^b \exp(-c/(kT_i))$, we can obtain

$$\lambda_i = a_1 \cdot G_i, \sigma_i^2 = a_2 \cdot G_i \tag{16}$$

Substitute Eq. (16) into Eq. (15)

$$\ln L(\Theta \mid Z) = -\frac{1}{2}\sum_{i=1}^{m}\sum_{j=n_{i-1}+1}^{n_i}\sum_{k=1}^{L}(\ln 2\pi + \ln\left(a_2 \cdot G_i(t_k{}^o - t_{k-1}{}^o)\right) + \frac{\left[z_{ijk} - a_1 \cdot G_i(t_k{}^o - t_{k-1}{}^o)\right]^2}{a_2 \cdot G_i\left(t_k{}^o - t_{k-1}{}^o\right)}) \tag{17}$$

Because Eq. (17) is complex, and there are 5 unknown parameters, it is difficult to estimate parameters directly. Therefore, we introduce a particle swarm optimization (PSO) algorithm to solve the maximum value of the likelihood equation. If you want to know more about PSO algorithm, see [16].

After calculating with PSO algorithm, the unknown parameters can be estimated and most articles use those parameters directly to predict the reliability and lifetime of products (e.g. [16]) without considering the errors. In this paper, a new method is proposed to further reduce the errors of parameters estimation.

Suppose that the parameters calculating with PSO are $a_{10}, b_0, c_0, a_{20}, \theta_0$ which indicate the initial value of the iteration. Taking those parameters into Eq. (7), we can obtain the acceleration factor between different working conditions.

$$AF_{f,h} = \frac{y_f}{y_h} = \frac{(RH_f)^{b_0}\exp\left(-\frac{c_0}{kT_f}\right)}{(RH_h)^{b_0}\exp\left(-\frac{c_0}{kT_h}\right)} \tag{18}$$

The method of adding pseudo samples has been presented to estimate the parameters accurately:

Step 1: Let $f=h+1$, and obtain the AF thought the parameters estimated by PSO in cycle n-1.

$$AF_{h+1,h,n} = \frac{(RH_{h+1})^{b_{n-1}}\exp\left(-\frac{c_{n-1}}{kT_{h+1}}\right)}{(RH_h)^{b_{n-1}}\exp\left(-\frac{c_{n-1}}{kT_h}\right)} \tag{19}$$

where the $AF_{h+1,h,n}$ denotes acceleration factor in cycle n between adjacent stresses S_{h+1} and S_h .

Step 2: Calculate the $y_{h+1,n}{}'$ thought $AF_{h+1,h,n}$.

$$y_{h+1,n}{}' = AF_{h+1,h,n} \cdot y_{h,n} \tag{20}$$

where $y_{h+1,n}{}'$ denotes the values of pseudo samples under S_{h+1} conversed from S_h in cycle n.

Step 3: Calculate the new degradation data.

$$y_{h+1,n} = \left(\alpha y_{h+1,n}{}' + \beta y_{h+1,n-1}\right)/(\alpha + \beta)$$

$$\alpha, \beta \le 100 \tag{21}$$

where $y_{h+1,n}$ and $y_{h+1,n-1}$ denote the new degradation data after nth and (n-1)th times cycles, the weight values are denoted by α, β which equal the ratio of the number of samples and the number of pseudo samples.

Step 4: Calculate the new parameters of cycle $n+1$ $\{a_{1,n+1}, b_{n+1}, c_{n+1}, a_{2,n+1}, \theta_{n+1}\}$ by PSO.

Step 5: Back to step 1 and cycle, until the values of parameters are constant or the values of change can be ignored.

What must be noted is that in the cycling, the number of pseudo samples shows exponential growth, so the maximum value of the weight should be set for avoiding overflow. The maximum value of the weight can be set according to your requirement. In this paper, the maximum value of the weight is set to 100.

4. Experiment Studies

4.1. *A simulation study*

In order to validate the algorithm based on MLE, a simulation test was conducted.

Let $\Delta y_{ijk,n}$ denote at the nth cycle, the degradation data of the jth sample at time t_k under stress S_i, t denote the real time, $\Lambda(t)$ denote the calculating time, and the $\Delta y_{ijk,n} = y_{ij(k+1),n} — y_{ijk,n}$ denote the degradation increment. Without loss of generality, we denote $\Lambda(t) = t^2$ and generate data. The simulation degradation data were generated from the following model

$$
\begin{aligned}
&\lambda_i = F(a_1, b, c) \\
&\sigma_i^2 = F(a_2, b, c) \\
&\Delta y_{ijk,0} - N\left(\lambda_i \Delta\Lambda(t), \sigma_i^2 \Delta\Lambda(t)\right)
\end{aligned}
\tag{22}
$$

where F denotes the acceleration function, in this paper F is Peck model. We set the initial values of parameters of model as $(a_1, b, c, a_2, \theta) = (8.15e+05, 3, 1.04e+04, 2.79e+05, 2)$, the number of acceleration stresses is m=6, the number of samples under S_i is n_i=15, the total number of samples is $N = m \times n = 6 \times 15 = 90$, the times of corresponding observed is L=20, and the time increment is $\Delta\Lambda(t) = 2$.

The steps of simulation are illustrated as following

(1)Generate the simulation degradation data $\Delta y_{ijk,0}$, $\Delta\Lambda(t)$ at t_k under S_i. The degradation process under S_i has been showed in Figure. 1

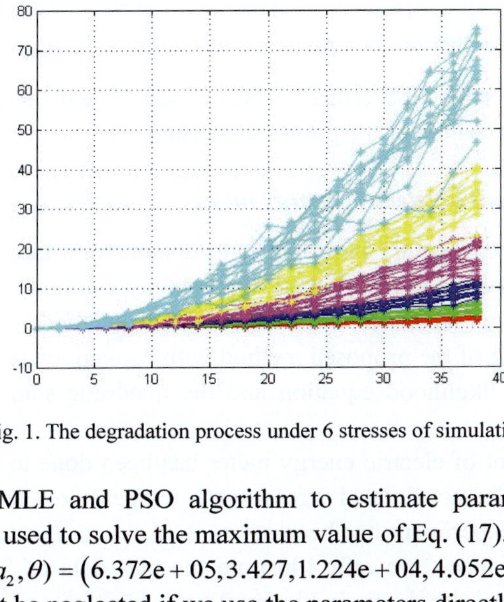

Fig. 1. The degradation process under 6 stresses of simulation

(2)Use the MLE and PSO algorithm to estimate parameters. The PSO algorithm can be used to solve the maximum value of Eq. (17). The result of this step is $(a_1, b, c, a_2, \theta) = (6.372e+05, 3.427, 1.224e+04, 4.052e+05, 2.416)$. The error of Θ cannot be neglected if we use the parameters directly.

(3)The result of step (2) can be used to obtain *AF*. The value of *AF* in first cycle has been illustrated in Table 1

Table 1. The value of AF in first cycle

Stresses	$S_1 \to S_2$	$S_2 \to S_3$	$S_3 \to S_4$	$S_4 \to S_5$	$S_5 \to S_6$
AF	2.715	2.610	2.518	2.435	2.360

Then we can obtain the conversed data with AF and get the new data with conversed data and initial data.

(4)Back to step (2) and obtain the new values of parameters. Cycle until the value of parameter is constant or the change can be ignored. The final values of the parameters are $(a_1, b, c, a_2, \theta) = (6.935e+05, 3.147, 1.183e+04, 3.474e+05, 2.123)$.

(5)Calculating the errors and comparing. The result has been illustrated in Table 2

Table 2. Comparisons of two methods with the simulated degradation data

Parameters		a_1	b	c	a_2	θ
Real value		8.15e+05	3	1.04e+04	2.79e+05	2
Basic method (B)		6.372e+05	3.427	1.224e+04	4.052e+05	2.416
Proposed method (P)		6.935e+05	3.147	1.183e+04	3.474e+05	2.123
Error	**B**	21.81	14.24	17.78	31.15	20.8
Comparing (%)	**P**	14.91	4.92	13.79	24.53	6.15

Table 2 shows that the errors of basic method and the proposed method which proves the credible of the proposed method.

4.2. *An experiment on electric energy meter*

In this section, a case study is provided to demonstrate the application of the proposed ADT model and the method of parameter estimation and compare the performance of our method with conventional method without cycle. To compare the fitting of the proposed method with conventional method, the value of the maximum likelihood equation and the quadratic sum of the errors are used.

An experiment of electric energy meter has been done to study its stability and reliability. The accelerated stresses are temperatures and humidity. The condition of the experiment has been set as $m=8, n_i=10, L=20, \Delta t=0.5$. Because of the limited of space, we only illustrate the part data of S_4 in Table 3, the complete data have been drawn in Figure. 2

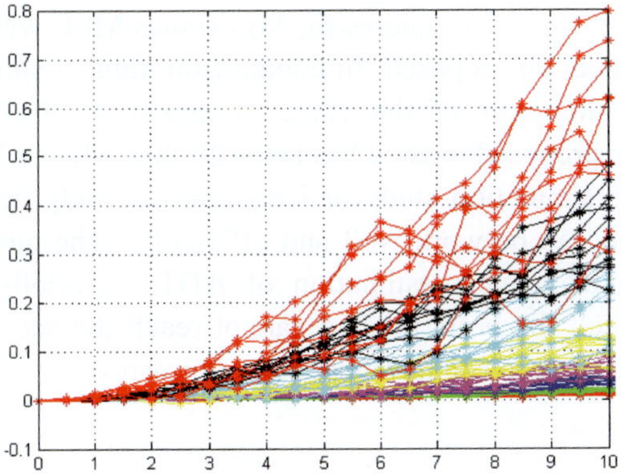

Fig. 2. The degradation process under 8 stresses of experiment

Table 3. Part degradation data of electric energy meter under S4

Time(h)	0.5	1	…	9.5	10
1	-0.0002299	-0.0002342	…	0.06654	0.07439
2	0.0002547	-0.0004398	…	0.04843	0.05299
3	0.0001819	0.0002873	…	0.06414	0.06371
4	0.0002322	0.0011793	…	0.05020	0.05462
5	0.0004026	0.0005513	…	0.07148	0.07505
6	0.0002663	0.0007589	…	0.03436	0.04652
7	-0.0034048	0.0024413	…	0.06296	0.08597
8	-0.0001206	0.0004945	…	0.05591	0.05754
9	0.0001977	0.0006210	…	0.07589	0.08814
10	0.0074136	0.0011997	…	0.05279	0.06220

We use Peck model to deal with the data, and compare their estimated parameters. The result has been illustrated in Table 4

Table 4. Comparisons of three methods with the degradation data of electric energy meter

Parameters	M_1	M_2	M_3
a_1	7.256e+04	9.756e+04	8.874e+04
b	2.742	2.842	2.715
c	6.358e+03	7.479e+03	7.795e+03
a_2	8.517e+03	5.517e+03	6.120e+03
θ	2.778	2.879	3.045
Log-MLE	4.7676e+08	5.4876e+10	5.9525e+11

where M_1 denotes least squares fit, M_2 denotes MLE without cycle, and M_3 denotes the method we proposed. In comparison, table 4 shows that M_3 clearly outperforms M_2 in terms of the value of maximum likelihood equation. It indicates that the proposed method has better fit than M_1 and M_2.

Overall, the simulation study and experiment study demonstrate that the proposed method can be work well and efficiently. The method can solve the problem of the parameters estimation of ADT, especially for the complex acceleration model, the basic method cannot reach the accuracy requirements, and the proposed method can have a good performance.

5. Conclusion

The paper has proposed a helpful method that can be used to exactly estimate the parameters of Wiener process and acceleration model. The objective is to accurately extrapolate the reliability information of products under normal operating conditions by properly modeling the accelerated degradation data which can be helpful for reliability Prognostics. The nonlinear Wiener process has been selected to describe the degradation process of product. The drift parameter and diffusion parameter are both modeled by acceleration model. Then a cycle method based on MLE and PSO has been proposed to estimate the parameters. At last, the simulation test validates that the method is credible.

We primarily discuss the issue associated with the accelerated degradation modeling and parameters estimation in this paper. Some other issues need to be further exploited. Firstly, we only use the time-transformed Wiener process to model ADT. However, the time-transformed Wiener process could not be appropriate for all the nonlinear degradation process. Therefore, using other types of nonlinear degradation process to model ADT data is needed. Second, we only discuss the issues regarding how to model the ADT data. However, many researchers are concerned with how to conduct a degradation test efficiently. Thirdly, the proposed method requires studying the direction of transformation, which means we must know that if we convince the stresses from low levels to high levels or reversing in advance. It depends on the property of the acceleration model which will be expounded in the future research.

References

1. Li Rui, Wang Li xin, Liu Gang, Zhou Zhijie, "Nonlinear Characteristic Analysis and Storage Life Forecast for Accelerometer based on Accelerate Degradation Model," Journal of Chinese Inertial Technology Journal of Chinese Inertial Technology, vol. 22, pp. 125-131, February 2014.
2. Chao Daihong, Wang Tao, Ma Jing, Zhang Chunxi, "Degradation Failure Modeling of SLD based on one-dimensional Brown Motion," Infrared and Laser Engineering, vol. 41, pp. 1848-1853, July 2012.
3. S.T.Tseng and C.Y.Peng, "Stochastic diffusion modeling of degradation data," Journal of Data Science, vol. 5, pp. 315-333,2007.
4. C.-Y. Peng and S.-T. Tseng, "Mis-specification analysis of lineardegradation models, "IEEE Transactions on Reliability, vol. 58,no. 3, pp. 444-455, 2009.
5. X.-S. Si, W. Wang, C.-H. Hu, and D.-H. Zhou, "Remaining useful life estimation—a review on the statistical data driven approaches, " European Journal of Operational Research, vol. 213,no. 1, pp. 1 - 14, 2011.
6. Z.-S. Ye, Y. Shen, and M. Xie, "Degradation-based burn-in with preventive maintenance," European Journal of Operational Research, vol. 221, no. 2, pp. 360-367, 2012.
7. G. Jin, D. E. Matthews, and Z. Zhou. A Bayesian framework for on-line degradation assessment and residual life prediction of secondary batteries inspacecraft,"Reliability Engineering & System Safety, vol. 113, pp. 7–20, 2013.
8. S. Tang, X. Guo, Z. Zhou, B. Zhang, "Real time remaining useful life prediction based on nonlinear Wiener based degradation processes with measurement errors," Journal of Central South University. In press.
9. C.-M. Liao and S.-T. Tseng, "Optimal design for step-stress accelerated degradation tests," *IEEE Transactions on Reliability*, vol. 55, no. 1, pp. 59–66, 2006.
10. S. T. Tseng and C.Y. Peng, "Stochastic diffusion modeling of degradation data," *Journal of Data Science*, vol. 5, pp. 315–333,2007.
11. G.A.Whitmore and F. Schenkelberg, "Modelling accelerated degradation data using Wiener diffusion with a time scale transformation," *Lifetime Data Analysis*, vol. 3, pp. 27–45, 1997.
12. A. Hoyland, M. Rausand, System Reliability Theory: Models and Statistical Methods, vol. 420, JohnWiley & Sons, New York, NY, USA, 1994.

13. Hao-Wei, Wen-Jun Xi. Acceleration Factor Constant Principle and the Application under ADT. Quality and reliability engineering international.2016.
14. Zhou YQ, Weng CX, Ye XT. Study on accelerated factor and condition for constant failure mechanism. Systems Engineering and Electronics, vol. 18, pp. 55–67,1996.
15. Shengjin Tang, Xiaosong Guo, Chuanqiang Yu, Haijian Xue, and Zhijie Zhou. Accelerated Degradation Tests Modeling Based on the Nonlinear Wiener Process with Random Effects. Mathematical Problems in Engineering. vol. 43, pp. 1-11, May 2014.
16. Ni Qingjian, Xing Hancheng. Survey of Particle Swarm Optimization Algorithm. PR&AI. vol. 20, pp. 349-357, June 2014.
17. Li Yifei, Zou Zhanming, Qi Bangyan. Research on ALT of Intelligent Electricity Meter Based on "Life-stress" Model. Modern Electronics Technique. vol. 34, pp. 167-170, 2011.

The Research on Early Warning Helicopter's Position Deploy for Aircraft Carrier's Sea Battle

Jian-Guo Wang[a], Jin-Zhu Meng, Ke-Ming Yao and Qun E

Dalian naval academy,

Dalian 116018, China

E-mail: [a]wangjianguo1981@163.com

According to ship-borne early warning helicopters position deploy problem for the aircraft carrier in sea combat, a position deploy method is proposed. Based on analysis of the process aircraft carrier's anti-sea combat, combined with combat background, the paper constructs the position deploy mode for early warning helicopter on the aircraft carrier's anti-sea battle, including distance deploy model, bearing deploy model and height deploy model. Finally, using example to calculate the model simulation to verify it. The conclusion can provide useful reference for the aircraft carrier formation in the actual use of early warning helicopters.

Keywords: Aircraft Carrier Formation; Anti-sea Combat; Early Warning Helicopter; Position Deploy.

1. Introduction

Formation of aircraft carrier battle on the sea is mainly refers to the enemy warship reconnaissance, attack recognition and, its purpose is the enemy surface threat for the aircraft carrier formation before, detection, identification, calibration and successfully fought, to the safety protection for the aircraft carrier formation, to seize command of the sea. Carrier AWACS is a major force in the formation of remote sea exploration, because the fixed wing carrier AWACS aircraft carrier catapult takeoff in need, at present, for small and medium sized aircraft, fixed wing AEW is not on the ship. And ship-borne AEW helicopters because of its small size, detection distance, can carry on small and medium-sized aircraft carriers and large destroyer, become the major airborne early warning and reconnaissance forces. Location is using ship-borne AEW helicopter combat an important decision factors, both at home and abroad this in-depth study, but the focus or focus on air defense warning helicopter location, such as literature [1-4], or focus on fixed wing carrier AWACS for naval warfare location, such as literature [5-6]. For AEW helicopters in the aircraft carrier formation in location research is relatively small. This article in the analysis based on the using process of early warning helicopter sea combat helicopter alert location model is constructed to discuss research for the aircraft carrier formation of naval warfare ship-borne AEW helicopters location method.

2. Analysis on the Use of Aircraft Carrier Formation for Early Warning Helicopter in Sea Warfare

In naval warfare, the main using of the ship-borne AEW helicopters is by selecting the appropriate warning position and force, the appropriate way to enemy's maritime target search, recognition and the strength to guide, to ensure the formation of sea combat, successfully completed.

Equipped with ship-borne AEW helicopter aircraft carrier formation or frigate formation in the sea combat, combat process can be described as: after received other reconnaissance and early warning system of target roughly target information or fleet commander determines the main reconnaissance and early warning area according to the battlefield situation, along with threat axis, sent ship-borne AEW helicopters, before a certain distance to search, the airborne early warning radar found the target. After identification and judgment, through the data chain returned to the Fleet Command or command air and surface forces to attack.

3. Early Warning Helicopter Location Model

In almost known target information of AEW helicopters location is to determine helicopter alert the forward distance, azimuth, patrol mode detection warning related elements.

3.1. *Distance deploy*

The distance deploy model as shown in Fig. 1, among them: d is the position of enemy warship formation, w is the position of aircraft carrier formation, d_{dw} is the distance between the aircraft carrier formation and the enemy warship formation; d_{wyxkz} is the distance for formation to control the Ship-borne AEW helicopters, general for the communication distance between the two. d_{dfk} is the maximum missile range of enemy anti-aircraft carrier; and d_{wld} is the maximum range for Ship-borne helicopter radar could detection the enemy warship.

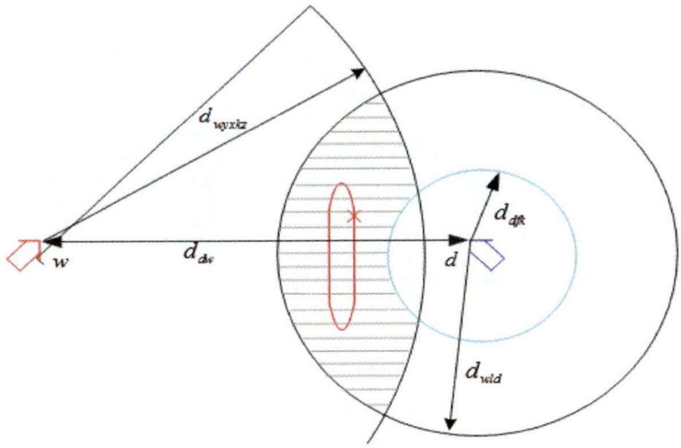

Fig. 1. Distance deploy model

In order to avoid damage by the enemy, the distance warning before the helicopter could be Eq.(1):

$$d_{dw} - d_{wld} < d_{qc} < \min(d_{dw} - d_{dfk}, d_{wyxkz}) \tag{1}$$

3.2. *Bearing deploy*

When finished before determining a carrier-based early warning helicopters from detectable distance determined single carrier-based early warning helicopters hovering probe can cover detection angle based on shipborne radar early warning helicopters. Here consider only the carrier early warning helicopters sea search, assuming guard helicopter search depth is 0, which means that from the radar and the target for the first time able to come into contact with the proper target identification and tracking stability of the minimum distance.

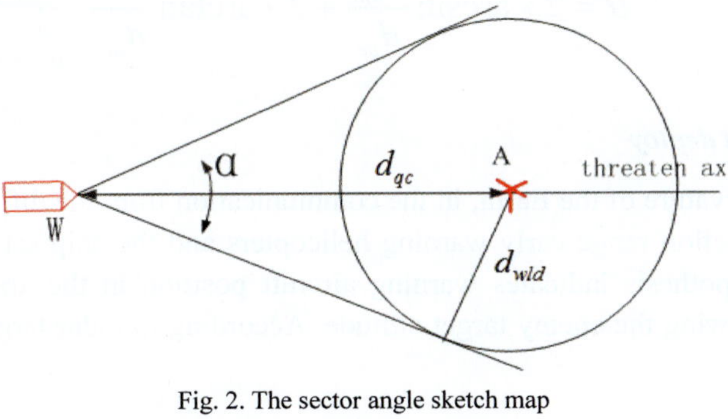

Fig. 2. The sector angle sketch map

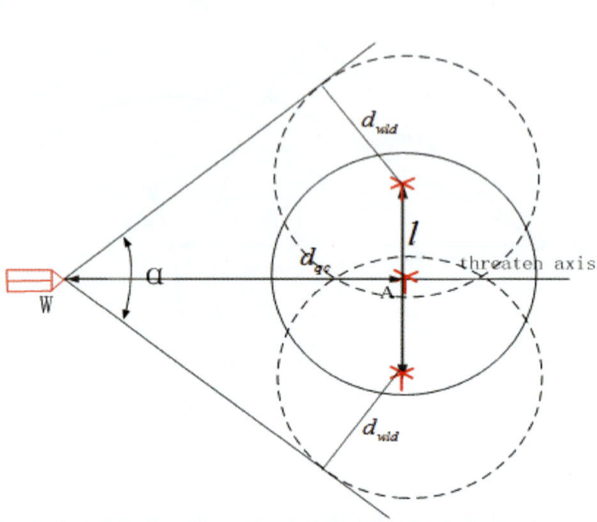

Fig. 3. The sector angle when the helicopter is in patrol

Then, as shown in Fig. 2, the warning sector angle is as Eq.(2):

$$\alpha = 2 \times \arcsin \frac{d_{wld}}{d_{qc}} \tag{2}$$

When the warning provided by the size of the fan angle cannot meet the requirements of both sides to detect early warning helicopters circle will appear a certain blind spot detection, as shown in Fig. 3. At this point need to alert helicopters to patrol airspace axis perpendicular to the threat of a "donut" or "∞" shape patrols to expand the search for a positive fan width, set patrol line length l, then the fan angle of warning is Eq.(3):

$$\alpha = 2 \times \arcsin \frac{d_{wld}}{d_{qc}} + 2 \times \arctan \frac{l/2}{d_{qc}} \tag{3}$$

3.3. *Height deploy*

Affected curvature of the Earth, in the communication from the different heights, and the detection range early warning helicopters and the ship set between the different hypothesis indicates warning aircraft position in the array of cruise altitude, showing the enemy target altitude. According to radar target geometric look into the distance, the detection distance as Eq.(4):

$$D_t = 4.12(\sqrt{H} + \sqrt{h_d}) \tag{4}$$

Among them, D_t the unit is km, H and h_d the unit is m.

The following table lists the horizon detection range early warning helicopters at different heights in the front position on the warning time is in Table 1.

Table 1. At different heights on the target detection range, the target height of 10 meters

Height (m)	6000	5000	4000	3000	2000	1000	500
Detect distance (km)	332	304	274	239	197	143	105

According to the formula, you can determine the maximum guard helicopter cruising height.

4. Application Case Study

According combat scenarios, assumptions about the parameter values as shown in Table 2.

Table 2. The correlation setting of aircraft carrier group in the battle on the sea

The initial distance between our formation and enemy surface ship formation	450km	The effective control distance of the ship formation can control the ship-borne warning helicopter	300km
the maximum range of enemy ship's anti-aircraft missile	100km	The max detection range of our ship-borne warning helicopter's radar	200km
the average speed of enemy surface ship formation	35kn	The max speed of our ship formation	35kn

The current distance of 280 kilometers, which patrol the line length of the longest, up to 212 km; Under the former distance of 270 kilometers premise patrol its maximum length is 210 km. Its length and warning patrol sector angle magnitude relationship as shown below. As can be seen from the figure, the current output from the constant, the size of the patrol line length is proportional to the angle of the fan warning and, when the patrol line length is 0, that is when hover detection, warning its fan angle of 95 degrees; maximum fan warning angle up to 138 degrees. In this case, to achieve 110-degree fan angle warning, according to the length of the model, patrol line is 68 kilometers. The result as shown in Fig. 4.

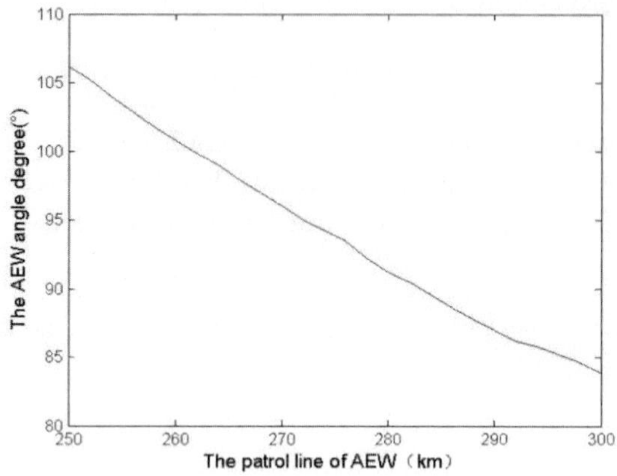

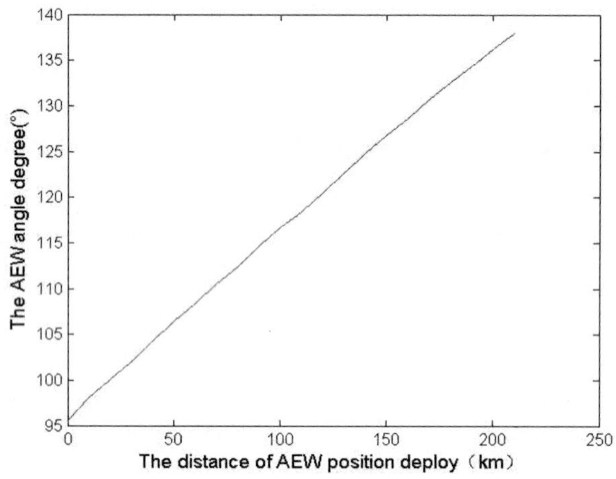

Fig. 4. The aew angle with the distance of position deploy

5. Conclusion

Array-bit configuration warning helicopter aircraft carrier battle groups to the sea combat important tactical elements, the paper surface ships for the Battle Field sea combat early warning helicopters configuration problems have been studied, a mathematical model of early warning helicopters bit array configuration, including early warning before the helicopter range, azimuth and highly configurable model and case analysis of the interaction model position of Early Warning factors, the conclusions drawn. Thesis validated the model proved correct and practical models, early warning aircraft carrier battle groups in the helicopter sea combat tactics used have a guiding role. Of course, these conclusions only considered the warning helicopter sea combat tactics used, without considering air defense operations. In actual combat, the array bit early warning helicopters configuration needs to consider the need for a comprehensive sea and air defense operations, in particular air strikes against the enemy troops and weapons early warning and detection, the next step will be based on this, considering the air defense of operational sea warning needs to study in the comprehensive combat situations early warning helicopters array bit configuration.

Acknowledgments

This paper is funded by the three period of Dalian naval academy 2110, and also funded by the scientific research and development funds of Dalian naval academy.

References

1. Yao Xiao-bai, Zhao Xiao-zhe. *Use of carrier based helicopters in early warning of low altitude air defence targets of warship formation* [J]. Modern defence technology, 2002, 30(3): 6-9. (in Chinese)
2. Shen Xiao-jun, Ju Hong-bin, Zhang Hui-hui, et.al. *Research on Disposition of Air Early Warning Ability For Carrier Helicopters on Warship Formation* [J]. Command Control & Simulation, 2007, 29(2): 52-59. (in Chinese)
3. Tan An-sheng. *Warship Formation Combat Operations Research Analysis* [M]. BeiJin: National Defense Industry Press, 2008. (in Chinese)
4. Xu Sheng-liang, Wu Xiao-feng, Zhao Xiao-long. *Research on the Position of Early Warning Aircraft Carrier Formations in Navigation* [J]. Command Control & Simulation, 2007, 29(1): 56-59. (in Chinese)
5. She Zhan-sheng, Xia Hui-cheng, Xu Ya-guang. *Research on the position deploying of early warning aircraft of air craft carrier group in the battle on the sea* [J]. Ship Science And Technology, 2011, 33(7): 115-118. (in Chinese)
6. Ma Liang, Zhang Lin, Wang Long-tao. *Optimization Design of Ship-Borne Warning Helicopters Search Parameters* [J]. Fire Control & Command Control, 2014, 39(2): 135-138. (in Chinese)

Design and Development of Well Site Drilling Information System Used in South Azadagan

Zhi-Kun Liu[a], Xiao-Bo Shen[b] and Mehmood Aayz[c]

Engineering Research Center of Development and Management for Low to Ultra-Low Permeability Oil & Gas Reservoirs in West China, Ministry of Education
Shannxi Xi'an 710065, China
Institute of Petroleum Engineering in Xi'an Shiyou University
Shannxi Xi'an 710065, China
E-mail: [a]Lzk12431@xsyu.edu.cn, [b]534521875@qq.com, [c]mehmood.gailani@gmail.com

Based on the experience and successes in the development of drilling information management software as well as the understanding of the South Azadagan well site situation in Iran, the South Azadagan Well Site Drilling Information Management System has been designed. Through the establishment of database of DIMS, the integrated well site drilling information management and application system is developed. In the process of collaborative information management under network environment, a convenient and unified data manage and analysis platform for well site drillers in different Rigs has been provided. This paper describes the design and development of South Azadagan Well Site Drilling Information Management System in detail.

Keywords: Drilling Information System; Data Warehouse; Collaborative Work; Azadagan.

1. Introduction

The improvement of scientific drilling level, to some extent, depends on the improvement of drilling information application level[1-3]. It requires a large number of reliable data to improve drilling information application level, and it must fully consider the data sharing among drilling engineers, mud logging engineers and rig supervisor, realizing collaborative drilling information management and application[2-5]. So it put forward a higher demand to convenience and flexibility of data organization. In traditional database management system, data has a low correlation between each other, lack effective centralized storage and management mechanisms of information, and can't provide the required comprehensive and statistical data for collaborative drilling information management and application[6-8]. Therefore, how to make full use of various kinds of data resources and to get accurate and scientific data timely is very important for engineers and supervisor at South Azadagan well site. For this reason, we propose to use data warehouse technology to build integrated drilling information system, providing a convenient and unified data analysis and processing platform for collaborative drilling information application among specialists and engineers from well site and drilling company office.

2. Well Site Drilling Data Management Function

Well site Drilling Data Management Module mainly provides an information management platform for the drilling supervisors in such operations as drilling, mudding, logging and cementing. At the same time, to satisfy the drilling supervisors' need in the management of the materials and costs in the well site, the module is designed to includes such 6 main functions (as show in fig. 1) as data input, daily reports, end well report, other regular reports, operation analysis and data query, according to the drilling operation process and the responsibility of the inspector in the well site.

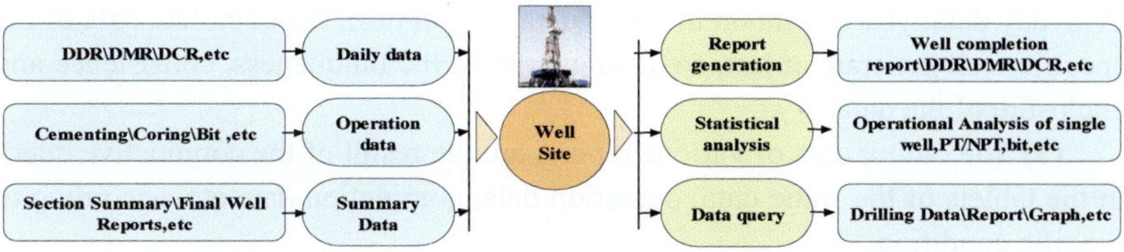

Fig. 1. The function list of Well Site Drilling Data Management System

2.1. *Data input*

Data input module can enter in various on-site drilling data in such simple and convenient ways as code input, record copy and paste, online calculation, automatic unit switch, auto-draft (wellbore structure, wellhead equipment diagram etc.) so as to provide data support for the daily report, final report, statistical analysis, cost control and project management.

The data inputted in are divided into 4 main categories:

(1) Static data: the records of the basic condition of the well in operation such as the fundamental data, casing program, geological introduction etc.

(2) Daily operation data: the records of the drilling operation, property of drilling fluid, consumption of materials, the utilization of diesel and water, costs etc.

(3) Operation data: the records of various procedures filled in operation rather than in each day, for example, pre-drilling acceptance, drilling machine examination, bit records, BHA log, borehole deviation log, casing log, cement log etc.

(4) Well completion data: including the filling of the handover book and completion operation information, drawing of the completion pipe string, and writing of the completion summary.

The logic organization of drilling data to organize numerous static data, daily operation data, operation data and completion data into reasonable structures, so as to optimize the data storage and avoid data redundancy(as show in fig. 2). The logic relationship of data includes:

(1) All the data tablets are associated through the number of the wells and operations like addition and revision of the data of a specific well are only allowed when there is the record of the well in the general data. In the same way, if the records of the data of a specific well are to be deleted from the general data, all the corresponding data of the well in all the data tablets will be deleted.

(2) A large number of the drilling data are generated automatically and progressively. That is, monthly data generate automatically based on the everyday data, yearly data on monthly data, and in turn, the complete data of the specific well generate at last, so as to guarantee the uniqueness, consistence and enclosure of the data.

(3) The output data of various reports are the result of the conjunctive query in the tablets of the static data, operation data, completion data etc. according to specific condition.

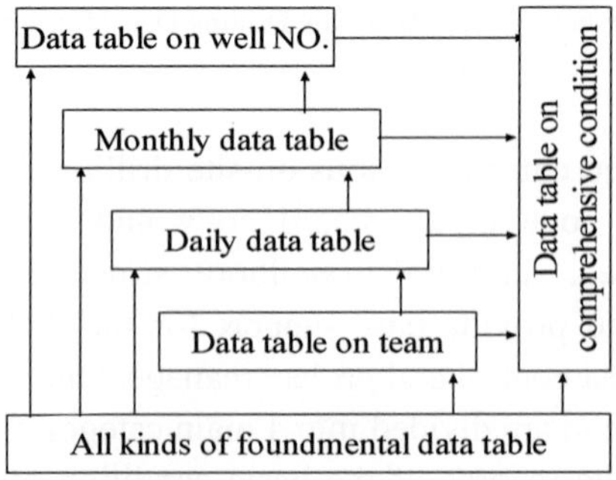

Fig. 2. Data flowchart of drilling database

2.2. *Daily reports*

Daily Reports can be generated automatically according to the required format and distributed to the related departments. The data (parameters and diagrams etc.) in the report will be derived from the data input module. Daily reports primarily include Daily Drilling Report, Daily Mud Report, Daily Completion Report, Daily Geological Report, Daily Directional Drilling Report, Daily Mud Logging Report and Daily Drilling Brief etc.

2.3. *End well report*

This module can provide auto-generated end well reports by the drilling crew immediately after the completion of the well drilling. End well report is summative technical document provided after the well completion. According to the requirement of South Azadagan drilling department, it includes 6 sections(show in table 1): general information, performance review, drilling data, completion data, HSE summary report, highlights and lessons learnt, as is shown in the following diagram.

Table 1. End well report contents

1. General Information	3.6 Casing Tally Report
1.1 Well parameters/overview	3.7 Casing make-up torque record
1.2 Well montage	3.8 Casing pressure test
1.3 Location map	3.9 Formation Fracture Pressure Test Report(FIT)
1.4 Brief summary of operation	3.10 Deviation Survey Data
1.5 Formation tops	3.11 Cementing Report
1.6 Well Schmatic	3.12 Coring Report
2. Performance Review	3.13Material consume
2.1 Section summary	4. Completion Data
2.2 Time Versus Depth Chart	4.1 Completion procedure
2.3 Mud weight curve	4.2 Completion fluid
2.4 ROP Chart	4.3 Perforations
2.5 Drilling time breakdown	4.4 Completion String
2.6 Daily operation summary	4.5 Temporary Well Suspension
3. Drilling data	4.6 Well head and X-tree
3.1 BOP Stack Arrangement	5. HSE Summary report
3.2 Bit report	HSE Summary report
3.3 BHA Serialized Components	6. Highlights and Lessons learnt
3.4 Mud Report	Highlights and Lessons learnt
3.5 Downhole Accident/Complication Report	Appendix: Service Company information etc.

2.4. *Other regular reports*

Other Regular Reports module can provide auto-generated any report required by the drilling crew immediately during drilling.

Other Regular Reports include various reports submitted according to the operation and management requirements in the whole duration of the drilling. According to the requirement of South Azadagan drilling department, it includes 14 types of reports(show in table 2) including weekly rig checklist, BOP test report, H_2S/fire drill report etc. The specific information is shown in the following table.

Table 2. Other regular reports contents

1.Weekly Rig Checklist	8. Kick and well loss data sheet.
2.BOP Test Report	9.Mud loss Record
3. H2S/Fire Drill Report	10.Lesson Summary Report
4. Pre-spud Inspection Report	11.Weekly Cost Report
5.Medical/Incident/Accident Report	12. Formation Fracture Pressure Test Report
6.Equipment TPI Report	13.HSE Summary Report
7. Perforation Report	14. MR/SR

2.5. *Operational analysis*

Operational analysis module can extract the required data according to the searching requirement selected by the users. The data can be proposed automatically and filled into corresponding forms. The statistical searching condition can be combined freely according to the time, regions, units and drilling crews, such as drilling bit analysis shown in fig. 3. Both the single and multiple wells can be selected.

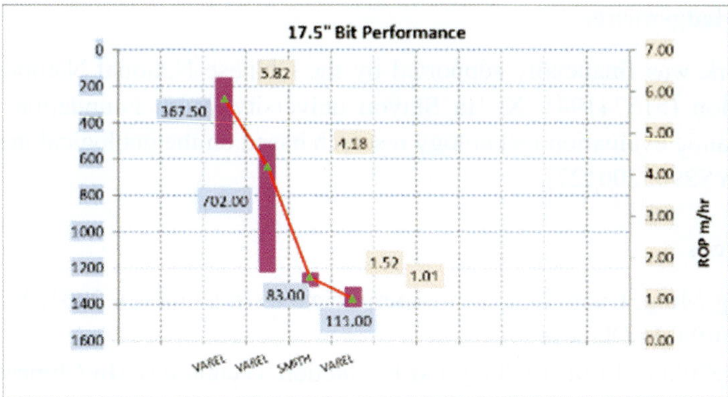

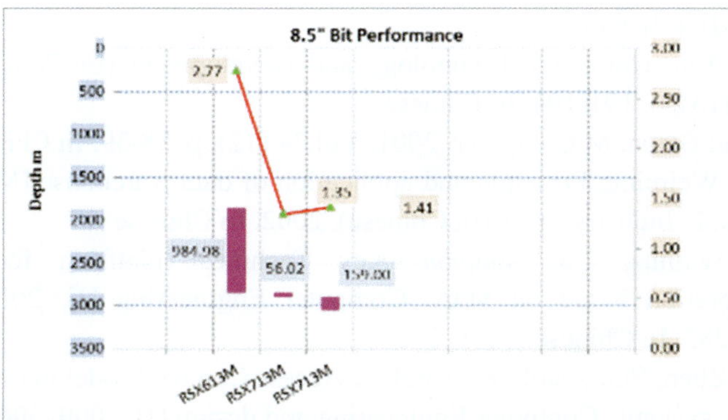

Fig. 3. Drilling bit analysis

3. Conclusion

In drilling engineering operation, it is necessary to convert, centralize and manage the various drilling data in South Azadagan through data warehouse technology and generate various type report automatically based on data warehouse according to the requirement of well site. The data warehouse system supports various types of data query, analysis and decision-making, facilitates data query and analysis for engineers of different levels, has overcome the problem of insufficient data use existing in traditional database system, and has provided an effective way to realize integration and collaboration of drilling information management.

Acknowledgements

This work was financially supported by the Chinese National Natural Science Foundation (51574194), Xi 'an Shiyou university youth Foundation: Drilling risk dynamic evaluation technology research based on the geological mechanical model (YS2903200127).

References

1. Fang Ming, Cuan Ying: Petroleum Science (In Chinese), 2005, Vol.26 (3), p. 90-94. In Chinese
2. Liu Zhikun, Li qi: Drilling and Production Technology (In Chinese), 2007, Vol.30 (3), p. 13-15. In Chinese
3. Yin Yuanfen, Zhang Zili: Computer Science (In Chinese), 2010, Vol.37(5), p. 162-164. In Chinese
4. Wang Tao: Computer Technology and Development (In Chinese), 2010, Vol.20 (5), p. 191-194. In Chinese
5. Micheal Blaba: M Computer, 2001, Vol.34 (12), p. 38-39. In Chinese
6. Zhang Weiming. Principle and application of data warehouse [M]. Beijing: Electronic Industry Press (In Chinese), 2002. In Chinese
7. Mao Weihua, Gao shujuan. Key Technical platform for business collaboration based on SOA. Computer Engineering [J], 2009, 35(19), p.280-283. In Chinese
8. Wang Zhen, Sun Xiaoli. Research of Access Control Model in collaborative design systems. Computer Engineering and design [J], 2009, 30(8), p.1836-1839. In Chinese

Have a Deep Look at Deformable Part Models for Cyclist Detection

Xiao-Ping Du[1,2,a], Hui Xiong[1,b,*] and Yang Li[1,c]

[1]School of Software, Beihang University, Xueyuan Road, Haidian District, No. 37 Beijing, Haidian District, China

[2]Key Laboratory of Advanced Manufacturing Technology for Automobile Parts, Ministry of Education, Chongqing University of Technology, Red Road, Banan District, No. 69 Chongqing, Banan District, China

E-mail: [a]xpdu@buaa.edu.cn, [b]tomxiong@buaa.edu.cn, [c]contactliyang@buaa.edu.cn

Compared with relatively mature pedestrian detection, cyclist detection lacks extensive research for vulnerable road users (VRUs) protection. In this paper, Deformable Part Models (DPMs) for cyclist detection on Tsinghua-Daimler Cyclist Benchmark is proposed, including training strategies, data clustering, deformable parts and component elements. The key contributions that DPMs have in cyclist detection to further improve its performance is researched, and the optional configuration is 8 or 10 deformable parts with 3 or 4 flipped components. To solve its speed bottleneck, a fast cyclist detection method that speeds up ten times based on upper body proposal and cascade framework is proposed, which can be extended easily to other VRUs detection.

Keywords: Cyclist Detection; Deformable Part Models; Vulnerable Road Users; Detection Proposals.

1. Introduction

For VRUs protection, though pedestrian detection has achieved great progress over the last few years [1,2], it is still a troublesome puzzle due to the large variability in appearance, body pose, occlusion and cluttered backgrounds. For cyclist detection, it not only has similar problems even worse, but also multiple viewpoints and rapid movements bring in more challenges. Therefore, the task of detecting cyclists needs to be given more care and support.

*Corresponding author.

In detecting cyclists, DPMs have a slight performance advantage over other promising methods by evaluating on the new cyclist detection dataset, refers to our joint research [6,7]. Therefore, in this paper, firstly we want to find the key contributions that DPMs have in cyclist detection, then to further improve its performance. And finally we propose a fast detection method based on upper body proposal and cascade framework to deal with its speed bottleneck problem of the state-of-the-art method.

2. Previous Work

Among VRUs protection, pedestrian detection has sufficient research resources. Cyclist detection is highly related to pedestrian detection, and we also can share ideas of feature extraction and classification methods [3,8,9]. However, before Tsinghua-Daimler Cyclist Benchmark is made public, there is no challenging cyclist dataset publicly available, except the KITTI object detection benchmark [10]. More details see [6]. Compared to cyclists, there are already many publicly available pedestrian datasets. Therefore, we serve the new cyclist detection dataset as a common point of reference for cyclist detection research.

3. How to Learn DPMs?

3.1. *Training strategies*

Different training strategies might achieve different performance even with high-quality data. We choose training set 1 as positive sample set, non-VRU as negative sample set, and training set 2 as the validation set. Positive and negative sample set is used to train the model, and the validation set is utilized to deepen the model. Unlike mining hard negative samples as in the original DPM-V5 method [4], in this paper we try to mine hard negative samples from both the validation set and non-VRU set, with maximum overlap of 0.3 Intersection over Union (IoU) with ground truths (GT).

3.2. *Data clustering*

By statistics, we note that the majority of the head/bike orientations distribute around 0 or 180 degrees. The difference between head and bike is very small. In our data clustering, we choose bike orientation as the basis for data clustering, because of better stability in motion.

However, due to the orientation information is not public this time [6], we divide cyclists' training data based on the aspect ratio of bikes to approximate the orientation classification results of bikes for data clustering. We divide the cyclist samples into three classes: narrow, intermediate and wide. We set standards of orientation classification as in Eq. (1).

$$\begin{cases} narrow, & if\ bo \in \left(0, {}^{45}/_{2}\right] \cup \left(360 - {}^{45}/_{2}, 360\right] \cup \left(180 - {}^{45}/_{2}, 180 + {}^{45}/_{2}\right] \\ wide, & if\ bo \in \left(90 - {}^{45}/_{2}, 90 + {}^{45}/_{2}\right] \cup \left(270 - {}^{45}/_{2}, 270 + {}^{45}/_{2}\right] \\ interme, & others \end{cases} \quad . \quad (1)$$

Here, *bo* stands for the orientation of the bike. According to this criterion, we get 1352 narrow, 2559 intermediate, 12291 narrow bikes, the majority of bike orientations distribute around 0 or 180 degrees.

3.3. *Deformable parts and components*

The idea of deformable parts makes great contributions to deformable part models (DPMs) [4]. However, the haze is that a different version of DPM has different numbers of parts, not saying the best disposition strategy of deformable parts and how much contribution to cyclist detection performance.

Components mean the mixture model with multi-view submodules in DPMs. There are two uncertainties about them: (1) the number of components; (2) how to split data into multiple-view components with one certain number, like three in section 3.2, where we solve the latter uncertainty.

4. Proposed Fast Detection Method

We achieve a fast method based on upper body proposal [7] and cascade framework to detect cyclists. The flowchart is shown in Figure 1, where UBD is the short name of upper body detection.

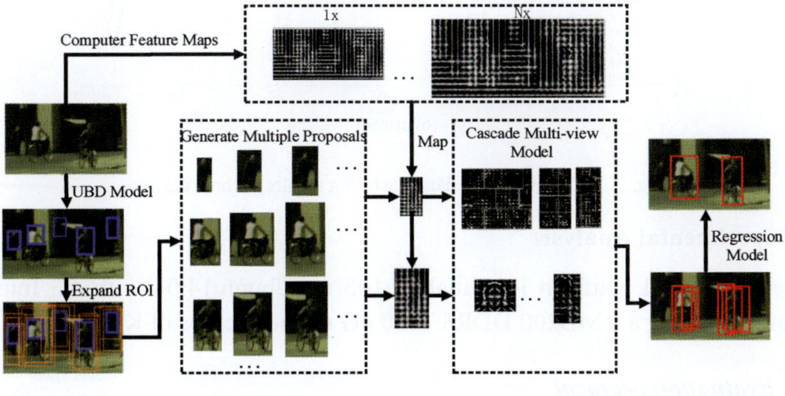

Fig. 1. The flowchart of proposed fast detection method

The upper body detection model was trained based on ACF framework [5, 7] to extract upper body candidates of person (pedestrians, cyclists and other riders), and then expand candidates' region of interest (ROI) to generate multiple proposals which cover the whole person. The cascade multi-view model was achieved by the thoughts of [11]. The regression model was trained by the ground truth of bounding boxes to output precise localization. Besides, it includes a greedy procedure via non-maximum suppression (NMS) to eliminate repeated detection with low scores.

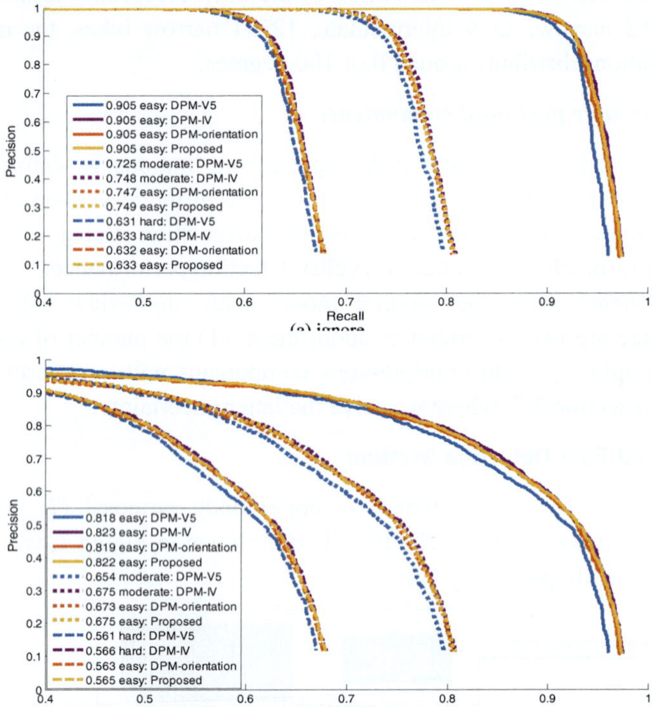

(b) discard

Fig. 2. Different cyclist data clustering results of three classes

5. Experimental Analysis

The experimental platform is Matlab 2014b on Ubuntu14.04 with 4G Intel i5 processor, adding a RMB200 DDR3 1600 4G memory chips of Kingston.

5.1. *Evaluation protocol*

For a fair comparison, we choose the well-established methodology [6], specifically precision/recall curve and mean average precision (AP). Other configurations are kept just as [6]. Besides, we use processing time per frame to verify the time performance of proposed fast detection method.

5.2. *Focus on DPMs*

Firstly of all, we verify the effectiveness by making a comparison between hard negatives mining method of the DPM-V5 [4] and proposed training strategies. The mean AP result is given in Table 1.

Table 1. Evaluation of proposed training strategies in three difficulty levels when ignoring or discarding pedestrians and other riders.

Methods	Easy	Moderate	Hard
DPM-V5 [4]	0.904/0.819	0.746/0.672	0.631/0.563
Proposed	0.905/0.823	0.748/0.675	0.633/0.566

In Figure 2, we make a comparison of four different data clustering methods. From the results in three difficulty levels, and when ignoring or discarding pedestrians and other riders, we can note that the performance of the proposed method is close to that of DPM-IV, and is better than that of DPM-V5. The conclusion is that the method of data splitting based on the aspect ratio of bikes, adjusting to the orientation classification result is effective. And when the classification result based on the aspect ratio of bikes is close to the orientation classification result, the holistic performance is basically stable.

Figure. 3 shows the performance comparison of different deformable parts configuration with other configurations kept as DPM-IV which has eight parts. We observe that DPM only with root has the worst performance. And the conclusion is that deformable parts are one of the key contributions for the success of DPMs when detecting cyclists. DPMs with ten parts lightly outperforms the other numbers of parts, achieving a 0.906 AP which outperform a 0.905 AP of the state-of-the-art method [6], even though it decreases to 0.811 AP when evaluating the ability of the detectors to distinguish cyclists from pedestrians or other riders in easy level. And opposed to the change of APs in Figure 3, we can conclude that with the subset becoming harder, mean APs of all the detectors decrease gradually, where cyclists are at a lower resolution and under partial occlusion. Additionally, the results indicate that bounding box regression still works on the new cyclist dataset.

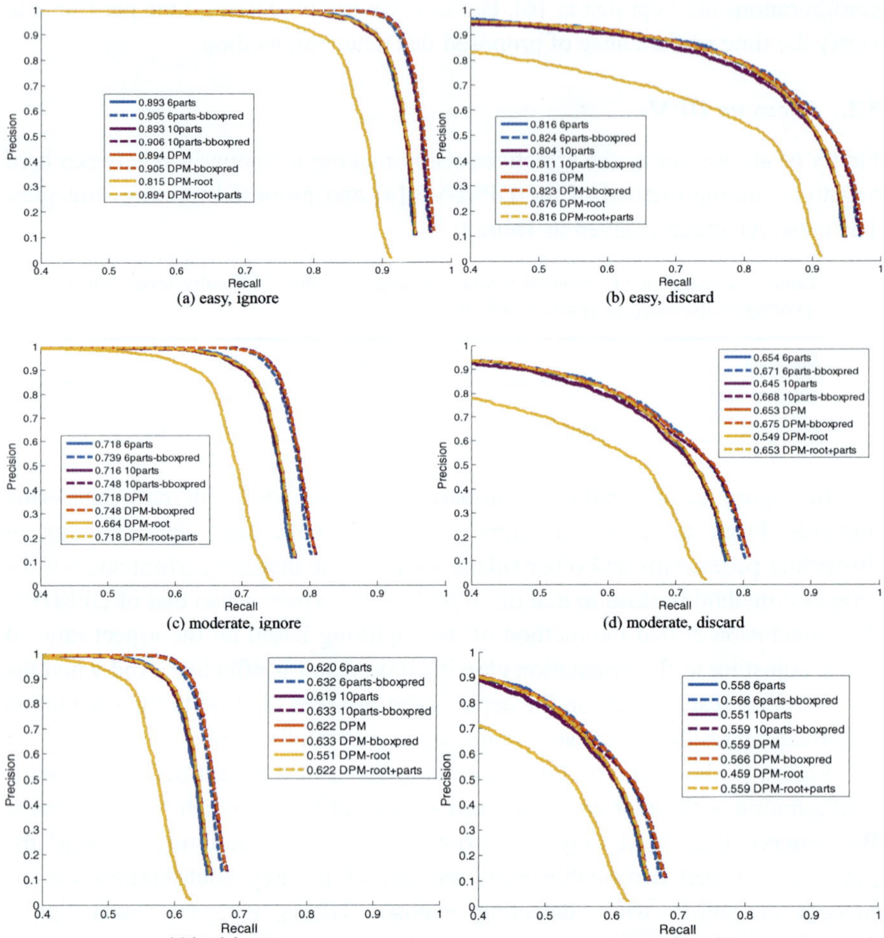

(a) easy, ignore

(b) easy, discard

(c) moderate, ignore

(d) moderate, discard

(e) hard, ignore

(f) hard, discard

Fig. 3. Performance evaluation with different number of deformable parts

Besides, by experimental comparisons, we can conclude that for cyclist detection, performance improves when the number of components increases from 1 to 3 (we use the flipped models) based on clustering method of DPM-V5, because the variety of models allows for more recall. However, performance drop when the number is over 3, the reason is that too many templates bring in confusion between multi-view models. What's more, the processing time cost increases as the component number grows.

5.3. *Evaluation of speedup methods*

The image of the new cyclist dataset is 2048*1024, with width 2048 pixels. Instead of compressing or cutting the image to speed up the method, we use the full size image and focus on the improvement of the method.

By comparing DPM-IV method and our speedup methods, the average processing time per frame is reducing from 20s to 2s. All the models are there classes with flipped and are trained by bounding box regression with 8 parts. The highest mean AP goes down from 0.905 to 0.814. The reason may be that trade-offs between performance and speed, multiple extended proposals lost the part accuracy, and bounding box regression doesn't work well, which will be considered and redesigned in forthcoming work. In this paper, we just focus on the method of a novel speedup strategy.

6. Conclusion

In this paper, we have found the fundamental contributions that DPMs have in cyclist detection. By experimental analysis, we know that training strategies, data clustering, deformable parts and component elements, and bounding box regression can all improve its performance, with deformable parts and component elements most important. More deeply, the optional configuration is 8 or 10 deformable parts with 3 or 4 flipped components. And the method of data splitting based on the aspect ratio of bikes, adjusting to the orientation classification result is applicable.

In addition, we have realized a fast detection method to deal with the speed bottleneck problem of the state-of-the-art method, however, the mean APs decrease. In further research, we need to consider additional speedup strategies, like other methods of proposals and feature extractions. It's still a challenging task to reach the balance of performance and speed.

Acknowledgments

This research was supported in part by the Opening Foundation of Key Laboratory of Advanced Manufacturing Technology for Automobile Parts, Ministry of Education.

References

1. R. Benenson, M. Omran and J. Hosang, et al, Ten Years of Pedestrian Detection, What Have We Learned?, Computer Science, 2014, pp: 613-627.

2. J. Hosang, M. Omran and R. Benenson, et al, Taking a Deeper Look at Pedestrians, in Proc. IEEE Conference on Computer Vision and Pattern Recognition (CVPR'2015), (Boston, USA, 2015).
3. W. Tian and M. Lauer, Fast Cyclist Detection by Cascaded Detector and Geometric Constraint, in Proc. IEEE 18th International Conference on Intelligent Transportation Systems (ITSC'2015), (Las Palmas, Spain, 2015).
4. P. F. Felzenszwalb, R. B. Girshick and D. McAllester, et al. Object Detection with Discriminatively Trained Part-based Models, in IEEE Transactions on Pattern Analysis and Machine Intelligence, Vol. 32, 2010, pp. 1627-1645.
5. P. Dollár, R. Appel and S. Belongie, et al, Fast Feature Pyramids for Object Detection, in IEEE Transactions on Pattern Analysis and Machine Intelligence, Vol. 36, 2014, pp. 1532-1545.
6. X. F. Li, F. Flohr, Y. Yang, H. Xiong, et al. A New Benchmark for Vision-Based Cyclist Detection, in Proc. IEEE Intelligent Vehicles Symposium (IV'2016), (Gothenburg, Sweden, 2016).
7. X. F. Li, L. X. Li, F. Flohr, J. Q. Wang, H. Xiong, et al, A Unified Framework for Concurrent Pedestrian and Cyclist Detection, IEEE Transactions on Intelligent Transportation Systems, 2016 (Accepted).
8. K. Yang, C. Liu and J. Y. Zheng, et al. Bicyclist Detection in Large Scale Naturalistic Driving Video, in Proc. 17th International IEEE Conference on Intelligent Transportation Systems (ITSC'2014), (Qingdao, China, 2014).
9. H. H. Chen, C. C. Lin and W. Y. Wu, et al, Integrating Appearance and Edge Features for on-road Bicycle and Motorcycle Detection in the Nighttime, in Proc. 17th International IEEE Conference on Intelligent Transportation Systems (ITSC'2014), (Qingdao, China, 2014).
10. A. Geiger, P. Lenz and R. Urtasun, Are We Ready for Autonomous Driving? The Kitti Vision Benchmark suite, in Proc. Computer Vision and Pattern Recognition IEEE Conference on, (CVPR'2012), (Providence, USA, 2012).
11. P. F. Felzenszwalb, R. B. Girshick and McAllester D, Cascade Object Detection with Deformable Part Models, in Proc. IEEE conference on Computer vision and pattern recognition, (CVPR'2010), (San Francisco, USA, 2010).

An Improved Particle Swarm Algorithm Based on the Siege Strategy

Qing Guo[1,a,*], Xiao-Bin Hui[1,b], Ping-Ping Wu[2,c] and Yu Zhao[1,d]

[1]*College of Equipment and Safety Engineering, Air Force Engineering University Xi'an 710051, China*

[2]*94188 forces, Xi'an 710077, China*

E-mail: [a]781106222@qq.com, [b]blue_seaing@126.com, [c]172141063@qq.com, [d]1803192468@qq.com

In order to deal with multi-dimensional functions optimization, an s-Particle Swarm Optimization(s-PSO) derived from the Local Siege Strategy was proposed. In s-PSO, each generation global optimal particle abandoned the traditional way to update the position instead of some siege particles was generated around it and then these particles approached it in a dynamic way to update its position. Experiments of several various multi-dimensional test functions were carried out to verify the validity of s-PSO and the results showed that they were able to handle with multi-dimensional function optimization with high success rate under 100 dimensionalities and its success rate was less than 50% for more than 100 dimensionalities.

Keywords: Particle Swarm Optimization; Local Siege Strategy; Local Exploitation Ability; Multi-dimensional Function Optimization.

1. Introduction

Particle Swarm Optimization algorithm (PSO) has been proposed by the American social psychologist Kennedy James and electrical engineer Eberhart Russell in 1995[1~3]. It is a new kind of intelligent stochastic swarm optimization algorithm simulated the foraging behavior of birds, which is suitable for solving a large number of complex optimization problems of non-linear, non-differentiable and complex optimization problem with multi peak value[2]. The PSO algorithm has the advantages of less parameters, intrinsic parallelism, simple principle, easy implementation, quick convergence to the global optimal solution area and so on. Therefore, PSO algorithm has been

---

*Corresponding author.

attracting extensive attention of many scholars since it was proposed, and has been universally used in numerous field of science and engineering, such as numerical optimization, image segmentation, pattern classification, training the neural network and fuzzy control system.

PSO algorithm is similar to other evolutionary algorithms. Owing to the declining of population diversity in the process of evolution, PSO algorithm has the following defects: easy to fall into the local optimal solution, bad local exploitation ability, easy to premature convergence and poor performance about high-dimensional function optimization. In order to solve this problem, most scholars have been improving the PSO algorithm in the following two aspects: Firstly, a variety of advanced theories, such as chaos optimization, reverse learning optimization, neural network technology, grey theory and adaptive technique, are introduced into the PSO algorithm to enhance spatial ergodic and population diversity of the algorithm; Secondly, Some scholars combine the PSO algorithm with other intelligent stochastic optimization algorithms to study the hybrid optimization algorithm.

Inspired by the siege behavior of Wolf Pack Algorithm (WPA) [4], this paper proposed a local siege strategy based on the global optimal particle. And it was applied to particle swarm optimization algorithms. This paper is organized as follows: In Section 1, the formation and development of PSO are briefly introduced; In Section 2, local siege strategy is described; In Section 3, the basic PSO and s-PSO algorithm are narrated; In Section 4, several standard functions are tested and the results are discussed; In Section 5, some conclusions are proposed.

2. Local Siege Strategy

The idea of local siege strategy is as follows: In the PSO algorithm, each generation global optimal particle i abandon the traditional way to update the position, but is viewed as a target T to be attacked. Some siege particles where is $A=\{A_1,A_2,\cdots,A_M\}$ are randomly generated around the target T according to Eq. (1~2), and the position of the particles are $A_m = (A_{m1}, A_{m2}, \cdots , A_{mD})$. $Z_m=f(A_m)$ is the function value of the siege particle M. If Z_m is better than the function value of the target T where is Y_T, both of them are exchanged. Then, the siege particles A attack the target T according to Eq. (3). Similarly, during the siege, if Z_m is better than Y_T, the siege particle is exchanged with the target T. After the siege, the update position and function value of the target T are returned to the particle i, and the rest of particles remains to be explored on the basis of the traditional way. In the iterative process of PSO algorithm, if the next global optimal particle is still particle i, it is not necessary to generate the siege particles, only to continue the siege on the basis of the previous generation of siege particles.

$$S_d^R = \left|\max_d(X) - \min_d(X)\right| \tag{1}$$

$$A_{md}^k = x_{Td}^k + \sin(\gamma) \times S_d^R \tag{2}$$

For m=1,2,$\cdots$,M. Where S^R is siege radius, M is the size of siege particle, γ is a random number of evenly distributed and $\gamma \sim U(-0.1, 0.1)$.

$$A_{md}^{k+1} = A_{md}^k + \lambda \times \left(x_{Td}^k - A_{md}^k\right) \Big/ \left|x_{Td}^k - A_{md}^k\right| \tag{3}$$

Where x_{Td} is the position of the global optimal particle i in the d dimensional space. λ is a random number of evenly distributed and $\lambda \sim U(0, 2)$. It shows that the exploitation behaviour of the siege particles can not only be in the front of the x_T, but also can be in the rear of the x_T.

3. S-Particle Swarm Optimization

For the sake of explaining s-PSO, it is necessary to give a concise outline of the basic PSO firstly.

3.1. *Basic PSO*

PSO is stochastic optimization technique. The algorithm is mainly composed of velocity and position updated formula. They had been first proposed by Kennedy and Eberhart[1], and have been improved by Shi and Eberhar[4~5]. They are described in vector notation as follows:

$$v_{id}^{k+1} = \omega v_{id}^k + c_1 r_1 \left(P_{id}^{best} - x_{id}^k\right) + c_2 r_2 \left(G_d^{best} - x_{id}^k\right) \tag{4}$$

$$x_{id}^{k+1} = x_{id}^k + v_{id}^{k+1}, \quad d = 1, 2, \cdots, D \tag{5}$$

For i=1,2,$\cdots$,N. where N is the swarm size; ω is inertia weight coefficient; c_1 and c_2 are learning factors and also known as acceleration coefficients; r_1 and r_2 are random numbers in the (0,1) region. Shi and Eberhart recommended to take the ω=0.7298 and c_1=c_2=1.49618[5] in the calculation.

3.2. *S-PSO*

To search the maximum value of test function as an example, this paper design a new PSO algorithm that is called s-PSO algorithm based on the local siege strategy. s-PSO algorithm process is as follows:

***Step*1:** Set the initial value of the inertia weight coefficient ω, learning factors c_1 and c_2, particle swarm size N, siege particle size M, the maximum number of iterations K_{max} and other initial parameters.

***Step*2:** Initialize the initial position X and velocity V of the particle swarm, and calculate the function value Y of each particle.

***Step*3:** The position of each particle is set to the personal best position that is recorded as P_{best}, and the maximum function value of the particle swarm is set to the global best position that is recorded as G_{best}.

***Step*4:** The global best particle i is viewed as a target T to be attacked. Some siege particles where is $A=\{A_1,A_2,\cdots,A_M\}$ are randomly generated around the target T according to Eq. (1~2).

***Step*5:** The siege particles perform local siege strategy on the target T according to Eq. (3). During the period, if the function value of the siege particle is greater than the function value of the target T, both of them are exchanged. Other particles adjust the position and velocity according to Eq. (4~5). If the function value of the particle is larger than the function value before the adjustment, the personal best position of the particle is be updated.

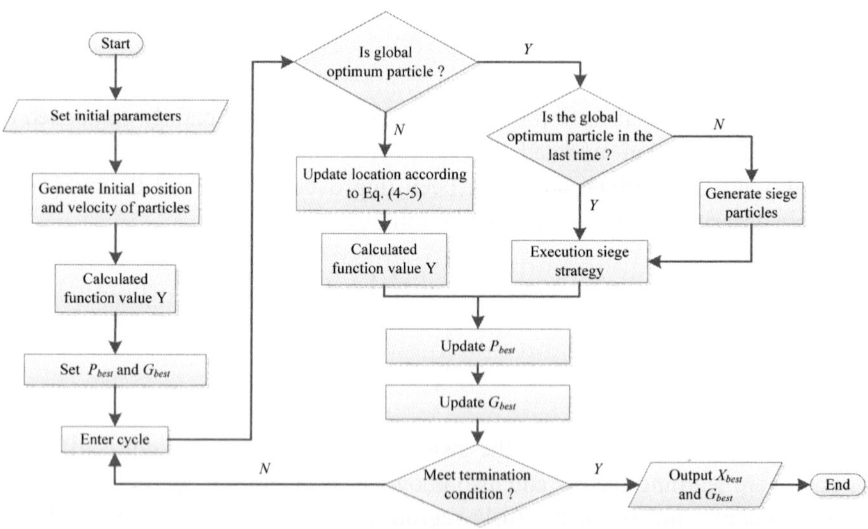

Fig. 1. Flow chart of s-PSO algorithm

Step6: The position X_T of target T is assigned to X_{best} and the Y_T is assigned to G_{best}. If the rest of the particle's P_{best} is greater than G_{best}, the X_{best} and G_{best} is be updated.

Step7: If the calculation results meet the requirements of the optimization accuracy or $K>K_{max}$, X_{best} and G_{best} are output. Otherwise, the algorithm is back to *step4*.

The flow chart of s-PSO algorithm is shown in Figure 1. This section describes the application of local siege strategy in the PSO algorithm, and then other PSO algorithm can according to the process to design the correspondingly improved PSO algorithm based on local siege strategy.

4. Experiments for s-PSO

In order to verify the validity of s-PSO, several standard test functions, named "Sphere", "Jason", "Sumsquares", "Quadric", "Griewank", "Ackley" and "Rosenbrock", were used in the optimization experiments. The detailed information of several standard test functions is summarized in Table 1. The choice of parameters recommended in published paper with ω=0.7298 and c1=c2=1.49618[5] were used. Each experiment was ran at least 20 times with a random initial manner in order to obtain the objective result. The comparison results of experiment were listed in Table 2. Moreover, another experiments were carried out using "Sphere" to verify the effect of the dimension. The comparison results of experiment were given in Table 3. Finally, experimental evolution curves of several test functions were showed in Figure 2

Table 1. List of standard test functions

Function	Formula	Solution domain	Optimal value	Optimal location
Sphere	$f(X)=\sum_{i=1}^{D} x_i^2$	$[-100,100]^D$	Min= 0	$[0,0,\ldots,0]^D$
Jason	$f(X)=\sum_{i=1}^{D} (x_i - i)^2$	$[-100,100]^D$	Min= 0	$[1,2,\ldots,D]^D$
Sumsquares	$f(X)=\sum_{i=1}^{D} i x_i^2$	$[-100,100]^D$	Min= 0	$[0,0,\ldots,0]^D$
Quadric	$f(X)=\sum_{i=1}^{D} \left(\sum_{k=1}^{i} x_k\right)^2$	$[-30,30]^D$	Min= 0	$[0,0,\ldots,0]^D$
Griewank	$f(X)=\sum_{i=1}^{D} x_i^2/4000-\prod_{i=1}^{D}\cos\left(x_i/\sqrt{i}\right)$	$[-20,20]^D$	Min= 0	$[0,0,\ldots,0]^D$
Ackley	$f(X)=-20e^{-0.2\sqrt{\sum_{i=1}^{D} x_i^2/D}}-e^{\sum_{i=1}^{D}\cos(2\pi x_i)/D}+20+e$	$[-10,10]^D$	Min= 0	$[0,0,\ldots,0]^D$
Rosenbrock	$f(X)=\sum_{i=1}^{n-1}\left[100\left(x_{i+1}-x_i^2\right)^2+\left(1-x_i\right)^2\right]$	$[-10,10]^D$	Min= 0	$[1,1,\ldots,1]^D$

Table 2. Comparison results of experiment for optimizing 20 dimensionalities test functions using s-PSO

Function	Algorithm	Size	Iterations	Best	Mean	Time	SR
Sphere	s-PSO	50+10	8000	4.04E-29	1.11E-14	4.13	100%
	PSO	60	8000	14.29	75.57	3.27	—
	s-PSO	100+20	8000	1.01E-71	2.15E-23	8.17	100%
	PSO	120	8000	0.37	2.09	6.22	—
Jason	s-PSO	50+10	8000	1.51E-17	7.69E-13	4.39	100%
	PSO	60	8000	13.36	150.72	3.79	—
	s-PSO	100+20	8000	3.16E-30	2.61E-21	9.31	100%
	PSO	120	8000	0.50	6.94	7.27	—
Sumsquares	s-PSO	50+10	8000	4.13E-25	3.08E-13	4.24	100%
	PSO	60	8000	931.85	6.99E+03	3.37	—
	s-PSO	100+20	8000	6.73E-38	1.77E-23	8.39	100%
	PSO	120	8000	7.20	2.12E+03	6.37	—
Quadric	s-PSO	50+10	10000	8.41E-15	1.15E-03	5.61	100%
	PSO	60	10000	8.96	176.57	4.51	—
	s-PSO	100+20	10000	1.36E-33	5.04E-04	11.20	100%
	PSO	120	10000	3.38	36.75	8.75	—
Griewank	s-PSO	50+10	1000	0.00E+00	1.63E-03	0.91	33.33%
	PSO	60	1000	4.55	6.43	0.61	—
	s-PSO	100+20	1000	0.00E+00	6.90E-05	1.74	35%
	PSO	120	1000	2.82	5.38	1.18	—
Ackley	s-PSO	50+10	1000	7.27E-12	2.98E-04	0.76	30%
	PSO	60	1000	5.65	8.02	0.61	—
	s-PSO	100+20	1000	0.00E+00	4.56E-08	3.05	33.33%
	PSO	120	1000	3.33	5.04	1.18	—
Rosenbrock	s-PSO	50+10	20000	1.56E-16	1.06E-05	12.06	75%
	PSO	60	20000	258.49	2.26E+04	9.41	—
	s-PSO	100+20	10000	1.44E-18	5.33E-05	11.61	80%
	PSO	120	10000	23.70	4.17E+03	9.72	—

Note: 50+10, '50' is particle swarm size; '10' is siege particles size. 'SR' is success rate.

Table 3. Comparison results of experiment for optimizing 20-120 dimensionalities Sphere function using s-PSO

Dimension	Algorithm	Size	Iterations	Best	Mean	Time	SR
20	s-PSO	50+10	10000	3.99E-188	4.34E-19	5.34	100%
40	s-PSO	50+10	15000	3.96E-09	1.26E-05	8.72	100%
60	s-PSO	80+15	20000	1.79E-06	6.01E-04	20.3	95%
80	s-PSO	80+15	25000	1.26E-05	2.63E-03	27.7	90%
100	s-PSO	100+20	30000	8.68E-05	2.62E-03	47.2	60%
120	s-PSO	100+20	40000	1.01E-03	3.01E-03	68.1	45%

Note: 50+10, '50' is particle swarm size; '10' is siege particles size. 'SR' is success rate.

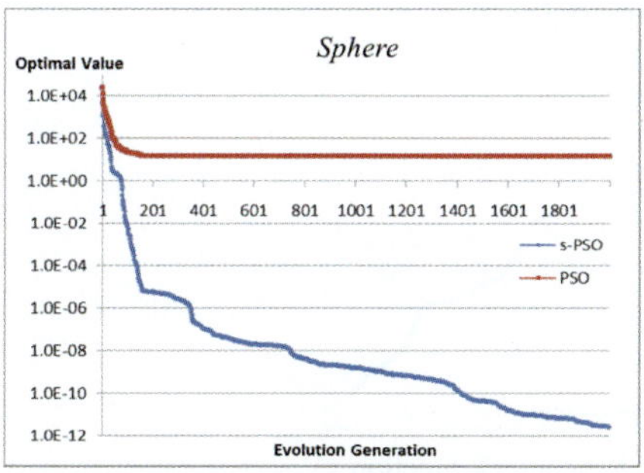

(a)20 dimensionalities Sphere function

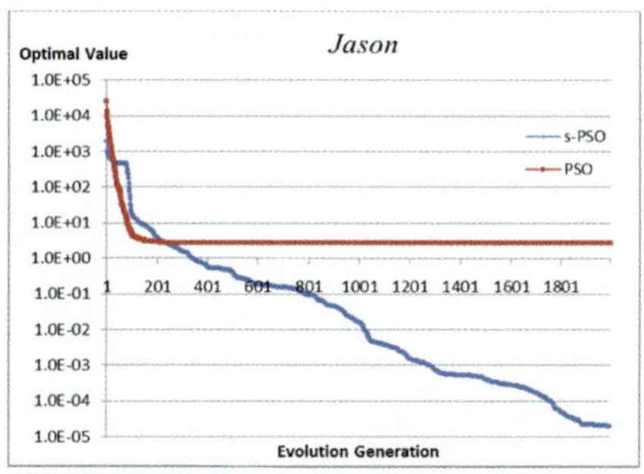

(b)20 dimensionalities Jason function

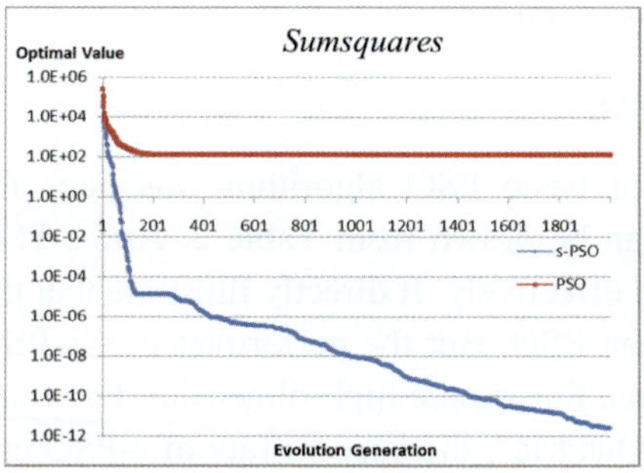

(c)20 dimensionalities Sumsquares function

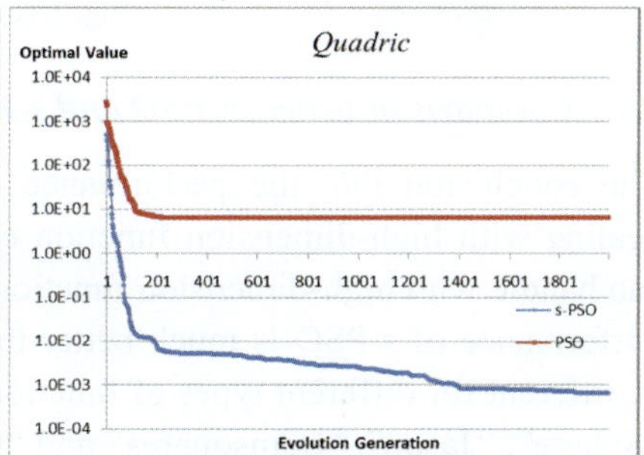

(d)20 dimensionalities Quadric function

Fig. 2. Evolution charts of experiment of above seven test function

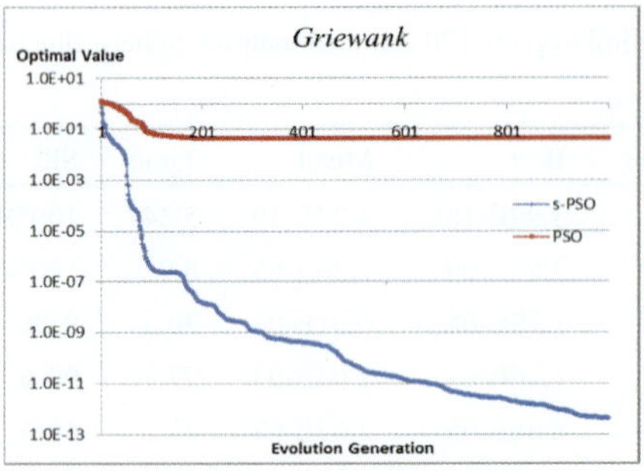

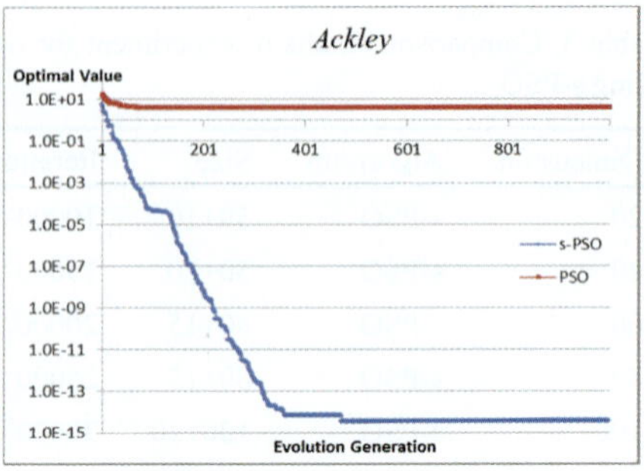

(e)20 dimensionalities Griewank function (f)20 dimensionalities Ackley function

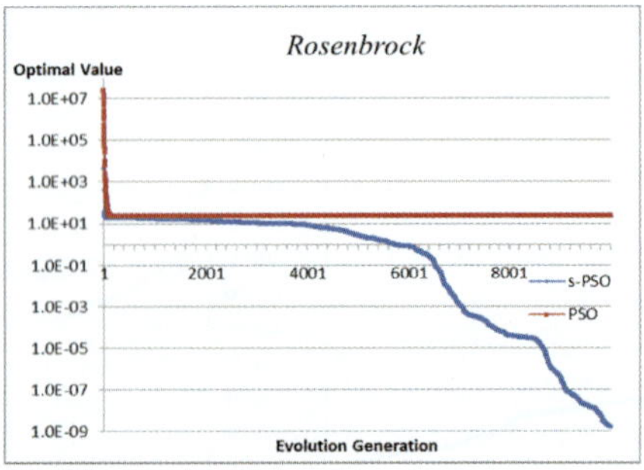

(g)20 dimensionalities Rosenbrock function

Fig. 2. (*Continued*)

4.1. *Comparison between PSO and s-PSO*

The conclusion that the performance of basic PSO algorithm was poor for dealing with high-dimension function can be drawn from Table 2. And s-PSO can handle with high-dimension function effectively. It directly illustrate that the performance of s-PSO is much better than PSO. But the performance of s-PSO is different for different types of functions. For simple high-dimension functions "Sphere", "Jason", "Sumsquares" and "Quadric", the success rate of s-PSO can reach 100%. However, the success rate of s-PSO is lower than 80% for complex and multi-peak functions "Griewank", "Ackley" and "Rosenbrock". This result indicates that s-PSO is also unable to avoid local optimal.

Furthermore, PSO algorithm is prone to premature convergence from Figure 2. And the accuracy of s-PSO algorithm is increasing with the iteration process. It is more intuitive to show the effectiveness of s-PSO algorithm compared with PSO algorithm. Overall, the performance of algorithm is markedly improved after using local siege strategy.

4.2. *Discussion of swarm size*

All discussion are based on data in Table 2-3. The influence of swarm size on the algorithm can be discussed from the following three aspects: In terms of time consumption, it varies linearly with the swarm size; In respect of computational accuracy, it increases with the increase of swarm size; As for the success rate of s-PSO, it is improved with more swarm size. So, the choice of swarm size needs to be combined with the complexity of function.

4.3. *Discussion of dimension*

From Table 3, we can draw a conclusion that s-PSO can be able to solve high-dimension function optimization. Its success rate can reach above 90% for less than 100 dimensionalities, and its success rate is less than 50% for more than 100 dimensionalities. The reason is that computational complexity increases exponentially with the increase of the dimension. This is the curse of dimensionality.

5. Conclusions

The experiments of s-PSO algorithm were carried out to compared with PSO algorithm. The comparison results show that the comprehensive performance of s-PSO is significantly better than PSO. It shows that the local exploitation ability of the algorithm is dramatically improved and the algorithm can avoid premature convergence and other defects by the introduction of the local siege strategy in the PSO algorithm. Therefore, this strategy can be applied to improve the local exploitation ability of PSO algorithm and the improved PSO algorithm based on this strategy can solve multi-dimensional functions optimization.

References

1. J. Kennedy and R. C. Eberhart. Particle swarm optimization[A]. Proc IEEE International Conference on Neural Networks[C]. USA: IEEE Press, 1995.1942-1948.
2. R. C. Eberhart and J. Kennedy. A new optimizer using particle swarm theory[A]. Proc Sixth International Symposium on Micro Machine and Human Science [C]. Nago ya, Japan: IEEE Press, 1995.39-43.
3. R. C. Eberhart, P. K. Simpson and R. W. Dobbins. Computational Intelligence PC Tools[M]. Boston, MA: Academic Press Professional, 1996.

4. Husheng Wu, Fengming Zhang and Lushan Wu. New swarm intelligence algorithm-wolf pack algorithm[J]. Systems Engineering and Electronics, 2013, 35(11): 2430-2438(In Chinese).
5. Y. Shi and R. C. Eberhart. Parameter selection in particle swarm optimization[A]. Proc 7th Annual Conference on Evolutionary Programming [C]. Washington DC: IEEE Press, 1998.591-600.
6. Y. Shi and R. C. Eberhart. A modified particle swarm optimizer[A]. Proc IEEE International Conference on Computation Intelligence[C]. Anchorage: IEEE Press, 1998.69-73.
7. Y. Shi and R. C. Eberhart. Fuzzy adaptive particle swarm optimization[A]. Proceedings of the IEEE Congress on Evolutionary Computation[C]. Piscataway, USA: IEEE Service Center, 2001.101-106.
8. M. Clerc and J. Kennedy. The particle swarm: Explosion, stability and convergence in a multi-dimensional complex space. IEEE Trans on Evolutionary Computation, 2002, 6(1): 58-73.
9. F. D. Bergh and A. P. Engelbrecht. A study of particle swarm optimization particle trajectories[J]. Information Science, 2006, 176(8): 937-971.
10. B. Y. Qu, P. N. Suganthan and S. Das. A distance-based locally informed particle swarm model for multimodal optimization[J]. IEEE Trans on Evolutionary Computation, 2013, 17(3): 387-402.
11. Z. Beheshti and S. M. Hj Shamsuddin. CAPSO: Centripetal accelerated particle swarm optimization[J]. Information Sciences, 2014, 258: 54-79.
12. V. Nedic, S. Cvetanovic, D. Despotovic and et al. Data mining with various optimization methods[J]. Expert Systems with Applications, 2014, 41(8): 3993-3999.
13. F. Han and Q. Liu. A diversity-guided hybrid particle swarm optimization based on gradient search[J]. Neurocomputing, 2014, 137: 234-240.
14. J. Sadeghi, S. Sadeghi and S. T. A. Niaki. Optimizing a hybrid vendor-managed inventory and transportation problem with fuzzy demand: An improved particle swarm optimization algorithm[J]. Information Sciences, 2014, 272: 126-144.
15. Kun Li, Ming Li and Hao Chen. Particle Swarm Optimization with Exhaustive Disturbance Based on Exploration-Exploitation Balance Theory[J]. PR&AI, 2015, 28(7): 603-612(In Chinese).

Theory and Practice of the Electronic Data Forensics of the Panda Case

Yong-Hao Mai[a], Jun Zhang[b] and Shu-Fang Yang[c]

Hubei University of Police, 99 Nanniwan Avenue
Wuhan, Hubei 430000, China
E-mail: [a]myh9999@163.com, [b]413794175@qq.com, [c]1127000510@qq.com

This paper introduced the dynamic of electronic forensic identification both in China and abroad and proposed its categories and hierarchies. By analyzing the three legal bases and three technical foundations of electronic forensic identification, it indicated that this kind of examination could be both quantitative and qualitative, and its process could be precisely reproduced. This paper mainly discussed the legal scheme, technical scheme, and practical implementation plan in handling the case, as well as the identification working environment, and the supervision of the chain of evidence. The architecture of electronic forensic identification was proposed, which could unite the legal and technical aspects of this type of identification.

Keywords: Electronic Data Forensics; Categories and Hierarchies; Architecture; Panda Case.

1. Introduction

Digital forensics is key to the trial and measurement of penalty in computer-related crimes, thus it is a hot issue in the digital era. With its high-tech properties such as modifiability, instantaneity, reliance on the equipment, and its precise repeatability, electronic forensic identification is both a legal and technical issue. We should integrate its particularity with its universality, and study on the evidence investigation, acquisition, preservation, application, examination and conformation, to secure the objectivity, legality and relevancy of the electronic evidence.

1.1. *Legal foundation of the electronic evidence identification*

The amended *Criminal Procedure Law*, and *Civil Procedure Law of the PRC* were enacted since January 1st, 2013. The amended *Administrative Procedure Law of PRC* took effect since May 1st, 2015. These laws confirmed that digital evidence is considered as evidence in any legal proceeding.

Article 285 and 286 of the *Criminal Law of PRC* stipulate the following six computer-related crime charges:(1) crime of illegal intrusion into computer information system;(2) crime of sabotaging functions of a computer information system;(3) crime of damaging computer information system data and application program;(4) crime of producing, disseminating of computer viruses and other destructive procedures;(5) crime of being hackers;(6) crime of providing hacking tools. Article 287 illustrates and summarizes other crimes involving the use of computer to commit crimes such as fraud, theft, corruption, embezzlement, stealth of State secret. There are more than a hundred kinds of such crime charges. Besides, the *Civil Procedure Law* and *Administrative Procedure Law* are facing increasing social demands. Areas such as E-government, E-commerce, network finance, industrial and agricultural production, social service, people's livelihood and privacy are calling for legal protection from the government.

1.2. *Technical basis electronic forensic identification*

The authors believe that the technical basis of the forensic identification of electronic data includes three technical methods: read only, cloning and verification.

Read-only can be realized through the method of software and hardware. The purpose is only to read the test material, without changing it. And it is designed to protect electronic data from being altered, so as to ensure that the primitiveness of the data for further retest.

Cloning is to clone the content of the hard disk to the clone hard disk with the help of the hard copy machine, during which the integrity of the original data will not be damaged or modified.

Hash check refers to transforming an arbitrary length of input into a very short fixed length output, through the hash algorithm. We can check whether the file or the hard drive has been tampered at any time in the case, simply by comparing the Hash values of the same file, hard disk partition or the entire hard disk.

2. Identification of the Case

2.1. *The identification of "production" of the virus*

Using hard disk copy machine, we copied the data from the original hard disk to a new hard disk without any data, and found in the Code Source directory a large number of source code files of virus and Trojan programs written in VB, VC and Delphi, which covered almost all the aspects of the network attack viruses and Trojans.

In the "\Source Code\Delphi\My_Work\chuangran" directory, we found a number of versions of the virus source code file. According to the time sequence, the code content was basically the same, and the function was gradually improved, which reflected the basic track of the author's maintenance and improvement process.

2.2. *The identification of "dissemination" of the virus*

In "**'s file", we found a large number of IP addresses, computer names, as well as user names and passwords for online games (such as "Hangame","Itembay", "Zhengtu (Warpath)"," Maple Story"). Combining with the related information found in the "readme.txt" (which appeared multiple times) under the "\Source Code\Delphi\My_Work\chuangran" directory, we concluded that the ultimate goal of the producer of the Trojan virus " whboy " (i.e. the Panda virus) was to obtain economic benefits through the sale of "the Trojans they designed and the information obtained by the Trojans. In addition, from the chat retrieved from the hard disk we could see that there were a lot of people who knew what the virus producer was doing, and they demanded for the virus. Therefore, the writer of the "whboy" was not writing this Trojan program simply out of interest.

2.3. *The identification of "intention"*

At the early stage, the virus producer gave out the virus to the Internet users, and then together with other defendants, he rented a server with 1600 yuan to set up a website, and enabled the affected computers to visit this website automatic ally. Then they could sell the site traffic, and implanted in the web server the Trojan program, which could steal the online game account and password by steps such as automatic detection and electronic envelope. Then the other defendants sold the information elsewhere. This series of behavior has constituted the main body of subjective "intention" in the production and dissemination of the virus.

2.4. *The identification of "consequence"*

Affected by the "whboy" Trojan, the running speed of the computer dropped, with blue screen and frequent restart of the system, and the hard disk data file was damaged. Meanwhile, the computer will become the "chicken" controlled by the Trojan writer, and would download files from specified website, which caused the failure of the computer system. Under "MyHacker\articles frequently read\bill", we found the billing information from January 2005 to July 2006, a total amount of about 400,000 yuan.

The behavior of the defendants is in full compliance with the constitutive elements of the crime of destroying computer information system. The identification of the four aspects: production, dissemination, intention and the consequences conform strictly to the relevant content of the criminal law, and the expert opinion has been admitted by the court: "Defendants Li and Lei intentionally produced computer virus; Defendants Li, Wang, and Zhang intentionally disseminated the computer virus which affected the normal operation of many computer systems with serious consequences. Their behavior has constituted the crime of destroying computer information system, thus should bear criminal responsibility."

3. Conclusion and Prediction

Generally speaking, the research on and development of digital forensics in and out of China is unbalanced, the criteria disunited. There is an urgent need to study digital forensics from the basic theory, structure model, and practical application to perfect its structure, and lay a theoretical foundation for the future standard setting and platform integration. This paper is a preliminary discussion based on this conclusion and prediction, which sets foot into an interdisciplinary, frontier and innovative research area.

Acknowledgments

This research is funded by *National High Technology Research and Development Program of China (863 Program)* (No. 2015AA017204).

References

1. The Scientific Working Group on Digital Evidence (SWGDE), *Digital Evidence: Standards and Principles, Proposed Standards for the Exchange of Digital Evidence*. (1999). London:nternational Hi-Tech Crime and Forensics Conference.

2. Dan Farmer, Wietse Venema. (2011). *Forensic Discovery, Computer Forensics Analysis Class Handouts*. Retrieved on August 6 from http://www.porcupine.org/forensics/handouts.html.
3. Chris Prosise, Kevin Mandia. (2001). *Incident Response: Investigating Computer Crime*, New York: McGraw-Hill Companies.
4. Technical Working Group for Electronic Crime Scene Investigation. (2001). *Electronic Crime Scene Investigation: A guide for responders, Washington*, DC: The U. S. Department of Justice (DOJ).
5. Dennis McGrath, Vincent Berk, Shu-kai Chin, etc. (2001). *A Road Map for Digital Forensic Research*, New York: Digital Forensic Research Workshop (DFRWS).
6. Sun Bo. (2004). *Research on key aspects of computer forensic methods.* Beijing: Chinese Academy of Sciences.
7. Standing Committee of NPC. (2005). Decision of the Standing Committee of NPC on the Administration of Forensic Authentication.
8. NPC. *Criminal Procedure Law of the People's Republic of China.*
9. Marcus K. Rogers, James Goldman, Rick Mislan, Timothy Wedge, eve Debrota. (2006). *Computer Forensics Field Triage Process Model,* Las, gas: Conference Digital Forensics, Security and Law.
10. Peter Sommer. (1998). *Digital Footprints: Assessing Computer Evidence*, London: Criminal Law Review Special Edition. NPC. Criminal Law of the People's Republic of China.
11. Wang, Wenqi, Miao, Fengjun, Pan Lei, Zhang Shuqin. (2010). *Research on the Integrity of Network Forensics.*

An Algorithm of the Conceptual Design Solution Evaluation and Selection Based on Trustworthiness

Dian-Ting Liu[1,a], Chao-Yang Li[2,b], Quan-Yong Zhang[2,c], Zheng-Feng Wang[2,d] and De-Jian Zhou[3,e]

[1]College of Mechanical and Control Engineering Guilin University of Technology Guangxi Guilin, China

[2]College of Information Science and Engineering Guilin University of Technology Guangxi Guilin, China

[3]Mechanical and Electrical Engineering Institute Guilin University of Electronic Technology, Guangxi Guilin, China

E-mail: [a]365565379@qq.com, [b]872896291@qq.com, [c]1370006407@qq.com, [d]wangzhengfeng171@163.com, [e]emezdj@guet.edu.cn

In order to evaluate and select the conceptual design solution better, the concept of trustworthiness is introduced, and proposes a conceptual design solution evaluation and selection algorithm based on trustworthiness. That is to get the comprehensive score by related trustworthiness computation, and then the preferable solution is ultimately selected. Finally, two experiments prove the necessity and feasibility of the algorithm, and it has a certain useful value.

Keywords: Conceptual Design Solution; Evaluation and Selection; Trustworthiness.

1. Introduction

The conceptual design is the core stage of the production innovation[1]. However, there are several design schemes during the conceptual design, and the key is how to evaluate and choose one of them. There are many solutions such as fuzzy number introduced [2-4], analytic hierarchy process based [3-4], weight discrimination-filter based on weights calculation [5], evaluation index weight calculation by entropy method [6] or combination of the methods mentioned above. Where the fuzzy number denotes the fuzzy processing of the evaluations of all levels, analytic hierarchy process is the evaluation index of stratification, weight discrimination-filter process and entropy method is to calculate the weight values of each evaluation index[7]. The grade and knowledge quantity of each expert is different, so the credibility of them varies from person to person. I.e. It is essential to take the credibility of scheme evaluation made by expert into consideration, when we make the group decision evaluation for the scheme of the conceptual design. According to the different trust values made by the expert from different grades, we proposed an algorithm of the conceptual design solution evaluation and selection based on trustworthiness. Firstly, we divided conceptual design solution into several indexes by analytic hierarchy process, and treated the each index of the evaluation items with fuzzy number. Then, we calculated the trustworthiness of the each expert's evaluation, and eventually calculate the comprehensive score of scheme evaluation from all experts in order to choose the best scheme. And we did some experiments about this algorithm, proved its feasibility and reasonability.

2. Relation Work

We supposed that the conceptual design of product was based on the environment of enterprise network community. Each user in network community can evaluate the conceptual design scheme of a product because of its timelessness, across localization and interaction etc. At the same time, the different grade users have the different trustworthiness for the conceptual design scheme of a product.T1, T2, T3...denotes, respectively, the index of the conceptual design scheme of a product. "Perfect", "Excellent", "Good", "Moderate", "Ordinary", "Bad", "Worse" and "Worst" describe the evaluation set of each index, and denote fuzzy interval number [10, 10], [9, 10) , [8, 9), [7, 8), [6, 7), [5, 6), [3, 5), [0, 3) respectively. Users evaluate the scheme by choosing one of the evaluation items.

2.1. *Data representation*

According to the factors such as activity, behavior and the time in community etc, we divided the network community into five ranks: "Special expert (H1)", "Senior expert (H2)", "Expert (H3)", "Civilian (H4)", "Newbie (H5)". It's important to notice that the rank of the users in community is float up or down with the behavior of the users. So, the different rank of users will select the different evaluation item when they evaluate the scheme evaluation in the community. $R(c,e,t) \in [0,1]$ denotes the credibility of users' evaluation, where c denotes one of level users, e denotes one of the evaluation items and t denotes the time.

2.2. *Symbolic interpretation*

$\gamma_D^{(x)} = \begin{cases} 0, & \text{if } x \in D, \\ 1, & \text{else} \end{cases}$ Where D denotes an integer set, $0^0=1$.

2.3. *Algorithm rule of fuzzy interval numbers [8]*

Interval numbers have its own binary algorithm which is similar to the real numbers' algorithm. If A=[aL,aP] and B=[bL, bP] respectively denote the two interval numbers and λ∈R, the corresponding binary algorithm is as follows.

(1) A-B=[aL-bL, aP-bP];

(2) λA= [λaL, λaP];

(3) A+B=[aL+bL, aP+bP];

If U(x) denotes the deterministic and objective function of interval numbers.

$$U(x) = [x^L, x^P] = \frac{x^L + x^P}{2} \tag{1}$$

Where x^L and x^P respectively denote the upper bound and lower bound of the interval, which is not distinguish between closed and open.

2.4. *The correlation matrix of data*

Matrix T denotes the relationship between indexes of a scheme and correlative evaluation items.

$$T = \begin{bmatrix} T_{11}, & T_{12} & \cdots & T_{1n} \\ T_{21}, & T_{22} & \cdots & T_{2n} \\ \vdots & & & \\ T_{m1} & T_{m2} & \cdots & T_{mn} \end{bmatrix} \tag{2}$$

Where T_{ij} denotes the trustworthiness expectation of the jth evaluation item of the ith index's evaluation set. Matrix R denotes the trustworthiness of different evaluation, which made by users with different grades, in different evaluation sets.

$$R = \begin{bmatrix} R_{11}, & R_{12} & \cdots & R_{1n} \\ R_{21}, & R_{22} & \cdots & R_{2n} \\ \vdots & & & \\ R_{s1} & R_{s2} & \cdots & R_{sn} \end{bmatrix} \tag{3}$$

Where R_{ij} denotes the trustworthiness of the ith grade users to the evaluation set and the jth evaluation item, s and n respectively denote the numbers of user levels and evaluation items in index evaluation set. Matrix K denotes the number of experts in each scheme index chose by the different grade experts.

$$K^m = \begin{bmatrix} K_{11}^m, & K_{12}^m & \cdots & K_{1n}^m \\ K_{21}^m, & K_{22}^m & \cdots & K_{2n}^m \\ \vdots & & & \\ K_{s1}^m, & K_{s2}^m & \cdots & K_{sn}^m \end{bmatrix} \tag{4}$$

Where K_{ij}^m denotes the number of the experts, who evaluate the jth evaluation item about the mth index, from the grade i. We can calculate the total number of experts about the scheme by function Eq. (5).

$$P = \sum_{l=1}^{m} \left(\sum_{i=1}^{n} \sum_{j=1}^{s} K_{ij}^{l} \right) \tag{5}$$

3. The Model of the Conceptual Design Scheme

We can initialize the matrix R on the basis of the different management system in different network community. We can also initialize the matrix k based on the users' evaluation on the scheme. So, we can calculate the trustworthiness expectation T_{ij} of the scheme, which is the jth evaluation item under the ith index, by Eq. (6).

$$T_{ij} = \frac{\sum_{l=1}^{s} (R_{lj} * K_{lj}^{i})}{\sum_{l=1}^{s} K_{lj}^{i}} * \gamma_{\{0\}}^{(\sum_{l=1}^{s} K_{lj}^{i})} \tag{6}$$

And we can calculate the average T^i, which is the ith index of scheme based on trustworthiness and evaluation item quantization, by Eq. (7). Where U(j) denotes the deterministic and objective function of interval numbers about the jth item in evaluation set.

$$T^i = \frac{\sum_{j}^{n} (U(j) * T_{ij})}{n} \tag{7}$$

We can also calculate the synthesis score ST of the scheme based on the trustworthiness and evaluation item quantization by Eq. (8). ω_i denotes the weight of coefficient of the ith child pointer.

$$ST = \sum_{i=1}^{m} (\omega_i * T^i) \tag{8}$$

4. Algorithm of the Conceptual Design Solution Evaluation and Election Based on Trustworthiness

4.1. *The basic idea*

According to these evaluations, firstly, we calculate the trustworthiness of the each evaluation item in every index. On this basis, we calculate the average values, which is the each index of scheme based on trustworthiness and evaluation item quantization. Then, we calculate the synthesis score of each scheme on the basis that the weight for index. Finally, according to the synthesis score of each scheme, we sorted it in descending order and chose the optimization.

4.2. *Algorithm*

The algorithm of the conceptual design solution evaluation and selection based on trustworthiness, we proposed, its process is mentioned below:

Step 1: Initial the matrix R and K. Solutions={ solution1,...,solutionN} denotes the conceptual design scheme set of the product, where N denotes the number of the schemes. SynthesisScores={Φ} denotes the synthesis score set of the scheme. We supposed the minimum threshold of the number of evaluation experts was min_amount. We defined one-dimensional array temp[N] and variate z=0.

Step 2: The first element of the Solutions set is chose. Then, it is delete and variate z pluses 1. Calculate the total number P of its experts by function 5, if p<min_amount, turn to the step 2. Otherwise, turn to the next step.

Step 3: for(int i=1;i<=m;i++)

for(int j=1;j<=n;j++){

Calculate T_{ij} by function (6);

}

for(int k=1;k<=m;k++){

Calculate T^k by function (7);

}

Step 4: Calculate the ST by function(8), temp[z]=ST, where z denotes the zth scheme. Then, add the ST into the set of SynthesisScores. if the number of the elements in the set of SynthesisScores is greater than 0, turn to the step 2. Otherwise, turn to the next step.

Step 5: If the number of elements in the set of SynthesisScores is greater than 1, they are sorted in descending order.

Step 6: Output the set of SynthesisScores. According to the values of its elements, we can get the relevant scheme ID from the array temp.

5. Theorems and Proofs Experimental Verification and Result Analysis

5.1. *Experimental verification*

To avoid the large amount of data statistics by analytic hierarchy process, when the indexes are too much, and weight is difficult to determine. So as to the spatial confined of the paper. Three concepts about smart phone examples were given in the experiment. And each conceptual design scheme of the smart phone is divided into three evaluation indexes: "function", "cost" and "appearance". The specific experimental data based on the survey of the network community is shown from table 1 to table 4. The evaluation expert quantity distribution of each data in the table is a set. Three elements of the set respectively denote three indexes of the scheme. For example, the first item {2, 4, 2} in table 2 denotes the number of special experts, who respectively evaluate the three indexes (function, cost and appearance) “perfect”.

Table 1. Trustworthiness

	Perfect	Excellent	Good	Moderate	Ordinary	Worse	Bad	Worst
H1	0.96	0.95	0.93	0.91	0.98	0.90	0.97	0.90
H2	0.95	0.93	0.87	0.81	0.92	0.80	0.91	0.80
H3	0.85	0.80	0.78	0.75	0.88	0.76	0.87	0.81
H4	0.60	0.58	0.53	0.51	0.62	0.50	0.61	0.50
H5	0.45	0.44	0.43	0.41	0.50	0.41	0.49	0.40

Table 2. The number of expert distribution for scheme 1

	Perfect	Excellei	Good	Moderate	Ordinary	Worse	Bad	Worst
H1	{2,4,2}	{6,7,5}	{12,13,10}	{7,8,6}	{4,6,4}	{2,4,3}	{2,1,1}	{1,2,2}
H2	{3,5,3}	{10,9,9}	{15,16,13}	{12,12,11}	{8,9,8}	{4,5,3}	{3,2,4}	{1,5,2}
H3	{5,7,5}	{13,14,12}	{20,22,19}	{14,15,13}	{25,28,24}	{10,24,12}	{18,22,20}	{12,25,10}
H4	{10,9,8}	{34,40,32}	{45,55,43}	{46,60,45}	{50,54,48}	{28,20,30}	{8,10,15}	{4,15,8}
H5	{15,14,14}	{38,45,36}	{42,53,41}	{50,56,44}	{55,58,50}	{30,18,32}	{5,9,17}	{3,12,10}

Table 3. The number of expert distribution for scheme 2

	Perfect	Excellent	Good	Moderate	Ordinary	Worse	Bad	Worst
H1	{15,14,14}	{30,44,35}	{40,45,41}	{45,50,43}	{50,55,46}	{30,16,28}	{8,10,16}	{5,10,9}
H2	{9,10,8}	{32,34,40}	{42,54,43}	{45,47,60}	{52,50,53}	{26,30,20}	{15,8,10}	{8,15,5}
H3	{7,5,6}	{14,12,13}	{18,20,22}	{15,13,14}	{26,24,28}	{22,14,12}	{18,20,23}	{10,12,25}
H4	{5,4,4}	{11,10,10}	{16,15,13}	{11,12,11}	{10,8,10}	{5,4,5}	{3,4,3}	{2,5,1}
H5	{2,2,4}	{6,5,8}	{10,12,14}	{5,6,8}	{5,4,6}	{3,2,4}	{2,1,3}	{1,1,1}

Table 4. The number of expert distribution for scheme 3

	Perfect	Excellent	Good	Moderate	Ordinary	Worse	Bad	Worst
H1	{4,3,6}	{9,11,9}	{14,17,12}	{13,11,12}	{6,10,7}	{3,6,5}	{4,4,3}	{2,6,2}
H2	{5,8,6}	{12,15,13}	{20,18,24}	{14,12,16}	{26,24,25}	{24,12,10}	{22,20,16}	{12,14,25}
H3	{16,14,15}	{36,46,39}	{55,40,41}	{49,55,45}	{56,59,53}	{35,20,33}	{16,10,6}	{10,8,8}
H4	{8,12,10}	{32,38,36}	{44,56,40}	{45,60,42}	{46,52,54}	{26,24,32}	{14,12,6}	{12,10,5}
H5	{2,3,2}	{5,6,7}	{10,12,8}	{5,7,9}	{3,7,4}	{3,4,2}	{1,32}	{1,1,2}

Experiment (1): We programmed the algorithm we proposed, where m=3, s=5, ω1=0.4, ω2=0.4, ω3=0.2, min_amount=2000, N=3. The results are mentioned below.

temp[3] = {4.08, 5.54, 4.87}. The total number of the expert for scheme 1, 2 and 3, respectively, are 2139, 2107 and 2162, and their synthesis scores are 4.08, 5.54 and 4.87 respectively. The result of the final output is {5.54(scheme 1), 4.87(scheme 2), 4.08(scheme 3)}.

Experiment (2): Take scheme 3 as an example, we studied the change of average score of the index of function based on trustworthiness and evaluation item quantization. Along with the "special expert users" and "newcomers" respectively in each evaluation item on increasing 25 people (i.e. growing 200 people) at the same time. The result is shown in Figure. 1.

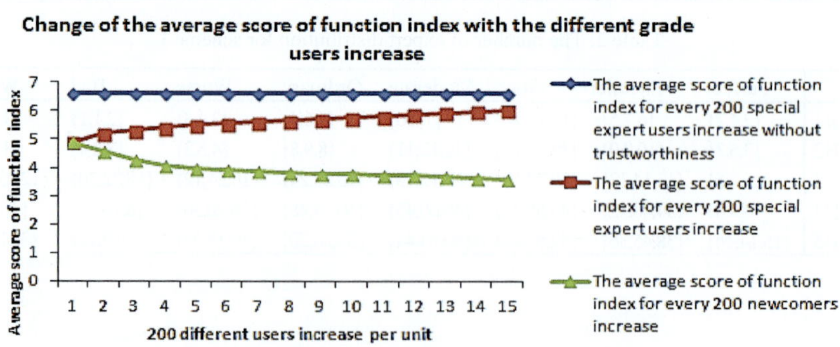

Fig. 1. The average score of objective function

5.2. *Result analysis*

From the result of experiment (1), the total number of three schemes is basically same. According to the synthesis scores of schemes in descending order, the sort is scheme 2, scheme 3 and scheme 1. I.e. the optimization is scheme 1, the second is scheme 3 and the scheme 2 is the worst. Actually, according to the number of expert distribution tables of three schemes, it is not hard to know that. Although the total number of evaluation people of schemes is basically same, the number of "special expert users", "senior expert users" and "expert users" of scheme 2 is apparently larger than other two schemes'. And that of scheme 3 is larger than scheme 1's. So, we can get the result of the experiment (1). It also demonstrates the algorithm, we proposed, feasibility and reasonability.

From the result of experiment (2), i.e. figure 1. The synthesis score of index of "function" is proportional to the number of special expert users. On the contrary, it is no longer proportional to the number of newcomers. That's to say, different grade users have different evaluation trustworthiness. And it is essential to set the different trust values for the different grade users. At the same time, we concluded that the broken line of special expert users and newcomers under the environment that there is no trustworthiness. I.e. it is unfair to choose the optimal scheme in this environment, and it is essential to set the different trust values for the different grade users from sides.

Experiment (1) and (2) amply demonstrate that, it is essential to propose the algorithm of the conceptual design solution evaluation and selection based on trustworthiness. The algorithm is feasibility and reasonability. Compared with no trustworthiness in conceptual design solution evaluation and selection, the algorithm is sensitive to the grade of the evaluation experts, and it helps to select the superior ones in the conceptual design scheme.

6. Conclusion

We proposed an algorithm of the conceptual design solution evaluation and selection based on trustworthiness. We considered the condition that different evaluation users have different trustworthiness. The higher grade of users, the more credible they have. The algorithm divides conceptual design scheme into several indexes through the analytic hierarchy process, and treated the each index of the evaluation items with fuzzy number. Then, we calculated the trustworthiness of the each expert's evaluation, and eventually calculate the comprehensive score of scheme evaluation from all experts in order to choose the best scheme. The experiment (1) and (2) demonstrate its feasibility and reasonability. Compared with no trustworthiness in conceptual design solution evaluation and selection, the algorithm is sensitive to the grade of the evaluation experts, and it helps to select the superior ones in the conceptual design scheme. At the same time, it can apply into the network community. It can also avoid the harmful effect, which made by online water army, in conceptual design scheme evaluation. It has certain practical value.

Acknowledgments

This research work was supported by National Natural Science Foundation of China (51165004) and Guangxi Science and Technology Development Program (1598007-15).

References

1. ZHENG Hao, Yixiong Feng, Jianrong Tan. An integrated cognitive computing approach for systematic conceptual design[J]. Journal of Zhejiang University-Science A(Applied Physics & Engineering), 2016(4) (in Chinese).
2. Ruifeng Bo, Ruiqin Li. Application of Fuzzy Data Envelopment Analysis Model in Concept Evaluation of Mechanical Product[J]. Machine Design & Research ,2011,27(3):18-23(in Chinese).
3. Fengqiang Zhao,Yi Xu, Guangqiang Li. System Integration Technology for Integrated Project Design and Evaluation of Products[J]. Computer Applications and Software, 2011,28(2):22-24(in Chinese).
4. Juan Pu; Yong Chen;Yan Xiong; Bing Li. Products Conceptual Design and Evaluation Based on TRIZ Theory and Fuzzy AHP Approach[J]. Manufacturing Automation, 2014,36(1):14-17(in Chinese).
5. Zhimin Liu, Kaidi Liu. The Evaluation Model of Reducer Design Scheme Based on Distinguishing Weight[J]. Journal of Taiyuan University of Technology, 2012,43(1):40-46(in Chinese).
6. Fuhong Zheng, Gang Guo. Evaluation System of Products Design Oriented to KBE[J]. Machine Tool & Hydraulics, 2011,39(1):59-61(in Chinese).
7. Hang Wang; Chao Zhang; Xiangxiao Zhu; Zhixin Sun. A Website Trust Comprehensive Evaluation Model Based on Fuzzy Theory [J]. Computer Technology and Development, 2015(6):119-123(in Chinese).
8. Haoping Hu; Dianting Liu. CNC Machine Tool Spindle Green Configuration Design Optimization under Uncertainty and Model Establishment[J]. Modular Machine Tool & Automatic Manufacturing Technique, 2014,(1)39-41(in Chinese).

The Application Research of Artificial Neural Network in the Transformer Fault Diagnosis

Jian-Li Yu[a,*], Hong-Qi Huang[b] and Hong-Gen Chen[c]

School of Management Engineering, Zhengzhou University of Aeronautical
Zhengzhou, China
E-mail: [a]yjl837@163.com, [b]760990540@qq.com, [c]microwr@163.com

In the transformer fault diagnosis, the span of the real amount of gas dissolved in transformer is greater than the training sample. Therefore, small sample training cannot meet the practical requirements of transformer fault diagnosis. But large sample size which is wide range and dispersion will reduce the generalization ability of neural network. Therefore, in view of the problems such as large amount of data and sample dispersion, it built the RBF neural network and GRNN (General regression neural network) neural network fault diagnosis model for the simulation results compared before and after the data standardization by using the cumulative frequency normalization processing on the data standardization and putting gathered all 441 groups of DGA data into network training and network detection. The results were as follows: cumulative frequency normalized data standardization method improved the neural network in different degrees of transformer fault diagnosis effect, and increased the value of practical application of transformer fault diagnosis.

Keywords: Fault Diagnosis; Cumulative Frequency Normalization; Neural Network.

1. Introduction

Power transformer is an important hub of power system. In order to improve the quality of the transformer monitoring ability, research of transformer fault diagnosis is more and more important[1, 2]. Dissolved gas Analysis in oil (DGA) is one of the important means of detection for the oil-immersed power equipment, namely the type and severity of fault diagnosis is identified according to the various gases dissolved in transformer oil composition and its relative content.

---

*Corresponding author.

Artificial neural network is a complex network system through a large number of neurons connected to each other, which have self-organizing, adaptive, self-learning, fuzzy information processing ability[3,4] and high generalization ability. Its structure and network training is simple and have high approximation ability and learning speed[5]. What's more, there is a good prediction effect for complex nonlinear factors affected by multiple factors outside[6]. Therefore, diagnosis effect of artificial neural network is ideal in fault diagnosis[7, 8].

Transformer fault diagnosis mainly use the generalization ability of neural network. To ensure a good network generalization ability, the selected appropriate sample should have ability to reflect all the information. Training samples of neural network are usually selected representative and compact samples in the current study of transformer fault diagnosis[9, 10]. However, the reality of various gas into dissolved in transformer oil component may be beyond the scope of the training sample that difficult to diagnosis accurately the faults type of transformer. Therefore, the size and coverage of the training sample should be as large as possible. The research how to improve the diagnostic efficiency has greater practical significance on this basis.

2. Data Processing Steps Based on the Cumulative Frequency Normalization

(1) Data collection. Raw data includes seven kinds of gases, H_2, CH_4, C_2H_6, C_2H_4, C_2H_2, CO, CO_2, a total of 441 sets. The content distribution of the gases is shown in Figure 1. The content of dissolved gas in transformer oil are widely distributed according to Figure 1. There are many compact district which represent the typical sample, but there are also numerous scattered points deviate from compact district of the gases. If these scattered points not be taken into account, misdiagnosis may emerge in the real diagnosis that is unfavorable to the transformer fault diagnosis model based on neural network method in the practical application.

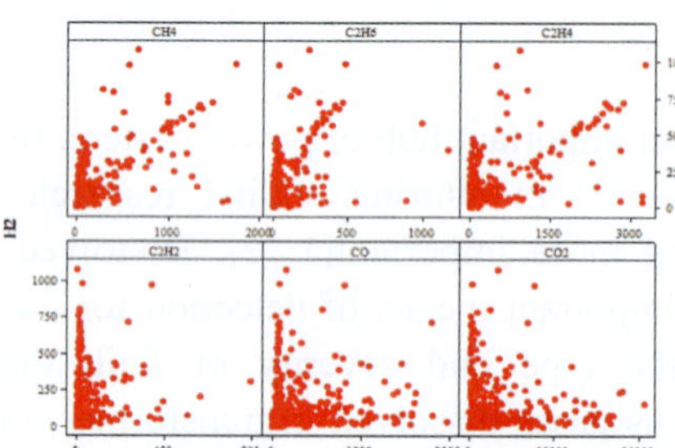

Fig. 1. The scatter plot of dissolved gas content

(2) Data grouping. According to the content of each gas distribution (shown in Table 1), when setting group number in each group, the standard deviation of gas content is relatively small which the group of data is a relatively small number; the standard deviation of gas content is relatively big which the group of data is a relatively big number. Therefore, seven gas data is grouped respectively to 200, 500, 200, 500, 100, 500, 100.

Table 1. The statistical results

	H_2	CH_4	C_2H_6	C_2H_4	C_2H_2	CO	CO_2
Mean	135.13	173.50	65.0659	335.26	35.5721	338.54	2936.5
Standard deviation	178.906	314.395	124.855	620.985	79.1513	391.360	3723.15
Minimum	0	0	0	0	0	0.5	20
Maximum	1080.00	1743.00	1171.90	3258.20	800.00	1981.00	20600

(3) The data standardization. According to the cumulative frequency normalization method, using the Matlab program count quantity and frequency of each group respectively, then calculate the cumulative frequency value to replace the original data of the gas content as input of neural network.

(4) The transformer fault diagnosis data included six kinds of fault types, such as low-energy discharge(A), high-energy discharge(B), middle temperature overheat(C), high temperature overheat(D), low-energy discharge and high temperature overheat(E), high-energy discharge and high temperature overheat(F). The normalized data draw out 10, 10, 5, 10, 5, 5 groups at random as testing data, namely 396 group for training and checking back and 45 groups for detecting (shown in Table 2).

Table 2. Grouping network training samples and testing samples

Sample types	A	B	C	D	E	F	The total number
Training sample	114	59	27	142	24	30	396
Testing sample	10	10	5	10	5	5	45
The total number	124	69	32	152	29	35	441

3. Simulation of the Transformer Fault Diagnosis

The six fault types of the transformer fault diagnosis data included is coded respectively as 1 0 0 0 0 0, 0 1 0 0 0 0, 0 0 1 0 0 0, 0 0 0 1 0 0, 0 0 0 0 1 0, 0 0 0 0 0 1. The H_2, CH_4, C_2H_6, C_2H_4, C_2H_2, CO and CO_2 data calculated by the method of cumulative frequency normalization act as network input variables, and the fault type encoding act as the output variable of the network. By constructing fault diagnosis model based on RBF neural network and GRNN neural network, it processes comparative study to find the influence of the cumulative frequency normalization, and the fault diagnosis accuracy is regarded as the evaluation standard of fault diagnosis.

3.1. *Fault diagnosis simulation based on RBF neural network*

Fault diagnosis model select strict RBF neural network model. The spreading constant of the RBF neural network standardization diagnosis model is set to 1, 5, 10, 15, 20, 25. The spreading constant of the RBF neural network unstandardization diagnosis model is set to 0.5, 1, 5, 10, 15.

Standardization diagnosis results of the RBF neural network is shown in Figure 2. When spread is 5, accuracy rate of checking back and detection is 98.23% and 77.78%. However, detection accuracy of unstandardization diagnosis results of the RBF neural network is 35.56% (shown in Figure 3).

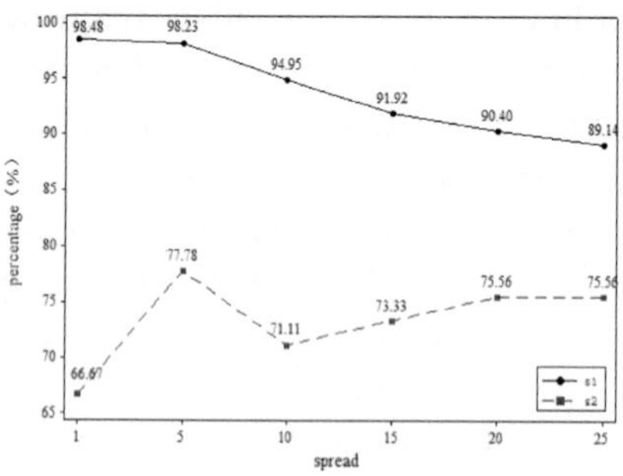

Fig. 2. Standardization diagnosis results of the RBF neural network

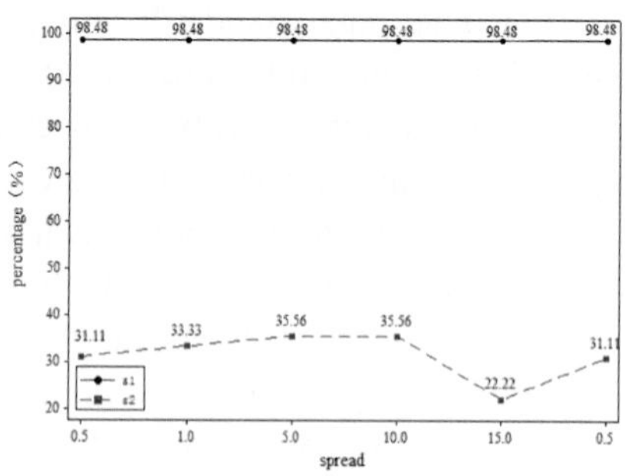

Fig. 3. Unstandardization diagnosis results of the RBF neural network

3.2. *Fault diagnosis simulation based on GRNN neural network*

The spreading constant of the GRNN neural network standardization diagnosis model is set to 0.005, 0.01, 0.05, 0.1, 0.11, 0.5, 1. The spreading constant of the GRNN neural network unstandardization diagnosis model is set to 1, 5, 10, 15, 20.

Standardization diagnosis results of the GRNN neural network is shown in Figure 4. When spread is 0.11, accuracy rate of checking back and detection is 96.97% and 80%. However, detection accuracy of unstandardization diagnosis results of the GRNN neural network is 57.78% (shown in Figure 5)

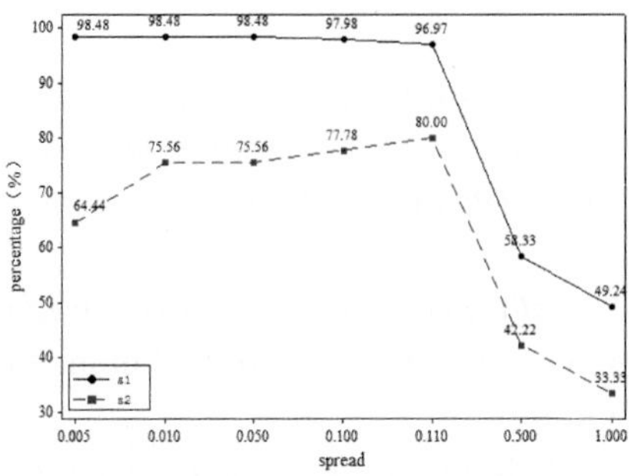

Fig. 4. Standardization diagnosis results of the GRNN neural network

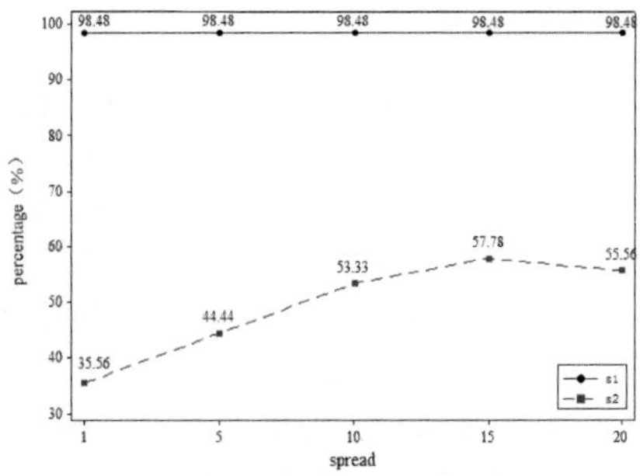

Fig. 5. Unstandardization diagnosis results of the GRNN neural network

4. The Comparison of Experimental Results

Based on RBF neural network and GRNN neural network, the simulation results of data standardization and unstandardization is shown in Table 3. The accuracy rate of checking back achieves a higher level before and after the cumulative frequency normalization that shows the neural network has better approximation ability. When data is not normalized by method of the cumulative frequency normalization, RBF neural network and GRNN neural network detection accuracy is not ideal. However, under the cumulative frequency normalization, the detection accuracy of RBF neural network and GRNN neural network respectively up 35.56%, 57.78% to 77.78%, 80%. Therefore, the cumulative frequency normalization method can improve the accuracy of the neural network fault diagnosis.

Tab. 3. The simulation results contrast

RBF			GRNN		
Data processing	s_1	s_2	Data processing	s_1	s_2
Standardization	98.23%	77.78%	Standardization	96.97%	80.00%
Unstandardization	98.48%	35.56%	Unstandardization	98.48%	57.78%

Acknowledgments

The research work was supported by National Natural Science Foundation of China under Grant No. U1404702, Aviation Science Fund under Grant No. 2014ZG55021, Nature Science Foundation of Henan Province under Grant No. 162102210083.

References

1. C. X. Dai, Z. G. Liu, K. T. Hu, et al, *Fault Diagnosis for Traction Transformer of High Speed Railway on the Integration of Model-based Diagnosis and Fuzzy Petri Nets*, Vol.44 (Power System Protection and Control, 2016), pp. 26-32. (In Chinese)
2. X. Shi, Y. L. Zhu, X. G. Ning, et al, *Transformer Fault Diagnosis Based on Deep Auto-encoder Network*, Vol.36 (Electric Power Automation Equipment, 2016), pp. 122-126. (In Chinese)
3. Q. J. Wang, Y. N. Du, J. Liu, *Introducing Atmospheric Angular Momentum into Prediction of Length of Day Change by Generalized Regression Neural Network Model*, Vol.21 (Journal of Central South University, 2014), pp. 1396-1401.
4. F. Yu, X. Z. Xu, *A Short-term Load Forecasting Model of Natural Gas Based on Optimized Genetic Algorithm and Improved BP Neural Network.* Vol.134 (Applied Energy, 2014), pp.102-113.
5. K. Ceryan, U. Okkan, A. Kesimal, *Application of Generalized Regression Neural Networks in Predicting the Unconfined Compressive Strength of Carbonate Rocks*, Vol.36 (Rock Mechanics and Rock Engineering, 2012), pp.86-96.
6. M. S. Rahman, Y. Park, K. D. Kin, *RSS-Based Indoor Localization Algorithm for Wireless Sensor Network Using Generalized Regression Neural Network*, Vol.37 (Arabian Journal for Science and Engineering, 2012), pp. 1043-1053.
7. D. J. Chen, Y. Z. Ye, R. Hua, *Fault Diagnosis System for NPC inverter based on Multi-layer Principal Component Neural Network*, Vol.8 (Journal of Computers, 2013), pp.1464-1471.
8. J. L. Yu, S. Bian, *Fault Diagnosis Model of Transformer Based on BP Neural Network*, Vol.26 (Journal of System Simulation, 2014), pp. 1343-1349. (In Chinese)
9. Z. C. Du, G. Y. Niu, *Transformer Fault Diagnosis Based on Weighted Fuzzy Clustering Algorithm*, Vol.50 (High Voltage Apparatus, 2014), pp. 42-48. (In Chinese)
10. L. Zhu, L. Wang, F. Pan, *Fault Diagnosis of Transformer Based on BP Neural Network*, Vol.11(Journal of Jiangnan University (Natural Science Edition), 2012), pp. 262-266. (In Chinese)

Study on Fault Diagnosis for Transformer Based on PCA and BP Neural Network

Jian-Li Yu[a,*], Xiao-Tian Pan[b] and Hong-Gen Chen[c]

School of Management Engineering, Zhengzhou University of Aeronautical Zhengzhou, China

E-mail: [a]yjl837@163.com, [b]332827678@qq.com, [c]cmicrowr@163.com

In order to improve the efficiency and accuracy of transformer fault diagnosis, a new fault diagnosis method based on PCA and BP neural network is proposed. The proposed method used PCA to reduce the data of fault messages dimensions through matrix conversion, and then used BP neural network for transform fault diagnosis. Illustrated by examples, in the fault diagnosis of transformer, the PCA can concentrate fault information without influencing analysis results under the condition that the loss of useful messages is relatively small. Based on that, compared with RBF and GRNN neural network, the BP neural network has a higher accuracy for transform fault diagnosis. As a consequence, combination of PCA and BP neural network is a practical and feasible method in transform fault diagnosis.

Keywords: PCA; BP Neural Network; Fault Diagnosis; Transformer.

1. Introduction

With the demand of power is increasing rapidly, as one of the most important equipment in electrical power system, the working performance of transformer has play a important role in our production and life. Apparently, the traditional fault diagnosis method can't meet the requirement of complicated transform. The three ratio method has a disadvantage of code absence, which is not suitable for the diagnosis of mixed fault[1]. And the characteristic gas method is difficult to diagnose the transformer in the case of less dissolved gas[2]. In recent years, a variety of intelligent technologies are proposed, such as expert system[3], fuzzy mathematics[4] and artificial neural network[5]. It is of a great importance for the research of transform fault diagnosis method. In fact, it is difficult to achieve

---

*Corresponding author.

the purpose of fault diagnosis only by one method. For example, the BP neural network is the one of the most widely used artificial neural network. It can independently complete the nonlinear mapping from input space to the output space, but it cannot simplify the input data. When the data dimension is high, it will cause the network structure complex and reduce the training speed[6]. Principal component analysis (PCA) is one of data dimension reduction method, it can get rid of the noise information and retention data which has a big variance contribution rate. Besides, PCA can effectively remove the correlation between the data[7]. Therefore, considering the characteristics of these intelligent diagnosis method. This paper use a method of PCA combined with BP neural network in the transformer fault diagnosis. By DGA method collected 441 groups data, after using PCA reduce their dimension and put them into BP neural network training procedure. Compare with the experimental result of RBF and GRNN. The PCA combine with BP method not only simplify the large capacity sample data, but also achieve higher diagnostic accuracy.

2. Principal Component Analysis

2.1. *Data preprocessing and principal component analysis*

Due to the quantity of gas concentration varies widely, if the original data are input directly, BP algorithm may not be sensitive to small data, and some important features will be difficult to be obtained. In order to fully exert effective information, this paper adopt the standardized data processing method.

According to dissolved gas analysis, gas generated by the transformer fault can be roughly divided into two categories, hydrocarbon and oxygen compounds. Therefore, there must be some correlation between the different gases. So it is necessary to use the PCA to eliminate the correlation and reduce dimension. The principal component analysis is shown in table 1 and table 2.

Table 1. Principal Component Analysis

Principal Component	Eigenvalue	Accumulating Contribution rate
PC1	3.2493	0.464
PC2	1.7272	0.711
PC3	1.0558	0.862

Table 2. The Eigenvector of Principal Component

	H_2	CH_4	C_2H_6	C_2H_4	C_2H_2	CO	CO_2
PC1	0.405	0.527	0.495	0.521	0.002	-0.135	-0.153
PC2	-0.172	-0.102	-0.071	-0.073	-0.113	-0.693	-0.676
PC3	-0.266	0.030	0.146	0.095	-0.935	0.049	0.144

From table 1 and table 2, the cumulative contribution rate of first three principal components are 0.862>0.85. So select three principal components[8]. The calculated result of the principal component Z_1, Z_2 Z_3 are in table 3.

2.2. *Construction of the BP neural network fault diagnosis model*

2.2.1. *Input layer*

The neural network input layer is the gas concentration data matrix. After the principal component analysis, seven kinds of gas are reduced to the three principal components. Putting the collected 441 groups of gas concentration data into the vector $Z = (z_1, z_2, z_3)^T$, to construct a 441×3 sample matrix as the BP neural network input layer.

2.2.2. *Output layer*

The neural network output layer is the transformer fault type. But the fault type has no specific numerical value, it is needed to translate the fault types into specific values. The method used in this paper that is "take 1" in "n" to encode the six fault types. The six types of faults respectively corresponding to the encoding rule are shown in table 3.

Table 3. Principal component analysis calculated results and code rule

No.	[Z_1; Z_2; Z_3]	Fault types	Code rule
1	[-0.67, -0.53,0.44]	Low energy discharge	[1,0,0,0,0,0]
...	... ...	... ...	... ...
21	[-0.64,-0.81,-0.21]	High energy discharge	[0,1,0,0,0,0]
...	... ...	... ...	... ...
229	[0.22,0.48,-0.49]	Middle temperature overheating	[0,0,1,0,0,0]
...	... ...	... ...	... ...
257	[0.43,0.35,-0.21]	High temperature overheating	[0,0,0,1,0,0]
...	... ...	... ...	... ...
388	[0.14,0.81,-0.73]	Low energy discharge and overheating	[0,0,0,0,1,0]
...	... ...	... ...	... ...
441	[0.46,0.64,-0.55]	High energy discharge and high temperature overheating	[0,0,0,0,0,1]

2.2.3. *Hidden layer*

The number of hidden layer neurons is related to the performance of the BP neural network. Too little will affect the learning ability of the BP neural network, and unable to accurately obtain samples rule. Too much will prolong the network learning time, even causing the over learning on the sample data, affecting the network generalization ability and fault tolerance. In the transformer fault diagnosis, the choice of the number of hidden can be based on many times experiments to determine the best performance.

3. Transformer Fault Diagnosis Based on BP Neural Network

In order to test the generalization ability of the BP neural network model, the 441 groups of sample data should be divided into 376 groups of straining sample and 65 groups of test sample.

The traditional BP neural network algorithm with poor anti-interference ability, low learning rate and easy to fall into local minimum value. In this paper, an improved BP neural network based on Levenberg-Marquardt algorithm is adopted. The principle of Levenberg-Marquardt algorithm is to make each iteration no longer along a single direction of the negative gradient, but allows errors to search along the direction of deterioration. At the same time, by the steepest gradient descent method and Gauss-Newton method to optimize the weights of network[9]. As a consequence, compared with the traditional BP neural network, the LM-BP neural network has the advantages of less iteration times, faster convergence speed and higher accuracy.

In this paper, an improved BP neural network based on Levenberg-Marquardt algorithm is adopted. The simulation software is MATLAB 2008a. Setting the training goal is 0.01 and the epochs is 300. The training statement is $net = newff(\min\max(p),[4,t],\{'\tan sig','\log sig'\},'trainlm')$ [10].The results are shown in table. 4.

Table 4. The results of the experiment

The number of Hidden neurons	4	5	6
Diagnostic accuracy of training samples	75.00%	73.94%	77.66%
Diagnostic accuracy of test samples	72.31%	70.77%	66.15%

Through the trial and error correction method to adjust the number of neurons in the hidden layer, and according to the maximum subordination principle, output the network. From table 4, when the number of hidden layer neurons is 4, the result is better than other hidden notes. And the average accuracy of the model is more than 70%, the network performance is well.

4. Compare the Result with Other Neural Network

4.1. *Compared with RBF neural network*

Assuming the input matrix p and the output matrix t are same with the BP neural network. The RBF training statement is $net = newrbe(p, t, spread)$. The results are shown in table 5.

Table 5. The results of the experiment

spread	18	19	20
Diagnostic accuracy of training samples	71.28%	71.01%	70.84%
Diagnostic accuracy of test samples	69.23%	70.77%	69.23%

As can be seen from table 5. When the spread is 19, the accuracy is higher than other. Not only the spreads in table 10, other spreads also lower than this parameter. But, the diagnostic accuracy of the RBF neural network is lower than the BP neural network based on principal component analysis.

4.2. *Compared with GRNN neural network*

The training statement is $net = newrgrn(p, t, \sigma)$.The results of the experiment are shown in table 6.

Table 6. The results of the experiment

σ	0.09	0.1	0.2
Diagnostic accuracy of training samples	94.15%	92.55%	85.37%
Diagnostic accuracy of test samples	64.62%	66.15%	60.00%

As can be seen from table 6. The diagnostic accuracy of training samples and test samples differ widely, it shows that the GRNN network model has been over trained, so its generalization ability is poor.

5. Conclusion

In this paper, PCA not only effectively reduce the data redundancy, but also eliminate the correlation, ensuring the reliability of the fault diagnosis results. Besides, the BP neural network realized the diagnosis of mixed fault types. And the diagnosis accuracy is higher than the results of RBF and GRNN, which is a practical and feasible new method for transformer fault diagnosis.

Acknowledgments

The research work was supported by National Natural Science Foundation of China under Grant No. U1404702, Aviation Science Fund under Grant No.

2014ZG55021, Nature Science Foundation of Henan Province under Grant No. 162102210083.

References

1. Z. X. Liu, B Song, E. W. Li, et al, *Study of "code absence" in the IEC three-ratio method of dissolved gas analysis,* Vol.31 (IEEE Electrical Insulation Magazine, 2015), pp. 6-12
2. A. X. Zhao, X. J. Tang, Z. H. Zhang, et al, *The DGA interpretation method using relative content of characteristic gases and gas-ratio combinations for fault diagnosis of oil-immersed power transformers,* (International Symposium on Electrical Insulating Materials, 2014), pp. 124-127.
3. D. Ma, W. Zhang, W. Yao, *Establish Expert System of Transformer Fault Diagnosis Based on Dissolved Gas in Oil,* (Information Science and Cloud Computing Companion (ISCC-C), 2014), pp. 681-685.
4. S. K. Tyagi, D. Pandey, V. Kumar, *Fuzzy Fault Tree Analysis for Fault Diagnosis of Cannula Fault in Power Transformer,* Vol.2 (Applied Mathematics, 2011), pp. 1346-1355.
5. J. L. Yu, S. Bian, *Fault Diagnosis Model of Transformer Based on BP Neural Network,* Vol.26 (Journal of System Simulation, 2014), pp. 1343-1349.(In Chinese)
6. J. B. Yang, C. H. Zhang, P. Chen, *Network Fault Diagnosis Based on Improved BP Neural Network,* Vol.40 (Computer & Digital Engineering, 2012), pp. 65-67. (In Chinese)
7. X. T. Zhu, J. B. Xiong, *Fault diagnosis simulation system based on PCA and BP neural network,* (Automation & Instrumentation, 2015), pp. 47-48+51. (In Chinese)
8. X. Q. He(eds.), *Applied Multivariate Statistical Analysis,* (China Statistics Press, 2010). (In Chinese)
9. W. Q. Xiang, H. Zhang, H. Wang, et al. *Application of BP neural network with L-M algorithm in power transformer fault diagnosis,* Vol.88 (Power System Protection & Control, 2011), pp. 170-174.
10. X. C. Wang, F. Shi, L. Yu, Y. Li(eds.), *43 Case Analysis of MATLAB Neural Network,* (Beijing University of Aeronautics and Astronautics Press, 2013). (In Chinese)

Monocular Vision Distance Measurement Based on Angle Error Compensation

Zheng-Guang Xu[a], Yan Zheng[b] and Jin-Jun Wang[c]

School of Automation and Electrical Engineering, University of Science & Technology Beijing, College Road, Haidian District, Beijing No. 30

Beijing, 100083, China

E-mail: [a]xzg_1@263.net, [b]zymingyuan1993@163.com, [c]tonyjinjun@163.com

Based on the distance measurement prototype, this paper proposes an angle error compensation method with monocular vision techniques for warehouse management system. To compensate the error of the distance estimation caused by pitch-down angle, the backward inference method for pitch-down angle calculation is given. Through analysis of factors affecting pitch-down angle calculation, a loop algorithm is designed for parameter optimization. The experiment result shows that the distance estimation error ratio is lower than 2%, which means that the optimal model is much better than the original one.

Keywords: Warehouse Management System; Monocular Vision Distance Measurement; Pitch-down Angle; Error Compensation.

1. Introduction

In recent years, with the rapid development of e-commerce industry and supplier logistics, there's an urgent need to adopt Warehouse Management System (WMS) of intelligent [1]. The intelligent WMS focuses on the research of the path navigation and accurate positioning of warehouse robot [2]. When the robot approaches designated goods shelf via path-planning, it needs to know the accuracy distance between pallet fork and objective goods for precise grasp. Based on the monocular vision system, this paper studies the measurement of the distance between pallet fork and objective good using only intrinsic parameters of the camera and projective geometry. This provides precise input parameters for accurate positioning of the warehouse robot.

Firstly, an archetype of distance measurement based on monocular vision is introduced. Theoretical analysis shows that pitch-down angle of camera has a great effect on algorithm accuracy. A pitch-down angle evaluating method by backward inference is given in this paper which also analyses the factors affecting the accuracy of pitch-down angle, and optimizes the method to obtain more accurate target depth information. At the end of the paper, the experiment results verify that the method can be used to implement precise object distance measurement.

2. Distance Measurement Model

Image acquisition means that 3D scene in objective world projects to 2D image plane (photosensitive matrix) in CCD camera[3]. The projection is normally described by geometry transformation. Article[4] discusses the perspective transformation based on pinhole imaging model. Since the heights of pallet fork are accurate mechanic parameters, which need to match the level heights of the goods shelf, it can be considered that pallet fork and the bottom layer of goods are at the same level. The distance measurement model based on monocular vision is established as Figure 1.

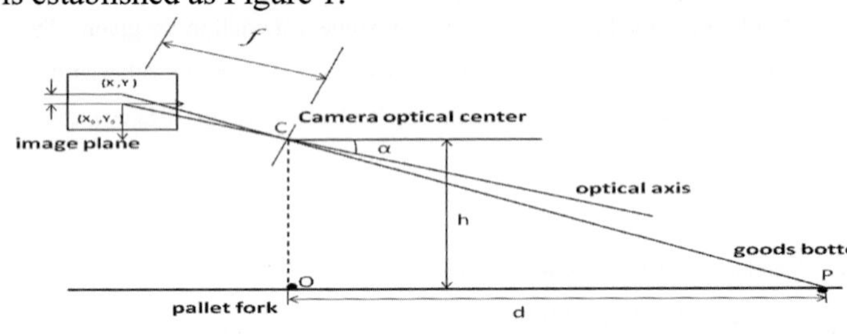

Fig. 1. The distance measurement model based on monocular vision

As is shown in the Figure 1, f is the effective focal length of CCD camera and α is the angle between camera optical axis and horizontal plane, which is called the camera's pitch-down angle[5]. Pallet fork is on the position O that is the vertical projection of camera optical center C on the ground, and the distance between C and O is h. (X_0,Y_0) is the intersection point of optical axis and image plane, which is also the center of image coordinate system.(X, Y) is the coordinate that point P on the goods bottom projects on the image plane.

According to the geometrical relationship, the computational formula is derived to calculate the distance d between point P and pallet fork O.

$$d = h/\tan\{\alpha + \arctan[y - y_0/f]\}. \quad (1)$$

In the camera imaging model, the external parameters describe the rotation and translation relationship between camera coordinate and world coordinate, and the internal parameters, including an image center, a focal length and distortion coefficients, describe the internal geometric properties and optical properties [6][7]. In the distance measurement model, f and y_0, the internal parameters, which do not change with the movement of camera position, can be obtained by a calibration algorithm in advance. The value of y can be got directly by the coordinate that is corresponding to the projection of P on the image plane. Therefore, there are two external factors affecting the accuracy of the algorithm results: one is the accuracy of camera height h, and the other is the accuracy of pitch-down angle α [8]. To test the influence of two factors, two sets of the results can be compared, which are shown in Table 1 and Table 2.

Table 1. Fix camera pitch-down angle and other parameters constantly, and change height of camera only. We get a set of distance data.(f:1315 α:0.39° y0:246)

h (m)	0.5	0.6	0.7	0.8	0.9	1.0	1.1
d (m)	16.7789	16.8375	16.9287	16.0247	16.1247	16.2383	16.3754

Table 2. Fix camera height and other parameters constantly, and change pitch-down angle of camera only. We get a set of distance data. (f:1315 h:1m y0:246)

α (°)	0.36	0.41	0.67	0.94	1.13	1.24	1.45
d (m)	16.2383	16.1465	15.0407	14.1453	13.4125	13.0748	12.4729

When the camera height range is 60cm, the range of distance is 0.904m; when the camera pitch-down angle range is 1.09, the range of distance is 3.7654m. Then we get the conclusion that the influence caused by height is less significant than it caused by pitch-down angle. The accuracy of pitch-down angle does a great impact on the accuracy of the measurement model.

3. Pitch Angle Measurement Method and Error Analysis

3.1. *Analysis the effect of the error of α*

To analyze the influence on the accuracy in different distance ranges, caused by the error of α, we analyze the following formula.

$$\theta = \arctan(h/d) \tag{2}$$

$$\theta - \alpha = \arctan[\tfrac{y-y_0}{f}] \tag{3}$$

According to formula (1), the accuracy of distance d has a certain relationship with α variation. If α proportion of Θ is large enough, a small change on α could cause a great change of b value[9]. And the proportion will increase while the distance increases. Therefore, even a small error on α will be continuously amplified with the increases of distance[10]. This is one of the factors effecting the accuracy of our measurement model.

We built a testing platform in the laboratory, installing h=1m, f=1340, y0=244, and α is approximately equal to 0.39. To show the inaccuracy, we got the following data which is analyzed later, based on the platform.

If the error of α is 0.1°, 0.01°, the inaccuracy is shown on Table 3.

Table 3. The inaccuracy data caused by the error of α

Measurement rang (m)	Proportion ($\frac{\alpha}{\Theta}*100\%$)	0.1°	0.01°
5	3.52%	3.49%~3.55%	3.51%~3.52%
10	6.83%	6.71%~6.95%	6.82%~6.84%
20	13.64%	13.18%~14.13%	13.59%~13.68%
30	20.53%	19.05%~21.67%	20.42%~20.63%
40	27.27%	25.49%~29.49%	27.08%~27.46%
50	34.21%	31.45%~37.50%	33.91%~34.51%

It can be seen from the table that if we use protractor to measure the angle, there will be about 1° error. While α is a small value, the error will be more than 1%.

3.2. *Pitch-down angle measurement method*

According to the above, manual measurement obviously can't satisfy the precision requirement of pitch-down angle measurement. Therefore, the paper, based on the original measurement model, proposes a method to backward calibrate α via a group of distance-known image. The formula is as follows.

$$\alpha = \arctan\left(\frac{h}{d_i}\right) - \arctan[(y_i - y_0)/f] \quad (4)$$

In theory, even if the objective is put in different positions, α is a fixed value. When we change the position of the objective, we get image i and (d_i, y_i). We can acquire a uniquely determined value of α theoretically, but actually α will change because of the inaccuracies of (d_i, y_i).

3.3. *Error analysis*

In theory, α is a single fixed value. But due to the existence of the measurement error of d_i and y_i, the obtained values of α are different. d_i and y_i measurement errors can be considered as a normal distribution, which means EΔd=0 and EΔy = 0. The α_i that we acquire from image i should be equally located on both sides of real α. If the quantity of the calibration image is enough and a suitable characteristic value (mean value, mode etc.), a more accurate value of α can be obtained.

On the other hand, the paper use Z. Y. Zhang's thesis——two steps calibration based on a plane to calibrate camera[11]. The method just needs a size-known chessboard. Using images captured from at least 3 different orientations, we can calibrate the internal parameters of the camera. The method is simple and flexible, suitable for the distance measurement model of warehouse robot. But the camera calibration precision in this method is also affected by many factors, such as the number of images, the luminance of light, the size of square on calibration board and so on. In the process of calibration, we choose the best calibration conditions according to the literature[12][13], which can make the calibration result accurate as far as possible. But there is still errors on the result.

Based on the analysis as above, the major factors of pitch-down angle measurement are from two aspects. The first one is (d_i, y_i) measurement errors on different images, and the second one is the error of internal parameters(f and y_0)caused by the calibration.

4. Error Compensation and Optimization

4.1. *The range of calibration distance*

By the formula (1), we can see that the proportion will increase with the increase of d. Even a small error on α will be continuously amplified with the increase of distance. When d is large enough, the error of α caused by the measurement inaccuracy of d can be ignored. Thus comes to conclusion 1: d cannot be too small when we calibrate α.

By the formula (4), we can get another conclusion. There is probably a 2-pixel error on the measurement of y_i. While d is too large, even a small change on y_i will cause a large Δd. Thus comes to conclusion 2:d cannot be too large when we calibrate α.

We got a distance range for calibration by the following calculation.

The lower limit: d=8m

θ=arctan(h/d)=7.125°, Δα = 0.01°, Δθ = 0.01°, θ'=7.1125°, d'=8.011m, Δd = 0.01m and the measurement error by a tapeline is about 1cm.

Therefore, the lower limit is d=8m.
The upper limit:d=20m
$\tan(\theta-\alpha)=dy/f$ dy=yi-y0
$\Delta y=2$ (the measurement error of y is about 2 pixel), $f*\tan(\theta-\alpha)\approx 70$
$\Delta y/dy=2/70=0.0286<3\%$
When d=20m, the influence by y error could be accepted.
Therefore, the upper limit is d=20m.
Thus, we designate the distance range as d~ [8m, 20m]

4.2. *Parameter optimization*

Observing the formula (1),we can find that the accuracy of the measurement model is determined by three parameters(α, y_0, f). y_0 and f can be obtained by calibration algorithm. By doing experiments, we know that the parameters we obtain are not precise values but range values actually. While the value of α was obtained by backstepping based on y_0 and f, the value of α we calculate is also a range value.

Firstly, we defined the value——the squared sum of the differences[15] between the actual measuring distance Li and the model measuring distance di, to express the accuracy of our distance measurement model.

$$\delta=\sum_{i=1}^{m}(d_i-L_i)^2 \tag{5}$$

We did an experiment with a group of experimental data. Firstly, we presume that the value of f is accuracy while the value of y_0 is not. We obtained α with the initial value of f and y_0. Secondly, we renew the measurement model with f and α. Finally, we changed the value of y_0, and get a series of δ value. As shown in the Figure 2.

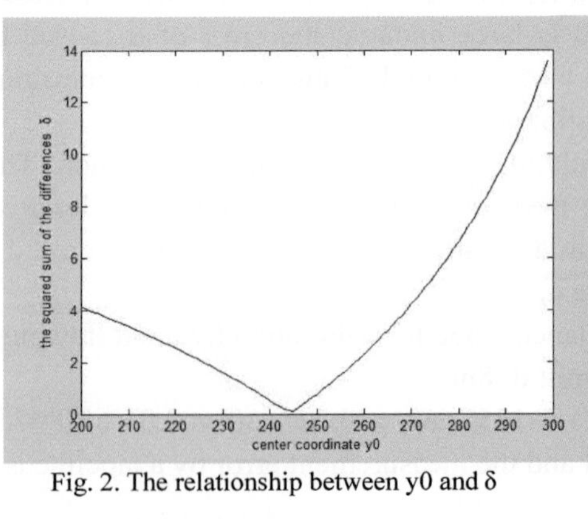

Fig. 2. The relationship between y0 and δ

The figure shows that there exists a better value of y_0 to match the model. Similarly, if we fix y_0 and α, we can obtain a better value of f; if we fixe f and y_0, we can obtain a better value of α. The conclusion is shown in Figure 3 and 4.

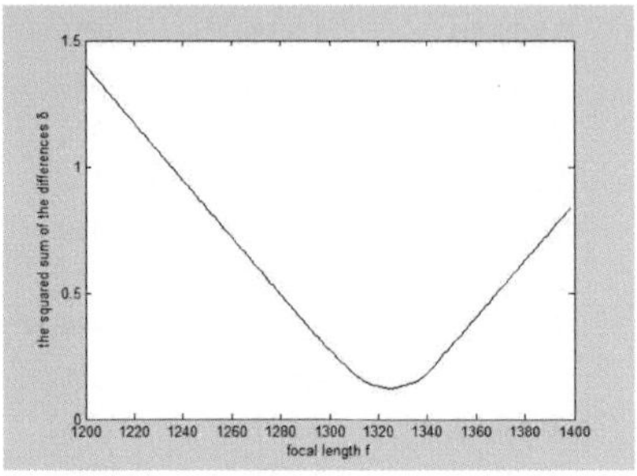

Fig. 3. The relationship between f and δ

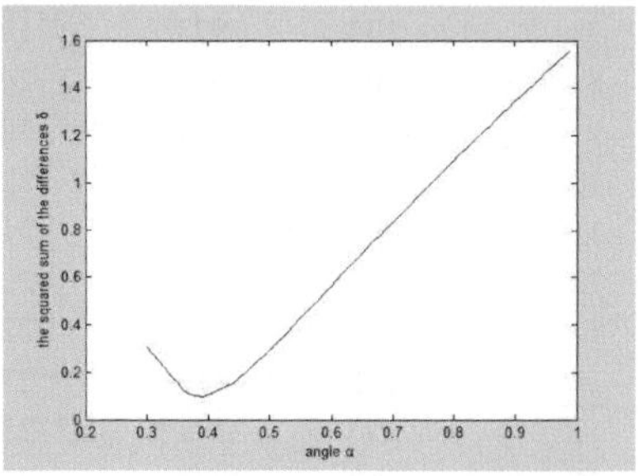

Fig. 4. The relationship between α and δ

This paper designed a method of parameter optimization[15] according to the conclusion above. Fixed two parameters A, B, and then optimize the other parameter C. Then use the optimized parameter C and the left parameter A to optimize the parameter B. Finally use the optimized parameter B and C to optimize parameter A. Then do the same again. After some cycles, the three parameters A, B and C will be convergent to optimal values. The comparison of original value and the optimal value is shown in Table 4

Table 4. The comparison of original value and the optimal value

original value	α=0.33	y0=242	f=1331
optimal value	α=0.39	y0=245	f=1315

5. Experimental Results

Finally, we do some experiments to test the optimization. We compare the distance errors produced by the improved method and original method. The data Table 5 is as follows

Table 5. Comparison of original results and optimal results

number	Y	L(mm)	Original d(mm)	Optimal d(mm)	Original error	Optimal error
1	370	973	979.13	971.07	0.63%	0.20%
2	362	1033	1040.92	1043.42	0.77%	1.01%
3	340	1273	1259.48	1264.40	1.06%	0.68%
4	331	1393	1377.81	1384.31	1.09%	0.62%
5	319	1573	1595.10	1584.66	1.40%	0.74%

Table 5. Comparison of original results and optimal results (Cont.)

number	Y	L(mm)	Original d(mm)	Optimal d(mm)	Original error	Optimal error
6	317	1633	1613.61	1623.83	1.19%	0.56%
7	307	1873	1838.30	1852.80	1.85%	1.08%
8	301	1993	2015.88	2024.01	1.15%	1.56%
9	298	2113	2081.68	2122.06	1.48%	0.43%
10	296	2173	2206.79	2192.88	1.55%	0.91%
11	295	2233	2177.07	2230.09	2.50%	0.13%
12	293	2293	2204.41	2308.43	3.86%	0.67%
13	292	2353	2280.59	2349.70	3.08%	0.14%
14	291	2413	2315.22	2392.47	4.05%	0.85%
15	290	2473	2378.36	2436.83	3.83%	1.46%
16	288	2533	2400.54	2520.67	5.23%	0.49%

6. Conclusion

Observing the original errors, we can see that the data errors are increasing with the growing of measuring distance. Therefore, the conclusion is that the original parameters (f, y0, α) is limited, which means that these parameters can't fit the real model faultlessly. But if we use the model with the parameters optimized, the whole error reduces. Even if there is some errors are bigger than original errors, we can conclude that the optimized parameters are more adaptable and global, and these bigger errors are caused by inaccuracies of y_i and di. Our new model can reflect the inaccuracies of partial y_i and d_i, only if we provide a sufficient amount of y_i and d_i and most of these data have little measuring errors. This method is equal to least square method which has the function of error correcting. So, as we optimize the parameters this way, our model can solve the distance more precisely.

References

1. Tianjian L I, Wang H, Huang M. Research on control method of storage robot based on computer vision [J]. Journal of Beijing Information Science & Technology University, 2015.
2. Baofeng Wang, Zhiquan Qi, Guocheng Ma. Robust lane recognition for structured road based on monocular vision [J]. Journal of Beijing Institute of technology, 2014, 23:345-351.
3. Houyun Yu, Weigong Zhang. Method of vechicle distance measurement for following car based on monocular vision [J]. Journal of Southeast University, 2012.

4. Rongben Wang, Bin Li, Jiangwei Chu, et al. Study on the method of measuring the leading vehicle distance based on the on-board monocular camera [J]. Journal of Highway and Transportation Research and Development, 2001, 18(6): 94-98. (in Chinese)
5. Masafumi Tsuji, Ryota Shirato, Hiroshi Furusho, et al. Estimation of road configuration and vehicle attitude by lane detection for a lane-keeping system [A]. In: SAE 2001 World Congress Intelligent Vehicle Initiative (IVI) Vehicle Navigation Systems (Part A&B) [C]. Detroit, Michigan, USA, 2001.
6. Feilu LUO, Enxi FU. A fast and accurate calibration method of intrinsic and extrinsic parameters of CCD camera [J]. Journal of Hunan University, 1997, 24(2): 71~74.
7. Feilu LUO, Tao Ji, Dixiang CHEN. Programmed correction of camera distortion[J]. Journal of National University of Defense Technology, 1997,19(1): 77~82(in Chinese).
8. Lei Guo, Youchun Xu, Keqiang Li, Xiaomin Lian. Study on Real-time Distance Detection Based on Monocular Vision Technique [J]. Journal of Image and Graphics, 2006, 11(1): 74-81(in Chinese).
9. Geng L, Xiao Z, Wu J, et al. Monocular Vision Distance Measurement Method Based on Dynamic Error Compensation [J]. International Journal of Digital Content Technology & Its Applications, 2013, 7(5):230-239.
10. Fernandes J C, Neves J A B. Angle Invariance for Distance Measurements Using a Single Camera [C]// IEEE International Symposium on Industrial Electronics. 2006:676-680.
11. ZHANG Z Y.A Flexible new technique for camera calibration [J]. IEEE Transactions on Pattern Analysis and Machine Inteligence, 2000, 22(11): 1330-1334.
12. Hongtao Yin, Cheng Liu, Yibing Li, et al. Analysis of Factors on the Error of the Camera Calibration [J]. INFORMATION & COMMUNITIONS, 2012, 12(1):28-30. (in Chinese)
13. Yuan Ming, Su Xianyu, Liu Xiaoqing, et al. Analysis of Factors on the Precision of the Camera Calibration [J]. OPTIC & OPTOELECTRONIC TECHNOLOGY,2010,8(4):18-21. (in Chinese)
14. Pang H, Li J, Chen D, et al. Calibration of three-axis fluxgate magnetometers with nonlinear least square method [J]. Measurement, 2013, 46(4):1600-1606.
15. Latry C, Despringre V, Valorge C. Automatic MTF measurement through a least square method[C]// Remote Sensing. International Society for Optics and Photonics, 2004:233-244.

Research on Visual Methods in Bibliometrics — Surveying and Mapping Journals

Jing Li[a], Hai-Yan Liu[b], Sen Che, Rui-Jie Yang and Wen-Yue Guo

Institute of Geospatial Information, Information Engineering University, Zhengzhou
Zhengzhou, Henan, China
E-mail: [a]brandy12367@sina.cn, [b]liu2000@ vip.sina.com

This paper proposes from the angle of data types and research contents in bibliometrics, Visualization as a widely used technology draws more and more attention in the field of bibliometrics. Some reasonable and effective visualization methods are proposed in accordance with the characteristics such as data types and the contents in bibliometric research through the way of analyzing Chinese surveying and mapping journals.

Keywords: Visualization; Bibliometrics; Tag Cloud; Textual Data.

1. Introduction

Bibliometrics is a quantitative analysis method, with various external feature as the research object, using mathematical and statistical methods to describe, and it is quantity analysis method using in analyzing the external features of the literature. It focuses on the analysis of the literature form features of "quantity", analyzing of the law of literature from a quantitative point, and indirect reflecting the relationship. Recently, with the growing number of academic papers, effective and reasonable analysis are needed to realize the development of a subject from the qualitative to quantitative.

The original bibliometrics is to analyze the data through the statistical methods without combining any graphics. With the increasing of analysis methods, the expression of complex data is limited, some significant information will be hided under the large numbers of statistical data without visualization. In 1970s, Dinsmore drew citation data in the social sciences of various fields to subject structure diagram. It was the first time that bring the concept of visualization into bibliometrics. At present, visualization technology is used more and more widely in the field of bibliometric research.

According to the characteristics such as data types and the contents in bibliometric research, we propose some reasonable and effective visualization methods in this paper.

2. Characteristics in Bibliometric Research

The academic paper is the main object in bibliometric research. The academic paper is different from the general text data, it has the certain structure, which belongs to the semi structure data. The academic paper consists of title, author, abstract, keywords, and main body, etc. According to the constitution of academic paper, three contents in bibliometric research are identified: keywords analysis, author analysis and the amount of published paper analysis.

On the basis of the three contents above, we choose three data types to visualize: textual data, attribute data of time, and attribute data of location. The specific contents of this paper are as follows:

- Visualization of word based on word frequency
- Visualization of textual data based on the time attribute
- Visualization of location attribute

3. Visualization Methods

3.1. *Visualization method of word based on word frequency —Tag cloud*

Word frequency analysis is an important research method in the research of bibliometrics. Through the statistics of the word frequency to reveal the rules. For example, the high-frequency keywords could reflect the hot topic in the research field in some degrees. Involves two ingredients of vocabulary level text and word frequency, Tag cloud is the most simple and commonly used visualization method.

Tag cloud arrange the words on the screen orderly with some orders, rules or constraints. Highlighting the importance of word in the way of setting different font sizes of words.

In the paper, we count the keywords in Chinese surveying and mapping journals from 2006 to 2015. We display the top 20 keywords in the order of word frequency from high to low in Table 1.

Fig. 1 will be the content of Table 1, with the frequency of the tag cloud as the constraint conditions. It can be seen that the larger font size and the central location of the keywords show the higher importance.

Table 1. Top 20 keywords in Chinese surveying and mapping journals from 2006 to 2015 ordered by word-frequency

Ranking	Name	Word-frequency
1	cartographic generalization	116
2	visualization	111
3	spatial analysis	96
4	topological relationship	80
5	spatial data	77
6	geographic information	74
7	electronic map	74
8	spatial database	71
9	DEM	61
10	3D visualization	58
11	database	53
12	geographic information service	51
13	spatio-temporal data model	48
14	remote sensing	45
15	digital city	44
16	3D GIS	42
17	map	40
18	spatial relationship	38
19	Mobile GIS	37
20	Ontology	36

Fig. 1. Tag cloud of top 20 keywords in Chinese surveying and mapping journals from 2006 to 2015

3.2. *Visualization method of textual data based on the time attribute*

In the research of bibliometrics, it is an important content for researchers to observe the changes of hotspots in terms of time. Publication date of academic papers provides the opportunity for researchers to find out the rules of discipline development over time. There are two factors should be considered: time, and high frequency keywords (which are usually used to present the hotspots).

In the time series analysis, a time bar is a straightforward way to look at data over time. In this paper, we display the top 10 keywords ordered by word frequency from high to low each year from 2006 to 2015 in Fig. 2.

2006	2007	2008	2009	2010
geographic information service	spatio-temporal data model	data model	spatial analysis	spatial analysis
spatial data	electronic map	database	database	visualization
spatial database	spatial data	spatial database	visualization	3DGIS
visualization	spatial analysis	spatial data mining	spatial database	electronic map
geographic information	topological relationship	3Dvisualization	spatial data	DEM
object-oriented	DEM	spatial data	DEM	remote sensing
map	spatial database	geographic information	electronic map	spatial data
spatial analysis	database	spatial analysis	map making	geographic information service
spatial relationship	spatial relationship	DEM	map	ontology
electronic map	map making	virtual reality	remote sensing image	spatio-temporal data model

(1)

2011	2012	2013	2014	2015
visualization	visualization	spatial data	visualization	visualization
topological relationship	cartographic generalization	cartographic generalization	geographic information	geographic information
spatial database	spatial database	topological relationship	geographic information service	spatial analysis
spatial analysis	electronic map	visualization	cartographic generalization	database
cartographic generalization	spatial analysis	point-cloud	topological relationship	cartographic generalization
electronic map	topological relationship	digital city	spatial analysis	big data
3DGIS	spatial data	geographic information	big data	cloud computing
3D modeling	map	electronic map	digital city	smart city
spatial data mining	geographic information	mobileGIS	remote sensing	Tile Map
3DGIS	geographic information service	spatial analysis	spatial data	geographic information service

(2)

Fig. 2. The top 10 keywords from 2006 to 2015

It's difficult to find out information from Fig. 2. Then considering about the continuity of keywords on the time dimension, we draw the continuous appeared keywords with shining colors(the same key words with the same color) in Fig. 3.

From Fig. 3, we can easily find out that five keywords , "spatial data", "spatial analysis", "visualization", "electronic map", "cartographic generalization", are continuous appeared in Chinese surveying and mapping journals during this period.

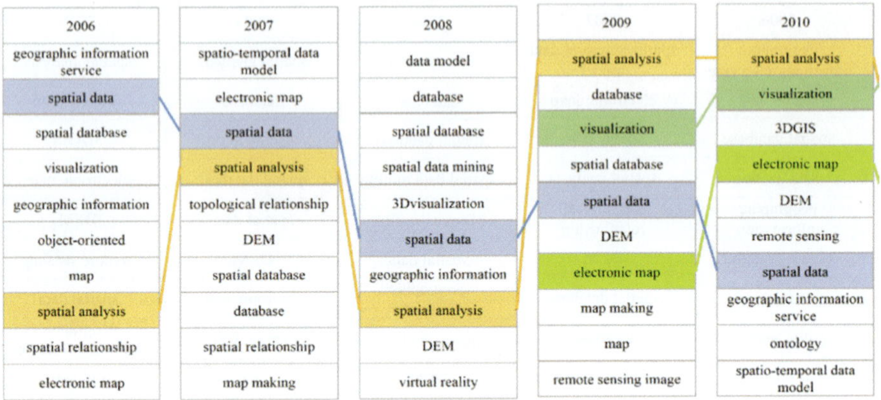

(1)

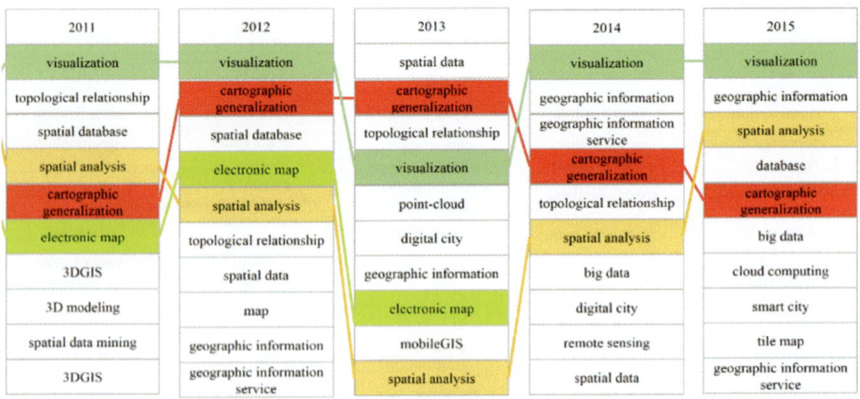

(2)

Fig. 3. The continuous appeared keywords from 2006 to 2015

But it is still too complex to find out useful information in Fig. 3. So we simplify Fig. 3 to Fig. 4 by deleting some useless keywords to highlight what we exactly focus on.

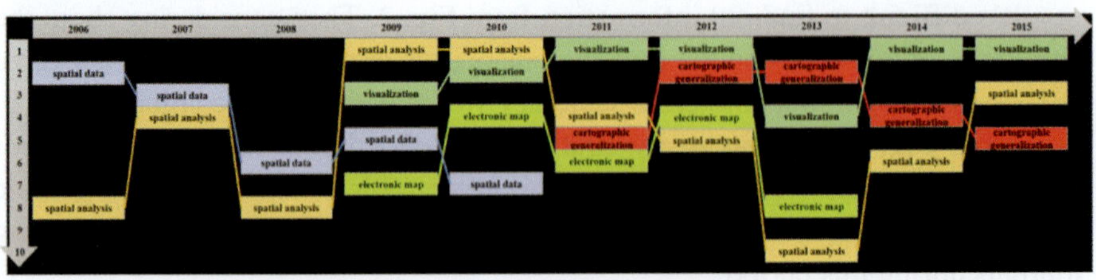

Fig. 4. The simplified graph of continuous appeared keywords from 2006 to 2015

Fig. 5 is the decomposition of Fig. 4. From Fig. 5 (1), we can find out that spatial data once was a hotspot in the field of surveying and mapping in the early years during 2006 to 2015. From Fig. 5 (2), we find that in the middle stage, the study of electric map drew more attentions of surveying and mapping researchers. And in the later years, research of cartographic generalization has been increased.

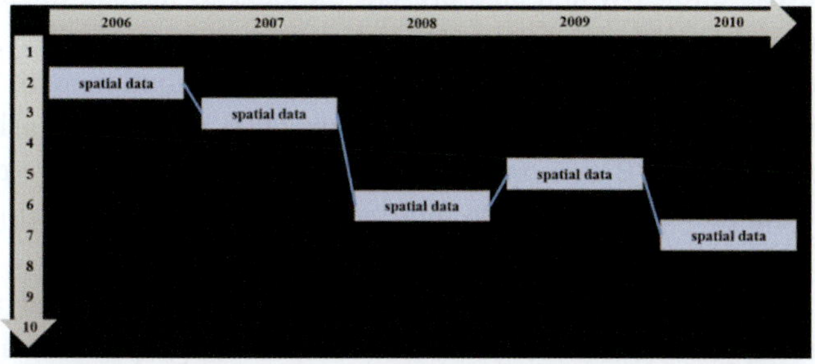

(1)

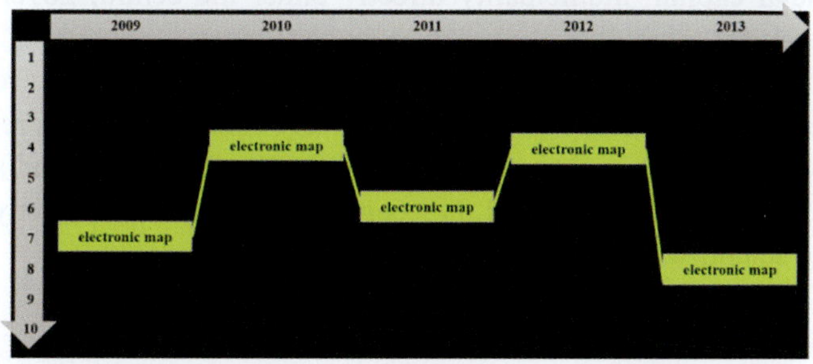

(2)

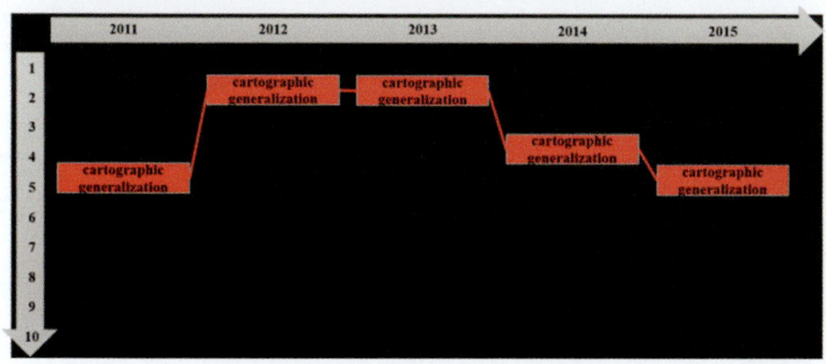

(3)

Fig. 5. Three period of Chinese surveying and mapping research(the decomposition of Fig. 4)

3.3. *Visualization method of location attribute*

In bibliometrics, distribution of academic paper publishing is another important content to consider of. Through the analysis of geographic distribution, researchers could identify the core research area.

There are two factors to visualizing: location information and the number of paper publishing. In our study, we choose cartogram to visualizing those two factors. We use circles which size present the data to instead of physical area using shapes.

Figures 6 and 7 are drawn the geographical distribution with the data of Chinese surveying and mapping journals from 2003 to 2013 by using Tableau visualization software. Based on 5 article number for the node, we consider the place paper number above 5 as the high post area, less than 5 and greater than zero as the low post area.

From Fig. 6, the high post area mainly distribute in central and eastern regions, and only Urumchi is in the west of China. High post areas are mainly the provincial capital, municipality directly under the central government and other large cities.

From Fig. 7, the low post areas are also in central and eastern regions, and southeastern coastal cities. The scale is relatively smaller. Overall, regardless of the high post or the low post areas, they mainly distribute in central and eastern regions. The scale of the city and the economic development directly affect the level of the scientific research.

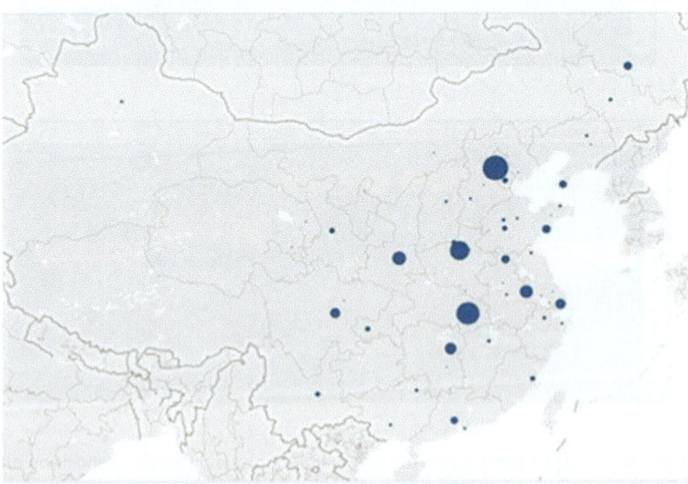

Fig. 6. Geographical distribution(the number of paper publishing >5)

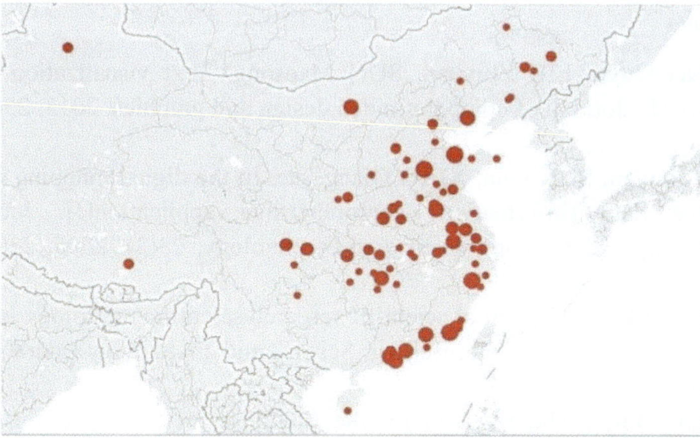

Fig. 7. Geographical distribution (the number of paper publishing ≤5)

4. Conclusion

Visualization can be a great tool to explore data, and the key to getting the most out of the data——to understand what it represent and what it means. In this paper, according to the data types and research contents, we propose some visualization methods in bibliometrics. Through the way of visualizing the paper data of surveying and mapping, we can draw the following conclusion:

(1) In bibliometrics, words analysis is a significant part. Tag cloud is a simple and useful method of visualizing words.

(2) In the time series analysis, a time bar is a straightforward way to look at data over time. And when the picture is too complex, simplifying it will help.

(3) Cartogram is a method of visualizing the combination of statistics and spatial data. It ignores the physical area and makes entire regions sized by data.

Acknowledgments

This work is funded by State Key Laboratory of Geo-information Engineering (NO. SKLGIE2015-M-3-1) and the National Natural Science Foundation of China (Nos. 41471387, 41501446).

References

1. TANG Guyu, LIU Zhiyuan, SUN Maosong. Text visualization research review[J]. Journal of computer-aided design and graphics, 2013, 25(3): 273-285
2. LIU Haiyan, SUN Qun, XIAO Qiang, etc. In the digital mapping of multi-source data (information) comprehensive application[J]. Journal of surveying and mapping science and technology, 23(3), 2006, 23(3): 161-164.
3. WINKLER. Evaluation of scientific research scientific metrology index [M] Translated by MA Zheng, Beijing: Science and Technology Literature Press, 2014.12
4. JIANG Ying. The research on the literature metrology in the field of Humanities and social sciences[M]. Beijing: Social Science Literature Press
5. L. Lamport, *LaTeX, A Document Preparation System*, 2nd edn. (Addison-Wesley, Reading, MA, 1994).
6. CHEN Sheng, ZENG Xingji, LIANG Jun. Based on statistical data of GIS visualization study. Computer engineering and design, 2008, 29(14): 3757-3759.
7. WANG Yuefen, The comprehensive research of literature metrology and content analysis [D]. Nanjing university of science and technology. 2007
8. LIN Hongfei, GAO Tian. The visual representation of Chinese text. Journal of northeastern university: natural science edition, 2000, 21(5): 501-504.
9. JIANG Chunlin, LIU Shengbo, DING Kun. Research hotspot and the evolution of knowledge map in China of the Journal of science and technology [J]. Journal of environmental science, 2008,06:954-958.

A Comparative Study of Algorithms on Project Scheduling Problem with Uncertain Resource Constraints

Chuan-Liang Jia[a], Jia-Li Tan[b] and Jie Su[c]

Central University of Finance and Economics, 39 South College Road, Haidian District Beijing, 100081, P. R. China

E-mail: [a]cnbjjcl@163.com, [b]tjl_carly@163.com, [c]sujiesu@126.com

In realities, many project scheduling problems involve uncertain resources. In this paper, on the basis of the resource project scheduling problem, scenario sets are used to describe the upper limit of available resources and the uncertainty of arrival time and build a robust optimization model for URCPSP. Since the model involves uncertainties of double resources constrained scenarios and cannot be solved easily, a genetic algorithm is designed and an ant colony algorithm to approximate the robust solution. In the case analysis, the quality of two algorithms is compared which includes the optimal solution and the efficiency of solving, weighing the pros and cons, and solutions to the procedure.

Keywords: URCPSP; Robust Optimization; Algorithm Comparison.

1. Introduction

Traditional project scheduling is usually carried out in a deterministic environment. However, the actual project environment is full of uncertainty, risk and interference. In order to ensure that the project is implemented successfully and smoothly, we must consider various uncertain factors and assess related risk advance, and give timely response to the occurrence of an uncertain event.

As an effective approach to solve project scheduling problem in uncertain environments, robust optimization has developed a lot since Soyster first proposed a robust linear optimization method to solve the problem of uncertainty of linear programming constraint matrix column in 1970s [1]. Ben-Tal, Ghaoui, Bersimas, Sim, Nemirovski, El Ghaoui, Lebret and other scholars made a lot of contributions to establishing robust optimization theory. Ling Zhang et al. established a robust optimization model for emergency relief network [2]. Lei Zhu et al. establish a network robust optimization model for configuration issues on multifunctional human resources [3].

Although robust optimization have been applied in many fields, robust project scheduling just gradually rises in the last decade. After W. Herroelen and R. Leus, professors of University of Leuven, cooperatively published two review articles about project scheduling in an uncertain environment and robust project scheduling in 2004 [4]and 2005 [5], robust project scheduling research was springing up.

Demeulemeester E. et al. proposed a three-stage method to solve the robust project scheduling problem [6]. Van de vonder et al. compared the trade-off between robustness and duration of the scheduling in the absence of resource constraints [7] and in the presence of resource constraints [8]. Lambrechts et al. put forward a proactive resource scheduling method under the condition of uncertainty of various resources [9]. Yongyi Shou et al. designed a genetic algorithm to solve project scheduling problem on the uncertainty of duration [10].

In this paper, we design a genetic algorithm and an ant colony algorithm for a robust optimization model that applied to uncertainties of double resource constrained scenarios and compare the two algorithms.

2. Resource Constrained Project Scheduling Problem(RCPSP)

The typical RCPSP is described as follows: a project includes J tasks and some tasks exist precedence relationships because of technical requirements. P_j represents the preceding task set of task j and S_j represents the following task set of task j. The acyclic directed graph $G(V, E)$ shows the relationship between project tasks, where V represents the node set, namely, the task, and E represents the arc set, that is, the time sequence relationship between the task. Task J (j=1,... , J) must be implemented in one pattern which is selected from M_j patterns (patterns provide a certain resource requirements and an execution time). Once the task is executed, and the pattern that is chosen cannot be changed or interrupted. In the selected m pattern of execution, the demand of the task J for k renewable resource is r^{ρ}_{jmk}, the demand of the task J for n unrenewable resource is r^{ν}_{jmn}, and the execution time is d_{jm}. Task 1 and Task J are respectively the only first beginning and the only late completion of the project, and both them are virtual tasks (which mean that they do not consume resources and their execution time is zero), indicating the beginning and the end of the whole project. Throughout the whole duration, the available amount of the k renewable resource and n unrenewable resource on each stage respectively are a constant R^{ρ}_{k}(k=1,…,K) and a constant R^{ν}_{n}(n=1,…,N).

If each execution pattern is feasible, the task J will satisfy:

$$r^{\rho}_{jmk} \leq R^{\rho}_{k}, m = 1, \dots, M_j, k = 1, \dots, K \tag{1}$$

$$r^{\nu}_{jmn} \leq R^{\nu}_{n}, m = 1, \dots, M_j, n = 1, \dots, N \tag{2}$$

The uncertain resource constraints are added to the typical RCPSP issue with limited discrete values or discrete interval values to generate a uncertain resource constrained project scheduling problem(URCPSP).

3. The Model of Resource Constrained Project Scheduling Problem

In this paper, scenario set $\Omega = \{1,2,3,\dots,\Phi\}$ represents randomness of the uncertainty of resource supply project, that is, all possible supply portfolios of resources. In the scenario $\varphi \in \Omega$, R^{φ}_{k} represents the arrival time and the amount of available resources $< r^{\varphi}_{gk}, a^{\varphi}_{gk} >$ of k resource in scenario φ, and changes of standard supply of resource, R_k, represents uncertainty of resource supply of this kind resource:

$$R^{\varphi}_{k} = R_k + \Delta R_k \tag{3}$$

where

$$\Delta R_k = \begin{cases} 0, t < a^{\varphi}_{g} \\ r^{\varphi}_{gk}, t \epsilon [a^{\varphi}_{g}, a^{\varphi}_{g+1}) \end{cases} \quad g = 1,2,3,\dots, \forall k, t \tag{4}$$

$$r^{\varphi}_{gk} \in [r^{k}_{min}, r^{k}_{max}], a^{\varphi}_{gk} \in [a^{k}_{min}, a^{k}_{max}] \ \forall g \tag{5}$$

Vectors $R^{\varphi} = \{R^{\varphi}_{1}, R^{\varphi}_{2}, R^{\varphi}_{3}, \dots, R^{\varphi}_{K}\}$ can denote the amount of resources in scenario φ. The goal of the above-mentioned URCPSP is to find a suitable schedule $S^{\varphi} = (s^{\varphi}_{1}, s^{\varphi}_{2}, \dots, s^{\varphi}_{J})$, so that all resource requirements do not exceed R^{φ}_{k}, to ensure that the project schedule satisfies both precedence relations and resource constraints, and thus to complete the project as short as possible. In scheduling scheme S, the duration of the project is equal to the latest finish time of all the tasks. It not only depends on project scheduling scheme S, but also depends on the arrival time and the amount of available resources. There is an optimal scheduling scheme which makes the duration of the project minimum in each scenario. Therefore, the stochastic scheduling method is designed to find a scheduling scheme which makes the expected value of the duration of project in all scenarios.

$$\min E^{\varphi}(CT_J) = \frac{1}{|\Omega|}\max_{\varphi}\{ST_j + p_j\} \tag{6}$$

Given a schedule S, the average duration $E(CT_J)$ in all scenarios and variance of time $V(CT_J)$ can be obtained. If $E(CT_J)$ and $V(CT_J)$ is relatively small, it indicates that the scheduling scheme is excellent and robust; on the contrary, that the scheduling scheme lacks robustness in a variety of scenarios.

$$V(CT_J) = \frac{1}{|\Omega|}\sum[CT_J - E(CT_J)]^2$$

Accordingly, URCPSP robust optimization model can be described as:

$$min\left\{E(CT_J) + \frac{1}{|\Omega|}\sum\left[CT_J - E(CT_J)\right]^2\right\} \tag{7}$$

s.t.

$$ST_j \geq CT_h, \forall j, h\in P_j \tag{8}$$

$$\sum_{j\in I_t(S^{\varphi})} r_{jk} \leq R_k^{\varphi}, \forall k, t \tag{9}$$

$$R_k^{\varphi} = R_k + \Delta R_k \tag{10}$$

$$\Delta R_k = \begin{cases} 0, t < a_g^{\varphi} \\ r_{gk}^{\varphi}, t\in[a_g^{\varphi}, a_{g+1}^{\varphi}) \end{cases} \quad g = 1,2,3,\ldots, \forall k, t \tag{11}$$

$$r_{gk}^{\varphi} \in \left[r_{min}^{k}, r_{max}^{k}\right], a_{gk}^{\varphi} \in \left[r_{min}^{k}, r_{max}^{k}\right] \forall g \tag{12}$$

Formula (7) indicates the expected value of objective function, and duration CT_J , is minimum under the premise of the robustness of the model. Formula (8) denotes precedence constraints, that is, task can only be started after the completion of all the precedent tasks. Formula (9) represents resource constraints, namely, demand for resources cannot exceed the supply of resources on any time of scenarios. $I_t(S^{\varphi})$ demonstrates the ongoing task of scheduling scheme S in scenario φ on time t. Formula (10), (11), (12) respectively indicate the uncertainty of resources, that the amounts of resources that arrive vary within $[r_{min}^{k}, r_{max}^{k}]$, and that arrival time varies within $[a_{min}^{k}, a_{max}^{k}]$.

4. Algorithm Design

In this paper, we design a genetic algorithm and an ant colony algorithm to solve the model.

4.1. *Genetic algorithm(GA)*

(i) project scheduling coding

Each gene represents a task and the completion time of task 0 (virtual task) is zero, and local schedule is generated during initialization. At the beginning of each phase, a task j^* is selected from the feasible task set according to the specific rules. Then calculate the finish time CT_j which satisfies the precedence relationships and resource constraints.

(ii) determine the fitness function

f(i) is fitness function of chromosome i in the current generation, and can be calculated as follows:

$$f(i) = \frac{1}{E(CT_J)} \tag{13}$$

(iii) determine the initial population

Assuming that arrival time and the amount of resources is full of uncertainty, the initial population is generated completely randomly, that is, each task is distributed random values between a earliest start time and latest start time.

(iv) determine the selection operator

By using roulette selection method, the survival probability of the individual is determined according to the proportion of each individual fitness:

$$p(i) = \frac{f(i)}{\sum_j f(j)} \tag{14}$$

(v) determine the crossover operator

Select a point randomly and exchange the two chromosomes after the point.

(vi) determine the mutation operator

(vii)Do random perturbation on the value of original gene and take the results after disturbance as the new values of mutated gene.

4.2. *Ant colony algorithm(ACA)*

(i) determine the initial node that can be selected

(ii) m ants select the task node according to the probability function to complete their traversal

(iii) calculate the probability distribution of the nodes to be selected $pheromone^{its\ own\ coefficient} * heuristic\ factor^{its\ own\ coefficient}$

(iv) select the next task point according to the probability

(v) find the best route of the current iteration and its total duration

(vi) update the pheromone by using ant_cycle model

(vii) clear the tabu list, repeat iterations and do not stop until iterations reach the required number

(viii) output the optimal task list and the minimum duration

5. Case Analysis

This study uses MATLAB2013a language to write the codes and test cases in Matlab2013a environment in window7.0. To test the effect of algorithms on solving URCPSP, we use case part 9 which is picked from Patterson sample library. The project of this case is a single project. There are 18 tasks totally, including the virtual start task 0 and end task 17. Only one renewable resource is involved, namely, human resources and the weekly standard capacity of resource supply is 8 hours.

The solving process of GA and ACA is as shown in Figure. 1. In GA, the value of the objective function (the average duration) to tend to be stable after the number of iteration equals approximately to 50,which is the same as ACA, and it is completely stable while the number of iteration equals approximately to 200 while it is approximately 125 in ACA. The optimal robust task chain is (2-16-17-9-10-11-7-13-14-15-5-6-8-12-4-3) in GA and (2-16-17-7-8-11-12-13-14-15-8-9-3-4-5-6) in ACA. The minimum average duration of GA and ACA respectively are 8 and 9.2 approximately, which shows that the optimal solution of GA is better than ACA obviously.

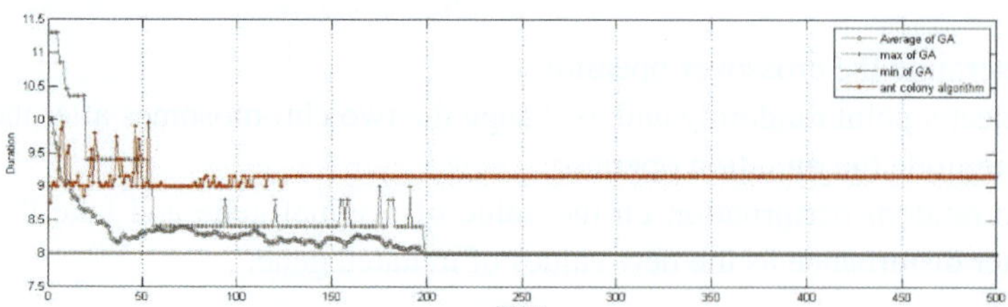

Fig. 1. The solving process of algorithms

In order to compare the efficiency of the algorithm, we takes the solving time as a standard measure. Both two algorithms iterate 100 and 500 times, and the results are shown as follows in Table. 1:

Table 1. Comparison of the iterative efficiency of the algorithm

	The time of iteration(seconds)	
Algorithm	The number of iteration = 100	The number of iteration = 500
GA	86	318
ACA	35	72

As can be seen from the table 1, the GA consumes more time than ACA. With the increase of the number of iterations, this disadvantage of GA is more obvious. Although the iterative efficiency of ACA is higher than GA, ACA is easy to fall into local optimum because of its own limitation. Therefore, the optimal solution of ACA is inferior to GA.

6. Conclusions

On the basis of resource constrained problem, this paper explores the uncertain resource constrained project scheduling problem. We use scenario sets to describe the upper limit of available resources and the uncertainty of arrival time and build a robust optimization model for URCPS. We respectively design a genetic algorithm and an ant colony algorithm to solve the model and also compare the solving quality of two algorithms. We find that although the time of iteration of genetic algorithm has a poor performance, but its optimal robust solution is significantly better than the optimal solution of ant colony algorithm. Thus, weighing the pros and cons, using genetic algorithm to solve URCPSP is proper.

Acknowledgements

This study is supported by the National Natural Science Foundation of China(91324203): The Theory and Methods of Unconventional Emergency Case Reasoning for Emergency Decision Support.

References

1. Soyster A. Convex programming with set-inclusive constraints and applications to inexact linear programming[J]. Operations Research, 1973, 21 (6): 1154-1157.

2. Ling Zhang, Tao Chen, Jun Huang. Robust optimization model and algorithm for emergency disaster relief network based on min max regret value [J]. Chinese Journal of Management Science, 2014, 22(7):131-139.
3. Lei Zhu, Jianqiang Li, Ming Wang. Robust Optimization for supply chain of Emergency Multi-functional Human Resource Management under Uncertainty [J]. Systems Engineering-Theory & Practice, 2015(3):736-742.
4. Herroelen W, Leus R. Robust and reactive project scheduling: a review and classification of procedures[J]. International Journal of Production Research, 2004, 42(8):1599-1620.
5. Herroelen W, Leus R. Project scheduling under uncertainty: Survey and research potentials[J]. European Journal of Operational Research, 2005, 165(2):289-306.
6. Demculemeester E, Herroelen W. Robust Project Scheduling[J]. Foundations & Trends® in Technology Information & Operations Management, 2013, 3:201-376.
7. Vonder S V D, Demeulemeester E, Herroelen W, et al. The use of buffers in project management: The trade-off between stability and makespan[J]. International Journal of Production Economics, 2005, 97(2):227-240.
8. Vonder S V D. Proactive-reactive procedures for robust project scheduling[J]. 2006.
9. Lambrechts O, Demeulemeester E, Herroelen W. Time slack-based techniques for robust project scheduling subject to resource uncertainty[J]. Annals of Operations Research, 2010, 186(1):443-464.
10. Yongyi Shou, Wei Wan.g. Genetic Algorithm to the Project Scheduling Strategy Based on Robust Optimization Model [J]. Journal of Industrial Engineering and Engineering Management, 2009, 23(4):148-152.
11. Ying Ying. Project Scheduling Problems with Uncertain Resource Constraint [D]. Zhejiang University, 2010.

Research on the Vulnerability Detection Approach Based on Program Slicing Similarity

Jie Gong[1,a], Xiao-Hui Kuang[1,b] and Qiang Liu[1,c]

Group National Key Laboratory of Science and Technology on Information System Security, Beijing Institute of System Engineering

Beijing, 100101, China

E-mail: [a]gongjie.cs@gmail.com, [b]xiaohui_kuang@163.com, [c]liuqiang_xjtu@163.com

The unknown vulnerability detection methods based on known vulnerabilities make an important significance. Since the code complexity, scientific extraction vulnerability related information is the key of the similarity matching methods to discover vulnerabilities. Dimensionality reduction based similarity matching function is one of the commonly used methods. However, faced with the choice of feature dimension reduction leads to bad arbitrary accuracy. To solve this problem, vulnerability discovery method based on the similarity of the program slicing, which slice through the promotion of a function expression vulnerability context information to enhance the accuracy of vulnerability discovery purposes. This paper also proposes a vulnerability detection framework based on program slicing similarity. It also solves the slicing feature points for vulnerability discovery labeling, automatic slicing etc. Thesis on open source projects Joern improves to achieve the above-described methods. Experimental verification shows that the method can significantly improve the accuracy of vulnerability discovery and improve the efficiency of vulnerability discovery, and demonstrates the effectiveness of the method and framework adopted.

Keywords: Program Slicing; Software Vulnerability Analysis; Machine Learning.

1. Introduction

The vulnerability of software system has become one of the main risks affecting information security. How to discover vulnerability automatically and efficiently has aroused concern and attention now. However, due to the increasing of the size and complexity of software systems [1], the machine learning methods to analysis vulnerability are proved to be useful and effective [2].

To discover vulnerability based on function similarity match, firstly we have to learn the known vulnerabilities sample database[3], extract features, and analyze in the program matching features, and identify known vulnerabilities similar to the pattern, and then verify the suspect vulnerability[4]. However, as a function of the vulnerability of the training set input is not targeted at the code generating intermediate expression analysis will generate a lot of redundant information, and will bring greater interference to subsequent analysis[5]. Therefore, our analysis is a particular kind of vulnerability, so before we extract feature of the program, we can use program slicing, and then discover the vulnerability through machine learning methods.

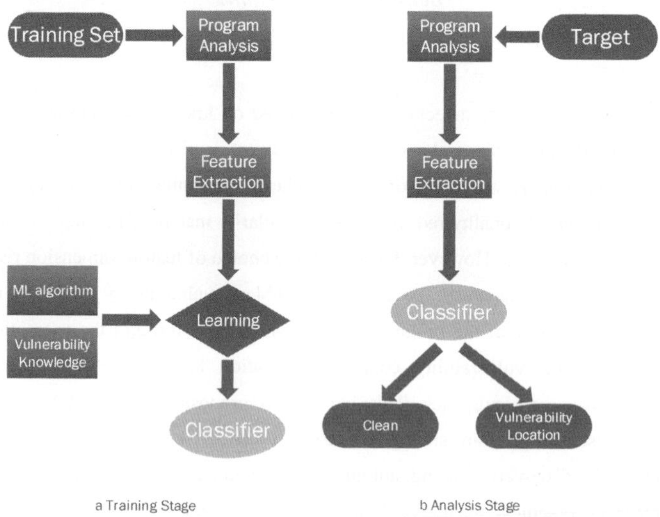

Fig. 1 Software vulnerability analysis framework based on machine learning

Program slicing is a program analysis and program understanding technology [6], it is widely used in program testing, debugging, field engineering, and anti-static analysis. A program slicing is some statements and determined expression consisting of a collection [7]. These statements and expressions that may affect the determination of a location in the program (common line number identification) defined by p and the values of variables defined by v. In this paper, we design a specific program slicing method towards vulnerability detection. And then we use our framework in an open source project OPENSSL, and find two vulnerabilities including Heartbleed.

2. Vulnerability Discovery Framework Based on Program Slicing Similarity

In addition to the exist framework, we made a research about discovering vulnerability based on program slicing. Because if we extract the feature direct from the source code, we will get lots of "noise"[9] that will disturb our detection. Therefore, as Figure 2 shows, first we do some pre-Analysis to the source code, that is program slicing, then extract feature which is API symbols [8] from the program slicing output, and embedding them into vector space. After that we choose a function F that is shown to be vulnerable, and use KNN to find the nearest neighbors of F, that is a set of suspect vulnerabilities.

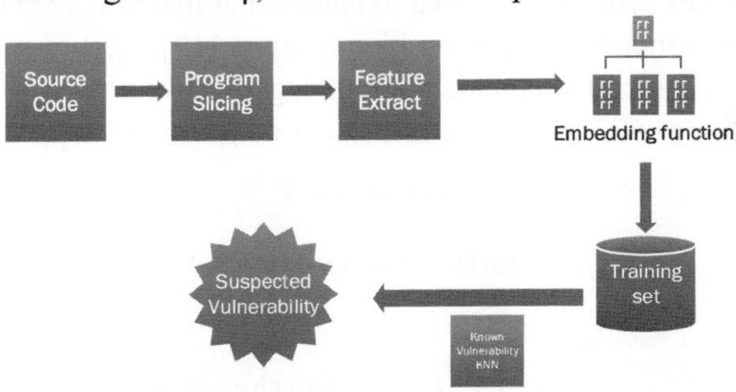

Fig. 2 Software vulnerability analysis framework based on program slicing similarity

2.1. *Towards vulnerability detection program slicing approach*

Definition 1. Program slicing is the computation of the set of programs statements that may affect the values of interest point which called slicing criterion. Especially for backward slicing, we choose the slicing criterion as: <V, p> which p is an interest point and V is a set of variables, and a backward slice of Program P[10] is a function that can make the same affection to p with any value of V.

Definition 2. Key point is used to describe the path to trigger vulnerability. A CVE demo always contains how a vulnerability can be triggered, normally, there is an entrance point E and a sink point S and the Key point is in the path between E and S[11].

Definition 3. Normal backward slicing may get different path from E to S, but there is only one path can trigger the vulnerability, and this path is described with K point, so we get a slicing criterion <V, p, K>.

2.2. *Extract feature*

We use lexical analysis to extract the feature of a function. After the last step, the source code has been sliced, then we tokenized each function to get API symbols. [9] The API symbols contain the names of types, names of functions and type casts such as "int", "if", "sizeof", "memcpy". Based on this symbols, we can use this API to reflect the behavior of a function, so that we extract the feature of a function12.

2.3. *Embedding function feature to vector space*

After we get API symbols, we need to embedding that into vector space so that we can use it as training set for machine learning [13]. First, we define $\Omega = \{f_1, f_2, \ldots, f_n\}$ is the sct of functions after slicing from source code. Then we can define a mapping ψ from Ω to S-dimensional vector space[14];

$$\psi : \Omega \longrightarrow S \tag{1}$$

$$\psi_S(f) := I\,(s, f)\ \mathrm{TFIDF}(s)$$

where I is

$$I\,(s, f) = \begin{cases} 1, & f \text{ contains the symbol } s \\ 0, & f \text{ doesn'tcontain the symbol } s \end{cases} \tag{2}$$

After that we get a matrix that every raw is a function that contains different symbols which looks like:

$$\mathrm{Raw}(j) = \{\text{function ID: } S_1 : V_1, \ldots, S_i : V_i, \ldots, S_s : V_s\} \tag{3}$$

$$\begin{pmatrix} \boldsymbol{Raw(1)} \\ \ldots \\ \mathbf{Raw(j)} \\ \ldots \\ \boldsymbol{Raw(n)} \end{pmatrix} \tag{4}$$

Then we embed the source code into vector space as the input of machine learning step [15].

2.4. *Machine learning*

In machine learning step, first we need to choose a function F that has known vulnerability as the analysis target. Then we get a vector:

$$F = \{F\text{-ID: } S_1 : V_1, \ldots, S_i : V_i, \ldots, S_s : V_s\} \tag{5}$$

then we calculate the distance between F and each function[9]:

$$Di = |F - fi| \tag{6}$$

Later we sort D_n in ascending order, we get a list based on the similarity. And we choose top k functions as suspect vulnerabilities.

3. Evaluation

We proceed to evaluate the practical efficacy of our approach in open source project OPENSSL. We choose the CVE-2016-2105 as the target vulnerability. First we choose the sink memcpy as interest point, then we get the slicing output as Table 1. [16]

Table 1. The EVP_EncodeUpdate in CVE-2016-2105 and its' slicing output

```
void EVP_EncodeUpdate(EVP_ENCODE_CTX *ctx, unsigned char
*out, int *outl, const unsigned char *in, int inl)
        {
        int i,j;
                unsigned int total=0;
                *outl=0;
                if (inl == 0) return;
                OPENSSL_assert(ctx->length <= (int)sizeof(ctx-
>enc_data));
                if ((ctx->num+inl) < ctx->length)
                        {
                                memcpy(&(ctx->enc_data[ctx-
>num]),in,inl);
                                ctx->num+=inl;
                                        return;
                        }
                if (ctx->num != 0)
                        {
                                i=ctx->length-ctx->num;
                                memcpy(&(ctx->enc_data[ctx-
>num]),in,i);
                                in+=i;
                                inl-=i;
                                j=EVP_EncodeBlock(out,ctx-
>enc_data,ctx->length);
                                ctx->num=0;
                                out+=j;
                                *(out++)='\n';
                                *out='\0';
                                total=j+1;
                        }
                while (inl >= ctx->length)
                        {
j=EVP_EncodeBlock(out,in,ctx->length);
                                in+=ctx->length;
                                inl-=ctx->length;
                                out+=j;
                                *(out++)='\n';
                                *out='\0';
                                total+=j+1;
                        }
                if (inl != 0)
                                memcpy(&(ctx-
>enc_data[0]),in,inl);
                        ctx->num=inl;
                *outl=total;
                }
```

```
void EVP_EncodeUpdate(EVP_ENCODE_CTX *ctx, unsigned char const
*in, int inl)
{
 int i;
 if (inl == 0) goto return_label;
 if (ctx->num + inl < ctx->length) {
  memcpy((void *)(& ctx->enc_data[ctx->num]),(void const *)in,
    (unsigned long)inl);
  goto return_label;
 }
 if (ctx->num != 0) {
  i = ctx->length - ctx->num;
  memcpy((void *)(& ctx->enc_data[ctx->num]),(void const *)in,
    (unsigned long)i);
  in += i;
  inl -= i;
 }
 while (inl >= ctx->length) {
  in += ctx->length;
  inl -= ctx->length;
 }
 if (inl != 0)
      memcpy((void *)(& ctx->enc_data[0]),(void const *)in,
        (unsigned long)inl);
 return_label: /* internal */ return;
}
```

After extracting the feature and embedding them into vector space, we use KNN To find the 10 most similar function with EVP_EncodeUpdate, and 2 among them are vulnerable, one is CVE-2016-2106 and the other is CVE-2014-0160 (Heart bleed).

Table 2. The suspected vulnerabilities discovered using our framework

Function Name	Location	CVE-ID
EVP_EncryptUpdate	crypto/evp/evp_enc.c	CVE-2016-2106
engine_des_init_key	demos/engines/zencod/hw_zencod.c	
aes_gcm_ctrl	crypto/evp/e_aes.c	
CMAC_CTX_copy	crypto/cmac/cmac.c	
uufread	crypto/des/des.c	
ssl3_send_finished	ssl/s3_both.c	
dtls1_send_finished	ssl/d1_both.c	CVE-2014-0160
engine_des_ede3_init_key	demos/engines/zencod/hw_zencod.c	
cfbr_encrypt_block	crypto/modes/cfb128.c	
uufwrite	crypto/des/des.c	

4. Conclusion

This paper analyzes the current vulnerability analysis framework based on similarity matching, and makes specific vulnerability analysis slicing, after then, it theoretically reducing the subsequent analysis of interfering factors. And we apply this framework into real project, and proved to be useful to find two real vulnerabilities. Besides, the efficiency and accuracy of the analysis have also been improved verified by experiment.

References

1. Wijayasekara, Dumidu, et al. "Mining bug databases for unidentified software vulnerabilities." Human System Interactions (HSI), 2012 5th International Conference on. IEEE, 2012.
2. Neuhaus, Stephan, et al. "Predicting vulnerable software components."Proceedings of the 14th ACM conference on Computer and communications security. ACM, 2007.
3. Grieco, Gustavo, et al. "Toward large-scale vulnerability discovery using Machine Learning."
4. Medeiros, Ibéria, Nuno F. Neves, and Miguel Correia. "Automatic detection and correction of web application vulnerabilities using data mining to predict false positives." Proceedings of the 23rd international conference on World wide web. ACM, 2014.

5. Shar, Lwin Khin, and Hee Beng Kuan Tan. "Predicting SQL injection and cross site scripting vulnerabilities through mining input sanitization patterns."Information and Software Technology 55.10 (2013): 1767-1780.
6. Alomari, Hakam W., Michael L. Collard, and Jonathan I. Maletic. "A very efficient and scalable forward static slicing approach." 2012 19th Working Conference on Reverse Engineering. IEEE, 2012.
7. Schoenig, Stéphane, and Mireille Ducassé. "A backward slicing algorithm for Prolog." International Static Analysis Symposium. Springer Berlin Heidelberg, 1996.
8. Balzarotti, Davide, et al. "Saner: Composing static and dynamic analysis to validate sanitization in web applications." Security and Privacy, 2008. SP 2008. IEEE Symposium on. IEEE, 2008.
9. Yamaguchi, Fabian, Felix Lindner, and Konrad Rieck. "Vulnerability extrapolation: Assisted discovery of vulnerabilities using machine learning."Proceedings of the 5th USENIX conference on Offensive technologies. USENIX Association, 2011.
10. Alpuente, María, et al. "Backward trace slicing for conditional rewrite theories." International Conference on Logic for Programming Artificial Intelligence and Reasoning. Springer Berlin Heidelberg, 2012.
11. Jaffar, Joxan, et al. "Path-sensitive backward slicing." International Static Analysis Symposium. Springer Berlin Heidelberg, 2012.
12. Yamaguchi, Fabian, Markus Lottmann, and Konrad Rieck. "Generalized vulnerability extrapolation using abstract syntax trees." Proceedings of the 28th Annual Computer Security Applications Conference. ACM, 2012.
13. Yamaguchi, Fabian, et al. "Chucky: exposing missing checks in source code for vulnerability discovery." Proceedings of the 2013 ACM SIGSAC conference on Computer & communications security. ACM, 2013.
14. Yamaguchi, Fabian, et al. "Modeling and discovering vulnerabilities with code property graphs." Security and Privacy (SP), 2014 IEEE Symposium on. IEEE, 2014.
15. Yamaguchi, Fabian, et al. "Automatic Inference of Search Patterns for Taint-Style Vulnerabilities." (2015).
16. Kirchner, Florent, et al. "Frama-C: a software analysis perspective." Formal Aspects of Computing 27.3 (2015): 573-609.

A Global Motion Compensation Algorithm Based on Sub-Block Feature Match

Jun-Yong Ma[1,2,a], Yin-Ji Hu[1,2] and Fei-Ran Jie[1,2]

[1]*Science and Technology on Electro-Optical Control Laboratory*
Luoyang, 471000, China
[2]*Luoyang Institute of Electro-optical Equipment, AVIC*
Luoyang, 471000, China
E-mail: [a]majunyongzhangduo@126.com

Motion estimation is a crucial technology in dynamic scene analysis. Firstly, it estimates the motion parameters based on sub-block feature matching. Then, the motion parameters are utilized to compensate the global motion of the background. At last, it detects the moving targets by inter-frame difference in the stabilized image sequences. The algorithm is verified in different dataset. The results are analyzed qualitatively and quantitatively, which validate the improved performance of the proposed motion estimation algorithm.

Keywords: Feature Tracking; Motion Estimation; Target Detection.

1. Introduction

As an important situational awareness system in the battlefield, the primary task of airborne downward-looking electro-optical reconnaissance system is detect effectively the long-range point targets from the complex ground background. However, flight attitude variation of the diagnostic instrument manipulator often causes the image dithering, and this decrease severely the detection and tracking precision. Therefore, the utmost assignment is to tackle the problem of motion estimation and background compensation.

In the imaging process, the imaging platform translates and rotates inevitably. The motion of the platform will cause that the image background is moving and the target position varies in different time. Usually, it is difficult to detect the targets in the complex ground background unless eliminate the global motion firstly. The global motion refers to the background motion caused by the camera motion. The global motion estimation aims to find the motion law of the background, to estimate the global motion parameters and compensate the background, thus eliminate the effect of background motion.

The current motion estimation algorithms are categorized into image feature matching method[1-2], transform domain method[3], image block method[4-5], and optical flow method[6-7] and so on.

2. Global Motion Compensation

The common global motion estimation methods conclude block matching, gray-level projection, and feature matching. Block matching is the most habitual motion vector estimation, searching rapidly and correctly the best matching block to acquire the motion vector. Although, the block matching method only estimate the translate motion vector. Rotation and scaling of the camera will result in worse matching precision even mismatching. The gray-level projection has high computation efficiency, but the acute gray variation is necessary, or else the curve variation of the gray-level projection is not evident and the result motion vector is not correct enough. The feature matching method has higher matching precision. Acquire firstly the main feature like spot feature, corner feature and so on. Then execute feature matching to compute the transformation parameters. In this study, the motion estimation is performed based on feature tracking. The block diagram of the algorithm is seen as figure 1.

Fig. 1. Block diagram of global motion compensation

2.1. *Sub-block feature detection*

SURF(Speed Up Robust Features)is an efficient and robust feature extraction algorithm proposed by Bay[10] in 2006. It resembles SIFT [11].

Because of the complex variation of scenery and the distribution difference of image texture, the distribution of extracted feature point is not uniform and present in cluster. This imposes larger error on motion parameter estimation. In this paper, image is separated into constant number of blocks. Feature points in each sub-block are sorted by response intensity. Only the feature points having larger response intensity are reserved. In addition, neighborhood selection strategy is applied to prevent more feature points from presenting in the same neighborhood. This will bring feature points with more uniform distribution.

The feature detection algorithm is described as follows:

(1) Compute Hessian matrix on every image pixel, and construct the Gaussian pyramid scale space;
(2) Perform feature detection in scale space and compute the response value of every candidate feature point.
(3) Divide the image into n×n sub-blocks.
(4) Select feature point in every sub-block. Employ mask of 3×3 or5×5 to slide in the sub-block and preserve the feature point with maximum response value.
(5) Sort the maximum response values in decreasing order, and select the first m feature points.

2.2. *Feature tracking*

To enhance real-time performance of global motion compensation, we apply feature-tracking method to track feature point in short time and acquire feature-matching correspondence. Because the time consuming of feature tracking is less than that of feature extraction, feature extraction can be executed without feature description and its matching. This reduces the parameter estimation time greatly.

We apply sparse optical flow pyramids LK [12] to track feature points.

2.3. *Motion parameter estimation*

After feature extraction and feature tracking, we can calculate motion parameters from feature matching pairs. RANSAC(Random Sample Consensus)algorithm is applied to eliminate the mismatch and filter out the global error brought by the local motion of foreground objects so that the feature matching pairs thoroughly denote the background motion.

Consider the tradeoff of the motion complexity and time efficiency, we choose affine transform model of six parameters to describe the background motion.

3. Change Detection

It is critical to evaluate the motion estimation and background compensation algorithm. Currently, the common evaluation indexes are accuracy and running speed of the algorithm. Accuracy indexes include MSE, PSNR and difference image method. The difference-image analysis mainly apply the difference image between adjacent frames to determinant the efficiency of eliminate the movement among frames. The smaller mean and variance of difference, the smaller deviation of the two images is. Actually, the difference-image analysis method is the simplification of MSE method. It also considers the difference variation of corresponding pixels. We choose difference-image analysis to evaluate the motion estimation and background compensation algorithm.

4. List Experiment and Analysis

In our experiment, VIVID dataset is used for test. The proposed feature tracking algorithm is compared with traditional feature matching method in several aspects. As a result, traditional feature matching method has less efficiency. It has less interior points involved in the model calculation, increasing the model error. In contrast, the proposed algorithm can enhance the feature matching efficiency and it has less time in computing feature descriptor.

As shown in figure 2, inter-frame difference are applied for change detection. Figure 2(b) is the image after global motion compensation. We can see from figure 2(d-e), image background are aligned and the image difference are decreased after global motion compensation. Finally, the isolated noise is eliminated by median filtering.

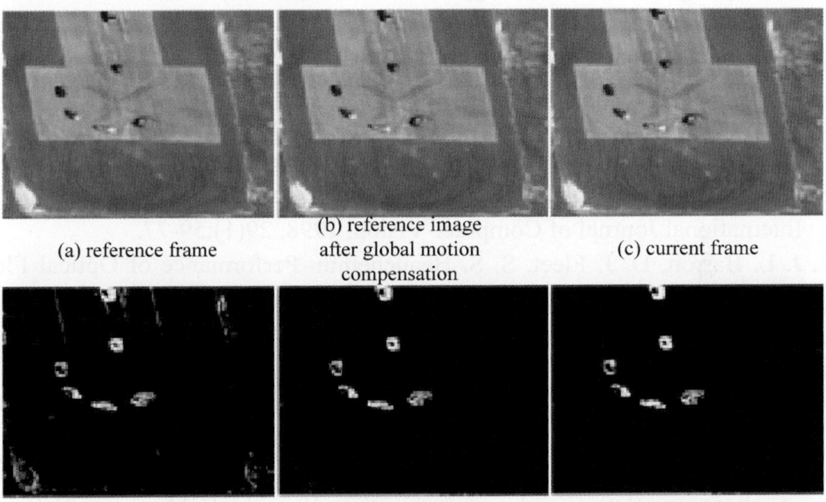

(a) reference frame; (b) reference image after global motion compensation; (c) current frame

(d) difference binary image without compensation; (e) difference binary image after compensation; (f) result after median filtering

Fig. 2. Results of change detection

5. Conclusion

Considering the efficiency and real-time characteristics of the algorithm, SURF is applied to extract features. And the inter-frame feature tracking are utilized to form feature matching pairs. It enhances the feature matching efficiency and has less time in computing feature descriptor. Resolve the motion parameters, which are utilized to compensate the global motion of the background. It eliminates the effect of ego motion and acquire more accurate motion of the moving object. Different datasets are used to test the proposed algorithm. The results are analyzed qualitatively and quantitatively, which validate the improved performance of the proposed motion estimation algorithm.

References

1. Q. Zheng, R. Chellappa. A computational vision approach to image registration[J]. IEEE Trans. on Image Processing,1993, 2:432-437.
2. Joon Ki Paik, Yong Chul Park, Dong Wook Kim. An adaptive motion decision system for digital image stabilizer based on edge pattern matching[J]. IEEE Trans. on Consumer Electronics,1992,38(3):521-530.
3. Hill L, Vlachos T. On the estimation of global motion using phase correlation for broadcast Application[J].IEEE,Proc.1999,465:725~732.
4. Ko Young-ki, Kim Hyun-gyun, Lee Jong-wook, et al. New motion estimation algorithm based on bit-plane matching and its VLSI implementation[J]. Proceedings of the IEEE Region 10 Conference,1999,2:848-851.
5. Christoph Stiller, Janusz Konrad. Estimating Motion in Image Sequences[J]. IEEE Signal Processing Magazine, July 2000.
6. Alireza Bab-Hadiashar, David Suter. Robust Optical Flow Computation[J]. International Journal of Computer Vision, 1998, 29(1):59-77.
7. J. L. Barron, D. J. Fleet, S. S. Beauchemin. Performance of Optical Flow Techniques[J]. International Journal of Computer Vision, 1994, 12(1):43-77.
8. Yong-Xiang Z, Jian W, Wei-Gong Z, et al. An improved algorithm of electronic image stability based on block matching[C]. 2010 5th IEEE Conference on Industrial Electronics and Applications. 2010: 1924-1927.
9. Liu Y, Jifu D, Li B, et al. Real-time global motion vectors estimation based on phase correlation and gray projection algorithm[C].Image and Signal Processing, 2009. CISP'09. 2nd International Congress on. IEEE, 2009: 1-5.
10. Bay H, Tuytelaars T, Van Gool L. Surf: Speeded up robust features[M]. Computer vision–ECCV 2006. Springer Berlin Heidelberg, 2006: 404-417.
11. D. Lowe. A. Distinctive Image Features from Scale-invariant Keypoints[J]. International Journal of Computer Vision, 2004, 60(2): 91-110.
12. Tomasi C, Kanade T. Detection and tracking of point features[M]. Pittsburgh: School of Computer Science, Carnegie Mellon Univ., 1991.

Vehicle Target Attitude Estimation Based on Motion Information

Duo Zhang
Science and Technology on Electro-Optical Control Laboratory
Luoyang, 471000, China
Luoyang Institute of Electro-optical Equipment, AVIC
Luoyang, 471000, China
E-mail: zhangduomajunyong@126.com

For vehicle target, such information as motion direction of target, geometry main axis, and vehicle type are critical for target identification and classification. Local feature tracking can be conducted by using KLT-algorithm in the target region with the help of local feature, and vehicle target motion direction can be estimated by point motion. First extract strong response corner point in the target region based on images after compensation for global motion, then Local feature tracking can be conducted by using KLT-algorithm in the target region, and vehicle target motion direction can be estimated by point motion. The proposed method and various main axis has been compared in the experiment, and the result shows that the proposed method has the higher accuracy.

Keywords: Main Axis Analysis; Motion Estimation; Target Identification.

1. Introduction

Automatic target identification plays an important role in the threat estimation, attacking target choice and attacking effect analysis, and also the critical link for target image interpretation. As target imaging result has the high sensitivity to target azimuth change, for specific target of each kind, a large amount of module library of different angles must be included based on target identification method of module; target image of each angle must be calculated aiming at target concept model in the database based on the identification method of model, if specific azimuth of target can be calculated in advance, which shall effectively reduce searching time for module library and calculate the times for target prediction image, so that improve efficiency of the whole automatic target identification system effectively. Therefore target image azimuth estimation is a very important issue for automatic target identification research[1-3].

Target position description can be acquired by motion target detection, for vehicle target, such information as target motion direction, geometry main axis, and vehicle type are critical for target identification and classification. Vehicle target attitude estimation can be generally classified into method based on geometry description and method based on motion information with the help of information as target mask, edge and local feature.

The thesis calculates vehicle motion attitude by using motion direction extraction method based on local feature, and makes a comparison with common main axis analysis method, the experiment result shows the method proposed by this thesis can accurately estimate the attitude for vehicle motion target.

2. Main Axis Based on PCA

Principal component analysis PCA[4] is a common data analysis method. It can save the major information of original data as a group of weighted array of optimal unit orthogonal vector by linear transformation, and make mean square error between transformed data and original data minimum. PCA saves most feature of original data, at the same time removes correlation between data. It can be used for extracting main feature vector of data, and often used for dimension reduction of high-dimensional data.

The estimation of geometry main axis is conducted by using PCA algorithm, which is to analyze main direction of target region in the two-dimension plane, which turns geometry problem into data analysis problem. Finding main axis direction of data is equivalent to find a new coordinate system, when original coordinate system data projects onto new coordinate system, actual distribution of original data still can be shown better. Here dimensionality of coordinate can be lower than that of original coordinate, and the process of projection can be understood as the process of dimension reduction.

3. Main Axis Analysis Based on RANSAC

When matching straight line by RANSAC[5], first assume to change model, then take samples at random, iterate continuously, and calculate largest consistent set conforms to this model.

4. Main Axis Analysis Based on Hough

Hough transform[6] can be used to detect a certain specific geometry object effectively, and to detect straight line, circle and ellipse by the way of voting.

Hough transform converses into point peak inside another space through specific geometry object of the coordinate space, to speculate geometry by peak statistics. Extracting target main axis by using Hough transform is conducted under the assumption of vehicle target conforms to the physical model of approximate rectangle shape. The main thought in the experiment is to detect two long straight lines on the edge of vehicle target by Hough transform, and then estimate the main axis direction of target through these two straight lines.

5. Main Axis Analysis Based on Motion Direction

Main axis analysis based on motion direction is to replace target main axis according to displacement of target in the adjacent frame. Assume that corresponding image frame of t is $\mathrm{I(x, y, t)}$, corresponding image frame of $\mathrm{t} + \Delta\mathrm{t}$ is $\mathrm{I(x, y, t + \Delta t)}$, the motion displacement between them is $\mathrm{d} = (\Delta\mathrm{x}, \Delta\mathrm{y})$,then

$$\mathrm{I(x, y, t + \Delta t) = I(x, y, t)} + \vec{\mathrm{d}} \tag{1}$$

The direction of $\vec{d}$ can be approximately equal to main axis direction of target when Δt is very small. Thus the extraction to main axis of target can be turned into motion displacement of seeking target. Because the center-of-mass position for the target of adjacent frame is generally stable, motion displacement $\vec{d}$ can be got by subtracting between the center-of-mass coordinate of previous frame and that of back frame. Due to the influence of various errors and noise during the process of target extraction, perhaps it is not so accurate to get motion displacement only by image centroid masked by target. Therefore, This research makes use of local feature, adopts KLT -algorithm to conduct Local feature tracking in the target region, and then estimates vehicle target motion direction by point motion. First extract strong response corner point by the method of Good Feature in the target region based on images after compensation for global motion, then track in the local region, and motion vector $\vec{d}$ can be calculated to analyze main axis direction of target.

6. Experimental Comparison for Main Axis Analysis

Test data in the experiment is 6148 target mask images extracted from image sequence of egtest01 in VIVID dataset. Because there is position displacement between target mask image and corresponding gray-scale artwork, the size of target mask image in the experiment shall be unified as 90*90 (the size is enough to surround target, and meanwhile avoid irrelevant interference.) for the convenience of marking in the gray-scale artwork.

(1) Main axis comparison extracted from various methods

Main axis comparison pictures are extracted by using the above methods(part frames), shown as Fig.1(a)~(c), in which the picture of every line from left to right respectively represents the main axis schematic diagram of the same target mask image extracted by the method of PCA, RANSAC, Hough and based on motion direction, and the red line is the target main axis got by algorithm.

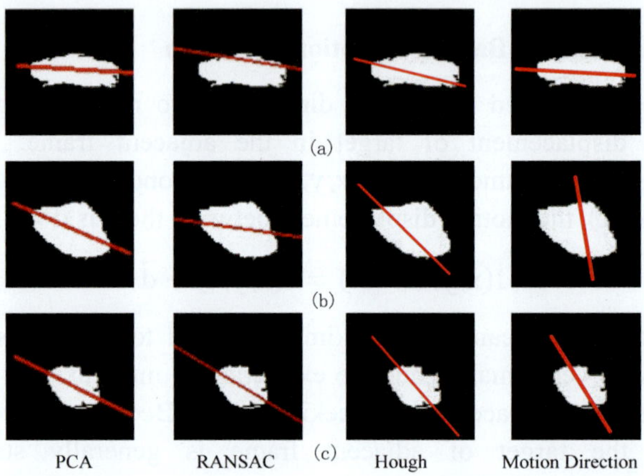

Fig. 1 Main axis comparison extracted from various methods

(2) Error deviation angle

For quantitative analysis of effect on target main axis extracted by various algorithms, the definition of error deviation angle is the difference of inclination angle between extracted target main axis and actual main axis on image coordinate system. During the experiment, all of actual main axes are marked by hand.

Take 6148 target mask images extracted from image sequence of egtest01 for example during the experiment, calculate error deviation angle of each image with various algorithm, and statistic analysis of images with scope of $0^{\circ}\sim10^{\circ}, 10^{\circ}\sim20^{\circ}, 20^{\circ}\sim30^{\circ}$, and $\geq 30^{\circ}$, as shown in Table 1.

Table 1 The percentage of error deviation angle within each scope

	PCA	RANSAC	HOUGH	Motion Direction
$0^{\circ}\sim10^{\circ}$	39.66%	25.07%	1.77%	78.53%
$10^{\circ}\sim20^{\circ}$	30.55%	16.74%	2.57%	18.49%
$20^{\circ}\sim30^{\circ}$	6.57%	13.10%	2.70%	2.42%
$\geq 30^{\circ}$	23.23%	45.09%	92.96%	0.56%

7. Conclusion

Estimate of vehicle motion can be conducted by using the method of motion information based on local feature. Local feature tracking can be conducted by using KLT-algorithm in the target region with the help of local feature, and vehicle target motion direction can be estimated by point motion. The comparison with various main axis methods has been made during the experiment, the result shows the proposed method has a higher accuracy, and it can precisely estimate the attitude of vehicle motion target.

References

1. PRINCIPE Jose C,XU Dong-xin, JOHN W F, Pose estimation in SAR using an information theoretic criterion[J], SPIE, 1998,3370(19) : 218-229.
2. DONG Yan-ting, CARIN L, Rate-distortion analysis of pose estimation via multi-aspect scattering data[J],IEEE Trans on Pattern Analysis and Machine Intelligence, 2003, 25(7): 872-883.
3. GAO Gui, HE Juan, KUANG Gang-yao, et al, A survey of target's orientation estimation in SAR image[J], Signal Processing, 2008, 24(3): 438-443.
4. Yang J, Zhang D, Frangi A F, et al. Two-dimensional PCA: a new approach to appearance-based face representation and recognition [J].Pattern Analysis and Machine Intelligence, IEEE Transactions on, 2004, 26(1):131-137.
5. Xu M and Lu J. Distributed RANSAC for the robust estimation of three-dimensional reconstruction[J]. IET Computer Vision,2012, 6(4): 324-333.
6. XU Mu, WANG Xue-song, XIAO Shun-ping, Target aspect estimation in SAR imagery based on Hough transform and major axis extraction[J], Journal of Electronics & Information Technology, 2007, 29(2):370-374.

System Contribution Rate Evaluation of the Equipment System Based on Rough Set and Neural Network

Hui-Wen Lv[a] and Wei Zhang

Department of Command, Equipment Academy
Beijing, 101416, China
E-mail: [a]oec_ljw2009@163.com

In order to estimate the system contribution rate of a certain equipment, the rough set theory and neural network are introduced into the evaluation of contribution rate of weapon equipment system, and it proposes the evaluation method of weapon system contribution rate combining with the rough set and neural network. It applies the training sample data set of rough set to simplify neural network, and eliminates the redundant data on the premise of keeping the important information. The simulation experiment shows that this method can achieve a better evaluation result. It takes the system contribution evaluation of a certain type of self-propelled artillery as an example. It constructs the evaluating model of the system contribution rate, the evaluation method of system contribution rate based on the rough set and neural network are presented and the basic steps and of the assessment method are also introduced.

Keywords: Weapon Equipment; System Contribution Rate; Rough Set; Neural network; Evaluation.

1. Introduction

In the demonstrating process of the weapon and equipment, the relevant demonstration department pays more attention to the demonstration of development model of weapon equipment and operational effectiveness of equipment system, but the index named total contribution rate of equipment system has not been got enough attentions [1, 2].The operational effectiveness evaluation is an important work in the demonstration of weapon equipment, and the evaluate conclusion is an important reference for the construction and acquisition decision of weapons and equipment [3]. The impact of the evaluation results usually includes guiding the decision makers to assess the weapon equipment project whose the evaluation conclusion of operational effectiveness is good, or convince the decision makers to give up the weapon equipment project whose the evaluation conclusion of operational effectiveness is bad. And usually the decision-making department takes the conclusion of equipment operational effectiveness as a powerful decision support and basis, and in the reality of operational effectiveness evaluation for equipment, the demonstration and research of system contribution rate of this equipment in the whole weapon and equipment system has not been done.

The contribution rate of weapon system is the contribution to the entire operation under the specified operational conditions, which should be the goals and overall requirements of demonstrating, designing, producing and using the weapons and equipment. At present, there is not much research on the system contribution rate, and even some research points are still in the blank stage. And now the commonly used assessment methods are the expert assessment method, experimental statistics, combat simulation method, index method, analytic hierarchy process and analytical method, et.al [4]

With the development of artificial intelligence technology, many researchers begin to introduce the artificial intelligence technology into the system evaluation [5,6]. At present, the domestic researchers have introduced rough set [7] and neural network [8] into the system efficiency evaluation. In the paper, it points out the weaknesses of the complex structure, low computational efficiency, low generalization ability, and it combine the neural network and the rough set to assess the contribution rate of weapon equipment system, it takes a certain type of self-propelled gun system for example. Among them, the rough set is used to reduce the unnecessary attributes, and the trained neural network is used to evaluate the system contribution rate of the self-propelled gun [9].

The simulation results show that this method is feasible and effective, and it has positive guidance function to the system contribution rate evaluation of weapon system and the development of weapon system.

2. Working Principle of Rough Set and Neural Network

2.1. *Rough set theory*

The rough set theory is a new mathematical tool for dealing with fuzzy and uncertain knowledge, which is proposed by Poland mathematician. Pawlak Z., The main idea is based on the non distinguishable relation by introducing the upper approximation set and the lower approximation set to describe a set;

Under the premise of keeping the classification ability of the information system, the knowledge reduction is carried out, and the decision or classification rules for the classification of the problem are finally obtained. The rough set theory compared to the others to deal with imprecise problems have obvious advantages, which is mainly seen in without any data set of prior information, the rough set can objectively deal with the uncertainty and from massive historical data discover the implicit knowledge to reveal potential rules.

A knowledge representation system can be viewed as a relational data table. Its formalization definition is as: Set s= (U, R, V, f) as a knowledge expression system, Among them: the field U={x1, x2, x3,..., n x} is a non empty finite set; R is a non null attribute set, R includes the condition attribute D and the result attribute C, that is $C \bigcup D = R$;V represents the range of properties a R; f :U×R→V is a single shot information function, which is the attribute value of any element in the specified domain. This definition makes it be easy for the knowledge of the object to be described in the form of a data table, which is called the knowledge representation system.

2.2. *Neural network theory*

Artificial Neural Network(ANN) is a description of the first order characteristic of the human brain system. Simply speaking, it is a mathematical model, which can be achieved through the electronic circuits and can also be simulated by the computer program. It is a research method of artificial intelligence. The neural network has its unique advantages in solving the complex nonlinear problems such as the effectiveness evaluation and system contribution rate of weapon system. The network model is as shown in Figure 1. It need to take the tactical and technical indicators whose contribution is larger as the input of the neural network and the system contribution rate of equipment as the output of the neural network.

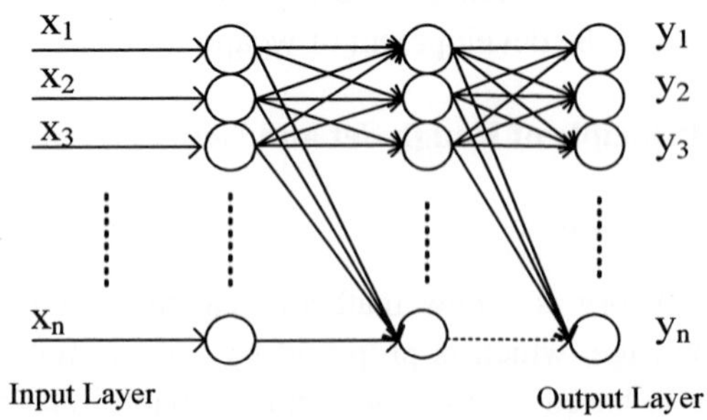

Fig. 1. Artificial neural network diagram

It uses the enough samples to train the network, through the dynamic adaptive adjustment, the weight and threshold value belonging to the trained network is the internal representation of the nonlinear relationship between the system contribution rate and the characteristics parameters. The Neural network in dealing with this problem has a unique advantage, and it mainly reflects as follows: first of all, the combat system is generally nonlinear system, which is not conducive to the establish the mathematical model, and the neural network don't need to establish the mathematical model, it just need to put on the collated data into the network, the network will establish the model through training to find out the law existing in the data. Secondly, the fault-tolerant ability is strong. Because in the process of evaluation of contribution rate of equipment system, the collected large amounts of data have a lot of noise, and the neural network algorithm compared with other evaluation methods can tolerate the noise interference to get the ideal evaluation results.

3. The Evaluation Model Based on the Rough Set Neural Network

3.1. *Data preprocessing*

The finite discretization data is the base of rough set analysis, and the original data contains a large number of continuous data in the engineering field .Therefore, before using the rough to reduction, it must first do the discrete normalization processing for the data, whose purpose is to reduce the loss of useful information in massive data as less as possible, while reducing system spatial dimension and the species of index. Now the discrete methods mainly includes the interval division method, S method, L method and equal frequency division, but no matter what kind of discrete method must ensure the dimension of discrete data as less as possible, each quality has the kinds of attribute values as less as possible and the loss of data information as less as possible.

3.2. *Rule extraction*

In the whole knowledge expression system, all attributes are not equally important, there may be a large number of redundant of attributes, so the attribute reduction is essential. However, the minimal reduction attribute of the conditional attribute C is not the only one, there may be a number of attribute sets, and the minimum attribute set taking problem has been proved to be a NP problem. In the practical engineering field, it only need to figure out the minimal reduction attribute set with practical application. The rules may too much or too little directly affect the accuracy of evaluation results of neural network. In the paper, it takes the table logical data analysis tool ROSETTA based on the rough set theory framework in paper [9] to get the most simple rules, whose decision rule extraction steps are as follows:

(1)Completion of the data.

(2) Discretizating of the data.

(3) The attribute reduction.

(4)Generating of the rule

(5)Reducing of the rule

3.3. *Evaluation model*

The main idea of assessment method of network security situation based on the rough set neural network is as follow: first, the intrusion detection data collected is pretreated to extract the useful data set to obtain the decision table of original information. Second, the original data set is discredited and normalized, and the original data are divided into two groups, one group is the training sample data, the other is the test sample data. Third, based on the attribute reduction ability of rough set theory, it can obtain the minimal decision rule set with complete original sample feature, and the rule number of neural network is determined by using the simplest index rule. Fourth, the rough set neural network is trained by the training data, and the evaluation indexes corresponding to minimum rule set can be obtained, and the input node number of the system is optimized.

Finally, it determines the network structure, relevant membership function and inference rules of input and output of evaluation model, and the test sample data are input to the evaluation system, through the rule inference made up by the rough set theory and professional knowledge to determine the running status of current network security.

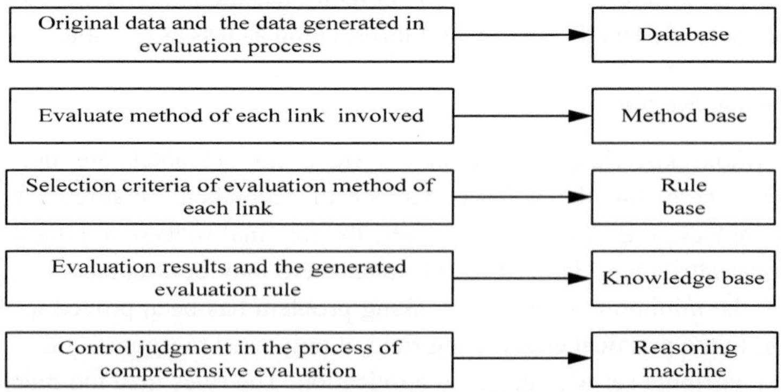

Fig. 2. Comprehensive evaluation system based on rough set and artificial neural network

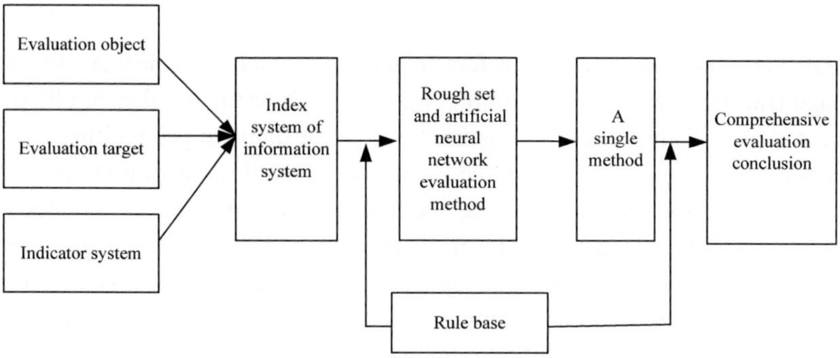

Fig. 3. Evaluation system operating mode based on rough set and artificial neural network

4. Evaluation on the Contribution Rate of a Certain Type of Self Propelled Artillery Weapon Equipment System

4.1. *Analysis of evaluation index*

4.1.1. *Operational efficiency index*

The Combat efficiency index mainly refers to the indexes which can measure the attack combat time, defense combat time and meet demand of time window, such as the suppressing enemy airport time, suppressing enemy air defense fire time, suppressing enemy carrier or land-based radar time, allied maneuver (boost) time, allied fighting window length .Selecting a baseline level (average or minimum value) of the operation time (including motor (boost) time and operational window time, it sees the operational time under the baseline level as a reference benchmark, then the operation time supported by evaluated weapon equipment is compared with the reference benchmark.

4.1.2. *The indicators of operational effectiveness*

The operational effect index mainly refers to the indexes which can measure the victories, the task completion rate or the task completion effectiveness. In the paper, it emphasizes the operational support effect of evaluated weapon equipment, such as the probability, the number and percentage damaging the enemy various types of targets or equipment, the casualties, captured personnel, destruction equipment and assets of the enemy, or the decline degree of connectivity, robustness and fragile, survivable of enemy combat system.

4.1.3. *Index of operational cost*

Operational cost index mainly refers to indexes which can measure the battle damage (ratio), price index of completing task, such as the number of allied with various types of ammunition consumption, battle damage probability quantity, percentage of goals or equipment, allied casualties, captured personnel, destruction equipment and assets, or the decline degree of connectivity, robustness and fragile, survivable of allied combat system etc. In the paper, it takes the battle self-propelled gun as example, and it only compared with the contribution rate of weapon equipment system of self-propelled artillery from the performance, and the following evaluation index system is formed as shown in figure 3. Real contribution rate of the weapon system is closely related to the training, security, personnel morale and so on [11].

According to the above evaluation index system, according to the rough set theory, we set up a system as for $T=\langle U,R\rangle$, the object set $U=\{D1,D2,D3,......,M122,M152\}$ represents the eight kinds of self-propelled artillery set, the attribute set $\mathrm{R}=\mathrm{C}\bigcup\mathrm{D}$, the condition attributes set $\mathrm{C}=\{\mathrm{C1},\mathrm{C2},\mathrm{C3},.....\mathrm{C10}\}$ represents the initial velocity, direct distance, penetrating target thickness and other factors respectively, the decision attribute set $\mathrm{D}=\{\mathrm{g}\}$ represents the final total score. The raw data are as shown in table 1.

Table 1. The raw data of self-propelled guns

Model / Attribute	D1	D2	D3	D4	D5	D6	M122	M152
C1	2000	1800	1750	1500	1300	1450	1500	1650
C2	2800	1800	1750	1500	1300	1450	1500	1650
C3	2000	1800	1750	1500	1300	1450	1500	1650
C4	2000	1800	1750	1500	1300	1450	1500	1650
C5	2000	1800	1750	1500	1300	1450	1500	1650
C6	2000	1800	1750	1500	1300	1450	1500	1650
C7	2000	1800	1750	1500	1300	1450	1500	1650
C8	2000	1800	1750	1500	1300	1450	1500	1650
C9	2000	1800	1750	1500	1300	1450	1500	1650
C10	2000	1800	1750	1500	1300	1450	1500	1650
g	0.88	0.8	0.76	0.6	0.45	0.33	0.6	0.65

Table 2. Data after discretization processing

Model / Attribute	D1	D2	D3	D4	D5	D6	M122	M152
C1	0.5	1	2	0.5	1	2	2	1
C2	1	1	1	1	2	1	1	2
C3	2	0.5	1	1	2	1	1	2
C4	1	1	1	1	0.5	1	1	0.5
C5	0.5	0.5	1	2	1	2	0.5	0.5
C6	1	0.5	0.5	2	2	1	0.5	1
C7	1	1	0.5	1	1	0.5	1	2
C8	2	2	2	0.5	2	2	2	2
C9	0.5	2	2	0.5	0.5	0.5	1	1
C10	1	1	2	2	0.5	2	2	2
g	2	1	0.5	0.5	1	2	1	1

4.2. *Data discretization*

The Rough set theory is an effective tool to deal with the discrete attributes. Unfortunately, it cannot directly deal with the continuous attributes. Therefore, through using rough set to deal with the decision table with continuous attributes, it is necessary to discrete the continuous attribute value. The discrete process of continuous attribute value directly influences the result of rough set theory analysis, and it has been widely recognized. In the existing research paper, there are several methods to deal with continuous attributes, such as the isometric method, S method, H method, L method, etc.. In this paper, we try to use the equal frequency method to discrete the original data in the table. After the discretization process, the knowledge expression system is obtained, as shown in table 2.

4.3. *Reduction of attribute*

The attribute reduction is a very important research topic in the rough set theory. In general, the attributes in the knowledge base are not equally important, and even some of them are redundant, which is not conducive to do the correct and concise decision. The attribute reduction requires keeping the classification ability of the knowledge base to delete the unnecessary, unimportant or irrelevant attributes. According to the attribute reduction steps of rough set theory, here it first delete the duplicate object and attribute value. D4 and D5 repeat, so it delete D5 and then doing classification, the genetic algorithm is adopted to reduction, getting rid of the redundant attributes. After Reduction, we can get the set for {C2, C3, C4, C5, C7, C9, C10}. It gets rid of the redundant attributes of {C1, C6, C8}, which greatly reduces the input dimension of the following neural networks.

4.4. *Neural network prediction of the reduced data*

The minimal conditional attribute set and the corresponding original data which are obtained by reduction are used to reform a new learning sample set. The sample removes all unnecessary condition attributes and it only retains the important attributes which can impact classification. it randomly selects D1, D2, D3, D4, M122, M152 as the training samples and the rest of the M5 and M6 as the prediction sample. The BP network is used to predict the performance of the network. The structure of the network uses 3-layer BP network of $N*(2N+1)*M$ M as the state classifier based on the Kolmogorov theorem. Among them, N represents the number of components of the input feature vector, M indicates the total number of output state categories. Then the input sample is 12 dimensional vector, so N =12, the middle layer has 25 neurons (it can be adjusted according to the generalization ability of network in the training process).

5. Conclusion

The comprehensive evaluation of contribution rate of weapon equipment system of weapon system is a complicated research topic, evaluating contribution rate of weapon equipment system of weapon system can provide a scientific basis for the rational development and planning the weapon system, which has the important theory significance and practical value.

Setting the rough set as the front system of BP neural network, the initial structure of the BP neural network is simplified, through the attribute reduction, it reduces the system index and the number of samples in the model evaluation and improves the efficiency of assessment; at the same time the method can obviously improve the prediction accuracy than simply using BP neural network. The assessment model of contribution rate of weapon system based on rough set and neural network effectively combines the advantages of two kinds of intelligent methods of the rough set and neural network, which is a new attempt of the comprehensive evaluation of contribution rate of weapon system.

References

1. [1] Gao jian, Tong Ming-an. *Extracting decision rules for cooperative team air combat based on rough set theory.* Chinese Journal of Aeronautics, 2003, 16(4): pp.233-228.
2. [2] Liu Xiaowu, Wang Huiqiang, Yu Hongwu, et al. *Quantitative Awareness of Network Security Situation Based on Fusion.* Journal of Jilin University: Engineering and Technology Edition, 2013, vol.43, no.6, pp.1650-1657.
3. [3] Huang C C, Tseng T L B, Fan Y N, et al. *Alternative Rule Induction Methods Based on Incremental Object Using Rough Set Theory.* Applied Soft Computing, 2013, vol.13, no.1, pp.372-389.
4. [4] Jan G B, Bazan-Socha S, Buregwa-Czuma S, et al. *Classifiers Based on Data Sets and Domain Knowledge*: A Rough Set Approach. Intelligent Systems Reference Library, 2013, vol.43, no.2, pp.93-136.
5. [5]Xie Lixia,Wang Yachao, Yu Jinbo. *Network Security Situation Awareness Based on Neural Networks.* Journal of Tsinghua University: Natural Science Edition, 2013, vol.53, no.12, pp.1750-1760.
6. [6] Wang Hong, Gong Zhenghu. Algorithm Based on Entropy for Finding Critical Traffic Matrices. Journal of Software, 2009,vol.20, no.5, pp.1377-1383.
7. [7] Zhuo Ying, Gong Chunye, *Gong Zhenghu. Research and Implementation of Network Transmission Situation Awareness.* Journal on Communications, 2010, vol.31, no.9, pp.54-63.
8. [8] Wang Gang, Zhang Zhiyu. *Rough Set Method Combined with BP Neural Network Data Fusion.* Journal of Xi'an University of Technology, 2006, vol.22, no.3, pp. 311-314.
9. [9] Gai Weilin, Xin Dan, Wang Lu, et al. *Data Fusion and Decision Methods of Situation Awareness.* Computer Engineering,2014, vol.40, no.5, pp.21-26.

An Improved Apriori Algorithm for Mining of Association Rules

Ji-Shuai Li[a] and Su-Juan Qin[b]

State Key Laboratory of Networking and Switching Technology, Beijing University of Posts and Telecommunications
Beijing, 100876, China
E-mail: [a]sky_lee1990@163.com, [b]qsujuan@bupt.edu.cn

The association rule mining is an important topic in the data mining. Association rule mining aims to find rules in the transaction database with the minimum support and minimum confidence which are user given. Apriori algorithm is one of the most influential algorithms for mining Boolean association rules, but it is ineffective because of large candidates and ineffective calculation for support. In order to find all the frequent item sets from the transaction database efficiently and quickly, an improved Apriori algorithm is presented to solve the bottleneck problems of the traditional Apriori algorithm. First of all, frequent item format is necessary, aiming to reduce the rate of memory occupancy in the process of frequent item generation, and then convert the storage structure of transaction records. Finally, it divides frequent 1-item into different groups in order to implement parallel computing. The experiment results show the improved Apriori algorithm can improve the efficiency of the original algorithm effectively.

Keywords: Association Rule; Apriori Algorithm; Storage Structure; Parallel Computing.

1. Introduction

Association Rules[1] plays an important role in data mining, is used to mining relationships from a large amount of data between valuable items. Association Rules is widely applied in the consumer market price analysis[2], analysis of customer spending habits and other fields. Apriori Algorithm[3] is one of the most popular algorithm in data mining for learning the concept of association rules, was proposed in 1993 by R. Agrawal. It is the recursion algorithm based on two phase frequency set.

Traditional Apriori algorithm has two fatal bottlenecks[2], one is a great.I/O operations are needed and another is a lot of candidates of frequent item sets may be produced. For the above mentioned problems, lots of algorithms were proposed in later. R.Agarwal puts forward AprioriTid[3] and AprioriHybird algorithms[3]. AprioriTid algorithm will calculate the support degree of frequent item sets while scanning. AprioriHybird is a combination of Apriori algorithm and AprioriTid algorithm. Mahesh Balaji and G Subrahmanya VRK Rao[4] proposed Adaptive Implementation of Apriori Algorithm for Retail Scenario in Cloud Environment which solves the time consuming problem for retail transactional databases. Yanbin Ye, Chia Chu Chiang[5] proposed a parallel Apriori algorithm for frequent item sets mining. Feng Wang, Yong-Hua Li[6] improved Apriori algorithm based on the matrix by using the "AND operation" to deal with the matrix to generate the largest frequent itesets. Honglie Yu, Jun Wenb[7] proposed an algorithm based on matrix storage and using Hadoop parallel computing.

On the basis of above algorithms, We improved the traditional algorithm by data formatting, storage structure transformation, concurrent computing and was proved efficiently by experiment and results.

The rest of the paper is organized as follows: in 2nd section, the concept and description of the improved algorithm is introduced; in 3rd section, an analysis of the efficiency of the improved algorithm by experiment; in 4th section, a conclusion is made.

2. Improved Apriori Algorithm

2.1. *The notion of the improved algorithm*

The improved algorithm puts forward in this paper mainly optimize the traditional Apriori algorithm through three aspects:

(1) The preprocessing of transaction datasets. For a given transaction, if the format of item was not shown by integer, normalize it using consecutive numbers and store it by bit set.

(2) The conversion of storage format. Traditional algorithm storage transaction records by using format like (Tid: A, B, C, D, E)[8], but the improved Apriori algorithm storage transaction records by the format like (A: Tid1, Tid2, Tid3).

(3) Grouping and parallel. The transformation of storage format reduce the cost of computing time on the one hand, and on the other hand make it possible to parallel operation in generation process of frequent items.

2.2. *The description of the improved algorithm*

The description of the improved algorithm is as follows, see Figure 1.

```
Improved Apriori Algorithm

Input:
    Transaction database D and min-support minsup
Output:
    All the frequent item sets in database D
Scan D
If item in D is Integer type
   Continue
Else
   Convert item into presentation of Integer type
Generate L1 and convert item storage format
L1 = {Item1:[Tid1,Tid2 ...],Item2:[Tid1,Tid3…] ...}
Divide L1 into different group
Parallel generate Lk according to Lk-1
  While len(Gi) > 1:
     Itemk = Itemi join Itemj
     TidSet(Itemk) = TidSet(Itemi) ∩ TidSet(Itemj)
     Support(Itemk) = len(TidSet(Itemk))
End
```

Fig. 1. The description of the improved algorithm

Suppose a database D have eight transaction records as shown in Table 1.

Table 1. Transaction database D

TID	Item set
1	A, B, E
2	B, D
3	B, C
4	A, B, D
5	A, C
6	B, C
7	A, C
8	A, B, C, E

Assuming the minimum support degree is 20%. The process of frequent item mining is as follows:

Step 1: Scan transaction database D to find frequent item set L_1 and store them by way as shown in Table 2.

Step 2: Transform item representation to storage and compute by using bit set, for example, transform [A, B, C, D, E] to [1, 2, 3, 4, 5]. Because the step is acting on algorithm implementation, so we use the original format.

Table 2. L_1

Item	TidSet	Support
A	1, 4, 5, 7, 8	5
B	1, 2, 3, 4, 6, 8	6
C	3, 5, 6, 7, 8	5
D	2, 4	2
E	1, 8	2

Step 3: According to the rule of frequent item set L_2, group L_1 as follows.

G_1: [A, B, C, D, E]

G_2: [B, C, D, E]

G_3: [C, D, E]

G_4: [D, E]

Therefore,

TidSet(AB) = TidSet(A) ∩ TidSet(B)

Support(A, B) = Len(TidSet(A,B))

Step 4: The complete frequent items mining process of G_1 as shown Figure 2, and other group is similar, not burdensome.

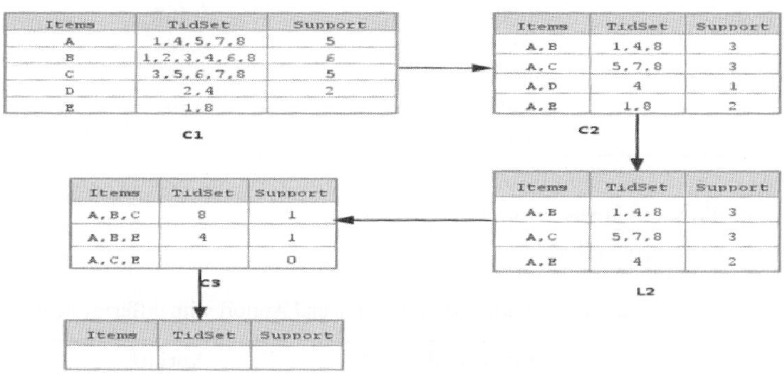

Fig. 2. Mining process of G_1

3. Case Analysis

The FP-Growth[9] is an association algorithm put forward by Han based on depth-first and greatly improved the efficiency compared with traditional frequent item sets mining algorithm. In this paper, we will compare the improved Apriori algorithm with FP-Growth on size of transaction, size of item sets and support degree to verify the feasibility and efficiency of algorithm.

Case 1:

Condition: Item = 100, Support = 20%, Unit of transaction: K, Unit of time: S

The result is shown in Table 3.

Tab. 3. The execution time of FP-Growth and Apriori with different transaction records

Trans	FP-Growth	Apriori
60	1.172	0.362
80	1.272	0.41
100	1.946	0.472
200	1.838	0.77
300	5.388	1.06
400	7.988	1.38
500	11.09	1.65

Case 2:

Condition: Item=100, Trans=200K

The result is shown in Table 4.

Tab. 4. The execution time of FP-Growth and Apriori with different support

Support	FP-Growth	Apriori
20	1.95	0.468
30	1.919	0.624
40	1.903	0.468
50	1.887	0.484
60	1.903	0.452
70	1.95	0.39
80	1.935	0.468

Case 3:

Condition: Trans = 300K, Support=30%

The result is shown in Table 5.

Tab. 5. The execution time of FP-Growth and Apriori with different item

Item	FP-Growth	Apriori
100	1.934	0.468
200	1.856	0.562
300	1.966	0.842
400	1.887	0.655
500	1.888	0.67
600	1.95	0.702
700	1.763	0.609

4. Conclusions

In this paper, we improve the traditional Apriori algorithm for mining association rules from three aspects. First, normalizes items using consecutive numbers at first to reduce the rate of memory usage in generation process of candidate datasets. Next, convert storage transaction records to reduce scan times for generate frequent items and computing support degree. At last, group items and make it possible to parallel operations to improve execution efficiency. Experiments show that our improvement strategy is feasible and effective.

Acknowledgments

This work is supported by NSFC (Grant Nos. 61300181, 61502044), the Fundamental Research Funds for the Central Universities (Grant No. 2015RC23).

References

1. Agrawa R, Srikant R, Fast algorithms for mining association rules in large database, In: VLDB, p.497-99,1994.
2. Mohammed Al-Maolegi, Bassam Arkok, An Improved Apriori Algorithm for Assocaition Rules, IJNLC, Vol.3, No.1,2014.
3. F.H.AL-Zawaidah, Y. H. Jbara, and A.L.Marwam, An Improved Algorithm for Mining Association Rules in Large Databases, Vol.1,7,311-316,2016.
4. Balaji Mahesh, VRK Rao G Subrahmanya, An Adaptive Implementation Case Study of Apriori Algorithm for a Retail Scenatio in a Cloud Envrioment, pp.625-629,2013 13th IEEE/ACM International Symposium on Cluster, Cloud, and Gridc Computing ,2013.
5. Akshita Bhandari, Ashutosh Gupta, Debasis Das, Improvised Aprori algorithm using frequent pattern tree for real time applications in data mining, Science Direct, Procedia Engineering 46 644-651, 2015.
6. Tassa T, Secure Mining of Association Rules in Horizontally Distributed Database, in IEEE Transaction on knowledge and data Engineering, Vol 26, No.4, April 2014.
7. Honglie Yu, Jun Wen, Hongmei Wang and Li Jun, An Improved Apriori Algorithm Based On the Boolean Matrix and Hadoop, Science Direct, Procedia Engineering 15 1827-1831, 2011.
8. Rao S, Gupta R, Implementing Improved Algorithm Over Apriori Data Mining Association Rule Algorithm, International Journal of Computer Science and Technology, pp.489-493, Mar. 2012.
9. Rui Chang, Zhiyi Liu, An improved Apriori algorithm, Electronics and Opttoelectronics,2011 International Conference, vol 1, pp. V1, V1-476-478,29-31 July 2011.

Decision-Making on the optimal Evasion Course of Escort Fleet's Collision Avoidance

Shu-Xiao Wang[a], Ke Wang[b] and Qian Huang[c,*]

Dept. of Navigation, Dalian Naval Academy
Dalian 116018, China
E-mail: [a]wangshx2006@sina.com, [b]123680323@qq.com, [c]finalfanst@163.com

In order to insure the validity of the escort fleet's actions for collision avoidance at sea, it is important that considering every vessel's requirement when adopt the optimal evasion course, and the fleet should keep original formation as far as possible. The paper introduces the basic principle of the fleet's relative motion, then imports the conceptions of Formation Relative Movement Belt (*FRMB*), and uses the method to calculate the evasion course that refers to the datum vessel's motion and the *FRMB*. A method is put forward to obtain the Distance of Closest Point of Approach (*DCPA*) and the Distance of Safe Point of Approach (*DSPA*), and a mathematical model is presented to decision-making of the optimal evasion course that fills the whole formation's requirement. The results obtained lay a foundation for escort fleet's collision avoidance.

Keywords: Evasion Course; Formation Relative Movement Belt (*FRMB*); Escort Fleet; Distance of Closest Point of Approach (*DCPA*); Distance of Safe Point of Approach (*DSPA*).

1. Introduction

A large scale convey fleet of naval ship is composed usually in the escort mission, for the safety of the fleet and to maintain the necessary ability of attack and defense and coordinated action. All ships in fleet should sail coordinated and keep original formation pattern as far as possible to avoid unnecessary disorder or to bring accident to the system of attack and defense. Zou[1] discussed the security related situation during the escort mission in the maritime, summed up security experience in the escort mission in the maritime and put

*Corresponding author.

forward the shortcomings. In this paper, we consider the formation as an integral whole when choosing an evasion course, which is plotted by the guide ship and satisfy the evasion demand of the whole formation. All the guard ships should follow the instructions of the guide ship.

2. Description and Modeling of the Problem

2.1. *Description of relative movement*

The own ship is regarded as an immobile point in radar plotting, and other ship moves on the relative course line relative to own ship. Or we can also regard the other ship as an immobile point and own ship moves on the relative course line[2]. In the analysis of formation movement, every ship in the formation is an own ship. So in order to describe the problem, the latter method is adopted.

As shown in figure. 1, own ship locates at point M_0, measures a ship locates at T_0. Two ships all move with fixed course and speed. If we take other ship as a stationary point, own ship's relative course and relative speed can be calculated by the speed triangle equations[3]:

$$\begin{cases} V_r = \sqrt{V_m^2 + V_t^2 - 2V_m \cdot V_t \cdot \cos(C_m - C_t)} \\ C_r = C_t \pm \left[180 - \cos^{-1}\left(\dfrac{V_r^2 + V_t^2 - V_m^2}{2V_rV_t}\right) \right] \end{cases} \tag{1}$$

Where C_m is own ship's course; V_m is own ship's speed; C_t is other ship's course; V_t is other ship's speed; C_r is own ship's relative course to the other ship; V_r is own ship's relative speed to the other ship.

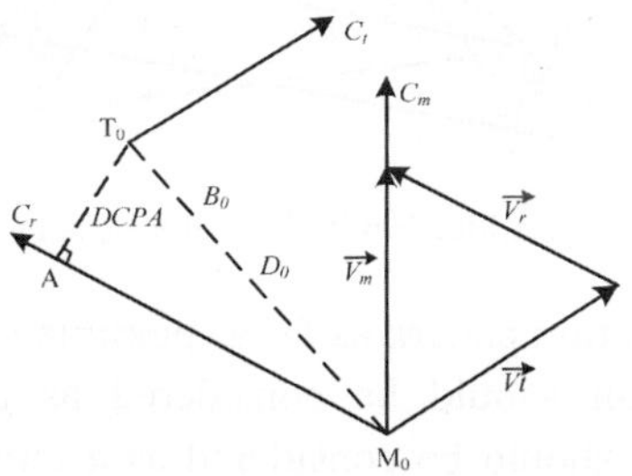

Fig. 1. Relative motion posture between ships of orientation and constant speed

If we regard the own ship as a stationary point, the other ship's relative speed to the own ship equals to the V_r in the Eq. (1), but the relative course differs by 180° from the C_r in the Eq. (1).

2.2. *Calculation model of DCPA*

According to the principle of relative movement, point A in figure 1 is the closest point of approaching (CPA), the length of T_0A is the *DCPA*[2]:

$$DCPA = D_0 \cdot \sin(B_0 - C_r) \tag{2}$$

Where B_0 is the bearing of other ship; D_0 is the distance between two ships; C_r is own ship's relative course. If *DCPA*=0, other ship will collide with own ship; If *DCPA*>0, other ship will pass right side of own ship's relative course line; If *DCPA*<0, other ship will pass left side of own ship's relative course line.

2.3. *Calculation model of FRMB*

In figure 2, two ships compose a single column sailing with course C_m and speed V_m, the leading ship locates at M_{10}, the rear ship locates at M_{20}, distance between ships is D_1. The other ship coming from point T_0, with course C_t and speed V_t. Known from the principle of relative movement, relative courses of all ships in formation are C_r, T_0A is *DCPA* of the leading ship, T_0F is *DCPA* of the rear ship. These two *DCPAs* are not equal, so the movements of collision avoidance will not be same, which means the formation pattern will not be maintained well.

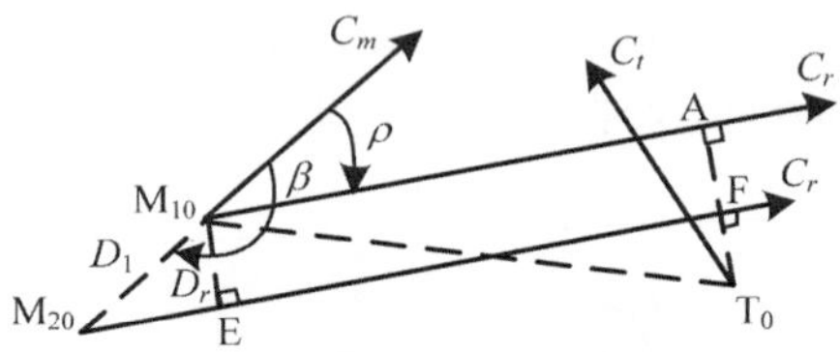

Fig. 2. Fleet's relative motion posture

So to keep the formation pattern as far as possible in the collision avoidance maneuver, the formation should be considered as an integral whole. The movement of formation should be considered as a movement of a belt having certain breadth. Then the belt can be named *FRMB* (Formation Relative Movement Belt) [4,5]. As shown in figure 2, the *FRMB* is the zone between the relative course lines passed M_{10} and M_{20}, and its width is:

$$D_r = D_1 \cdot \sin(\beta - \rho) \tag{3}$$

Where D_l is the formation length; β is the angle between guide's course line and formation line ; ρ is the angel between own ship's course line and the relative course line. If $D_r<0$, *FRMB* diverge to left side of the guide's course; If $D_r>0$, *FRMB* diverge to right side of the guide's course line.

3. Solving Algorithm of Formation Evasion Course

3.1. *Calculation of formation DCPA*

All ships in formation should be taken into account when estimate the collision situation between the other ship and the formation. Theoretically, *DPCA* of each ship can be plotted respectively, and the minimum *DCPA* can be taken as the formation *DCPA*. But that will bring discordance to formation, so the formation *DCPA* should be calculated by the width of *FRMB*.

$DCPA_2$ of the rear ship can be calculated by the following equation:

$$DCPA_2 = DCPA_1 - D_r \tag{4}$$

Where $DCPA_1$ is the *DCPA* of the leading ship; D_r is the width of *FRMB*.

The formation *DCPA* should choose the minimum absolutely value of $DCPA_1$ and $DCPA_2$. If the signs of $DCPA_1$ and $DCPA_2$ are opposite, the other ship will pass through the formation, and the formation *DCPA* should be 0.

$$DCPA=\begin{cases} 0 & DCPA_1 \text{ different name as } DCPA_2 \text{ or } DCPA_1 = 0 / DCPA_2 = 0 \\ DCPA_1 & DCPA_1 \text{ same name as } DCPA_2 \text{ and } |DCPA_1| < |DCPA_2| \\ DCPA_2 & DCPA_1 \text{ same name as } DCPA_2 \text{ and } |DCPA_1| > |DCPA_2| \end{cases} \tag{5}$$

Formation should carry out evade maneuver according to the COLREGS (Convention on the International Regulation for the Preventing Collision at Sea) [6], when the formation *DCPA* does not satisfy the safety conditions.

3.2. *Calculation of DSPA*

Three elements should be confirmed firstly in radar plotting[2]: time of evasion maneuver, amplitude of evasion maneuver, result of evasion maneuver. Result of evasion maneuver can be expressed by the *DSPA* (distance of safe point of approach) after taking the evasion maneuver. The amplitude is decided by the *DSPA* defined beforehand.

The *DSPA* should be more than 2 n mile according to the COLREGS[6]. So based on the theory mentioned above, the defined *DSPA* should satisfy the demand of formation. Taking the calculation principle of formation *DCPA*, the leading ship *DSPA* can be calculated by the following equation:

$$DSPA_1 = \begin{cases} DSPA_0 & (DSPA_0 \text{ different name as } D_r) \\ DSPA_0 + D_r & (DSPA_0 \text{ same name as } D_r) \end{cases} \tag{6}$$

If *DSPA*>0, other ship will pass right side of own ship's relative course line;
If *DSPA*<0, other ship will pass left side of own ship's relative course line.

3.3. *Calculation of evasion course*

The principle of calculate the evasion course at designated moment is:

Step1: Confirm the formation $DSPA_0$,then calculate the evasion course of the leading ship with the method of single ship evasion maneuver[3];

Step2: Calculate D_r after altering course according to C_{m1} and Eq. (3);

Step3: Calculate the $DSPA_1$ of the leading ship according to Eq. (6).

Step4: Calculate the evasion course C_{m2} of the leading ship, which is also taken as the formation evasion course, according to Eq. (7).

$$\begin{cases} C_r = B_1 \pm \arcsin\left(\left|\frac{DSPA_0}{D_1}\right|\right) \\ C_{m1} = C_r \pm \arcsin\left[\frac{V_t}{V_m} \cdot \sin\left(\left|C_r - C_t\right|\right)\right] \end{cases} \tag{7}$$

Strictly, D_r used in calculating $DSPA_1$ should be calculated by C_{m2}, since the difference between C_{m1} and C_{m2} is less, so error of the width of RFMB can be ignored.

4. Scenario and Analysis of Result

A single column is composed of three ships, distance between ships is 5 cab, course is 050°.0, speed is 12 kn. The leading ship gets a series of data with radar:

t=1200 B_0=030°.0 D_0=90Cab; t=1206 B_1=030°.0 D_1=70Cab

Formation plans to alter course at 1209 to evade the target ship. The process of evasion maneuver is shown in figure 3, taking the leading ship as stationary point. C_{r1} and C_{r2} are the relative course lines of the other ship relative to the leading ship.

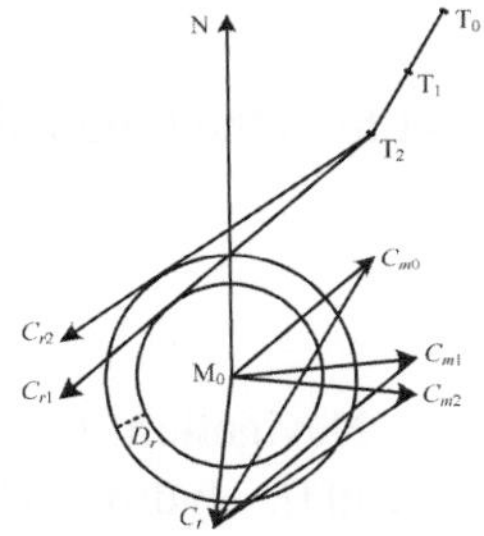

Fig. 3. Plotting course of vessel fleet's collision avoidance

Step1: Plotting the other ship's positions at time 1200(T_0) and 1206(T_1),then calculate the C_t =185°.0, V_t =9.6kn, D_r =-3.4Cab,formation $DCPA$=0. Based on rules of COLREGS [6], the other ship should evade to starboard and meet us port to port. To coordinate with the other ship, our formation alter course to starboard and make the formation $DSPA_0$ = -2.0 n mile;

Step2: Plotting the position of the other ship at time 1209(T_2): B_1 =030°.0, D_1=50Cab;

Step3: Calculate the evasion course of the leading ship according to $DSPA_0$ and Eq.(7): C_{m1} =083°.5;

Step4: Calculate the D_r according to C_{m1} and Eq.(3), and the $DSPA_1$ according to Eq.(6): $D_r = -6$ Cab , $DSPA_1 = -2.6$ n mile ;

Step5: Calculate the formation evasion course according to $DSPA_1$ and Eq.(7): C_{m2} =094°.5。

From the result of plotting, $DCPA$ of the rear ship is only 1.4 n mile after altering to evasion course 083°.5. So evasion course 094°.5 should be taken to guarantee all ships in formation pass the other ship beyond 2 n mile.

5. Conclusion

The paper proposed a method of calculating the evasion course based on width of *FRMB*, to confirm the effectiveness of evasion maneuver of the escort fleet, and to make sure the evasion maneuver satisfy the evasion demand of formation. This method, has been proved by practice, can be used in various of situation at sea. Meanwhile, the evasion maneuver mathematical model, which can be used in computer programming, can improve the degree of automatic evasion operation. Nonetheless, the method plotting the variation of the situation during the altering process need to be studied further.

Acknowledgment

This work is supported by project from the National Natural Science Foundation of China (Grant No. 60572160).

References

1. Fuquan Zou. Analysis on Navigation Guarantee Work in Escorting Operation in the Gulf of Aden[J]. Hydrographic Surveying and Charting. 2011,31(6):1-4.(In Chinese)
2. Jianguo Zhu, Jianjun Wong. Radar Observation and lotting[M].Wuhan: Wuhan University of Technology Press， 2010. (In Chinese)
3. Guijun Wang, Shu-xiao Wang. Military Navigation [M]. Beijing: Hai Chao Press， 2009. (In Chinese)
4. Cheng-xiang Hua. Warship Formation Military Navigation Theory and Methods [M]. Beijing： Hai Chao Press， 2010. (In Chinese)
5. Wei Li, Cheng-tao Yi, Shu-xiao Wang. An optimum seeking method of azimuth formation evasion course[J]. Journal of Transport Science and Engineering. 2015, 31(1): 103-107. (In Chinese)
6. Convention on the International Regulation for the Preventing Collision at Sea,1972[S]， International Maritime Organization. (In Chinese)

Evolving Support Vector Regression by Hybrid PSO and SA for Rainfall-Runoff Forecasting

Jian-Sheng Wu

Department of Mathematics and Computer, Guangxi Sciences & Technology Teachers University Liuzhou, Guangxi, 545004, China

E-mail: wjsh2002168@163.com

In this paper, an effective hybrid optimization strategy is employed to simultaneously optimize the type of kernel function and the kernel parameter setting of Support Vector Regression (SVR), namely SVR-HPSOSA. This hybrid algorithm focuses on combining the advantages of PSO (fast calculation and easy mechanism) and SA (ability to jump away from local optimum solutions and converge to the global optimum solution). The HPSOSA algorithm combined the metropolis processes of SA into the movement mechanism and parallel processing of PSO. By combining the two methods, the PSO-SA algorithm has the advantage of both fast calculation and searching in the direction of the global optimum solution, helping PSO jump out of local optima, avoiding into the local optimal solution early and leading to a good solution quality. Compared with SVR-HPSOSA and pure SVR, results show that the SVR-HPSOSA model can successfully identify the optimal type of kernel function and all the optimal values of the parameters of SVR with the lowest prediction error values in rainfall-runoff forecasting, can significantly improve the rainfall-runoff forecasting accuracy. Experimental results reveal that the predictions using the proposed approach are consistently better than those obtained using the other methods presented in this study in terms of the same measurements.

Keywords: Rainfall-Runoff; Support Vector Machine; Particle Swarm Optimization; Simulated Annealing; Hybrid Optimization.

1. Introduction

Rainfall-runoff forecasting is very important for Water Resources Management because accurate and timely prediction can avoid accidents, such as the life risk, economic losses[1]. Developing a rainfall-runoff modeling has been a difficult subject in hydrology due to a variety of non-linear factors involved, such as, rainfall characteristics, watershed morphology, water level and soil moisture, etc. In addition, the deficiencies in data like missing data, noisy data, and insufficient data in rainfall-runoff modeling[2]. Neural Networks (NNs) have been found to be a useful technique for modeling rainfall-runoff forecasting due to their ability to capture subtle functional relationships among the empirical data even though the underlying relationships are unknown or hard to describe. However, NNs also suffers from a number of shortcomings such as the need for a large number of controlling parameters, difficulty in obtaining a stable solution and the risk of model over-fitting[3].

Support Vector Regression (SVR) has also been receiving increasing attention to solve nonlinear regression problems due to its many attractive features and promising generalization performance. When using SVR, two problems are confronted: how to choose the type of SVR kernel function and how to set the best parameters of SVR kernel function. Proper type of SVR kernel function and the parameters of SVR kernel function can improve the SVR regression accuracy. Inappropriate parameters in SVR lead to over-fitting or under-fitting[4,5]. The effects of SVR applications strongly depend upon operators experience the main reason optimal hyper-parameters are obtained by the trial-and-error. If carelessly used, it can easily learn irrelevant information in the system (over-fitting). Such a model might be doing well in predicting past incidents, but unable to predict future events[6,7].

Recently, several studies have proposed the parameter optimization of Gaussian kernel function by evolutionary optimization, such as Genetic Algorithm (GA), Particle Swarm Optimization (PSO). This proposed a novel and specialized hybrid optimization strategy to simultaneously optimize both the type of SVR kernel function and all the SVR parameters, namely SVR-HPSOSA. Our approach simultaneously determines the appropriate type of kernel function and optimal kernel parameter values for the SVR model. The runoff data of Liuzhou, Guangxi, China, is predicted as a case study for our proposed method. An actual case of forecasting daily rainfall-runoff is illustrated to show the improvement in predictive accuracy and capability of generalization achieved by our proposed SVR-HPSOSA model.

The rest of this study is organized as follows. Section 2 describes the related works including the basic SVR concepts. Section 3 describes the SVR-HPSOSA, ideas and procedures. For further illustration, different model are used to employ for runoff forecasting analysis in Section 4 and conclusions are drawn in the final Section.

2. Support Vector Regression and Kernel Parameters

The brief ideas of SVR for the case of regression is introduced. Suppose we are given training data $(x_i, d_i)_{i=1}^{N}$, where $x_i \in R^n$ is the input vector; d_i is the output value and n is the total number of data dimension. The linear regression function is formulated as follows:

$$f(x) = \omega\phi(x_i) + b, \quad \phi: R^n \to F, \omega \in F \tag{1}$$

Where ω and b are coefficients; $\phi(x)$ denotes the high dimensional feature space, which is non-linearly mapped from the input space x. According to Ref.[8], the SVR function is given by:

$$f(x, \alpha_i, \alpha_i^*) = \sum_{i=1}^{N} (\alpha_i - \alpha_i^*) K(x, x_i) + b \tag{2}$$

Where $K(x, x_i)$ is defined as kernel function. SVR has recently emerged as an alternative and highly effective means of solving the nonlinear regression problem. When designing an effective SVR model, values of the four essential parameters in SVR have to be chosen carefully in advance. Different parameter settings can cause significant difference in performance. The parameters include:

(1) *Kernel function type:* The kernel function is used to construct a nonlinear mapping between the input space and feature space.

(2) *Kernel function parameter:* t represents the intercept of the polynomial kernel, d represents the degree of the polynomial kernel, δ represents the bandwidth of the Guassian kernel function, α and β are parameters of Sigmoid kernel function.

(3) *Regularization parameter* C: determines the trade-off cost between minimizing the training error and minimizing the model's complexity.

(4) *The tube size of* ε *-insensitive loss function*: It is equivalent to the approximation accuracy placed on the training data points.

Types of various kernel function, kernel function parameters and SVR parameters are shown in Table 1.

Table 1. Types of kernel function, function and SVR parameters.

Kernel Type	Kernel Parameters		SVR Parameters	
Linear	γ	$-$	C	ε
Ploy	d	t	C	ε
RBF	C	δ	C	ε
Sigmoid	α	β	C	ε

3. Hybrid PSOSA Strategy for SVR

3.1. *Particle swarm optimization and simulated annealing*

Particle swarm optimization (PSO) was a global optimization technique, which is more powerful, robust and able to provide accurate solution in nonlinear optimization problems[9]. Simulated Annealing (SA) is a stochastic global searching algorithm for optimization problems, which is based on the statistical thermodynamics to simulate the behavior of atomic arrangements in liquid or solid materials during the annealing process[10]. SA includes a rather simple optimization strategy. The SA algorithm simulates this process of slow cooling of molten metal to achieve minimum function value in the minimization problem.

3.2. *Hybrid PSOSA for SVR's parameters optimization*

To obtain the global or near global optimum solutions, this paper proposes a hybrid Particle Swarm Optimization with Simulated Annealing (HPSOSA) algorithm in order to combine the advantages of SA (ability to jump away from local optimum solutions and converge to the global optimum solution) and the advantages of PSO (fast calculation and easy mechanism). The HPSOSA has the characteristics that is easily realizable, and has the advantages of both PSO and SA algorithms.

In this paper, HPSOSA algorithm is employed to simultaneously optimize the type of kernel function and the kernel parameter setting of Support Vector Regression (SVR), namely SVR-HPSOSA. The developed SVR-HPSOSA model is being applied for daily rainfall-runoff forecasting in Liuzhou of Guangxi, China.

3.3. *Chromosome representations*

The chromosome is comprised of three parts; Kernel Type (integer-valued), Kernel Parameters and SVR Parameter (real-valued). Chromosome 00,01,10,11 represents the kernel function type, which the values zero, one, and two denote that the system will choose 'Linear kernel', 'Polynomail kernel', 'Gaussian (RBF) kernel' and 'Sigmoid function', respectively. Real value chromosome $\{x_{i,1}, x_{i,2}\}$ represents the valued of kernel parameter. Real value chromosome $\{x_{i,3}, x_{i,4}\}$ represents the valued of the penalty parameter and insensitive loss function, respectively.

3.4. *SVR-HPSOSA model*

Generally, when selecting the parameters based on a small and appropriate feature subset, most researchers still follow the trial-and-error procedure, first building a few SVR models based on different parameter sets, testing them on a validation set to obtain optimal parameters. However, this procedure is time-consuming and requires some luck. With a small and appropriate feature subset, the rationale for regression decision can be realized. In addition to feature selection, proper type of kernel function, optimal parameter setting can improve SVR accuracy. Because feature subset selection influences kernel type and kernel parameters, obtaining the proper feature subset, SVR kernel function and the optimal SVR parameters must occur simultaneously.

Fig. 1 illustrates the process of the SVR-HPSOSA algorithm for SVR optimization. Details of our proposed SVR-HPSOSA are described as follows:

1. Particle initialization and PSO parameters setting: Generate initial particles comprised of the SVR's kernel type and parameters. Let $k = 0$, and randomly initialize PSO's position s_i^0, and PSO's velocity.

2. Input training data and calculate the fitness of each chromosome according to Eq. (3)

3. Evaluate the fitness value of all particles, which determine Gbest and Pbest by a simple comparison of their fitness values. The fitness function is defined as the $Mape_{cross\ validation}$ validation of the 5-fold cross validation method on the training data set, as follows:

$$Mape_{cross\ validation} = \frac{\sum_{i=1}^{l} |a_i - p_i|}{a_i l} \times 100\% \qquad (3)$$

Where l is the number of training data samples; a_i is the actual value, and p_i is the predicted value. In this study, the 5-fold cross validation which offers the best compromise between computational cost and reliable parameter estimates is used to evaluate fitness on the training data set. For each particle, evaluate its fitness by formula (3). Note that the accuracy i in formula (3) is set as average CV accuracy obtained in the previous step.

4. Perform PSO operators. Update the global and personal best according to the fitness evaluation results. Record the average training CV accuracy and validation accuracy for the global and personal best.

5. Evaluate $\Delta Fitness = Fitness(s_i^{k+1}) - Fitness(s_i^k)$, and then randomly select a number $R \in [0,1]$. If $\Delta Fitness > 0$ meaning that, the new position is improved for increasing fitness function, then position s_i^{k+1} is accepted according to the following criterion: $\exp(\Delta Fitness / T_i) > R$. Proceed to Step 6 when the velocity of all particles are determined, or return to Step 2 for those particles failing to be accepted, and generate new velocities using the same evaluation process. Too many failures (i.e., 100 in our study) for the same particle will force the last velocity to be accepted, in consideration of CPU time, thereby prevent entering into an endless loop. However, this did not occur during our study and simulation.

6. Renew each particle to the new position and modify G_{best} and P_{best} by simple comparison their fitness values.

7. When the evolution process has achieved a satisfactory condition (or maximum evolution number is reached), proceed to Step 3, otherwise, modify the inertia weight, and annealing temperature $T_{i+1} = k * T_i$, let $k = k+1$, and return to Step 2.

8. Output the best solution G_{best} and its fitness value. With the stopping training iteration determined in the previous step, recall the type of kernel and the parameter value of SVR in the stopping iteration.

9. Retrain and build the SVR on the larger training set based on the type of kernel and the parameter value of SVR. Finally, measure testing accuracy on testing set via the trained SVR model.

4. Experiments Analysis

In this paper, PSO parameters are set as follows: the iteration times are 100; the population is 100; the minimum inertia weight is 0.1; the maximum inertia weight is 0.9 and the learning rate is 2.0. Initial temperature is 5000; termination temperature is 0.9 and temperature reduction factor 0.001.

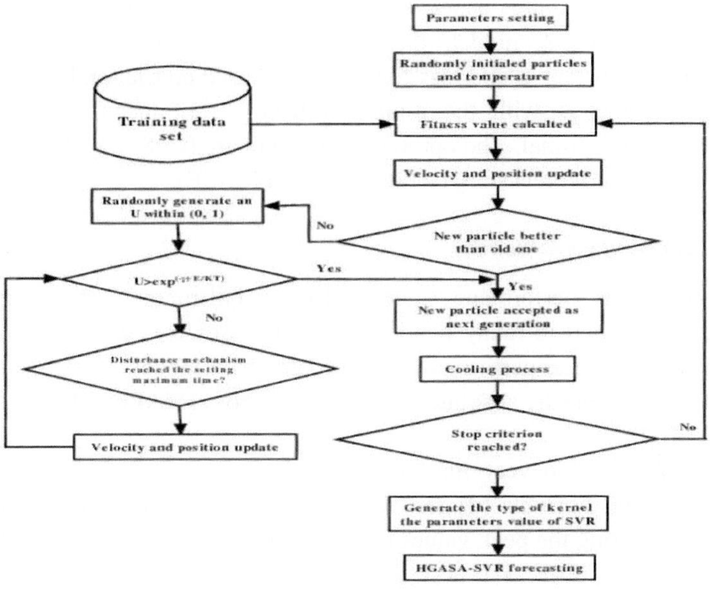

Fig. 1. Flowchart of the HPSOSA optimization SVR.

4.1. *Empirical data*

The data were divided into two parts, a total of 821 data for modeling training from January 1, 2008 to March 31, 2010, and the remaining 183 samples (the main flood season from April 1, 2011 to September 30, 2011) for model testing. Daily water level as runoff data from Daqiao stream flow gauging stations, were obtained from the observation archives of Liuzhou Water Management Information System. The collected data were prepared for the period from January 1, 2008 to September 30, 2010, a total of 1004 data points.

According to the literature(~see Ref.[11]), runoff at time steps $t-1(X_{t-1})$, $t-2(X_{t-2})$, $t-3(X_{t-3})$, $t-4(X_{t-4})$ and rainfall at time step $t-1(R_{t-1})$ are considered as inputs to the model by the step-wise regression method to eliminate low impact factors and choose the most influential factors.

4.2. *SVR model*

The forecasting results of the proposed SVR-PSOSA model are compared to the SVR model using the same forecasting variables. For building SVR forecasting model, the LIBSVM package proposed by Chang and Lin is adapted in this study.[11] For simplifying the setting of parameter, the RBF kernel function with

$\sigma = 0.75$ is applied in this paper, which the width of the RBF is the same value in the SVR-HPSOSA model, the selection of the other two parameters, regularization constant C and loss function ε is based on trial-and-error method. The best parameters with the minimum testing root mean square error is considered to be optimal. The optimal parameters are (C=8, $\varepsilon = 0.07$) based on the best testing and forecasting result (minimum RMSE).

4.3. *Performance evaluation*

There were many performance indexes for rainfall-runoff forecasting model, which can be found in many paper. This paper uses the following evaluation metric to measure the performance of the proposed model: Root mean square error (RMSE), Mean absolute percentage error (MAPE), Coefficient of efficiency (CE).

Moreover, due to very importance of the extreme values in the rainfall runoff modeling, Formula (4) can be used to compare the ability of different models in capturing the peak values in runoff time series for the total runoff data.

$$CE_{peak} = 1 - \frac{\sum_{i=1}^{n} (x_{pi} - x_{pi}^{*})^2}{\sum_{i=1}^{n} (x_{pi} - \bar{x}_p)^2} \tag{4}$$

Where CE_{peak} is coefficient of efficiency for peak values, x_{pi}, x_{pi}^{*}, $\bar{x}_p$ and n are the observed values, the forecast value, the average of observed value, and the number of observed data for peak values, respectively.

5. Results Analysis

Fig. 2 shows the observed runoff and the forecast runoff by the proposed SVR-HPSOSA model with pure SVR models for runoff less than 4000 from April 1 to September 30 in 2010. Fig. 3, the observed peak values and the forecasted peak values obtained by the proposed SVR-HPSOSA model with pure SVR models from April 1 to September 30 in 2010. From the graphs, we can generally see that the results of SVR-HPSOSA model are closer to the corresponding observed water level values than those of the SVR models. Especially, the SVR-HPSOSA model produced better forecasting for the runoff peak values, while other models were slightly overestimated or underestimated.

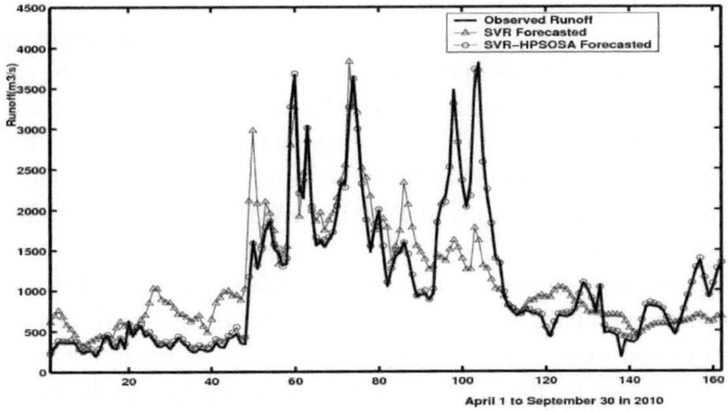

Fig. 2. Results comparison between observed and predicted of two models for runoff less than 4000.

Table 2 illustrates the fitting and forecasting accuracy and efficiency of the model in terms of various evaluation indices for SVR and SVR-HPSOSA, respectively. As shown in Table 2, for the tanning data, the RMSE for SVR model is 167.863; while for SVR-HPSOSA model, RMSE reaches 74.218. Similarly, for the testing data, the RMSE for the SVR model is 909.564; while for the SVR-HPSOSA model, RMSE reaches 201.723. Focusing on the MAPE indicator of the training case and testing data, the SVR-HPSOSA model is also less than the SVR models. These results indicate that the deviations between observed and forecasting value are very small. In addition, the CE of SVR-PSOSA is the maximum in all models. This also means that SVR-HPSOSA is capable to capture the average change tendency of the daily runoff.

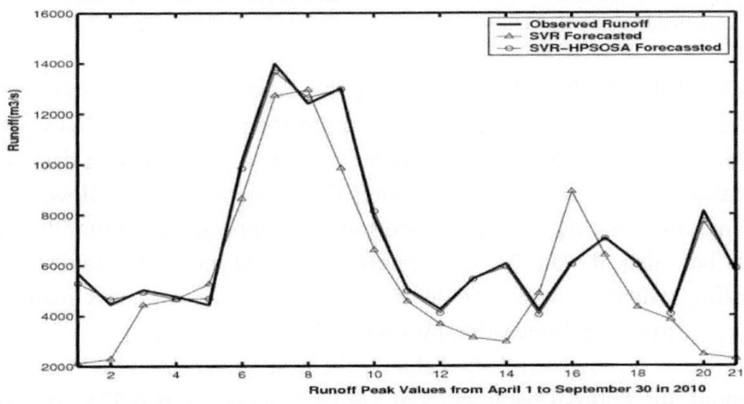

Fig. 3. Results comparison between observed and predicted of two models for runoff more than 4000.

The empirical results show that the SVR-HPSOSA model are very promising in the runoff forecasting under the research where either the measurement of fitting performance is goodness or where the forecasting performance is effectiveness. It also can be seen that there was consistency in the results obtained between the training and testing of the SVR-HPSOSA model. To summarize, the SVR-HPSOSA model is superior to the other two models presented here in terms of RMSE, MAPE and *CE* for runoff prediction under the same input.

The more important point in the runoff modeling which makes sure that our model is most promising when comparing with different models is the capability of the proposed model in estimating peak values. Whereas the estimation of peak values is usually the most important part of the flood mitigation program for actual rainfall-runoff application, as final step of the modeling process.

Table 2. Comparison the results of rainfall--runoff values, Kernel function type.

Fitting values (January 1, 2008-March 31, 2009)				
Model	MAPE	RMSE	*CE*	CE_{peak}
SVR	15.758%	167.863	0.987	0.929
SVR-HPSOSA	3.734%	74.218	0.997	0.984
Forecasting values (April 1, 2010-September 30, 2010)				
SVR	25.881%	909.564	0.822	0.482
SVR-HPSOSA	5.284%	201.723	0.992	0.977
Kernel function type and parameters				
	α	β	C	ε
Sigmoid	0.325	0.0264	18.60	0.1059

Note: Table notes. The runoff peak values is 48 samples in fitting model, the runoff peak values is 21 samples in forecasting model. The runoff value more than 4000, is defined as the peak values.

From Table 2, it is found out that the capability of the SVR-HPSOSA model for predicting extreme runoff is more than SVR. The CE_{peak} of SVR-HPSOSA model is 0.984 in training data, and it is 0.977 in testing data. There is an identical high capability of our models for prediction of peak flows in testing data. Therefore, not only the proposed model is appropriate in monitoring peak values, but also it can be considered as almost powerful tool for runoff forecasting which is necessary in the water resources systems management, where it is directly in forecasting by stream flow forecasting.

Further it can be seen from Table 2, the best choice of kernel function type is Sigmoid, the optimal parameters of kernel function α is 0.325, β is 0.0264, the optimal parameters of SVR C is 18.60, ε is 0.1059 for runoff modeling.

6. Conclusion

The rainfall-runoff system is one of the most active dynamic weather systems. In this paper, the advantages and the key issues of the PSO and SA evolve the type and the parameters of SVR kernel function have been presented to model the runoff forecasting. The experiment with real rainfall-runoff data have showed that the SVR-HPSOSA can be of high precision, even better than those of pure SVR, by setting proper values for all parameters (parameter values and type of kernel function) in the SVR model. According to the results obtained in this paper, the SVR-HPSOSA method has the following characteristics:

Remark 1. The HPSOSA algorithm enables the solution to jump out of local optima, and decreases the vibration near the end of locating a solution by incorporating the metropolis acceptance criterion of SA into PSO randomly acceptance rule. The rule determines whether to accept the new position or recalculate another candidate position according to the fitness function difference between the new and old positions. This enables the solution to jump out of local optima, and decreases the vibration near the end of locating a solution. These characteristics improve the quality of the solution and increase the rate of convergence.

Remark 2. The HPSOSA algorithm has the advantage of both fast calculation and searching in the direction of the global optimum solution, leading to a good solution quality by combining the PSO characteristics of movement mechanism and parallel processing into the disturbance mechanism and solution searching procedure of SA.

Remark 3. According to the results obtained in this paper, we can draw the following conclusions that the SVR model with Sigmoid kernel function can be used as an alternative tool for actual runoff forecasting application to obtain better forecasting accuracy and improve the prediction quality further in view of empirical results.

Acknowledgments

The authors would like to express their sincere thanks to the editor and anonymous reviewer's comments and suggestions for the improvement of this paper. This work was supported by the Natural Science Foundation of Guangxi Province under Grant No. 2014GXNSFAA118027, and by the Guangxi Education Department under Grant YB2014467, and Key Laboratory for Mixed and Missing Data Statistics of the Education Department of Guangxi Province under Grant No. GXMMSL201405.

References

1. J. Wu, J. Long and M. Liu, A hybrid support vector regression approach for rainfall forecasting using particle swarm optimization and projection pursuit technology, *Int. J. Comp. Intel. Appl.* **9**, 87 (2010).
2. V. Nourani and M. Komasi, Two hybrid Artificial Intelligence approaches for modeling rainfall-runoff process, *J. Hydrol.* **402**, 41 (2011).
3. K. Ozgur, S. Jalal, T. Mustafa, Modeling rainfall-runoff process using soft computing techniques, *C. Geosci.* **51**, 108 (2013).
4. J. L. Chi, S. L. Tian and C. C. Chih, Financial time series forecasting using independent component analysis and support vector regression, *Decis. Support Syst.* **47**, 115 (2009).
5. W. C. Hong, Application of seasonal SVR with chaotic immune algorithm in traffic flow forecasting, *Neural Comput. Appl.* **21**, 583 (2012).
6. S. W. Lin and K. C. Ying, S. C. Chen, Particle swarm optimization for parameter determination and feature selection of support vector machines, *Expert Syst. Appl.* **35**, 1817(2008).
7. K. Y. Chen and C. H. Wang, A hybrid SARIMA and support vector machines in forecasting the production values of the machinery industry in Taiwan, *Expert Syst. Appl.* **32**, 254(2007).
8. B. Paola and R. Dario, Support vector regression for link load prediction, *Comput. Netw.* **53**, 191(2009).
9. C. Oysu and Z. Bingul, Application of heuristic and hybrid GASA algorithms to tool-path optimization problem for minimizing airtime during machining, *Eng. Appl. Artif. Intel.* **22**, 389(2009).
10. H. M. Rabie, E. Ihab and T. Assem, Particle Swarm Optimization algorithm for the continuous p-median location problems, in *Proc. Comput. Eng. Confer.* 81-86, 2014.
11. C. C. Chang, C. J. Lin, LIBSVM: A Library for Support Vector Machines, 2001, `http://www.csie.ntu.edu.tw/~cjlin/libsvm.`

An Improved FFT Method for Determining the Period of a Torsion Pendulum

Feng-Jiao He[a] and Jia-Hao Xu[b]

School of Mechanical Engineering and Electronic Information,
China University of Geosciences
Wuhan 430074, China
E-mail: [a]hefengjiao32@163.com, [b]xujiahaothanks@163.com

Measuring the period of a torsion pendulum is of great importance for most gravitational experiments. The improved fast Fourier transformation (FFT) method which was proposed by Barry G. Quinn can be used to determine the period of a torsion pendulum precisely. In this paper, several factors affecting the precision of the period estimation are discussed. The period of a sinusoidal signal subject to the window effect and the phase effect is estimated. Meanwhile, the effects are evaluated on the period determination due to other disturbances that would be present in a real oscillator, such as, higher harmonic, the damping, the monotonic drift and the white noise. The computer simulation experiments show that it is effective to overcome the disturbances mentioned above, and this method can be used to determine the period of a torsion pendulum with high accuracy.

Keyword: Period Estimation; The Improved FFT Method; Disturbances; Accuracy.

1. Introduction

In gravitational experiments, particularly in the measurement of the Newtonian gravitational constant *G*, determining the period of a torsion pendulum with high precision plays a very crucial role because the accuracy in measuring the period greatly affects the experimental results[1][2]. In the experiment for determining *G*, the period used to be measured by the time-of-swing method[2] which is based on detecting the change in the periods of the pendulum at different configurations can be expressed as in Eq. (1)

$$G = \frac{4\pi^2 I}{C_g}\left(\frac{1}{T_2^{\ 2}} - \frac{1}{T_1^{\ 2}}\right) \tag{1}$$

Where T_2 and T_1 represent the periods of the pendulum at different configurations, respectively, I is the moment of inertia of the pendulum, and C_g is a coupling constant[3]. In this case, in order to obtain realistic G, we need to determine the periods of the pendulum with high precision from the experimental data. Traditional methods such as the fast Fourier transform method[4], the ''all-poles'' method[5], and the nonlinear least-square fitting method[6] are different varieties of methods to extract the period of torsion pendulum.

It is known that the fast Fourier transform method is the popular method to determine the period. The period of the torsion pendulum is determined by calculating the fundamental peak of a power spectrum which had been computed from the angular position of the suspended beam using a fast Fourier transform[4]. However, there are some limitations in the FFT method. It is known that the accuracy of the FFT method is proportional to the number of sinusoidal cycles involved in the experimental data. What is more, the window effect and the phase effect lead to a serious deviation of the period in the FFT method[7]. Although Goldblum and Ritter have done some beneficial work on this problem, the two effects cannot be eliminated[4].

In this paper, we use the improved FFT method to estimate period of the sinusoidal signal[8]. The result of processing experimental data shows that the improved FFT method is an effective method to determine the torsion pendulum's period accurately, which is significant for the determination of the gravitational constant G.

2. The Improved FFT Method

The improved FFT method proposed by Barry G. Quinn can be used to determine the period of a torsion pendulum. As show in [9], we consider the estimation of the frequency parameter ω in the model, as in Eq. (2)

$$y_t = \mu + \bar{y}_t + \varepsilon_t = A\sin(\omega t + \varphi) + \varepsilon_t\,,\ t=0,1,...,T\text{-}1 \tag{2}$$

Where $\{\varepsilon_t\}$ represents some random noise sequence μ is the mean or DC term, $\bar{y}_t$ is the ideal signal, A is the amplitude and φ_0 is the initial phase of the signal. As shown in [9], The Fourier coefficients of $\{y_t\}$ and $\{\varepsilon_t\}$ is expressed as in Eq. (3) and Eq. (4)

$$Y_j = \sum_{t=0}^{T-1} y_t \exp(-i2\pi jt/T) \tag{3}$$

$$U_j = \sum_{t=0}^{T-1} \varepsilon_t \exp(-i2\pi jt/T) \tag{4}$$

Then

$$\begin{aligned} Y_j &= U_j + A/2\exp(i\varphi)[\exp(iT\omega)-1]/\{\exp[i(\omega-2\pi j/T)]-1\} \\ &+ A/2\exp(-i\varphi)[\exp(-iT\omega)-1]/\{\exp[-i(\omega+2\pi j/T)]-1\}. \end{aligned} \tag{5}$$

Thus, when ω-$2\pi j/T$ is $O(T^{-1})$

$$Y_j = U_j + TA\exp(i\varphi)[\exp(iT\omega)-1]/\{4\pi i(T\omega/(2\pi)-j]\} + O(1) \tag{6}$$

Let $\delta=T\omega/(2\pi)$-j and considering only the case where $\delta \in (-1,\ 1)$, we have, for k=-1,0,1, as show in [7]

$$Y_{j+k} = U_{j+k} + Tc\delta/(\delta-k) + O(1) \tag{7}$$

$$\frac{Y_{j+k}}{Y_j} = \frac{\delta}{\delta-k} + \frac{1}{c}T^{-1}U_{j\text{-}k} - \frac{\delta}{c(\delta-k)}T^{-1}U_j + O(T^{-1}\log T) \tag{8}$$

Where $c = A\exp(i\varphi)[\exp(i2\pi\delta)-1]/(4\pi i\delta)$, almost surely, as $T\to\infty$. As the error term in the above equation is of small order, the term may be estimated by the real part of the left side of (8), as in [8], the modified algorithm for estimating δ is proposed as follows:

1)Put k_T equal to the maximizer of $\left|Y_j^{\,2}\right|$, $1 \le j \le [(T\text{-}1)/2]$.

2)Let $s_a = \operatorname{sgn} R(Y_{k_T+a}\overline{Y}_{k_T})$. Let $\hat{a}=1$ if s_{-1}=1 and s_1=-1 and let $\hat{a}=-1$ otherwise.

3)Estimate ω by $\hat{\omega}_T = 2\pi(k_T+\hat{\delta})/T$, where $\hat{\delta} = \hat{a}\dfrac{R_T}{1+R_T}$ and $R_T = -\,S_{\hat{a}}\left|\dfrac{Y_{k_T+\hat{a}}}{Y_{k_T}}\right|$

.

2.1. *The window effect*

We use a computer simulation to test the impact of the window function on the period of a torsion pendulum. In this article, the performance of Rectangular, Triangle, Hamming, Hanning and Blackman window is compared, considering their magnitude response, phase response, equivalent noise bandwidth, side lobe transition width, response in time and frequency domain using MATLAB simulation. Comparing simulation results with different window function, we can found rectangular window with best performance among them which is also expected from the theory in this paper. Figure 1 shows the window function responses in time domain. The function of the sinusoidal signal can be expressed as $y=a_0\sin(\omega t+\varphi_0)$, where a_0=1rad, the initial phase $\varphi_0=0$. The expression of the output signal with different window function is $y_0=y\times w(\text{n})$, where $w(n)$ is the expression of different window function[7]. A computer simulation experiment is performed to test the fundamental frequency dependency on the window effect. The results are shown in Table 1.

The period of an oscillator is estimated from a 200000-points FFT of a 537.024385s sinusoidal signal with an amplitude of 1rad by the improved FFT method, with a sampling interval of 0.5s. The impact of the Rectangular window on the period estimate is less than other window function by comparing the period with the window function. The corresponding deviation of the period is about 0.063ppm.

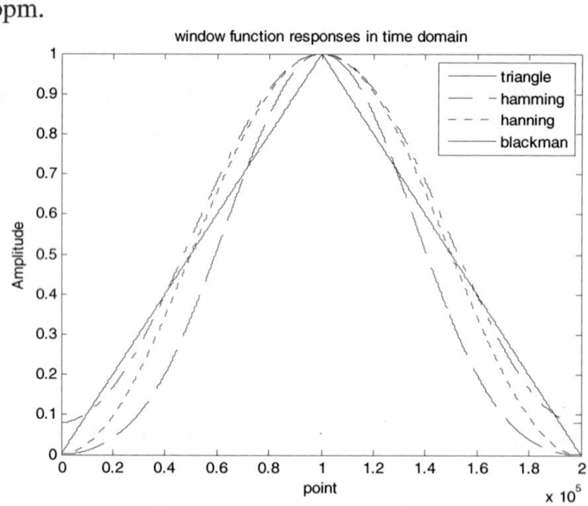

Fig. 1. Window function responses in time domain. The frequency of an ideal sine wave for a standard 200000-points FFT algorithm, with T=537.024385s.

Table 1. The deviation of $\tilde{T}_0$ due to the window effect by the improved FFT method.

Window function	Rectangular window	Triangle window	Hamming window	Hanning window	Blackman window
$\tilde{T}_0$ (s)	537.024351	537.167149	537.172074	537.190328	537.209976
deviation of $\tilde{T}_0$ (ppm)	0.063	265	275	309	346

2.2. *The phase effect*

In the FFT method, the starting phase of the sampled data has a crucial effect on the accuracy of the periods[7]. The frequency of the measured sine wave with different initial phase is obtained. The improved FFT method is performed on different starting phases from 0° to 360° with results showed in Table 2. The conclusion that the different initial phase of the sinusoidal signal have little impact on the estimate of the frequency is drawn. The relative deviation of the result of the improved method is less than 0.121ppm.

Table 2. The deviation of $\widetilde{T}_0$ due to the phase effect by the improved FFT method.

φ_0	0°	60°	120°	180°	240°	300°	360°
$\widetilde{T}_0$ (s)	537.024351	537.024326	537.024323	537.024344	537.024379	537.024417	537.024443
deviation of $\widetilde{T}_0$ (ppm)	0.063	0.110	0.121	0.076	0.011	0.060	0.108

3. Deviations to the Disturbances

In a real experiment, the improved FFT method suffers various interferences such as a monotonic drift, the interference of high-order harmonics, amplitude damping, the white noise, and so on[7]. Allowing for some systematic disturbances such as the harmonic oscillation, the damping and the monotonic drift, the output signal from the oscillator can be expressed as in Eq. (9)

$$y(t) = (1-\beta t)\sum_{l=1}^{L} a_l \sin(l\omega t + \varphi_l) + kt + b \tag{9}$$

Where β, k and b are the damping factor, the slope and the intercept of the monotonic drift, respectively and a_l, ω and φ_l are fundamental frequency and phase of the harmonic oscillation of the oscillator, respectively. l is the order of the harmonic oscillation of oscillator.

3.1. *Deviation to the high order harmonic frequency oscillation*

There is the interference of high-order harmonic frequencies included in this residual curve. Now, the effect of the high order harmonic frequency due to the heterogeneity of the gravitational field outside is taken into consideration. If T is the period of the fundamental frequency oscillation $y_1 = a_1\sin(\omega t+\varphi_1)$, it means that the points at the time span of T have the same value. According to the character of the harmonic frequencies oscillation, we know that the points at the time span of T in the twice order harmonic $y_2 = a_1\sin(\omega t + \varphi_1)$ also have the same value, and so in triple order harmonic $y_3 = a_3\sin(3\omega t + \varphi_3)$ and in the i-th order harmonic $y_i = a_i\sin(i\omega t + \varphi_i)$. Besides, the points at the time span of T in their synthetic oscillation $y = y_1 + y_2 + y_3 +...+ y_i+...$ also have the same values. Therefore, we should use the ideal function $y = a_1\sin(\omega t + \varphi_1) + a_1\sin(\omega t + \varphi_1) + a_3\sin(3\omega t + \varphi_3)$[1]. The fundamental period is set to be 537.024385s, a sampling interval of 0.5s was chosen, and 200000 points were generated. Table 3 shows the deviation of $\tilde{T}_0$ in the improved FFT algorithm, from which we know that the deviations are up to 0.009ppm. As a comparison, the deviations by means of the FFT method are about 1543ppm, which is independent of the influence of the high order harmonic.

3.2. *Deviation to the weak damping*

If β is the coefficient of the damping of the amplitude, the function of the output signal can be expressed as $y=(1-\beta t)\sin(\omega t+\varphi_0)$. A computer simulation experiment is performed to obtain the fundamental frequency dependency on the influence of the damping. Table 4 illustrates the result that the less β is, the least deviation of $\tilde{T}_0$ is by means of the improved FFT method. In addition, the deviations are also about 1543ppm by means of the FFT method. From the results, we can see that the improved FFT method is more insensitive to the amplitude damping than the FFT method.

3.3. *Deviation to the monotonic drift*

Due to the creep of the suspension fiber and the change in the experimental environment of an oscillator, there is always a monotonic drift in the experimental data. Regarding the drift as a linear change, we can use a straight line $kt+b$ to express it, where k is the rate of drift and b is the initial equilibrium position. The function $y=a_0\sin(\omega t+\varphi_0)+kt+b$ is used to generate a data-series by the computer. The generated sinusoidal data has the same characteristics as the above simulation, and namely $T = 537.024385$s, $a_0=1$rad, $\varphi_0=0$, respectively. A group of simulation experiments are carried out to evaluate the effect of such a drift on the period of a sinusoidal signal and give the period of torsion pendulums, as Table 5 shows. In the determination of the Newtonian gravitational constant G[7], long-term observations show that the linear drift of the fiber is about 0.0001 times the amplitude of the signal per hour. The corresponding deviation of the period is about 0.061ppm. The results given by the FFT method are also listed in Table 5, and the deviation is 1543ppm while the drift is about 0.0001 times of its amplitude.

3.4. *Deviation to the white noise*

The noise interference is inevitable in the experiment. Much experimental noise can be seen as white noise. A computer simulation experiment is also performed to calculate the influence of the white noise on the fundamental frequency. The motion signal of torsion pendulum subject to the white noise is given $y=a_0\sin(\omega t+\varphi_0)+\varepsilon_t$. The generated sinusoidal data has the same characteristics as the above experiment, the values of T, a_0 and φ_0 are the same as that in the above simulation experiment, where the sinusoidal data are generated with the magnitude of the white noise of 0.2, 1 and 2mV, respectively. The results are shown in Table 6. The simulation experiment results show that the relative uncertainty of the period is less than 0.1ppm with the improved FFT method, but that of FFT method is 1543ppm. As shown in Table 6, the oscillators have a small magnitude of the white noise and then the deviation due to it can be ignored.

Table 3. The deviation of $\widetilde{T}_0$ due to the high order harmonic frequencies oscillation

The high order harmonic frequencies	The FFT method $\widetilde{T}_0$ (s)	The improved FFT method $\widetilde{T}_0$ (s)	deviation of $\widetilde{T}_0$ by the FFT method (ppm)	deviation of $\widetilde{T}_0$ by the improved FFT method (ppm)
a2/a1=0.1,a3/a1=0	536.195710	537.024370	1543	0.028
a2/a1=0,a3/a1=0.1	536.195710	537.024361	1543	0.045
a2/a1=0.1,a3/a1=0.1	536.195710	537.024380	1543	0.009
a2/a1=0.01,a3/a1=0.01	536.195710	537.024353	1543	0.060

Table 4. The deviation of $\widetilde{T}_0$ due to the damping of amplitude.

The damping of amplitude	The FFT method $\widetilde{T}_0$ (s)	The improved FFT method $\widetilde{T}_0$ (s)	deviation of $\widetilde{T}_0$ by the FFT method (ppm)	deviation of $\widetilde{T}_0$ by the improved FFT method (ppm)
10^{-8}	536.195710	537.024352	1543	0.061
10^{-7}	536.195710	537.024455	1543	0.130
10^{-6}	536.195710	537.038102	1543	26

Table 5. The deviation of $\widetilde{T}_0$ due to the monotonic drift.

The monotonic drift (of amplitude per second)	The FFT method $\widetilde{T}_0$ (s)	The improved FFT method $\widetilde{T}_0$ (s)	deviation of $\widetilde{T}_0$ by the FFT method (ppm)	deviation of $\widetilde{T}_0$ by the improved FFT method (ppm)
0.000001	536.195710	537.024446	1543	0.114
0.0000001	536.195710	537.024360	1543	0.047
0.00000001	536.195710	537.024352	1543	0.061
0.00000005	536.195710	537.024355	1543	0.056

Table 6. The deviation of $\widetilde{T}_0$ due to the white noise

Magnitude of the white noise(V)	The FFT method $\widetilde{T}_0$ (s)	The improved FFT method $\widetilde{T}_0$ (s)	deviation of $\widetilde{T}_0$ by the FFT method (ppm)	deviation of $\widetilde{T}_0$ by the improved FFT method (ppm)
0.0002	536.195710	537.024380	1543	0.009
0.001	536.195710	537.024397	1543	0.022
0.002	536.195710	537.024420	1543	0.065

3.5. *Conclusions*

The computer simulation experiments show that the improved FFT method can determine the period of a physical oscillator with a relative bias of 10^{-7} orders, while the standard FFT method can only determine it with a relative bias of 10^{-3} orders. Therefore, we can conclude that the improved FFT method can determine the period of a torsion pendulum with high accuracy. Through the above simulation results, we can also see that the window effect and the phase effect have an important effect on the accuracy of the period extraction of torsion pendulum.

Acknowledgments

This work is partially supported by the Natural Science Foundation of Key Projects of Hubei province in China (2013CFA045).

References

1. Z. K. Hu, J. Luo, *Rev, Sci. Instrum,* 70(11): 4412. (1999).
2. J. Luo, Z. K. Hu, X. H Fu, S. H Fan and M. X Tang, *Phys. Rev. D,* 59(4): 042001. (1999)
3. J. Luo and D. H. Wang, *Rev. Sci. Instrum,* 79(9): 094705. (2008)
4. C. E. Goldblum and R. C. Ritter, *Rev. Sci. Instrum,* 59(5): 778. (1988)
5. J. J. Snyder, *Applied Optics,* 19(8): 1223-1225. (1980)
6. X. H Fu, J. Luo, Z. K. Hu and M. X Tang, *Acta Phys. Sin,* (1998) (overseas Edition)
7. Z. K. Hu, Precise determination of the gravitational constant *G* and study on the properties of torsion balance, *doctoral dissertation,* Huazhong University of Science and Technology (2001).
8. B. G. Quinn. Estimation of frequency, amplitude, and phase from the DFT of a time series[J]. *IEEE Transactions on Signal Processing,* 45(3): 814-817. (1997)).
9. B. G. Quinn. Estimating frequency by interpolation using Fourier coefficients[J]. *IEEE Transactions on Signal Processing,* 42(5): 1264-1268. (1994)

Novel Object Tracking Method Based on Bayesian Framework

Qin-Jun Zhao[a], Jun Wei[b], Qin Zhang[c] and Yuan Xu[d]

School of Electrical Engineering, University of Jinan

Jinan, 250022, China

E-mail: [a]cse_zhaoqj@ujn.edu.cn, [b]cse_wj@ujn.edu.cn, [c]cse_zhangq@ujn.edu.cn, [d]cse_xuy@ujn.edu.cn

In order to solve the problem of object tracking in practical application, this paper proposes a method of target tracking based on Bayesian framework. When the object appearance model is established, the background around the object is also used as a part of the model, which can solve the problem of appearance change and occlusion in a certain degree. In addition, since the phase of the image's Fast Fourier Transform contains the texture information of the image, it is used to deal with the illumination change of object. Compared with the existing optical flow method, the usage of Fast Fourier Transform improves the real-time performance of the proposed object tracking method.

Keywords: Object Tracking; Occlusion; Bayesian Framework.

1. Introduction

Object tracking[1] in image sequences is one of the hot spots in the field of computer vision. With the development of computer vision technology and computer hardware technology, object detection and tracking in image sequences is more and more widely used in the military and civilian fields, such as intelligent surveillance, human-computer interaction, visual navigation, assistant driving, etc.

With a simple background and little change in object appearance, most tracking methods have good tracking effects. But in practical applications, due to the complexity of the external environment and the diversity and variation of the characteristics of the target[2], the object tracking technology is still a big challenge. For example, in the process of tracking, the appearance of a target is often changed. There are two main changes, internal and external. The internal changes include posture change, deformation of non rigid object and changes in object appearance profiles[3]. The external changes mainly include the impact of environmental changes on the appearance of the target, and the partially or completely occluding by other objects[4]. Therefore, in practical applications, a good tracking method is required to be able to adapt to changes in the appearance of the target[5].

The current object tracking method can be divided into two categories, the discriminative model and the generative model[6]. The generative model needs to set up an appearance model to represent the object, and then the area of image that matches the appearance model is searched in the whole frame. But this method ignores the useful information around the target, which can help to distinguish target and background. The discriminative model is considered as a two classification problem, which determines whether an image area is a target or a background. But the goal of this method is to predict the category of the target, which is different from the purpose of tracking.

2. Proposed Algorithm

In this section, details of the proposed algorithm are presented. The main steps of the algorithm are as follows.

(1) Generating kernel function template

In the object image area being tracked, the closer to the center of the object area, the greater the possibility of being part of the target, thus the greater the contribution should be to the target template. In order to generate a better target template, these areas should be given larger weights. On the contrary, the further away from the center of target image, the smaller the possibility of being part of the target, the smaller the contribution should be to the target template, thus the smaller weight should be given to these regions.

Therefore, firstly, we need to create a kernel function template to highlight the center of object image area and weaken the edge area. We use the two-dimensional Hanning window $w_2(n)$ as the kernel function template.

$$w_2(n) = w_1(n) * [w_1(n)]^T \tag{1}$$

where is the one dimensional Hanning window:

$$w_1(n) = \frac{1}{2}\left(\cos\left(\frac{2\pi n}{L-1}\right)\right), 0 \le n \le L-1 \tag{2}$$

where L is the length of Hanning window, n is the element number of the vector, which starts from 0.

(2) Calculating Fast Fourier Transform (FFT) of the object's confidence map template.

The confidence map of the target $c(z)$ is the probability map of the element as part of the target at each position.

$$c(z) = P(z \mid o) = be^{-\frac{|z-z^*|}{2*\alpha}} \tag{3}$$

where b is a normalized constant, α =2.25, $z \in R^2$ is the coordinates of the points in the template, z^* is the coordinate of the center point in the template. Then we calculate the FFT of confidence map template indicated by $F(c)$.

(3) Get the initial position of the target in the first frame

Read the first frame image in the video, suppose the initial position of the target in the first frame image is known, which can be given by the target detection method or manual label. The initial location and size of the object is represented by a rectangular.

(4) Get spatial context image of the object

If the image is a color image, it should be converted to a gray image first. Suppose the width and height of the target in the previous image are w_{t-1} and h_{t-1}, and the coordinate of the center point is z^*_{t-1}. Take z^*_{t-1}, $2w_{t-1}$ and $2h_{t-1}$ as the center, width and height of the target context image respectively. In order to get the normalize context image I_{norm}, we should scale its resolution to 101×101 pixels, and then the value of each pixel in the context image is subtracted by the average value of all the pixels in the context image. This process can reduce the influence of the illumination change.

In order to strengthen the influence of pixels near the center of the target image and weaken the influence of edge pixels in the target image, we calculate the spatial context image of the current target h^{sc} as:

$$h^{sc} = I_{norm} w_2(n) \tag{4}$$

(5) Calculate the max confidence point

Since the phase of the image's FFT contains the texture information of the image, it can be used to deal with the illumination change of object. So we calculate the FFT of the target spatial context image of the current frame by:

$$FFT(h^{sc}) = M_h e^{j\theta_t} \tag{5}$$

where $e^{j\theta_t}$ is the phase of the image's FFT.

Then we calculate the confidence map's FFT of the spatial context image of the current frame by:

$$FFT(c_t) = e^{j\theta_t} e^{j\theta_{t-1}} \tag{6}$$

where $e^{j\theta_t}$ is the phase of the object spatial context image's FFT in the current frame, and $e^{j\theta_{t-1}}$ is the phase of the object spatial context image's FFT in the previous frame. The confidence map of the current frame image c_t is obtained by Inverse Fourier Transformation (IFFT) of $FFT(c_t)$. Take the Dudek sequence as an example, the confidence map of the 100th frame is shown in Figure 2.

(6) Update the spatial-temporal context model

Take the max value point in the confidence map $z(c_{\max})$ as the new target location z_t in the current image, and calculate the final object spatial context image h^{sc} in the current frame, which can be used to update the spatial-temporal context model H_t^{stc} .

$$H_{t+1}^{stc} = (1-\rho)H_t^{stc} + \rho h_t^{sc} \tag{7}$$

where ρ is the update ratio.

Then we calculate the phase $e^{j\theta_{t+1}}$ of the spatial-temporal context model's FFT.

$$F(H_{t+1}^{stc}) = Me^{j\theta_{t+1}} \tag{8}$$

(7) Predict the phase of target spatial context image in the next frame

The phase of target spatial context image in the next frame $e^{j\theta_p}$ can be predicted by:

$$e^{j\theta_p} = \frac{F(c)}{e^{j\theta}} \tag{9}$$

3. Experiments and Analysis

Two experiments of the proposed tracking algorithm are shown in this section. For the David sequence, the tracking results are shown in Figure 1. From Figure 1, we can see that in the David indoor sequence, though there are great change in the background and illumination, David also took off and wear glasses, the proposed tracking algorithm can track David's face correctly.

For the Dudek sequence, the tracking results are shown in Figure 2. From Figure 2 we can see that in the Dudek sequence, although both Dudek's expression and pose change a lot, the proposed algorithm can track his face correctly.

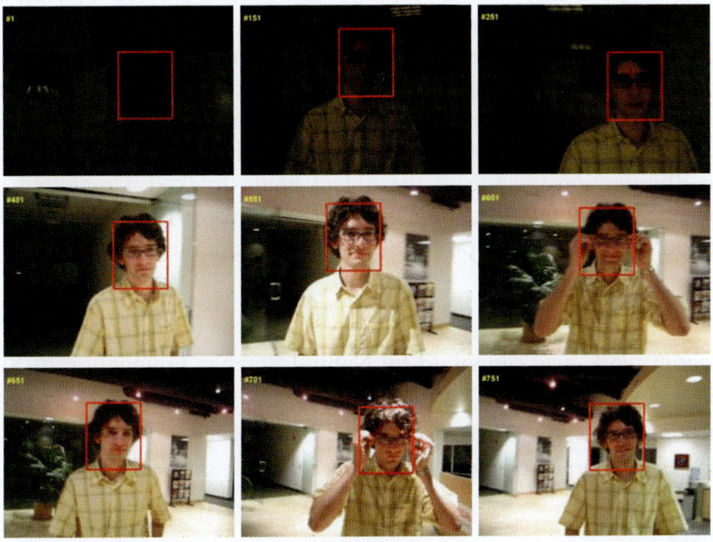

Fig. 1. Tracking results of the David indoor sequence

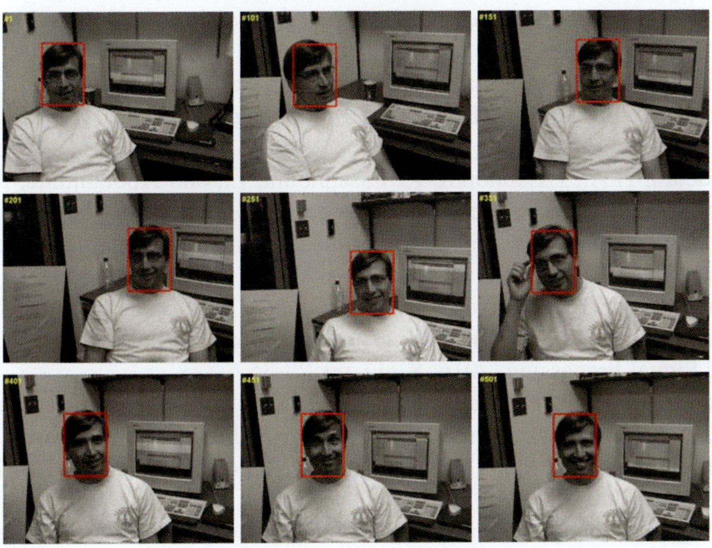

Fig. 2. Tracking results of the Dudek sequence

4. Conclusion

In this paper, a novel object tracking method based on Bayesian framework is proposed. When the object appearance model is established, the background around the target is also used as a part of the model. It's can be seen from the experiments that, in the process of tracking, although the appearance of the target changes, including expression and pose change, and in both of the experiments, the person being tracked took off and wear his glasses, their faces are occluded in several frames, the proposed method can handle these situations well. In addition, the phase of the image's Fast Fourier Transform is used to deal with the illumination change of the object being tracked. Compared with the existing optical flow method, the usage of Fast Fourier Transform improves the real-time performance of the proposed object tracking method.

Acknowledgments

The research work was supported by Natural Science Foundation of Shandong Province under Grant No. ZR2013FL004, ZR2013HM013 and ZR2014FP010, National Natural Science Foundation of China under Grant No. 61503153, and Doctoral Foundation of University of Jinan under Grant No. XBS1503.

References

1. Čehovin, L., Leonardis, A., and Kristan, M.: ‘Visual object tracking performance measures revisited’, IEEE Transactions on Image Processing, 2016, 25, (3), pp. 1261-1274
2. Sui, Y., and Zhang, L.: ‘Visual tracking via locally structured gaussian process regression’, IEEE Signal Processing Letters, 2015, 22, (9), pp. 1331-1335
3. Abdelali, H.A., Essannouni, F., Essannouni, L., and Aboutajdine, D.: ‘Fast and robust object tracking via Accept–Reject color histogram-based method’, Journal of Visual Communication and Image Representation, 2016, 34, pp. 219-229
4. Ramaravind, K., Shravan, T., and Omkar, S.: ‘Scale Adaptive Object Tracker with Occlusion Handling’, International Journal of Image, Graphics and Signal Processing, 2016, 8, (1), pp. 27-35
5. Zhang, S., Zhou, H., Jiang, F., and Li, X.: ‘Robust visual tracking using structurally random projection and weighted least squares’, IEEE Transactions on Circuits and Systems for Video Technology, 2015, 25, (11), pp. 1749-1760
6. Zhang, K., Zhang, L., and Yang, M.-H.: ‘Fast compressive tracking’, IEEE Transactions on Pattern Analysis and Machine Intelligence, 2014, 36, (10), pp. 2002-2015.

Sybil Attack Group Detection Scheme in ZigBee Network

Yi-Cai Huang[1], Mei-Gen Huang[1,a], Bin Yu[1] and Zhi-Yin Kong[2,b]

[1]*Zhengzhou Institute of Information Science and Technology, Zhengzhou, 450001, China*

[2]*Science and Technology on Information Assurance Laboratory Beijing, 100000, China*

E-mail: [a]huang_meigen@163.com, [b]kongwanghui@sohu.com

Aiming at the problems of Sybil attack group damaging routing protocol and positioning mechanism in ZigBee network, a Sybil attack group detection scheme is proposed. In the scheme, an available channel list structure algorithm and a Sybil group attack discovery algorithm was designed, and based on channel access fairness, Sybil attack groups was detected with anomaly traffic in the fixed time. Experimental results show that the scheme has a lower storage and computing overhead while efficiently detecting Sybil attack groups in ZigBee network.

Keywords: ZigBee; Sybil Attack; Attack Detection; Multi-Channel; Neighbor Node.

1. Introduction

ZigBee as an emerging short-range wireless communications technology, low-power and self-organization features make it unique in the field of wireless sensor networks [1]. Sybil attack is an identity-based attack, launched by malicious nodes, and generates a plurality of false identities called Sybil nodes. Depending on whether malicious node is conspiracy, Sybil attack can be divided into conspiracy attack and non-conspiracy attack. Conspiracy attack is usually more dangerous to the network, and more difficult to prevent.

Sybil attack was proposed by the Douceur [2] in 2002. In 2004, Newsome et al [3] considered Sybil attack prevention in wireless sensor networks for the first time, followed by the emergence of a large number of Sybil attack detection scheme [4-6], which cannot prevent the conspiracy Sybil attack. Therefore, [7] proposes the use of a wireless link characteristics to defense Sybil attack, and [8] proposes a non-encrypted Sybil attack authentication scheme, both of which can effectively prevent the conspiracy attack, but there are disadvantages of higher legitimate node misjudgment rate and illegal node missing rate.

In summary, there are issues of not preventing conspiracy Sybil attack, lower node detection rate and so on in the above schemes. Therefore, the paper designs a Sybil attack group discovery algorithm, improving Sybil attack detection rates while reducing node resource requirements by contrasting free communication records in multiple channels and finding abnormal Sybil attack groups.

This paper is organized as follows. Section 1 introduces some related work about Sybil attack prevention. Two algorithms are presented in Section 2. Scheme process is built in Section 3. The experiment and analysis are made in Section 4. And in Section 5, a conclusion is drawn.

2. Model Building

2.1. *Network structure*

Mesh is a basic topology in ZigBee, with features of easy expansion and self-healing. This paper establishes a mesh network structure, as shown in Figure 1.

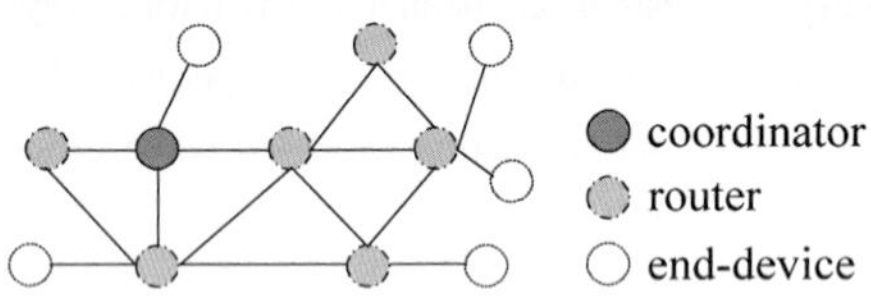

Fig. 1 Structure of mesh network

In the mesh network structure of Figure 1, there is only one coordinator, responsible for establishment, maintenance and management of the entire network. The routers mainly implement forwarding network messages, assuming there is *m*, recorded as $R_p\left(p \le m, p \in N^*\right)$. The end-device mainly completes the practical functions such as sensor monitoring and industrial control, assuming there is *n*, denoted $E_q\left(q \le n, q \in N^*\right)$.

2.2. *Available channel list*

In ZigBee network, the communication band is divided into several channels, node communication doesn't disturb each other on different channels, so that set of channels where nodes can be communicated are called available channel list, wherein the router available channel list and end-device available channel list are denoted as UCL_R and UCL_E. The list construction process is as **algorithm 1**.

Algorithm 1 Available channel list construction algorithm

Step1: Coordinator obtain the average number of router nodes and the average number of end-device nodes in the router neighbor table based on network topology, which are denoted as $|RNR|$ and $|RNE|$.

Step2: The coordinator performs channel scan, to obtain idle channel list ICL, within which the number of channels is recorded as $|ICL|$.

Step3: Coordinator calculates the number of router available channels $|UCL_R| = \min\{|ICL|, \lfloor |RNR|/2 \rfloor\}$ and the number of end-device available channels $|UCL_E| = \min\{|ICL|, \lfloor |RNE/2| \rfloor\}$, where the symbol $\lfloor \ \rfloor$ represents rounded down.

Step4: coordinator respectively randomly selected $|UCL_R|$ and $|UCL_E|$ channels from ICL to structure UCL_R and UCL_E.

2.3. *Sybil attack group*

Sybil attack group is a collection of a plurality of interconnected conspiracy malicious nodes and the fake Sybil nodes, which are illegal node set in the network, denoted *SybilGroup*. After the coordinator complete record and collection of the communication between nodes, Sybil attack group consists of two parts, part of the collection of nodes with significantly smaller traffic, and the other part of the set of nodes with significantly larger traffic between each other which forged by malicious nodes. This paper designs Sybil attack group discovery algorithm is shown in **Algorithm 2**.

Algorithm 2 Sybil attack group discovery algorithm

Step1: Coordinator constructs $m \times (m+n)$ communication matrix based on collected communication record, and the row is composed of *m* router and column is composed of *m* routes and *n* end-device, and cell represents the number of communications between row node $N_i^r (i \in N)$ and column node $N_j^c (j \in N)$, denoted as $E_{i,j}$,as shown in the formula (1).

$$E_{i,j} = \begin{cases} Num_R & i < j < m \\ Num_E & m \le j < m+n \\ 0 & j \le i \end{cases} \tag{1}$$

Num_R is the number of communications between router N_i^r and router $N_j^c (j < m)$, and Num_E is the number of communication for router N_i^r to listen to the end-device $N_j^c (m \le j < m+n)$.

Step2: The coordinator calculates the number of communications for each node, wherein the number of router communications referred to as $\left|N_j^c\right|_R$, and the number of end-device communications referred to as $\left|N_j^c\right|_E$. At the same time, it calculates the average number of communications between the router nodes and end-device nodes, which are denoted as $\left|\bar{N}_j^c\right|_R$ and $\left|\bar{N}_j^c\right|_E$. The formula (2) is shown below.

$$\begin{aligned}
\left|N_j^c\right|_R &= \sum_{i=0}^{m-1}\left(E_{i,j}+E_{j,i}\right) && (j<m) \\
\left|N_j^c\right|_E &= \sum_{i=0}^{m} E_{i,j} && (m \le j < m+n) \\
\left|\bar{N}_j^c\right|_R &= \frac{1}{m}\sum_{j=0}^{m}\left|N_j^c\right|_R && (j<m) \\
\left|\bar{N}_j^c\right|_E &= \frac{1}{n}\sum_{j=m}^{m+n}\left|N_j^c\right|_E && (m \le j < m+n)
\end{aligned} \qquad (2)$$

Step3: Coordinator sets the traffic deviation threshold (α,β). α is smaller threshold value, β is larger threshold, $0<\alpha<0.5<\beta<1$. For router, if $\left|N_j^c\right|_R \le \alpha\left|\bar{N}_j^c\right|_R$ or $\left|N_j^c\right|_R \ge \beta\left|\bar{N}_j^c\right|_R$, add it into *SybilGroup* ; for end-device, if $\left|N_j^c\right|_E \le \alpha\left|\bar{N}_j^c\right|_E$ or $\left|N_j^c\right|_E \ge \beta\left|\bar{N}_j^c\right|_E$, add it into *SybilGroup.*

3. The Process of Scheme

The scheme in this paper is based on channel access fairness. In a period of time, node free access channel and select the neighbor node to communicate with, and finally identify Sybil attack groups with abnormal traffic by matching the communication record. Thus, scheme assumes that all the nodes in the network can only receive or send data in one channel at the same time.

In ZigBee network, the end-device node can only communicate with the router nodes, so the scheme is divided into two steps: the first step is to test router nodes, freely choose channel to communicate with their neighborhood router nodes within the available channel list and record communication data; the second step is to test end-device nodes, freely choose the channel broadcasting existing information in its list of the available channels. All router nodes are monitoring in promiscuous mode, and recording monitor data. Therefore, the coordinator needs to set three thresholds, namely router testing time, end-device testing time and channel waiting time.

Sybil attack group testing process:

Step1: Coordinator executes **Algorithm 1** to construct list UCL_R and UCL_E.

Step2: the coordinator broadcast start detecting commands $Cmd_{begin} = \{T_R, UCL_R; T_E, UCL_E; T_W\}$ in the whole network.

Step3: After receiving the command, the end-device node start timing T_R and sleep; router random sets antenna state to receive or transmit, and randomly selects channel to communicate with their neighborhood router nodes within UCL_R, recording all communication data. When node successfully communicates or fails to establish communication with the other nodes in T_W time, re-select and switch to the new channel and antenna status.

Step4: After time T_R, the end-device nodes automatically wake up, and randomly select channel to broadcast existing packets based on UCL_E, and router nodes open promiscuous mode and randomly select channel to monitor based on UCL_E, and record existing packets broadcasted by end-device nodes.

Step5: After time T_E, all router nodes report route communication data and monitored end-device existing information.

Step6: After receiving the record, the coordinator performs **algorithm 2** to construct $SybilGroup$, then broadcast end command $Cmd_{end} = \{SybilGroup\}$.

Step7: All nodes store $SybilGroup$, and add it to the blacklist.

4. Experiments and Results Analysis

Experiments are based on TI's CC2530 development platform, using mesh to deploy 56 nodes, where the coordinator 1, legitimate router node 12, malicious router node 3, legal end-device nodes 30, malicious end-device nodes 10, and each malicious node creates five Sybil nodes. Experimental environment is a typical office space, where nodes are in the same plane. The nodes are identified by MAC address. Communication band is 2.4GHz, and the other parameters as follows, (α, β) is $(0.2, 0.8)$, T_R is 6s, T_E is 16s, T_W is 50ms.

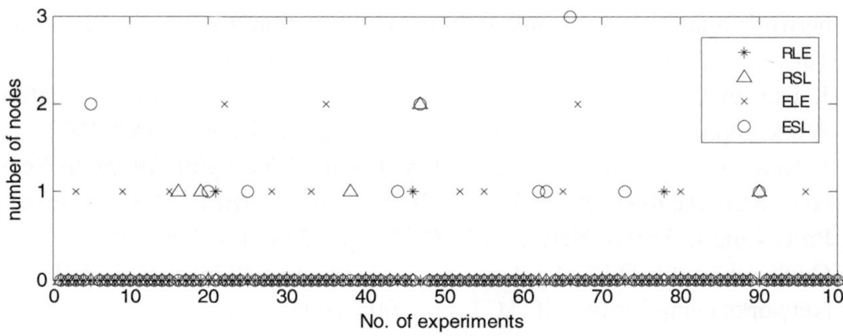

Fig. 2 Experimental results

Experiments are carried out 100 times independently. Randomly move node location after each experiment to change the network topology, and re-establish the network after a power-on reset. Experimental results are summarized as shown in Figure 2, where RLE, RSL, ELE, ESL respectively represent the legal route misjudgment, illegal router Missing, legal end-device misjudgment and illegal end-device missing. The horizontal axis shows the serial number of experiments, and the vertical axis represents the number of nodes. Figure 2 shows the proportion of RLE, RSL, ELE, ESL is respectively 0.25%, 2.0%, 0.53%, 1.4%, reaching the expected detection results.

5. Conclusions

On the basis of in-depth study of the characteristics of Sybil attack and ZigBee technology, this paper first proposes an available channel list construction algorithm, and then design a Sybil attack group discovery algorithm based on channel access fairness, and gives Sybil attack group detection scheme process. Finally, the scheme is verified by experiments. Experimental results show that the proposed scheme can be achieved less costly and has high Sybil node detection rate, and can prevent conspiracy Sybil attack, which effectively enhances the security performance of ZigBee network in practical applications.

Acknowledgments

This work is supported by Science and Technology on Information Assurance Laboratory.

References

1. Tseng H W, Lee Y H, Yen L Y, et al, ZigBee (2.4 G) wireless sensor network application on indoor intrusion detection//Consumer Electronics-Taiwan, 2015 IEEE International Conference on, pp. 434-435, 2015.
2. J. Douceur, "The sybil attack", Peer-to-Peer Systems: First International Workshop, Lecture Notes, Springer-Verlag, pp. 251-260, March 2002.
3. J. Newsome, E. Shi, D. Song, and A. Perrig, "The Sybil Attack in Sensor Networks: Analysis & Defenses", In Proc.of 3rd IEEE/ACM Information Processing in Sensor Networks(IPSN'04), pp. 259-268, April 2004.
4. Gunhee Lee, J.L.D.K., An Approach to Mitigating Sybil Attack in Wireless Networks using ZigBee. ICACT, pp. 1005-1009, 2008.
5. H. Yang, J. Zhang, Y. Zhao, J. Han, Y. Lin, and Y. Lee, "SUDOI: software defined networking for ubiquitous data center optical interconnection," IEEE Communications Magazine, vol. 54, no. 2, pp. 86-95, Feb. 2016.

6. H. Yang, J. Zhang, Y. Zhao, Y. Ji, J. Han, Y. Lin, and Y. Lee, "CSO: Cross Stratum Optimization for Optical as a Service," IEEE Communications Magazine, vol. 53, no. 8, pp. 130-139, Aug. 2015.
7. Xiao L, Greenstein L J, Mandayam N B, et al, Channel-based detection of Sybil attacks in wireless networks, Information Forensics and Security, IEEE Transactions on, vol. 3, no. 4, pp. 492-503, 2009.
8. Zeng K, Govindan K, Mohapatra P, Non-cryptographic authentication and identification in wireless networks, Network security, pp. 3, 2010.

Research on Improvement of DV-Hop Localization Algorithm in WSN

Xi Li[a], Lu Wang and Ai-Zhen Liu
Information Engineering Department, Ordnance Engineering College, Shijiazhuang, Hebei, China
E-mail: [a]lixi7780@aliyun.com

DV-Hop localization algorithm is an important location algorithm for Wireless Sensor Networks. To solve the problem of large error on specific network, an improved algorithm about selecting shortest hop beacon node and computing the average hop distance is proposed. Simulation results show that it is useful for declining error rate of localization, and it is better for complex network especially.

Keywords: WSN; DV-Hop; Localization Accuracy; Node Localization.

1. Introduction

Wireless sensor network [1] due to its real-time perception and communication, can be widely used in the field of transportation, agricultural irrigation, city surveillance, military reconnaissance etc.. In the practical application, the location information is an important parameter used in WSN, accurate localization can enable WSN to achieve better monitoring results. Therefore, in recent years, localization technology has attracted much attention in the study of wireless sensor networks.

WSN localization technology [2, 3], according to whether need to beacon nodes, can be divided into beacon node localization technology and self localization technology of coordinate system, according to whether need to range, can be divided into range-based localization technology and range-free localization technology. This paper mainly study a kind of DV-Hop location technology with beacon nodes and range-free localization. Firstly, analyzing the composition and characteristics of the existing DV-Hop location algorithm, focus on factors affecting localization deviation, then improving the algorithm, and through the experiment to verify it.

2. DV-Hop Location Algorithm

DV-Hop algorithm [4-7] is one of a series of distributed localization algorithms proposed by Dragos Niculescu et al., which uses the principle of distance vector routing and GPS location. It includes 6 kinds of localization algorithms: DV-Hop, DV-distance, Euclidean, DV-coordinate, DV-Bearing and DV-Radial. DV-Hop localization algorithm is the most successful and widely used in the APS (Ad hoc localization System) series [8]. There are three main steps in the DV-Hop algorithm:

The first step: distributing a plurality of nodes in wireless sensor networks, in which the beacon node use distance vector exchange protocol packet to the neighbor nodes broadcast their location information, so that all nodes in the network obtain the information of minimum hop counts distance from beacon nodes.

The second step: each beacon node uses the location information of other beacon nodes and the minimum hops to compute average distance per hop. The beacon node in the network broadcast the average distance per hop. After receiving the information, Ordinary nodes calculate the distance to the beacon node by using the shortest hop distance multiplied by the network average hop distance. Average hop distance is as shown in the Eq. (1).

$$C_{ij} = \frac{\sum_{i \neq j} \sqrt{(x_i - x_j)^2 + (y_i - y_j)^2}}{\sum_{i \neq j} hops_{ij}} \quad (1)$$

Among them, (x_i, y_i), (x_j, y_j) are the coordinates of i and j, $hops_{ij}$ is the hops between i and j.

The third step: when the nodes to be positioned to obtain three or more beacon nodes in the distance, the unknown information can be calculated by three sided measurement or the maximum likelihood estimation method.

In summary, it can be seen that the DV-Hop algorithm is a kind of algorithm locating by the beacon node, the principle is to calculate the distance between the unknown node and the three beacon nodes, and to estimate the coordinates of the unknown nodes on the basis of the three side measuring method or the maximum likelihood estimation method. At the same time, the DV-Hop algorithm is a kind of non ranging algorithm, the distance between the unknown node and the beacon node is estimated by the shortest hop distance between them multiplied by the average distance of each hop. At present, there are some improvements for DV-Hop algorithm, such as Yu Ning et al. proposed improved algorithm based on using hop count to adjust the packet reception [9]; Shuang Tian et al. Proposed the combination of ranging technology and non ranging technology RDV-Hop algorithm [10], etc..

3. DV-Hop Error Factor Analysis and Algorithm Improvement

3.1. *Error factor analysis*

Analysis of DV-Hop algorithm shows that the distance between the unknown node and the beacon node is estimated distance, since it is estimated that the distance will produce error. To improve the localization accuracy of the algorithm, it is necessary to reduce this error. The error factors of DV-Hop algorithm are analyzed in detail in the following example.

If there is a wireless sensor network topology is shown in Figure 1, S1, S2, S3 are the beacon nodes, A is one of the nodes to be positioned.

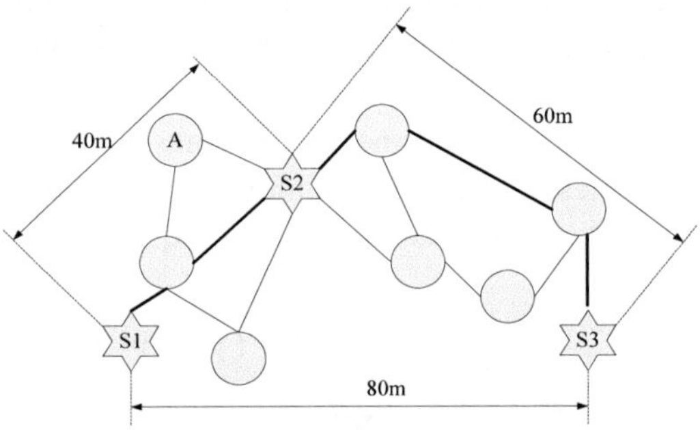

Fig. 1. Schematic of DV-Hop algorithm

From the figure, the minimum number of hops between S1 and S2 is 2, the minimum number of hops between S2 and S3 is 3, the minimum number of hops between S1 and S3 is 5. At this time, measuring the distance that S1 and S2 are 40m, S2 and S3 distance is 60m, S1 and S3 distance is 80m.

According to the algorithm, the beacon node S1 the average distance per hop is (40+80) / (2+5) =17.14, the beacon node S2 the average distance per hop is (40+60) / (2+3) =20, the beacon node S3 the average distance per hop is (60+80) / (3+5) =15. The node to be positioned A distance S2 1 hop, hop at least, so average hop distance of node A is 20. average hop distance from the beacon node S2 the average hop distance is 20, therefore, the distances between A,S1,S2,S3 are 40, 20, 80, according to the three sided measurement or the maximum likelihood estimation method can estimate the coordinate of A.

In summary, the typical factors affecting the accuracy of WSN localization are three points:

(1) Node density. In general, when the number of nodes in a limited area is more, the precision of DV-Hop algorithm is relatively high. However, simply

increase the number of network nodes means increasing the hardware equipment, thereby increasing the cost of localization

(2) Number of beacon nodes. Different from the ordinary nodes, because the beacon node comes with satellite localization system, thus increasing the beacon node will increase the cost of communication.

(3) The position of the beacon node and the nodes to be positioned. This relative position can affect the determination of the average hop distance of the network, which can affect the calculation of the distance. During the operation process, the reasonable choice of beacon node can improve the accuracy of the algorithm.

Analysis of these factors, the influence on the localization accuracy of node density and the number of anchor nodes was not a completely linear, rush to improve node density or increase the number of beacon nodes does not necessarily improve the localization precision of a network. The purpose of improving the accuracy is the value of the shortest hop multiplied by the average hop distance as close as possible to the true distance between the node and the beacon node. The improvement of the algorithm is aimed at the two aspects of the shortest hop count and the average hop distance of the network.

3.2. *Improved algorithm*

Based on the above analysis, the improvement of DV-Hop algorithm is mainly aimed at the selection of beacon nodes in the network topology. The selection of the beacon node will have two effects: one is the selection of the shortest hop beacon nodes, the two is the calculation of the average distance of each hop.

3.2.1. *The shortest hop beacon node selection*

The selection of the minimum hop beacon node is obtained by distance vector protocol of DV-Hop algorithm. After the node to be positioned to obtain the shortest hop of neighboring beacon nodes, the average distance of each hop is determined as the average hop distance of each hop.

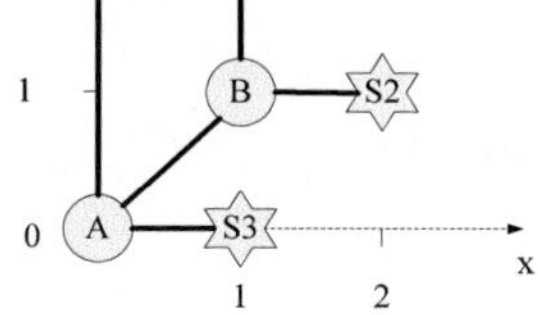

Fig. 2. Topology problem 1

This problem can be shown in Figure 2. A, B are the common to be localization nodes, S1, S2, S3, S4 are the beacon nodes. The solid line represents the network connection, the dotted line represents the two-dimensional coordinate system. The node A for localization, running the first step to find S1, S3 to the node A are 1 hop, the least number of hops. According to the coordinate system, the beacon node coordinates are S1 (0, 2), S2 (2, 1), S3(1, 0), S4 (1, 2). If the S1 is selected as the shortest hop beacon node, the average hop distance of S1 can be calculated according to the Eq. (1).

$$C_{S1} = \frac{d_{S1S2} + d_{S1S3} + d_{S1S4}}{hops_{S1S2} + hops_{S1S3} + hops_{S1S4}} = \frac{\sqrt{5} + 1 + \sqrt{5}}{3 + 2 + 3} \approx 0.684$$

If the S3 is selected as the shortest hop beacon node, the average hop distance of S3 can be calculated according to the Eq. (1).

$$C_{S3} = \frac{d_{S3S1} + d_{S3S2} + d_{S3S4}}{hops_{S3S1} + hops_{S3S2} + hops_{S3S4}} = \frac{\sqrt{5} + \sqrt{2} + 2}{2 + 3 + 3} \approx 0.706$$

Thus, when a node to be positioned with multiple shortest hop beacon nodes, which beacon nodes as the shortest hop beacon nodes to be chose will effect on average hop distance, and this distance will affect the localization accuracy. Therefore, it is very important to select the minimum number of hops.

Firstly, using the Eq. (1) to calculate the average hop distance of all the beacon nodes with the shortest hop to the nodes to be located. Secondly, using the Eq. (2) for calculating the average value of the beacon node average hop distance. The denominator is the number of beacon nodes to the node to be positioned in the shortest hops, the numerator is the sum of the average value of the beacon nodes with the shortest hops to the node to be positioned. Finally, using the Eq. (3) to select the ideal shortest hop beacon node. By comparing the absolute value of the difference, the error caused by the selection of beacon nodes is reduced.

$$\overline{C}_{Sshort} = \frac{\sum_{i \neq j} C_{Sshortij}}{N_{Sshort}} \tag{2}$$

$$\min | C_{Sshorti} - \overline{C}_{Sshort} | \tag{3}$$

3.2.2. *Improved calculation method of average distance per hop*

The average hop distance is obtained by the Eq. (1). Eq. (1), the numerator is the sum of the true distance from the selected beacon node to the other beacon nodes, the denominator is the sum of hops from the selected beacon node to the other beacon nodes. In the actual network, because the network topology is random, when the distance from a beacon node to the selected beacon nodes far greater or far less than the distance from other nodes to the selected node, but the hops are not much different, which will have a greater impact on the average hop distance of the selected node.

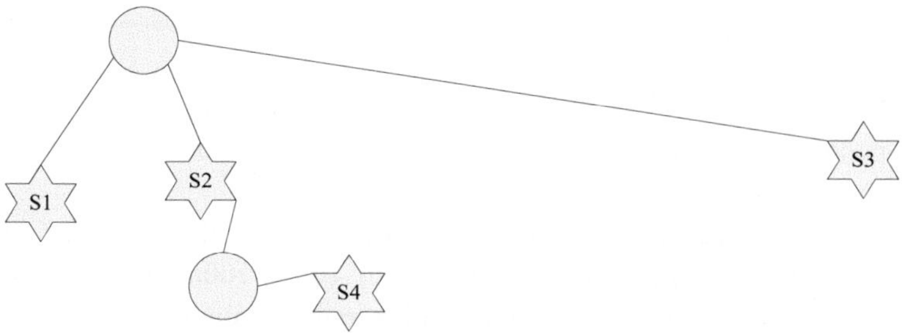

Fig. 3. Topology problem 2

This problem is shown in Figure 3 Among them, S1, S2, S3, S4 represent beacon node. S1 to S2 is 2 hops, S1 to S3 is 2 hops, S1 to S4 is 4 hops, but the distance from S3 to S1 is far greater than the distance from S2,S4 to S1.In this case, using Eq. (1) to calculate the average hop distance of S1 will have a large deviation.

Needle to this can improve the DV-Hop algorithm. After running the improved algorithm to select the shortest hop beacon node, using the Eq. (1) to calculate the average hop distance from each beacon node to the node to be positioned. The average hop distance is multiplied by the hops to each beacon node, which is the distance from beacon node to the node to be positioned, as shown in the Eq. (4).

$$\tilde{d}_i = C_i \times Hops_i \tag{4}$$

If the number of the beacon nodes is greater than 4, according to the calculation results of the Eq. (4) to remove the maximum distance of the beacon node and the shortest one. Thereafter, using Eq. (1) to calculate the average hop distance of the remaining nodes.

4. Experimental Validity and Analysis

Localization error rate is used to measure the localization accuracy in the evaluation of the node localization accuracy. The localization error of a node e_i is the difference between the estimated position and the actual position. Localization error rate $\overline{R}_e$ is the number of nodes with the average localization error divided by node communication radius, as shown in the Eq. (5).

$$\overline{R}_e = \frac{\sum_{i=1}^{N_a} \sqrt{(\tilde{x}_i - x_i)^2 + (\tilde{y}_i - y_i)^2}}{N_a \times r} \tag{5}$$

Among them, $(\tilde{x}_i, \tilde{y}_i)$ is the estimated position coordinates, (x_i, y_i) is the actual position coordinates, r is the node communication radius, N_a is the number of non beacon nodes.

The DV-Hop algorithm and the improved DV-Hop algorithm are analyzed and simulated by using Matlab7.0. Establish 100m*100m environment area. Test in two groups, different communication radius values were selected, and each group was tested for several times, and the localization error rate of different beacon node density was tested.

First group, random distribution of 100 nodes, including the beacon node and the common to be positioned nodes, set the communication radius of 10m. The ratio of the beacon node is adjusted, and the results of the test are shown in Figure 4.

Second group, random distribution of 100 nodes, including the beacon node and the common to be positioned nodes, set the communication radius of 20m. The ratio of the beacon node is adjusted, and the results of the test are shown in Figure 5.

The experimental results show that the improved algorithm can effectively reduce the localization error rate and improve the localization accuracy when the communication radius is 10m and 20m. The effect of improved algorithm in the node communication radius of 20 meters is more obvious. Moreover, when the number of beacon nodes is large in unit range, the advantage of the improved algorithm can be better reflected. This shows that the improved localization algorithm is superior to the complex topology network.

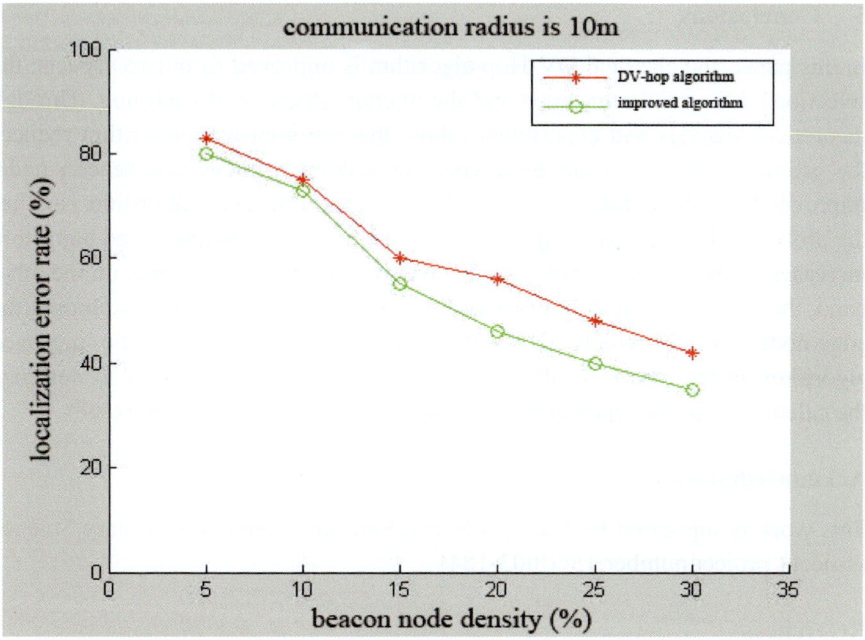

Fig. 4. Comparison of the localization error rate when the communication radius is 10m

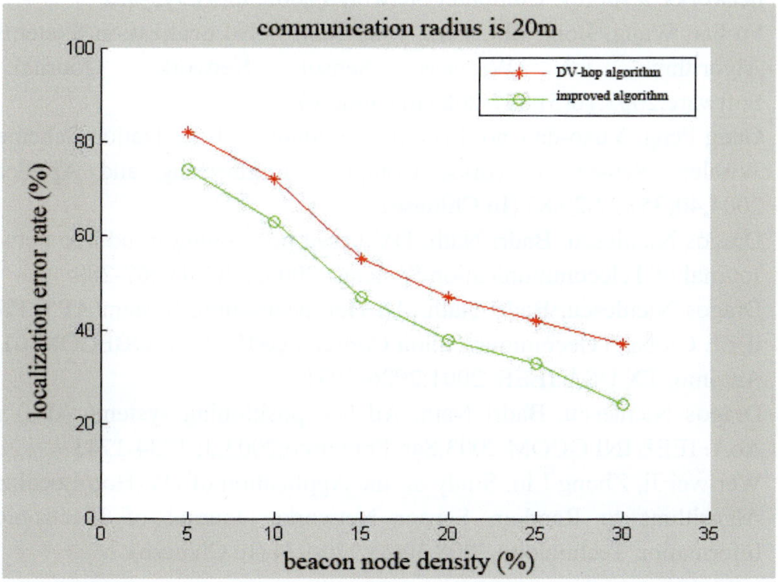

Fig. 5. Comparison of the localization error rate when the communication radius is 20m

5. Conclusions

In this paper, the classical DV-Hop algorithm is improved from two aspects: the selection of the minimum hops and the average distance of each hop. Through theoretical analysis and experiments show that the improved algorithm reduces the estimate error of distance between the unknown nodes and beacon node, improves the localization accuracy. However, the improved algorithm also has the problem of increased computation. On the one hand, the improved algorithm increases the traversal operation of the average distance of the node, on the other hand, the improved algorithm increases the repetitive operation of excluding the edge nodes, both of which increase the amount of computation of the improved algorithm. In the next step of work, we will continue to study how to optimize the calculation of the algorithm, while achieving better localization results.

Acknowledgments

This work is supported by National Social Science Foundation-Military Science Project.(project number:15GJ003-184)

References

1. Akyidiz IF, Su W, Sankarasubramaniam Y, et al. Wireless sensor networks: a survey. Computer Networks,2002,38(4):393-422
2. Fu-bao Wang, Long Shi, Feng-yuan Ren. Self-Localization Systems and Algorithms for Wireless Sensor Networks. Journal of Software,2003,16(5):857-868 (In Chinese)
3. Gang Peng, Yuan-da Cao, Li-min Sun. Study of Localization Schemes for Wireless Sensor Nerworks. Computer Engineering and Application, 2004,40(35):27-29,83 (In Chinese)
4. Dragos Niculescu, Badri Nath. DV based positioning in ad hoc networks. Journal of Telecommunication Systems, 2003, 22(1/4):267-280
5. Dragos Niculescu, Badri Nath. Ad Hoc positioning System(APS).Proc of IEEE Global Telecommunication Conference(IEEE GLOBECOM 01).San Antonio, TX,USA:IEEE, 2001:2926-2931
6. Dragos Niculescu, Badri Nath. Ad hoc positioning system(APS) using AoA. IEEE INFOCOM 2003,San Francisco,2003,3: 1734-1743
7. Wei-wei Ji, Zhong Liu. Study on the Application of DV-Hop Localization Algorithms to Random Sensor Networks. Journal of Electronics & Information Technology,2008,30(4):970-974 (In Chinese)

8. Nasipuri A, Li Kai. A directionality based location discovery scheme for wireless sensor networks. Proc of the 1st ACM International Workshop on Wireless Sensor Networks and Applications. New York, NY, USA: ACM, 2002: 105-111.
9. Ning Yu, Jiang-wen Wan, Qing Song, et al. An improved DV-Hop localization algorithm in wireless sensor networks. Proc of IEEE International Conference on Information Acquisition. Shandong: IEEE, 2006: 638-643.
10. Shuang Tian, Xin-ming Zhang, Peng-xi Liu, et al. A RSSI-based DV-hop algorithm for wireless sensor networks. Proc of International Conference on Wireless Communications, Networking and Mobile Computing (WiCom '07) . Shanghai: IEEE, 2007: 2555-2558.

Parallel Multi-Pattern Matching Algorithm Based on CUDA

Jie Wang[1,a], Hui Wang[2,b,*], Wei-Hao Chen[1] and Ji-Wei Liu[1]

[1]*School of Software Technology, Dalian University of Technology, Dalian, 116024, China*

[2]*Lab, CNCERT/CC, Yumin Road No. 3A Beijing, 100029, China*

E-mail: [a]wang_jie@dlut.edu.cn , [b]wh@cert.org.cn

As a classical problem in computer sciences, the multi-pattern matching algorithm has been widely researched and derives a lot of different matching algorithms. With the arrival of the age of big data and explosion of network information, original pattern-matching algorithm can no longer meet the need of practical application. This paper designed and implemented the parallelization of AC algorithm and WM algorithm based on GPU, proposed solutions to solve the problems of thread junction, optimized multi-pattern matching algorithm and tested the time consuming of these algorithm. The efficiency of coarse-grained thread-parallel AC algorithm is 20 times as much as serial algorithm, and improved when the size of test string and pattern set increases. The efficiency of coarse-grained parallel WM algorithm is 2 times as much as serial algorithm when the size of shortest pattern string is 2. At the same time, comparing the acceleration performance on GPU and FPGA, it further proves the superiority of GPU on pattern-matching algorithm.

Keywords: GPU; Multi-Pattern Matching; Coarse-Grained Parallel.

1. Introduction and Background

Data analysis is the core of the whole processes in recent age of big data, which attracts scholars pay more and more attention to multi-pattern matching algorithm. Traditional multi-pattern matching algorithm can no longer meet the need of practical application. W. Zhang [1] *et al.* focused on large data set on virus scanning, their research was based on Map Reduce and Hadoop platform,

*Corresponding author.

and the experiment showed that parallel scanning was more efficient than traditional stand-alone scanning. P. Yang [2] *et al.* adopted the Uq-grams and the hash method on the one of the fastest multi-pattern string matching algorithm BG, and results showed that BGqus is faster than BG in most of case. There are also other multi-pattern matching algorithms [3, 4] have been researched, the thoughts of them were based on software-matching.

However, on the side of hardware, general calculation based on GPU is becoming a new trend in the development of computing. Recently, for high-level single-chip GPU, the ability of processing single-precision float point comes to 1 Tflop/s, storage bandwidth also comes to 141GB/s, which has more than 10 times of mainstream CPU [5]. At the same time, software based on GPU has advantages on costs and cycles [6].

Recently, the acceleration of pattern-matching algorithm obtained good efficiency on CUDA. For example, D. L. Xu etc. successfully transplanted WM algorithm to GPU, which made the speedup ratio 12 times as much as original serial algorithm [7]; G. B. Zhang *et al.* designed and implemented AC algorithm based on CUDA, experiment showed that the speedup ratio of parallel algorithm was 22 times as much as original serial algorithm [8].

This paper designed parallel AC and WM multi-pattern matching algorithm based on CUDA, considered the problems in thread junction and analyzed the complexity of the algorithms.

2. The Basic Principle of Multi-Pattern Matching Algorithms

2.1. *The basic principle of AC multi-pattern matching algorithm*

Classical AC algorithm [9] generates finite-state machine in the preprocessing stage, which includes *goto*, *failure* and *output* functions. For pattern set P{*he*, *she*, *his*, *hers*}, the corresponding state machine is shown in Figure 1.

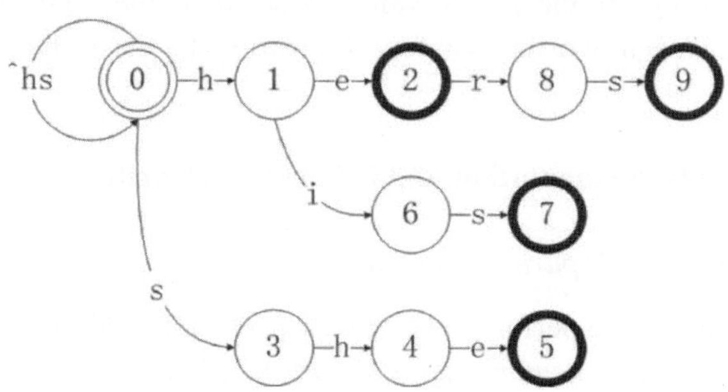

Fig. 1. State machine of pattern set.

goto function indicates what state will arrival when reading a character from the text in the current state; *failure* function indicates the next state when the character reading form the text is mismatching the state; *output* function indicates what mood will be output when the character reading from the text is matching. The pattern-matching stage of AC algorithm is shown below: it starts at state 0, each time picks out one character from the test, uses *goto table* transfer to the next state based on current state and scanned character. If the *failure* function of the current state is not *null*, then jump in accordance with the failure value, else if the *output* function of the current state is not *null*, then record the current matched position.

2.2. *The basic principle of AC multi-pattern matching algorithm*

WM [10] algorithm combined the filter and the thought of BM [11] algorithm, which is also divided into pre-processing stage and pattern-matching stage. In the pre-processing stage, three tables are constructed: *shift table*, *hash table* and *prefix table* [12]. *Shift table* stores the distance that should move when the block-string appeared. *Hash table* stores the string which has the same hash value at the end of the block-string in the matching window. While *Prefix table* stores the string which has the same hash value of the start of the block-string in the matching window.

If the size of the matching window T is m, the size of the block-string B is 2, matching process will look like the following:

(1)Calculate the hash value h at the end of the block-string,

(2)Research the *shifttable* to find out the value of *shift*[h], if it cannot be found, then first move the window $m - B + 1$ positions to the right, then jump to (1), else if *shift*[h] > 0, then move the window *shift*[h] positions to the right then jump to (1), else jump to (3),

(3)Pick out the *prefix* of the block-string, calculate the *prefix* value of the start of the block-string. If the *prefix* value exists then the value is the matched pattern string. We move the window 1 position to the right and continue to match.

3. Design and Implementation of AC Parallel Algorithm

3.1. *The design of AC parallel algorithm*

In order to optimize the performance of GPU, we first need to consider 3 factors, they are *datastructure*, *memoryaccess* and *threadallocation*.

The design of data structure: here we use a type of uint4 *StateTable* to store *goto*, *failure*, *output* values. The design of memory access: since the storage space of shared memory and constant memory is limited, it cannot meet the demand of *StateTable* for storage space. For global memory, its storage is large enough to meet the demand for storage space, but the AC algorithm accesses to the *StateTable* is random, it may cause serious efficiency drops. For texture memory, it not only can meet the demand of *StateTable* for storage space, but also has an ideal memory access speed [13]. The design of thread allocation: if the pattern set is divided into several small sets, then each thread has to do part of the pattern-matching. Since it is difficult for the scale of divided pattern to achieve GPU full-load and thread balance-load, it is not suitable to do in this way when the size of the pattern set is small. If the text string is divided into several pieces, then each thread has to do part of the text string matching. It can ensure to achieve GPU full-load and thread balance-load for massive data. The analysis result indicates that it is suitable to divide the text string.

3.2. *The implement of AC parallel algorithm*

AC algorithm can be divided into two parts: pre-processing and pattern-matching. Since preprocessing is a serial process which make it difficult to transplant, so this paper focuses on pattern-matching process parallelization when transplant to GPU [14].

Pattern-matching process, each thread process 1KB consecutive data:

Algorithm 1 The auto search function 0 of AC state-machine

Require: g idata
Ensure: g_odata, g_valid
  s_idata[32][132]
  currentState.w=0
  FOR each i ∈ [0, 7]
    FOR each j ∈ [0, 31] do
      read 128B data;
    ENDFOR
    FOR each k ∈ [0, 127] do
      read currentState
      if it need output ,**then** output the result and record the index;
      if fail, **then** jump according to failure function
    ENDFOR
  ENDFOR

Due to each thread starts from state zero, matched pattern may lose at the junction of the thread. In order to avoid data lose, the *autosearch* function 1 is added to process the 64B data at the junction of the thread.

Algorithm 2 The auto search function 1 of AC state-machine

Require: g idata
Ensure: g_odata, g_valid

```
s_idata[32][132]
currentState.w=0
FOR each i ∈ [0, 31]
   do read 64B data
ENDFOR
FOR each i ∈ [0, 31]
   do calculate the state at the junction of thread
ENDFOR
FOR each i ∈ [0, 31]
   do calculate the output at the junction of the thread
ENDFOR
```

3.3. *The time complexity analysis of AC parallel algorithm*

On the stage of pattern-matching, it supposes the time of pattern-matching is T_1 before parallelization in Eq. (1), T_2 after parallelization in Eq. (2). The time when put the text string and *jumptable* into video memory is c, the number of thread-block is k, the speedup ratio is R_1, it is found that:

$$T_1 = n \tag{1}$$

$$T_2 = \frac{(n+c)}{k} \tag{2}$$

$$R_1 = \frac{T_1}{T_2} = k * \frac{1}{1+\frac{c}{n}} \tag{3}$$

Eq. (3) shows that: because of the existence of acceleration performance of parallel AC algorithm reflected when the length of the text string reached to a certain scale. In addition, when the length of the text string rises, the performance of acceleration increases the same.

4. Design and Implementation of WM Parallel Algorithm

4.1. *The design of data structure*

Here we focus on the design of data structure, because the AC and WM algorithm are the same in memory access and thread allocation, we use a type of uint4 *StateTable* to store *shift*, hash, and *prefix* value. Another data structure is an array composed of pattern set. If the max length of pattern string in the pattern set is *LenMax*, then the length of the array is *LenMax* + 1. The last bit of each pattern records the number of the next pattern which has the same *prefix* value as the current pattern. If the current pattern is the last which has the same *prefix* value, then the last bit of the current pattern will be *NULL*.

4.2. *The implementation of WM parallel algorithm*

Algorithm 3 The auto search function 0 of WM state-machine

```
Require: g idata
Ensure: g_odata, g_valid
  s_idata[32][132]
  FOR each i ∈ [0, 31]
    read 128B data;
  ENDFOR
  FOR each k ∈ [0, 127] do
      do pick out the string-block
      if the shift value is 0, then record the matched index, move the window 1 position
      else if the shift value not exist, then move the window m-B+1 positons
      else move the window shift value positions
  ENDFOR
```

The parallel process approach between AC and WM algorithm are different, because there are no state changes during the execution of WM algorithm, just need to search the *StateTable* constantly. Therefore, when dealing with the junction of thread, only need to change *LenMax* to 2 ∗ *LenMax*. Here do not give the function, because the process approach is the same as the function WMkernel_0.

4.3. *The time complexity analysis of WM parallel algorithm*

The average time complexity of WM serial algorithm is O(*Bn*/*m*). In the practical application $B < m$, so the time complexity of WM algorithm is lower than AC algorithm at the pattern-matching stage. Suppose the matching time is T_3 before parallelization in Eq. (4), T_4 after parallelization in Eq. (5), the time when put the text string and *StateTable* into video memory is *c*, the number of thread is *k*, the speedup ratio is R_2, it is found that:

$$T_3 = \frac{Bn}{m} \tag{4}$$

$$T_4 = \frac{Bn}{mk} + c \tag{5}$$

$$R_1 = \frac{T_3}{T_4} = k * \frac{1}{1 + \frac{mkc}{Bn}} \tag{6}$$

Eq. (6) shows that: because of the exits of *c*, acceleration performance of parallel WM algorithm reflects when the length of the text string reaches to a certain scale. In addition, the acceleration of performance increases when the length of the text string rises or the size of the pattern set decreases. The max speed up ratio is k in theory.

5. The Testing and Analysis of the Parallel Algorithm

This paper implement the parallel pattern-matching algorithm based on CUDA, and tests the speedup ratio. Experiment environment is as Table 1:

Table 1. The experiment environment.

Item	Content
Operating System	Window 7
CPU	AMD
GPU	NVIDIA
Programming	Platform
CUDA	Version
RAM	2GB
Video	Memory

5.1. *The testing and analysis of AC parallel algorithm*

In this paper, we test the performance of AC algorithm in the size of text string and pattern set two aspects, the results are as Figure 2:

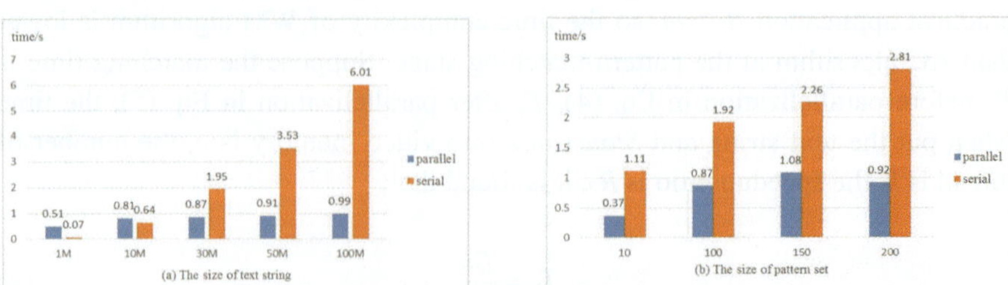

Fig. 2. The test results of AC serial implementation and parallel implementation.

Figure 2(a) shows the time consumed when the pattern set is 100, the test string increases from 10M to 150M. The result shows that the time consumed of both algorithms increased with the growth of the length of text string, but the growth trend of the parallel algorithm is smaller than the serial algorithm.

Figure 2(b) shows the time consumed when the size of test string is 100, the pattern set increase from 10 to 150. The result shows the size of the pattern set for AC parallel algorithm does not have a big impact on the acceleration performance.

5.2. *The testing and analysis of WM parallel algorithm*

For WM algorithm, we also test the size of text-string and pattern-set two aspects. The results are as Figure 3:

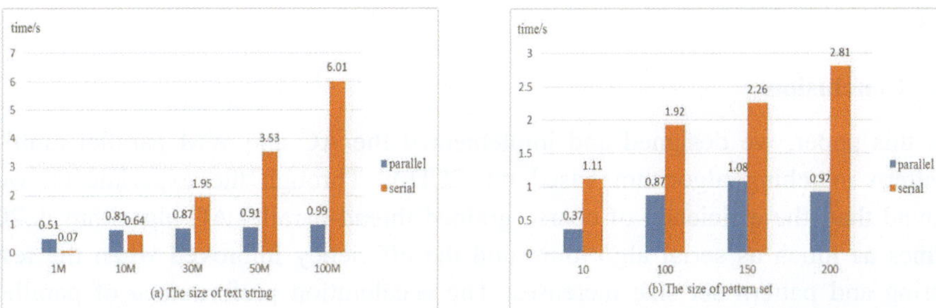

Fig. 3. The test results of WM serial implementation and parallel implementation.

Figure 3(a) shows the time consumed when the pattern set is 100, the test string increase from 1M to 100M. Figure 3(b) shows the time consumed when the size of test string is 100, the pattern set increases from 10 to 200. The result almost the same as AC algorithm, but the efficiency of WM algorithm is higher than AC algorithm.

5.3. *The analysis of multiple matching-pattern algorithms*

This paper also analysis the speedup ratio on different devices, or in different application backgrounds. Among them, the results of the AC algorithm and WM algorithm are applied on regular expression based on GPU, and the AC algorithm based on FPGA [15] all come from documents. The contrast result showed in Table 2.

By analyzing the above data, we found that: whether the application background is a regular expression or a simple text, the acceleration performance of AC algorithm on the GPU is better than that on the FPGA. It proves the superiority of GPU as the speed up platform of the pattern matching algorithm.

Table 2. The comparison of acceleration performance.

algorithm	Device	Application	background
AC	NVIDIA GeForce GTX 480	regular expression	22[13]
AC	NVIDIA GeForce GTX 460	simple text	20
AC	FPGA	regular expression	10[15]
WM	NVIDIA GeForce GTX 570	GeForce	12[7]
WM	NVIDIA GeForce GTX 460	GeForce	2

6. Conclusion

In this paper, we designed and implemented the AC and WM parallel multi-pattern matching algorithm based on CUDA. Through the experiments, we found that, the efficiency of coarse grained thread-parallel AC algorithm is 20 times as much as serial algorithm, and the efficiency improved when the test string and pattern set size increases. The acceleration performance of parallel WM algorithm is most influenced by the length of the shortest string in the pattern string. Compared to serial algorithm, the shorter execution time, faster processing speed and easier configuration made the system have great performance boosting.

These algorithms implemented in this paper also have many deficiencies. The one hand, we have to adopt the method of processing batches, because of the restriction of equipment resources; on the other hand, CPU is in idle state when GPU is in pattern-matching stage, it is clearly a waste of resource. Adding CPU in the system to form a heterogeneous acceleration platform can be a promising direction area to improve the system performance. Beside, how to implement fine-grained parallelism will be our main effort for work in the future.

Acknowledgments

Work partially supported by Grant 2015QN-12 of Youth Foundation of National Computer Emergency Response Team/Coordination Center of China and Grant 61472100 of National Nature Science Foundation of China.

References

1. W. Zhang, B. Li and K. Li, Multi-pattern matching algorithm based on MapReduce and Hadoop, in Proc. Int. Conf. Mechatron. Sci., Electric Eng. Comput. (MEC'13), (Shenyang, China,2013).
2. P. Yan, L. Liu, H. Fan, et al. Fast multi-pattern string matching algorithms based on q-grams bitparallelism filter and hash, in Proc. Int. Conf. Info. Tech. Soft. Eng. , (Springer Berlin Heidelberg, 2013) , pp. 487-495.
3. Yang G, Li S, Tan Z, et., A New Multi-pattern Matching Algorithm Based on Frequently Used Group, in Proc. IEEE Int. Conf. Comput. Inf. Technol.(CIT'12), (Chengdu, China, 2012).
4. L. Jun, Z. Zhuo, M. Juan et al., Multi-pattern Matching Methods Based on Numerical Computation, Telkomnika Indonesian J. Elect. Eng., 11, 1497(2013).
5. NVIDIA Corporation, CUDA Programming Guide Version 5.0,(NVIDIA Corporation , California , 2012).
6. G. G. Zhao, C. G. Wu. Research on Multiple Pattern String Matching with Bit-parallelism Based on GPU, Comput. eng., 37,265(2011).
7. D. L. Xu, H. L. Zhang and Y. J. Fan, The GPU-based High-performance Pattern-matching , J. Comput. Inf. Syst., 9, 3791(2013).
8. Giorgos Vasiliadis, Spiros Antonatos, Michalis Polychronakis, et High Performance Network Intrusion Detection Using Graphics Processors, Lect. Notes Comput. Sci., (MA, United states, 2008).
9. A. Aho, M. Corasick, Efficient string matching: an aid to bibliographic search, Commun. ACM, 18, 333(1975).
10. S. Wu, U. Manber, A fast algorithm for multi-pattern searching, Technical Report TR-94-17, University of Arizona(Tucson, Arizona, 1994).
11. R. S. Boyer, J. S. Moore, A fast string searching algorithm, Commun. ACM, 20,762(1997).
12. J. Ma, G. P. Wang and M. Yang, Wu-Manber Multi-pattern Matching algorithm based on CUDA, Comput. Syst. App, 3, 11(2012).
13. G. G. Zhang, W. S. Xie and H. W. Wu, Multi-pattern Matching Technology Based on CUDA, in Proc. netinfo security acad. commun. Conf., (Mount wuyi, China,2011)

14. S. Zhang, Y. L. Chu, K. Y. Zhao, et al., GPU high performance computing based on CUDA, (China Water Power Press, Beijing, 2009), pp. 227-236.
15. S. Dharmapurikar, J. Lockwood, Fast and Scalable Pattern Matching for Content Filtering, Symp. Archit. Networking Commun. Syst.,(ANCS'05), (Princeton, United states, 2005).

Research on the CORBA Implementation of the PL-ISEE Broker

Jian-Li Dong[1,a] and Wen Dong[2]

[1]*School of Computer Engineering, Huaihai Institute of Technology*
Lianyungang, Jiangsu, 222005, P. R. China
[2]*28th Subsection of United Logistics, Lanzhou Military Region of PLA*
Xi'an, 710043, P. R. China
E-mail: [a]dongjl1019@sina.com

With the research and development of software engineering, the industrialization production technology and method of software products have become the hot topics in software engineering field. The main problems facing software industrialization production are the research and implementation of software product line and PL-ISEE. In the paper, a new industrialized PL-ISEE model is proposed. One of the main parts framed the new PL-ISEE is the core asset and COTS component agent bus. To realize the agent bus and component based software assembly line, the broker idea and architecture based on CORBA are introduced, and the broker architecture and basic framework model adapted to the new PL-ISEE agent bus requirements are created, and then its CORBA based implementation mechanism and method are systemically discussed. The PL-ISEE realized by the broker architecture will have more advantages on the locating transparency, dynamic updates and expansion of the COTS servers, and interoperability and interactivity between different agent systems. These advantages are very useful to realize the new PL-ISEE and industrialization production of software products.

Keywords: Broker Architecture; Software Component; Software Product Line; PL-ISEE (Product Line Based Integrated Software Engineering Environment); CORBA; Agent Bus.

1. Introduction

In the heterogeneous network environment, so as to make full use of the extensive network resources and collaboration to resolve the complex distributed computing problems effectively, the researches and applications on software component, software middleware, Internet ware, and software Agent technologies have made rapid progress. In order to achieve the interoperability and communication between components and component-based application software development under such a heterogeneous network environment, the agent/broker technique and method have become the research hot points of the current heterogeneous networks, distributed computing and communication, software product line and so on fields. This paper will mainly study the framework model and implementation mechanism of software component broker architecture in a new industrialized PL-ISEE (product line based integrated software engineering environment). The aim is to create a feasible theory and technology support for industrialized assembling production of application software products in distributed network [1-3].

2. The Design of PL-ISEE Broker System

We have proposed a new industrialized PL-ISEE model shown as the Figure 1 in the paper [4]. This new industrialized PL-ISEE model is a multi-layer architecture model on the basis of unified product line engineering conceptual model, large-granularity reusable asset data model, component assembly behavior model, iterated evolution model of core assets developing and application software producing. Here, we create a broker architecture model such as shown in Figure 1 to suit to the PL-ISEE model in the paper [4]. The broker architecture generally consists of the following six parts: client, server, broker, bridge, client-side broker, and server-side broker, and in which the component parts of the role are discussed below [5-8]:

Server/component server: The server is responsible for achieving various

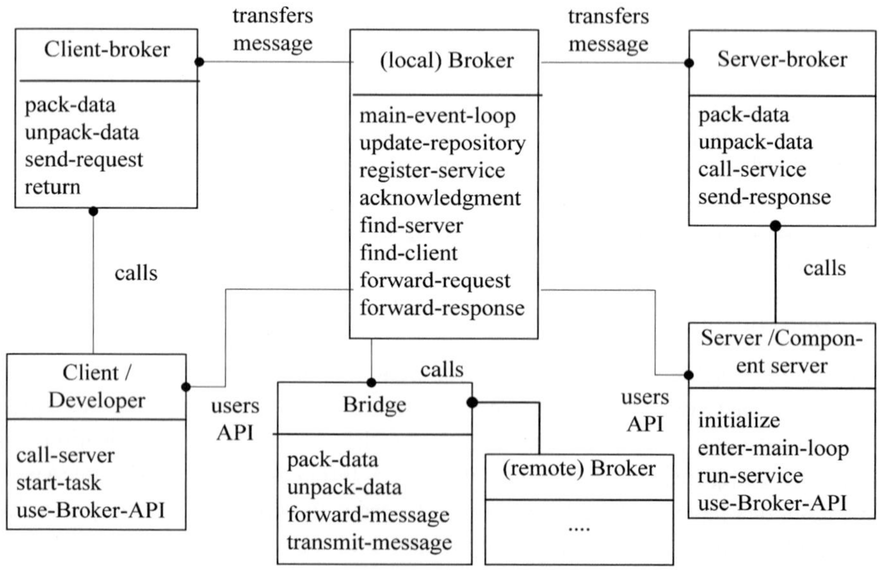

Figure 1. Broker architecture system model

function services of the server-side and registering the services to brokers, and then displays and provides its functions through its interfaces [9-10].

Client/developer: The client is an application program to complete specific problem solving by accessing one or more servers. In the broker architecture, the client's requests will be transmitted to the server by the broker.

(local or remote) Broker: The broker is responsible for transmitting the client requests to the server side and the server result data to the client side.

Client-broker: The client-broker is the isolated layer adding between client and broker, taking charge of communication between client and broker.

Server broker: The server broker is responsible for receiving the requests sent by the broker, analyzes the received message, unpacks parameters, locates and calls the appropriate service, completes operation requested by the client. At the same time, result data to return to the client should be packaged in accordance with the data semantics.

Bridge: that is a communication bridge between two different network systems.

3. The CORBA Implementation of the PL-ISEE Broker System

According to the requirements of the new PL-ISEE model in paper [4] and PL-ISEE broker architecture shown in Figure 1 as well as the CORBA (Common Object Request Broker Architecture) architecture and its function configuration, we design an implementation framework of the PL-ISEE broker system and PL-ISEE component database system platform based on the CORBA. This framework model is shown in Figure 2. In Figure 2, in addition to retaining ORB functions of the CORBA, that is, retaining ORB to be responsible for the communication and interoperability between customers and server objects in heterogeneous network environments, the component model and component assembly capability provided by CORBA V3.0 cluster could be used. Furthermore, "core asset component and its agent bus" in the PL-ISEE model shown in paper [4] can be implemented by ORB. In fact, ORB acts a dual role in the framework of PL-ISEE based on CORBA: one is ORB role in the original CORBA architecture; another is product line core asset component and its agent bus which is also called CAB (Component Agent Bus) [10-13].

The essence of PL-ISEE is to realize the assembly production of software products with product line core asset components (such as architecture, framework, component and connector). Therefore, in the product line development environment based on CORBA shown in Figure 2, the left part consists of the client-side and client broker, it actually is a work environment of all developers (such as analysis, design, programming, testing and management personnel) who produce the software products with the core asset components requested by client broker from the component object server through the broker (ORB) and server broker. The right part consists of the server-side (including server-broker, server objects, etc.), its main function is to receive the requests form the broker (ORB) and achieve the location and return of the requested component object in software product line core asset database system. At the same time, it achieves a lot of work about the organization, saving, issuance, distribution, search, selection and management of the asset component objects in the environment database system.

Generally, production and management of product line core assets called COTS components will be completed by assets manufacturers or the third-party component providers. The communication, interoperation and component-entity transmission between client side and server side are achieved by object request broker (ORB) and ensure the transparency of these works or computing in heterogeneous network environment.

Figure 2 shows that client-side environment framework mainly contains various types of development tools using software product line core asset components to assembly application software products, such as product line analysis, design, implementation and management tools. These tools would be integrated on the CORBA architecture according to the three-dimensional integrated model with interface, tool and data. It must be emphasized that the integration of client data (core asset components) appears at client side in the way of agent, which is only the registration and identification of components data. And actual component data is all saved in the server side which will provide the retrieval, query, classification and management of component data by corresponding server object. The interface between ORB and client should be expressed by the interface definition language (IDL) provided by CORBA architecture, mainly including CS (Client Stubs), DII (Dynamic Invocation Interface), and IR (Interface Repository). CS is static interfaces provided by object server to client, that is, client local agent (called as client-broker) of server side object services, and clients call the services provided by service object through the interface or client-broker. DII (Dynamic Invocation Interface) and IR (Interface Repository) can be used to dynamically call services provided by service objects under running status. Here, the DII and IR are also collectively called the dynamic client-broker). On the server side (the right part in the Figure 2), object adapter, product line object skeleton, DFI (Dynamic Framework Interface), component object server and its component implementation database, architecture object server and its implementation database, management object server and management assets implementation database and other facilities are all configured.

When the client users or developers use the services provided by the component, architecture and management object server in server side, they could inquire and access the various services provided by service-side object implementation by two ways: One is that they could send the requests to the object server side through client-side CS (Client Stubs, that is the client broker)) service agents of object implementation. Another is that they can use routines in IR (interface library) and send requests to service-side object implementation by calling DII (Dynamic Invocation Interface). Once object calling requests arrive at ORB, ORB is responsible for the requests and their parameters conversion, and sends the requests to the Server-Broker and appropriate object adapter. After receiving the requests, the object adapter determines whether there is corresponding skeleton for the requested object implementation. If there is corresponding skeleton, object adapter call the operation in object implementation library through the skeleton. Otherwise, the object adapter calls the operations in object implementation library through the dynamic implementation routines in DFI (Dynamic framework interface). After finishing the service of object implementation, the results would be reversed back to client according to object request transmission and executing path. Here what

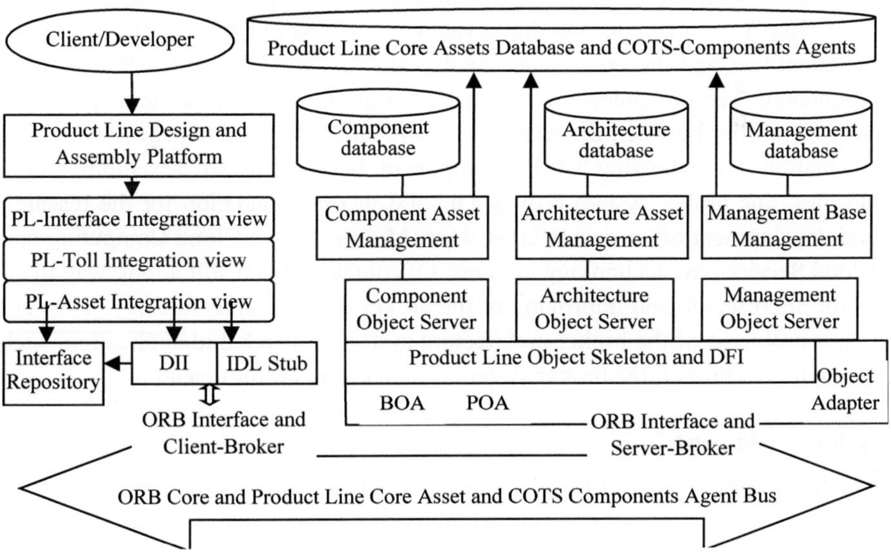

Figure 2. The framework of PL-ISEE broker system based on CORBA

must be noted is that object implementation or services of service-side mainly provide the search and acquisition of software product line core asset components and return to client-side developers through ORB in order to achieve the assembling production of product line application software [13-14].

4. Conclusions

The broker architecture is an inevitable model to realizing distributed computing in heterogeneous network environments. In today's Internet application information system, many systems use the broker architecture model. For example, the Common Object Request Broker Architecture (CORBA: Common Object Request Broker Architecture) developed and promulgated by OMG, which gets widely industry support and application, is becoming a standard broker architecture and object oriented technology realizing distributed computing in heterogeneous network environment.

The CORBA architecture and technology are employed as the broker of the product line core asset and COTS component agent bus in the new PL-ISEE model, so as to realize the complex component broker system of the integrated component assembling environment/line of the software product line in heterogeneous network. The implementation of the PL-ISEE system based on the CORBA architecture has the advantages of location transparency between the client side and the server side, the dynamic updating and extensibility of the component server, independence and portability of the system platform, interoperability between different broker systems. These advantages lay a solid foundation for achieving COTS component based software assembling line. Besides, this broker system provides a solid theory foundation for the research and development of current Internet ware, Mobile-Agent, Cloud Computing and Cloud Service, etc. technology systems. Of course, there is still a long way to go as for the research and improving of the broker theory and technology. They are major problems of the broker architecture system research and application, such as intelligent broker, the broker system efficiency and error detection.

Acknowledgment

This project is supported by Fund of Jiangsu University Natural Science Basic Research Project, Grant No. 08KJD520013 and Jiangsu Key Built Discipline Project—Computer Application Technology.

References

1. Zhang Xinyu, Zheng Li, Sun Cheng, "The research of the component-based software engineering", 6th International Conference on Information Technology: New Generations, pp.1590-1591, 2009.
2. YANG Fuqing, LV Jian, MEI Hong, "Internet ware technology System: A Approach centered Architecture", Science in China (Series E: Information Sciences), Vol.38, No.6, pp.818-828, 2006.
3. Thurimella Anil-Kumar, Padmaja Maruthi T., "Software product line engineering: A review of recent patents," Recent Patents on Computer Science, vol.3, no.2, pp.148-161, 2010.
4. Jianli DONG, Ningguo SHI. "A study on framework and realizing mechanism of ISEE based on product line," Journal of Software, Vol.5, No.10, p.1077-1083, 2010.
5. Zhijian WANG, Yukui FEI, Yuanqing LOU, Software Component technology and Application. Beijing: Science Press, April 2004.
6. HE Tian-zhang, WANG Pan-qing, LI Xiao-hui, "Research and Application on CORBA Component Assembly", Science Technology and Engineering, Vol.8, No.1, pp.84-86, 2008.
7. CHANG Bing-guo, WANG Xiang-zong, "Research and development of component integration support platform", Computer Engineering and Design, Vol.32, No.8, pp.2712-2715, 2011.
8. Jainli DONG, Ningguo SHI, "Research on the CORBA Implementation Mechanism of a New Industrialized PL-ISEE", Journal of Software, Vol.7, No.5, pp.1171-1176, 2012.
9. Jianli DONG, Ningguo SHI, Yong ZHANG, "Research and Implementation on an Ideal Industrialized PL-ISEE and Its Database Supporting Platform", JCIT, Vol.7, No.13, pp.206-214, 2012.
10. Longye Tang, Yukui Fei, Zhijian Wang, "Service-Oriented Component Model", IJACT- International Journal of Advancements in Computing Technology, Vol.3, No.1, pp.68-79, 2011.
11. Li Na, Wang Weizhe, "ON CORBA BASED ACCESS MIDDLEWARE OF HETEROGENEOUS DATABASE AND ITS IMPLEMENTATION", Computer Applications and Software, Vol.27, no.5, pp.162-164, 2012.
12. YU Bin, HUA Qingyi, "Analysis and practice of distributed heterogeneous computing environment based on CORBA", Journal of Northwest University (Natural Science Edition), vol.30, no.2, pp.113-117, 2000.
13. YAN Juan, ZHANG Lifang, CAI Xuqing, "Research and Development of CORBA", Software Guide, Vol.8, No.6, pp.41-43, 2009.
14. Jianli DONG, "Research on the Realizing Mechanism of PL-ISEE Broker Architecture", Journal of Software, Vol.8, No.3, pp.579-586, 2013.

Development of Brain Extraction Methods for MRI

Shao-Feng Jiang[a], Su-Hua Yang, Zhen Chen and Cong-Xuan Zhang

Key Laboratory of Nondestructive Testing (Nanchang Hangkong University), Ministry of Education, Nanchang, Jiangxi 330063, China

E-mail: [a]jsphone@163.com

Brain extraction or skull stripping is an important pre-processing step in neuroimaging analysis. This review summarizes the current research efforts in the area of automatic or semi-automatic brain extraction from MRI volumes. The review firstly gives a full description of the various brain extraction methods based on categorization, then addresses the key problems (boundary leakage, local convergence and sensitivity to parameter setting) in brain extraction. The paper analyses how well these problems were dealt with in recent researches.

Keywords: Brain Extraction; MRI; Categorization of Methods; Comparison Between Methods; Challenges.

1. Introduction

Segmenting brain from non-brain tissue (eyeballs, skin, fat, muscle, skull, etc.) named brain extraction or skull stripping is needed before most of neuroimaging analyses, such as registration between fMRI and T1-Weighted MRI, measurement of brain volume, brain tissue classification and cortical surface reconstruction. The similarity in brightness between brain tissue and nearby non-brain tissue, such as dura, makes distinguishing between such tissues on a local level very difficult [1]. As manual Brain extraction, requiring the operator with professional knowledge about cerebral anatomy is extremely time-consuming and hard to obtain objective result, in recent decades, automatic or semi-automatic brain extraction methods (BEM) have become the choices for fast brain extraction. These techniques can generally be categorized: region-based, boundary-based, atlas-based, and hybrid methods. In this paper, we will simply introduce these methods and give a comparison between some of above methods.

2. Classification of BEM

2.1 *The region-based methods*

The region-based methods first use thresholding or clustering techniques to divide cerebral image into several regions by the observation that intensities of the voxels in the same tissue are similar. Then, the brain region can be extracted from these regions by morphological operations and region merging. Lemieux [2] proposed an algorithm which utilized several intensity thresholds and morphological operations to remove non-brain areas. Coxs [3] used Gaussian mixture model to estimate an intensity range to extract the brain areas in a slice-by-slice manner. Hahn and Peitgen [4] presented a pre-flooding height based watershed algorithm to group image voxels with similar intensities and merged the largest connected component as the brain volume. The region-based methods are usually sensitive to image processing parameters and image artifacts, such as noise and intensity inhomogeneity. Therefore, the region-based methods usually require the user to determine the proper parameters.

2.2 *The boundary-based methods*

The boundary-based methods are used to locate a closed contour which partitions the cerebral image into internal part (brain) and external part (non-brain). Smith [5] proposed a well-known boundary-based method called Brain Extraction Tool (BET). BET initialized the brain contour with a tessellated mesh and pushed the mesh to the brain boundary with some smoothing forces and a pushing force. The main drawback of BET is that the brain boundary is usually over-smoothed due to the global pushing force. Another widely used boundary-based method is Brain Surface Extraction (BSE) [6]. BSE used a series of processes to separate brain and non-brain tissues. The parameter of morphological operators has extremely influence on the extraction. Zhuang [7] developed an active contour model based level set method (MLS) which defined the image data function according to the pushing force used in BET and the smoothing function according to the mean curvature of the evolving curve. MLS can get good result in most cases. However, MLS easily leaks through a weak boundary. Liu [8] and Zhang [9] developed a similar method as MLS with more accuracy.

2.3 *The atlas-based methods*

The atlas-based methods register the brain volume to an atlas using registration techniques before performing brain extraction. Rex [10] developed a brain extraction meta-algorithm (BEMA), which executed four extraction algorithms to obtain individual extraction results in concert with an atlas-based registration procedure and combined them to achieve the final improved brain extraction result by using a variety of anatomically specified Boolean functions. It is obvious that BEMA costs a lot of time. Wang [11] warped an atlas to the brain volume to obtain the initial brain mask, and then refined the mask with a deformable-surface similar with BET. Eskildsen [12] proposed an atlas-based method with nonlocal segmentation technique, without the need for time-consuming non-rigid registrations. By using registration techniques, the atlas-based methods can address the problem of variability in anatomy and modality and produce more robust results. However, the registration in atlas-based methods is usually time-consuming and if the registration fails, bad result may be obtained.

2.4 *The hybrid methods*

The hybrid methods try to integrate above mentioned methods to improve the extraction result. Most of the hybrid methods are from coarse to fine. In early hybrid methods, usually the region-based method severs as pre-process to obtain a rough brain region or boundary. Next, the boundary-based method is carried out with the initial contour obtained in the pre-process. The extraction result in the hybrid methods is more accurate since the initial contour is close to the brain boundary at the beginning of the boundary-based stage. Ségonne [13] proposed a hybrid watershed algorithm (HWA) applying the watershed algorithm to get an initial brain volume for deformable model. Meanwhile, an atlas-based force was added to ensure that the deformed template possesses the shape of a brain within certain tolerance. Huang [14] employed the expectation-maximization algorithm on a mixture of Gaussian models to determine the initial brain contour for the geodesic active contour evolution. Sadananthan [15] used intensity thresholding to generate a preliminary binary mask ideally including the brain tissues, the skull and some thin connections between them. Then, a graph cuts based image segmentation (GCUT) was used to remove narrow connections. Jiang[16] used BET to obtain a rough brain surface, and then refined the brain surface by performing level set in its neighborhood.

3. Comparison Between Some BEM Methods

To measure the extraction accuracy of BEMS, we used 18 normal T1-weighted MR Image datasets with expert segmentations, obtained from the Internet Brain Segmentation Repository (IBSR, https://www.nitrc.org/projects/ibsr) developed by the Centre for Morphometric Analysis (CMA) at Massachusetts General Hospital. Each volume has around 128 coronal slices, with 256 × 256 pixels per slice and 1.5mm thickness. The DICE coefficient was used as the evaluation metric, which is defined in Eq.(1).

$$DICE = \frac{2|M \cap N|}{|M|+|N|} \tag{1}$$

Where, the ground truth M is the set of voxels that are labelled as brain by the expert, and N is the set of voxels that are labelled as brain by the algorithm or method being tested.

Table 1. The comparison result on IBSR data between different BEM methods

Methods	Type	DICE	Time	Parameter setting	Robustness
BET[5]	boundary	0.941	<10S	Manual	good
BSE[6]	boundary	0.913	<10S	Manual	bad
MSL[7]	boundary	0.936	4Min	Manual	bad
Liu[8]	boundary	0.956	30S	Manual	good
GCUT[15]	hybrid	0.911	4Min(matlab)	Manual	bad
Jiang[16]	hybrid	0.96	10Min(matlab)	Manual	good
Beast[12]	atlas	0.967	20Min	Auto	best

In Table 1, the atlas based method, Beast obtained the best DICE coefficient with high robustness, however the computational time is too long; The boundary based method, BET obtained good balance on accuracy and computational time; Jiang's hybrid method achieved high accuracy with less time than Beast, however the parameters need to be set manually.

4. The Challenges in BEM

The above mentioned methods have achieved great improvements in the accuracy and robustness for brain extraction. However, these methods can not completely substitute for manual method for the appearances of over-smoothness, leakage through a weak boundary and missing brain tissues caused by local convergence. Unfortunately, it is a conflicting problem to improve all of them. Brain extraction is a compromised problem where a semi-global understanding of the image is required as well as a local understanding [6]. For example, it is effective that using local region features to obtain sharp brain boundary and eliminate the leakage, but easy to lead to local convergence at the edges between the white matter and gray matter.

Smith [6] used a semi-global designed force in BET to push the contour to the brain boundary. and can be considered the semi-global items in the force, because and are the minimum and maximum intensity values along a line pointing inward from the current vertex to the center. This force is well designed so that BET became one of the widely used brain extraction tools and liu [8], Wang [11], Jiang [16], Zhuang [7] and Ségonne [13] used the similar forces in their proposed BEMS. The main drawback of BET is that the brain boundary is usually over-smoothed due to the global pushing force. To obtain a more sharp brain surface, Jiang[16] used BET to obtain a rough brain surface, and then refined the brain surface by performing level set in its neighborhood; GCUT[15] used graph-cut to refine the brain boundary after initializing the boundary by thresholding and atlas registration respectively. To overcome leakage of boundary, Liu[8] and Zhuang [7] detected the leakage of boundary first, then modified the parameters in level set to eliminate leakage of boundary. The most effective way to overcome leakage of boundary and local convergence is to use atlas, however this way is time consuming as mentioned in previous sections. Thus, a fast atlas-based BEM method is needed in the future to obtain the brain fast, accurately and stably. One way for fast brain extraction could be using GPU-based parallel computing technique for registration to atlas and segmentation. Another way could be incorporating the grid based feature matching technique to detect leakage of boundary and local convergence in the boundary based BEM methods.

5. Conclusions

In the past 20 years, the techniques of BEM have achieved great improvement from semi-automatic performance to full, from low accuracy to high accuracy. However, the conflict between the accuracy and computational time still occurs, which limits the application of BEM in clinic and brain researches. To develop a fast and accurate BEM method is the key task in the future.

Acknowledgments

This work was supported by the National Natural Science Foundation of China (No. 61162023 and No. 61163046).

References

1. B. P. Sutton and A. T. Van. "Multicontrast 3D structural imaging to improve automatic brain extraction and segmentation," ISMRM-ESMRMB Joint Annual Meeting. vol.4, pp.3005, 2010.
2. L. Lemieux, G. Hagemann, K. Krakow, F. G. Woermann, "Fast, accurate, and reproducible automatic segmentation of the brain in T1-weighted volume MRI data," Magnetic resonance in medicine, vol. 42, no. 1, pp. 127-135, 1999.
3. R. W. Cox, "AFNI:Software for analysis and visualization of functional magnetic resonance neuroimages," Comput Biomed Res, vol. 29, no. 3, pp. 162-173, 1996.
4. H. K. Hahn, H. O. Peitgen, "The Skull Stripping Problem in MRI Solved by a Single 3D Watershed Transform," Springer-Verlag. In Proceedings of the Third International Conference on Medical Image Computing and Computer-Assisted Intervention, pp. 134-143, 2000.
5. S. M. Smith, "Fast robust automated brain extraction," Human brain mapping, vol. 17, no. 3, pp. 143-155, 2002.
6. D. W. Shattuck, S. R. Sandor-Leahy, K. A. Schaper, D. A. Rottenberg, R. M. Leahy, "Magnetic resonance image tissue classification using a partial volume model," NeuroImage, vol. 13, no. 5, pp. 856-876, 2001.
7. A. H. Zhuang, D. J. Valentino, A. W. Toga, "Skull-stripping magnetic resonance brain images using a model-based level set," NeuroImage, vol. 32, no. 1, pp. 79-92, 2006.
8. J. Liu, Y. Chen, L. Chen, "Accurate and robust extraction of brain regions using a deformable model based on radial basis functions," Journal of Neuroscience Methods, vol. 183, no. 2, pp. 255-266, 2009.
9. H. Y. Zhang, J. F. Liu, Z. X. Zhu, H. Y. Li. "An automated and simple method for brain MR image extraction," Biomedical Engineering Online, 10:81, 2011.
10. D. E. Rex, D. W. Shattuck, R. P. Woods, K. L. Narr, E. Luders, K. Rehm, S. E. Stoltzner, D. A. Rottenberg, A. W. Toga, "A meta-algorithm for brain extraction in MRI," NeuroImage, vol. 23, no. 2, pp. 625-637, 2004.
11. Y. Wang, J. Nie, P. T. Yap, F. Shi, L. Guo, D. Shen, "Robust Deformable Surface Based Skull Stripping for Large-Scale Studies," In Proceedings of MICCAI. pp. 635–642, 2011.
12. S. F. Eskildsen, P. Coupé, V. Fonov, et al, "BEaST: Brain Extraction based on nonlocal Segmentation Technique," NeuroImage, vol. 59, no.3, pp. 2362–2373, 2012.

13. F. Segonne, A. M. Dale, E. Busa, M. Glessner, D. Salat, H. K. Hahn, B. Fischl, "A hybrid approach to the skull stripping problem in MRI," NeuroImage, vol. 22, no. 3, pp. 1060-1075, 2004.
14. A. Huang, R. Abugharbieh, R. Ram, A. Traboulsee, "MRI brain extraction with combined expectation maximization and geodesic active contours," In proceedings of IEEE International Symposium on Signal Processing and Information Technology, pp. 107-111,2006.
15. S. A. Sadananthan, W. Zheng, M. W. Chee, V. Zagorodnov, "Skull stripping using graph cuts," NeuroImage, vol. 49, no. 1, pp. 225-239, 2010.
16. S. Jiang, W. Zhang, Y. Wang, Z. Chen, "Brain extraction from cerebral MRI volume using a hybrid level set based active contour neighborhood model," BioMedical Engineering OnLine. 12: 31, 2013.

Research on Communication Anti Jamming System Based on Multitier Architecture

Ai-Rong Yu[1,a], Jun Wang[2,b], Yan-Jie Niu[1], Guo-You Chen[1] and Yong Wang[1]

[1]*Institute of Command Information Systems, PLA University of Science and Technology, Nanjing 210007, China*

[2]*Nanjing Telecommunication Institute, Nanjing 210007, China*

E-mail: [a]498067717@qq.com, [b]intraweb@163.com

This paper proposes and designs a testing framework for the whole network based on the multi-layer software architecture. System based on TCP protocol and socket interface command flow, implementation of all kinds of network test equipment centralized control and status monitoring, improve the accuracy and efficiency of data transmission test system of anti-jamming in the field of communication.

Keywords: Multitier Architecture; Anti-Jamming Communication; Integrated Test.

1. Introduction

1.1. *Multitier architecture*

In software engineering, multitier architecture (often referred to as n-tier architecture) is a client–server architecture in which presentation, application processing, and data management functions are physically separated. The most widespread use of multitier architecture is the three-tier architecture.

N-tier application architecture provides a model by which developers can create flexible and reusable applications. By segregating an application into tiers, developers acquire the option of modifying or adding a specific layer, instead of reworking the entire application. A three-tier architecture is typically composed of a presentation tier, a domain logic tier, and a data storage tier.

While the concepts of layer and tier are often used interchangeably, one fairly common point of view is that there is indeed a difference. This view holds that a layer is a logical structuring mechanism for the elements that make up the software solution, while a tier is a physical structuring mechanism for the system infrastructure [1] [2].

1.2. *Communication equipment network test system*

At present, network technology represented by TCP/IP, with its mature, open and other advantages, is being applied in automation in various fields, to replace the traditional mainstream serial communication automation system communication.[3] In order to ensure the normal operation of communication equipment, emerge as the times require monitoring system of communication equipment, but with the communication equipment, instrument automation, large-scale, high speed and complexity, as well as the communication network scale is more and more big, [4] connected to the communication network in the communication equipment of various kinds and number of rapid growth, which makes the structure of the communications network is more complex, state monitoring communication equipments becomes very complex.

In recent years, with the development of automatic testing and integration testing of communication anti jamming techniques, in anti-jamming communication integration testing type communication equipment, instrument relates to many kinds of type, variety, the equipment monitoring and testing system has put forward higher requirements. But the equipment monitoring and testing system previously developed mostly for single or single class network equipment, scalability, flexibility, [5] generality, and between each equipment monitoring and testing system are independent of each other, the data format and communication format is not the same, the "information island" effect greatly limits the equipment monitoring and testing the scope of application system anti-jamming communication, and caused a huge waste of resources.

2. Anti Jamming System Architecture

The system in this paper realizes Communication Anti-jamming infield test. Anti jamming capability of communications equipment in field test is divided into basic technical parameter test and ability of anti disturbance simulation performance tests. The basic technical indicators testing is mainly refers to the use of various instruments on the sensitivity, selectivity, double signal frequency rejection ratio, mirror frequency suppression ratio, blocking, reciprocal mixing, the average transmission power, [6] frequency hopping rate were measured; the anti-interference ability simulation performance tests are tested in the simulation of interference environment loading under the communication efficiency the communication equipment, instrument, including data communication frame loss, error test, speech communication vocabulary definition, sentence intelligibility test.

The system is divided into interface layer, testing process monitor layer, data layer and intelligent equipment control layer, interface layer, the testing process monitor layer needs to be able to obtain real-time data intelligent device control layer, and the analysis of control strategy, control commands through communication equipment network to intelligent equipment control layer, control of intelligent equipment implementation, this is the monitoring system data exchange function. From the longitudinal data interaction, including the interface layer and control layer between the test processes, test the communication between process control layer and the intelligent equipment control layer; from the horizontal data interaction, communication test process monitoring layer internal. [7] Figure 1 for anti jamming system architecture diagram.

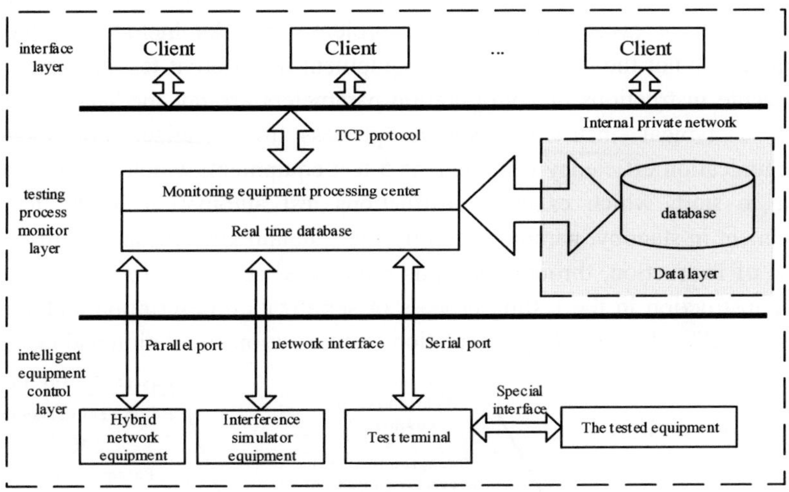

Fig. 1 Anti jamming system Architecture

The working flow of the system: the client monitor equipments by certain time-frequency, equipment monitoring center receives the query or command, it will be a combination of query or command and control sequences, thereby forming device control instruction stream, and then follow each device control protocol instruction stream send to the end of each device via Ethernet. Through the use of instruction serialization, we can greatly reduce the difficulty of unified control different devices [8].

3. Realization of Network Communication Based on Serialization Process Instruction

In this paper, the Anti jamming system uses the tcp protocol to build a basic network communication to ensure accurate data transmission. Specific programming communication is achieved by the socket. To accomplish this goal, we use a technique called as object serialization. For example, in the communication device simulation and control system, various exchanges between systems inside the device control information, parameter information, status information and data information, after using serialization technology, information is becoming binary serialized bytes sent over the network to facilitate [9].

Serialization steps flow instructions in simulation test system is divided into three parts: Project serialization, equipment instructions and instruction serialization, as shown in Figure 2. Since an automation communication equipment testing will be in accordance with the timing has to perform multiple test projects or tasks [10], each test projects or tasks included in the test equipment is not the same, and each equipment in different test scenarios need to execute instructions or configuration parameters are not the same, Figure 2 gives a typical instruction stream process to serialize. For example, communication efficiency test contains 5 test equipment, which are arranged in order to start, which executes instructions test automation in the terminal equipment in standby, parameter setting, start, obtain and termination of these 5 forms of instruction, through take this multi-level serialized form [11], can be every instruction in the testing process of serialization description and storage, so as to realize the rapid implementation of automation simulation and testing.

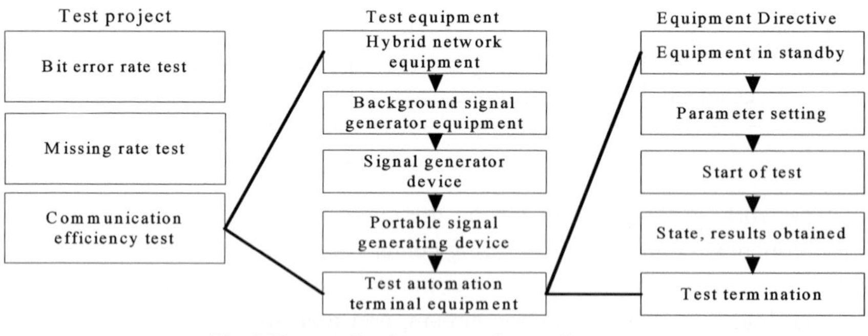

Fig. 2 The serialization process instruction stream

After serialize the monitoring equipment instructions, the byte code of parameter configuration instructions will be stored into database, by this way the user can set a good test content, test environment configuration, etc. information is stored, to facilitate the bulk, mass communications test [12]. During the test, we just read from the database in the data stream forms of instruction out of the frame, converting a simple byte memory space that can continuously send data directly to the network.

In anti jamming system, internal equipment exchange of various monitoring information including control information, parameter information, the state information and data information, transfer to a frame of information form. Frames of information from various information items according to certain structure mode combination, called the information frame structure. [13] The information from the frame header contains information frame it and it appears in the information frame in the position to jointly determine the physical meaning, information items using some type of data to express [14].

Information can be utilized in a variety of data types are used to express the information. In order to reduce the pressure on the communication channel, information storage, computing equipment as far as possible, to improve system's real-time performance [15], information data types used in the system of unified communication protocol using a binary data format, a binary data format generated provides precondition for instruction stream. Figure 3 shows a typical message frame structure.

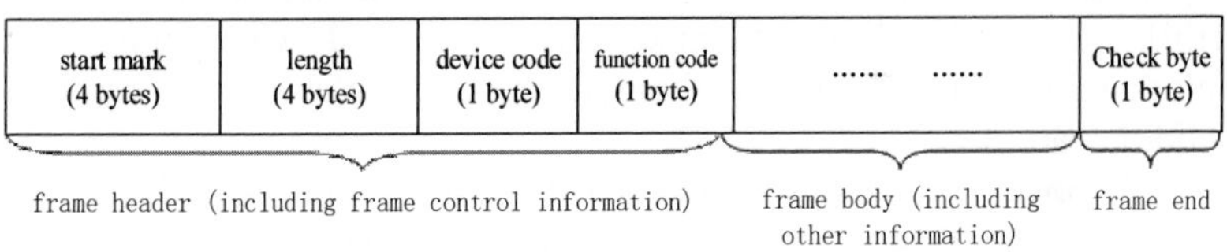

Fig. 3 Information frame structure

4. Conclusion

The practical application shows that, by adopting multi tier architecture, the system has good expansibility. Based on the combination of TCP protocol, designed to unify all equipment centralized monitoring framework, realize centralized monitoring of equipment, instrument data and status of communication anti jamming, while meeting the correct safety monitoring data transmission.

References

1. Deployment Patterns (Microsoft Enterprise Architecture, Patterns, and Practices)
2. Fowler, Martin "Patterns of Enterprise Application Architecture" (2002). Addison Wesley.
3. J. Hellerstein, Y. Diao, S. Parekh, and D. Tilbury, Feedback Control of Computing Systems. John Wiley & Sons, 2004.
4. Oracle Sun Developer Network (SDN) "http://java.sun.com/developer/technicalArticles/Programming/serialization/" (accessed on Feb 14, 2012)
5. Axel Naumann; Philippe Canal"C++ and Data", Proceedings of Science, FERMILAB-CONF-08-692-CD
6. G. Jung, K. Joshi, M. Hiltunen, R. Schlichting, and C. Pu, "A cost-sensitive adaptation engine for server consolidation of multi-tier applications," in Proc. of Middleware, 2009.
7. Ross, J.C.; Chandran, P , "Object Serialization support for object oriented java rocessors" International Symposium on Information Technology, 2008. ITSim 2008.
8. How to marshal an object to a remote server by value by using Visual Basic 2005 or Visual Basic .NET […] Because the whole object is being serialized to the server (marshaling by value), the code will execute in the server's process.
9. Opyrchal, L.; Prakash, A.; ,"Effective Object Serialization in Java", 19th IEEE International Conference on Distributed Computing Systems Workshops on Electronic Commerce and Web-based Applications/ Middleware, 1999.
10. Java™ObjectSerialization Specification, Revision 1.4.4, http://java.sun.com/j2se/1.4/pdf/serial-spec.pdf. (Accessed on Feb 14, 2012)
11. Y. Lu, D. H.-C. Du, C. Liu, and X. Zhang, "Qos scheduling for networked storage system," in Proc. of ICDCS, 2008
12. Y. Lu, T. F. Abdelzaher, and A. Saxena, "Design, implementation, and evaluation of differentiated caching services," IEEE Trans. on Parallel and Distributed Systems, vol. 15, pp. 440– 452, 2004.
13. Kazuaki Maeda; " Comparative Survey of Object Serialization Techniques and the Programming Supports", World Academy of Science, Engineering and Technology 60 2011
14. C. Krasic, M. Saubhasik, A. Sinha, and A. Goel, "Fair and timely scheduling via cooperative polling," in Proc. of Eurosys, 2009
15. C Sharp Corner "http://www.c-sharpcorner.com/interviews/Answer/499/what-is-serialization-in-net-types-of-serialization-and-wh" (accessed on Feb 20, 2012)

A New Hierarchical Testing Model in Software Reliability Testing

Lei Yu[1,a], Wei-Shan Xu[1], Shao-Fan Hou[1] and Jun-Chi Feng[2]

[1]State Key Laboratory of Mathematical Engineering and Advanced Computing,
Zhengzhou, 450001, China
[2]Logistics Software Testing and Evaluating Center
Beijing, 100071, China
E-mail: [a]yljacky8@hotmail.com

Software reliability testing based on the traditional Markov chain usage model does not consider the software structural information, so it has a low ability of finding software defects. To solve this problem, a new reliability testing model is proposed in this paper. It contains the interaction information between software and environment, and the software structural information. The algorithm to generate test data set based on the Hierarchical Model is also provided. Testing based on the new model satisfies the software reliability testing request. It also improves the test data set's ability of finding faults. Finally, a case study of demonstration software is presented to verify the effectiveness of the method.

Keywords: Software Reliability Testing; Hierarchical Testing Model; Test Data Generation.

1. Introduction

With the widespread use of the software system, software quality gets more attention, especially in the safety critical field. Software testing as an effective means to ensure the quality of software, has been more and more researched. Different from traditional software testing technology, software reliability testing technology uses the model of software to generate the test data, and uses the statistical results of failures to evaluate the reliability of the software. Commonly in software reliability test, people use the Markov Chain Model (MCUM) [1] [2] [3] to describe the real software Usage and generate test data close to the real use, to find the defect with a greater influence on the reliability. Relative to the random test, this technology saves the test time and improves the software reliability.

Along with the increase of the complexity of software, the relationship between the code structure and the reliability of software gradually obtained the more attention [4]. Studies have been shown that software reliability has obvious correlation with test coverage [5]. Statistical structure test takes more defects found as the goal [6] [7], generates test data on the basis of the probability distribution of input, according to the adequacy criteria such as condition coverage, etc.

Traditional reliability test uses the software as a black box, does not consider the logical structure of software. Because of the complexity of the software [8], some failures will only be exposed when performing a certain path in specific operating conditions. So taken structure information into account in reliability testing is very important to improve the quality of software [9] [10].

To solve the above problem, we proposed a new software reliability testing model, Software Hierarchical Testing Model (SHTM). The model includes two levels: the usage model and the input data distribution model. Usage model corresponds to software function and behavior, ant the input data distribution model is associated with the code structure of the software. As shown in Figure 1, the usage model describes the change process of state due to the interaction between software and external environment. The input data distribution model describes the input data range corresponding to the code execution path. The input data distribution model is refinement of state transfer in usage model.

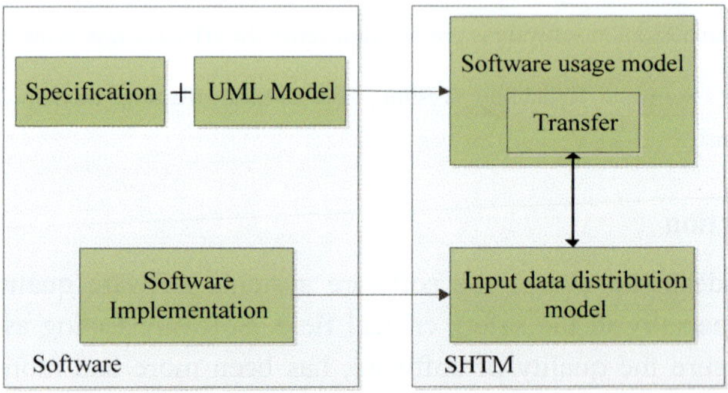

Fig. 1. Software hierarchical testing model

2. Software Hierarchical Testing Model

Software hierarchical testing model is defined as a quintuple (S, T, δ, q_0, f). S is a collection of software state, q_0 is the initial state, f is a termination condition, T is a collection of transfer between two states, each transfer $t \in T$ is a binary group ($p_{\text{Transition}}$, I_{Iddm}), $p_{\text{Transition}}$ is the probability for transfer, the sum of transition probability of all the edge to particular state equals to 1. Transfer between states meets Markov character. I_{Iddm} is the input data distribution model. δ is the transfer relationship between state $S \times T \rightarrow S$.

The input data distribution model describes the value scope of input parameter and its probability distribution. The scope of the input data is classified into different input fields. Each input field is endowed with certain probability, representing the possibility of corresponding execution path.

If suppose that there are n transfer paths and m input parameters, the input data distribution model is defined as an tuple $(D_1^{\mathrm{CombVar}}, D_2^{\mathrm{CombVar}}, \ldots, D_n^{\mathrm{CombVar}})$. Compound data domain D^{CombVar} was said the combination of variable input data fields and defined as $(D^{\mathrm{Var}}{}_1, D^{\mathrm{Var}}{}_2, \ldots, D^{\mathrm{Var}}{}_m, p_{\mathrm{Path}})$. p_{Path} means probability of the Path. The sum of the probability of all the complex data fields in the model adds up to 1. The compound data domain D^{CombVar} contained many variable input data domain D^{Var}. D^{Var} described the constraints which the input variables should satisfy. This paper adopts the way of mathematical expressions to describe the constraint. Mathematical expression is consists of operands and operators. Table 1 showed the common operators, including attribute operator used to retrieve member variable values in an object.

Table 1. Operands

Type	Operands
Arithmetic operator	+, -, ×, /, %
Function operator	min(*a*,*b*), max(*a*,*b*), abs(*a*)
Relational operator	==, !=, >, <, >=, <=
Logical operator	&&, ||, !
Attribute operator	.

Operands contain constants and variables, such as class member variables. Object variables, refers to the member variables in the method of an object, in the form "self + attribute operator + a variable name" as representation. Class variables, referring to the static member variables in the class, are in the form "class name + attribute operator + a variable name" as representation.

```
class Test{
    int a,b;
    void test(int c){
      if(c<=a){
        if(c<=b){ ...; }
      } else ...;
```

Fig. 2. A program example

For the method "test" shown in Figure 2, The method includes three paths. If the probability of each execution path is equal, the input data distribution model is expressed as:

{{c:self.b<c<=self.a,1/3},{c:0<c<=min(self.a,self.b),1/3},{c:self.a<c,1/3}}.

3. Test Data Generation Based on SHTM

In the test data generation process based on software hierarchical testing model, there are two key points. The first is to satisfy the statistics requirement of the software reliability test which tests need to accord with the actual use of the software. The second is to improve the defect detection ability of test data which the test needs to try to cover more execution paths.

The usage model hierarchy describes the usage of software, starting from the initial state, according to the transfer probability to choose the next state, ends until the state of termination; the resulting transfer sequence is test sequence of software running.

The input data distribution model hierarchy describes the mapping between the input data and software execution path. When the input parameters in the test sequence is generated, we get test data in accordance with the input data distribution model.

The Algorithm of generating test data based on the model needs to meet two adequacy criteria: usage stop criterion τ_{Usage} and structure stop criterion $\tau_{Structure}$. The τ_{Usage} refers to the usage model's statistical properties which test data set need to meet. According to the generated test sequence set, counting up each state transfer frequency as transition probability can build a Markov chain, called the test chain, the original usage model of Markov chain is called usage chain. Reliability test requires generating test data continuously until the relevant mathematical characteristics of the test chain achieving the coverage criterion. Generally we used Discriminant value to assess the similarity between test chain and usage chain. Adequacy criterion $\tau_{Structure}$ refers to the input data distribution model's coverage criteria, which test data set need to meet. $\tau_{Structure}$ points to the input data distribution model of each transfer and makes the test data have the same opportunity in each compound input field, which covers the probability of each path as same as possible, so that the test data can cover all the test path as soon as possible.

In the progress of test data generation, firstly we generated test sequence by traversal using model until meeting the stop criterion τ_{Usage}. Then for the transition set of each test sequence, we generated the input data in accordance with $\tau_{Structure}$: We Adopted the method of roulette, selected the non-empty input field randomly according to the probability and selected input values randomly from the input field. Execute the software method, and transfer into the next state, repeated the above process and generated the input data for all transfer. Finally we combined all the test sequence with the corresponding input data, respectively test data set that reliability testing required was generated.

4. Experiment and Analysis

In order to verify the effectiveness of the proposed method in this paper, an ATM simulation software is selected as tested software for experiments. The operations that users use the ATM to withdraw, to transfers accounts and other operations can be simulated with using the software. We built the SHTM for the software and did test data generation experiment based on it.

The test data generation technology based on SHTM and MCUM were used to generate test data set for ATM software respectively. In the test data generation based on traditional MCUM technology, the parameter of the test methodological sequence is assign a random value in the range of the input variable.

With different Discriminant value restrictions, two methods were used respectively to generate test data sets, and then assess their ability of defect discovery through mutation test. In addition, two different usage profile of the ATM software are experimented, i.e. the experimental results are observed in different probability distribution. It is assumed in Table 2 that the transfer probability in the usage profile I and II differs. Experiment results can be seen in Figure 3-4, in which dis means the Discriminant value. Moreover, in order to show the results conveniently the horizontal axis is expressed by –lg(dis).

Table 2. The probability of transition of the use model

Transition	I	II	Transition	I	II
InsertCard	0.95	0.95	DoWithdrawal	0.5	0.5
DoTransfer	0.5	0.5	WithdrawErr	0.2	0.3
VerifyAccountErr	0.05	0.1	Withdraw	0.8	0.7
VerifyAccount	0.95	0.9	Quit(13-14)	0.9	0.8
TransferErr	0.2	0.3	DoAnother	0.1	0.2
Transfer	0.8	0.7	Quit(2-14)	0.05	0.05

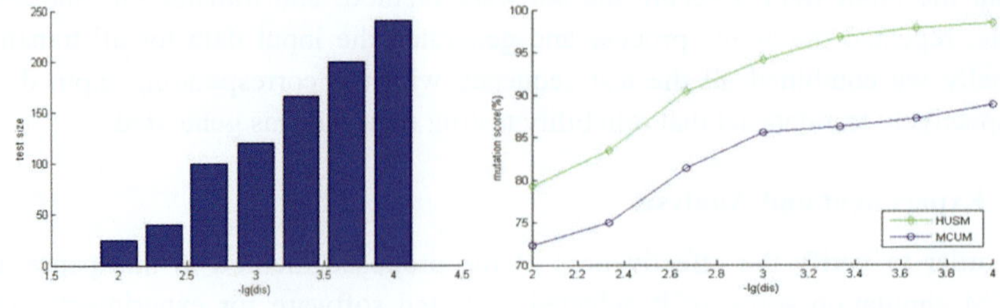

a) Number of test data b) Mutation score

Fig. 3. The experimental results of usage I

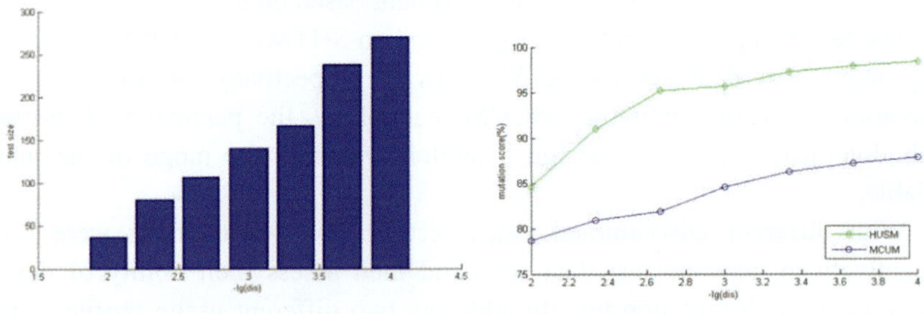

a) Number of test data b) Mutation score

Fig. 4. The experimental results of usage II

With the same Discriminant value, mutation score of the test data set generated based on SHTM were apparently larger than the set based on MCUM. When mutation score were same, the number of test data generated based on MCUM was larger than the set based on SHTM. Along with the mutation scores tend to be stable, for usage profile I, mutation score of test data set generated by SHTM was close to 99%, while by MCUM was close to 88%; for usage profile II, mutation score of test data set generated by SHTM was close to 99%, while by MCUM was close to 86%.

By the above analysis we can see that under the same adequacy criterion, the defect detection ability of test data set generated based on SHTM is obviously better than the set based on MCUM. To achieve the same defect detection ability, much more test data must be generated based on MCUM. When the sufficiency criteria is satisfied, such as Discriminant value in this paper, the generated test data set based on SHTM can detect most of the mutations injected in the software. Compared with the traditional reliability test data generation method, our new method based on SHTM can obtain better defect detection ability. In the case of that test resources are limited, the new method can help to improve the reliability of the software.

5. Conclusion

In this paper, the internal structure information of software is taken into account in the software reliability test, the concept of hierarchical software test model is put forward and the reliability test data generation algorithm based on the model is given. Through the ATM simulation software testing, the results show that compared with the method based on the Markov chain use model, the new method has higher ability of defect detection, can detect software defects effectively and improve the level of software reliability.

Acknowledgement

This work is supported by project 61402525 of Chinese National Natural Science Foundation.

References

1. Meitner M, Saglietti F. Software reliability testing covering subsystem interactions[M]//Schmitt J B. Measurement, Modelling, and Evaluation of Computing Systems and Dependability and Fault Tolerance, Vol. 7201. Berlin: Springer, 2012: 46-60
2. Shuanqi Wang, Yumei Wu, Minyan Lu. An approach of software reliability accelerated testing and assessment[J]. Journal of Harbin Engineering University, 2012, 33(11): 1358-1365(in Chinese)
3. Caihua Wu, Juntao Liu, Shirui Peng, et al. Deriving Markov chain usage model from UML model[J]. Journal of Computer Research and Development, 2012, 49(8): 1811-1819(in Chinese)
4. Hsu C J, Huang C Y. An adaptive reliability analysis using path testing for complex component-based software systems[J]. IEEE Transactions on Reliability, 2011, 60(1): 158-170
5. Malaiya Y K, Li M N, Bieman J M, et al. Software reliability growth with test coverage[J]. IEEE Transactions on Reliability, 2002, 51(4): 420-426
6. Denise A, Gaudel M C, Gouraud S D. A generic method for statistical testing[C]//Proceedings of the 15th International Symposium on Software Reliability Engineering. Los Alamitos: IEEE Computer Society Press, 2004: 25-34

7. Poulding S, Clark J A. Efficient software verification: statistical testing using automated search[J]. IEEE Transactions on Software Engineering, 2010, 36(6): 763-777
8. Caliebe P, Herpel T, German R. Dependency-based test case selection and prioritization in embedded systems[C]//Proceedings of the 5th IEEE International Conference on Software Testing, Verification and Validation. Los Alamitos: IEEE Computer Society Press, 2012: 731-735
9. Kicillof N, Grieskamp W, Tillmann N, et al. Achieving both model and code coverage with automated gray-box testing[C]//Proceedings of the 2nd Workshop on Advances in Model Based Testing. New York: ACM Press, 2007: 1-11
10. Qiuying Li, Haifeng Li, Gang Xu. Software reliability growth testing practice based on coverage[J]. Application Research of Computers, 2010, 27(7): 2594-2597(in Chinese)

An Effective Fault Localization Approach Based on Weighted Test Cases

Yi-Han Li[a], Ji-Cheng Chen and Ya-Qian Zhao

State Key Laboratory of High-end Server & Storage Technology, Inpsur
Beijing, 10085, China
E-mail: [a]liyihannew@126.com

Spectrum based fault localization techniques have shown promising results in assisting developers to find the possible locations of faults. These techniques employ the number of failed tests as well as the number of passed tests that cover statements to distinguish faulty statements and non-faulty statements. However, these techniques essentially assume the same importance for all the test cases, which ignore fault diagnosis ability for individual test cases. In this paper, an approach is proposed to quantify fault diagnosis ability for failed tests and passed tests. Two fault localization techniques are then proposed based on the approach to calculate the suspiciousness of statements for further ranking. Experimental results on Siemens Test Suite programs show that the proposed fault localization techniques are significantly more effective than traditional techniques.

Keywords: Fault Localization; Debugging; Test Cases.

1. Introduction

Software debugging is an import activity in the life cycle of software as bugs are more or less introduced by developers during software development processes. Typically, debugging consists of locating faults, repairing faults and verifying. According to a previous study, locating faults have been recognized as one of most expensive tasks [1]. Thus, in order to reduce the cost of debugging, many different fault localization techniques [2-5] have been proposed to guide developers to the possible locations of faults in recent years.

Among the proposed techniques, spectrum-base fault localization (SFL) techniques have shown promising results in locating faults. The basic idea behind them is that they utilize execution traces collected from a dynamic analysis of a faulty program to exploit how program entities are correlated with program failure. Those program entities that are more likely to be faulty are supposed to have high scores using statistical models and are ranked high for first examination. Following the idea, many different statistical models have been proposed to measure program entities how they are correlated with faults based on coverage information, such as Tarantula [2], Ochiai [3] and Jaccard [3].

SFL have shown promising results in locating faults. However, these techniques essentially assume the same importance for all the test cases, which ignore fault diagnosis ability for individual test cases. Due to that, some statements may not be distinguished from each other. For example, if two statements are both exercised by the same number of passed tests and the same number of failed tests, the current SFL techniques, such as Ochiai [3], Wang3[4] and etc., assigns same suspiciousness score to these two statements and therefore fails to distinguish these statements, which may decrease accuracy in locating faults.

In this paper, we propose an approach to quantify fault diagnosis ability for failed tests and passed tests respectively. The approach assumes that statements involved in the execution of test cases make different contributions to the results of tests. For each passed test, different weights are assigned according to how similar the passed tests is with failed tests. For each failed test, different weights are assigned according to both coverage information of the failed test and status of tests with respect to each statement. Two fault localization techniques are then proposed based on the approach to calculate the suspiciousness of statements for further ranking. The empirical results show that our techniques are promising at locating faults on the studied subject programs.

2. Proposed Approach

In the following subsection, for the convenient discussion, we supposed the faulty program P consists of n executable statements and m basic blocks, which can be denoted as $P = \{s_1,s_2,s_3,\ldots,s_n\}$ and $P = \{b_1,b_2,b_3,\ldots,b_m\}$ respectively. Also consider that the program P is tested against a test suite T, which comprises of w different test cases that are denoted as $T = \{t_1,t_2,t_3,\ldots,t_w\}$. The test suit T can be partitioned into two disjoint subsets T_p and T_f according to the passed/failed status of test cases.

2.1. *Weights of failed test*

2.1.1. *Weight of coverage of tests with respect to each statement*

Suppose there is one failed test case t_i, and the coverage of basic block for t_i can be denoted as $<z_{i1},z_{i2},z_{i3},\ldots,z_{iw}>$. If block b_j is covered by test t_i, then the value for z_{ij} is 1 otherwise 0. Then the following formula is used to measure the weights of coverage of test t_i with respect to statements:

$$\mathrm{TC}(t_i) = \frac{1}{\sum_{r=1}^{w} z_{ir}} \tag{1}$$

The value of $\mathrm{TC}(t_i)$ varies inversely with the number of basic block covered by t_i. That is, the less basic block covered by t_i, the stronger fault diagnosis t_i reveals.

2.1.2. *Weight of status of tests with respect to each statement*

Suppose the number of failed tests that cover the statement s_j is a_{ef}. Therefore the number of failed tests that do not cover s_j is equal to $|T_f|-a_{ef}$. Let G denotes the event that the statement s_j do not covered by failed tests. According to coverage information, the probability of G can be calculated as: $(|T_f|-a_{ef})/|T_f|$. Then the information quantity of the event can be measured as: $-\log((|T_f|-a_{ef})/|T_f|)=\log(|T_f|/(|T_f|-a_{ef})) = \log(a_{ef}/(|T_f|-a_{ef})+1)$. When the probability of G grow smaller, the statement s_j will be executed by more failed tests. In this case, G will contain more information quantity and s_j will be more suspicious. Thus, in this paper the following formula is used to calculate the fault diagnosis of the failed test t_i for its coverage:

$$\mathrm{TS}(t_i, s_j) = \log(\frac{a_{ef}}{|T_f|-a_{ef}+0.1} + 2) \tag{2}$$

According to the above analysis, the following formula is used to calculate the suspicion of statement s_j introduced by test t_i:

$$\mathrm{FW}(t_i, s_j) = \mathrm{TC}(t_i) * \mathrm{TS}(t_i, s_j) \tag{3}$$

2.2. *Weight of passed tests*

Suppose the statement coverage vector for test t_i can be denoted as $<c_{i1}, c_{i2}, \ldots ,c_{in}>$. According to above analysis, the following formula is used to measure the similarity of two tests:

$$Sim(t_i, t_j) = \frac{n(t_i \cap t_j)}{\sqrt{n(t_i) \times n(t_j)}} \quad (4)$$

where $n(t_i)$ represents the number of elements that are not zero in the vector of t_i. And $t_i \cap t_j = \{c_{iu} | c_{iu} \neq 0 \wedge c_{ju} \neq 0, 1 \leq u \leq n\}$. The Sim formula measures the ratio of the number of statements covered by both two tests to that of statements covered by either test.

If the similarity between one passed test and one failed test is great, that is they both cover many same statements, since the failed test must execute the faulty statements, thus the passed test has great probability in the execution of covering the faulty statements. Thus, such passed test will reduce the probability of statements involved being correct. According to the above analysis, the following equation is employed to quantify the fault diagnosis of test t_i:

$$W(t_i) = \frac{\sum_{j \in T_f}(1 - Sim(t_i, t_j))}{|T_f|}, where\ t_i \in T_p \quad (5)$$

The statements involved in the execution of the passed test all have impact on the result of the test. Thus, for the statement s_j executed by the passed test t_i, we use the following equation to calculate the likelihood of the statement to correct:

$$PW(t_i, s_j) = W(t_i), where\ c_{ij} \neq 0 \quad (6)$$

2.3. *Suspicion calculation*

We first present the following notations to denote impact of statements involved in the executions:

$N_{ef}(s)$: the weights of all the failed tests that cover the statement s

$N_{ep}(s)$: the weights of all the passed tests that cover the statement s

Therefore, the two notations can be represented using the following equations:

$$N_{ef}(s) = \sum_{t_i \in T_f} FW(t_i, s) \quad (7)$$

$$N_{ep}(s) = \sum_{t_i \in T_p} PW(t_i, s) \quad (8)$$

If the statement s is covered by many failed tests and the fault diagnosis of failed tests is strong, then the statement is likely to contain fault. Therefore, the suspiciousness of statements is positively correlated with the number of failed tests that covered the statements. Furthermore, the faulty statements may be executed by a few passed tests. Therefore, the suspiciousness of statements is inversely correlated with the number of passed tests that covered the statements. Based on the above analysis, we proposed the first method to calculate suspiciousness of statements:

$$H1 = N_{ef}(s) - N_{ep}(s) \tag{9}$$

Additionally, the suspiciousness of statements may be proportional to the number of failed tests that covered the statements, and inversely proportion to the number of passed tests that covered the statements. Based on the above analysis, we proposed the second method to calculate suspiciousness of statements:

$$H2 = \frac{N_{ef}(s)}{(N_{ep}(s)+N_{ef}(s))} \tag{10}$$

3. Experiment Results and Analysis

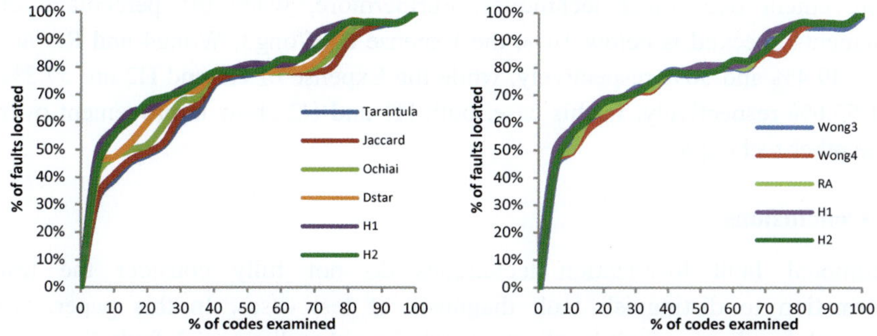

(a)Tarantula, Jaccard, Ochiai and Dstar (b)Wong3, Wong4 and RA

Fig. 1. Comparison with seven other fault localization techniques

This paper uses 7 programs from Siemens Test Suite [11] as subject programs. The test suite has been widely used to verify the effectiveness of fault localization [3-8]. To validate the effectiveness of the proposed method, seven related fault localization techniques are used to make comparison, including Tarantula [2], Jaccard [3], Ohiai [3], Dstar [5], Wong3 [4], Wong4 [6] and RA [7].

To improve readability of graphs, seven fault localization techniques are divided into two groups for comparison. The results are listed in Figure 1.

From the Figure 1(a), it can be seen that H1 and H2 can locate more faults than Tarantula, Jaccard and Ochiai on the subject programs. The curves of H1 and H2 are close, and they are above those of three other techniques in most cases. When the percentage of statements checked is below 40%, H1 and H2 both have great improvement over three other techniques. As with the checked statements increasing, the curves of Tarantula, Jaccard and Ochiai get close to that of H1 and H2. This is due to that some types of faults, such as faulty statements executed by all of the test cases, it requires more statements to be check for these techniques to locate. It can also be seen that compared with H2, the improvement of H1 over three others techniques is more clear and stable.

Then, we compare out methods with the techniques that distinguish fault diagnosis. Figure 1(b) lists the experimental results. From the figure, it can be seen that on Siemens subject programs H1 gets a litter improvement over three other techniques, while H2 does not always show improvement over three other techniques. For example, when the percentage of statements checked is below 5%, the Expense of Wong3, Wong4 and RA are 44.5%, 45.5% and 46.6% respectively, and the Expense of H1 and H2 are 48.9% and 43.8% respectively. In such case, H1 is the most effective technique, while H2 shows no improvement over other techniques. Furthermore, when the percentage of statements checked is below 10%, the Expense of Wong3, Wong4 and RA are 50%, 49.4% and 50% respectively, while the Expense of H1 and H2 are 57.3% and 55.6% respectively. In this case, both H1 and H2 show improvement over three other techniques.

4. Conclusions

Traditional fault localization techniques do not fully consider the test information to distinguish fault diagnosis of test cases. In this paper, we proposed an effective fault localization technique that distinguish fault diagnosis of test cases based on test information. To verify the effectiveness of our method, comparison with seven other fault localization techniques are conducted on the subject programs from Siemens Test Suite. The experimental results indicate that H1 is more effective than seven other techniques and H2 reveals improvement over other techniques for most programs. In the future work, we will explore more factors [9-10] that may impact the fault diagnosis of test cases so as to improve the effectiveness of fault localization.

References

1. I. Vessey, "Expertise in Debugging Computer Programs: A Process Analysis", ;presented at International Journal of Man-Machine Studies, 1985, pp.459-494.
2. A. Jones, M. J. Harrold, and J. Stasko, “Visualization of test information to assist fault localization,” in ICSE ’02: Proceedings of the 24th International Conference on Software Engineering, Orlando, Florida, 2002, pp.467–477.
3. R. Abreu, P. Zoeteweij, R. Golsteijn, and A.J.C.V. Gemund, "A practical evaluation of spectrum-based fault localization", presented at Journal of Systems and Software, 2009, pp.1780-1792.
4. W.E. Wong, Y. Qi, L. Zhao, and K. Cai, "Effective Fault Localization using Code Coverage", in Proc. COMPSAC (1), 2007, pp.449-456.
5. Wong, W. E., Debroy, V., Gao, R., & Li, Y. (2014). The DStar Method for Effective Software Fault Localization. IEEE Transactions on Reliability, 2014,1(63), 290-308.
6. Eric Wong, W., Vidroha Debroy, and Byoungju Choi. "A family of code coverage-based heuristics for effective fault localization." Journal of Systems and Software 83, no. 2 (2010): 188-208.
7. University N, Nanjing. Spectra-Based Fault Localization by Increasing Marginal Weight[J]. Chinese Journal of Computers, 2010, 33(12):2335-2342.
8. J.A. Jones and M.J. Harrold, "Empirical evaluation of the tarantula automatic fault-localization technique", in Proc. ASE, 2005, pp.273-282.
9. A. Bandyopadhyay and S. Ghosh, "Proximity based weighting of test cases to improve spectrum based fault localization", in Proc. ASE, 2011, pp.420-423.
10. H. Cleve and A. Zeller. Locating causes of program failures. In Proceedings of the International Conference on Software Engineering, pages 342-351, St. Louis, Missouri, May 2005.
11. [Online]. Available: http://sir.unl.edu/portal/index.html

A Kind of Hierarchical Network Vulnerability Assessment Model Based on Attack Graph

Jun-Chun Ma[a], Shan Chen, Min Li and Jun-Ping Yao

Research Inst. of High-tech Hongqing Town,
Xi'an, Shanxi, China
E-mail: [a]chenshan1223@126.com

Assessing the existing vulnerability in the target network, and establishing corresponding assessment model are the key to network vulnerability assessment. Aiming at the problem that the network vulnerability assessment involves many factors which are difficult to quantify, a kind of Hierarchical Network Vulnerability Assessment Model based on Attack Graph (AG-HNVAM) is proposed. This model combines with the Common Vulnerability Scoring System (CVSS), and adopts the idea of bottom-up and local-whole, which gives the vulnerability assessment value of three levels (service, host and network) intuitively. Experimental results show that this method is feasible and effective.

Keywords: Network Security; Network Vulnerability Assessment; Attack Graph.

1. Introduction

In recent years, researchers have proposed a variety of network vulnerability assessment methods, but the existing methods generally lack the ability to reveal the deeper nature of the vulnerability. And network vulnerability refers to many factors, not only includes the vulnerability of critical network nodes line, the host vulnerability, the service vulnerability, but also includes the vulnerability brought by firewall policies, router configuration and so on. Therefore, the network vulnerability assessment model should consider a variety of factors, and can be portrayed from different perspectives.

Based on the above considerations, this paper proposed a kind of Hierarchical Network Vulnerability Assessment Model based on Attack Graph (AG-HNVAM). By comparison with the existing assessment methods, AG-HNVAM has advantages of objectivity, comprehensiveness and practicality.

2. Method of Assessing the Vulnerability Index

2.1. *Method of assessing the service vulnerability index*

The service vulnerability assessment model divided various factors which affect the service vulnerability index into three parts: the vulnerability relationship, the vulnerability own characteristics and the network environment factors.

2.1.1. *Factors affect the service vulnerability index*

From the viewpoint of the vulnerability relationship, because vulnerabilities in the target network is not isolated, this paper analyzes the relationship between them based on attack graph [1-2]. The degree of vulnerability dependence is the number of vulnerabilities in Pre(V)(Pre(V) is a set of parent nodes), when one vulnerability in Pre(V) is used, V has the possibility to be attacked, so if the degree of vulnerability dependence is higher, V has greater possibility to be attacked. At the same time, the degree of vulnerability dependent is the number of vulnerabilities in Post(V)(Post(V) is a set of sub nodes), if the degree of vulnerability dependent is higher, V has greater damage. Therefore, the vulnerability relationship considers two factors: the degree of vulnerability dependence and the degree of vulnerability dependent.

From the viewpoint of the vulnerability own characteristics, for some vulnerability, only a very few attackers know how to attack, while attackers can get some vulnerability exploit code on the Internet. Therefore, the vulnerability own characteristics considers two factors: exploit code and remedial measures, which describes the degree of attack difficulty using the vulnerability, and its value reflects the possibility which the vulnerability is exploited by attackers.

From the viewpoint of the network environment factors, on the one hand, if the critical hosts, servers or routers are attacked, its impact and losses caused will be huge, so if the asset is more critical, which expresses the vulnerability existing on it has greater potential impact; on the other hand, some of the target network require higher confidentiality, while some need higher availability and so on. Therefore, the network environment factors considers four factors: equipment assets, region of influence, the security requirements of the target network and the destructiveness of security requirements, its value reflects the degree of destructiveness after vulnerabilities are exploited.

2.1.2. *Value of factors affect the service vulnerability index*

Since CVSS is a recognized vulnerability assessment system, it has better compatibility, and its value related to factors affect the service vulnerability index can be found in CVE [3]. Therefore, there are four factors: exploit code, remedial measures, the security requirements of the target network and the destructiveness of security requirements, their value directly use the value in CVSS [4].

For the value of equipment assets and region of influence, in recent years, there is no influential and persuasive method. Therefore, in order to make the assessment more objective, this paper uses the expert evaluation method, that is, according to ten experts' evaluation score to determine its value. Table 1 shows the value of equipment assets, and table 2 shows the value of region of influence.

Table 1. The value of equipment assets.

Classification	Description	Value
Unimportant	After being used, the loss is very little	0
Not important	After being used, the loss is lower	0.5
Important	After being used, the loss is moderate	0.75
Very important	After being used, the loss is serious	1.00

Table 2. The value of region of influence.

Classification	Value
The distribution scope of vulnerability is 0%~9%	0
The distribution scope of vulnerability is 10%~30%	0.25
The distribution scope of vulnerability is 31%~69%	0.75
The distribution scope of vulnerability is more than 70%	1.00

Set the number of vulnerabilities is n, and make the vulnerability dependence, make the vulnerability dependent Dependence, table 3 shows the value of dependence, table 4 shows the value of dependence.

Table 3. The value of equipment assets.

Classification	Value
dependence≤(n-1)/4	0.25
(n-1)/4<dependence≤(n-1)/2	0. 5
(n-1)/2<dependence≤3(n-1)/4	0.75
dependence>3(n-1)/4	1.00

Table 4. The value of region of influence.

Classification	Value
Dependence≤(n-1)/4	0.25
(n-1)/4<Dependence≤(n-1)/2	0. 5
(n-1)/2<Dependence≤3(n-1)/4	0.75
Dependence>3(n-1)/4	1.00

2.1.3. *Method of calculating the service vulnerability index*

Firstly, using Nessus [5] to obtain the service vulnerability information in the target network, secondly, assessing the value of various factors affect the service vulnerability index, lastly, calculating the service vulnerability index (vulasset), its computational formula as follows:

value of the vulnerability own characteristics= f(exploit code, remedial measures)

value of the security requirements=(the security requirements of the target network)•(the destructiveness of security requirements)/3

value of the network environment factors= f(equipment assets and region of influence, value of the security requirements)

value of vulnerability relationship=f(vulnerability dependence, vulnerability dependent)

vulasset=f(value of the vulnerability own characteristics, value of the network environment factors, value of vulnerability relationship)

Where f represents to polymerize various factors by adopting the idea of bottom-up, this paper introduces weighted average method, and vi represents the weight of xi. There are:

$$f(x_1, x_2 \cdots x_n) = \sum_{i=1}^{n} v_i \times x_i \qquad (1)$$

Where in: $\sum_{i=1}^{n} v_i = 1$.

2.2. *Method of calculating the host vulnerability index*

According to BS7799[6-7], the host is consist of system software, application software, services running on the host and so on, after calculating the service vulnerability index vulasset, depending on the host to polymerize them, the host vulnerability index hostasset will be obtained.

hostasset =f(vulasset1, vulasset2, …vulassetn)

Where f represents to polymerize the existing vulnerabilities in the host, and its formula is the same with formula (1).

2.3. *Method of calculating the network vulnerability index*

The network concludes hosts, routers, routing strategies and so on, after calculating the host vulnerability index hostasset, depending on the routers to polymerize them, the network vulnerability index netasset will be obtained.

netasset = f(hostasset1, hostasset2, ...hostassetn)

Where f represents to polymerize the hosts in the network, and its formula is the same with formula(1).

2.4. *The network vulnerability assessment*

In order to facilitate the National Computer Network Emergency Response Technical Center and related network security manager to understand the network vulnerability index, this paper divides the network vulnerability index into five grades: "excellent, good, fair, poor, dangerous", table 5 shows the specific meaning of each grade.

Table 5. Qualitative description of the network vulnerability index.

Range of index	Level	Description
(0.9,1]	excellent	Network security situation is excellent, the lost caused by network vulnerability is negligible.
(0.7,0.9]	good	Network security situation is good, the lost caused by network vulnerability is smaller, and the influence to the normal operation is very small.
(0.3,0.7]	fair	Network security situation is fair, the lost caused by network vulnerability is large, and the influence to the normal operation is large.
(0.1,0.3]	poor	Network security situation is poor, the lost caused by network vulnerability is larger, and the influence to the normal operation is larger.
(0,0.1]	dangerous	Network security situation is at risk, the lost caused by network vulnerability is particularly large, and the influence to the normal operation is particularly severe.

3. Experimental Results and Analysis

In order to verify feasibility and effectiveness of AG-HNVAM, taking some network for example.

The first step: calculating the value of factors affecting the service vulnerability index in turn

The second step: using weighted average method to polymerize various factors, and the service vulnerability index vulasset will be obtained.

The third step: using weighted average method to polymerize vulnerabilities in the host, and the host vulnerability index hostasset will be obtained.

The fourth step: using weighted average method to polymerize hosts in the network, and the network vulnerability index netasset will be obtained, it's 0.63.

According to table 5: the network security situation is fair. If attackers exploit the vulnerabilities to attack, the lost will be large, and the influence to the normal operation is large too, so network security manager should pay attention to it, and take effective security measures to ensure it operating normally and safely.

4. Conclusion

Assessing the vulnerabilities in the network, and establishing network vulnerability assessment model are so important to network assessment. In order to make the assessment more objective and accurate, this paper presents a kind of hierarchical network vulnerability assessment model based on attack graph, By comparison with the existing assessment methods, AG-HNVAM has objectivity, comprehensiveness and practicality advantages.

References

1. Ma Chunguang, Wang Chenghong, A dynamic network risk assessment model based on attacker's inclination[J], journal of computer research and development.2015,52(9):2056-2068
2. Liu Weixin, Zheng Kangfeng, Alert processing based on attack graph and multi-source analyzing[J].journal on communications.2015,36(9):135-144
3. CHEN F, SU J S, ZHANG Y. A scalable approach to full attack graphs generation[C]. Proc. of 1st International Symposium on Engineering Secure Software and Systems, 2008, 150-163.5
4. IGOR Anikin. Vulnerability risk assessment method based on fuzzy logic[C]. Proceedings of the 2nd national conference on information technology and computer science(CITCS2015),2015,
5. Mu Huina, Wen Yang, Reliability design and optimization of a retracting actuator based on NESSUS[J].Chinese journal of energetic materials,2015,23(1):85-88
6. BS 7799-1. Code of Practice for Information Security Management Systems[S]. Information Security Management, Institute British Standards, 1999.
7. BS 7799-2. Code of Practice for Information Security Management Systems[S]. Information Security Management, Institute British Standards, 1999.

An Effective 3D Printing Placement Algorithm

Gong-Hai Xie[a] and Ruo-Mei Wang*

School of Data and Computer Science, Sun Yat-sen,
Guangzhou, Guangdong, China
E-mail: [a]xiegh3@mail2.sysu.edu.cn

3D printer becomes popular and has great applications in many areas. An efficient placement algorithm in an available space of a 3D printer to print multiple 3D objects is important for the printing time cost. In this paper, a 3D model placement algorithm base on model's contour is proposed. First, a robust algorithm is proposed to exacting the contour from 3D model. Second, the proposed algorithm adopts the bottom-left strategy combined with dynamic alter rotation to optimize the contour placement result. Moreover a tabu search is used to guide the search to get better results. Some 3D models are used to evaluate the algorithm, the experiment results show that the proposed algorithm can obtain optimal placement results.

Keywords: 3D Printing; Placement Algorithm; Contour; Tabu Search.

1. Introduction

With the development of 3D printing technology, 3D printer becomes popular and has great applications in many areas. In order to obtain high quality 3D printing product, the researches of printing material, printing device, 3D object design and analysis are key problems.

Considering the time cost and efficiency, how to optimize an available space of a 3D printer to print multiple 3D objects is important. That is significant to design an automatic placement algorithm.

The irregular strip packing problem is a NP-hard combinatorial optimization and a review of approaches to this problem is in Dowsland and Dowsland [1]. Bennell and Oliveira [2] reported and analyzed the geometric representations. Adamowicz and Albano [3] proposed an algorithm that the given polygons are partitioned into several subsets of polygons then a layout of

---

*Corresponding author.

these enclosures is obtained. Albano and Sapuppo [4] reported an algorithm that places each shape at the bottom-left position. A feasible layout of the given polygons is obtained by bottom-left heuristic and this layout is optimized by compaction algorithm to get a locally optimal solution. Gomes and Oliveira [5] proposed a separation algorithm to locally optimize the placement based on linear programming models, they further incorporated the method with simulated annealing to guide this search. Egeblad et al. [6] presented a fast neighborhood search to obtain minimum overlap through only vertical and horizontal translation, then it can get a feasible layouts. López-Camacho and Ochoa [7] proposed an effective heuristic for the two-dimensional irregular bin packing problem.

In this paper, we present an effective automatic 3D objects placement algorithm. Firstly a robust algorithm is designed that is used to exacting the contour of 3D model. Secondly, our algorithm adopts the bottom-left strategy combined with dynamic alter rotation are used to optimize the placement result, moreover a tabu search is used to guide the search to get more better results.

2. Algorithm of Extract Contour for 3D Object

In order to place a set of 3D model on an available space to finish the printing in one printing processing, how to arrange these model is a placement problem. Consider the requirement of 3D printing, these 3D models are needed to process to obtain their 2D contour. So the first step is to extract contour.

Some concepts relevant to the contour are defined. Here, a 3D object is constructed by a series of connected triangular facets.

Definition 1 A 3D model named *M*, if the normal vector of one triangular facet *F* named n , v is the viewing direction, if $v \cdot n \leq 0$, *F* is the Front facet. If $v \cdot n > 0$, *F* is the back facet.

Definition 2 e is the Contour Edge if e is the common edge of a Front facet and a Back facet.

Definition 3 Contours of one 3D object may be consist of many polygons, the max polygon is the Outer Loop.

Definition 4 If the contour of a 3D model consist of a number of polygons, the inner polygon named Inner Loop. Inner Loops are holes of one 3D model's projection.

There have different representations of one irregular shape. Considering the representation accurate, we representing the contour as polygons, the amount of information is proportional to the number of vertices and does not depend on the absolute size of the pieces or the layout.

The algorithm of extract contour for 3D object can be described as follows:

Algorithm 1. Extract contour from 3D model
1.Read 3D model from file(standard file type is stl).
2.Set the viewing direction $v = (0, 0, -1)$, it means that viewed from the model's top to bottom.
3. $fset$ is the index set of font facet, $bset$ is the index of back facet.
4.**For** each facet of all facets **Then**
5. **If** $v \cdot n_i <= 0$ **Do**
6.Push back the ID of current facet id to the $fset$
7.**Else** push back the ID of current facet id to the $bset$
8.Set Subject paths to null.
9.**For** each facet in the $fset$ **Do**
10.Using vatti's polygon clipping algorithm [8] to get an union path of subject paths and the current facet; Save the result to subject paths.
11.**End For**
12.**For** each polygon of Subject paths **Do**
13. Compute the area of each path of contours and save the one has max area
14.**End For**
15.The path that has max area that is outer loop of the 3D model.

Figure 1 shows part of results obtained by our algorithm. The blue path represents outer loop and the red path represents inner loop :

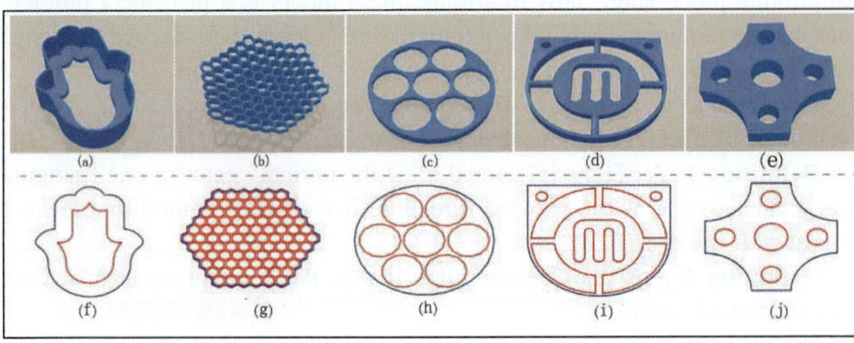

Fig. 1. Exacting contour from 3D model

3. 3D Objects Placement Algorithm

In order to printing a lot of 3D models in a printer, an efficient placement algorithm is designed: firstly, according to the algorithm 2, the outer loop of each model's contour is computed. Secondly, our algorithm finds an initial legal placement through bottom-left strategy based on piece orderings, while in the process our algorithm adopts the strategy of dynamically rotating the models by 90 or 180 degrees according to current effective utilization rate. If the current layout solution is better than last layout solution, using the strategy of swapping two objects and randomly shuffle operation to get more neighbors sequence to go next run. Moreover a tabu search is used to avoid the search going into minima. It's worth noting that when we used Graham [9] algorithm to get the closure of each outer loop of 3D model, our algorithm would expand closure to a bigger one, so the final nesting result could keep each 3D model separate from each other absolutely. The entire algorithm is formally described in Algorithm 2.

Algorithm 2. Entire 3D models placement algorithm
1.Using Algorithm 1 to extract contours from each model.
2.Using Graham [9] algorithm to get the closure of each contour of 3D model.
3.Let's every model's closure to expand an fixed distance.
4.Finding an initial legal placement through bottom left-fill strategy based on piece large area first, Get current maximum height and length, then obtain the initial effective area utilization rate.
5.**While** in a time limit **Do**
6. Using Swapping and randomly shuffle to get the current neighbors of current sequence list.
7.Setting the target list to null.
8.**While** each list in the current neighborhood list **do**
9.For a sequence of models and the sequence not in the tubu list **do**
10.Putting first models to lower left corner of the container.
11.Computing the efficient rate and let the model rotate 90 or 180 degrees counterclockwise, record
the best rotate angle, adding the best sequence and it's effective area utilization rate to target list.
12.Setting the model to the best orientation.
13.End For
14.Save the best sequence and recording every transformation matrix that each model's contour done.
15.Swap in the new sequence to the tubu list and swap out the old sequence according to target list.
16.End While
17. **End While**
18.Recording the final contour placements result and do the transforming on the total set of 3D models
according to its transformation matrix.

---

4. Experiments

In order to evaluate the algorithm proposed above, different kinds of 3D models are used. Figure 2 shows a set of 3D models:

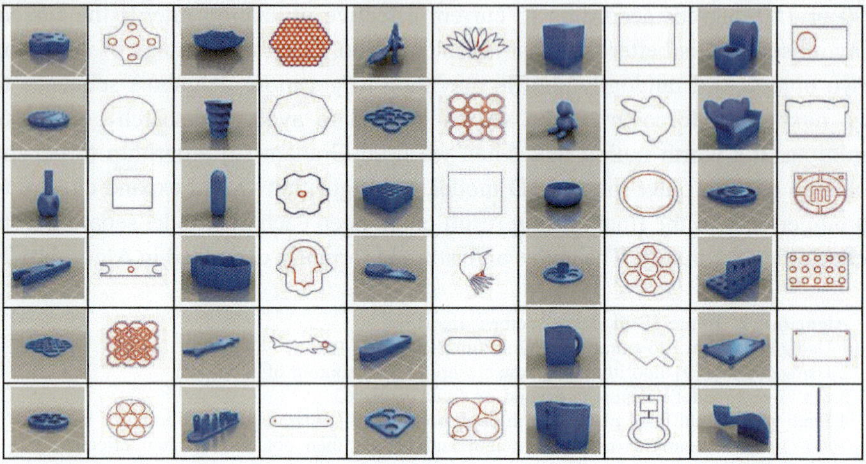

Fig. 2. Set of 3D models

There are total 150 3D models need to printing, and different layout is generated in different 3D printers, Figure 3 shows the placement results on the 3D printer with big size(Object-1000 is made by the stratasys company (1000mm*800mm)), two layouts are needed.

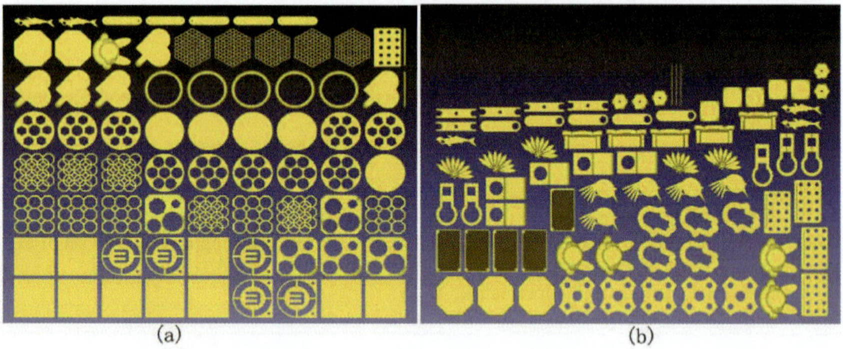

Fig. 3. Two layouts the algorithm produce

Figure 4 shows the placement result on the 3D printer with small size(Object-500 is made by the stratasys company(490mm*390mm)), seven different layouts are needed.

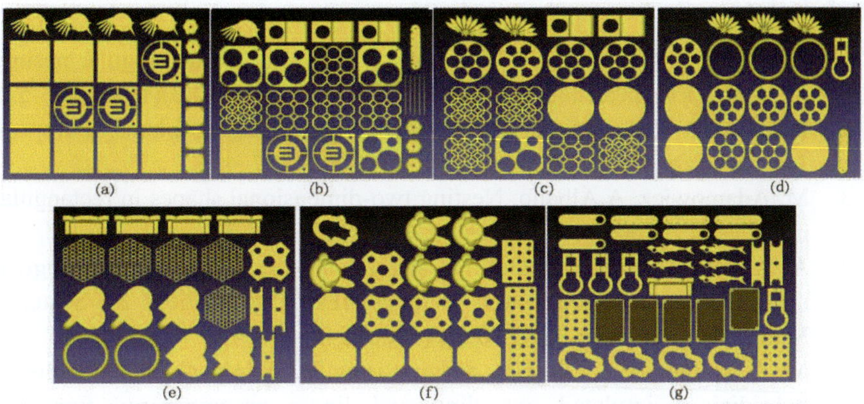

Fig. 4. Seven layouts the algorithm produce.

Figures 3 and 4 show that when the total 150 3D models place on different 3D printers, our algorithm can obtain corresponding local optimal layouts and its optimal printing times.

These final 3D models can be put into the 3D printing system, as for the object series, it adopts PolyJet technology [10], the process contains three steps, first doing pre-processing to calculates the placement of photopolymers and support material from final 3D models we generate. Second, The 3D printer jets and instantly UV-cures tiny droplets of liquid photopolymer. Finally the user removes the support material by hand, with water or in a solution bath.

5. Conclusions

Through testing on different type of 3printers, our algorithm can generate different optimal placement results automatically instead of adjusting multiply models manually, when users print models according to the final placement 3D models layouts can reduce average 50 to 60% total printing time than printing these models single by single.

Acknowledgments

We would like to thank the anonymous reviewers for their valuable comments. We were supported by the National Natural Science Foundation of China (61432003, 61272192).

References

1. Dowsland K A, Dowsland W B. Solution approaches to irregular nesting problems, European Journal of Operational Research,84(3)(1995):506-521.
2. Bennell JA, Oliveira JF. The geometry of nesting problems, European Journal of Operational Research, 184(2)(2008):397–416.
3. M. Adamowicz, A.Albano, Nesting two-dimensional shapes in rectangular modules, Computer-Aided Design, 8 (1) (1976):27–33.
4. A. Albano, G. Sapuppo. Optimal allocation of two-dimensional irregular shapes using heuristic search methods, IEEE Transactions on Systems, Man and Cybernetics SMC-10 (5) (1980):242–248.
5. M. A. Gomes, J. F. Oliveira. Solving irregular strip packing problems by hybridizing simulated annealing and linear programming, European Journal of Operational Research, 171 (3) (2006):811–829.
6. Egeblad J, Nielsen BK, Odgaard A. Fast neighborhood search for two and three-dimensional nesting problems, European Journal of Operational Research , 183(2007):1249–66.
7. López-Camacho E, Ochoa G, Terashima-Marín H, et al. An effective heuristic for the two-dimensional irregular bin packing problem, Annals of Operations Research, 206(1)(2013):241-264.
8. Vatti B R. A generic solution to polygon clipping, Communications of the Acm, 35(7)(1992):56-63.
9. Graham R L, Yao F F. Finding the convex hull of a simple polygon, Journal of Algorithms, 4(4)(1983):324-331.
10. Ionita C N, Mokin M, Varble N, et al. Challenges and limitations of patient-specific vascular phantom fabrication using 3D Polyjet printing, Proceedings of SPIE--the International Society for Optical Engineering, 9038(16) (2014):90380M-90380M-12.

A Programming Abstraction for R in Distributed Parallel System

Xin Zhao[a], Kai Lu and Xiao-Ping Wang

College of Computer, National University of Defense Technology
Science and Technology on Parallel and Distributed Procession Laboratory
Collaborative Innovation Center of High Performance Computing
Changsha, 410073, China
E-mail: [a]zhaoxin10@nudt.edu.cn

This paper comes up with Rdp, a novel implementation of programming abstraction for R language under the circumstance of distributed parallel system. It keeps the traditional programming habits of R users and use MPI underneath to accelerate the execution performance. Furthermore, experiments are taken to prove the efficiency and usability of the new method.

Keywords: R Language; High Performance Computing; Runtime; MPI.

1. Introduction

R is one of the most popular statistic language at present which is developed by two statisticians, Ross Ihaka and Robert Gentleman from the University of Auckland. R language is an implementation of S language, so it mainly depends on command lines. Its flexibility, openness and widely community support help R's development and improvement. As it is a typical functional and interpreted language, it occurs to a bottleneck in performance when the data volume takes on a trend of explosive growth. The ever-growing size and complexity of modern data sets in statistical analysis constantly challenge the capabilities of existing statistical computing methods.

In this paper, we proposed Rdp, a distributed parallel programming system specifically designed for R. Here are the main contributions in the paper:

(1) A deep study into R's original runtime;

(2) Abstraction and implementation for R in distributed parallel environment;

(3) Optimization in memory management and load balance performance.

2. Approach

In this section, we are going to cover several design key points of Rdp including its programming model and API design.

2.1. *Application scenarios and concept of Rdp*

As big data becomes a main trend of present society, R language becomes a focus to many research institution. In order to deal with the increasing volume of data, high performance computing methods and arithmetic appear so that parallel programming and computing turn out to be a common solution for improving traditional serial arithmetic.

Rdp is a system which can be understood as a programming abstraction and is aim to shorten the gap between parallel programming and arithmetic design as well as keeping the usability.

2.2. *Layered view of Rdp*

Runtime is a mechanism that combines operating system with programming model. There are two main tasks that a runtime needs to complete: one is to help high-level programs interact with the environment including access to the underneath software layer and the machine. The other is to hide the implementation details from the programmers.

In other words, the more flexible the language is, the more complex task the runtime needs to handle. Generally, it contains garbage collection, JIT, memory mapping, task scheduling and so on. As R is an interpreted language, the codes will not be complied until they are executed.

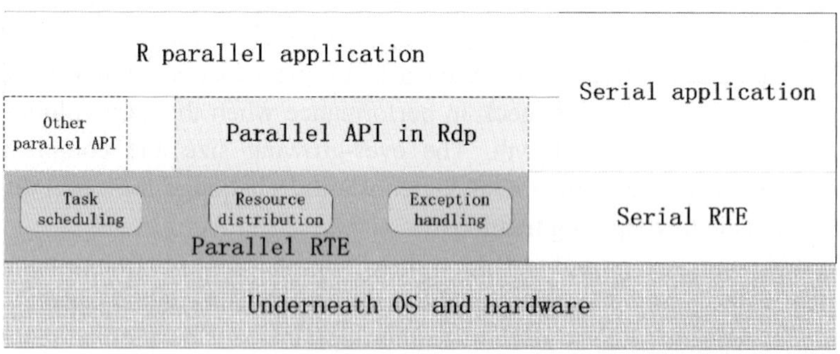

Fig. 1. A hierarchical execution framework of Rdp. The runtime environment (RTE) could be divided into two parts, one for parallel applications and one for serial applications respectively.

In order to do some optimization work, we focus on R's runtime environment (RTE), and divide it into parallel runtime environment and serial runtime environment.

As Figure 1 shows above, the parallel RTE is in charge of task scheduling, resource distribution and exception handling. The unit of task scheduling is a thread, each contains a queue. In order to improve the utilization of a cluster, we choose to use the MPI standard as the basic communication method combining with multi-threaded programming to complete the inter-communication between different cores and processes without modifying R's original execution environment.

2.3. *Programming model of Rdp*

2.3.1. *MapReduce-like programming style*

We choose the mapreduce-like programming style because there is a corresponding relationship between vectorization programming and mapreduce framework.

Take apply(x, fun) for instance, a function fun applies to every single element in vector x can be analogous to a task maps to different nodes in one cluster and the results return of apply () can be analogous to the reduce process.

So the whole process will be like follows:

(1) Start M working threads, doing some necessary initialization;

(2) Divide tasks into M data blocks and then send the data to these threads;

(3) Wait until all the threads finish computing;

(4) Repeat (2) (3) until all the tasks are being completed;

(5) Close working threads.

2.3.2. *Task scheduling framework*

When the user starts running an R script, the node with MPI rank 0 is regarded as the master node, the others are corresponding slave nodes. In these kind of master-slave structure, all nodes are equipped with R environment and those parallel tool packages. Master node takes control of all the other nodes with MPI implementing communication underneath.

As Figure 2 shows below, the master node and slave nodes are running with different routes. But at the initialization stage, they all load Rdp package with R runtime and C/MPI runtime set up. Slave nodes use a simple loop to wait data and scheduling messages from the master through MPI. Parallel processing will be triggered when the message arrives and all the nodes begin to execute at the same time.

The design of the parallel framework make it possible for the system to allocate data and counting numbers to working process at a appropriate time. As far as the user concerns, they do not need to do anything related to manually divide data and collect results. The underneath implementation by C is sure to gain a great improvement compared with present Rmpi approach.

There is another scenario that deserve discussing is when tasks are much larger than the available nodes. Here we come up a load balance strategy which will allocate the first available node to the coming task so as to reduce the total execution time of the system. All the performance will be tested in the next testing section.

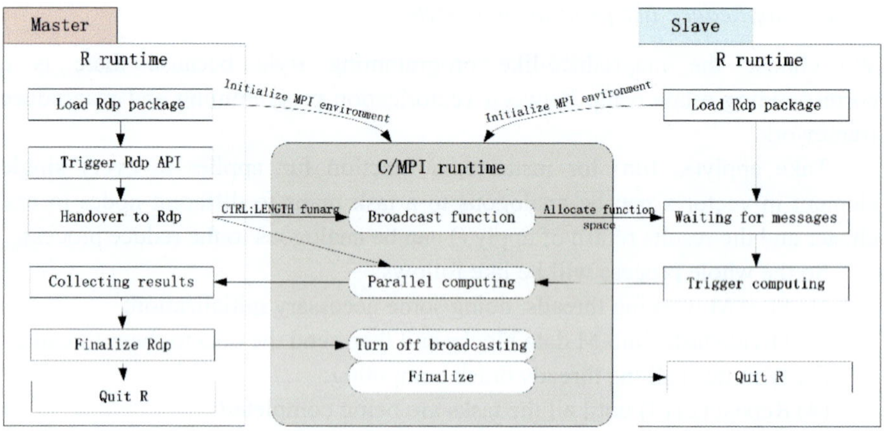

Fig. 2. A parallel task scheduling framework of Rdp. The process of distribute tasks are being done by MPI which is implemented in C.

2.4. *API of Rdp*

Here is a simple example of Rdp's function in order to briefly show how to use Rdp's and what are its programming abstractions like. The bold phrases are the essential APIs that are used in Rdp.

```
library(Rdp)
//initialize MPI environment
Rdp_initialize()
cl<-Rdp_getHandle()
set.seed(123)
N<-17e3
M<-matrix(runif(N^2),N,N)
sum(M)
system.time(Rdp_Export(cl,"M"))
//finalize MPI environment
Rdp_finalize()
```

The example is to create a random matrix M and the allocates its related computation to a cluster sized Rdp_ get Handle (). All the APIs' functions are referred to the existing API in parallel package (now available in >= R2.14.0) but are implemented in a different and more effective method.

Figure 3 shows execution schematic diagram of the function Rdp_lapply (). Vector X will be divided into smaller units and communicate with slave nodes by asynchronous methods. Space for function string and other arguments will be allocated at the beginning of collective communication without double transfer. We can also see a loop in slave node which is used when the computing task needs to be done circularly.

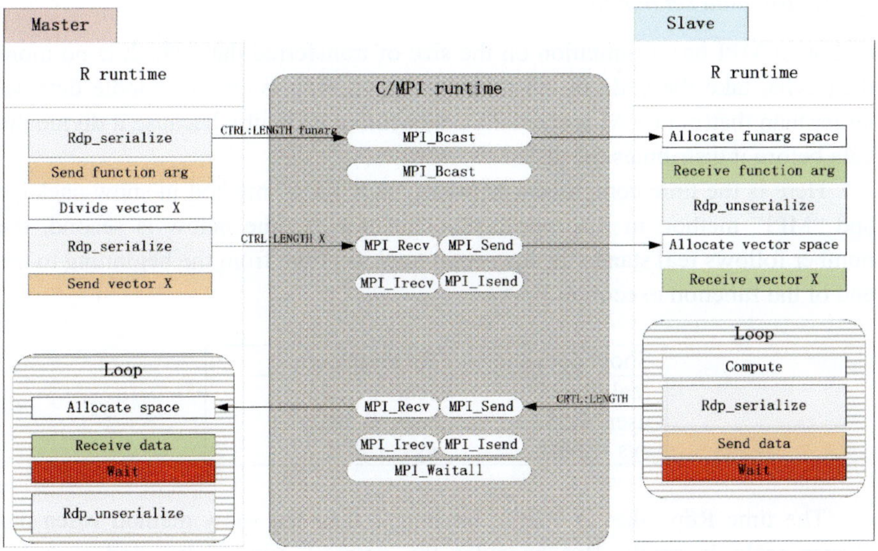

Fig. 3. A parallel task scheduling framework of Rdp. The process of distribute tasks are being done by MPI which is implemented in C.

3. Experimental Results

3.1. *Testing environment setup*

The experiments are set in order to test the handling ability of big data set, scalability and load balance performance compared with the corresponding function in snow package. The results are average number that are get after 10 times measurements. We use the following command to run the R scripts:

```
mpiexec -n PROCNUM ~R/x86-linux/Rdp/Rdp -q --no-save Rscript.R
```

The testing platform are set up as Table 1 shows:

Table 1. A general view of testing platform configuration.

Name	Configuration
ThinkPad T430u	2 cores, i5-3317U, 1.7GHz, RAM 4.00GB
Dell desktop	2 cores, i5-4570, 3.2GHz, RAM 4.00GB
Server	8 cores, 2 CPUs, E5-2670, 2.60GHz
OS	Ubuntu 14.04, version 3.16.0-30

3.2. *Performance comparison*

3.2.1. *Big data set handling*

Although MPI has a limitation on the size of transferred data which is no more than 2GB, take the code in 2.3 as an example, Rdp is able to handle data set larger than that(matrix M is sized 2.2GB) without difficulty because it divide the data before it distributes the tasks.

Here is the time comparison between "SOCKET" method in snow package and "MPI" method in Rdp package. (The unit of time below is second, the number follows real stands for the actual total run time from the beginning to the end of the function execution.)

Snow package	Rdp package
real 8.535	real 11.243
user 4.553	user 9.301
sys 1.660	sys 1.822

The time Rdp takes is a little bit longer than the snow method when our cluster scale is small. But consider the network time delay and complex interconnect when the cluster becomes larger, there is surly a performance advantage using MPI methods in Rdp.

3.2.2. *Scalability & load balance performance*

In this part, we increase the number of process from 2 to 16 and Figure 3 below shows the comparison curve.

As we can see from Figure 4, the functions in Rdp have stable performance while the ones in snow are not. One possible reason is that it takes some time for snow cluster to initialize, so when the scale of cluster increases, the initial time will be longer and cause a decrease in system performance.

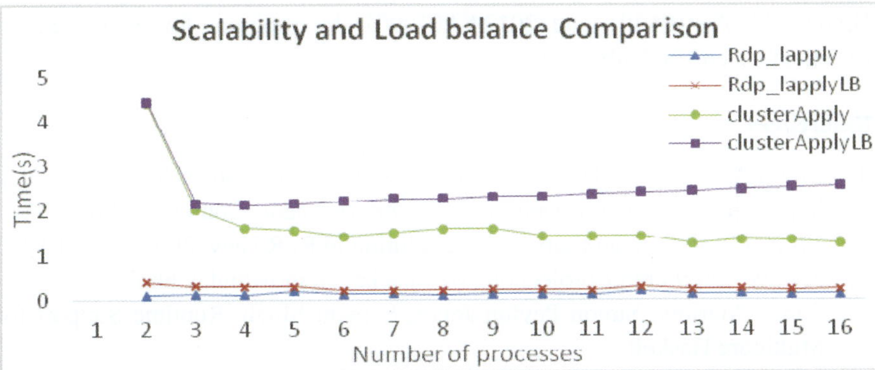

Fig. 4. Scalability and load balance comparison among Rdp_lapply, Rdp_lapplyLB, clusterApply and clusterApplyLB.

4. Related Work

Parallel packages for R: There is a CRAN R[1] high performance and parallel computing task view giving a brief summary and classification on those parallel packages targeting to improve R's performance and increase abilities to deal with big data, including Rmpi[2], snow[3], multicore[4], parallel[5] and so on.

JIT Compilation optimization: Some optimization aim to extend the R performance without sacrificing compatibility. Presented work are Renjin[6], Riposte[7], pqR[8].

VM-level optimization: This method is to build a brand new R VM and is now the most effective way to address some of the most significant performance problems of R. Pioneering early work in VM-level optimization includes OBRIT[9] and RABID[10].

5. Conclusion

In this paper, we have designed Rdp, a distributed parallel framework for R which provides a convenient programming methods for statisticians. We focus on optimizing the implementation of apply-like function family, and the experiments show that the method outperforms in big data set handling, scalability and load balance. However, our methods are now limited to several APIs and we are looking forward to further completeness of the whole system.

Acknowledgments

This work is partially supported by National Science Foundation (NSF) China 61272142, by National Hightech R&D Program of China (863 Program) under Grants 2012AA01A301 and 2012AA010901, by program for New Century Excellent Talents in University.

References

1. Cran R. Task View: High Performance and Parallel Computing with R[OL]. http://cran.r-project.org/web/views/HighPerformanceComputing.html
2. Yu H. Rmpi: Parallel Statistical Computing in R. R New, 2002, 2(2): 10-14.
3. SNOW, http://cran.r-project.org/web/packages/snow/index.html
4. Simon Marlow, Simon Peyton Jones, Satnam Singh. Runtime Support for Multicore Haskell.
5. Vera G, Jansen RC, Suppi RL. R/parallel-speeding up bioinformatics analysis with R. BMC Bioinformatics, 2008. http://www.rparallel.org/
6. Bertram A. Renjin: JVM-based interpreter for the R language for statistical computing; 2014. Available from: http://www.renjin.org.
7. Talbot J, DeVito Z, Hanrahan P. Riposte: a trace-driven compiler and parallel VM for vector code in R. In Proceedings of the 21st international conference on parallel architectures and compilation techniques. PACT'12, Minneapolis, Minnesota, USA. New York, NY: ACM; 2012: 43-52
8. Neal R. pqR-a pretty quick version of R. Dept. of Statistics and Dept. Of Computer Science, University of Toronto, 2014.
9. Wang H, Wu P, Padua D. Optimizing R VM: allocation removal and path length reductional via interpreter-level specialization. In Proceedings of the international symposium on code generation and optimization(CGO), CGO'14, Orlando, Florida; 2014.
10. Hao Lin, Shuo Yang, and Samuel P. Midkiff. RABID: A Distributed Parallel R for Large Datasets. In Big Data (BigData Congress), 2014 IEEE International Congress on, June 2014: 725-732.
11. R.Ihaka and R.Gentleman. R: A language for data analysis and graphics. Journal of Computational and Graphical Statistics, 5(3), 1996.

Design of Reconfigurable Data Processing Software Based on Component

Guo-Hua Wang[a], Wei-Shuo Zhang[b] and Si-Chen Xu

Instrumentation Science and Opto-electronics Engineering, Beihang University, Beijing, China

E-mail: [a]wgh@buaa.edu.cn, [b]buaazws@buaa.edu.cn

The Satellite Condition Monitoring System (SCMS) plays a crucial role in ensuring the reliability and stability of satellite operation, however the design method of existing data processing software of SCMS requires the developers to redesign for a specified satellite model from scratch. Due to the different models and functional requirements between satellites, this development mode leads to a large amount of repetitive work, increases the development cost and declines the design efficiency. To overcome this development challenge, a component-based software architecture is proposed to achieve reconfigurable development of the data processing software. This paper first presents the unified component interface model, and then introduces the configuration description language to model the data processing flow. At last, a reconfiguration support software is designed to facilitate the developers to implement reconfiguration visually.

Keywords: Data Processing; Software Reconfiguration; Component-based Development; Satellite Condition Monitoring System.

1. Introduction

With the booming development of aerospace technology, the function and structure of spacecraft represented by satellite is becoming increasingly complex and huge [1]. As the key technique to keep the reliability and stability of satellite platform, satellite condition monitoring system (SCMS) checks the satellite status accurately in real-time and make correct fault diagnosis strategy through effective data processing for a large amount of operating parameters [2]. The current data processing software in realm of SCMS was developed for specific satellite product, which lead to high development cost and period due to the diverse satellite models and functional requirements that result in the differences of spacecraft parameters and their processing methods. Thus, it is imperative to improve the development efficiency and quality of data processing software in the domain of SCMS [3.4.5].

Component-based reconfiguration is an engineering technology that deals with cost-effective, quick reaction to market changes[6], in which the component, as a unit of composition with contractually specified interfaces and explicit context dependencies only, can be deployed independently and is subject to composition by third parties [7]. In recent years, a number of methods about the development of reconfigurable application based on component have been developed. For instance, OpenRec proposed by Hillman and Warren is a framework which comprises a reflective component model plus an open and extensible reconfiguration management infrastructure [8.9]. Batista and Rodriguez also proposed an approach for dynamic reconfiguration of applications based on CORBA components running in an environment called Lua Space that is composed by the dynamically typed language Lua and a set of tools based on Lua [10.11.12]. Inspired by these applications, a component-based reconfigurable software architecture for data processing software is proposed to meet the current urgent requirements.

The remainder of this paper is organized as follows: Section 2 introduces the unified component interface model and reconfiguration model described by configuration description language. Section 3 presents the reconfigurable software architecture of the data processing software. Section 4 presents the reconfiguration support software to facilitate the developers to achieve reconfiguration visually and a conclusion is drawn in Section 5.

2. The Reconfiguration Framework

The reconfiguration framework is designed to support the reconfigurable development of component-based data processing software for the domain of SCMS. The implementation of reconfiguration is controlled and sequenced by the reconfiguration framework. Our reconfiguration framework is mainly divided into two parts: the component interface model and the reconfiguration model.

2.1. *The component interface model*

Components are encapsulated units of functionality and deployment that interact with their environment exclusively through well-defined interfaces [13].

Developers only need to know the functionality of a software component and how it interfaces with its environment, and don't need alter the component's internal logic and code [14]. Thus, component model must be standard in order to help developers design self-defined components and make components' use more convenient. Besides, the unified component model is conducive to effectively achieve reconfiguration of data processing software for SCMS.

The key interfaces of component model are split into three types, as illustrated in Figure 1.

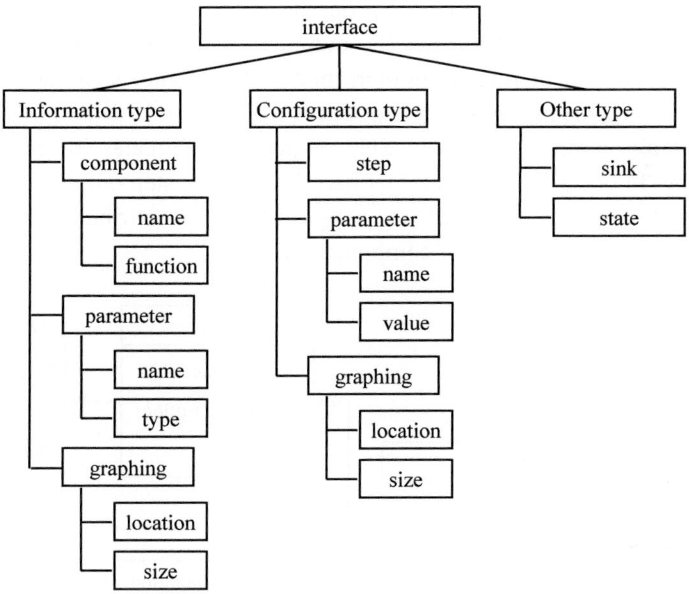

Fig. 1. The component interface model.

Information type interfaces take charge of providing required information to user. Among them, graphing information interface is used for reconfiguration support software introduced in Chapter 4. Configuration type interfaces are generic processing services for component settings in the procedure of reconfiguration. Step configuration interface is aimed at step concept which will be detailedly recommended in reconfiguration model. Moreover, other type interfaces that mainly include sink interface and state interface are equally important. When component needs to generate new output, sink interface will be called to update the calculated result to the receiving component. And state interface can control the executing status of any object instantiated from component.

2.2. *The reconfiguration model*

A reconfiguration is defined as a set of components which are connected to each other by interfaces [15]. The loose coupling between components means that, in principle, the reconfiguration can be achieved. However, component model cannot entirely express all information owned by a reconfiguration. Therefore, it is necessary to build reconfiguration model using XML-based reconfiguration description language.

According to the execution order of each component, a flow describes a sequence of steps that configure the properties through corresponding interfaces of component model and transfer the output to the next component. Figure 2 shows the structure of reconfiguration model. There into, step can be divided into four parts in detail. Step part introduces the basic information of every step corresponding component model. Step output part indicates the properties of each output in one step. Output target part shows what step outputs to. And step configuration part is intended to assign values to attributes through the configuration type interfaces of component model.

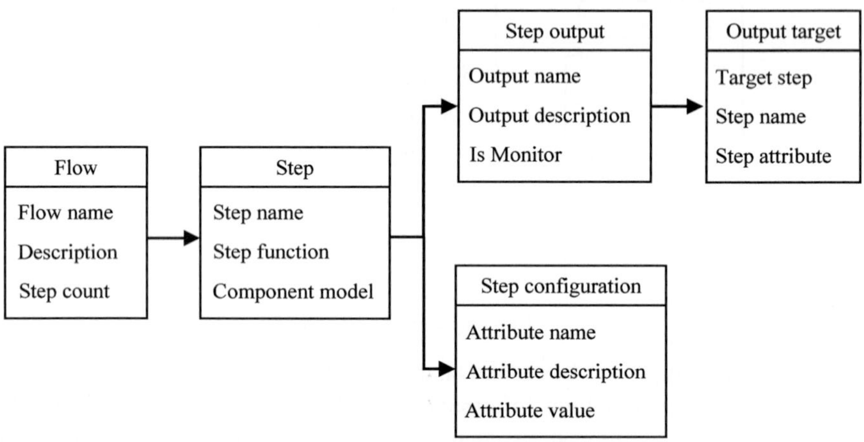

Fig. 2. Structure of reconfiguration model.

3. Software Architecture

The data processing software of SCMS is responsible for analyzing and computing the collected telemetry data, thus providing data support for the further condition monitoring and fault diagnosis [16.17]. Relying on the reconfiguration framework, the architecture of data processing software is presented in Figure 3.

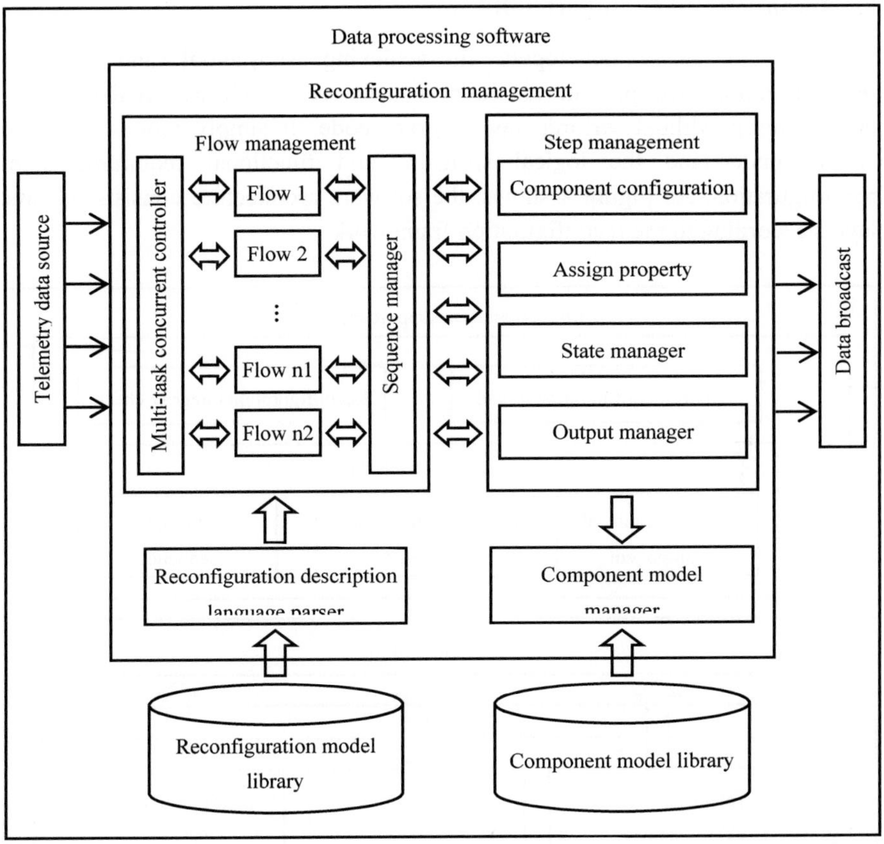

Fig. 3. The architecture of data processing software.

Reconfiguration management is the core of this structure. On one hand, reconfiguration description language parser analyzes reconfiguration models and transfers the consequence to flow management. According to the telemetry data acquisition, flow management creates tasks set in which each task represents a flow through multi-task concurrent controller. Then sequence manager controls each flow task to execute every step on the basis of sequence. On the other hand, with the request from sequence manager, step management calls the relevant component acquired by component model manager. The concrete operation includes configuration of component, property assignment, component's executing state management and management of component's output. All these management are implemented through the interfaces of component models.

4. Reconfiguration Support Software

In order to assist developers in achieving substantial and complex reconfiguration, we present an support software which can realize visual programming without writing any program code. It simply request users to clearly understand the logical structure and functional requirements of reconfiguration. As Figure 4 shows, the software architecture consists of three layers according to the reconfiguration framework.

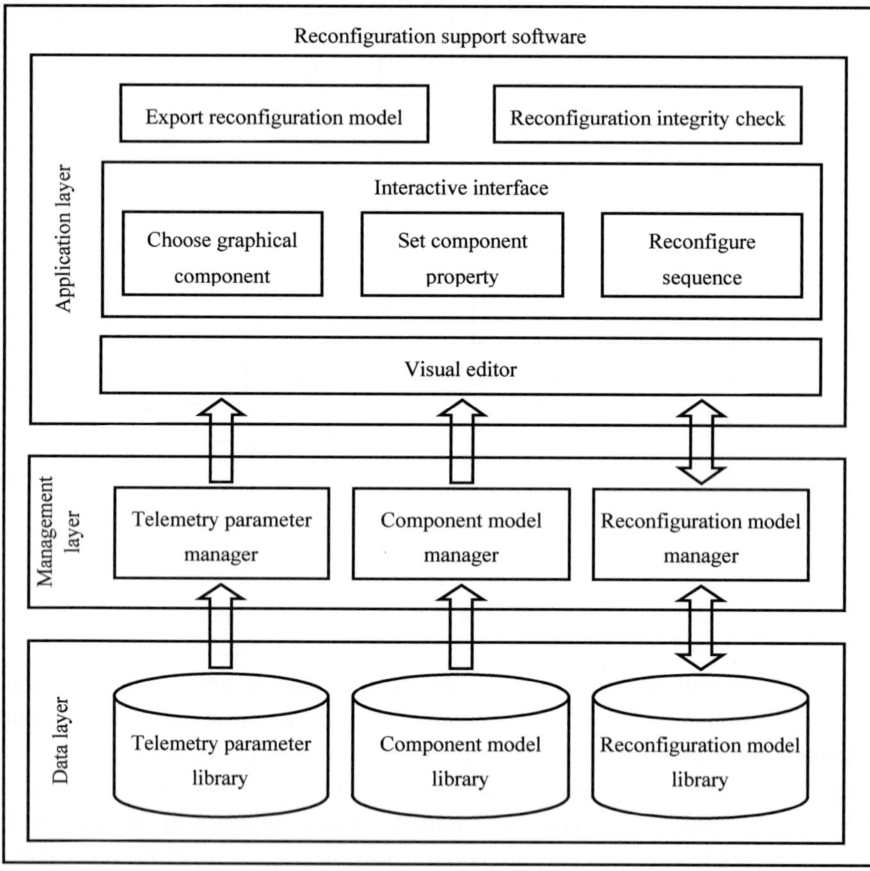

Fig. 4. The architecture of reconfiguration support software.

Data layer is a container of databases including telemetry parameter library, component model library and reconfiguration model library. Management layer provides access service for each database in the data layer, and then individually selects and analyzes information about parameters or models to promote application layer invoke the underlying data source.

Application layer transforms components into corresponding graphic objects through the visual editor. By means of interactive interface, user can choose graphical components, then set their properties, and finally adjust the sequence between components so as to compose a complete reconfiguration model. Meanwhile, application layer supply other services including reconfiguration model export and reconfiguration integrity check which can automatically examine whether the reconfiguration model is complete.

5. Conclusions

In this paper, a component-based reconfigurable software architecture is proposed for the data processing software to improve the development efficiency and quality. Moreover, a reconfiguration support software is developed to assist the reconfiguration development visually. Practices indicate that the proposed reconfigurable development approach based on component is feasible. It brings significant improvement in declining repetitive work, reducing development difficulty, shorting design period and upgrading efficiency.

References

1. A. Ahmadi, T. Fransson, A. Crona, M. Klein and P. Soderholm, Integration of RCM and PHM for the next generation of aircraft, in 2009 IEEE Aerospace Conference (IEEE, 2009).
2. S. Dyne, P. Collins and D. Tunbridge, Satellite mechanical health monitoring, in Advanced Vibration Measurements, Techniques and Instrumentation for the Early Prediction of Failure, IEE Colloquium on (IET, London, 1992).
3. A. Serov, THE PROBLEMS OF AUTOMATIC DATA PROCESSING AT THE SYSTEMS OF CONDITION MONITORING OF INDUSTRIAL EQUIPMENT.
4. ISO 13374-2, Condition monitoring and diagnostics of machines - Data processing, communication and presentation - Part 2: Data processing.
5. J.T. Malin and P. Oliver, Making Technology Ready: Integrated Systems Health Management, in AIAA Infotech@ Aerospace 2007 Conference and Exhibit (AIAA, Reston, 2007).

6. Y. Koren, U. Heisel, F. Jovane, T. Moriwaki, G. Pritschow, G. Ulsoy and H. Van Brussel, Reconfigurable manufacturing systems, CIRP ANN-MANUF TECHN, **48**, 527 (1999).
7. C. Szyperski, J. Bosch and W. Weck, Component-oriented programming, in European Conference on Object-Oriented Programming (Heidelberg, Germany, 1999).
8. J. Hillman and I. Warren, An open framework for dynamic reconfiguration, in Proceedings of the 26th International Conference on Software Engineering (Washington, USA, 2004).
9. I. Warren, J. Sun, S. Krishnamohan and T. Weerasinghe, An automated formal approach to managing dynamic reconfiguration, in 21st IEEE/ACM International Conference on Automated Software Engineering (Tokyo, Japan, 2006).
10. J. Siegel, CORBA: Fundamentals and Programming (John Wiley & Sons, Ltd, Manhattan 1996).
11. T. Batista and N. Rodriguez, Dynamic reconfiguration of component-based applications, in Software Engineering for Parallel and Distributed Systems, 2000. Proceedings. International Symposium on (Limerick, Ireland, 2000).
12. J.P.A. Almeida, M. Wegdam, M. Van Sinderen and L. Nieuwenhuis, Transparent dynamic reconfiguration for CORBA, in Distributed Objects and Applications, 2001. DOA'01. Proceedings. 3rd International Symposium on (Rome, Italy, 2001).
13. T. Batista, A. Joolia and G. Coulson, Managing dynamic reconfiguration in component-based systems, in Software Architecture (Pisa, Italy, 2005).
14. T. Ravichandran and M.A. Rothenberger, Software reuse strategies and component markets, Commun. ACM, **46**, 109 (2003).
15. M.C. Eddin and Z. Mammeri, Preserving the global consistency of dynamic reconfiguration, in Software Engineering, Artificial Intelligence, Networking and Parallel/Distributed Computing (SNPD), 2013 14th ACIS International Conference on (Honolulu, USA, 2013).
16. M. Pecht, Prognostics and health management of electronics (John Wiley & Sons, Ltd, Manhattan, 2008).
17. A.J. Guillen, J.F. Gomez, A. Crespo and A. Guerrerro, A. Sola, Advances in PHM Application Frameworks: Processing Methods, Prognosis Models, Decision Making, Chem. Eng. Trans. **33**, 391 (2013).

Equipment Attitude Monitoring System of the Railway Transportation Based on WSN

Gui-Xing Zheng[a], Ya-Hui Che, Yue-Ming Li and Peng Wang

Military Transportation University,
Tianjin, 300161, China
E-mail: [a]zgx_cn@163.com

In order to improve the unsatisfied function of equipment attitude monitoring facilities, the equipment attitude monitoring system of the railway transportation based on WSN is designed. The framework of the software and the structure of the hardware had been studied and designed. The low pass filter has been applied to process the data of equipment's attitude. The calculation algorithm of equipment attitude had been worked out and tested by using the models. Incidents caused by unexpected shift of equipment transported by train will be decreased, owing to this monitoring facilities.

Keywords: Railway Transportation, Equipment Attitude, WSN, Monitoring System.

1. Introduction

Railway transportation is an important type of shipping, by which large amount of people and goods can be carried. It's cheaper, safer and more reliable. The train can keep moving on the railway regularly and durably despite the bad weather and nature condition.

Railway flatcar, a kind of railway wagon, can carry different kinds of equipment. When the train is moving, the equipment may be made glide or turn around by various many kinds of mechanical force, even though the equipment is fastened well. Once the equipment slips a small distance or turns a small angle, it may lead serious accidents and large economic losses. Therefore, it is necessary to monitor the movement attitude of the equipment during all the travel time by using some kind technique method[1]. Only in this way the safety of transportation can be ensured.

Recently, video is used to monitor the attitude of equipment[2-5], especially when the equipment is expensive. This video monitoring depends on the work of the escort workers. The escort workers have to stare the TV screen. When they see something happen on the screen, they have to make sure whether it is an accident. Under bad weather and night condition, escort workers cannot have a rest. It is weary and exhausted for the escort workers to concentrate on the full-time monitoring job during a long time travel. Under this situation, it is more difficult to make sure that every unexpected change of the equipment can be found promptly and precisely by the escort workers. Meanwhile, the facilities of video monitoring needs strong power supply, which the train cannot provide easily. At the same time, the facilities of video monitoring also needs bandwidth to fit the large data transport.

The equipment monitoring system of the railway transportation, which is based on wireless sensor network (WSN), can automatically oversee the state of equipment all the daytime and night. Compared with video monitoring system operated by escort workers, the equipment monitoring system itself can intelligently give an alarm at the very time when the state of equipment changes. With the application of equipment monitoring system, the safety of the equipment and the informatization level is advanced significantly.

2. Design of the Hardware

The equipment attitude monitoring system of the railway transportation consists of altitude monitoring unit (AMU), altitude reference unit (ARU) and monitoring terminal, are shown in Figure 1 and Figure 2.

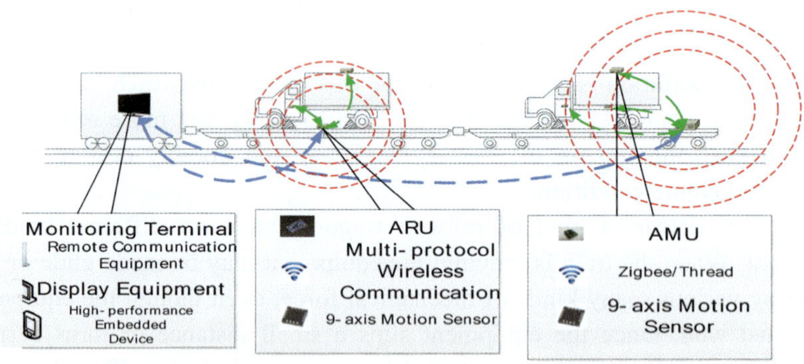

Fig. 1 Sketch of equipment attitude monitoring system

The AMU is put on the particular position of the equipment. When this position moves, the movement information is transferred to relevant electronic signal by AMU. And then, the AMU sends this electronic signal to ARU wirelessly.

The ARU is put on the particular position of the flatcar. When the flatcar moves, the movement information is transferred to relevant electronic signal by ARU. Then, ARU get two signal. One received from the ARU; the other is produced by itself. Usually, the two signals are the same, because the equipment didn't move. While the ARU tells the two signals are not the same, it tells that the equipment have some movements. Finally, ARU give the information to the monitoring terminal.

Monitoring terminal, communicates with ARU by Sub-G wirelessly, which can send security early warning signal to escort with the preset threshold.

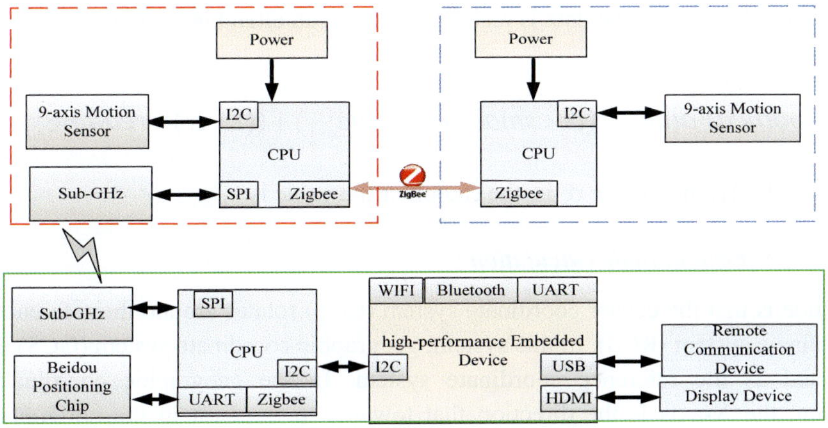

Fig. 2 Framework of the system

3. Algorithm Design

3.1. *Preprocessing of data*

9–axis motion sensor consists of 3-axis accelerometer, 3-axis gyroscope and 3-axis magnetometer, sense the movements of the equipment. But, because of the mechanical vibration caused by various reason, such as bad weather, the sensor itself and the movement of the train, the output signal will have noises. Therefore, the system has to filter the noise signal to improve the precision of monitor and the dynamic function of the system.

The signal-noise ratio (SNR) of measure values of pitch and roll can be large, when the accelerometer is resting or moving slightly. The magnetometer is used to measure the geomagnetic intensity. The output signal vary slowly, that's to say that the frequency of the signal is low. Because the bulky and weighty equipment is well fastened on the railway flatcar, the state of equipment is steady. That's why that the output signal of 9–axis motion sensor is almost low-frequency signal. Therefore, low-pass filter and average filter can be used to preprocess the output signal. In that way, the SNR can be improved.

There exists a particular critical frequency value of every low-pass filter. The signal whose frequency is higher than the critical frequency value will be cut off by low-pass filter, while the low-frequency signal will not to be influenced. Most MCUs have a hardware average filter themselves. The average filter can process the signal as low-pass filter do, so that the amount of calculating is reduced.

Therefore, when the data is read, it should be an alterable average, as in Eq. (1).

$$smoothedValue_n = (\alpha \times smoothedValue_{n-1}) + ((1-\alpha) \times reading_n) \quad (1)$$

$\alpha \in [0,1]$, the bigger α is, the smoother the value is.

3.2. *Movement attitude calculation*

Attitude is that the carrier coordinate system (CCS) rotates around the reference coordinate system (RCS). In this system, geographic coordinate system (GCS) is selected as the reference coordinate system. In the geographic coordinate system, the X-axis is the direction that towards to the East in the horizontal plane. The Y-axis is the direction of geomagnetic north. The Z-axis is the up direction perpendicular to the horizontal plane.

In the carrier coordinate system, the base point o is the geometrical center point. The x-axis, the horizontal axis, is the direction that the train moves toward. The y-axis is the vertical axis. The z-axis is the up direction perpendicular to the oxy plane within the Right-handed Role. The three attitude angles are like this:

Pitch θ, The angle between y-axis of CCS and its projection in the OXY plane of GCS, the range is -90~90°.

Yaw φ, The angle between the projection of y-axis of CCS in the OXY plane of GCS and Y-axis of GCS, the range is0~360°.

Roll γ, The angle between x-axis of CCS and its projection in the OXY plane of GCS, the range is -180~180°.

CCS is rotated according to the order of z-x-y, and the attitude transformation matrix, as in Eq. (2).

$$C=\begin{bmatrix}\cos\gamma\cos\varphi-\sin\gamma\sin\theta\sin\varphi & \cos\gamma\sin\varphi+\sin\gamma\sin\theta\cos\varphi & -\sin\gamma\cos\theta\\ -\cos\theta\sin\varphi & \cos\theta\cos\varphi & \sin\theta\\ \sin\gamma\cos\varphi+\cos\gamma\sin\theta\sin\varphi & \sin\gamma\sin\varphi-\cos\gamma\sin\theta\cos\varphi & \cos\gamma\cos\theta\end{bmatrix} \tag{2}$$

The measured value of 3-axis accelerometer is $G=|g_x, g_y, g_z|$, so that the pitch θ and the roll γ are shown in Eq. (3).

$$\theta=\arcsin(g_y)$$
$$\gamma=\arctan(-\frac{g_x}{g_z}) \tag{3}$$

The measured value of 3-axis magnetometer is $H=\left[h_x,h_y,h_z\right]^T$, so that the yaw is φ, as in Eq. (4).

$$\varphi=\arctan(\frac{h_y}{h_x}) \tag{4}$$

The 3-axis gyroscope can process the calculation of attitude angle independently. The result can be set up as the default value of last filter.

The attitude angle of equipment is θ,φ,γ, the attitude angle of flatcar is θ',φ',γ', as in Eq. (5).

$$\Delta\theta=\theta-\theta'$$
$$\Delta\varphi=\varphi-\varphi' \tag{5}$$
$$\Delta\gamma=\gamma-\gamma'$$

Usually, the value of $\Delta\theta,\Delta\varphi$ and $\Delta\gamma$ are 0°. The changes of their value indicate that the movement of the equipment and the movement of the flatcar are not the same. The movement of the equipment can be calculated. An early warning can be given according to the results.

4. Experiment Test

The experiment uses a 1:100 flatcar model and a 1:100 equipment model to test the algorithm, is shown in Figure 3. The frequency of sampling is 50Hz.

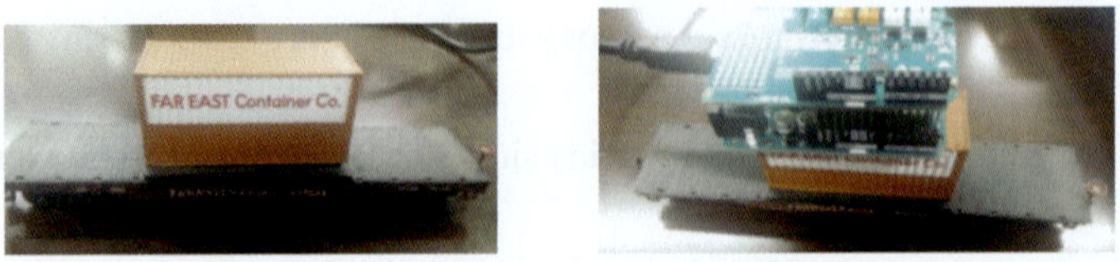

Fig. 3 The sketch of the models

The initial data of sampling is shown in Figure 4.

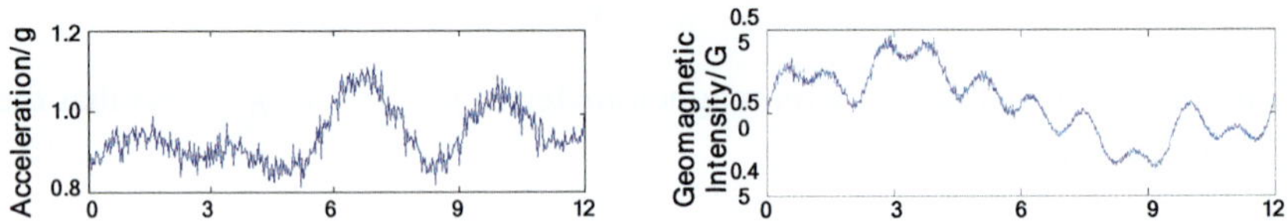

Fig. 4 The data before filter

The data after low-frequency filter are shown in Figure 5. Figure 6 shows that the value pitch and the roll were almost 0°. And the yaw has been changed when the flatcar was swerved. These indicate the change of equipment attitude angle. In the same way, the attitude angle of flatcar almost keeps pace with the equipment's.

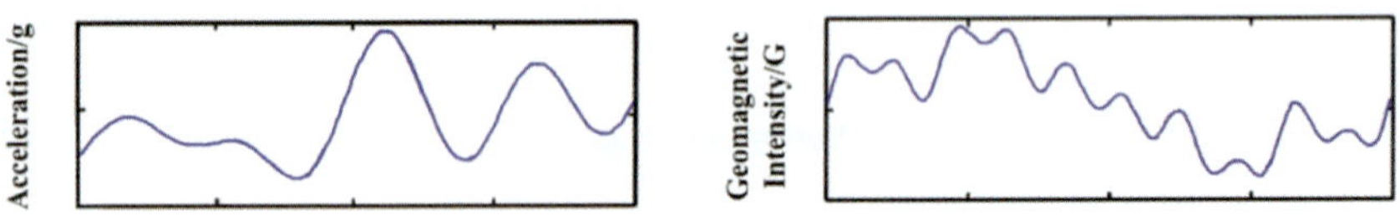

Fig. 5 The data after filter

Movement attitude calculation:

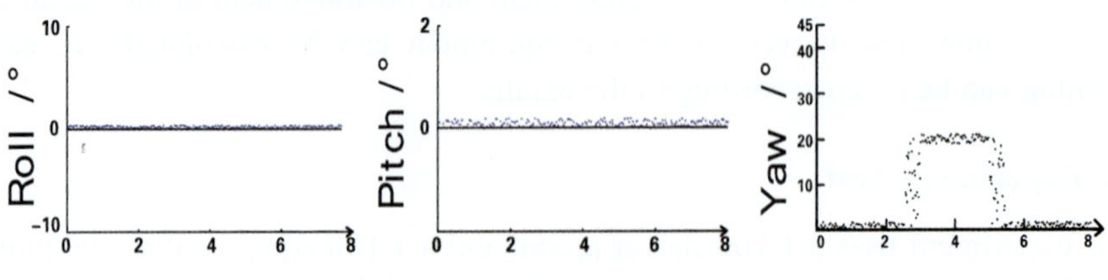

Fig. 6 The sketch of the attitude angle

5. Conclusion

The equipment attitude monitoring system for the railway transportation has been designed. The system is tested using flatcar model and equipment model. It shows that the data preprocessing and attitude calculating algorithms are effectiveness. According to the calculation of real-time attitude data, the equipment position offset can be estimated.

References

1. Hai Jun. *Thoughts on Strengthening the Construction of Military Railway Transportation Equipment*. China Railways ,2014, Vol.8, pp.16-18.
2. Zhang Yawei, Lv Xiaojun. *The Analysis of the Train Operation Environment Monitoring System and Application.* Proceedings of the 10th Annual Conference of ITS China. (ITS China, 2015).
3. Li Hui, Research on Energy and Routing for Wireless Sensor Network, Master's thesis, Lanzhou Jiaotong University (2014).
4. Yu Shanshan, Research of rail transit intelligent supervisory control based on RFID and WSN, Master's thesis, Hefei University of Technology (2015).
5. Chen Wei, Research and application of attitude angle estimation algorithm based on quaternion and Kalman filter, Master's thesis, Yanshan University(2015).

A Study on Transformation Practice of Real-Time Probe Vehicle System Architecture in Beijing

Li-Yun Zhu[a], Yang-Lin Hu, Jian-Ping Sun and Peng Zhang

Beijing Transportation Research Center,
Beijing, 100073, China
E-mail: [a]zhuly@bjtrc.org.cn

With the development of the Internet of Things, the influx of mass sensed data, and the bottleneck of relational databases in functions, performance and stability, the industry's leading IT companies have started to abandon the technical architecture of single relational databases, and the upgrade, transformation and migration of the software and hardware architecture of existing systems with a soaring size data for processing. Storage in the information systems of the transportation industry have also become a priority. Taking the upgrade and transformation project for the real-time probe vehicle system of Beijing for instance, this paper describes the real-time computing and storage management dilemma in the traditional architecture of the urban transportation core business system, new architecture solutions, and the effect of enhancement after upgrade and transformation.

Keywords: Probe Vehicle; Big Data; Hadoop; Storm; Open-Source GIS; Upgrade and Reconstruction.

1. Introduction

With the rapid development of Internet and networking technology, the scale of data to be processed by software systems have been rapidly expanded, and cloud computing with grid computing, parallel computing and virtualization technology has promoted the processing of mass data to a new era. The open source, high fault tolerance and cross-platform and other features of Hadoop have made it the preferred technology for building cloud platforms [1]. The industry's leading IT companies have started to abandon relational databases and explore new data storage and computing solutions, and in education, medicine, finance, manufacture and other industries, new architectures have also been adopted for cost control and efficiency enhancement so as to cope with the new big data situation. For the time being, most of the solutions for big data processing are characterized by: A hardware platform is built with a cluster of a large number of middle-end and low-end machines (blade computers), and a software platform is built with relevant open-source software [2].

Beijing Transportation Operations Coordination Center (TOCC) is also facing the same problem. Since it was established in 2010, TOCC has integrated nearly 3,000 data, accessed 20,000 video channels and 19 application systems [3]. For the time being, the existing systems were built based on traditional relational databases. In the PC times, the data size processed by an IT system is limited, and a software architecture based on relational databases could meet most of the demands for information systems of the transportation industry. However, with the development of the Internet of Things and the influx of a huge size of traffic operation and operation monitoring data, in the processing of mass data, a bottleneck has appeared in relational databases in terms of functions, performance and stability. Therefore, the upgrade, restructuring and migration of the software and hardware architecture of existing systems with soaring data size for processing and storage step by step according to priorities have become a priority.

2. Problems

The road network operation monitoring and intelligent analysis platform of Beijing is one of the core decision-making support systems of TOCC. In the probe vehicle system, information about vehicle positions, directions and speed recorded on a regular basis when probe vehicles with vehicle-borne global positioning systems are moving is processed by map matching, path speculation and other computing models and algorithms, so that the position data of the probe vehicles are related to urban roads in time and space, and speed of each vehicle on the roads each probe vehicle passes by, running time on the roads and other traffic congestion information can be finally obtained. If there are enough probe vehicles in place in the city, and the position data of such probe vehicles are transmitted to an information processing center via a wireless communications system on a regular basis in real time for the information center to process in a centralizes manner, the dynamic and real-time traffic congestion information of the whole city can be obtained [4].

This system, since 2007, has a soaring size of probe vehicle satellite positioning data and map data that have been accessed and to be assessed. See Table 1 and Table 2 below for details.

Table 1 Growth of probe vehicle data in previous years

Year	Number of Vehicles	GPS Uploading Interval (second)	Daily Record Number (10,000)	Daily Data Size (GB)
2008	8000 taxis	60	1100	0.8
2009	12000 taxis	60	1800	1.2
2012	40000 taxis	60	5760	4
2013	40000 taxis +10000 buses	60, 40\20	8640	6
2015	40000 taxis +23000 buses	60, 40\20	12500	8.6
2016	40000 taxis +23000 buses +30000 social vehicles	60, 40\20, 9	41300	29
2017	40000 taxis +23000 buses +13000 vehicles for energy saving and emission reduction monitoring	60, 40\20, 1	118000	82

Table 2 Growth of road network factors that match GIS base maps in previous years

Year	Geographic Scope of Analysis	Analysis Target	Scale of Analysis	Spatial Coverage (km^2)
2008	Within the Fifth Ring	Road network	28414 road sections	700
2012	Downtown area (including the six major districts and the Fifth Ring)	Road network	40419 road sections	2400
2015	Administrative region of the city	Road network	465240 road sections	16000
2015	Administrative region of the city	Road section + bus network	465240 road sections+2300 bus lines	16000

As described above, since the Olympic system in 2008, the probe vehicle system of Beijing has been developed from satellite positioning data for 8,000 vehicles with one piece of position status information uploaded every minute into 40,000 taxis with one piece of position status information uploaded every minute, 23,000 buses with one piece of position status information uploaded every 40 or 20 seconds and 30,000 volunteer vehicles with one piece of position status information uploaded every 9 seconds in 2016, and even 13,000 energy saving and emission reduction monitoring vehicles collecting position and motor work condition information every second in 2017. Besides, the data size of electronic base maps as core data of the probe vehicle system, which have direct impact on the volume of matching computing has been developed from more than 28,000 links in the Olympic system in 2008 into nearly 500,000 links. The real-time requirement for the system has been enhanced all the time as is shown in Table 3. Due to the dramatic growth of the data size and the enhancement of the requirement for real-time performance, the designed computing performance of the original system is not enough any longer, and the real-time system is unable to fulfill real-time computing tasks.

Table 3 Change in the demand for road condition update in previous years

Year	Name of the System	Interval of Update
2008	Probe vehicle system	5 minutes
2013	Probe vehicle system	1 minute
2015	Bus system	10 seconds
2017	Energy saving and emission reduction monitoring and statistic platform	1 second

On the other hand, due to the query demand in the transportation industry, all data results in the system from 2007 on involve historic road conditions in various time granularity, historic speeds on nearly 10,000 roads, traffic target systems of each region, distribution of road sections where traffic congestion often occurs and other mass data, all of which need online query, the system storage has failed to meet the actual demand for administration long before, and the traditional system architecture based on relational databases cannot cope with the existing data computing and storage calling demand by any means, so that the platform is almost about to collapse.

3. Practice

Considering the functional demand and computing and storage pressure of the original system as well as the further growth trend of data size in the future, the upgrade and restructuring project for the existing system finally adopts a technology architecture of Storm streaming platform + Hadoop database source platform + open-source GIS development based on Linux, and the basic storage and computing functions of the system are based on the building of an open-source software architecture, including:

i.Compute real-time data by streamlining method with the Storm system architecture

(a)Real-time road conditions and targets
(b)Microscopic short-term prediction
ii.Analyze and manage historic data with the Hadoop system architecture
(a)Complement computing and analysis of historic data of probe vehicles
(b)Bid data storage and management platform
iii.Realize analysis and computing and map release based on spatial locations with the open-source GIS development technology architecture of GeoServer, Geotools and OpenLayers.
(a)Map matching computing
(b)Spatial overlay analysis
(c)Thematic map generation, rendering and release

Among others, the core computing and storage system structure drawing based on Storm and Hadoop is shown in Figure 1:

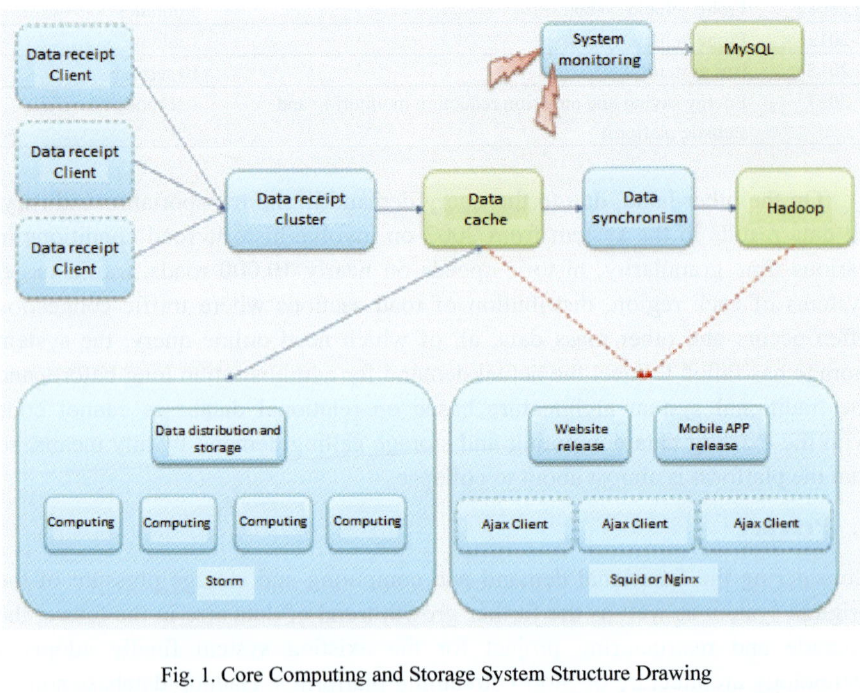

Fig. 1. Core Computing and Storage System Structure Drawing

For the matching computing and thematic drawing rendering based on spatial locations as a core technology of the probe vehicle system, most of the traditional systems use secondary development packages of ARCGIS Engine, ARCGIS Server, Map X and other mature GIS software for realizing the development of analysis business processes. However, due to the functional packaging of secondary development packages, some of them cannot support the Storm steaming computing mode while realizing real high performance. Instead, the upgrade and restructuring project replaces the secondary development technology with ARCGIS Engine in the core computing system, which significantly enhances the realization performance of the spatial analysis algorithm.

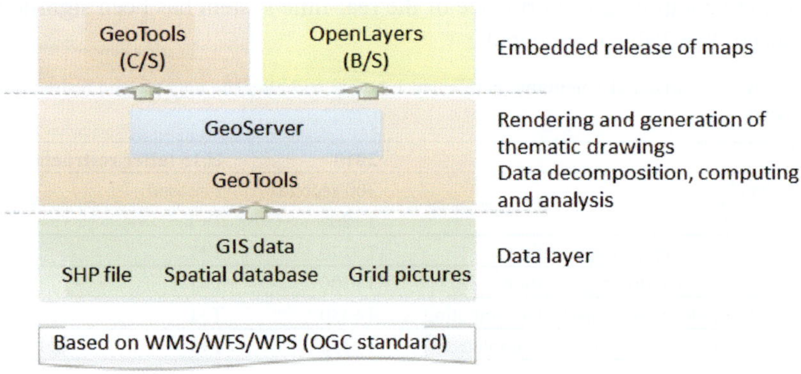

Fig. 2. Open-source GIS System Technology Architecture Drawing

The current open-source GIS map processing, spatial analysis and thematic map release are designed based on the GIS agreement released by a standard organization OGC (Open Geospatial Consortium). The development realization of the system is completely based on the OGC standard for WMS, WFS and WPS. See Figure 2 for the technology architecture drawing. See the description of the technology system of each layer as follows:

• On the data layer, the supplementation, editing, modification, deletion and storage of geographic information data are processed, and vectorized geographic information is stored in SHP files and spatial databases (such as PostGIS, MySQL, etc.) and graphic geographic information is stored in grid files.

• The decomposition, computing and analysis of data based on spatial locations are realized by the GeoTools development, result data are extracted after computing, and the rendering and generation of thematic maps are mainly realized by GeoServer development under the frame of GeoTools, so as to complete the storage of coverage information, factor information and rendering pattern information and connect them to the release service on the upper layer.

• Map release is realized in two patterns, including the embedded release in C/S system and the embedded release in B/S system. In the CS pattern that is designated for professional analysis, the processing and rendering service of geographic information is provided on JVM with GeoTools; in the BS pattern that is designed for comprehensive and general application, key geographic information is displayed mainly with OpenLayers embedded in business web pages.

• Through the upgrade and restructuring of the new technology architecture above, the computing performance of the real-time system has been significantly enhanced. See Table 4 for details:

Table 4 A Comparison of computing performance before and after the upgrade and restructuring of the system

	2010	**2015 (after restructuring)**
GPS batch	300 seconds	1 second
GPS reading	T+20	T+1
One-time matching path generation	T+270	T+1
Real-time road condition generation	T+300	T+1
The traffic index system starts the computing	T+330	T+1
The computing of each index is completed	T+350	T+1

5 servers with 2*8 core and 12G memory are used for the assessment of the historic data computing performance, which takes about 5 minutes for computing data of taxis and probe vehicles in one day in road networks of downtown areas of Beijing, while under the same hardware conditions, it takes about 30 hours for computing data of one day in the original system [5].

In the system, storage management of primary satellite positioning data is carried out with HDFS files. The storage management of result data for online query required for the system is carried out with HBASE. Sqoop provides a convenient import tool for connecting HBase to the RDBMS data in the upper layer application system. This architecture guarantees a quite good online response and horizontal expansion capacity for system storage management.

4. Conclusion

With the development of the Internet of Things, the influx of mass sensed data, not only the industry's leading IT companies have started to abandon the technology architecture with single relational databases, the transportation industry, as a key development field of the Internet of Things, also has to start exploring new data storage and computing solutions for upgrade and restructuring of the existing traditional systems in dilemma.

With the restructuring of the original system with a new technology architecture of Storm streaming computing + Hadoop data source platform + open-source GIS development based on Linux, the real-time probe vehicle system of Beijing is significantly benefited in the following aspects:

- The storage capacity of the system is improved and a larger size of incremental data can be supported;
- The computing performance is enhanced, so that the real-time requirement for computing and analysis can be met better.
- The concurrent service capability of the system is enhanced, so that more users and more application systems can access the system.
- More importantly, when facing the influx of more data, the above service capability can continue to be expanded horizontally to solve the problem, which lays a solid foundation for the long-term development of the system and the support for more complex future demands.

Acknowledgements

This work is supported by grant 61572069 and grant 71501014 of the China National Natural Science Foundation.

References

1. Wang Yanming, Feng Guohe & Xue Yun, Summary of Hadoop Research in Recent Years in Foreign Countries, Computer Systems & Applications, Issue 6 of Volume 22, 2013(In Chinese).
2. Chen Jirong & Le Jiajin, An Overview of Big Data Solutions Based on Hadoop Ecological System, Computer Engineering and Science, Issue 10 of Volume 35, October 2013(In Chinese).
3. Chen Zhihong, Current Situation of the Intelligent Transportation of Beijing, China Urban Intelligent Transport Forum, December 2012(In Chinese).
4. Probe vehicle, Baidu Baike, http://baike.baidu.com/link?url=XEQHUpNBiNmIZ7vCt2bI1QEc2Aub5-DOBp5eSMcbaURBG_M6_y61BjB0WkaWpB9PlyLjdxT_yw7l0nx0LGNtK(In Chinese).
5. Beijing Transportation Research Center, Final Inspection Report for the Upgrade and Restructuring Project for Traffic Operation Monitoring and Intelligent Analysis Platforms, December 2015 (In Chinese).

Session II

Computational Intelligence

Robust D-Stable Pole Assignment Fuzzy Control of Nonlinear Systems Subject to Bounded Input Bounded Output Constraints

Hong-Yu Qiao[1,a] and Wen-Jer Chang[2,b,*]

[1]*Department of Marine Engineering, Nantong Vocational Technical Shipping College*
No.185, Tong-Sheng Avenue, Nantong 226010, Jiangsu, China
[2]*Department of Marine Engineering, National Taiwan Ocean University*
No. 2, Pei-Ning Road, Keelung 20224, Taiwan
E-mail: [a]*qhy@ntsc.edu.cn,* [b]*wjchang@mail.ntou.edu.tw*

A novel robust fuzzy controller design of nonlinear systems is investigated with assigning all poles into a specified disk, while the norms of input and output are bounded. Firstly, sufficient conditions are derived in terms of linear matrix inequalities (LMI) based on the Lyapunov theory. Secondly, a fuzzy controller based on parallel distributed compensation has been designed to meet all the desired control requirements via solving the corresponding sufficient conditions. Finally, control effect of a two-link robot system is proposed as a numerical example to illustrate the advantages of the proposed method.

Keywords: Pole Assignment; Takagi-Sugeno Fuzzy Model; Bounded-Input Bounded-Output.

1. Introduction

In the past couple of years, Takagi-Sugeno (T-S) fuzzy control methods have been widely and successfully applied to many industrial processes. Recently, various performance constraints, including pole assignment constraint [1], covariance constraint [2], control input and output constraint [3], and so on, have been considered in T-S fuzzy model to obtain better performance. There has been much research on pole assignment to achieve good transient behavior [4]. In fact, placing all the eigenvalues of the T-S model in a region of the left half-plane, can improve system performance, particularly in terms of response time and damping ratio. D-pole assignment, assigning all poles of T-S fuzzy system in a specified disk, has been considered in [5]. Recently, the problem of

*Corresponding author.

Bounded Input Bounded Output (BIBO) stabilization for many kinds of control systems has recently been extensively investigated [6]. Fuzzy output-feedback controllers are designed to achieve a BIBO stabilization of T-S fuzzy systems under persistent perturbations in [7].

The BIBO problem is studied associating with pole assignment in this paper. By combining the characteristics of pole assignment and T-S fuzzy control, the contribution of this paper is to develop a fuzzy controller such that the stability of T-S fuzzy model can be guaranteed while BIBO constraint and pole assignment can be fulfilled, simultaneously.

2. System Descriptions

The T-S fuzzy model is considered as follows:
Rule *i*: IF $z_1(t)$ is M_{i1} and … and $z_{ip}(t)$ is M_{ip} THEN

$$\dot{x}(t) = \mathbf{A}_i x(t) + \mathbf{B}_i u(t) \tag{1a}$$

$$y(t) = \mathbf{C}_i x(t) \tag{1b}$$

where $i = 1, 2, \cdots, r$ and r is the number of IF-THEN rules, M_{ip} are fuzzy sets, p is the premise variable number, $x(t) \in \Re^n$ is the state vector, $u(t) \in \Re^m$ is the input vector, $y(t) \in \Re^q$ is the output vector, the matrices $\mathbf{A}_i \in \Re^{n\times n}$, $\mathbf{B}_i \in \Re^{n\times m}$, $\mathbf{C}_i \in \Re^{m\times n}$ are constant.

Given the pair $(x(t),\ u(t))$, the overall fuzzy model can be described as follows:

$$\dot{x}(t) = \sum_{i=1}^{r} h_i(z(t))\{\mathbf{A}_i x(t) + \mathbf{B}_i u(t)\} \tag{2a}$$

$$y(t) = \sum_{i=1}^{r} h_i(z(t))\mathbf{C}_i x(t) \tag{2b}$$

where $h_i(z(t)) = \prod_{j=1}^{p} \mathrm{M}_{ij}(z_j(t)) \Big/ \sum_{i=1}^{r}\prod_{j=1}^{p} \mathrm{M}_{ij}(z_j(t))$, $h_i(z(t)) \geq 0$, $\sum_{i=1}^{r} h_i(z(t)) = 1$, $\mathrm{M}_{ij}(z_j(t))$ is the grade of the membership of $z_j(t)$ in M_{ij}.

For the T-S fuzzy model in (1), one can construct the fuzzy controller via parallel distributed compensation concept. Then, one obtains the following closed-loop system.

$$\dot{x}(t)=\sum_{i=1}^{r}\sum_{j=1}^{r}h_i(z(t))h_j(z(t))\{(\mathbf{A}_i+\mathbf{B}_i\mathbf{F}_j)x(t)\} \tag{3}$$

3. Stability Analysis with BIBO Constraints and Pole Assignment

The well-known sufficient stability conditions for ensuring stability of T-S fuzzy system (3) have been derived by using Lyapunov approach [3]. Moreover, the purpose of pole placement constraints is to place all the closed-loop poles into a circle region D, which is defined as follows [1]:

$$D=\left\{x+jy\in C:(x+q)^2+y^2<r^2\right\} \tag{4}$$

which means centered at the point $(-q,0)$ with $-q+r<0$ and radius $r>0$.

Lemma 1 [5]

If and only if there exists a positive definite matrix $\mathbf{Q}$ such that

$$\begin{bmatrix} -r\mathbf{Q} & q\mathbf{Q}+\mathbf{Q}(\mathbf{A}_i+\mathbf{B}_i\mathbf{F}_j)^{\mathrm{T}} \\ q\mathbf{Q}+(\mathbf{A}_i+\mathbf{B}_i\mathbf{F}_j)\mathbf{Q} & -r\mathbf{Q} \end{bmatrix}<0 \tag{5}$$

The matrix $(\mathbf{A}_i+\mathbf{B}_i\mathbf{F}_j)$ is D-stable and this leads to all the poles will be lying in region D described in (4). The sufficient conditions for ensuring D-stability of T-S fuzzy system (3) and satisfying BIBO constraint are given by the following theorem.

Theorem 1

Assuming that the initial condition $x(0)$ is known, if there exist a positive definite matrix $\mathbf{Q}>0$, $\mathbf{T}_i$ satisfying the following sufficient conditions, then the closed-loop system (3) is D-stable while control input constraint $\|u(t)\|\leq\mu$ and output constraint $\|y(t)\|\leq\lambda$ are enforced simultaneously.

$$\mathbf{A}_i\mathbf{Q}+\mathbf{B}_i\mathbf{T}_i+\mathbf{Q}\mathbf{A}_i^{\mathrm{T}}+\mathbf{T}_i^{\mathrm{T}}\mathbf{B}_i^{\mathrm{T}}<0,\ i=1,2,\ldots,r \tag{6}$$

$$\left(\frac{\mathbf{A}_i\mathbf{Q}+\mathbf{B}_i\mathbf{T}_j+\mathbf{A}_j\mathbf{Q}+\mathbf{B}_j\mathbf{T}_i}{2}\right)+\left(\frac{\mathbf{Q}\mathbf{A}_i^{\mathrm{T}}+\mathbf{T}_j^{\mathrm{T}}\mathbf{B}_i^{\mathrm{T}}+\mathbf{Q}\mathbf{A}_j^{\mathrm{T}}+\mathbf{T}_i^{\mathrm{T}}\mathbf{B}_j^{\mathrm{T}}}{2}\right)<0,\ \text{for } i<j \tag{7}$$

$$\begin{bmatrix} 1 & x^{\mathrm{T}}(0) \\ x(0) & \mathbf{Q} \end{bmatrix} \geq 0 \tag{8}$$

$$\begin{bmatrix} \mathbf{Q} & \mathbf{T}_i^{\mathrm{T}} \\ \mathbf{T}_i & \mu^2 \mathbf{I} \end{bmatrix} \geq 0 \tag{9}$$

$$\begin{bmatrix} \mathbf{Q} & \mathbf{Q}\mathbf{C}_i^{\mathrm{T}} \\ \mathbf{C}_i\mathbf{Q} & \lambda^2 \mathbf{I} \end{bmatrix} \geq 0 \tag{10}$$

$$\begin{bmatrix} -r\overline{\mathbf{X}} & q\overline{\mathbf{X}} + \overline{\mathbf{X}}\mathbf{A}_i^{\mathrm{T}} + \mathbf{T}_i^{\mathrm{T}}\mathbf{B}_i^{\mathrm{T}} \\ q\overline{\mathbf{X}} + \mathbf{A}_i\overline{\mathbf{X}} + \mathbf{B}_i\mathbf{T}_i & -r\overline{\mathbf{X}} \end{bmatrix} < 0 \tag{11}$$

where $\mathbf{T}_i = \mathbf{F}_i\mathbf{Q}$ and $\mathbf{F}_i$ are the feedback gains, the values of μ and λ are preset as the performance parameters.

Proof:

Firstly, let us choose a Lyapunov function as $V(x(t)) = x^{\mathrm{T}}(t)\mathbf{P}x(t)$. According to [3], the closed-loop system (3) is stable and $\dot{V}(x(t)) < 0$ if conditions (6) and (7) are satisfied.

Secondly, let us give an assumption as $x^{\mathrm{T}}(0)\mathbf{P}x(0) \leq 1$. Then, one has

$$1 - x^{\mathrm{T}}(0)\mathbf{Q}^{-1}x(0) \geq 0 \tag{12}$$

where $\mathbf{Q} = \mathbf{P}^{-1}$. Therefore, the inequality (12) is transformed into (8) by the Schur complement procedure. Then, the derivation of (10) is given as follows. From $\|u(t)\| \leq \mu$, one has

$$u^{\mathrm{T}}(t)u(t) = \sum_{i=1}^{r}\sum_{j=1}^{r} h_i(z(t))h_j(z(t))x^{\mathrm{T}}(t)\mathbf{F}_i^{\mathrm{T}}\mathbf{F}_j x(t) \leq \mu^2 \tag{13}$$

Therefore, one has

$$\sum_{i=1}^{r}\sum_{j=1}^{r} h_i(z(t))h_j(z(t))x^{\mathrm{T}}(t)\left(\frac{1}{\mu^2}\mathbf{F}_i^{\mathrm{T}}\mathbf{F}_j - \mathbf{Q}^{-1}\right)x(t) \leq 0 \tag{14}$$

The inequality (14) can be transformed into (15) as follows.

$$\sum_{i=1}^{r} h_i^2(z(t))x^{\mathrm{T}}(t)\begin{bmatrix}\mathbf{Q}^{-1} & \mathbf{F}_i^{\mathrm{T}} \\ \mathbf{F}_i & \mu^2\mathbf{I}\end{bmatrix}x(t) \ge 0 \tag{15}$$

Multiplying both sides of the inequality (20) by $diag[\mathbf{Q} \quad \mathbf{I}] < 0$, then

$$\sum_{i=1}^{r} h_i^2(z(t))\begin{bmatrix}\mathbf{Q} & \mathbf{T}_i^{\mathrm{T}} \\ \mathbf{T}_i & \mu^2\mathbf{I}\end{bmatrix} \ge 0 \tag{16}$$

Then, one can arrive at the condition (9). Therefore, it is proved that if conditions (8) and (9) hold, control input constraint $\|u(t)\| \le \mu$ is enforced at all times $t \ge 0$. Similarly, output constraint $\|y(t)\| \le \lambda$ can be enforced at all times $t \ge 0$ if conditions (8) and (10) hold.

At last, let us consider the pole placement constraints. In Lemma 1, the task is to find a positive definite matrix, which can guarantee (5). For this reason, one can set $\mathbf{Q} = \overline{\mathbf{X}}$ so as to ensure the D-stability and satisfy multiple constraints. Then, set $\mathbf{T}_i = \mathbf{F}_i\overline{\mathbf{X}}$ and (5) can be expressed as (11). Therefore, the T-S fuzzy system (3) is stable subject to various constraints. □

4. Applications to a Nonlinear Two-Link Robot System

The dynamic equations of a two-link robot system have been described in [8]. The stochastic T-S fuzzy system can be established as Itô form in [9]. Thus, the T-S fuzzy model for the two-link robot system can be found in [9]. By applying the proposed design technique, the fuzzy controller can be obtained to guarantee the achievement of D-stable and BIBO constraint simultaneously. In the proposed design, the circle region D is selected as $(q,r) = (10,8)$.

Solving the sufficient conditions of Theorem 1 via MATLAB LMI-Toolbox, the positive definite matrix $\overline{\mathbf{X}} = \overline{\mathbf{X}}^{\mathrm{T}} > 0$ and $\mathbf{F}_i$ can be obtained to construct the fuzzy controller as follows:

$$u(t) = \sum_{i=1}^{9} h_i(x(t))\mathbf{F}_i x(t) \tag{17}$$

Applying the fuzzy controller (17), one can obtain the response comparisons of states between the proposed design method and the method presented by [9], which are shown in Figs. 1-4 with the initial condition $x(0) = [88° \quad 0 \quad -88° \quad 0]^{\mathrm{T}}$. It is obvious that the performance of T-S fuzzy systems controlled by the proposed fuzzy controller is better than the method presented by [9]. Therefore, the closed-loop nonlinear two-link robot system can achieve stability constraint, pole placement constraint and BIBO constraint by the proposed fuzzy controller.

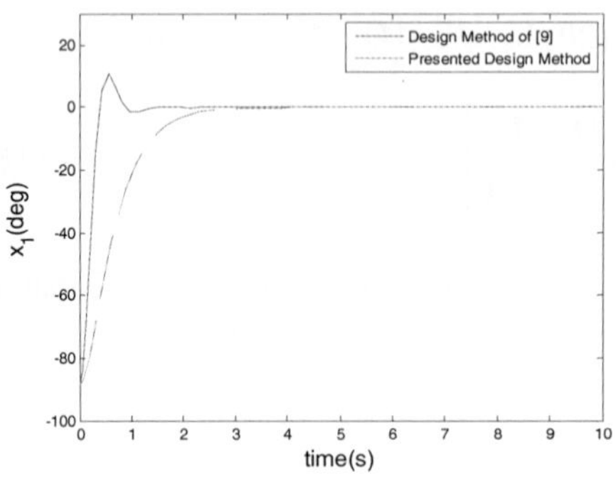

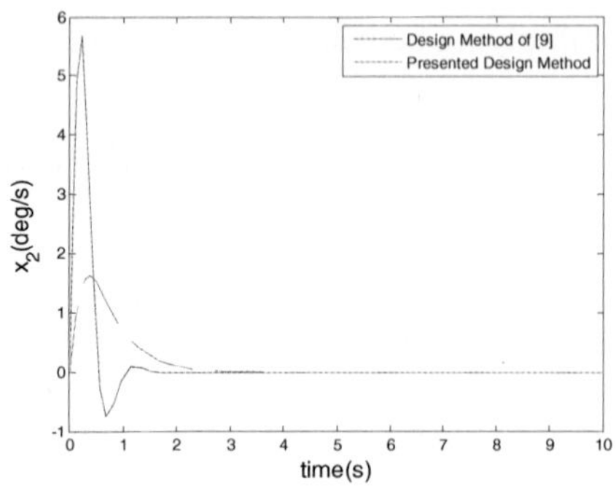

Fig. 1. The responses comparison of state $x_1(t)$ Fig. 2. The responses comparison of state $x_2(t)$

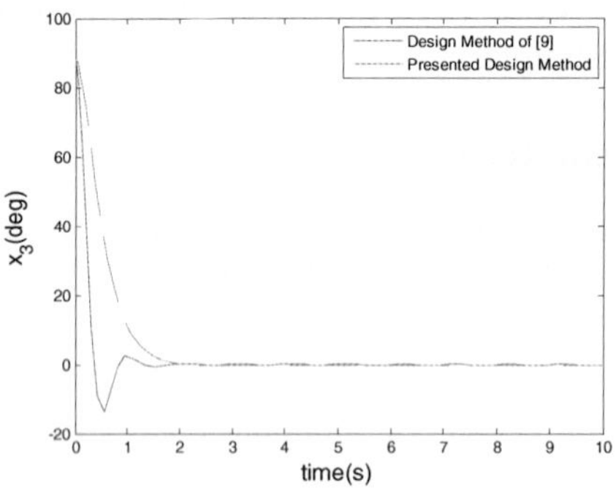

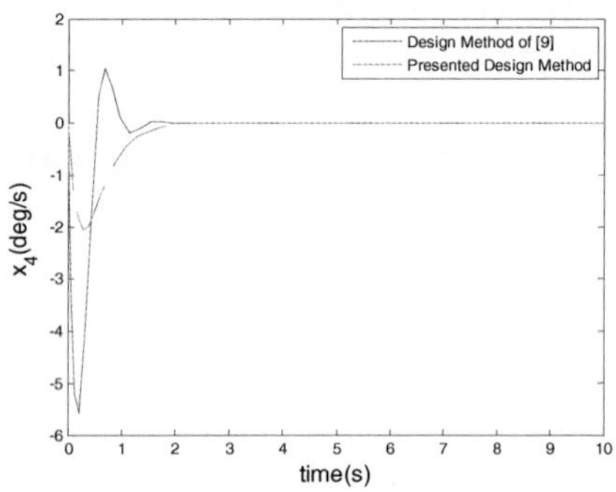

Fig. 3. The responses comparison of state $x_3(t)$ Fig. 4. The responses comparison of state $x_4(t)$

5. Conclusions

In this paper, a fuzzy controller design methodology has been investigated to achieve multiple performance constraints for a continuous-time T-S fuzzy model. The performance constraints considered in this paper included stability constraint, bounded input bounded output constraint and pole placement constraint. The LMI technique was employed to solve proposed fuzzy control problem to achieve the above performance constraints. Finally, a nonlinear two-link robot system was provided to show the application of the proposed fuzzy control method. The advantage of the proposed design method has been illustrated by comparing the proposed design method with a previous method.

References

1. S. K. Hong, and Y. Nam, "Stable Fuzzy Control System Design with Pole-Placement Constraint: an LMI Approach", *Computers in Industry*, Vol. 51, pp. 1-11, 2003.
2. W. J. Chang and C. C. Shing,"Fuzzy-Based Upper Bound Covariance Control for Discrete Nonlinear Perturbed Stochastic Systems", *International Journal of Fuzzy Systems*, Vol. 5, No. 1, pp. 11-21, 2003.
3. W. J. Chang, and S. M. Wu, "Continuous Fuzzy Controller Design Subject to Minimizing Control Input Energy with Output Variance Constraints", *European Journal of Control*, Vol. 11, No. 3, pp. 269-277, 2005.
4. D. Henrion, M. Sebek, and V. Kucera, "Robust Pole Placement for Second-Order Systems: an LMI Approach", *Kybernetika*, Vol. 41, No. 1, pp.1-14, 2005.
5. I. Abidi, J. Bosche, A. El Hajjaji, and A. Aguilera-Gonzalez, "Fuzzy Robust Tracking Control with Pole Placement for a Turbocharged Diesel Engine", *2013-21st Mediterranean Conference on Control & Automation (MED)*, Crete, Greece, pp.1417-1422, 2013.
6. F. Zhou, and Z. J. Wang, "Containment control of linear multi-agent systems with directed graphs and multiple leaders of time-varying bounded inputs", *IET Control Theory Appl.*, Vol. 9, No. 16, pp. 2466-2473, 2015.
7. J.V. Salcedo, and M. Martinez, "BIBO stabilisation of Takagi-Sugeno fuzzy systems under persistent perturbations using fuzzy output-feedback controllers", *IET Control Theory Appl.*, Vol. 2, No. 6, pp. 513-523, 2008.
8. C.S. Tseng, B.S. Chen and H.J. Uang, "Fuzzy tracking control design for nonlinear dynamic systems via T-S fuzzy model", *IEEE Trans. on Fuzzy Syst.*, Vol. 9, No. 3, pp. 381–392, 2001.
9. C. C. Ku, P. H. Huang and W. J. Chang, "Passive Fuzzy Controller Design for Nonlinear Systems with Multiplicative Noises", *Journal of the Franklin Institute-Engineering and Applied Mathematics*, Vol. 347, No. 5, pp. 732-750, 2010.

Fuzzy Sliding Mode Controller with Integral Sliding Surface for Permanent Magnet Synchronous Motor

Jing Wang[1,2,3,a], Sheng-Wei Zhang[1,2,b] and Yu Zhang[1,2,c]

[1]*Key Laboratory of Microwave Remote Sensing, CAS*
Beijing 100190, China
[2]*National Space Science Center, CAS*
Beijing 100190, China
[3]*University of Chinese Academy of Sciences*
Beijing, 100190, China
E-mail: [a]wangjingcoral@126.com, [b]zhangshengwei@mirslab.cn, [c]zhangyu@mirslab.cn

In this paper, sliding mode controller with integral sliding surface is proposed to reject the system disturbances for permanent magnet synchronous motor (PMSM) speed regulation system. To reduce the chattering phenomenon, the signum function is replaced by the saturation function and fuzzy module is introduced in sliding mode controller. Simulation results show that the proposed control method can obtain satisfactory tracking performance and dynamic performance with smaller chattering.

Keywords: Permanent Magnet Synchronous Motor (PMSM); Speed Regulation System; Fuzzy Sliding Mode Controller (FSMC); Integral Sliding Surface.

1. Introduction

Permanent magnet synchronous motor (PMSM) has been widely used in many fields due to its high power density, high efficiency, low inertia and reliable operation. The method of speed regulation system is important to improve the dynamic performance. The Field Orientation Control (FOC) strategy is used in speed system regulation, and there are many different forms for FOC strategy [1,2]. The FOC strategy always includes speed loop and current loop. In this paper, Current Hysteresis Band Pulse Width Modulation (CHBPWM) is introduced to control the three-phase stator current and its structure is shown in Figure 1. CHBPWM is the fastest strategy in current closed-loop controlling.

In PMSM system, there are many disturbances and uncertainties such as load disturbances, friction force and parameter uncertainties. Therefore, many intelligent algorithms and nonlinear control strategies are introduced to improve the system performances, e.g., artificial neural network (ANN) [3], fuzzy control [4], active disturbance rejection control (ADRC) [5], sliding mode control (SMC) [6], and so on. The SMC is widely used for its invariant property to uncertain internal parameter variations and external disturbances. However, the SMC has a chattering phenomenon which can excite high frequency dynamic performance. In [7], a new exponential reaching law of sliding mode control is proposed to reduce the chattering. In [8], sliding mode based model predictive controller is proposed to track the desired currents in finite time.

In this paper, fuzzy sliding mode controller with integral sliding surface is proposed to suppress chattering and improve the reaching speed. Simulation results show that the proposed method is able to improve the dynamic performance and robustness characteristics of speed servo system compared with the PI controller.

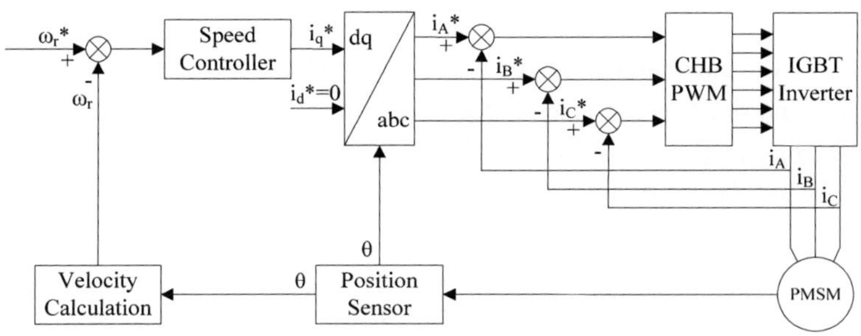

Fig. 1. The structure of PMSM speed regulation system.

2. Model of PMSM System

Assume that magnetic circuit is unsaturated, hysteresis and eddy current lose are ignored, the distribution of the magnetic field is sine space and the variations of the motor parameters are ignored. In the d-q rotor reference frame, a surface-mounted PMSM can be expressed as the following dynamic equations.

(i) Voltage dynamic equations:

$$\begin{aligned} u_d &= R_s i_d + \frac{d\psi_d}{dt} - \omega_e L_q i_q \\ u_q &= R_s i_q + \frac{d\psi_q}{dt} + \omega_e L_d i_d + \omega_e \psi_f \end{aligned} \tag{1}$$

where u_d, u_q are the d-axis and q-axis stator voltages; i_d, i_q are the d-axis and q-axis stator currents; ψ_d, ψ_q are the d-axis and q-axis stator flux linkage; L_d, L_q are the d-axis and q-axis stator inductances and $L_d = L_q = L$; R_s is the stator resistance; ψ_f is the rotor flux linkage; ω_e is the electrical angular velocity.

(ii) Flux linkage dynamic equations:

$$\begin{aligned} \psi_d &= L_d i_d + \psi_f \\ \psi_q &= L_q i_q . \end{aligned} \tag{2}$$

(iii) Electromagnetic torque dynamic equation:

$$T_e = 1.5 n_p [\psi_f i_q + (L_d - L_q) i_d i_q] = 1.5 n_p \psi_f i_q \tag{3}$$

where n_p is the number of pole-pairs, T_e is the electromagnetic torque.

(iv) Mechanical dynamic equation:

$$T_e = J \frac{d\omega_r}{dt} + T_L + B\omega_r \tag{4}$$

where ω_r is the mechanical angular velocity and $\omega_r = \omega_e / n_p$; J is the system moment of inertia; B is the viscous friction coefficient; T_L is the load torque.

According to Eq. (1) to Eq. (4), the d-axis reference current i_d^* is set to zero, and we can get the following relationship between $\dot{\omega}_r$ and i_q:

$$\dot{\omega}_r = \frac{1.5 n_p \psi_f}{J} i_q - \frac{B}{J} \omega_r - \frac{T_L}{J}. \tag{5}$$

To obtain the relationship between $\dot{\omega}_r$ and i_q^*, Eq. (5) is rewritten as:

$$\dot{\omega}_r = \frac{1.5 n_p \psi_f}{J} i_q^* + d(t) \tag{6}$$

where i_q^* is the q-axis reference current; $d(t)$ is the disturbance of the system and it is defined as:

$$d(t) = -\frac{1.5 n_p \psi_f}{J} (i_q^* - i_q) - \frac{B}{J} \omega_r - \frac{T_L}{J}. \tag{7}$$

3. Design of Fuzzy Sliding Mode Speed Controller

3.1. *Design of sliding surface*

In [6]-[8], the sliding surface contains the differential of speed error. In some low speed servo systems, the differential operation will introduce high frequency noise. This may cover the real speed error and the whole system will be unstable. In this paper, the integral of speed error is added to the sliding surface as shown in Eq. (8). Torque is more smooth and steady state error is reduced by adopting integral sliding surface [9].

$$s = e + c\int_0^t e(\tau)d\tau \tag{8}$$

where $s \in R$ is the sliding surface, e is the speed error which is defined as $e = \omega_r^* - \omega_r$, ω_r^* is the reference mechanical angular velocity, c is a design positive value which is met the Hurwitz condition.

3.2. *Design of sliding mode control law*

The control law $u(u = i_q^*)$ contains equivalent control law u_{eq} and switching control law u_{sw}, and $u = u_{eq} + u_{sw}$. Equivalent control law controls the certainty of system and maintains the system states on the sliding surface. Switching control law forces the system states to approach the stable point by high-frequency switching. By setting $\dot{s} = 0$ and $d(t) = 0$, we can get u_{eq} just as shown in the following equation:

$$\begin{aligned} \dot{s} &= \dot{e} + ce \\ &= \dot{\omega}_r^* - \dot{\omega}_r + ce \\ &= \dot{\omega}_r^* - \frac{1.5n_p\psi_f}{J} i_q^* - d(t) + ce = 0 \end{aligned} \tag{9}$$

hence

$$u_{eq} = \frac{cJ}{1.5n_p\psi_f} e + \frac{J}{1.5n_p\psi_f} \dot{\omega}_r^* . \tag{10}$$

Switching control law u_{sw} is selected as:

$$u_{sw} = \frac{J}{1.5n_p\psi_f} \eta \cdot sign(s) \tag{11}$$

where $\eta > |d(t)|$, $sign(\cdot)$ is a signum function. To reduce the chattering, the signum function is replaced by the saturation function $sat(\cdot)$, shown as:

$$sat(\mathrm{s}) = \begin{cases} s/\Delta & (|\mathrm{s}| \leq \Delta) \\ sign(s) & (|\mathrm{s}| > \Delta) \end{cases} \tag{12}$$

where *Δ* is the thickness of the boundary layer neighboring the sliding surface, and this is a design parameter. Therefore, the control law is written as:

$$i_q^* = u = u_{eq} + u_{sw} = \frac{cJ}{1.5n_p\psi_f}e + \frac{J}{1.5n_p\psi_f}\dot{\omega}_r^* + \frac{J}{1.5n_p\psi_f}\eta \cdot sat(s). \tag{13}$$

3.3. *Stability analysis*

To set up the existence condition of the sliding mode, the Lyapunov function candidate is defined as:

$$V = \frac{1}{2}s^2. \tag{14}$$

Taking the derivation of V with respect to time domain:

$$\begin{aligned} \dot{V} &= s\dot{s} \\ &= s(\dot{e} + c\mathrm{e}) \\ &= \mathrm{s}(\dot{\omega}_r^* - \frac{1.5n_p\psi_f}{J}i_q^* - d(t) + ce) \\ &= \mathrm{s}\{\dot{\omega}_r^* - \frac{1.5n_p\psi_f}{J}[\frac{cJ}{1.5n_p\psi_f}e + \frac{J}{1.5n_p\psi_f}\dot{\omega}_r^* + \frac{J}{1.5n_p\psi_f}\eta \cdot sat(s)] - d(t) + ce\} \\ &= \mathrm{s}[-\eta \cdot sat(s) - d(t)] \\ &= -\eta \cdot \mathrm{s} \cdot sat(s) - sd(t) \\ &\leq -\eta|\mathrm{s}| + |d(t)||s| \leq 0. \end{aligned} \tag{15}$$

Lyapunov function is less than or equal to 0 and when $\dot{V} \equiv 0$, $\mathrm{s} \equiv 0$. Therefore, the control system is stable and the system states will converge towards the sliding mode surface in the limited time.

3.4. *Design of fuzzy sliding mode controller*

Sliding mode control causes chattering phenomenon in the switching control law, and the chattering phenomenon can excite high frequency dynamics. In order to reduce the chattering and improve the control performance, the fuzzy module is introduced in switching control law. That is to say, when the disturbance is larger the switching control law is larger; when the disturbance is smaller the switching control law is smaller. The control law is designed as:

$$u = u_{eq} + a \cdot u_{sw} \tag{16}$$

where a is the output of fuzzy module. The input of fuzzy module is sliding surface function s. The membership functions of s and a are shown in Figure 2.

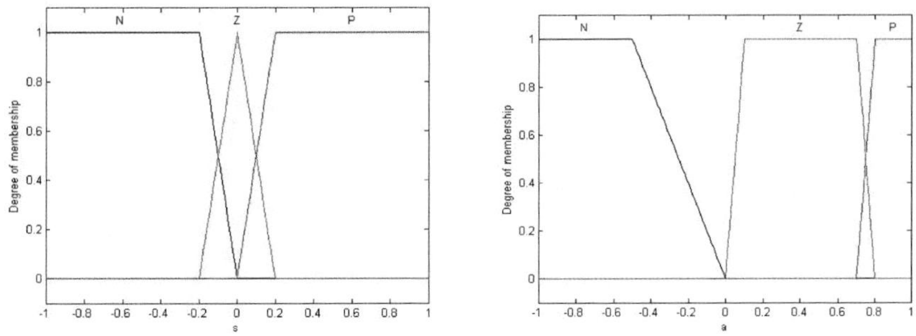

Fig. 2. Membership functions of s and a.

If the system states are near the sliding surface, a will become smaller. If the system states are far away from the sliding surface, a will become larger. This strategy will reduce chattering and ensure that the system states will reach the sliding surface. The fuzzy rules are described as:

- If s is N then a is P,
- If s is Z then a is Z,
- If s is P then a is P.

4. Simulation Results

In this section, the simulation is implemented in MATLAB/Simulink to validate the feasibility and effectiveness of the proposed method. The parameters of the PSMS system are as follows: the stator resistance $R_s = 2.875\Omega$; the rotor flux linkage $\psi_f = 0.175Wb$; the d-axis and q-axis stator inductances $L_d = L_q = 8.5mH$; the number of pole-pairs $n_p = 4$; the system moment of inertia $J = 7.7 \times 10^{-3} kg \cdot m^2$; the viscous friction coefficient $B = 0N \cdot m \cdot s$; the load torque $T_L = 0.3N \cdot m$; the rated DC voltage $U_d = 27V$; the saturation limit of i_q^* is $\pm 1.5A$. With these parameters, the disturbance of system $d(t)$ is estimated as $30sin(t)$. The reference mechanical angular velocity ω_r^* is set to $sin(2\pi t)$. In CHBPWM, the time constant of current filter t_{oi} is 5×10^{-5} and the width of current hysteresis band β is 0.05.

The comparative simulation results of the PI speed controller and fuzzy sliding mode speed controller are shown in Figure 3. For PI speed controller, the proportional gain $K_p = 0.5$ and the integral gain $K_i = 2.0$. For fuzzy sliding mode speed controller, $c = 30$, $\eta = 30.2$ and the thickness of the boundary layer $\Delta = 0.006$. It indicates that the dynamic performance is improved based on the fuzzy sliding mode speed controller.

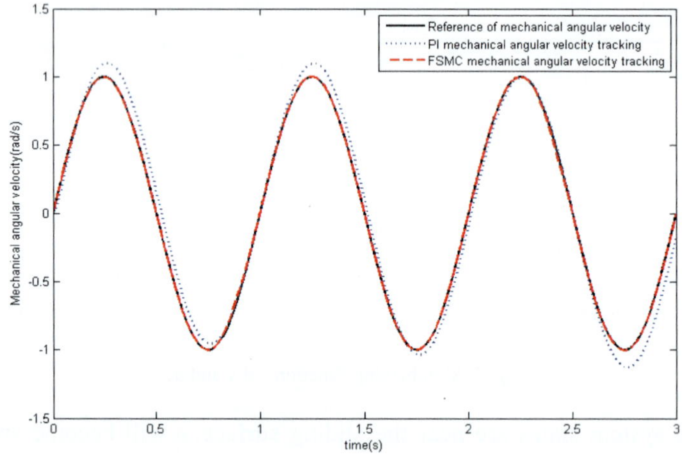

Fig. 3. Speed tracking curves with PI controller and FSMC.

In order to reduce the chattering, the signum function is replaced by the saturation function and fuzzy module is introduced in sliding mode controller. The control outputs of SMC, SMC with saturation function and FSMC with saturation function are shown in Figure 4. It shows that the control output has the smallest chattering with the proposed method.

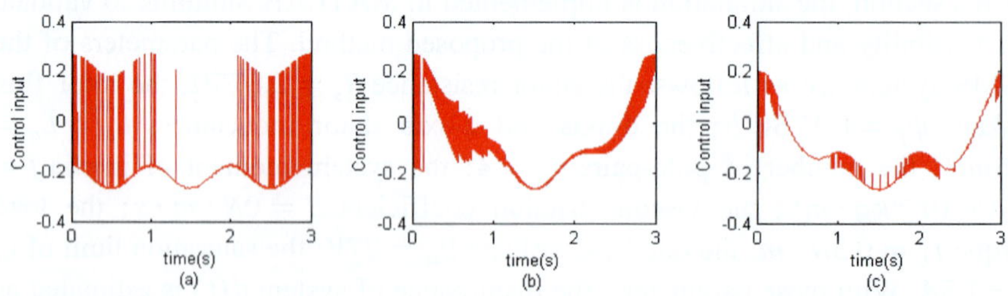

Fig. 4. The control output with different methods. (a) SMC. (b) SMC with saturation function. (c) FSMC with saturation function.

5. Conclusions

This paper has proposed a SMC with integral sliding surface to enhance the robustness of the PMSM speed regulation system. In order to suppress the chattering, the signum function is replaced by the saturation function and fuzzy module is introduced in sliding mode controller. Comparative simulation results have validated the proposed method.

References

1. Li L B, Sun L L, Zhang S Z, et al. Speed tracking and synchronization of multiple motors using ring coupling control and adaptive sliding mode control[J]. ISA transactions, 2015, 58: 635-649.
2. Saghafinia A, Ping H W, Uddin M N, et al. Adaptive fuzzy sliding-mode control into chattering-free IM drive[J]. Industry Applications, IEEE Transactions on, 2015, 51(1): 692-701.
3. Pajchrowski T, Zawirski K. Application of artificial neural network for adaptive speed control of PMSM drive with variable parameters[J]. COMPEL-The international journal for computation and mathematics in electrical and electronic engineering, 2013, 32(4): 1287-1299.
4. Wang L, Tian M, Gao Y. Fuzzy self-adapting PID control of PMSM servo system[C]//Electric Machines & Drives Conference, 2007. IEMDC'07. IEEE International. IEEE, 2007, 1: 860-863.
5. Zhang J, Kang L. A sensorless vector control system of permanent magnet synchronous motor based on line active disturbance rejection controller[C]//Electrical Machines and Systems (ICEMS), 2014 17th International Conference on. IEEE, 2014: 1140-1144.
6. Yang J, Li S, Su J, et al. Continuous nonsingular terminal sliding mode control for systems with mismatched disturbances[J]. Automatica, 2013, 49(7): 2287-2291.
7. Wang A, Jia X, Dong S. A new exponential reaching law of sliding mode control to improve performance of permanent magnet synchronous motor[J]. Magnetics, IEEE Transactions on, 2013, 49(5): 2409-2412.
8. Lee I, Lee Y, Shin D, et al. A sliding mode based model predictive control structure for permanent magnet synchronous motor[C]//Control, Automation and Systems (ICCAS), 2015 15th International Conference on. IEEE, 2015: 550-555.
9. Du Z, Chen Z, Liu X, et al. Adaptive switch gain time-varying sliding mode controller design for the low speed servo system in a control moment gyroscope[C]//Mechatronics and Automation (ICMA), 2015 IEEE International Conference on. IEEE, 2015: 935-940.

An Investigation of charged Particle Identification with Totally Depleted SSB Detectors Using Artificial Neural Networks

Li-Feng Ji[a], Gu-Fu Liu[b], Jun Yang[c], Jin-Tao Zhu[d], Xiao-Liang Luo[e] and Lei Zhang[f]

College of Mechatronics and Automation, National University of Defense Technology Changsha 410073, China

E-mail: [a]841679571@qq.com, [b]lgflh@163.com, [c]jyang@nudt.edu.cn, [d]henanzhujintao@163.com, [e]delongtmac@163.com, [f]15262248772@163.com

The identification of charged particles with totally depleted Silicon Surface Barrier (SSB) detector under the deployment of front-side injection is more difficult than that of rear-side injection, for the pulse shape of latter deployment is more sensitive to charge and mass of the detected ions than that of former deployment. Considering the successful application of the Artificial Neural Networks (ANNs) method on the discrimination of neutrons and gamma rays, the ANNs method is firstly introduced to identify charged particles with a totally depleted SSB detector under the deployment of front-side injection in the paper. Compared with the Pulse Shape Analysis (PSA) method, the experimental results show that the ANNs method is feasible and effective according to the value of Figure-Of-Merit (FOM).

Keywords: Charged Particle Identification; Totally Depleted Silicon Surface Barrier; Pulse-Shape Analysis; Artificial Neural Networks.

1. Introduction

Identification of charged particles by atomic mass number A and atomic charge Z is one of the key requirements in many nuclear physics experiments and the fields of radiation detection. In the past, a number of techniques, such as the time-of-flight (TOF) method, the ΔE-E telescope method, and the pulse shape analysis (PSA) method, have been investigated with varying degrees of success in the classification of charged particles.[1] Actually, the TOF method can only confirm the mass number A, and the ΔE-E telescope method needs the particles to have enough energy to punch through the ΔE detector [1-4] As for the PSA method, which is based on the idea that the pulse shape represents a complete signature (mass, charge and energy) of the detected ions and mainly uses a totally depleted silicon surface barrier (SSB) detector [2], although it has the advantage of handiness and convenience, its performance of identification depends mainly on the different injection direction towards the detector, i.e., front-side injection or rear-side injection [5].

It has been found that the pulse shape of a rear-side injection deployment is more sensitive to charge and mass of the detected ions than that of a front-side deployment [6], so the rear-side injection deployment is usually used to identify charged particles [7]. But the energy resolution under the rear-side deployment is lower than that of a front-side deployment [5], so the front-side deployment is widely used in the situation of energy measurement of charged particles.

Since recently, artificial neural network has been successfully used in many fields by taking advantage of its parallel processing, non-linear mapping and huge scale calculation capability, and flexible network construction [8]. Under the enlightenment of the feasible application of the artificial neural networks (ANNs) method on the discrimination of neutrons and gamma rays [9], we decided to try using the ANNs method to identify charged particles with a totally depleted SSB detector under the deployment of front-side injection in this study.

According to the above considerations, we will use the ANNs method to discriminate the alpha particle and the proton under the front-side injection deployment. This paper is organized as follows: in Section 2 the experimental set up is outlined, in Section 3 the detailed description of the ANNs method, the result of verification and the experimental process are outlined, and in Section 4 the conclusion is given.

2. Experiment

2.1. *Experimental equipment*

The data for this research were obtained at the Institute of Nuclear Physics and Chemistry, the Chinese Academy of Engineering Physics. Figure 1 shows the schematic layout of the measurement system. The alpha particles were produced from a uranium-plating copper slice while the protons were obtained via the reaction of neutrons emitting from 252Cf bombarding polythene. The energy of the particles was about several MeV.

A 2GS/s-14-bit ADC, CAEN v1729A digitizer was used to collect thousands of alpha particle and proton pulses. The data were produced by exposing an ORTEC B-017-150-300 totally depleted silicon surface barrier detector to the radiation from above sources. The detector has an area of 150 mm^2 and is made of 300 micron thickness silicon. In order to ensure the normal operation of the detector, it was mounted in reverse configuration with an applied voltage of 200V, while the depleted voltage is 72V. The high voltage was provided by the ORTEC 556 high voltage power supply. The signal of the detector is processed in a preamplifier, CANBERRA Model 2003BT, which provides two output signals, including an energy output indicating the energy information and a timing output indicating the current shape of detected particles. Since the current signal is too weak, the timing output should pass through a fast amplifier ORTEC 9302.

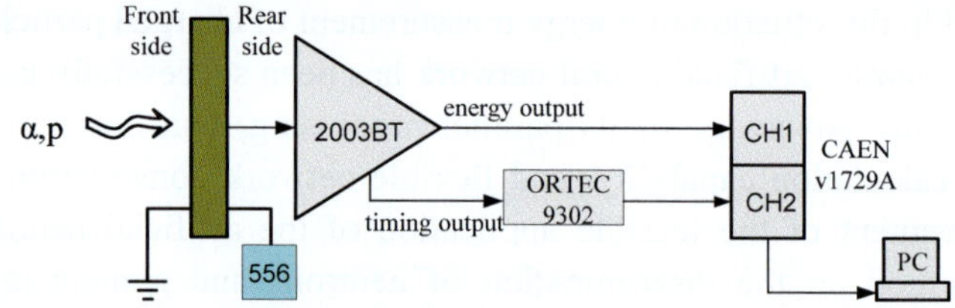

Fig. 1. Schematic layout of experimental setup

2.2. *Typical pulse waveform*

The main energies of alpha particles leaving from the uranium used in this experiment are 4.196MeV and 4.776MeV, which can be used to calibrate the energy. As shown in Figure 2(a), there are two Gaussian peaks in the ADC spectrum corresponding to the two energy values mentioned above for front-side injection. Because of the linear relationship between the energy and the ADC channel, these two energy points are enough to accomplish the calibration. We can get the energy calibration as Figure 2(b).

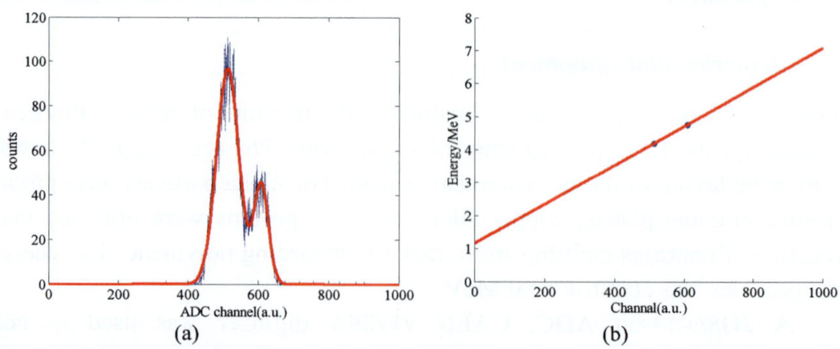

Fig. 2. (a) Relationship between counts and ADC Channel numbers (b) Energy calibration of the ADC

The typical current pulse waveforms of protons and alpha particles with the same energy were shown in Figure 3. Figure 3(a) shows that the peak value of the proton current pulse of rear-side injection particles is obviously larger than that of the alpha particle current pulse. Whereas, Figure 3(b) shows that there is no obvious difference between the current pulse waveform of the proton and the alpha particle of front-side injection, which is consistent with the viewpoint given by G. Pausch that the pulse shape of rear-side injection are much more sensitive to charge and mass of the detected ions than front-side injection [6].

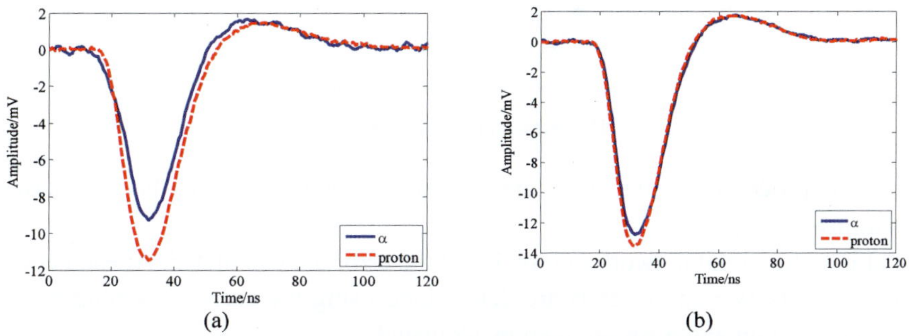

Fig. 3. Typical current pulse waveform of protons and alpha particles with the same energy. (a) The incident on rear side of the detector and (b) the incident on front side of the detector

3. Artificial Neural Networks

3.1. *Principle*

Artificial Neural Networks, a complex system which consists of several processing units called neurons and mathematical models that mimic the human brain, have been widely used in many fields including automatic, robot technique, artificial intelligence and pattern recognition by taking advantage of its parallel processing, non-linear mapping and huge scale calculation capability and flexible network construction. With the help of ANNs, a number of problems which cannot be solved by means of traditional functions have already been figured out smoothly [10].

The Back Propagation (BP) network is most widely and successfully applied in the field of pattern recognition among many kinds of ANNs. The BP is a supervised learning technique which is capable of computing some functional relationship between its input and output. The steepest descent technique computes the interconnection weights that minimize the total squared output error between the desired and the actual net outputs. In general, the BP network is a multilayered, fully connected, feed-forward network. The first layer is called input layer and the last layer is called output layer. The layer(s) between the input layer and the output layer is(are) called hidden layer(s). The nodes in the hidden layer(s) organize themselves to recognize different features in the input domain. The topology construction is shown in Figure 4 [11].

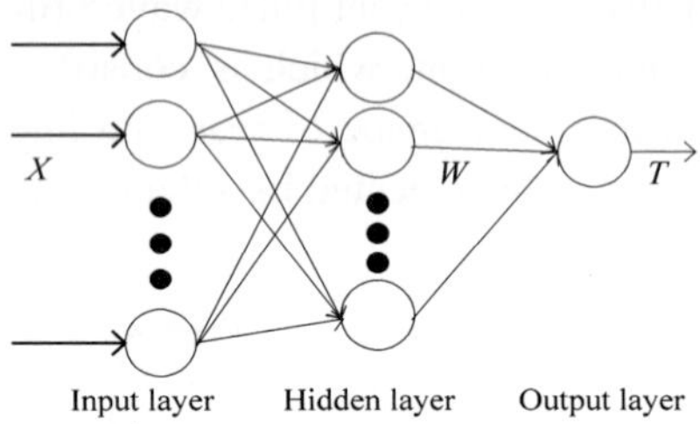

Fig. 4. The architecture of the BP neural network

The procedure of the BP adaptive learning techniques may be summarized as follows: [12]
(1) First, the initial network output T and the error are calculated. At each epoch, new weights W and biases B are determined using the current learning rate η. The new output and error are then recalculated.
(2) If the new error exceeds the old error by more than the maximum error ratio (ER_{max}), the new weights and biases are discarded. In addition, η is decreased by the decrement factor.
(3) If the new error is less than the old error, η is increased by the increment factor.
(4) This procedure is repeated to increase η, but only to the extent that the network can learn without increase in error. Thus a near optimal η is obtained at each epoch.
(5) When η is too high to guarantee a diminution in error, it gets decreased until stable learning resumes.

3.2. *Training and testing*

The performance of BP is dependent on several factors, e.g. the number of the neurons in hidden layers, learning rate, momentum, and training data. [8]At the first step of the simulations, the structure of the networks should be determined. The ANNs train and test datasets used in this work were produced by the experimental equipment which is mentioned in Section 2. The data were divided into two separate sets, one is training step (about 50% of all data) and the rest is for the test step. The alpha particle experimental data and the proton experimental data were generated separately mainly for training stage.

The frequency magnitude spectrum of the two kinds of particles was showed in Figure 5. Analyzing the frequency magnitude spectrum and looking for the differences between the two particles, we propose to train and test the ANNs with the frequency spectrum. The former 20 lower frequency components were selected as the input layers neurons. One input layer with 20 neurons, one hidden layer with 8 neurons and one output layer with one neuron BP neural network topology (20-8-1) were selected for discrimination of the alpha particles and protons of the front-side injection. In this training step, we let the output of the ANNs be 1 or 0 according to whether the input event is an alpha particle event or a proton event.

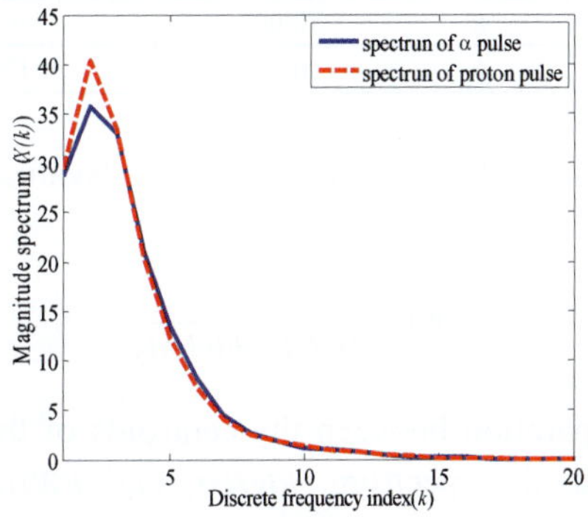

Fig. 5. Frequency spectrum of the proton and the alpha pulse

3.3. *Performance of ANNs*

After training of the networks, the ANNs method was tested over testing data including alpha particle and proton events together for classification. In the event classification stage of the work, we let the output of the ANNs be 1 or 0 according to whether input is an alpha particle event or a protons event, respectively. The Figure 6 (a) shows the output of the ANNs method for rear-side injection particles. The performance of this method is really satisfied. As indicated in Figure 7 (a), the networks classify different events with a similar success of rear-side injection.

Misdiagnosis rate (MR) is defined as the ratio of the number of events incorrectly discriminated by the ANNs to the total number of events. The MR of alpha particle, proton and total events is calculated with the following equations:

$$MR_{\alpha}=\frac{N_{\alpha}\text{-}N_{\alpha\_out}}{N_{\alpha}}\times 100\%,\ MR_{p}=\frac{N_{p}\text{-}N_{p\_out}}{N_{p}}\times 100\%$$

$$MR_t = \frac{(N_\alpha - N_{\alpha\_out}) + (N_p - N_{p\_out})}{N_\alpha + N_p} \times 100\% = \frac{N_\alpha}{N_\alpha + N_p} MR_\alpha + \frac{N_p}{N_\alpha + N_p} MR_p \quad (1)$$

where N_α and N_p are the total numbers of alpha particle pulses and proton pulses respectively. The output numbers of discriminated accurately by ANNs unit are N_{α_out} and N_{p_out}. Table 1 shows the misdiagnosis rate of the ANNs method used in this work.

Table 1. Discrimination results of the ANNs method used in this work.

Mounting	n	MR_α	MR_p	MR_t
Rear-side	8	0.002	0	0.0010
Front-side	8	0.097	0.129	0.113

The figure-of-merit (FOM) is widely used to evaluate the discrimination performance and is defined as:

$$FOM = \frac{S}{FWHM_\alpha + FWHM_p} \quad (2)$$

where S is the separation between the centroids of the alpha particle peak and the proton peak in the spectrum, $FWHM_\alpha$ and $FWHM_p$ is the full-width-half-maximum (FWHM) of the spread of events classified as alpha particle and proton events respectively.[13] If the probability distribution function of each event is consistent with the Gaussian distribution, Eq.(2) becomes:

$$FOM = \frac{|\mu_\alpha - \mu_p|}{2.35(\sigma_\alpha + \sigma_p)} \quad (3)$$

where μ_α μ_p σ_α and σ_p are mean values of the two Gaussian fits corresponding and standard deviations of the two Gaussian fits. As shown in Figure 7 (b), it is obvious that there are two peaks, the left one corresponding to the proton events and the right one corresponding to the alpha particle events. The sum of Gaussian distributions is expressed as

$$f(x) = A_\alpha \exp\left[-\frac{(x-\mu_\alpha)^2}{2\sigma_\alpha^2}\right] + A_p \exp\left[-\frac{(x-\mu_p)^2}{2\sigma_p^2}\right] \quad (4)$$

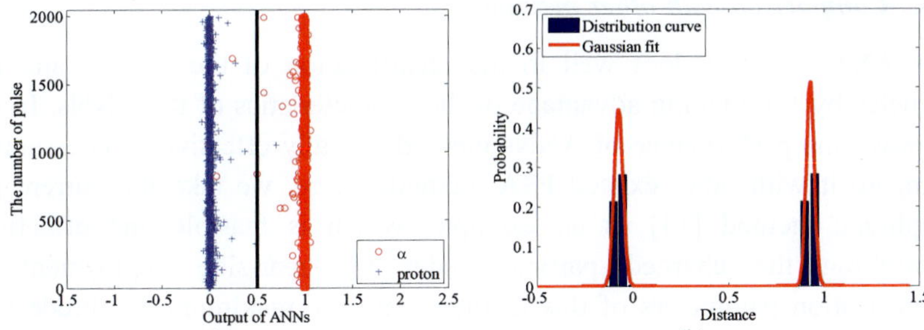

Fig. 6. The discrimination results of the ANNs method of rear-side injection. (a) The discrimination outputs of ANNs. (b) Probability distribution histograms with fitted Gaussian distributions for the ANNs method.

where μ_α, μ_p, σ_α and σ_p are the same as those in Eq. (3), while A_α, A_p are the scale factor for alpha particle events and proton events respectively.[13] Table 2 presents the means and standard deviations with uncertainties for the Gaussian fits shown in Figure 7(b). In summary, the feasibility and effectiveness of the ANNs method are verified with a good identification performance.

Table 2. Values of parameters in Eq. (4) for the ANNs method

Mounting	n	μ_1	σ_1	μ_2	σ_2	FOM
Rear-side	8	0.9281 ±0.0004	0.0210 ±0.0014	-0.0772 ±0.0005	0.0201 ±0.0024	10.4198 ±0.0263
Front-side	8	-0.0396 ±0.0061	0.0260 ±0.0049	0.8891 ±0.0047	0.0313 ±0.0033	6.8910 ±0.0726

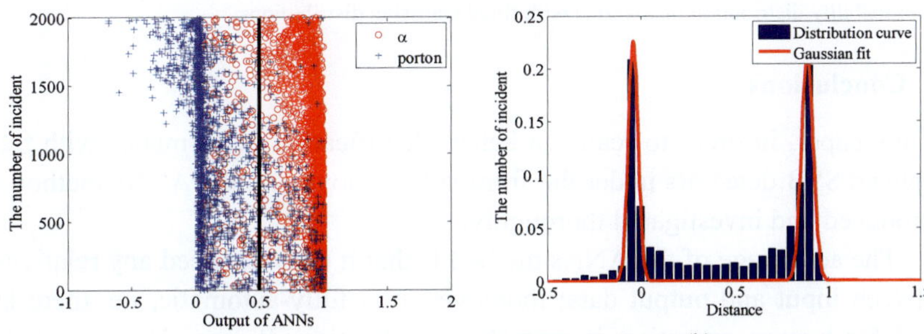

Fig. 7. The discrimination results of the ANNs method of front-side injection. (a) The discrimination outputs of ANNs under different conditions. (b) Probability distribution histograms with fitted Gaussian distributions for the ANNs method.

3.4. *Comparison with other methods*

The ANNs method does well in the identification of the protons and alpha particles by fully taking advantage of the characteristics of the ANNs. In order to prove the performance of ANNs method is really effective, it is essential to compare it with other existed PSA methods. Here, we take the current pulse amplitude method [14] as an example, which is feasible and effective in identifying the charged particle under the rear-side deployment. The identification parameters of this method were the maximum amplitude of the current pulse. Figure 8 shows the result of this method. As listed in Table 3, the FOM of the current pulse amplitude method is 0.1154, means that this method can hardly identify the alpha particles and the protons of front-side injection.

Table 3. The values of parameters in Eq.(3) for current pulse amplitude method

μ_1	σ_1	μ_2	σ_2	FOM
-0.2157 ±0.0074	0.0722 ±0.0144	-0.1602 ±0.0066	0.2173 ±0.0088	0.1154 ±0.0206

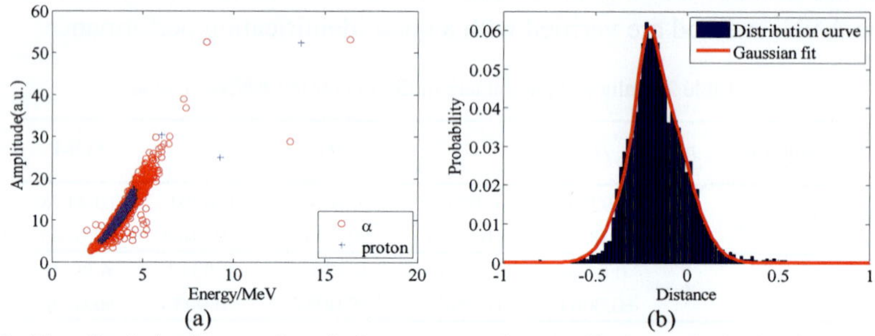

Fig. 8. The discrimination results of the current pulse amplitude method. (a) Scatter plots. (b) Probability distribution histograms with fitted Gaussian distributions.

4. Conclusions

In this paper, in order to realize a better identification performance with totally depleted SSB detectors under the front-side deployment, the ANNs method was introduced and investigated thoroughly.

The advantage of the ANNs method is that it does not need any relationship between input and output data; moreover, it is fully-automatic, i.e. there is no need for human operation in particle classification. It was also seen that the ANNs method is very successful in event classification. In this study, by using the frequency magnitude spectrum of these two kinds of particles training and testing ANNs, showed that this method was feasible and effective in discrimination between alpha particles and protons. The value of FOM of this method is acceptable. For the front-side injection, the misdiagnosis rate was nearly 0.1, means that the performance was really satisfied. With the development of digital system, it is possible to enhance the detection efficiency and analysis performance. Combining ANNs method with digital system will make it possible for real-time processing.

Acknowledgments

This project is supported by the National Natural Science Foundation of China under Grant no. 11375264.

References

1. S. Barlini, R. Bougault, Ph. Laborie, et al. New digital techniques applied to A and Z identification using pulse shape discrimination of silicon detector current signals, *J. Nucl. Instr. and Meth. A*600,644(2009)
2. N. Le Neindre, R. Bougault, S. Barlini, et al., *J Nucl. Instr. and Meth. A***701,**145 (2013)
3. L. Bardelli, M. Bini, G. Casini, et al. Progresses in the pulse shape identification with silicon detectors within the FAZIA Collaboration ,*J Nucl. Instr. and Meth. A***654,** 272(2011)
4. S. Carboni, S. Barlini, L. Bardelli, et al., *J Nucl. Instr. and Meth. A***664**,251 (2012)
5. M. Alderighi, F. Amorini, A. Anzalone, et al., *J IEEE Trans. Nucl. Sci***NS-52**,1624 (2005)
6. G. Pausch, W. Bohne, D. Hilscher, Particle identification in solid-state detectors by means of pulse shape analysis- results of computer simulations *J Nucl. Instr. and Meth. A***337**, 573 (1994)
7. M. Mutterer, W.H. Trzaska, G.P. Tyurin, et al. Breakthrough in Pulse-Shape Based Particle Identification, *J IEEE***NS-9**, 148 (2000)
8. P.F. Castelaz. Neural networks in defense applications, *IEEE Int. Conf. Neural Networks 2*, 473 (1988)
9. G. Liu, M.D. Aspinall, X. Ma, M.J. Joyce, et al. An investigation of the digital discrimination of neutrons and γ rays with organic scintillation detectors using an artificial neural network *J Nucl. Instr. and Meth. A***607,**620 (2009)
10. J.H. John, Artificial Neural Networks J *IEEE Circuits And Devices Magazine* **88**,3 (1988)

11. O. Colin, L. Benjamin, Chi. Sheng-Chai, et al. Comparing BP and ART II neural network classifiers for facility location ,*J Neural Network classifiers***28**,43(1995)
12. E.A. Mohamed, N.D. Rao. Artificial neural network based fault diagnostic system for electric power distribution feeders, *J Electric Power Systems Research***35**,1 (1995)
13. R.A. Winyard, J.E. Lukin, B.W. McBeth et al. Pulse shape discrimination in inorganic and organic scintillators, *J Nucl. Instr. and Meth***95**,141 (1971)
14. G. Pausch, H.-G. Ortlepp, W. Bohne, et al. Identification of light charged particles and heavy ions in silicon detectors by means of pulse-shape discrimination, *J IEEE Trans. Nucl. Sci***43**,1097 (1996)

Deep Learning Based Disease Mention Recognition

Yu-Xin Zhou[1,2,a], Yi-Nan Lu[1,b,*], Zhi-Li Pei[2,c], Yang Lu[1,2] and Xiao-Lei Ma[1,2]

[1]College of Computer Science and Technology, Jilin University
Changchun, 130012, China

[2]College of Computer Science and Technology, Inner Mongolia University for the Nationalities Tongliao, 028000, China

E-mail: [a]szhyx76@163.com, [b]luyn@jlu.edu.cn, [c]zhilipei@sina.com

With the rapid growth of the biomedical literature volume, the development of biomedical text mining technology is becoming more and more important. But the research progress of other semantic type such as disease has been hindered because of the lack of adequately availability annotated corpora. For all of disease centric information extraction task, the correct identification of disease entity is the key issue for further improvement. In this paper, a machine learning based approach that uses deep belief network as basic architecture, combining some simple orthographic features for disease mention recognition is proposed, which achieves comparable or better results than the state-of-the-art results on Arizona Disease Corpus. The paper also discusses why simple orthographic features can improve the performance under deep belief network architecture.

Keywords: Machine Learning; Disease Mention Recognition; Arizona Disease Corpus; Deep Belief Network; Named Entity Recognition; Deep Learning.

1. Introduction

With the rapid growth of the biomedical literature volume, the development of biomedical text mining technology is becoming more and more important. Among these, biomedical named entity recognition plays a very important role. Most previous work focused on gene/protein mention recognition, however, the research progress of other semantic type biomedical named entity, such as

[*]Corresponding author.

disease, has been hindered because of the lack of availability of adequately annotated corpora [6, 8].

In this paper, we proposed a deep learning based disease named entity approach. Our system achieved comparable or even better results than state-of-the-art approach on Arizona Disease Corpus (AZDC), which is particularly designed for disease mention recognition. There is an important difference between our approach and previous methods, that is, we introduced a number of biomedical related features into deep learning. Experimental results show that our system achieved comparable or even better results than state-of-the-art machine learning based approach, but our system does not need to combine too many complex artificial features.

The remaining of the paper is organized as follows. Section 2 introduces previous related work on disease mention recognition briefly. Then, section 3 describes our system. And section 4 shows the experimental data, results and analysis. At last, section 5 discussion concludes the paper, and outlines our future work.

2. Related Work

Named entity recognition is the task of locating named entity boundaries in a text, and tagging them with their corresponding semantic type, such as person, location, and gene and so on. Existing named entity recognition methods can be divided into three categories. (1) Dictionary based approach, (2) rule/pattern based approach and (3) machine learning based approach.

To date, there have been lots of Named Entity Recognition Systems, they all focus on gene/protein mention recognition, and almost all of the best machine learning based Biomedical Named Entity Recognition Systems are built on the basis of Support Vector Machines (SVMs) or Conditional Random Fields (CRFs) [2,4]. Although there are some deep learning based Named Entity Recognition Systems [3], almost all of them identify entity mentions in the texts such as News. These biomedical named entity recognition systems either need specific gene/protein features, or do not execute good on disease mention recognition.

After Hinton et al. proposed the concept of deep learning [5], many researchers start to devote to the research of deep learning. In the aspect of NER, Bengio et al. proposed a neural probabilistic language model [1], which gives distributed representations of each word and probability functions of the word sequences that represented by these representations. Ronan Collobert and Jason Weston (2008) proposed a unified architecture for natural language processing, using deep neural network with multitask learning. They all achieve the best performance on NLP corpora, such as Brown Corpus, and so on, but they are suitable for biomedical named entity recognition.

In the field of biomedical named entity recognition, Leaman, Gonzalez (2008) and Leaman et al., (2009) developed a system named BANNER. By using a set of complex features, like orthographic, contextual and syntactic dependency features [10]. It achieves 86.43% F-score on BioCreative II GM corpus, which is the best result on this corpus. But it only gets 54.84% F-score on another corpus, BioText corpus [10]. This corpus is not suitable for the comparison of systems. A modified version of BANNER achieved 77.9% F-score on AZDC [8]. Md. Faisal Madhbub Chowdhury and Alberto Lavelli proposed a machine learning based approach, which takes advantage of features customized for disease mention recognition, using conditional random fields, achieves 81.08% F-score on AZDC [2].

3. Description of Our System

Previous biomedical named entity recognition mostly extracts a rich set of hand-craft features, and then passes them to a classification algorithm. The selected features are task dependent, which means we need extra research.

We adopt a deep belief network based approach. The input sentences are processed by some feature extraction layers. Our proposed architecture is shown in Figure 1.

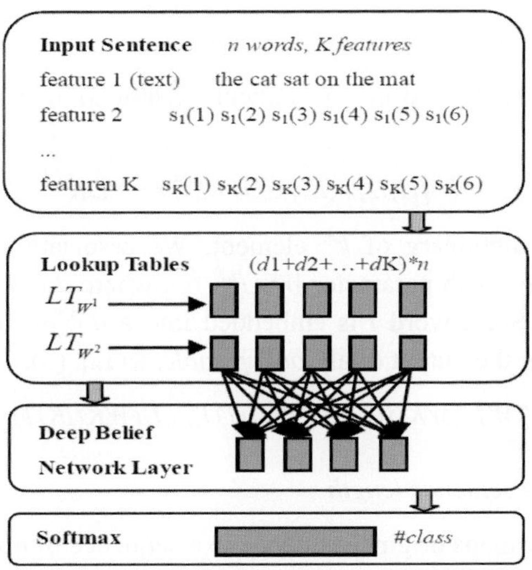

Fig. 1. The deep-learning based architecture for Biomedical named entity recognition

3.1. *Pre-processing*

Before the input sentence is processed, the system first tokenizes the input sentence. And then, the tokens are further processed using the following generalization and normalization steps, as Leaman et al. and Chowdhury et al. did (2010) [2].

3.2. *Convert words into vectors*

To process words in deep learning based approach, the first layer of network must map words to real valued vectors, so that the following layers can process them. The words are seen as the indexes of vocabulary D in a limited dictionary, which is a limited word subset.

3.2.1. *Words to vectors layer*

In this layer, each word i in D is embedded into a d-dimensional space, using a *lookup-table* $LT_W(\cdot)$ [3], as in Eq. (1).

$$LT_W(\cdot)=W_i \tag{1}$$

where $W\in R^{d\times|D|}$, is a parameter matrix to be learning, $W_i\in R^d$ is the ith column of W, d is the word vector size (*wsz* for short) that user selects. For an input sentence $\{s_1,s_2,...,s_n\}$, the first layer applies *lookup-table* to every word in this sentence to convert it into a sequence of vectors $\{W_{s_1},W_{s_2},...,W_{s_n}\}$.

3.2.2. *Variations on word representations*

When a word is decomposed into K elements (features), it can be represented as Eq. (2).

$$i=\{i1,i2,...,iK\}\in D1\times D2\times...\times DK \tag{2}$$

where D^K is the dictionary of kth element. We associate each element to a lookup-table $LT_{W^k}(\cdot)$ with parameter $W^k\in R^{d^k\times|D^k|}$, where $d_k\in N$ is a user specified word vector size. So, a word i is embedded into a $d=\sum_k d^k$ dimensional space, through connecting the output of all *lookup-table,* as Eq. (3).

$$LTW1...WK(i)T=(LTW1(i1)T,...,LTWK(iK)T) \tag{3}$$

3.2.3. *Variable sentence length*

Lookup-table layer maps original sentence to a sequence of n $x(\cdot)$, with the same size, $(x_1,x_2,...,x_n)$ $\forall t\ x_t\in R^d$

Obviously, the size n of sequence changes depending on sentence. Unfortunately, normal neural network can not handle sentence of variable length. We use window approach to resolve this problem, by considering a window with fixed size ksz around each word that we want to label. Because the output of layer is fixed dimensional (sentence size independent), the following layers can be traditional neural network layers.

3.2.4. *Deep learning architecture*

Our system uses hyperbolic tangent function tanh as activation function in the input layer. In the lth layer that contains n_{hu_l} hidden units, the system uses Eq. (4)

$$ol=tanh(Ll \cdot ol\text{-}1) \tag{4}$$

to compute the output of lth layer, where the matrix of parameter $L^l \in R^{n_{hu_l} \times n_{hu_{l-1}}}$ is trained through backward propagation.

The size o^{last} of the output of last layer is the class number to be considered. The following layer is a *softmax* layer, which ensures that the output is positive and the sum is 1.

3.2.5. *Features for disease recognition*

Although, there have been many work on named entity recognition system, but most of them mainly focus on news et al. fields, and achieve satisfying results in related fields. But the features in those systems are not equally effective in biomedical literature. Some deep learning based named entity recognition system achieves satisfying effect on free texts, but cannot get corresponding good performance in biomedical named entity recognition. We introduce some simple orthographic features into deep learning, as shown in Table 1.

Table 1. Orthographic features for token

Feature Names	Description
InitCap	Is initial letter capital
AllCap	Are all letters capital
MixCase	Dose contain mixed case letters
SingLow	Is a single lower case letter
SingUp	Is a single upper case letter
Num	Is a number
PuncChar	Is a punctuation character
PreCharAN	Is previous character alphanumeric

4. Experiments

4.1. *Data*

We have carried out experiments on AZDC [8], we employ IOB2 format to label corresponding disease annotation. The following table shows various characteristics of the corpus.

We employ the same way as Chowdhury et al. to treat overlap annotations. In our experiments, we only consider the larger annotations. There remain 3,244 disease mentions after resolving overlaps according to the aforementioned criterion, as shown in Table 2.

Table 2. Various characteristics of AZDC

Item Name	Total Count
Abstracts	793
Sentences	2,783
Total disease mentions	3,455
Disease mentions without overlaps	3,093
Disease mentions with overlaps	362

4.2. *Results*

We performed 10-fold cross validation on AZDC in such a way that all sentences of the same abstract are included in the same fold. The results of all folds are averaged to obtain the final outcome. Table 3 shows the results of the experiments using the exact matching criterion.

Table 3. 10-fold cross validation results using exact matching criteria on AZDC (the numbers inside the brackets is the word vector dimensions)

System	Note	P	R	F-score
BANNER	(Leaman et al., 2009)	80.9	75.1	77.9
BioEnEx	Md. Faisal Mahbub Chowdhury(2010)	83.21	79.06	81.08
Our System(50)	Deep Belief Network	72.73	60.92	66.3
Our System(100)	After adding orthographic features	82.98	78.84	80.86
Our System(150)	After adding orthographic features	**83.65**	**79.62**	**81.59**

As we can see, our approach achieves comparable or better result than state-of-the-art biomedical named entity recognition system. Firstly, when we apply deep belief network to biomedical named entity recognition, if each word is represented with 50 dimensional vectors, the system only gets 66.3% F-score, which is far below what we expected. After some simple orthographic features are added into the system, with the gradually increase of word features, the obtained precision, recall both have greatly improvement. In our deep belief network architecture, combining some simple orthographic features, the system gets 81.59 F-score with representing each word as 150 dimensional word vectors.

5. Conclusions

In this paper, we proposed a deep belief network based biomedical named entity recognition approach to identify disease mention. We employ deep belief network as our basis architecture, and introduce some simple orthographic features into the system when we carry out biomedical named entity recognition, which greatly improve precision and recall of biomedical named entity recognition. We evaluate our approach on AZDC corpus, and it achieves comparable or better results than state-of-the-art machine learning based approach.

Our future work includes introducing other features or employing other deep learning architecture to improve our current approach.

Acknowledgments

This work was carried out in the context of the project of the Science and Technology Department of Jilin Province "Research on Text Mining Based Biomedical Information Extraction, 20140101195JC", "Research on Deep Learning and Topic Model Based Text Feature Extraction Methods, 61373067", and "Research on the Key Network Public Opinion Analysis Based Technology, 2013MS0911".

References

1. Bengio Y, Ducharme R, Vincent P, et al. 2003. A neural probabilistic language model. The Journal of Machine Learning Research, 3:1137-1155.
2. Chowdhury M, Lavelli, A. 2010. Disease mention recognition with specific features. Proceedings of the 2010 Workshop on Biomedical Natural Language Processing. Association for Computational Linguistics, 83-90.
3. Collobert R, Weston J. 2008. A unified architecture for natural language processing: Deep neural networks with multitask learning. Proceedings of the 25th international conference on Machine learning. ACM: 160-167.
4. Dai, H., Chang, Y., Tsai, R., Hsu, W. 2009. New challenges for biological text-mining in the next decade. Journal of Computer Science and Technology, 25(1): 169-179.

5. Hinton G E, Salakhutdinov R R. Reducing the dimensionality of data with neural networks. 2006. Science, 313(5786): 504-507.
6. Jimeno, A., Jimnez-Ruiz, E., Lee, V., Gaudan, S., Berlanga, R., Rebholz-Schuhmann, D. 2008. Assessment of disease named entity recognition on a corpus of annotated sentences. BMC Bioinformatics, 9(S-3).
7. Leaman, R., Gonzalez, G. 2008. Banner: An executable survey of advances in biomedical named entity recognition. In Proceedings of Pacific Symposium on Biocomputing, volume 13, 652-663.
8. Leaman, R., Miller, C., Gonzalez, G. 2009. Enabling recognition of diseases in biomedical text with machine learning: Corpus and benchmark. In Proceedings of the 3rd International Symposium on Languages in Biology and Medicine, 82-89.

A New Structure-Preserving Method for Recognition of Color Face Images

Zhi-Gang Jia[1,a], Ru-Ru Ma[1,b] and Mei-Xiang Zhao[2,c]

[1]School of Mathematics and Statistics, Jiangsu Normal University & Jiangsu Key Laboratory of Education Big Data Science and Engineering Xuzhou, 221116, China

[2]School of Information and Electronic Engineering, China University of Mining and Technology, Xuzhou, 221116, China

E-mail: [a]jiazhigang1980@126.com, [b]maruru@126.com, [c]zhmx79@126.com

This paper presents a new structure-preserving method for color face recognition based on quaternion model. Inputting a new color face from the testing set, its projection is computed onto the chosen eigen-subspace, and then identify it by comparing its distance with the projections of known color face images. The processing is completed by a new fast structured method, in which only real computations are needed though the face images and the eigenface images are represented in quaternion forms. The experiments are conducted on color face databases: Faces95 and Georgia Tech face database, and the numerical results show that they achieved high level in both the performance and the efficiency in the proposed methods.

Keywords: Color Face Recognition; Eigenface; Quaternion Matrix; Color PCA.

1. Introduction

Face recognition is one of the most important topics in the field of pattern recognition, and has been successively applied in many practical fields, such as law enforcement, driver license and passport card identification. To improve the ratio of face recognition, many models start to make use of the color information of face images, while the fundamental mathematics theory and fast algorithms are great in need.

As a widely used linear subspace transformation method for recognizing faces, principal component analysis (PCA) [4] can maximize the variance of the transformed features in the projective subspace. Recently, there are many works applying color information to recognize color faces. Torres, Reutter, and Lorente [3] extended traditional PCA to color face recognition by using the R, G, B color channels, respectively. Face recognition is conducted on each color channel and the final result comes from the fusion of the three color channels. Yang and Liu [6] presented a general discriminant model for color face recognition. The model uses a set of color component combination coefficients to convert three color channels of the face image into one channel to represent color face images in the form of one-dimensional vector for recognition. Xiang, Yang and Chen [5] utilized color images matrix representation model based on the framework of PCA. All these methods have improved the robust and the ratio of face recognition with applying the color information. To simultaneously and mathematically deal with the three channels of color image, the quaternion was applied to represent the color pixel consisting of three components [2].

This paper is organized in the following way. In section 2, we recall the quaternion matrices and introduce new structure-preserving methods for solving the Hermitian eigenvalue problem of quaternion matrices. In section 3, we generate a new method for the color face recognition. Two experiments are given in section 4. The conclusion is presented in section 5.

2. Quaternionic Eigenvalue Problem

In this section we present a new structure-preserving method for computing the eigenvalue problem of quaternion matrix.

Let H denote the quaternion skew-field. A quaternion matrix is denoted by $Q = Q_0 + Q_1 i + Q_2 j + Q_3 k \in H^{m\times n}$. Its real counterpart Υ_Q is defined as in [1]. A pure imaginary quaternion is a quaternion with its real part being zero, it can *represent one pixel of the color image by the expression: Ri+Gj +Bk, where R, G*, and *B* stand for the values of red, green and blue color channels. The RGB information of each color image can be stored in one pure quaternion matrix [2]. Based on these, we present the mathematical theory required to develop and analyze algorithms for solving the Hermitian eigenvalue problem.

Theorem 2.1. *(Hermitian Schur Decomposition) If* $Q \in H^{n\times n}$ *is Hermitian, then there exists a real orthogonal matrix X and a unitary quaternion matrix W such that* $Q = W^* X diag(\lambda_1, \cdots, \lambda_n) X^T W$, *where* $\lambda_1 \geq \ldots \geq \lambda_n$ *are eigenvalues of Q. Moreover,* $W^* X(:,s)$ *is the eigenvector corresponding to* λ_s *for s=1...,n.*

The eigenvalues of an Hermitian quaternion matrix have a minimax characterization that resolves around the quadratic form v^*Av/ v^*v.

Theorem 2.2. *(Courant-Fischer Minimax Theorem) Suppose* $Q \in H^{n\times n}$ *is Hermitian and has the unitary tridiagonalization* $WQW^* = D \in R^{n\times n}$*. Then the s-th largest eigenvalues of* Q *is* $\lambda_s(Q) = max_{dim(S)=s} min_{0\neq y\in S} \frac{v^*Qv}{y^*y}$*, for* $s=1,\ldots,n$*, where* $S \subset R^n$ *and* $v=W^*y$*.*

Now a structured method can be designed for computing the first t largest eigenvalues and corresponding eigenvectors of an Hermitian quaternion matrix.

Algorithm 2.1. *A structure-preserving method for computing the first* t $(\leq n)$ *largest eigenvalues* $\Lambda = diag(\lambda_1, \ldots, \lambda_t)$ *and corresponding eigenvectors* $V \in H^{n\times t}$ *of an Hermitian quaternion matrix* $Q = Q_0 + Q_1 i + Q_2 j + Q_3 k$*, where* $Q_s \in H^{n\times n}$*,* $s=0,1,2,3$*.*

(1) Compute the tridiagonalization of Q: $D = WQW^*$ *with* $W = W_0 + W_1 i + W_2 j + W_3 k$*.*

(2) Compute the first t largest eigenvalues, saved in a diagonal matrix Λ_D*, and corresponding eigenvectors, saved in* Λ_D*, of D.*

(3) Compute $V = \Lambda_D^T (W_0 + W_1 i + W_2 j + W_3 k)$ *and let* $\Lambda = \Lambda_D$*.*

3. Face Recognition in Color

Suppose that the training set contains ℓ known color face images, denoted by $T = \{F_1, \ldots, F_\ell\}$, and the testing set contains m color face images to be recognized, denoted by $S = \{G_1, \ldots, G_m\}$. Here F_s $(s = 1, \ldots, \ell)$ and G_t $(t = 1, \ldots, m)$ are $mn \times \ell$ pure quaternion vectors, representing $m \times n$ color face images. Now we present a new method for face recognition based on quaternion model.

Algorithm 3.1. *Input the color face images in T and S, and compute the average face image of T by* $\Psi = \frac{1}{\ell}\sum_{s=1}^{\ell} F_s$ *.*

(1) Compute the covariance matrix of l known color face images from the training set T :

$$C = \frac{1}{\ell}\sum_{s=1}^{\ell} \Phi_s \Phi_s^*$$

where $\Phi_s = F_s - \Psi$*,* $s = 1, \ldots, \ell$*.*

(2) Compute the first r $(1 \leq r \leq \ell)$ *largest eigenvalues of C and their eigenvectors (called eigenfaces), denoted by* $(\lambda_1, v_1), \ldots, (\lambda_r, v_r)$ *by Algorithm 2.1. Define an* $mn \times r$ *quaternion matrix* $V = [v_1, \ldots, v_r]$ *as a projection operator.*

(3) Compute the projections of ℓ *known face images in T,*

$$P_s = V^* \Phi_s,\ s=1,\cdots,\ell,$$

and the projections of $\tilde{\ell}$ given face images in S

$$\tilde{P}_t = V^* (G_t - \Psi). \qquad \square$$

(4) For a chosen color face image $G_t \in S$, find out the nearest face image $F_s \in T$ which satisfy $\| P_s - P_t \|_2 = min$. Such P_s is output as the one from the same the person with G_t, $t = 1,\ldots,\ell$.

The core work of face recognition in color is computing the eigenface subspace, which is spanned by part of the eigenvectors of $C = AA^*$ with defining an $mn \times l$ quaternion matrix $A = [\Phi_1, \ldots, \Phi_\ell]$. An interesting notation is that the covariance matrix C and the vectors in the eigenspace V are not surely with zero real part, although each Φ_s is a pure quaternion vector. An eigenface has two parts: color information and grey information (see Figure 1). In Algorithm 3.1, we make use of both parts without overlooking any information.

4. Experiments

Example 4.1. *Take three sets of 128 × 128 face images in color of 32 people from Faces95 [7], denoted by $T_s = \{F_{1,s}, \cdots, F_{32,s}\}$, s=1,2,3, where $F_{t,1}$, $F_{t,2}$ and $F_{t,3}$ are three different face images of the t-th person. We take T_1 as the training set, from which the eigenface subspace (see Figure 1 for color parts and grey parts) is generated, and T_2 and T_3 as testing sets. Algorithm 3.1 is applied to recognize the color faces from T_2 and T_3.*

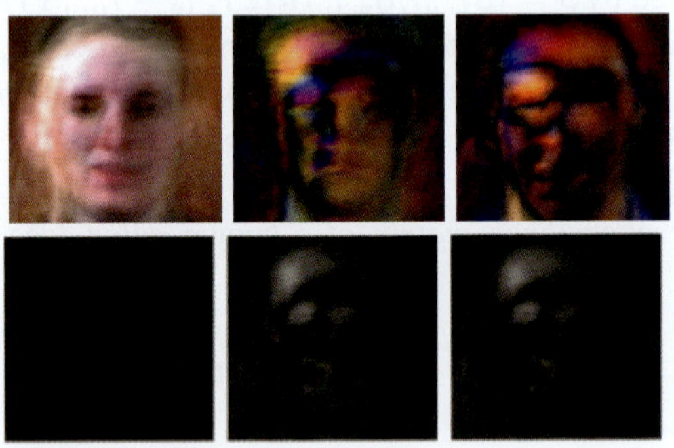

Fig. 1. Color parts (top) and grey parts (bottom) of three main eigenfaces

The numerical results are presented in Tables 1 and 2, where r denotes the number of chosen eigenfaces, CPU time is the total time to recognize all the faces in the testing set T_2 or T_3, RecRatio is the ratio of recognition, FailedFcs contains all the indexes of the faces which cannot be recognized.

Table 1. Test results for T_2

r	CPU time	RecRatio	FailedFcs($F_{t,2}$)
3	0.0745	0.9375	t=5,21
7	0.1170	0.9688	t=23
13	0.1242	1	-

Table 2. Test results for T_3

r	CPU time	RecRatio	FailedFcs($F_{t,2}$)
3	0.0748	0.9062	t=5,9,23
9	0.1103	0.9375	t=9,23
16	0.1733	0.9688	t=9

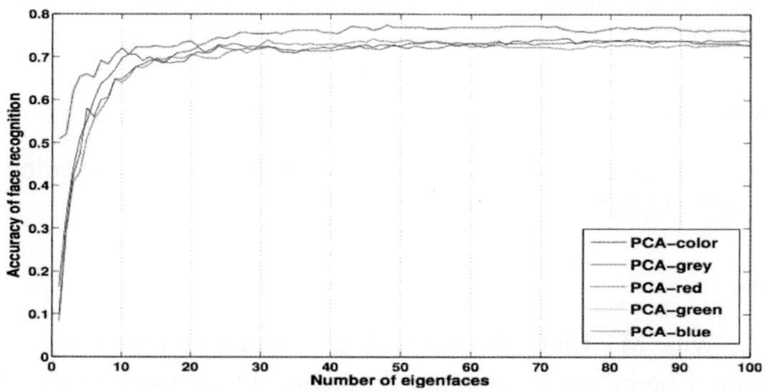

Fig. 2. Ratios of face recognition based on the Georgia Tech database

Example 4.2. *Georgia Tech face database [8] contains various pose faces with different expressions on cluttered background. In this experiment, we use the first x images of each individual as the training set and the remaining 15 − x images as the testing set. Now we compare the five PCA-like methods with each other under the same setting x = 8; and compare PCA-color with two recent approaches: CPCA [5] and CPCA-long [3]. The computational results are shown in Figure 2 and Table 3, where MR denotes the maximal face recognition ratio and CPU denotes the total computation time.*

Table 3. Maximal face recognition ratio and average CPU time (seconds)

x	CPCA		CPCA-long		Color PCA	
	MR	CPU	MR	CPU	MR	CPU
11	80%	0.0575	78%	0.0041	80%	0.0079
16	87%	0.1297	87%	0.0070	88%	0.0195

This example indicates that
(1) color PCA always reaches a higher recognition ratio than PCA, PCA-red, PCA-green and PCA-blue;
(2) color PCA costs less CPU time than CPCA but more CPU time than CPCA-long;
(3) when $x \geq 11$, color PCA has a higher recognition ratio than CPCA-long and CPCA.

5. Conclusions

In this paper, we introduce new structure-preserving methods for color face recognition to save the storage space and the computational time. The proposed fast and robust algorithms make it possible to treat the large scale color images in face recognition.

Acknowledgments

This paper is supported in part by National Natural Science Foundation of China under grants 11201193.

References

1. Jia, Z., Wei, M., Ling, S., 2013. A new structure-preserving method for quaternion hermitian eigenvalue problems. J. Comput. Appl. Math. 239, 12–24.
2. Pei, S.C., Chang, J.H., Ding, J.J., 2003. Quaternion matrix singular value decomposition and its applications for color image processing. Image Process. ICIP 2003, I –805–8.
3. Torres, L., Reutter, J., Lorente, L., 1999. The importance of the color information in face recognition. IEEE Int. Conf. Image Process. 3, 627–631.
4. Turk, M., Pentland, A., 1991. Eigenfaces for recognition. J. Cognitive Neurosci 3(1), 71–76.
5. Xiang, X., Yang, J., Chen, Q., 2015. Color face recognition by pca-like approach. Neurocomputing 152, 231–235.
6. Yang, J., Liu, C., 2007. A general discriminant model for color face recognition. IEEE 11th International Conference on Computer Vision , 1–6.
7. Spacek, L., 2007. Collection of facial images: Faces95. http://cswww.essex.ac.uk/mv/allfaces/faces95.html.
8. Nefian, A.V., 1999. The georgia tech face database. http://www.anefian.com/research/ facereco.htm.

Design of Intelligent Alarm System for Fire Based on Microcontroller

Gai-Lian Zhang

School of Applied Technology, Xi'an International University,
Xi'an, Shaanxi,PR. China, 710077
E-mail:zhglian@126.com

The AT89C51 microcontroller is regarded as the control center in intelligent alarm system for fire, and the system can receive and take a treatment on the concentration and temperature signal of smoke output by the fire detector with sound-light alarm. It can monitor the temperature and smoke concentration, etc. by sending inspection signal to the site continually, and have a feedback to alarm controller constantly. The controller compares the accepted signal with the normal value in storage to judge and determine whether there is a fire. When the smoke and temperature in site are anomalies, or fire occurs, it can realize sound-light alarm, the set of alarm limit of smoke concentration and temperature, self-diagnosis breakdown, delayed alarm, etc., which has a certain practical value.

Keywords: AT89C51 Microcontroller; Intelligent Alarm; Sensor; Controller.

1. Introduction

For the past few years, with the rapid development of China's economy and the speeding up of urbanization, when the convenience and efficient for people have arrived, the trouble has always befallen, especially in the densely populated cities. And the density of fire and power utilization is great, the precaution of fire is more difficult. Therefore, the alarm on fire has become more important [1]. Automatic alarm system for fire can monitor the fire quickly and the early characteristics of fire can be found which is not easy to find by person, and it can reduce losses of life and property brought by the fire to a minimum. Intelligent alarm system for fire is the system which is a collection of signal detection, transmission, processing and alarm. With the rapid development of economy and construction of city, high-rise, underground construction and large comprehensive buildings are increasing day by day in the city, fire hazard also increased greatly and the number of fires and the damage caused by it have a rising trend year by year. Therefore, intelligent alarm control system for fire with a large capacity, high reliability and a simple operation is needed urgently by the market. Based on the requirement of social and economic, this design aims to develop an intelligent alarm system for fire which has a capable of the real-time monitoring and alarm.

2. Alarm System for Fire and the Design of Entirety Scheme

2.1. *Function and types of alarm system for fire*

Generally, the fire alarm system consists of fire detector, regional and centralized alertor. Fire detector is based on the detection of physical and chemical phenomena from the fire, which is gas (burning gas), smoke (particles of smoke), heat (temperature) and light (fire), and the fire signal detected by it can be changed to electrical signal transmitted to the fire alarm controller. Sound-light alarm will be send out by analyzing signal of regional alertor after receives the fire signal, warning the operator on duty in fire protection control center, and showing the room number with fire on the screen. Centralized alertor is to express the received signal in the form of light-sound, it's also shows the floor and room number with fire on the screen, using the dedicated telephone also can rapidly give the instructions and alarm to the fire brigade. In addition, it can also control the fire extinguishing system or transmit the signal to fire protection control room. The entirety circuit diagram is shown in Figure1.

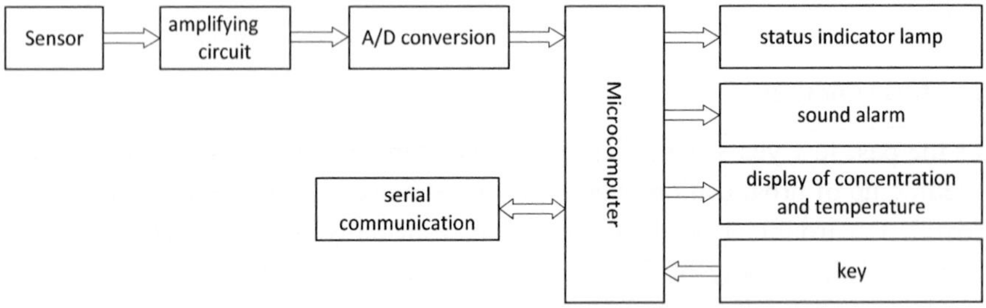

Fig. 1. Block diagram of intelligent alarm system for fire

2.2. *Hardware architecture of the system*

2.2.1. *Configuration of hardware system*

Alarm system for fire consists of the following several parts: module of system control, module of fire detection, module of data conversion and alarm module. The core of the control system of this design is microcontroller, and the sensor is regarded as its temperature measuring device to realize the design of fire alarm system [2]. The design can be real-time acquisition of indoor and outdoor temperature and smoke, when the measured temperature or smoke concentration is higher than the critical temperature, it alarms automatically. After acquisition of temperature signal or smoke concentration signal, the circuit transmits the signals in the form of a digital signal into the microcontroller. The digital signal is filtered by microcontroller, and the data is analyzed after filtering to estimate whether it is greater than or equal to a preset value, that is the critical temperature or smoke concentration of alarm. If greater, the alarm circuit can be started to give out alarm sound and display abnormal state, the opposite to normal state.

2.2.2. *Design of the control scheme of hardware system*

Alarm system is mainly composed of three modules of data acquisition, microcontroller control and sound-light alarm. The structure diagram of alarm system for fire is shown in Figure 2.

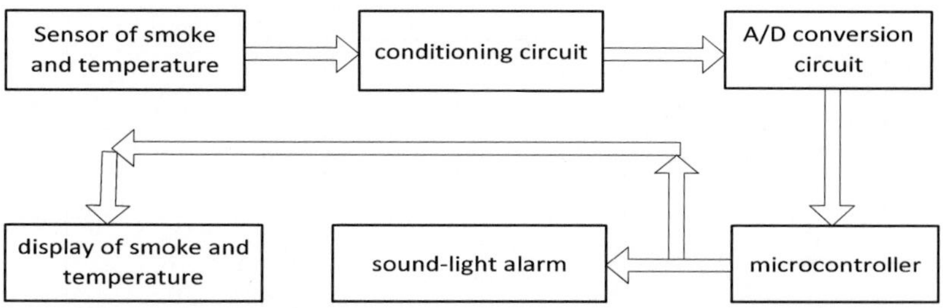

Fig. 2. The total structure diagram of alarm system for fire

Alarm system for fire is mainly to realize the test work of fire in scene, so as to start the fire alarm system. It mainly consists of data acquisition programs of smoke sensor, temperature sensor and sound-light alarm, and so on. Among them, data collection procedure of smoke sensor is to complete the acquisition of smoke concentration and transfer of data; temperature collection procedure shows collecting the temperature on site. The working principle of system is: firstly, the temperature and smoke signals in the field which is not the electrical signal can be converted to electrical signals through the sensors (including temperature and smoke); secondly, conditioning circuit is to regulate (amplifying, filtering, etc.) signals output by sensor to make them meet the requirements of A/D conversion; finally, the conversion from analog signal output by temperature and smoke sensor to digital signal is completed by circuit of A/D conversion, and microcontroller can make a judgment whether there is a fire at the scene. Alarm program sets up the lower limit of alarm, when the index outside is beyond limit, it will carry out sound-light alarm.

3. Design of Every Circuit Module

3.1. *A/D converter circuit*

The voltage signal detected by gas sensor is analog signal, which it is not directly identified by microcontroller. As a result, A/D change of signal is to carry out after amplifying circuit to transform the analog signal to digital signal and to input it into microcontroller. The circuit of A/D conversion uses the chip ADC0809 in analog-to-digital conversion commonly which has 8-bit and 8 channels, and the output ends of the smoke and temperature sensors are contacted to IN0 and IN1 of ADC0809 respectively. The circuit of A/D conversion is shown in Figure 3.

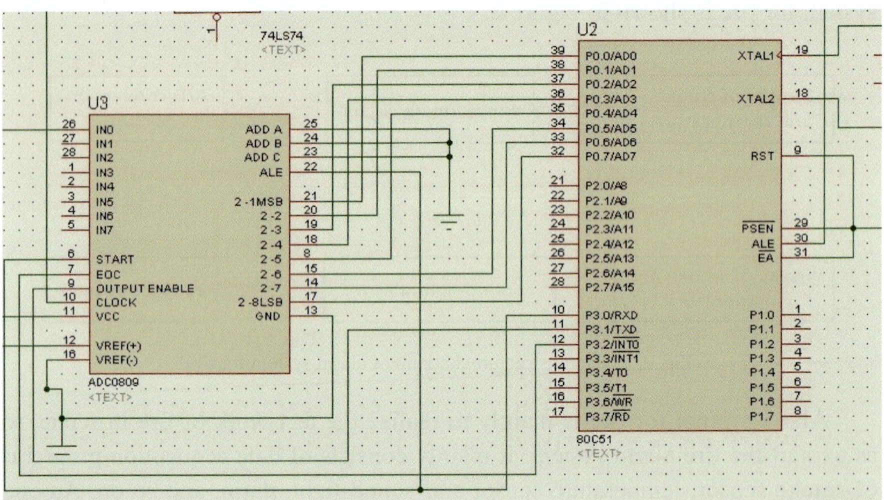

Fig. 3. A/D conversion circuit

This design uses the 74LS373 as the latch of address, when the OE which is tri-state allowed control side is low level, the output ends O0~O7 is the state of normal logic, and it can be used to drive load or bus [3]. When the OE is high level, O0~O7 is in high impedance state, and neither drive bus, nor for the load of bus. But the logic operation of latch inside is not affected. The OE which is tri-state allowed control side connected to ground expresses that tri-state door has always been opened. When the allowed end of latch, LE is high level, the output ends O0~O7 is the same as the input ends O0~O7; when LE changes from "1" to "0", data is input into the latch. The end of LE is connected to the ALE which is the allowed port of latch of microcontroller.

3.2. *Conditioning circuit of smoke signal*

Filter circuit can make useful frequency signal pass, at the same time suppress unwanted components of frequency and filter or attenuate useless frequency signal into small enough. Transition zone of first order filter circuit is wide; the biggest attenuation frequency of amplitude-frequency characteristic is only -20 db/ten times' frequency. In order to make the filtering properties of filter be close to ideal features, that is to say that in the same frequency band, the characteristic curve is gentler; and in the external of same frequency band, attenuation of characteristic curve is steeper. Only increasing network series, the system uses second-order filter circuit to arrive the ideal state. In the early time of fire, smoke and temperature signals is a graded signal, so the system put to use a second-order active low-pass filter circuit (Low Pass Filter, LPF). Two low-pass networks RC connected in series is directly connected with the follower circuit of reverse voltage, the simple second-order LPF circuit of smoke and temperature conditioning circuits can be composed. Figure 4 is conditioning circuit of smoke signal.

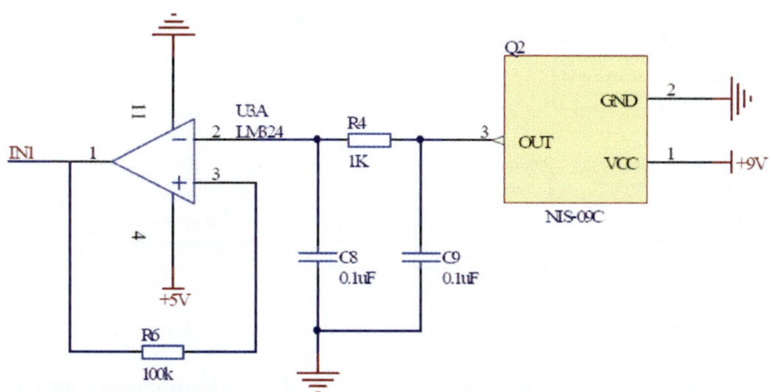

Fig. 4. Conditioning circuit of smoke signal

4. Program Design of Alarm System for Fire

4.1. *Master flowchart*

In order to facilitate system maintenance, the design of software in fire alarm system adopts the modular program design method; the function of each module of system is implemented through subroutine call [4]. It makes the program structure be clear, and be easy to further expand its function in the future. This system mainly includes the main program, the subroutine of data acquisition of smoke and temperature, subroutines of determination for fire and alarm, etc. Flow chart of system program is shown in Figure 5.

The main program is an infinite loop; which flow path is as follows. Firstly, after power on, system parts including output and input ports of the microcontroller, data storage circuit and peripheral driving circuit has totally completed the initialization. Then the programs of data acquisition, determination for fire and alarm of alarm system for fire are executed. After system initialization, P2.5 of microcontroller is low level; P2.2, P2.3 and P2.4 are high level, so only the green light is on, red light and yellow light is not bright, buzzer is no-alarm.

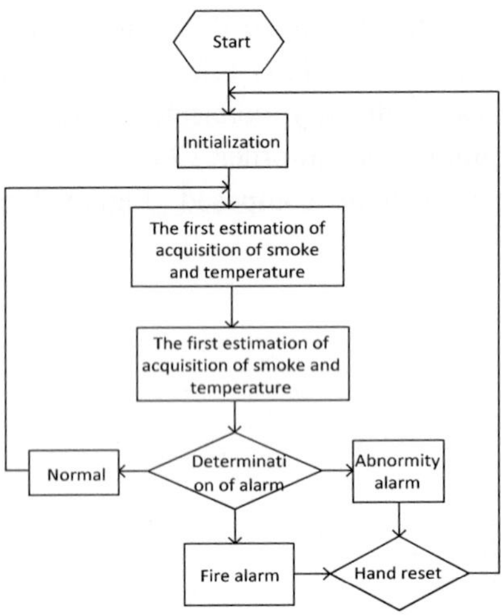

Fig. 5. Flow chart of system program

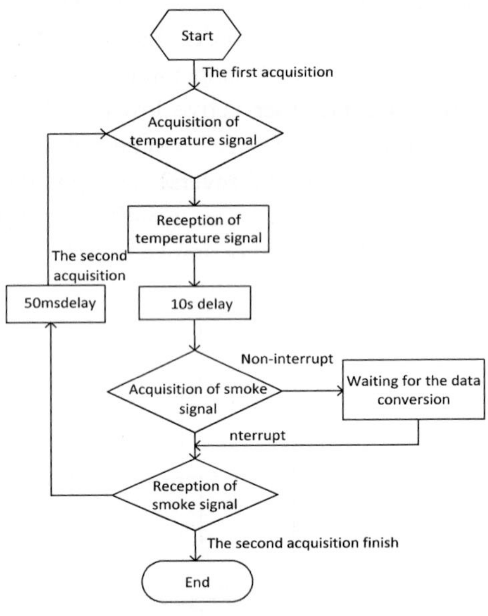

Fig. 6. Flow chart of data acquisition

4.2. *Determination for fire and design of alarm program*

System carries out data collection and judgment twice for temperature and smoke, after each signal acquisition according to the data, comparison with the given threshold value has been completed. Synthesize twice acquisition of temperature and smoke signals, according to the variables and status of register of temperature and smoke, the situation on the ground can be judged. After the alarm judgment for the field by system and after the interval of 20s (which is implemented by the time delay procedures of system), collect the temperature and smoke signal in site to estimate again, which is to say that the voice alarm is 20s continual every time until the system making the next judgment result. The flow chart of data collection is shown in Figure 6.

5. Conclusions

In this paper, the alarm system for fire in this paper has used the AT89C51 as the controlling part, it can judge whether there is fire disaster through the real-time collection of the signals of smoke and temperature in site, and also it can enhance the accuracy of the system prediction [5]. The system is safe and reliable, also has low rate of misinformation, easy operation and low cost. It adopts multisensory detection method combining the temperature sensor DS18B20 and smoke sensor NIS – 90C to make the system own high sensitivity and short response time, and can alarm accurately in the early stages of the fire. In the software design of system, it adopts the modularized program design method; the specific function of each module of system is implemented through subroutine call. Not only make the program structure be clear, but easy to expand its function further, and also facilitate maintenance of the system. The research of alarm system on fire disaster is the urgent demands for the economic interest and social stability, and this research and development has an important implication [6].

References

1. B. W. Cheng, L. Liu, C. M. Yang, etc. The design of alarm system on fire smoke based on microcontroller [J]. *Journal of Hunan Institute of Science and Technology (Natural Sciences (atural science)*, 2014, 27(3): 41-44.
2. Y. Zhang. Design Ideas of Fire Alarm System [J].*Value Engineering*, 2012, (13): 160~161.
3. Y. C. Sun, MCS-51 microcontroller and its application [M]. *Southeast University Press*, 2006.
4. Q. S. Fu. Design and realization of automatic fire alarm system [D]. *Wuhan University of Technology*, 2009.
5. Y. H. Song, D. X. Cai. Design of intelligent alarm system for fire of building based on microcontroller [J]. *Mechanical & Electrical Engineering Technology*, 2011(01):45-48.
6. J. Wang, H. F. Tian, Z. Y. Zhou. Synthetic Design of Distributed Intelligent Alarm System for Fire [J]. *Microcomputer Information*, 2012, 08(12):43-45.

Evolutionary Process of Vibration Trajectory Based on Hydraulic Excitation

Hui-Xian Zhang[a] and Ling-Xia Miao[b]

College of Mechanical Engineering, Luoyang Institute of Science and Technology
Luoyang, Henan 471023, China
E-mail: [a]zhxsky2008@163.com, [b]miaolx2009@163.com

This paper researches on the vibration characteristics of hydraulic excitation system based on the fluid-filled pipe and a hydraulic excitation testing system is established and an elastic plate connected with the pipe is served as a vibrating unit. Its mathematical model is established and the evolutionary process of the three-dimensional and two-dimensional vibration trajectories is simulated. By comparison, the vibration trajectories of the two-dimensional vibrating screen are regular, and that of the three-dimensional vibrating screen is confused, but which has higher screening efficiency. Serving as a new vibration mode, the three-dimensional vibration trajectory is based on the hydraulic excitation, has more advantages than that of the planar.

Keywords: Hydraulic Excitation; Vibration Trajectory; Evolutionary Process; Resultant Vibration.

1. Introduction

Nowadays, hydraulic excitation mechanism has been used in many industrial fields and much effort has been obtained. Schmitt et al [1] established a numerical model to simulate the propagation of pressure waves in water networks. The water hammer caused the maximum pressure values at the closing valves in the network, and then the influence of a defect such as a corrosion crater (pit) was estimated by computing a safety factor for the stress distribution at the defect tip. Per-Anders et al [2] carried out finite element analysis for one-dimensional fluid flow under the action of fluid structure interaction, and the transient response of free vibration of pipe was obtained by the numerical simulation. Jin et al [3] studied stability and parametric resonance of a clamped-clamped pipe conveying fluid. The results revealed the relationships between fluid and fluid-filled pipe, providing some theoretical foundation for the design of a stable pipe. Bao et al [4] studied dynamic characteristics of a pipe conveying fluid with elastic support. The numerical results showed that its natural frequency increased with the increasing elastic supporting stiffness and axial tension, but decreased with the increasing fluid flow velocity, the fluid pressure and its axial compressive force.

Most of the researchers above mainly devoted their attentions on how to reduce the damages from shock wave resulted from fluid-filled pipe. Up to now, little work has rarely been done on how to generate available hydraulic excitation wave by the fluid-filled pipe and make use of it. For the field, Kou et al [5] studied the dynamic characteristics of the fluid in the hydraulic excitation system by the method of characteristics (MOC). Zhang et al [6][7] developed a fluid-structure interaction model for the fluid-filled pipe, then the kinematic properties of the pipe were simulated by the MOC and the finite element method (FEM).

In this study, to uncover the dynamic characteristics of hydraulic excitation resulted from the fluid-filled pipe, a vibration testing system is developed. The resultant three-dimensional and two-dimensional vibration trajectories are simulated. And the comparisons between three-dimensional and two-dimensional vibrating signals are presented.

2. Principle of Hydraulic Excitation

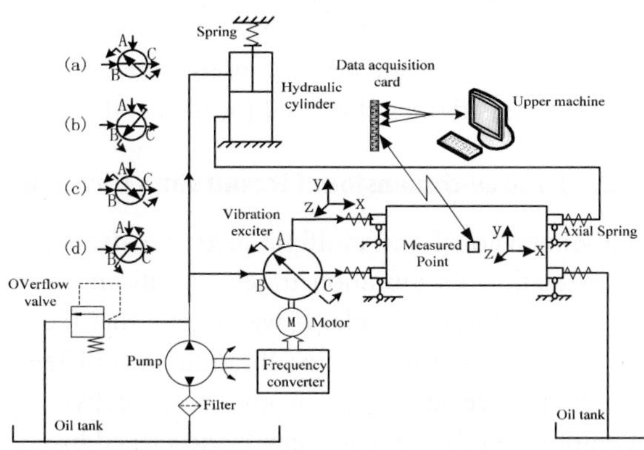

Fig. 1. The principle of hydraulic excitation system

The developed hydraulic excitation system shown in Fig. 1, which consists of pump, hydraulic cylinder, vibration exciter, pipe network, rectangular elastic plate, axial spring and frequency converter, etc. Vibration exciter serves as a valve which can open and close rapidly, which is driven by a motor and controlled by frequency converter. There are three ports, A, B and C connected to the external pipe respectively. When the valve of the vibration excitation rotates to the position shown in Fig. 1(a), high pressure oil will flow into the hydraulic cylinder from the pump, and then the piston will move downward until the valve rotates to the horizontal position BC. At this moment the oil inlet B is closed and the piston reaches the bottom of cylinder. Once the valve rotates to the position shown in Fig. 1(b), the piston will move upward until the valve rotates to the vertical position. Then port A is closed and the piston reaches the top of the cylinder, consequently a vibration cycle is completed. With rotating of the vibration exciter, the same motion will repeat periodically, thus the piston will run two cycles when the valve completes one cycle. As the valve rotating, pulsating pressure wave from fluid between the hydraulic cylinder and the vibration exciter will excite the pipe network to vibrate. Thus, the elastic plate connected with the pipe network will vibrate together with the fluid-filled pipe. So, the vibration mode can be utilized and the vibration mechanism should be revealed.

The main design parameters of the developed hydraulic excitation system are as follows: the pipe length is 2000mm, its external diameter is Φ34mm and its wall thickness is 5mm, mid-diameter of axial spring is Φ38mm and its steel wire diameter isΦ3.5mm, pump rated speed is 1500r/min, its rated pressure is 31.5MPa and its nominal discharge is 63mL/r, power of frequency converter is 3kW and vibration exciter motor is 1.5kW, its pole pairs are 3. In addition, three-axis acceleration transducer is used for displacement amplitude measurement, and acquisition card is used for data collection.

3. Simulation of Three-dimensional Resultant Vibration

Served as three-dimensional and multiple-degree-of-freedom vibrations, for the purpose of investigating its vibration trajectory, the measured point shown in Fig. 1 can be simplified as a particle. If we assume that the particle of Cartesian coordinates xyz is in simple harmonic vibration with different frequencies, and $\vec{i}$, $\vec{j}$, $\vec{k}$ represent unit vectors in x, y and z respectively, then the resultant displacement amplitude of the particle can be described by

$$\vec{r} = \sum_{l=1}^{n} \vec{r}_l = \sum_{l=1}^{n} A_{xl} \cos(\omega_1 t + \varphi_1)\vec{i} + \sum_{l=1}^{n} A_{yl} \cos(\omega_2 t + \varphi_2)\vec{j} + \sum_{l=1}^{n} A_{zl} \cos(\omega_3 t + \varphi_3)\vec{k} \qquad (1)$$

where $\vec{r}$ is resultant displacement amplitude, A is displacement amplitude, subscripts x, y and z are coordinate axis, l is 1, 2,$\cdots$, n, ω is angular frequency,

φ is initial phase and t is time. Eq. 1 indicates the resultant vibration in three-dimensional space shows further complicated motion. To the same point, we suppose there are n different vibrations frequencies will participate in motion at the same time, and then the respective vibration equation can be depicted in Eq. 2.

$$\vec{r}_1 = A_1 \cos(\omega_1 t + \varphi_1)(\cos(\alpha_1)\vec{i} + \cos(\beta_1)\vec{j} + \cos(\gamma_1)\vec{k}) \quad (2)$$

$$\vec{r}_2 = A_2 \cos(\omega_2 t + \varphi_2)(\cos(\alpha_2)\vec{i} + \cos(\beta_2)\vec{j} + \cos(\gamma_2)\vec{k})$$

$$\vec{r}_3 = A_3 \cos(\omega_3 t + \varphi_3)(\cos(\alpha_3)\vec{i} + \cos(\beta_3)\vec{j} + \cos(\gamma_3)\vec{k})$$

$$\cdots\cdots$$

$$\vec{r}_n = A_n \cos(\omega_n t + \varphi_n)(\cos(\alpha_n)\vec{i} + \cos(\beta_n)\vec{j} + \cos(\gamma_n)\vec{k})$$

where A_1, $\cdots$, A_n are displacement amplitudes, ω_1, $\cdots$, ω_n are angular frequencies, and $\varphi_1, \cdots, \varphi_n$ are initial phases, α, β and γ are included angle between resultant amplitude and coordinate axis x, y, and z. If n=5, indicating that the simple harmonic vibrations with five different frequencies. Supposing each frequency ratio from ω_1 to ω_5 in pairs is irrational number, such as $\omega_1 = 10\sqrt{3}$, $\omega_2 = 10\sqrt{5}$, $\omega_3 = 10\sqrt{7}$ and $\omega_4 = 10\sqrt{11}$, the corresponding amplitudes is A_1 =0.8, A_2 =1.0, A_3 =1.2 and A_4 =1.4, and the corresponding phase is $\varphi_1 = \pi/6$, $\varphi_2 = \pi/9$, $\varphi_3 = \pi/12$ and $\varphi_4 = \pi/15$, then the resultant trajectories are shown in Fig. 2(a) and Fig. 2(c). Additionally, if each frequency ratio is rational number, such as $\omega_1 =$ 10, $\omega_2 =$ 30, $\omega_3 =$ 50 and $\omega_4 =$ 70, and the other parameters remain unchanged, then the resultant trajectory is shown in Fig. 2(b) and Fig. 2(d)

Fig. 2 is Evolutionary Process of three-dimensional resultant vibration, where Fig. 2(a) and Fig. 2(b) are vibration trajectories when time t is 0~0.5s, and the frequency ratio correspond to irrational number and rational number respectively. Evidently, when the frequency ratio is an irrational number, the vibration trajectory is an unclosed spatial curve, whereas once the frequency ratio is rational number, then the vibration trajectory is closed. Fig. 2(c) and Fig. 2(d) are vibration trajectories when time t is 0~12s. Similarly, the different frequency ratios correspond to different vibration trajectories. It is shown that, with the increasing time, the vibration trajectory will become more complicated.

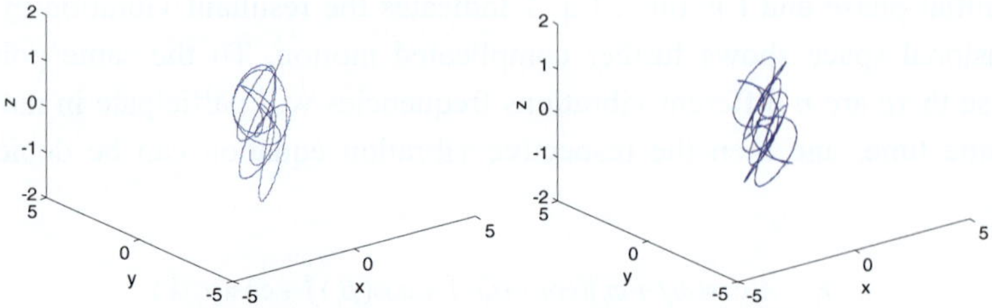

(a) frequency ratio is irrational number (t =0~0.5s) (b) frequency ratio is rational number (t =0~0.5s)

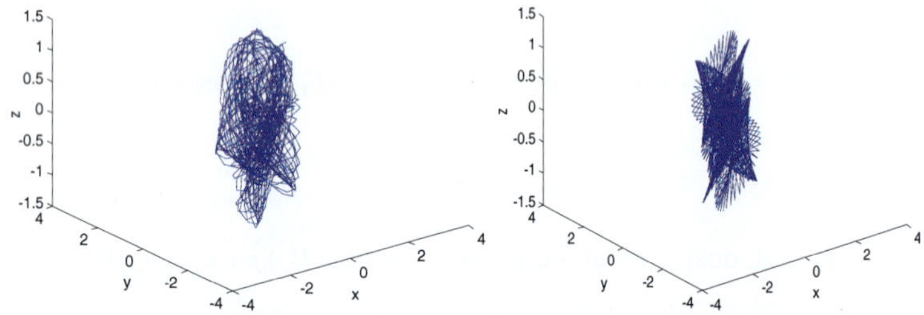

(c)frequency ratio is irrational number (t =0~12s) (d) frequency ratio is rational number (t =0~12s)

Fig. 2. Evolutionary Process of three-dimensional resultant vibration

4. Comparisons with Two-dimensional Resultant Vibration

For the two-dimensional vibrating unit, because there are two excitation sources, it can be regarded as the resultant vibration with two different displacement amplitudes, two different vibration frequencies and two different initial phases. Thus, Eq. 1 can be simplified as

$$\vec{r} = A_{x1}\cos(\omega_1 t + \varphi_1)\vec{i} + A_{y1}\cos(\omega_2 t + \varphi_2)\vec{j} \tag{3}$$

If the frequency ratio is an irrational number, where $A_{x1}=2$, $A_{y1}=3$, $\omega_1=30$, $\omega_2=30\sqrt{3}$, $\varphi_1 = \pi/3$, $\varphi_2=\pi/6$, then the resultant trajectory in different times are shown in Fig. 3(a) and Fig. 3(c) respectively. Additionally, if the frequency ratio is a rational number, such as $\omega_1 = 30, \omega_2 = 40$, and the other parameters remain unchanged, then the resultant trajectories are shown in Fig. 3(b) and Fig. 3(d).

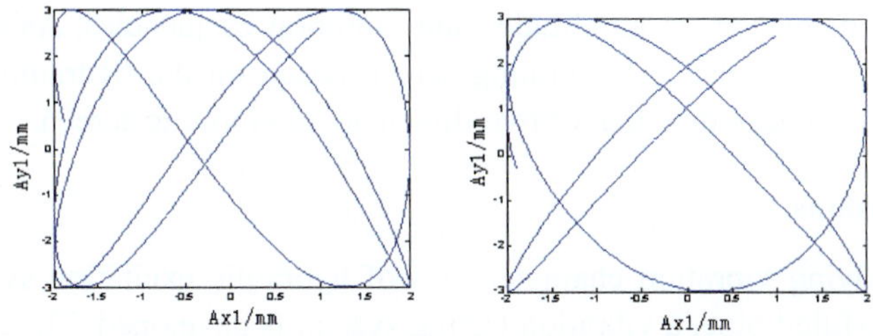

(a) frequency ratio is irrational number(t =0~0.5s) (b) frequency ratio is rational number(t =0~0.5s)

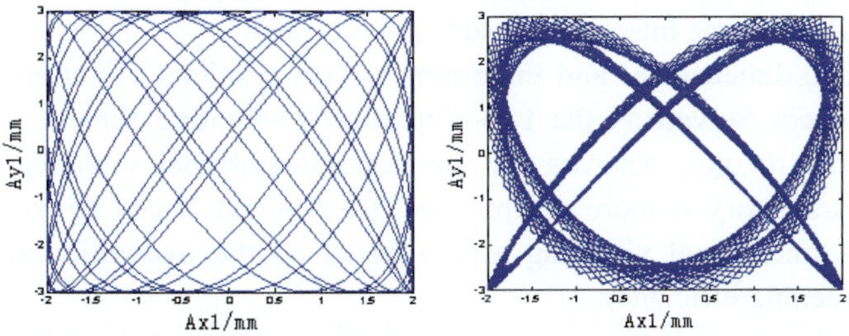

(c)frequency ratio is irrational number(t =0~12s) (d) frequency ratio is rational number(t =0~12s)

Fig. 3. Evolutionary Process of Two-dimensional Resultant Vibration

Served as the plane vibration, Fig. 3(a) and Fig. 3(b) are vibration trajectories when time t is 0~0.5s, and the corresponding frequency ratios are irrational number and rational number respectively. Fig. 3(c) and Fig. 3(d) are vibration trajectories when time t is 0~12s Similarly, the different frequency ratios correspond to different vibration trajectories. Evidently, with the increasing time, the vibration trajectories become more complicated. By comparison with the three–dimensional resultant vibration shown in Fig. 2, the vibration trajectories shown in Fig. 3 are more regular. If we take the elastic plate shown in Fig.1 as a vibration screen, according to the screening mechanism of materials, the more complicated vibration trajectories will benefit materials to pass through the screening surface and can result in higher screening efficiency. On the contrary, the regular vibration trajectories will lead to some uneasy screened materials through the screening surface difficultly. It is shown that the vibration trajectory of three-dimensional vibrating screen based on hydraulic excitation shown in Fig. 2 has more advantages than that of two-dimensional vibrating screen shown in Fig. 3.

All the research above can verify that the hydraulic excitation system can generate three-dimensional and multiple-degree-of-freedom vibration. Furthermore, different excitation pressure distributing along the pipe can result in different displacement amplitudes and vibration frequencies. As a result, we have demonstrated that the vibrating screen based on the hydraulic excitation has more advantages than that of two-dimensional vibrating screen.

5. Conclusions

(1) For studying vibration characteristics of hydraulic excitation system based on the fluid-filled pipe, a vibration testing system is developed. The elastic plate connected with the fluid-filled pipe is served as a vibration screen, and its mathematical model is established. Meanwhile, the numerical simulations are carried out and some interesting results are revealed.
(2) The two-dimensional and three-dimensional resultant vibration trajectories are compared. Served as the two-dimensional vibrating screen, its vibration trajectory is regular, whereas for the three-dimensional vibrating screen, its vibration trajectory is more complicated. By contrast, it can be concluded that the three-dimensional vibrating screen based on the hydraulic excitation has higher screening efficiency.
(3) According to evolutionary process of vibration trajectory, it is verified that the vibration mode based on hydraulic excitation has a better screening ability for materials. So, as a new vibration mode, we can demonstrate that the three-dimensional vibrating screen based on the hydraulic excitation has more advantages than that of the planar.

Acknowledgments

The project is supported by The National Natural Science Foundation of China (NSFC) & The Talent Cultivation Funds of Henan Province of China (U1404513).

References

1. C. Schmitt, G. Pluvinage. Water pipeline failure due to water hammer effects [J]. Fatigue and Fracture of Engineering Materials and Structures, 2006, 29(12): 1075-1082.
2. Per-Anders Hansson. Göran Sandberg. Dynamic finite element analysis of fluid-filled pipes [J]. Computer Methods in Applied Mechanics and Engineering, 2001, 190: 3111-3120.
3. JIN Jiduo, SONG Zhiyong, YANG Xiaodong. Stability and parametric resonances of a clamped-clamped pipe conveying fluid [J]. Journal of Vibration Engineering, 2004,17(2):190-195.

4. BAO Ridong, Feng Ying, Bi Wenjun Bangchun. Dynamic characteristics of pipeline conveying fluid with elastic supports[J]. Journal of Vibration and Shock, 2010, (3):129-131.
5. KOU Ziming, ZHANG Huixian, LIAN Hongzhen, et al. Design and simulation of an active hydraulic excitation system based on frequency conversion[J]. Transactions of Chinese Society for Agricultural Machinery, 2011, 42(5):226-230.
6. ZHANG Huixian, KOU Ziming, Wu Juan, et al. Dynamic Modeling and Experiments for Fluid. Structure Interaction in Pipe under Hydraulic Shock Wave [J]. Journal of Xi'an Jiaotong University, 2012, 46(3):94-99.
7. ZHANG Huixian, KOU Ziming, Lu Chunyue, et al. Kinematic Analysis and Experimental Research of Pipe Vibration Control Based on an Active Hydraulic Excitation Force [J]. Journal of Mechanical Engineering, 2012, 39(2): 94-99.

Face Detection Based on Method Combined RVM and SVM

Zhen Zhang[1,a], Cheng-Long Gong[2,b] and Rui-Ming Liu[2,c]

[1]Institute of Information and Electrical, China University of Mining and Technology
Xuzhou, 221008, China
[2]Institute of Electronic Engineering, Huaihai Institute of Technology
Lianyungang 222005, China
E-mail: [a]zzhenxuexi@163.com, [b]GongCL126@126.com, [c]nanjue1975@gmail.com

Face detection in complex background is widely used in face recognition, video retrieval, and human-computer interaction, etc. It is one of the hot topics in the study of computer vision and pattern recognition. A new method of face detection based on Relevance Vector Machine (RVM) and Support Vector Machine (SVM) is developed. First, the template matching based on average-face is used to eliminate a lot of simple background images, and then RVM classifier and nonlinear SVM classifier are combined to classify face and nonface images. The experiments show that this algorithm is effective.

Keywords: Face Detection; Relevance Vector Machine; Support Vector Machine.

1. Introduction

Human face detection is a process of segmenting all the faces, and finding the location, size of faces in a given image, if there are any faces in it. It is extensively applied in fields of identity authentication, video surveillance, semantic image annotation and retrieval, centralized control and human-computer interaction. However, due to the posture, facial expression, illumination and obstructions (glasses, beard and hair, scarf, etc.), the influence of such factors causes great difficulties, which also makes human face detection as a challenging research topic. To resolve the above questions, there have been many methods applied to face detection, which can be roughly divided into two broad categories: knowledge-based methods and appearance-based methods. The former includes Support Vector Machine (SVM) [1,2], neural network [3],

Adaboost [4,5], etc. SVM is an effective method of face detection, which can effectively resolve the small sample problem in practice. However, there are also some shortcomings, such as high computation cost, too much support vectors, the huge memory demand, if SVM directly is applied to detect faces.

Relevance Vector Machine (RVM) was proposed by Michal E. Tipping in 2000. RVM and Support Vector Machine (SVM) have the same function form and base on the kernel function. The difference is that RVM is training under the Bayesian framework and can obtain more sparse model, and RVM uses the number of the relevance vectors are far less than the number of support vectors and is not restricted by Mercer conditions. So, this paper introduces the RVM algorithm in face detection and proposes the method combined template matching based on average-face, RVM classifier and nonlinear SVM classifier. The method uses average-face based template matching and RVM classifier as the classification of coarse classifier, and it uses "bootstrap" technique within the limit of subspace to collect nonface training samples of nonlinear SVM classifier, which can decrease train difficulty and speed up the testing. Experiments show the effectiveness of the algorithm.

2. Support Vector Machine

SVM is a kind of statistical learning theory based on the structural risk minimization principle. Its basic idea can be summarized as: a nonlinear transformation to map the input space to a high-dimensional space to obtain the optimal classification hyperplane in the high dimensional space by defining appropriate inner product function.

Let $S=(x_i, y_i)$, $i=1,\cdots,n$, $y_i=\{-1,+1\}$ be the training set where y_i is the corresponding label of x_i. The input vectors are mapped to high dimensional space with kernel functions satisfying the Mercer condition to ensure them is Linearly Separable in high dimension space. In the high dimensional space to calculate a optimal hyperplane to maximize the distance of two classes.

The above problem equals to solving a quadratic programming problem:

$$\begin{aligned} &\min \quad W(\alpha)=\frac{1}{2}\sum_{i=1}^{n}\sum_{j=1}^{n}\alpha_i\alpha_j y_i y_j\left(x_i \bullet x_j\right)-\sum_{i=1}^{n}x_i \\ &subject \quad to \quad \sum_{i=1}^{n}\alpha_i y_j=0, \quad 0\le\alpha_i\le C \end{aligned} \tag{1}$$

where α_i is the Lagrange multipliers, and C is the penalty parameter.

A series of the corresponding vectors can be got from the training sample set when solving the quadratic programming problems. These vectors are the support vectors which decide the optimal hyperplane:

$$u = \operatorname{sgn}\left|\sum_{x_i \in sv} y_i \alpha_i K\left(x_i \bullet x\right) + b\right| \tag{2}$$

where sv is the support vector set.

3. Relevance Vector Machine

RVM is a learning method based on Bayes' estimation theory, suitable for pattern classification and function regression problems. Its sparsity and generalization performance is better than those of SVM, and it has the advantage of probability prediction. The mathematical model of RVM is similar to the SVM. Let $\{t_n, x_n\}$ be the training set and the model output of RVM is given by

$$y\left(x, w\right) = \sum_{i=1}^{N} \omega_i K\left(x, x_i\right) + \omega_0 \tag{3}$$

where ω_i is the corresponding weight of x_i, and $K\left(x, x_i\right)$ is the kernel function.

We conclude that

$$t_n = y\left(x_n + \omega\right) + \varepsilon_n \tag{4}$$

where x_n is the input parameter, and ε_n is the noises.

If we assume that the noise ε_n follows the Gaussian distribution whose mean is zero and variance is σ^2. We can conclude that.

$$p\left(t_n \middle| \omega, \sigma^2\right) = N\left(y\left(x_i, \omega_i\right), \sigma^2\right) \tag{5}$$

If t_n is independent identical distribution, it can show the likelihood function of training sample set. If directly using the maximum likelihood method to get σ^2 and ω, we will make the most elements of ω usually are not zero, which will result from the problem of over learning. To solve this problem, we add prerequisite to ω. The probability distribution is the normal distribution around zero, namely the prior probability distribution.

$$p\left(\omega_i \middle| \alpha_i\right) = N\left(\omega_i \middle| 0, \alpha_i^{-1}\right) \tag{6}$$

where α_i is the corresponding parameters of ω_i.

So, we can get ω by solving α, and when ω is tending to zero, and α goes to infinity.

4. Face Detection based on Method Combined RVM with SVM

The face detection method based on a method combined RVM with SVM is proposed in this paper. First of all, some preprocessing is performed, which includes the illumination gradient correction [3,6] and histogram equalization [7]. To solve the problem of facial multiple scales, the input images to be detected width is reduced by a factor of 1.2 to produce a series of image pyramid, then a 19 * 19 pixel mask moves 2 pixels by 2 pixels to scan all the pyramid images. Each image window is detected in turn by template matching based on average-face, RVM classifier and nonlinear SVM classifier. We record the location of the image windows classified as faces by the three layers classifier. Finally, we merge the overlapping position.

The face detection process of three layers classifier is as follows. Firstly, each image window is matched by template matching based on average-face. If the value of correlation coefficient is greater than the threshold value (the value is 0.1 in the experiment), we think that the image window pass the coarse screening of template matching based on average-face, then it is detected by the RVM classifier. Otherwise we detect the next image window. Secondly, image window passing the coarse screening of template matching based on average-face after grayscale average and masking is classified as the RVM classifier, if the output value is greater than the set threshold value (the value is –0.7 in the experiment), we think that the image window pass RVM classifier, then it is detected by the nonlinear SVM classifier. Otherwise we detect the next image window. Finally, if it is classified as the face image by the nonlinear SVM classifier, we can record its location to join the list of chosen face. The frame diagram of the detection windows is shown in Figure 1.

Every image window classified by the RVM and nonlinear SVM classifier is needed to normalize by grayscale average for reducing the influence of illumination, skin color and other factors. The normalization means: If the average gray level of the image window more than 155 which will be normalized to 155; if the average gray level of the image window less than 140 which will be normalized to 140; If the average gray level of the image window between 155 and 140 which will keep unchanged.

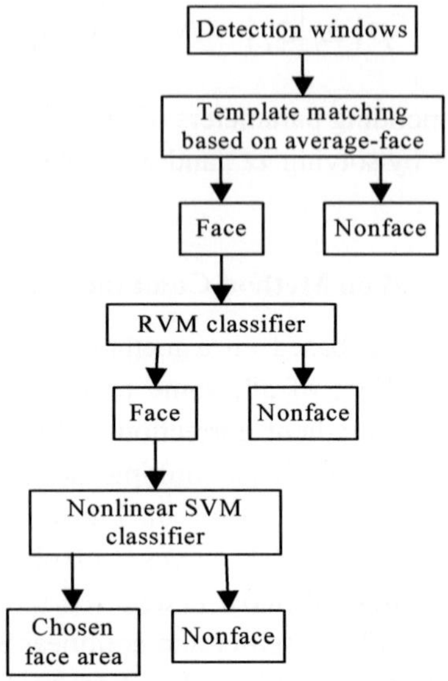

Fig. 1. This is the frame diagram of the detection windows.

4.1. *Template matching based on average-face*

If RVM and SVM is used in face detection, how to generate the face training samples is the primary problem. We select face samples from the MIT, BioID and ORL face database, and we take pictures and download images from the Internet. The pictures contain a variety of age, expression and posture.

After the pictures being normalized by histogram equalization and illumination gradient correction, we calibrate square face (including the pupil and the corners of the mouth) in these image. Then the pictures are transformed into 19 * 19 pixel by the geometric correction and are normalized by grayscale average. To improve the generalization ability of the classifier, we carry on the geometric correction as follows.

(1) For upright human faces, rotating them randomly [8] by -10° and $+10^{\circ}$,
(2) For non-upright human faces, mirroring them,
(3) For all of the human faces, scaling up 1.2 times.

After masking, more than 4400 face samples are generated to train our classifiers.

Average Face is obtained from selecting the portion of face data sets (note that these images are without masking processing). For further improving the speed of face detection, each image window first is matched by template matching based on average-face. Set $T[M][N], \sigma_t, m_t$ and $R[M][N], \sigma_r, m_r$, respectively for the gray matrix, the gray variance and the gray average of the average-face and the image window. The correlation coefficient [9] is given by

$$r(T,R) = \frac{\sum_{i=0}^{M-1}\sum_{j=0}^{N-1}\left(T[i][j]-m_t\right)\left(R[i][j]-m_r\right)}{M \bullet N \bullet \sigma_t \bullet \sigma_r} \tag{7}$$

When we detect the image, each image window firstly is matched by the template matching based on average-face. If the value of correlation coefficient is greater than the threshold value (the value is 0.1 in the experiment), we think that the image window pass the coarse screening of template matching based on average-face, then it is detected by the RVM classifier. Otherwise we detect the next image window.

4.2. *The training of RVM classifier*

The face samples are selected from the face sets. The uncertain factors of nonface samples are more than those of face samples. It is more difficult to collect them. This paper applies the "bootstrap" technique to collect the nonface training samples of RVM classifier. The specific steps are as follows.

Step1 Some images are selected as the training image library. These images should include the common background in our daily life, such as house, grassland, mountain, water, etc,

Step2 The above images are preprocessed by the illumination gradient correction and histogram equalization,

Step3 The above images are detected by the template matching based on average-face, and we collect a certain number of nonface samples which are false positives and they are used as the initial nonface training samples of the RVM classifier,

Step4 Train the RVM classifier,

Step5 Detect the training samples by the combined method of template matching based on average-face and RVM. The false positives are collected to contract the nonface samples set to train the RVM classifier,

Step6 Repeating steps 4 and 5, until the average-face based template matching and RVM classifier combination method can eliminate a certain amount of background windows, we eliminate 99% of the total number of image windows in the experiment.

We use Gaussian radial basis function as the kernel function. After masking processing and PCA dimension reduction, the input samples are the 88 dimension. In the end, more than 1700 nonface samples and the above more than 3500 face samples are collected to train the RVM classifier.

4.3. *The training of nonlinear SVM classifier*

The above more than 4400 face samples are used as the face training samples of the nonlinear SVM classifier, and we apply the "bootstrap" technique to collect the nonface training samples. The specific steps are as follows.

Step1 The training images were preprocessed by the illumination gradient correction and histogram equalization,

Step2 The above images are detected by the combined method of template matching based on average-face and RVM, and we collect a certain number of nonface samples which are false positives and they are used as the initial nonface training samples of the nonlinear SVM classifier,

Step3 Train the nonlinear SVM classifier,

Step4 Detect the training samples by the combined method of template matching based on average-face, RVM and nonlinear SVM. The false positives are collected to contract the nonface samples set to train the nonlinear SVM classifier,

Step5 Repeating step 3 and 4 until the number of false detections is smaller than a certain value (the value is 30 in the experiment).

We use Gaussian radial basis function as the kernel function. After masking processing and PCA dimension reduction, the input samples are the 88 dimension, and constrained optimization conditions $C = 200$. In the end, more than 5600 nonface samples and the above more than 4400 face samples are collected to train the nonlinear SVM classifier.

5. Experimental Results

To test the effectiveness of the proposed face-detection algorithm, we selected the two test sets which are separate from the training images. Test set 1 from CMU data set contains of 65 images including 248 faces, and test set 2 contains of 110 images including 406 faces. In order to reveal the effectiveness of the proposed face-detection algorithm, the algorithm of face detection based on template matching and Support Vector Machines [9] (the correlation coefficient of average-face is 0.08, and the correlation coefficient of average-eye is 0.15 in the experiment) is compared in the experiments. Figure 2 shows some face-detection results by our algorithm.

Fig. 2. Some typical results on test set 1 and 2.

Can be seen from the Figure 2, the proposed algorithm has good robustness and can detect faces with glasses and near-frontal faces.

Table 1. Results from our method along with that from "average-eye + average-face + nonlinear SVM" method.

	Test set 1			Test set 2		
Method	Faces detected	False detections	Detection rate (%)	Faces detected	False detections	Detection rate (%)
average-face + RVM + SVM	225	13	90.7	387	14	95.3
average-eye + average-face + SVM	213	20	85.9	380	18	93.4

The statistical results of test set 1 and 2 are given in Table. 1. 7110712 image windows are searched on the test set 1. 7033947 image windows are eliminated by the template matching based on average-face and RVM classifier, which approximately account for 99% of the total number of image windows. Only 76765 image windows are detected by the nonlinear SVM classifier, which approximately account for 1% of the total number of image windows. Thus it can be seen that template matching based on average-face and RVM classifier can eliminate most of the background windows, which can improve the detecting speed. The picture with 338*490 pixel is detected by our algorithm, the processing time for 12.63 seconds. If it is detected by the method based on template matching and Support Vector Machines, the processing time is 14.18 seconds. If it is detected by only nonlinear SVM, the processing time is 4022.37 seconds.

The testing results show that the proposed algorithm is better than the face-detection algorithm based on template matching and Support Vector Machines, and our algorithm has higher detection rate and lower false detections.

6. Conclusions

This paper introduces the RVM algorithm in face detection and proposes the method combined template matching based on average-face, RVM classifier and nonlinear SVM classifier. Detection precision of the frontal view upright face in complicated background is improved. As the first level classifier, template matching based on average-face has the advantage of simple algorithm and fast testing velocity. It can eliminate many simple background images under the premise of ensuring that human faces are exactly detected. So the detecting speed is improved, and the training difficulty of RVM classifier and nonlinear SVM classifier is reduced.

Because the computation complexity and detection precision of template matching based on average-face is low, template matching based on average-face can only eliminate a part of nonface images under the premise of ensuring that human faces are exactly detected, otherwise it maybe eliminate the human face windows. In this case, if nonlinear SVM is directly used as the core classifier, the memory demanding and the number of support vectors can't be underestimated. In order to solve the above problems, this paper regard RVM classifier as the second level classifier. When RVM is used in face detection, its the number of relevance vectors is considerably lower than the number of support vectors used by the nonlinear SVM. The precision of RVM is slightly lower than the SVM. So we choose RVM classifier to be the second level classifier, which can eliminate almost all simple background image windows under the premise of ensuring that human faces are exactly detected. Nonlinear SVM classifier only need to confirm a small number of candidate regions. Thus the detection speed and precision is improved. The experiments show that this algorithm is effective.

References

1. Peichung Shih, Chengjun Liu. Face detection using discriminating feature analysis and Support Vector Machine[J]. Pattern Recognition, 2006, 39(2):260-276.
2. TENG Shaohua, CHEN Haitao, ZHANG Wei. Multi-pose cooperative face detection based on hypersphere support vector machine[J]. Journal of Computer Applications, 2015,36(4):1355-1360 (In Chinese).
3. Rowley H A, Baluja S, Kanade T. Neural network-based face detection[J]. IEEE Trans Pattern Analysis and Machine Intelligence, 1998, 20(1):23-38.
4. XU Xin S, HAO Xiao-li, WANG Fang. Long distance face detection based on Adaboost algorithm[J]. COMPUTER ENGINEERING AND DESIGN, 2015,36(4):1355-1360 (In Chinese).
5. JIANG Weijian, GUO Gongde, LAI Zhiming. An improved adaboost algorithm based on new Haar-like[J]. JOURNAL OF SHANDONG UNIVERSITY(ENGINEERING SCIENCE), 2014,44(2):43-48 (In Chinese).
6. Sung K, Poggio T. Example-based learning for view-based Human face detection. IEEE Trans Pattern Analysis and Machine Intelligence, 1998, 20(1):39-51.
7. Shu Zhan, Qin-Qin Tao, Xiao-Hong Li. Face detection using representation learning [J]. Neurocomputing, 2016, 187:19-26.
8. Waring C A, Xiuwen L. Face detection using spectral histograms and SVMs[J]. IEEE Transactions on Systems, Man and Cybernetics, Part B, 2005, 35(3):467-476.
9. LIANG Lu-Hong, AI Hai-Zhou, XIAO Xi-Pan, et al. Face detection based on template matching and Support Vector Machines [J]. CHINESE J.COMPUTERS, 2002, 25(1):22-29 (In Chinese).

Multi-Exposure Images Fusion Based on IHS Transformation

Nan Li[a], Jian-Xian Zhang[b] and Duan Zhou[c]
School of Computer Science and Technology, Xidian University
Xi'an 710071, China
E-mail: [a]lndawn@163.com, [b]jianxianzhang@mail.xidian.edu.cn, [c]dzhou@xidian.edu.cn

Due to the traditional multi-exposure images fusion method performed in the RGB color space and cannot manipulate the intensity information conveniently, this paper proposes a new IHS color space based multi-exposure image fusion method, which transforms the input origin images from RGB color space to IHS color space and deal with the intensity and chrominance information separately. The fused intensity component is achieved by weighted sum in multi-resolution fashion and the weight map is estimated by the quality measures: local contrast and saturation. For the saturation and hue components, the best chosen pixel on the same location used the "winner-take-all" manner to recover the fused chrominance. Experimental results demonstrate the superiority and effectiveness of this method in term of subjective and objective evaluation.

Keywords: Multi-exposure Fusion; High Dynamic Range; IHS Transformation; Pyramid Fusion.

1. Introduction

In general, natural scene has a wide dynamic range and human eyes can adapt the similar dynamic range. But the most of image capture and display devices are difficult to restore the real scene due to the limited dynamic range. The single photograph captured by the common digital camera systems is not capable to obtain the whole dynamic range information. High dynamic range (HDR) imaging is used to solve this problem, which can preserve the natural color without the loss of details and abundant textural features[1]. In recent years, the HDR imaging technique is applied widely and has attracted many researchers. There are two different methods to display the HDR-like low dynamic range (LDR) image: tone mapping method[2] and image fusion method[3]. Image fusion method is directly fuse the many different exposure images to obtain a more detailed LDR image, which avoid the camera response function (CRF) estimation, radiance map reconstruction[4] and tone mapping. Thus, the multi-exposure fusion can effectively reproduce the satisfactory natural scenes and becomes an important technique to capture the HDR scenes.

For now, multi-exposure fusion methods based on weight term are applied widely. The weight map decision has a great influence on the quality of the fusion result. The fusion algorithms can be generally classified into multi-scale fusion and single scale fusion. Three quality measures, namely, contrast, saturation and well-exposure is used to construct the weight map for input source images, then combine the input images decomposed by Laplacian pyramid and the weight maps defined by Gaussian pyramid into the final result in a multi-resolution fashion. The final image can preserve the global contrast but will lose the details in the bright and dark regions[5]. Based on the fusion method [5], other researches has made some improvement from different aspects and obtain a more pleasing results [6-9], and the method of the ghost detection and removal is applied to fuse the input images which exist moving object. Li .et[10] used the edge-preserving recursive filter to refine the final weight map, and employed the median filter to detect the ghost. Although the approach can deal with both the static scenes and the dynamic scenes, it is difficult to preserve the content in the under-exposure or over-exposed areas. Liu .et[11] proposed a DSIFT-based multi-exposure fusion method, they also refined the weight map with recursive. The result can preserve more details but would appear brightness inverse. In addition, many different approaches have been proposed such as supervised learning based[12], variance based[13] and probabilistic model-based methods[14]. Optimization problem solution can improve the quality of the fused result but increase the time complexity and is difficult to achieve a good performance and efficiency tradeoff.

In this paper, we proposed a simple yet effective multi-exposure fusion scheme. The proposed method is different from the traditional multi-exposure method completed in the RGB color space, which transforms the source images from RGB color space into the IHS color space and deal with the intensity and chrominance separately. The intensity fusion employ the weighted sum of the original images in multi-scale fashion, the weight map is estimated by the two quality measures: local contrast and saturation. The chrominance is recovered with the best pixel on the same location, which usually own the best hue and saturation. The proposed method produces visually pleasing fused image with better color appearance and more texture details. The results of experiments demonstrate the superiority of the proposed method in the terms of subjective and objective assessment.

The rest of this paper is organized as follows. Section 2 describes the proposed method in detail. The experimental results are presented in Section 3 to verify the efficiency of the proposed approach. Finally, the conclusion remarks are listed in Section 4.

2. Fusion Model based on IHS Color Space

Figure. 1 shows the flowchart of the proposed multi-exposure fusion algorithm based on IHS transformation. Input images is transformed from RGB color space to IHS color space so that the intensity and chrominance can be processed separately. Intensity fusion is achieved by multi-scale fusion based on weight term. The weight map is estimated by the quality measures: local contrast and saturation, Laplacian-Gaussian pyramid method is employed to blend the input intensity images and the weight map to generate the fused intensity image. For the different input images sequence, the normal exposure pixels on the same location have the similar hue, so we select corresponding hue to the best saturation to obtain the final chrominance, which can preserve the rich color information. Finally, IHS inverse transformation are applied to obtain the fused RGB image.

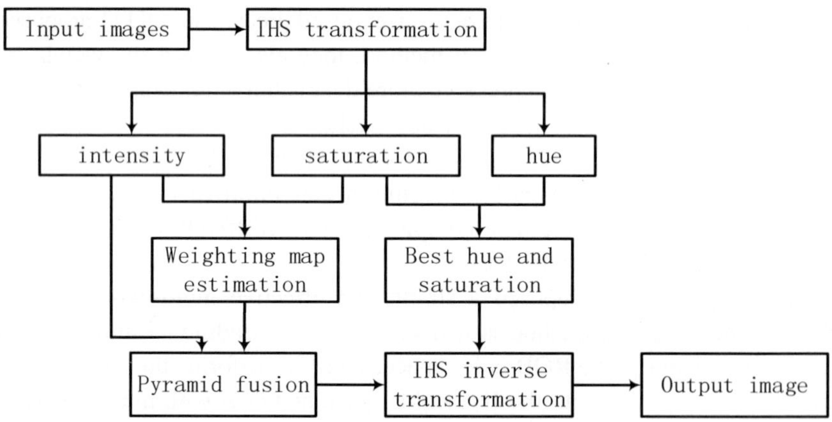

Fig. 1. The flowchart of the proposed method

2.1. *Intensity fusion*

2.1.1. *Local contrast*

Local contrast and brightness can represent the structure information of the image. The basic structure of the image can be preserved by fusing the edges features extracted by the local contrast and intensity image. The local contrast of the each pixel is calculated as follows:

$$C_n(x,y) = h * I_n(x,y) \tag{1}$$

Where h is the Laplacian operator, I_n is the intensity component of the nth source image after IHS transformation. $*$ denotes the convolution operation. There are two distribution strategies for fusing the images: "weighted-average[5-7]" and "winner-take-all[10, 11]", which can be employed to construct the local contrast weight term. Here, "winner-take-all" strategy is employed to enhance the global contrast of the image and emphasize the detail information, which is defined as in Eq. (2):

$$C_n(x,y) = \begin{cases} 1, & C_n(x,y) = \max\{C_n(x,y), n = 1,2,...,N\} \\ 0, & otherwise. \end{cases} \tag{2}$$

2.1.2. *Saturation*

When the photograph has been captured in a longer exposure time, the resulting colors become degraded and eventually clipped. To pursue better preserve the region with perfect information, saturation is considered as a weight term to conduct the fusion process. While the saturation component transformed is directly involved in the fusion process, the details in dark and bright area will be lost, the resulting intensity image yet contain the over-exposed or under-exposed pixels. In order to preserve the details in visible area, the origin saturation component is adjusted by Eq. (3):

$$S_n(x,y) = \begin{cases} S_n(x,y) & T < I_n(x,y) < 1-T \\ 0 & otherwise. \end{cases} \tag{3}$$

Where T is a threshold value for the normal exposure usually between 0.05~1.0, when T is too small, the details in dark and bright region is not obvious, when too large, the origin basic structure will be distorted.

2.1.3. *Intensity fusion*

According to the two quality measures is calculated by the approaches mentioned above, the weight map of nth input image is calculated by Eq. (4):

$$W_n(x,y) = C_n(x,y) \times S_n(x,y) \tag{4}$$

In theory, the result image can be obtained by a linear combination of normalized weight map and intensity image, if follow this way, which will introduce the seam and artifacts such as black halos and contrast reversal. Researchers have attempted to refine the weight maps or fuse at the multi resolutions that solve this problem. The presented pyramid fusion approach has achieved a satisfactory result and plays an important role in multi-exposure fusion study. Thus, we choose the pyramid fusion to obtain the resulting image, which is defined as in Eq. (5):

$$L\{R\}_{xy}^{l} = \sum_{n=1}^{N} G(W)_{xy,n}^{l} L(I)_{xy,n}^{l} \tag{5}$$

Where $G\{W\}$ is the Gaussian pyramid of weight map, $L\{I\}$ is the Laplacian pyramid of intensity images. $L\{R\}$ is the fused Laplacian pyramid image and be constructed to generate the resulting intensity component.

Multi scale pyramid fusion can preserve the local and global contrast of original images and enhance the details that avoid the introduction of the artifact and noise. Multi-resolution fusion is more consistent with the human visual characteristics and can achieve visually pleasing result.

2.2. *Chrominance fusion*

The saturation has a difference in one image sequence captured by different exposure time. In normal exposure range, it is found the hue for the different images sequence on the same location are similar to each other, that the saturation is larger, the color looks more vivid. However, the relation of saturation and hue will not be satisfied in under-exposed and over-exposed regions. Here, the guided pixel are selected which has the best saturation on the same location for the input image sequence, the saturation and hue corresponding to the pixel will be the fused feature component to recover chrominance of the intensity image.

$$S(x,y) = \max\left(S_n(x,y)\right),\ n = 1,2,...,N \tag{6}$$

$$H(x,y) = H_{select}(x,y) \tag{7}$$

Where *select* is the guided pixel on the same location. As mentioned above, the "take-winner-all" manner is employed again to choose the best saturation and hue component avoid the loss of the color information in the image obtained by "weighted-average" strategy, which can increase the saturation of the resulting image and preserve the vivid color information of original images.

3. Experiments Results and Discussions

To verify the effectiveness of the proposed fusion method, we have tested for eight different datasets, the results are compared against the results of the exposure fusion (EF) [5] method, the FMMR [10] method and the DSIFT based fusion method [11]. EF approach is widely used in multi-exposure image sequence taken in static scenes. The latter two are all used to fuse images captured at both static and dynamic scenes. Here, we only manipulate image sequence taken in static scenes to access the performance of the proposed method.

Figure. 2 shows the results of the multi-exposure image sequence of "Memorial church" and partially enlarged view of window, it can be seen that the detail in result of the EF and FMMR methods have suffered a heavy loss. The result of the DSIFT preserve the most of the detail, but involved the problem as luminance reversion. By contrast, the proposed method well preserve the details of origin images and rich color.

Fig. 2. Comparison results to other recent methods on the "Memorial church" image sequence, (a) EF, (b) FMMR, (c) DSIFT, (d) the proposed method

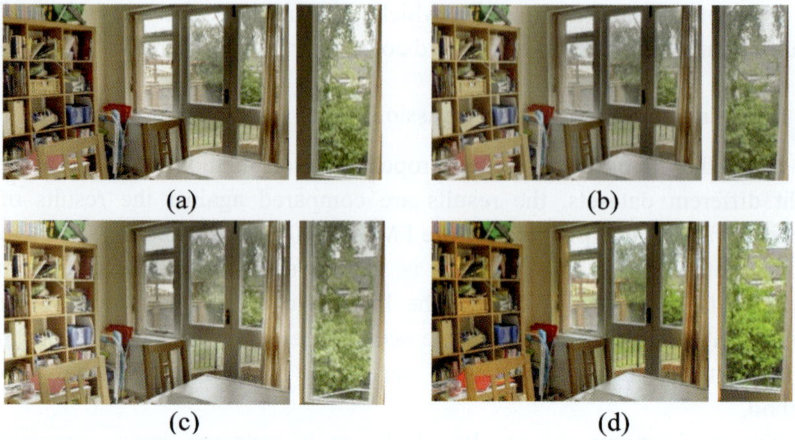

Fig. 3. Comparison results to other recent methods on the "house" image sequence, (a) EF, (b) FMMR, (c) DSIFT, (d) the proposed method

Figure. 3 is the result of the "house" image sequence, which are captured at the sunny indoor and outdoor scenes and has the wider dynamic range. The result obtained with the FMMR and DSIFT methods can be seen "washed-out" and degrade the visual quality. The EF method has better performances but the outdoor region with tree and grass suffer from over-exposure. The fusion result of the proposed method is satisfactory with a more complete edge information and a better color appearance.

To evaluate the validity of the proposed method objectively, the fusion performance evaluation index is employed to access the fused result. Owing to there has been no available ideal image as the reference, we only use the no reference evaluation index: entropy, average gradient and spatial frequency to evaluate the quality of fused result.

The image entropy is an important index to measure the amount of information in the image, a larger entropy value indicates a better fusion result. Table. 1 is the performances of different methods using entropy, the proposed method has close performance with other fusion methods in most cases, for several sequence, such as "memorial" and "venice", which obtains the highest value, but for the "outdoor" and "gate" sequences, which contain too much under-exposed pixels without involved in the fusion, which leads to a reduction in information of the resulting image to preserve the details in the dark area.

Table 1. Performances of different methods on the eight image sequences using the image entropy.

Images	EF	FMMR	DSIFT	Proposed
Example1	7.56	7.65	**7.71**	7.65
House	**7.68**	7.48	7.53	7.62
Memorial	7.49	7.40	7.41	**7.50**
Outdoor	7.30	7.30	**7.51**	7.14
Venice	7.53	7.36	7.36	**7.69**
Gate	6.94	7.05	**7.16**	6.87
Office	7.17	7.22	**7.56**	7.36
Pond	7.71	7.68	**7.74**	7.69

The average gradient reflects the sharpness of the image. Obviously, a higher value indicates a better result. Table. 2 shows the performances of the different methods using average gradient, it can be seen the proposed method obtain higher scores than the other methods in all datasets except "gate" sequence. For the "example1" sequence, the average gradient of the proposed method is improved by 7%, 19% and 13% compared with the EF, FMMR and DSIFT methods, respectively, and for the "pond" sequence, which is increased by 9%,44% and 18%. For the "gate" sequence, the result using the proposed method is lower than the EF method, but outperforms the FMMR and DSIFT methods and yet improved by 11% and 3%.

Table 2. Performances of the different methods on the eight image sequences using average gradient.

Images	EF	FMMR	DSIFT	Proposed
Example1	15.75	14.98	16.68	**17.83**
House	10.37	8.11	9.29	**10.83**
Memorial	11.88	10.01	11.92	**13.91**
Outdoor	11.28	10.06	11.15	**12.23**
Venice	6.25	4.78	5.70	**7.29**
Gate	**6.72**	6.04	6.50	6.69
Office	7.05	6.13	6.87	**7.70**
Pond	12.82	9.73	11.87	**14.02**

The spatial frequency reflects the activity of an image in the spatial domain, that is larger, the quality of the image is better. The proposed method obtained the highest scores listed in the Table. 3, but the FMMR method gets the lowest scores in all the eight sequences. For the different sequences, EF method and DSIFT method have both advantages and disadvantages. For the "memorial" sequence, the spatial frequency using the proposed method is improved by 20%,

38% and 13% compared with the EF, FMMR and DSIFT methods, respectively. And for the "office" sequence, which is improved by 6%, 25% and 8%.

Table 3. Performances of the different methods on the eight image sequences using spatial frequency.

Images	EF	FMMR	DSIFT	Proposed
Example1	35.33	34.00	37.86	**40.17**
House	24.08	18.99	21.87	**25.18**
Memorial	24.18	21.02	25.56	**28.93**
Outdoor	30.57	27.49	30.52	**34.17**
Venice	16.15	12.03	14.79	**18.92**
Gate	19.18	17.90	18.82	**20.11**
Office	16.76	14.26	16.44	**17.84**
Pond	30.96	23.25	28.93	**36.60**

In summary, the proposed method have the better scores than the other methods in the average gradient and spatial frequency and the very close scores to the optimal value in the entropy. Both the subjective visual perception and objective evaluations show the proposed method outperforms those of three comparison methods, which can produce the visually pleasing result with a better color appearance and a more detail texture.

4. Conclusions

In this work we proposed a multi-exposure images fusion method based on IHS color space. The input images are transformed from RGB color space into the IHS color space, the intensity components fusion employ the multi resolution schema based on the weighted sum. For the saturation and hue components, we choose the best pixel on the same location used the "winner-take-all" strategy to involve in the final fusion. Experimental results show the effectiveness of the proposed method, which can preserve the origin rich color information while reproduce the details in the dark and bright areas and generate a pleasing resulting image. The proposed approach outperforms the other multi exposure fusion method in terms of objective evaluation. So far the proposed method is only employed in the image sequence captured at static scenes, we plan to develop the effective ghost-free fusion schema to fuse the image sequence taken in dynamic scenes based on the proposed approach.

Acknowledgment

This work was supported in part by the National Natural Science Foundation of China under Grant No. 61474087, and the Fundamental Research Funds for the Central Universities under Grant No. JB150315.

References

1. E. Reinhard, *High dynamic range imaging: acquisition, display, and image-based lighting*. (Morgan Kaufmann, 2005).
2. E. Reinhard, Photographic tone reproduction for digital images. *ACM Trans. Graph.* **21**, 367(2002).
3. A. A. Goshtasby, Fusion of multi-exposure images. *Image Vision Comput.* **23**, 611(2005).
4. P. E. Debevec and J. Malik, Recovering high dynamic range radiance maps from photographs. in *Proc. ACM SIGGRAPH* (1997), pp. 369–378.
5. T. Mertens, J. Kautz and F.V. Reeth, Exposure Fusion, in *Proc. Pacific Graphics* (2007), pp. 382–390.
6. H.-C. Tsai, H.-J. Lin and J.-J. Leou, Multiexposure image fusion using intensity enhancement and detail extraction. *J. Vis. Comun. Image Represent.* **33**, 165(2015).
7. A. V. Vanmali, S. G. Kelkar and V. M. Gadre, Multi-exposure image fusion for dynamic scenes without ghost effect, in *Proc. IEEE National Conf. on Communications (NCC),* (IIT Bombay, 2015), pp. 1-6.
8. W. Zhang and W. K. Cham, Reference-guided exposure fusion in dynamic scenes. *J. Vis. Commun. Image Represent.* **23**, 467(2012).
9. A. Jaehyun, H. Seong Jong and C. Nam Ik, Reduction of ghost effect in exposure fusion by detecting the ghost pixels in saturated and non-saturated regions, in *Proc. IEEE Int. Conf. on Acoustics, Speech and Signal Processing (ICASSP*), (Kyoto, Japan, 2012), pp. 1101-1104.
10. L. Shutao and K. Xudong, Fast multi-exposure image fusion with median filter and recursive filter. *IEEE Trans. Consum. Electron.* **58**, 626(2012).
11. Y. Liu and Z. Wang, Dense SIFT for ghost-free multi-exposure fusion. *J. Vis. Comun. Image Represent.* **31**, 208(2015).
12. M. E. Moumene, R. Nourine and D. Ziou, Generalized Exposure Fusion Weights Estimation. in *Canadian Conf. on Computer and Robot Vision (CRV)* (2014), pp. 71-76.
13. M. Bertalmio and S. Levine, Variational Approach for the Fusion of Exposure Bracketed Pairs. *IEEE Trans. Image Process.* **22**, 712(2013)
14. S. Mingli, et al., Probabilistic Exposure Fusion, *IEEE Trans. Image Process.* **21**, 341(2011).

Binocular Vision System for a Four Legged Robot

Long Han

Tieling normal College, Tieling City,
Liaoning Province, China
E-mail: holms8105@163.com

Aiming at the positioning problem of a four legged robot, a mobile robot localization method based on robot binocular vision system and landmark information is proposed in this paper. The parallel binocular vision system is composed of two C270 cameras and a horizontal scale bar, and the mathematical model of the camera is established. The calibration experiment to the established camera model is done by using Zhang Zhengyou calibration method, to solve camera internal and external parameters. A target recognition algorithm based on color feature is proposed.

Keywords: Hand/Foot Fusion; Binocular Stereo Vision; Color Recognition; Camera Calibration.

1. Introduction

In 1977, Professor Marr proposed his vision theory: Marr vision theory and extensive influence [1-2]. In 2000, the Zhejiang University adopted the binocular vision to obtain the image, the coordinates of the feature points extracted from the two images can be achieved on the Stewart platform of the dynamic, pose detection [3][4]. In 2002, Beijing Institute of Technology researchers used a wearable visual system to track the methods of hand and hand gesture recognition. The proposed method can achieve the tracking of the depth and the gray level information of the Wearable vision system [5]. In 2003, the Harbin Institute of Technology adopted a heterogeneous binocular vision system to achieve a full autonomous soccer robot navigation [6].

2. The Basic Principle of Binocular Vision System

Binocular vision system is the use of the visual sensor to identify objects in the environment, the external features of the object-color as the visual system to identify the main characteristics of different objects, and then the use of binocular vision technology to identify the target location. According to the 3D space coordinates of the object, the robot's self localization is realized.

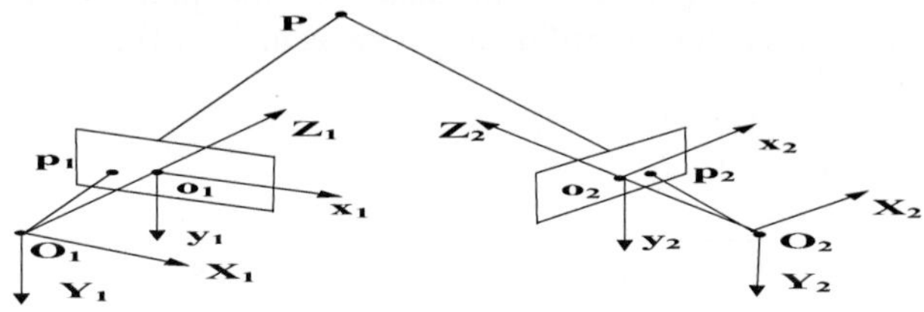

Fig. 1. Coordinate calculation of spatial points in binocular vision

Binocular vision is based on parallax, as shown in Figure 1. Set the left camera coordinate system $O_1-X_1Y_1Z_1$, At the origin of the world coordinate system, and there is no rotation transformation between the world coordinate system. Image coordinate system is $O_1-x_1y_1$. Set the right camera coordinate system $O_2-X_2Y_2Z_2$. Image coordinate system is $O_2-x_2y_2$. Two camera projection center line distance, that is, the baseline distance is B. Two camera at the same time to detect the center of mass points of space objects P. $P_1(X_1,Y_1,Z_1)$, $P_2(X_2,Y_2,Z_2)$ are the coordinates of the point P in the camera coordinate system. $p_1(x_1,y_1,z_1)$, $p_2(x_2,y_2,z_2)$ are respectively in the left and right camera imaging point, f_1, f_2 ,respectively, the effective focal length of the left and right cameras.

From the pinhole imaging principle, the camera coordinate system and the physical coordinates of the space point P are met as in Eq. (1) and Eq. (2).

$$z_1\begin{bmatrix}x_1\\y_1\\1\end{bmatrix}=\begin{pmatrix}f_1&0&0\\0&f_1&0\\0&0&1\end{pmatrix}\begin{bmatrix}X_1\\Y_1\\Z_1\end{bmatrix}=M_1\begin{bmatrix}X_1\\Y_1\\Z_1\end{bmatrix}\tag{1}$$

$$z_2\begin{bmatrix}x_2\\y_2\\1\end{bmatrix}=\begin{pmatrix}f_2&0&0\\0&f_2&0\\0&0&1\end{pmatrix}\begin{bmatrix}X_2\\Y_2\\Z_2\end{bmatrix}=M_2\begin{bmatrix}X_2\\Y_2\\Z_2\end{bmatrix}\tag{2}$$

But the position relationship of the coordinate system $O_1-X_1Y_1Z_1$ and $O_2-X_2Y_2Z_2$ can be expressed by the space transformation matrix:

$$\begin{bmatrix}X_2\\Y_2\\Z_2\end{bmatrix}=[R|T]\begin{bmatrix}X_1\\Y_1\\Z_1\\1\end{bmatrix}=\begin{pmatrix}r_{11}&r_{12}&r_{13}&t_x\\r_{21}&r_{22}&r_{23}&t_y\\r_{31}&r_{32}&r_{33}&t_z\end{pmatrix}\begin{bmatrix}X_1\\Y_1\\Z_1\\1\end{bmatrix}=M_{12}\begin{bmatrix}X_1\\Y_1\\Z_1\\1\end{bmatrix}\tag{3}$$

In the expression:

R-Rotation transformation matrix between coordinate system.

T-Coordinate system and translation vector.

By Eq. (1) ~ Eq. (3), the coordinates of the point P (X_1, Y_1, Z_1) can be expressed in the left camera coordinate system as in Eq. (4) :

$$\begin{cases} X_1 = Z_1 x_1 / f_1 \\ Y_1 = Z_1 y_1 / f_1 \\ Z_1 = \dfrac{(f_2 t_x - x_2 t_z) f_1}{(r_{31} x_1 + r_{32} y_1 + r_{33} f_1) x_2 - (r_{11} x_1 + r_{12} y_1 + r_{13} f_1) f_2} \\ \quad = \dfrac{(f_2 t_y - y_2 t_z) f_1}{(r_{31} x_1 + r_{32} y_1 + r_{33} f_1) y_2 - (r_{21} x_1 + r_{22} y_1 + r_{23} f_1) f_2} \end{cases} \quad (4)$$

Therefore, when the focal length f_1, f_2 and the image coordinates of the spatial points are known, the 3D coordinates of the measured points can be obtained by the R and T.

3. Target Location Experiment

3.1. *Hardware components of binocular vision system*

The binocular vision system is composed of two C270 cameras, and their main function is to capture the original image from multiple angles. Camera through the diameter of 4mm screw and the horizontal scale bar connected, and horizontal scale bar by three 5mm screw fixed on the robot, in order to form a binocular vision system.

3.2. *Perspective transformation calibration method*

The calibration method of the perspective transformation matrix is used as the reference of 3 3D to calibrate the camera. Reference vertex of the dice is seen to feature points for processing, production and need precise determination of these feature points relative to the world coordinate system of position, by their coordinates in the image and the world coordinate system to compute the camera's parameters.

The X-ray transform method is also used in linear pinhole imaging model, and the parameters are calibrated by using the projection transformation matrix. It will be written:

$$s\begin{bmatrix} u \\ v \\ 1 \end{bmatrix} = \begin{bmatrix} m_{11} & m_{12} & m_{13} & m_{14} \\ m_{21} & m_{22} & m_{23} & m_{24} \\ m_{31} & m_{32} & m_{33} & m_{34} \end{bmatrix} \begin{bmatrix} X_W \\ Y_W \\ Z_W \\ 1 \end{bmatrix} \quad (5)$$

In Eq. (5):

(XW, YW, ZW, 1)T - the world coordinate of reference point.

(u, v, 1) - the image coordinates of the feature points.

m_{ij} -Elements of the irow j column of the projection matrix M_{12}.

By Eq. (5), we can get three equations:

$$\begin{cases} su = m_{11} X_W + m_{12} Y_W + m_{13} Z_W + m_{14} \\ sv = m_{21} X_W + m_{22} Y_W + m_{23} Z_W + m_{24} \\ s = m_{31} X_W + m_{32} Y_W + m_{33} Z_W + m_{34} \end{cases} \tag{6}$$

Finishing (6) type, elimination of S, we can get two linear equations on m_{ij} :

$$\begin{matrix} m_{11}X_w + m_{12}Y_w + m_{13}Z_w + m_{14} - m_{31}uX_w - m_{32}uY_w - m_{33}uZ_w - m_{34}u = 0 \\ m_{21}X_w + m_{22}Y_w + m_{23}Z_w + m_{14} - m_{31}uX_w - m_{32}uY_w - m_{33}uZ_w - m_{34}u = 0 \end{matrix} \tag{7}$$

By Eq. (7), it can be known that the two coordinates of the feature points, if the transformation matrix is unknown, there are 12 unknowns to solve. And the constant of the M_{12} multiplied by any of the zero does not affect (X_w, Y_w, Z_w) and (u, v) So we assume $m_{34} = 1$. Then there are only 11 unknowns. These 11 parameters have the constraint relationship among the variables. That is to say, by the space of more than 6 points and their image points coordinates, using the least square method, we can solve them. Then according to the variables of the 11 unknown parameters, the internal and external parameters of the camera are solved. The process is not required to solve the nonlinear equations, and the calculation accuracy is also higher.

4. Nonlinear Optimization Method

The experimental results show that the linear model does not consider the lateral and tangential distortion of the camera, in practice, the imaging geometry can not be clearly expressed. So the nonlinear optimization method considering the distortion is produced, and the following Eq. (8) is used to describe the nonlinear distortion:

$$\begin{cases} \overline{x} = x + \delta_x(x, y) \\ \overline{y} = y + \delta_y(x, y) \end{cases} \tag{8}$$

In Eq. (8):

($\overline{x}$, $\overline{y}$)- the ideal value of the coordinates of the image points.

(x, y) - the coordinates of the actual image points.

δ_x, δ_y The nonlinear distortion values are related to the position of the image points in the image. A formula is expressed as in Eq. (9):

$$\begin{cases} \delta_x(x,y) = k_1 x(x^2+y^2) + (p_1(3x^2+y^2) + 2p_2 xy) + s_1(x^2+y^2) \\ \delta_y(x,y) = k_2 y(x^2+y^2) + (p_2(3x^2+y^2) + 2p_1 xy) + s_2(x^2+y^2) \end{cases} \tag{9}$$

In Eq. (9):

$k_1 x(x^2+y^2)$, $k_2 y(x^2+y^2)$ -Radial distortion.

$(p_1(3x^2+y^2)+2p_2 xy)$, $(p_2(3x^2+y^2)+2p_1 xy)$ -Centrifugal distortion.

$s_1(x^2+y^2)$ - thin prism distortion.

$k_1, k_2, p_1, p_2, s_1, s_2, s_2(x^2+y^2)$ -Nonlinear distortion parameter.

Therefore, the nonlinear distortion and the parameters of the linear model a_x, a_y, u_0 and v_0, are the internal parameters of the nonlinear model. To solve this model, we use the linear model to calculate the initial parameters, and then use the iterative method to calculate the exact solution of these parameters.

5. Conclusion

In this paper, the color of artificial landmark is used as the basis of image segmentation, and its shape features are identified, which makes up for the deficiency of gray level segmentation, and captures the essential information of target extraction process, and improves the accuracy of recognition.

Object recognition based on prior knowledge is extracted from the image. Target recognition requires the use of different characteristics of the comprehensive feature comparison to overcome the use of a single feature caused by inaccurate identification.

Figure 2 represents the flow chart of object recognition based on color and shape features as follows:

(1) using the color feature to extract the target region, in the next step, the feature extraction is performed in the target area;

(2) the feature of target region is obtained by using the method of the target region extraction based on connectivity, and the shape feature is extracted by Hough transform;

(3) the recognition of the ball: according to the color and shape of the ball in the environment, it is necessary to judge whether the target's characteristic is in accordance with the characteristics of the ball. The condition is that the color is yellow, the region characteristic is $area > T_{area}$, the shape feature is $Num\_circle = 1$.

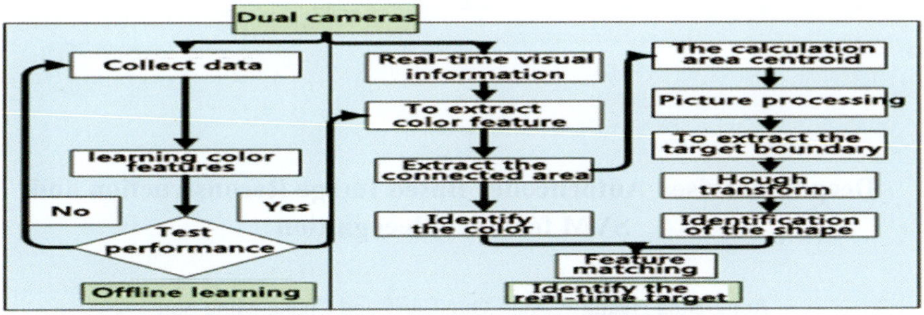

Fig. 2. Target recognition process chart

Experimental results are shown in Figure 3:

(a)Source image (b)Color recognition image (c)Image preprocessing (d)Shape extraction results

Fig. 3. Shape feature extraction results

References

1. Bamard S, etal. Computational stereo. ACM Computing Survegs, 1982, 14:553-572
2. Li Qi, Feng Huajun, Xu Zhihai, Huang Hongqiang. The computer deals with South Korea, stereo vision technology [J]. optical technology, 2007(5):71-73
3. Zuo Aiqiu,Wu Jiangning,Li Shilun,Luo Hanxiu.Binocular stereo vision measurement of the position and pose of Stewart platform[J]. Chinese term Journal Abstracts,Vol.5-1,1999
4. Stewart D. A platform with six degrees of freedom. Proc Inst Mech Eng, 1965/1966;180
5. Gao Qingji, Hong Bing Rong, Yu Feng Ruan. Based on heterogeneous binocular vision of autonomous soccer robot navigation [J]. Journal of Harbin Institute of technology.2003:35(9):21-24
6. Gao Qingji, Hong Bingrong, Ruan Yufeng. Navigation of autonomous soccer robot based on heterogeneous binocular vision [J]. Journal of Harbin Institute of Technology, 2003:35(9):21-24

Deep Supervised Autoencoder Based Image Reconstruction and SVM for Face Recognition

Rong-Bing Huang[1,a], Xiao-Qun Liu[2,b] and Chang-Ming Shu[1,c]

[1]*Key Laboratory of PR & IIP, Chengdu Univ*
Chengdu 610106, China
[2]*Psychological Health & Education Center, Chengdu Univ.,*
Chengdu 610106, China
E-mail: [a]huangrb2006@126.com, [b]xiaoqunliu118@126.com, [c]cmshu@cdu.edu.cn

In this paper, a novel method is proposed based on a deep supervised autoencoder (DSAE) image reconstruction for face recognition. Unlike conventional deep autoencoder based face recognition method, the label information and the reconstruction residual information are taken into account in the learning procedure. First, an Adaptive Deep Supervised Network Template (ADSNT) with the supervised autoencoder is defined which is trained for labeled face images. Then, ADSNT is performed on face images to obtain the residual images which are computed by subtracting reconstructed images from original images. Furthermore, the residual images are applied by LDA to derive the compact discriminant feature representation. Finally, the features are used to train and test SVM for classification. The experiments demonstrate that the proposed method achieves promising performance.

Keywords: Stacked Autoencoder; Image Reconstruction; Face Recognition.

1. Introduction

The face images in real world are affected by illuminations, poses, occlusions, and expressions. What's more, the difference of face images from the same person could be even larger than that from different ones[1]. Therefore, how to extract robust and discriminant features that make the intraspace compact and enlarge the margin between different people is a critical and difficult problem in face recognition. Up to now, various face representation methods have been introduced, including classical subspace-based dimension reduction approaches like principal component analysis (PCA), linear discriminant analysis (LDA), independent component analysis (ICA), and so on[1].

Currently, deep learning has demonstrated its great success in image representation[2],[3], and their fundamental ingredient is the training of a nonlinear feature extractor at each layer[4],[5]. After the layer-wise training of each building block and the building of a deep architecture, the output of the network is used for the image representation in the subsequent task. As a typical building block in deep neural networks, denoising auto-encoder (DAE)[6] extracts the features through a deterministic nonlinear mapping, and it is robust to the noises of the data. Image representations based on the DAE have shown good performance in many tasks, like object recognition, digit recognition, etc. Motivated by the success of DAE based deep neural networks, Gao et al.[3] proposed a supervised auto-encoder(SAE) to build the deep neural network, which firstly treated the faces with all type of variants like illuminations, expressions, poses as images contaminated by noises. With a SAE, the face without the variants can be recovered, meanwhile, robust features for image representation are also extracted.

Inspired by SAE, in this paper, we propose a novel method based on adaptive deep supervised auto-encoder image reconstruction and SVM for face recognition.

2. Work Related to DAE

DAE is an one-layer neural network, which is a recent variant of the conventional AE. It learns to try to recover the clean input data sample from its corrupted version. Let there be a total of k training samples. For the ith sample, let x_i denote the original input data. In DAE, the input data x_i is first corrupted by some pre-defined noise such as Gaussian noise or salt-and-pepper noise. Such a corrupted $\tilde{x}_i$ is used as the input of the encoder $h_i = f(\tilde{x}_i) = s_f(W\tilde{x}_i + b_f)$. Then the output of encoder h is input into the decoder $\hat{x}_i = g_i(h_i) = s_f(W'h_i + b_g)$. Here s_f and s_g are predefined activation functions of encoder and decoder respectively. $W \in R^{d_h \times d_x}$ and $W' \in R^{d_x \times d_h}$ are the network weights which denotes the weights for the encoder and decoder, respectively. $b_f \in R^{d_h}$ and $b_g \in R^{d_x}$ refer to the bias terms. d_x and d_h are the dimensionality of input data and the number of hidden nodes respectively. Based on the above definition, a DAE learns by solving the following (regularized) optimization problem:

$$\min_{W,W',b_f,b_g} \sum_{i=1}^{n} \left\| x_i - \hat{x}_i \right\|_2^2 + \frac{\lambda}{2}(\|W\|_F^2 + \|W'\|_F^2) \quad (1)$$

Here $\|\cdot\|_2^2$ is the reconstruction error and $\|\cdot\|_F$ denotes the Frobenius norm, λ is a parameter which balances the reconstruction loss and weight penalty terms. By reconstructing the clean input data from a corrupted version of it, a DAE is more effective than the conventional AE in discovering more robust features by preventing the AE from simply learning the identity mapping.

After learning f and g, the output of encoder h is used as the input of the next layer. By training such DAE layer by layer, stacked denoising auto-encoders (SDAE) are built.

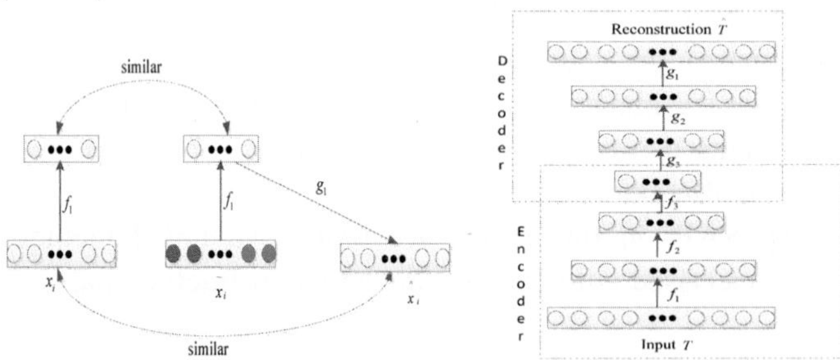

(a) (b)

Fig. 1. (a)Supervised auto-encoder(SAE) (b)Adaptive Deep Supervised Network Template

3. Proposed Method

3.1. *The adaptive deep supervised network template (ADSNT)*

As depicted in Figure 1(b), similar to [7], our ADSNT is a deep supervised auto-encoder(DSAE), which consists of two parts: an encoder and a decoder. Both of them have three hidden layers each, with a shared third layer (the central hidden layer). The basic SAE shown in Figure 1(a)[3] is comprised of the clean/"corrupted" data.

3.2. *Formulation of image reconstruction based on ADSNT*

Given a set of k classes training images which contain the gallery images (called clean data), probe images (called corrupted data) as well as their corresponding class labels y_c=[1,2, …,k]. We will use the data set to train ADSNT for feature extraction. We denote each probe image in this dataset as $\tilde{x}_i$, and its corresponding gallery image as x_i (i=1,2,…, N). It is desirable that x_i

and $\tilde{x}_i$ should be similarly. Therefore, following the work[4], we obtain the following formulation:

$$\arg\min_{\theta_{ADSNT}} J = \frac{1}{M}\sum_i \left\| x_i - \hat{x}_i \right\|_2^2 + \frac{\lambda_{\theta_W}}{M}\sum_i \left\| f(x_i) - f(\tilde{x}_i) \right\|_2^2 + \varphi\left(\left\|\theta_W\right\|_F^2 + \left\|\theta_W'\right\|_F^2 \right) \quad (2)$$

where $\theta_{ADSNT}=\{\theta_W,\theta_b\}$ are the parameters of ADSNT which is fined tune by learning. $\hat{x}_i$ is the reconstruction image of the corrupted image $\tilde{x}_i$. Like regularization parameter, λ_{θ_W} balances the similarity of the same person to preserve $f(x_i)$ and $f(\tilde{x}_i)$ as similarly as possible. $f(\cdot)$ is a non-linear activation function(typically a sigmoid or tangent hyperbolic). Similar to DAE, we introduce sparsity constraint on the activation of the hidden layer to enhance learning meaningful features. Then, we further obtain the following objection formulation:

$$\arg\min_{\theta_{ADSNT}} J_{reg} = J + \gamma(KL(\rho_x \,\|\, \rho_0) + KL(\rho_{\tilde{x}} \,\|\, \rho_0)) \quad (3)$$

where $\rho_x = \frac{1}{n}\sum_i f(x_i)$, $\rho_{\tilde{x}_i} = \frac{1}{n}\sum_i f(\tilde{x}_i)$, $KL(\rho \| \rho_0) = \sum_j (\rho_0 \log(\frac{\rho_0}{\rho_j}) + (1-\rho_0)\log(\frac{1-\rho_0}{1-\rho_j}))$

To solve above optimization problem, we employ the L-BFGS to learn parameters $\theta_{ADSNT}=\{\theta_W,\theta_b\}$.

After the parameters θ_{ADSNT} are learnt, we can use them to reconstruct the images. Then the residual images will be obtained by subtracting the reconstructed image $\hat{x}_i$ from the original image $\tilde{x}_i$, namely $\bar{x}_i \equiv \tilde{x}_i - \hat{x}_i$. It contains rich information for the individual identities, so we further extract face features from these residual faces.

3.3. *Flowchart of the proposed face recognition approach*

Our proposed face recognition flowchart is shown in Figure 2. To better train ADSNT, all images are needed to preprocess to remove the illumination effects possibly. Then, the preprocessed images are input to the ADSNT. After that, one can obtain the residual images, which are further applied by LDA[8] that can extract discriminative information and reduce the dimension to obtain the coefficient matrices. Finally, the features are utilized to train a classifier such as SVM for face recognition.

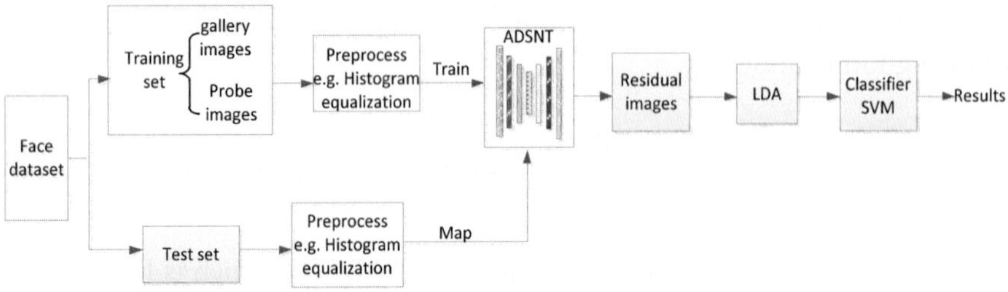

Fig. 2. Flowchart of the proposed ADSNT image reconstruction for face recognition

4. Experimental Results

In this section, we preliminarily make experiments on AR[9] face dataset which contains over 4,000 frontal faces taken from 126 subjects(70 men and 56 women) in two different sessions, and the images contain variances in occlusion, expression, and illumination. We randomly choose a half number of images from each subject to compose the training set, and the remaining images to compose the testing set.

4.1. *Experimental setup*

All the face images from the AR are cropped and converted to gray scale levels. The cropped gray scale images are then resized to 32×32. Thus the dimensionality of the input vector is 1024. Each image is preprocessed with histogram equalization to minimize illumination variations. For ADSNT, we train our deep model with 3 layers, where the number of hidden nodes for these layers are empirically set as [1024->800->300->40]. Because our experiments show that three hidden layers can get a sufficiently good performance. The parameter λ , ε are empirically set as 5, 0.001 and the weight corresponding to the *KL* divergency term γ is empirically set to be 0.01. We used the hyperbolic tangent function as the non-linear activation function. In our experiments, for each subject in the training set, we use the face images taken with the frontal or near frontal pose, neutral expression, and normal lighting condition as the galleries, and use the rest of the images as probes. For classification technique, we use SVMs with RBF kernel function to recognize face images.

4.2. *Results comparing with other methods*

We compare our proposed approach with several recently proposed methods including DAE with 10% masking noises followed by SRC[6], Template Deep Reconstruction Model(TDRM)[7]. We use the implementations of these compared methods provided by the respective authors. For all the compared methods, we use the default parameters recommended by the corresponding papers.

Table 1 tabulates the average identification rates with standard deviations of different methods. The results from Table 1 suggest that the proposed method outperforms the other methods and achieves the best average identification rates for most of the configurations of the training and testing set lengths.

Table 1 Comparisons of the mean identification rate and standard deviation(%)

Method	Identification rate(%)
DAE[6]	47.56 ± 2.2
TDRM[7]	84.70 ± 1.6
Our method	87.52 ± 1.6

References

1. W. Zhao, R.chellappa, P. Phillips, A. Rosenfeld. Face recognition: a literature survey, *ACM comuting surveys*, 35(2003)399-458.
2. A. Krizhevsky, I. Sutskever, G.E. Hinton, ImageNet classification with deep convolutional neural networks, *In: proc. Adv. Neural Inf. Process syst.* , 2012, pp.1527-1554.
3. S. Gao, Y. Zhang, K. Jia, J.Lu, Y. Zhang. Single sample face recognition via learning deep supervised autoencoders, *IEEE trans. Information forensics and security*, 10(10)(2015)2108-2118.
4. G.E.Hinton, R.R. Salakhutdinov, Reducing the dimensionality of data with neural networks, *Science*, 313(5786)(2006)504-507.
5. Y.Bengio, Practical recommendations for gradient-based training of deep architectures, In neural networks: tricks of the trade. Berlin, Germany: *Springer-Verlag*, 2012, pp.437-478.
6. P.Vincent, H. Larochelle, I.Lajoie, Y.Bengio, P.-A. Manzagol, Stacked denosing autoencoders: learning useful representations in a deep network with a local denoising criterions, *J. Mach. Learn. Res.* 11(5)(2010)3371-3408.
7. M. Hayat, M. Bennamoun, S. An, Learning non-linear reconstruction models for image set classification, *In CVPR*, 2014, pp.1915-1922.
8. P.N.Belhumeur, J.P.Kriegman, D.J. Kriegman, Egienfaces vs. Fisher faces: recognition using class specific linear projection, *IEEE Trans. Pattern Anal. Mach. Intell.* 19(7)(1997)711-720.
9. A. Martinez, R. Benavente, The AR face database, *CVC Tech. Rep.* #24, Jun. 1998.

Research on a New User Authentication Strategy for Rabbit Farm in the Context of Internet of Things

Zhi-Hui Wang[a], Jing-Jing Yang[b] and Ben-Zhen Guo[c]

School of Information Science and Engineering, Hebei North University
Zhangjiakou, Hebei, 07500, China
E-mail: [a]iowzh@126.com, [b]78z-yang@126.com, [c]996735169@qq.com

Aiming at the high overhead cost in a single-chip system when the traditional internet security strategy is used in a rabbit farm environmental monitoring system. This paper proposes an improved scheme to realize asymmetrical bi-directional security authentication and key negotiation based on a third party in the system. The experiment proves that such a design scheme can meet the design requirement of bidirectional authentication and key negotiation between the IoT gateway and the client APP with the aid of the central server of the system without the need to increase the single-chip computing capacity of the gateway and the system construction cost.

Keywords: Internet of Things; Security; User Authentication; Key Negotiation.

1. Introduction

In a rabbit farm environmental monitoring system designed based on the internet of things (IoT) technology, a large number of devices including the sensors and the environmental intervention controllers used in the rabbit hutches are connected to the internet [1-3] through the IoT gateway to realize the automatic acquisition of the environmental parameters in the rabbit hutch such as the temperature, the humidity and the concentration of harmful gases, which will also be submitted to the system server for storage. The server will automatically analyze the variation trend of the environmental parameters in the rabbit hutch and send the warning message to the users as soon as an unfavorable change, such as the temperature higher than 30°C [4-5], occurs to affect the normal growth of the rabbits. The users can receive the warning message from the system at anytime and anywhere through their mobile apps or on the web pages. Also they can impose a remote intervention to the internal environment of the rabbit hutch. For example, they can turn on the cooling fan to reduce the temperature in the rabbit hutch and control the temperature between 20°C and 30°C [6-7] that is favorable to the rabbits. Or they can turn on the ventilator fan to reduce the impact of the adverse environmental factors on the normal growth of the meat rabbits by reducing the ammonia concentration within the rabbit hutch.

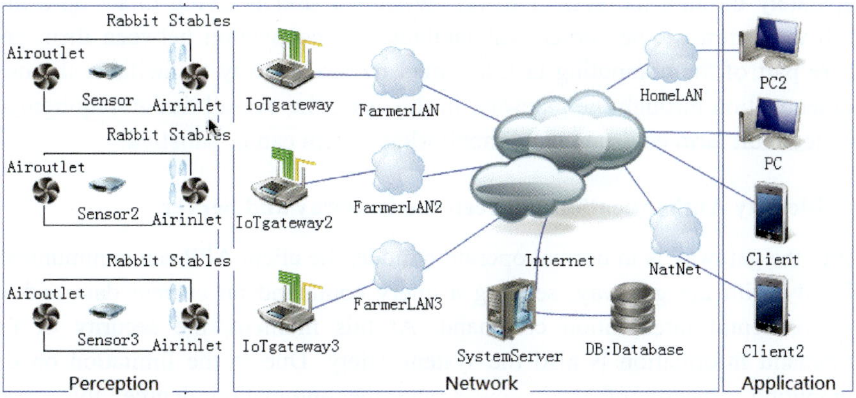

Fig. 1. Architecture diagram of the rabbit farm environmental monitoring system

Figure 1 shows the architecture of the rabbit farm environmental monitoring system. It consists of three layers, separately including the perception layer that is composed of different types of sensors and controllers, the application layer that is comprised of the early warning server and the client terminals as well as the network layer that consists of the IoT gateway, the system server and the network transmission at the client. All of these three layers collaborate closely with each other to achieve the system design objectives.

As the core activity of the IoT gateway doesn't require high computing power of the hardware, then a small embedded system will do. However in this way, the three main hardware devices including the client APP, the system server and the IoT gateway that constitute the network layer of the system will show the asymmetry in computing capacity. As the adoption of the traditional Internet-based system authentication strategy, such as vpn and ssl, will increase the traffic load on the gateway, then it's necessary to improve the computing power of the CPU on the gateway, expand the memory space and increase the amount of code for the gateway application program. Also the development efficiency must be enhanced for less maintenance cost.

2. Asymmetric User Authentication Strategy

In view of the deficiency of the traditional authentication strategy in solving the gateway-based user authentication problem found in a rabbit hutch environmental monitoring system, this paper proposed an improved strategy for user authentication based on the system server with the core idea provided as below: Firstly, complete the user authentication and gateway authentication separately through the system server. When the user is trying to set up a link with the gateway, the server will facilitate the connection between them and share part of the computing task assumed by the gateway to facilitate the user authentication through the gateway. In this way, the overall design requirement of the rabbit farm environmental monitoring system can be satisfied.

3. Identity Authentication Between the Gateway and Server

After the gateway is in normal operation mode, the client APP can communicate directly with the gateway, sending a query command on current data and an environmental intervention command. At this moment, the security of the command information is also the system safety. Due to the limitation on the computing capacity of the gateway and the automation degree, this paper systematically designs a user-gateway authentication flow based on the system server with the specific process provided as below.

(1) The client APP sends a request to the server for the linkage.

(2) The system server generates the gateway authentication information for the client and sends it to the client APP and the corresponding IoT gateway through the existing channel.

(3) After the client APP receives the user's gateway authentication information, use the message key to encrypt the user authentication information for the connection with the gateway of the appointed IP address.

(4) If the gateway verifies that the user authentication information matches, it will return TRUE and turn to the next step.

(5) The client will send command to the gateway via an encrypted message.

(6) The purpose of gateway decryption is to verify the validity of the command. If it's verified true, continue to execute the command and return the result. Otherwise, the command will be discarded.

4. Experiment

Figure 1 shows the system architecture of the rabbit farm environmental monitoring system for the construction of an experimental test platform in this paper. The system server is connected to the Internet via the 10MP dedicated fiber optic line with a fixed IP address. Also use the cell phone installed with Android 4.2 and the windowsPC to serve as the client platform. Deploy totally three sets of IoT gateways and perception subsystems in Yongli Meat Rabbit Farm located in Xuanhua County, Guoqiang Rabbit Farm located in Huai'an County and Hebei North University Meat Rabbit Breeding Lab. Both of the client terminal and gateway are connected to the Internet through ADSL. They are located behind the NAT device with a dynamically changeable IP address.

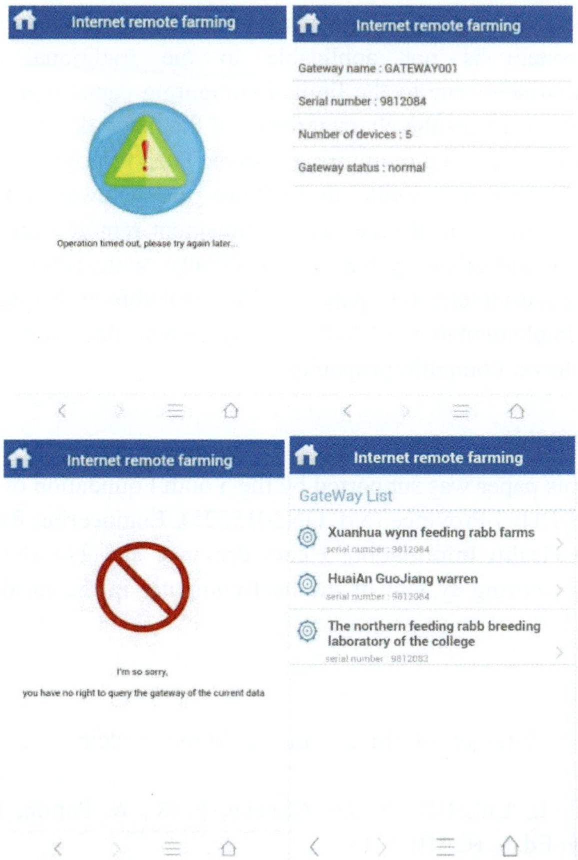

Fig. 2. Identity Authentication Between the Gateway and Server

Fig. 2 reveals the user authentication process through the gateway with the aid of the system server. The first picture shows a list of gateway that the Client APP is authorized for direct connection. The second picture prompts that the users are not allowed to query the current data from the appointed gateway. The third picture provides the current data information queried from the appointed gateway through the direct connection. The fourth picture shows a system prompt that the fan is turned on after the user has begun the ventilation operation. The fifth picture is a prompt about the operation timeout on the Client APP after the invalid request has been discarded by the gateway.

5. Conclusions

In view of the fact that the IoT gateway used in a rabbit farm environmental monitoring system is not applicable to the traditional internet-based authentication strategy due to the limited computing capacity and cost control, this paper firstly analyzes the characteristics of the network layer information in a rabbit farm environmental monitoring system. Then it proposes to use the APP installed in an Android mobile to facilitate the gateway authentication in addition to the utilization of gateway to implement remote user authentication strategy with the aid of the system server. Finally, with the construction of an experimental environment, this paper verifies that this authentication solution works in the implementation of IoT gateway design objectives on a hardware platform with lower computing capacity.

Acknowledgements

The work of this paper was supported by the Youth Foundation of the Education Department of Hebei Province (No. QN2015225), Engineering Research Center of Population Health Information, Hebei Province and The development and research of monitoring system of the host computer in the local area network (0801113B).

References

1. Kopetz, H. Internet of things. In Real-time systems. Springer US 307 (2011).
2. McNitt, J. I., Lukefahr, S. D., Cheeke, P. R., & Patton, N. M. Rabbit production Ed. 9. (CABI,2013).
3. G.Mingming,S. Liangshan.The Design of Wireless Smart Home System based on ZigBee. IACSIT. proceedings of 2010 3rd International Conference onComputer and Electrical Engineering **(2010).**
4. Chen zanmou. " The Influence of temperature factor on the fecundity of female rabbit meat " Livestock ecology,**(1994),** Vol.15, No. 4:9-11.

5. Ye, J., Wang, Y., & Long, N. Farmer initiatives and livelihood diversification: From the collective to a market economy in rural China. Journal of Agrarian Change, 9(2), 175 (2009).
6. Nolan, S., Unkovich, M., Yuying, S., Lingling, L., & Bellotti, W. Farming systems of the Loess Plateau, Gansu Province, China. Agriculture, ecosystems & environment, 124(1), 13(2008).
7. Cartuche, L., Pascual, M., Gómez, E. A., & Blasco, A. Economic weights in rabbit meat production. World Rabbit Science, 22(3), 165 (2014).
8. Apori, S. O., Hagan, J. K., & Osei, D. The growth and reproductive performance of different breeds of rabbits kept under warm and humid environments in Ghana. Online Journal of Animal and Feed Research, 4(3), 51(2014).

Optimize Choice Method of the Mission Load for Unmanned Ship-Based Helicopter

Jin-Zhu Men[a], Ke-Ming Yao[b] and Jian-Guo Wang[c]

Dalian Navy Academy, No. 667 Jiefang Road

Dalian, Liao Ning, China

E-mail: [a]mjzh_tougao@163.com, [b]seafish12@sina.com, [c]wangjianguo1981@163.com

The employment of mission load is very important to operational application of unmanned ship-based helicopter. Firstly, the actuality of unmanned ship-based helicopter and styles of anti-submarine load are analyzed, and then the fuzzy AHP is applied to resolve the problem. Furthermore, under the settled tactics background, the applied problems of anti-submarine load are optimized, and the feasibility and validity of the method are validated. It is a reference value to study on optimized choice of the mission load for unmanned ship-based helicopter.

Keywords: Mission Load; Unmanned Ship-based Helicopter; Fuzzy AHP.

1. Introduction

As the mission load of UAV has been modularized, there is no problem in the technique area to alter and transform different mission loads. Furthermore, considering anti-submarine operation is more complex than other combat mission, e.g. sea surveillance, the optimize choice method of the anti-submarine mission load for unmanned ship-based helicopter is focused on in the paper.

Anti-submarine search equipments: dipping sonar and sonobuoy.

Anti-submarine attack weapons: airborne torpedo and aerial depth bomb.

Although tactics and technique performances are different, the weight of the same type weapon is relative consistent. For example, airborne torpedo developed and used by different countries are almost 324mm light torpedo, their weight is about 200kg. Similarly, the weight of single sonobuoy is about 10kg, and the weight of single dipping sonar is 200kg approximately.

According to analysis above, it is assumed that the suitable research object is the unmanned ship-based helicopter with the ability of carrying 250kg mission load. Meanwhile, some types of anti-submarine mission load suited to unmanned ship-based helicopter have been chosen as follows.

The research type: 1 dipping sonar, or 25 sonobuoys.

The attack type: 1 airborne torpedo.

The research and attack combined type: 1 airborne torpedo and a few sonobuoys.

2. Optimize Choice Method

2.1. *Choice plan of mission load under tactics background*

Because the mission includes search and attack tasks, there must be two helicopters, one loads search equipments, the other loads airborne torpedo. "HA" represents one unmanned ship-based helicopter, and "HB" represents the other. Therefore, there are some projects about mission loads as follows.

Project I: HA carries one dipping sonar, and HB carries one torpedo.

Project II: HA carries 25 sonobuoys, and HB carries one torpedo.

Project III: HA carries one dipping sonar, and HB carries one torpedo and 5 sonobuoys.

Project IV: HA carries 25 sonobuoys, and HB carries one torpedo and 5 sonobuoys.

2.2. *Introduction of optimize choice method*

2.2.1. *Layer structure chart construction*

According to their properties, factors above-mentioned need to be layered to produce layer structure. The first layer is goal layer. There is only one goal in the layer. The second layer is middle layer, also can be called criterion layer in this problem. The last layer is called project layer, which is composed by preparative project, optional result, and index.

2.2.2. *Judgment matrix construction*

Interval number $\alpha=[\alpha^-,\alpha^+]=\{x|0<\alpha^- \leq x \leq \alpha^+\}$ can be regarded as a kind of special trapezoid fuzzy number $(\alpha^-,\alpha^-,\alpha^+,\alpha^+)$. The vector or matrix whose elements are interval number, is called interval number vector or interval number matrix.

On the basis of interval number, $A=(\alpha_{ij})_{n\times n}$ is constructed interval number judgment matrix, $\alpha_{ij}=(\alpha_{ij}^-,\alpha_{ij}^+)$, $\alpha_{ij}=1/\alpha_{ij}$. The bigger of value of α_{ij} represents that under the same criterion, compared between two projects, one with "i" is more important than the other with "j". The interval number judgment matrix is expressed,

$$A^- = (\alpha_{ij}^-)_{n\times n},\ A^+ = (\alpha_{ij}^+)_{n\times n},\ A = [A^-, A^+]$$

2.2.3. *Weight of each project to criterion establishment*

To the given interval number judgment matrix, $A = [A^-, A^+]$

1) solve normalized feature vector with positive component corresponding to the maximum eigenvalue of A^-, A^+, that is, x^-, x^+.

2) calculate α and β,

$$\alpha = \left[\sum_{j=1}^{n} \frac{1}{\sum_{i=1}^{n} a_{ij}^+}\right]^{1/2},\ \beta = \left[\sum_{j=1}^{n} \frac{1}{\sum_{i=1}^{n} a_{ij}^-}\right]^{1/2} \tag{1}$$

3) calculate weight coefficient vector $\omega = [\alpha x^-, \beta x^+]$.

2.2.4. *Interval number calculation and rank*

L_k is settled as certain layer, $2 \le k \le m$, m is the number of layers. All elements of L_k are $L_k = \{e_1^k, e_2^k, \cdots, e_{n_k}^k\}$.

Corresponding to each criterion $e_l^{k-1}(l = 1,2,\cdots,n_{k-1})$ in the superior layer $L_{k-1} = \{e_1^{k-1}, e_2^{k-1}, \cdots, e_{n_{k-1}}^{k-1}\}$, rank weight number in the L_k is $\omega_{il}(i=1,2,\cdots,n_k)$.

After the total weight of the supreme layer has been achieved, each interval number composed weight can be also achieved, $g_1^{k-1}, g_2^{k-1}, \cdots, g_{n_{k-1}}^{k-1}$. It can be inferred that the total composed weight in the L_k is

$$g_i^k = \sum_{j=1}^{n_{k-1}} g_j^{k-1}\omega_{ij}, (i = 1,2,\cdots,n_k) \tag{2}$$

According to uniform distribution situation of probability distribution method in the fuzzy ranking method, ranking exponential express of fuzzy number can be ranked. The ranking exponential of $g_i = [g_i^-, g_i^+]$ can be achieved.

$$m_u(g_i) = (g_i^- + g_i^+)/2, (i = 1,2,\cdots,n_m) \tag{3}$$

$$\sigma_u(g_i) = (g_i^+ - g_i^-)/(2\sqrt{3}), (i = 1,2,\cdots,n_m) \tag{4}$$

According to expressions (3) and (4), each preparative element can be ranked and optimized.

3. Mission Load the Calculation Example

3.1. *Element simulation*

The four projects mentioned in Section II are settled as PI, PII, PIII and PIV. Four indexes shown in the table 1 are analyzed and compared. Simultaneously, these four projects are simulated, also shown in the table 1.

Table 1. The simulation of load applying factors

	Search time	Find probability	Cooperation difficulty	Hit probability
PI	90	0.65	level 1	0.8
PII	120	0.68	level 2	0.8
PIII	80	0.76	level 4	0.8
PIV	100	0.72	level 3	0.8

3.2. *FAHP algorithm implement*

3.2.1. *Layer model construction*

Decision-making goal: optimal implement of mission load.

Criterion layer: {search time, find probability, cooperation difficulty, hit probability}. Project layer: {PI, PII, PIII, PIV.}.

The layer model chart is shown in Figure 1.

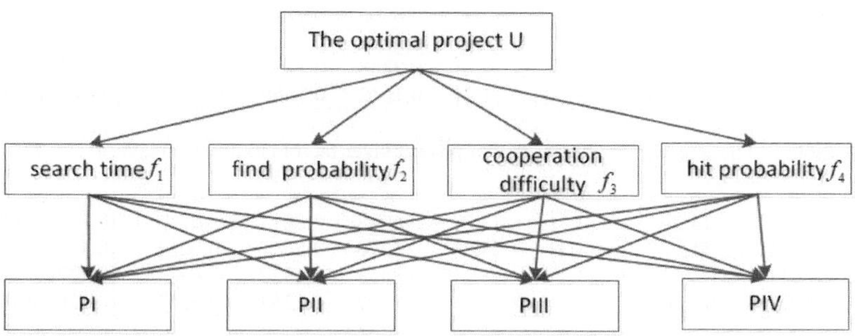

Fig. 1. The simulation of load applying factors

3.2.2. *Judgment matrix construction*

According to the importance of four indexes of criterion layer to the optimal project, the interval number judgment matrix of project layer to goal layer is achieved by compared between two projects, shown in the table 2.

Table 2. The interval number judgment matrix of criterion layer f to decision-making layer u

u	f_1	f_2	f_3	f_4	x^-	x^+	α, β	g_j
f_1	[1,1]	[2,3]	[5,3]	[3,4]	0.8305	0.8429	$\alpha =$	[0.8158,0.8364]
f_2	[1/2,1/3]	[1,1]	[4,3]	[1,2]	0.4450	0.4343	0.9823	[0.4371,0.4310]
f_3	[1/5,1/3]	[1/4,1/3]	[1,1]	[1,3]	0.1774	0.2751	$\beta =$	[0.1743,0.2730]
f_4	[1/3,1/4]	[1,1/2]	[1,1/3]	[1,1]	0.2841	0.1586	0.9924	[0.2791,0.1574]

According to simulation result, under the restriction of every index of criterion layer, the interval number judgment matrix of criterion layer is achieved by compared between two projects, shown in the table 3 to table 6.

3.2.3. *Weight calculation*

Weight vector of each interval number judgment matrix can be calculated, shown in relevant tables.

Table 3. The interval number matrix of project layer facrors to criterion layer factor f1

u	f_1	f_2	f_3	f_4	x^-	x^+	α, β	g_j
f_1	[1,1]	[5,3]	[2,3]	[4,5]	0.8801	0.8576	$\alpha =$	[0.8717,0.8453]
f_2	[1/5,1/3]	[1,1]	[1,2]	[3,4]	0.3043	0.4194	0.9905	[0.3014,0.4134]
f_3	[1/2,1/3]	[1,1/2]	[1,1]	[2,3]	0.3308	0.2732	$\beta =$	[0.3277,0.2693]
f_4	[1/4,1/5]	[1/3,1/4]	[1/2,1/3]	[1,1]	0.1532	0.1181	0.9856	[0.1517,0.1164]

Table 4. The interval number matrix of project layer facrors to criterion layer factor f2

u	f_1	f_2	f_3	f_4	x^-	x^+	α, β	g_j
f_1	[1,1]	[6,7]	[3,5]	[2,3]	0.8605	0.9157	$\alpha =$	[0.8115,0.8464]
f_2	[1/6,1/7]	[1,1]	[3,4]	[4,5]	0.3931	0.3454	0.9431	[0.3707,0.3196]
f_3	[1/3,1/5]	[1/3,1/4]	[1,1]	[5,4]	0.2868	0.1757	$\beta =$	[0.2705,0.1624]
f_4	[1/2,1/3]	[1/4,1/5]	[1/5,1/4]	[1,1]	0.1512	0.1060	0.9234	[0.1426,0.0980]

Table 5. The interval number matrix of project layer facrors to criterion layer factor f3

u	f_1	f_2	f_3	f_4	x^-	x^+	α, β	g_j
f_1	[1,1]	[4,3]	[2,1]	[3,2]	0.8018	0.6813	$\alpha =$	[0.7425,0.6371]
f_2	[1/4,1/3]	[1,1]	[5,3]	[4,3]	0.5270	0.5647	0.9261	[0.4881,0.5281]
f_3	[1/2,1]	[1/5,1/3]	[1,1]	[3,4]	0.2453	0.4322	$\beta =$	[0.2272,0.4042]
f_4	[1/3,1/2]	[1/4,1/3]	[1/3,1/4]	[1,1]	0.1387	0.1753	0.9351	[0.1285,0.1639]

Table 6. The interval number matrix of project layer facrors to criterion layer factor f4

u	f_1	f_2	f_3	f_4	x^-	x^+	α, β	g_j
f_1	[1,1]	[1,1]	[1,1]	[1,1]	0.5000	0.5000	$\alpha =$	[0.5000,0.5000]
f_2	[1,1]	[1,1]	[1,1]	[1,1]	0.5000	0.5000	1.0000	[0.5000,0.5000]
f_3	[1,1]	[1,1]	[1,1]	[1,1]	0.5000	0.5000	$\beta =$	[0.5000,0.5000]
f_4	[1,1]	[1,1]	[1,1]	[1,1]	0.5000	0.5000	1.0000	[0.5000,0.5000]

3.2.4. *Rank*

According to equation (2), the total composed weight to the goal layer can be calculated.

$g_1 = [0.6063, 0.6022]$ $g_2 = [0.2109, 0.1913]$

$g_3 = [0.1103, 0.0365]$ $g_4 = [0.1318, 0.1016]$

According to equations (3) and (4), the rank exponential calculated.

PI: $m_u(g_1) = 0.6043$, $\sigma_u(g_1) = 0.0012$ PII: $m_u(g_2) = 0.2011$, $\sigma_u(g_2) = 0.0057$

PIII: $m_u(g_3) = 0.0734$, $\sigma_u(g_3) = 0.0213$ PIV: $m_u(g_4) = 0.1167$, $\sigma_u(g_4) = 0.0087$

3.3. *The result analysis*

Compared data above, the rank result of four mission load applied projects to the goal is, PI, PII, PIV, PIII. Therefore, under the given tactics background, the optimal project is PI, that is, HA carries one dipping sonar, and HB carries one torpedo. Contrast to table 1, it can be found that the calculation result is similar to people's intuitive thinking.

4. Conclusion

On the basis of unmanned ship-based helicopter current situation, the problem of application of the mission load has been researched with FAHP. Four anti-submarine load have been optimized chosen under certain tactics background. While, it is hard to confirm many factors in the actual operation, for example, environment, opponent, etc. Furthermore, the search method and probability may be different in distinct situation. It is worth to further research. The research is supported by Dalian Naval Academy Scientific Research Foundation under grant 2015026.

References

1. B. Han. "Task load and development analysis of tactical UAV", in Ship Electronic Engineering, vol. 27, no. 3, pp. 31-35, Mar. 2007.
2. Z. H. Cai, R. Y. Yan, and Y. X. Wang. "Task planning method for muti-payload remote sensing UAV", in Journal of Shanhai Jiaotong University, vol. 45, no. 2, pp. 267-271, Feb. 2011.
3. Y. Y. Hua, Y. J. Wu, and X. M. Dong. "A new method of variable structure control system based on lines cluster approaching theory", in *Proc. 2014 IEEE Chinese Guidance, Navigation and Control conf.* pp.468-473.
4. J. J. Zhang. "Fuzzy analytical hierarchy process", in Fuzzy Systems and Mathematics, vol. 12, no. 2, pp. 80-88, Jun. 2000.
5. Y. M. Zhou and W. H. Li. "Enhanced FAHP and its application to task scheme evaluation", in Computer Engineering and Application, vol. 44, no.5, pp. 212-214, May. 2008.

Research of Robot Tutorial Software Systems

Huan-Xia Feng[1,a] and Jian Zhang[2,b]
[1]Foshan Ebell science and technology co. Ltd, No. 133 Jihua Road Foshan, Guangdong, China
[2]Guangdong Vocational Technology Institute, No. 28 Jiangwan three-way Foshan, Guangdong, China
E-mail: [a]67222896@qq.com, [b]zj3319896@163.com

An independent server program of drawing panel based on the original software system of SCARA2-DOF Googol robot is developed in this paper through utilizing the common module mode of Windows platform — DLL (Dynamic Linked Library). It is not only complex mathematic graph but also arbitrary hand drawing with mouse can be realized conveniently. This software operating system has good expansibility and widespread applicability. Besides complex mathematic 2-dimension graph, arbitrary hand drawing with mouse can be realized conveniently comparing with the original simple tutorial function.

Keywords: Two Dimension of Freedom Robot; Dynamic Linked Library; Man-machine Interface; Tutorial Function; Hand Drawing.

1. Introduction

In 1960, American Unimation Corporation developed the first robot prototype according to Devol's controllable mechanical arm idea and manufactured Unimate robots. Meanwhile, AMF Corporation designed and manufactured another programmable robot Versatran in a form of cylindrical coordinate. As the first most famous industrial robots applied till now, the above two robots successfully replace workers for transfer, welding, painting, etc. in the automobile production line through "tutorial reproduction", and present good economic benefit, reliability and flexibility in operation. In 80s of the 20th century, development and wide application of computer technology and power electronics greatly widely and deeply extended the robot technology. Currently, the widely applied robots include the industrial mechanical arm manufactured by American Adept Corporation, Motoman series industrial mechanical arm manufactured by Japanese YASKAWA, industrial mechanical arm manufactured by Swiss ABB Corporation, etc. For high system safety & reliability and convenient use, closed architecture, dedicated control software and hardware are adopted for these industrial robot systems mainly oriented to industrial application[1]. Joint structure design similar to Adept SCARA robot is adopted for GRB200 robot manufactured by Googol Technology (Shenzhen) Ltd., and simple point-to-point transfer can be finished with such device and supporting software, but it is fairly difficult to realize complex tutorial task due to software system limitation, so it is necessary to extend tutorial function maximally without changing the original system. Based on original software system of 2-DOF robot, utilizing the standard Windows operating system environment, an individually and easily extendable man-machine interface and convenience operations are provided by means of dynamic-linked-library. Not only complex mathematic 2-dimension graph but also arbitrary hand drawing with mouse can be realized conveniently comparing with the original simple tutorial function.

1.1. *Operating principle of mechanical arm*

2-DOF mechanical arm composed of two rotary joints, is driven by AC servo motor and harmonic reducer. Together with incremental photoelectric coded disk on the motor, the joint control axis installed with photoelectric limit switch is used to relatively locate the robot control axis so as to ensure joint axis travel range. The robot motion control system includes such hardware as universal PC, DSP high-performance multi-axis motion controller, motor driver, interface circuit board control cabinet and robot body[2].

For the projection of 2-DOF mechanical arm into plane coordinates as shown in Figure 1, the solid line represents the mechanical arms — mechanical arm 1 started from the origin and mechanical arm 2 connected thereto, wherein the drawing pen installed at the top end of mechanical arm 2 is used for drawing. The combined motion of two mechanical arms must be analyzed and controlled for correct locus motion. Limited to plane motion, the plane geometry method can be directly used for finding the joint angle for the mechanical arms.

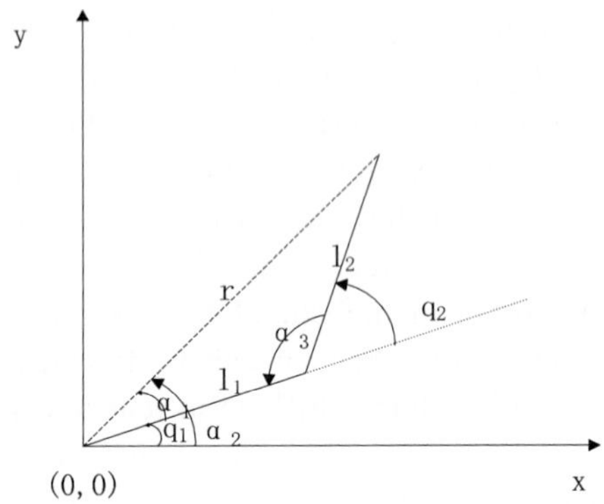

Fig. 1. Projection of 2-DOF mechanical arm in plane coordinates

The kinematic positive solution of the endpoint coordinate of mechanical arm 2 can be obtained according to Figure 2:

$$\begin{cases} l_1\cos q_1 + l_1\cos(q_1 + q_2) \\ l_1\sin q_1 + l_2\sin(q_1 + q_2) \end{cases} \tag{1}$$

Where l1 and l2 are respectively the connecting rod lengths of robot joints 1 and 2, mm; q1 and q2 are radians. The kinematic inverse solution is as in Eq. (2):

$$\begin{cases} r^2 = x^2 + y^2 \\ l_1^2 + l_2^2 - r^2 = 2l_1l_2\cos\alpha_3 \\ \sin\alpha_3 = \sqrt{1 - \cos^2\alpha_3} \\ \sin\alpha_1 = \frac{l_2\sin\alpha_3}{r} \\ r^2 + l_1^2 - l_2^2 = 2ri_1\cos\alpha_1 \\ \alpha_1 = \mathrm{atan2}(\sin\alpha_1, \cos\alpha_1) \\ \alpha_2 = \mathrm{atan2}(y, x) \end{cases} \tag{2}$$

Accordingly, the kinematic inverse solution expression is obtained as in Eq. (3):

$$\begin{cases} q_1 = \alpha_1 - \alpha_2 \\ q_1 = \mathrm{atan2}\big((y - l_1\sin q_1), (x - l_1\cos q_1)\big) - q_1 \end{cases} \tag{3}$$

Where α tan2(y, x) is the mathematical function for calculating the arc tangent of y/x (unit: radian), with value range of $(-\frac{\pi}{2}, \frac{\pi}{2})$.

The original system is only provided with several kinds of simple drawing demo software. We expect to add other curvilinear equations and functions in the original man-machine interface to make users select the added curvilinear equations and freely draw in the effective range even with mouse so as to finish the designated tasks through such mechanical arm. Theoretically, for a given group of rectangular coordinate data, the system obtains interpolation position sequence p[n]=(x[n], y[n]) and interpolation speed sequence in the rectangular coordinate space through locus interpolation, and then formula (2) is adopted for the kinematic inverse solution of each pairs of interpolation position and speed to obtain target joint position q[n]=(q1[n], q2[n]) and speed of the robot. Finally, joint position and joint speed are input as the reference signal into the motion driver to drive the motion platform. According to previous and current q1 and q2, formula (1) is adopted to obtain the rectangular coordinate data for current position through the kinematic positive solution.

2. Graphical Tutorial System Design

Hierarchical structure is adopted for the whole system, as shown in Figure 2. Universal PC is taken as the master controller and the main control program of the robot runs thereon to provide user interface, finish task planning, kinematic positive/inverse solution, coordinate transformation, etc., and issue robot joint tasks (speed and acceleration for the motion to a certain position) to the motion controller. As a subordinate controller, DSP high-performance motion controller employs certain control strategy to control joint motor motion.

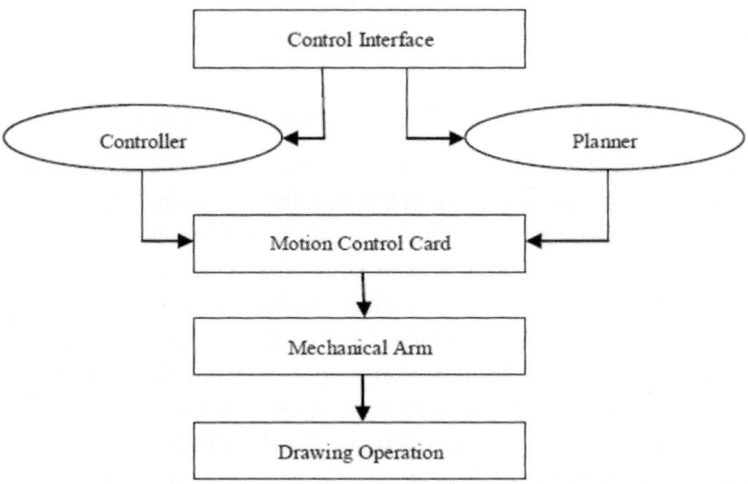

Fig. 2. Schematic diagram of graphical tutorial system structure

PC master controller communicates with DSP subordinate motion controller through PC bus, wherein the motion controller provides the drive program function library in the operating system and the master controller calls the function library to issue tasks and detect the command execution state. The control signal of DSP controller is sent to various joint motor drivers in the control cabinet for driving the robot joint motor after operational amplification. Hierarchical independence is realized in the motion control system through such hierarchical structure design. The controlled objects of the master controller and DSP motion controller are respectively robot joint and specific motor control axis between which the corresponding relationship is determined by robot model, thus realizing motion controller universalization.

It is not easy for general mechanical arms able to realize point-to-point motion to finish the motion among multiple points. Similarly, 2-DOF mechanical arm must be moved to corresponding coordinate positions by the sequence contrary to the practical operations, and these coordinates should be recorded to realize point-to-point motion through playback. In tutorial process, for moving the mechanical arms to accurate coordinate points, mechanical arms 1 and 2 must be cooperatively moved, usually for several times. In case of complex operation tasks (dozens of tutorial points or with the requirements for the curvilinear motion of the mechanical arm), the tutorial process will become very long and tedious. For tutorial process simplification, an independent drawing panel is added to the original control panel to make the mechanical arms not only conveniently finish common tutorial tasks but also have the ability for complex mathematic arbitrary hand drawing, thus becoming more competent for more complex operation tasks.

3. Software Implementation of Arbitrary Graphical Tutorial System

Software principle diagram of the graphical tutorial system is as shown in Figure 3. Through function addition, the robot has three drawing operation modes: tutorial playback, standard curve drawing and mouse drawing[3]. In any above mode, a group of rectangular coordinate data is finally given after corresponding operation. Specifically, the interpolation position sequence and the speed sequence are obtained in the rectangular coordinate space through the locus interpolation of this group of data, then target joint position and speed of the robot are obtained through the kinematic inverse solution, and finally joint position and speed are input as the reference signals into the motion controller to drive the motion platform. Before tutorial playback, the joint position of current mechanical arm must be obtained through Record button in order to obtain the tutorial points through the kinematic positive solution[4].

For convenient updating and function extension in future, the designed drawing panel with new functions is independent of the original control system.

Utilizing common module idear of Windows system, this drawing panel is designed in Visual C++ programming environment as MFC based DLL (Dynamic Linked Library) service program. If such function is needed during original control system operation, this service program can be dynamically loaded and automatically unloaded after drawing operation. DLL service program mainly includes a property sheet (CPropertySheet) CPaneSheet with two property pages — (CPropertyPage) CDrawPane and CNormalPane, wherein the former one is the dialog box for drawing free curves and the latter one is the dialog box for drawing standard curves. As extension classes, classes CPaneSheet, CDrawPane and CNormalPane must be manually modified in the generated DLL project, and AFX-EXT-CLASS should be added during class declaration. Head files of pane.h (head files of classes CDrawPane and CNormalPane) and panesheet.h must be copied under the directory of the project files of the original control system.

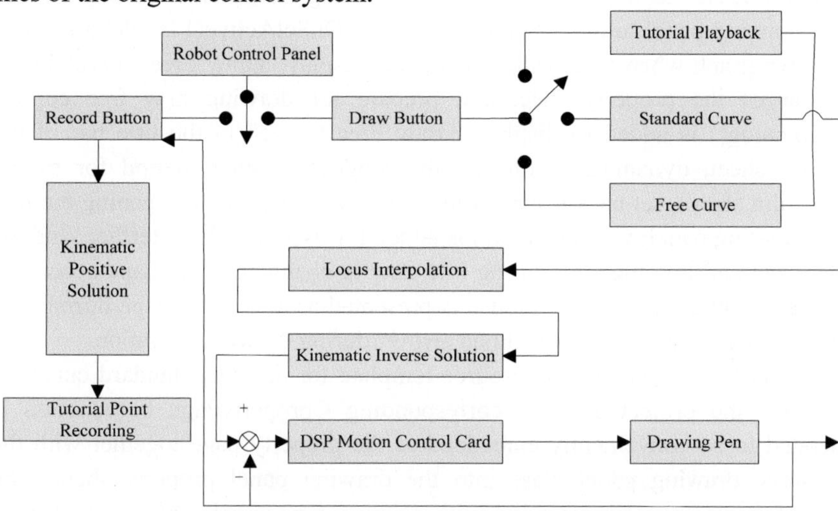

Fig. 3. Software principle diagram of graphical tutorial system

Firstly, after the establishment of MFC based extended DLL project, the dialog box resource template for drawing free curves is added to the project and the corresponding CpropertyPage based class is generated to be conveniently embedded as the property page into the property sheet in future for processing. If not starting drawing in the free curve drawing panel, the user can click the mouse and move it for drawing operation, and clear the existing graph; during drawing operation, the user can click the mouse to finish the drawing operation and it is forbidden to move the graph with mouse. If drawing is allowed at present, the user can move the mouse in the free curve drawing panel to save the product of the scale factor and the difference between current mouse coordinate and drawing start point (the coordinate point of the first mouse click point is regarded as the start point, namely zero point) in arrays posInfoX and posInfoY, and meanwhile display the title bars thereof in the property sheets for user's convenient observation, wherein posInfoX and posInfoY are dynamically adjusted according to the number of the locus points currently obtained. When the point number is over the maximum value (MAXLEN, set by the developer) allowed by the system, current drawing operation will be forced to be ended. Therefore, OnLButtonDown() and OnMouseMove() are added to realize above function. The free curve drawing panel is a property page of the whole drawing panel property sheet, so it is necessary to consider the cases of switching this page to other pages or reactivating this page. Specifically, OnKillActive() is added to release memory space and clear some flag bits when switching the free curve drawing panel to another property page; OnSetActive() is added to clear the drawn graph when reactivating this page, display "Draw Free Curve" in the title bar of the property sheet and prepare for drawing new free curves; OnInitDialog() is added to display "Draw Free Curve" in the title bar of the property sheet, dynamically allocate the program running period for saving locus point arrays, set background color, etc. at the first time of opening the free curve drawing panel; OnSetCursor() is added for user-friendly interface, and the system can call this function during idle time to change mouse shape according to current operation state: the mouse is presented as a "cross" shape during idle operation but as an "upwards inclined arrow" during drawing operation.

Secondly, the dialog box resource template for drawing standard curves is added for the project and the corresponding CpropertyPage based class is generated to be conveniently embedded as the property page together with the free curve drawing panel class into the drawing panel property sheet. The standard curve panel is provided with a curve type combo box and a graph preview window, and the user can freely select curve types in the combo box, and the panel can call corresponding curve function according to user's current choice to obtain a series of discrete points and finally display the graph corresponding to current curve type. Therefore, OnSelchangeComboNormal Sel() and OnUpdatePrev() and the following six drawing functions are added: OnDrawCircle(), OnDrawFourrose(), OnDrawHeart(), OnDrawSquare(), OnDrawEllipse() and OnDrawTriangle(). The above drawing functions can obtain the discrete points according to the corresponding curvilinear equation and save them in the standard arrays; OnUpdatePrev() function is used to update the graph in the preview window according to the data in current locus array.

OnInitDiaLog(), OnKillActive() and OnSetActive() of this standard curve drawing panel are similar with those of the free curve drawing panel.

Then, the drawing panel property sheet class is established, and the property pages of above free curve drawing panel and standard curve drawing panel are embedded into this property sheet. "Apply" button on the drawing panel is selected to activate OnApply() to send corresponding drawing operation command to the main window of the original control system according to current active page. For obtaining the main window handle of the client program to realize the communication between DLL service program and the client program of the original control system, GetClientWnd() member function is added and the client program can call this function during running to obtain the main window of the original control system.

Finally, the project files of the original control system are slightly modified. First, a new menu item is added in the project, the message processing function is also added, and the drawing panel service program is loaded in this function. Second, OnDrawPaneApplied() and OnNormalPaneApplied() for processing the drawing commands are added respectively for the free curve drawing panel and the standard curve drawing panel, and they can start the mechanical arm to draw in the control platform according to current curve locus. Third, the head files (Pane.h and PaneSheet.h) of the extended class, library file (*.LIB) and DLL files (*.DLL) under the directory of the drawing panel service project are copied to the directory of the control system service project. Fourth, the project is recompiled and reconnected. In future, under the condition of not changing the head files ---- Pane.h and PaneSheet.h of the extended class, it is only necessary to modify the drawing panel service project and then update *.LIB and *.DLL files under the directory of the original control system project to update the drawing panel.

4. Conclusion

An independent server program of drawing panel based on the original software system of SCARA 2-DOF Googol robot is developed in this paper through utilizing the common module mode of Windows platform ---- DLL (Dynamic Linked Library). Not only complex mathematic graph but also arbitrary hand drawing with mouse can be realized conveniently. Furthermore, this control system has good expansibility and widespread applicability, network and vision function can be further added with the same idea.

References

1. Yin Jiying, He Guangping, Joint Robot [M]. Beijing: Chemical Industry Press, 2003.
2. Du Haofan, Cong Shuang, Li Zexiang, et al. A 4-DOF Robot System for Handling and Assembling Operations [J]. Manufacturing Automation, 2003, 25(7): 33-37.
3. Googol Technology (Shenzhen) Ltd., User Manual for Mechanical Arm [Z]. 2003.
4. Xiong Youlun. Robot Operation [M]. Wuhan, Hubei Science & Technology Press, 2002

Big Data Local-Loop Particle Filter Based on the Artificial Fish Algorithm

Jian Yu[1,a] and Yu Yan[2,b]

[1]Education Technology College, Shenyang Normal University
Shenyang, China
[2]Software College, Shenyang Normal University
Shenyang, China
E-mail: [a]davidyu0566@sina.com, [b]ybrady1234@126.com

In this paper, a big data novel filtering method is proposed– Local-loop Particle Filter Based on the Artificial Fish Algorithm (LPF-AF) for nonlinear dynamic systems. Particle filtering algorithm has been widely used in solving nonlinear/non Gaussian filtering problems. The proposal distribution is the key issue of the particle filtering, which will greatly influence the performance of algorithm. In the proposed LPF-AF, the local searching of AF is used to regenerate sample particles, which can make the proposal distribution closer to the poster distribution. There are mainly two steps in the proposed filter. In the first step of LPF-AF, extended Kalman filter was used as proposal distribution to generate particles, then means and variances of the proposal distribution can be calculated. In the second step, some of the particles move toward to the particle with the biggest weights. The proposed LPF-AF algorithm was compared with several other filtering algorithms and the experimental results show that means and variances of LPF-AF are lower than other filtering algorithms.

Keywords: Big Data; Filtering Algorithm; Particle Filtering; Extended Kalman Filter; Artificial Fish Algorithm.

1. Introduction

In the filtering field, Kalman filtering is the most famous filtering method solving linear gauss issues. But in the real world, most filtering problems are non-linear, and non-linear filtering has a wide range of applications in many filed such as statistical signal processing [1], finance [2], target tracking [3], et al. Extended Kalman filtering (EKF) is a important non-linear filtering method, which uses the 2-order truncation of Kalman filtering to draw up to the non-linear feature of some problems. Due to the 2-order truncation in EKF, the accuracy is low, in some high linear environment, the EKF often fails. Particle filtering (PF) is a new type of filtering method, which samples points to draw up to the poster distribution. The key issue of PF is the choice of proposal distribution. Until now, many methods, such as EKF, UKF and some mixed algorithms are used to generate proposal distribution, which greatly improve the performance of PF. Artificial Fish (AF) is a new type of swarm intelligence algorithm. In the AF, every fish has a certain view sight range and only can get information from other fishes in this range. After defining the fitness, these fishes always try to get the better region using try-out method, which means that when a fish wants to move, it tries to move several times and choose the best destination it can get. This process can be regarded as 'local only' (compared to the well known 'social only') model with try-out action.

In this paper, we proposed big data's novel filtering method – Local-loop Particle Filter Based on the Artificial Fish Algorithm (LPF-AF) for nonlinear dynamic systems. Particle filtering algorithm has been widely used in solving nonlinear/non Gaussian filtering problems. The proposal distribution is the key issue of the particle filtering, which will greatly influence the performance of algorithm. In the proposed LPF-AF, the local searching of AF is used to regenerate sample particles, which can make the proposal distribution more closed to the poster distribution. There are mainly two steps in the proposed filter. In the first step of LPF-AF, extended filter was used as proposal distribution to generate particles, then means and variances of the proposal distribution can be calculated. In the second step, some particles move to toward the particle with the biggest weights. The proposed LPF-AF algorithm was compared with other several filtering algorithms and the experimental results show that means and variances of LPF-AF are lower than other filtering algorithms.

The remaining of the paper is organized as follows: a brief description of GPF is presented in Section 2. The details of the new PF this paper proposed – LPF-AF is presents in Section 3. In Section 4 the proposed algorithm is compared to other several different filtering algorithms, finally, we give some concluding remarks in section 5.

2. Generic Particle Filter and Artificial Fish

2.1. *Generic particle filter*

The problem being addressed here is an estimating problem of the state of a system as a set of observations becomes available on-line, which can be expressed as follows:

$$x_t = f(x_{t-1}) + w_{t-1}$$
$$y_t = h(u_t, x_t) + v_t \tag{1}$$

$x_t \in \Re^{n_x}$, $y_t \in \Re^{n_y}$, $u_t \in \Re^{n_u}$, $v_t \in \Re^{n_v}$ are the state of the system, the output observations, the input observations, the process noise and the measurement noise. The mappings:

$f : \Re^{n_x} * \Re^{n_x} \mapsto \Re^{n_x}$ and $h : \Re^{n_x} * \Re^{n_v} \mapsto \Re^{n_y}$ represent the deterministic process and measurement models. In the filtering paradigm, the posterior distribution is updated recursively over the current state x_t given all observations $Z_t = \{z_i\}_{i=1}^{t}$ up to and including time *t*. Using Monte Carlo sampling points, particle filter executes the filtering process by generating weighted sampling points of state variances recursively. Generic particle filter algorithm can be predicted as follows [6]:

Initialization

For each particle

draw the states $x_0^{(i)}$ from the prior $p(x_0)$;

End

For each loop

importance sampling step

For each particle

sample $\hat{x}_0^{(i)} \sim q(x_t \mid x_{0:t-1}^{(i)}, y_{1:t})$

End

For each particle

evaluate the importance weights up to a normalizing constant:

$$w_t^{(i)} = w_{t-1}^{(i)} \frac{p(y_t \mid x_t^{(i)}) p(\hat{x}_t^{(i)} \mid x_{t-1}^{(i)})}{q(\hat{x}_t^{(i)} \mid \hat{x}_{0:t-1}^{(i)}, y_{1:t})} \tag{3}$$

For each particle, normalize the importance weights:

$$\tilde{w}_t^{(i)} = w_{t-1}^{(i)}[\sum_{j=1}^{N} w_t^{(j)}]^{-1} \tag{4}$$

// Re-sample

Eliminate the samples with low importance weights and multiply the samples with high importance weights, to obtain N random samples $x_{0:k}^{(i)}$ approximately distributed according to $p(x_{0:k} \mid z_{1:k})$.

Assign each particle an equal weight: $w_t^i = 1/N$.

When executing particle filtering, the choice of the proposal distribution is very important. Usually, the transition prior distribution is chosen to be the proposal distribution:

$$q(x_t \mid X_{t-1}, Y_t) = p(x_t \mid x_{k-1}) \tag{5}$$

2.2. *Artificial fish algorithm*

Artificial Fish (AF) is a new type of swarm intelligence algorithm. In the AF, every fish has a certain view sight range and only can get information from other fishes in this range. After defining the fitness, these fishes always try to get the better region using try-out method, which means that when a fish wants to move, it tries to move several times and choose the best destination it can get. This process can be regarded as 'local only' (compared to the well known 'social only') model with try-out action. Artificial fish state is denoted by $X = (x_1, x_2, ..., x_n)$; the density of food of the current location is denoted by $Y = f(x)$. The distance of any two fishes is denoted by $d_{i,j} = \| X_i - X_j \|$. The view range of fish is Visual. And the max speed of fish is denoted by Step. There are four typical actions of fish in the AF:

- Searching food: fish always wants to move the location with higher density of food, and it sees the range of Visual, and can try some predefined time, if finally it cannot get a better location, it will move randomly.
- Assembling: if there are some other fishes in Visual, and the density of fishes is smaller than some predefined threshold, the fish will move to the center of these fishes, otherwise it will conduct the action of searching food.
- Chasing: if there are some fishes in the Visual, and the density of fish A of the location with highest density of food, the fish will move to the fish A, otherwise it will conduct the action of searching food.
- Randomly moving: it is the simplest method, the fish chooses a direction, and move along this direction.

From the actions of AF, it can be clearly that, the most importance features in AF are the re-trying process and local searching – Visual. In the proposed algorithm, we will introduce these concepts into the particle filtering process.

3. The LPF-AF Algorithm

3.1. *The local-loop process in particle filtering*

In the proposed algorithm, after calculating the weights of particles before the re-sampling process in the general particle filtering, the mean of weights M and the particle with biggest weight A will be calculated. For each particle with weight smaller the M, it will move toward A for a random distance. If the weight of new location is bigger than the former one, the particle will move to the new location. Each particle can move predefined times to find a better location. And if finally it cannot find a better one, it will not move. This process can be depicted as follows:

Step.1: calculate the mean of weights M

Step.2: identify the weight and location of the particle with biggest weights.

Step.3:

```
For each particle
        If weightP < M
          For i=1 to threshod
            newLocation =
 orginalLocation+rand*(location of M - orginalLocation);
            if weight of newLocation > weightP
              orginalLocation = newLocation;
break;
            end if
          end for
        end for
```

After the Local-loop process, the weights will be normalized again as follows:

$$\tilde{w}_t^{(i)} = w_{t-1}^{(i)}[\sum_{j=1}^{N} w_t^{(j)}]^{-1} \tag{6}$$

3.2. *The LPF-AF algorithm*

Basing on the Local-loop process and general particle filtering algorithm, the proposed LPF-AF can be depicted as follows:

```
    Initialization
    For each particle
  draw the states x_0^(i) from the prior p(x_0);
End
For each loop
  importance sampling step
  For each particle
     sample x̂_0^(i) ~ q(x_t | x_{0:t-1}^(i), y_{1:t})
  End
  For each particle
evaluate the importance weights up to a normalizing constant:
```

$$w_t^{(i)} = w_{t-1}^{(i)} \frac{p(y_t \mid x_t^{(i)}) p(\hat{x}_t^{(i)} \mid x_{t-1}^{(i)})}{q(\hat{x}_t^{(i)} \mid \hat{x}_{0:t-1}^{(i)}, y_{1:t})}$$

```
    Calculate the mean of weights M
    Identify the weight and location of the particle with biggest weights.
    For each particle
      If weightP < M
         For i=1 to threshod
            newLocation =
orginalLocation+rand*(location of M - orginalLocation);
            If weight of newLocation > weightP
               orginalLocation = newLocation;
              break;
            end if
         end for
      end for
    For each particle, normalize the importance weights:
```

$$\tilde{w}_t^{(i)} = w_{t-1}^{(i)} [\sum_{j=1}^{N} w_t^{(j)}]^{-1}$$

```
  // Re-sample
```

Eliminate the samples with low importance weights and multiply the samples with high importance weights, to obtain N random samples $x_{0:k}^{(i)}$ approximately distributed according to $p(x_{0:k} \mid z_{1:k})$.

Assign each particle an equal weight: $w_t^i = 1/N$.

4. The Simulation Experiments

4.1. *Benchmark function*

In this paper, the following benchmark function [10] was chosen to test the proposed algorithm.

Bechmark:

$$x_t = 1 + \sin(w\pi(t-1)) + \frac{1}{2}x_{t-1} + u_t$$

$$y_t = \begin{cases} \frac{1}{5}x_t^2 + v_t, & t \le 30 \\ \frac{1}{2}x_t - 2 + v_t & t > 30 \end{cases}$$

Where $w_t \sim \gamma(3, 0.5)$, $v_k \sim N(0, 1e-4)$, particle number N=100, sample time T=30, which the results were the average of 50 times of experiments. $R = 1e-4$, $Q = 0.75$; $\alpha = 1$, $\beta = 0$, $k = 2$, $threshold = 3$. All experiments were tested in MATLAB7.0.

In this paper, the proposed algorithm was compared to other several filtering algorithm – EKF, UKF, GPF, , EKFPF, , UPF, Experimental settings are shown in the table 1.

The settings of other six filtering algorithms are the same as [4-8].

4.2. *Experimental results and some remarks*

Experimental results are shown in fig. 1~fig. 2 and table 1. All results are the means of 100 runs, as the results of sa are close and far different with others, a enlargement fig was drawn as fig. 3.

As shown in the experimental results, it is clear that, EKF has the worst mean and var results, but has the best running time. While the proposed algorithm has the best mean and var result, but has longer running time.

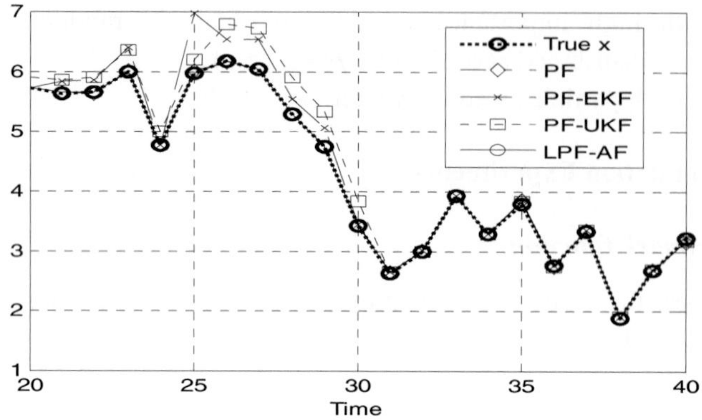

Fig. 1. Results on benchmark

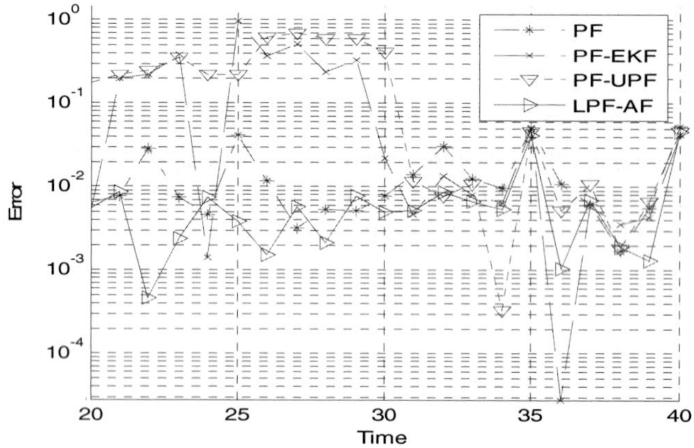

Fig. 2. Results of errors on bechmark

Table 1. Results On Benchmark 1

	MSE		Mean Run Time
	Mean	Variance	
EKF	0.6075	0.1138	-
UKF	0.2644	0.1297	-
PF	0.1601	0.1047	0.4034
PF-EKF	0.1126	0.2157	5.1792
PF-UKF	0.10339	0.1207	6.1134
LPF-AF	0.02218	0.03459	7.2126

5. Conclusion

In this paper, we proposed big data novel filtering method – Local-loop Particle Filter Based on the Artificial Fish Algorithm (LPF-AF) for nonlinear dynamic systems. Particle filtering algorithm has been widely used in solving nonlinear/non Gaussian filtering problems. The proposal distribution is the key issue of the particle filtering, which will greatly influence the performance of algorithm. In the proposed LPF-AF, the local searching of AF is used to regenerate sample particles, which can make the proposal distribution more closed to the poster distribution. There are mainly two steps in the proposed filter. In the first step of LPF-AF, extended Kalman filter was used as proposal distribution to generate particles, then means and variances of the proposal distribution can be calculated. In the second step, some particles move to toward the particle with the biggest weights. The proposed LPF-AF algorithm was compared with other several filtering algorithms and the experimental results show that means and variances of LPF-AF are lower than other filtering algorithms, but the running time is higher than others. It is clear that a suitable proposal distribution will improve the performance of particle filtering algorithm greatly. But as shown in the simulation results, the performance on the mean and var error results were improved greatly, so this cost is deserved.

References

1. der Merwe R V, Doucet A. The Unscented Particle Filter[DB/OL]. Http://cslu.cse.ogi.edu/publications/ps/UPF_CSLU_talk.pdf.
2. Riget. J. A Diversity-guided Particle Swarm Optimizer-the ARPSO. EVALife Technical Report 2002-02, Dept. of Computer Science, University of Arhus, 2012:
3. D.Guo, Wang X, and Chen R., New sequential monte carlo methods for nonlinear dynamic systems, Statistics and Computing, vol. 15, no 2, pp, 135-147, 2010.
4. O. Cappe, S.J. Godsill, and E. Moulines, An overview of existing methods and recent advances in sequential monte carlo, IEEE Proceeding, vol. 95, no.5, pp.899-924, 2007.
5. D. Guo and X. Wang, Quasi-monte Carlo Filtering in nonlinear dynamic systems. IEEE Trans. Signal Process. vol 54, no.6. pp. 2087-2098, 2010.
6. Bar-Shalom Y, Li X R, Kirubarajan T. Estimation with Applications to Tracking and Navigation: Theory, Algorithm and Software [M]. New York: Wiley, 2011.

7. Arulampalam M S, Maskell S, Gordon N, et al. A Tutorial on Particle Filters for Online Nonlinear/Non-Gaussian Bayesian Tracking [J]. IEEE Trans on Signal Processing, 2012, 20(2): 174-188.
8. Crisan D, Doucet A. A Survey of Convergence Results on Particle Filtering methods for Practitioners [J]. IEEE Trans on Signal Processing, 2014, 50(3): 736-746.
9. Anderson, B. D. and Moore, J.B. Optimal Filtering, Prentice-Hall, New Jersey, 2013.
10. Julier, S.J. and Uhlmann, J.K. A new extension of the Kalman filter to nonlinear systems, Proc. of AeroSense: The 11th International Sysmpsium on Aerospace/Defence Sensing, Simulation and Controls, Orlando, Florida, 2010. Vol. Muti Sensor Fusion, Tracking and Resource Mangement II p.182-193.
11. Shi Y, Eberhart R.C. A Modified Particle Swarm Optimizer. In: Proceedings of the IEEE International Conference on Evolutionary Computation. Piscataway, NJ: IEEE Press, 2015, 69-73.

The Detection of Buddha's Circle Head Light and Backlight in Thangka Image

Wen-Tao Shen[a] and Wei-Lan Wang[b,*]

Department of Math and Computer Science, Northwest University for Nationalities, Lanzhou City, China

E-mail: [a]shenwentao54321@163.com, [b]wangweilan@xbmu.edu.cn

According to the feature of Buddha's head light and backlight area is circle in Thangka image, so a method is proposed for detection of circle head light and backlight. Firstly, a method of morphology in edge extraction to get image edge is used, and by removing the edge connection point to get edge segment image. Secondly, through least square circle detection and verification condition of target circle to get the precise position of circle head light and backlight in Thangka image. The experimental results show that the method is with high accuracy and accurate positioning features in the detection of Buddha's circle head light and backlight in Thangka Image.

Keywords: Circle; Buddha; Head Light and Backlight Detection; Edge Extraction; Least Square method; Thangka.

1. Introduction

Thangka is a unique art form of painting in Tibetan culture. The objects, colors and shapes are given a certain symbolic significance, and convey spirit and thought of Buddhism in the painting. Its material contents involve history, politics, culture and social life as well as many other fields of Tibetan, which with high cultural heritage value and rich cultural information.

Head light and backlight is a bright area which approximate circular in silent Thangka Buddha's head and back, and it reflects the status and sacredness of Buddha. In the context of traditional culture, round head light and backlight is a symbol for completeness, tact, harmony. There are all kinds of icons with approximate circular backlight in Thangka, and they have calm and gentle expression, which on behalf of all kinds of Buddha, Tara, Bodhisattva, Grand

*Corresponding author.

master, Reverence, Arhat, historical figures and so on. The full picture is a distinct feature of Thangka, so there is no obvious foreground and background for Thangka image. We detected Buddha's head light and backlight in complex Thangka image, we through its boundary to split out Buddha's approximate location, and shielding its complex background patterns, in order to further lay the foundation for extract Buddha's headwear, gesture, musical instruments, clothes, which is various pixel with religious information. Meanwhile, we also can retrieve the silence Thangka image in the image library by circular feature of head light and backlight.

Research of circle detection in the image, Hough through the transform algorithms converts detection problem of the image space into parameter space. Methods that conduct a simple statistical accumulated for peak accumulator in the parameter space has well detection effect, but its computation is huge, which requires a large storage space[1]. Xu et al. has presented randomized Hough transform (RHT) that three points were randomly selected to map to the parameter space in edge image. Accumulation in the parameter space, which significantly reduces the amount of computation and storage of Hough transform, but it has higher demand to original edge image [2]. In recent years, researchers aimed at RHT algorithm that proposes many improved algorithm to reduce the amount of computation and useless accumulation[3-4]. Qing Huang et al. have come up with circle detection method that based on curvature estimation[5]. The method applies fuzzy line theory to curvature estimation in the edge line segment. To begin with filtering the curvature curve, and split possible edges, then through the mean curvature to point-selection to calculate the circle parameters. This method has the anti-interference ability. Yunchu Zhang has proposed circle detection method that based on existence probability map[6]. The method transforms image edge point co-circular structure information into peak of existence probability map, and confirms circle parameters by peak detection. The detection results are stable and occupy less memory, but its computational efficiency is poor. Jia Cai et al. have put forward rapid detection method that based on region growing and distance histogram of gradient [7]. The method that based on gradient region growth to get a number of arc line segment support area, and through three coordinates points of arc line segment to calculate the center and radius. Then the center coordinates as the center for each calculated circle, and the radius is the length of square, which adapt to each point in the region. Finally carry on projection and calculate distance accumulation value, and synthesize the cumulative distance of map information to get the center and radius. But detection effect for smaller circles and concentric circles is poor. Xiang Fei determined headdress scope by uses

RHT algorithm to locate head light position in Thangka portrait image headdress segmentation algorithm[8].

In the aspect of Thangka digital protection, our research includes different categories of Thangka image detection, semantic annotation and retrieval and so on[9-12]. Head light and backlight detection is difficult, because the background of head back light is complicated and it even covers the head back light. Edge integrity is too low, and most of them are approximate circles when extract edges. In this paper, we propose edge extracting of Buddha's circle head light and backlight and the detection method based on least square method in Thangka image. We use method of morphology in edge extraction to get image edge in the image red channel, and then through remove the edge connection point and short edge points to get required edge image. Finally, calculate the center and radius of edge circle by least square method. This method that can be effectively detects Buddha's circle head light and backlight in Thangka image.

The second part is image edge extraction; the third part is detection method of head light and backlight in Thangka image; the fourth part is the analysis of the experimental results; the last part is the conclusion.

2. Image Edge Extractions

The content of Thangka image is various and has a rich variety of composition. Edges are complicated; especially there are a lot of small edges when using the conventional edge extraction algorithm. Because we mainly concern the contour edge of head light and backlight in Thangka image, and its contour edge is longer and smoother. For the concern object, the edge of the residual background can be regarded as the edge noise. The image edge, which extracted by candy and other edge operators, has complex structure and lots of edge data to handle. Through a lot of experiments show that morphological edge detection algorithm has better results for contour edge detection of head light and backlight in Thangka image.

Extraction steps of image edge are as follows:

(i) Input image as shown in figure 1a, extracting the R component from RGB components of input image.

(ii) Through morphological edge detection algorithm to extract R component image edge, and get the binary image, the edge detection formulas such as in Eq. (1).

$$\beta(A) = A - (A \ominus B) \tag{1}$$

(iii) Carry median filter on binary image, and eliminating isolated edge noise points.

(iv) Extracting all connected components of edge image, and calculate the number of pixels point in each connected component. If the number C, of pixels in the connected component is less than threshold T_c, then delete the connected component. After handle by steps 2, 3, 4, the results as shown in Figure 1b.

(v) Edge image thinning, as shown in Figure 1c. Eliminate all connection points of edge lines in the edge image, as shown in Figure 1d. The connection point is defined as edge lines that exists bifurcation. As shown in Figure 2a is the edge line connection. Figure 2b is an image that eliminating the connection point and 8 neighborhood of all the connecting point.

(vi) Edge tracking for the image which eliminating edge connection points. Find the starting point of the edge segment, then recording the position $(X_i, Y_i) i \in (1,2,3\ldots N)$ of the pixels and the number N of pixels in the edge lines from the start point. If the number of pixels is less in the edge segment, (If the N is less than the threshold T_n, then delete the edge segment) which can consider that the pheromones contained in the edge segment is small, and then delete this line segment. Edit all line segments in the image, and the results as shown in Figure 1e.

Through the above steps that extract the edge contour image and it can be seen that the contour of Buddha's head light and backlight is more obvious. These steps lay a good foundation for following detecting the position information of head light and backlight.

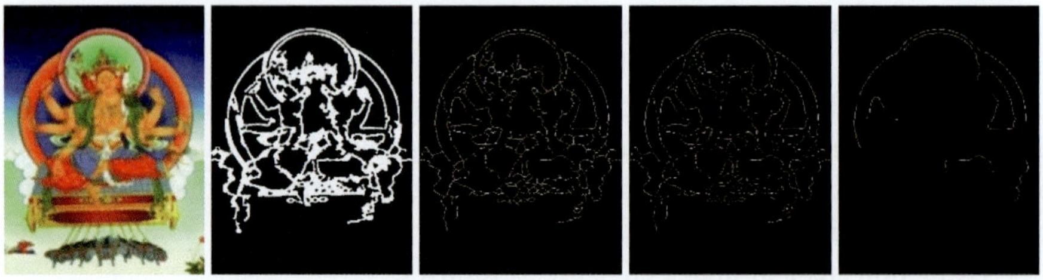

a b c d e

Fig. 1. Process and results of image edge extraction

a b

Fig. 2. Edge line connection and eliminating connection point

3. Detection Methods of Thangka's Head Light and Backlight

According to the feature of Buddha's head light and backlight geometry is circle in Thangka image, so we use least square method to detect center and radius of Buddha's head light and backlight in Thangka image. Then judge the correctness of position information by check the verification condition of target circle.

3.1. *Least square methods for circle detection*

The least square method is a mathematical optimization technique, which through minimizing the squared error and finding optimal functions matching in a set of data. Find some unknown true value with the simplest method, and Sum of squared error is the minimum. The following is the principle of least square circle detection.

The circular curve equation is shown as in Eq. (2):

$$R^2 = (X - A)^2 + (Y - B)^2 = X^2 - 2AX + A^2 + Y^2 - 2BY + B^2 \tag{2}$$

$$\text{Order(2)}\begin{cases} a = -2A \\ b = -2B \\ c = A^2 + B^2 - R^2 \end{cases} \tag{3}$$

By Eq. (2),(3) can get another form of circular curve equation, as in Eq. (4).

$$X^2 + Y^2 + aX + bY + c = 0 \tag{4}$$

The circle center and radius parameters is the Eq. (5), when the parameter a, b, c is known.

$$\begin{cases} A = \dfrac{a}{-2} \\ B = \dfrac{b}{-2} \\ R = \dfrac{1}{2}\sqrt{a^2 + b^2 - 4c} \end{cases} \tag{5}$$

The distance square of point to the center is d_i^2 in pixel point set $(X_i, Y_i)\,\mathrm{i} \in (1,2,3\ldots\mathrm{N})$ of edge segment, as in Eq. (6).

$$d_i^2 = (X_i - \mathrm{A})^2 + (Y_i - \mathrm{B})^2 \tag{6}$$

The difference of radius square to the distance of point $(X_i, Y_i) i \in (1,2,3\ldots N)$ to the center is the Eq. (7).

$$\delta_i = d_i^2 - R^2 = (X_i - A)^2 + (Y_i - B)^2 - R^2 = X_i^2 + Y_i^2 + aX_i + bY_i + c \tag{7}$$

Let $Q(a,b,c)$ be the sum of δ_i^2, as in Eq. (8).

$$Q(a,b,c) = \Sigma\delta_i^2 = \Sigma\left[X_i^2 + Y_i^2 + aX_i + bY_i + c\right]^2 \tag{8}$$

Function parameters of circle with pixel point set is a,b,c, when the value of parameter $Q(a,b,c)$ is the minimum. From the Eq.(8) we can know that $Q(a,b,c)$ is greater than 0, therefore, the function has minimum with greater than 0 or equal to 0, and the maximum value is infinite. Take the derivative of $Q(a,b,c)$ to a,b,c, and make the derivative equal to 0, which can get the Eq. (9). It can find that circular function parameters is Eq. (10), in which the values of $C,\ D,\ E,\ G,\ H$, as shown in Eq. (11).

$$\begin{cases} \dfrac{\partial Q(\mathrm{a,b,c})}{\partial a} = \sum 2(X_i^2 + Y_i^2 + aX_i + bY_i + c)X_i = 0 \\ \dfrac{\partial Q(\mathrm{a,b,c})}{\partial b} = \sum 2(X_i^2 + Y_i^2 + aX_i + bY_i + c)Y_i = 0 \\ \dfrac{\partial Q(\mathrm{a,b,c})}{\partial c} = \sum 2(X_i^2 + Y_i^2 + aX_i + bY_i + c) = 0 \end{cases} \tag{9}$$

$$\begin{cases} a = \dfrac{HD - EG}{CG - D^2} \\ b = \dfrac{HC - ED}{D^2 - GC} \\ c = -\dfrac{\sum(X_i^2 + Y_i^2) + a\sum X_i + b\sum Y_i}{N} \end{cases} \tag{10}$$

$$\begin{cases} C = N\sum X_i^2 - \sum X_i \sum X_i \\ D = N\sum X_i Y_i - \sum X_i \sum Y_i \\ E = N\sum X_i^3 + N\sum X_i Y_i^2 - \sum(X_i^2 + Y_i^2)\sum X_i \\ G = N\sum Y_i^2 - \sum Y_i \sum Y_i \\ H = N\sum X_i^2 Y_i + N\sum Y_i^3 - \sum(X_i^2 + Y_i^2)\sum Y_i \end{cases} \tag{11}$$

Plug Eq. (10) into Eq. (5), we can get the value of parameters *A,B,R* of circle with edge point set in which required.

3.2. *Target circle verification*

After using the least square method to calculate the circle parameters, it does not representative that the edge line segment is a part of circle in the image. And the line segment can be any shape, so it is necessary that verify the detected circle, whether it is true circle.

Calculate the distance d_i $i \in (1, 2, 3, \ldots N)$ between all points $(X_i, Y_i)\, i \in (1,2,3\ldots N)$ of edge line segment and the center (A, B) of fitting circle. Take the radius R of fitting circle as average value, which is the distance form line edge to center. Calculate its standard deviation and the calculation formula such as in Eq. (12), if the standard deviation is less than threshold that can be consider edge line segment as circular, otherwise non circle.

$$\sigma = \sqrt{\frac{\sum(\sqrt{(X_i - A)^2 + (Y_i - B)^2} - R)^2}{N}} \tag{12}$$

Make a judgment about center position (A, B) and radius R of the edge segment. According to the feature of Buddha generally located in the middle of the image in Thangka image, and then stipulate the scope of circle center and radius. Set w for the width and h for the height of the image; the constraint condition of circle center (A, B) and radius R as shown in Eq. (13-14).

$$\begin{cases} \frac{h}{5} < A < \frac{2h}{3} \\ \frac{w}{3} < B < \frac{2w}{3} \end{cases} \tag{13}$$

$$\begin{cases} \frac{w}{10} < R < \frac{w}{2}, & h < w \\ \frac{h}{10} < R < \frac{h}{2}, & h > w \end{cases} \tag{14}$$

4. Experimental Results and Analysis

The detection process of Buddha's circle head light and backlight in Thangka Image as shown in Figure 3. The Thangka image that need to be detected, which through edge extraction steps to get the binary edge segment image, and meanwhile get the position information of edge segment. We through the least square method for circle detection to get circle center and radius of each edge in the binary edge image. After the target circles pass the verification step, we make a judgment that standard deviation between centers distance of all points of edge segment and radius of corresponding circle whether less than the threshold. If the standard deviation is less than the threshold, that continue to make a judgment that whether the center and radius accords with Eq.(13) (14). If accords with Eq.(13) (14), and then record the center coordinates and radius.

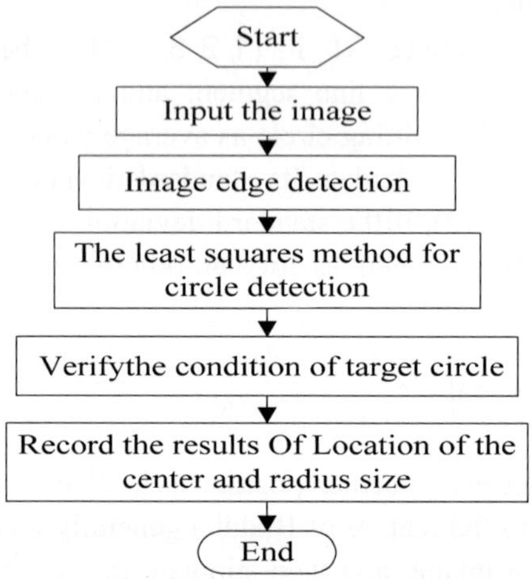

Fig. 3. Detection processes of Buddha's circle head light and backlight in Thangka Image

Experiments on the computer with 4.0 internal storage, Core(TM)i5-2004 CPU @3.10GHz with Matlab programming. In order to verify effectiveness of the method, and a lot of experiments were carried out. Make Description by the following three groups of experimental results. Figure 4 a(1), Figure 4 b(1), Figure 4 c(1), respectively, for the input image that to be detected. Figure 4 a(2), Figure 4 b(2), Figure 4 c(2), respectively, for the edge segment image, which after image edge extraction. In the process of image edge extraction, Threshold T_c of pixels number of connected region is 11000, and the threshold T_n of the edge segment length is 70. The article uses edge extraction method that can reduce the impact of complex background in Thangka image. This method can extract image edges of Buddha's circle head light and backlight effectively. Moreover, the method for extracting edge segment has strong purpose. Take all points in each line as data of circle parameter fitting, which can well reduce the missing rate. Eliminating the short edge line segment can reduce the computation and improve the detection efficiency.

The detection results show that method of circle detection and target circle verification can well detected the Buddha's circle head light and backlight in Thangka image. Figure 4 a(3), Figure 4 b(3), Figure 4 c(3) respectively as the result image, which passed the least square method circle detection and the target circle verification. The circle area with black line segment is the Buddha's circle backlight area in Thangka image. Table 1 is the center position and radius of a circle where the Buddha's head light and backlight in Thangka image.

Fig. 4. The detection results of Buddha's head light and backlight in Thangka image

Table 1. Center position and radius of Buddha's head light and backlight in Thangka image

Input image	*Image size*	*Head light center coordinates (A,B)*	*Head light radius R*	*backlight center coordinates (A,B)*	*backlight radius R*
a	650*509	(186,255)	67	(283,257)	163
b	1024*641	(257,326)	136	(411,319)	260
c	536*359	(132,179)	83	(233,183)	152

5. Conclusions

According to the approximate circular contour feature of Buddha's head light and backlight in Thangka image, so we put forward the edge extraction method for Thangka image which based on morphology, and the least square method for circle detection. The method not only has fast computing speed and use small memory, but also can effectively detect the Buddha's circle head light and backlight in Thangka image. Experimental results show that the detection effect is well enough for the Buddha's head light and backlight contour image, when the image is complete or have a certain cover in. Detection will be affected when the head light and backlight is covered more, further research is needed to solve such problem.

Acknowledgements

This work was supported by the National Natural Science Foundation of China (No.61162021, No. 61561042), the personnel training program of State Ethnic Affairs Commission, and also was supported by graduate research and innovation projects of Northwest University for Nationalities(Yxm2015176).

References

1. Hough PVC. Methods and means for recognizing complex patterns: US, 3069654 [P]. 1962.
2. Xu L, OJA E. Randomized Hough transform (RHT): basic mechanisms, algorithms, and computational complexities [J]. CVGIP: image Understanding, 1993,57(2):131-154.
3. Xianquan ZHANG, Qin SU, Lianyuan JIANG, Guoxiang Li. Fast algorithm for circle detection using randomized Hough transform[J]. Computer Engineering and Applications, 2008, 44(22):62- 64.

4. Yongliang Zhou, Yan Jin, Ping He, Qiang Chen. Accelerated Randomized Hough Transform for Cicle Detection Using Effective Accumulation Strategy [J]. Journal of Computer-Aided Design & Computer Graphics, 2014, 26(4):574-580.
5. Lianyuan JIANG, Qin Su, Yingjun Zhu. Fast multi-circle detection algorithm with randomized hough transform [J]. Computer Engineering and Applications, 2009, 45(17): 163-166.
6. Qing Huang, Biao Li. Circle detection based on curvature estimation[J]. Infrared and Laser Engineering, 2007,36:250-253.
7. Yunchu Zhang, Hongming Wang, Zize Liang, Tan Min, Ye Wen- bo, Lian Bo. Existence Probability Map Based Circle Detection Method[J]. Computer Engineering and Applications, 2006, 29:49-51.
8. Jia Cai, Panfeng Huang, Bin Zhang. Fast Cicle Detector Based on Region-Growing of Gradient and Histogram of Euclidean Distance [J]. ACTA OPTICA SINICA, 2015,35(3): 0315001-1~ 0315001-10.
9. Yin Lu. A study on Automatic Annotation of Thangka Image Based on Graph Learning [D]. Lan Zhou: Northwest University for Nationalities, 2011.
10. Yin Lu, Weilan Wang. Headdress Detection Based on Saliency Map for Thangka Portrait Image. MVA2011 IAPR Conference on Machine Vision Applications, 2011, Nara, Japan, pp 14~18.
11. Xiang Fei, Chuansheng Liu, Fang Miao. Headdress Segmentation Algorithm for Thangka Portrait Image Based on Circular Region Location [J]. Computer & Telecommunication, 2013, 09:27~44.
12. Ru Xue, Li Xu, Yong Hu. Study of Line Drawing Extraction Method Based on Thangka Image [J]. Science Technology and Engineering, 2014,14(16): 107~111.

Multi-Frames Pedestrian Recognition Via Deep Learning

Kun Zhang[a], Cui-Rong Wang[b] and Bing-Yu Liu[c]

Northeastern University at Qinhuangdao, NO.143. Taishan Road, Economic and Technological Development Zone

Qinhuangdao, Hebei, China

E-mail: [a]zkhbqhd@163.com, [b]qhd_wcr@163.com, [c]liuby78@163.com

In this paper, a pedestrian recognition algorithm of Multi-frame based on deep learning is proposed. First, a pedestrian image is adjusted to the same size, through image augmentation, make available information increases for different pedestrians. Second, a five layer CNN network is designed for pedestrian recognition, including two convolution layers, two pool layers, a whole connected layer, use softmax regression for multiple classes division in the last layer. Finally, experiments of different parameter settings are conducted, comparing with the Depth Belief Networks (DBN) and Depth Fully Connected Network (DFCN). The experimental results show that better pedestrian recognition rate can be obtained, even under insufficient pedestrian images or low resolution conditions.

Keywords: Pedestrian Recognition; Multi-Frames; Convolution Neural Network; Softmax Regression.

1. Introduction

Target Recognition, which aims at distinguishing a specific target from other targets effectively, is a classical problem in computer vision. Previous works on this problem mainly concentrate on metric learning or feature design and selection [1-8]. In [1], Yang et al. research on the algorithm of pedestrian recognition in front of the vehicle based on SVM, mainly studies the efficient algorithms of splitting pedestrian target from other non-pedestrians. In [3], Liu et al. introduced a man-in-the-loop method to improve the performance of metric learning. Feature matching-based algorithms [4-6] mainly focus on designing or selecting discriminative features. [7] transfer attributes information from existing scene segmentation datasets to the pedestrian dataset, by proposing a novel deep model to learn high-level features from multiple tasks and multiple data sources.

Recently Deep learning [8-11] has been widely applied to computer vision, target recognition and natural language processing etc. Convolution Neural Network (CNN) is applied in computer vision and works well in object recognition, few parameters and easy training is the most obvious advantage. So in this paper we design a CNN network to complete Multi-frames pedestrian recognition.

2. Preprocessing of Pedestrian Dataset

In order to identify pedestrians on Multi-frames appearing in the video, it need to obtain lots of pedestrians pictures from the video frames firstly. The ETHZ dataset contains lots of pedestrians images taken from the video, so in this paper we mainly use ETHZ dataset to get our experimental dataset (shown in Figure 1).

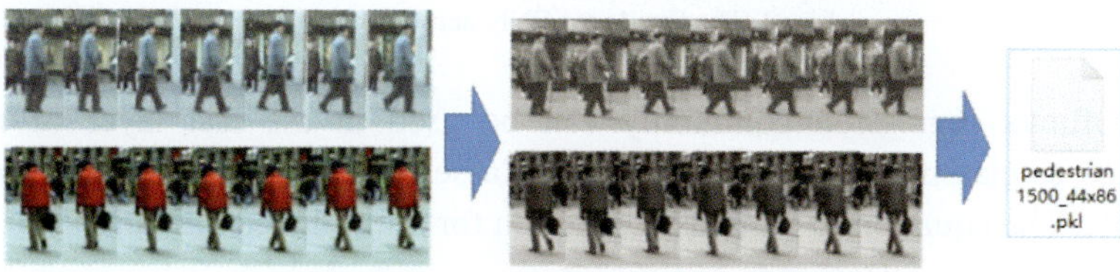

Fig. 1. The preprocessing of pedestrian dataset

Images in ETHZ dataset are different in size, their storage format is not suitable for deep learning experiment, so preprocessing of pedestrian dataset are need. Each pedestrian image should be adjusted to the same size and converted to gray scale, then saved as pkl format file. Using the image augmentation to extended input data, there are five modes: upside down, left and right flip, flip up and down and the image cutting-out (around 4 pixels will be set to 0).

3. Multi-frames Pedestrian Recognition

Here we design a five-layer CNN network (shown in Figure 2), including two convolution layers, two pool layers, a whole connected layer, without simgoid and tanh as activation function, but with ReLU as activation function, finally we use the softmax regression classifier to obtain classification results. In Figure 2, layer-C1 is a convolution layer, its input is an image, its size is $r \times c$, and has f_1 kinds of $n_1 \times n_1$ convolution kernel. f_1 feature maps can be obtained after this layer, size of each feature map is $(r - n_1 + 1) \times (c - n_1 + 1)$. Layer-S2 is a subsampling layer, also known as pooling layer, taking the maximum from every four points and sampling one point finally. The output is f_1 feature maps, size of each feature map is $(r-n_1+1)/2\times(c-n_1+1)/2$. Layer C3 is convolution layer too, but it has f_2 kinds of $n_2\times n_2$ convolution kernel, size of each feature map is $((r-n_1+1)/2-n_2+1)\times((c-n_1+1)/2-n_2+1)$. Layer S4 is the subsample layer just like Layer S2, the output is f_2 feature maps. Layer C5 is the fully connected layer, it has f_3 output points. Finally using softmax regression classifier, the number of the output point that can be set belonging to the number of categories.

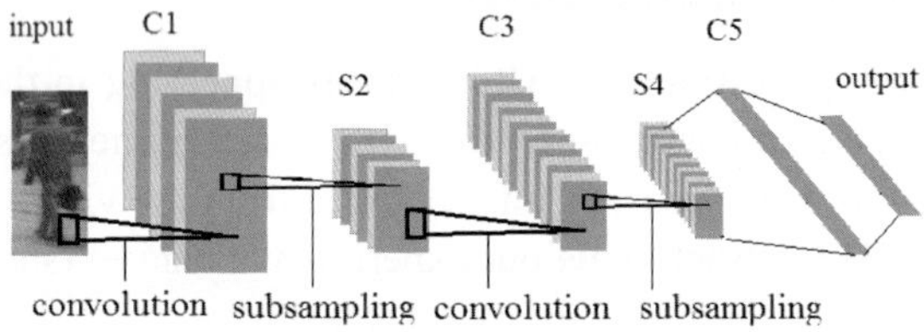

Fig. 2. The five-layer CNN network design

Softmax regression commonly can be used in the last layer of neural network as classifier. In case of multiple classes division, softmax regression is suitable. The equation of softmax regression for multiple classification is:

$$h_\theta(x^i)=\begin{bmatrix} p(y^i=1\mid x^i;\theta) \\ p(y^i=2\mid x^i;\theta) \\ \vdots \\ p(y^i=k\mid x^i;\theta) \end{bmatrix}=\frac{1}{\sum_{j=1}^{k}\exp(-\theta_j{}^T x^i)}\begin{bmatrix} \exp(-\theta_1{}^T x^i) \\ \exp(-\theta_2{}^T x^i) \\ \vdots \\ \exp(-\theta_k{}^T x^i) \end{bmatrix} \tag{1}$$

Here θ is a matrix, each row respectively corresponding to every sub-class parameters, the number of rows is k, then the loss function is:

$$J(\theta)=-\frac{1}{m}\left[\sum_{i=1}^{m}\sum_{j=1}^{k}1\{y^i=j\}\log\frac{\exp(\theta_1{}^T x^i)}{\sum_{l=1}^{k}\exp(\theta_l{}^T x^i)}\right] \tag{2}$$

If $y^i=j$ is true, the result of $1\{y^i=j\}$ is 1, otherwise it is 0. Using the gradient descent method, then the loss function is:

$$\nabla_{\theta_j}J(\theta)=-\frac{1}{m}\sum_{i=1}^{m}\left[x^i\left(1\{y^i=j\}-p\left(y^i=j\mid x^i;\theta\right)\right)\right] \tag{3}$$

Here $\nabla_{\theta_j}J(\theta)$ is the parameter derivation of class j, its result is a vector. To get specific derivative of one parameter, it should be re-evaluated for the parameter, then get $\partial J(\theta)/\partial\theta_{jl}$ further.

4. Experiments

We select 30 different pedestrians and more than 100 pictures of the same pedestrian as training dataset for our experiment, extract 1000 pedestrian pictures randomly from the training dataset as the test set. We adjust the input image to the same size of 44×86 ($r = 44, c = 86$), after the image augmentation, the training dataset has more than 15000 pictures. Firstly we set $n_1 = n_2 = 5$ $f_1 = 15$, $f_2 =, 30$, $f_3 = 400$ to complete the experiment. After learning and training, according to the saved parameters, input a picture, we can extract the corresponding image feature maps (shown in Figure 3).

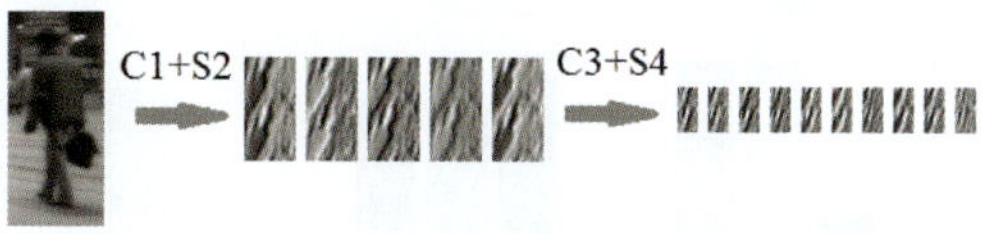

Fig. 3. Image feature maps

Under the same parameters, kinds of convolution kernel for layer C1-C3 are set as 5-10, 6-12, 15-30 and 32-64 differently, then compare their experimental results (shown in Figure 4-(a)). The results showed that the highest recognition accuracy obtained in the case of 15-30. Fixed convolution kernel number as 15-30, we do the comparison of different convolution kernel sizes (shown in Figure 4-(b)). It can been seen that recognition accuracy changing around 93.3%.

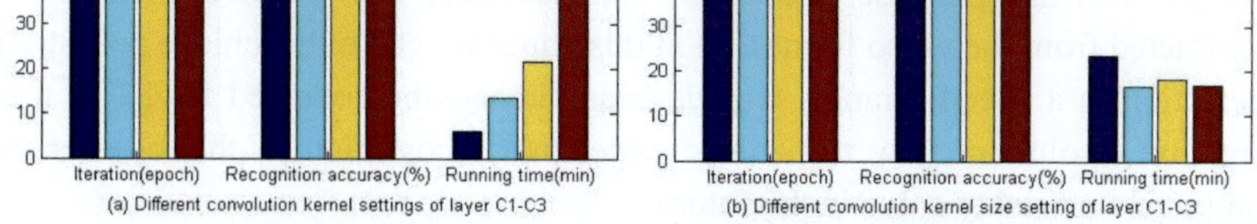

Fig. 4. Comparison the experimental results of different convolution kernel setting

Comparing with the Depth Belief Networks (DBN) and Depth Fully Connected Network (DFCN) respectively on the same training data, we set the number of convolution kernel is 6-12, the convolution kernel size is 3-2 for layer C1-C3, the experimental results are shown in the Figure 5. As can be seen, DBN has maximum epoch number of iteration and the longest running time, DFCN has the minimum running time, CNN network requires 483575 parameters, but DFCN requires 2161615, ours has highest recognition accuracy and minimum number of iterations, on the whole, our model is better than the other two networks.

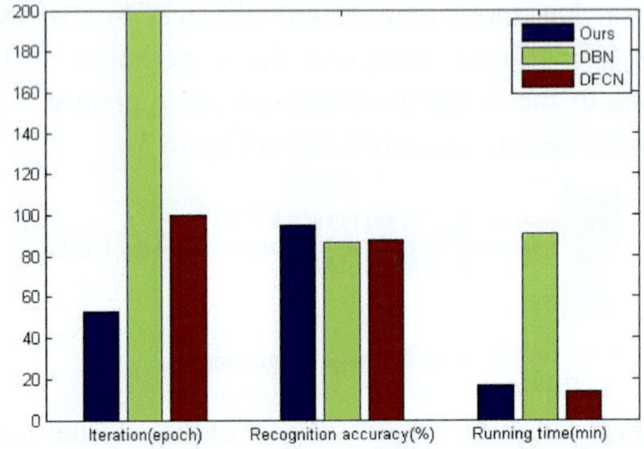

Fig. 5. Experiment Comparison with DBN and DFCN neural network

5. Conclusions

In this paper, through preprocessing of pedestrian ETHZ dataset, we design a five-layer CNN network and use softmax regression classifier finally to achieve the multi-frame pedestrian recognition. A large amount of experimental results indicate that we can get ideal recognition accuracy, even under the condition of video frame sequence may missing some important data. By comparing with the Depth Belief Networks (DBN) and Depth Fully Connected Network (DFCN), CNN network has better results with these two advantages: local perception and weight sharing. Because pedestrians images have the location particularity (extracted from the video frame), so in this paper we can only achieve pedestrian detection in a specific range. If pedestrians images be collected fewer, or they are low resolution, how to achieve pedestrian recognition in this case is the problem we need to solve in the future.

Acknowledgments

Specialized Research Fund for the Doctoral Program of Higher Education: Dr. Fund (XNB2015006) of Northeastern University at Qinhuangdao. Hebei province science and technology research fund (QN2016310).

References

1. Yang, Y., Liu, W., Wang, Y., & Cai, Y. Research on the algorithm of pedestrian recognition in front of the vehicle based on SVM. In *Distributed Computing and Applications to Business, Engineering & Science (DCABES), 2012 11th International Symposium on* (Guilin, China, 2012), pp. 396-400.
2. Xie, Y., Yu, H., Gong, X., Dong, Z., & Gao, Y. Learning visual-spatial saliency for multiple-shot person re-identification. *IEEE Signal Processing Letters, 22*(11) (2015), pp. 1854-1858.
3. Liu, C., Change Loy, C., Gong, S., & Wang, G. POP: Person re-identification post-rank optimisation. In *Proceedings of the IEEE International Conference on Computer Vision* (Sydney, VIC, 2013), pp. 441-448.
4. Zhao, R., Ouyang, W., & Wang, X. Unsupervised salience learning for person re-identification. In *Proceedings of the IEEE Conference on Computer Vision and Pattern Recognition* (Portland, OR 2013), pp. 3586-3593.
5. Zhao, R., Ouyang, W., & Wang, X. Learning mid-level filters for person re-identification. In *Proceedings of the IEEE Conference on Computer Vision and Pattern Recognition* (Columbus, OH, 2014), pp. 144-151.
6. Su, C. L., Chang, Y. H., Chen, K. P., & Wu, J. H. Pedestrian recognition using feature extraction. In *Consumer Electronics-Taiwan (ICCE-TW), 2015 IEEE International Conference on* (Taipei 2015, June), pp. 274-275.
7. Tian, Y., Luo, P., Wang, X., & Tang, X. Pedestrian detection aided by deep learning semantic tasks. In *Proceedings of the IEEE Conference on Computer Vision and Pattern Recognition* (Boston, MA, 2015), pp. 5079-5087.
8. LeCun, Y., Bengio, Y., & Hinton, G. Deep learning. *Nature, 521*(7553), (2015), pp. 436-444.
9. Hinton, G. E., Osindero, S., & Teh, Y. W. A fast learning algorithm for deep belief nets. *Neural computation, 18*(7) (2006), pp. 1527-1554.
10. He, K., Zhang, X., Ren, S., & Sun, J. Delving deep into rectifiers: Surpassing human-level performance on imagenet classification. In *Proceedings of the IEEE International Conference on Computer Vision* (Santiago, Chile, 2015), pp. 1026-1034.
11. Ouyang, W., Wang, X., Zeng, X., Qiu, S., Luo, P., Tian, Y., ... & Tang, X. Deepid-net: Deformable deep convolutional neural networks for object detection. In *Proceedings of the IEEE Conference on Computer Vision and Pattern Recognition* (Boston, MA, 2015), pp. 2403-2412.

Imbalanced Learning Based Sentiment Classification of Stock Reviews

Guo-Xun Wang[1,2,4,a], Min Tian[3,4,b] and Ya-Chen Lin[4,c]

[1]*Research Center on Fictitious Economy and Data Science, Chinese Academy of Sciences, Beijing, China*

[2]*Key Laboratory of Big Data Mining and Knowledge Management, Chinese Academy of Sciences, Beijing, China*

[3]*Lingnan College, Sun Yat-Sen University, Guangzhou, China*

[4]*Post-Doctoral Research Station, China Guangfa Bank, Guangzhou, China*

E-mail: [a]guoxunwang@163.com, [b]tianmin_2005@qq.com, [c]linyachen2@cgbchina.com.cn

The stock reviews are important professional advice for stock traders. Based on the massive stock reviews available online, an automatic approach which can identify the emotional tendency hidden in stock reviews will provide tremendous help to stock traders. A sentiment classification strategy is proposed for stock reviews analysis. Firstly, stock reviews are collected from the Internet and construct a labeled corpus. Secondly, a feature extraction approach is designed which can effectively map the corpus into a structured matrix. Finally, four classifiers are evaluated on multiple criteria. The synthetic oversampling approach is utilized to overcome the imbalanced distribution of positive and negative reviews. The experimental results demonstrate that the SVM algorithms coupled with SMOTE can achieve the highest performance for sentiment classification on the real world Chinese stock review corpus.

Keywords: Imbalanced Learning; Sentiment Classification; Stock Reviews; Oversampling.

1. Introduction

With the continuous development of information technology, more and more institutions and individuals are able to share their viewpoints on the Internet.

The latest online news and research articles provided by the authority and experts becomes the vane of the changes in the financial industry. As the core of the financial world, stock market draws a lot attention from people no matter which field they are worked in. Studies have shown that stock price fluctuations are sensitive to the influence of financial news and research reports [1, 2]. Therefore, it becomes very significant and valuable to analyze and summarized the huge online information in time. The good news is that the availability of online newspaper made it possible for us to easily access news articles relating to business and financial news. However, due to the large volume of news articles, one needs text mining software or techniques to analyze the data in order to arrive to a certain trade decision.

Sentiment analysis is a subfield of text mining, including a serials of tasks like extracting, clustering, classifying, and summarizing sentiment from text [3, 4]. For the stock traders, the sentiment analysis can be restricted to judge the attitudes hidden in the stock reviews, either bullish, bearish and neutral. The mainly used approaches applied for the automatic sentiment analysis can be divided into three categories: lexicon based approach, machine learning approaches and hybrid methods [5]. Lexicon based approach and machine learning are two main ways to do sentiment analysis. Machine learning approach for sentiment classification involves building classifiers based on labeled instances of a group of texts [6]. Naïve Bayes, Decision Tree, SVM and regression are popular methods to do classification. However, bore in mind the fact that the Chinese stock market does not have the short mechanism, the financial research reports online are mainly bent on preaching some public company, rather than preach them down [7, 8]. This results in a huge gap between the number of stock reviews in various categories. The data set for supervised learning are very imbalanced, resulting in traditional classification methods cannot be implemented directly.

Imbalanced datasets pose challenges to standard classification algorithms as the results would be dominated by the majority categories while overlooking the minority categories. Imbalanced classification generally refers to the problem that the number of samples in one category is far less than the number of samples in other categories. Widely used methods for unbalanced classification include: sampling [9], cost sensitive learning [10], One-way learning [11] and ensemble techniques [12]. We take oversampling methods for imbalanced learning in this research.

Another challenge in Chinese sentiment classification is that there is no qualified domain dictionary. Traditional words segmentation tools and technology will separate some idiomatic structure, or mismatch some independent words, and lead to ambiguity or misunderstanding [13]. We define a serials of feature structures to extract and filter the words in stock reviews in order to map the texts to vector space effective.

To the best of our knowledge, this is the first study to use synthetic minority oversampling approach to sentiment classification of Chinese stock reviews. The main contributions of this work including the following three aspects, e.g., overcome the difficulty of imbalanced learning by taking oversampling techniques, build an effective feature expression rule to map the texts to vector space, identify a suitable way to do sentiment classification of Chinese stock reviews.

2. Sentiment Classification for Stock Reviews

2.1. *Dataset*

We download all news and articles published on HIBOR in the year 2015 as the main source of financial news by employing the R packages RCurl [14, 15]. We form a subset of all data available in the datasets by choosing only the stock reviews related to public finance companies, because most important for us is building a professional and relatively regular texts. At last, we build a corpus with 7850 research articles, consist of 6315 strongly recommended, 600 preached down, and 935 are neutral rated. Considering the reality of Chinese stock markets, neutral rating is another saying of not recommend to buy. So the group preached down and neutral rating has been merged into one. In the following parts, strongly recommended 6315 articles are named as negative instance, and the others are named as positive instance. The imbalanced rate of the dataset is around 4.1.

2.2. *Feature extraction*

Once these stock research articles have been gathered they need to be represented in machine-friendly form. There are multiple techniques available to convert plain text documents to structure dataset, i.e., tokenize the file and use tokens as feature space, writing style analysis and parts of speech methods. We take unigram, syntactic features and domain specified lexicon to build the feature space of the corpus.

2.2.1. *Unigram*

N-gram model is a very simple and powerful approach applied in natural language processing. A n-gram is a set of consecutive tokens with length n from a sequence of data [16]. We take unigram in our research, so the tokens can be any single Chinese character or word in a plain text. The software ICTCLAS is used to segment the stock reviews corpus in to unigram format [17]. We focus on the classification of sentiment hidden in the stock reviews, therefore, nouns with neutral meaning and stop words are removed from the unigram set. And only adjectives, adverbs and verbs are retained as the basic feature of this work. Considering the question mark, exclamation mark usually contain strong emotion, so punctuation also taken as alternative feature sets.

2.2.2. *Syntactic features*

Unigram model cannot reflect the sequence relationship among words, and will lose some information about the sentiment in the corpus [4]. Compare to unigram, the syntactic of individual components of the sentence and the order of their arrangement contains more message about the sentient in the documents. Part of speech, as an important element of a sentence, directly affects the representation of the sentence. Such as "good", "bright" and "excellent" these adjectives express obvious positive emotional tendency. In addition, some fixed collocation like "Substantial rise", "terribly slow" and "lose declining" express apparent opinion trend. On the other word, negative expression is a type of commonly used sentence pattern and are used to express destructive meaning. Therefore, in this paper, we also take into account the extraction of the negative structure in the corpus. In this research, we design 8 kinds of fixed collocations in total as showed in Table 1.

2.2.3. *Lexicon features*

Some specific expressions such as "asset restructure" and "merger and acquisition", are widespread used in the security industry, and have relatively fixed emotional tendency. As a consequence, we extract 145 fixed expressions with special meaning as the lexicon feature space in this work.

After data preprocessing as mentioned before, we select 1734 features in total to convert the corpus into vector space. The classifications, properties and amount detail of the selected features are presented in Table 1.

Table 1. The classifications, properties and amount of the selected features

Classification	Property	Amount
Unigram	Adjective, Adverb, Verbs, Nouns with positive or negative meaning	1265
Syntactic	(Privative +) Adverb + Verbs (Privative +) Adverb + Adjective (Privative +) Adjective + Verbs Privative + Verbs Privative + Adverb + Nouns	324
Lexicon	Dictionary of specific expression in security industry	145

2.3. *Feature selection*

Feature selection approach can be divided into lexicon-based approach and the statistical approach. As lexicon based methods usually need human annotation, the automatic statistical methods are more frequently used in text mining task. The feature selection techniques treat the documents either as a group of words, e.g., Bag of Words (BOWs), or as a string which retains the sequence of words in the document. BOW is utilized more often because of its simplicity for the classification process [4]. We take the Chi-square method as the feature selection method as they are reported effectively when identifying the key features.

Let n be the total number of documents in the collection, $p_i(w)$ be the conditional probability of class i for documents which contain w, P_i be the global fraction of documents containing the class i, and $F(w)$ be the global fraction of documents which contain the word w [18, 19]. Therefore, the Chi-square statistic of the word between word w and class i is defined as in Eq.(1):

$$\chi_i^2 = \frac{n \cdot F(w)^2 \cdot (p_i(w) - P_i)^2}{F(w) \cdot (1 - F(w)) \cdot P_i \cdot (1 - P_i)} \tag{1}$$

Chi-square and PMI are two ways of measuring the correlation between terms and categories. Chi-square is preferable to PMI because it is a normalized value which are more comparable across terms in the same category [18, 19].

2.4. *Synthetic minority oversampling techniques*

Techniques such as oversampling the minority class samples have been used to deal with imbalanced learning. However, these approaches may lead to overfitting as the decision regions for minority samples are specified strictly. Synthetic minority oversampling technique (SMOTE) was proposed to reduce the unequal distribution of majority and minority samples [20], which is useful in dealing with unbalanced classification. It generates synthetic instances for the minority class in the feature space rather than reuses the minority data.

The SMOTE works as the following approach. Given training data samples T with m samples $\{x_i, y_i\}, i = 1...m,$ where x_i is an instance in n dimensional feature space X, and $y_i \in \{-1,1\}$ is the class label associated with x_i. Define m_p as the number of minority class samples. K_s is the parameter used to control the number of samples generated. $(K_s - 1) * m_p$ minority samples will be created after the generation process. For each minority sample x, the SMOTE first find its k nearest neighbors in minority class, then randomly select one from them i.e. s

and a synthetic sample g will be generated by the linear interpolation of x and S as in Eq.(2):

$$g_i = x_i + (S_i - x_i) * \alpha,\ i = 1...n \tag{2}$$

Where α is a random number in the range [0, 1]. A mechanism derived from the SMOTE is set to make punishments on the noises in existing minority class and avoid creating false minority samples from them. This can be achieved by assigning different weights to each existing minority sample based on the density of samples around it and the position where it locates.

2.5. *Classification techniques*

Machine learning based methods, lexicon based methods and hybrid methods are the mainly used techniques for sentiment classification [4]. Machine learning method relies on the general data mining algorithms to solve the sentiment classification as a regular text classification problem that makes use of syntactic and linguistic features. Furthermore, text classification methods using the machine learning approach can be roughly divided into unsupervised and supervised learning methods. Unsupervised methods are used when it is difficult to find these labeled training documents. Supervised methods make use of a large number of labeled training documents. Three kinds of supervised learning methods are employed in this work.

The Naive Bayes classifier is the most commonly used probabilistic classifier. It computes the posterior probability of a class, based on the distribution of the words in the document. Naïve Bayes predict the probability that a given feature set belongs to a particular label based on Bayes theorem. However, Naïve Bayes classifiers assumes that the features are independent of each other, which may not be fulfilled in some corpus. A Bayesian Network model is a directed acyclic graph whose nodes represent random variables, and edges represent conditional dependencies [21]. It is envisaged a complete model for the variables and their relationships. Therefore, a complete joint probability distribution over all the variables, is specified for a model.

Support vector machine classifiers (SVM) transform the training data into a higher dimension space and search for the linear optimal separating hyperplane. SVM classifiers are appropriate for text data because the sparse nature of the text document matrix, where features tend to be correlated with each other and generally organized into linearly separable categories [19].

Decision tree classifier applies a hierarchical decomposition of the training set in which a condition on the attribute value is utilized to partition the data. The partition is recursively done until the leaf nodes contain minimum numbers of records which are utilized for the classification. Random Forests classifiers are a combination of decision tree predictors, in which each tree depends on the values of a random vector samples independently and with the same distribution for all trees in a forest [22]. Random forests are more robust than a single decision tree with respect to noises.

2.6. *Performance criteria*

When the distributions of different categories' samples or the cost of two types of errors are significantly imbalanced, single predicting accurate measure may not be appropriate to evaluate the classification models [23]. Therefore, we choose several widely used performance criteria to make the evaluation. These criteria are defined by the confusion matrix. Weighted accuracy is a tradeoff between sensitivity and specificity. For weighted accuracy, we set w at 0.7 to indicate higher weights for accuracy on the positive instance.

Overall accuracy is one of the most widely used classification performance metrics, which measures the percentage of correctly classified instances. True Positive (TP, sensitivity) measures how well a classifier can recognize positive instances. False Positive (FP) measures the percentage of negative instances that were incorrectly classified as positive. True Negative (TN) is also called specificity, measures how well a classifier can recognize negative instances. False Negative (FN) measures the percentage of positive instances that were incorrectly classified as negative.

Precision: $TP/(TP + FP)$.

Recall: $TP/(TP + FN)$.

F-measure: $2*Precision*Recall/(Precision + Recall)$

Weighted accuracy (WA): $w*sensitivity+(1-w)*specificity$.

3. Results and Discussion

We choose the naive estimator to estimate the conditional probability tables and set the alpha as 0.5 for the Bayesian network classifier. The polynomial kernel is used in the SVM classifier. For the random forests, the number of trees to be generated in a single forest is placed at 5. We provide simulation in Table 2 where each result is the average value after a five-fold cross-validation.

We also take the five-fold cross -validation procedure to examine the SMOTE oversampling techniques. Synthetic minority oversampling approach is done on the training sets in each fold. The oversampling rate is set at 4 in order to balance the positive and negative instance. Parameters for classification algorithms are set to the same values as mentioned above.

Table 2. Performance of SOMTE and baseline classifiers on stock reviews corpus

Algorithms	Methods	Accuracy	Precision	Recall	F measure	Weight accuracy
Naive Bayes	Base	0.925	0.768	0.652	0.705	0.747
	SMOTE	0.929	0.722	0.722	0.722	0.793
Bayesian network	Base	0.928	0.738	0.701	0.719	0.779
	SMOTE	0.929	0.755	0.707	0.731	0.784
SVM	Base	0.939	0.799	0.734	0.765	0.805
	SMOTE	0.934	0.801	0.738	0.768	0.807
Random forests	Base	0.920	0.744	0.674	0.707	0.760
	SMOTE	0.925	0.750	0.711	0.730	0.786

There are several interesting findings in table 2. First, even the eight algorithms get extremely close value on criterion overall accuracy, there is a great difference on other indicators. This demonstrates that we should take a group of performance criteria rather than single accuracy when evaluating a series of algorithms. This finding is in agreement with the literature [23]. Second, the synthetic oversampling approach can make some improvements on the performance for the given classifiers. Furthermore, the synthetic oversampling approach together with the SVM algorithm gets the best performance on every criterion in our experiment. Therefore, it confirms that the synthetic oversampling approach is suitable for the applications in which the minorities are more concerned. Considering that the models will be used to assist the stock traders to make a decision on stock market, it should be paid much more attention on the models' ability of identifying "bad news", in other words, the precision criterion. At last, we will employ the SVM classifier with the synthetic minority oversampling technique to analyze the sentiment tendency hidden in the huge amount of stock research articles.

4. Conclusion

This paper applies sentiment classification technique to analyze the emotional tendency of the stock reviews. A real world dataset from a shared financial website in China is used in this study. We design a feature extraction approach which draws unigram, syntactic and lexicon feature from the stock reviews. The oversampling method is put in place to balance the distribution of negative and positive reviews. Four classification algorithms including Naïve Bayes,

Bayesian network, SVM and Random Forests are used to analyze the sentiment trend in the reviews. The results indicate that the synthetic minority over-sampling approach makes notable improvements on criteria precision, recall, F-measure and weighted accuracy. Finally, the SVM classifier with the SMOTE is chosen to make further analysis for stock review corpus.

Further researches will be explored in different directions. First, other fixed structures in stock review will be investigated to enhance the efficiency of feature extraction. Second, algorithms suitable for large scale sparse data may be adopted in order to improve the precision of the classifiers.

References

1. Xiaodong Li, Haoran Xie, Li Chen, Jianping Wang, Xiaotie Deng, News impact on stock price return via sentiment analysis, Knowledge-Based Systems, Volume 69, October 2014, pages 14-23.
2. Thien Hai Nguyen, Kiyoaki Shirai, Julien Velcin, Sentiment analysis on social media for stock movement prediction, Expert Systems with Applications, Volume 42, Issue 24, 30 December 2015, pages 9603-9611.
3. Chun Liao, Chong Feng, Sen Yang, Heyan Huang, Topic-Related Chinese Message Sentiment Analysis, Neurocomputing, Available online 29 June 2016.
4. Kumar Ravi, Vadlamani Ravi, A survey on opinion mining and sentiment analysis: Tasks, approaches and applications, Knowledge-Based Systems, Volume 89, November 2015, pages 14-46.
5. Pang Bo, Lee Lillian, Opinion mining and sentiment analysis, Foundations and Trends in Information Retrieval, Volume2(1-2), 2008, pages 1-135.
6. Kumar Ravi, Vadlamani Ravi, A survey on opinion mining and sentiment analysis: Tasks, approaches and applications, Knowledge-Based Systems, Volume 89, November 2015, pages 14-46.
7. Zhong-Xin Ni, Da-Zhong Wang, Wen-Jun Xue, Investor sentiment and its nonlinear effect on stock returns—New evidence from the Chinese stock market based on panel quantile regression model, Economic Modelling, Volume 50, November 2015, pages 266-274.
8. Qing Li, TieJun Wang, Ping Li, Ling Liu, Qixu Gong, Yuanzhu Chen, The effect of news and public mood on stock movements, Information Sciences, Volume 278, 10 September 2014, pages 826-840.
9. Muhammad Atif Tahir, Josef Kittler, Fei Yan, Inverse random under sampling for class imbalance problem and its application to multi-label

classification, Pattern Recognition, Volume 45, Issue 10, October 2012, pages 3738-3750.

10. Xingyu Gao, Zhenyu Chen, Sheng Tang, Yongdong Zhang, Jintao Li, Adaptive weighted imbalance learning with application to abnormal activity recognition, Neurocomputing, Volume 173, Part 3, 15 January 2016, pages 1927-1935.
11. F. Dufrenois, J.C. Noyer, One class proximal support vector machines, Pattern Recognition, Volume 52, April 2016, pages 96-112.
12. José F. Díez-Pastor, Juan J. Rodríguez, César I. García-Osorio, Ludmila I. Kuncheva, Diversity techniques improve the performance of the best imbalance learning ensembles, Information Sciences, Volume 325, 20 December 2015, pages 98-117.
13. Qiudan Li, Zhipeng Jin, Can Wang, Daniel Dajun Zeng, Mining opinion summarizations using convolutional neural networks in Chinese microblogging systems, Knowledge-Based Systems.
14. http://www.hibor.com.cn/
15. https://cran.r-project.org/web/packages/RCurl/
16. Abinash Tripathy, Ankit Agrawal, Santanu Kumar Rath, Classification of sentiment reviews using n-gram machine learning approach, Expert Systems with Applications, Volume 57, 15 September 2016, pages 117-126.
17. Hua-Ping ZHANG, Hong-Kui Yu, De-Yi Xiong, Qun LIU, HHMM-based Chinese Lexical Analyzer ICTCLAS, Second SIGHAN workshop affiliated with 41th ACL; Sapporo Japan, July, 2003, pages 184-187.
18. Aggarwal Charu C, Zhai Cheng Xiang, Mining Text Data, Springer New York Dordrecht Heidelberg London: Springer Science+Business Media, LLC'12; 2012.
19. Medhat W, Hassan A, Korashy H, Sentiment analysis algorithms and applications: A survey, Ain Shams Engineering Journal, Volume 5(4), 2014, pages 1093-1113.
20. Chawla, N., Bowyer, K., Hall, L. and Kegelmeyer, W., Smote: synthetic minority over-sampling technique, Journal of Artificial Intelligence Research, Volume 16, 2002, pages 321–357.
21. Friedman N, Geiger D, Goldszmidt M, Bayesian network classifiers, Machine learning, Volume 29(2-3), 1997, pages 131-163.
22. Breiman, L., Random Forests, Machine Learning, Volume 45, 2001, Pages 5-32.
23. Peng, Y., Wang, G., Kou, G., and Shi, Y., An Empirical study of Classification Algorithm Evaluation in Financial Risk Management, Applied Soft Computing, Volume 11, Issue: 2, 2011, pages 2906–2915.

Echo-Based Image Watermarking Scheme in the Wavelet Domain

Huang-Nan Huang[1,a], Der-Fa Chen[2,b], Chiu-Chun Lin[2], Jun-Jin Xie[2,c] and Shuo-Tsung Chen[1,a]

[1]*Department of Applied Mathematics, Tunghai University*
Taichung 40704, Taiwan (ROC)
[2]*Department of Industrial Education and Technology,*
National Changhua University of Education Changhua 500, Taiwan (ROC)
E-mail: [a]nhuang@thu.edu.tw, [b]wdfchen@cc.ncue.edu.tw, [c]anvy651018@yahoo.com.tw

An image watermarking scheme is developed with echo-based hiding technique in the wavelet domain. In the embedding process, DWT coefficients with echo delay are utilized for watermarking. During the detection process, detect echo delay is first detected by the concept of image similarity and thus the embedded watermarks are extracted by the inverse procedure of embedding process. Experimental results confirm the watermarked image can keep high PSNR and high embedding capacity.

Keywords: Wavelet; Watermarking; Image; Echo.

1. Introduction

With the rapid development of activity on the internet, much digital information is widely spread. Digital watermarking was developed to hide digital information and protect the copyright of multimedia, like audios, images, etc. Due to the fact that discrete-time wavelet transform (DWT) provides an useful platform, numerous DWT-based algorithms for digital watermarking have been proposed in recent years [1-5].

Wanga et al. [6] proposed a fuzzy self-adaptive digital audio watermarking method based on a time-spread echo hiding algorithm which perform in the impulse response domain using PN sequences to achieve good robustness of echo hiding and high secrecy of spread spectrum with Fuzzy theory to control the embedded power of the watermark. Hua et al. [7] proposed time-spread echo-based audio watermarking with optimized imperceptibility through based finite-impulse-response filter design and robustness with the aid of the auto-correlation function of the echo filter coefficients as the constraint in the formulation. Hua et al. [8] started from noting inappropriate cepstral analysis from existing works, and provides rigorous derivations to reveal the advantages of using real cepstrum than complex cepstrum in echo-based audio watermark detection. Furthermore, they introduce a joint detection scheme based on real and imaginary parts of cepstrum.

In this study, an echo-based image watermarking scheme by using the DWT quantization idea is proposed. In the embedding process, DWT LH2 and HL2 coefficients with echo delay in an image are used to embed watermarks. In the detection process, we first detect echo delay by the concept of image similarity and thus extract the embedded watermarks by the inverse procedure of embedding process. Peak Signal to Noise Ratio (PSNR) and bit error rate (BER) is used to measure the quality and robustness of an indicator image watermarking scheme. Experimental results show that the watermarked image using the proposed scheme can keep high PSNR and better BER.

2. The Proposed Watermarking Scheme

The wavelet is used to transform the host image into the orthogonal DWT domain by two-level decomposition. DWT has local analysis of frequency in space and time domain and it gets image multi-scale details step by step. If the scale becomes smaller, every part gets more accurate and ultimately all images details can be focalized accurately. If DWT is applied to an image, it will produce high-frequency parts, middle-frequency parts, and a lowest-frequency part which is a square coefficient matrix. In the embedding process, DWT LH2 and HL2 coefficients with echo delay are utilized for embedding watermarks. In the detection process, we first detect echo delay by the concept of image similarity and thus extract the embedded watermarks by the inverse procedure of embedding process.

2.1. *Embedding process*

First of all, the watermark B=$\{\beta_{i,j}\}$ is randomly generated using a binary PN sequence so that the watermark values belong to the set $\{1,0\}$ and is adopted as the secret key. To embed this watermark in the wavelet domain, the host image **I** is transformed to **C** by applying two-level DWT. The proposed embedding technique is given as $\hat{\mathbf{C}}(i,j)=\mathbf{C}(i,j)+\alpha_{i,j}\mathbf{C}_d(i,j)$ where **C** is the transformed image; $\mathbf{C}_d$ is the transformed image with echo shift (which is called delay in the present study) $d \in \mathbb{N}$ in both image directions which is adopted as another secret key; $\alpha_{i,j}$ is the corresponding weighting of the (i,j) location $\mathbf{C}_d$; $\hat{\mathbf{C}}$ is the watermarked image. The proposed embedding rules are in the following, $q \in \mathbb{R}^+$:

- If $\beta_{i,j}$=1 is embedded, the weighting $\alpha_{i,j}$ is assigned to $\alpha_{i,j} = -1/q$,
- If $\beta_{i,j}$=0 is embedded, the weighting $\alpha_{i,j}$ is assigned to $\alpha_{i,j} = 1/q$.

2.2. *Extraction process*

To detect the watermark, the received watermarked image $\hat{\mathbf{I}}$ is first transformed to $\hat{\mathbf{C}}$ by applying two-level DWT. Then, we detect echo delay *d* by the concept of image similarity which is introduced as follow:

$$\text{Similarity}\left(\mathbf{C},\hat{\mathbf{C}}\right) = \sum_{i=1}^{M}\sum_{j=1}^{N}\mathbf{C}(i,j)\hat{\mathbf{C}}(i,j) \Big/ \sum_{i=1}^{M}\sum_{j=1}^{N}[\hat{\mathbf{C}}(i,j)]^2$$

With the detected delay *d* and the original image $\mathbf{C}$ in the DWT domain, binary bits of PN sequence are extracted by using the following rules.

- If $(\hat{\mathbf{C}}(i,j) - \mathbf{C}(i,j)) / \mathbf{C}_d(i,j) > 0$, then the extracted value $\hat{\beta}_{ij}$=1 .
- If $(\hat{\mathbf{C}}(i,j) - \mathbf{C}(i,j)) / \mathbf{C}_d(i,j) < 0$, then the extracted value $\hat{\beta}_{ij}$=0 .

Finally, the hidden watermarks are extracted as $\hat{\text{B}}=\{\hat{\beta}_{i,j}\}$.

3. Experimental Results

To evaluate the performance of the proposed scheme, four images, Lena, Jet, Peppers, Cameraman, each of size 512×512, are adopted as the example images. The four host images are decomposed into two levels by applying DWT, and then the watermark is embedded into the LH2 and HL2 coefficients with very high capacity. Generally, the quality of a watermarked image is evaluated by peak signal to noise ratio (PSNR) which is defined as

$$PSNR = -10\log_{10} \sum_{i,j=1}^{i=m,n=n} [\hat{\mathbf{I}}(i,j) - \mathbf{I}(i,j)]^2 \Big/ 255^2 mn$$

where m and n represent the height and width of the image and $\mathbf{I}(i,j)$ and $\hat{\mathbf{I}}(i,j)$ denote the values of original and the watermarked images, respectively. Table 1 shows the PSNR of each watermarked image under fixed echo delay *d* is increasing as parameter *q* increases. Moreover, Figure 1 shows the PSNR under different delay *d* and we found that PSNR is regardless of the value *d* when *d* is in the range of between 2 to 8. In other words, the increasing parameter *q* has the increasing PSNR for each watermarked image when d is in the range from 2 to 8. In addition, we extract the watermark and shows zero bit error rate before any attack is applied when $1 \le q \le 6$. There is no error in detect the echo delay by using the concept of similarity between the watermarked and original images no matter the watermarked image is under the attack or not. The robustness is measured by bit error ratio (BER) defined by $B_{error} / B_{total} \times 100\%$ where B_{error} and B_{total} denote the number of error bits between B and $\hat{\mathrm{B}}$, and the number of total bits, respectively. Table 2 shows the BER under the attacks JPEG2000 compression and Gaussian noise. The average of BER in JPEG2000 compression and Gaussian noise are about 40 and 30. Our experiment shows that the high BER is due to the magnitude of LH2 and HL2 is not enough to resist the effect of adding echo-image.

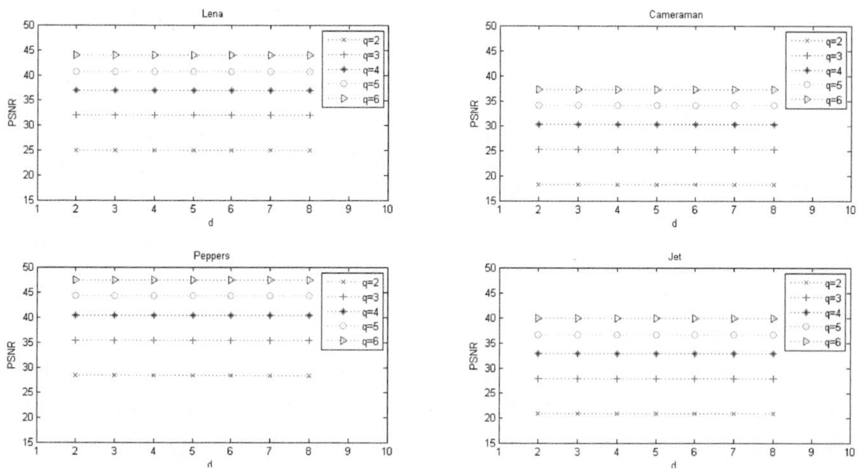

Fig. 1. PSNR of each watermark image embedded with different delay *d*.

Table 1. PSNR of each watermarked image vs parameters q with capacity 128*128*2 bits.

Image Type	PSNR(dB), q=4	PSNR(dB), q=5	PSNR(dB), q=6
Lena	36.89	40.77	43.94
Cameraman	30.25	34.13	37.30
Jet	32.83	36.71	39.87
Peppers	40.44	44.31	47.48

Table 2. BER (%) under the JPEG2000 compression and Gaussian noise attacks.

Image type	Parameters	JPEG Quality factor			Gaussian noise dB		
		30	20	12	35	30	25
Lena	$1 \leq d \leq 6$, $q=4$	38.960	40.14	41.29	27.14	33.19	37.92
	$1 \leq d \leq 6$, $q=5$	41.96	44.55	46.83	29.41	35.12	39.63
	$1 \leq d \leq 6$, $q=6$	43.12	45.35	47.72	31.30	36.56	40.88
Cameraman	$1 \leq d \leq 6$, $q=4$	37.98	40.25	42.42	26.89	31.92	36.37
	$1 \leq d \leq 6$, $q=5$	39.29	41.24	43.05	28.78	33.89	38.03
	$1 \leq d \leq 6$, $q=6$	40.19	42.00	43.46	30.59	35.09	39.13
Jet	$1 \leq d \leq 6$, $q=4$	39.27	41.63	44.19	29.92	34.82	38.84
	$1 \leq d \leq 6$, $q=5$	40.68	42.75	45.05	31.82	36.48	40.24
	$1 \leq d \leq 6$, $q=6$	41.75	43.52	45.56	33.48	37.75	41.34
Peppers	$1 \leq d \leq 6$, $q=4$	38.27	41.36	44.31	25.81	32.07	37.57
	$1 \leq d \leq 6$, $q=5$	39.18	42.56	45.28	28.44	34.45	39.11
	$1 \leq d \leq 6$, $q=6$	40.43	43.39	45.16	30.24	36.00	40.36

4. Conclusion

An echo-based scheme is presented for image watermarking with the DWT quantization idea. The watermark is embedded in LH2 and HL2 coefficients of DWT. Experimental results show that the watermarked image can keep high PSNR but limited robustness.

Acknowledgments

This work of H.-N. Huang was partially supported by Ministry of Science and Technology of Taiwan under the grand MOST No. 104-2115-M-029-004.

References

1. S.-T. Chen, H.-N. Huang, C.-J. Chen, and G.-D. Wu, "Energy-proportion based scheme for audio watermarking," *IET Proceedings on Signal Processing*, vol. 4, no. 5, pp. 576-587, 2010.

2. S.-T. Chen, G.-D. Wu, and H.-N. Huang, "Wavelet-domain audio watermarking scheme using optimization-based quantization," *IET Proceedings on Signal Processing*, vol. 4, no. 6, pp. 720-727, 2010.
3. S.-T. Chen, C.-Y. Hsu, and H.-N. Huang, "Wavelet-Domain Audio Watermarking using Optimal Modification on Low-Frequency Amplitude," *IET Proceedings on Signal Processing*, vol. 9, no. 2, pp.166 – 176, 2015.
4. S.-T. Chen, H.-N. Huang, W.-M. Kung, and C.-Y. Hsu, "Optimization-Based Image Watermarking with Integrated Quantization Embedding in the Wavelet Domain," *Multimedia Tools and Applications*, doi:10.1007/s11042-015-2522-8.
5. H.-N. Huang, D.-F. Chen, C.-C. Lin, S.-T. Chen*, W.-C. Hsu, "Improving SVD-Based Image Watermarking via Block-by-Block Optimization on Singular Values," *EURASIP Journal on Image and Video Processing*, 25, 2015 (DOI 10.1186/s13640-015-0073-6.
6. H. Wanga, R. Nishimurab, Y. Suzukib, L. Mao, "Fuzzy self-adaptive digital audio watermarking based on time-spread echo hiding," *Applied Acoustics*, vol. 69, no. 10, pp. 868–874, 2008.
7. G. Hua, J. Goh, V. L. L. Thing, "Time-Spread Echo-Based Audio Watermarking With Optimized Imperceptibility and Robustness," *IEEE Transactions on Audio, Speech, and Language Processing*, vol. 23, no. 2, pp. 227–239, 2015.
8. G. Hua, J. Goh, V. L. L. Thing, "Cepstral Analysis for the Application of Echo-Based Audio Watermark Detection," *IEEE Transactions on Information Forensics and Security*, vol. 10, no. 9, pp. 1850–1861, 2015.

A Research on Uyghur Semantic Text Classification

Gui-Xian Xu, Zhi-Yuan Chen, Lei Shen, Rui She, Jian-Lin Wang,
Zhen-Zi Jia and Shu-Qi Yan

Minzu University of China
Beijing, China
E-mail: xuguixian2000@sohu.com

The research is designed to improve the result of Uyghur text classification. Based on current semantic text classification, this paper uses information gain and the KNN algorithm. Besides, it also provides an improved semantic text algorithm. And this algorithm has better results than the non-semantic algorithm.

Keywords: Semantic Text Classification; Uyghur Language Information.

1. Introduction

Since the 1980s, the development and application of Xinjiang ethnic characters on computer has become a social system engineering promoting ethnic Chinese modernization and informationization[1]. However, compared with English and Chinese, Uyghur natural language processing technology is not mature enough, and the research now also does not reach the level of available tools[2].

Text classification based on semantic relation of words can classify texts more efficiently and accurately. The difference between Uyghur and Chinese is mainly manifested in that the weaving of the original feature space dimension is bigger, and that the part of speech change is more flexible and so on. Therefore, according to the different characteristics of the text, such as speech or meaning, this study divides texts into semantic and non-semantic part. Then the study will use two different methods applying in processing the two parts.

2. Background

Nowadays, all kinds of text files and information online have proliferated. So there is a huge applicable value in text auto classification.

In text classification, how to present texts is a basic and important issue. Vector space model (VSM) is still the main method of text representation, and relative researches are still concentrated on using what units as the feature on the issue. Paper[3] concludes a lot of researches about how to choose feature unit in Chinese and English text classification. In paper[4], the authors point out that the phrase refers to multiple words appearing in texts consecutively, which have syntactic or statistical meaning. And they propose an algorithm of English phrase extraction based on statistical methods. Paper[5] points out that use the phrase as text feature can improve the efficiency of English text classification. In paper[6], the experiment indicates we can get the same classification result using Chinese character directly as using phrases.

Now there are many studies on text classification. For example, support vector machines theory Vapnik V[7] proposed is a binary classification method based on statistical learning theory. The basic idea is to find an optimal hyperplane which can correctly classify samples. An optimal hyperplane is the hyperplane can not only separate the two types of sample point correctly, but make the classification spaces between the two types maximum.

3. The Proposed Algorithm

Based on the non-semantic algorithm, we provide an improved semantic one. The process is shown in Figure. 1.

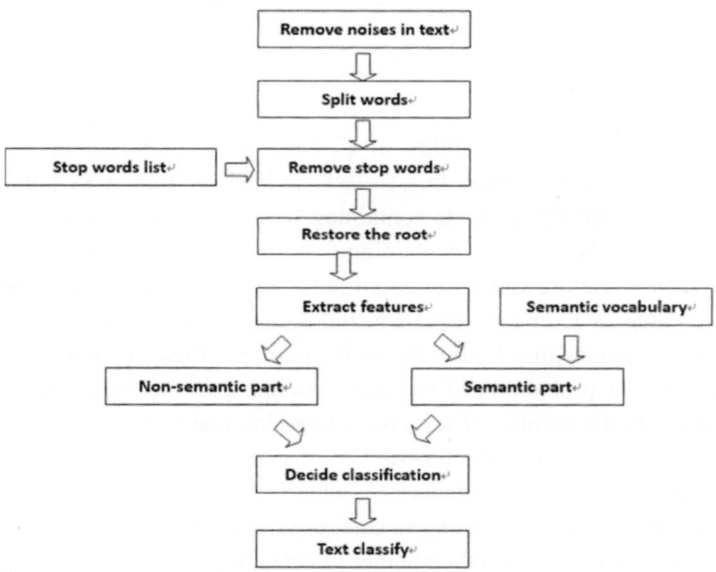

Fig. 1. The process of Uyghur text classification

3.1. *Text preprocessing*

Text preprocessing is to turn the text into the sequence of elements in the original feature space. Its function is to provide a simple set of elements for feature extraction and text classification. Uyghur text preprocessing generally includes noise reduction, splitting words, removal of stop words, root reduction and so on. And it finally generates the original word sequence.

3.2. *Feature extraction*

Information gain is the difference between information entropies and indicates the information obtained after the elimination of uncertainty.

Aiming at each feature item, it calculates the information gain of feature item t to category C by counting the quantity of files that include feature item t or not in category C, and it is defined as the difference in entropies considering the appearance of feature item t before and after, as in Eq. (1):

$$\mathrm{IG(T) = H(C) - H(C|T)}$$
$$= \sum_{i=1}^{a} P(C_i)\log_2 P(C_i) + P(t)\sum_{i=1}^{n} P(C_i|t)\log_2 P(C_i|t)$$
$$+ P(\bar{t})\sum_{i=1}^{n} P(C_i|\bar{t})\log_2 P(C_i|\bar{t}) \quad (1)$$

$P(C_i)$ indicates the probability of C_i class texts appearing in the corpus, which equals to text number in C_i class divided by total text number; P(t) indicates the probability of texts containing feature item t in the corpus, which equals to the number of texts containing feature t divided by total text number; $P(C_i|t)$ indicates the probability of condition that texts contain feature item t and belong to category C_i, which equals to the number of texts containing feature t and belonging to category C_i divided by the number of texts containing feature t; $P(\bar{t})$ indicates the probability of texts not containing feature item t in the corpus, which equals to the number of texts not containing feature t divided by total text number; $P(C_i|\bar{t})$ indicates the probability of condition that texts don't contain feature item t but belong to category C_i, which equals to the number of texts not containing feature t but belonging to category C_i divided by the number of texts not containing feature t; m is the number of category.

Obviously, the bigger an information gain value of a feature item is, the more contribution it gives and the more important it is to the classification. Therefore, we usually select several words with high information gain value to form feature vector of texts. According to the training data, we calculate the information gain of each feature item, delete some small ones and sort the rest in terms of information gain from the largest to the smallest.

3.3. *Text classification*

This system divides the text into the semantic part and the non-semantic part.

3.3.1. *The algorithm for the non-semantic part*

We use KNN algorithm[8] to deal with the non-semantic part, and we do not introduce the details of KNN algorithm here anymore.

3.3.2. *Calculation method of classification based on semantics*

The similarity of concepts is determined by several parameters such as Semantic Depth, Superposed Degree and Dissimilitude Degree. We provide the semantic depth of the root node in semantic vocabulary is 0, and the depth of its child node is 1. The others is followed by analogy.

1)Semantic Depth: It refers to the level position of the concept P in the semantic vocabulary, noted as Depth.

2)Superposed Degree: It refers to the length of the path of the same parent nodes of the concepts of P_1 and P_2 in the semantic vocabulary, noted as $Spd(P_1,P_2)$.

3)Dissimilitude Degree: It refers to the length of the shortest path of the concepts of P_1 and P_2 along their parent nodes gradually moving to their first common node in a semantic vocabulary, noted as $Dsd(P_1,P_2)$. In fact, Dissimilitude Degree and Semantic Distance is equivalent.

Then we calculate the similarity between two texts: $Sim(D_1,D_2)$. Text similarity is composed of two parts. Sim_1 stands for semantic similarity, and Sim_2 stands for non-semantic similarity. Calculation methods is as Eq. (2)(3)(4)(5) show:

$$Sim(S_i,S_j) = \frac{-\alpha \times Spd(S_i,S_j)}{(Distance(S_i,S_j)-\alpha)\times \max(Depth(S_i),Depth(S_j))} \quad (2)$$

$$Sim_1(d_1,d_2) = \sum_{i-1}^{m}\sum_{j-1}^{m}\frac{Sim(S_i,S_j)}{a\times b} \quad (3)$$

$$Sim_2(d_1, d_2) = \frac{x_1 \times u_1 + x_2 \times u_2 + \cdots + x_p \times u_p}{\sqrt{x_1^2 + x_2^2 + \cdots + x_p^2} \times \sqrt{u_1^2 + u_2^2 + \cdots + u_p^2}} \tag{4}$$

$$Sim(d_1, d_2) = Sim_1(d_1, d_2) + Sim_2(d_1, d_2) \tag{5}$$

S_i indicates concepts in Text D_1, and S_j indicates concepts in Text D_2. Depth(S) indicates the Semantic Depth of the concept in a semantic vocabulary, and Distance(S_i,S_j) indicates the Superposed Degree of two concepts in a semantic vocabulary, and Spd(S_i,S_j) indicates the Dissimilitude Degree of two concepts in a semantic vocabulary, and α is a parameter used to adjust. The letter "a" is the number of non-zero concepts in Text D_1 in the semantic space, and the letter "b" is the number of non-zero concepts in Text D_2 in the semantic space.

3.3.3. *The classification decision*

The classification decision is based on the similarity weighting decisions, and its rule function is as the following Eq. (6)(7)(8) show:

$$S(d) = argmax\ score(d, c_i) \tag{6}$$

$$score(d, c_i) = \sum_{d_j \epsilon KNN(d)}^{i=1} sim(d, d_j)\delta(d_j, c_i) \tag{7}$$

$$\delta(d_j, c_i) = \begin{cases} 1 & d_j \in c_i \\ 0 & d_j \notin c_i \end{cases} \tag{8}$$

S(D) indicates the highest scoring category, which is also the decision category for the Document D. Score(D,C_i) stands for the score which D get in the Ci category, and Sim(D,D_j) stands for the score of the similarity of D and D_j, and KNN(d) stands for the k-nearest neighbors of the document d. δ(D_j,C_i) indicates whether D_j belongs to the C_i category.

4. Conclusion

Existing algorithms of text classification generally describe text resources with keywords, which, obviously, does not apply to Uyghur text classification, and is inefficient. While our approach is effective in reducing vector model dimensions and has a good performance on the efficiency and accuracy of text classification.

Acknowledgments

This work was supported by the National Key Technology Research and Development Program of the Ministry of Science and Technology of China (No.

2014BAK10B03), the Beijing Social Science Foundation (No. 14WYB040), and the National Natural Science Foundation of China (No. 61309012, No. 61331013).

References

1. Maimaitiabudula. Technical information processing and retrieval based on database-specific format [D]. Software College of Tongji University, 2007. (In Chinese)
2. Zulipiya·maimaitiming. Uyghur language verb phrase recognition [D]. University of posts and telecommunications, 2012. (In Chinese)
3. Jinshu Su, Bofeng Zhang, Xu Xin. Research progress on techniques of text categorization based on machine learning [J]. Journal of software, 2006, 17 (9): 1848-1859. (In Chinese)
4. Caropreso M F, Matwin S, Sebastiani F. Statistical phrases in automated text categorization, Statistical Phrases in Automated Text Categorization [R]. Paris: Centre National de la Recherche Seientiflque, 2000:78-102.
5. Koster C, Beney J. Phrases—based document categorization revisited [C]. Proceedings of the 2nd International Workshop on Patent Information Retrieval. New York: ACM, 2009: 49-55.
6. Aihua Zhang, Jiwu Jing, Ji Xiang. Text representations of Chinese text classification [J]. Journal of the Graduate School of Chinese Academy of Sciences, 2009, 26 (3): 400-407. (In Chinese)
7. Vapnik V. The Nature of Satistical Learning Theory [M]. New York; Spring-Verlag, 1995.
8. Huailiang Liu, Zhiguo Zhang, Zhihui Ma, Lei Sun. Empirical Study of the Comparison of SVM and KNN-based Categorization of Chinese Text. Theory & Application, 2008, 31(6): 941-944. (In Chinese)

Temperature Recognition Based on Infrared Images of Electric Power Equipment

Bin Yu, Yu Zhong, Dan-Lei Shan, Jie-Qiong Jin and Wei Qi

State Grid Hangzhou Xiaoshan Power Supply Company
JinCheng Road, Hangzhou 311200, China
E-mail: binyu87125296@163.com

Infrared imaging detection is widely applied in power equipment maintenance. In this paper, the temperature recognition based on infrared images of electric power equipment is proposed to obtain the temperature automatically to replace the time-consuming and error-prone manual way. Image enhancement and the morphological processing are adopted first to help the segmentation. Then, multi-segmentation based on prior knowledge is applied to get the temperature value region and the character region sequentially. The temperature value is obtained by the comparison of the character region and the standard character templates. The experiment is conducted on infrared images collected from the a power plant. The experimental results demonstrate the effectiveness and the practicability of the proposed method on automatic recognition of infrared image temperature of electric power equipment.

Keywords: Image Enhancement; Morphological Processing; Segmentation.

1. Introduction

The safe operation of electrical power equipment and power grid is not only related to the daily lives of people, but also seriously affects social and economic activities of society[1]. Many electrical power equipment operating conditions are very poor and easily lead to the failure of electrical power equipment, which makes the power equipment daily inspection indispensable. The thermal effect of electrical equipment is a precursor to many faults [2], [3]. The real-time monitoring of the temperature of the electrical equipment is helpful to ensure the normal operation of the power equipment.

There are many ways to detect temperature, which can be divided into contact type and non-contact type [4]. The scope of contact temperature measurement application is limited because of its non-sensitivity and large measurement error [5]. In recent years, a non-contact temperature measurement based on infrared imaging detection is widely applied to overhaul the electric power equipment. This detection technique has unexampled advantages compared to the past contact detection method, such as live detection, no need of contact, fast scanning and imaging, which make it the most effective means of power system state maintenance [6]. However, the final failure judgment need read the temperature of the image. The complexity of the captured image apparently led to an oversight or a misjudgment in some cases. Considering the inspection workload, the workers cannot guarantee the timely read a large temperature value of the images.

In this paper, the temperature recognition based on Infrared images of electric power equipment is proposed to obtain the temperature automatically to replace the time-consuming and error-prone manual way. According to the characteristics of infrared images returned by the infrared thermometer, the method uses the infrared image enhancement, the morphological processing and segmentation of image processing technology to generate temperature value area feature descriptor. The temperature value is obtained by the comparison with standard character templates.

This article is organized as follows. The problem statement is described in Section 2. The temperature recognition method is illustrated in Section 3. In Section 4, experimental results are presented to demonstrate the effectiveness and the practicability of the proposed method. Finally, Section 5 concludes the paper.

2. Problem Statement

Infrared images are widely applied in military, scientific, medical and other fields. However, infrared images have shortcomings of noise, low contrast and blurred texture details due to the uneven photosensitive response of infrared detector and non-ideal optics system [7]. Image enhancement techniques are used to improve the image quality, enrich the amount of information, and enhance the image interpretation and recognition results [8]. Typically infrared thermometer photographed images are color images, which contain a large amount of color information with red, green, blue three layer dimension. Gray is used to convert the original three-dimensional color images into two-dimensional grayscale images [9]. Then, binarization is adopted to turn the grayscale images to binary images. The process of gray and binarization eliminates a lot of useless information, improves computational efficiency and saves storage space, which is necessary for a real-time system. Image segmentation is an important preprocessing of image recognition and computer vision. The only basis for segmentation is the brightness and color of pixels in an image. When the computer is automatically processed, it will encounter various difficulties, such as non-uniform illumination, unclear portion and shadow in the image. It is a promising way to correct some errors in the segmentation by introducing some artificial knowledge oriented and artificial intelligence methods.

3. The Proposed Method

For the temperature recognition of the infrared images, some prior are introduced. The prior that the temperature region is a connected region whose area is greater than a certain value is employed to eliminate some noise. The prior that the region of the temperature of the electrical equipment is consisted of five words and the temperature values exits in 3rd and 5th subregions is the guidance for the segmentation. The temperature recognition is in the following:

Procedure The Temperature Recognition Algorithm:

Input Infrared images of electric power equipment.

Output t the temperature of electric power equipment.

Step 1 Gray. The infrared images taken by infrared thermometers are usually color images, which represents by the value of R, G, B, $f(x,y)=\begin{cases} R \\ G \\ B \end{cases}$. Convert the RGB image into the gray image using the weighted average method: $\mu(x,y)=0.3R+0.59G+0.11B$

Step 2 Binarization. Convert the gray image into binary image by adaptive threshold, $\mu(x,y)=\begin{cases} 0, \mu(x,y)\le T \\ 1, \mu(x,y)\ge T \end{cases}$

Step 3 Connected-component labeling (CCL). CCL is adopted in computer vision to detect connected regions in binary images [10]. Obtain connected region and delete the connected regions the area of which is less than 1000. If $\mu(x,y)\in S$,where $A(S)<1000$,then $\mu(x,y)=0$.

Step 4 Dilation and segmentation. Dilation adds pixels to the boundaries of objects in an image that connect the regions with small intervals [11]. In this paper, erosion and CCL are used to find the temperature regions. The dilation factor is set to 4 to make the word a whole. Segment the connected regions and find the region which contains 5 non-zero connected subregions, S_1, S_2, $\cdots$, S_5. Each subregion represents a word.

Step 5 Erosion and segmentation. Erosion removes pixels on object boundaries that split a connected object into several mutually independent connected domains [12]. Erosion and CCL is applied to obtain the separate characters. Segment the 3rd and 5th subregions and obtain 4 part, P_1, P_2, P_3, P_4. Each part represents a character.

Step 6 Resize the character part according to the size of standard templates and obtain C_1, C_2, C_3, C_4.

Step 7 Compare C_1, C_2, C_4 with the standard templates and achieve character recognition.

Step 8 Compute the temperature of electric power equipment,

$$t = 10C_1 + C_2 + 0.1C_4$$

Based on the above algorithm, we can automatically identify the temperature in the infrared images of the electrical equipment.

4. Experimental Results

The effectiveness and the practicability of the proposed method is demonstrated by the experiment on an infrared image of the electrical equipment. The infrared image, the corresponding gray image and the binary image are shown sequentially in Figure 1. Figure 2 shows the obtained temperature area after the process of dilation and segmentation. Figure 3 shows the obtained character region after the process of erosion and segmentation. The recognition temperature is shown in Figure 4.

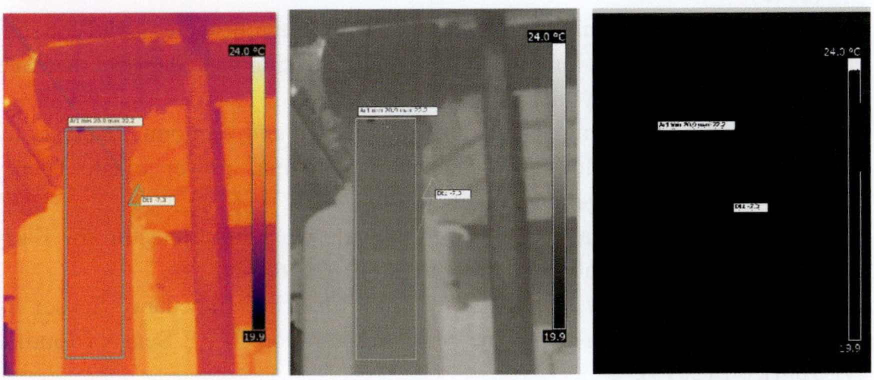

(a) (b) (c)

Fig. 1. a. The original color image b. The gray image c. The binary image

Fig. 2. Dilation and segmentation

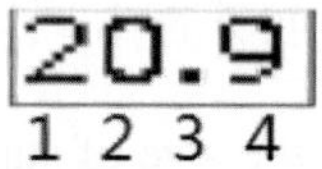

Fig. 3. Erosion and segmentation

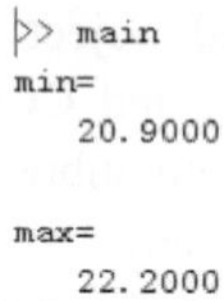

Fig. 4. The temperature of the electrical equipment

5. Conclusions

The temperature recognition based on Infrared images of electric power equipment is proposed to obtain the temperature automatically to replace the time-consuming and error-prone manual way. The experimental results on infrared images demonstrate the effectiveness and the practicability of our proposed method.

Acknowledgment

This work is supported by Technology Project Smart Gird Zhejiang Electric Power Company.

References

1. Bai J, Gu W, Yuan X, et al. Power Quality Prediction, Early Warning, and Control for Points of Common Coupling with Wind Farms. Energies, 8(9) (2015).
2. Moghaddam I G, Saniei M, Mashhour E. A comprehensive model for self-scheduling an energy hub to supply cooling, heating and electrical demands of a building. Energy, 94:157-170 (2016).
3. Budisulistyo D, Krumdieck S. Thermodynamic and economic analysis for the pre-feasibility study of a binary geothermal power plant. Energy Conversion & Management, 103:639-649 (2015).
4. Kai Y, Zhang R, Yang J, et al. A Novel Arc Fault Detector for Early Detection of Electrical Fires. Sensors, 16(4) (2016).
5. Durante G, Becari W, Lima F A S, et al. Electrical Impedance Sensor for Real-Time Detection of Bovine Milk Adulteration. IEEE Sensors Journal, 16(4):1-1 (2015).

6. Dankert A, Kamalakar M V, Dash S P, et al. Room Temperature Electrical Detection of Spin Polarized Currents in Topological Insulators. Nano Letters(2015).
7. Liu D, Lu W, Lei S, et al. Low-noise readout circuit for thermo-electrical cooler-less uncooled microbolometer infrared imager. Electronics Letters, 52(9):705-706(2016).
8. Li Y, Zhang Y, Geng A, et al. Infrared image enhancement based on atmospheric scattering model and histogram equalization. Optics & Laser Technology, 83:99-107(2016).
9. Charbal A, Dufour J E, Guery A, et al. Integrated Digital Image Correlation considering gray level and blur variations: Application to distortion measurements of IR camera. Optics & Lasers in Engineering, 78:75-85(2016).
10. Liu L, Zhang Y J, Liu J, et al. Application of Infrared Binocular Vision for Monitoring Moving Target in Por. Applied Mechanics & Materials, 678:155-161(2014).
11. Chen J W, Vakil-Gilani K, Williamson K L, et al. Infrared pupillometry, the Neurological Pupil index and unilateral pupillary dilation after traumatic brain injury: implications for treatment paradigms. Springerplus, 3(3):1-10(2014).
12. Sabri T, Baratta G A, Jäger C, et al. A laboratory study of ion-induced erosion of ice-covered carbon grains. Astronomy & Astrophysics, 575(1):419-419(2015).

Research on the Control of the Crazyfile based Open Source Unmanned Aerial Vehicle

Xia Gao[1,2,a], Hai-Feng Lu[1,2,b], Fang-Qin Xu[2,c]

[1]*College of Computer Science and Technology, Donghua University Shanghai, 201620, China*

[2]*College of Information Technology, Shanghai JianQiao University Shanghai, 201306, China*

E-mail: [a]14080@gench.edu.cn, [b]1771097725@qq.com, [c]xufqin@gench.edu.cn

Intelligent UAV(Unmanned Aerial Vehicle) as a new field of artificial intelligence and robotics technology, which has widely received attention by the domestic and foreign industries. In view of the problem of the single function and the poor stability of flight that is widely known, this paper researches on the flight attitude of UAV based on IDE Arduino development platform, and the flight stability of UAV which is optimized through the PID control algorithm and fuzzy control method. At the same time, combined with the open source of Arduino, all kinds of sensors are installed on the UAV to carry out the underlying call, and finally, to realize the intelligent and stable flight control.

Keywords: UAV; Crazyfile; Arduino IDE; PID.

1. Introduction

The concept of UAV started from Britain, which mainly located in military applications, such as investigation, and it is designed to reduce the cost of human resources. With the reform and the change of the times, UAV gradually spread to civil. The United States as the most mature technology, it has been used widely in agriculture, news, rescue and other fields[1]. The UAV started late in China, a few domestic authoritative company also has a single function, the code is not open source and other issues, such as the DaJiang UAV, although the technology has matured in the flight attitude, but because it does not share the source code, resulting in third party developers is difficult to make a difference on this basis, which results in the development of the UAV has been stagnant. Even some people think that the UAV is the aerial photo machine, and the development and application of UAV has been greatly restricted[2].

In order to solve the above situation, open source hardware platform of the crazyfile2.0 is used to study the realization of the flight attitude. Through the modification of UAV on this basis, so as to realize the UAV detection, data collection, take things and other functions.

2. Related Technologies

2.1. *Crazyfile2.0*

Crazyfile is a general-purpose hardware development platform, in addition to light weight, small size and other features, it also supports low power Bluetooth connectivity, greatly enriched the developer's control device selection. In addition, PCB board of Crazyfile is used in the design of welding without welding, so beginners can also be simple assembly and start quickly[3].

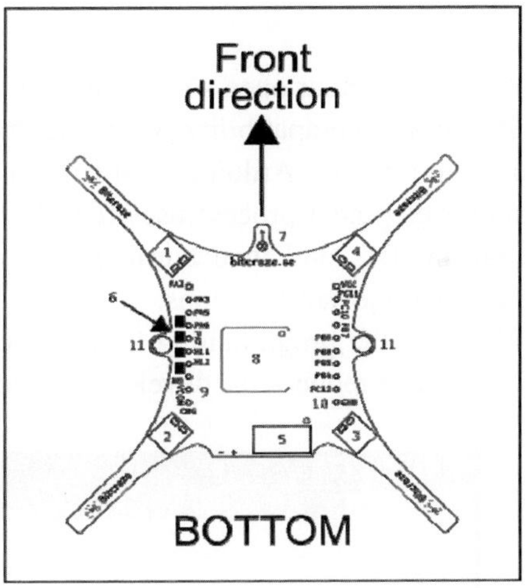

Fig. 1. Schematic diagram of Crazyfile circuit board

As shown in Figure 1, PCB board of Crazyfile integrates the LED indicator light (show the current state of Crazyfile), expansion connector (used to connect the various extension panel), STM32F405 controller, nRF51822 controller (used to debug access), motor connector (used to connect four motors use).

As shown in Figure 2, it is the same as the vast majority of four axis aircraft on the market. Crazyfile uses the method that the diagonal of the Deputy motor rotates in different directions but the same speed, which enables the lift of aircraft is greater than gravity, so as to achieve the effect of rising, and it can also decrease and hover.

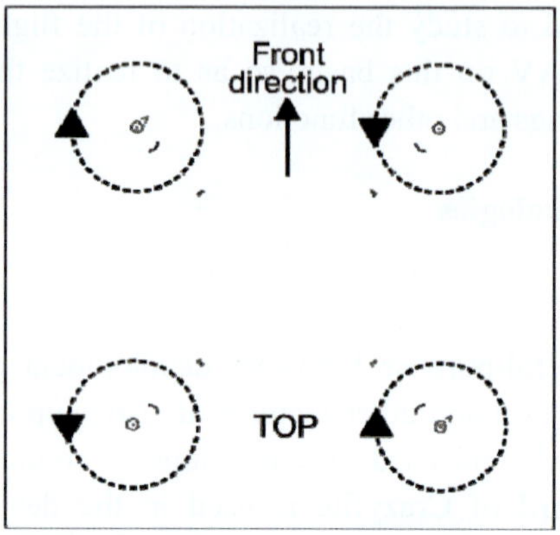

Fig. 2. The flight principle of Crazyfile

2.2. *Arduino*

Arduino is one of the most popular open source electronic prototype platform in the market, and its strong compatibility won the majority of developers. Traditional Arduino refers to the Arduino board (hardware) and the Arduino IDE (software). And development process uses IDE Arduino this time, through writing program code in IDE, and then burning the program into the circuit board, that can achieve the relevant functions.

As shown in Figure 3, the programming language of Arduino IDE is built on the basis of C/C++, which reduces the developer's study requirements.

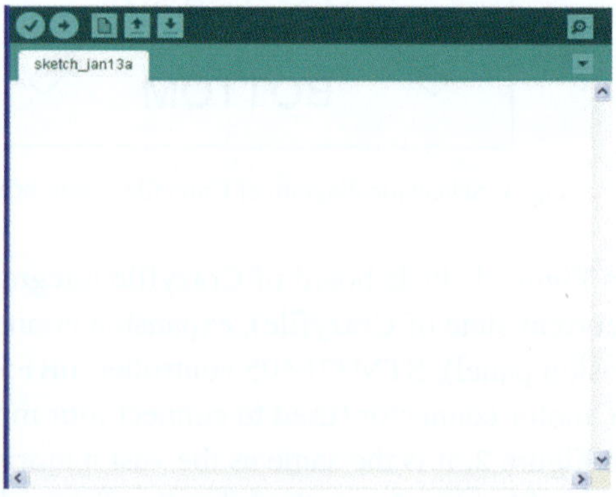

Fig. 3. The interface of Arduino IDE

2.3. *PID*

PID algorithm is a common control method, its advantage is that each parameter in the calculation process is independent, which P represents the proportion, I represents the integral, D represents the differential. PID algorithm is relatively simple in the selection of parameters, so in the process of control, the structure change is flexible, it can meet the requirements of general control.

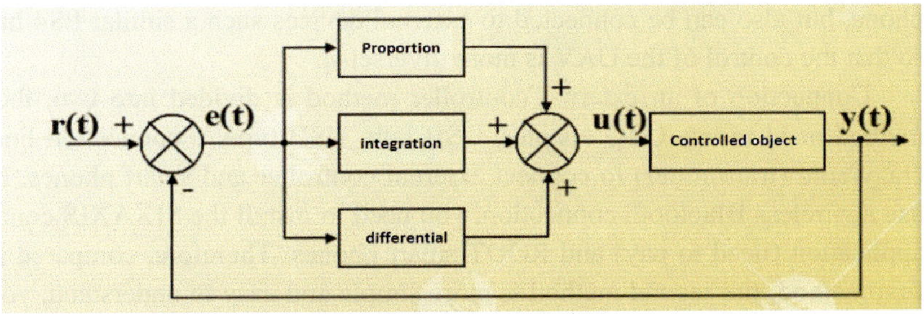

Fig. 4. PID algorithm control principle

As shown in Figure 4, r(t) is the standard value that is set firstly, e(t) is the deviation value, u (t) is the new numerical value through the PID algorithm calculates. This value is returned to the control object to adjust, and final y(t) is the actual value. That is r(t) - y(t) = e(t), the set value minus the actual value is equal to the deviation value, the deviation value of the PID algorithm is controlled to adjust the object.

3. Implementation and Experiment

3.1. *Implementation process*

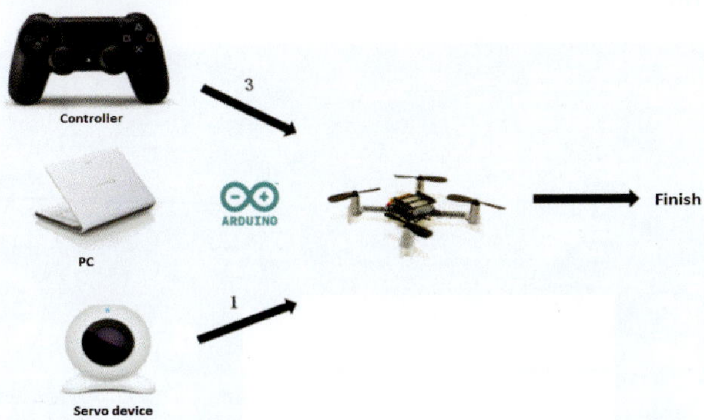

Fig. 5. Implementation process

As shown in Figure 5. First of all, the required equipment is installed in the UAV platform, like the camera, temperature and humidity sensor. Then using the Arduino IDE of computer write programming code into PCB circuit board of Crazyfile. This step is mainly through the code to call the serial port on the various devices. At the same time it contains the PID value to make the UAV flight attitude to achieve a smooth. In the end, the controller can be connected with the crazyfile client. The controller can choose the common Android smart phone, but also can be connected to external devices such a similar PS4 handle, so that the control of the UAV is more diverse[4].

Connection of an external controller method is divided into two, the first method need to use OTG adapter, USB hub, USB type Y connection line and crazyradio (transmitter) to connect external controller and smart phones. If you use a wireless Bluetooth connection, you need to install the SIXAXIS controller application (need to pay) and ROOT smart phones. Therefore, compared to the first method, the second method is more simple and easy to understand, you can directly choose the product line of SONY, SONY XPERIA series of smart phones can be directly connected to the Station Play handle.

3.2. *PID numerical acquisition*

3.2.1. *Multiwiiconf*

Multiwiiconf referred to MWC, which is currently the most popular open source debugging software of flight control on the market. At first it was used to develop the control handle to support the Japanese Nintendo game console Wii. Because of its strong compatibility and easy to understand the structure, it is populated by the majority of developers. As shown in Figure 6 is the interface for multiwiiconf 2.4.

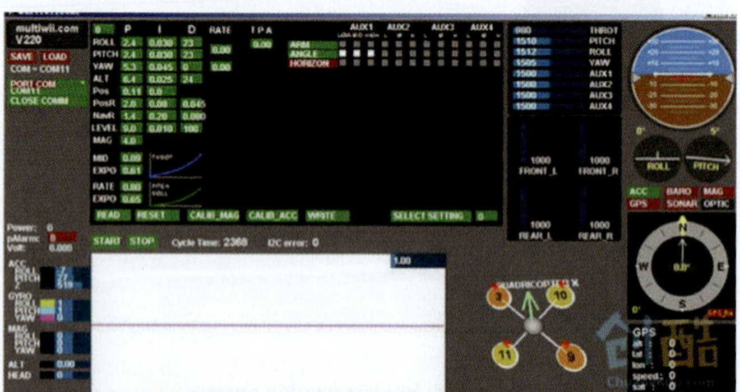

Fig. 6. The interface of multiwiiconf

3.2.2. *Experimental procedure*

Under the condition of without shutting down the power to test compatibility and stability of the hardware; In order to obtain the stable numerical PID. First crazyfile is suspended by two ropes. Then through the PID of the current multiwiiconf value to change the debugging, the edge of the flying edge to adjust the value, so as to observe the crazyfile flight attitude, get the final PID value[5].

P (ratio): is a gain factor, the main expression of the degree of resistance to the outside world; The larger the value of P, the greater the degree of resistance of the UAV; But the big value will lead to UAV bumping and trembling, even rollover; I (integral): it is a sensitive response to the error of the UAV, if I is too small will lead to the extreme reaction of the UAV; If value I is too large, it will lead to a slow response to the error of the UAV, and it cannot be made in a timely manner to correct the attitude of the flight. D (differential): when the UAV tilt and other flying pose problems, the appropriate D value can play a role in the inhibition[6].

Tab. 1. Final PID value

	P	I	D
ROLL	1.8	0.025	35
PITCH	1.8	0.025	35
YAW	1.1	0.015	25
ALT	0.0	0.000	0
Pos	0.15	0.0	
PosR	3.4	0.14	0.053
NavR	2.5	0.33	0.083
LEVEL	3.1	0.000	100
MAG	0.0		

As shown in Table 1, ROLL, PITCH, YAW respectively represent the pitch, roll, the direction, in general it is the X, Y, Z axis when fly. Usually X axis and Z axis are as a horizontal plane of real flight, so ROLL and PITCH use the same value. ALT and LEVEL represent the attitude stability and automatic balance. Pos and PosR are the fixed point function service for the UAV, the former is the correction, the latter is the correction rate[7]. After many experiments, the PID values of Table 1 are obtained; After obtaining the PID ratio coefficient, as shown in Figure. 7, IDE defines various functional functions, so that the UAV can reach a certain height, fixed position and other flying attitude[8].

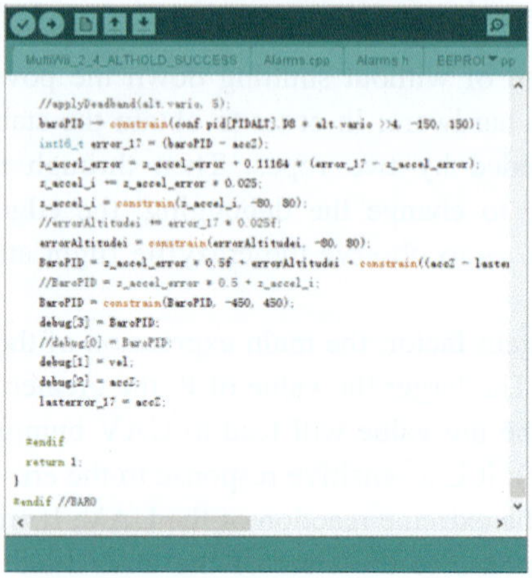

Fig. 7. Fixed height PID algorithm

On this basis, the function of the UAV can be expanded the use of this open source development platform, such as the installation of cameras, all kinds of sensors, using tongs to achieve the detection, data acquisition, sending things and other functions, the UAV functions market is from the original aerial extended to all areas of life[9].

4. Conclusion

In this paper, through the study of crazyfile open source UAV to put forward innovation and reform of current market, break the traditional single function, the source code is closed and so on[10]. Autonomous research and complete calculation of the UAV flight attitude. Through the PID to combine multwiiconf algorithm, in order to complete the multi function UAV flight, such as set high, fixed flight. These experimental values allow crazyfile UAV to achieve a smooth flight attitude such as DaJiang UAV. UAV brings convenience to people's lives at the same time, but also to reduce human resources and costs, to improve the safety and efficiency of high-risk work. So open source UAV has a strong application value and development prospects.

References

1. Malatinec T, Popelka V, Huba M, et al. Laboratory model helicopter control using a lowcost Arduino hardware[C]// Control Conference. IEEE, 2014:326-331.

2. Liu W, Peng C, Wang F, et al. Design of UAV Airborne Reconnaissance and Rescue Based on ATMEGA2560[C]// International Conference on Education, Management, Commerce and Society (EMCS-15). Atlantis Press, 2015.
3. Helland A S. UAV anti-icing system based on conductive coating[J]. Institutt for Teknisk Kybernetikk, 2014.
4. Liu J C, Li-Bin L U, Tan L N. Implementation of remote control servo motor based on Arduino[J]. Information Technology, 2015.
5. Zhu L, Xu J, Yan L. Design of Four Axis Aircraft Based on Arduino Used in City-wide Food Delivery[J]. Advance Journal of Food Science & Technology, 2016, 11.
6. Koszewnik A. The Parrot UAV Controlled by PID Controllers[J]. Acta Mechanica Et Automatica, 2014, 8(2):65-69.
7. Misra D, Bhattacharjee S, Goswami B, et al. Guaranteed performance PID controller for UAV pitch control[C]// IEEE First International Conference on Control, Measurement and Instrumentation. IEEE, 2016.
8. Katigbak C N R, Garcia J R B, Gutang J E D, et al. Autonomous trajectory tracking of a quadrotor UAV using PID controller[C]// International Conference on Humanoid, Nanotechnology, Information Technology, communication and Control, Environment and Management. IEEE, 2015.
9. Zhou D, Geng Q. Multi-model And Fuzzy PID Control for Fixed-wing UAV[J]. 2015.
10. Lin F, Wang X, Qu X. PID parameters tuning of UAV flight control system based on artificial bee colony algorithm[C]// International Conference on Electrical, Computer Engineering and Electronics. 2015.

An Analysis of BDS-Based High Precision Positioning System for Autonomous Driving

Jia-Wei Yu[a] and Feng Luo[b]

School of Automotive studies, Tongji University, Cao'an Highway No.4800
Shanghai, 201804, China
E-mail: [a]14_joy@tongji.edu.cn, [b]luo_feng@tongji.edu.cn

With the advent of the Chinese new BeiDou Navigation Satellite System (BDS), multisystem Real-Time Kinematic (RTK) high precision positioning service can be possible and available almost everywhere. This study aims to give an initial view of a BDS-based RTK positioning system combined with a path tracking algorithm. Application and tests will be carried out in Shanghai, China, on a real vehicle to analyze the feasibility of a high precision system to be equipped on an autonomous vehicle.

Keywords: BeiDou Navigation Satellite System; High Precision Positioning; Path Tracking; Autonomous Driving.

1. Introduction

In recent years, rapid development of internet industry has provided automotive industry revolutionary opportunities. Artificial-Intelligence based driving behavior decision, multi-sensors based environment detecting methods and other new technology have become a heated focus in autonomous driving fields. The Global Positioning System is also widely used as a component in land vehicle navigation systems. However, such positioning systems can hardly provide high positioning accuracy and continuous positioning information enough to make a self-driving vehicle to find its way. The BeiDou Navigation Satellite System(BDS) in China now can serve as an alternative to provide space-time reference.

Space constellation of global BeiDou system consists of five Geostationary Earth Orbit (GEO) satellites, twenty-seven Medium Earth Orbit (MEO) satellites and three Inclined Geosynchronous Satellite Orbit (IGSO) satellites[1].

The construction of BeiDou regional satellite navigation system (also known as BeiDou-2) started in 2004. Since 2011, the BDS has been providing open service in Asian-Pacific areas. By 2016, there have been altogether 22 satellites in orbit. In four years, the BDS will construct to a global satellite navigation system with a fully operational constellation of 35 satellites, which will provide global high precision, high reliability of the positioning, navigation, timing and short message communication service. So far, regional BDS has been applied in many fields to provide critical support, including precision agriculture[2] and intelligent driving test system. Due to high precision positioning capability, stability and compatibility with other satellite systems, the BDS shows its potential in lane-level autonomous driving applications.

The rest of this paper goes as follows. Important performance requirements for automotive application are discussed in Section 1. Basic composition of a high precision positioning system is presented in Section 3. Next, a simple BDS-based trajectory-tracking system is introduced in Section 4. After that, test results are analyzed and summarized in Section 5. The conclusion of this paper comes in Section 6.

2. Performance Requirements

Before analysis, it is necessary to make clear some performance requirements of positioning system to be applied in autonomous vehicles. To realize self-driving function, autonomous vehicles need to know where they are (Position), where to go (Destination) and how to go (Direction and Route).

To answer the first question, detailed requirements of positioning system are as follows.

- Accuracy:

Despite computer vision can help improve positioning performance by detecting lane line, a satellite-based positioning system still need to work as an independent system with high level(cm-level) positioning precision, especially when the lines are obscure or even do not exist, to guarantee safety-related in-lane driving or lane changing.

- Real-Time:

Since vehicles often run at a relatively high speed and road conditions change all the time, real-time positioning ability is crucial for on-road self-driving vehicles to make real-time driving behavior decisions. With higher real-time data updating frequency, the driving system can achieve more accurate position control at every moment.

- Continuity:

  Continuity means the positioning information should be both time-related continuous and space-related smooth. Due to speed is transitional, vehicles positioning points shift should be restrained by some fitting methods to eliminate and correct fault positioning data.
- Stability and environmental adaptability:

  Autonomous vehicles required high stability to deal with complicated self-conditions of vehicles such as large temperature difference, electromagnetic compatibility environment and shock and vibration. Besides, urban-roads environment with large mansions, leaves-sheltered avenues and tunnels is a great challenge for satellite-based positioning.

3. Basic Concept of a High Precision Positioning System

Commonly, there are three ways of point positioning: pseudorange positioning, pseudorange relative positioning and carrier phase positioning. According to the study of Shi C [3], the results show that:

(1) the accuracy of pseudorange point positioning is less than 20 m;

(2) the accuracy of pseudorange relative positioning are 3.0 m for the vertical component, 1.5 m for north component and 0.6–0.8 m for east component;

(3) based on the carrier phase and pseudorange observations, precise relative positioning (short baseline) can obtain an accuracy better than 1 cm for east component, 2 cm for north component, 4 cm for up component;

(4) the accuracy of BeiDou and GPS combined precise relative positioning has an improvement of 20% over GPS alone.

In this paper, a BDS&GPS integrated high precision positioning system is adopted. The system mainly consists of two parts: a local reference station and mobile user stations. The local reference station, which observes and tracks both BDS and GPS satellites signals, provides reliable differential correction and initial coordinates to mobile user stations through wireless digital radio. The mobile user stations, which receive the space-time information from satellites and corrections from the local reference station, conduct RTK coordinate calculation and output centimeter-level precision positioning results. The system topology is shown in Figure 1.

Fig. 1. A high precision positioning system topology

Normally the results are presented in the format of NMEA standard. Known as National Marine Electronics Association, NMEA (or NMEA 0183) is also a communication standard for navigation devices with messages like GGA, RMC and VTG, in which geographic coordinates, course heading, ground speed and positioning status are included.

4. A Simple Trajectory-tracking System

The high precision positioning system is to give precise information about vehicles' location and motion state. To realize basic autonomous driving function, a trajectory-tracking system is designed to tell the vehicle where to go and how to go. The system shown in Figure 2 is composed of BDS, vehicle control unit(VCU), steer-by-wire system(SBW), drive-by-wire(DBW) system and brake-by-wire system(BBW).

Stored in VCU, a planned trajectory is described by a set of pre-collected road-points coordinates. A trajectory-tracking algorithm is then introduced in VCU to compare the difference between the current vehicle position data and the target point data on planned trajectory. Given the condition that the autonomous vehicle operates at a low-and-steady speed, the deviation is mainly azimuth-oriented. Then, the deviation is put to a PID controller to calculate steering angle. Finally, commands are sent to SBW, DBW and BBW for steering, speed and brake control. For better comprehension, See Figure 3 and Figure 4.

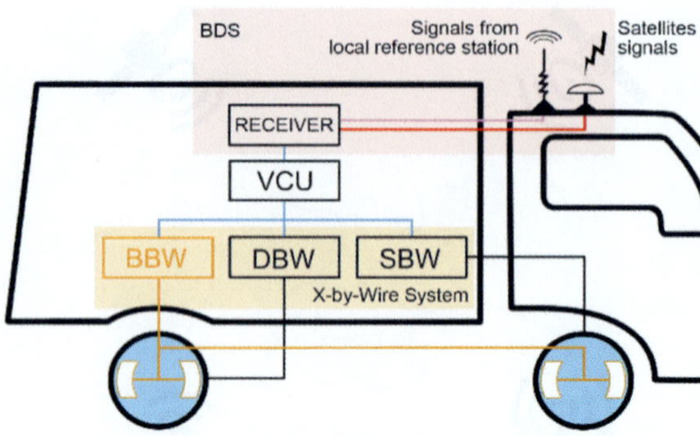

Fig. 2. Structure of a trajectory-tracking system

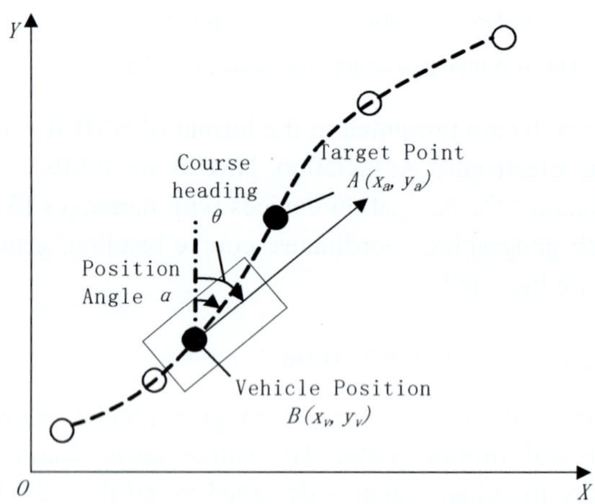

Fig. 3. A simple trajectory-tracking algorithm

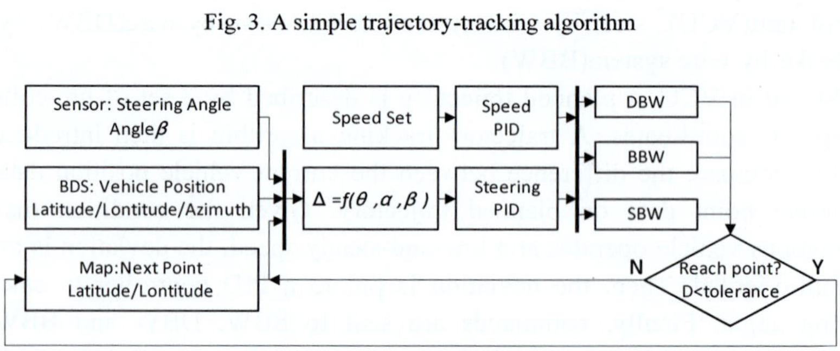

Fig. 4. Algorithm flow chart

5. Test Analysis

A BDS-based autonomous electric vehicle in Figure 5 was developed in 2015. The vehicle in test operated at a relatively low speed for special use in Tongji University Jiading Campus. A circular path was designed in the test field.

Fig. 5. Appearance of the BDS-based test vehicle

The circular path is described by 58 high precision points in counterclockwise direction with longitude, latitude and altitude information.

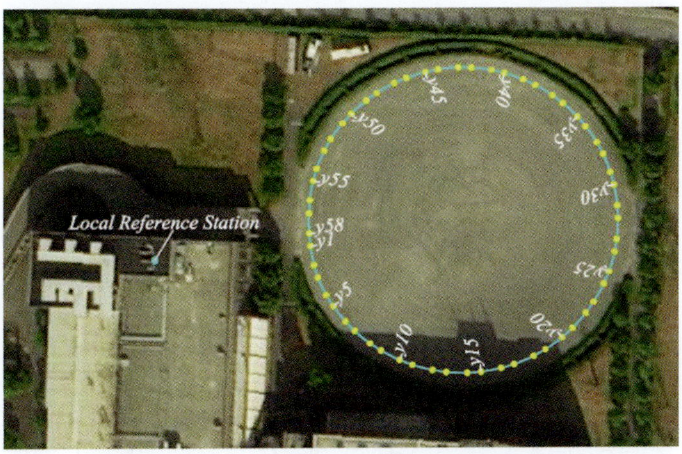

Fig. 6. Test field in Tongji University

Figure 6 shows the points position and the local reference station position matched with a satellite map in test field. The local reference station was installed on the roof and the radio signal coverage can reach up to 5km.

To validate the performance of BDS-based high precision positioning system and evaluate the feasibility of application in autonomous driving, a suitable receiver is picked out and installed on the test vehicle with a GNSS antennae and a radio antenna. Besides, the receiver will also observe GPS satellites for better performance. Main parameters of employed receiver are shown in Table 1.

Table 1. Parameters of the employed receiver

Parameter names	Value
Channels	120, BDS B1/B2, GPS L1/L2
Update Rate	5Hz
Positioning Accuracy	Horizontal: ±(10+0.5×10-6×D[a])mm
	Vertical: ±(20 +1×10-6×D)mm
Data Format	NMEA-0183/ RTCM3.X
Communication	RS232/CAN

Note: [a] D is the distance between mobile user station and local reference station.

Results of trajectory-tracking test on May 13, 2016 are presented. The speed was set to 5km/h.

Figure 7 shows the satellite visibility of BDS and GPS satellites during the test. The average satellite number is 15.8, which is better than GPS or BDS works alone compared to the research by Liu J[4].

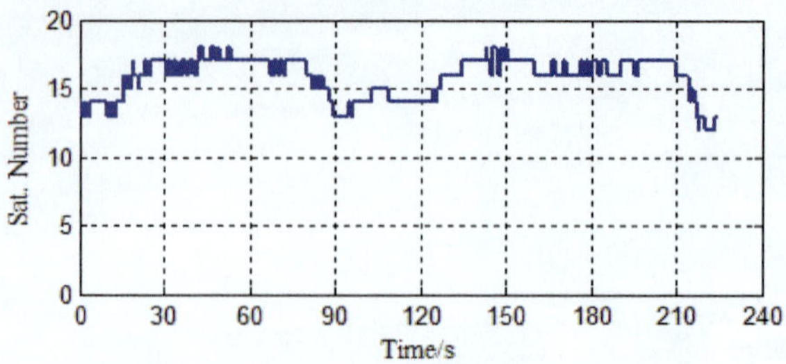

Fig. 7. Numbers of visible BDS and GPS satellites

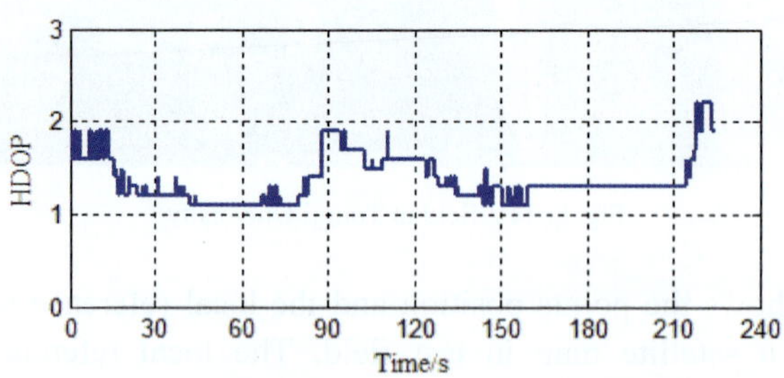

Fig. 8. Fluctuation of HDOP value

Horizontal Dilution Of Precision(HDOP) value reflects the quality of satellite distribution and positioning accuracy. Lower value represents better positioning accuracy performance. Figure 8 shows the HDOP value fluctuation with an average of 1.37. Evidently, the HDOP is highly affected by the number of available satellites.

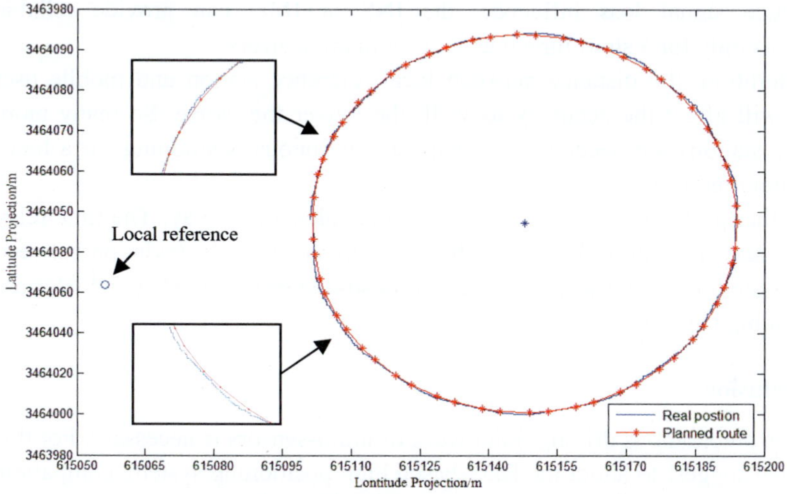

Fig. 9. Comparison of real position and planed route

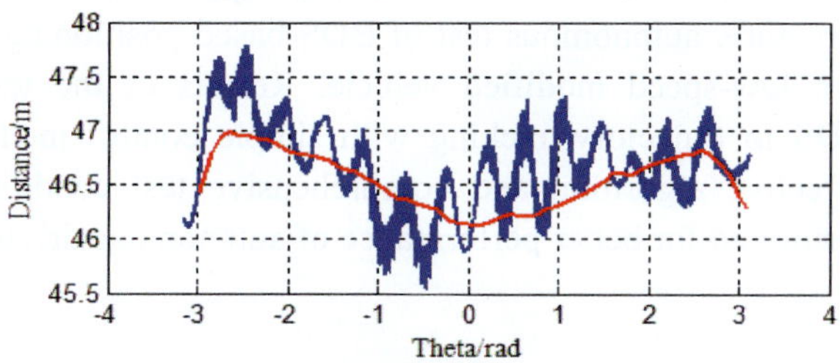

Fig. 10. Comparison in Polar coordinates

Figure 9 shows the vehicle's real position and the planned route under the Descartes coordinates, adopting the simple track algorithm. Figure 10 compares the position points (smooth line for planned route) in Polar coordinates. Considering the response delay of mechanical system and the room for algorithm improvement (1m algorithm tolerance in test), the BDS-based high precision positioning system turns out to be a feasible navigation equipment for low speed automated vehicle.

Although the high accuracy feature is attractive, there is still many problems need to discuss. The main drawback of the high precision positioning system is its environmental suitability. As one of the common problems of GNSS positioning, loss of available satellite signals or reference station signals is a remarkable problem in traditional vehicles operation conditions, such as tunnels, forests, near large mansions, etc. Despite that Inertial Measurement Unit(IMU) has been introduced into mobile user station receivers to improve performance and reduce signal loss influence, the INS or IMU can provide reliable corrections only for a short time due to accumulative errors.

In addition, the distance between local reference station and mobile user stations will affect the accuracy as well, the longer the worse. So many more reference stations are needed to accomplish continuous positioning for a long-range autonomous driving.

Another problem is positioning signal and calculation relay. The time relay currently may up to 200 MS. That is to say, there is a notable deviation between the data output to vehicles and their actual position especially when vehicles are driving at high speed.

6. Conclusion

To realize autonomous driving, joint work of multi-sensors is necessary. For this reason, we suggest to adopt the BDS-based high positioning system, compatible with GPS, to serve as a navigation sensor. Given the requirements and application difficulties, further study is needed to supplement deficient aspects. Based on EV structure, autonomous test of BDS-based positioning system was carried out on a low-speed modified vehicle. Results of the test show the capability of BDS in trajectory-tracking with simple control method. In near future, more effective algorithm and comprehensive test conditions will be designed and performed for better performance of autonomous driving.

References

1. Sun, F., Liu, S., Zhu, X., & Men, B. (2012). Research and progress of BeiDou satellite navigation system. *Science China Information Sciences*, 55(12), 2899-2907.
2. Caojun, H., Jing, Z., Chen, Z., Boshi, L., & Dekui, X. (2015). BeiDou-GPS integrated dual-system with multi-satellites for positioning and navigating farm vehicles. *International Journal of Agricultural and Biological Engineering*, 8(5), 79.
3. Shi, C., Zhao, Q., Hu, Z., & Liu, J. (2013). Precise relative positioning using real tracking data from COMPASS GEO and IGSO satellites. *GPS solutions*, 17(1), 103-119.
4. Liu, J., Cai, B., & Wang, J. (2013, June). An analysis of BeiDou Navigation Satellite System (BDS) based positioning for train collision early warning. *Intelligent Vehicles Symposium (IV)*, 2013 IEEE (pp. 1065-1070). IEEE.

Detection of Behavior Based on Image Analysis

Tian-Zheng Wang[1,a], Gang Yang[1,b], Hai-Fang Li[2,c], Xing-Zhong Zhang[2,d], Hong-Xia Deng[2,e] and Xiao-Feng Yang[2,3,f,*]

[1]Electric Power Research Institute, Shanxi Electric Power Company Taiyuan 030001, Shanxi Province, China

[2]College of Computer Science and Technology, Taiyuan University of Technology Yuci 030600, Shanxi Province, China

[3]Department of Computer Engineering, Shanxi Architectural College Yuci 030600, Shanxi Province, China

E-mail: [a]wtz2000@163.com, [b]syanggang9800@163.com, [c]lihaifang@tyut.edu.cn, [d]1659898176@qq.com, [e]denghongxia@tyut.edu.cn, [f]18817710@qq.com

In order to monitor and alert the abnormal behavior of distraction, this paper proposes a method to detect the head behavior based on facial feature extraction. This method uses the ASM algorithm to obtain the facial feature points, calculates the head posture description on the position information of the face feature points, and draws the conclusion of head posture classified by SVM from the above information. Finally, experimental results show that the method proposed can effectively detect the abnormal behavior and the average detection rate is above 94%.

Keywords: ASM; Facial Feature; Abnormal; Distraction; Behavior.

1. Introduction

A lot of drivers develop a habit of watching the phone while driving. Poor performance on a peripheral detection task (PDT) [1] is caused by using mobile while driving, which is an important reason of traffic accidents. Particularly that is the most harmful in the public transport.

*Corresponding author.

Currently, the method of driver's fatigue detection or calling detection while driving is more common, however, the detection method of driver's looking down during driving is rare. Using ASM[2] driver's state detection algorithms are as follows: fatigue fuzzy inference infers the driver's state through feature extraction from eyes and mouth based on ASM[3]; ASM-based fatigue detection by tracking eye[4]; ASM-based discriminant of the behavior making a phone call during driving by tracking color area of ears and hands[5].

There are also methods about the head pose detection, which are required to calculate three offset angles (roll, pitch, and yaw) of the head position. These methods have amount of calculation and week real-time ability, which are as follows: dual camera method based on AAM algorithm[6]; head posture analysis by ICP and the depth map[7]. The method proposed by Hua Shi does not use the iterative method to get the head pose. But when looking up at the angle greater than 30°, the highest detection rate is only 43.33% [8] that is not suitable for the real-time detection.

The methods related from foreign experts are as follows: algorithm based on infrared camera and binocular camera[12] proposed by Breitenstein, which is basically for the real-time head pose estimation, but it need high hardware equipment. The algorithm based on a simplified AAM algorithm combines ZNCC for head tracking proposed by KoiChi and Yasue[11]. The algorithm uses two adjacent frames for head pose calculation, while it's not effective for the static image. But calculation of local square texture mapping of this algorithm is greater than the amount of ASM algorithm which has gray texture mapping in normal direction. The method using mobile APP application to detect driving safety proposed by Wang Yang[13], and the similar method made by Yantao Li[14]. These methods above based on a variety of sensors in your phone are different from the idea in this article.

This paper proposes a method for detecting the driving behavior based on ASM algorithm, which is available for static images and dynamic images. The average detection rate is over 94%, and the highest detection rate is above 97%. Another work in this paper is redundant design of head posture detection parameters to overcome the accuracy of ASM algorithm or the improved[10] that is not high for this experiment, and to increase the robustness of this method.

2. Detection Scheme

In the detection scheme, placement of the camera are shown in Fig. 1. Because the camera is placed below the eye level, the face relative to the camera is looking up state when normal driving (Fig. 2). In this paper, it is considered to bow to play the phone that the camera displays looking ahead or head-down which are all abnormal driving state (Fig. 3 and Fig. 4).

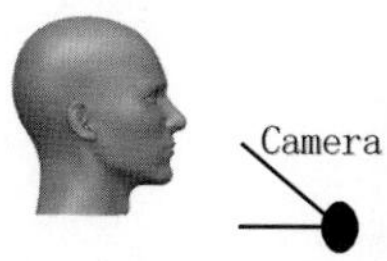

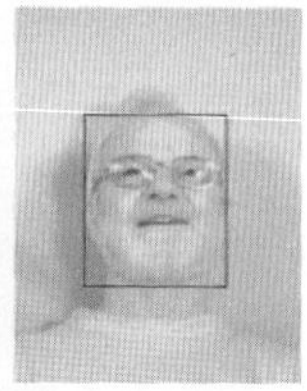

Fig. 1. Camera's Place Fig. 2. Normal Fig. 3. Abnormal Fig. 4. Abnormal Fig. 5. Face Detection

3. Get Information of Facial Feature Point

In order to improve the convergence speed of ASM, and to avoid reaching local optima causing the failure of the search, this method uses the cascade Adaboost algorithm for rapid face detection based on a simple Haar-like features proposed by Viola[9](Fig. 5). However, if Adaboost algorithm cannot detect the driver's head[5], it can be simply considered as abnormal driving behavior, which also does not affect the accuracy in this paper.

The faces to be detected is regarded as a shape vector, which is coordinate information of a number of key facial feature points in series[13], used by ASM algorithm. The shape vector can be used to figure out head posture in this article.

4. Processing of Feature Point and Behavior Detection

The point set (shape vector) $\mathrm{S} = ((x_1, y_1)^{\mathrm{T}}, (x_2, y_2)^T, \cdots, (x_n, y_n)^T)^T$ can be gotten by using ASM to fit any image.

The point set S should be pretreated to get the set of point $S^{'}$:

$$\bar{S} = (\bar{\mathrm{x}}, \bar{\mathrm{y}}) \tag{1}$$

$$\sigma_x = \sqrt{\frac{\sum(x_i-\bar{x})^2}{n}} \tag{2}$$

$$\sigma_y = \sqrt{\frac{\sum(y_i-\bar{y})^2}{n}} \tag{3}$$

Let $\sigma^{-1} = (\frac{1}{\sigma_\mathrm{x}}, \frac{1}{\sigma_\mathrm{y}})^\mathrm{T}$

$$S^{'} = (S - \bar{S})\sigma^{-1} = ((x_1^{'}, y_1^{'})^T, (x_2^{'}, y_2^{'})^T, \cdots, (x_n^{'}, y_n^{'})^T)^T \tag{4}$$

After pretreatment, 14 points could be used, shown in Fig. 6 and Fig. 7. Seven point pitches L_k (k is 1, 2, 3, 4, 5, 6 or 7, shown in Fig. 6 and Fig. 7), according to the 14 feature points coordinates, are the square of the distance between two feature points$(x_i^{'}, y_i^{'})$, $(x_j^{'}, y_j^{'})$ in the 14 points.

$$L_k = L_{ij}^2 = (x_i^{'} - x_j^{'})^2 + (y_i^{'} - y_j^{'})^2 = \left(\frac{x_i - \bar{x}}{\sigma_x} - \frac{x_j - \bar{x}}{\sigma_x}\right)^2 + \left(\frac{y_i - \bar{y}}{\sigma_y} - \frac{y_j - \bar{y}}{\sigma_y}\right)^2 = \frac{(x_i - x_j)^2}{\sigma_x^2} + \frac{(y_i - y_j)^2}{\sigma_y^2}$$

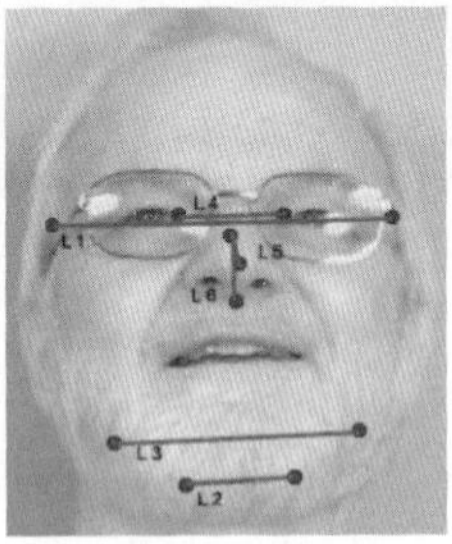

Fig. 6. Parameters on The Face (1)

Fig.7. Parameters on The Face (2)

The head posture detection parameter is the ratio of above two is as follows.

$$\mathrm{x} = \frac{L_{ij}^2}{L_{nm}^2} = \frac{\frac{(x_i - x_j)^2}{\sigma_x^2} + \frac{(y_i - y_j)^2}{\sigma_y^2}}{\frac{(x_n - x_m)^2}{\sigma_x^2} + \frac{(y_n - y_m)^2}{\sigma_y^2}} = \frac{\sigma_y^2 (x_i - x_j)^2 + \sigma_x^2 (y_i - y_j)^2}{\sigma_y^2 (x_n - x_m)^2 + \sigma_x^2 (y_n - y_m)^2}, x \text{ is } a, b, c \text{ or } d$$

$$\left(a = \frac{L1^2}{L2^2}, b = \frac{L3^2}{L4^2}, c = \frac{L5^2}{L6^2} \text{ and } d = \frac{L2^2}{L7^2}\right)$$

The head posture can be obtained by SVM and 4 parameters (a, b, c, and d).

5. Experiment Results and Analysis

1037 images are manually selected from MUCT, including 161 normal driving (positive) images and 876 non-normal driving (negative) images.

50 positive images and 100 negative images are selected as the training data set, and the remaining images (111 positive images, 776 negative images) are selected as the test data set. The test results are shown in Table 1, where the average prediction accuracy is 94.29%. So, the method is to be proved effectively. Compared to other similar findings[13][14], the proposed method has reached a good level. Comparative results are shown in Table 2.

Based on the first test group, classification performance tests are also done between the 4 detection parameters for SVM. In the tests, 2, 3 and 4 parameters used by SVM are selected for testing. Results are shown in Fig. 8. As can be seen from Fig. 8, the multi parameters increases prediction accuracy of SVM.

Although the accuracy improved by the multi parameters is limited, the robustness of this method can be increased. For example, the result of the test parameter b & parameter d(lower than others) doesn't affect the final result. In this experiment, the main effort is to select valid parameters and to analyze the classification performance of the parameters for optimal solution.

Table 1. Test result of subgroup

Sub-group	Training Set (Image ID) Positive	Negative	Test Set (Image ID) Positive	Negative	Forecast Accuracy
1	1-50	1-100	51-161	101-876	97.07%
2	51-100	101-200	1-50, 101-161	1-100, 201-876	94.59%
3	101-151	201-300	1-100, 201-161	1-200, 301-876	91.21%

Table 2. Comparison of results

	Reference 14	Reference 13	This paper
Accuracy	87%	90%(Up to 97%)	94.29%

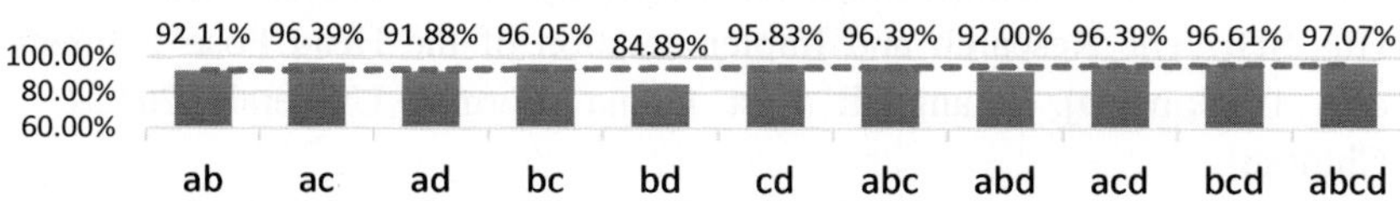

Fig. 8. Analysis of detection parameters for head posture

6. Conclusions

Facial feature is derived based on ASM, head posture can be effectively detected from facial feature based on redundant parameter selection, and the highest prediction accuracy is up to 97.07% finally. Other behavior can be detected in the subsequent work in view of the success of this experiment.

Acknowledgments

This research was supported by Science and Technology Project of China State Grid Corp No.52053015000W.

References

1. Jan Tornros, Anne Bolling. Mobile Phone Use -Effects of Conversation on Mental Workload and Driving Speed in Rural and Urban Environments[J]. Transportation Research Part F: Traffic Psychology and Behaviour, 2006, 9(4):298-306.

2. Cootes T, Taylor C, Cooper D et al. Active shape models-their training and application[J]. Computer Vision and Image Understanding, 1995, 61(1): 38-59.
3. Zhonghao BAI, Yinghao JIAO, Fanghua BAI. Driving fatigue detection based on active shape model and fuzzy inference[J]. Chinese Journal of Scientific Instrument, 2015,4:768-775, (In Chinese).
4. Zhiyong YANG, Yifei PU, Xiaoqian GONG, Jiliu ZHOU. Eye Location and Tracking for Fatigue Driving Detection[J]. Microelectronics & Computer, 2014,8:115-122, (In Chinese).
5. Bo ZHANG, Wenjun WANG, Minkooc WEE, Bo CHENG. Detection handled phone use by driver based on machine vision[J]. Journal of Jilin University(Engineering and Technology Edition), 2015,9: 1688-1695, (In Chinese).
6. Kan WANG. Attitude Parameters Measurement of The Human Head[D]. Xi`an: Xi`an Technological University, 2015,4, (In Chinese).
7. Bo-wen ZHANG. The Driver Head Pose Estimation Method Based on Depth Image[D]. Dalian: Dalian Maritime University: 2015,4, In Chinese.
8. Hua SHI. The Research and Implementation of the Head Pose Estimation and Tracking[D]. Shanghai: East China Normal University,2015,I, (In Chinese).
9. VIOLA P, JONES M J. Robust real- time face detection[J]. International Journal of Computer Vision, 2004, 57(2): 137-154.
10. Hua TIAN, Tianyin PU. Improved ASM localization method for human facial features[J]. Journal of Chongqing University of Posts and Telecommunications(Natural Science Edition), 2014, 26(1), (In Chinese).
11. Koichi Takahashi, Yasue Mitsukura Head Pose Tracking Based on Optimizing Normalized Cross-Correlation[J] 5 SICE 2013,2513-2517.
12. Michael, D, Breitenstein, Daniel, Kuettel, Thibaut, Weise, Luc, van, Gool. Real-time face pose estimation from single range images[C]. Anchorage, AK:CVPR 2008, 2008. 1-2.
13. Yan Wang, Yingying Chen, Jie Yang, Marco Gruteser, Richard P. Martin, Hongbo Liu, Luyang Liu, Cagdas Karatas. Determining Driver Phone Use by Exploiting Smartphone Integrated Sensors[J]. IEEE Transactions on Mobile Computing (TMC), 2015, (9): 1-1.
14. Yantao Li, Gang Zhou, Yue Li, Du Shen. Determining driver phone use leveraging smartphone[J/OL]. http://link.springer.com/content/pdf/10.1007%2Fs11042-015-2969-7.pdf, 2015-08-09.

Fault Location Based on Support Vector Machine

Ya Li[a], Shao-Bin Huang[b] and Yan-Mei Li[c]

College of Computer Science and Technology, Harbin Engineering University
Harbin, 150001, China
E-mail: [a]liya_heu@163.com, [b]huangshaobin@hrbeu.edu.cn, [c]liyanmei@hrbeu.edu.cn

This study proposes an automatic fault location approach combining support vector machine. Different from the usual fault localization approach, the support vector machine is applied to classify the program statement into two classes. If there is only one class, the classification probability is used to rank the statements. If a statement has a minimum probability, it will have a maximum probability to be a fault. And empirical results of applying SVM are also presented to locate the fault and compare them against the results of other algorithms for the JTCAS program.

Keywords: Debugging; Fault Location; SVM; Statistical Analysis.

1. Introduction

Diagnosing faults during debugging of hardware and software may take a long time [1]. And a significant manual effort may be required. Fault localization intends to automatically locate the faults in software, which improves software quality and reduces the cost of software debugging. Therefore, research on fault localization is of great significance.

During the last few years, several fault location algorithms have been developed and significant progress has been achieved. The methods used can be divided into three categories: the methods based on program slicing [2, 3], coverage-based fault localization [4,5], and others. Error location technique based on program slicing can be used to locate the error by analyzing program's data dependence and control dependence to extract error related program fragments. The coverage-based fault location technique usually collects coverage information of program code from the passed test runs and failed test runs. Then based on the analysis of the program code, the error location technique can calculate the probability of error of each element in the program.

In this paper, we show how SVM can be utilized to locate the faults. The key feature of this algorithm is binary classification for the program statement. First, obtain training data and testing data depending on the running of test case, and obtain the classifier; and second, classify the testing data. If all the testing data are in the same class, the probability of a statement belongs to the class will be used to rank the statement. If a statement has lower probability, then it has higher probability to be a suspect.

2. SVM-Based Fault Location

In this section, we describe the details of how SVM can be used to locate faults in the software. In particular, we explain how to obtain train data and the prediction data.

2.1. *Support vector machine*

Support Vector Machines is a new classic of machine learning algorithm based on the statistical learning theory. It has standout learning capability when solving small-samples, nonlinear and complex pattern recognition problems and can be generalized to other machine learning problems such as function fitting [6]. In this paper, we use the two-class SVM, as an example to illustrate the principle of the support vector machine method.

Given n points of the form $(\overrightarrow{x_1}, y_1), (\overrightarrow{x_2}, y_2), \cdots, (\overrightarrow{x_n}, y_n)$, where $\overrightarrow{x_i} \in R^n$, $y_i \in \{-1, +1\}$ and $i = 1, 2, \cdots n$, each y_i indicating the class to which the point $\overrightarrow{x_i}$ belongs. Each $\overrightarrow{x_i}$ is an m-dimensional real sample vector. We want to find a "hyperplane" that divides these sample points into two classes, and make the distance between the hyperplane and the nearest sample-point $\overrightarrow{x_i}$ from either class is maximized. So any hyperplane can be written as the set of points $\overrightarrow{x_i}$ satisfying:

$$y_i\left(\vec{w}^T \overrightarrow{x_i} + b\right) \geq 1, i = 1, \cdots, n \tag{1}$$

Where $\vec{w}$ is the normal vector to the hyperplane. The two-classification problem can be translated into a minimum constrained optimization problem:

$$\begin{aligned} & min \frac{1}{2} \| \vec{w} \|^2 \\ & s.t., y_i(\vec{w}^T \overrightarrow{x_i} + b) \geq 1, i = 1, \cdots, n \end{aligned} \tag{2}$$

However, there are noises in the data which diverge far from the normal position, and we call them outliers. Generally, because of the hyperplane is formed by only a few support vectors, so the existence of outliers may have a significant effect. In order to deal with this situation, the SVM introduces the variable ξ, which the data points are allowed to deviate from the hyperplane at a certain distance. However, the value of this slack variable cannot be arbitrary; otherwise any hyperplane would be eligible. Thus the sum of the primary objective function and the slack variable ξ_i must be minimal, and the objective function can be rewritten as follows:

$$min\frac{1}{2}\|\vec{w}\|^2 + C\sum_{i=1}^{n}\xi_i \tag{3}$$

Where C is a parameter and is used to control the weight between "seeking a hyperplane with maximum margin" and "ensuring the data points with minimum offset". So the two-classification problem can be rewritten as follows:

$$\begin{aligned} & min\frac{1}{2}\|\vec{w}\|^2 + C\sum_{i=1}^{n}\xi_i \\ & s.t., y_i(\vec{w}^T \vec{x_i} + b) \geq 1 - \xi_i, \\ & \quad \xi_i \geq 0, i = 1, \cdots, n \end{aligned} \tag{4}$$

That is

$$\begin{aligned} & min\frac{1}{2}\sum_{i,j=1}^{n}\alpha_i\alpha_j y_i y_j \kappa(x_i, x_j) - \sum_{i=1}^{n}\alpha_i \\ & s.t., 0 \leq \alpha_i \leq C, i = 1, \cdots, n \\ & \sum_{i=1}^{n}\alpha_i y_i = 0 \end{aligned} \tag{5}$$

Where $\kappa(x_i, x_j)$ is the kernel function, and calculates the inner product of the two vectors in the space after the implicit mapping. The most common kernel functions are polynomial kernels, Gaussian kernels and linear kernels. Solving this optimization problem, the two parameters w and b of the hyperplane can be determined. For those samples that have not been classified, we can determine their classification by the SVM classification function Eq. (6).

$$f(x)=\sum_{i=1}^{n}\alpha_i y_i \kappa(x_i,x)+b \tag{6}$$

Due to the fact that the statement of the program can only be right or wrong, it can be considered to be a typical two classification problem. As mentioned above, the samples are m dimensional vectors, so how a statement can be expressed as an m dimensional vector, to facilitate a more accurate classification? We discuss this in more detail later in the next section.

2.2. *Data preprocessing*

The research object is the program statement, so the sample feature is the characteristic of each statement in the program, and then the feature of each statement is expressed in the form of multidimensional characteristic matrix. At present, the following intuition experience is used by many researchers to calculate the suspicion degree of the program statement *s*, it is:

(i) Positively related to the number of times it has been covered by the failed execution, which is represented as n_{ef}.
(ii) Negative correlation with the number of times it has not been covered by the failed execution, which is represented as n_{uf}.
(iii) Negative correlation with the number of times it has been covered by the passed execution, which is represented as n_{ep}.
(iv) Positively related to the number of times it has not been covered by the passed execution which is represented as n_{up}.

In addition if a statement only appeared in the successful execution path, it must be right. A statement is said to be irrelevant if it does not appear in the successful execution trace, or in the failed execution trace. And it can be ignored. As stated preciously, a statement can be represented by an eight-dimensional vector $\vec{x}=\{n_{ef},n_{uf},n_{ep},n_{up},n_{op},n_{of},n_{ob},n_{ub}\}$, where n_{op} and n_{of} indicate whether the statement only appears in the successful execution path or in the failed execution path, and n_{ob} indicates whether the statement both appears in the successful execution path and in the failed execution path. Conversely, n_{ub} indicates whether the statement neither appears in the successful execution path nor in the failed execution path.

After getting the characteristic vector of the sample, it is divided into two parts, testing data and training data. And then the training data is used to train the classifier. Finally using the testing data as input of the classifier, the statements were divided into two classes, which is the result of the error location.

3. Experimental

In this section, we experimentally demonstrate the effectiveness of the fault location methods based on SVM by showing the results from the JTCAS program of the Siemens test suite [7]. The JTCAS task is a Java version of the TCAS program consists of 197 lines of code and 1600 test cases. And the authors have created 41 versions of the program by injecting one or more faults.

In order to evaluate the effectiveness of fault location methods, a scoring function was proposed by Renieris and Reiss [8], see Eq. (7). It gives an estimate of the amount of code that can be ignored when looking for the actual fault with the help of the diagnosis information provided, and higher numbers are better. We compare our approach with another seven methods [9, 10, 11], and the results show in Figure 1. And the vertical axis is the T-score. Clearly, our approach BSVM resulted in a median of 0.97 for the five versions of JTCAS and it is higher than the other seven methods. The figure shows the performance improvement obtained by using SVM. In particular, the average performance of the SVM-based fault location method is stable compared to the other algorithms.

$$\text{T-score} = 1 - \frac{\text{the number of suspects}}{\text{the total number of lines}} \times 100\% \tag{7}$$

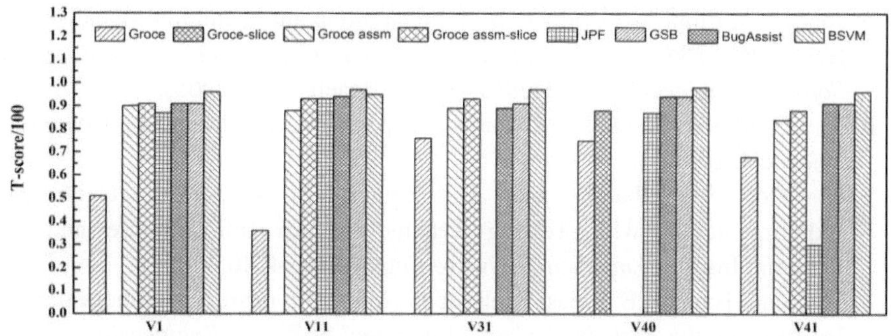

Fig. 1. Comparisons of the effectiveness of each fault localization technique.

4. Conclusion

In this paper, we have presented a SVM-based method for fault location. The approach constructs the training data and testing date from the program execution with the test cases; and then constructs a classifier to classify the testing data. If there is only one class, the probability of a statement belongs to a class will be used to rank the statements. The smaller the probability, the more likely it is to be a fault. We have demonstrated the applicability of the approach on five examples. We have demonstrated the applicability of the approach on seven examples. Although our experimental results are still preliminary, the experimentation shows the algorithm is correct and efficient.

References

1. U. Ali and B. Raif, Real-time condition monitoring and fault diagnosis in switched reluctance motors with Kohonen neural network, *J. Zhejiang U-Sci C* **12**, 941 (2013).
2. Y. Lei, X. Mao, Z. Dai and C. Wang, Effective Statistical Fault Localization Using Program Slices, *IEEE 36th Annual Computer Software and Applications Conference*, (Izmir, turkey, 2012).
3. X. Zhang, H. He, N. Gupta and R. Gupta, Experimental evaluation of using dynamic slices for fault location, in *Proc. the sixth international symposium on Automated analysis-driven debugging(AADEBUG'05)*, (New York, USA, 2005).
4. Abreu R, Zoeteweij P and Van Gemund A J C, On the Accuracy of Spectrum-based Fault Localization, *Testing: Academic and Industrial Conference Practice and Research Techniques – Mutation(TAICPART-MUTATION),* (Windsor, England, 2007).
5. Jones J A, Empirical evaluation of the tarantula automatic fault-localization technique, *20th IEEE/ACM International Conference on Automated Software Engineering (ASE 2005)*, (Long Beach, USA, 2005).
6. M. A. Mathias and C. Mohamed, Support Vector Machine, *Computer Science* **4**, 1(2002).
7. H. Do, S. Elbaum and G. Rothermel, Supporting Controlled Experimentation with Testing Techniques: An Infrastructure and its Potential Impact, *Empirical Software Engineering* **4**, 405(2005).
8. M. Renieris and S.E. Reiss, Fault localization with nearest neighbor queries, In *Proc. of the 18th Int'l Conf. Automated Software Engineering (ASE)*, (2003).
9. Groce A, Error explanation with distance metrics, Tools and Algorithms for the Construction and Analysis of Systems **8**, 229(2004).
10. A. Groce and W. Visser, What went wrong: explaining counterexamples, *International Conference on Model Checking Software* (*SPIN'03)*, (Berlin, Heidelberg, 2003).
11. A. Griesmayer, S. Staber and R. Bloem, Fault localization using a model checker, *Software Testing Verification \& Reliability* **20**, 149(2010).

Ant Colony Optimization Metaheuristic for Shortest Path of Directed Graph Passing Through Specified Nodes

Di Zhong[1,a], Long-Bin Zhang[2,b] and Ping-Jian Zhang[1,c]

[1]*Software Engineering, South China University of Technology, Guangzhou, Guangdong, China*

[2]*College of Automation Science and Engineering, South China University of Technology, Guangzhou, Guangdong, China*

E-mail: [a]289528475@qq.com, [b]zhanglongbin9155@126.com, [c]pjzhang@126.com

Finding the shortest loopless path of directed graph passing through specified nodes is the main purpose in this paper. The algorithm for the problem is a challenging work due to the fact that calculating the shortest path visits specified nodes is at least as difficult as the traveling salesman. To avoid duplicate search for invalid path in this paper, a new version of ant colony optimization metaheuristic is presented to ensure the extensive and convergence of the search, using priority queue to select paths and adopt Dijkstra algorithm to optimize the results of path which speeds up the generation of an optimal path. By utilizing ant colony optimization metaheuristic, priority queue and Dijkstra algorithm, the accuracy and efficiency of the algorithm is guaranteed, and the experimental results demonstrate the proposed method is effective.

Keywords: Ant Colony Optimization; Priority Queue; Dijkstra; Shortest Loopless Path; Specified Nodes.

1. Introduction

In technology age, using heuristic algorithms to find the shortest loopless path passing through specified nodes have attracted an increasing interest. Now, many methods about finding shortest path have been proposed [1-7], however, there are few approaches for the problem and slowly. Thus, finding shortest path passing through specified nodes should be further researched. To effectively find it, some scholars begin to study the ant colony optimization algorithms [8-11]. From the motivation above, this paper addresses an improved ant colony optimization for the problem. Compared with the previous works, we avoid duplicate search for invalid path and guarantees the extensive and convergence of the search and differs from the primitive ant system. To select paths effectively, priority queue is used, and Dijkstra algorithm is adopted to optimize the results of path which speeds up the generation of an optimal path. The organization of this paper is as follows. Section 2 presents the problem statement. Section 3 describes primitive ant system. Section 4 describes the details about ant colony optimization metaheuristic algorithm. Experimental results are given in Section 6 to demonstrate the effectiveness of the proposed approach. Finally, the conclusion of this paper is given in Section 7.

2. Problem Statement

In this work we will solve the problem in graph G = (V, E) where V is defined as nodes set, E is a set of directed arcs, and Each arc has it own value. At the beginning, we could catch Start node named s and teriminal node named t. What's more, the subset of V named V' is most important in the problem, because the aim of the problem is to find a loopless path from s to t which passed all of nodes in V' (the order of node in V' is not limited) and the value of all arcs is minimal. Arcs (v_i, v_j) is different from Arcs (v_j, v_i) and Multiple paths exist in Arcs (v_i, v_j).

3. Ant System

Early Ant Colony algorithm using the elite strategy and it's easy to achieve, it also has been used in the TSP. However this problem is not only rely on it, but for all optimal path it has been found that additional enhancement will be given in the algorithm (Eq.(1)). To further enhance the performance of algorithm, the negative feedback mechanism will be in use. In path search process, using the roulette way to choose the path where selection probability of each path is determined by the information, such as Eq.(2). Besides, enhance and volatile all the pheromone after all of ants are completed it search for path (Eq.(3)).

$$P_k(r,s) = \begin{cases} \frac{[\tau(r,s)]^\alpha[\eta(r,s)]^\beta}{\sum_{\mu\in J_k(r)}[\tau(r,s)]^\alpha[\eta(r,s)]^\beta}, & x < 0 \\ 0, & otherwise \end{cases} \tag{1}$$

where τ is the pheromone, $\eta = 1/\delta$ is the inverse of the distance $\delta(r, s)$, $J_k(r)$ is the set of cities that remain to be visited by ant *k* positioned on city *r* (to make the solution feasible), and β is a parameter which determines the relative importance of pheromone versus distance ($\beta > 0$).

$$\tau(r,s) \leftarrow (1-\alpha)\tau(r,s) + \sum_{k=1}^{m} \Delta\tau_k(r,s) \tag{2}$$

where

$$\Delta\tau_k(r,s) = \begin{cases} \frac{1}{L_k}, & if(r,s) \in tour\ done\ by\ ant\ k \\ 0, & otherwise \end{cases} \tag{3}$$

$0 < \alpha < 1$ is a pheromone decay parameter, *Lk* is the length of the tour performed by ant *k*, and *m* is the number of ants.

4. Ant Colony Optimization Metaheuristic

4.1. *Maxcmin ant system and pheromone trail updating*

Information will be completely volatile when connectivity of a graph is not so good. To avoid it, we will limit the pheromone to an interval $[\tau_{min}, \tau_{max}]$. To avoid the useless search using the following failing updating rule to change the pheromone,

$$\tau_{ij}(t+1) = \delta\tau_{ij}(t) \tag{4}$$

where δ is the attenuation parameter, and the arc(i, j) belongs the failing path to the destination. And the pheromone level is updated by applying the following updating rule

$$\tau_{ij}(t+1) = (1-\alpha)\tau_{ij}(t) + \alpha\Delta\tau_{ij}^{k}(t) \tag{5}$$

Where

$$\Delta\tau_{ij}^{k} = \begin{cases} \frac{G}{L_k(t)}, & if\ arc(i,j) \in tour\ done\ by\ ant\ k \\ 0, & otherwise \end{cases} \tag{6}$$

$0 < \alpha < 1$ is a pheromone decay parameter, others have been shown above.

The partial adjustment rule of pheromone is

$$\tau_{ij}(t+1) = (1-\rho)\tau_{ij}(t) + \rho\tau_0 \tag{7}$$

where $0 < \rho < 1$ is a parameter, and τ_0 is the initial pheromone level.

Compared to Ant System rule, this choice amplifies the pheromone on the arcs which have get to the destination, and expands the range of solutions. As a result, it can have an impact on the ants' movement for the next time.

4.2. *Selection operation*

In ant system, the probability to destination is quite small. Thus, in this paper, we proposed the following cost function

$$\mathrm{F} = \left(\mathrm{M} + \frac{W}{L_c}\right) * \tau_c \tag{8}$$

where F is the cost weight of one path, W is the pheromone quality coefficient, M is the number of specified nodes of the path from the beginning of the trial.

We utilize priority queue to store these trails, as shown in Figure 1. To begin with, there is just one node (start node), and then according to the node, we can expand the trails to next different nodes and we store these trails into priority queue which uses the preferred way of storing larger weights.

According to the cost weight of different path, we choose X trails from the priority queue whose cost weight is higher. And we select another Y random trails from the rest paths of the priority queue. Then, take the X + Y trails into next iteration.

Through using the priority queue, we don't need to sort all paths to find X trials of higher cost weight and Y random trails, which makes algorithmic complexity far less than the sort $O(N^2)$, and avoid moving large amounts of data.

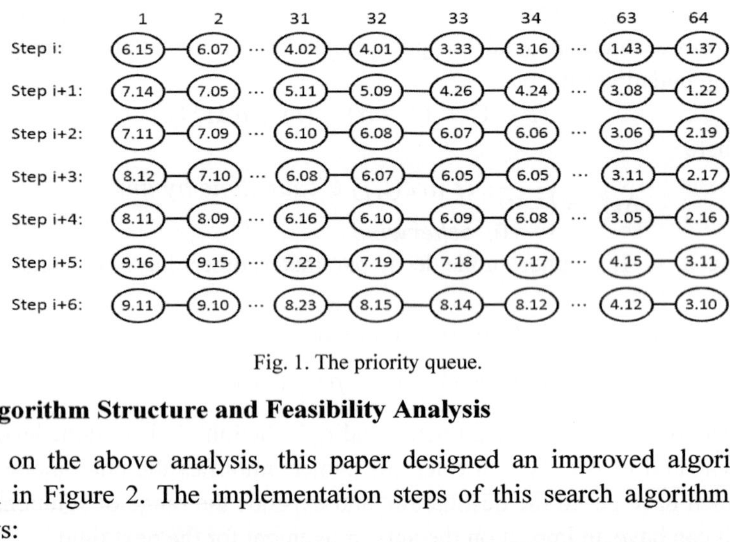

Fig. 1. The priority queue.

5. Algorithm Structure and Feasibility Analysis

Based on the above analysis, this paper designed an improved algorithm as shown in Figure 2. The implementation steps of this search algorithm are as follows:

(i)Ant colony initialization: We set the Maximum Iterations T_{max}, and let the initial pheromone of all sides $\tau_{ij} = 1.0$, the number of iteration $T_i = 0$;

(ii)Initialize the map information: Initialize the search trails, and set the current path length $= 1$, the node-sets of trails path $=$ S, the cost of paths weight $=$ 0, the access token of nodes vis $= \phi$;

(iii)Route search: pull out the paths R_i successively from the current path sets, find the nodes set Next $= E_1, E_2, \ldots, E_k$ that the terminal nodes R_{ij} of node E_i can get. If Next $= \phi$, skip to (ix) or execution (iv).

(iv)Path extension: R_i combine with nodes of Next set and form a new path $newR_i$ in sequence, and add $newR_k$ into the priority queue Q.

(v)Path judgment: Determine whether $newR_k$ passes through the whole specified nodes, if it is, use the Dijkstra algorithm reach the destination and execution (vi) or skip to (vii).

(vi)Path optimization: use the Dijkstra algorithm to optimize the trails between specified nodes, and update the optimal paths and pheromone.

(vii)Update negative pheromone: Decay the Pheromone that $newR_k$ passes through.

(viii)Path decisions: Choose X trails from the priority queue whose cost weight is higher and select another Y random trails from the rest paths of the priority queue, then add X + Y trails into path sets.

(ix)(ix) End of iteration: Determine if the iteration is complete. If $T_i < T_{max}$, back to (ii), or the end of the algorithm.

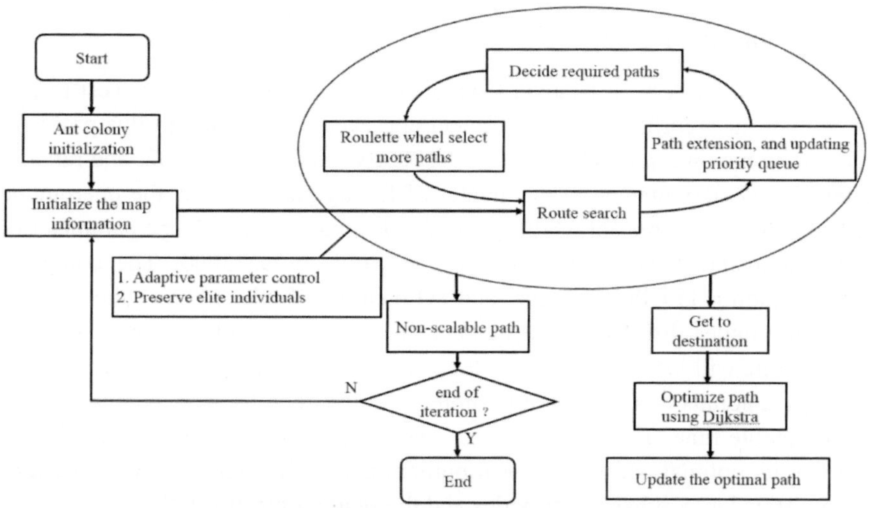

Fig. 2. The algorithm structure of the improved algorithm.

On the whole, this design uses the priority queue algorithm to do the breadth first search, which ensures the breadth of search results. For the path of diffusion, we put ant pheromones into path choice, which can improve the likelihood of shortest path. Finally, to optimize the current shortest path, we use the Dijkstra algorithm to optimize the path between specified nodes in turn, and this ensure the optimal path. Pruning is used to narrow the search field in the search process, so as to reduce the search time. Theoretically, algorithm has the possibility to be realized. We note that: K: search popularity, V : a set of nodes,

A: a set of arcs, Q:number of paths stored in the priority queue, L: number of edges of shortest paths. The space complexity of the algorithm is $\Omega(K * V + V * A)$, and the storage space of this algorithm consists of adjacency list $\Omega(V * A)$ and store path $\Omega(K * V)$, so the storage space meets the actual requirements. The time complexity of algorithm is $O(L * log_2^Q)$, and the main time consuming are:

(i) update priority queue $O(log_2^Q)$;

(ii)updating pheromone $O(L)$;

(iii) Dijkstra algorithm is adopted to optimize the path$O(V^2)$.

Compared to other algorithms, the algorithm does not limit to the number of specific nodes, and the number of specific nodes in the algorithm have little impact on time consuming. The restrictions on the number of specific nodes has made a great improvement.

6. Experimental Results

In this paper, we test on Huawei Code Craft official test data sets. Test results show that our algorithm can be efficient and accurate solution to this problem. We set the maximum iterations T_{max} = 1000, required paths X = 32, and random paths Y = 32, the attenuation parameter of failing path $\delta = 0.9$, the pheromone decay parameter of the ant which found the destination $\alpha = 0.5$, the parameter of partial adjustment rule $\rho = 0.5$, and the path sets as 3000. The computer configuration is i5 CPU, 3.2 Ghz, and 8G memory. Table. 1 shows the solution efficiency under different scale of data, and as the complexity increases, the solving time will increase, but amplitude of time increases slowly. When applied to larger amounts of data, the algorithm can guarantee the convergence within an acceptable time. The search time of data 12 dropped significantly due to the fact that its optimal path is the local optimal path. Although the nodes and arcs of data 16 is large, it has fewer nodes and the search time also fell sharply.

Figure 3 shows the algorithm execution results which contrast with the Code Craft best results qualifying in 10 seconds. The convergence process of finding the optimal path of data 16 is shown in Figure 4. The experimental results have indicated that the proposed algorithm have satisfactory performance, better convergence, stability and feasibility of practical application.

Table 1. The solution efficiency under different scale of data.

Data ID	Nodes	Arcs	Specified nodes	Average time(ms))	Length of path
1	17	44	6	1	71
2	19	88	8	20	95
3	49	174	10	202	99
4	50	254	15	1123	193
5	60	297	15	2792	254
6	70	347	15	7894	182
7	80	370	15	8001	225
8	90	444	15	10082	240
9	100	483	15	11514	275
10	150	767	18	12470	376
11	200	952	20	12700	322
12	280	1377	23	7680	404
13	300	1561	27	11240	439
14	400	2188	30	15010	484
15	460	2611	34	18531	527
16	500	2000	21	9016	468
17	500	2847	40	22115	645
18	560	3195	44	24147	737
19	600	3372	50	25004	792

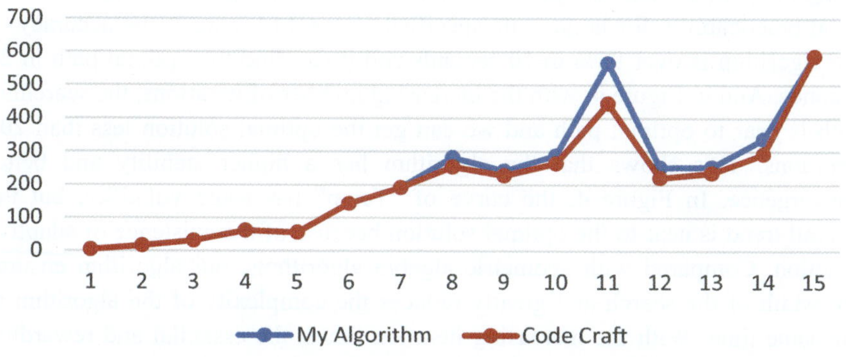

Fig. 3. The algorithm execution results and the Code Craft-best results qualifying in 10 seconds.

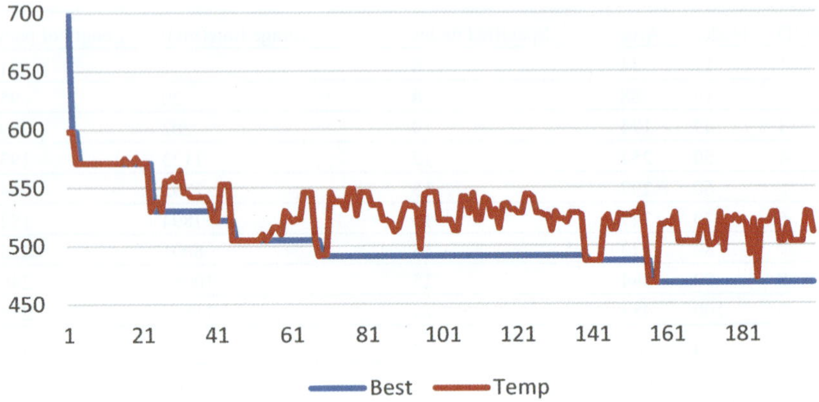

Fig. 4. The convergence process of finding the optimal path of data 16.

7. Conclusions

According to the experimental results, we can see that the number of nodes, path complexity and the number of specified nodes all have impacts on the efficient execution of algorithms. In our algorithm, the influence of specified node number does not show exponential growth like other algorithms, for example, using the permutations of specified nodes to solve it [13]. So our algorithm has good practicability for large scale specified nodes. In Figure 3, the accuracy of the algorithm is over 95% in 10 seconds and it can find the optimal path in 20 seconds. And in Figure 4, with the increasing number of iterations, the searching path is near to optimal path and we can get the optimal solution less than 200 iterations. This shows that the algorithm has a higher stability and better convergence. In Figure 4, the curve of "Temp" has some volatility, but the overall trend is near to the optimal solution because of the existence of adaptive function. Compared with geometric algebra algorithms, our algorithm ensures the width of the search and greatly reduces the complexity of the algorithm at the same time. With the increasing iteration times, the essential and rewarding effects of pheromone become apparent, and make the path more close to the optimal solution, but are still volatile after getting the optimal solution, which shows the algorithm can meet the convergence criteria and ensure a wider range of search. The complexity of the algorithm is $O(V^2)$, and the algorithm is able to meet the actual needs, if it adds multithreaded searches, we will increase the practicability of this algorithm further more.

References

1. S. Zhu, G. M. Huang, "A new parallel and distributed shortest path algorithm for hierarchically clustered data networks," *IEEE Transactions on Parallel and Distributed Systems*, vol. 9, no. 9, pp. 841 - 855, 1998.
2. B. Linkai, C. Tzi-Dar, "Solving the shortest path problem using an analog network," *IEEE Transactions on Circuits and Systems I: Fundamental Theory and Applications*, vol. 46, no. 11, pp. 1360 - 1363, 1999.
3. F. Gang, K. Turgay, "Finding Multi-Constrained Multiple Shortest Paths," *IEEE Transactions on Computers*, vol. 64, no. 9, pp. 2559 -2572, 2015.
4. R. Gbor, J. B. Jzsef, C. Tibor, "On Shortest Path Representation," *IEEE/ACM Transactions on Networking*, vol. 15, no. 6, pp. 1293 - 1306, 2007.
5. S. Misra, B. J. Oommen, "Dynamic algorithms for the shortest path routing problem: learning automata-based solutions," *IEEE Transactions on Systems, Man, and Cybernetics, Part B (Cybernetics)*, vol. 35, no. 6, pp. 1179 - 1192, 2005.
6. M. Saad, Z. Q. Luo, "Design of WDM networks under economy of scale pricing and shortest path routing," *IEEE Journal on Selected Areas in Communications*, vol. 24, no. 4, pp. 36, 2006.
7. E. P. Chan, Y. Yang, "Shortest Path Tree Computation in Dynamic Graphs," *IEEE Transactions on Computers*, vol. 58, no. 4, pp. 541 -557, 2009.
8. C. F. Juang, C. W. Hung, C. H. Hsu, "Rule-Based Cooperative Continuous Ant Colony Optimization to Improve the Accuracy of Fuzzy System Design," *IEEE Transactions on Fuzzy Systems*, vol. 22, no. 4, pp. 723 -735, 2014.
9. C. Blum, M. Dorigo, "The hyper-cube framework for ant colony optimization," *IEEE Transactions on Systems, Man, and Cybernetics, Part B (Cybernetics)*, vol. 34, no. 2, pp. 1161 - 1172, 2004.
10. M. Dorigo, M. Birattari, T. Stutzle, "Ant colony optimization," *IEEE Computational Intelligence Magazine*, vol. 1, no. 4, pp. 28 - 39, 2006.
11. S. L. Huang, D. S. Hu, Y. M. Jiang, "Algorithm for finding shortest path which must go through specified intermediate node set," *Computer Engineering and Allpications*, vol. 51, no. 11, pp. 41 - 46, 2015.

An Optimization Scheme for Intelligent Material Delivery Based on Omni-Directional Vehicle

Shang-Jie Pan[a], Lu Zhao and Hao Fu

Beijing Institute of Spacecraft Environment Engineering,
Beijing 100094, China
E-mail: [a]njtupp@163.com

In this paper, an omni-directional vehicle with mecanum wheel is designed for material delivery in the process of satellite assembly. Considering the character of mecanum wheel and environment of assembly hall, both machine vision navigation and magnetic tape are used on the omni-directional vehicle. An intelligent step length adjustment strategy is proposed for angle and displacement deviation, and is applied in the process of material delivery. Experiments demonstrate that the vehicle can deliver materials from warehouse to operation station automatically and accurately.

Keywords: Material Delivery; Omni-Directional Vehicle; Step Length Adjustment.

1. Introduction

In the process of satellite assembly, a great deal of material need to be delivered from warehouse to assembly stations. With the rapid growth in the number of satellite assembled, the amount, volume and weight of material increase quickly, and the manual delivery greatly reduces the efficiency of assembly. Therefore, an intelligent material delivery scheme is necessary to improve the efficiency of satellite assembly. In this paper, we take advantage of omni-directional vehicle with mecanum wheel and propose an intelligent step length adjustment strategy to deliver material from warehouse and assembly stations. The environment of satellite assembly hall is complex, in which the narrow aisles, cracked ground, serious electromagnetic interference, and uneven lighting condition make high requirement for automatic material delivery.

Common wheeled vehicle needs a large space for movement posture adjustment, and is not fit for the narrow aisles in satellite assembly hall. In this implementation, the omni-directional vehicle is applied as the platform for intelligent manual delivery, which can move and turn to any direction freely along the narrow aisles through the coordination with different rotation speed and direction of mecanum wheel group [1]. The above kinematic properties are fit for the material delivery in the satellite assembly hall.

Automatic guidance and deviation adjustment are the main problems for intelligent delivery, and many techniques are utilized for it, such as machine vision guidance, magnetic tape guidance, electromagnetic guidance, laser guidance, etc. Compared with other methods, both machine vision guidance and magnetic tape guidance are simple and easy to be implemented with low costs [2-3]. However, the machine vision guidance can be severely influenced by uneven lighting condition and cracked ground [4], and magnetic tape guidance can be influenced by electromagnetic signal from environments [5]. The combination guidance of machine vision and magnetic tape can overcome the above disadvantages, and thus are suitable for the application of satellite assembly. In the process of assembly, the angle and displacement deviation are collected in real-time, and are adjusted step by step through mecanum wheel. The combination guidance method and step adjustment strategy are applied to make sure that the materials are delivered from warehouse to assembly stations efficiently and accurately.

2. Control for Omni-Directional Vehicle

The four mecanum wheels of omni-directional vehicle are installed at the bottom of the vehicle symmetrically, and each of them is controlled by an AC motor independently, as shown in Figure 1.

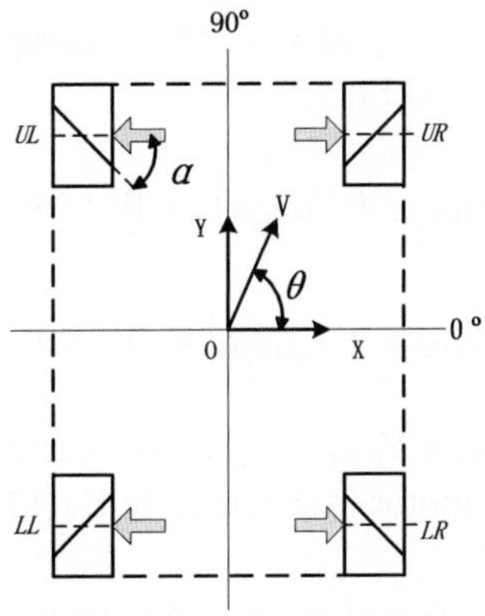

V: velocity of omni-directional vehicle
θ: angle of vehicle's velocity with X axis
α: installing angle of rollers's axis with X axis
Fig. 1. The sample of omni-directional vehicle.

When the mecanum wheel rotates, one of the rollers around the wheel which touches the ground both bears the friction F_a from hub along the roller's axis direction and friction F_r from ground along the roller's vertical axis direction [6-7]. Because of the structure characteristic of mecanum wheel, the actual velocity of each wheel is always along the axis of the roller [8].

In this implementation, we adopt a mutual exclusion control strategy between move and rotation on omni-directional vehicle. When moving, the velocity of the two wheel on the diagonal is same, and the velocity of four wheels can be simplified as $V_{(UL)}$ and $V_{(UR)}$, according to the vector superposition method, as shown in Figure 2.

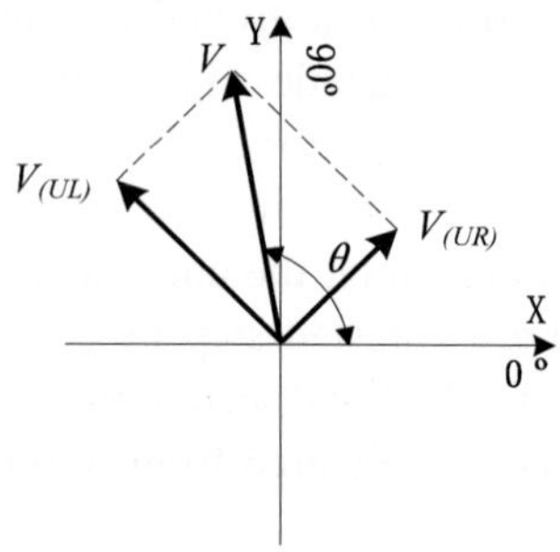

Fig. 2. Vector synthesis of $V_{(UL)}$ and $V_{(UR)}$ when moving.

The omni-directional vehicle can move along any direction within 0 degrees to 360 degrees throughout coordination between rotation rate and direction about four wheels. The relationship between omni-directional vehicle's velocity V and its decomposition velocity of $V_{(UL)}$, $V_{(UR)}$ along X and Y coordination axis can be shown as in Eq. (1) and Eq. (2).

$$|V_{(UL)X} + V_{(UR)X}| = |V \cdot \cos\theta| \quad (1)$$

$$|V_{(UL)Y} + V_{(UR)Y}| = |V \cdot \sin\theta| \quad (2)$$

The relationship between $V_{(UL)}$, $V_{(UR)}$ along X and Y coordination axis and the rotation rate about AC motor is shown as in Eq. (3) and Eq. (4).

$$|V_{(i)X}| = \omega_{(i)} \cdot K \cdot \cos\alpha. \quad (3)$$

$$|V_{(i)Y}| = \omega_{(i)} \cdot K \cdot \sin\alpha. \quad (4)$$

$i=(UL,UR,LR,LL)$

in which K is constant for the mecanum wheel whose structure is fixed. Its value is shown as in Eq. (5).

$$K = N \cdot \varepsilon \cdot L. \tag{5}$$

in which N is the number about roller of each mecanum wheel; ε is the motion continuity ratio of each mecanum wheel; L is the length helical line of the roller.

When the vehicle moves along θ degrees according to the established velocity V, the rotation rate of each AC motor can be written as in Eq. (6).

$$\begin{pmatrix} \omega_{(UL)} \\ \omega_{(UR)} \\ \omega_{(LR)} \\ \omega_{(LL)} \end{pmatrix} = \frac{V}{2 \cdot K \cdot \cos\alpha} \begin{pmatrix} \sin\theta + \cos\theta \\ \sin\theta - \cos\theta \\ -\sin\theta - \cos\theta \\ -\sin\theta + \cos\theta \end{pmatrix}. \tag{6}$$

When the vehicle rotates, the velocity of the four wheels on the diagonal is same, which can be simplified as $V'_{(UL)}$. The vehicle can rotate in clockwise or anti-clockwise direction according to the established velocity V through changing the rotating direction synchronously, as shown in Figure 3.

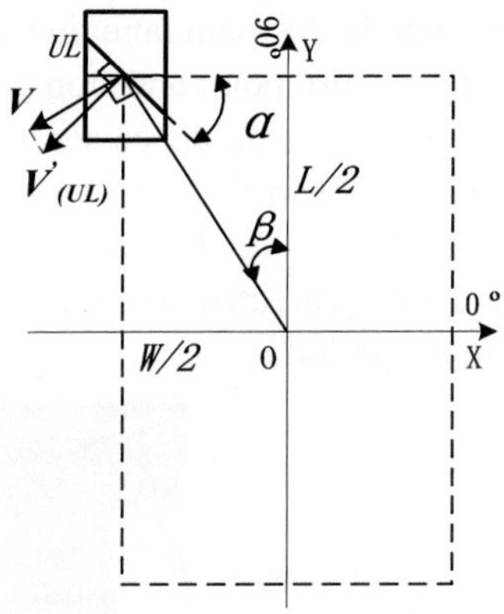

W:center distance of wheels along X axis
L: center distance of wheels along Y axis
β:half of diagonal angle
Fig. 3. Vector synthesis of $V'_{(UL)}$ when rotating.

The relationship between V and $V'_{(UL)}$ is given as in Eq. (7).

$$V_{(UL)}' = \frac{V}{\cos(\pi/4 - \alpha - \beta)}. \tag{7}$$

The relationship of rotation rate about AC motor and macanum wheel' velocity is brought into the formula and simplified. When the vehicle rotes according to *V*, the rotation rate about each AC motor is given as in Eq. (8).

$$\begin{pmatrix} \omega^T{}_{(UL)} \\ \omega^T{}_{(UR)} \\ \omega^T{}_{(LR)} \\ \omega^T{}_{(LL)} \end{pmatrix} = \frac{1}{K} \cdot \left(\frac{V \cdot \sqrt{L^2+W^2}}{L \cdot \sin\alpha + W \cdot \cos\alpha} \right) \begin{pmatrix} (-1)^j \\ (-1)^j \\ (-1)^{j+1} \\ (-1)^{j+1} \end{pmatrix} j = (0,1). \tag{8}$$

in which,

$$\mathrm{K} = \mathrm{N} \cdot \varepsilon \cdot \mathrm{L}. \tag{9}$$

The omni-directional vehicle can move and turn freely within 0 - 360 degrees by making coordination between the rotation rate and direction.

3. Guidance and Deviation Adjustment Strategy

3.1. *Layout of guidance device*

In this implementation, guidance magnetic tape is used as lay lane line. There are two kinds of lane line, one is the main lane line for guidance, the other is the remark lane line for indicating turn point and stop point.

The CCD camera and magnetic guidance sensor are used to detect the lane for the vehicle. They are installed in the front and at the bottom of the vehicle, respectively, as shown in Figure 4. The collected data are transmitted to computer to process, and the generated reference data are used to adjust the deviation for the next control period.

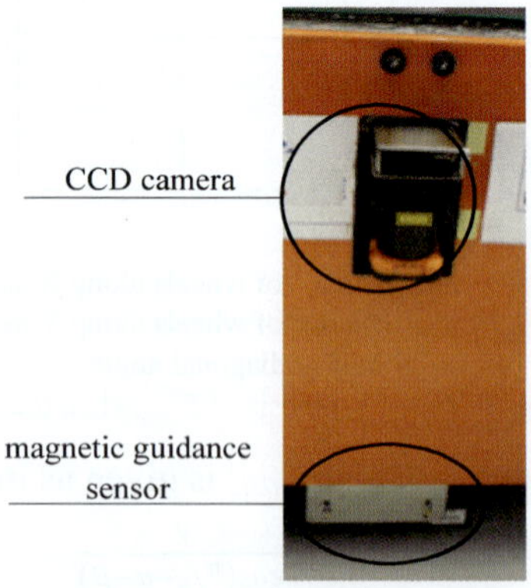

Fig. 4. The CCD camera and magnetic guidance sensor on the vehicle.

3.2. *Basic control strategy*

The control strategy based on state switching is used for omni-directional vehicle. According to the delivery procedure, the statuses of vehicle can be defined as: Start, Track, Turn-left, Turn-right, Pause and Stop. A delivery procedure is beginning with Start-status and ending with Stop-status. The vehicle can accomplish all the delivery procedure in the hall of satellite assembly through the coordination among Track, Turn-left, Turn-right and Pause. The Stop-status should be start manually, and the other statuses switch automatically.

The deviation adjustment strategy is a key technology in motion control. There are two kinds of deviations in the process of delivery, one is lateral deflection deviation Δd and the other angle deviation $\Delta\theta$. The deviation is collected and analyzed automatically, and the adjustment parameter and strategy are drafted in the next control period until the deviation reaches the established targets range. The deviation about Δd and $\Delta\theta$ are defined as shown in Figure 5.

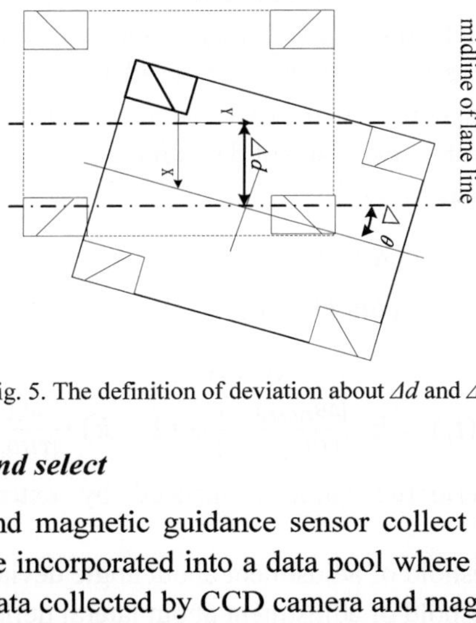

Fig. 5. The definition of deviation about Δd and $\Delta\theta$.

3.3. *Data process and select*

The CCD camera and magnetic guidance sensor collect the real-time data of lane, and the data are incorporated into a data pool where the data are stored in certain period. The data collected by CCD camera and magnetic guidance sensor are processes by different methods. At last, two lane lines can be obtained.

The image captured by CCD camera is processed by using denoising, distortion correction, edge detection algorithm, etc. A Chess Board correction method is used to remove the camera's distortion. The deformation coefficient is got according to the three images of Chess Board. Images before and after correction are as shown in Figure 6 for comparison. And the binary edge image of the lane is extracted by exploiting Sobel operator with 8-direction templates. The slope of lane centerline is calculated relative to the centerline of vehicle.

Fig. 6. Image comparison before and after correction.

When the magnetic guide sensor is working, the potential information from different sampling points is extracted. Let L_1 be the closest triggered sampling point to the left of the vehicle and R_1 the closest point to the right, the position information about L_1 and R_1 are collected. And the position of the center of the lane relative to the current magnetic guide sensor is calculated [9]. Through collecting the information of two magnetic guidance sensors installed in front and behind of the vehicle, the $\Delta d_M(t_i)$, $\Delta\theta_M(t_i)$ are calculated.

The principle of weighted maximum is used for deviation selection. When one kind of deviation collected by CCD camera or magnetic guide sensor is incorrect or immeasurable, the value of deviation gets to 0. The final deviation at any moment is shown as in Eq. (10).

$$\begin{pmatrix}\Delta\theta(t_i)\\ \Delta d(t_i)\end{pmatrix} = \begin{cases}(\Delta\theta_V(t_i), \Delta d_V(t_i))w_{(V)}(t_i) \geq w_{(M)}(t_i)\\ (\Delta\theta_V(t_i), \Delta d_V(t_i))w_{(V)}(t_i) < w_{(M)}(t_i)\end{cases}. \tag{10}$$

$$(i \in N)$$

$$w_{(V,M)}(t_i) = k \cdot \frac{|\Delta\theta_{(V,M)}(t_i)|}{|THD_{(ST)}(\theta)|} + (1-k) \cdot \frac{|\Delta d_{(V,M)}(t_i)|}{|THD_{(ST)}(d)|}. \tag{11}$$

$k \in (0,1)$: experiential value influenced by external environment of ground;

$THD_{(ST)}(\theta)$: threshold of adjustment about angle deviation;

$THD_{(ST)}(d)$: threshold of adjustment about lateral deflection deviation.

3.4. *Deviation adjustment algorithm*

The deviation between omni-directional vehicle and center of the lane can be divided into two categories: one is lateral deflection deviation *Δd* and the other angle deviation *Δθ*. In this application, we experientially set the adjustment starting threshold value of angle deviation as $\pm 10°$, and the adjustment ending threshold value of angle deviation is set as ±3°. And the adjustment starting threshold value of lateral deflection deviation is ±80mm, with the adjustment ending threshold value of lateral deflection deviation is ±20mm. When both the lateral deflection deviation and angle deviation get greater than the threshold value, the adjustment about angle deviation is exploited first. In a certain adjustment period, only one adjustment of angle deviation or lateral deflection deviation is applied. The deviation adjustment algorithm is presented as in Figure 7.

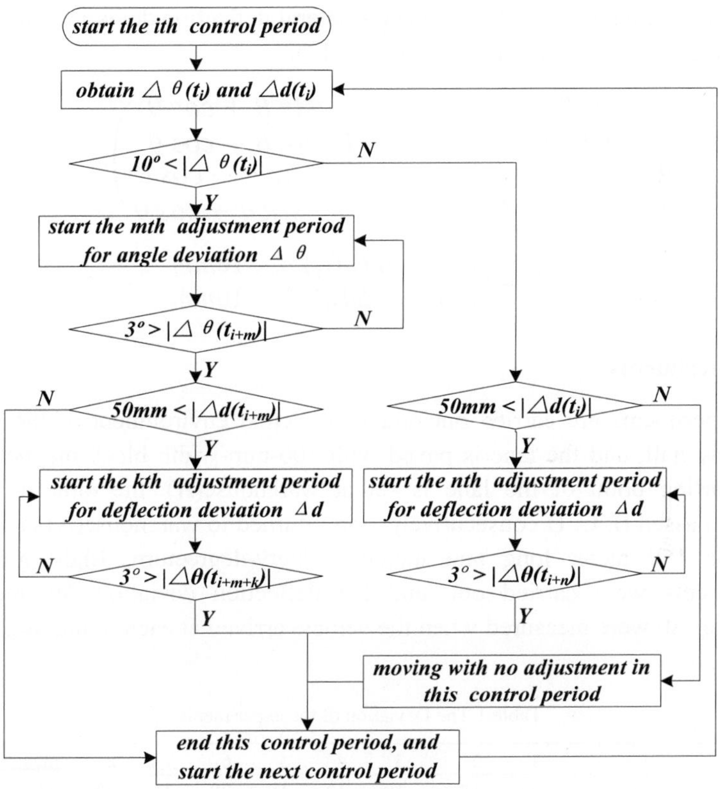

Fig. 7. The algorithm about deviation adjustment.

In a certain adjustment period about angular deviation, the angular velocity of each wheel is shown as in Eq. (12).

$$\begin{pmatrix} \omega^T{}_{(UL)} \\ \omega^T{}_{(UR)} \\ \omega^T{}_{(LR)} \\ \omega^T{}_{(LL)} \end{pmatrix} = \frac{1}{K} \cdot \left(\frac{V \cdot \sqrt{L^2+W^2}}{L \cdot \sin\alpha + W \cdot \cos\alpha} \right) \begin{pmatrix} (-1)^j \\ (-1)^j \\ (-1)^{j+1} \\ (-1)^{j+1} \end{pmatrix}. \quad (12)$$

$$j = \begin{cases} 0 & \Delta\theta_M(t_i) < 0° \\ 1 & \Delta\theta_M(t_i) > 0° \end{cases}$$

In a certain adjustment period about lateral deflection deviation, the angular velocity of each wheel is shown as in Eq. (13).

$$\begin{pmatrix} \omega_{(UL)} \\ \omega_{(UR)} \\ \omega_{(LR)} \\ \omega_{(LL)} \end{pmatrix} = \frac{V}{2 \cdot K \cdot \cos\alpha} \begin{pmatrix} \sin\theta + \cos\theta \\ \sin\theta - \cos\theta \\ -\sin\theta - \cos\theta \\ -\sin\theta + \cos\theta \end{pmatrix}. \quad (13)$$

$$\theta = \begin{cases} 45° & \Delta d_M(t_i) < -10mm \\ 135° & \Delta d_M(t_i) > 10mm \end{cases}$$

4. Experiments

The experiments are carried out under the actual environment of the satellite assembly hall, and the lane is paved with 100-mm-width black magnetic tape. The starting point of the lane is set at warehouse(A), the omni-directional vehicle passed B, C, D consecutively, and returned to warehouse(A) at last. The route is 150 meter long and includes3ninety-degreeturn. Eight groups of experiments were carried out, and the deflection deviation Δd and angle deviation Δθ were measured when the vehicle arrived at each point, as shown in Table 1.

Table 1 The Deviation of the experiments.

		1	2	3	4	5	6	7	8	mean value
B	*Δd(mm)*	23	35	19	12	16	28	31	20	23
	Δθ(°)	8	4	7	6	5	4	3	6	5
C	*Δd(mm)*	39	19	42	35	29	17	33	31	31
	Δθ(°)	7	3	6	7	8	6	4	8	6
D	*Δd(mm)*	26	32	41	19	25	38	34	44	32
	Δθ(°)	5	8	5	7	4	6	8	8	6
A	*Δd(mm)*	41	38	21	13	27	32	38	30	30
	Δθ(°)	3	8	7	7	5	4	8	3	6

Experiments results prove that the accuracy of delivery automatically is accord with the design index, it can meet the delivery demand of satellite assembly.

5. Conclusion

In this paper, we utilize the omni-directional vehicle for material delivery in satellite assembly, which can move along any direction and is fit for the complex environment in satellite assembly hall.

The proposed method of machine vision and magnetic tape can overcome the influence of multiple external environment factors and collect the real-time information of lane line accurately. Through the detected lane line, the deviation is collected and analyzed automatically, and step adjustment strategy for angle and displacement deviation is applied. Experiments demonstrate that, by using the proposed method, the vehicle can deliver material from warehouse to operation station robustly and accurately.

References

1. Zheng-jia Guan. The Research on Significance and Application of Omni-Directional Platform with Mecanum Wheel[D]. Zhejiang: Zhejiang University, 2012.
2. Kelly A., Nagy B., Stager D., et al. An Infrastructure-free Automated Guided Vehicle based on Computer Vision[J]. IEEE Robotics and Automation Magazine. 2007, 14(3): 24-34.
3. Qian-yi Chen. The Research of the Magnetic Guided AGV (Automated Guided Vehicle) Central Control System[D]. Wuhan: Wuhan University of Technology, 2014.
4. Milan Sonka, Vaclav Hlavac, Roger Boyle. Image Processing Analysis and Machine Vision[M]. Tsinghua University Press, 2011.1.
5. Xian-long Yang. Design of Structure and Control for Two-wheel difference Speed Steering AGV with Magmetic Navigation[D]. Hefei: Hefei University of Technology, 2014.
6. Wen-lv Wei. The Structure Analysis and Design of Omni-Directional Mobile Robot[D]. Nanjing: Southeast University, 2006.
7. Liang-shi Wei, Song-wang Xing, Jia Qian, et al. Development of Omni-Directional Mobile Robot Based on Mecanum Wheel[J]. Mechanical Engineer, 2007,9:18-21.

8. Diegel O, Badve A, Bright G, et al. Improved Mecanum Wheel Design for Omni-directional Robots[C]. Proc. of 2002 Australasian Conference on Robotics and Automation. Auckland, New Zealand: [s. n.], 2002: 117-121.
9. Bing Wang, Bin Hu, Xiang-wang Chun. Research and Design of the Onboard Controller for Automated Guided Vehicles[J]. Process Automation Instrumentation, 2013,34(5): 1-4.

A Double Time-Slot RFID Anti-Collision Algorithm Based on Gray Code

Hong-Wei Deng[1,2,a], Hui Wang[1,b] and Lang Li[1,c]

[1]*School of Computer Science and Technology, Hengyang Normal University, Hengyang, Hunan 421002, China*

[2]*School of Information science and Engineering, Central South University, Changsha, Hunan 410083, China*

E-mail: [a]dhwwhd@163.com, [b]wanghui18188@hotmail.com, [c]lilang911@126.com

This paper aims at RFID problem, propose an Anti-Collision Algorithm based on Gray Code. This algorithm simplifies the reader to search tag prefix by Gray Code regulation and to enhance the identification speed through efficient division of the collision tags. Branch the tag colliding efficiently to enhance the identification speed of tag. The findings from analysis of algorithm and simulation result demonstrate that BSGC can reduce the number of collision and transmission delay, enhance throughput rate and increase the efficiency of tag identification.

Keywords: Gray Code; Extra Code; Time-Slot Control Code; Double Time-Slot; Anti-Collision

1. Introduction

In the Internet of things at present, the application of RFID technology ever more widely, on account of the characteristic of reading data is convenient, without interact directly and can work on various severe environment et. RFID are widely used in various industry sectors. But in the practical application environment, multiple tags vie channel to transmit data at the same time cause the problem of collision, affect the accuracy and efficiency of data transmission in the overall system and transmission efficiency. So in order to solve the problem of data collision. To tackle the problem of data collision, so anti-collision algorithm of RFID system become a hot research spot right now.

2. The Correlation of RFID Anti-Collision Algorithm

At present, Time Division Multiple Address algorithms is easy to implement and more popular, it is mainly divided into ALOHA algorithm and binary search tree algorithm. Pure ALOHA is easy to implement, and in the case of the number of tags is small can identify tag efficiently, but the throughput rate is low, only up to 18.4%. Dynamic frame slot ALOHA algorithm [1], according to the number of tag determine the slot number in the frame dynamically to maximize the throughput. A binary search tree algorithm [2] is composed of query command and response command of the multicycle reader, algorithm steps is similar to a tree structure of data structure. Correlation algorithm include BBT (bit-by-bit tree) algorithm [3], the binary search algorithm based on regressive [4], ABS (adaptive binary splitting) algorithm [5], Q- tree algorithm [6], the dynamic binary search algorithm [7] [8].Tag only transfer the L-K bit data out of command, reduce the redundant data in the information transmission broadly. the tree structure of RFID collision algorithm of being improved [9], the binary tree is divided into several small branches, reduce the number of search, optimize the number of idle time slot, improve the efficiency of recognition greatly, but the algorithm is still inadequacy, on this basis, putting forward a double time-slot RFID anti-collision algorithm based on Gray Code.

3. Algorithm Principle

3.1. *The introduction of gray code*

Gray Code is a kind of binary cyclic code, Frank Gray was named by the application of patent in 1953 and the name and used in analog digital conversion and angle conversion in present. Gray Code is belongs to reliability codes, and is a coding scheme with minimize mistakes. The conversion between gray code and binary code: supposing a natural code is $B=B_{n-1}\ldots B_{i+1}B_{i}\ldots B_0$, the corresponding gray code is $G=G_{n-1}\ldots G_{i+1}G_{i}\ldots G_0$, the transformation formula can be expressed as in Eq. (1).

$$G_{n-1}=B_{n-1},\ G_i=B_{i+1}\oplus B_i\ (n-1\geq i\geq 0) \quad (1)$$

3.2. *Algorithm instruction constraint*

The algorithm utilize the gray code to improve the original algorithm in instruction as follows:

(1) Setting extra code M and time slot control code N. When the tag is

activated, firstly, top three collision bits of itself convert into gray code, gray code number is three. Setting tag extra code M, the initial value is 0000, from left to right is 3, 2, 1, 0 in sequence, extra code M have but one "1", the position of "1" according to the gray code decimal value of two digits after to determine. If the gray code after two of tag collision bit is 00, then the zeroth position of corresponding extra code M's value is 0, means M=0001. Similarly, 01 corresponds to M=0010, 10 corresponding to M =0100, 11 corresponding to M=1000. Setting time slot control code N, the value is the first value of gray code. An accumulator C is set to each tag, the value corresponding time slot control code N to control the response time slot of tag.

(2) Query instruction REQUEST. The parameters of REQUEST instructions are divided into three forms: a single parameter, three-parameter and the value of extra code, which is REQUEST (bit), REQUEST (D1, D2, D3) and REQUEST (EC) instructions. REQUEST (bit) is the initial query instructions, all tags in the reader should respond; REQUEST (EC) instructions is the extra code of query tag; D1, D2 and D3 in the REQUEST (D1, D2, D3) is the collision bit of tag. Queue stored in the REQUEST instruction, when the queue is empty, the algorithm is finish.

(3) Select instruction SELECT. SELECT (ID) select number for the ID tag is prepare for read or write data.

(4) Reading instruction READ. READ (ID) read out numbers for ID tags in the data.

(5) Shield instruction UNSELECT. UNSELECT (ID) let the number of ID tags in inactivated state, REQUEST instruction receiving not to respond.

3.3. *Tag code conversion relationship*

Table 1 Tag code table

Tag identification code (The top three collision positions)	Gary code	Slot control code N	Additional code M
000	0 00	0	0001
001	0 01	0	0010
010	0 11	0	1000
011	0 10	0	0100
100	1 10	1	0100
101	1 11	1	1000
110	1 01	1	0010
111	1 00	1	0001

The code conversion relationship of tag is showed in Table 1.

The algorithm agreement: each query is divided into two time slots response : 0 and 1, response time slot is determined by the time slot control code N. Tags will response in the first time slot when N=0 , while tags will response in the second time slots when N=1. It can be seen from table1 that tags have the same extra code M, but with the different time slot control code N. In the process of tag identification, reader can identify the corresponding tag identification code (three collision bits) in different time slots by the extra code M. Then insert the tag identification code (three collision bits) into the queue, and then according to the FIFO method, construct a new query instruction to identify the tags.

3.4. *Algorithm description*

Algorithm flow chart is showed as Figure 1.

Step 1: Reader sends initialization query instruction REQUEST (bit).

Step 2: Responding the tag Matching the query instruction, if colliding, jump to step 3; if only one tag respond reader, then, identify the tag directly.

Step 3: If only one collision, then, identify two tags at the same time; if have two collision bits, reader using quad-tree identify tag directly; if the collision number is more than two, according to the information of tag time slot control code N, tag of N is 0 should be put in the first time slot, extra code of N is 1 put in the second slot response. If the slot is also colliding, then, according to the extra code M's information, reader confirm the three identification code of time slot, and inserts into the queue.

Step 4: According to the queue information, reader constructs a new query instruction, if the queue is not empty, then jump to step 2; if the queue is empty, the recognition process is over.

3.5. *Algorithm example*

Here to explain the realization process of the algorithm by an example, assume that reader have eight tags waiting for identified in the range of identification, tag's ID number is six digits, as shown in Table 2.

The realization process of the algorithm is as follows:

(1) Reader to initialize bit=111111.

(2) The reader sends the REQUEST (bit), and all the tags are respond in the scope of reader, according to the principle of Manchester encoding, we can get the decoding information is X0XXXX, as shown in Table 3. The positions of the top three collision are respectively 1, 3, 4, reader generates new query instruction REQUEST (D1, D3, D4) and sends to the tags. At the same time, the

tag will convert their top three collision into a gray code, and set the time slot control code N, the value is the first bit of gray code. Each tag sets an accumulator C, N values is stored in its own accumulator C, according to the values of C response to a reader in the corresponding time slot. As shown in Table 4.

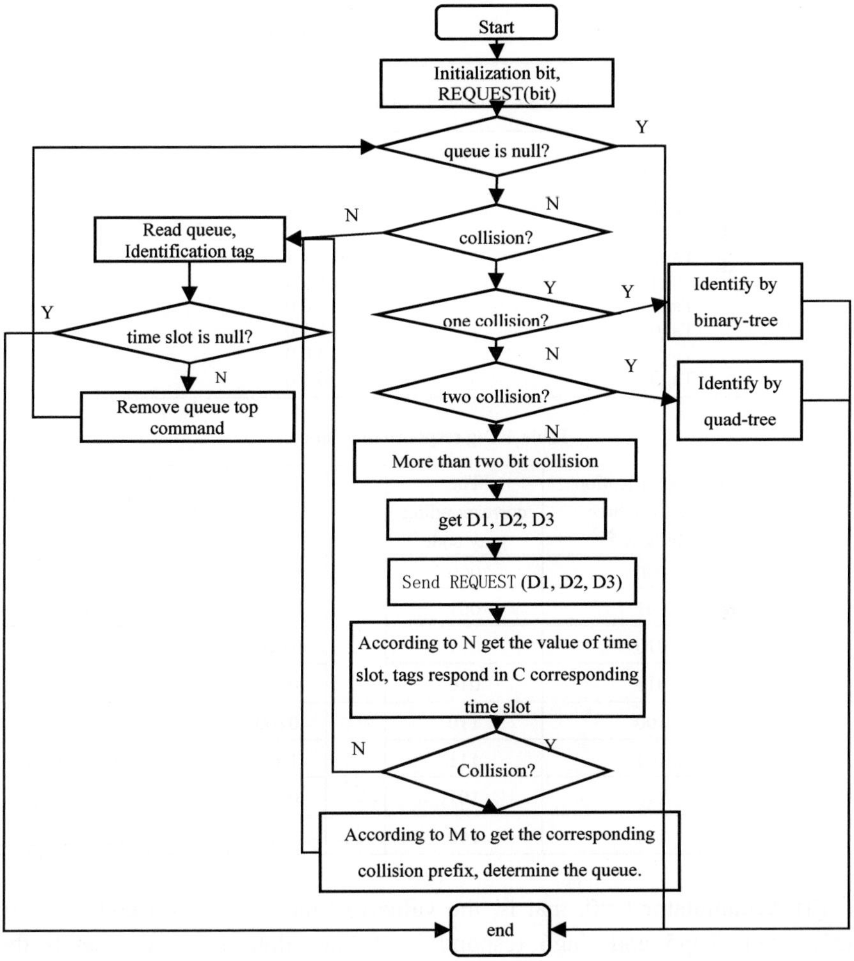

Fig. 1. Flow chart

Table 2 Manchester coding

Tags	Manchester coding
Tag1	1 0 0 1 0 1
Tag2	1 0 0 1 1 1
Tag3	0 0 0 0 1 1
Tag4	0 0 0 1 0 0
Tag5	0 0 1 1 0 0
Tag6	0 0 1 1 1 0
Tag7	1 0 1 0 0 0
Tag8	1 0 1 0 1 0

Table 3 Collision bit of information

Position	1 2 3 4 5 6
Information	X 0 X X X X
Tag1	1 0 0 1 0 1
Tag2	1 0 0 1 1 1
Tag3	0 0 0 0 1 1
Tag4	0 0 0 1 0 0
Tag5	0 0 1 1 0 0
Tag6	0 0 1 1 1 0
Tag7	1 0 1 0 0 0
Tag8	1 0 1 0 1 0

Table 4 Tag response time slot

Time slot	Tag identification code (top three collision)	The corresponding gray code	N	M	C	In response to the tag
a0	000	000	0	0001	0	Tag3
	001	001		0010		Tag4
	010	011		1000		
	011	010		0100		Tag5, Tag6
a1	100	110	1	0100	1	
	101	111		1000		Tag1, Tag2
	110	101		0010		Tag7, tag8
	111	100		0001		

(3) Accumulator C=0, that is, the value of time slot control code N is 0, Tag3, Tag4, Tag5 and Tag6 respond in 0 time slot, the reader sends the REQUEST (EC) instruction to query the value of extra code M inside of tag, obtain the collision information of M is 0XXX, as shown in Table 5. According to table 4, there can be four different situations of M in 0 time slot (0001, 0010,

1000, 0100), whereas, M collision information 0XXX, there may be only three scenarios (0001, 0010, 0100), and their corresponding tag collision bit information is (000, 001, 011). To push the three prefix REQUEST instructions into the "queue", in turn, call and send REQUEST (000), REQUEST (001), can identify Tag3 and Tag4 respectively. When the reader sends REQUEST (011), receives the collision information as shown in Table 6, it is only one has collision, according to the query tree algorithm, and can identify Tag5 and Tag6 directly. At this point, tag in zero time slot have identified.

Table 5 M collision information (first round)

Position	1 2 3 4 5 6	M
Information	0 0 X X X X	0 X X X
Tag3	0 0 0 0 1 1	0 0 0 1
Tag4	0 0 0 1 0 0	0 0 1 0
Tag5	0 0 1 1 0 0	0 1 0 0
Tag6	0 0 1 1 1 0	0 1 0 0

Table 6 M collision information (second round)

Position	1 2 3 4 5 6	M
Information	0 0 1 1 X 0	0 1 0 0
Tag5	0 0 1 1 0 0	0 1 0 0
Tag6	0 0 1 1 1 0	0 1 0 0

(4) Accumulator C becomes 1, judging the institution of collision in 1 time slot, judging steps in accordance with the above method.

(5) After the reader identifies all tags, judging have or not REQUEST instruction in the queue, if not, identification is ends.

4. Performance Analysis

4.1. *The query command times analysis of reader*

The definition of parameter names is as follows:

K:Tag length

L:the top L bit of tag collision (L<K)

N:The total number of Query tags

P(c):In N tags, probability of collision which prefix's long is L

P(s): In N tags, probability of recognition which prefix's long is L
P(i):In N tags, probability of free which prefix's long is L
n(c):Number of collision prefix
n(s):Number of successful recognition prefix
n(i):Number of idle prefix
Q: The total number of query instructions that Reader needs to transmit

In practical applications, the number of tags to be identified is massive, that is, N is very large. In the definition stage of tag prefix, the reader transmits a command REQUEST (bit) , all tags are respond, reader obtain the information of tag collision, suppose there are K bit collision, get the top L collision bits, there may be 2^L prefix. As in Eq. (2)~ Eq. (7).

$$P(i)=(1-1/2^L)^N \tag{2}$$

$$P(s)=N/2^L*(1-1/2^L)^{N-1} \tag{3}$$

$$P(c)=1-P(s)-P(i)=1-(1-1/2^L)^N-N/2^L * (1-1/2^L)^{N-1} \tag{4}$$

$$n(i)=2^L* P(i) =2^L* (1-1/2^L)^N \tag{5}$$

$$n(s)=2^L* P(s)=2^L*N/2^L* (1-1/2^L)^{N-1} \tag{6}$$

$$n(c)=2^L* P(c)=2^L*(1-(1-1/2^L)^N-N/2^L* (1-1/2^L)^{N-1}) \tag{7}$$

When $N>>2^L$,$(1-1/2^L)^N \rightarrow 0$, $(1-1/2^L)^{N-1}\rightarrow 0$,we can know, $n(i)\rightarrow 0$, $n(s)\rightarrow 0$, $n(c)\rightarrow 2^L$.It is shown that when the number of tags is very large, there is almost no free prefix and successful identification prefix, and almost all the prefix collide.

BSGC algorithm is divided into two stages: tag prefix determination and time slot query.

(1)The stage of prefix determination: readers need to broadcast one query instruction REQUEST (bit) to obtain the tag information, and then send 2 command REQUEST (EC) to obtain the collision bit information.

(2)The stage of Time slot query: according to the analysis, the two time slots of 0 and 1 have 2^L branches in all, each of which has $(2^{K-L} *2^{L-1})$ branch. In the one of time slot, reader sends to query instruction number of Q_{one} for each branch is:

$$Q_{one}=2^{K-L}-1 \tag{8}$$

To query a time slot, From Eq. (8) ,the number of query instructions Q_0 can be expressed as in Eq. (9).

$$Q_0=2^{L-1}*Q_{one}=2^{L-1}*(2^{K-L}-1) \tag{9}$$

Similarly, the same query instruction number of Q_0 is needed for another time slot. Therefore, Eq. (10) means the query instruction number of Q which reader sends.

$$Q=3+2Q_0 =3+2^k-2^L,\ 1<2^L \leq K \tag{10}$$

4.2. *The analysis of transmission delay*

In the stage of prefix determination, firstly, the reader broadcast a REQUEST (bit) query instruction which length is R, tag responds K bit collision information. The reader determine the prefix which length of tag is L, and continue to broadcast a query instruction which length is L, after the tag receives the order, it responds the information of extra code collision which length is 2^{L-1}. Therefore, in the stage of prefix determination, the length of transmission channel L_1 can be expressed as in Eq. (11).

$$L_1=2*(R+L+2^{L-1}) \tag{11}$$

In the stage of time slot identification, the sum length of the query instruction send by reader and the reply by tag is equal to K. Therefore, the length of transmitted data in each branch L_d is equal to the multiple of the number of query instruction send by reader and K. L_d can be expressed as in Eq. (12).

$$L_d=KQ_{one}= K*(2^{K-L}-1) \tag{12}$$

We can get 2^L branch of search, and the total number L of bits in the transmission channel is:

$$L_2=2^L*L_d =2^L*K*(2^{K-L}-1) \tag{13}$$

From Eq. (12) and (13) , the total number L of bits in the transmission channel of BSGC algorithm can be expressed as in Eq. (14).

$$L=L_1+L_2 = 2*(R+L+2^{L-1})+2^L *K*(2^{K-L}-1) \tag{14}$$

Assume that the data transmission rate in the channel is V bit/s, so the transmission delay of the BSGC algorithm can be expressed as in Eq. (15).

$$T=L/V= (2*(R+L+2^{L-1})+2^L *K*(2^{K-L}-1))/V \tag{15}$$

4.3. *The analysis of throughput rate*

If the number of the tag is N and the times of query of query tag by Reader is Q, the system of throughput is defined as in Eq. (16).

$$S=N/Q*100\% =N/(3+2k-2L) *100\% \quad (16)$$

The throughput rate is determined by the number of searches, so when the length of the tag prefix is getting closer to the tag length, the throughput will be increased accordingly.

5. The Algorithm Emulation

Through the platform of MATLAB emulation, and put the BSGC algorithm, the query tree algorithm (QT) algorithm and hybrid query number (HQT) together to emulation, can be seen from Figure 2, when the tag number is larger, more and more time is needed for QT algorithm and HQT algorithm, the efficiency is lower than BSGC obviously.

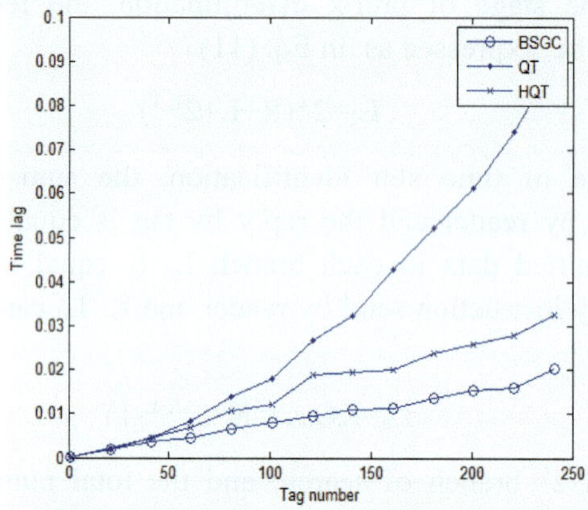

Fig. 2 The comparison of transmission delay

From Figure 3, you can see that the query tree algorithm (QT) and hybrid query number (HQT) to compared with BSGC algorithm, there is a clear gap in search times, in the case of the same number of tag, the performance of BSGC algorithm is better than the query tree algorithm (QT) and hybrid number query algorithm (HQT).

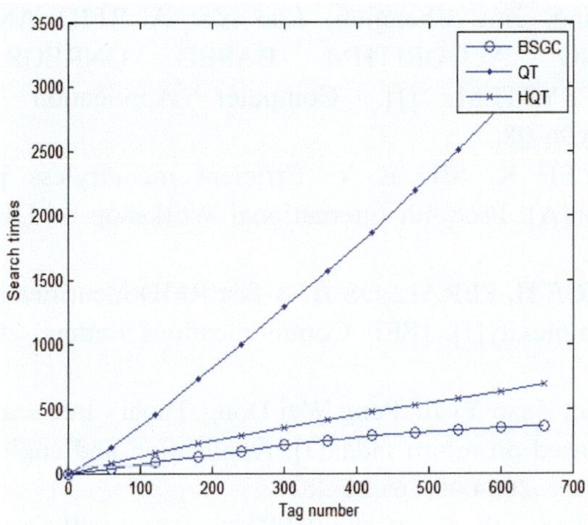

Fig. 3 Compare of searches

Through the above algorithm emulation, it is clear indicate that BSGC algorithm is better than query tree algorithm (QT) and hybrid query number (HQT) in transmission delay and the average of searching times. Thus, the proposed of algorithm in this paper reduces the transmission delay and the number of search, to optimize the overall running time, performance is obviously improved.

Acknowledgements

This research was financially supported by the National Natural Science Foundation of China (NO:61572174) and Science and technology project of Hunan Province (NO:2013SK3178).

References

1. Cheng Wen Qing, Zhao Meng Xin et. An Improved RFID dynamic framed slot ALOHA algorithm [J]. Journal of Huazhong University of Science and Technology: Humanities and social edition, 2007,35(6):14-16.
2. FINKENZELLER K. RFID Handbook: Radio-Frequency identification Fundamentals and Applications(2nd ed.)[M]. John Wiley and Sons Ltd, 2003.
3. Dennis Connors, Gregoryj. A Medium access control protocol for real time video over high latency satellite channels [J]. Mobile networks and applications, 2002, 7(1): 9-20.

4. Li Bingzhang, Jing Zhengjun, Luo Ye. A RFID ANTI-COLLISION SEARCHING ALGORITHM BASED ONREGRESSIVE-STYLE BINARY SYSTEM [J]. Computer Application and Software. 2009,26(12):96-98.
5. LAW C, LEE K, SIU K Y. Efficient memoryless protocol for tag identification[A]. Proc 4th International Workshop on DIALM[C].Boston, 2000.75-84.
6. LANDALUCE H, PERALLOS A. A fast RFID identification protocol with low tag complexity[J]. IEEE Communications Letters, 2013,17(9): 1704-1706.
7. Yu Song Sen, Zhan Yi Ju, Peng Wei Dong. Binary tree search anti-collision algorithm based on return index[J]. Application and engineering of Single Chip processor ,2004,40(16):26-28.
8. Ye Chuan Ling. Study of the RFID tag Anti-collision Algorithm [D]. Nanjing :Nanjing University of Posts, 2013.
9. LIU X H, QIAN Z H, ZHAO Y H, et al. An adaptive tag anti-collision protocol in RFID wireless systems[J]. Communications China, 2014,11(7):117-127.
10. Wang Xue, Qian Zhi Hong, Liu Xiao Hui, Cheng Chao. An Improved RFID Anti-collision Algorithm In tree structure[J]. Journal Communication, 2015,36(7):129-137.

Spoken Term Detection Based on Neural Network Front-Ends in Reverberant Environments

Zhen Zhang[a] and Peng Li[b]

National Computer Network Emergency Response Technical Team/Coordination Center of China, Beijing, China

Email: [a]zhangzhen@cert.org.cn , [b]lipeng@cert.org.cn

This paper presents an investigation of reverberant Spoken Term Detection (STD) using frond-ends based methods. A 2-channel dereverberation method is adopted to achieve robust dereverberation under different reverberant conditions. A 2-channel spectral enhancement method is also used where the gain of each frequency bin is controlled by acoustic scene, which is detected based on the analysis of full-band coherent property. Deep Neural Network (DNN) as a feature extractor is used. The DNN based front-end allows a very flexible integration of meta-information. Bottleneck features are extracted in place of MFCC features used in HMM-GMM system which generates the lattice structure. The spoken terms are detected on lattice. The methods on the data provided by REVERB challenge are evaluated. On the corpus, the DNN front-end yields huge relative reduction in Equal Error Rate (EER).

Keywords: REVERB Challenge; Deep Neural Networks; Der-Everberation; Spoken Term Detection.

1. Introduction

The speech in reverberant environments is a big challenge to traditional spoken term detection. Reducing the spoken term detection performance gap between reveberant speech and close-talking recordings has been an important research topic for a long time. Lots of researches have proved that audio processing methods are helpful in improving the quality of the reverberant speech. Among the front-end signal processing technologies, three categories of dereverberation methods are generally applied: 1) beamforming using microphone arrays, 2) spectral enhancement, 3) blind system identification and inversion[1].Spectral enhancement based dereverberation shows superiority due to its robustness in both reverberant and noisy environment [2].Fractional time delay alignment filter is applied to the reverberant signal, and the acoustic scene is classified by analyzing the coherent component. Based on the acoustic scene, an appropriate spectral enhancing scheme is selected to eliminate the interference as much as possible while keeping the speech distortion always in a low level.

Recently, acoustic model based on the Deep Neural Networks (DNNs) has gained popularity with the consistent improvement in both automatic speech recognition(ASR) and spoken term detection (STD) performance over earlier Neural Network based front-ends (e.g. [3]). DNNs are either deployed as the front-end for standard Hidden Markov Model based on Gaussian Mixture Models (HMM-GMMs), or in a hybrid form to directly estimate state level posteriors. As noted in several publications [4, 5, 6, 7], DNNs show general equal error rate (EER) improvements on the order of 10-30% relative across a variety of tasks when compared with HMM-GMMs built on classic features (e.g. MFCC, PLP). Neural network based features have long been used successfully in ASR and STD[8,9,10]. While the early research did not involve deep layers [4], the path towards deep learning was laid in the stacking of bottleneck networks [9]. A DNN is a conventional Multi-Layer Perceptron (MLP) with many internal or hidden layers. The BottleNeck (BN) features extracted from the internal layer with a relatively small amount of neurons have been shown to effectively improve the performance of ASR systems. It is possibly due to the limited number of units which creates a constriction in the network and further forces the information pertinent to classification into a low dimensional representation [11, 5, 12]. In many STD systems, the neural network based features performs better than the cepstrum or spectrum based features (e.g. MFCC, PLP).

According to REVERB challenge, the reverberant data is simulated in various rooms with different distances between source and microphones[13, 14, 15] and three kinds of utterance are provided: 1-channel, 2-channel and 8-channel. We choose the 2-channel dereverberation method for both Speech Enhancement (SE) task and Spoken Term Detection (STD) task. Work in this paper aims to extend and enhance the preliminary work in [16] with advanced DNN based feature extraction. We followed the standard strategies where the DNN includes one input layer, three hidden layers, another bottleneck layer and one output layer. The BN features are extracted from the bottleneck layer of DNN trained to predict the context-dependent clustered triphone states.

The rest of this paper is organized as follows. Section II introduces the STD system structure and algorithms of 2-channel dereverberation and DNN based feature extractor. Section III presents experiment results. Finally, section IV concludes the paper and discusses future work.

2. Spoken Term Detection of Reverb Speech

Figure 1 shows the overall spoken term detection system proposed for REVERB challenge. It contains two basic modules, front-end module and back-end spoken term detection module [17]. In the front-end module, different from our previous system, we adopt a DNN based feature extractor. For consistent comparison, we use the same recognizer provided by REVERB challenge organizer.

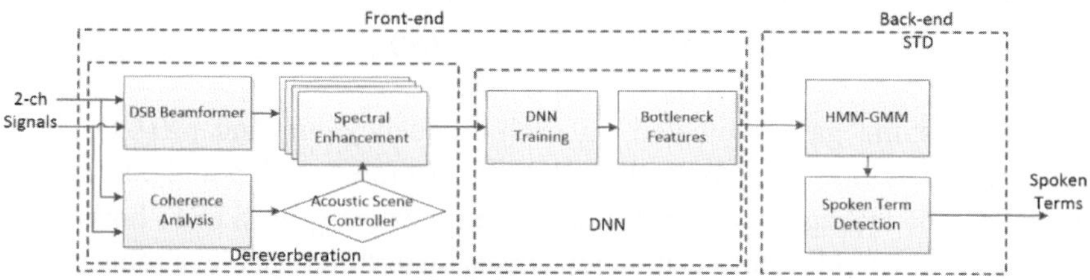

Fig. 1. System structure

2.1. *Dereverberation and noise reduction*

Spectral enhancement methods show their priority on the robustness in the condition of both noise and reverberation. In this section, an acoustic scene aware dereverberation method is utilized for the purpose of achieving environmental adaptation [16]. Two sensors are utilized since it is the basic topology of all microphone arrays and can be generalized to any other microphone arrays conveniently.

2.1.1. *Signal model*

Let *s(n)* represents the target clean signal, and $x_m(n)$ is the time-aligned signal at sensor $m(m=1,2)$. $n_m(n)$ is the noise of environment. $h_m(t)$ can be seen as the time-delayed RIR which is the convolution of real RIR from target signal to sensor $m(m=1,2)$ and alignment filter where the alignment filter is designed to steer the direction of target speech signal. The observed signal each channel can be expressed as follows.

$$x_m(n) = h_m(t) * s(n) + n_m(n) \tag{1}$$

Applying STFT to the 16kHz time-aligned signal, we have sinal expression at l th frame and k th frequency bin in time-frequency domain.

$$x_m(l,k) = H_m(l,k)S(l,k) + N_m(l,k) \tag{2}$$

2.1.2. *Spectral enhancement*

Spectral Enhancement method has a generalized form. The estimate of the amplitude spectrum of the target signal can be expressed as follows.

$$|\hat{S}(l,k)| = G(l,k)|\hat{X}(l,k)| \tag{3}$$

$G(l,k)$ is the gain estimated on each frequency bin and $|\hat{X}(l,k)|$ is the amplitude spectrum of signal to be enhanced. Before overlap-and-add scheme, regard-less of leakage between frequency bins causing by STFT, both $G(l,k)$ and $|\hat{X}(l,k)|$ should choose cautiously versus distortion to achieve robustness.

2.1.3. *Environmental adaptation based processing*

Reverberation, especially late reverberation, shows isotropic property as well as the environmental diffuse noise, while the direct sound shows strong coherent property [18]. There are two main acoustic scenes of the room we should blindly aware.

One is the reflection condition which can be interpreted by reverberation time (T60) and the other one is the speake-mic distance. By estimating the proportion of coherent component, the effects of two are synthesized. All the diffuse part can be seen as noise to be filtered. We follow the Coherent-to-Diffuse energy Ratio (CDR) estimation in [19], which is expressed as follows.

$$\varepsilon(e^{j\Omega}) = \frac{|\sin c(\Omega f_S d_{mic}/c)|^2 - |\Gamma_{X_1X_2}(e^{j\Omega})|^2}{|\Gamma_{X_1X_2}(e^{j\Omega})|^2 - 1} \tag{4}$$

$\varepsilon(e^{j\Omega})$ is CDR estimator of each frequency bin and $\Gamma_{X_1X_2}$ is the expression of complex coherence function [20]. And a Wiener filter can be formed based on the estimation of CDR which can filter the non-coherent part. According to [19], it's more accurate when CDR is relatively large. Furthermore, We use global CDR, denoted by $\hat{\varepsilon}$, as an full-band acoustic scene aware controller indicating the level affected by reverberation and diffuse noise which can be interpreted as a direct sound activity detector to achieve environmental adaptation.

Up to now, lots of 1-channel and 2-channel dereverberation methods are proved efficiency under the framework of spectral enhancement and achieve robustness to noise compared with the methods using inverse filtering. Fixed beamforming, such as Delay-and-Sum Beamformer (DSB), helps to suppress the reverberation based on priori DOA information though its suppression ability is limited. Late reverberaion suppressing method using generalized statistic model of reverberation [21] shows outstanding performance especially when reverberation is strong. Based on the controller mentioned above, we compared $\hat{\varepsilon}$ with three constants σ_1, σ_2, σ_3 (from large to small, chosen 15dB, 10dB, 5dB).

Spectral enhancement strategy suggested above separates the acoustic scene into four cases. In the first case, the acoustic scene is ideal so that the speech signal recorded is very close to clean speech. In the second and third cases, a moderate tradeoff between dereverberation and signal distortion is achieved. In the last case, more reverberation reduction means better performance when reverberation is strong enough.

To avoid music noise, both time recursive and adjacent frequency gain smoothing are conducted. The recovered signal is obtained by inverse STFT and overlap-and-add scheme. The phase of recovered speech signal equals the noisy phase of beamformer output. All the processing is with windows of 512 points and step-size of 256 points which means the result of a DFT with length 512 (32 ms) at a shift of 16 ms.

2.1.4. *DNN based features*

Figure 2 shows the architecture. It is similar to those in[3,22,23]. All DNNs are trained feed-forward with the TNET[1] on GPUs. In a default TNET setup, 31 adjacent frame MFCC features are decorrelated and compressed with DCT into a dimension of 624 $(31\times 39 \rightarrow 16\times 39)$. Global mean and variance normalization are performed on each dimension before feeding as the DNN input. The 6 layered DNN structure is shown in Figure 2. On average 10% data in training set is reserved for cross validation in DNN training. The training stops automatically when the improvement of frame-based target classification accuracy on the cross validation set drops to below 0.1%.

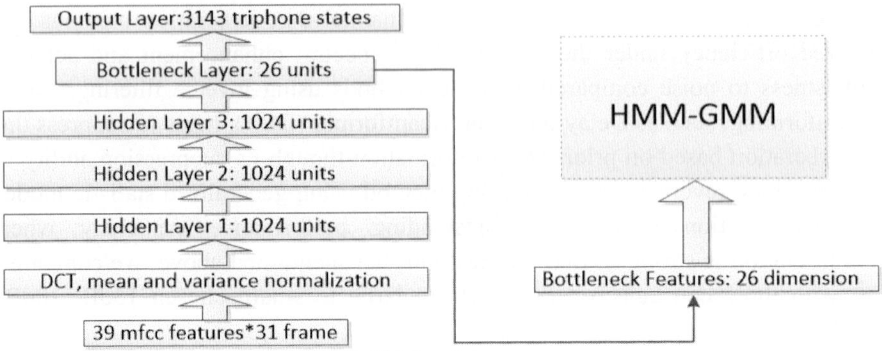

Fig. 2. DNN module structure

The bottleneck layer is placed just before the output layer, as in our initial experiments this topology gives the best performance. We set to 26 dimension according to our experiments. DNNs are trained on classification targets of 3143 triphone states. In the bottleneck layer, linear BN features are extracted before the sigmoid activation.

3. Experiment

3.1. *Data and system set*

In the REVERB challenge, we conducted the experiments on two real recorded mandarin sets. The speakers read texts in different rooms and the speech is recorded to build the testsets. Set1 is 1 hour long, and a hundred keywords are selected from this corpus with 397 occurrences. This set is recorded in labortory environment and the speakers do not have strong accent. Set2 is 10 hours long CTS set with a hundred key-words and 1934 occurrences. In this set, the speakers have strong accent. The reverberation time of the rooms are 250ms, 500ms and 700ms respectively. Recorded background noise is added to the reverberant data at a fixed signal-to-noise ratio (SNR) of 20dB. The test data are from the databases under the following important assumptions. First, there is no drastic change in RIR within an utterance. Second, relative speaker-microphone posit-ion changes from utterance to utterance, which means the direction of arrival (DOA) of the target speech signal is uncertain, and this is essential to our derev-erberation method. The recording 8-channel cicular array has diameter of 20cm and the 2-channel microphone distance, denoted by d_{mic} , can be calculated.

Under the framework of HTK based recognizer organizer provided, we re-train the acoustic model of "multi-condition" using HMMs structure and DNN respectively. The proper starting point is that the artificially distorted training signals are mismatch with the enhanced ones. Therefore, Substituting the reverberant noisy training data by the enhanced signal and enlarging the re-training data with enhanced convolving data, we provide STD result of this re-trained acoustic model. Then the five possible cases are:

Clean+ noEnh: "clean-condition" HMMs without dereverberation;

Multi+ noEnh: "multi-condition" HMMs without dereverberation;

Clean+ Enh: "clean-condition" HMMs with dereverberation;

Multi+ Enh: "multi-condition" HMMs with dereverberation;

ReTrn+ Enh: re-trained "multi-condition" HMMs with dereverberation;

DNN+ Multi+ Enh: "multi-condition" HMMs with features from DNN;

DNN+ ReTrn+ Enh: re-trained "multi-condition" HMMs with features from DNN;

The system performance of spoken term detection is measured in Equal Error Rate(EER): It is defined as a point in DET curve where False Alarm rate(FA) equals to False Reject rate(FR).

3.2. *Baseline experiments*

For the STD task, we use the WFST decoder [24]. The acoustic model is trained with 400 hours of CTS data. Baseline models as well as re-trained model are provided in this section. The "clean-condition" baseline system uses 39 dimension mel-frequency cepstral coefficients (MFCCs) including Delta and Delta-Delta coefficients as features. As acoustic models, it employs tied-state HMMs with 32 Gaussian components per state trained according to the maximum-likelihood criterion [25]. Further, the model is re-trained using the features of artificially distorted data to form the "multi-condition" HMMs. The utterances are in mixture with 24 kinds of RIRs and 6 kinds of noises. We test the enhanced signals on the two baseline systems both using and not using the unsupervised CMLLR model adaptation.

Table 1. Equal error rate of baseline.

Test Data		Equal error rate(%)							
		Room 1		Room 2		Room 3		Ave.	
		Set1	Set2	Set1	Set2	Set1	Set2	Set1	Set2
Clean+noEnh	nocmllr	25.43	37.86	36.22	50.64	42.65	59.73	34.76	49.41
	cmllr	19.95	34.53	31.67	47.23	37.97	56.45	29.86	46.07
Multi+noEnh	nocmllr	22.66	30.85	32.95	45.61	40.85	56.37	32.15	44.27
	cmllr	17.44	26.95	29.06	42.31	36.99	52.26	27.83	40.51

Tables 1 shows the EER results on the 2 datasets respectively. It includes the STD results of "clean-condition" model, "multi-condition" model. As we can seen, "multi-condition" model performs better than "clean-condition" model. It achieves decrease on EER from 34.76% to 32.15% on average of set1 and from 49.41% to 44.27% on average of set2. Consistent improvement across all recording conditions is achieved by using CMLLR which results in EER 27.83% on set1 and 40.51% on set2.

3.3. *2-channel dereverberation*

Performance of dereverberation is examined using both "clean-condition" and "multi-condition" acoustic model. According to table 2, recognizing the test set with "clean-condition" model without CMLLR adaptation, the dereverberation method achieves decrease on EER from 34.76% to 30.26% on average of Set1 and from 49.41% to 45.89% on average of Set1. Consistent improvement across all recording conditions is achieved by using CMLLR which results in EER 25.27% on Set1 and 36.94% on Set2. However, recognizing with "multi-condition" model without CMLLR adaptation, the performance (Set1: 33.81%, Set2: 46.02%) is worse than the "multi-condition" baseline (Set1: 32.15%,Set2: 44.27%) because the recognizing enhanced data is mismatch with the reverberant data used to train the "multi-condition" acoustic model, though using CMLLR gives a little improvement.

Table 2. Equal error rate of 2-channel dereverberation.

Test Data		Equal error rate(%)							
		Room 1		Room 2		Room 3		Ave.	
		Set1	Set2	Set1	Set2	Set1	Set2	Set1	Set2
Clean+noEnh	nocmllr	20.43	28.25	30.85	52.48	39.51	56.94	30.26	45.89
	cmllr	17.47	22.47	24.19	37.86	34.16	50.50	25.27	36.94
Multi+noEnh	nocmllr	23.64	32.46	34.72	46.69	43.08	58.91	33.81	46.02
	cmllr	19.93	28.04	31.91	43.84	39.95	56.33	30.59	42.73
ReTrn+Enh	nocmllr	18.64	21.76	22.79	31.56	27.01	37.15	22.81	30.15
	cmllr	**17.76**	**19.52**	**21.23**	**27.79**	**24.09**	**34.50**	**21.03**	**27.27**

To overcome the mismatch, the re-trained "multi-condition" HMMs gives a better result. The optimized one has a EER 22.81% on average of Set1 and 30.15% on average of Set2 without CMLLR and finally 21.03% of Set1 and 27.27% of Set2 with CMLLR.

3.4. *Bottleneck features from DNN*

Table 3 shows the results for BN features based decoding. All the DNNs are trained with the triphone state targets force-aligned using training set. The decoding is performed on the test set. We achieved different performance without CMLLR and with CMLLR. On Multi+ Enh" case, we got 23.86% on average of Set1 and 30.70% on average of Set2 without CMLLR and finally 20.03% of Set1 and 26.11% of Set2 with CMLLR. To overcome the mismatch, we re-trained "multi-condition" HMMs, then, we got the result 19.07% on average of Set1 and 24.34% on average of Set2 without CMLLR and finally 18.02% of Set1 and 22.04% of Set2 with CMLLR. The further experiments will be investigated.

Table 3. Equal error rate of bottleneck features from DNN.

Test Data		Equal error rate(%)							
		Room 1		Room 2		Room 3		Ave.	
		Set1	Set2	Set1	Set2	Set1	Set2	Set1	Set2
DNN+Multi +Enh	nocmllr	17.67	23.36	23.56	29.39	30.35	39.36	23.86	30.70
	cmllr	14.72	19.23	19.95	25.07	25.42	34.02	20.03	26.11
DNN+ReTrn +Enh	nocmllr	16.89	18.25	18.68	23.80	21.64	27.97	19.07	24.34
	cmllr	15.69	16.82	17.83	22.74	20.53	26.55	18.02	22.04

4. Conclusions

We have presented out dereverberation approach to the RE-VERB challenge based on spectral enhancement. An acoustic scene aware technique is proposed to make dereverberation robust to different conditions. For STD task, when it is combined with back-end ASR with matched training, it produces a significant decrease on EER.

The DNN based front-end was tested in the context of reverberant speech recognition. Experiments showed that on both testsets, BN features gave an relative EER reduction over using MFCC features without CMLLR. Retraining did not give as much gain as we got on MFCC features. We also need to do further experiments about the performance difference between MFCC features and BN features.

References

1. P. A. Naylor and N. D. Gaubitch, "Speech dereverberation," in Proc. Int. Workshop Acoust. Echo Noise Control, 2005.J. Clerk Maxwell, A Treatise on Electricity and Magnetism, 3rd ed., vol. 2. Oxford: Clarendon, 1892, pp.68-73.
2. T. Yoshioka, T. Nakatani, and M. Miyoshi, "Integrated speech enhancement method using noise suppression and dereverberation," Audio, Speech, and Language Processing, IEEE Transactions on, vol. 17, no. 2, pp. 231–246, 2009.K. Elissa, "Title of paper if known," unpublished.
3. F. Grezl, M. Karafiat, S. Kontar, and J. Cernocky, "Probabilistic and bottle-neck features for LVCSR of meetings" in Acoustics, Speech and Signal Processing, 2007.ICASSP2007. IEEE International Conference on, vol. 4, 2007, pp. IV–757–IV–760.
4. H. Larochelle, Y. Bengio, J. Louradour, and P. Lamblin, "Exploring strategies for training deep neural networks," J. Mach. Learn. Res., vol. 10, pp. 1–40, Jun. 2009. [Online]. Available: http://dl.acm.org/citation.cfm?id=1577069.1577070
5. F. Seide, G. Li, and D. Yu, "Conversational speech transcription using context-dependent deep neural networks," in INTERSPEECH, 2011, pp. 437–440.
6. P. Swietojanski, A. Ghoshal, and S. Renals, "Hybrid acoustic models for distant and multichannel large vocabulary speech recognition," in Automatic Speech Recognition and Understanding (ASRU), 2013IEEE Workshop on, Dec 2013, pp. 285–290.
7. Y. Liu, P. Zhang, and T. Hain, "Using neural network front-ends on far field multiple microphones based speech recognition," in ICASSP2014 - Speech and Language Processing (ICASSP2014 - SLTC), Florence, Italy, May 2014, pp. 5579–5583.
8. A. Stolcke, X. Anguera, K. Boakye, O. Cetin, A. Janin, A. Mandal, B. Peskin, C. Wooters, and J. Zheng, "Further progress in meeting recognition: The ICSI-SRI spring 2005 speech-to-text evaluation system," in Machine Learning for Multimodal Interaction, ser. LNCS. Springer Verlag, 2005, no. 3869, pp. 463–475.
9. F. Grezl, M. Karafiat, and L. Burget, "Investigation into bottle-neck features for meeting speech recognition," in Proc. Interspeech 2009, no. 9, 2009, pp. 2947–2950.
10. T. Hain, L. Burget, J. Dines, P. N. Garner, F. Grezl, A. el Hannani, M. Huijbregts, M. Karafiat, M. Lincoln, and V. Wan, "Transcribing meetings

with the AMIDA systems," Transactions on Audio, Speech and Language Processing, Aug. 2011.
11. D. Yu and M.L. Seltzer, "Improved bottleneck features using pretrained deep neural networks," in INTERSPEECH, 2011, pp. 237–240.
12. Z. Tüske, R. Schlüter, and H. Ney, "Deep hierarchical bottleneck MRASTA features for LVCSR," in IEEE International Conference on Acoustics, Speech, and Signal Processing, Vancouver, Canada, May 2013, pp. 6970–6974.
13. T. Robinson, J. Fransen, D. Pye, J. Foote, and S. Renals, "Wsjcamo: A british english speech corpus for large vocabulary continuous speech recognition," in Acoustics, Speech, and Signal Processing, 1995. ICASSP-95., 1995 International Conference on, vol. 1. IEEE, 1995, pp. 81–84.
14. M. Lincoln, I. McCowan, J. Vepa, and H. K. Maganti, "The multichannel wall street journal audio visual corpus (mc-wsj-av): Specification and initial experiments," in Automatic Speech Recognition and Understanding, 2005 IEEE Workshop on. IEEE, 2005, pp. 357–362.
15. D.B. Paul and J. M. Baker, "The design for the wall street journal-based csr corpus," in Proceedings of the workshop on Speech and Natural Language. Association for Computational Linguistics,1992,pp.357– 362.
16. X. Wang, Y. Guo, X. Yang, Q. Fu, and Y. Yan, "Acoustic scene aware dereverberation using 2-channel spectral enhancement for reverb challenge," REVERB (REverberant Voice Enhancement and Recognition Benchmark) Challenge, May 2014.
17. Mamou J, Ramabhadran B, Siohan O. Vocabulary independent spoken term detection[C]//Proceedings of the 30th annual international ACM SIGIR conference on Research and development in information retrieval. ACM, 2007: 615-622.
18. H. Kuttruff, Room acoustics. Taylor & Francis, 2000.
19. Jeub, Marco, et al. "Blind estimation of the coherent-to-diffuse energy ratio from noisy speech signals." Signal Processing Conference, 2011 19th European. IEEE, 2011.
20. I. A. McCowan and H. Bourlard, "Microphone array post-filter based on noise field coherence," Speech and Audio Processing, IEEE Transactions on, vol. 11, no. 6, pp. 709–716, 2003.
21. E. A. Habets, S. Gannot, and I. Cohen, "Late reverberant spectral variance estimation based on a statistical model," Signal Processing Letters, IEEE, vol. 16, no. 9, pp. 770–773, 2009.

22. F. Grezl and P. Fousek, “Optimizing bottle-neck features for LVCSR,” in Acoustics, Speech and Signal Processing, 2008. ICASSP2008. IEEE International Conference on, 2008, pp. 4729–4732.
23. K. Veselý, M. Karafiát, and F. Grézl, “Convolutive bottleneck network features for LVCSR.” in ASRU, D. Nahamoo and M. Picheny, Eds. IEEE, 2011, pp. 42–47. [Online]. Available: http://dblp.unitrier.de/db/conf/asru/asru2011.html#VeselyKG11
24. Hori T, Hori C, Minami Y, et al. Efficient WFST-based one-pass decoding with on-the-fly hypothesis rescoring in extremely large vocabulary continuous speech recognition[J]. Audio, Speech, and Language Processing, IEEE Transactions on, 2007, 15(4): 1352-1365.
25. K. Kinoshita, M. Delcroix, T. Yoshioka, T. Nakatani, E. Habets, R. Haeb-Umbach, V. Leutnant, A. Sehr, W. Kellermann, R. Maasetal., “Proceedings of the ieee work shop on applications of signal processing to audio and acoustics (waspaa-13),” THE REVERB CHALLENGE: A COMMON EVALUATION FRAME WORK FOR DEREVERBERATION AND RECOGNITION OF REVERBERANT SPEECH, May 2013.

A Secure Permutation-Substitution Based Color Image Encryption Scheme Using Exchanging Strategy

Rui-Song Ye[a], Jun-Ming Ma, Xing Zhang, Ming Ye and Ya-Fang Li

Department of Mathematics, Shantou University,
Shantou, Guangdong, 515063, China
E-mail: [a]rsye@stu.edu.cn

An efficient color image encryption scheme with permutation-substitution architecture is proposed. The discrete generalized Arnold map is applied to disorder pixel positions and exchange the pixel gray values using exchanging strategy in the permutation process. The continuous generalized Arnold map is employed to generate pseudo-random sequences to realize the diffusion effect in the substitution process. One round of permutation and substitution can obtain perfect security effect. The security and performance of the proposed image encryption scheme have also been analyzed. Experimental results demonstrate that the proposed image encryption scheme is secure and effective for practical application.

Keywords: Bit Plane; Generalized Arnold Map; Permutation; Substitution; Image Encryption.

1. Introduction

Thanks to the rapid developments of innovative technologies in information and computer science in the last decades, vast amounts of digital multimedia data like images, videos, audios is being stored on different media, increasingly shared and transmitted over the Internet and wireless networks. As a result, protection of digital information data against illegal copying and distribution has become extremely urgent. Encryption is a powerfully direct and efficient way to protect the information from unauthorized eavesdropping [1]. In order to meet the needs of practical image encryption application, chaos-based image encryption schemes are extensively studied and developed. Chaos theory has been successfully introduced to modern cryptography thanks to its fantastic features, such as ergodicity, high sensitivity to initial conditions and control parameters, pseudo-randomness which are consistent with the fundamental requirements like confusion and diffusion in cryptography. As a result, chaotic systems provide potential candidates for constructing cryptosystems [2-6].

In this paper, we present an efficient color image encryption scheme with permutation-substitution architecture instead of permutation-diffusion one. Permutation-substitution architecture has been an effective architecture for designing cryptosystems [7]. The permutation operation is performed in two manners. One exchanges the pixel intensity values of red channel component R and green channel component G, while the other exchanges the lower 4 bit planes part B_1 and the higher 4 bit planes part B_2 of blue channel component B. B_1, B_2 are then with the same size $H \times W$ and 16 gray levels. They consist of the 1-4, 5-8 bit planes of blue channel component B respectively. As we know, the exchanging operation between B_1 and B_2 can not only disorder the pixel positions, but also change their intensity values. On the other hand, the exchanging between R component and G component will perform by one round of discrete generalized Arnold map, and therefore improve the execution rate. To achieve large key space and good performance, one substitution process is designed using pseudo-random gray value sequences generated by a continuous generalized Arnold map with positive real number parameters. Thanks to generalized Arnold map's perfect chaotic natures, we apply the discrete version in permutation process while the continuous version in substitution process to realize the encryption effect. The security and performance analysis of the proposed image encryption are carried out in detail. All the experimental results show that the proposed image encryption scheme is highly secure and demonstrates excellent performance.

2. The Proposed Image Encryption Scheme

2.1. *Generalized arnold map*

The chaotic generalized Arnold map is defined by

$$\begin{pmatrix} x_{n+1} \\ y_{n+1} \end{pmatrix} = \begin{pmatrix} 1 & a \\ b & 1+ab \end{pmatrix} \begin{pmatrix} x_n \\ y_n \end{pmatrix} \mod 1. \tag{1}$$

In this paper, we are concerning the color image encryption, where the color plain-image is modeled by three channel components R, G, B, which are of size $H \times W$ and 256 gray levels. For the sake of application of generalized Arnold map, we assume $H = W$. We will apply the generalized Arnold map in both the permutation process with the discrete version Eq. (2) and the substitution process with the continuous version Eq. (1). The discrete version of generalized Arnold map is expressed by

$$\begin{pmatrix} s \\ t \end{pmatrix} = \begin{pmatrix} 1 & p \\ q & 1+pq \end{pmatrix} \begin{pmatrix} i \\ j \end{pmatrix} \bmod H, \tag{2}$$

where the integer parameters $p, q \in \{1, \cdots, H-1\}$ and (i, j), (s,t) are the pixel positions.

2.2. *Permutation process*

The detail permutation process is described as follows.

Step 1. Read the color plain-image I and get the red, green, blue channel components R, G, B. The blue channel component B is then separated into two parts: one consisting of the lower four bit planes and the other consisting of the higher four bit planes. We denote them by B_1, B_2 respectively, which are both of 16 gray-level image.

Step 2. Exchange the gray values of pixel pairs between B_1 and B_2 as well as the gray values between R and G. The generalized Arnold map Eq. (2) is applied to confuse the pixel positions. The pixel positions and gray values exchanging operation are defined by $R(i, j) \leftrightarrow G(s,t), B_1(i, j) \leftrightarrow B_2(s,t)$ $i, j = 0,1,\cdots, H-1$.

Step 3. Integrate the exchanged matrices B_1 and B_2 together to be one new matrix B by $B(i, j) = B_1(i, j) + B_2(i, j) \times 16,\ i, j = 0,1,\cdots, H-1$.

Step 4. Integrate the yielded three channel components R, G, B together to be one permuted color image I.

2.3. *Substitution process*

The substitution process is outlined as follows.

Step 1. Place matrices R, G, B orderly together to be one large matrix denoted by $C = [R, G, B]$ with size $H \times 3W$.

Step 2. Generation of pseudo-random gray value vectors SVR, IVC with length H . With initial conditions x_0, y_0, control parameters a, b and one positive integer N, we iterate Eq. (1) for N times and reject the transient points $\{(x_k, y_k) : k = 0,1,\cdots, N-1\}$ to improve the chaotic nature. The values of (x_N, y_N) are set to be the new initial values (x_0, y_0) and we iterate Eq. (1) to generate SVR, IVC by $SVR(i) = floor(x_{i+1} \times 256), IVC(i) = floor(y_{i+1} \times 256)$, $i = 0,\cdots, H-1$, where $floor(x)$ returns the largest integer not larger than x. Transpose IVC to get one column vector IVC with H elements.

Step 3. Generation of pseudo-random gray value vectors IVR, SVC with length $3H$. We still denote (x_H, y_H) as (x_0, y_0) for simplicity. Another two pseudo-random gray value vectors IVR, SVC are generated by iterating Eq. (1) and $IVR(i) = floor(x_{i+1} \times 256), SVC(i) = floor(y_{i+1} \times 256),\ i = 0, \cdots, 3 \times H - 1$.

Step 4. Substitute the 2D matrix C row-by-row for $i = 2, \cdots, H$ and column-by-column for $j = 2, \cdots, 3 \times H$ by

$$C(1,:) = C(1,:) \oplus IVR \oplus SVR(1);\ C(i,:) = C(i,:) \oplus C(i-1,:) \oplus SVR(i),$$

$$C(:,1) = C(:,1) \oplus IVC \oplus SVC(1);\ C(:,j) = C(:,j) \oplus C(:,j-1) \oplus SVC(j),$$

where "$\oplus$" represents the bitwise XOR operation, and $C(i,:), C(:,j)$ denote the i th row and j th column of matrix C. The resulted C is finally converted to be one color image. Encrypt the color plain-image Lena one round with cipher keys $p = 67, q = 146$, $x_0 = 0.17, y_0 = 0.56$, $a = 22.73, b = 17.0$ and $N = 133$, the resulted cipher-image for plain-image Lena (Figure 1(a)) is shown in Figure 1(b).

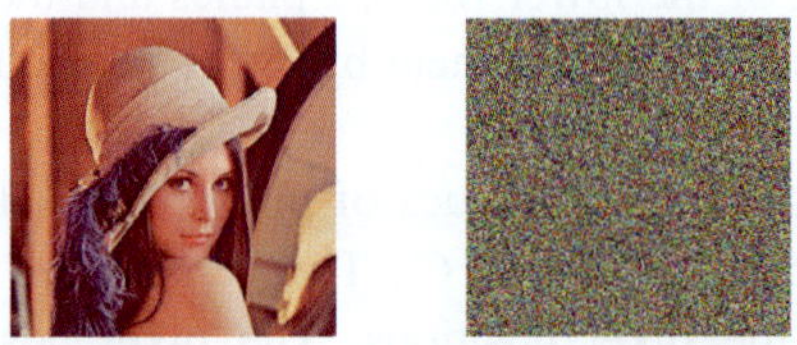

(a) (b)

Fig. 1. The encrypted results: (a) plain-image Lena, (b) cipher-image.

3. Performance Analysis

3.1. *Correlation coefficient analysis*

An ideal cipher should yield cipher-images with less correlation in the adjacent pixels. To quantify the correlations of adjacent pixels in images, we randomly select T pairs of horizontally, vertically and diagonally adjacent pixels from red, green, blue channel components respectively and calculate the correlation coefficients. In the simulation, we set $T = 6000$. The correlation coefficient of the chosen pairs is calculated by Eq. (3):

$$Cr = \frac{cov(x,y)}{\sqrt{D(x)}\sqrt{D(y)}},\ cov(x,y) = \frac{1}{T}\sum_{i=1}^{T}(x_i - E(x))(y_i - E(y)), \qquad (3)$$

where x_i, y_i form the ith pair of horizontally, vertically or diagonally adjacent pixels, $E(x) = \frac{1}{T}\sum_{i=1}^{T} x_i$, $D(x) = \frac{1}{T}\sum_{i=1}^{T}(x_i - E(x))^2$. The correlation coefficients of horizontally, vertically, diagonally adjacent pixels for plain-images Lena and its corresponding cipher-images are shown in Table 1. It is clear from Table 1 that the proposed image encryption technique significantly reduces the correlation between the adjacent pixels of the plain-image.

Table 1. Correlation coefficients between adjacent pixels.

		Correlation between adjacent pixels		
		Red	Green	Blue
Horizontal	Plain-image	0.9510	0.9382	0.9166
	Cipher-image	-0.0144	-0.0026	0.0111
Vertical	Plain-image	0.9770	0.9649	0.9551
	Cipher-image	0.0028	-0.0099	-0.0066
Diagonal	Plain-image	0.9262	0.9063	0.8967
	Cipher-image	-0.0017	0.0140	0.0038

3.2. *Information entropy analysis*

Information entropy is a criterion to measure the uniformity of image histograms. The entropy $H(m)$ of a gray image I can be measured by

$$H(I) = -\sum_{i=0}^{L-1} p(r_i)\log_2(p(r_i)) \text{ (bits)} \quad (4)$$

where L is the number of gray levels of image, $p(r_i)$ stands for the probability of occurrence of gray value r_i. For a random gray image with 256 gray scale levels, its entropy is $H(I) = 8$ bits. We have calculated the information entropy values for plain-image Lena and its cipher-image by Eq. (4). The results for red, green, blue channel components of Lena are 7.2494, 7.5891 and 6.9289, while for red, green, blue channel components of its cipher image are 7.9973, 7.9971 and 7.9974 respectively. The values of information entropy for the cipher-image are all very close to the expected value 8 of truly random image. The proposed encryption scheme is extremely robust against information entropy attacks.

3.3. *Differential attack analysis*

Two most common measures NPCR (number of pixel change rate) and UACI (unified average changing intensity) are calculated to measure the robustness of image cryptosystems against the differential cryptanalysis. If $C^{R/G/B}$ and $\overline{C}^{R/G/B}$ represent the red, green, blue channel components for two cipher-images, then NPCR and UACI for each color channel are defined by

$$\mathrm{NPCR}^{R/G/B} = \frac{\sum_{i=1}^{H}\sum_{j=1}^{W} D_{i,j}^{R/G/B}}{W \times H} \times 100\%, D_{i,j}^{R/G/B} = \begin{cases} 0, & if\ C_{i,j}^{R/G/B} = \bar{C}_{i,j}^{R/G/B}, \\ 1, & if\ C_{i,j}^{R/G/B} \neq \bar{C}_{i,j}^{R/G/B}, \end{cases}$$

$$\mathrm{UACI}^{R/G/B} = \frac{1}{W \times H} \sum_{i=1}^{H}\sum_{j=1}^{W} \frac{|C_{i,j}^{R/G/B} - \bar{C}_{i,j}^{R/G/B}|}{2^{L^{R/G/B}} - 1} \times 100\%, \tag{5}$$

where $L^{R/G/B}$ is the number of bits used to represent the red, green or blue channels of the considered image. For a 24-bit true color image (8 bit for each color channel) $L^{R/G/B}=8$. We choose 100 pixels in the plain-image randomly and calculate the 100 NPCR and UACI values by Eq. (5) whose average values are shown in Table 2. They are very close to the expected values 99.6094 and 33.4635, implying that proposed image encryption technique shows good sensitivity to plaintext and hence invulnerable to differential attacks.

Table 2. Difference analysis.

Average NPCR (%)			Average UACI (%)		
Red	Green	Blue	Red	Green	Blue
99.6205	99.6186	99.6083	33.3957	33.5403	33.4093

4. Conclusion

In this paper, we present an efficient color image encryption scheme with permutation-substitution architecture instead of permutation-diffusion one. Permutation-substitution architecture has been an effective architecture for designing cryptosystems.

The security and performance of the proposed image encryption scheme have also been analyzed. Experimental results demonstrate that the proposed image encryption scheme is secure and effective for practical application.

Acknowledgements

This research is supported by Innovation and Entrepreneurship Training Program of Guangdong College.

References

1. B. Schiener, Applied Cryptography: Protocols, Algorithms and Source Code in C. (John Wiley and sons, New York, 1996).
2. J. Fridrich, Symmetric ciphers based on two-dimensional chaotic maps, International Journal of Bifurcation and Chaos, 8, 1259-1284 (1998).
3. F. Huang and Z.-H. Guan, A modified method of a class of recently presented cryptosystems, Chaos, Solitons and Fractals, 23, 1893-1899 (2005).
4. N. K. Pareek, V. Patidar, and K. K. Sud, Image encryption using chaotic logistic map, Image and Vision Computing, 24, 926-934 (2006).
5. R. Ye, A novel chaos-based image encryption scheme with an efficient permutation-diffusion mechanism, Optics Commun., 284, 5290-5298 (2011).
6. R. Ye, A novel image encryption scheme based on generalized multi-sawtooth maps, Fundamenta Informaticae, 133, 87-104(2014).
7. Vinod Patidar, N. K. Pareek, G. Purohit, and K. K. Sud, A robust and secure chaotic standard map based pseudorandom permutation-substitution scheme for image encryption, Optics Commun., 284, 4331-4339 (2011).

Application and Research on Gesture Recognition by Kinect Sensors

Ze-Sheng Yu[a], Wen-Hua Cui and Tian-Wei Shi
University of Science and Technology Liaoning
Anshan, 114000, China
E-mail: [a]525358121@qq.com

To solve the problem of complex operations in the current smart home system, acquire a simple control method and increase feeling experience for users, the gesture recognition method based on Kinect was researched and integrated into the Human-Computer Interaction (HCI) system in smart home. Users can customize the gestures to realize the intelligent control of household equipment. The utilized template matching gesture recognition method is accomplished based on the Dynamic Time Warping (DTW) algorithm. The results of actual gesture recognition experiments show that the gesture recognition based on DTW is feasible and effective. The best identification distance is in the range of 2 - 2.5 m in front of Kinect and the highest recognition accuracy is reached on 96%.

Keywords: Kinect; Gesture Recognition; DTW Algorithm; Human-Computer Interaction.

1. Introduction

The smart home is the living environments for people. To make the domesticity smarter, more convenient and comfortable, it utilizes the advanced computer technology, network communication technology and medical electronic technology etc to realizes the comprehensive intelligent controls and managements. The Human-computer Interaction (HCI) is an information interchange process between people and computer to accomplish specific tasks. Nowadays in family, people may control the equipment by using the voice recognition, gesture recognition, face recognition and other wireless control modes [1]. With the development of the society, the intelligent household equipment are used more widely and the demands of natural living environment for people are also more intense. In these cases, the design of intelligent HCI system with friendly environment has become an inevitable trend. To solve the current problem of complex operations of the intelligent household system and the low gesture recognition accuracy of conventional gesture recognition technologies [2], an intelligent gesture control system is researched based on Kinect sensor in this paper. To achieve the gesture recognition and devices control, the proposed system applies the Dynamic Time Warping (DTW) algorithm.

The outline of this paper is as follows: Section II presents the process of skeleton-data acquisition. Section III describes the technical methods for gesture recognition. Section IV and Section V introduce the experiments and conclusions respectively.

2. Skeleton-Data Acquisition

The gesture data is obtained through Kinect published by Microsoft. It is an ideal motion-sensing peripheral device for gesture recognition. Moreover, it uses three cameras to get the RGB image, depth image and human body skeleton image simultaneously [4]. To enable the Kinect to recognize three-dimensional (3D) space, the infrared transmitter and receiver are composed of infrared projector and monochrome CMOS sensor. In addition, it has a multi-array microphone which is mainly used to input voice, positioning and filter ambient noise. Figure 1 shows the exterior of Kinect.

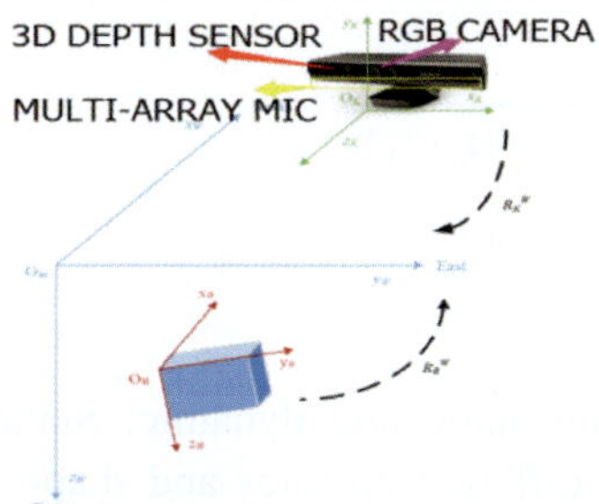

Fig. 1. Observation coordinates and Object coordinates

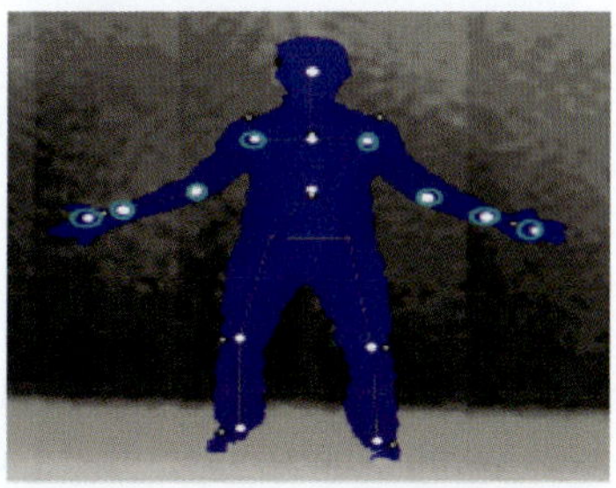

Fig. 2. Skeleton map of human body

2.1. *Skeleton tracking technology*

The Kinect mainly uses the infrared transmitter and 3D depth sensors to acquire space images. It utilizes the optical encoding technology to project laser speckle into space, which is different from the traditional Time of Flight (TOF) or structured light measurement technology. The speckle has high randomness and also transforms the patterns with different of distances. According to the speckles on objects, the actual depth of objects can be inferred [5]. The skeletal tracking technology calculates the position information of each joint point by processing the depth information [6]. The positions are expressed as (x, y, z) in the Cartesian coordinate system. Since different development platforms have different number of positioning joint points, in this study, the published Microsoft SDK v1.8 is utilized to get 3D coordinates of 20 joint points. Figure 2 shows the skeleton map of human body.

2.2. *Gesture feather extraction*

In the sample space, the gesture feature vector has the translation invariance and scalability properties. How to extract the active gestures feature is one of the key researches on gesture recognition [7], which directly affect the effectiveness of recognition algorithm. The skeleton coordinate is shown in Figure 2. Since the differences of body and position for users, the joint point position may also have significant changes. It is not feasible to use the joint point positions as the recognition criteria directly. Thus, the relative position between the skeleton points was used to describe the gesture features. In this paper, the eight of twenty skeleton points were selected to extract the dynamic gesture features (green circles in Figure 2).

Set (x_0, y_0, z_0) is the right-hand position of one frame of skeleton diagram. (x_n, y_n, z_n) is the position of joint point *n*. Thus, the distance between them is modeled as Eq. (1).

$$D_n = \sqrt{(x_n - x_0)^2 + (y_n - y_0)^2 + (z_n - z_0)^2} \tag{1}$$

where *n* denotes the number of gesture features.

3. Technical Methods

Normally, the hand gesture is divided into static and dynamic. Static hand gesture means that fingers and palm make different postures and shapes in the case of hand do not move. Dynamic hand gesture is refers to the change of hand over time, namely the position and shape of hand change simultaneously. It can better express the intention of users [8]. The gesture recognition algorithms are mainly divided into three kinds: Dynamic programming, Vector Quantization (VQ) and Hidden Markov Models (HMM). Table 1 displays the comparison of the recognition methods.

As shown in Table 1, the HMM and DTW algorithms were widely used in dynamic gesture recognition. For the simple and independent recognition, the effect of HMM and DTW algorithm is not very different. Since the large computational complexity and combined with the application requirements, this paper mainly research on the dynamic gesture recognition.

Table 1. Comparison of the recognition methods

Method	Advantages	Disadvantages
VQ	Easy to understand	Low rate of accurate
HMM	High rate of accuracy	Complex calculation process
DTW	Simplicity, high efficacy	Vulnerable to environmental impact

3.1. *DTW algorithm*

Since applying the dynamic programming, the DTW algorithm can solve the problem of time axis distortion [9]. In gesture recognition, the key of gesture recognition is not the gesture movement speed, but the gesture movement trajectory.

Let $F=\{F(1),F(2),...,F(n)\}$ is the dynamic time warping function, where $F(n)=(i(n),j(n))$ is the n-th matching point. $i(n)$ and $j(n)$ are the eigenvectors of time sequences R and T respectively. Define $L=(R_{i(n)},T_{j(n)})$ is the matching distance between R and T. According to the dynamic programming principle of DTW, namely it minimizes the sum of weighted distance D between the feature vectors for all matching points, it can be obtained by using the Eq. (2).

$$D = \min \sum_{n=1}^{N} d(R_{i(n)}, T_{j(n)}) \tag{2}$$

To improve the gesture recognition accuracy, it is necessary to add Continuity constraints and Monotonicity constraint for the warping function F [10]. Combining with the above conditions, the optimal path and the determined template matching gesture can be obtained by using Eq. (3).

$$D(R_{i(n)}, T_{j(n)}) = L(R_{i(n)}, T_{j(n)}) + \min \begin{pmatrix} D(R_{i(n+1)}, T_{j(n)}), \\ D(R_{i(n+1)}, T_{j(n+1)}), \\ D(R_{i(n)}, T_{j(n+1)}) \end{pmatrix} \tag{3}$$

4. System Realization and Experimental Results

4.1. *Gesture recognition system based on Kinect*

The main interface of gesture recognition system proposed in this paper and process of gesture recognition are shown in Figure 4 and Figure 5 respectively. Firstly, the user stands in front of the sensor in range of 1.5 - 2.5 m. Next, click on the "input motion" to begin. Then, the motion input hint is display and the skeleton becomes red. During this period, the user should perform a predetermined dynamic gesture and the background of main display interface become green. Finally, the interface will display the corresponding result.

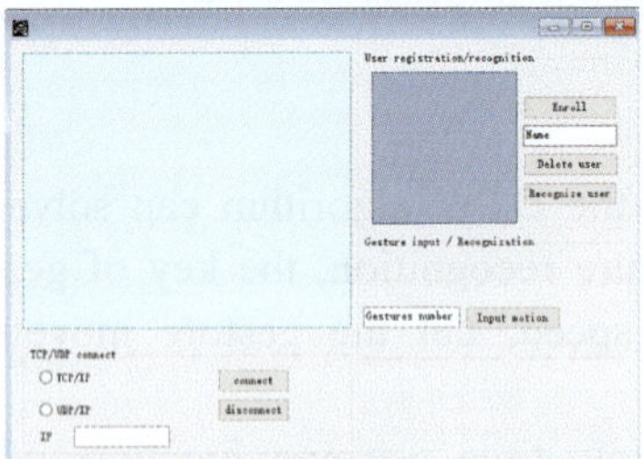

Fig. 4. Main interface of gesture recognition system

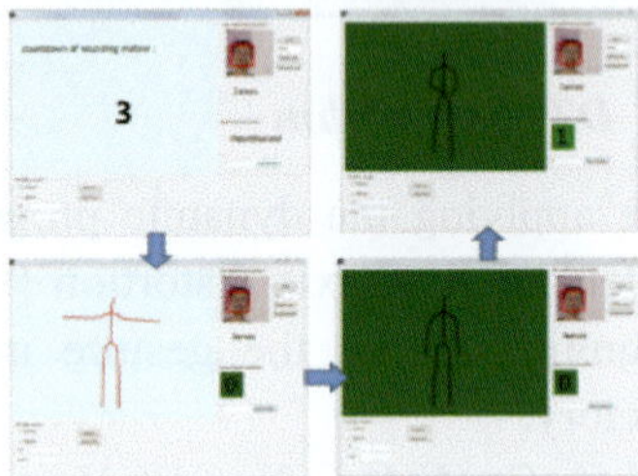

Fig. 5. Process of gesture recognition

4.2. *Experiments and results*

To verify the feasibility and effectiveness of DTW algorithm and proposed gesture recognition system, and to find the best distance for gesture recognition, five healthy subjects (three males and two females, aged 31 ± 1.5 years, heighted 170 ± 2.5 cm) participated in the actual gesture recognition verification experiment. Each subject performed predetermined dynamic gestures (see Figure 6) in the effective recognition distance. Subjects completed the predetermined dynamic gestures (each 10 times) at each specified distance and get the average accuracy (mean ± S.D.). Figure 7 displays the processes and recognition results. Table 2 and Figure 8 describes the recognition accuracy at different distances (mean ± S.D.).

Fig. 6. Predetermined gestures

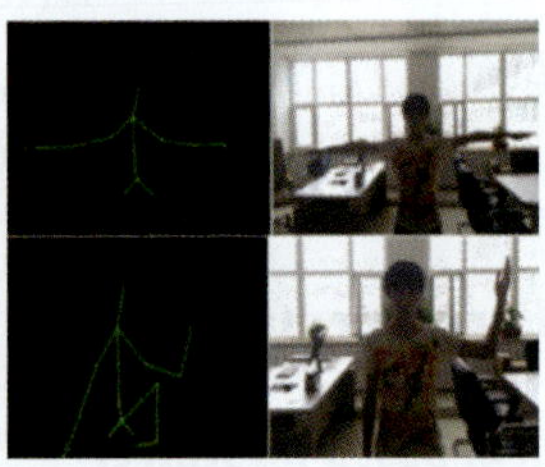

Fig. 7. Experimental process

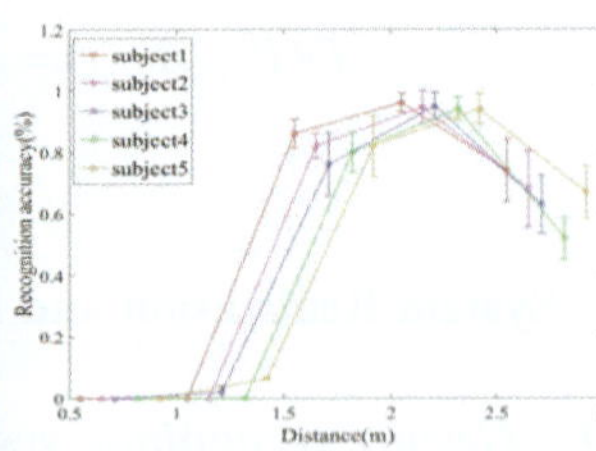

Fig. 8. Recognition accuracy

Table 2. Recognition accuracy

Distance (m) / Subjects	0-1	1-1.5	1.5-2	2-2.5	2.5- 3
Subject 1	0	0	76%±4.6%	96%±4.9%	64%±10.2%
Subject 2	0	0	72%±4%	93.6%±5.3%	58%±12.5%
Subject 3	0	2%	76%±10.2%	92%±7.4%	43%±9.4%
Subject 4	0	0	70%±6.3%	94%±3.27%	52%±6.8%
Subject 5	0	4%	72%±9.8%	94%±4.9%	67%±8.7%

The experimental results show that the best distance is in range of 2 - 2.5 m. In the case of less than 1.5 m and more than 2.5 m, it appears the recognition error and memory deficiency. Similarly, they should pay attention to position of their hands also when they are standing.

5. Conclusions

This paper mainly proposes a smart home system for gesture recognition based on Kinect. It establishes the gestures template library and implements the matching process between dynamic gesture and template library using the DTW algorithm. The results of actual gesture recognition verification experiments show that the DTW algorithm and proposed system is feasible and effective. The best distance for gesture recognition is in range of 2 -2.5 m. The recognition accuracies for all subjects are all more than 91% and the highest recognition accuracy is 96%.

Acknowledgements

This research is financial supported from Project of Education Department of Liaoning Province.

References

1. A. Blandford, Intelligent interaction design: the role of human-computer interaction research in the design of intelligent systems[J]. Expert Systems, 2001, 18(1):3–18.
2. S. Mitra, T. Acharya, Gesture recognition: a survey IEEE transaction on systems, cybernetics-part C: applications and review 2007, 37(3): 2127-2130.
3. A.S. Dong, X. Liu, H. Y. Jiang, Gesture Recognition Research Based on Kinect[J]. Advanced Materials Research, 2014, 971-973:1928-1931.

4. Q.W. Shi, Research on the Application of Motion Capture of Kinect Technology in the Sport Training[J]. Advanced Materials Research, 2014, 926-930(9):554–564.
5. J. Webb, J. Ashley, Skeleton Tracking[M]. Apress, 2012.
6. M. Tang, Recognizing Hand Gestures with Microsoft's Kinect[J]. 2011.
7. K. Oka, Y. Sato, H. Koike, Real-time fingertip tracking and gesture recognition[J]. IEEE Computer Graphics &Applications, 2002, 22(6):64-71.
8. C.J. Su, C.Y. Chiang, J. Y. Huang, Kinect-enabled home-based rehabilitation system using Dynamic Time Warping and fuzzy logic[J]. Applied Soft Computing, 2014, 22(5):652-666.
9. Z. Hong, Key techniques of real-time dynamic gesture recognition[D]. South China university of technology, 2011. (in Chinese)

Task Planning of spaced Early Warning System Based on Mixed Discrete Particle Swarm Optimization

Ping Jian[1,a] and Lin Guo[2]

[1]*Science and Technology on Complex Electronic System Simulation Laboratory, Beijing 101416, China*

[2]*Group, Laboratory, Equipment Academy, Beijing 101416, China*

E-mail: [a]jianping85730@sina.com

According to the task planning problem of early warning system, the task planning model is set up, including the optimizing indexes of the tracking precision, task completing rate, resource laxity and sensor switching rate . A mixed Discrete Particle Swarm Optimization (DPSO) and Simulated Annealing (SA) algorithm is proposed to solve the task planning model. In the mixed algorithm, the ways of checking the restriction are proposed. Simulation results in the task planning instance show that the DPSO-SA algorithm is available and improves the planning quality.

Keywords: Spaced Warning System; Task Planning; Mixed Discrete Particle Swarm Optimization.

1. Introduction

1.1. *Index of task planning*

The aim of task planning is assigning the sensors to observe and positioning the targets rationally according to some rules. The optimizing indexes of the tracking precision, task completing rate, resource laxity are modeled in the paper.

(1)The tracking precision. The tracking precision can be measured by geometric dilution of precision, so in the task planning of spaced warning system, the paper modeled the racking precision E_{GDOP} as formula (1):

$$E_{GDOP} = \sum_{i=1}^{N_t}\left(\sum_{j=1}^{NT_i} P_i^j \times (GDOP_i^j)_{avg}\right) \Bigg/ \sum_{i=1}^{N_t} NT_i \quad (1)$$

In the formula (1), $(GDOP_i^j)_{avg}$ is the average tracking precision of the of the missile i, it can be calculated by uniform sampling. P_i^j is the priority the subtask j of the missile i, NT_i is the number of subtask of the missile i, N_t is the number of the missiles. $GDOP$ is calculated by the formula (2), and θ is the relative angle between missile and sensors.

$$GDOP_\theta = \sqrt{Trace(P_\theta)} = L\sigma_\theta \sqrt{\frac{\sin^2\theta_1 + \sin^2\theta_2}{\sin^4(\theta_2 - \theta_1)}} \quad (2)$$

(2)The task completing rate. In the task planning, the task with higher priority may be scheduled easily, so the task completing rate can not only reflect the number of subtask, but also the synthesis priority of the task. The paper defines the task completing rate E_{Task} as formula (3):

$$E_{Task} = \sum_{i=1}^{N_t}\sum_{j=1}^{NT_i}(X_i^j / P_i^j) \Bigg/ \sum_{i=1}^{N_t}\sum_{j=1}^{NT_i}(1/P_i^j) \quad (3)$$

In the formula(3), P_i^j is the priority the subtask j of the missile i, the less value of P_i^j delegates the higher priority. NT_i is the number of subtask of the missile i, N_t is the number of the missiles. If $X_i^j = 1$, then the subtask j of the missile i is scheduled completely, If $X_i^j = 0$, then the subtask j of the missile i is not scheduled completely.

(3)resource laxity. For the stability and using lifetime factors of satellite and, the sensor of satellite needs work symmetrically, so the paper defines the resource laxity as formula(4):

$$E_{Lax} == \frac{\sqrt{\sum_{i=1}^{N_r}(T_{si} - E(T_s))^2 / (N_r - 1)}}{|T_{planning}|} \quad (4)$$

In the formula(4), T_{si} is the total working time of the sensor, $E(T_s)$ is the average working time of all sensor, N_t is the number of the missiles, $\left|T_{planning}\right|$ is task planning cycle, and $\left|T_{planning}\right| = T_{end} - T_{begin}$. Apparently, the less E_{Lax} is, the more uniform the sensor works.

1.2. *Task planning model*

Task planning of early warning system is a constrained multi-object optimization problem, the problem has many Pareto optimal solutions theoretically. But in the paper's problem, it needs one and only scheme to supervise the sensors to track the missile. So, in the paper, task planning of early warning system is transformed to single objective optimization problem by weighting and adding up the optimizing indexes of the tracking precision, task completing rate, resource laxity and sensor switching rate. The task planning model is set up as formula (5) - (16):

$$\begin{cases}
Min: \\
f = \dfrac{1}{(E_{Task})^{\lambda_3}} \bullet (E_{GDOP})^{\lambda_1} \bullet (E_{Lax})^{\lambda_2} \bullet (5) \\
Constrants: \\
\lambda_1 + \lambda_2 + \lambda_3 = 1 \quad (6) \\
(work_i^r)_j \in 0,1 \quad (7) \\
X_i^j \in 0,1 \quad (8) \\
\sum_{i=1}^{M} \sum_{j=1}^{NT_i} (work_i^r)_j \le 1 \quad (9) \\
(work_i^r)_j = 0, \ if \ sensor_r \notin Rsc_i^j \quad (10) \\
\sum_{r=1}^{N_t} (work_i^r)_j = 2 \ || \ \sum_{r=1}^{N_t} (work_i^r)_j = 0 \quad (11) \\
X_i^j = 1, \ if \sum_{r=1}^{N_t} (work_i^r)_j = 2 \ \&\& \ [GDOP_i^j] \le \delta_{\min} \quad (12) \\
\dfrac{\sum_{j=1}^{NT_i} X_i^j \bullet \Delta t_i^j}{Wmax_i - Wmin_i - T_A} \ge \lambda_{\min} \quad (13) \\
Tbeg_i^j = Wmin_i + \sum_{k=1}^{j-1} \Delta t_i^k \quad (14) \\
Tend_i^j = Wmin_i + \sum_{k=1}^{j} \Delta t_i^k \quad (15) \\
Tend_i^j = Tbeg_i^{j+1}, Tend_i^{j-1} = Tbeg_i^j \quad (16)
\end{cases}$$

The formula (5) is the objective function. In the formula (6), the sums of the vertex-weights the index of E_{GDOP}, E_{Lax}, E_{Task} is 1. In the formula (7) and (8), $(work_i^r)_j$ is the decision variable, X_i^j is completion of tracking task, the two formulas define the value range of $(work_i^r)_j$ and X_i^j. The formula (9) and (10) express the constraint of sensors, which is one sensor can only be assigned to a missile at the same time when it is visible to the missile. The formula (11) and (12) express that two sensors are assigned to detect the missile and the tracking accuracy must should be less or equal to $\delta_{\min}$. The formula (13) expresses that the tracking time of the missile must be greater or equal to $\delta_{\min}$. In the formula (14), (15) and (16), it is defined the begin and end time of subtask.

2. Solving for the Task Planning Model

Discrete Particle Swarm Optimization (DPSO) is easy to fall into the defect of local optimum, this paper intends to combine simulated annealing algorithm with the Particle Swarm Optimization to put forward an improved DPSO. Based on the fast optimization ability of DPSO, the mutation and crossover operation of genetic algorithm would be introduced to make the particle swarm gain the ability of aberrance. In the meantime, the Metropolis criterion of simulated annealing algorithm would also be introduced to allow particles to deteriorate within a limited range of the objective function and prevent local optimum, thus forming a new algorithm model that can be applied to solve task planning problem of early warning system. Its solving process is as Figure 1.

3. Example of Task Planning

In order to validate the task planning method, the paper sets the typical simulation situation and analyzes the example of task planning. The constellation of spaced early warning system is selected, in which the constellation configuration is Walker-δ (24/3/2), the orbit height is 1577.93 km, the orbit inclination is 51.856°, the longitude ascending node of the first satellite of the first orbit plane, and the latitude amplitude is 29.694°. In the initial parameters of DPSO-SA, the particle size is 50, the learning factor is 2, the weight coefficient is 0.8, the initializing temperature and cooling coefficient of simulated annealing optimization is 2000 and 0.9. In the parameters of the task planning model, $\lambda_1 = 0.4$, $\lambda_2 = 0.3$, $\lambda_3 = 0.3$. And in the parameters of the incoming missile, the point of launch position is N30.2, E125.6, the point of fall is N45.56, E140.5, the apogee is 1024.5km, the tracking task to the missile is divided into 11 subtasks.

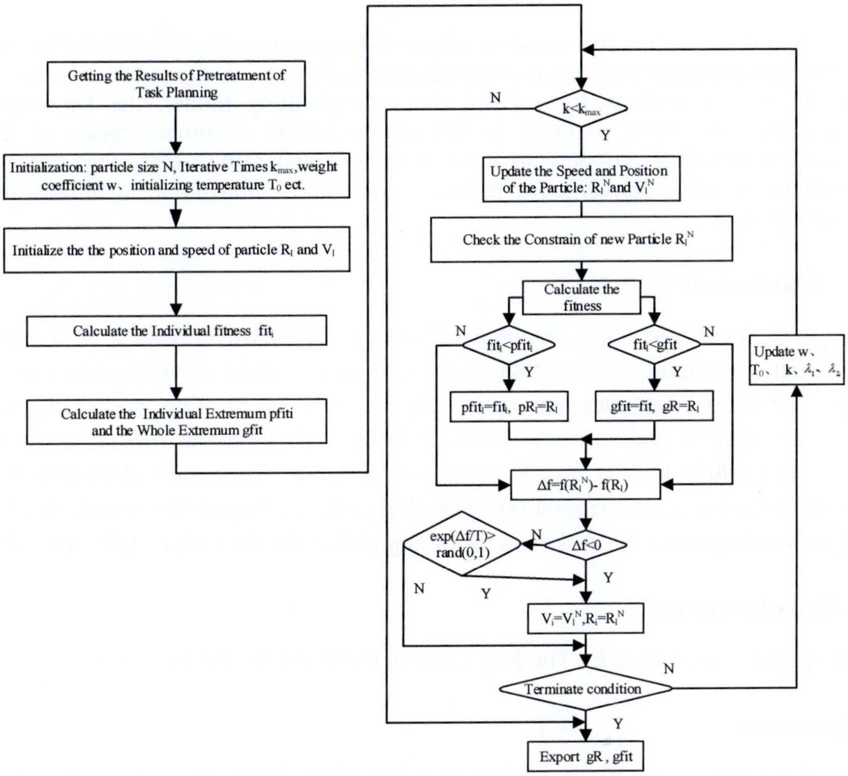

Fig. 1. Solving process of DPSO-SA algorithm

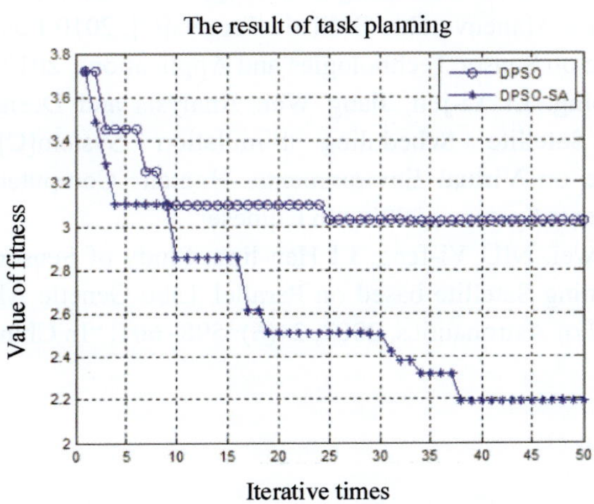

Fig. 2. The iterative progress of the two algorithms

Under the simulation situation above, the planning effect of DPSO-SA and DPSO are comparatively analyzed in the paper. Figure 2 is the iterative progress of the two algorithms for solving the task planning model, the DPSO-SA algorithm can allow particles to deteriorate within a limited range of the objective function and prevent local optimum, and DPSO algorithm has the problems of slow convergence in later period and being prone to falling into local optimum.

4. Conclusions

In order to improve the resource efficiency for missile tracking with early warning system, the original task planning model of early warning system is set up. The model includes the optimizing indexes of tracking precision, task accomplishment and resource slack is built. Based on the model, a mixed discrete particle swarm optimization and simulated annealing algorithm was proposed to solve the original task planning problem. Simulation results that the algorithm improves the seeking and solving ability for the global optimal result.

Acknowledgments

The paper is supported by The Key Lab Fund (DXZT-JC-ZZ-2013-008).

References

1. Tang Shao-xun, Yi Xian-qing, Luo Xue-shan. Research on Early-Warning Detecting Tasks Re-scheduling and Sensor Resources Allocation Strategy of Midcourse Maneuverable Ballistic Targets[C]. 2010 Fourth International Conference on Sensor Technologies and Applications, 2010.
2. Luo Kai-ping, Li Yi-jun, Jiang Wei. Analysis and Design of the early-Warning Satellite Scheduling Simulation System[C]. International Conference on Virtual Environments, Human- Computer Interfaces and Measurements Systems, 2009. “In Chinese”.
3. YAN Zhi-wei, NIU Yi-feng, LI Han-ling. Study of Sensor Scheduling for Early Warning Satellite based on Parallel Tabu Genetic Algorithm(PTGA) [J]. Journal of Astronautics, 2003, 24(6): 598- 601. “In Chinese”.

4. Guo Hao-bo, WANG Ying-long, ZENG Hui. Sensor Scheduling for Missile Early-warning Satellite based on Genetic and Simulated Annealing Algorithm [J]. ELECTRONICS 0PI1CS & C0NTR0L, 2006, 13(4):72-74. "In Chinese".
5. FENG Ming-yue, TANG Shao-xun, HE Jun et al. Resource Scheduling for Space-based Early Warning System Based on Improved Particle Swarm Optimization[J]. Journal of CAEIT, 2010, 5(1): 97-101. "In Chinese".

Task and Scale Variable Focus of Attention Based Visual Attention Method

H. Wang[1,a], Z. C. Li[1] and H. C. Ke[2,b]

[1]*College of Computer Science and Engineering, Changchun University of Technology, Changchun, 130012/Jilin province, China*

[2]*School of Computer Technology and Engineering, Changchun Institute of Technology Changchun, 130012/Jilin province, China*

E-mail: [a]wanghui1982@ccut.edu.cn, [b]kehongchang1981@163.com

Information extraction of visual attention can focus on the key areas of an image or video, which has important implications for target search, image search and other image processing algorithms. In this paper, a task and scale variable focus of attention based visual attention method is proposed. The proposed method top-down selects feature channels based on the key features of task target calculated by current task scenarios reasoning. Meanwhile, the scale variable round is used as focus of attention. The proposed method can have practical meaning, and universally meet the complex situations that the size of task target is not fixed in order to improve the hit rate of targets.

Keywords: Visual Attention; Feature Channel Selection; Scale Variable; Knowledge Base.

1. Introduction

The computer model of visual attention can take advantage of the limited system resources on the priority focus areas of the image to increase the efficiency of target searching, target tracking and other image or video processing [1].

In recent years, there are some representative computer models of visual attention. Sun et al. proposed and implemented a hierarchical selection mechanism based on grouping target saliency calculation and attention transfer combined the eye movement and kinetics perceptual coding [2]. Gao et al. proposed the target detection method based on hierarchical noted, after obtaining a saliency region, with classifier fusion strategic to guide task target detection [3]. Bruce and Tsotsos proposed AIM model, which can calculate the visual saliency information of input image based on the principle of maximizing the amount of information [4]. K. Lee et al. proposed the method which can use the bottom-up feature maps such as skin color, facial features and other features, top-down prompt maps combined integrated map with neural network to guide visual search task [5]. Qiaorong Zhang et al. proposed the method which can combine the spatial saliency map calculated by intensity features and color features with temporal saliency map calculated by extracting motion features of adjacent frame image, then detect the salient targets of video images, and each saliency target of adjacent frame image would do feature matching to achieve target tracking [6]. Jinkui Chu et al, proposed the robot target tracking model with the topological perception theory who use a top-down guidance of topological map to accelerate to find the region that the target may exist [7]. Sun et al, proposed the method which use the heuristic knowledge priori interaction, combined motion saliency to the human body in real-time monitoring and tracking, and achieved good results [8]. Ma et al. proposed the method which can obtain the using the weight coefficients of each channel feature map by Logistic regression analysis in the training stage to do top-down guide [9].

Previous work has achieved good results. However, visual attention takes time in the calculation, if we can ensure hit rate as much as possible to shorten the calculation time of visual attention which will be exciting. Features channel selection which is based on the key features of the task targets of the task scenarios reasoning is a good choice. Therefore, the paper proposed key feature inference rule of task target based on task scenario and setting the size of the focus of attention with scalable scale round focus of attention fell on a meaningful space of the region. The task and scale variable focus of attention based visual attention method is proposed to minimize the time of generating visual attention saliency map with ensuring the premise of the target hit rate and to improve the efficiency of visual attention intelligence application.

2. The Task and Scale Variable Focus of Attention Based Visual Attention Method

Initially, the system input includes the current task scenario, to be processed image and trained knowledge base (training methods see next section). The system determines whether the interfering target is known in current task scenario. If unknown, the distance between task target and the feature information of image will be calculated based on the knowledge base information; if known, the distance of between task target and interfering target will be calculated. Then, a key feature matrix and feature weights of the task target can be obtained.

Analyzing whether the weight difference of the first key feature and the second key feature of target is greater than a given threshold, if meeting, key feature of the channel is calculated as saliency map; if not meeting, the feature channel of the first key feature and the second key feature is calculated to weight and generate saliency map. Finally, the variable scale focus of attention of the saliency map is used to guide target identifying, if hit the target, ending; otherwise, return and modify key feature matrix of target, recalculate saliency map. System workflow is shown in Figure 1.

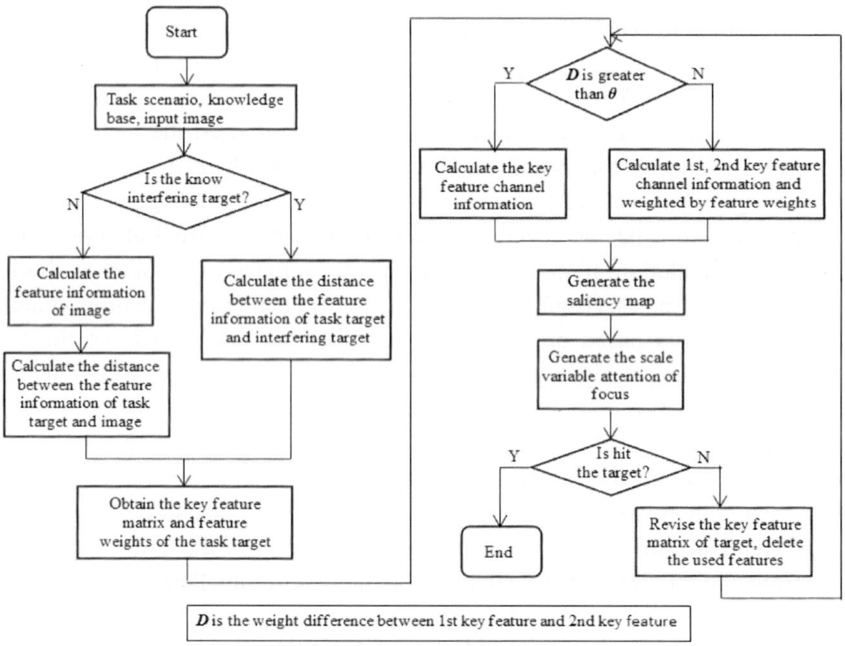

Fig. 1 The flowchart of the system

3. The Key Algorithm

3.1. *Feature channel saliency map generation*

Intensity, color and orientation features which are more sensitive for visual are selected to involve in testing. The intensity map I, red and green color channels feature map *RG*, blue and yellow feature map *BY*, the direction of the channel feature map $O(\theta)$ can be calculated. Where $\theta = 0°, 45°, 90°, 135°$. 7 feature maps of three channels are respectively be filtered by 9 layers Gaussian pyramid, the second and third layer of the pyramid is selected to normalize them into uniform scale as the feature vectors. Based on Markov Chain activity diagram generation and the integration algorithm are used to calculate activity diagram of the corresponding channel, which can be seen in Ref [10].

3.2. *Knowledge base training*

Set the form background of specific task scenario is (U,A,I), where $U=\{x_1,x_2,\cdots,x_n\}$ is the object set, A is the attribute set. I is the relation among the attributes. $L(U,A,I)$ stands for the whole concept of (U,A,I). The feature information of target x_i meets $(x_i,l_i,rg_i,by_i,o_{1i},o_{2i},o_{3i},o_{4i})\in L(U,A,I)$.

Where x stands for the name of target concept, *l*, *rg*, *by*, O_1, O_2, O_3, O_4 are respective the features of intensity, RG, BY, $0°,45°,90°,135°$ local orientation. Where, the features matrix of rg channel is:

$$rg=\begin{bmatrix} rg_{\min} \\ rg_{\max} \end{bmatrix}^{\mathrm{T}} \tag{1}$$

Where, $rg_{\max}$, $rg_{\min}$ are the maximum value, minimum value of rg features of target.

Other target feature matrix methods is similarly defined.

n is used to record the number of targets x which have been fused in the knowledge base.

When there is new information of the target x add to the knowledge base, the new features $(x,l,rg,by,o_1,o_2,o_3,o_4)$ are fused into the original features of target x in base which is $(x_i,l_i,rg_i,by_i,o_{1i},o_{2i},o_{3i},o_{4i})\in L(U,A,I)$, then the new features $(x,l',rg',by',o_1',o_2',o_3',o_4')$ can be obtained where,

$$rg'=\begin{bmatrix} \dfrac{rg_{i\min}\times n+rg_{\min}}{n+1} \\ \dfrac{rg_{i\max}\times n+rg_{\max}}{n+1} \end{bmatrix} \tag{2}$$

Other feature fusion method of targets is similar, no longer tired. At the same time, the counter n is incremented by 1.

3.3. *Target key feature queen generation and scale variable focus of attention*

The generation method of target key feature queen can be seen in Ref [11].

The study of correlation psychology shows that the size of the visual focus of attention in visual attention processing may vary with the actual situation. In order to make the attention focus on a meaningful region of image to improve the hit rate of target, different with the traditional focus of visual attention which is fixed size, scalable scale circle is defined as the focus of attention proposed in the paper. Considering the inside color of most objects have the phenomenon of continuity, the space color continuity and the closed contour together are important indicators for judging whether there is a meaningful target in the region.

The improved Fuzzy C-means clustering algorithm with spatial information involved is used to make color clustering on the winner region, then adjust the size of FOA(focus of attention) to cover the regional block after clustering. Based on the traditional fuzzy C-means clustering algorithm, the proposed algorithm combined the spatial location information so that the neighbor pixels tend to cluster together. Based on the principle of color continuity of inside objects, the regional block obtained can contain meaningful object as far as possible, which can improve the hit rate of target.

4. Conclusions

Visual attention makes the target match and other operations do not have to perform on the whole image, but on several key regions. Therefore obtains a high degree of attention. Based on key feature of task target under special task scenario, the feature channel filtering method of visual attention is proposed in this paper to improve efficiency of attention. Meanwhile, a scalable size round focus of attention is proposed to increase the hit rate of the target.

The proposed method can shorten the generating time of visual attention saliency map while ensuring the hit rate of task targets. However, the proposed algorithm has some shortcomings, such as, the algorithm use the stationary distribution of Markov chains to simulate the visual competition result in order to increase the hit rate, which is also more time-consuming. How does not reduce the premise of hit rate and further improve the efficiency of visual attention is the direction of next effort.

Acknowledgments

This work is supported by project of science and technology development of Jilin provincial education department, China (No. 2016346, No. 2016310).

References

1. L. Elazary and L. Itti. *Vision Research*, 2010, 50(14): pp. 1338-1352.
2. Y. R. Sun, R. Fisher, F. Wang and H. M. Gomes. *Computer Vision and Image Understanding*, 2008, 112: pp. 126-142.
3. L. N. Gao, F. K. Bi and J. Yang. *Journal of Systems Engineering and Electronics*, 2011, 22(1): pp. 150-156.
4. D. Neil, B. Bruce and K. John. *Journal of Vision*, 2009, 9(3): pp. 1-24.
5. K. Lee, Guiding Attention by Cooperative Cues. *Journal of computer science and technology*, 2008, 23(5): pp. 874-884.
6. Q. R. Zhang and H. J. Zhang. 2014, 36(8): pp.1549-1554.
7. J. K. Chu, R. H. Li, Q. Y. Li and H. Q. Wang. *International Journal of Automation and Computing*, 2010, 7(1): pp. 39-46.
8. Y. R. Sun, X. G. Hu, J. H. Zeng and Z. Zhang, Tracking humans in real-time by opponent-motion and visual attention. 2010 WASE International Conference on Information Engineering, 2010, pp. 230-233.
9. L. L. Ma, J. Cheng, J. Liu, J. Q. Wang and H. Q. Lu, Visual attention model based object tracking. *In Proceedings of the 2010 Advances in Multimedia Information Processing, and the 11th Pacific Rim Conference on Multimedia*. 2010, pp. 483-493.
10. X. L. Zhang, H. W. Zhao, H. Wang and J. B. Dai. *ACTA ELECTRONICA SINICA*, 2010, 38(2A), pp. 213-217.
11. H. Wang, L. J. Tian, H. C. Ke. The top-down visual attention method with known interference target. The International Conference on Electronic, Information Technology and Intellectualization (ICEITI 2016).

RNASIM: A Simulation Tool for Solexa Transcriptome Sequencing

You-Jie Zhao[1], Yong Cao[1], Fei Xiong[1] and Zhi Xiong[2,a]

[1]*Department of Computer and Information Sciences, Southwest Forestry University, Kunming, 650224, China,*

[2]*Department of graduation, Southwest Forestry University, Kunming, 650224, China*

E-mail: [a]bioala@swfu.edu.cn

DNA sequencing technology has played an important role on life sciences, especially Illumina's solexa sequencer. It was used for more and more transcriptome projects. In this paper, a tool named as RNASIM is developed, which can simulate solexa transcriptome sequencing based on the reference sequences. The tool RNASIM can actually simulate random gene expression and insert size of library with normal distribution in solexa pair-end sequencing. In order to validate the tool, three times of experiments were simulated based on the reference Arabidopsis transcripts and produced total reads' length of 1Gb, 2Gb and 4Gb. Simulated reads were assembled and compared with original reference sequences. There were respectively 19,704, 20,376 and 20,692 transcripts aligned to one assembled contig. And there were only 1,071(3.2%), 849(2.5%) and 778(2.3%) original transcripts were not found related contigs in three assembled transcripts. Others were assembled multiple copy because of alternative splicing or gene duplication.

Keywords: Illumina Solexa; Transcriptome Sequencing; Computer Simulation; Normal Distribution.

1. Introduction

DNA sequencing technology has played an important role on life sciences. It was more obvious when the next generation sequencing technology come into the world [1]. The next generation sequencing can parallelize the sequencing process, producing thousands or millions of sequences at once, and then it was also known as high-throughput sequencing. Today, there are four commercially available systems: 1) Illumina's Genome Analyzer (Solexa sequencing, now part of Illumina), 2) Life Technologies' SOLiD System, 3) Roche's 454 GS FLX, and 4) Helicos' Heliscope Sequencer. Illumina's Genome Analyzer was highly welcomed by biologists in view of cost and application, more and more projects of transcriptome sequencing had used it [2, 3].

Simulated data is indispensable for guiding tool development and evaluating tool performance, and therefore it is essential to develop simulation software that can produce next-generation sequencing reads that captures the most essential characteristics of real data. In the pioneer papers, a multitude of computational tools have been developed to simulate solexa data based on the reference genome. MetaSim [4] is a sequencing simulator for genomics and metagenomics. Wgsim is a small tool for simulating sequence reads from a reference genome in SAMtools [5]. Simulate is a tool of simulate pair end reads in MAQ [6]. ART [7] is a set of simulation tools that supports the major commercial next-generation sequencing platforms.

Although these programs work well in their domain, there is a need for a special read simulation program used to transcriptome that can generate sequence reads with random gene expression and different insert size consistent with normal distribution. Here we developed a tool named as RNASIM, which can specially simulate solexa transcriptome sequencing based on the reference sequences.

2. Data and Methods

2.1. *Data selected and downloaded*

Arabidopsis thaliana is a small flowering plant, and that is widely used as a model organism in plant biology. It has a genome size of 125-megabase and contains about 25,498 genes. Transcript sequences of arabidopsis thanliana were downloaded from TAIR (http://www.arabidopsis.org/). Since one gene maybe have multiple alternative splicing, these genes were shown to form about 33,410 different transcripts in the GFF annotation. Arabidopsis thaliana has experienced at least three WGD events, and then there were many single-gene and transposed gene duplications in the genome. In this paper, Arabidopsis was selected as reference sequences to be simulated and validated.

2.2. *Simulation of transcriptome sequencing*

2.2.1. *Related definitions in solexa sequencing*

DNA firstly was successfully extracted by experiment, and broken into DNA fragment with different length. The length of DNA fragment is known as insert size. Insert size is always followed by normal distribution. The pair end of DNA fragment would be sequenced by certain cycles. The length of pair end sequenced DNA fragment is read length. Solexa read length is always from 35bp-150bp. Average sequenced time of every hit is called depth.

We need simulate random solexa data, which has certain depth, read length, insert size and error rate (follow the normal distribution) based on the reference genome sequence.

2.2.2. *Calculate the count of reads*

Depth is a random value affected by gene expression. Different gene maybe has different sequencing depth. If we know the options of depth, read length and reference sequence length, so then the count of reads could be calculated by the expression(Eq.(1)).

$$\text{count of reads} = \frac{\text{reference sequence length} * \text{depth}}{\text{read length}} \tag{1}$$

2.2.3. *Random insert size followed normal distribution by Box-Muller*

Normal distribution could be produced by Box-Muller method, and the number of normal distribution sample equals to half of the count of reads.

The Box–Muller transform (by George Edward Pelham Box and Mervin Edgar Muller 1958)[1] is a pseudo-random number sampling method for generating pairs of independent standard normally distributed (zero expectation, unit variance) random numbers, given a source of uniformly distributed random numbers.

Suppose U1(Eq.(2)) and U2(Eq.(3)) are independent random variables that are uniformly distributed in the interval (0, 1). Let

$$Z_0 = R\cos(\theta) = \sqrt{-2\ln U_1 \cos(2\pi U_2)} \tag{2}$$

$$Z_1 = R\sin(\theta) = \sqrt{-2\ln U_1 \cos(2\pi U_2)} \tag{3}$$

Then Z0 and Z1 are independent random variables with a normal distribution of standard deviation 1. We can always construct another normal random variable with specific mean μ and variance σ2(Eq.(4)).

$$X = \sigma Z + \mu \tag{4}$$

2.2.4. *Error rate of solexa data*

According to Illumina's figures, the error rate of solexa sequencing was closed related to sequencing quality . The default error rate is set to 0.1 percent, because quality was always cut off from 20 in the earlier selection. Meanwhile uncertain sequencing base N is produced, and the number of N is numerically equal as error bases.

2.3. *Transcriptome assemble and validate*

The public tool Trinity was used to assemble the simulated reads of transcriptome sequencing. Main options were as *--max_memory 80G --left simulate_1.fa --right simulate_2.fa --seqType fa --CPU 8*. In order to assess the results of transcriptome assembling, assembled contigs were aligned and clustered to original sequences by Cdhit tool using the default options.

According to the result of alignment, six different types ('1to1', '1toN', 'Nto1', 'NoN', 'segment' and 'noseq') were characterized by a perl script. '1to1' means that one original transcript was assembled to one contig. '1toN' means that one original transcript was assembled to multiple contigs. 'Nto1' means that multiple original transcripts were assembled to one contig. 'NtoN' means that multiple original transcripts were assembled to multiple contigs. 'Segment' means that one original transcript was assembled to multiple fragments. 'Noseq' means that original transcript was not found related assembled sequence.

3. Results

3.1. *Simulate solexa transcriptome sequencing*

We develop a perl script tool named as RNASIM to simulate random solexa library with random depth and certain insert sizes followed by normal distribution based on the reference sequence.

In order to test the script RNASIM, we simulated three times of transcriptome sequencing with max depth of 50X, 100X and 200X. Arabidopsis's transcripts was set to the reference sequences. Insert size of pair-end was set to the usage length 200bp, read length was 100bp. The standard deviation of normal distribution was set to default value 10. The error rate of sequencing was set to default 0.1 percent. As is shown (Tab. 1), three simulated samples obtained total size of 1.02G, 2.03G and 4.03G reads respectively.

Table 1 Simulation of transcriptome sequencing in Arabidopsis thaliana

Sample	Max depth(X)#	Count of reads	Total size of simulated data	GC%
Expriment50	50	10,281,040	1.02G	45.32
Expriment100	100	20,324,850	2.03G	45.25
Expriment200	200	40,337,442	4.03G	45.57

#Max depth means genes have a random sequencing depth [1, max].

3.2. *Transcriptome assemble and validate*

A total of 36.9, 37.5 and 37.9Mb sequences were respectively assembled with three samples of simulated reads, and N50 sizes were up to 1372, 1382 and 1390bp (Tab. 2). Assembly of reads resulted in *36,504, 36,261 and 36,455* contigs with different mean sizes of 1011, 1033 and 1040bp. Any number of total assembled contigs were higher than original number of 33,410. One obvious possible reason is that some gene had been assembled to multiple shorter fragment sequences.

Table 2 Results of transcriptome assembly of simulated reads

Sample	Assembled length	Number of assembled transcripts	Min length	Mean length	Max length	N50
Expriment50	36.9M	36,504	201	1,011	15,989	1,372
Expriment100	37.5M	36,261	201	1,033	15,996	1,382
Expriment200	37.9M	36,455	201	1,040	16,004	1,390

In order to validate the simulation and assembly, all assembled contigs of three samples were aligned to original Arabidopsis transcript sequences (Tab. 2). There were respectively 19,704, 20,376 and 20,692 transcripts aligned to only one assembled contig (1to1). And 8,342, 7,738 and 7,562 transcripts were found to align to multiple fragment sequences (Segement). There were 1,071(3.2%), 849(2.5%) and 778(2.3%) transcripts were not found perhaps because of lower depth of random sequencing. Other types of 1toN, Nto1 and NtoN, one gene was assembled multiple copy perhaps because of alternative splicing and gene duplication.

Table 3 Comparition of assembled and original transcripts

Sample	1to1	1toN	Nto1	NtoN	Segment	Noseq
Expriment50	19,704	2,630	353	225	8,342	1,071
Expriment100	20,376	2,761	384	237	7,738	849
Expriment200	20,692	2,730	368	244	7,562	778

4. Conclusions

In this paper, we developed a tool named as RNASIM, which can simulate solexa transcriptome sequencing based on the reference sequences. The tool can actually simulates random gene expression and insert size of library with normal distribution in solexa pair-end sequencing. In order to validate the tool, three times of experiments were simulated with total reads' length of 1Gb, 2Gb and 4Gb based on the Arabidopsis transcripts. Simulated reads were assembled and compared with original reference sequences. And there were only 1,071(3.2%), 849(2.5%) and 778(2.3%) original transcripts were not found related contigs in three assembled transcripts. Meanwhile, we found some genes were assembled to multiple fragments or gene copy perhaps because of alternative splicing or gene duplication in the Arabidopsis genome.

Acknowledgments

This work is supported by Project of Education Department of Yunnan Province(2015Y287), Project of Breeding and functional gene cloning and identification of Pinus kesiya (201304105), Key Disciplines (Biology) Project of Yunnan Education Department and Research Center of Kunming Forestry Information Engineering Technology and Project of Eduation Reform of Southwest Forestry University (YB201416).

References

1. Schuster S C, Next-generation sequencing transforms today's biology, Nature, 2008, 200(8): 16-18.
2. Maher CA, Sinhal CK, Cao XH, et al, Transcriptome sequencing to detect gene fusions in cancer, Nature, 2009, 458: 97-101.
3. Wang Z, Gerstein M, Snyder M, RNA-Seq: a revolutionary tool for transcriptomics, Nat Rev Genet, 2009, 10(1):57–63. [4]
4. D.C. Richter, F. Ott, A.F. Auch, et al, MetaSim: a sequencing simulator for genomics and metagenomics, PLoS One, 2008, 3 :e3373.

5. H. Li, B. Handsaker, A. Wysoker, et al. The Sequence Alignment/Map format and SAMtools, Bioinformatics, 2009, 25: 2078-2079.
6. C. Kumps, N. Van Roy, L. Heyrman, et al, Multiplex Amplicon Quantification (MAQ), a fast and efficient method for the simultaneous detection of copy number alterations in neuroblastoma, BMC Genomics, 2010,11: 298.
7. Huang W, Li L, Myers JR, Marth GT, ART: a next-generation sequencing read simulator, Bioinformatics, 2012, 28 (4): 593-594.

Program Repair Via Code Block Mutation Operator

Lin-Xin Wang, Yong Liu[a] and Yang Xu

College of Information Science and Technology, Beijing University of Chemical Technology, Beijing 100029, China

E-mail: [a]lyong@mail.buct.edu.cn

This paper proposed an automated repair method based on mutation testing, specifically for mutating code blocks of program. The code block mutation operator is designed and applied this mutation operator to repair defects caused by incorrect code formatting in C/C++ language programs. The empirical study was conducted and the results showed that 28,765 of 29,202 faulty programs caused by incorrect block of code formatting in the database were repaired automatically. The empirical result indicates that the designed mutation operator is highly effective.

Keywords: Automatic Program Repair; Mutation Operator; Online Judge System.

1. Introduction

With the arrival of information society, there is a growing emphasis on the application and development of the computer software. Much effort have been spent on software testing which is an indispensable part during the software development activity. It appears to be a fact of life that researchers have devoted a certain degree of attentions on the area of Automated Program Repair (APR) techniques.

The concept of APR is automatically fixing faults in source code level, not binary files or run-time patching [1]. In general, automated program repair is a three-step procedure: fault localization [2], [3], patch generation and patch validation. Recently, APR techniques have received much attention of researchers [4]. Debroy and Wong present a generate-and-validate approach with two modifications: replacement of an operator with another from the same class, and condition negation [5], [6].

Recently, APR mainly targets specific types of faults, data structure and memory overflow [7]. However, there are few program repair methods aiming at defects due to poor programming experiences and inadequate habit. Code standardization is the foundation of programming, and suitable programming habits could enhance the readability and maintainability of the program [8]. On the contrary, programmers have paid more attention on the algorithms and correctness rather than the code standardization, so it consumes a lot of time in the process of software debugging [9]. This paper was depended on the code database from the Online Judge System of Beijing University of Chemical Technology, and did statistical analyses on non-standardization degrees of the submitted programs of the code database. Besides, this paper designed a code block mutation operator focusing on repairing the defects caused by the incorrect block of code.

The main contributions of this paper are as follows:

(1) This paper utilizes regular expression and edit distance to calculate the non-standardization degree of program, and conducts a statistical analysis to prove the prevalence of non-standard programs developed by beginners.

(2) This paper designs and implements a code block mutation operator to mutate non-standard programs.

(3) This paper conducts an empirical study to demonstrate that the code block mutation operator can precisely repair the program faults caused by incorrect block of code.

2. Statistical Analysis of Program Faults Due to Incorrect Code Formatting

2.1. *Algorithm of code formatting standardization*

For the purpose of helping programming beginners to learn more about the correctness and standardization degree of the code, this paper utilizes the code database from Online Judge System of BUCT, gives statistical analyses to the submitted programs, and integrates the Python scripts with the Astyle tool to calculate the non-standardization degree.

2.1.1. *Preprocessing of programs by regular expression*

In Python, Regular expression [10] is called model which matches some string or not. While there are infinite strings at present, we may divide them in two groups: matched string and mismatched string.

(1)'.*? +' Use this model to delete the extra space, and notice that there is a space between '?' and '+';

(2)'[,!=<>\+\-*\/]+[A-Za-z0-9]+|[A-Za-z0-9]+[,!=<>\+\-*\/]+'. Use this model to add a space between identifier and operator.

2.1.2. *Edit distance of standard program and non-standard program*

The similarities between two strings can be quantified by the edit distance [11] [12]. We proceed Dynamic Programming (DP) based on edit distance. The edit distance algorithm has optimal time complexities in *O(m, n)* and spatial activity in *O(m, n)*. If the order of the edit distance doesn't need to be saved, then the algorithm's spatial activity will be *O(m, n)*, m denotes the length of the source string S and n denotes the length of the target string T. The Eq. (1) as follows is the equation set of edit distance:

$$\begin{aligned} &D_{[i,j]} = 0 \ if\ (i == 0\ or\ j == 0) \\ &D_{[i,j]} = Min(d_{[i-1,j]} + 1, d_{[i,j-1]} + 1, d_{[i-1,j-1]})\ if\ (S_i == T_j) \\ &D_{[i,j]} = Min(d_{[i-1,j]} + 1, d_{[i,j-1]} + 1, d_{[i-1,j-1]} + 1)\ if\ (S_i\ != = T_j) \end{aligned} \tag{1}$$

2.1.3. *Algorithm of code formatting standardization*

Algorithm 1 Algorithm of code formatting standardization

```
Input: incorrect formatting program OriginCode;
Output: program after code formatting standardization EndCode;
the incorrect code formatting degree Degree;
While (OriginCode <- InputFromDataBase())
Begin // Extract the code from database
    code <- PreparedforMoldesign(originCode); // Pre-Processing, Pre-Standardization
    endCode <- NormalizeCode(code); // Code Standardization
    tempCode <- endCode;
    tempCode <- DeleteSomeSub(tempCode);
    Degree <- CalculateNormal(tempCode); // Calculate Degree
    OutputToDatabase(EndCode,percentOfNormal);
End // End while
```

2.2. *Statistics of non-standard programs from OJ*

This paper analyses and calculates the non-standardization degree of 135,556 C/C++ programs from OJ. The result shows in Figure 1, where the vertical axis denotes the different non-standardization degree spans referring to different edit distances, and the horizontal axis denotes the amount of the corresponding programs. In Figure 1, we can find that fewer than 11,000 programs are in standardization. The prevalence of non-standard programs developed by beginners can be proved.

Furthermore, this paper analyses the 87,933 faulty programs on OJ independently in order to learn more about the effect on the correctness of codes by different non-standardization degrees. Figure 2 shows the number of failed codes in different non-standardization degrees.

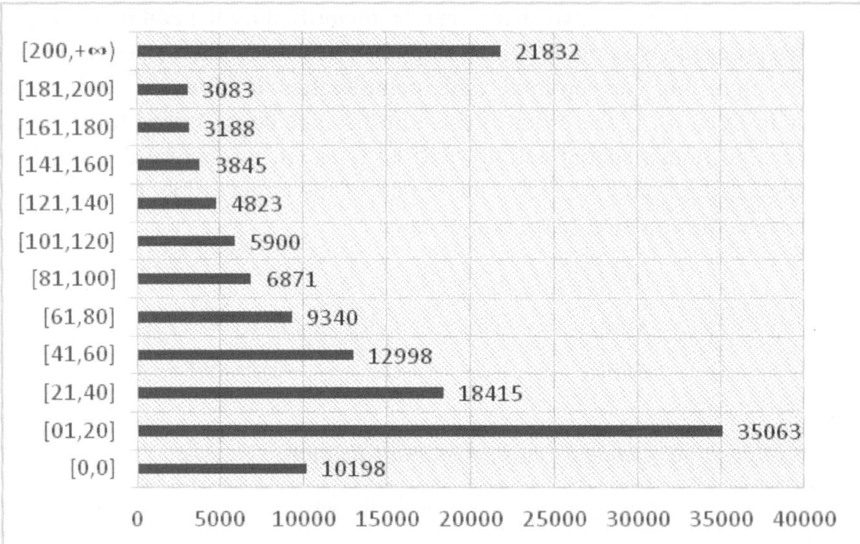

Fig. 1. Number of OJ code database in different non-standardization degrees

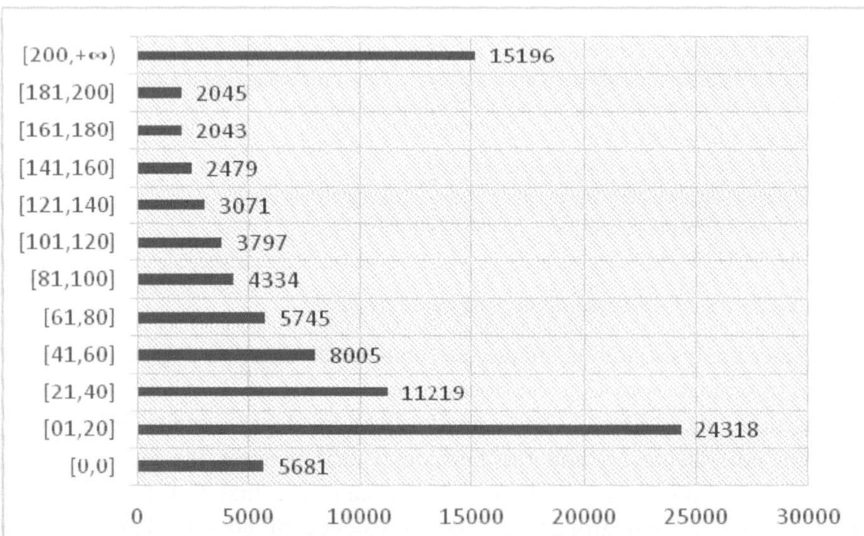

Fig. 2. Number of failed codes in different non-standardization degrees

Compared comprehensively, this paper finds that the number of incorrect code formatting programs is in positive correlation with the number of failed programs. In particular, we get the Table 1 according to classifying the different fault types of faulty programs.

During our manual classification, we find that the trend of fault types in C/C++ programs is similar to the result proposed by Pan in 2008 [13]. Moreover, we have counted the amount of the faulty programs caused by the incorrect block of code formatting, the result shows that there are 29,202 programs reaching 33.21% of the OJ database. Then, this paper designs the code block mutation operator for code block standardization focusing on repairing the defect caused by incorrect block of code.

Table 1 Classification of different fault types

Fault Type	**Number of faulty programs**	**Percentage of faulty programs**	**Number of faulty programs caused by incorrect block of code formatting**	**Percentage of faulty programs caused by incorrect block of code formatting**
If related	26,257	29.86%	10,525	11.97%
Method call related	11,528	13.11%	809	0.92%
Loop related	29,202	33.21%	13,911	15.82%
Assignment related	9,479	10.78%	1,460	1.66%
Method declaration related	7,412	8.43%	1,574	1.79%
Others	4,055	4.61%	923	1.05%
Total	87,933	100.00%	**29,202**	**33.21%**

3. Designing and Implementation of Code Block Mutation Operator

Automated program repair via mutation testing is an approach that using some mutation operators to mutate an already faulty program. If there exists a mutant which is un-killable with respect to all test cases in the available test set, then such a mutant might represent a fix to the fault, i.e., a possibly correct version of the program.

At present, mutation operators based on mutation testing are still in the operator stage, like arithmetic operators {+, −, /, ×, %}, relational operators {>, <, ==, >=, <=, !=}, logical operators {&&, ||}, i.e., {AND, OR} and so on.

Besides, there are few mutation operators aiming at code block formatting standardization, especially aiming at the faults caused by incorrect location of code blocks. So we propose a novel mutation operator especially for code block standardization.

3.1. *Designing of code block mutation operator*

Different from the traditional mutation operators, code block mutation operator focuses on the basic bit. Consider each '{' in a program, code block mutation operator first deletes the corresponding '}', and then replaces every '\n' behind the ';' to '}'. While this paper includes the case that programmers forget to add both the blocks of code at the end of the loop statements as follows:

for (int i = 0; i < 10; i++)
....
....
	for (int i = 0; i < 10; i++) {
	....
	}

while (i < 10)
....
....
	while (i < 10) {
	....
	}

In order to simplify the understanding of the algorithm, we eliminate the non-line break characters except for blocks of code and semicolons in program. These characters' exist doesn't affect the correctness of mutation, because we just consider the mutation of character '\n'. Meanwhile, duplicate check plays an important role in solving the problem of large amount of mutants, we should also proceed the syntax check to guarantee the mutants will be compiled successfully.

3.2. *Syntax check*

Step 1: Check the missing block of code behind the loop statements

Add the missing block of code behind the loop statements and it will not affect the result of the program even if adding the block of code at the first correct statement.

Step 2: Delete the redundant characters

Traverse the entire code and delete all characters except for '{', '}', and ';', at the same time mark on the deleted code in modified code.

3.3. *Algorithm of code block mutation operator*

Algorithm 2 Algorithm of code block mutation

```
Input: A failed program due to incorrect block of code formatting OriginCode;
Output: A passed program or NULL
originCode <- InputFromDataBase(); // Extract the code from database
tempCode <- CheckWhetherOmitBrace(originCode); // Step 1
tempCode <- ClipCode(tempCode); // Step2
Q = Queue.new;
Q.push(tempCode);
While (!Q.empty())
Begin
  tempCode = Q.pop();
  variantCode[] = VariantCode(tempCode);
  for_each(eachVariantCode in variantCode)
  Begin
  if (CheckComplie(eachVariantCode) == True && CheckUnique(eachVariantCode) == True) // duplicate check and syntax check
    Begin
    if (CheckRight(eachVariantCode) == True)  // check whether the mutants are the patches or not
    return eachVariantCode; // return correct mutants
    else
    Q.push(eachVariantCode); // prepare for next mutation
    End
  End // END for_each
End // END while
return NULL;
```

4. Experiment

4.1. *Preparation of experiment*

4.1.1. *Experimental environment*

The experiment runs on the computer with Intel Core (TM) i7-4510U 2.60GHz CPU and 8GB memory. The operating system (OS) is Ubuntu14.04. The experiment relies on the software My SQL and Sublime.

4.1.2. *Experimental data:*

There are 135,556 subject programs come from BUCT Online Judge (OJ), including 1,604 problems of C/C++ programming language, data structure, dynamic programming and so on.

4.2. *Experiment result*

In Table 2, we find that 28765 of 29,202 faulty programs caused by incorrect block of code formatting are repaired automatically, the repair efficiency reaches to 98.50%. The empirical result indicates that code block mutation operator is highly effective in repairing program faults caused by incorrect position of code blocks.

Table 2 Percentage of repaired code

Fault Type	**Number of faulty programs**	**Number of faulty programs caused by incorrect block of code formatting**	**Number of repaired programs**	**Ratio between repaired programs and incorrect formatting programs**	**Ratio between repaired programs and total faulty programs**
If related	26,257	10,525	10,323	98.08%	39.31%
Method call related	11,528	809	750	92.71%	6.51%
Loop related	29,202	13,911	13,879	99.77%	47.53%
Assignment related	9,479	1,460	1,456	99.73%	15.36%
Method declaration related	7,412	1,574	1,478	93.90%	19.94%
Others	4,055	923	879	95.23%	21.68%
Total	**87,933**	**29,202**	**28,765**	**98.50%**	**32.71%**

5. Conclusion

This paper proposed an automated repair approach based on mutation testing, especially for the block of code. And this approach was applied to repair defects of incorrect code formatting in C/C++ language programs. Regular expression and edit distance were utilized to design the code block mutation operator for code block standardization, and syntax check was proceeded to guarantee that the mutants are grammatical correct. The empirical study was conducted and the results were promising, the efficiency of designed automated repair approach is up to 98.5%. In future work, we'll further analyze the habits of programmers and will focus on code formatting in Java, C# and other language programs.

Acknowledgments

This work is supported by the Fundamental Research Funds for the Central Universities in China (PT1613-09). Work partially supported by grant 2-4570.5 of the Swiss National Science Foundation.

References

1. Qi Y, Mao X, Lei Y, Using automated program repair for evaluating the effectiveness of fault localization techniques[C]//Proceedings of the 2013 International Symposium on Software Testing and Analysis. ACM, 2013: 191-201.
2. X. Xie, T. Y. Chen, F.-c. Kuo, and B. Xu. A theoretical analysis of the risk evaluation formulas for spectrum-based fault localization. ACM Transactions on Software Engineering and Methodology (TOSEM), 22(4):Article 31, 2013.
3. W. Jin and A. Orso. F3: fault localization for field failures. In International Symposium on Software Testing and Analysis (ISSTA), pages 213–223, 2013.
4. M. Monperrus. A critical review of "automatic patch generation learned from human-written patches": an essay on the problem statement and the evaluation of automatic software repair. In International Conference on Software Engineering (ICSE), 2014.
5. Debroy V, Wong W E. Using mutation to automatically suggest fixes for faulty programs[C]//Software Testing, Verification and Validation (ICST), 2010 Third International Conference on. IEEE, 2010: 65-74.
6. Debroy V, Wong W E. Combining mutation and fault localization for automated program debugging[J]. Journal of Systems and Software, 2014, 90: 45-60.
7. MA Chun-yan, LIU Jie, LAI Wen-yu. Method for repairing program automatically with mutation[J]. Application Research of Computers, 2014, 31(1):177-181. (in Chinese)

8. WANG Yan-qing, WANG Jian-zheng, ZHANG Li-jie. A Framework for Quantitative Evaluation of Coding Standards in Programming Language Teaching [J]. Journal of Hefei University of Technology (Social Sciences), 2008(6):67-71. (in Chinese)
9. Tom Schorsch. CAP: An Automatic Self-assessment Tool to Check Pascal Programs for Syntax, Logic and Style Errors[A]. Proceedings of the 26th SIGCSE technical symposium on Computer science education, USA.1995:168-172.
10. Brzozowski J A. Derivatives of regular expressions[J]. Journal of the ACM (JACM), 1964, 11(4): 481-494.
11. Levenshtein V I. Binary codes capable of correcting deletions, insertions, and reversals[C]//Soviet physics doklady. 1966, 10(8): 707-710.
12. Godfrey J J, Holliman E C, McDaniel J. SWITCHBOARD: Telephone speech corpus for research and development[C]//Acoustics, Speech, and Signal Processing, 1992. ICASSP-92., 1992 IEEE International Conference on. IEEE, 1992, 1: 517-520.
13. Pan K, Kim S, Whitehead Jr E J. Toward an understanding of bug fix patterns[J]. Empirical Software Engineering, 2009, 14(3): 286-315.

Head Detection by PCA-based CNN with Multi-Stage Features Integration

Jian-Chao Fei[1], Jun-Hua Zou[1,a], Ting Rui[1,2], You Zhou[3] and Qi-Yu Gao[1]

[1]*College of Field Engineering, PLA University of Science and Technology, Nanjing, China*

[2]*State Key Lab. for Novel Software Technology, Nanjing University, Nanjing, China*

[3]*Jiangsu Institute of Commerce, Nanjing, China*

E-mail: [a]278287847@163.com

Head detection plays an important role in pedestrian detection for the unique feature of human head. The existing methods of head detection mainly use the features of contour, color and template, which usually have low accuracy and robustness of detection. In this paper, a novel method based on CNN with multi-stage feature integration to detect head in complex background is proposed. This method combines the shallow and deep feature of CNN which can increase the completeness and comprehensiveness of image description. Meanwhile, the computation cost is decreased by reduced high dimensional features with PCA. The experimental results show that the proposed method has high detection accuracy, which is better than the existing methods.

Keywords: Head Detection; CNN; Multi-Stage Feature Integration; PCA.

1. Introduction

Pedestrian detection is an important and challenging task in surveillance video analysis. Human bodies are probably occluded too much because of the shooting angle. On the contrary, human head is less possible to be occluded in crowd, which is an obvious detection target and contains unique information [1-3]. Due to various challenges, head detection becomes a challenging task.

Convolutional neural network (CNN), as a kind of deep learning model, usually takes the pooling features of the last layer as the basis of classification

[4]. Different levels of abstract play different roles and make different contributions to feature abstract. Therefore, we combine the abstracted features of different layers, and find it can improve the integrity of the feature expression and increase the classification accuracy. Based on the above observations, we propose a novel head detection method using PCA based CNN with features Integration. The main contribution of our method includes:

(1) We enrich the features in detection by integrating the multi-stage features, which makes full use of all features of all subsampling layers.

(2) We reduce the feature dimension and keep principal component to solve the problem of the complexity of the classifier design, the calculation quantity and the redundant information.

2. Related Work

Object detection is usually formulated as a classification task which scans an image with sliding windows. Generative methods calculate the probability of a window enclosing the pedestrian [5]. And the discriminative classifiers, such as SVM [6] and boosting classifiers [7], separate samples into positive and negative ones.

Deep models have achieved spectacular progress in computer vision [8]. In recent years, they have been widely used in object detection because of its fantastic performance in feature extraction and representation. In the existing CNN model, only the feature of the last layer would be the basis of classification.

There are many other methods in head detection. In [9], Kinect camera was used to detect head. In [10], a new spherical mixture model was proposed for head detection. In [11], a method using skeleton graph was described for head detection.

In our previous research, we proposed multi-stage CNN with voting strategy [12]. In this paper, we firstly used features which had been abstracted by multi-stage CNN from different layers to classify respectively, and then we got the final the final classification through voting strategy.

3. The Multi-Stage CNN Feature Integration

Considering that human takes advantage of abstracting information of different levels to make a comprehensive conclusion when detecting targets, we combine abstract results of different convolutional layers to form a multi-stage features to improve the detection effect of CNN.

We take the head test sample as an example. The sample size is 64×64, and the CNN has seven layers including one input layer (I), three convolutional layers (C), and three pooling layers (P). We put the single sample into the network in order to make the size of feature maps in P1, P2, P3 to be 30×30, 13×13 and 3×3 respectively, and then convert each feature map to a column vector P_{ij}, here i represents number of pooling layer and j represents number of feature map. In the end, we connect all the column vectors P_{ij} of each layer to form a column vector respectively:

$$\begin{aligned} v_{P1} &= [p_{11};\ p_{12};\ p_{13};\ \cdots] \\ v_{P2} &= [p_{21};\ p_{22};\ p_{23};\ \cdots] \\ v_{P3} &= [p_{31};\ p_{32};\ p_{33};\ \cdots] \end{aligned} \quad (1)$$

In the last layer, we connect v_{p1}, v_{p2} and v_{p3}:

$$V = [v_{P1};\ v_{P2};\ v_{P3}] \quad (2)$$

In consequence, the last column vector V contains feature information from different layers after processing. This network mentioned above is called CNN with multi-stage feature integration.

From the result, we can get the column vector V. We can find V is a very high dimension feature. The high dimension feature greatly increases the number of network parameters and the computational complexity, forms the redundant features, wastes the calculating process and eventually does harm to the improvement of the object detection accuracy. We utilize PCA to handle feature columns vectors, and then reduce the dimension and reserve the main information of feature.

The calculation of multi-stage features Integration is as follow:

1) Process v_{p1}, v_{p2}, v_{p3} with PCA to obtain feature vector v_{p1}', v_{p2}', v_{p3}';

2) Connect v_{p1}', v_{p2}', v_{p3}' to form $V' = [v_{P1}';\ v_{P2}';\ v_{P3}']$;

3) Put the feature column vector V' into SVM to complete classification.

The difference between the structure and the traditional CNN is that PCA-based CNN with multi-stage feature integration combines global features and local features, which enriches the feature information by integrating the multi-stage features. The structure of PCA-based CNN with multi-stage feature integration is shown in Figure 1:

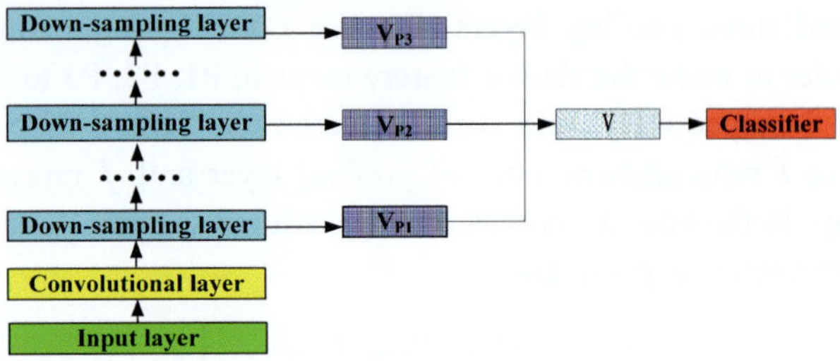

Fig. 1. The structure of PCA based CNN with multi-stage feature integration

4. Experiments and Analysis

4.1. *Data set and experiment setting*

To validate the performance of the proposed method, we collect a large number of positive and negative samples from surveillance videos. The positive samples include heads in bright or dim natural light, heads with supplementary light or without supplementary lighting at night. Negative samples which do not contain head are arbitrarily extracted from the rest parts of video frames.

We normalize the sizes of samples into 64×64. The training set contains 4,800 samples including 2,400 positive samples and 2,400 negative samples. The test set contains 3,524 samples including 1,762 positive samples and 1,762 negative samples. Some examples of positive samples and negative samples are shown in Figure 2

(a) positive samples (b) negative samples

Fig. 2. Examples of positive samples and negative samples in data set

4.2. *Experimental results*

Convolutional kernels and the layers of network are two important parameters for CNN. The experiments is performed for these two parameters.

(1) Determining the convolutional kernel

The scale of convolutional kernel is determined by the size and complexity of detection object. As for the self-built database, the scale of convolutional kernel is set to 3×3, 5×5 and 7×7 respectively in the experiment, and the visualization results of the second layer are shown in Fig. 3. We find that the effect of 5×5 convolutional kernel is the best.

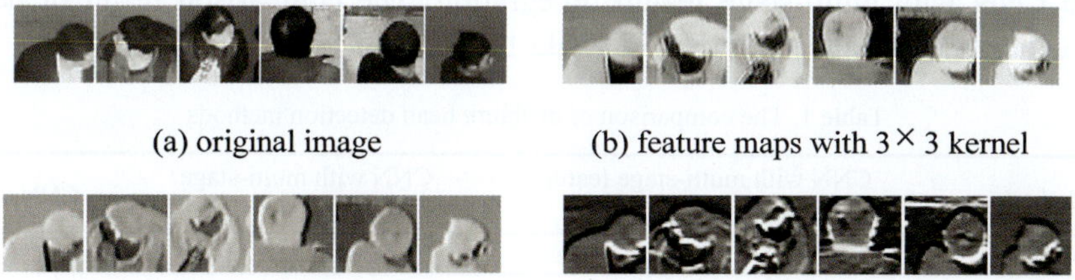

(a) original image (b) feature maps with 3×3 kernel

(c) feature maps with 5×5 kernel (d) feature maps with 7×7 kernel

Fig. 3. Feature maps generated by different convolutional kernels

(2) Determining the layers of network

As a model of CNN, deeper model can describe feature more abstract and represents feature more thoroughly, and excessive layers result over-fitting. Suitable layers have better detection result. We use 3, 5, 7 layers CNN and the scale of convolutional kernels are all 5×5 in the experiments. From Fig. 4, we find the effect are the best and the error is the smallest when the number of layers is 7. So the scale of convolutional kernel is 5×5 and the number of layers is 7.

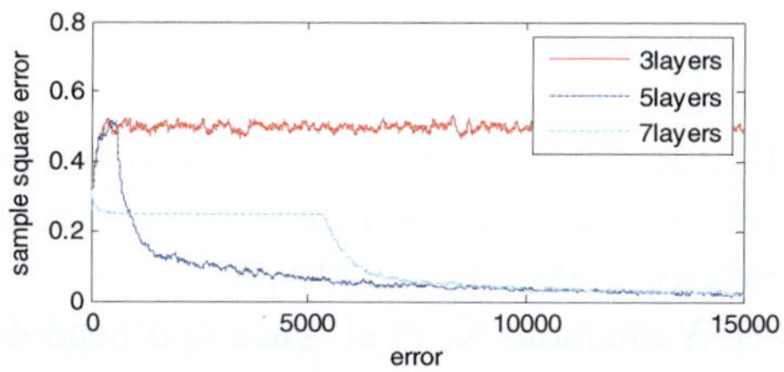

Fig. 4. Mean square error graph experiments and results

After using the network determined above, the accuracy of the test database reaches 98.3%. Figure 5 shows the detection result on one frame of a video.

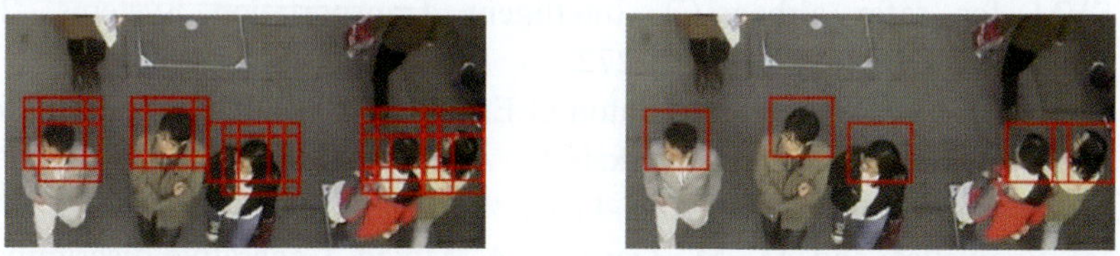

(a) Primary detection result (b) Detection result after removing duplicates

Fig. 5. Example of head detection result

In order to validate the advantage of the proposed structure and increase the persuasiveness and integrity, we compare the proposed method to original CNN and CNN with multi-stage feature integration. The comparison result of head detection performance is shown in Table 1.

Table 1. The comparison of different head detection methods

Method	CNN with multi-stage feature Integration based on PCA	CNN with multi-stage feature Integration	CNN
Detection rate	98.3%	96.6%	94.2%

5. Conclusions

In this paper, we propose a novel head detection method with Multi-stage CNN, which uses PCA to reduce the dimension of high-dimensional features and regards the multi-stage features as the foundation of SVM. The experimental results show that the PCA-based CNN with multi-stage feature integration can obtain higher detection accuracy than the existing methods.

Acknowledgments

This work was supported in part by National Natural Science Foundation of China (Grant No.61472444, 61472392).

References

1. Lu W, Tan J, Floyd R. Automated fetal head detection and measurement in ultrasound images by iterative randomized Hough transform [J]. Ultrasound in medicine & biology, 2005, 31(7): 929-936.
2. Ishii Y, Hongo H, Yamamoto K, et al. Face and head detection for a real-time surveillance system[C]. Pattern Detection, 2004. ICPR 2004. Proceedings of the 17th International Conference on. IEEE, 2004, 3: 298-301.
3. Reyna R, Giralt A, Esteve D. Head detection inside vehicles with a modified SVM for safer airbags[C]. Intelligent Transportation Systems, 2001. Proceedings. IEEE, 2001: 268-272.
4. Krizhevsky A, Sutskever I, Hinton G E. Image net classification with deep convolutional neural networks[C]. Advances in neural information processing systems. 2012: 1097-1105.
5. M. Enzweiler and D. M. Gavrila. A Mixed Generative-discriminative Framework for Pedestrian Classification[C]. Computer Vision and Pattern Recognition, 2008. CVPR 2008. IEEE Conference on. IEEE, 2008: 1-8.

6. P. F. Felzenszwalb, R. B. Girshick, D. Mcallester, and D. Ramanan. Object detection with discriminatively trained part-based models[C]. IEEE Transactions on Pattern Analysis and Machine Intelligence. IEEE, 2010, 32(9): 1627-1645.
7. P. Dollar, R. Appel, and W. Kienzle. Crosstalk cascades for frame-rate pedestrian detection[C]. Computer Vision-12th European Conference on Computer Vision, 2012: 645-659.
8. Wanli Ouyang, Xingyu Zeng, Xiaogang Wang. Learning Mutual Visibility Relationship for Pedestrian Detection with a Deep Model [J]. International Journal of Computer Vision, 2016: 1-14.
9. Anh Tuan Nghiem, Edouard Auvinet, Jean Meunier. Head Detection using Kinect Camera and its Application to Fall Detection[C]. Information Science, Signal Processing and their Applications (ISSPA), 2012 11th International Conference on. 2012: 164-169.
10. Denis Brazey, Bruno Portier. A New Spherical Mixture Model for Head Detection in Depth Images [J]. SIAM J. Imaging Sci., 2014, 7(4): 2423–2447.
11. Kheireddine Aziz, Djamal Merad, Rabah Iguernaissi, Pierre Drap, Bernard Fertil. Head Detection based on Skeleton Graph Method for Counting People in Crowded Environments [J]. J. Electron. Imaging. 25(1), 013012 (Jan 27, 2016). doi:10.1117/1.JEI.25.1.013012.
12. Ting Rui, Jianchao Fei, You Zhou, Jian Tang, Husheng Fang. Human Head Detection Based on Multi-stage CNN with Voting Strategy [C]. ICIMCS '15 Proceedings of the 7th International Conference on Internet Multimedia Computing and Service, 2015.

Evaluation of Multi-Boreholes Heat Exchanges Based on Optimization Model

Yong Li[1], Hui-Liang Lian[1,a], Fu-Sheng Peng[1], Xu Han[1], Hai-Bo Liu[1] and Ludan Zhang[2,b]

[1]*Institute of military environmental teaching and research, PLA Univ. of Sci. & Tech. Nanjing 210007, PR China*

[2]*Ding Chen architectural design co., LTD Nanjing 210007, PR China*

E-mail: [a]lgdxbing121@126.com, [b]hvac_121@163.com

Based on the Moving Finite Lines Source (MFLS) model, the heat transfer model for multi-boreholes fields was established, combined with quasi three-dimensional model of the circulating flow in the pipe of the borehole, the optimization model for multi-BHEs was established to guiding design. With the arrangement optimization, the utilization rate of the allowable area and the COP of the GSHP could be improved by 12.5% and 10%, respectively.

Keywords: MFLS; Multi-Boreholes Heat Exchangers; Optimization.

1. Introduction

The infinite line source model (ILS) [1], cylindrical heat source model[2] and finite line source model (FLS) [3][4] were derived to analyze the heat transfer around the BHE. But if groundwater flow is present, it means that heat is also transported by the moving water, the moving infinite line source model (MILS) for evaluating the effects of groundwater flow on the heat transfer into the BHE was discussed by Wang [5], Raymond [6] and Diao [7].

Based on a three dimensional computational fluid dynamics model and the second-order Response Surface Model, how the parameters affect on the total heat transfer efficiency of the BHEs in cooling mode was probed by Vahid. Khalah [8] and the optimum combination parameters for optimum total heat transfer efficiency was given. Markus Beck [9] gave the measures including operation mode adjustment and geometric arrangement to optimize performance of the multi-BHEs, but the groundwater flow was not taken into account.

In the present study, based on the MFLS model and temperature superposition. Combined with the quasi three-dimensional model of the circulating fluid in the pipe, the outlet temperature could be attained, the lower the outlet temperature lead to the higher heat transfer efficiency of the GSHP system, then outlet temperature was taken as the optimized objective to establish the optimization model for multi-BHEs, which was applied to the cases of arrangement optimization and load optimization pattern.

2. Methods

2.1. *Moving finite line source model (MFLS)*

The axial effects are taken into account for moving infinite line source model, then the temperature response of MFLS model [10] with the x-direction groundwater flow could be attained as Eq. (1).

$$\Delta T_{MFLS} = T(x,y,z,t) - T_{ground} = \frac{q_L}{2\pi\lambda_{por}} \exp\left(\frac{v_T x}{2a_{por}}\right) \left\{ \int_0^H (f_1(x,y,z,t) - f_2(x,y,z,t)) dh \right\} \quad (1)$$

$$f_1(x,y,z,t) = \frac{1}{4r}\left[\exp\left(-\frac{v_T\sqrt{r^2+(z-h)^2}}{2a_{por}}\right) erfc\left(\frac{\sqrt{r^2+(z-h)^2}-v_T t}{2\sqrt{a_{por}t}}\right) + \exp\left(\frac{v_T\sqrt{r^2+(z-h)^2}}{2a_{por}}\right) erfc\left(\frac{\sqrt{r^2+(z-h)^2}+v_T t}{2\sqrt{a_{por}t}}\right)\right]$$

$$f_2(x,y,z,t) = \frac{1}{4r}\left[\exp\left(-\frac{v_T\sqrt{r^2+(z+h)^2}}{2a_{por}}\right) erfc\left(\frac{\sqrt{r^2+(z+h)^2}-v_T t}{2\sqrt{a_{por}t}}\right) + \exp\left(\frac{v_T\sqrt{r^2+(z+h)^2}}{2a_{por}}\right) erfc\left(\frac{\sqrt{r^2+(z+h)^2}+v_T t}{2\sqrt{a_{por}t}}\right)\right]$$

$$r = \sqrt{x^2 + y^2}$$

Table 1 Parameters of BHEs

Parameter	Symbol	Value	Unit
Undisturbed soil temperature	T_{ground}	[℃]	17.4
Borehole diameter	d_b	[m]	0.12
Branch pipe outer diameter	d_p	[m]	0.032
Grout thermal conductivity	λ_g	[W/m.K]	2.4
Grout vol. heat capacity	$\rho_g c_g$	[J/m^3/k]	3.2*10^6
Soil thermal conductivity	λ_s	[W/m.K]	2.0
Subsurface vol. heat capacity	$\rho_s c_s$	[J/m^3/k]	4.8*10^6
Heat flux per unit length	q_L	[W/m]	40
Groundwater flow velocity	u	[m/s]	$2*10^{-8}$~$2*10^{-6}$
Porosity	φ	-	0.25

2.2. *Comparison of different models*

According to the parameters in Table 1, Figure 1 showed the vertical temperature profile at the radial distance r=1 m (x-direction), after 90 days, in this case the borehole length was 60 m, groundwater velocity (Darcy velocity) was 2e-7 m/s.

In Figure 1, the temperature response of MFLS model is nonlinear along the borehole, especially at the beginning and ending part. The temperature response of MILS model is 0.5°C higher than the MFLS model at the middle of the borehole with the radial distance r=1 m. It indicates that the axial effects would play a non-ignorable role on the heat transfer of BHEs.

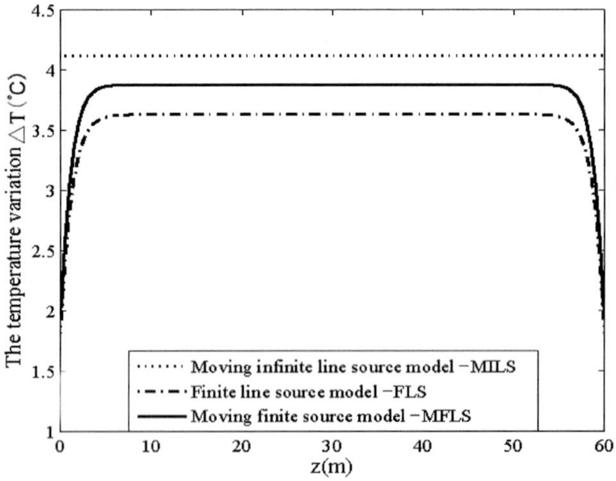

Fig. 1 The vertical temperature profile of different models at the radial distance r=1 m (q_L=40 W/m, u=2e-7 m/s, t=90 days)

3. MFLS Multi-BHEs Model

Based on the MFLS model Eq. (1), the temperature variation at any arbitrary point in the soil of multi-BHEs fields could be attained by applying superposition principle to Eq. (2) as:

$$\theta(x,y,z,t)_{MFLS} = \sum_{j=1}^{n} \frac{q_j}{2\pi\lambda} \exp\left(\frac{v_T X_T}{2a_{por}}\right) \left\{ \int_0^H (f_1(x,y,z,t) - f_2(x,y,z,t)) dh \right\} \quad (2)$$

$$r_{ij} = \sqrt{(x-x_i)^2 + (y-y_j)^2}$$

$$X_T = (x - x_i)$$

Where $\theta(x, y, z, t)_{MFLS}$ is the superposition temperature change of arbitrary point (x, y) in depth z caused by every borehole with an energy transfer rate q_j at the time of t. j is the borehole number, q_j is the given energy transfer rate per unit length of the BHE j#, X_T is the distance in x-direction to arbitrary point (x, y) with respect to the BHE located at (x_j, y_j).

4. Optimization Model for Multi-BHEs

Zeng et al. [7] developed a quasi three-dimensional model for BHEs taking into account the heat capacity of the materials inside borehole and the short circuiting between legs. With the aid of Multi-BHEs model (Eq. (2)) and quasi three-dimensional model of the circulating fluid, an optimization function is formulated as:

$$\text{minimize}(\sum_{j=1}^{n} t_{fo_j} / n) \tag{3}$$

Where t_{foj} is the outlet temperature of the BHE $j\#$ with the energy transfer rate q_j, the optimized solution is the optimized arrangement or the load distribution or the operation model for BHEs, the aim is to keep the average outlet circulating fluid temperature as small as possible, thus, a higher COP would be attained for GSHP system.

5. Application of Optimization Model

5.1. *Arrangement optimization*

The number of the BHEs n, the horizontal spacing $x_c=x_{j+1}-x_j$ and longitudinal spacing $y_c=y_{j+1}-y_j$ between boreholes are taken as the control objective, with the aid of Eq. (6), the arrangement optimization model for BHEs could be expressed as:

$$\text{minimize}(\sum_{j=1}^{n} t_{fo_j} \Big/ n = f(n, x_c, y_c)) \tag{4}$$

With constraint condition:

$$N_1 < n < N_2$$
$$3 \le x_c < \sqrt{S}$$
$$0 < y_c \le x_c$$

Where N_1 is minimum allowable number of BHEs, and N_2 is maximum allowable number of BHEs, *S* is the allowable area for BHEs fields.

The case of BHEs arrangement optimization was done in a square of 16×16 m^2 shown as Figure 2, considering the far field condition, the square for finite element numerical simulation was set 25×25 m^2. The total rejection load for the multi-BHEs was 57.6 KW, the installation depth was 60 m, the soil and grout thermal parameters was shown as Table 1 with the groundwater velocity u=2e-7 m/s, the inlet temperature was 32°C with the running time of 90 days. The number of optimized multi-BHEs in Figure 2.a is 18 with horizontal spacing x_c=5.3 m and longitudinal spacing y_c=2.65 m, the routine practice BHEs is 4×4 square lattice arrangement shown in Figure 2b.

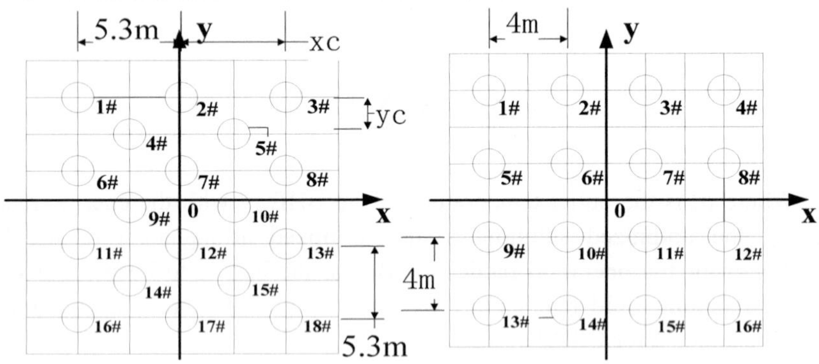

(a) Optimized 18 multi-BHEs (b) Routine 16 multi-BHEs

Fig. 2 Comparison diagram between optimized and non-optimized arrangement

With the aid of parameter in Table 1, the average outlet temperature change with groundwater flow velocity of optimized 18 multi-BHEs was compared with the routine 16 multi-BHEs shown in Figure 3, it shows that with the same total energy rejection load, the average outlet temperature of optimized 18 multi-BHEs is about 0.4 to 0.8°C lower than the routine 16 multi-BHEs.

Figure 4 showed the soil temperature distribution of the optimized 18 multi-BHEs fields and routine 16 multi-BHEs with the groundwater velocity (*Pe*=1.26) u=2e-7 m/s after 90 days running.

In Figure 4, it shows that the optimized soil average temperature of the multi-BHEs fields is about 1.0°C lower than the non-optimized fields; this indicates that the optimized multi-BHEs have a greater heat transfer capacity. It could be also found that the temperature of BHE 8# (Figure 2a) is only 1.75°C higher than the temperature of BHE 6# (Figure 2a) in the optimized BHEs fields, but the temperature of BHE 8# (Figure 2b) is 2.4 higher than the temperature of BHE 5# (Figure 2b) in the non-optimized BHEs fields, the temperature rise of downgradient BHE decreases 27%, therefore, the optimized arrangement could relieves the heat accumulated in the downgradient BHEs fields, which results from the groundwater flow.

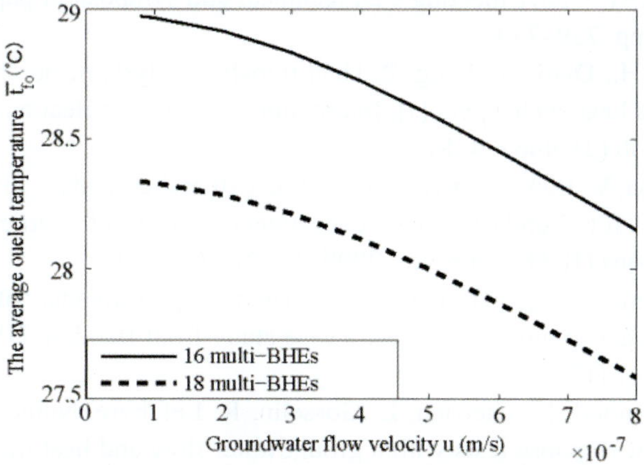

Fig. 3 Average outlet temperature change with groundwater flow velocity

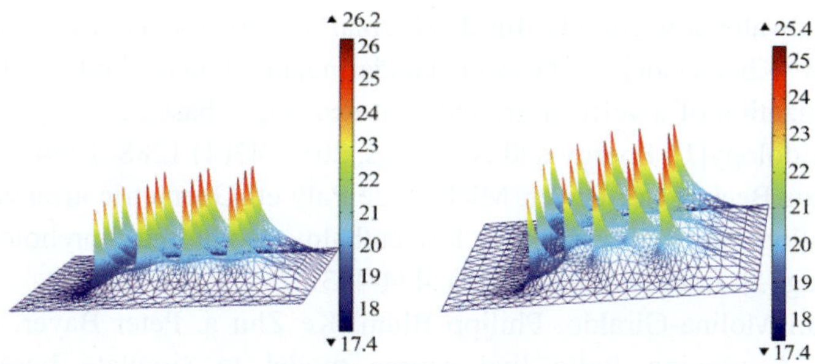

Fig. 4 Temperature distribution of the optimized and non-optimized arrangement multi-BHEs

6. Conclusions

Assuming the groundwater flow only in x-direction, which would improve heat transfer along the flow direction, the arrangement optimization was applied in a square of 16*16 m^2, the optimized 18 BHEs would make the average outlet temperature decrease 0.4 to 0.8°C and the average soil temperature fields decrease about 1°C compared to the routine 16 BHEs.

References

1. Ingersoll LR, Adler FT, Plass HJ, Ingersoll AC. Theory of earth heat exchangers for the heat pump [J]. ASHVE Trans 1950, 56:167–88.
2. Bernier MA. Ground-coupled heat pump system simulation [R]. In: ASHRAE winter meeting CD, technical and symposium papers. ASHRAE; 2001. pp. 739–750.
3. Zeng, H., Diao, N., Fang, Z. Heat transfer analysis of boreholes in vertical ground heat exchangers [J]. International Journal of Heat and Mass Transfer, 2003, 46 (3): 4467–4481.
4. Tatyana V. Bandos, alvaro Montero, Esther Fernandez. Finite line-source model for borehole heat exchangers: effect of vertical temperature variations [J]. Geothermics, 2009, 38 (2): 263–270.
5. H. Wang, C. Qi, H. Du, J. Gu, Thermal performance of borehole heat exchanger groundwater flow: a case study from Baoding [J]. Energy Build. 2009, 41 (12) :1368-1373.
6. J. Raymond, R. Therrien, L. Gosselin, R. Lefebvre, Numerical analysis of thermal response tests with a groundwater flow and heat transfer model [J]. Renew. Energ. 2011, 36 (1):315-324.
7. N. Diao, Q. Li, Z. Fang, Heat transfer in ground heat exchangers with groundwater advection [J] Int. J. Thermal Sci. 2004 43 (12):1203-1211.
8. Vahid Khalajzadeh, Ghassem Heidarinejad, Jelena Srebric Parameters optimization of a vertical ground heat exchanger based on response surface methodology[J]. Energy and Buildings, 2011, 43(4) 1288–1294.
9. Markus Beck, Peter Bayer, Michael de Paly etl Geometric arrangement and operation mode adjustment in low-enthalpy geothermal borehole fields for heating [J]. Energy, 2013, 49 (2) :434-443.
10. Nelson Molina-Giraldo, Philipp Blum, Ke Zhu a, Peter Bayer, Zhaohong Fang A moving finite line source model to simulate borehole heat exchangers with groundwater advection[J] International Journal of Thermal Sciences 2011, 50: 2506-2513.

Mitosis Detection in Breast Cancer Using Histological Images

Chao Li[1,a], Chu-Qing Cao[1,b] and Yun-Feng Gao[2,c]

[1]*HIT Wuhu Robot Technology Research Institute Laboratory, Wuhu, Anhui Province, China*

[2]*School of Mechatronics Engineering, Harbin Institute of Technology Harbin, Heilongjiang Province, China*

E-mail: [a]cynthia0217@163.com, [b]caochuqing@hitrobot.com.cn, [c]gfy@hit.edu.cn

In this paper, a scheme for mitosis detection in breast cancer histological images is proposed. The whole scheme includes three main stages, images pre-processing stage, feature extraction stage and classification stage. In the candidate detection phase, morphological operation and marker-controlled watershed segmentation algorithm to generate candidates are performed. In the feature extraction stage, a total of 90 features including conventional morphological features and circular Gabor features of the candidate region is extracted and circular Gabor filter banks are designed for feature extraction. In classification stage, three different AdaBoost algorithms are employed to classify the candidates, the results shows that Modest AdaBoost achieves highest accuracy of 73.2%.

Keywords: Marker-Controlled Watershed; Circular Gabor Filter; AdaBoost; Mitosis.

1. Introduction

To diagnose breast cancer, samples of tissue are removed from breast. From these samples, histology slides are produced. These slides are stained generally with H&E. Pathologists analyze breast biopsy slides and give them a grade according to some grading systems [1]. Mitotic count is an important parameter in breast cancer grading as it gives an evaluation of the aggressiveness of the tumor.

Detection of mitosis is a very challenging task, since in images, they appear as small objects which have a large variety of shapes. The four main phases of a mitosis are prophase, metaphase, anaphase and telophase. Figure 1 shows examples and description of the mitosis phases. The shape of the nucleus is very different depending on the phase of the mitosis. On its last stage, the telophase, a mitosis has two distinct nuclei, but they are not yet full individual cells. A mitosis in telophase must be counted as one single mitosis, it should not be miscounted as two mitosis. Artifacts are also common and should not be confused with mitosis.[2]

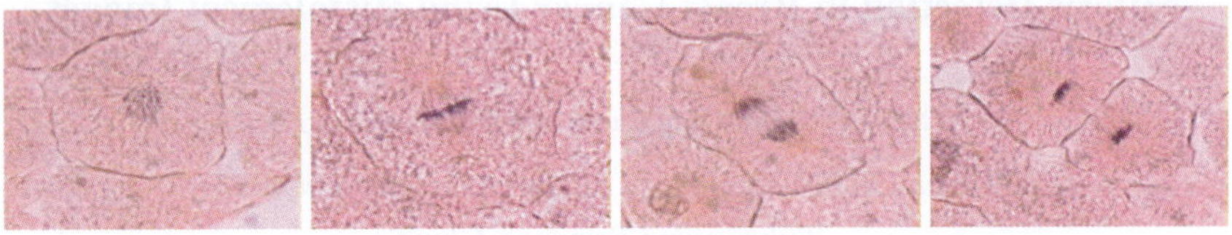

(a) (b) (c) (d)

Fig. 1. Four mitosis phases (a) Prophase (b) Metaphase. (c) Anaphase (d) Telophase

A Computer Aided Detection (CAD) system with computer vision algorithms would help the doctors use the computer output as a "second opinion" which would greatly save the doctors' efforts[3-6]. Firstly, segmentation of nucleus, cytoplasm of the cells is a very complicated task and is error prone owing to overlapping cells and not clear boundaries of cells. In this paper, we proposed a scheme for mitosis detection in breast cancer histological images. The whole scheme includes four stages, images pre-processing stage, feature extraction stage and classification stage.

2. Proposed Mitosis Detection Scheme

2.1. *Image pre-processing*

Figure 2 illustrates the original image of the mitosis and ground truth of the corresponding image. The main step of marker-controlled watershed segmentation are described as follows, and the flowchart is shown is Figure 3:

Step 1: Read in the single plane of each color image.

Step 2: Use the gradient magnitude as the segmentation function.

Step 3: Mark the foreground objects.

Step 4: Compute background markers.

Step 5: Compute the watershed transform of the segmentation function.

Follow these steps, figure 4 illustrates the intermediate results of the whole process.

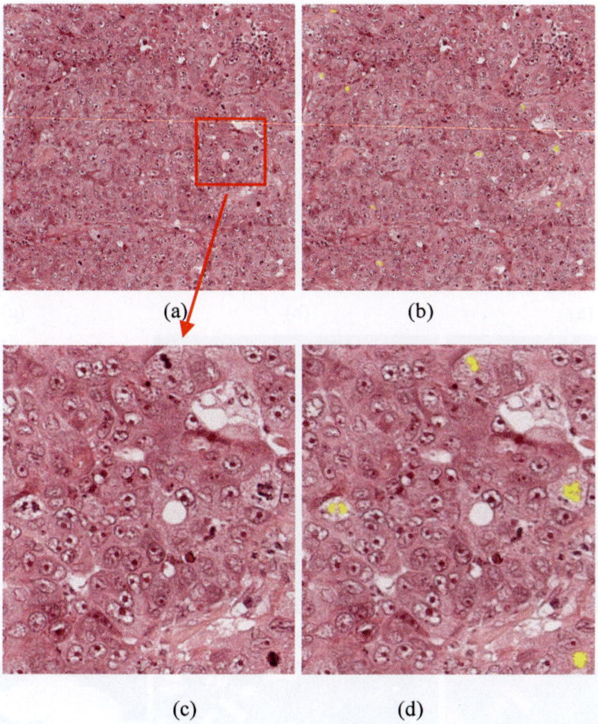

Fig. 2. (a) Shows original image of the mitosis (b) Shows the ground truth of the corresponding image (c) and (d) are the enlarged part in picture (a) and (b) respectively

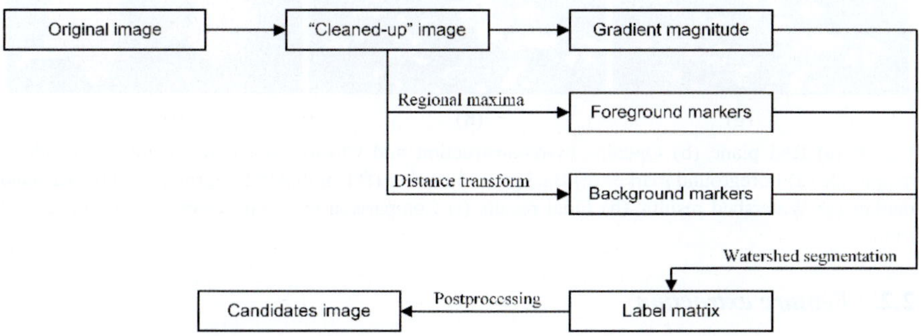

Fig. 3. The flowchart of marker controlled watershed segmentation

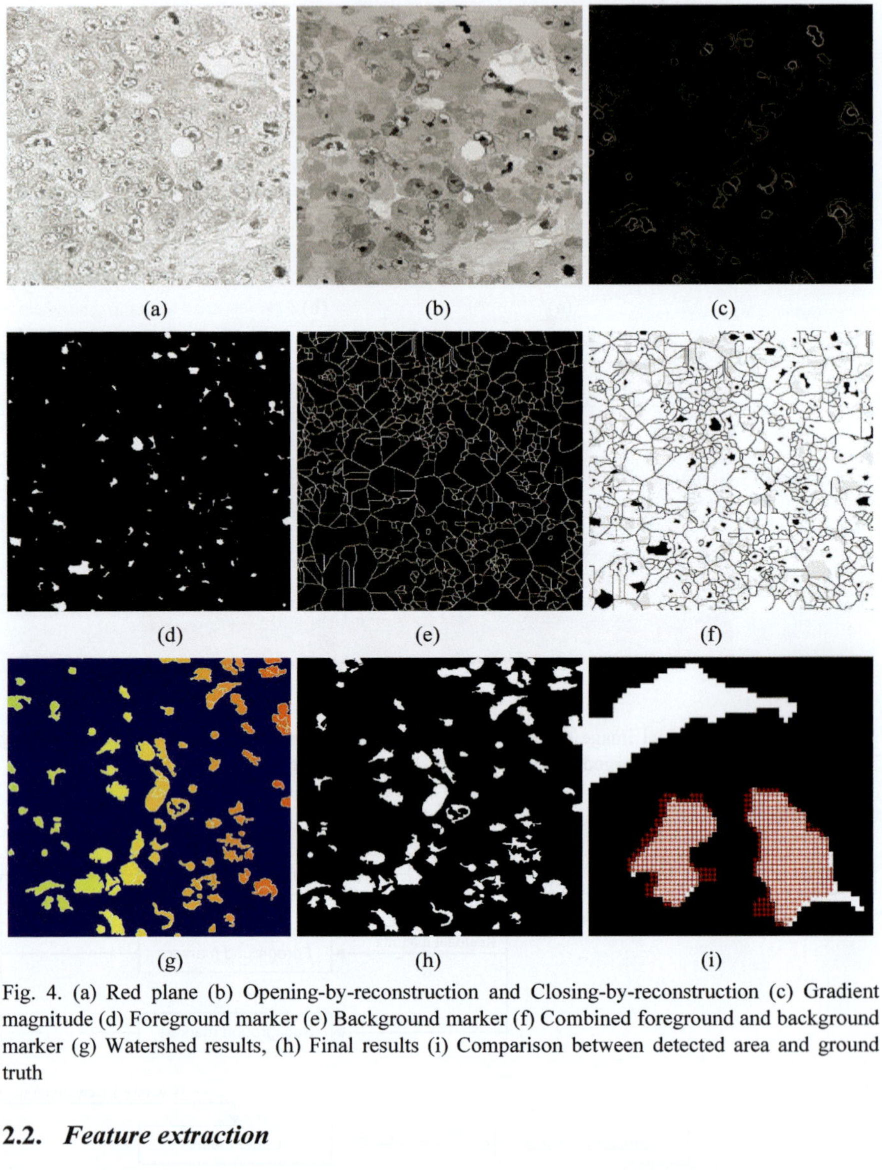

Fig. 4. (a) Red plane (b) Opening-by-reconstruction and Closing-by-reconstruction (c) Gradient magnitude (d) Foreground marker (e) Background marker (f) Combined foreground and background marker (g) Watershed results, (h) Final results (i) Comparison between detected area and ground truth

2.2. *Feature extraction*

After image pre-processing step, we extracted the useful features in the next stage. The full feature list (as shown in Table 1) includes commonly used conventional features and circular Gabor features. For common features, we extract 14 features including Area, Major and Minor axis length, eccentricity, elliptical deviation, Equivalent diameter, sphericity, compactness, shape, Mean,

Variance, energy, entropy, and homogeneity for each channel of RGB image. All the features used in this study must be strictly rotation invariant ones. Traditional Gabor filters are well known as orientation detectors. Traditional Gabor filters are well known as orientation detectors. But in the application of extracting orientation invariant features, their main advantages become vital disadvantages. Circular Gabor filters get rid of the property of orientation selectivity, and go in for extracting rotation invariant features [7]. While Circular Gabor filters get rid of the property of orientation selectivity, and go in for extracting rotation invariant features, which can be written as Eq.(1).

$$G(x,y)=g(x,y)\exp\left(2\pi F\sqrt{x^2+y^2}\right) \tag{1}$$

Where F is the radial frequency and $g(x,y)$ is a 2-D Gaussian envelope assumed to be isotropic as Eq.(2):

$$g(x,y)=\frac{1}{2\pi\sigma^2}\exp\left[-\frac{x^2+y^2}{2\sigma^2}\right] \tag{2}$$

While Circular Gabor filters (CGF) get rid of the property of orientation selectivity, and go in for extracting rotation invariant features. Figure 5 shows the 2-D views of the real and imaginary part and Fourier transform of the CGF.

Table 1. The extracted feature list

Category	Features
Size and Shape	Area
	Major and Minor axis length, eccentricity, elliptical deviation
	Equivalent diameter, sphericity, compactness, shape
Statistical (moments)	Mean, Variance
Texture	Energy, entropy, homogeneity, circular Gabor features

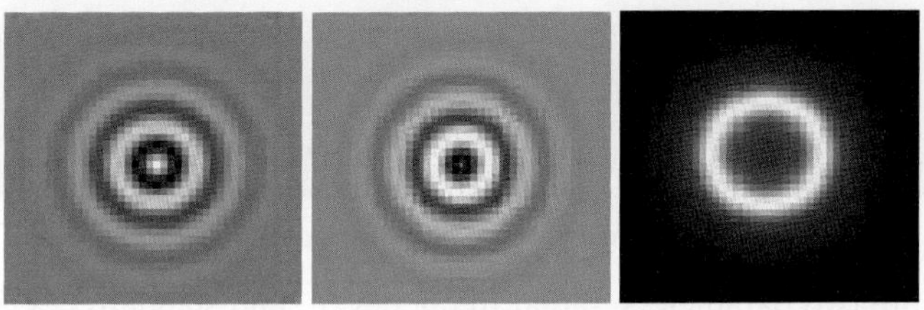

(a) (b) (c)

Fig. 5. (a) and (b) are the 2-D views of the real and imaginary part of a CGF (c) is the Fourier transform of the CGF

2.3. *Classification*

In the classification stage, we compare three AdaBoost methods, that is Real Ada Boost, Gentle AdaBoost and Modest AdaBoost. Real AdaBoost is the generalization of a basic AdaBoost algorithm first introduced by Fruend and Schapire [8]. Gentle AdaBoost is a more robust and stable version of real AdaBoost. So far, it has been the most practically efficient boosting algorithm. Generally, Gentle AdaBoost performs slightly better than Real AdaBoost on regular data, but is considerably better on noisy data, and much more resistant to outliers. Modest AdaBoost – regularized tradeoff of AdaBoost, mostly aimed for better generalization capability and resistance to overfitting [9].

3. Experiments and Results

In this study, the dataset we tested are the RGB images of H&E stained slides of breast cancer downloaded from ICPR 2012 contest [10]. The dataset include 35 RGB images and the images were provided with manually marked ground data. There are 1 to 17 mitosis in single image, and the total ground truth mitosis are 226.

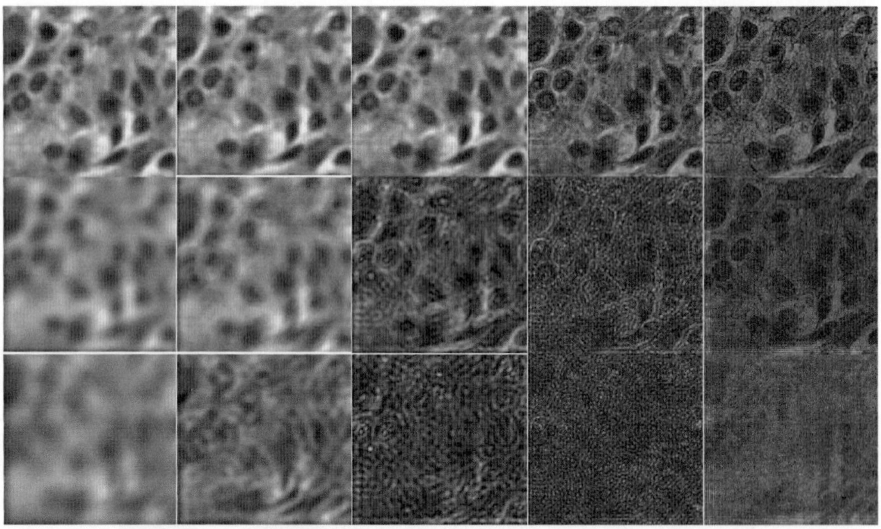

Fig. 6. Circular Gabor filters bank of 3 scales.

There are two parameters, radial frequency F and standard deviation σ for circular Gabor filter, which are needed to be specified. It is a lot easier compared with the design of traditional Gabor filters. Various combinations of the two parameters produce a set of circular Gabor filters. The parameters are chosen according to Jain's method [37]. Figure 6 shows the results of circular Gabor filter bank filtered histological images at 5 frequencies, 3 scales [3, 7, 11].

Central Frequencies are selected as follows (N is the matrix size):

$$2\left\{1,2,4,8,16,\ldots,\frac{N}{4}\right\}/N$$

For each candidate, extract 3×5 circular Gabor feature vector.

We extracted 90 features including conventional features and circular Gabor features in total.

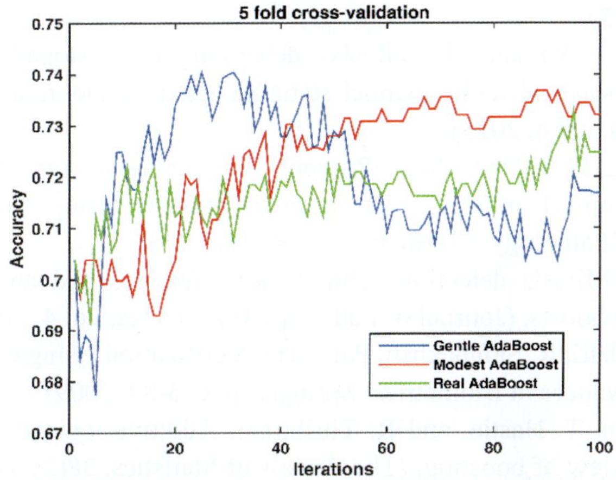

Fig. 7. The accuracy of three algorithms, Real AdaBoost, Modest AdaBoost and Gentle AdaBoost.

The experimental results of three different boosting algorithms are shown in Figure 7. Among three methods, the Modest AdaBoost algorithm achieves the highest accuracy of 73.2% which is comparable to state-of-art methods presented in the literature [3-7]. And moreover, the experiments show that in terms of accuracy and overfitting Modest AdaBoost outperforms both Real and Gentle AdaBoost.

4. Conclusions

The proposed method applied the combination of conventional and circular Gabor features and ensemble of AdaBoost classifiers to the mitosis detection problem. The circular Gabor features were employed for texture feature analysis. The technique exploits the local characteristics of cells. Modest AdaBoost algorithm obtained the highest accuracy of 73.2%.

References

1. M.N. Gurcan, L.E. Boucheron, A. Can, A. Madabhushi, N.M. Rajpoot, and B. Yener, Histopathological Image Analysis: A Review, (IEEE Reviews in Biomedical Engineering, vol. 2, pp 147-171, 2009).
2. Pathology Reporting of Breast Disease, (NHS Cancer Screening Programmes and The Royal College of Pathologists, 2005).
3. C.D. Malon, E. Cosatto, Classification of mitotic figures with convolutional neural networks and seeded blob features(Journal of Pathology Informatics. Vol. 4, 2013).
4. H. Irshad, Automated mitosis detection in histopathology using morphological and multi-channel statistics features, (Journal of Pathology Informatics. vol 4, 2013).
5. A.M. Khan, H. ElDaly, N.M. Rajpoot, A gamma-gaussian mixture model for detection of mitotic cells in breast cancer histopathology images (Journal of Pathology Informatics. vol 4, 2013).
6. F.B. Tek, Mitosis detection using generic features and an ensemble of cascade adaboosts, (Journal of Pathology Informatics. vol 4, 2013).
7. A. Ghandehari, R. Safabakhsh, Palmprint Verification Using Circular Gabor Filter. (Advances in Biometrics: Springer; p. 675-84, 2009).
8. J. Friedman, T. Hastie, and R. Tibshirani. Additive logistic regression: A statistical view of boosting. (The Annals of Statistics, 38(2):337–374, April 2000).
9. A. Vezhnevets, V. Vezhnevets, Modest AdaBoost- Teaching AdaBoost to Generalize Better. (Graphicon-2005, Novosibirsk Akademgorodok, Russia, 2005).
10. L. Roux, D. Racoceanu, N. Loménie, M. Kulikova, H. Irshad, J. Klossa, F. Capron, C. Genestie, G.L. Naour, M.N. Gurcan, Mitosis detection in breast cancer histological images: An ICPR 2012 contest (http://ludo17.free.fr/mitos_2012/ , 2012)

Tunnel Lighting System Control Design and Research

Wei-Sheng Liu[1,a], Yan-Jun Liu[2,b,*] and Yi-Ping Zhang[3,c]
[1]*Heibei University of Technology,*
Tianjin, China
[2]*University of Jyvaskyla, Jyvaskyla,*
Finland
[3]*Tianjin Heping District Xinhua Worker University,*
Tianjin, China
Email: [a]ws.liu@163.com, [b]435155208@qq.com, [c]935507994@qq.com

By using the studies of highway tunnel as research background, a tunnel lighting energy-saving LED lamp control system is designed, which according to the requirements of highway tunnel lighting safety, comfort level and energy-saving. The system uses monitor computer as the operation control core, and median machine as the local output controller. By using CAN bus control, going through the sensor module to collect vehicle flow rate, the speed and the brightness information. Subsequently, the system input control parameters as the control signal output to the lighting equipments from the operation control center are collected. Therefore, the command to the microcontroller and control the real-time automatic switch to on-off state in the different sections of the tunnel lighting is implemented. Based on the development of the lightings intelligence control system of CAN bus technology, to improve the lighting scalable class, the control precision, and the lighting continuity. In the meantime, it also saves the electric energy of the operation system. This paper includes the diagram for the tunnel control system, the research on the structure of the control system, and the usage analysis of the features and requirements of the control system.

Keywords: Tunnel Lighting; CAN Bus Control; Low Energy Consumption; Security; System Composition.

*Corresponding author.

1. Introduction

The LED energy-saving tunnel lighting demonstration project explored new options for highway tunnel lighting, energy saving and increased cost-efficiency [1]. In the field of highway tunnel lighting, LED lights have broad application prospects. The implementation of this project provided the basis for promoting and applying LED lighting to the national related departments so they could formulate relevant policies and the corresponding technical standards for the field of highway tunnel lighting. The lab result verified this design scheme's maturity and reliability. By using LED lighting we were able to save electricity by 50%~70% when compared to the traditional high pressure sodium lamps (HPSL).

The basic tunnel lighting system design is drafted under the condition of the safety driving assurance and standard driving comfort level. The design also simplified the control method of lighting circuit, prioritize the maintenance conviniency and in the mean while to save as much as energy as possible. The LED light control system can raise the human recognition ability and driving reaction speed, as a result efficiently decrease the occurrence of traffic accidents. Under the circumstances of keeping the persistence of the intensity of illumination, and that increased the visual brightness of the pavement, improved the driving safety. The features of the lighting product is glare free, uniformity of road surface illumination, and also conducively reduce the Zebra Effect. LED's have the following advantages:

Wide range of the working voltage

Longer operational life

Lower energy consumption

Reduce certain amount of costs of cables and electrical equipments

2. The Design for the Tunnel Lighting Control System

Based on the requirements of energy saving and the safety of tunnel lighting, this design for the tunnel lighting system uses the monitoring system as a control core, and uses a microcontroller to set up local area network. It can update the control method base on the measurements of the parameters outside the tunnel, for example like the change of brightness, car speed, traffic flow, therefore to implement the real time automation control of tunnel lighting system and also achieve the efficiency of safe energy saving. LED tunnel lighting system is using more advanced intelligence control technology, as a result decreased the cost of lighting. The lighting drive can receive the real-time control signals, by turning on-and-off state in different parts of the tunnel to save energy resource efficiently. The LED tunnel lighting control system mainly uses the surveillance center to control computers, illuminance transducers, pressure coils and the preinstalled LED tunnel lighting controller. It also handles the data communication. The system communication method uses CAN buses as a result of an improvement of the system anti-interference performance and also increase the reliability of the system [2]. The tunnel lighting control system is shown in Figure 1:

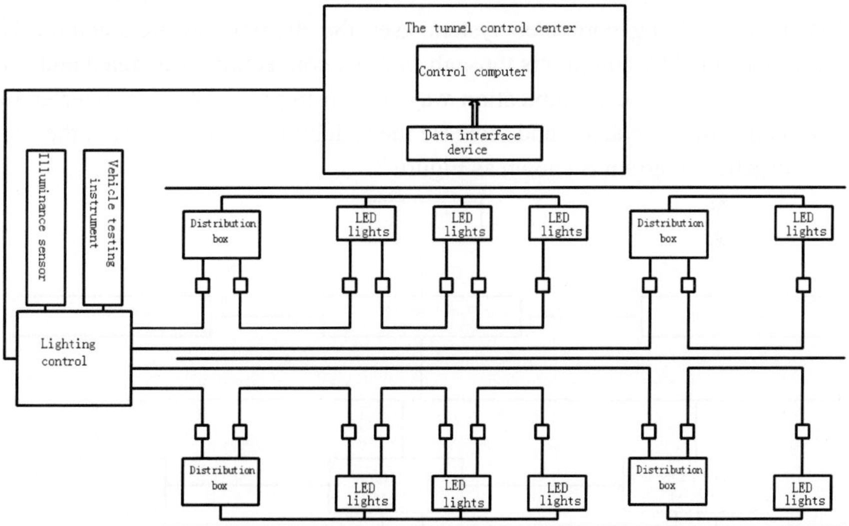

Fig. 1 The tunnel lighting control system schematic diagram

Lighting control system collect the information from the sensor, pressure coil, gathering outside the tunnel illumination value, tunnel illumination value, flow, speed and other values. After this, upload the information to the control center for analysis and process. According to the features of tunnel, using the single-chip microcomputer control the lighting of entrance section, transition section, the basic section and exit section.

In accordance with the master control computer requirements, tunnel lighting control system uses the field bus to distributed control commands to the lightings microcontroller [3]. The LED lighting control unit changes its corresponding working status according to the control command to control the tunnel lighting brightness in different sections. In the mean time, the master control computer can detect the intensity of illumination by using the outdoor illumination sensors. Therefore, determined base on whether the current system of illuminance level can meet the requirements of the tunnel lighting or not. If it does not meet, then it has to go through the tunnel lighting controller again, where the controller generates new control commands, to control LED tunnel light in real-time and change the illuminance in the tunnel in time. Master control computer achieve the functionality of the data preservation, discriminate, sampling, and so on.

3. Tunnel Lighting System Bus Structure Design

LED tunnel lighting computer system uses the distribution architecture. The system is formed by computers through Internet connection. It selected and used the CAN bus as the communication way, which improves the anti-interference performance of the system, and increase the reliability of the system at the same time. Structure diagram is shown as Figure 2.

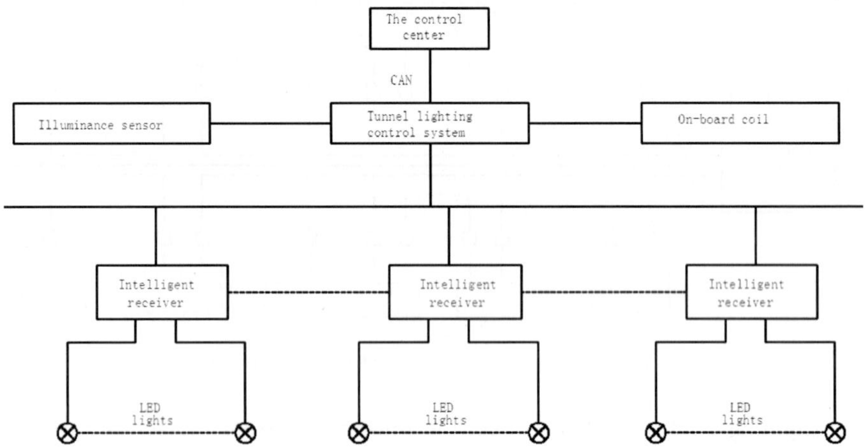

Fig. 2 The structure diagram

CAN bus has excellent communication protocol, and the signal transmission speed is larger than RS-485. Under serious error cases, the CAN node has a self-closing output functionality to eliminate the impacts on the operation of the rest of the other notes on the bus. The area controlled by the control system is divided into five sections: the entrance section, transition section I, transition section II, intermediate section and exit section. And it meets the standard regulations for different sections of the lighting illumination.

Whenever there is a vehicle entering the tunnel, the vehicle detector sends a signal to the control system. Then the system activates the tunnel lighting and checks whether there is vehicle following the car that caused the first signal to be sent, and then turn off the other corresponded lighting [4]. In the mean time, tunnel lighting control system will detect the weather outside the tunnel whether it is sunny, cloudy, heavy overcast according to the detected light intensity value outside the tunnel which is provided by the luminance sensor. This function increases efficiency by turning off the corresponding lights that are not needed at that specific time. This synchronism control strategy analyze the real time situation and make the right adjustment for the configuration.

Tunnel lighting is divided into six different grades of control levels to make the control commands. The six different control level grades are defined by the weather situation: sunny day, cloudy day, overcast sky, heavy cloudy day, night, late night. Each of them are assigned with a different circuit. Also, the basic LED lighting in the tunnel can be used as emergency lighting by using an uninterrupted power system (UPS) to supply the power. The lightings can achieve the automatic control by the collected data and analysis through illuminance transducer and pressure coil. Moreover, lights conduct the real time control on the lights indifferent sections in the tunnel so that saved the energy resources efficiently.

The lighting reinforcement at the tunnel entrances, that to strengthen lighting therefore turn on all LED lights at sunny day, the interval decrease by half at cloudy day, the interval decrease by other half at overcast day, turn on only 1/8 of the entrance section (the rest of the full closed) at heavy cloudy day, and shut down all the time at night and late night. Power for the emergency lighting is turned on all the time. The street lights that outside of the tunnel are turned on during the evening and late night and fully turned off the rest of the time. Tunnel lighting electric power distribution system uses the "emiting + trunk system" distribution method.

The benefits of the LED tunnel lighting control system: First of all it makes the wiring design for the lighting much more simplified and the costs of laying down the wiring are significantly reduced. When comparing the use of LED lighting and the use of HPSL's in traditional tunnel lighting, LED lights use about 50% less electricity. Plus if used in junction with the tunnel lighting control system, there can be an about 20% decrease in electricity usage.

Along with the development of modern science and technology, the advanced LED lightings and control technologies will be widely implemented in tunnel lighting system. This technology will also present a significant role in improving tunnel operation efficiency, travel safety and reducing the maintenance cost.

4. Economic and Social Benefits Evaluation

The use of LED tunnel lighting control system, first of all make the lamps and lanterns lighting wiring design greatly simplified, wiring construction costs are greatly reduced. Using the control system of LED tunnel lighting and tunnel lighting without tunnel lighting control system of LED tunnel lighting, compared to saving electricity about 30%, compared with the traditional tunnel lighting of high pressure sodium lamp can power saving about 80% less. With the development of modern science and technology, LED lighting equipment and control technology because of their excellent characteristics, will get more extensive application in the tunnel lighting system, to improve the efficiency of the operation of the tunnel, reduce running cost, improve the driving safety play a bigger role.

5. Conclusions

Nowadays, most of the tunnels requires huge amount of lighting for long time illumination. By using the traditional way of continuous lighting or voice control lighting, it is difficult to implement the automatic control of lighting system. Therefore it is a waste of valuable energy resources and also causes the damage to the equipments. There are already some similar lighting intelligence control system exist in domestic and overseas. But due to the expensive costs of such kind of products, so that the implementation is limited. Base on the lighting intelligence control system of the design and development of CAN bus technology, it solves the issues of automatic control and reduce the wiring complexity inside the tunnel. Also the work of maintenance and maintenance costs is reduced.

References

1. Wei-sheng Liu, Dan Sun, Yi-ping Zhang, Tunnel lighting system unit emergency lighting control design and research, ICCEA2014.
2. Wei-qing Tao, High-level protocol for CAN bus CAN open, Automation technology, 51:2642 Mongolia, 2004
3. Ji-qiang Xia, Chun Xiang Xing, Field bus, industrial control network technology, Beijing university of aeronautics and astronautics press, 2003
4. Xiao-jiang Xiang, De-xing Wu, etc. Road and tunnel lighting analysis system (R&TLAS), Highway, 10.1999

An Error Classification-Based Query Error Correction Method in Chinese Search Engine

Feng-Qi Li and Jian Shen

School of Software Technology, Dalian University of Technology, Dalian, Liaoning, China

E-mail: dllgsj@mail.dlut.edu.cn

Search engine, as a common tool in people's daily life, can bring users better experience with its automatic error correction for the input, which is an indispensable function of the current search engines. This paper proposes an error classification-based method to correct the various query errors which usually happen in Chinese search engines by analyzing the online users' query logs. To solve pinyin problem, training Hidden Markov model is explored. Experimental results demonstrate that appropriate methods in this paper acting on different error types can effectively improve the precision of error correction.

Keywords: Chinese Search Query Logs; Query Error Correction; Hidden Markov Model.

1. Introduction

There are more than 10%~15% queries with spelling errors by analyzing the query log of the search engine[1]. Although the pattern of Chinese is different from that of English language, using the Chinese input method does not normally occur the non-word, however, in the Chinese search engine query errors reach to 10 percents [2]. Users want to get good results that are returned, but due to a spelling error or having no idea about the correct spelling, if a search engine does not have good error correction process, the user is likely to get very few search results or there will be larger gaps between search results and the target query. There has been a long history of spelling correction research in natural language processing and information retrieval[3], but its application in Chinese search engine query correction is still a challenge. Many methods and techniques used in English spelling correction are often difficult to be used in Chinese due to differences in language structures and grammatical rules. It is particularly important to design a Chinese search engine query error correcting model to solve the query error effectively.

In this paper we propose a query correction processing method based on data dictionary and edit distance algorithm. At the same time, the hidden Markov model is applied to query correction processing of pinyin, and further enhance the search engine query accuracy rate and the recall rate.

The rest of the paper is structured as follows: Section 2 introduces other related work already existing in the error correction processing; Section 3, describes our approach. Section 4 shows our experimental results and analyze performance. Section 5 concludes the paper and put forward the direction of future work.

2. Related Work

Spelling correction is well developed in the field of computational linguistics, and dictionary based query error correction method has been proposed [4]. The correction is found by comparing each query split into single words with a dictionary, to find out whether the word has one or more characters added or missing. Traditionally candidate ranking is based on scores such as weights to different edit operations or leveraging candidate frequencies [5]. Wagner and Fuscher [6] proposed a method of measuring the distance between strings, and a fixed operation is given a fixed value. Brill and Cucerzan [1] first used query log to help correct spelling mistakes. They also mentioned that using the traditional edit distance as error model may cause inappropriate corrections, so a weighted distance algorithm has been put forward. These methods are still used in the industrial field for a long period of time.

Many researchers are looking for new ways to have a better effect on the exploration of error correction. Ahmad and Kondrak [7] proposed to learn the edit distance weights in the query log to establish the error model by directly using Expectation Maximization algorithm. Duan et al. [8] proposed a generative model based on a noisy channel for the intended query, and trained a Markov n-gram transformation model to captures users' spelling behaviors. The query log can help to improve the error correction, but there are some rarely appeared words, under such a circumstance, only using search logs is difficult to solve problems. [9] Chen et al. added the search results of information to the error correction algorithm, which has been proved to achieve better effects.

The relevant work of query error correction in Chinese search engine includes integrating traditional way into training a Chinese character from n-gram language model on a large scale corpus, transforming corpus into pinyin to obtain pinyin model and the tone as the third model to improve spelling errors detection [10]. But this method is just for detection instead of correction. Besides being modeled by using language feature, how to add the feature of search engine to query error correction is also the key point of our research.

3. Method for Query Error Correction

3.1. *Motivation*

At present, there are many researches on query error correction in search engines, which aimed at exploring how to build a better model to identify errors. This direction evolved out a statistical context-sensitive spelling check [11] [12], by using morphological analyzer, dictionary lookup, and probability of similarity for error correction [9]. A method is proposed that integrating Hamming Distance and n-gram algorithms for typing errors[13]. In the above methods, however, the similarities between two queries are modeled on the average of many misspelling pairs, which cause that some kinds of spelling error can not be corrected, such as pinyin or acronym in Chinese search engines. By analyzing the query log, we summarize the query error types as follows:

Table 1. Query error types.

No.	Type
1	Full pinyin input
2	Mixture of Chinese and Pinyin
3	Homophone
4	Mixture of Chinese and Arabia numeral
5	Typos
6	Character added
7	Character missing

In this work, we design a kind of hybrid method which contains dictionary lookup, edit distance algorithm and HMM, striving to correct all kinds of query errors that appear in Chinese search engine. The workflow of the model is as follows: first, Pre-process the query to extract the core content of the query; use the common wrong dictionary based on query log for priority matching, which is for quickly identifying the error query and correction pairs to solve mixture of Chinese and Arabia numeral; then use the edit distance algorithm to correct the typos, characters added and characters missing errors; finally, from the table 1, we found that the first three are related to the pinyin. So the trained Hidden Markov model is used to solve the problem.

3.2. *Pre-processing the query*

In normal users' queries, it is inevitable that too long input and too many useless words will undoubtedly bring confusion and trouble for subsequent correction treatment. For a query, the early stage of query analysis is about word segmentation processing and word tagging. After analyzing a large number of queries, to search for relevant content (e.g. video search), users often input key words about video types or specific details before or after the name of a video such as "TV series", "the-film", "the third department", "second season" etc. It is clear that in this part there is no need for analysis and correction, so we can temporarily ignore these words before the formal error correction.

When a query arrives, the query result set $\{t_1, t_2, \ldots t_n\}$of the seg-words will be first obtained and checked, if $t_1$or t_n is a pre-set specific word, it will be temporarily stored, and the remaining seg-words will start for error correction as a whole query, after correction, the correction query together with the previously stored token will be returned for the senior processing of the search engine.

3.3. *Common query error correction*

Considering the actual situation, in many cases, some error correction task is very urgent, like sudden hot event or very popular video, which need fast processing, it may take several weeks by using the regular method, which obviously could not satisfy the requirement for some emergency query.

We use query log and artificial added way to establish a common query map, which has common errors and candidates. When a query starts for error correction, first in the map, if an error has been found, the corresponding error correction results will be returned, otherwise the error correction processing will go on for the next.

Another situation, users often input Chinese digital into Arabia digital. The program will traverse the query characters, and the number of Arabia will be replaced by the corresponding Chinese figures. After completion, the traversal will generate a new string result, and the error correction process continues.

3.4. *Edit distance query error correction*

To solve the query of typos, characters added and characters missing, we use edit distance algorithm for error correction. In our method the editing operation is allowed to replace a character, insert a character and delete a character. We define a function Eq.(1), which represents the string to string edit distance, the length of first string is i, the length of second string is j. Eq.(2) define $F(i, j)$.

$$\text{edit}(i,j) = \begin{cases} 0 & i = 0 \text{ and } j = 0 \\ j & i = 0 \text{ and } j > 0 \\ i & i > 0 \text{ and } j = 0 \\ \min\{F(i,j)\} & i \geq 1 \text{ and } j \geq 1 \end{cases} \quad (1)$$

$$F(i,j) = \text{edit}(i-1,j) + 1, \text{edit}(i,j-1) + 1, \text{edit}(i-1,j-1) + f(i,j) \quad (2)$$

Among this, when the first string i_{th} character is not equal to the second string j_{th} character, f(i,j)=1; else f(i,j)=0.

For a query Q, according to editing distance algorithm, the first step is to calculate editing distance between all the strings with Q, choose the query with minimum editing distance as the candidate, and then determine the most possible candidate word C according to search frequency of the candidate word. In order to improve the matching extent and the retrieval efficiency, the Trie tree is used to store and search.

3.5. *Hidden Markov model*

Hidden Markov model is used in this paper to deal with Pinyin queries. Training a Hidden Markov model needs to build three matrices: initial state matrix, state transfer matrix and the emit matrix.

The initial state matrix is constructed, based on queries input. The method proposed is first extracting queries from the query log and choosing the first character of each query. After processing, we can get the first character and its corresponding search frequency, C represents a character, n represents the search frequency of C, N represents the total search frequency of all characters, initial probabilities π of character C is calculated in Eq.(3):

$$\pi = P(C) = \frac{n}{N} \quad (3)$$

The state transition matrix also depends on the queries. Transfer search times of two adjacent characters are obtained by map/reduce from Hadoop. Assuming that the next state A of the character C has three candidates, and the corresponding search counts wereN_1, N_2, N_3, then we can get the state C transfer matrix, the corresponding transition probability α is calculated in Eq.(4):

$$\alpha_{A1} = P(A|C) = {N_1}/{(N_1 + N_2 + N_3)} \quad (4)$$

The emit matrix needs the Chinese character pinyin table, the common phrases and idioms table. In the map phase, each query acts as an input, and each character will get its correct pinyin through the above two tables. In the reduce stage, the results of map are used as the input to calculate the number of Chinese characters and corresponding pinyin, and then output the result. If a character C is a polyphone, with two pronunciation of C_1 and C_2, the number of C_1 appears as N_1, the number of C_2 appears as N_2, for characters C the emission probability P is calculated in Eq.(5):

$$P(C_1) = {}^{N_1}/_{(N_1 + N_2)} \tag{5}$$

Pinyin correction is the process of finding out the most possible Hidden state sequence according to the observation state sequence. Pinyin query is the observation state sequence. Viterbi algorithm is rewritten in this paper and with the help of the three trained matrix mentioned above, it can give a Chinese character sequence by dynamic programming algorithm, which has the maximum probability.

4. Experimental Results

4.1. *Dataset*

In this experiments, a dictionary set was established with 400473 pieces of data which are extracted for common query error correction and editing distance correction from tens of millions of pieces of data, based on query logs of a Chinese video website from March to June, 2016, and then the dictionary, together with Pinyin table, converse table between simplified Chinese and traditional Chinese, commonly used Pinyin table of phrases, are used for training the Hidden Markov Model.

4.2. *Results*

In order to test our method, 5000 query are randomly selected from the online query log selected as the test data, and 707 queries are found as error data after manual inspection, with the error rate being 14.14%. The 707 queries are classified according to error types.

Table 2. Query error distribution in test set.

No.	Type	Error number	Error rate
1	Full pinyin input	134	19.0%
2	Mixture of Chinese and Pinyin	22	3.1%
3	Homophone	103	14.7%
4	Mixture of Chinese and Arabia numeral	20	2.8%
5	Typos	155	21.9%
6	Character added	90	12.7%
7	Character missing	177	25.0%
8	Others	6	0.8%

From the table 2 we can see that the main error types are distributed in less characters, typos, and full pinyin input instead of Chinese characters. Our method achieves good results in the experiment, and the performance is evaluated by the following metrics:

Precision: the number of correct correlation results generated by the method divided by the total number of query which has results.

Recall: the number of correction for error queries generated by the method divided by the total number of error queries in the test set.

F-measure: F-measure integrated precision and recall results, when the F-measure is higher, it can be explained that the test method is more effective. We use F1 measure for our results.

Table 3. Performance results for different models.

Method	Precision	Recall	F-Measure
Baseline method	55.7%	75%	63.9%
Method proposed	88.1%	81.8%	84.8%

Baseline method is the traditional method which uses the corpus and editing distance algorithm to achieve query error correction. From the table 3, we can see that our method is better than the baseline method in terms of precision, recall, and F- measure.

On the other hand, through analyzing online search engine real-time search results during two months, the percentage of query errors for the search engine problems dropped down from 25% to 18% after query error correction method we proposed has been used.

5. Conclusions

This paper proposes a linear integrated method to solve several types of query errors of the Chinese search engine, the method for error correction proposed in this paper is better than the basic method in terms of recall rate and precision rate, and can also bring highly improved search engine performance.

In this method, all input query will get through the error correction process, including the correct queries, therefore it may happen that even the correct queries have to experience the error correcting process, so the future research will focus on and target at how to identify and classify errors, and reduce the processing time of the correct query. In addition, for those errors which still exists and can not be corrected, exploration in the future is suggested to focus on learning results of search engine returned and making full use of users' accurate judgment for query correction with better effect.

References

1. Cucerzan S and Brill E, Spelling Correction as an Iterative Process that Exploits the Collective Knowledge of Web Users,(EMNLP,2004), ACL, (Barcelona, Spain. 2004) pp.293-300.
2. Hu Y, Liu Y F et al, An Online System for Chinese Query Correction in Search Engine. Vol.1, in Proc. Journal of Chinese Information Processing, (2016)(In Chinese)
3. Kukich K, Techniques for automatically correcting words in text, in Proc. ACM Computing Surveys, 1992, 24(4) pp.377-439.
4. Damerau F J. A, Technique for Computer Detection and Correction of Spelling Errors, in ACM of Communications, 1964, 7(3) pp.171-176.
5. Levenshtein V I, Binary codes capable of correcting deletions, insertions and reversals, Doklady Akademii Nauk Sssr, 1965, 10(1) pp.707-710.
6. Wagner R A and Lowrance R, The String-to-String Correction Problem. Journal of the ACM, 1974, 21(1) pp.168-173.
7. Ahmad F, Kondrak G. Learning a Spelling Error Model from Search Query Logs.HLT/EMNLP (Vancouver, British Columbia, Canada. 2005) pp.955-962.
8. Duan H, Hsu B J. Online spelling correction for query completion, in Proc. WWW,(2011) pp.117-126.
9. Chen Q and Li M, Zhou M. Improving Query Spelling Correction Using Web Search Results, EMNLP-CoNLL (Prague, Czech Republic. 2007) pp.181-189.
10. Jin P, Chen X, Guo Z, et al, Integrating Pinyin to Improve Spelling Errors Detection for Chinese Language, in Proc. International Joint Conferences on Web Intelligence. IEEE (2014) pp.455-458.

11. Kim M, Choi S K, Kwon H C, Context-Sensitive Spelling Error Correction Using Inter-Word Semantic Relation Analysis. International Conference on Information Science and Applications. (2014) pp.1-4.
12. Kim M, Jin J, Kwon H C, et al, Statistical Context-Sensitive Spelling Correction Using Typing Error Rate, in Proc. IEEE of International Conference on Computational Science and Engineering. (2013) pp.1242-1246.
13. Hodge V J, Austin J. A, comparison of standard spell checking algorithms and a novel binary neural approach. Knowledge & Data Engineering IEEE Transactions on, 2003, 15(5) pp.1073-1081.

The Mathematical Model of Tunnel Lighting Brightness and Application

Wei-Sheng Liu[1,a], Yan-Jun Liu[2,b,*] and Yi-Ping Zhang[3,c]

[1]*Heibei University of Technology, Tianjin, China*

[2]*University of Jyvaskyla, Jyvaskyla, Finland*

[3]*Tianjin Heping District Xinhua Worker University, Tianjin, China*

Email: [a]ws.liu@163.com, [b]435155208@qq.com, [c]935507994@qq.com

Base on the growing technology of LED lighting which combined with intelligent control method in tunnel lighting. The performance of long working life, low consumption and good light stability will definitely become the future trend. Through reasonable lighting, not only to ensure the driver can obtain the quality of visual information, but also guarantee the comfortableness and safety during driving in the tunnel. This paper mainly focuses on the research about mathematical calculation model of highway tunnel lighting system. Base on the studies of lighting computational scheme, in order to determine the correct calculation method. The result can be applied to guidance for designing the tunnel lighting system.

Keywords: Tunnel Lighting System; Brightness; The Mathematical Model; Design.

1. Introduction

The number of high ways are increasing over the years, which high light the importance of the analysis and design in highway tunnel lighting. The structure of highway tunnel is tubular structure. Hence, the environment is relatively closed [1]. When car entered in the tunnel, the light in the tunnel comes from outside. After the visual adjutancy in the tunnel, then comes towards the brightness outside the tunnel. Because of the closed environment in the tunnel,

*Corresponding author.

the length of the road the drivers can perceive becomes shorter. And the environment in the tunnel is darker in general, which may cause claustrophobia or depression for a driver. It decrease the freedom and dexterity of driving which becomes a threat for traffic security and certainly increased the possibility of travel accident. Therefore, it is important to build a computable modal for tunnel lighting system.

2. The Tunnel Lighting Design Requirements

According to the lighting standard specification, the tunnel has to have lighting system if the length of the tunnel is more than 100m [2]. The tunnel lighting system include entrance stage, transition section, middle section and exit section, as the Figure 1 below shows the relationship between brightness and section length.

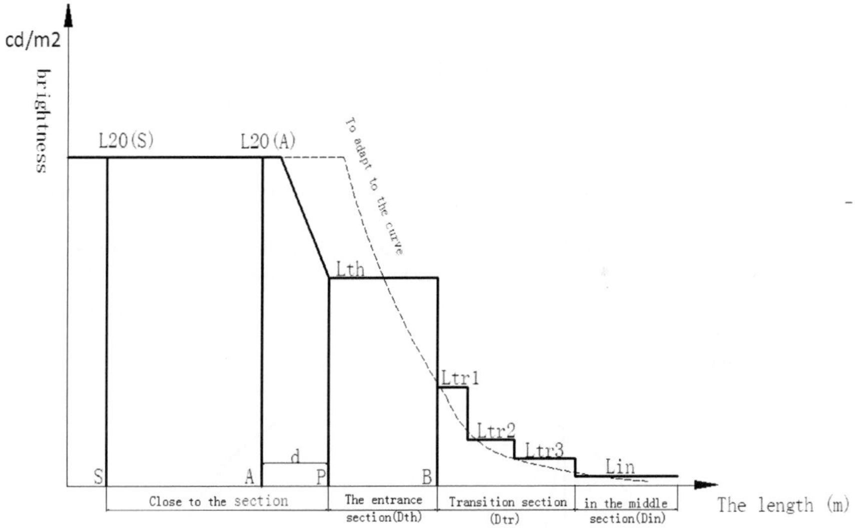

Fig. 1. The tunnel lighting brightness and paragraph length

S- close to the period of starting point; A-the starting point from adapting period; D- adapting distance; P- the starting point of the entrance of the cave; B-transition section starting point; L20 (S)- brightness outside the tunnel; L20 (A)-the brightness of adapting period; Lth-entry section brightness; Ltr1 Ltr2, Ltr3-transition section 1, 2, 3, segmented brightness; Lin-middle section (or basic) brightness [3].

The formula of calculating the brightness of entrance section is shown in Eq.(1).

$$L_{th} = k \times L_{20}(S) \quad (1)$$

$L_{20}(S)$ - brightness outside the tunnel (cd/m^2), value 4500 (cd/m^2); K-entrance section of luminance reduction factor, when driving speed of 60 km/h, design traffic volume(two-lane two-way traffic) N≥1300 cars/h, the desirable value of k = 0.022 [2]. According to the type (1) : Lth = 90(cd/m^2).

Transition section brightness: transition section by Ltr1, Ltr2, Ltr3 three lighting sections. Corresponding to the brightness value from table 1.

Table 1. The brightness of transition section values table

Lighting section	Ltr1	Ltr2	Ltr3
brightness	$L_{TR1} = 0.3L_{th}$	$L_{TR2} = 0.1L_{th}$	$L_{TR3} = 0.035L_{th}$

Therefore, the calculation result of different lighting sections are: the entrance section = 90 (cd/m^2), transition section Ltr1 = 27 (cd/m^2), Ltr1 = 9(cd/m^2), Ltr1 = 3.15 (cd/m^2), middle section = 2.5 (cd/m^2), exit section (by two-way entry section design) = 90(cd/m^2).

3. The Engineering Model and Design of the Tunnel Lighting Systems

Project case: This paper uses Cheng Qin highway Qing Long cable design as an instance. The width of the road is 10,8m, the height of lighting H=5,45m, installation angle $\alpha = 15°$, tunnel height 6,97m, the section Figure 2 shows below:

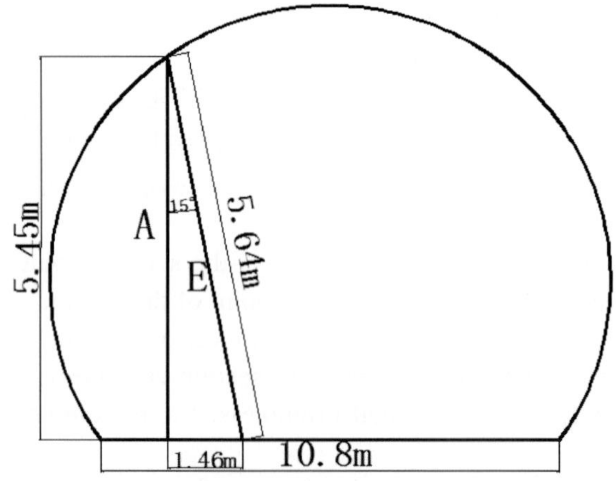

Fig. 2. Tunnel section

The triangle relationship for calculating brightness as shown in Figure 3.

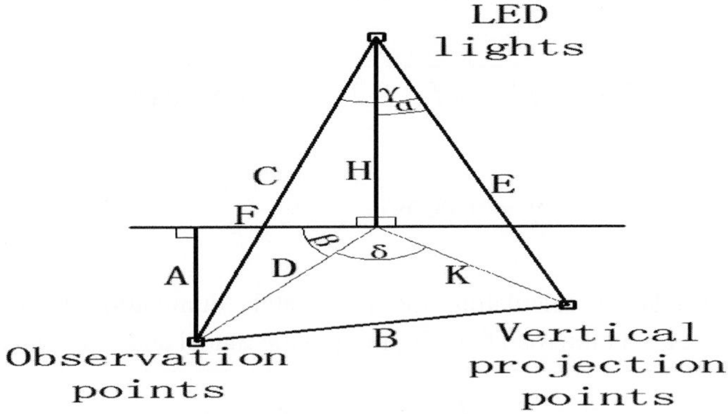

Fig. 3. The triangle diagram

Among A indicates the length between the observation point and the side of the road, B indicates the distance between the observation point and the projection point of vertical illumination on the road but is shown in Eq(7), C indicates the distance between the observation point and the lighting point but is shown in Eq(3), D indicates the distance between the lighting projection point and observation point but is shown in Eq(2), E indicates the lighting point to the vertical irradiation point, and F indicates the projection points of observation point on the side of the road and lighting projection point on the road, H the installation height of lightings, α indicates that the installation Angle of lightings, β indicates that the angle between C and D, γ- the lightings of observation points corresponding to the Angle of incidence of light and is shown in Eq(8), δ indicates that the angle between observation point and positive side of the project point but is shown in Eq(6) .

$$D = \sqrt{A^2 + F^2} \tag{2}$$

$$C = \sqrt{D^2 + H^2} \tag{3}$$

$$\beta = \arctan \frac{A}{F} \tag{4}$$

$$K = H \tan\alpha \tag{5}$$

$$\delta = 90° - \beta \tag{6}$$

$$B = \sqrt{D^2 + K^2 - 2 \times D \times K \times \cos\delta} \tag{7}$$

$$\gamma = \arccos\frac{C^2 + E^2 - B^2}{2 \times C \times E} \tag{8}$$

The formula of calculating the horizontal illumination which find by observation point on the road from lighting in the tunnel and is shown in Eq(9)

$$E_{pi} = \frac{I_{cr}}{H^2}\cos^3\gamma \bullet \frac{\phi}{1000} \bullet M \tag{9}$$

Type: E_{pi} - inside the tunnel horizontal illumination which find by observation point - O on the road from lighting in the tunnel

γ - observation points corresponding to the Angle of incidence of the ray of lighting

I_{cr}- brightness intensity value of lighting on the observation point

M- maintenance factor of lighting as 0.7

ϕ - rated luminous flux of the lightings, in 5600lm.

After obtained the brightness intensity of observation point E_{pi}, then calculate the average value which is the average intensity of illumination, and base on the computable relationship between the average intensity of illumination and the brightness intensity to obtained the coefficient[4].

The average illumination = average brightness intensity * coefficient

The coefficient values between 13 to 22, can press 18.5 $lx/cd \bullet m^2$ value [2], and then obtain the average brightness.

Entrance section observation points (calculation point) distribution design as shown in Figure 4.

Entrance section of the distribution of lighting for each observation point average brightness calculated values shows in table 2.

The average brightness calculation result of entrance section is 108.9 (cd/m^2), the national standard value is 90(cd/m^2), thus fully meet the design requirements.

Apply to these algorithms are able to calculate the average brightness of every other section, must refer to the national standard request and determine the parameters of the tunnel lighting.

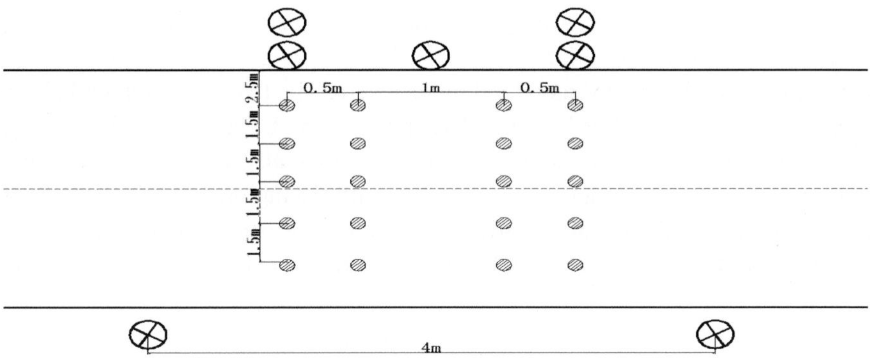

Fig. 4. Entry period of observation point distribution

Table 2 Entry section distribution calculated value at every points of lighting

183.5	142.46	142.46	183.5
149.44	131.9	131.9	149.44
126.64	101.94	101.94	126.64
76.68	64.85	64.85	76.68
58	53.14	53.14	58
	The average brightness of 108.9		

4. Conclusions

With the rapid increase of the numbers of the vehicles, the development of highway tunnel construction are extremely fast. When a car is driven into a tunnel, this sudden change of brightness difference makes driver can not adjust themselves into a darker environment. This phenomenon called black-hole phenomenon which would threaten the life safety of drivers. The risk coefficient increased especially for the fast speed of driving on the highway. Thus, the installation of lighting facilities in the tunnels is indispensable, the design of the tunnel lighting system including entrance section, transition section, middle section, exit section four parts. In addition, emergency lighting system shall be set up to implement the tunnel special function and to meet the using environment. Inside the tunnel should be guaranteed lighting is continuously throughout the whole day. Along with the tunnel operating time are increasing year by year, the safety of the tunnel lighting, economy and low energy consumption problems are more and more severe. The traditional tunnel lighting is using sodium lamp, but lighting efficiency is low. Because of LED lightings technology becomes more and more mature, gradually replace sodium lamp lighting. In this paper, strictly in accordance with the national lighting standards, and combined with actual situation, carries on the tunnel entrance section, transition section, the basic length design, and the results of tunnel lighting brightness.

References

1. Wei-sheng Liu, Dan Sun, Yi-ping Zhang, Tunnel lighting system unit emergency lighting control design and research, ICCEA2014.
2. General tunnel lighting standard-JTJ 026.1-1999.
3. Shanxi Province highway tunnel lighting system design guidelines,11. 2011.
4. Dong Liu. Yunnan phoenix mountain highway tunnel lighting system optimization research [D], Xian chang an university. 2009.

Session III

Cloud Computing

Design and Implementation of Financial Information System of Covering the Entire Business Process

Jian Jin[a], Cheng-Feng Ding, Hao Zhang, Xiao-Chuan Ma and Chang-Feng Jiang

Petro China West Pipeline Company

Urumqi, The Xinjiang Uygur Autonomous Region, China

E-mail: [a]clmjet@qq.com

Financial management business includes modules of budget management, cost management, fund management, asset management, general ledger management and decision support. With the increase of Western Pipeline Company's business expansion, increasingly complex financial accounting and financial set of books appeared, doubling the workload and other issues. To solve these problems, it is proposed through the information technology to implement financial information management system of covering the entire business processes to further regulate the financial management and reduce human intervention. The system completes integration of automated processes in the greatest degree, improves decision support, data sharing and improving financial management.

Keywords: Financial Information Management; Information System; Covering Entire Business Process.

1. Introduction

Western Pipeline company "The International Advanced Level of Pipeline Construction Company Rolling Plan (2014-2018)"[1], in the financial management section presents gaps in terms of information technology, analyze the current financial status of the company management[2], according to the proposed joint-stock company unified deployment, design and implement financial information management solutions which covers the entire business processes, including centralized accounting, asset management system, financial management system platform, ERP systems, integrated information systems integration, seamless docking with information systems management and financial business operations; combing the financial reporting system, improve reporting formula, fully automated preparation of monthly financial statements; enabled company reimbursement platform, self-development contract settlement system, the original documents to the accounting documents throughout the network processing; achievement of the various information systems can do their job and cooperate with each other through data sharing, reducing the risk of manual control, improve work efficiency and the quality of accounting information.

2. The System Target

It covers the entire business process through the establishment of financial information management solutions to achieve the following objectives:
Improve office efficiency: by means of information, solve different departments, different positions of office business processes, and effectively solve the information of quick communicating, sharing, enhance information flow; implement various posts through the system, the various departments of business collaboration to achieve cooperative office, information sharing provide accurate finance[3]. all related company for all levels of staff, and comprehensive information support, thus enhance the corporate financial management and control[4].

- Improve the execution: Because of the company management process ubiquitous operating system process is not standardized, resulting in differences in management behavior and inconsistency results, thereby resulting in inefficient management or even away from the goal[5]. Through the financial information system will assist the Western Pipeline Company organize management processes and management approach into information technology operating system[6], the company's management information system to solidify, the operation of the system to ensure that systems, processes strictly enforced to protect corporate governance practices, efficiency, process control, process traceability and improve the overall execution capability[7].
- Improve internal supervision capacity: The company treasury financial control management rely on manual operations, resulting in the company's internal supervision of the treasury in the working pressure is relatively heavy state[8]. Through internal control systems, which is required each time by starting the system of internal control testing, after completion of the test, perform different operations under different circumstances circulation, reach the target managed automatically[9].
- Achieving "generalization to fine management" business strategy: by covering the deployment and use of financial information management system-

wide business processes, support enterprise management to manage the company even generalization of the department of fine management transformation[10]. Systematic existing duplication of work, financial officers transferred to the mental valuable work from which the computer cannot be completed the contents, and truly achieve the goal of fine management and financial management of scientific, standardized procedures[11].

3. The System Design

3.1. *The overall design ideas*

Using technical means of information technology and perspective of systems engineering design the financial management of the whole process[12], integrates business data and related information and form a data sharing[13], covers the entire business processes of financial information management solutions[14]. Western Pipeline Company wants to solve budget management, cost management, fund management, asset management, general ledger management and decision support business processes. The program consists of subsystems and modules are: budget management subsystem, subsystem reimbursement system, subsystem contract settlement, compensation management module, treasury management platform, monitor accounts and General Ledger module, internal management subsystem, between sign and acknowledge management module, three gold resources management, investment project assistant management system, financial statements, management subsystem, account management subsystem management subsystem reporting and analysis.

3.2. *The system architecture*

Based on the database and network technology, the full use of data fusion, integration and management techniques, with using of B / S and C / S model, combines the financial business data and other relevant data to associated and forms the basis of data fusion sharing platform, in this platform based on the completion of the financial services sector with all relevant nodes makes the efficient and stable network platform, the basic structure of the system shown in Figure 1.

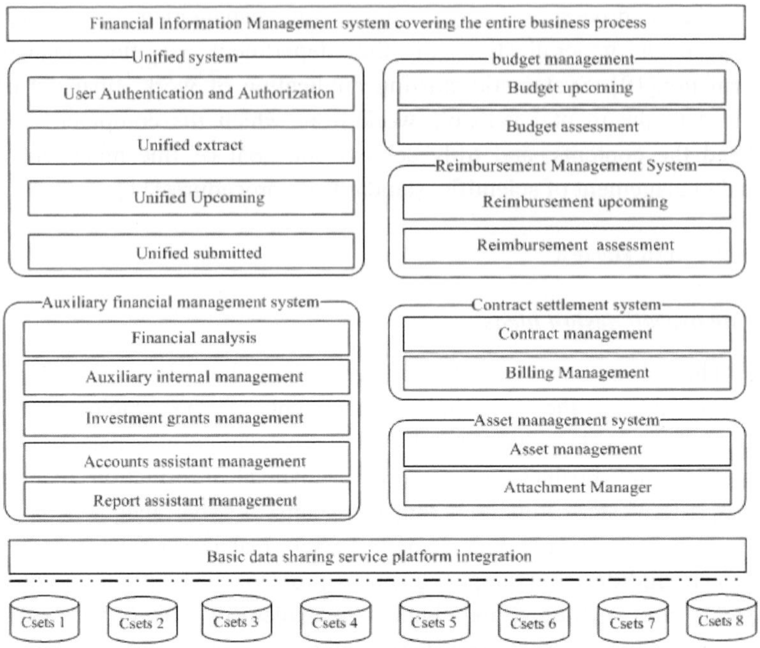

Fig. 1. The basic structure of the system

The basic structure of the financial information management system which covers the entire business process is divided into three parts.

- Data source layer: Data source layer provides data to support the application service layer. Data sources for business data includes sales pipeline Western Digital, the Western United Company data, northwest joint pipeline data, the western branch pipeline data, the western pipeline branch sales data, Group C set, Western Pipeline share data, Western Pipeline Group, 04- 06 C set data and the external data source.
- Basic data sharing service platform integration: Through data integration, data sharing and data fusion mechanism of heterogeneous data source data to associated with a data form the basis for the use of financial operations related systems integration services shared platform.
- Covering the entire business process application service layer: On the basis of data fusion based on shared service platform, the establishment of a business-oriented departments and personnel to cover the whole of the business processes of financial information management application service layer. Including budget management, claims management system, auxiliary financial management system, contract settlement systems and asset management systems.

4. Related Algorithms Design

4.1. *Improved minimum link load balancing scheduling algorithm*

To resolve the problem of rapid visit to the system in the same time, this paper design and implement a improved minimum link load balancing scheduling algorithm. Evaluates the performance of the transmission speed, loading users number and disk read speed and other aspects in the redundant resource sharing. The improved minimum link load balancing scheduling algorithm, expressed as follows:

Definition 1.1 Let C_i is the i-th access request quantity, R_i is the i-th quantity of resources service allocated to the request,N_j is the j-th server in the network throughput is the bandwidth of the entire network, P_j is the j-th server extreme value of processing power. Then the j-th server load rate can be represented as in Eq. (1):

$$M(j) = \{1 - \textstyle\sum_{i=1}^{c} R_i C_i \div P_j\} N_j \div G \tag{1}$$

Definition 1.2 Let P_{min} for the lowest extreme value of processing performance cluster servers processing power. This value characterizes the minimum value of the cluster server processing capacity, $P_{min} = \min(P_1, P_2, \ldots, P_n)$. Normalization of an access request is of the available load factor L can be represented as in Eq. (2):

$$L = R_i \div P_{min} \tag{2}$$

Load factor L indicates the current server load status, larger value of L are, the smaller the server load is, the greater the surplus processing capacity. It represent processing ability of accepting the new access request is stronger, also indicates that the server can be assigned the greater the probability to accept the new request. The step of the algorithm (ILVS) is as follows:

Step 1: Equalizer makes periodic assessments on the status of each server, including the load, the processing performance extremes and network status.

Step 2: Calculate statements all servers available load factor by definition1.1 and sorting, update load factor table.

Step 3: Listen to the new request, equalizer evaluate consumption of processing resources of a new request, by definition 2 and (2) to calculate the normalization of load ratio.

Step 4: Evaluate the normalized load rate of a new request. Compare available load factor of the table, if the load exceeds the maximum available rate, an error message is returned to the user; otherwise, assigned to server service witch at the first row of available load factor the table.

Step 5: Update served server load factor and switch to step1.

4.2. *Performance evaluation of transmission speed of system*

Test the server system in two ways, namely multi servers clustering and load testing under the traditional model and improving model, both simulate a large number of concurrent users access. The comparison result between two status is shown in Table1:

Table 1. Data of the speed of transmission of two ways

No.	Number of Node	speed of transmission of traditional way (Mbit/s)	speed of transmission of improved way (ILVS) (Mbit/s)
1	506	51	76
2	513	56	85
3	535	62	84
4	621	73	79
5	723	65	81
6	821	63	83
7	856	59	90
8	864	54	84

From the Table1 we can find that the average throughout of traditional way is about 60Mbit/s, the data of the improved way(ILVS) is about 82. The latter more than the former about 30%. From the testing result we can conclude that this financial system uses the ILVS algorithm to achieve expected result.

5. Conclusions

In this paper information technology is used to implement the financial information management system of covering the entire business processes to further regulate the financial management, reduce human intervention. The system complete integration of automated processes in the greatest degree, improve decision support, data sharing and improving financial management. Also using the ILVS algorithm to improve the attribute of the system's load balancing function.

References

1. J. Dvořáček, R. Sousedíková, L. Domaracká. Selecting indicators of future corporate business development[J]. Metalurgija, 2011, 50(1).
2. Bidisha Mukhopadhyay, Rudra P. Pradhan. Structural breaks in finance growth nexus: the study of Indonesia[J]. Journal of Economics and Behavioral Studies, 2011, 2(1).
3. Mirdala Rajmund. Interest rate transmission mechanism of monetary policy in the selected EMU candidate countries[J]. Panoeconomicus, 2009, 56(3).
4. Iuliana Carmen Bărbăcioru. Uncertainty functional differential equations for finance[J]. Surveys in Mathematics and its Applications, 2010, 5+(2010).
5. Catherine A McCarty. Vision-related research priorities and how to finance them[J]. Indian Journal of Ophthalmology, 2012, 60(5).
6. P du Toit, G Pienaar. Korporatiewe Identiteit as die Basis van Strafregtelike Aanspreeklikheid van Regspersone (2): Die Praktyk[J]. Potchefstroom Electronic Law Journal, 2011, 14(2).
7. Kožetinac Gradimir. The role of money in monetary policy design of modern central banks[J]. Medjunarodni Problemi, 2007, 59(4).
8. Remberto Rhenals, Juan Pablo Saldarriaga. Una regla de Taylor óptima para Colombia, 1997-2006[J]. Lecturas de Economía, 2008, 69(69).
9. Carlo Migliardo. Monetary Policy Transmission in Italy: A BVAR Analysis with Sign Restriction[J]. AUCO Czech Economic Review, 2010, 4(2).
10. Bin Lu, Xin-Yuan Song, Xin-Dan Li. Bayesian analysis of multi-group nonlinear structural equation models with application to behavioral finance[J]. Quantitative Finance, 2012, 12(3).
11. G.S. Lodha, Quantitative interpretation of ariborne electromagnetic responsefor a spherical model, Master's thesis, University of Toronto (1974).
12. D. Jones, The term 'phoneme', in *Phonetics in Linguistics: A Book of Reading*, eds. W.E. Jones and J. Laver (Longman, London, 1973) pp.187–204.
13. B. Davidsen, Netpbm(1993),ftp://ftp.wustl.edu/graphics/graphics/packages/NetPBM.
14. L. Lamport, *LaTeX, A Document Preparation System*, 2nd edn.(Addison-Wesley, Reading, MA, 1994).

Simulation Research of 1/2 Vehicle Based on Double Fuzzy Control of Semi-Active Suspension

Xiao-Peng Wang[1,2,a], Jian-Jun Liu[1,2,b], Hao Hong[2,c] and Long Wu[2,c]

[1]*School of Mechanical & Electronic Engineering, Sanming University*
Sanming 365004, China

[2]*Engineering Research Center in Fujian Province University for Modern Mechanical Design and Manufacturing Technology*
Sanming 365004, China

E-mail: [a]mrxp1984@163.com, [b]ljj9751@126.com, [c]su27smki@sina.com

Dynamic simulation model based on 1/2 of the vehicle is constructed by MATLAB software. With this model, centroid parameters of the vehicle body and elevation angle parameters are calculated. These data as inputs of the control systems, double fuzzy controllers is adopted in the active suspension system. Main power is controlled by elevation angle velocity and acceleration in front of the suspension system. Main force is controlled by centroid velocity and acceleration in rear suspension assembly. The results show that vehicle ride comfort and stability are improved significantly, through double fuzzy controllers, and optimizing these parameters of the body vertical acceleration, front and rear suspension stroke, elevation angle acceleration with performance rise by 23.8%, 47.0%, 67.3% and 23.8% respectively.

Keywords: Active Suspension; Vehicle Model; Fuzzy Control; Co-simulation Model.

1. Introduction

The suspension is a power transmission device between the wheel and the vehicle body, in the process of moving the vehicle only under special driving conditions, the state of passive suspension to achieve optimal state, when the condition of the road surface or driving speed changes, suspensions optimal state aircraft will destroy happen, so only the passive suspension design of a compromise approach to resolve. With microprocessor applications in vehicles becoming more common, according to a controllable suspension damping and stiffness of the shock absorber of the vehicle with the external signal adjustment of the spring, because of its regulatory function, thereby improving the suspension to a certain extent performance of the system, making the car ride comfort and handling stability are well improved. Controlled Suspension may be divided active suspension and semi-active suspension: Active suspension control law designed according to the output of a corresponding control signal to the actuator, the control body vibrations generated by the control actuator. Since the active control can use an external energy supply means for the vehicle in motion and the road surface excitation and inhibition take the initiative to respond to the vibration of the vehicle body, so it's good control effect, but the complex structure and high cost. Compared to its semi-active suspension, mainly by changing the damping characteristics of the shock absorbers, body and wheel vibration attenuation, simple structure, low energy consumption [1]. Fuzzy control compared with other control: use of language, and without the precise mathematical model; robust, suitable for solving highly nonlinear process control, time lag varying strong coupling problem; there is a strong fault tolerance, having adaptation controlled object dynamics, environmental characteristics and the ability to move the line conditions change; the operator through easy-to-person contact natural language man-machine interface [2-5]. In this paper, semi-active suspension, for example, the use of double fuzzy controllers for half car model simulation study and performance comparison with the passive suspension.

2. Car Model

Half car model with four degrees of freedom, namely: vertical vibration of the vehicle body, the front and rear of the vehicle body pitching motion and vertical motion. The following assumptions in the modeling process: 1) at a low frequency excitation pavement, road surface model input about two vehicle has a high correlation between left and right wheels can be considered consistent with the road surface input; taking into account the geometry of the vehicle and mass distribution is usually symmetrical, it can be considered way movement left and right sides of the vehicle in exactly the same. 2) In the high-frequency excitation, the vehicle suffered excited actually mostly involves only wheels beating, less impact on the body, the relative movement of the body on both sides can be neglected [6]. Half car model establish simplified shown in Figure. 1 Vehicle parameter table shown in Table. 1

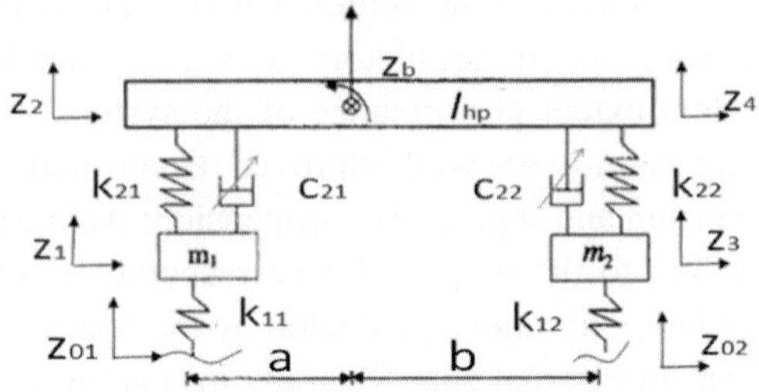

Fig. 1. Half car model

Semi-car movements equation as in Eq. (1-8).

$$m\ddot{z}_b = F_f + F_r \tag{1}$$

$$m_1\ddot{z}_1 = K_{11}\left(z_{01} - z_1\right) - K_{21}\left(z_1 - z_2\right) - C_{21}\left(\dot{z}_1 - \dot{z}_2\right) - U_1 \tag{2}$$

$$m_3\ddot{z}_3 = K_{12}\left(z_{02} - z_3\right) - K_{22}\left(z_3 - z_4\right) - C_{21}\left(\dot{z}_3 - \dot{z}_4\right) - U_2 \tag{3}$$

$$I_{hp}\ddot{\theta}_b = -aF_f + bF_r \tag{4}$$

$$F_f = K_{21}\left(z_1 - z_2\right) + C_{21}\left(\dot{z}_1 - \dot{z}_2\right) + U_1 \tag{5}$$

$$F_r = K_{22}\left(z_3 - z_4\right) + C_{21}\left(\dot{z}_3 - \dot{z}_4\right) + U_2 \tag{6}$$

Body centroid, pitch angular acceleration, there is a relationship between the front and rear suspension sprung mass:

$$\ddot{z}_2 = \ddot{z}_b - a\ddot{\theta}_b \tag{7}$$

$$\ddot{z}_4 = \ddot{z}_b + b\ddot{\theta}_b \tag{8}$$

Where: m is half body mass; I_{hp} is half-body moment of inertia; m_1 is front-wheel unsprung mass; m_3 is for the rear wheel unsprung mass; K_{11} is a front tire stiffness; K_{12} is after tire stiffness; K_{21} is the front suspension spring stiffness; K_{22} is the rear suspension spring stiffness; C_{21} and C_{22} are a front suspension damping and rear suspension damping; *a* is front axle distance of the centroid; *b* is the rear axle from the centroid.

Table 1. Vehicle parameters

Model parameters	Symbol	Numerical	Unit
1/2Body mass	m_{hb}	690	*kg*
1/2Moment of inertia	I_{hp}	1222	$Kg{\cdot}m^2$
Front wheel unsprung mass	m_1	40.5	*kg*
Rear unsprung mass	m_3	45.4	*kg*
Front tire stiffness	K_{11}	192	*kN/m*
After the tire stiffness	K_{12}	192	*kN/m*
Front suspension stiffness	K_{21}	17	*kN/m*
Rear suspension stiffness	K_{22}	22	*kN/m*
Front suspension damping	C_{21}	1500	$N/(s{\cdot}m^{-1})$
Rear suspension damping	C_{22}	1500	$N/(s{\cdot}m^{-1})$
Centroid distance to the front axle	a	1.25	*m*
Centroid distance to the rear axle	b	1.51	*m*

3. Road Surface Model

We need to enter the road surface model when the suspension performance analysis. According to national standards will be divided into eight kinds of road class, measured in different sections, the road is difficult to get two identical profile curve. The measurement is usually obtained by a large number of random road roughness data, obtained by the data processing power spectral density. Generating a random road roughness temporal profile in two ways, by the white noise generated by an integrator or white noise generated by a shaping filter. When the pavement domain model available equation:

$$\dot{q}(t) = -2\pi f_0 q(t) + 2\pi\sqrt{G_q V}w(t) \tag{9}$$

Where: *q(t)* is the road surface excitation; *w (t)* is the integral of white noise; f_0 is the time frequency; G_q of road roughness coefficient; *V* is the vehicle speed.

In the process of moving the vehicle, due to the presence of the wheelbase, the road entered the rear wheels relative to the front wheel to have a relative time lag. The wheelbase of 2.76 meters, the driving speed of 20*km/h*, the rear wheels calculated delay 0.138 seconds. According to the formula 9 set up road pavement Simulink model and delay shown in Figure. 2 Simulation time is 10 seconds, the front and rear wheels calculated to give input surface as shown in Figure. 3.

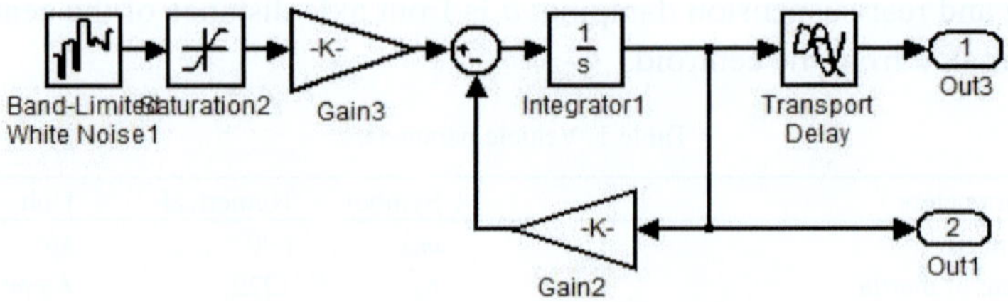

Fig. 2. Class B road time-domain models

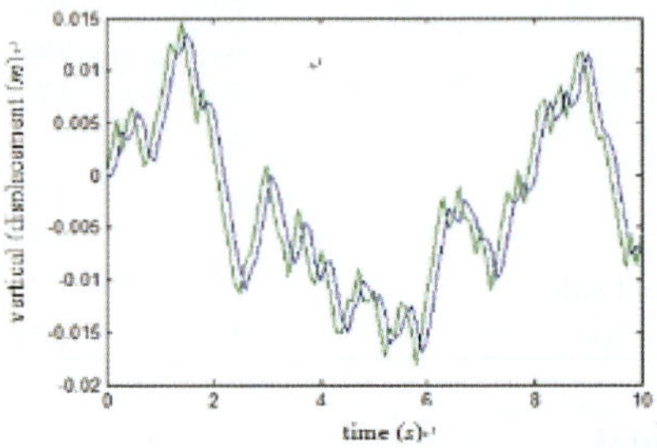

Fig. 3. The front and rear wheels pavement

According to the formula established 1-9 half-car model in the B-class road input simulation role simulation model 4, as shown in the calculation output acceleration and pitching angular body at the centroid, front and rear wheels and front and rear suspension dynamic travel itinerary fetal movement. Among them, the vehicle acceleration at the centroid, pitch angle, front and rear suspension dynamic travel as input active suspension.

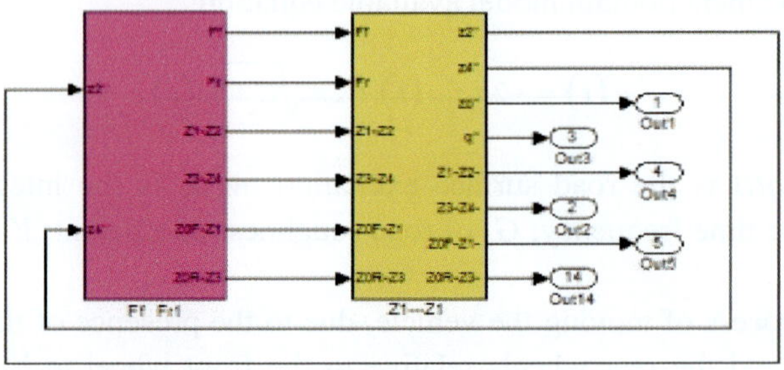

Fig. 4. Semi-passive suspension vehicle simulation model

4. Fuzzy Controller Design

Double fuzzy controllers are active on the front and rear suspension control U_1, U_2 control. For the front suspension: in the control process to error and its rate of change of vehicle speed and desired value as input fuzzy controller, U_{11} as an output fuzzy controller; and the angular velocity of the vehicle body pitch errors and expectations another change in the rate of output as input to another fuzzy controller, U_{12} as fuzzy control gas. For the rear suspension: in the control process to error and its rate of change of vehicle speed and desired value as input fuzzy controller, U_{21} as an output fuzzy controller; stroke to move the body and the body and between its error rate change expectations as another input fuzzy controller, U_{22} as another output fuzzy control gas. Wherein the front and rear suspension was a total control amount of the output of the fuzzy controller and the following formula:

$$U_1 = k_{11}U_{11} + k_{12}U_{12} \tag{10}$$

$$U_2 = k_{21}U_{21} + k_{22}U_{22} \tag{11}$$

According to the formula 10 set up the front suspension of double fuzzy controllers output control, simulation model is shown in Figure. 5

Fuzzy controller feature is not dependent on precise mathematical model, robust, suitable for solving highly nonlinear process control, time lag varying strong coupling problem; there is a strong fault tolerance; easy man-machine operator interface contact.

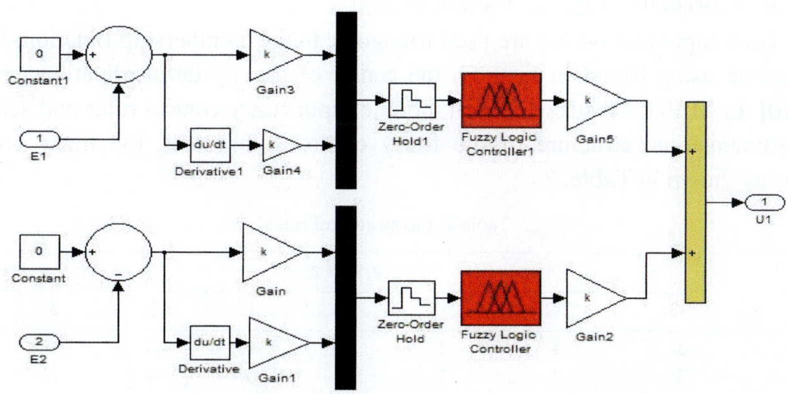

Fig. 5. Front suspension double fuzzy controllers

Fuzzy control rules is the core of the fuzzy controller, which in a way language depicts the relationship between the controller input and output quantities. Front and rear suspensions of the input variables were body mass and heart rate variation, the body pitch rate and the amount of change, after the suspension stroke and the amount of change move. 7 linguistic variables using rules to describe: big negative (-3), the negative (-2), small negative (-1), zero (0), is a small (1), middle (2), big (3) output variable control U also adopted seven fuzzy language to describe: big negative (-3), the negative (-2), small negative (-1), zero (0), is a small (1), middle (2), big (3). Wherein each of the fuzzy controller input error and change domain were taken:

Its error rate of change in the front suspension and body connection speed at the desired value, the quantization factors are:

E=[-0.06,0.06], EC=[-0.6,0.6];

K_e = 3/0.006=50, K_{ec}=3/0.6=5;

Body and pitch angular error and change rate expectations, quantization factors are:

E=[-0.025,0.025], EC=[-0.25,0.25];

K_e = 3/0.025=120, K_{ec}=3/0.25=12;

Error and its rate of change of the rear suspension and body connection speed at the desired value, the quantization factors are:

E=[-0.08,0.08], EC=[-0.8,0.8];

K_e= 3/0.08=37.5, K_{ec}=3/0.8=3.75;

Rear suspension and the error rate of change between the body and the body moving and travel expectations, quantization factors are:

E=[-0.0008,0.0008], EC=[-0.008,0.008];

K_e = 3/0.0008=375, K_{ec}=3/0.008=375;

Each input and output are used triangular fuzzy membership function, fuzzy inference using Mandain method, the center of gravity defuzzification method [7-10]. In MATLAB fuzzy control module input fuzzy control rules and set up a two-dimensional structure of the fuzzy control subsystem, the fuzzy control rules as shown in Table. 2

Table 2. Fuzzy control rules

$\dot{z}_2$ / $\dot{\theta}$ / $\dot{z}_4-\dot{z}_3$	$z_2/\theta/z_4-z_3$						
	-3	-2	-1	0	1	2	3
-3	3	3	2	1	1	-1	-2
-2	3	3	2	1	0	-1	-2
-1	3	2	1	1	-1	-2	-3
0	3	2	1	0	-1	-2	-3
1	3	2	1	-1	-1	-2	-3
2	2	1	0	-1	-2	-3	-3
3	2	1	-1	-1	-2	-3	-3

5. Simulation Analysis

According to semi-passive suspension vehicle simulation model with dual fuzzy controller model, built semi - active suspension vehicle simulation model as shown in Figure 6. On the B-class vehicles on our roads to 20km / h speed straight running, the body active and passive suspension calculate acceleration, pitch angle, dynamic travel front and rear suspension, front and rear wheels fetal stroke. Active and passive suspension results shown in Figure 7-12, where the blue line results for the passive suspension, active suspension for the red line and the results are displayed in the same graph. Simulation step of 0.005s, simulation time is 10s.

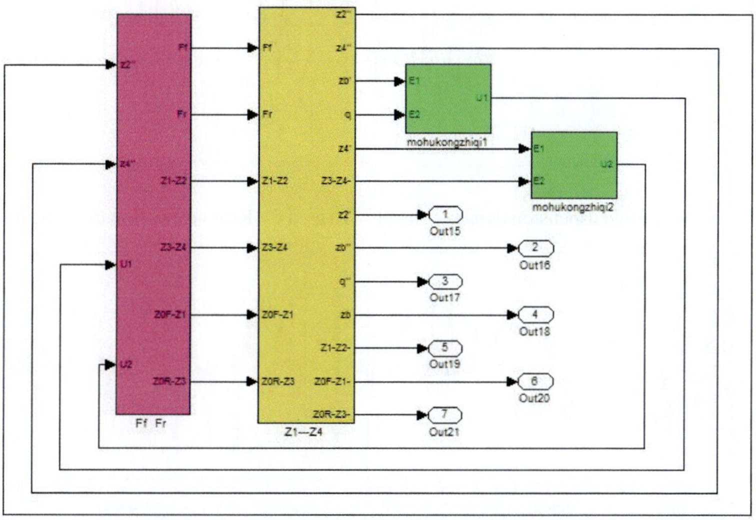

Fig. 6. Semi-active suspension car simulation model

As can be seen from the results, active suspension passive suspension on the overall performance has improved with respect. Wherein the vertical acceleration of the vehicle body, front and rear suspension dynamic travel performance significantly, but the stroke movement of the tire tends to deteriorate due to the change amount of the order of 10^{-3}, a very small amount of change, it can be ignored. Specific performance parameters as shown in Table. 3

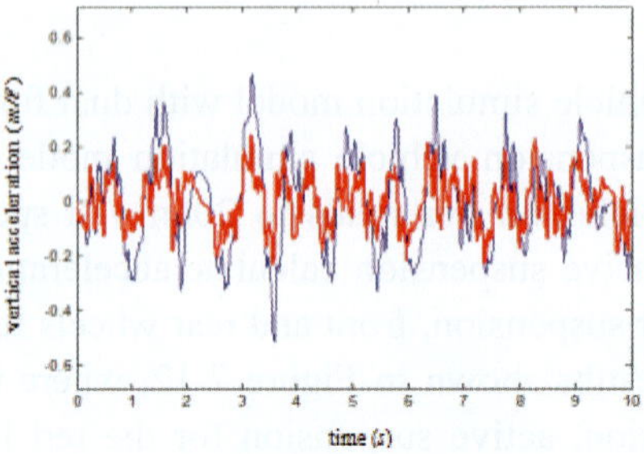

Fig. 7. Body centroid vertical acceleration

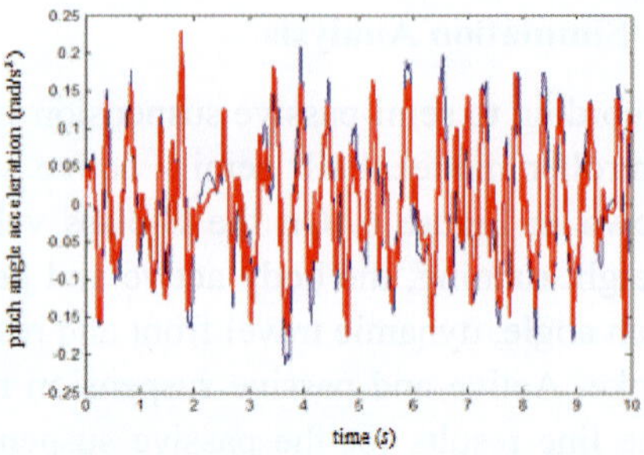

Fig. 8. Body centroid pitching angular

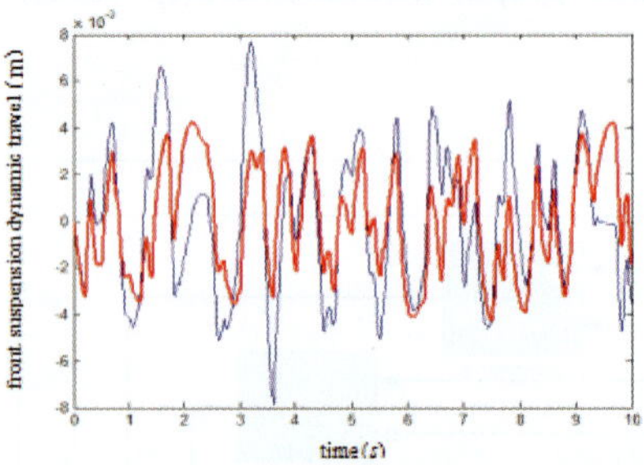

Fig. 9. Front suspension dynamic travel

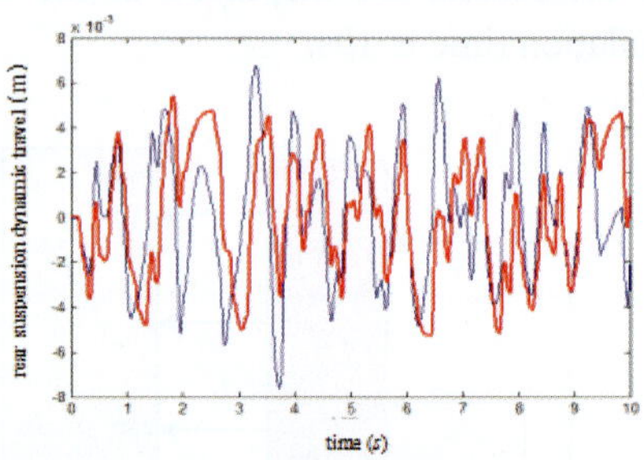

Fig. 10. Rear suspension dynamic travel

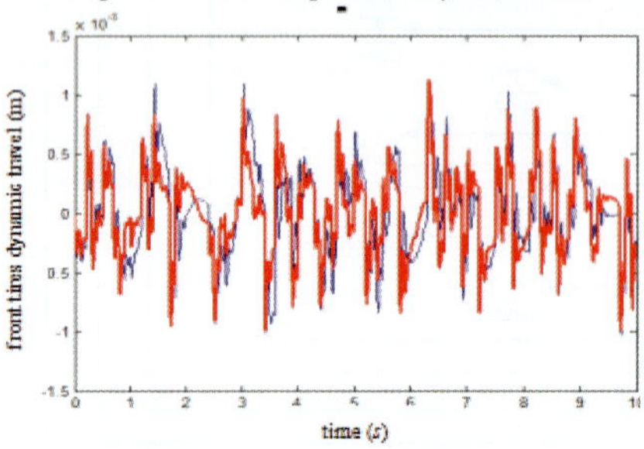

Fig. 11. Front tires dynamic travel

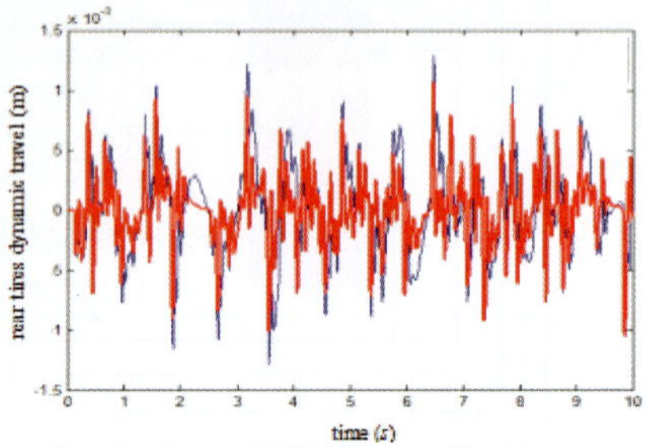

Fig. 12. Rear tires dynamic travel

Table 3. RMS value of such performance table

RMS	passive	initiative	Optimal alignment
Vertical acceleration (m/s^2))	4.49e-2	3.42e-2	23.8%
Pitch angle acceleration (rad/s^2)	1.07e-1	9.74e-2	8.97%
Front suspension dynamic travel (m)	3.51e-3	1.86e-3	47.0%
Rear suspension dynamic travel (m)	2.03e-3	6.63e-4	67.3%
Front tires dynamic travel (m)	3.96e-4	3.84e-4	3.03%
Rear tires dynamic travel (m)	2.79e-5	6.84e-5	-130.3%

6. Conclusions

This paper established a simulation model based on semi-passive suspension vehicle four degrees of freedom model to calculate the speed of the front and rear suspension joints and acceleration of dynamic travel front and rear tires and body pitch angular displacement and angular velocity as input controller; Active Suspension design double fuzzy control strategy, front suspension and body pitch velocity and the angular velocity of the body is connected as input, output force for the front suspension total control; rear suspension and speed of the vehicle body and suspension joints moving stroke as input fuzzy controller output force for the rear suspension total control. Semi-passive suspension vehicle simulation model for docking with double fuzzy controllers established semi - active suspension vehicle simulation model, calculation and analysis, the following conclusions can be drawn:

1) body vertical acceleration, pitch angular acceleration, dynamic travel front and rear suspension, the front tire has a very good improvement moving stroke, wherein the vertical body acceleration, front and rear suspension dynamic travel improved very significantly, enhance the performance were 23.8%, 47.0%, 67.3%.

2) fuzzy controller on the vehicle parameters relatively insensitive, except for the rear tire dynamic travel tends to deteriorate due to changes in the amount of the order of 10-3, the amount of change is extremely small, can be ignored. Dual fuzzy controller is superior overall comprehensive performance, robustness.

3) Simulation-based foundation for steering the vehicle dynamics model, ABS braking and other control systems integrated performance on the same model of follow-up.

Acknowledgments

China Fujian Province Department of Education-funded projects; Project name: Based on the H5 type of heavy trucks and flexible body isolated powertrain mounting system research and application; Item Number: (JK2014048).

References

1. Yang Likang. The Theoretical and Experimental investigation On Semi-active Vehicle Suspension Employing Magneto-rheo logical Technology [D]. Zhejiang University, 2003.

2. Kang Zhiqiao. Dynamics Simulation of half Vehicle Suspension System [J].Highways & Automotive Applications, 2015, 166(1):5-8+56.
3. Liu Jing. The skyhook active suspension Simulation Research of the half vehicle[J].Highways & Automotive Applications, 2015,166(3):15-20+80.
4. Zhang Jie. Studies on coupling vibration of highway vehicle-bridge system[D]. Southwest Jiaotong University, 2007.
5. Hrovat D. Optimal active suspensions for 3d vehicule models[C].Proc. of the American Control Conference, Arizona, USA.1991,2:1534~1541.
6. Yu Fan, Lin Yi. Automotive Systems Dynamics [M].Beijing, Machinery Industry Press, 2012.171-172.
7. Zhou Bing, Zhao Baohua. Simulation Study of Self-adaptive Fuzzy-PID Control of Active Suspension[J].JOURNAL OF HUNAN UNIVERSITY(NATURAL SCIENCES), 2009,36(12):27-30.
8. Zhang Kun, Xi Wenhui, DENG Wen-hua et al. Fuzzy Control Simulation of Full Vehicle Semi-Active Suspension Based on Carsim-Simulink Co-simulation[J].Faculty of Transportation Engineering, Kunming University of Science and Technology, 2015,40(1):39-44.
9. Sy Dzung Nguyen, Seung-Bok Choi. A novel minimum-maximum data-clustering algorithm for vibration control of a semi-active vehicle suspension system[J].Proceedings of the Institution of Mechanical Engineers, Part D. Journal of Automobile Engineering,2013,227(9):1242-1254.
10. Guan jifu, Gu liang, Hou Chaozhen, et al. Fuzzy Logic Control for Semi-Active Suspension System of Tracked Vehicle[J]. JOURNAL OF BEIJING INSTITUTE O F TECHNOLOGY,2004,13(2):113-117.

Competition Situation and Regulatory Strategy of Internet Access Market in Shaanxi Province

Ling-Yi Kong[a] and Wei-Feng Jia[b]

College of Economics and Management, Xi'an University of Post and Telecommunication
Xi'an, 710061, People's Republic of China
E-mail: [a]kly@xupt.edu.cn, [b]jia_wf@163.com

The competition intensity of internet access market has been ever-increasing in Shaanxi Province. Effective competition structure has not formed because of the backward supervision. Furthermore, internet access user loss was extremely serious because of many problems of upstream foundational network operators and downstream value-added service enterprise. In order to realize effective competition situation and promote vitality of the market, supervision department should relax restriction of market access and introduce competition, establish supervision system based on internet access service industry chain level, increase support for value-added service enterprise and strengthen supervision for interconnection, price and quality.

Keywords: Internet Access Market; Competition; User Loss; Interconnection; Regulatory Strategy.

1. Introduction

Internet access is the physical connection between the user and IP wan under the governmental regulation, using the transmission technology and specific information transmission channel. Because the market has been perfect, competition mechanism fully played the role of optimizing the resources allocation after relaxing the internet access regulation in the western developed countries.

Therefore, the western economists have focused mainly on service fees and network access pricing in internet access regulation research field. Sumanta Basu, etc. proposed effective element pricing rules[1]. Christos Bouras, etc. studied the fully distributable costs pricing[2].And then, Laffont, etc. proposed

Ramsey pricing for the network access[3]. Karl-Heinz Neumann, etc applied Ramsey pricing for the unbundled local loop[4]. Lisa Correa, etc applied Ramsey pricing for Broadband Internet in Ireland and the Netherlands[5]. Especially, La fon, etc. launched systematic analyses of service fees, network access pricing, universal service, regulation reform and other critical issues, based on which they provided new and inspiring ideas.

From the end of 1980s, especially after a series of reform in the telecommunications industry regulation in the nineties, Chinese academic circle also paid an intense attention to the internet access regulation researches, including market structure, price, general services, etc. Lin Huai-guo compared the status of telecommunications market before the reform with those afterwards by means of the SCP paradigm and found that Chinese telecom industry formed an effective competition situation preliminarily, but as the same time, Chinese telecom industry still had very big development space. Also, we must take valid measures to perfect the reform of our telecom industry[6]. Ao Yong-chun, etc. introduced market competition intensity factor in price ceiling regulation model. On the basis of telecom business cost, they linked the degree of competition in the market to regulated prices, and put forward the relevant countermeasures for the development of the telecom price regulation in the future[7]. Wang Wen-jing and Lv Ting-jie thought that the choice and implementation of competition regulatory policies and measures of telecom market were very important to promoting fairness and effectiveness in China's telecom market. They firstly introduced the problems existing in China's telecom market competition, then analyzed the current situation of supervision, and finally put forward suggestions on policy implementation in the China's telecom market[8]. In 2011, monopolistic conducts of China Telecom and China Unicom in the internet access market became burning issue, which was the first antitrust problem concerning the large public utility enterprises since the implement of antimonopoly law. The survey result would directly exert a far-reaching effect on the antitrust of monopolistic public enterprises. Ding Guo-feng proposed the cognizance analysis of the abusing dominant market position in the field of internet access of the telecom industry included many contents, but its core elements lie in suspected behavior confirmation of abuse dominant market position[9]. Guo Zong-jie, etc. thought Chinese monopolistic industries should apply cross subsidy as a transition in the near future, and gradually establish price compensation mechanism with a universal service fund as the core, in order to realize externalization, transparency and standardization of universal service price compensation[10].From the experience and lessons of governmental regulation for electricity, public enterprise and telecom industry in the United States, Liu Xin-yuan interpreted regulation economics in the field of natural monopoly, and provided the beneficial references for the natural monopoly regulation[11].

The common purpose of these experts and scholars is to provide constructive opinions about regulatory reform for China's telecom industry. They generally thought that China's government should adopt effective reform measures so as to introduce and establish effective and orderly competition. But as a part of China's telecom market, until now no field investigation of internet access market has been reported, much less to certain provincial internet access market. Therefore, internet access market in Shaanxi Province was systematically investigated in the paper, so as to discern several changes in recent years. On the basis of spot survey, competition situation of internet access market and the effects on website users were analyzed. Meanwhile, the reasons for website user loss and the difficulties to develop ISP business were explained. Thus, supervision countermeasures and some suggestions were put forward for supervision department of Shaanxi Province to realize effective competition in internet access market.

2. Development Situation of Internet Access Market in Shaanxi Province

Twenty years ago, Shaanxi internet access market was almost exclusively monopolized by Shaanxi Telecom. Based on its strong market power, monopoly ignored the various needs of user, only completed simple physical access to the Internet. The basic internet access services were not satisfied, much less to additional services. The fundamental operators might rarely feel competition pressure at that moment.

The competition in its true sense really appeared in Shaanxi internet access market since the broadband business started in 2003, especially since China Telecom completed the restruction in 2008. Only three domestic telecommunications operators had internet access business license — Shaanxi Telecom, Shaanxi Unicom and Shaanxi Mobile. Oligopoly market structure was formed with three major operators.

In the 21st century, with the Internet spreading and new telecom technology emerging endlessly, the status of the Internet is growing. Along with the coming of internet economy, network users are increasingly dependent on the ability to acquire information rapidly. Nowadays, fast, stable and affordable solution of internet access has become an important ability of network users to quickly deal with environmental changes. Therefore, monopolistic operators have to face unprecedented challenge in the Shaanxi internet access market. Network users have strong protest for expanding network bandwidth, strengthening interconnection and enhancing internet service quality. It has been to the fore that Shaanxi internet access market transforms from monopoly into competition in the near future.

In April 2016, three basic telecommunications enterprises have provided internet broadband access service for 7.314 million subscribers. At present, only 13,000 web users have accessed to internet in Shaanxi Province. However, up to 6 million Shaanxi website users preferred other provincial network operators to access internet. Obviously internet access user loss is very serious in Shaanxi Province. Meanwhile, more than 40 enterprises have been approved by Shaanxi Communication Administration to operate internet value-added service, including ISP and IDC business, but they rarely carry out the business, only 17 or so do.

Compared with other market, internet access market has chain features on the basis of the information products, achieve value appreciation. Rational division of upstream and downstream firms with cooperation plays an important role in value-added efficiency in such market. As the network users increasingly need personalized and applicative information service, the traditional value chain "operators — customers" is transforming to the new one, that is "foundational network operators — value-added service enterprise — the customer".

3. Competition Situation of Upstream Foundational Network Operators

In 2008, China Unicom and China Netcom joined together in internet access market to challenge China Telecom, but it was not a peer-to-peer competition because the internet access business of New Unicom was not mature. At that time China Netcom was called "Small Netcom" for its congenital deficiency in the internet infrastructure construction. Meanwhile the interconnection between "Small Netcom" network and Shaanxi Telecom network existed respectable problems. Therefore the ability of China Unicom and China Netcom was very weak, so that they were hard to compete with China Telecom even after their combination.

In addition, the interconnection between Mobile and Shaanxi Telecom also had a lot of problems, with the addition of congenital deficiency of the network facilities quality, so that the share of Shaanxi Mobile was rare to see in Shaanxi internet access market. On the contrary, Shaanxi Telecom took advantage of its original monopoly position so as to occupy obvious advantages, including the access pricing, network propaganda and the distribution channels, etc.

Hence there is obviously power imbalance between upstream foundational network operators. It is difficult to form real competition in the upstream of internet access market, still maintaining strong monopoly situation.

3.1. *High market concentration*

Currently there are three basic telecom enterprises in Shaanxi internet access market -- Shaanxi Telecom, Unicom and Mobile. According to internet access business sales income, Shaanxi Telecom occupied 90% market share. While Shaanxi Unicom had 9 percent. Shaanxi Mobile accounted for only 1%. Three operators carved up the entire internet access market.

According to the theory of modern market structure, an important market concentration index is Herfindahl Index (HHI), which is the sum of the squares of three companies' market shares. HHI may be calculated for 0.827. Visibly, this explains that market concentration is very high and manufacturer's forces are not balanced. Internet access market is almost completely monopolized by Shaanxi Telecom because of the tiny market share of Unicom and Mobile.

In fact, three basic operators also had no dedication to internet access market with all their strength in Shaanxi Province, but they could still get big profits. Especially the internet access business in the relevant department of Shaanxi Telecom could keep up to 33 percent of the annual business revenue growth rates and 13.34% profit margins, so this was breathtaking operational performance in the intensely competitive telecommunication market nowadays. Moreover according to the our survey, Shaanxi Telecom provided high prices to downstream value-added service enterprise for renting internet access resources, with no downward trend. Downstream access service providers needed rental price reduction urgently, but Shaanxi Telecom was unconcerned because of its dominance position in the internet access market. These facts have undoubtedly proved Shaanxi Telecom has strong monopoly position in Shaanxi internet access market.

3.2. *Service homogeneity*

Products of telecom enterprise are comparatively different from the tangible products of other industries, which consists of the network, special business and services. Production process and consumption process simultaneously occur in the telecom industry.

In Shaanxi Province, three basic operators have introduced advanced transmission equipment, cabinet and server, using an advanced network technology for network users, so their internet access service was no difference, and homogeneity phenomenon was serious.

Although in recent years the market competition pressure forced each big operators to positively develop all kinds of value-added service in the internet access business, value-added service income was always trivial compared with internet access resources rent income. Interdependency of the resource rent income was very high for foundation operators. For example, Shaanxi Telecom provided VIP customers (including Tencent, Sina, Grand, the ninth city and Shantong company, etc.) special line access or server hosting business, whose income was accounted for 80-90% of its ISP income of in 2015. From IDC income constitution, broadband rent income accounted for 93.4% of total income, whereas other value-added service income only accounted for less than 6%. It is obvious that the root causes is powerful market monopoly power. As the upstream of the internet access market, foundation operators control internet access resources absolutely, so they lack motive power to increase the service quality and improve the service quality.

3.3. *High barriers to entry and exit*

Foundation operators of internet access evolved from complete monopoly telecommunications industry in Shaanxi, and the establishment and development of China Unicom has obvious national policy overtones.

In recent years, through the establishment of modern enterprise system, major telecom enterprises have had absolute advantage in capital operation, capital, technology, the scale, the brand, etc. Along with China's entry into the WTO, agreements with members state that proportion of foreign capital in the basic telecom business (including internet access service) shall not exceed 50%, so the foreign-owned enterprises are difficult to enter into China’s internet access market.

Because the internet access industry has the characteristics of network industry, producers and consumers must use specific transmission network to produce and consume various products and services. In addition these network infrastructure assets possess strong specificity and comprehensiveness. So three foundation operators that manage internet access business, need great amount of initial capital for network infrastructure, and asset specificity is strong, sunk costs are high. Once they enter the internet access market, it is almost impossible to exit for them.

4. Competition Situation of Downstream Value-added Service Enterprises

Foundation operators will lease internet resource to downstream internet access service providers, which are small and medium-sized, in succession, value-added service enterprise provide internet access to end users after integration of internetwork hardware resources and value-added service, so that users can not only access to the internet, but also get value-added service provided by value-added service enterprise.

In the past two years, competition of Shaanxi internet access market has entered a new stage that shows a growing number of downstream value-added service enterprise and increasing competition.

4.1. *The simplification means of competition*

Internet access market competition promotes Shaanxi internet access market to transform from seller's market into buyer's market. The essence of buyer's market is an internet access service sales crisis, that is to say, value-added service enterprise service hardly sell, service capacity is relative surplus on the market, namely service supply is greater than service demand, eventually access service price will fall.

Because the amount of network users are rapidly increasing in recent decades, internet access market demand is huge. Many small and medium-sized private enterprises, tempted by the potential profit, blindly entered the Shaanxi internet access markets, so the market scale was enlarging and the current oversupply situation was forming. Because of the homogeneity of internet access service provided by downstream manufacturers, they had to take the direct competition means to lower price in order to fight for the customer, even launch a price war. But the price is "double-edged sword", if their competition relied solely on price, results were very cruel, failure rate was very high. Finally only several value-added service enterprises could survive, which bear lower operating costs than others and basically operated a break-even or meager profit business, consequently enterprise performance was difficult to boost, and they had no ability to carry out technical innovation and service innovation. Therefore the competition ability of value-added services enterprise is generally weak in the industry chain downstream. According to our survey, Among 11 value-added service enterprises in Shaanxi, only 3 made a profit, 6 operated a break-even business, and two operated in the red, i.e., 77.3% downstream enterprise was in the break-even or losses state.

4.2. *The backward management means*

According to our survey, the website users usually get the information of internet access service providers through the internet search and inquiry, so as to select becoming value-added service providers. This docking process most does without face-to-face negotiations.

Access service providers, which are located in Beijing, Shanghai, Jiangsu and many other developed provinces, have invested a lot of internet advertising expenses for propaganda, so that website users can easily find them through internet search. They are springing up enormously in Internet access to a vast emerging market like bamboo shoots after a spring rain. Shaanxi value-added service enterprise have hardly used advertising on the network, whose propaganda is small, so that website users in Shaanxi have great difficulties to search local value-added service providers through the internet. It is an important reason for a large number of Shaanxi personal website or enterprise website users to choose value-added service enterprise located in the developed area to access the internet. Therefore, Shaanxi value-added service enterprise's indifference to network marketing is one of the primary causes of Shaanxi website users outflow.

5. Internet Access Supervision Countermeasure to Realize the Effective Competition

5.1. *To establish supervision system for Shaanxi internet access service industry chain*

Based on above analysis, systematic supervision of local internet access market should be considered to break the strong monopoly and prevent internet access users outflow in Shaanxi Province, including strengthening supervision of each link in the internet access service industry chain, establishing universally compatible supervision system, balancing power of upstream and downstream internet access service enterprises, ensuring effective competition situation of upstream and downstream market, and providing terminal network users the biggest gains.

In order to break the strong monopoly of foundation operators, local regulators should relax market entry conditions as far as possible and allow more operators to participate in internet access business, including IDC and ISP business.

5.2. *To strengthen interconnection supervision*

The interconnection cannot depend on the market itself, but is realized by the government's control policies. the interconnection between the three foundation operators is fraught with obstacles and limits the normal development of internet access market in Shaanxi. Shaanxi Telecom is the leading operator in internet access market, whose motivation to promote network compatibility is not strong because keeping the network incompatible can suppress other disadvantaged companies and maintain its monopoly power. Meanwhile, the interconnection problems also bring about great resistance to downstream value-added service enterprise and lead to the high use-cost of website users, which is directly related to loss of the website users in Shaanxi Province. In a word, interconnection problems have seriously restricted the healthy development of local internet access market.

Therefore, the provincial communications administration should strengthen interconnection supervision of foundation operators, especially strengthen interconnection supervision of the leading telecom enterprise — Shaanxi Telecom. Through the establishment of effective supervision mechanism and strict rewards and punishment system, internet access resources allocation efficiency will surely be enhanced, and internet access resources will be efficiently allocated.

5.3. *To strengthen price supervision of leading operators*

The gloomy business of value-added service enterprise and high rents specified by foundation operators are inseparable. In other words, high rents have hindered the development of internet access market in Shaanxi Province.

Regulators should strengthen price supervision of leading operators, especially resources rental price. Firstly, price discrimination or unfair phenomenon should be eliminated. Secondly price cap should be formulated by reference to other provinces, so as to reduce resources rental prices. Finally provincial communication administration should speed up the construction of low-end machine rooms used for internet access. Such countermeasures can be conducive to reduce the cost of value-added service enterprise, afford value-added service enterprise enough profit space in the process of renting internet access resources from upstream foundation operators and providing value-added service to website users, stimulate enthusiasm of downstream value-added service enterprise, and attract more potential entrants to enter into access market.

5.4. *To strengthen internet access service quality supervision*

Because internet access service quality is low in Shaanxi, foundation operators and value-added service enterprises should strengthen service quality and set service quality as a key inspection index in enterprise management.

In order to improve service quality supervision, regulator should establish the supervision platform for internet access service quality, obtain terminal website users' service quality evaluation information at any time, and monitor customer complaints about internet access service. Whether the government or the internet access service providers shall change ideas, set up the guiding ideology centered on website users, and initiatively adapt to the requirements of the internet access market. To meet the needs of internet users should be the lifeline of foundation operators and value-added service enterprises and the only standard for supervising telecom enterprises.

5.5. *To increase support for value-added service enterprises*

Three basic operators are very strong with a strongly monopolistic position, but the market position of downstream private enterprises is quite low. Downstream enterprises cannot get the right position despite of their studious development. They lack proper protection and promotion measures from upstream operators or government. Even basic operators have robbed customers of value-added service enterprises more than once, however downstream value-added service enterprises have more and more responsibilities. So it's a huge obstacle that goes against the coordinated development of Shaanxi internet access industry chain and restricts the maturity of Shaanxi internet access market.

As mentioned previously, the propaganda of internet value-added service enterprise in Shaanxi Province is so weak that mass website users have run off, which must be paid high attention by Shaanxi Communication Administration. Government regulators gave value-added service enterprise less support in their initial phase and emphasized managerial control too much, which impeded their development.

Therefore, Shaanxi communication administration and local government should promote the development of private value-added service enterprise (revenue, preferential tax, human resources, control policies and public service platform, etc.) and encourage them to publicize their internet access business through network, broadcasting, television and newspapers and many other kinds of medium, so as to expand their internet access market share, restore the loss of customers and retain the existing customers.

6. Conclusions

- Based on classic Structure-Conduct-Performance paradigm of industrial organization theory, the paper analyzed market regulation institutions, upstream foundational network operators, downstream value-added service enterprises and website customer step by step.
- Spot survey was applied to evaluate development situation of internet access market in Shaanxi province, based on which we found serious user loss and gloomy ISP business.
- Further, as we discussed next, competition situation of upstream foundational network operators appeared high market concentration, service homogeneity and high industry barriers, while downstream value-added service enterprises adopted simplex competition means and backward management means.
- All results indicated that Shaanxi internet access market extremely lacked effective competition and vitality.
- Therefore, internet access supervision countermeasures were to realize the effective competition, including supervision system based on industry chain level, interconnection supervision, price supervision, quality supervision and government support.

Acknowledgments

The paper was sponsored by National Natural Science Foundation of China (Number: 71102149), Research project of humanities and social science on Young Fund of the Ministry of Education in China(Number: 12YJC790084): “Research on Interaction between Foreign Technology Diffusion and Domestic Enterprise's Research and Development Investment——based on the Perspective of Evolutionary Game Theory”, and New Star Team of Xi’an University of Posts & Telecommunications (Number: XY201406).

References

1. S. Basu, S. Chakraborty and M. Sharma, Pricing cloud services—the impact of broadband quality, *Omega*, **50**, 1 (2015).
2. C. Bouras, V. Kokkinos and G. Tseliou, Methodology for Public Administrators for selecting between open source and proprietary software, *Telematics and Informatics*, **30**, 2 (2013).
3. J. J. Laffont, J. Taylor and Hanhui Hu, etc., *Telecom Competition,* (The People's Posts and Telecommunications Press, Beijing, 2001). (In Chinese).

4. K. H. Neumann and I. Vogelsang, How to price the unbundled local loop in the transition from copper to fiber access networks? *Telecommunications Policy*, 37, 10 (2013).
5. L. Correa and P. Crocioni, Can evidence of pricing power help market power assessment? Broadband Internet in Ireland and the Netherlands, *Telecommunications Policy*, 36, 5 (2012).
6. H. G. Lin, Comparative analysis of the SCP of Chinese Telecom industry before and after the new round telecommunication reform, *Modern Finance and Economics-Journal of Tianjin University of Finance and Economics*, **1** (2012). (In Chinese).
7. Y. C Ao, G Wei and C. Z. Chen, Study on China telecom price regulation model, *Price: Theory & Practice*, **8** (2012). (In Chinese).
8. W. J. Wang and T. J. Lv, Research on Competition Regulatory Policies of China's Telecom Market, *Journal of Beijing University of Posts and Telecommunications(Social Sciences Edition)*, **14**, 1 (2012). (In Chinese).
9. G. F. Ding, The legal regulating of abusing dominant market position in the telecoms sector with suspected monopolistic conducts of China Telecom, China Unicom for example, *Jiang-huai Tribune*, **3** (2012). (In Chinese).
10. Z. J. Guo, and X. D. Sun, The price compensation mechanism of the universal service in monopoly industries with Posts and Telecommunications for example, *Price: Theory & Practice*, **10** (2014). (In Chinese).
11. X. Y. Liu, Interpretation of natural monopoly field based on regulation economics with American power, public enterprises and telecommunications industries for example, *Academic Forum*, **12** (2013). (In Chinese).

The Weak Signal Detection for Drill Pipe Acoustic Communication Based on Stochastic Resonance

Si-Min Kang[1,2,a], Fu-Cai Qian[1,b], Wei-Bin Cheng[2,c] and Yue-Long Wang[2,d]

[1]School of Automation and Information Engineering, Xi'an University of Technology Xi'an 710048, China

[2]School of Electronics Engineering, Xi'an Shiyou University Xi'an 710065, China

E-mail: [a]siminkang@xsyu.edu.cn, [b]fcqian@xaut.edu.cn, [c]wbcheng@xsyu.edu.cn, [d]ylwang@ xsyu.edu.cn

In this paper, the nonlinear SR system is introduced into the underground short-range sonic weak signal detection and successfully realized the drilling acoustic communication signal detection. It is better solved by the frequency modulation technology, introduced in the process of detection, that the SR system is not suitable for most impact attenuation signal and the SR system parameters are hard to match with the testing signals. Using stochastic resonance system has realized the drill pipe sound waves detection and parameter estimation under low SNR signal and the detection method breaks through the limitations of traditional detection method of weak signal by suppressing noise to improve the processing gain. Through the signal and noise and SR system to work together, it change part of the noise energy into signal energy, and produce resonance output similar to mechanics. This detection method greatly improves the effect of acoustic signal detection in weak signal environment and the purpose of the system outputting SNR to achieve identification of weak signals.

Keywords: Stochastic Resonance; Weak Signal Detection; Short-distance Communication of Downhole; Acoustic Wave; Noise.

1. Introduction

Downhole measurement and control technology's development is a major technological progress in the field of drilling. With the deepening of the oil and gas exploration and development, drilling technology step by step enters into the era of refinement, information and automation. It is hoped that more accurate and real-time understand in underground work status, and how to realize the two-way, fast borehole acoustic signal transmission is still the key which restrict the development of the downhole measurement and control technology[1]. Acoustic transmission mode is not limited by outside conditions such as drilling medium, formation. Not only it can transmit data, and meet the needs of drilling information transmission in conventional drilling, but also can satisfy the demand of drilling new technology, new process and the need of high-speed MWD information transmission[2].

Underground sound waves in the transmission will be influenced by bit vibration in the process of drilling, casing rotation collision with wall and its resonance noise, etc. Sound waves tend to drown in the noise in the transmission, and if the measurement data is very short, or noise frequency and signal frequency is close or overlap, the conventional signal analysis methods such as spectrum analysis, wavelet analysis or other noise suppression method will fail. So we must use effective signal processing method, extract effective acoustic information from the sound waves signals of downhole near-bit lateral, provide reliable basis for accurate judgment of downhole measurement information.

Although there are some research results about the theory of Stochastic Resonance in weak signal detection, the application of the technology for underground short-range sonic signal detection reports couldn't be seen. The SR is a kind of nonlinear algorithm using noise, in principle it can improve the signal-to-noise ratio at the same time maximize the retention of useful signal. The early stages of the SR research is aimed at the weak periodic signal[3], but in recent years the study found the SR can also be used to deal with non-periodic signal[5]. So some scholars began to think about using the SR to detect impact signal[6]. Under the idea put forward in this paper by using the theory of stochastic resonance to detect the short-range sonic weak signal in the downhole. Because only under the condition of small parameter could the bistable SR system make the moderate amount noises be chosen by the input signal and produce the SR phenomenon. In engineering practice, the received acoustic signal has large attenuation, and information such as the signal amplitude and noise intensity is unknown. Therefore, based on the basic principle of SR, frequency modulation technology is introduced, and make the periodic impact signal transform to the small parameter range, and then according to the actual situation of signal amplitude and noise intensity of unknown, adaptively adjust the system parameters, eventually make the system enter a state of optimal SR, so as to better detect the weak acoustic signals submerged in noise.

2. The Principle and Model for Detecting Weak Signal with SR

The SR theory was first put forward by Italian scholars Benzi[7], to explain the phenomenon that every 100000 years or so glacial and warm climate period appear alternately in the ancient earth weather. The theory expounds the idea: when the weak periodic signal submerged in strong background noise go through a nonlinear system and the system nonlinearity, signal and noise reach some kind of match, background noise can enhance the weak periodic signal transmission and make the system output signal-to-noise ratio strengthen.

Bistable system is the basis of the stochastic resonance phenomenon, and lang zhiwan equation which has the dual potential well nature is a typical model for describing the nonlinear bistable system. Nonlinear bistable system driven by external forces and gaussian white noise is one of the most frequently adoptive nonlinear systems, and the mathematical model[8] is given as:

$$\frac{dx}{dt} = ax - bx^3 + AS(t) + N(t) \tag{1}$$

Where a, b are the bistable system parameters. $S(t) = A\sin(2\pi f_0 t)$ is the measured signal, and can be a periodic or non-periodic signal. A is the signal amplitude. $f_0$is the signal frequency. $N(t)$ is background noise. It is Gaussian white noise whose variance is D and mean is 0. The statistical properties of $N(t)$ is given as:

$$\langle N(t) \rangle = 0$$

$$\langle N(t)N(t') \rangle = 2D\delta(t - t')$$

WhereDis noise intensity. Here, the expression of the potential function is as follows:

$$V(x) = -\frac{1}{2}ax^2 + \frac{1}{4}bx^4 \tag{2}$$

Where a, b are system parameters, and $a > 0, b > 0$. In the absence of incentives and noise, barrier height $\Delta V = a^2/4b$, and the two potential well of The potential function respectively is $X_{12} = \mp\sqrt{a/b}$, Potential well spacing is $\Delta x = 2\sqrt{a / b}$. When $S(t)$, $N(t)$ and non-linear system match in some way, $N(t)$ jumps in the two potential well with the change of $S(t)$, so as to achieve the effect of strengthening the $S(t)$. This is the basic principle of bistable system SR in the over damping state.

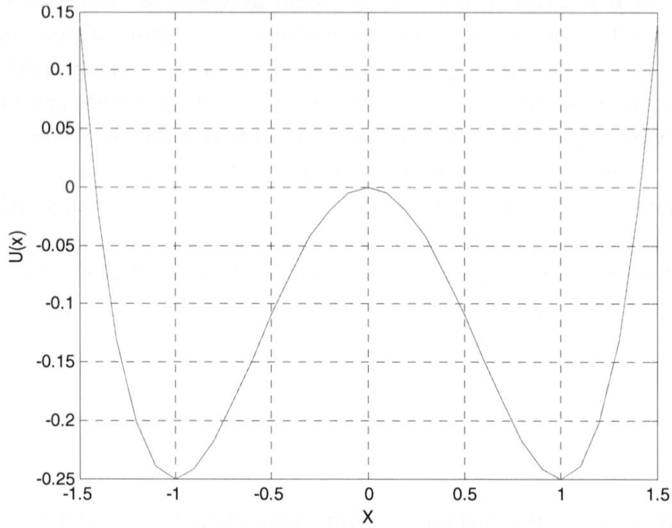

Fig. 1. Bistable potential system

To generate stochastic resonance, the key is that the system, signal and noise achieve a better match. In signal detection, generally the size of the signal cannot be changed, and only can change the size of the system parameters and noise intensity. The system parameter a directly determines the highest transition frequency of the system output, and the value is generally larger than the signal frequency values to one or two orders of magnitude. The value of the parameter a, b determines the barrier height of the system. When the value of the parameter a, b is determined, the noise intensity value D can be determined through the experiment. When the collaborative energy of the signal and the noise can overcome the barrier blocking and switch with signal frequency between the two steady states, system will achieve stochastic resonance state.

In order to analyze the bistable SR system's performance of detecting weak signals, we test for weak signal detection. The SR system equation of small signal detection method uses the fourth order Runge - Kutta method to solve the equation (1). It constructs a simulation signal polluted by noise:
$s = 0.6\cos(2\pi ft)$.

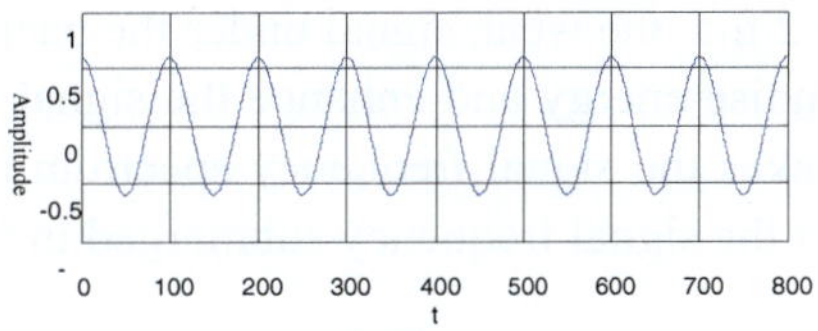

(a) Input signal

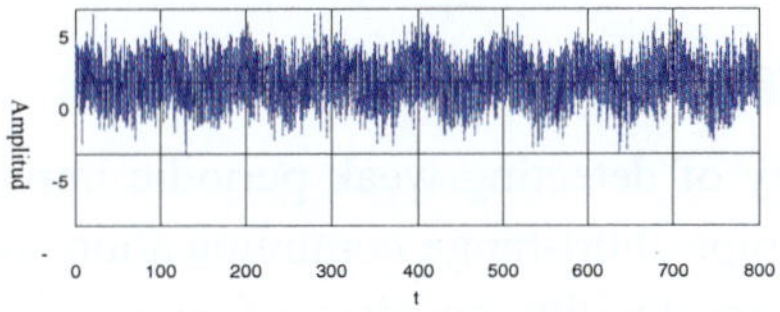

(b) Signal adding noise

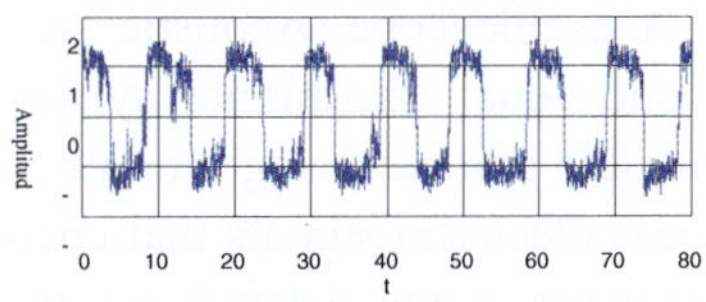

(c) The output signal time-domain plot

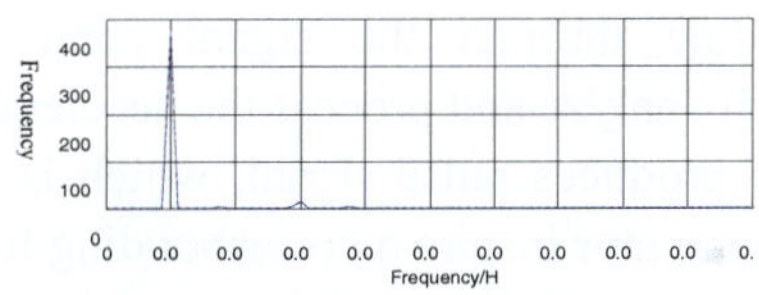

(d) The output signal spectrogram

Fig. 2. The stochastic resonance of cosine signal with noise

Note: Sampling frequency fs=10, The input signal frequency f=0.01, noise intensity D=0.8, the system parameters a=b=1, the sampling points N=8000, the input signal amplitude a=0.6

The stochastic resonance of the bistable system can detect the slim cosine drive signals which are submerged in the strong noise, as shown in figure 2. Figure 2 (a) is the original cosine signal; Figure 2 (b) is cosine signal submerging in strong noise; Figure 2 (c) is the output of the bistable system; Figure 2 (d) is the output signal spectrum. By the graph, you can see that through the bistable system, we can clearly see the waveform whose fundamental frequency is cosine signal frequency, and when the waveform signal peaks, particle is located at the positive potential well; when the waveform signal achieves the minimum, particle is located in the negative potential well. Parameters a = 1, b = 1, figure 2 is a bistable SR system input and output time-domain and frequency domain power spectrum diagram. It can be seen from the figure 2 that the weak signal under the background of strong noise inhibit some of the noise energy and enhance the signal energy, after through a bistable SR. This makes the signal frequency spectrum component highlighted, thus can easily detect the signal frequency submerged in the noise.

3. Experimental Model of Drill Pipe Acoustic Signal Detection

3.1. *Experiment design*

To check on the ability of detecting weak periodic impact signal for stochastic resonance in the drill pipe short-range communication, we design the following experiments: experiment facility consists of simulation drill pipe, XD2022 signal generator, excitation device (5-5000 H z), CA-YA-117 triaxial accelerometer, DTS403A oscilloscope. Acoustic signal transmission system is shown in Fig.3.the acoustic signal transmission system composes of transmitting module, transmission module and receiving module. First the pulse generator in the emission part produces electrical signals that encourage vibrator to generate acoustic signals, and acoustic signal through the transmission medium (pipe) transmit to receive accelerometer, then the acceleration signal is transmitted to data acquisition module through the signal conditioner, finally the data acquisition module will analyze and process the acceleration signal.

Emission module produces pulse signal, which is transmitted to the pulse generator, and pulse generator inspire a corresponding frequency acoustic signal. Through transmission to a receiving module, acoustic wave receiving transducer transform the acoustic signal into electrical signal, and the acoustic signal is transmitted to data acquisition module. Finally the data acquisition module will analyze and process the electrical signal.

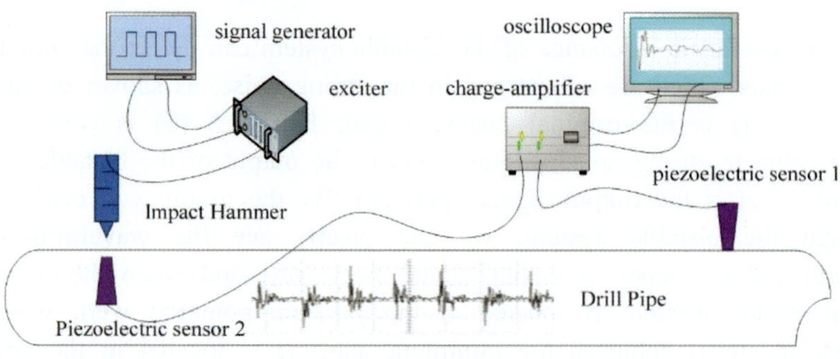

Fig. 3. Acoustic signal transmission system

Communication experiment was carried out on the drill pipe. In specific communication, in addition to the characteristics of the channel, the characteristic of transmitting and receiving devices, downhole noise etc need to be considered. Considering the above factors, use 10HZ acoustic wave to conduct the test. The signal form of incentive sound waves in the drill pipe is given as:

$$x(t) = A_0 e^{-\varepsilon t} \cos(\omega_d t + \varphi) \tag{3}$$

Where $\varepsilon = r_m/2m$, is the attenuation coefficient; r_m is the system resistance coefficient; the minus sign shows the damping force and movement are in the opposite direction; m is particle quality; $\omega_d = \sqrt{\omega_0^2 - \varepsilon^2}$, is the inherent circular frequencies of the damped vibration; A_0 and φ are two real constant determined by the initial conditions. Set the initial amplitude $A_0 = 1$, attenuation coefficient $\varepsilon = 0.1$, the initial phase $\varphi = 0$, the inherent circular frequency determining its damping vibration $\omega_d = 0.1$.

3.2. *Analog signal simulation results and analysis*

Construct a simulation signal polluted by noise and the signal amplitude, signal frequency. Make this simulation signal act on the bistable system, and set the bistable system parameter a=l, b=1, and Runge-Kutta calculate step length. The time domain can be seen as a periodic pulse signal, and each periodic pulse signal is composed of exponentially decaying cosine signal. Due to the pulse signals are positive pulse, so set iterative initial value to be 1, and the particle will oscillation in the negative potential well. the output of the bistable system is shown in Fig. 4.

When the simulation signal in Fig. 4 (a) is joined the noise of the strength D=0.08, the time-domain diagram will be difficult to identify the fault signal characteristic, as shown in Fig. 4(b). If the Fig. 4(b) with noise signal is input to bistable systems with all parameters the same, then get the system resonance output in Fig. 5. As is shown in Fig. 5, we can respectively clearly see the periodic pulse waveform of attenuation signal and frequency of communication and the characteristics of the times spectrum in the time-frequency diagram. It shows that the bistable system can deal with shock signal of periodic oscillation attenuation and other types, and the weak impact signal feature with noise polluting can be extracted effectively.

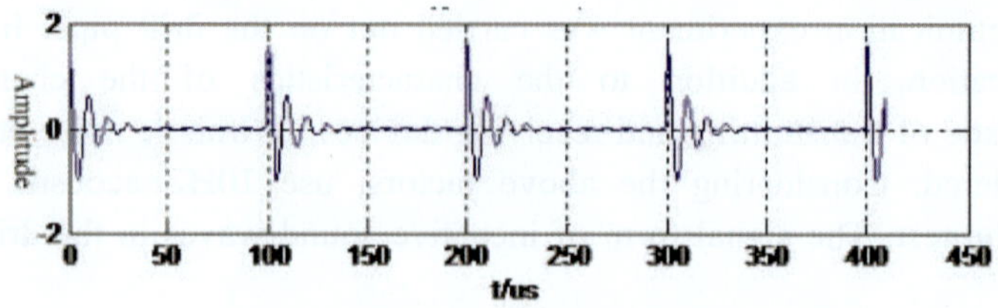

(a) Periodic attenuation Iutput signal

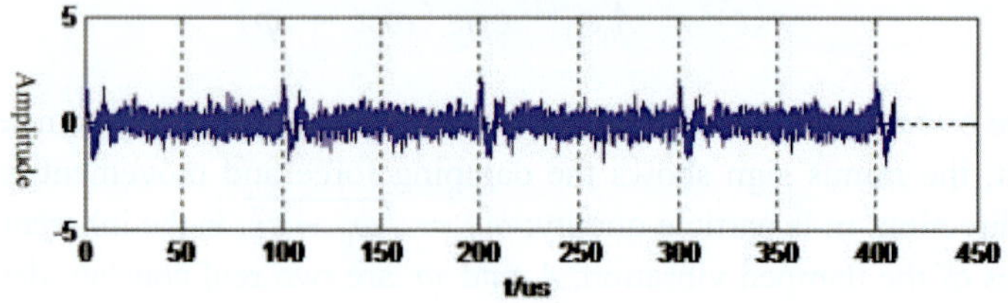

(b) Load noise periodic attenuation signal

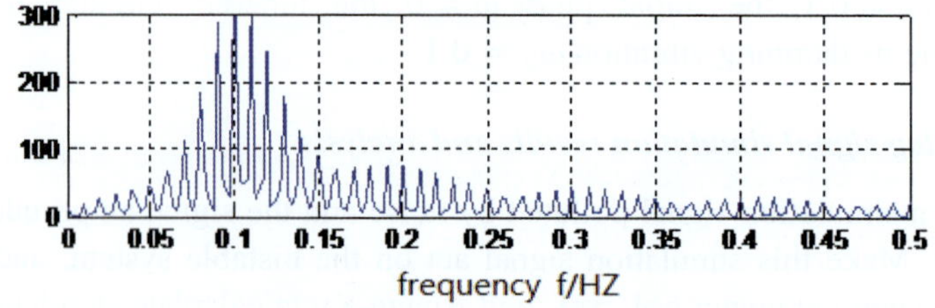

(c) Frequency spectrum of input signal

Fig. 4. Short-range communication acoustic wave analog signal time and frequency domain diagram

Compared with Fig. 4, the high frequency part of the output signal reduces and the low frequency part amplifies in Fig. 5.The main reason is that the stochastic resonance lorentz distribution of bistable system can damp the high frequency signal attenuation and amplificate the low frequency signal. The attenuation of high frequency components make the free oscillation part of domain waveform fast damped, and the energy increase of the low frequency components further highlight the characteristics of time domain pulse Periodic waveform. Under the resonance action of the negative potential well in a bistable system, the system output periodic pulse whose time domain signal presents the fast attenuation oscillation around steady state solutions 0.1.

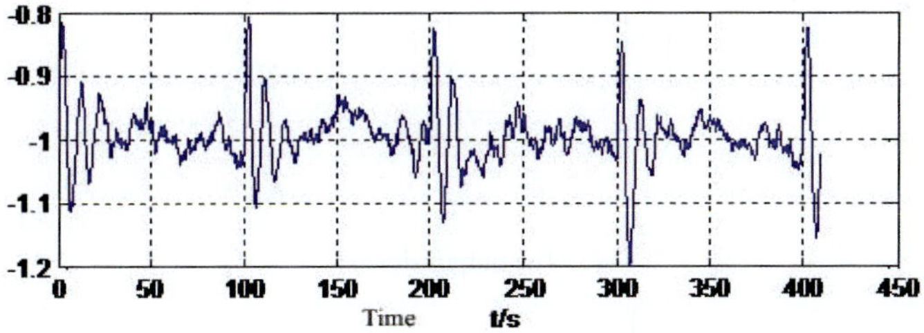

(a) Output signal amplitude chart

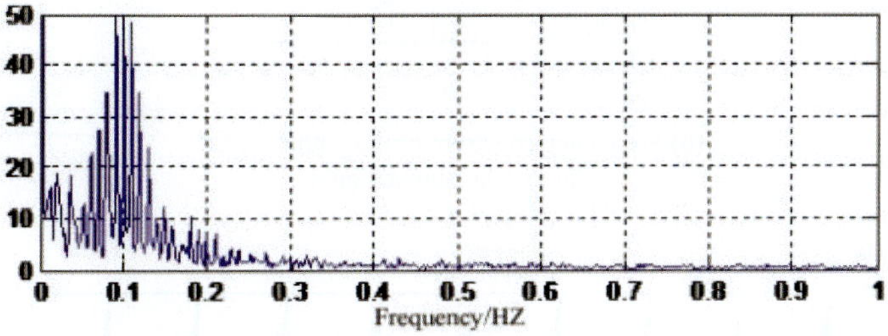

(b) Frequency spectrum of output signal

Fig. 5. Time and frequency domain diagram of short-range communication acoustic wave simulation signal after the dual stabilization system

4. Case Analysis

Experiments are conducted on the acoustic signal transmission system test bench. Acceleration sensor installed on the drill pipe vertical direction is used for data collection. Sampling frequency f is 2000 Hz and signal frequency is 10Hz. Time domain waveform and spectrum of the measured signal is shown in Fig. 6(a), Fig. (b). Some characteristic frequency of sound waves can be estimated when acoustic signal is detected. So the sampling frequency and the adjustment coefficient R can be correspondingly preset. Here set the sampling frequency $f_s = 2000Hz$, and 4096 data is collected. By the previous discussion, the acoustic frequency which may occur in the short-range sonic communications testing are mostly between a few Hertz to dozens of Hertz, and need to have a stochastic resonance treatment by frequency adjustment method. Now set frequency area contraction ratio R=100, sampling frequency $f_s = 2000Hz$. First pass through single stability nonlinear system, the system parameter a=100. b=106.The results are shown in Fig. 7.

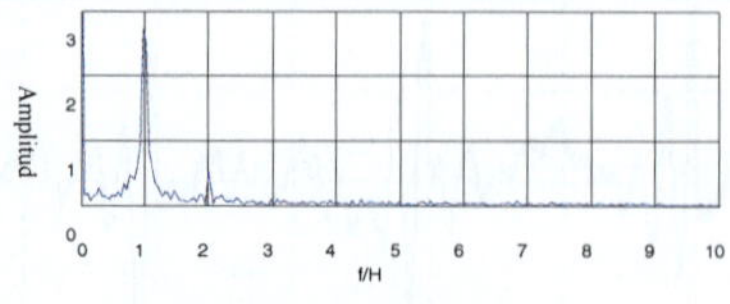

(a) The output signal

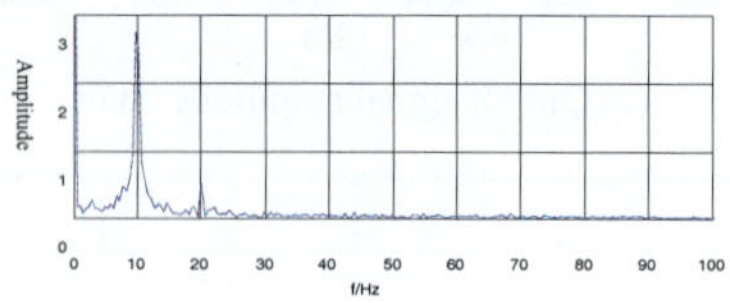

(b) Frequency spectrum of the output signal

Fig. 6. The output signal

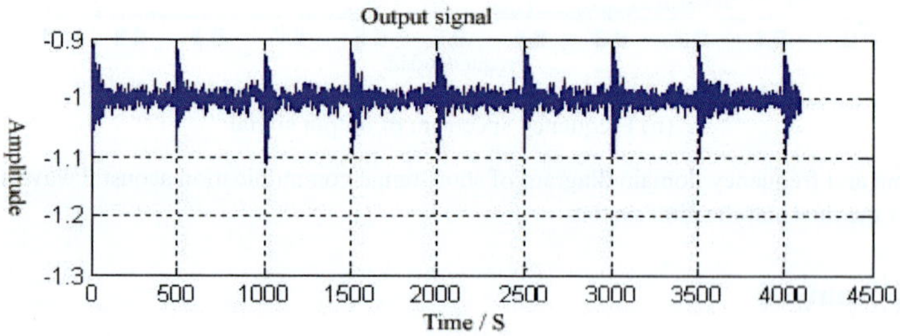

Fig. 7. The output signal

5. Conclusions

In view of the practical problems of weak signal detection for downhole short-range acoustic wave, based on the bistable system of small parameter stochastic resonance theory, this article uses the frequency modulation technology to realize the stochastic resonance of large parameter, and the method is successfully applied to the extraction of weak periodic impact signal in strong noise background. This study verifies the effectiveness of stochastic resonance for frequency adjustment in solving the signal problem of large parameters, provides a good solution for common problems of weak signal detection in engineering.

Acknowledgements

This work was financially supported by National Natural Science Foundation of China (61273127, U1534208, 61473222), Science and Technology Project of

Shaanxi Province (2016GY-108), The Key Laboratory for Fault Diagnosis and Maintenance of Spacecraft in Orbit(SDML_OF2015004) and The Key Program of National Natural Science Foundation of China (61533014).

References

1. Yan Wenhui, Peng yong, Zhang Shaohuai. Development Principle of rotary steering drilling tool [J]. Journal of oil, 2005, 26 (5): 94-97. In Chinese
2. Jing Yufu, cheng Weibin, Guo Yingna, Huo Aiqing. Wavelet denoising of Downhole casing acoustic communication [J]. Journal of petroleum machinery, 2011, 33 (6) 6: 33-35 In Chinese
3. Xia Junzhong, Liu Yuanhong, Ma Zongpo, etc. research of weak signal detection Based on the modulated stochastic resonance [J]. Journal of vibration and shock, 2012, 31 (3): 132-135 In Chinese
4. Fan Yangyu, Li Lipin, Dang Ruisheng. Research of any large frequency weak signal detection based on stochastic resonance method [J]. Journal of instruments and meters, 2013, (3): 566-572 In Chinese
5. Fan Shengbo, Wang Taiyong, Leng Yonggang, etc. detection of weak periodic impact signal Based on the stochastic resonance of variable scale [J]. China mechanical engineering, 2006 (4): 387-390 In Chinese
6. Shi Peng, Leng Yonggang, Fan Shengbo, etc. Research of processing weak shock signal in bistable system [J]. Journal of vibration and shock, 2012, 31 (6): 150-154 In Chinese
7. Beniz R, Sutera A, Vulpiani A. The mechanism of stochastic resonance [J]. The Journal of Physical A, 1981, 14(11): 4453-4572. In Chinese
8. Bruce M, Kurt W. Theory of stochastic resonance [J]. Physical Review A, 1989, 39(9): 4854-4869. In Chinese

The Differential Horizontal Well Design Method of Tight Sandstone Gas Reservoir

Tao Sun[1,a], Bin Fu[2,b] and Rong Xie[1,c]

[1]*School of computer science in Xi'an Shiyou University*
Shannxi Xi'an 710065, China

[2]*Sulige Research Center, PetroChina Chanqing Oilfield Company*
Xi'an 710018, China

E-mail: [a]765536036@qq.com, [b]fubin_cq@petrochina.com.cn, [c]xierong@xsyu.edu.cn

Horizontal well is an effective method to improve the recovery of tight sandstone gas reservoirs, but this kind of gas reservoir has strong heterogeneity with sandstone multiple stack and effective sandstone scattered development. During the implement of horizontal well, there are risk of lost circulation or sticking which will impair the gas field productivity. Besides, unreasonable design of well trajectories will cause insufficient development of reserves and loss of effective sandstone. In order to avoid the above phenomena, the geological study of tight sandstone reservoir need to be strengthened. Through long period field test of Sulige gas field, the differential geological design of unique well is determined. Then, the potential risk can be avoided based on well trajectories and the development of effective sandstone can be optimized. Using one well with the different horizontal well design ideas, from geological design to avoid risks. On the basis of abundant drilling geological parameters of Sulige gas field, this paper determines development characteristics of sandstone and effective sandstone using statistical method. Combined with previous research, three kinds of sand body stack types available for horizontal well development is proposed. Then on this basis, there are three kinds of well trajectories and effective sand body distribution characteristics. Base on this, three kinds of horizontal well trajectory and three-dimensional horizontal wells are designed to save the filed space and provide guarantee for improving the production efficiency of gas field.

Keywords: Horizontal Well; Tight Sandstone Gas Reservoir; Strong Heterogeneity; Geological Design.

1. Introduction

Tight sandstone gas reservoir derives from Natural Gas Policy Act of the United States in 1978, in which sandstone reservoir with natural gas permeability equal to or less than $0.1\times10^{-3}\mu m^2$ is defined as the tight sandstone gas reservoir. Industry standard of our country released in 2011, which defines tight sandstone gas reservoir as overburden pressure matrix permeability equal to or less than $0.1\times10^{-3}\mu m^2$, and usually without natural capacity or with natural capacity lower than inferior limit of industrial gas flow[1,2]. In this kind of gas reservoir, the sand body is usually layered or lenticular shaped development, and effective sand is multi-layered with small single layer thickness. The reservoir is with physical properties of low porosity and low permeability, low abundance, and no obvious features of gas-water interface. According to foreign development experiences, horizontal well is an important technical method to improve the recovery. Through optimizing the developing method, daily gas production can reach 3-5 times than vertical wells[4], but with sandstone multiple stack and effective sandstone scattered development, the tight sandstone gas reservoir is of strong heterogeneity, and easy to cause lost circulation or sticking and other engineering problems during the implementation as well as insufficient development of reserves. With the continuous improvement of horizontal well technology, three-dimensional horizontal well, extended horizontal well, stepped horizontal well and branch horizontal well technology have been developed. Therefore, fully understanding the geological characteristics of tight sandstone gas reservoir and strengthening horizontal well types design still need further exploration.

Since horizontal well test of in 2002, Sulige gas field has experienced four development stages and is in its scale application stage now. Through the analysis of sand body superposed relationship of braided river channel and space development characteristics of effective sandstone in the main gas-bearing layer, combined with the existing technology development of horizontal well, differential horizontal well design method of tight sandstone gas reservoir with strong heterogeneity is explored can play an important role in improving reserves development and enhance the recovery.

2. Development Characteristics of Sand Body and Effective Sand Body

2.1. *Development characteristics of sand body*

He-8 member is the main gas producing formation of Sulige gas field, composite sand body of braided river and meandering river developed under the control of the inland lake-delta depositional system[6-8]. Statistics suggest that the average drilling ratio of sand body is 94.81%. With the thickness of 9.8m and sand body drilling ratio of 83.71%, the second thin layer of lower He 8 member is the most important layer of sand body development and suitable for horizontal well development (Table 1). According to the sand body drilled characteristics, combined with the predecessors' study of sandy body distribution law in Sulige gas field, the stacked types of composite sand bodies suitable for drilling horizontal well can be summarized as: 1. Massive stacked sand bodies; 2. Multilayer stacked sand bodies; 3. Truncation stacked sand bodies. Massive stacked sand body refers to contiguous composite thick massive sandstone formed lateral migration of high-energy channel in low accommodation space. The thickness of sand body is 5-10m, mainly distributed in the second thin layer of lower He-8 member, and the mudstone layer inside is mainly dense thin layers formed by energy weaken of the water. Multilayer stacked sand body refers to vertically connected or pan connected thick sandstone formed by multi-stage high-energy channel erosion. The thickness of sand body is with a nonuniform distribution in the range of 4-20m. It is easy to meet lithology mutation during the implementation of horizontal well, then thick mudstone will be drilled. Truncation stacked sand bodies refers to vertical multi-stage channel sand body obstructed by thick mudstone or dense layer, which is hard to link in late reformation and cause the insufficient development of reserves.

Table 1 He-8 member sand thickness characteristic table

Segment \ Sand parm	Ave (m)	min (m)	max (m)	MSE (m)	Variance (m)	Sand drilling rate (%)
HE-8_{up}^1	5.99	0.4	27	3.71	13.78	66.58
HE-8_{up}^2	6.97	0.4	43.2	4.19	17.53	73.97
HE-8_{down}^1	8.85	0.4	24.3	4.57	20.92	82.46
HE-8_{down}^2	9.8	0.4	46.2	4.95	24.47	83.71

2.2. *Development characteristics of effective sand body*

The development of effective sandstone is mainly controlled by combination process of sedimentation and diagenesis. The vertical effective sandstone thickness of He-8 member is about 3.93m and the second thin layer of lower He-8 member is the thickest with the average thickness of 4.24m. The first thin layer of upper He-8 member has the minimum variance with a uniform thickness. In each layer the variance of effective sandstone thickness is smaller than that of sandstone thickness (Table 2), which shows that the thickness of effective sand body is more uniform and its distribution is relatively stable. In the plane, due to the complexity structure of the surface in Sulige gas field, high frequency components of seismic wave attenuations quickly (main distribution range of frequency band is 10-35HZ), which increases difficulty of predicting effective sandstone transverse distribution using the seismic data. In order to determine the lateral connectivity of effective sand bodies, effective sand body fine description is implement in the encryption area (well spacing < 600m, row spacing <800m) and interference test is used in the gas field[9].

The description result shows that single effective sand body is mainly irregular ellipse shaped which has the typical sedimentary characteristics of complex channel bar. With the well spacing of 500~600m in east-west direction and 600~800m in north-south direction wells are basically not connected, while with the well spacing of 300~400m in east-west direction and less than 600m in north-south direction wells well interference occur. Then the width of effective sand body can be determined below 500-600m, and length is below 600-800m. Suppose the length of horizontal segment is 1000m, implementation of horizontal well will drill non effective sandstone and connect 2-3 effective sand body. Through detailed geologic analysis, the design of horizontal well can be optimized. Then drilling length of non-effective sandstone can be reduced and reservoir drilling rate can be improved.

Table 2 He-8 member effective sand Thickness characteristic table

EF parm / Segment	average(m)	Min (m)	Max (m)	MSE(m)	variance(m)	Sand drilling rate(%)
HE-8up1	2.95	0.54	13.9	2.04	4.15	9.46
HE-8up2	3.35	0.6	23.24	2.45	6.02	19.37
HE-8down1	4.19	0.42	17.68	2.88	8.28	35.92
HE-8down2	4.24	0.48	37.52	2.82	7.93	44.43

3. Differential Geological Design

3.1. *Differential horizontal well geological design method*

In order to ensure the development effect of horizontal wells, the thought of determining the enrichment zone first and concentrated deployment of horizontal well is adopted. Based on the design foundation of six figures and one table(seismic profile, sand body thickness and effective thickness map of target layer, the top structure maps of sand body, horizontal well trajectory design section and horizontal section target spot design table), the differential horizontal well geological design thought is formed to design the well trajectory based on different stacks type of sand body (Figure 1).

(1) Massive stacked sand bodies: continuous distributed sand body through erosion and lateral erosion, beaded shaped effective sand body developed, using mature straight horizontal well design ideas; (2) Multilayer stacked sand bodies: labyrinth shaped effective sand body under different degrees of erosion , taking the effective sandstone top as target, steady dropped or high angle design the trajectory of horizontal well, adopted different well completion methods to develop different effective sandstone; (3) Truncation stacked sand bodies: vertical multi-stage sand body not connected, and the effective sandstone also isolated from each other, ladder typed horizontal well trajectory is adopted. To avoid engineering problems of lost circulation or sticking, drill the interlayer with rapid drop of inclination and control the well trajectory in about 82 degrees. When drilling the casing reservoir, increase the inclination under the consideration of thickness, drilling the reservoir in a stable inclination so as to achieve the purpose of increasing the discharge area.

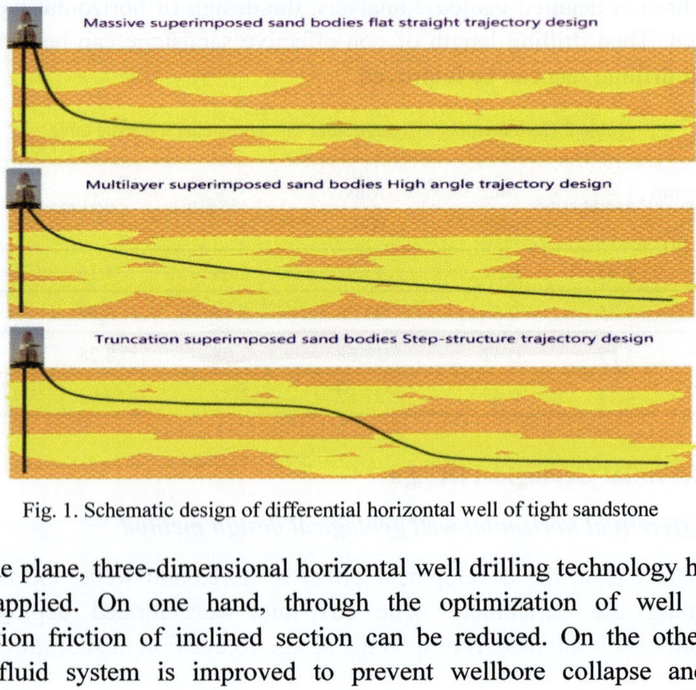

Fig. 1. Schematic design of differential horizontal well of tight sandstone

In the plane, three-dimensional horizontal well drilling technology has been widely applied. On one hand, through the optimization of well profile, construction friction of inclined section can be reduced. On the other hand, drilling fluid system is improved to prevent wellbore collapse and other accidents[10-11]. The maximum displacement of three-dimensional horizontal well reached 600m in the implementation of the Sulige gas field. To take the advantage of saving well field area and reduce environmental destruction and construction period, the design of three-dimensional horizontal wells group and large cluster horizontal well group design is prior to consider (Figure 2). In the new development area where well control degree is low and geological knowledge is relatively not clear, well trajectory is prior to drill the main gas layer and make the developing plan of substitution layer based on the vertical effective sand body distribution of controlled wells.

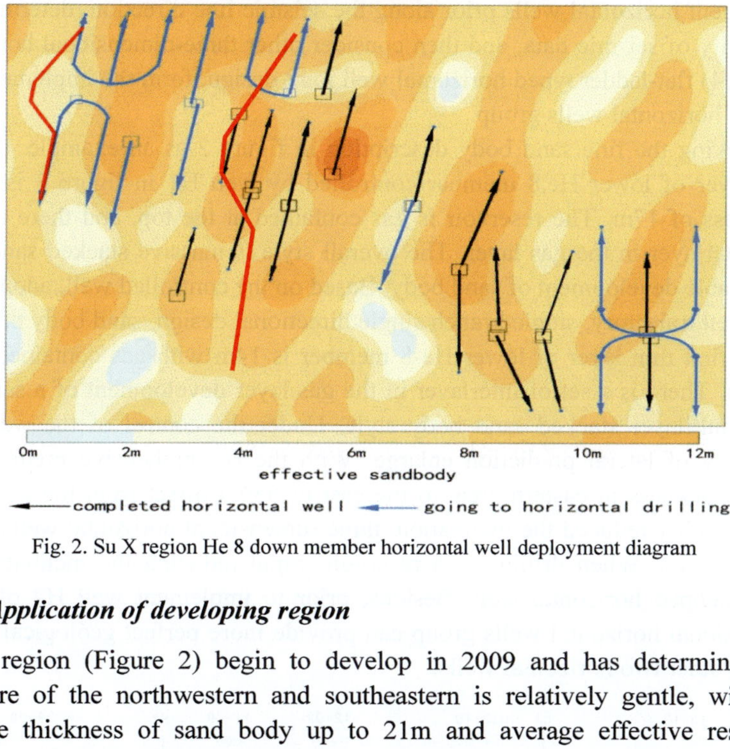

Fig. 2. Su X region He 8 down member horizontal well deployment diagram

3.2. *Application of developing region*

Su X region (Figure 2) begin to develop in 2009 and has determined the structure of the northwestern and southeastern is relatively gentle, with the average thickness of sand body up to 21m and average effective reservoir thickness greater than 5m. Sand bodies controlled by skeleton well, the second thin layer of lower He-8 member is developed by single branch single directional horizontal well and double branch bidirectional horizontal well. The stable production capacity is up to $2\times10^4 m^3$. However, further study of sand body by skeleton well found local enrichment zone also exist in the first thin layer of lower He-8 member expert for the continuous sand body in the second thin layer of lower He-8 member. The reservoir producing degree of simple straight horizontal well is low. Re-description of the sand body in the enrichment area shows that there are mainly massive stacked sand bodies and multilayer stacked sand bodies (Figure 3). Therefore differential horizontal well design method is used to make integral deployment of horizontal well. (1) horizontal well already drilled area: strengthen the geological and production dynamic understanding of adjacent region, extend the old field and form the horizontal wells group; (2) skeleton well controlled area: intensively deploy the horizontal wells, first implement the reliable horizontal well, then adjust the well trajectory design of other horizontal wells based on the implementation effect; (3) no skeleton well area: first design three-dimensional horizontal wells, implement horizontal wells prior along the seismic line direction, determine the reliability of seismic data, and then consider other three-dimensional horizontal wells; (4) flat-ladder typed horizontal well joint design, form the implementation plan of horizontal wells group.

Taking the fine sand body description in figure 2 as an example, the first thin layer of lower He.8 member controlled by well H1 in figure 3 is with a thickness of 17m. The reservoir is gas contained at the top, and there are two sets interlayer in the gas layer. The overall style is massive stacked sand body with stable development of sand body. Based on the controlled well, adopted flat type well trajectory, single branch single directional design, sand body thickness of the first thin layer of lower He-8 member is 14m with gas contained at the bottom. There is a set of interlayer in the gas layer development of a sandwich with multilayer stacked sand body style. Under the control of the wells, the difficulty of lateral prediction enlarge. With the comprehensive prediction of larger thickness in eastern area, to the east of 550m offset from the controlled well, steadily reduced the inclination, three-dimensional horizontal wells design is performed. When drilling non reservoir, rapid reducing the inclination can form stepped horizontal well. Besides, prior to implement well H2 of three-dimensional horizontal wells group can provide more perfect geological data is for the other two horizontal wells.

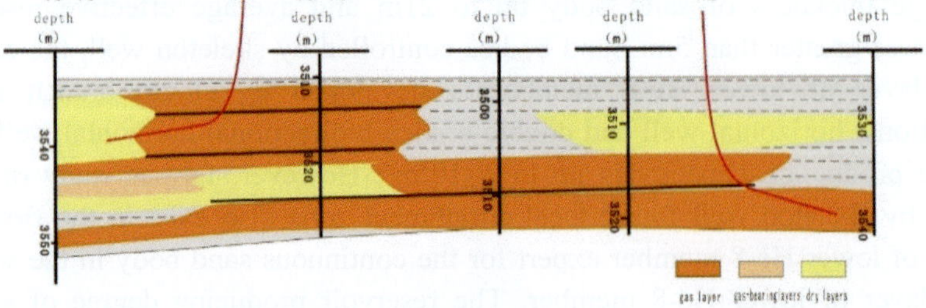

Fig. 3. Su X region Northwest He 8 down member section plane of gas layer

4. Application Effect

According to the geological characteristics of tight sandstone gas reservoir in Sulige gas field, in order to guarantee the reserves producing degree and improve drilling rate of effective sandstone, adopting the design thought of 'overall deployment and differential design' to optimize well patterns and types, with the increased difficulty to select the enrichment region, there are 94 flat typed horizontal wells, 33 horizontal wells with high angle and 15 ladder typed horizontal wells. It has not only greatly improved the producing degree of different reservoirs but also enhance the application space compared with only single branch single directional horizontal well and double branch bidirectional horizontal well design thought in the early application. Statistic shows the average length of differential designed horizontal segment is 1312.7m, sandstone drilling rate is 76.8%, and effective sandstone drilling rate is 60.2%. The average open flow capacity of gas testing is $40\times10^4 m^3/d$ and the average daily gas production of developed wells is $4.9\times10^4 m^3$, maintain development effect of flat typed horizontal well. At the same time, under the promotion of three-dimensional horizontal well design, the floor and road space of well field can be further reduced, and the cost of the investment can be dropped, providing a new method for long-term stable production. The practice proves that the overall implement effect is favorable.

5. Conclusions

(1) Tight sandstone gas reservoir is with strong heterogeneity and diversity sand body stack type. Combined with previous studies, do statistic of sand body development scale in the Sulige gas field and identify three stack types available for horizontal well development.

(2) Implementing fine sand body description and interference well test in encryption area, the effective sand body spatial distribution characteristics of tight gas reservoir in Sulige gas field is determined. The implementation of horizontal wells must drill several sets of effective sandstone. Make sure well trajectory inside the sand body at first, then consider the spatial combination relations of effective sandstone.

(3) Under the complex geological background, combined with the improvement of horizontal well technology, on the basis of the different geological conditions, differential design ideas of horizontal wells are formed to further guarantee the sustainable development of the gas field.

Acknowledgements

This work was financially supported by the Chinese National Natural Science Foundation (51574194), Xi 'an Shiyou university youth Foundation: Drilling risk dynamic evaluation technology research based on the geological mechanical model (YS2903200127).

References

1. Lei qun, wan. Development of tight sandstone gas reservoirs in the United States and Its Implications[J]. Natural gas industry,2010,30. (In Chinese)
2. Liu jiyu, ma zhixin. Research status and development prospect of tight gas bearing sandstone[J]. Natural Gas Geoscience,2008,19. (In Chinese)
3. Kang Yili. Current status and Prospect of key engineering technologies for exploration and development of tight sandstone gas reservoirs in China [J]. Petroleum exploration and development, 2007, 34. (In Chinese)
4. Lv zhikai. Tight gas reservoir horizontal well production capacity and application [J]. Special oil and gas reservoirs,2014,(6):105-108. (In Chinese)
5. lutao, zhangji, liyuegang. Development technology and Prospect of horizontal well in tight sandstone gas reservoir in Surig gas field [J]. Natural gas industry, 2013,33(8):38-43. (In Chinese)
6. Yang hua,fu jinhua,li uxinshe, fanliyong. Formation conditions and exploration technology of Sulige large tight sandstone gas reservoirs [J]. Acta petrolei sinica, 2013,33(S1):27-36. (In Chinese)
7. Fei shixing, wang dongxu, lingang. Technology - the key geological tight sandstone gas reservoir horizontal well integrated development as an example to Su southeast region [J]. Natural Gas Geoscience, 2014, 25(10): 1620-1629. (In Chinese)
8. He guanghuai, li jinbu. New development and Prospect of Surig gas field development [J]. Natural gas industry,2011,31(2)12-16. (In Chinese)
9. li yuegang, xu wen, xiao feng, liu lili, liu shixin, zhang wei. Based on the dynamic characteristics of the wells optimization - dense strong heterogeneous sandstone in Sulige gas field as an example [J]. Natural gas industry,2014,34(11):56-61. (In Chinese)
10. weiyunsheng, hedongbo, jiguang. Optimization of the length of horizontal well in tight sandstone gas [J]. Natural Gas Geoscience, 2012,23(4):775-779. (In Chinese)
11. li wenquan. Overall development technology of horizontal well in Su 53 block [J]. Special oil and gas reservoirs,2015,(1):107-110. (In Chinese)

An Impact of Consumer's Internet Information Adoption Through Electronic Word of Mouth Communication

Safdar Hussain[1,a], Wasim Ahmed[1,b], Rana Muhammad Sohail Jafar[1,c], Ambar Rabnawaz[2,d], Jian-Zhou Yang[1,e,*]

[1]*College of Economics, Fujian Agriculture and Forestry Fuzhou, 350002, China*

[2]*Department of Economics, Faculty of Management & Administrative Sciences, University of Sargodha 40100, Pakistan*

E-mail: [a]ranasafdar@uaar.edu.pk, [b]wasimtouseef@hotmail.com, [c]rana.sohail.jafar@gmail.com, [d]awanambar0@gmail.com, [e]yjianz2015@163.com

This study proposed electronic Word Of Mouth (eWOM) conceptual framework for food products information adoption on the internet. Literature review reveals some streams that affect in eWOM involvement such as reviews, reviewers, websites, online opinion seeking, source credibility and their effects on the process of decision-making in the food industry. The results revealed that there was positive influence of reading some reviews because of product popularity, consistency, regency, usefulness rating of reviewers, and website's reliability before information adoption on the internet. Likewise, eWOM involvement had a significant effect on online opinion seeking or leadership, source credibility and perceived risk. E-marketers need to encourage more on positive eWOM established discussion forums, emphasis on social networking sites, target the specific food products users to attract the customers, get consumers' opinion, and increase the level of information satisfaction which can influence the purchase decision.

Keywords: Perceived Risk; Purchasing Decision; Source Credibility.

1. Introduction

The Internet plays a significant role in marketing and communications. For the most part, internet users evidently participate in different online blogs or communities, either directly or indirectly[1]. Further, particular features of the

*Corresponding author.

Internet provide excellent information to consumers, have extensive collections of different products and brands, and facilitate in decisions regarding price and quality. Cyberspace offers a podium where consumers from all over the world can interact, not only with each other but also with companies [2]. These communications are carried out via e-mail, instant messaging, social blogs, social communities, newsgroups, online chats, review sites, networking sites, and other forums [3]. It is an acceptable central form of universal electronic word of mouth (eWOM) communication which refers to a statement in a positive or negative way about company or product [4-5]. eWOM provide consumers opportunities to extend the options for product information, such as comments posted by different people on the internet. Because of internet usage, people's decision behavior has been changing by eWOM from online opinions as posted by other consumers [6]. Different forms of online communications such as group discussions, social networking, and blogs have been monitored closely to observe how they facilitate eWOM and influence products and consumers [7]. With the increased recognition of information technology and online networking, conventional WOM has evolved into eWOM. Word Of Mouth (WOM) is no longer effective in conveying ideas only to known people. The Internet has facilitated the views of a single individual to be conveyed to anyone around the globe without any limitations.

Many researchers investigated the impact of eWOM behaviors such as perceived value and quality, satisfaction, commitment, information adoption, source credibility and others but not explained that why customers like to read eWOM [8]. It is interesting that writers and readers are not known by each other's but increasing day by day on eWOM platforms. Information sharing between them will not be credible because people don't trust each other's, but it's true that customers read the reviews on websites before making the right decision, so there is some impact or influence of eWOM on people [9].

The same reviews & comments can provoke different responses [9]. So it is interesting to investigate the extent of eWOM information influence on the people specifically comments readers [10]. The existing literature used dual process theories to explain how people get influenced by information [11] to investigate what factors of eWOM information lead to consumer's purchase decision [12]. In the context of China as one major developing country, this paper studies the effect of online analyses of purchasing decision that online reviews have an impact on consumer purchasing decision take attention the repute of reviewers' and the website's as a consistent source of information.

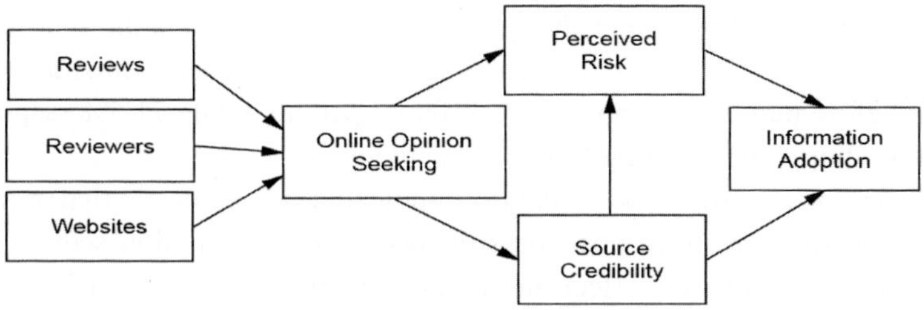

Fig. 1. The conceptual framework.

2. Methodology

To observe consumer reviews, reviewers and websites characteristics measured through the construct of Al Mana and Mirza [13]. Online opinion seeking is a dimension of eWOM where customers seek advice from opinion leaders to fulfill the purpose of purchasing decision. Construct of Flynn, Goldsmith [14] and Darden and Reynolds [15] have been used to measure to online opinion seeking. Source credibility has been used the construct of Cheung, Lee [12], Sussman and Siegal [11], Wu and Shaffer [16] and Wu [17] to measure it. Perceived risk is a dimension of eWOM communication which help in product selection and reduces the ambiguity, decrease the anxieties, and increase confidence in product choices, followed by the study of Bettman [18].

To test hypotheses, a quantitative method was chosen for this research, used convenience sampling to assess online shoppers of food products based on non-probability sampling. Three independent variables and two mediators have been observed the relationship with the dependent variable of the willingness of buy the food products. Three hundred and forty respondents were selected as a sample size from different regions of the People's Republic of China. Before entering the variables into regression model Confirmatory Factor Analysis (CFA) was used, for this purpose, AMOS was used to check CFA reliability and validity, while for the seven fit measures of Structure Equation Modeling (SEM) was checked the values of study model.

3. Results and Discussions

In this research, 43.8 percent (149 numbers) respondents are males, 56.2 percent (191 numbers) females respondents. On those surveyed' age ranges between 21 to 40 years were the highest frequency of 68%, while bachelor degree holders have taken part in this study with a high range of frequency i.e. 42.1% with total 143 numbers. The frequency of internet usage (range between 1-10 hours) in a week at a higher rate with 68.3% with a total number of 232 numbers and

82% respondents made online shopping and 18% respondents did not avail this facility. Seventy-four percent respondents read reviews/comments on the internet before purchase as posted by different people, while 71.5% respondents did online shopping regarding food product items.

Regression coefficients estimation indicated in Table 2 that consumer reviews and websites have positive influence on online opinion seeking, while reviewers have a negative effect on values of range 0.57, -.02 and 0.50. Online opinion seeking has a positive impact on source credibility and perceived risk with the value of 0.75 and 0.84. Source credibility has an adverse impact on perceived risk with the value range of -.07, while positively influence value reached 0.49 on information adoption, and perceived risk positively influence on internet information adoption with the value range of 0.76 respectively.

Table 1. Respondents demographics and search information (n= 340).

	Frequency	Percent		Frequency	Percent
Gender			The frequency of internet usage in a week?		
Male	149	43.8	1-5 hours	56	16.4
Female	191	56.2	6-10 hours	108	31.8
Age			11-20 hours	124	36.5
Under 20	18	05.3	21 hours or above	52	15.3
21-30	127	37.4	Ever shopped online before?		
31-40	104	30.6	Yes	278	82.0
41-50	63	18.5	No	62	18.0
51 and above	28	08.2	Read reviews/ comments before purchase?		
Education level			Yes	252	74.0
Diploma/ Certificate	36	10.6	No	88	26.0
Under bachelor degree	86	25.3	Ever shopped online food products?		
Bachelor degree	143	42.1	Yes	243	71.5
Master degree or above	75	22.0	No	97	28.5

Participants agreed with the statement that the consistency of the reviews that were posted on the website had an impact on online opinions. Concerning the importance of a website's product reviews on the decision making of consumers, participants agreed that such reviews are helpful when seeking the opinion. The top-ranked statement in this section of the questionnaire is the one related to the impact of highly rated products through online reviews and agreed with the value of such a rating in their decision-making process. It is suggested that other reviewers' evaluations of reviews should be presented to customers. Participants disagree with the fact that the nickname or the real name of the reviewers affected their purchase decision, the responses were more or less similar and followed a similar pattern. The reviewer gender has the least impact on purchasing decisions, agree that the reviewer's gender makes a big difference on their purchasing decision The factor of reviewer gender, nick or real names, and residence is assessed with the least influence on purchasing decisions. Participants agreed on the effect of the website popularity on the consumer purchasing decision. Therefore, it can be recommended that popularity, reliability, internationality, and ownership of the website are critical for Chinese consumer respectively. The role of retail websites varies rendering new sites and webpage's design characteristics also have an influence on consumers' purchasing decisions through locate and product selection. Many researchers explained factors like playfulness, information quality and service, system usage and design which are critical for website's success. Website contents offered by information and website design presented the way to customers are two essential roles of considerations for online retailers. Product purchasing or services associated with customers' views as consequences alter the risk perception in the shape of distinct of inherent and handled classes. Perceived risk is a major element in e-commerce for customers' perspective, while from managerial perceptive that business strategies can reduce the consumers' risk with the understanding of mitigate and consumer react, however, alternative payment method and comparison among product are most important for customers. It can be concluded that security or privacy are the key factors of perceived risk, and consumers' get more attention during online shopping.

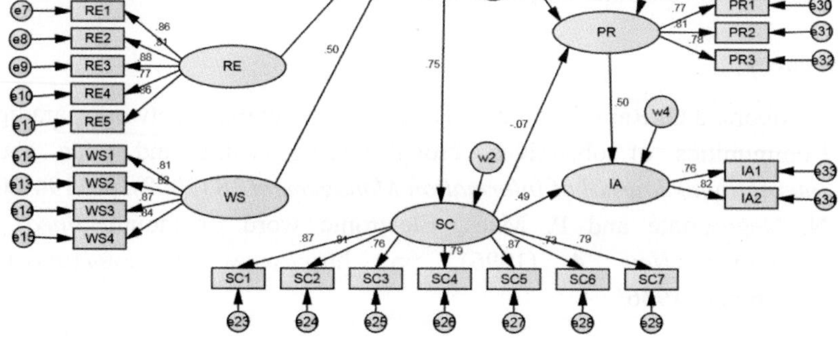

Fig. 2. Structural equation model fitness. ($\chi2$/df =2.141, GFI= 0.843, AGFI= 0.820, NFI= 0.905, TLI= 0.943, CFI = 0.947, while RMSEA = 0.056).

Table 2. Regression coefficients.

Casual Paths			Regression Coefficients	Results
OOS	<---	CR	0.57***	Accepted
OOS	<---	RE	-.02	Rejected
OOS	<---	WS	0.50***	Accepted
SC	<---	OOS	0.75***	Accepted
PR	<---	OOS	0.84***	Accepted
PR	<---	SC	-.07	Rejected
IA	<---	SC	0.49***	Accepted
IA	<---	PR	0.50***	Accepted

Note: *** p values ≤ 0.05

4. Conclusions

E-marketing is growing steadily and is saving consumers' time on shopping. Online shopping depends on product reviews, which are considered the most influential elements of eWOM. Recent reviews via eWOM are potentially more convincing in shaping consumers' purchasing behavior when they are very serious about making a purchase. Comments from the users of a product posted on an online forum or community are considered to be more influential than the information on a commercial website. Therefore, it is necessary to ensure that the information about a product available online is a credible and trustworthy resource. Consequently, more studies are required to improve the relevance, quality, and credibility of product information as they are evaluation parameters of customers' purchasing behavior. E-marketers would have to consider the credibility and trustworthiness of their product reviews. Further studies are required to consider the involvement of motivational factors and investigate motives such as consumer empowerment.

References

1. J. Albors, J.C. Ramos and J.L. Hervas, New learning network paradigms: Communities of objectives, crowdsourcing, wikis and open source, *International Journal of Information Management* **28** (2008), pp. 194-202.
2. N. Negroponte and P. Maes, Electronic word of mouth, *línea], On Newsstand Now* **4** (1996), pp. http://www.wired.com/1996/1910/ negroponte- 1946/.

3. R.E. Goldsmith, Electronic word-of-mouth, *Encyclopedia of e-commerce, e-government and mobile commerce* (2006), pp. 408-412.
4. T. Hennig-Thurau and G. Walsh, Electronic word-of-mouth: Motives for and consequences of reading customer articulations on the Internet, *International Journal of Electronic Commerce* **8** (2003), pp. 51-74.
5. A.A. Barreda, A. Bilgihan, K. Nusair and F. Okumus, Generating brand awareness in Online Social Networks, *Computers in Human Behavior* (2015).
6. C. Dellarocas, The digitization of word of mouth: Promise and challenges of online feedback mechanisms, *Management Science* **49** (2003), pp. 1407-1424.
7. M.R. Subramani and B. Rajagopalan, Knowledge-sharing and influence in online social networks via viral marketing, *Communications of the ACM* **46** (2003), pp. 300-307.
8. M. Khammash and G.H. Griffiths, 'Arrivederci CIAO. com, Buongiorno Bing. com'—Electronic word-of-mouth (eWOM), antecedences and consequences, *International Journal of Information Management* **31** (2011), pp. 82-87.
9. P. Racherla and W. Friske, Perceived 'usefulness' of online consumer reviews: An exploratory investigation across three services categories, *Electronic Commerce Research and Applications* **11** (2012), pp. 548-559.
10. S. Liu, C. Jiang, Z. Lin, Y. Ding, R. Duan and Z. Xu, Identifying effective influencers based on trust for electronic word-of-mouth marketing: A domain-aware approach, *Information Sciences* **306** (2015), pp. 34-52.
11. S.W. Sussman and W.S. Siegal, Informational influence in organizations: An integrated approach to knowledge adoption, *Information Systems Research* **14** (2003), pp. 47-65.
12. C.M. Cheung, M.K. Lee and N. Rabjohn, The impact of electronic word-of-mouth: The adoption of online opinions in online customer communities, *Internet Research* **18** (2008), pp. 229-247.
13. A.M. Al Mana and A.A. Mirza, The impact of electronic word of mouth on consumers' purchasing decisions, *International Journal of Computer Applications* **82** (2013), pp. 23-31.
14. L.R. Flynn, R.E. Goldsmith and J.K. Eastman, Opinion leaders and opinion seekers: Two new measurement scales, *Journal of the Academy of Marketing Science* **24** (1996), pp. 137-147.
15. W.R. Darden and F.D. Reynolds, Shopping orientations and product usage rates, *Journal of Marketing Research* (1971), pp. 505-508.

16. C. Wu and D.R. Shaffer, Susceptibility to persuasive appeals as a function of source credibility and prior experience with the attitude object, *Journal of Personality and Social Psychology* **52** (1987), pp. 677-688.
17. M.-H. Wu, Relationships among Source Credibility of Electronic Word of Mouth, Perceived Risk, and Consumer Behavior on Consumer Generated Media, (2013).
18. J.R. Bettman, Perceived risk and its components: a model and empirical test, *Journal of marketing Research* (1973), pp. 184-190.

Motion Trend Estimation of Track Vehicles Based on Micro-Motion Model

Xin-Yi Li[a], Yin-He Huang[b], Kui-Ying Yin[c] and Yin-Qi Qiao[d]

Nanjing Research Institute of Electronics Technology

Nanjing, 210000, China

E-mail: [a]lixinyichn@gmail.com, [b]yinhe_huang@sina.com, [c]yin_kuiying@sina.cn, [d]ffgg145236@163.com

This article presents an illustration of moving track vehicles, builds an echo model of scatter points on the track, and analyzes impacts of various motion trends on radar echo. Moreover, it conducts simulation study in vehicles with different attitude angles based on micro-motion feature. Experimental results validate the effectiveness of this model.

Keywords: Target Tracking; Micro-motion; Feature Extraction.

1. Introduction

Attitude angle reflects vehicle's movement tendency faithfully. Thus, it is of great significance in many fields such as security monitoring, target tracking and battlefield attack [1-6]. Moving targets can be categorized into sea targets, air targets and ground targets. As for sea target [3, 4], its moving attitude angle usually is acquired through track. For air target [5, 6], generally its track is calculated first, and then the angle between axial vector and radar line-of-sight (LOS). Ground target has neither high speed as air target does to form a track in limited time, nor ship wake as sea target. Currently, moving direction of ground moving target is mainly calculated based on static target image. Few studies focus on estimation of moving direction for moving ground vehicles.

When an object moves in radar LOS direction, it causes a frequency shift in return signal known as the Doppler Effect. If the object has micro-motion like vibration or spinning in addition to the transnational motion of the entire object, it causes additional shift in frequency and the Doppler shifted signal becomes modulated. This additional Doppler Effect causing the modulation of the signal is called the micro-Doppler effect [7-8]. This modulation can reflect the identity of specific object.

In battlefield, track vehicles are usually used for high-stress combat for its adaptability to various terrains, ability of barrier-crossing and good performance for both defense and strike. Therefore, estimation of track vehicle's moving trend offers great information support for air-to-ground and ground strike. Different parts of track have different return signal feature in different attitude angle. Compared with extracting motion trail of moving vehicle, our method of extracting vehicle's moving trend via building model of vehicles with different moving directions has more value of popularization and application.

2. Micro-motion Feature and Modeling

To simplify our modeling, radar is set stationary in this paper. Attitude angle of moving vehicles is the angle between direction of movement and radar LOS. We refine the attitude angle as shown in Fig. 1:

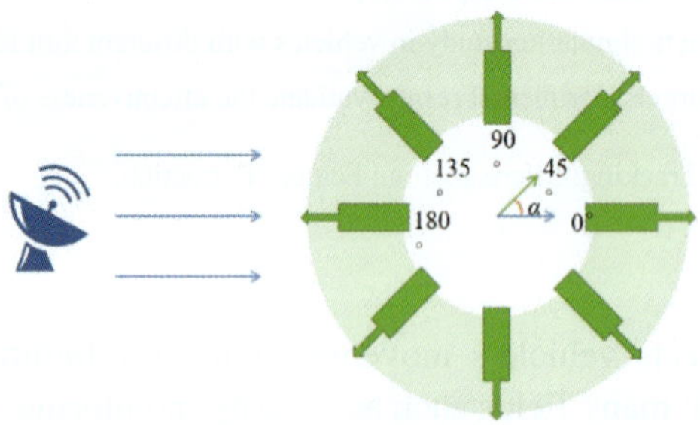

Fig. 1. Target attitude angle

2.1 *Micro-motion analysis in front view*

Take radar detect moving vehicle in front view for instance, as shown in Fig. 2. Irradiated zone of radar signal is between C and D. Signal wave length is λ, incident angel (pitch angle) is β, azimuth α is $180°$. Point P_1 on track front surface AC has a phase angle ofθ_1, point P_2 on track back surface BD has a phase angle of θ_2.

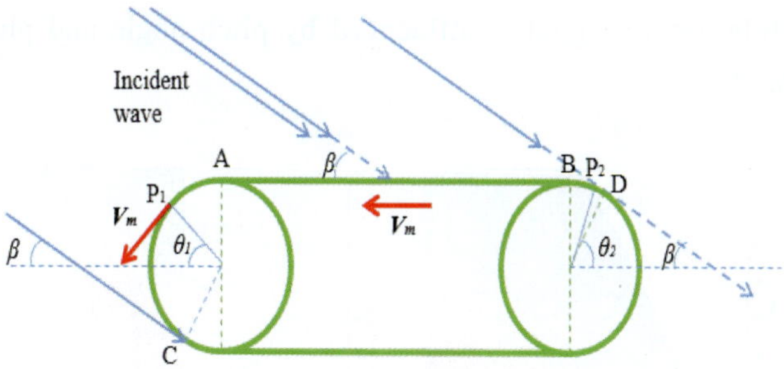

Fig. 2. Vehicle moving in front view

Track vehicle moves towards radar at velocityv_m. Despite of vehicle body moves in velocityv_m, vehicle track has a relative speed with respect to vehicle body. And this micro-motion modulates radar signal both in phase position and range.

Based on micro-Doppler analysis, frequency shift of vehicle body is calculated as:

$$f_{d\_body} = \frac{2v_m \cos\beta}{\lambda} \tag{1}$$

Frequency shift of track upper surface is calculated as:

$$f_{d\_AB} = \frac{4v_m \cos\beta}{\lambda} \tag{2}$$

Frequency shift of track front surface AC which is illuminated by radar signal is calculated as:

$$f_{d\_AC} = \frac{2v_{m(}\cos\beta + \sin(\theta_1 - \beta)}{\lambda}, \beta - \frac{\pi}{2} \leq \theta_1 \leq \frac{\pi}{2} \tag{3}$$

Frequency shift of track back surface BD (which is illuminated by radar signal) is calculated as:

$$f_{d\_BD} = \frac{2v_{m(}\cos\beta + \cos(\beta - \theta_2)}{\lambda}, 0 \leq \theta_2 \leq \theta \tag{4}$$

It is clear in above equations that track upper surface, back surface and part of front surface cause a greater frequency shift than that caused by vehicle body. This indicates that these parts have a higher velocity than body movement. However, part of lower half-track wheel leads to relatively smaller frequency shift compared to vehicle body. This is because these scattering points have relative backward velocity to vehicle body.

Meanwhile, return signal is influenced by pitch angle and phase angle as shown in Fig. 3:

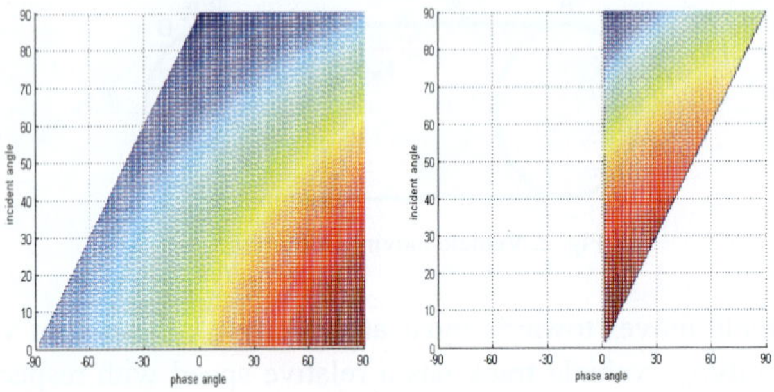

(a) Track front surface AC (b) Track back surface BD

Fig. 3. Projection of micro-Doppler distribution

Fig. 3(a) shows micro-Doppler distribution of track front surface AC. When incident angle increases, irradiated zone decreases, thus micro-Doppler bandwidth decreases accordingly. Fig. 3(b) shows micro-Doppler distribution of back surface BD. For BD, when incident angle increases, irradiated zone increases as well. Thus micro-Doppler bandwidth increases.

Micro-Doppler of track vehicle in front view can be considered as sum of four parts illustrated in Fig. 4:

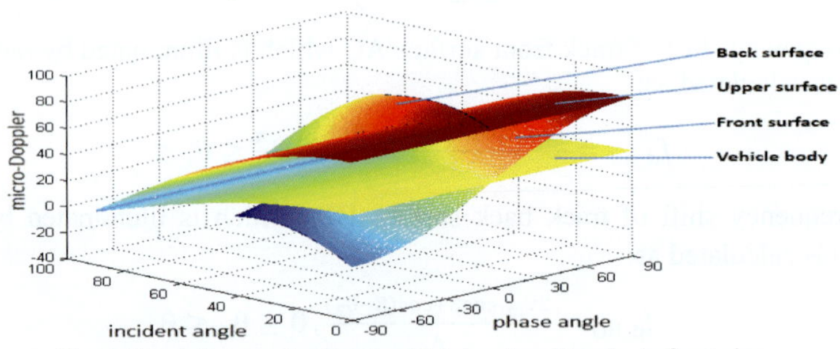

Fig. 4. Simulation result of track vehicle's micro-Doppler in front view

2.2 Micro-motion analysis in side view

In the condition that there is an angle between radar LOS and vehicle moving direction, shielding effect is eliminated. The whole track and track wheels scatter radar signal. Return signal differentiate from the case in front view.

As illustrated in Fig. 5, there is radar coordinates OXYZ where radar is located in the origin point O. Besides, there is target coordinates oxyz where track is located in yoz plane. And the origin point o of oxyz coincides with one of the wheel center. Radius of track wheel isr_0, length of track is b. Track vehicle moves in the direction of axis oy at velocity$\boldsymbol{v_m}$. Azimuth is α and incident angel (pitch angle) is β. OXYZ-coordinates of point o at time 0 is $\boldsymbol{R_0} = [X_0, Y_0, 0]$.

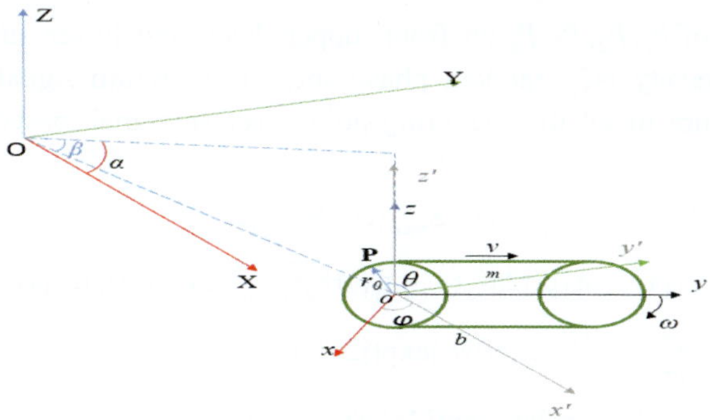

Fig. 5. Vehicle moving in side view

Scattering points in upper surface and lower surface of the track have a micro-motion of linear motion; scattering points in front and back of the circular arc have a micro-motion of rotation. Since the velocity of translational motion is $\boldsymbol{v_m}$, relatively, upper surface of track has a velocity of $\boldsymbol{v_m}$, lower surface has a velocity of$-\boldsymbol{v_m}$, and circular arcs on both ends have an angular velocity of $\boldsymbol{\omega} = \boldsymbol{v_m}/r_0$.

For scattering point on front surface of track, its initial phase angle is θ, oxyz-coordinates at time t is

$$\mathrm{r_t} = [0, \mathrm{r_0} \cos(\theta - \omega t), \mathrm{r_0} \sin(\theta - \omega t)] \quad (5)$$

For scattering point on upper surface of track, initial y-coordinate is y_0, oxyz-coordinates at time t is

$$\mathrm{r_t} = [0, \mathrm{y_0} + \mathrm{v_m t}, \mathrm{r_0}] \quad (6)$$

For scattering point on back surface of track, initial phase angle is θ, oxyz-coordinates at time t is

$$\mathrm{r_t} = [0, \mathrm{b} + \mathrm{r_0} \cos(\theta - \omega t), \mathrm{r_0} \sin(\theta - \omega t)] \quad (7)$$

For scattering point on lower surface of track, initial y-coordinate is y_0, oxyz-coordinates at time t is

$$\mathrm{r_t} = [0, \mathrm{y_0} - \mathrm{v_m t}, -\mathrm{r_0}] \quad (8)$$

In radar coordinates OXYZ, coordinates of scattering point P at time t is:

$$\mathrm{R_p} = \mathrm{R_t} + \mathrm{r_t} \cdot \mathrm{B_T} \quad (9)$$

where $\boldsymbol{R_t} = [X_0 + v_x t, Y_0 + v_y t, 0]$, $\boldsymbol{B_T} = \begin{bmatrix} cos\varphi & -sin\varphi & 0 \\ sin\varphi & cos\varphi & 0 \\ 0 & 0 & 1 \end{bmatrix}$.

Time delay of return signal of scattering point P is

$$\tau_P = \frac{2\|R_P\|}{c} \tag{10}$$

For any of P_1, P_2, P_3, P_4 on front, upper, back and lower surface of track, scattering intensity is ξ_i, random phase angle is ψ_i, return signal of the whole track is the sum of all the scattering points' return signal, based on scattering point model:

$$\begin{aligned} S_r(t) &= S_{front}(t) + S_{upper}(t) + S_{back}(t) + S_{lower}(t) = \\ &\sum_{i=1}^{n_1} \xi_i \exp(j\psi_i)\exp(j2\pi f_o(t - \tau_{p1})) + \sum_{i=n_1}^{n_1+n_2} \xi_i \exp(j\psi_i)\exp(j2\pi f_o(t - \\ &\tau_{p2})) + \sum_{i=n_1+n_2}^{n_1+n_2+n_3} \xi_i \exp(j\psi_i)\exp(j2\pi f_o(t - \tau_{p3})) + \\ &\sum_{i=n_1+n_2+n_3}^{n_1+n_2+n_3+n_4} \xi_i \exp(j\psi_i)\exp(j2\pi f_o(t - \tau_{p4})) \end{aligned} \tag{11}$$

Where $n_i (i = 1,2,3,4)$ stands for number of scattering points on each section of the track.

According to micro-Doppler theory,

$$f_{d\_body} = \frac{2v_m \cos\alpha \cos\beta}{\lambda} \tag{12}$$

$$f_{d\_uppersurface} = \frac{4v_m \cos\alpha \cos\beta}{\lambda} \tag{13}$$

$$f_{d\_wheel} = 2\int_0^{r_0} \int_{-\pi}^{\pi} \frac{(\frac{r}{r_0} v_m \sin\theta + v_m \cos\beta)\cos\alpha}{\lambda} d\theta dr = \frac{2v_m \cos\alpha \cos\beta}{\lambda} \tag{14}$$

$$f_{d\_lowersurface} = 0 \tag{15}$$

Distribution of micro-Doppler of scattering points on track wheels is shown as Fig. 6:

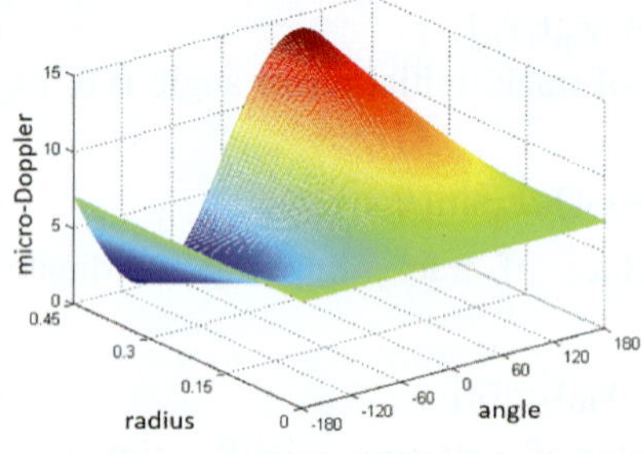

(a) 3-D

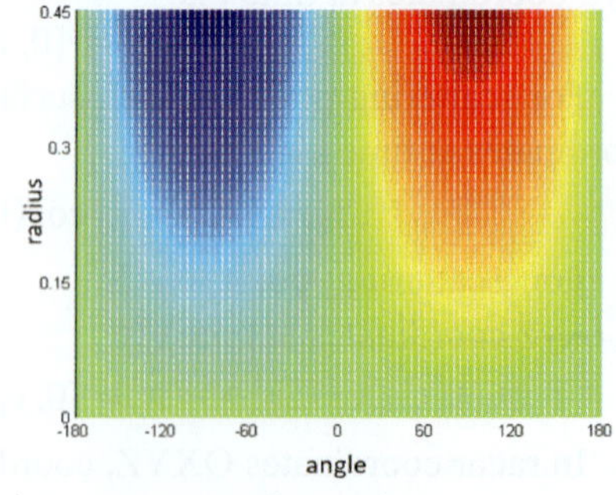

(b) x-y view

Fig. 6. Distribution of micro-Doppler of scattering points on track wheels

It is illustrated in Fig. 6 that micro-Doppler of all the scattering points on the wheel with the same radius follows distribution of sine function of phase angle θ. All of the scattering points on track wheel have a micro-Doppler frequency symmetric distribution centered at zero. What's more, intersection points of LOS normal direction and external margin of wheel has the biggest radial velocity, and then the biggest micro-Doppler frequency.

When azimuth increases, micro-Doppler distribution pattern does not change. So micro-Doppler shift and bandwidth decrease collectively as velocity component in radar LOS direction decreases, as shown in Fig. 7:

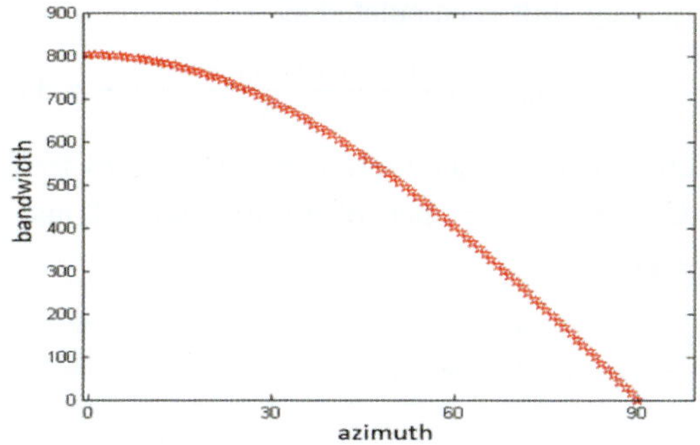

Fig. 7. Micro-Doppler bandwidth varying with azimuth

3. Simulation Experiments and Analysis

Radar transmits complex signal with single frequency. Carrier frequency is 1GHz, pulse repetition frequency is 2 kHz, pulse width is 32μs, and wave duration is 0.5s. Radius of track wheel is 0.45m, length of track upper and lower surface is 6m. Track vehicle moves in the direction of azimuthα.

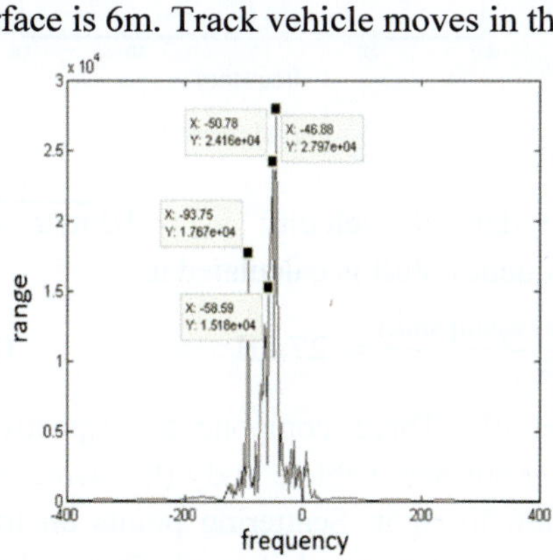

Fig. 8. α=0°

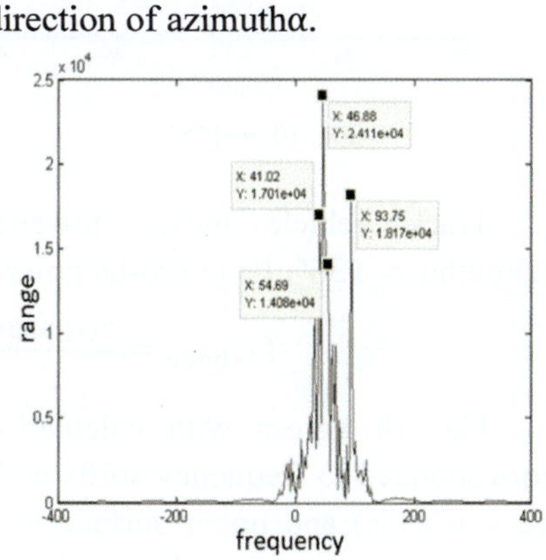

Fig. 9. α=180°

Track vehicle moves right away from radar at velocity$v_m = 10m/s$. Its micro-Doppler frequency shift is calculated as

$$f_{d-body} = \frac{2(v_x \sin\beta\cos\alpha + v_y \sin\beta\sin\alpha)}{\lambda} = -47.2\text{Hz} \quad (16)$$

Frequency components shown in Fig. 8 agree with calculation result. Four components respectively corresponded to frequency shifts of upper surface, part of trailing end BD, part of front end AC and vehicle body in Fig. 8 from left to right.

Track vehicle moves right towards radar at velocity$v_m = 10m/s$. Its micro-Doppler frequency shift is calculated as

$$f_{d-body} = \frac{2(v_x \sin\beta\cos\alpha + v_y \sin\beta\sin\alpha)}{\lambda} = 47.2\text{Hz} \quad (17)$$

Four components respectively corresponded to frequency shifts of part of front end AC, vehicle body, part of trailing end BD, and upper surface in Fig. 9 from left to right.

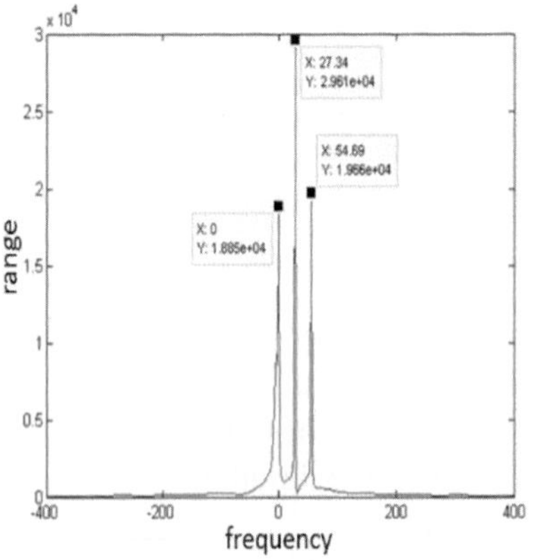

Fig. 10. α=135°

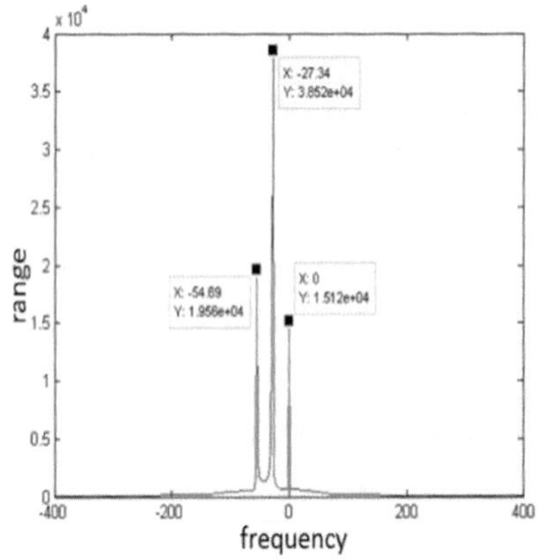

Fig. 11. α=45°

Track vehicle moves towards radar at velocity $v_m = 10m/s$ and azimuth$\alpha = 135°$. Its micro-Doppler frequency shift is calculated as

$$f_{d-body} = \frac{2(v_x \sin\beta\cos\alpha + v_y \sin\beta\sin\alpha)}{\lambda} = 27.2\text{H} \quad (18)$$

Fig. 10 agrees with calculation result. Three components respectively corresponded to frequency shifts of lower surface, vehicle body (the same with track wheels) and upper surface from left to right. Scattering points on track wheels have micro-Doppler distribution of sine function in [-π, π]. Thus, echo of all the scattering points have the same micro-Doppler frequency with vehicle body, shown as two overlapping frequencies in Fig. 10.

Track vehicle moves away from radar at velocity $v_m = 10m/s$ and azimuth$\alpha = 45°$. Its micro-Doppler frequency shift is calculated as

$$f_{d-body} = \frac{2(v_x \sin\beta\cos\alpha + v_y \sin\beta\sin\alpha)}{\lambda} = -27.2\text{Hz} \quad (19)$$

Fig. 11 agrees with calculation result. Three components respectively corresponded to frequency shifts of upper surface, vehicle body (the same with track wheels) and lower surface in from left to right. Like in Fig. 10, echo of wheel have the same micro-Doppler with vehicle body, shown as two overlapping frequencies.

It is validated from both theoretical analysis and simulation experiments that micro-Doppler distribution of track vehicle is function of its attitude angle. Due to shielding effect, micro-Doppler of track vehicle in front view has four major components which are corresponding to vehicle body, upper surface and part of both ends. However, entire track is illuminated in side view, including track wheels. And micro-Doppler frequency shift caused by wheels is the same as vehicle body due to its symmetry. Thus three major components in side view can be seen in simulation. Additionally, distribution of these frequency components agrees well with theoretical calculation. To summarize, estimation on attitude angle can be realized based on micro-Doppler feature.

4. Conclusions

Radar is able to work all day, regardless of weather and illumination. It is an ideal sensor which can detect target's moving trend based on Doppler Effect. Furthermore, radar is capable of distinguishing attitude angle in a range of 180°. Practically, because of the existence of blind area in vertical direction, at least two radars working cooperatively are needed to detect in fully 360° range.

References

1. Liu, X. M., & Shen, J. F. (2009). Research on Getting Aspect Angular for Radar/Infrared-Imaging ASM. Journal of Naval Aeronautical and Astronautical University, 24(3), 304-306.
2. Wang, H. M., Huo, L. L., & Zhang, J. (2011, May). Target tracking algorithm based on dynamic template and Kalman filter. In Communication Software and Networks (ICCSN), 2011 IEEE 3rd International Conference on (pp. 330-333). IEEE.

3. Dzvonkovskaya, A., Helzel, T., Petersen, L., Merz, C. R., Liu, Y., & Weisberg, R. H. (2014, June). Initial results of ship detection and tracking using WERA HF ocean radar with MIMO configuration. In 2014 15th International Radar Symposium (IRS) (pp. 1-3). IEEE.
4. Xu, H., Xie, W., Gao, F., Yuan, H., & Wang, Y. (2015, October). Sea surface multitarget track initiation for airborne radar. In IET International Radar Conference 2015 (pp. 1-4). IET.
5. Mohajerin, N., Histon, J., Dizaji, R., & Waslander, S. L. (2014, May). Feature extraction and radar track classification for detecting UAVs in civilian airspace. In 2014 IEEE Radar Conference (pp. 0674-0679). IEEE.
6. CUI, M., MA, T. H., & LIU, Y. J. (2014). Research for Using Improved Kalman Algorithm to Solve Small Missiles Attitude Angle. Fire Control & Command Control, 1, 031.
7. Chen, V. C., Li, F., Ho, S. S., & Wechsler, H. (2006). Micro-Doppler effect in radar: phenomenon, model, and simulation study. IEEE Transactions on Aerospace and Electronic systems, 42(1), 2-21.
8. Chen, V. C., Li, F., Ho, S. S., & Wechsler, H. (2003). Analysis of micro-Doppler signatures. IEE Proceedings-Radar, Sonar and Navigation, 150(4), 271-6.

A Novel Method of Test Case Generation for Embedded Software

Zheng-Wei Yu[a], Shuai-Shuai Yang[b,*], Yu-Mei Wu[c] and Bin Liu[d]

Beihang University, 37 Xueyuan Rd Haidian District

Beijing, 100191, China

Email: [a]buaayuzhengwei@163.com, [b]yss930819@163.com, [c]wuyumei@buaa.edu.cn, [d]liubin@buaa.edu.cn

With the development of software testing automation, the software test case generation based on modeling has become one of the key techniques. Now classic modeling has the limitations in the test case type and test case number. In this paper operation modeling is proposed to describe and model the use of the software in real life, based on which test case generation method is used to provide test cases of good quality for the embedded software.

Keywords: Test Case; Operation Modeling; Embedded Software.

1. Introduction

The embedded software is widely used in civil, military and aerospace fields and the testing of the embedded software is becoming more and more important. With the development of software testing automation, the software test case generation based on modeling has become one of the key techniques. Now classic modeling such as finite-state machines model[1], UML model[2], and Markov model[3], based on which the software test case generation method has the limitations in the test case type and test case number. The finite-state machines model has the problem of state space explosion and multi test unit synchronization. It is difficult to represent complex control problems for UML model. In the Markov model, it is difficult to determine the migration probability, and it is not enough to test the important operation with low risk. In this paper an embedded software test case generation model based on the use profile is proposed to solve these problems mentioned above.

---

*Corresponding author.

2. Operation Modeling

Three steps are included in the operation modeling: construction of system usage view, construction of function model and construction of operation model.

2.1. *Function and operation*

The construction of operation modeling starts from the software function (F), which can be extracted from the software requirements document. Each function is achieved and realized through the operation (O). The function should be a group of ordered sets of operations (O_1, O_2...O_n). The operation is the user's input to the software. In this paper, the operation mainly includes the input variables of the test case assignment information. A user can perform a task by performing a series of functions (F_1, F_2...F_n) of the software. Thus, the task is also a group of ordered set of operations.

2.2. *Construction of system usage view*

The system usage view can clearly show the relationship among the user, the participant and the system under test (SUT). Users reach their goal by using SUT. By extracting the user, the use of the tested system can be analyzed in the user's view and accordingly the tasks can be performed by SUT. Participants provide support for SUT to operate normally. For embedded software testing, simulation of these participants is used to provide data for the SUT to run. By extracting the participants, the input and output variables for SUT are analyzed. Constructing the system usage view is to analyze the whole operation/running process and distinguish the boundary between SUT and the outside related devices.

2.3. *Construction of function model*

The function module is the main component of the function model and the operation model. It encapsulates the functions that have the same characteristics. The function module can be divided into three layers: top-level module, middle-level module and bottom-level module. The top-level module is one of the most high-level functional modules of the software and includes all functions of the software. The middle-level module is a logical combination of functions. And it includes other middle-level modules, bottom-level modules and operations. The bottom-level module contains only the operation. Generally, when the function is described by the operation, the function is transformed into the bottom-level module. Construction of function model is to describe the relationship between function modules, and it can be divided into the following three steps: function capture, function module partition, and function module description.

Function capture: A list of functions can be obtained from the software requirements. The functions can be divided into two categories, direct use function and indirect use function. The indirect use function is not directly used by users, but it can ensure the normal use of the software. And the user uses these functions indirectly during software running. In software testing, the direct use function should be mainly considered.

Function module partition: From the user perspective, the direct use function is classified into different functional modules based on the characteristics. First, the bottom-level module is built on the consideration of the single use and the functions with the following characteristics can be captured into one function module:

- Relatively fixed functions;
- "Parallel" functions: the user can use any of them to complete one specified task;
- independent functions which can be used in any case without preconditions;
- functions with the same prerequisites;
- If there are some functions that are not included in any modules after the above process, these functions can be regarded as independent functional modules.

Then, higher-level module is built based on the bottom-level module until the top-level module is established, then the partition function module is completed. The top-level module should be the complete set of all modules.

Function module description: Step by step from the top-level module to describe the module. Description shows the relationship between the function modules or functions and it includes preconditions and post-conditions.

2.4. *Construction of operation model*

The operation model can be constructed based on the analysis of function model. The function module is not a real operational entity. In order to obtain a unit which can actually run, the function module needs to be decomposed into operations. A function may contain only one operation or a set of operations. To construct the operation model, all modules should be decomposed into operation.

An operation can be described by the input and output variables. The input and output variables are extracted from the system usage view and are the input and output of SUT. The variables which have common properties can be encapsulated in a class. For embedded software, the class is a data frame in the communication process.

3. Test Case Generation

The first step for test case generation is to traverse every operation in the operation model and get the sequences of operations. The test case is the instantiations of each specified sequence of the operations. The travers process follows the four criteria below:

- Node coverage criterion: each operation node is performed at least once.
- Migration edge coverage criterion: all edges are covered at least once.
- Logical path coverage criterion: all of the logical paths need to be executed at least once.
- Representative value coverage criterion: For each control point and control value a finite set of inputs need to be selected (representative value set). Each of the representative value set is to be tested at least once.

The model based on the use of profile has the following advantages.

- Through the analysis of the software functions, the test cases can reach 100% coverage of software requirements.
- The model is built from the user's point of view and it is possible to present the use of software in real life.
- It also aims for the important operation with low probability.

4. Case Study

Generating test cases for mission computer software (MC) is used as an example for analysis to verify the method proposed in this paper. The case is conducted as follows:

Construction system usage view

User: Pilot and DCMP

Participants: DCMP, SMP, INS, CNI, DTE.

Construction function model

From the software requirements the functions of MC are listed. The partial function list in Table 1. From the function list can get modules in Figure 1. In the end, the partial function module description in Table 2.

Table 1. Partial function list

Function	Function
Initialization	Comes into play mode -FAF mode
Into the "end of the flight" mode process	Comes into play mode -MLS runway model
Into the navigation or approach mode	Comes into play mode - TACAN runway model
Into the A / F or A / A integrated avionics fire control mode	Comes into play mode - autonomous runway model
Order waypoint navigation.	DST operation -CHK display.
Select waypoint navigation.	DST operating procedure -COPY operation.
Select route navigation.	DST operating procedure -TOT operation.
Compass navigation.	Maintenance display process
TACAN navigation	Exit from the maintenance display
Navigation data transmission (DT / NAV)	The execution MBIT
Find near navigation (HEP) navigation	MBIT fault detection process
DTC modify MC subsystem data file	……

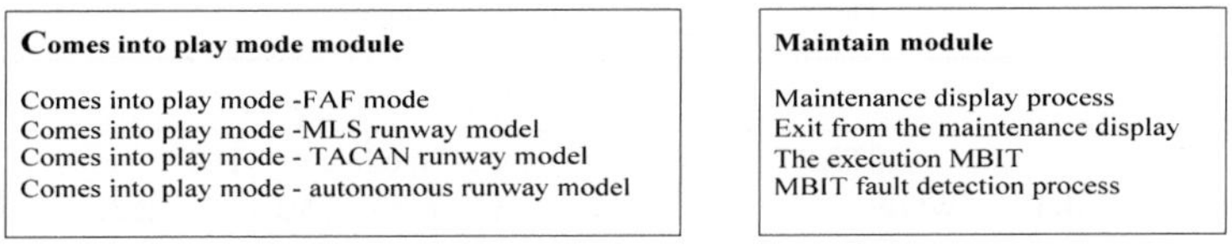

Fig. 1. Partial modules figure.

Table 2. Partial function module description

Module	Precondition	Postcondition
Navigation module	WOW==0	Attack module; Comes into play mode module; PUMARK module; Stop; Self
Maintain module	WOW==1	Stop

**WOW is wheel load status*

Construction of operation model

The operation model is shown in Figure 2

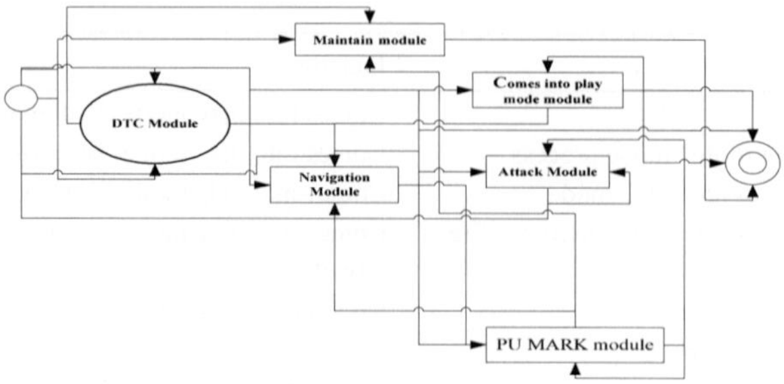

Fig. 2. Partial operation model figure.

Test Case Generation:

Traversing the operation model and then get the sequences of operations. Some operations sequences in Table 3.

Table 3. Partial operations sequences

NO	Sequence
1	START → [WOW == 1] DTC module → STOP
2	START → [WOW == 1] DTC module → [WOW == 1] Maintain module → STOP
…	…
n	START→ [WOW == 0] Navigation module{ START →TACAN navigation→ STOP }→ STOP

5. Conclusions

The software test case generation based on modeling is important for software testing automation. This paper proposed the operation modeling to generate test case for embedded software and the method has been used in the case study.

References

1. Chow, T. S. Testing Software Design Modeled by Finite-State Machines. in *IEEE Transactions on Software Engineering* 3 (1978), pp. 178-187.
2. OFFUTT, J., and A. ABDURAZIK. Generating tests from UML specifications. In *Lecture notes in computer science* (1999), pp. 416-429.
3. Whittaker, James A., and Michael G. Thomason. A Markov chain model for statistical software testing. in *IEEE Transactions on Software engineering* 20.10 (1994), pp. 812-824.
4. Yumei Wu, Zhengwei Yu, Zhifang Liu, Study of Task Profile Oriented Embedded Software Test Aimed to Improve Reliability, in *2nd International Conference on Future Computer and Communication*, Vol. 2, (2010), pp. 58-62.

Conditional Restricted Boltzmann Machines for Collaborative Filtering Based on GPU

Hong-Yi Su[a], Feng-Jiao Chen[b], Bo Yan[c] and Hong Zheng[d]

Beijing Institute of Technology, Key Lab of Intelligent Information Technology
Beijing, 100081, China
E-mail: [a]henrysu@bit.edu.cn, [b]chenfengjiao@bit.edu.cn, [c]yanbo@bit.edu.cn, [d]hongzheng@bit.edu.cn

Collaborative Filtering (CF) is one of the most popular algorithm used by many recommendation systems. However, there remain important research questions in overcoming the challenges such as cold startup, sparsity and poor prediction quality. In order to address these issues, Conditional Restricted Boltzmann Machines (CRBMs) which could take auxiliary information into account to collaborative filtering tasks are applied. The attributes of items are combined with the user's behavior in the training of model and show that CRBMs could improve the accuracy of the prediction. Furthermore, based on the programming mode of CUDA, the parallel implementation is realized. The experiment results indicate that the GPU implementation can yield very good speedups (up to 47x) as compared with CPU implementation.

Keywords: Collaborative Filtering; Restricted Boltzmann Machine; GPU.

1. Introduction

The CF[1] which was proposed in 1992 by Goldberg[2], has achieved a great success in information filtering. Nevertheless, memory-based approaches like GroupLens[3] do not scale without further approximation because they require access to the rating of the entire set community, what's more, sparsity is another great challenge for CF. Therefore, the model-based approaches such as singular value decomposition (SVD) have also been proposed[4]. However, this creates a difficult non-convex problem because most of data sets are sparse. As such, Hoffman proposed a formal statistical model of user preference using hidden variables over user-item-rating triples[5].

Hinton proposed a fast learning algorithm of RBMs named Contrastive Divergence (CD) in 2002[6]. Salakhutdinov et al. revised the classic RBMs into the collaborative filtering task in 2007[7], these models were trained using CD, which maximized an approximation to the true likelihood function. Furthermore, they also proposed a conditional RBMs model and report that the performance on the Netflix data set is superior to the competitive SVD model.

Recently, lots of accelerated implementations has been proposed for RBMs on GPU platforms. For instance, Ly[8] investigated the inherent parallelism in RBMs to provide a better performance. Y. Zhu[9] proposed a memory efficient algorithm on GPU which can train large-scale RBMs without size restriction.

2. Method

2.1. *Restricted Boltzmann machines*

RBM is an energy-based generative model. As showed in Figure 1, an RBM consists of two layers: visible variables v and hidden variables h with no intra-layer connections.

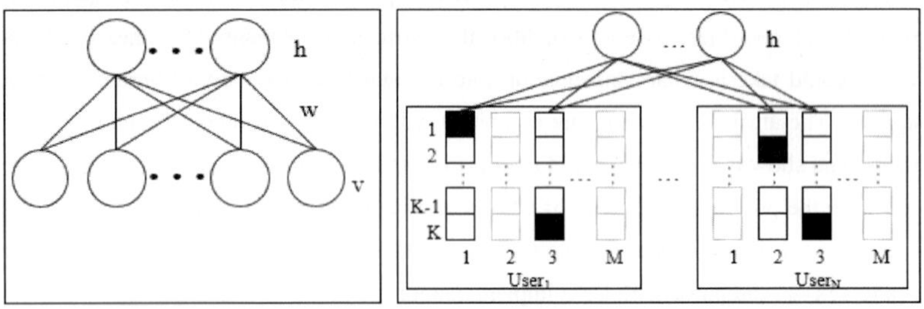

Standard RBM RBM for Collaborative Filtering

Fig. 1. Comparison between RBM and RBM in Collaborative Filtering.

The conditional probabilities of the visible unit and the hidden unit are:

$$p(v_i = 1 | h) = \sigma(b_i + \sum_j h_j w_{ij}) \tag{1}$$

$$p(h_j = 1 | v) = \sigma(c_j + \sum_i v_i w_{ij}) \tag{2}$$

Where σ(x) is the logistic sigmoid function.

In the collaborative filtering problem, we are presented with an N*M rating Matrix, where N represents the number of users, M represents the number of items and each item rated using integer values from 1 to K. As shown in Figure 1, the Collaborative Filtering RBMs uses a different RBM for each user, but shares weights and biases between users on commonly rated items.

We need to learn the RBM model by adjusting the weights and biases to lower the energy of that particular vector while raising the energy of other configuration. By using CD, Rules can be applied in order to update the weights and biases of the network by the following equation:

$$\Delta w_{ij} = \varepsilon(<h_j v_i>_{data} - <h_j v_i>_T) \tag{3}$$

$$\Delta b_i = \varepsilon(<v_i>_{data} - <v_i>_T) \tag{4}$$

$$\Delta c_j = \varepsilon(<h_j>_{data} - <h_j>_T) \tag{5}$$

Where ε is the learning rate. <.>data defines the expectations under the distribution of data, <.>T represents a distribution of samples from running the Gibbs sampler, initialized at the data, for T full steps.

2.2. *Conditional RBMs(CRBMs)*

Benefited from the Conditional Restricted Boltzmann Machines, we could easily take some extra information into account [10,11]. As shown in Figure 2, r is a binary vector, which denotes movie's feature, and affects binary states of the hidden units.

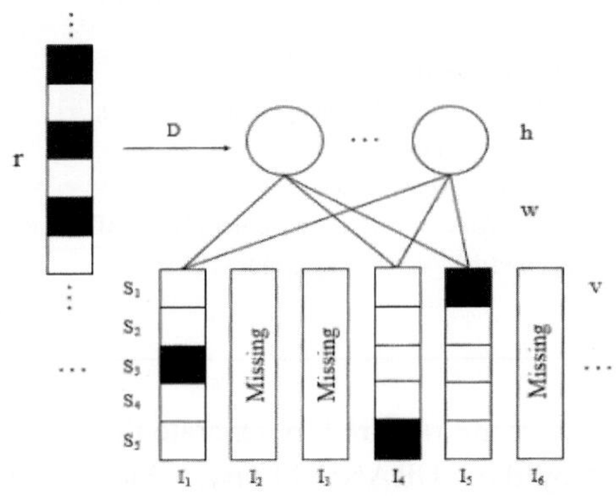

Fig. 2. Conditional RBM in collaborative filtering.

The conditional distribution takes the form

$$p(h_j = 1 | r, v) = \sigma(c_j + \sum_i v_i w_{ij} + \sum_k r_k D_{kj}) \tag{6}$$

The learning of the D using CD is similar to learning biases, in this paper, we used a penalty function to avoid large weights, the update rule becomes follows

$$\triangle D_{kj} = \varepsilon((< h_j >_{data} - < h_j >_T) r_k + \lambda D_{kj}) \tag{7}$$

2.3. *GPU-accelerated CRBMs*

Our training algorithm for CRBMs was implemented by using CUDA programming model. There are three major classifications of computational kernels were identified: multiplication of matrix (Eq.(6-7)), random number generation (Eq.(6)) and sigmoid transfer function (Eq.(6)). These three kernels were generated and tested separately and then integrated at a final stage.

We used the cublasSgemm function from CUBLAS library to implement these matrix operations as its excellent performance. Taking matrix v multipled by matrix w (Eq.(6)) as an example, details of multiplication of matrix is described in Algorithm 1.

Algorithm 1: GPU algorithm to calculate multiplication of matrix

Input:
    matrix v and matrix w
Output:
    matrix x, which equals matrix v multipled by matrix w
Begin
    cudaMalloc(dev_v, sizeof(v));
    cudaMemcpy(dev_v, v, cudaMemcpyHostToDevice);
    for (each slices w_i of w) **do**
        cudaMalloc(dev_w_i, sizeof(w_i))
        cudaMemcpy(dev_w_i, w_i, cudaMemcpyHostToDevice);
        cublasSgemv(dev_v, dev_w_i, x[index]);
    end for
End

The random numbers are required to generate the node states. In this paper, they were generated by the CURAND library, which is a part of the NVIDIA CUDA library.

There are two methods to implement sigmoid transfer function in CUDA, the first is to use _expf(x) function in CUDA, and the second is by using texture memory, the values were precalculated on the CPU and then loaded onto the texture. The result range was normalized to automatically by GPU to [0,1]. In this paper we used the former.

3. Results

3.1. *Experiment data sets*

We test our approach with the three data sets of MovieLens. The first set is called ML-100k, which contains 100,000 ratings including 943 users and 1682 movies, the second set is ML-1M, which consists of 1,000,209 ratings including 6040 users and 3952 movies, the last set is ML-10M, which has 10 million ratings including 72,000 users and 10,000 movies. We divided every data set into two parts: 10% of the ratings are deemed as the testing dataset and the remaining as the training dataset.

3.1.1. *The performance evaluation of the CRBM*

We illustrate the results on datasets ML-1M. For comparing the performance of the RBM and the CRBM, we introduces the root mean squared error (RMSE) to evaluate the referred models. To compare the models, we train RBMs with the number of hidden units F=100 firstly. The detailed results are shown in Figure 3:

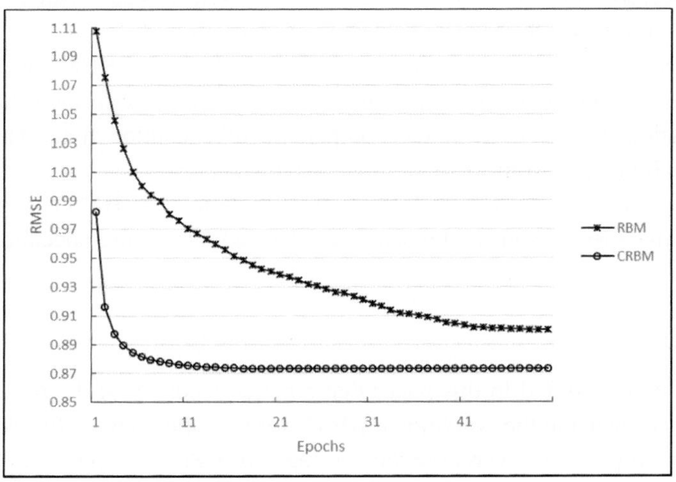

Fig. 3. Performance of different models.

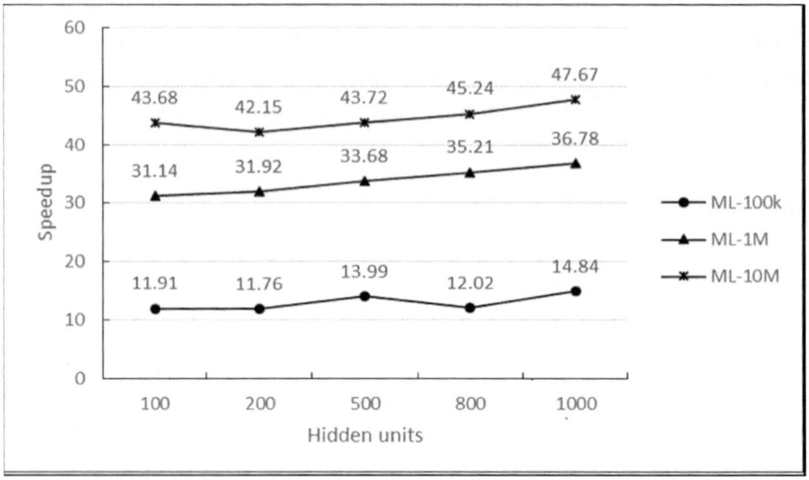

Fig. 4. Speedup comparison in different datasets.

Figure 3 shows the performance of the RBM and the CRBM. It reveals that using CRBM can obtain much faster convergence and better recommendation results by taking the attributes of items into account.

3.1.2. *The evaluation of the GPU-accelerated CRBM*

The performance of our implementations is evaluated on an Intel Core 6 Xeon 2620 processor with 16GB of RAM, an NVIDIA tesla k20c with 2496 stream and 5GB of onboard RAM. The CUDA version is 5.5.

To verify the efficiency of the GPU-Accelerated CRBM, we vary the number of hidden units and the scales of datasets and performed 20 tests per configuration. Figure 4 show the comparison of execution time. The running speed has improved from 11 to 47 times for three datasets.

As we can see from Figure 4, the GPU-Accelerated CRBM can significantly improve the speed. And as the scales of datasets grow, the speedups are also increased.

4. Conclusions

We have demonstrated in this paper that a better accuracy of the prediction can be achieved by using the conditional RBMs for CF, and then a GPU-Accelerated CRBM is proposed to overcome the shortages of CPU. The proposed algorithm can improve the accuracy of the prediction as well as accelerate the large scale datasets. As RBM-based model could be easily combined with deep models to extract more feature for recommendation, in future work we will use deep models to solve the CF problems.

References

1. J.S. Breese, D. Heckerman, C. Kadie.1998. Empirical analysis of predictive algorithms for collaborative filtering. Proceedings of the Fourteenth Conference on Uncertainty in Artificial Intelligence: 43–52.
2. Goldberg D, Nichols D, Oki B, et al. 1992. Using collaborative filtering to weave an information tapestry[J]. Communications of the ACM. Volume 35(12):61-71.
3. Resnick, P., Iacovou, N., Suchak, M., Bergstrom, P., Riedl, J.: Grouplens: an open architecture for collaborative filtering of netnews. In: Proceedings of the 1994 ACM conference on Computer supported cooperative work, ACM (1994) 175-186.
4. Goldberg, K., Roeder, T., Gupta, D., Perkins, C.: Eigentaste: A constant time collaborative filtering algorithm. Information Retrieval 4(2) (2001) 133-151.
5. Hofmann, T.: Latent semantic models for collaborative filtering. ACM Transactions on Information Systems (TOIS) 22(1) (2004) 89-115.
6. Hinton, G.E.: Training products of experts by minimizing contrastive divergence. Neural computation 14(8) (2002) 1771-1800.
7. Salakhutdinov, R., Mnih, A., Hinton, G.: Restricted boltzmann machines for collaborative filtering. In: Proceedings of the 24th international conference on Machine learning, ACM (2007) 791-798.
8. D.L. Ly, V. Paprotski, and D. Yen, "Neural networks on GPUs: Restricted Boltzmann Machines," Technical Report, Depl. of Electrical and Comp. Eng., University of Toronto, 2009.
9. Y. Zhu, Y. Zhang, Y. Pan, "Large-scale restricted boltzmann machines on single GPU", in Proc. of IEEE 1nl. Conf. Big Data, pp. 169-174, 2013.
10. Ilya Sutskever and Geoffrey E Hinton. Learning multilevel distributed representations for high-dimensional sequences. In International Conference on Artificial Intelligence and Statistics, pages 548-555, 2007.
11. GrahamWTaylor, Geoffrey E Hinton, and Sam T Roweis. Modeling human motion using binary latent variables. Advances in Neural Information Processing Systems, 19:1345, 2007.

Mirror Boundary Normal Modes Method of Atmospheric Acoustic Fields

Song Yin[1,a] and Zhi-Yuan Li[2]

[1]*School of Engineering, Anhui Agricultural University*
Hefei, Anhui 230036, China
[2]*School of Mechanical and Automotive Engineering, Hefei University of Technology*
Hefei, Anhui 230009, China
E-mail: [a]yinsong@189.cn

Normal modes method applies the technique of separation of variables to solve Helmholtz equations in computational acoustics, which is suitable for the sound fields with boundaries. The top boundary condition usually causes a singular case in atmospheric acoustics. The mirror boundary approach is that the sound field is placed, a mirror at the top to extend the original calculation area to an axisymmetric area with both rigid boundaries at the top and bottom. With a proper absorption coefficient assigned above the mirror position, the solution of the sound field below the mirror is correct. The approach is practical for normal modes method in atmospheric acoustics.

Keywords: Atmospheric Sound Field; Normal Modes; Separation of Variables; Boundary.

1. Introduction

In acoustics, the Helmholtz equation forms the theoretical basis for the important numerical methods, including the Wavenumber Integration (WI), Normal Mode (NM) and Parabolic Equation (PE) methods.[1,2] Salomons E M [3] and Xunren Y[4], in the milestone atmospheric acoustics works, reviewed all types of the numerical methods except for the NM model which is vital in underwater acoustics and geoacoustics.[3,4] The coupled NM model, is considered as the most accurate method in underwater acoustic[5]. Kobayashi N[6] develops a method which can directly dispose the open boundary at the upper atmosphere to calculate normal modes. Didier [7] introduced impedance boundary conditions. But the NM model has a boundary condition issue in atmospheric acoustics, especially in the small scale sound fields.

According the mathematical basis of normal modes, the boundary conditions should imply two boundaries. In atmosphere the top boundary locates out at infinity, which causes a singular case. This paper attempts to solve the boundary issue in atmospheric acoustics, discusses an approach of mirror boundary. The numerical calculations verified the correctness.

The derivation of the boundary conditions overcome the difficulty of numerical calculation, helpful to apply the normal modes model in atmospheric acoustics.

2. Normal Modes

A sound pressure field yields the so-called Helmholtz equation in two dimensions with sound speed and density depending only on depth z,[1]

$$\frac{1}{r}\frac{\partial}{\partial r}\left(r\frac{\partial p}{\partial r}\right)+\rho(z)\frac{\partial}{\partial z}\left(\frac{1}{\rho(z)}\frac{\partial p}{\partial z}\right)+\frac{\omega^2}{c^2(z)}p=-\frac{\delta(r)\delta(z-z_s)}{2\pi r} \tag{1}$$

2.1. *Non-singular case*

Using the technique of separation of variables, we shall take the Hankel function of the first kind, and obtain the pressure as [1]

$$p(r,z)=\frac{i}{4\rho(z_s)}\sum_{m=1}^{\infty}f_z^{[m]}(z_s)f_z^{[m]}(z)H_0^{(1)}\left(k_r^{[m]}r\right) \tag{2}$$

Here, $f_z^{[m]}(z)$ denotes the particular function $f_z(z)$ obtained with the separation constant $k_r^{[m]}$ which satisfied the modal equation[1]

$$\rho(z)\frac{d}{dz}\left[\frac{1}{\rho(z)}\frac{df_z^{[m]}(z)}{dz}\right]+\left[\frac{\omega^2}{c^2(z)}-k_r^{[m]2}\right]f_z^{[m]}(z)=0 \tag{3}$$

The approximations of the eigenfunctions of Eq. (3) evaluated at the mesh points composed the vector

$$\vec{f}_z=\left[f_z^{[0]},f_z^{[1]},\ldots,f_z^{[N]}\right], \tag{4}$$

an algebraic eigenvalue problem of the form can be obtained[1]

$$[I\lambda-A(\lambda)]\vec{f}_z=0\,,\ \lambda^{[m]}=k_r^{[m]2} \tag{5}$$

In non-singular case, the above problem is a standard algebraic eigenvalue problem and can be solved using standard routines. In general, only the lower-order modes will be sufficiently accurate; the higher-order modes are undersampled by the finite-difference mesh. Thus, routines which are designed to extract a subset of the eigenvectors and eigenvalues are desired, i.e. Sturm's method combined with inverse iteration.[1,8,9]

2.2. *Singular case*

In atmospheric acoustics, the boundary conditions should imply a perfectly rigid ground ($z = 0$) and a pressure-release interface located at $z = D$.

$$\left.\frac{df_z}{dz}\right|_{z=0} = 0, \quad f_z(D) = 0 \tag{6}$$

The ground condition is easy to satisfy; whereas the top boundary locates out at infinity, which would cause a singular case. The ground and top boundary conditions involve functions $f^{G,T}$ and $g^{G,T}$, which are independent of k_r as happens for the rigid ground and pressure-release interface conditions.[1,9] If the functions f^T and g^T are not independent of k_r, then the above problem is not a standard algebraic eigenvalue problem, what happens for the arbitrary interval (arbitrary D value) in calculations.

The atmospheric models in original physical boundary conditions are usually the singular case, which could not be calculated.

3. Mirror Boundary

3.1. *Virtual sources*

The virtual source concept is an approximate method for solving the integral equation. As Figure 1a, a sound field is produced by a real source O_{01} at a certain height above the ground, which satisfied a perfectly rigid boundary(solid line) condition. While the upper boundary is perfectly free boundary (Dirichlet boundary, dashed line), the waves to receiver P are reflected by both boundaries, as virtual sources distribute(O_{02},O_{03},...) at the symmetrical side of the boundaries and the images of the boundaries. While the upper boundary is transmitted boundary (dashed line), which causes the singular case, the wave is only reflected by the ground. There is still a virtual sources distribution, which the upper boundary reflections are absent, as Figure 1b. In Figure 1c, supposing that a mirror is placed at the original upper boundary to double the original calculation area, a new calculation area is symmetrical with two rigid boundaries. The virtual sources distribution is the same as Figure 1b. In other words, the normal modes of the mirrored calculation area are the same as the normal modes of the calculation area absent the top reflection.

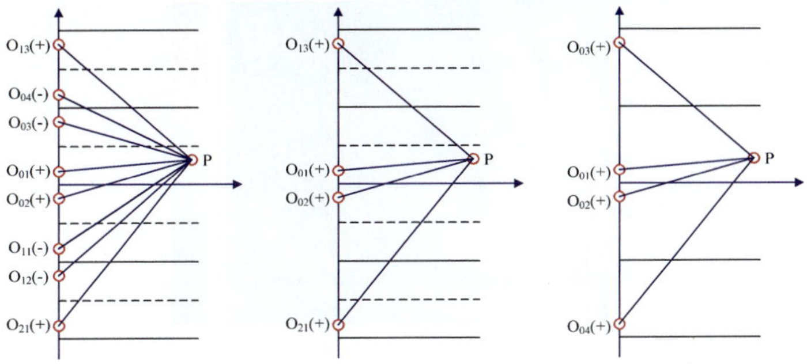

Fig. 1. Virtual source distribution a) rigid and free boundaries, b) rigid and transmitted boundaries, c) rigid boundaries

The mirror generates a top rigid boundary to avoid the singular case. The reasons that it can be introduced exist in two aspects in mathematics.

First, the solution function of wave equations could be analytical continuation. After the analytic continuation, the horizontal wavenumber of eigenvalues would include the original eigenvalues.

Second, the sound pressure of wave equation can be expressed as a sum of analytic functions of normal modes. The depth-separated Green's function can be derived,[1,10]

$$g(x)=\frac{1}{2\pi\rho(z_s)}\sum_m \frac{f_z^{[m]}(z_s)f_z^{[m]}(z)}{k_r^{\,2}-k_r^{[m]2}} \tag{7}$$

By the modal expansion of the Green's function, the mode set converges in the mean to an arbitrary piecewise continuous function, so the mirror position could be an arbitrary height not to be restrict at the local extreme points.

3.2. *Examples*

The approach is that a mirror was placed at the top of calculation area which would be extended to an axisymmetric area with both rigid boundaries at the top and bottom. While a proper absorption coefficient assigned above the mirror position, the sound field below the mirror was correct. The transmission loss

(TL) below 600m is as Figure 2. The sound source frequency is 500Hz, locates at the height of 1.5m, the sound field range is 2km in horizontal and 600m in height.

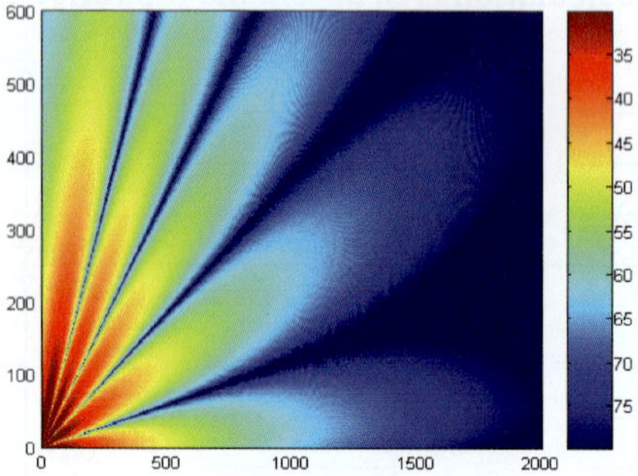

a)

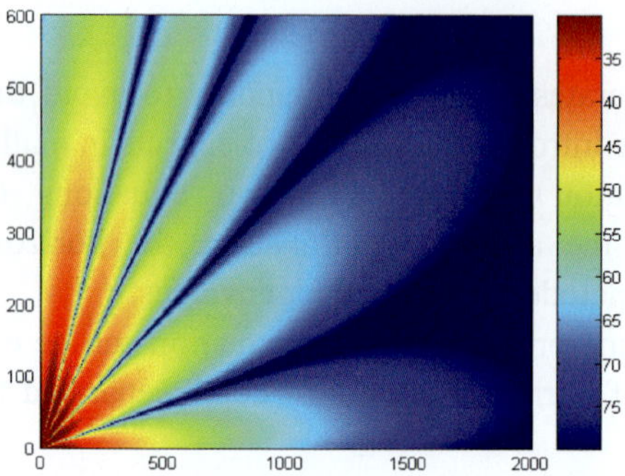

b)

Fig. 2. TL of a point source of 500Hz, mirror boundary at a)600m, b)1000m

If the calculation area had been enlarged, i.e. substituted 1km for 600m, the interference (wrong results) would decrease to an ignorable level.

4. Conclusions

Normal modes method applies the technique of separation of variables, which main problem involved eigenvalues and boundary conditions. This paper discusses the solutions for the singular case of the normal modes in computational atmospheric acoustics. By analysis and examples, a reasonable approach is derived to disposing boundary conditions. Some important conclusions are:

1 Normal modes method is suitable for the sound fields with boundaries. But at the top of the atmosphere, the original physical condition is a gradual change without a clear-cut interface. So the wave equations are usually the singular case, which could not be calculated.

2 The mirror boundary approach is that the sound field is placed a mirror at top to extend the original calculation area to an axisymmetric area with both rigid boundaries at the top and bottom. While a proper absorption coefficient assigned above the mirror position, the solution of sound field below the mirror is correct.

The approach is practical for normal modes method in atmospheric acoustics. It could be expected that normal modes acted as a standard method to verify the results of other methods as it be in underwater acoustics.

Acknowledgments

Project supported by the National Key Technology R&D Program of China (Grant No. 2006BAA02A21-8).

References

1. Jensen F B. Computational ocean acoustics [M]. Springer, 2011.
2. Dezhao W, Erchang S. Underwater acoustics [M]. Science press, 2013. (in Chinese).
3. Salomons E M. Computational atmospheric acoustics [M]. Springer, 2001.
4. Xunren Y, Yu C. Atmospheric acoustics [M]. Science press, 2007. (in Chinese)
5. Lianglong D. Modeling and application for ocean acoustics [M]. Science press, 2012. (in Chinese)
6. Kobayashi N. A new method to calculate normal modes [J]. Geophysical Journal International, 2007, 168(1): 315-331.
7. Didier Dragna, Benjamin Cotté, and Philippe Blanc-Benon. Time-Domain Simulations of Outdoor Sound Propagation with Suitable Impedance Boundary Conditions[C]. J AIAA, 2011, 49(7): 1420-28.
8. Porter M B. Acoustics Toolbox [OL]. http://oalib.hlsresearch.com/Modes/AcousticsToolbox/. 2010.
9. Dunren G. Mathematical physics methods [M]. Beijing: High education press, 1991(in Chinese)
10. Gonghuan D, Zhemin Z, Xiufen G. Acoustics fundamentals [M]. Nanjing University press, 2012. (in Chinese)

Tuning Pretty Fast Analysis on Heterogeneous Systems Equipped with GPUs

Xin-Biao Gan[1,2,a], Rui Liu[1,2], Jian-Zheng Sun[3] and Jie Liu[1]
[1]*School of Computer, National University of Defense Technology*
Changsha, 410073, China
[2]*Sate Key Laboratory of Space Weather, Chinese Academy of Sciences*
Beijing, 100190, China
[3]*Shijiazhuang Mechanized Infantry Academy,, Shijiazhuang, 050000, China*
E-mail: [a]xinbiaogan@163.com

Pretty Fast Analysis (PFA) is an important tool for analyzing large-scale molecular dynamics simulation trajectory data. However, accurate analysis of large-scale molecular dynamics simulation requires a large number of simulation trajectory data and time consumption. Therefore, PFA is benchmarked for profiling and tuning PFA on heterogeneous systems composed of CPU and GPU. Benchmarking results demonstrate that it is advisable to start specified number of processes for ensuring correctness of running PFA on heterogeneous systems equipped with GPU. Furthermore, optimization including eliminating redundant synchronization and reorganizing special branch selection into computation would increase PFA performance by 7.1%.

Keywords: Pretty Fast Analysis; Molecular Dynamics Simulation; GPU; Profiling; Optimization.

1. Introduction

Graphics Processing Unit (GPU) are increasingly being applied to scientific computations due to high GPU computing capability and low barrier to program GPU applications.

Pretty Fast Analysis (PFA) is computationally intensive software for analyzing large-scale Molecular Dynamics (MD) simulation trajectory data. PFA would Read either CHARMM or AMBER style topology or trajectory files as input [1-2], and PFA routines can scale up to thousands of compute cores or hundreds of GPU nodes. Fortunately, useful profiling including PFA communication patterns, PFA productivity and PFA optimizations have been concluded from homogeneous systems based on CPU clusters[3]. However, GPU have applied to high performance computing fields such as MD[4-5], while there is no available performance profiling on heterogeneous systems equipped with GPUs. Therefore, we test PFA on heterogeneous systems equipped with GPUs to examine its correctness when starting a variable number of processes and obtain useful information for tuning PFA.

This paper is organized as follows. Section 2 contains a short introduction to PFA software, main features of heterogeneous systems and execution model for GPU are introduced in Section 3. Section 4 presents benchmarking results and optimizations. Finally, conclusions with a perspective activity are given in Section 5.

2. Pretty Fast Analysis

PFA is a data analysis parallel software suite for analyzing large-scale MD simulation trajectory data on massively parallel supercomputers. PFA analysis routines can scale up to thousands of compute cores or hundreds of GPU nodes with either parallel or UNIX file I/O [1]. The pseudo-code of the PFA algorithm is illustrated in Fig. 1.

PFA has dynamic memory management, and each code execution can perform a variety of different structural, energetic, and file manipulation operations on a single MD trajectory at once. The code itself has been written in a combination of Fortan90 and C, and its GPU kernels are written with CUDA (Compute Unified Device Architecture) API to achieve maximum GPU performance. Fortunately, PFA has been carefully tested on CPU clusters and useful profiling and architectural optimization for CPU clusters have been obtained[2]. However, there is no available useful profiling on PFA running on GPU clusters, we benchmark PFA on heterogeneous systems equipped with GPUs.

```
if(node=master) then
        get inputs
        open output files
end if
        MPI_BROADCAST inputs to nodes
for(i=1;i= Nsteps - NCPUs ;i+= NCPUs ) do
    if( use MPI IO) then
            MPI_FILE_READ_AT a single frame
    else
        master reads NCPUs frames
        MPI_SCATER frames to nodes
    end if
// structrural  and enegetic caculations could be accelerated using GPU

    do structrural caculations
    MPI_GATHER output to master for writing
    do enegetic caculations
    MPI_GATHER output to master for writing
    if(writing output trajectory) then
            do any coordinate transforms
            MPI_FILE_WRITE_AT asingle frame
    end if
end for
    if(node=master) then
            close all output files
    end if
```

Fig. 1. PFA algorithm in master/slave mode

3. Architecture

3.1. *Heterogeneous systems architecture*

GPU architecture consists of a scalable number of streaming multiprocessors (SMs), each containing eight streaming processor (SP) cores and every three SMs constitute a threading multiprocessor cluster (TPC) in Nvidia GTX 280, a read-only constant cache, and a read-only texture cache. Additionally, Each SM has 16 KB read and write shared memory which is common to all 8 SPs inside it.

3.2. *CUDA execution model*

In CUDA-enabled GPU, instructions are structured in SPMD (Single Program, Multiple Data), and CUDA execution model provides three key abstractions, a hierarchy of thread groups, shared memories, and barrier synchronization. Threads have a three level hierarchy. A grid is a set of thread blocks that execute a kernel function, Each grid consists of thread blocks. Each block is composed of hundreds of threads. Threads within one block can share data using shared memory and can be synchronized at barrier, while redundant synchronization would severely damage GPU performance. All threads within a block are executed concurrently in a form called warp, which is composed of 32 parallel threads, and Instructions are scheduled and managed based on warp in SIMT (Single Instruction, Multiple Threads)[6].Therefore, thread-level parallelism is prone to exploited according to CUDA execution model, while threading divergence for would severely damage GPU performance.

Consequently, CUDA-enabled GPU is computing-intensive architecture, while redundant synchronization and threading divergence would severely damage GPU performance according to CUDA Execution Model.

4. Performance Results

In order to examine PFA correctness when starting a variable number of processes and obtain useful performance profiling for tuning PFA. We carefully benchmark PFA on heterogeneous systems equipped with GPUs. In this section, we first briefly introduce the experiment setup and benchmarks. Then performance evaluation and optimizations are presented.

4.1. *Experiment setup*

The experimental platform is composed of two servers inter-connected with infiniband. Configuration for each sever and selected benchmarks are listed in Table 1.

Table 1. Experimental configuration

Component	**Description**
CPU	2 * Intel xeon X5675 3.07 GHz
GPU	6 * NvidiaTesla C2070 1.15GHz
Mem	12 * 8G
OS	Linux redhat 5.5
MPI	Open MPI
Benchmarks	*Lysozyme*, known as muramidase or N-acetylmuramide glycanhydrolase, Lysozyme it is part of innate immune system[7]

4.2. *Methodology with optimizations*

Redundant Synchronization Elimination (**RSE**). In CUDA execution Model, sync threads( ) is used to coordinate threads communication in one thread block to avoid data hazard. However, redundant synchronization using sync threads( ) would damage system performance especially for threads in one warp because of implicit synchronization for threads in one wrap. Therefore, it is valuable to eliminate redundant synchronization in one warp that would improve system performance.

Branch selection Transform (**BST**). Similarly, branch selection would cause thread divergence and damage system performance. While branch selection for loop would be minimized based on loop unrolling and might reorganize into conditional computation in some special cases.

Based on RSE and BST optimization, PFA performance would increase by 7.1% when PFA running with 144 computing processes based on homogeneous systems equipped with GPUs, optimization techniques for performance improvement is described in Fig. 2.

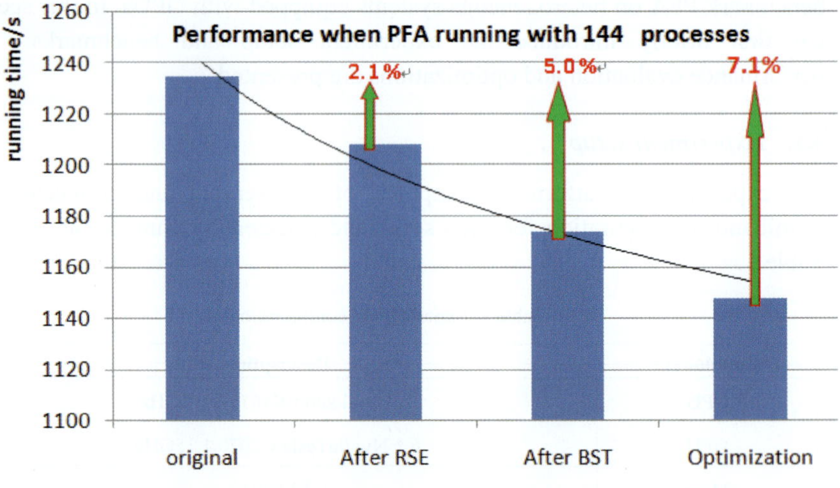

Fig. 2. Optimizations when PFA running with 144 processes

As demonstrated in Fig. 2, optimizations including RSE and BST would improve PFA performance by 2.1% and 5.0% than that of original PFA without any optimizations, respectively. Therefore, architecture-oriented optimizations would increase performance by 7.1% when PFA running with144 computing processes on homogeneous systems equipped with GPUs.

5. Conclusions

PFA is a computing-intensive data analysis parallel software suite for analyzing large-scale MD simulation trajectory data on massively parallel computer systems, and it is challengeable to accelerate and tune PFA on heterogeneous systems equipped with GPUs. Unfortunately, there is no available PFA profiling and optimization on heterogeneous systems equipped with GPUs. Accordingly, we benchmark PFA for useful profiling on heterogeneous systems composed of CPU and GPU. Moreover we tune PFA with architecture-oriented optimizations including RSE and BST and advance PFA performance by 7.1% expectably.

Acknowledgments

This work is partly supported by the Specialized Research Fund for State Key Laboratories, partly supported by the Open Research Fund of Key Laboratory of Spectral Imaging Technology, Chinese Academy of Sciences under Grant No. LSIT201602D, partly supported by Research Foundation of National University of Defense Technology under Grant No. ZK16-03-06 and partly supported by National Natural Science Foundation of China (Grant No. 61602495).

References

1. Lebard D N. Pretty Fast Analysis: An embarrassingly parallel algorithm for biological simulation analysis. arXiv preprint arXiv: 0808.2992, 2008.
2. Car R, Parrinello M. Unified approach for molecular dynamics and density-functional theory. Physical review letters, 1985, 55(22): 2471-2474.
3. HPC Advisory Council. PFA (Pretty Fast Analysis) Performance Benchmark and Profiling. Jun, 2011.
4. Plimpton S. Fast parallel algorithms for short-range molecular dynamics. Journal of Computational Physics, 1995, 117(1): 1-19.
5. Yang J, Wang Y, Chen Y. GPU accelerated molecular dynamics simulation of thermal conductivities. Journal of Computational Physics, 2007, 221(2): 799-804.
6. NVIDIA.CUDA Compute Unified Device Architecture Programming Guide, Version 2.0. 2008.
7. Shugar D. The measurement of lysozyme activity and the ultra-violet inactivation of lysozyme. Biochemical et biophysicaacta, 1952, 8: 302-309.

The Economic Design of ARMA Control Chart Based on Quality Loss Function

Li Zhang[a] and Xiao-Yang Dong[b,*]

School of Management Engineering, Zhengzhou University of Aeronautics Zhengzhou, Henan, China

Email: [a]lizhang89@hotmail.com, [b]13027618837@163.com

To improve the sensitivity of statistical process monitoring while reducing costs, the economic design model of Autoregressive Moving Average (ARMA) process was built. Monte Carlo was used to calculate the Average Run Length (ARL) of ARMA control charts. Genetic algorithm was used to search for the optimal combination of parameters and the minimum cost of the model. Finally, the sensitivity analysis was carried out, which provides the parameters related to the expected cost in per unit time in the monitoring process in order to reduce the loss of quality.

Keywords: ARMA Control Chart; Quality Loss Function; Economic Design; Genetic Algorithm.

1. Introduction

In the process of statistical process control, the basic premise of the Shewhtar chart is that the observed value is independent. While in reality, many processes have the characteristics of auto-correlation. In order to solve the monitoring problem of the self-correlation process, Jiang proposed the ARMA control chart in 2000[1]. But because of the influence of the relevant parameters on the cost of process quality control, the economic design of ARMA control chart must be considered. The economic design of the control chart was first proposed by Ducan in 1956[2]. Subsequently, Lorenzen et al proposed a general model for the economic design[3]. Chen et al proposed the economic design of cumulative conformance count chart[4]. Lin Songnong put forward the economic design of ARMA control chart[5].

It is traditionally believed that it will result in the quality loss if the quality characteristic beyond the limitation, while Taguchi thought that the quality loss

*Corresponding author.

arises as long as the quality characteristic value deviation from the target value[6]. He put forward the quadratic quality loss function, in order to approximately measure the quality loss caused by the deviation from the target value. Many scholars have applied the loss function in the economic design of control chart[7-10]. But few scholars have discussed the economic design of ARMA control chart based on the quality loss function. In this study the quality loss function and the economic design model of Lorenzen were combined to establish the economic design model of ARMA control chart.

2. The Economic Design of ARMA Chart

2.1. *Symbol description*

$1/\lambda$: The time of special cause occur
T_{12}: The total time required to find and eliminate the special cause
T_3: The unit time to sample and interpreter the result
T_4: When the control chart false alarm, the time required to confirm
C: Total cost of the economic model
C_4: Cost of false alarm per time
C_{12}: The cost to find and eliminate assignable causes in per unit time
a: Fixed cost per sample
b: Cost per unit of sampling
U: Number of manufactured products in per unit time
Q: Average quality loss cost per product, $Q = c_2 - c_1$
ARL_0: Average run length of control chart under controlled condition
ARL_1: Average run length of control chart under uncontrolled condition
τ: The time between the occurrence of a special cause and the previous sampling interval
h: Sampling interval

2.2. *The economic design of ARMA chart based on quality loss function*

The total cycle time is shown in Figure 1:

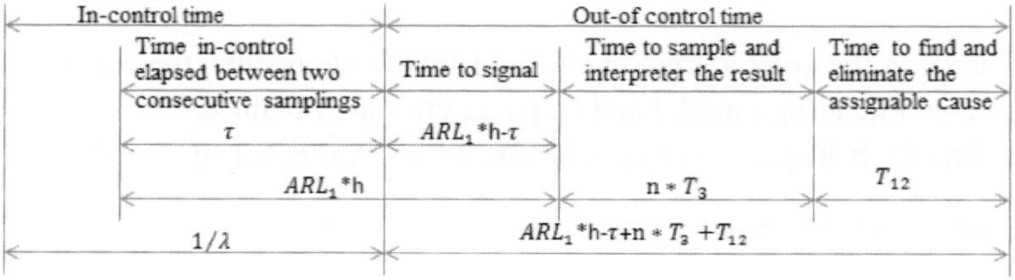

Fig. 1. Figure of a quality control cycle

The quality loss per unit can be calculated as:

$$\frac{L}{T}=\frac{QUT_2+C_{12}T_{12}+\frac{C_4T_4}{\lambda h(ARL_0)}}{\frac{1}{\lambda}+(ARL_1)h-\tau+nT_3+T_{12}}+\frac{(a+bn)}{h}.$$

3. Example

Using genetic algorithm to solve the optimal combination of five parameters of the ARMA control chart, getting the minimum cost per unit time.

3.1. *Solution procedure*

(1) Setting genetic algorithm parameters for initial solution as 40, crossover rate as 0.8, mutation rate as 0.1;
(2) Setting the parameter values as follows: $L = 1, \delta = 2, U = 10, A = 10, B = 50, T_{12} = 2, \lambda = 0.01, T_3 = 0.05, a = 0.5, b = 0.1, u = 0.5, v = 0.3, \sigma_0^2 = 1$;
(3) Using MATLAB programming, establishing the cost function. Monte Carlo method was used to calculate ARL_0 and ARL_1;
(4) Setting the search scope of the control chart parameters $[n, h, k, \phi, \theta]$: the minimum value [1 0.1 2 0.01 0.01], the maximum value [30 5 4 1 1];
(5) Using Matlab genetic algorithm toolbox to solve, and output the results.

3.2. *Solution result*

After 5 times to solve, the optimal parameter combination and the lowest total cost are obtained, as shown in Table 1:

Table 1. Table of solution result

Number	n	h	k	ϕ	θ	Total cost
1	6	0.211	2.009	0.619	0.167	55.310
2	6	0.205	2.008	0.687	0.281	57.081
3	8	0.208	2.024	0.467	0.151	54.863
4	4	0.203	2.002	0.55	0.177	54.7
5	5	0.206	2.039	0.576	0.118	54.117

Based on the comparative analysis of the above results, the minimum cost of the economic design model and its parameters are obtained:

$$\text{cost}(n, h, k, \phi, \theta) = \text{cost}(5, 0.206, 2.039, 0.576, 0.118) = 54.117$$

4. Sensitivity Analysis

The sensitivity analysis of the economic model was carried out with the orthogonal experiment design and regression analysis. 12 parameters and three levels for each parameter were selected, as shown in table 2. Using the $L_{27}(3^{13})$ orthogonal table. The experimental results were obtained by the matlab programming and the results are shown in table 3.

Table 2. Table of parameter levels of sensitivity analysis

Factor	Parameter	Parameter significance	Level 1	Level 2	Level 3
A	u	Auto regressive parameter	0.1	0.5	0.9
B	v	Average moving parameter	0.1	0.5	0.9
C	$1/\lambda$	The time of special cause occur	100	300	500
D	T_3	The time required for sampling and tracing	0.01	0.03	0.05
E	T_{12}	Time to find and eliminate the assignable cause	0.01	0.05	0.1
F	C_{12}	The cost to find and eliminate the assignable cause in per unit time	200	250	300
G	C_4	Cost of false alarm per unit time	40	50	60
H	T_4	When the control chart false alarm, the time required to confirm	1	5	10
I	U	Number of manufactured products in per unit time	20	25	30
J	a	Fixed cost per sample	0.5	2	5
K	b	Cost per unit of sampling	0.1	1	2
L	δ	Migration coefficient of process	2	3	5

Table 3. Sensitivity analysis of the experimental results table

Number	n	h	k	ϕ	θ	Cost
1	1	0.102	2.018	0.427	0.212	19.015
2	27	0.703	2.01	0.831	0.273	103.37
3	30	1.95	2.093	0.779	0.616	129.237
4	17	4.958	2.137	0.613	0.27	78.74
5	30	0.429	2.017	0.601	0.176	56.777
6	30	1.566	2.048	0.648	0.194	48.284
7	16	4.994	2.196	0.538	0.147	15.979
8	9	4.996	2.666	0.826	0.12	36.813
9	27	4.892	2.126	0.61	0.191	1.929
10	24	0.204	2.013	0.466	0.192	109.391
11	27	0.231	2.073	0.591	0.167	293.606
12	1	0.431	2.009	0.381	0.108	54.947
13	1	0.202	2.011	0.291	0.116	79.474
14	30	0.208	2.033	0.514	0.113	93.005
15	30	0.739	2.04	0.531	0.289	126.173
16	23	3.952	3.116	0.43	0.196	0.391

Table 3. Sensitivity analysis of the experimental results table (Cont.)

Number	n	h	k	ϕ	θ	Cost
17	30	4.978	2.016	0.601	0.118	21.013
18	26	4.903	3.378	0.714	0.741	4.283
19	23	0.201	2.209	0.421	0.109	209.775
20	4	0.853	2.027	0.494	0.19	54.149
21	2	0.206	2.009	0.56	0.163	129.321
22	2	0.319	2.003	0.397	0.165	78.389
23	14	0.213	2.016	0.544	0.155	115.663
24	2	0.25	2.026	0.561	0.109	39.484
25	1	0.2	2.007	0.173	0.107	54.855
26	1	0.211	2.005	0.429	0.177	73.097
27	30	0.585	2.092	0.609	0.199	41.142

In order to study the influence of the model parameters on the optimal solution of the economic model, we make a regression analysis for each parameter. The significant level is 0.05. The conclusions are as follows:

(1) n is negatively correlated with u and b, and is positively correlated with T_{12} , c_{12}, a and δ. (2) k is positively correlated with v and δ. (3) h is negatively correlated with u, and is positively correlated with v and T_3. (4) ϕ is negatively correlated with u and T_{12}. (5) The total cost of per unit time is positively correlated with u, E, U, b, δ, and is negatively correlated with v, T_{12}, $1/\lambda$ and a.

5. Conclusions

The economic cost model of ARMA control chart was constructed. Monte Carlo method was used to simulate the ARL, and the genetic algorithm was used to solve the model. Through the sensitivity analysis of the 12 parameters in the model, the impact of the parameters of the control chart on total cost per unit time are found out. In the practical application, we should pay special attention to the changes of these parameters in order to reduce the loss of quality and improve the quality of products.

Acknowledgments

This research was supported by the National Natural Science Foundation of China Grants U1204702 and U1404702, the Key Scientific Research Projects of Henan Province 17A630069 and the Graduate Education Innovation Fund of Zhengzhou University of Aeronautics 2016CX014.

References

1. W. Jiang, K. L. Tsui, Woodall, et al. A new SPC monitoring method: The ARMA chart, Technometrics. **42**, 04 (2000).
2. A. J. Ducan. The economic design of X-bar charts used to maintain current control of a process, Journal of American Statistical Association. **51**, 274 (1956).
3. T. J. Lorenzen, L. C. Vance. The economic design of control charts: A unified approach [J]. Technometrics. **28**, 1 (1986).
4. Y. K. Chen, C. Y. Chen. Economic design of cumulative conformance count charts with variable sampling intervals. Arabian Journal for Science and Engineering. **37**, 7 (2012).
5. S. N. Lin, C.Y. Chou, S. L. Wang, et al. Economic design of autoregressive moving average control chart using genetic algorithms, Expert systems with Applications. **39**,2 (2012).
6. G. Taguchi, E. A. Elsayed, T. C. Hsiang. Quality engineering in production systems, 5th edn (McGraw-Hill, New York, 1989).
7. A. S. Safaei, R. B. Kazemzadeh, S. T. A. Niaki. Multi-objective economic statistical design of X-bar control chart considering Taguchi loss function, The International Journal of Advanced Manufacturing Technology. **59**,9-12 (2012).
8. W. C. Yeong, M. B. C. Khoo, M. H. Lee, et al. Economic and economic statistical designs of the synthetic chart using loss functions, European Journal of Operational Research. **228**, 3 (2013).
9. A. A. Yazdi, M. S. F. Nezhad. Economic Design of Acceptance Sampling Plans Based on Conforming Run Lengths Using Loss Functions, Journal of Testing and Evaluation. **44**, 1 (2014).
10. S. T. A. Niaki, M. J. Ershadi. A parameter-tuned genetic algorithm for statistically constrained economic design of multivariate CUSUM control charts: a Taguchi loss approach, International Journal of Systems Science. **43**,12 (2012).

An Improved Bounded Rational Negotiation Model Based on Answer Set Program

Long-Yun Gao[a], Hui Wang[b] and Wu Chen[c,*]

College of Computer and Information Science, Southwest University,
No. 2 of Tiansheng Road in Beibei District, Chongqing, 400715, China
E-mail: [a]chopin.ring.ly@gmail.com, [b]2577455635@qq.com, [c]chenwu@swu.edu.cn

Recently, along with logic theories being used in science research, various works have been advancing in auto-negotiation field, where multi-agent automated negotiation is a new popular research area. However, nearly all negotiation models used in research are based on the hypothesis that agent is rational and the importance of knowledge have not been taken into consideration. Negotiation process based on this model, which loses efficiency in solution, is complicated. This paper proposes a bounded rational negotiation model based on answer set program. It is to redefine and classify negotiation demand, propose the concept of core demand, and analyze the importance of literals in order to figure out the importance of demand as well as answer set dynamically. A negotiation method based on the concept of core demand is adopted in the model, where elements of the set of core demands must remain and only put non-core demands into negotiation. This method reduces the complexity of negotiation process and improves the solving efficiency.

Keywords: Multi-agent Negotiation; Answer Set Program; Core Demand; Boundary Coefficient; Dynamic Sorting.

1. Introduction

Negotiation among several agents is common in real society. It is a repeated process. In each round of negotiation, deals will be made between two negotiation sides until they come to an agreement. Negotiation is an early topic which has been concerned in game theory and there are many formalized methods dealing with negotiation[1][2][3]. In recent years, especially, another formalized method has been proposed from the aspect of belief revision.

*Corresponding author.

Formalized method based on classic game theory is complementary with the one based on logic. The former one has the advantage of high abstract view of decision making, and the later could catch detail questions during reasoning process of agents.

Logic programming, as an important method of knowledge presentation, is widely used in AI area. Dongmo Zhang etc. have done research in the method of negotiation model presentation using classic logic[7][8][9][10][11]. However, human thinking is non-monotonic, which results in the fact that classic logic program could not present such non-monotonic thinking mode effectively. Vladimir Lifschitz et al. propose a declarative logic programming method based on non-monotonic reasoning, whose foundation is answer set semantics or stable model semantics[4][5][6], i.e. answer set programming (ASP for short). Some researchers use answer set to present human belief and use ASP in multi-agent negotiation, which provides a new path to this field. Chen, Tran Cao Son et al. search for supporting conditions by analyzing demands and backward recurrence algorithm[15]. This paper uses an ASP to represent the set of relation of negotiation knowledge of an agent.

Chen and Zhang et al. illustrate and prove the process of negotiation, but they have not considered the importance of negotiation demand, which makes difference between the negotiation results and real situation[12][13][14][15]. Li and He etc. have done research on the importance of demands and propose a sorting method based on derivation relation among demands[16].

In section two, we introduced the basic knowledge of ASP and forget theory. Modified negotiation model.

2. Preliminaries

Let Γ denote the language of ASP. The Herbrand base of Γ is a set of fundamental atoms which are formed from predicate symbols of Γ and items of Herbrand domain (as predicate parameters). We use $B\Gamma$ represent the Herbrand base of Γ. A rule is a formula as is shown in Eq.(1).

$$\mathrm{L_0} \leftarrow \mathrm{L_1}, \dots, \mathrm{L_m}, \mathrm{not}\ \mathrm{L_{m+1}}, \dots, \mathrm{not}\ \mathrm{L_n} \quad (\mathrm{n} \geq \mathrm{m} \geq 1) \tag{1}$$

Each $L_i (0 \leq i \leq n)$ is a literal of language Γ. Word 'not' stands for 'negative as failure (NAF)', and each literal is an atom or an atom with prepositive classical negative symbol '$\neg$'. The former is called positive literal while the latter is called negative literal. And they are a pair of complementary literals. A set S of literals is consistent if no pair of complementary literals is contained in it, otherwise, S is inconsistent. Also, we call a literal fundamental literal if the atom in it is a fundamental atom.

Let *Lit* be the set of literals in the underlying language of Π. Let *ANS*(Π) to denote the set of consistent answer sets of the ASP Π.

Forget theory is often used in giving up literals[6][7][8][9][10][11]. We use $SReduce(\Pi, L)$ and $WReduce(\Pi, L)$ separately to represent the modified programs with the methods above. Similarly, we use $SReduce(\Pi, X)$ and $WReduce(\Pi, X)$ to represent the new programs where some literals of set X have been given up using the methods above separately.

3. A Bounded Rational Negotiation Model Based on Answer Set Program

We mainly describe basic concepts and the process of answer set solving in previous sections. As what we say, we propose a heuristic method in bilateral negotiation. And this method mainly consists of two parts, selecting a pair of answer sets as demand in negotiation and updating trade sets of negotiators.

3.1. *Definition of negotiation model*

The negotiation model that we propose between two agents includes the following four parts. A negotiation set that represents the negotiation space of all agents; some negotiation termination conditions which determine the time of reaching the agreement and the agreement it already reached; some negotiation rules, which are put forward by the agent to define the legal demands; some strategies. Each agent puts forward a strategy. This strategy determines the demand that will be put forward. This paper mainly discusses the definition of rules and the negotiation strategies. Sort the answer sets of each negotiators in descending order. The rules of sorting is as below:

3.2. *Representation of demands and classification*

In this paper, it use $'not\ f(x)'$ to define the symbol "*not confirm*". To unify the representation of demand, the classification of negotiation demands is shown in Eq.(2).

$$\text{literal}\begin{cases}\text{assist literal}\\ \text{demand(literal)}\begin{cases}\text{potential demand}\\ \text{user demand}\begin{cases}\text{core demand}\\ \text{non}-\text{core demand}\end{cases}\end{cases}\end{cases} \quad (2)$$

In the above classification, this paper views the head literals of asp as demands. This article will regard the fact as the core demand, and other demands in the head literals set are non-core demand. With the symbol "*Cd*" represents the set of core demand set, $ANS_j(\Pi)$ represents an answer set of ASP Π. l_i is a literal of ASP, then $Cd = \{l_i | l_i \leftarrow . \in \Pi\}$. Every core demand is a fact literal, and it meets with the condition of Eq.(3).

$$\mathrm{l} \in \mathrm{Head}(\Pi), \mathrm{l} \in \mathrm{r}\ (\mathrm{r} \in \Pi, \mathrm{Neg}(\mathrm{r}) = \emptyset, \mathrm{Head}(\mathrm{r}) \neq \emptyset) \quad (3)$$

In which *l* is a literal, and *r* is a rule of Π.

3.3. *Termination conditions of negotiation*

In the process of multi-round negotiation, the termination conditions of negotiation can be divided into three categories. First categories is termination for success. In this situation, there exists same answer sets between these two ASPs. The second is termination for the fact conflicting which leads to the failure of negotiation. In this case, the facts that two ASP programs conflict and cause both sides of negotiation giving up their demand or accepting the other's demand will bring lots of losses. The last one is the situation in which the initial answer set of both sides is empty.

3.4. *Solution of demand conflict*

Demand conflict can be divided into three categories as below.

- Core demands and core demands
- Core demands and non-core demands
- Non-core demands and non-core demands

When non-core demands conflict with non-core demands, program works out the sort of importance among demands. Agent uses strong forget theory to deal with the answer set according to the importance of literals in it. Under this circumstance, literals with high priority block ones with lower priority.

3.5. *Multi-round negotiation model*

There are many ways now to sort priorities of answer sets. This paper introduces an different method.

Firstly we use symbol Ψ to express the priority relation among users' demands. Secondly, we calculate the importance among the characters based on the deriving relation in the answer sets. The real text's priority is the highest. Sorting is based on literals of own ASP. Thirdly, we should ensure the importance of users' demands according the importance of the text, such as the set of users' demands {a, b, c, d, e}. We can assume the priority relationship of the text in answer set: $\Psi = \{b \succ c \succ a \succ d \succ e\}$.Then the priority of answer set will be confirmed according the sort of text.

Negotiation of this paper is about two consultation participants' demand (answer set) mutually amend process. We divided demand modification process into two parts: the contraction and expansion. In other words, the negotiation gives up its own part of consultations first, and then accepts all or part of the other's demands.

The following will detail the consultation process.

Step1: Demand representation and answer set program build.

Step2: Calculation core demands (*Cd*) of answer set program (ASP).

Step3: Optimize answer set program. Before solving the answer set program, we can do the following operations: initial demands set text, facts set, initial set of non-facts, and then delete the rules that header text contains facts and rules body is not empty.

Step4: Before the first round of negotiations begins, we use the method above to resolve the program. The first round of negotiation accepts all the core needs of each other's core needs in the form of all the facts to add to your answer set programs, according to the fact that expanded, use of the method of appeal procedures for their modification.

Step5: Calculate each ASP answer set. Determine whether the two sides have same answer set (shown in Figure 1). If yes, go to step 6; or, go to step 7.

Step6: if parties have same answer set, do as follows.

If there is one set answer that is identical: according to the end of negotiation, negotiation reach an agreement and finish this round of negotiation.

If there is not only one set answer that is identical: select the bigger interests answer set as a result of a set of negotiation according to the interests with both sides cooperation.

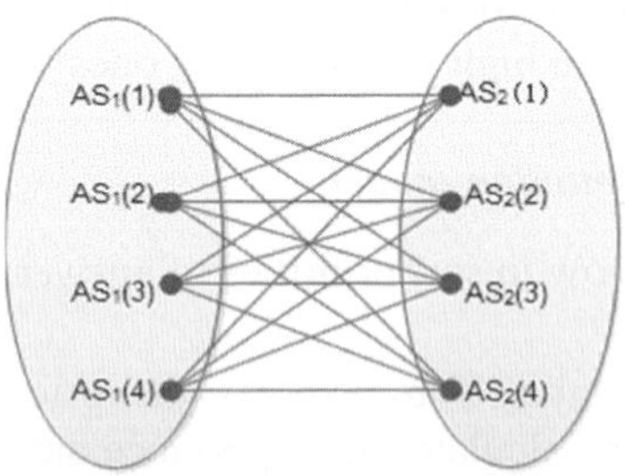

Fig. 1. Check whether there are the same answer sets

Step 7: If there is no same answer set, then agent gives up some demands or accepts some demands of counterpart selectively. Firstly, we work out the importance of all answer sets of agent 1 and 2 according to the sort of importance of literals, and sort them. Then we divide the issue into two situations.

(1) If one answer set is contained in the other, then add the derivation rules of literals that do not belong to the intersection of the two answer sets to the ASP whose answer set has less literals, and recalculate the answer sets of this ASP. If the answer set for less literals could be found, the result of negotiation is the answer set with less literals.
(2) If no inclusion relation exists, in order to make a deal, agents give up own demands to accept others' demands.

In our model, as shown in figure 2, agent chooses the best scheme after comparing demands of two sides. The times of comparison is $M \times N$ (M and N represent the numbers of answer sets of agent 1 and 2 respectively). We adopt bounded rational theory, so number of comparison here is $M + N - 1$.

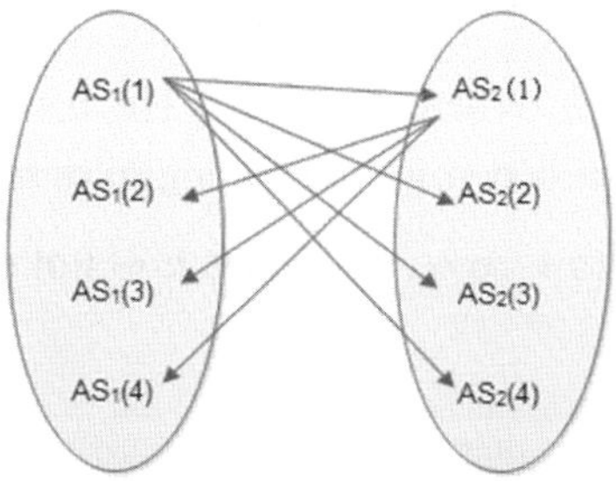

Fig. 2. Bounded rational negotiation

Step 8: Repeat from step 3 to step 7 until a deal is made. Many real life negotiations are the processes of multi-round activities. In each round, both sides give up own demands and accept some demands of the other agent. Multi-round negotiation proceeds in the selecting of each agent.

If two sets of answer set of ASP Π_1 and Π_2 do not contain the same set, then enter the next round. The necessary and sufficient condition of negotiation entering to the next round is as follows:

$$\mathrm{Fact}(\Pi_1 + \Pi_2) \neq \mathrm{Lit} \quad (4)$$

which means no conflict is found in facts. In general, negotiation has two main stages, tackling contradictions of core demands, contradicting between core demands and non-core demands. Table 1 shows ELP of negotiators.

Table 1. ELP of $\Pi_1$and Π_2

Π_1	Π_2
$a \leftarrow .\ b \leftarrow .$	$c \leftarrow .\ d \leftarrow .$
	$\neg b \leftarrow .\ \ \neg a \leftarrow not\ e.$

We can get results that $ANS(\Pi_1) = \{a, b\}, ANS(\Pi_2) = \{\neg a, \neg b, c, d\}$. $\neg b$ is the core demand of Π_2 which is in conflict with a, the core demand of Π_1, so this is the conflict between core demands, and this round of negotiation fails.

Research found that the only one round of negotiation could reach the tasks of the first stage in multi-round negotiation. After the first stage, no core demand conflict will exist. So in stage two, we have to deal with the conflict between non-core demands. Because of the dynamic change of non-core demands, work in this stage is more complicated.

In literature[5], the accepted demand is regard as fact. But we add corresponding rules and generative rules to own ASP. We propose the Trading Rules Set, and use symbol TRS represent selected trading set of answer sets.

As follow ASP Π : $a \leftarrow . b \leftarrow . c \leftarrow not\ d. d \leftarrow not\ c. e \leftarrow not\ d. f \leftarrow not\ d. h \leftarrow not\ c, g. g \leftarrow b$. Where $\mathrm{ANS}(\Pi) = \{\{a, b, c, e, f, g\}, \{\mathrm{a, b, d, h, g}\}\}$. If the chosen answer set is$\{\mathrm{a, b, d, h, g}\}$, the trading rules set is shown as Eq.(5).

$$\mathrm{TRS}(\Pi) = \{\mathrm{a} \leftarrow . \mathrm{b} \leftarrow . \mathrm{d} \leftarrow \mathrm{not\ c. h} \leftarrow \mathrm{not\ c, g. g} \leftarrow \mathrm{b.}\} \quad (5)$$

4. Conclusions

4.1. *Related work*

Currently, more and more scholars begin to use answer set program to study automatic negotiation, but only a few researchers consider the importance of the negotiation demands. Based on the answers programming, this paper put forward a negotiation model where the repeated negotiations between the two ASPs are formalized. In this paper, the demands are classified, thoughts of user demands, supplementary demands, core demand, non-core demands are put forward, and we study the conflicts deeply occurred in the negotiation process, especially analyze and solve the problem of "ring" of the answer set procedure.

4.2. *Future work*

The follow-up work is mainly to study further about non-core needs sorting and belief modifying. We will continue to study the way of calculating the importance among characters and the way that how it affects the negotiation result after agents accept and give up characters or rules. We will continue to optimize the negotiation model, with social networks, combining fractal mathematics research.

References

1. L. Michael, and S .Peter. Implicit negotiation in repeated games, Intelligent Agents VIII. (Springer Berlin Heidelberg,. 393-404, 2001).
2. H. Sabourian, and L. Jihong. Complexity and efficiency in repeated games with negotiation. *Econometric Society 2004 North American Summer Meetings*. No. 58 (2004).
3. Y. Zhang, and Y. F. Norman, Solving logic program conflict through strong and weak forgettings. *Artificial Intelligence* 170.8: 739-778(2006).
4. G. Michael, and V. Lifschitz. The stable model semantics for logic programming. *ICLP/SLP*. Vol. 88(1988).
5. G. Michael, and V. Lifschitz. Classical negation in logic programs and disjunctive databases. *New generation computing* 9.3-4: 365-385. (1991)
6. V. Lifschitz. Foundations of logic programming. *Principles of knowledge representation 3*: 69-127 (1996).
7. B. Chitta. Knowledge representation, reasoning and declarative problem solving. *Cambridge university press*, (2003) .
8. Dongmo Zhang, et al. Negotiation as mutual belief revision. *AAAI*. Vol. 4. (2004).
9. K. Rex and Dongmo Zhang. Logical foundations of negotiation: Outcome, *Concession and Adaptation.* (2003).
10. M. A. Thomas , et al. Logical Foundations of Negotiation: Strategies and Preferences. *KR*. (2004).
11. Dongmo Zhang, et al. Strategic trading agents via market modelling. *ACM SIGecom Exchanges 4.3* : 46-55(2004).
12. G. Wagner. Web rules need two kinds of negation. *Principles and Practice of Semantic Web Reasoning*. (Springer Berlin Heidelberg,.33-502003).
13. N. Boland, et al. New integer linear programming approaches for course timetabling. *Computers & Operations Research* 35.7: 2209-2233 (2008).
14. Jing Xiaoxin, Dongmo Zhang and Xudong Luo. A logical framework of bargaining with integrity constraints.*AI 2013: Advances in Artificial Intelligence*. (Springer International Publishing,1-13, 2013).
15. Wu Chen, Dongmo Zhang and Maonian Wu. A sequential model for reasoning about bargaining in logic programs. *Logic Programming and Nonmonotonic Reasoning*. (Springer Berlin Heidelberg,. 239-244, 2013).
16. S. C. Tran, et al. Formalizing negotiations using logic programming. *ACM Transactions on Computational Logic (TOCL)* 15.2: 12(2014).

Agricultural Data Integration and Storage with Cloud Services

Rong-Hua Gao[a] and Hua-Rui Wu[b,*]

Beijing Research Center for Information Technology in Agriculture, Beijing Academy of Agriculture and Forestry Sciences,
Beijing, 100097, China
National Research Center of Intelligent Equipment for Agriculture,
Beijing 100097, China
Key Laboratory for Information Technologies in Agriculture, Ministry of Agriculture,
Beijing 100097, China
Beijing Engineering Research Center of Agricultural Internet on Things,
Beijing 100097,China
E-mail: [a]gaorh@nercita.org.cn, [b]wuhr@nercita.org.cn

To solve the problem of multi-source agricultural data integration and storage, the integration and storage models are imposed, and mix with different agricultural production data, for meeting a large number of users access to massive agricultural data synchronously. The method of agricultural data integration and storage with cloud services is proposed in this paper. Modern networks and cloud computing technology are used to resolve problems of varied information structures, information integration of different standards in different period of the experimental area. Experimental results of this method can prove the effectiveness of utilizing parallel file transfer method for agricultural data storage with cloud services.

Keywords: Cloud Services, Information integration, Metadata, Service-oriented architecture.

1. Introduction

In recent years, information technology has made rapid development of the agriculture, but there are still many problems in the field of information technology: self-contained information system in different agricultural field, the lack of effective collaboration between them; small-scale and scattered

*Corresponding author.

information resources, uneven distribution; serious duplication of information, lack of deep excavation and development; information silos severe. With the development and application of artificial intelligence technology, China's information technology resources integration into the rapid development stage, the integration of research resources in terms of information theory, research experts to define its concepts, forming several representative view [1,2,3]. Information resources integration of different fields, which summarize different characteristics clusters [4,5,6]. Recently, some significant research results to integrate technology, system integration model and integration platform [7,8], and so on.

Horton proposed information resource management is a fusion of different technologies and the integration of technology areas, these technologies and areas, including management information systems, records management, automatic data processing and electronic communication networks et al [9]. With the acceleration of agricultural information, the process of information management and information service mode of agricultural resources urgently needed to change. In the past, the researchers are more concerned with the practices and learn from the experience of developed countries in the development of IT and information industry, and the development and sharing of information resources, inadequate attention, which resulting in different regions, different systems, different applications, and different technology platforms "islands of information".

To solve the interconnection of heterogeneous platforms, in this paper, agricultural information system based on the integration of technology of cloud services is be studied, and modern networks and cloud computing technology is used to resolve the problems of varied information structures, information integration of different standards in different period of the experimental area. Follow certain principles, norms, standards, discrete, diverse, heterogeneous distributed agricultural data together to build information services in the overall application integration of resources, to achieve the integration diversified, and unified description of multi type agricultural data.

2. Integration and Storage of Agricultural Data Based on Cloud Services

Cloud services mean services made available to users on demand via the Internet from a cloud computing provider's servers as opposed to being provided from a company's own on-premises servers. Cloud services are designed to provide comfortable, scalable access to applications, resources and services, and are fully managed by a cloud services provider.

A cloud service can dynamically scale to meet the needs of its users, and because the service provider supplies the hardware and software necessary for the service, there's no need for a company to provision or deploy its own resources or allocate IT staff to manage the service. Examples of cloud services include online data storage and backup solutions, Web-based e-mail services, hosted office suites and document collaboration services, database processing, managed technical support services and more.

2.1. *Integration model*

Under the impetus of information technology, database technology, data mining technology, artificial intelligence technology to support the theory, agricultural data integration need to analyze data according to user needs survey, based on the entire target targeted to collect data and information, and post-process feedback to the user, in order to achieve the best result of information integration, is shown in Figure 1.

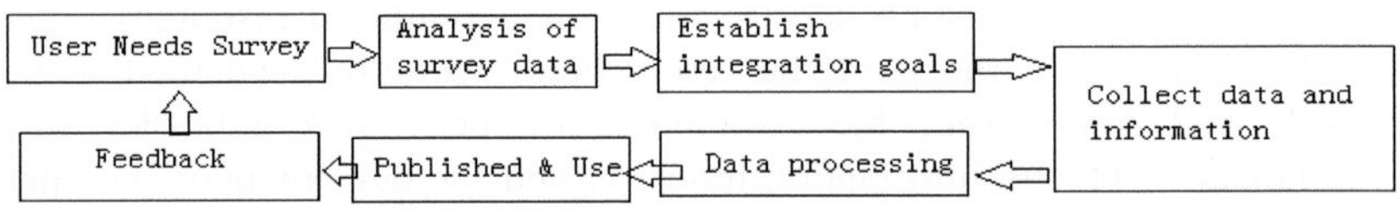

Fig. 1. Information resources flowchart

In this paper, cloud services agricultural data integration system model based on two-tier architecture is logically divided into: Background information resource consolidation level, cloud resources, heterogeneous data resources; intermediate level data fusion using fusion technology, that combined with cloud service, is shown in Figure 2.

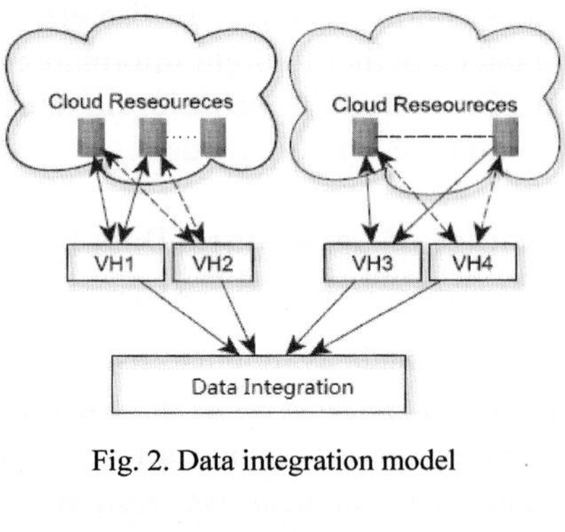

Fig. 2. Data integration model

Figure 2 shows the extraction of functional matrix from cloud service provider premises. The monitoring agent embedded with virtual host (VH1) measures the resource metrics from cloud infrastructure. For the disaster recovery, VH2 also measures the resource metrics from the same cloud infrastructure so that results will be accessed in case of VH1 fails. Similarly, it collects the resource metrics from another cloud infrastructure. All resource metrics measured from individual cloud infrastructure are collected in data Integration.

2.2. *Massive data storage model*

According to the characteristics of massive data, combined with cloud computing technology, the massive data storage model calculations, is shown in Figure.3.

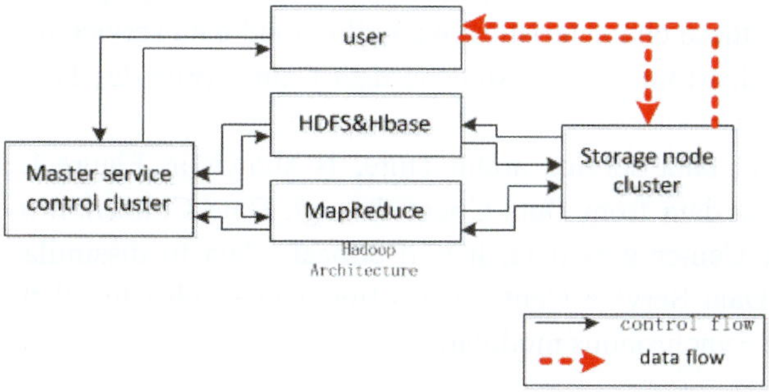

Fig. 3. Massive data storage model

In Figure 3, the master service control cluster is equivalent to the controller part, which responsibility is receiving application request and responds according to the type of demand. Storage node cluster is equivalent to the memory section, which composed of a large disk array system and having a mass data storage capability, the main function is to access process data resources. HDFS and Hbase be employed to store data or deployed on each compute node. Hadoop has as a master server for scheduling and managing other computers, and the master server can run on any computer. When scheduling and data management tasks, must be implemented in the data storage node. Map tasks and Reduce tasks distributed free task tracker, so that these tasks run in parallel, and are responsible for monitoring the operation of the task. If any of them are out of order, job tracker will be rerun by responsible to another task. The user does not directly read HDFS and Hbase access data by Hadoop architecture. Thus avoiding system congestion by reading a lot of data. Users read data from the storage node after transitional information to master service control cluster with Hadoop architecture.

3. Experiment and Results

An experiment is conducted to test the validity of integration and storage implemented in agricultural production including environmental parameters, production data, crop growth and so on. By testing with one, two, and four cloud storage providers, the application proves that it is possible use methods explained in the previous section to combine many cloud storages into a one big storage. For testing on upload time, we are able to prove the effectiveness of utilizing parallel file transfer method for agricultural data's cloud storage.

In this paper, three characteristics of a cloud computing environment: compute power are elastic, but only if the workload is parallelized, Data is stored as suspect host; Data is replicated, often across large geographic distances. According to these characteristics, we build cloud data service to handle elastic, security and distribute issue. And the data Center provides Data-as-Service to the user.

The cloud data service architecture, is shown in Figure.4. Data Service Center collects data from Data Client through Data Collection modular. When Data Service Center gets data, it will allocate data to dissimilar data servers. Since then, Data Service Center can offer data service to all the Data Client through Data Synchronous modular.

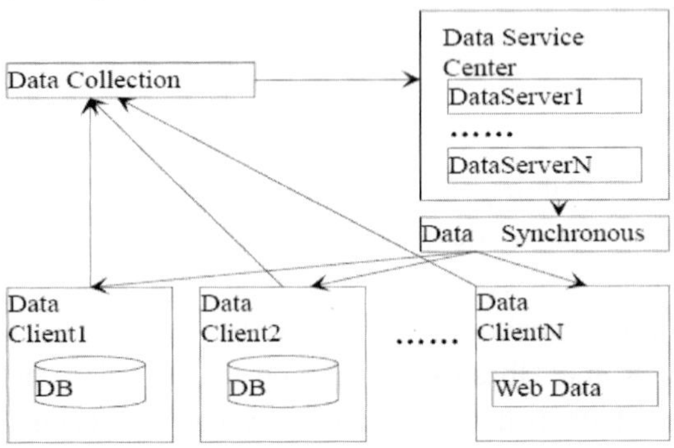

Fig. 4. Cloud data service architecture

4. Conclusions

For agricultural data obvious characteristics which have types complex and diverse, spatial and temporal variability, significant variation, strong randomness, discrete high, the scale effect and so on. Agricultural data lack of overall planning and effective integration of information resources in decentralized basis, independent of each other is simple, yet linked to form a complete network, and the lack of reference to the implementation of the standard system, the presence of system compatibility, interoperability of insufficient issue. To solve the problem of integration and storage of multi-source data, the integration and storage model is imposed, and mixes different agricultural production data, then meet a large number of users with concurrent access to massive agricultural data.

Acknowledgments

This work was supported by Beijing Municipal Natural Science Foundation (4151001).

References

1. Zhang Yunxing. Research on the Integration of Village Tourism Resources in Yuntai Mountain Area of Henan Province. Journal of Anhui Agricultural Sciences,2012, 40(2): 919-920. (In Chinese)
2. Qin Zhihua, Liu Chuanyou. Entrepreneurial Resource Acquisition Based on the Integration and Exploitation of Heterogeneous Resource. Journal of Renmin University of China, 2011, 6(6):143-150. (In Chinese)
3. Chu Dianhui, Wang Xianzhi, Wang Zhongjie, et al. Personalized Requirement Oriented Virtual Service Resource Aggregation Method. Chinese Journal of Computers, 2011, 34(12):2370-2380. (In Chinese)
4. Li Ruofang. Discussion and Research on County Agricultural Information Resource Integration Model in Yunnan Province. Journal of Anhui Agricultural Sciences, 2012, 40(20):10690-10691. (In Chinese)
5. Liu Xiuru, Yang Yongchuan, Yan Hongli. Research on the Application of Topic Maps in Public Security Information Resources Integration. Computer Applications and Software, 2012, 29(4):206-208.
6. Xu Can, Su Houqin. Study and Practice of an Information Resource Integration Platform. Computer Applications and Software, 2012, 29(4): 195-196.
7. EL K Duygu, EL Atilla. A Broker-based Semantic Agent for Discovering Semantic Web Services Through Process Similarity Matching and Equivalence Considering Quality of Service. Science China (Information Sciences), 2013, 56(24):1-24.(In Chinese)
8. Wang Zhen, Sun Fuchun, Liu Zhiyou. On Discovery and Composition of Resource Ontology-based Web Services. Computer Applications and Software, 2012, 29(3):191-194.
9. Casado Ruben, Younas Muhammad, Tuya Javier. Multi-dimensional Criteria for Testing Web Services Transactions. Journal of Computer and System Sciences, 2013, 79(7):1057-1079.

Measuring the Contribution of Developers in Open Source Projects

Yi-Ang Gan[a], Gang Yin[b], Yao Lu[c], Xiang Hou, Meng-Wen Chen and Tao Wang

National Laboratory for Parallel and Distributed Computing, School of Computer, National University of Defense Technology

Kaifu District, Changsha City, Hunan Province, China

E-mail: [a]ganyiang@outlook.com, [b]yingang@nudt.edu.cn, [c]yaolu_study@163.com

Measuring the contribution of individual developers is very important for the governance of open source projects. In this paper, combining techniques of data mining and visualization analysis to design the contribution characteristics models of open source developers are attempted and study the differences between the models in software evolution processes that are hosted on GitHub. The experiment results show that the rhythm of the entire software evolution is driven by the activities of the small portion of core developers, who contribute to the project continuously rather than most contributors. Coding activities are also found to be closely accompanied by other communication activities such as issues and comments. These findings provide a solid foundation for contribution measurement of individuals in open source development.

Keywords: Open Source Software; Mining Software Repositories; Software Contribution Metrics; Visual Analysis; Contribution Evolution.

1. Introduction

Open Source Software (OSS) development is a form of crowdsourcing in software production and innovation, and has made a tremendous impact on the development of IT industry. Developers from all around the world make their contributions to various OSS projects through the Internet, e.g., submitting code patches, reporting bugs, discussing feature enhancements, etc. These behaviors are recorded in software repositories. It is vitally important to comprehensively measure and visualize developers' contributions [1]. On the one hand, core developers can assign development tasks based on the developers' contribution history and their special area, thus improving development efficiency and software quality. On the other hand, the contribution history is a best resume for a developer, which facilitates companies to get a comprehensive understanding of job candidates.

GitHub provides development tools such as version control, issue tracking, and social communication tools [2]. Over 25 million repositories are hosted on GitHub, and more than 10 million active users are engaging in various activities of communities, which produce the big data of OSS. In this paper, we attempt to combine techniques of data mining and visualization analysis, to analyze GitHub developers' contribution characteristics, and study different contribution model of developers in software evolution progress. These are some of the most noteworthy contributions of this paper:

- Core contributors usually maintain a small number of core files, and they tend to use pull-request to collaborate.
- The evolution process of the entire software is driven by a small portion of core developers who contribute to the project continuously.
- Coding activities often accompanied by other communication activities such as issues and comments.

The rest of the paper is organized as follows. Section 2 describes the three research questions and the preliminary results. Section 3 introduces the closely related work. Section 4 describes our method. Section 5 presents the experimental results and section 6 concludes the paper.

2. Research Questions and Results

2.1. *RQ1: What factors have influence on developers' contribution?*

We make use of visualization techniques and correlation analysis in machine learning and find there exists correlation relationship with different strength between a developer's contribution and his code or after-code interactive development activity.

We also find that it is more scientific to use the number of bug fixed, the number of core files modified to measure the contribution, compared to the lines of code changed. And the influence of social contribution is not obvious. Core contributors tend to use pull-request, pull-request is one of contribution model in distributed software development [3].

2.2. *RQ3: What is the process of contribution evolution of developers in software life cycle like?*

We introduce novel visualization techniques such as annual ring chart and radar chart, to observe the changes of every developer in each dimension in accordance with the versions and compare with the whole process of software evolution. We find that open-source development model make software development become public collaborative development from minority elite development, but the whole development process is dominated by a small number of elite and the participation of most peripheral developers is random. And there is a linear relationship between early stage and late stage.

Meanwhile, we analyze the contribution evolution model of different contributors in communities and infer contribution type they are good to by using radar chart to measure the ability of developers in each observation index, which is used to identify developers with different abilities. The contribution of vast majority of contributors in the project is very small. And the larger the project, the more likely this is the case. And it is difficult to measure the contribution of vast majority of contributors independently. The larger the team, the more average that close to the overall average each contributor's contribution is.

2.3. *RQ3: What relationship between code contribution of developers and after-code interactive development activity?*

By using regression analysis, we find the number of issue and comments is correlated to the number of after-code activities. One explanation is that high contributors communicate with and give feedback to other developers actively in contribution process in communities. And from RQ2, we can also observe that the activities of issues and commits are accompanied by that of comments.

3. Related Work

Some important researches have been conducted on measuring contribution of developers in software projects.

In mining and analyzing the behavior characteristics of developers in open source paradigm, Gousions proposed a more complex system by combining code and non-code contributions [1]. This system summarizes various behaviors by using nearly 30 metrics including positive behavior and negative impacts and gives us a comprehensive method about personal contribution calculation. But there is also a disadvantage that Gousions just proposed. In fact, they only use the metrics related to code to measure the contribution.

In assessing developer contribution with repository, Jalerson Lima etc. proposed several indexes about measuring developers' contribution according to experience and gain some conclusions by communicating and discussing with seven leaders of developer teams [4]. These metrics are in four major areas including code contribution, average complexity per method, introduced bugs and bug fixing contribution. These leaders give positive feedback to code contribution and average complexity per method and negative feedback to the indexes related to bug, which have many limits. Meanwhile, the authors pointed that each metric cannot be measured independently and they must be together.

Minghui Zhou etc. proposed a research method of developers' contribution from three aspects including ability, willingness and environment [5]. They designed a series of metrics for Mozilla and Gnome projects. They discovered that the probability of becoming a long-term contributor for newly added developer is more related to his willingness and environment. In details, a long-term contributor in the future will be more active in the first adding month. This is just a kind of explanation.

In software evolution, Fisher etc combined software knowledge base and defect tracking system to study the macro changing process of different software versions [6]. Wang etc discovered the relationship between developer contribution of different types of work and evolution model, they extracted 5 types of developer evolution model in communities[7].

Sureka etc. divided developers into core, semi-edge and edge developers by mining the information in defect tracking system and finding out the onion structure of cooperation network of developers [8].

Ben Xu etc. studied the factors that affect developer contributions from the first code submission by using a variety of visualization techniques for analyzing the contribution in open source software repository. And they also worked on the partnership of developers. The conclusion they found is that the file modified when developers first submitted is modified more within a period of time before submitted, the contribution of developer is relative smaller [9].

Generally, recent works are mainly focused on code-related metrics (by analyzing source code) and commit-related metrics (by analyzing commit history), more researches should be conducted on the measurement of developer contribution based on more comprehensive activities.

4. The Approach

4.1. *Contribution measurement*

The classic way of measuring contribution is to use LOC (Line of Codes), which is the number of lines of all changed commit accumulated by each developer. Gousions and Minghui Zhou proposed a series of measurement metrics, which is very complex. Jalerson Lima also proposed four types of metrics. In our study, we make use of code contribution and after-code contribution. The former one includes the addition of code, the deletion of code, the number of file changed, the number of bug fixed and the number of pull-request. The latter one is the active situation of developers in GitHub, which is described by the number of issue and comment. The contribution of each developer should be calculated by Eq. (1).

$$\text{Contri(i)} = \alpha\frac{\text{Code(i)}}{\sum_{K=1}^{n}\text{Code(k)}} + \beta\frac{\text{After-Code(i)}}{\sum_{K=1}^{n}\text{After-Code(k)}}, 1 \leq i \leq n, \alpha + \beta = 1 \quad (1)$$

N is the number of developers, α and β is the weight of behaviors. It is difficult to set up the weight. This is because degree of different behaviors affecting on the project is not only related to the specific stage of the project progress, and even has a lot of contact with subjective feelings of evaluators. It is hard to judge the influence. We must gain specific calculation method through data mining automation as well as the knowledge and experience of the field experts.

4.2. *Contribution influencing factors*

Firstly, we propose several factors through heuristic method according to related references. And then, we divide them into two types: code and after-code. Code contribution is gained from log information of Git, and after-code contribution is gained from GitHub. We combine correlation and regression analysis with visual analysis methods. Correlation analysis is to analyze two or more variable elements with correlation in order to measure the correlation degree of these variables.

In our work, we focus on the impact of various variables on the contribution of commits. The contribution of commits is regarded as the contribution of the whole project referring to the ranking of contributors in GitHub. We make correlation analysis by using Spearman Rank Correlation. Spearman correlation coefficient is a non-parametric test method, which is used to measure the degree of the relationship between variables. At the time of regression analysis, we use linear regression of single variable and analyze each regression variance.

In this part, in order to verify the conclusion, we introduce the radar chart of contributor ability at the same time, which is a good representation of multivariate data. We can observe the deviation from the reference value and the actual value of the index by radar chart. We can also infer the types of contribution that developer prefers by focusing on analyzing the index of ability gap larger. The purpose of that is to identify developers with different abilities. The larger the area of the radar chart, the more the overall contribution is.

4.3. *Contribution evolution characteristics*

To model the evolution process of individual contribution, we propose to use annual ring chart to model version evolution, and use radar chart to model the capability of contributors. The former is like concentric ring pattern of trees in the main cross section on the tree, which is used to describe the situation of contribution evolution. The annual ring can be used to visualize the data of high latitude space on a map. We take the indexes to be measured as a line from center point radiating to the outward. The nodes represent the version number, which radiating to the outward orderly. This chart counts the contribution of each measurement index at the present time according to version time. And the most outer ring represents the most upper limit of each index version. In this chart, the gradient of the two circle represents the variation between the cross versions.

Through annual ring chart, we can observe metric change of all contribution during the period from developer adding to the version to the latest version. We can infer active period of developer by observing the early, middle and late contributions of developer. We can also find different types of developers and infer the status of developers in the project. compared annual ring chart of personal evolution process to that of the whole project's evolution, we can get the degree of contribution of each person in software evolution process. In order to observe conveniently, we use parallel coordinate line chart to conduct auxiliary observation at the same time, in which X axis is time series and Y axis is the value of measurement index. In this chart, each node represents a version, we standardize specific value into unified range and then map different contribution dimension to the color and the shape of the lines to draw a graph to observe the high dimensional coordinate space.

4.4. *Relation between code and after-code contribution*

We select valuable code and after-code variables to model according to RQ2 and experience an use regression analysis and visualization to analyze. We firstly check if there is a linear relationship. We consider code contribution and after code contribution as predictive variable and explanatory variable respectively to do multiple linear regression. After that we gain fitting model, conduct the significance test of model's coefficient and combine visualization to measure and explain this model.

5. Experiment

5.1. *Data set*

We use GitHub as the data source for our experiment. The data set of GitHub has been widely used in research studies. We choose a large scale project named Elasticsearch hosted on GitHub as the data source. This project has typical representative and represents a class of active development project. And it is not a separate case, which belongs to business-objected and is the same as docker, openstack and apache tomcat. It also have high followers. Therefore, we consider this project as the object of case study. elastic/elasticsearch is a Java project in GitHub with a lots of stars. As shown in table 1.

Table 1. Basic information of elasticsearch

Name	Commits	Contributors	Tags	Fork	Star	Watch
Elasticsearch	22438	664	152	5787	17093	1617

We completely clone repository to local and write vertical crawler system. We get the basic information and user information of projects by API of GitHub. In addition to this, we also obtain the information of issues and pull requests as well as their comments. The form of data gained by API is a JSON string. We need to use scripts to parse and extract useful information. In the local Git repository, we also extract the information related to the code by combining Git command and shell command, which is stored into database. These information include the number of times per developer submission, the lines of code addition and deletion, the number of files modified, the number of bug fixed and the number of issues closed by log.

In the process of continuous contribution, development may change your own Git email or author information. OSS contributors often use different aliases. And this is particularly likely to occur on the body of the long-term developer. We need to combine the contribution of the same developer with different identity, which is very complex. We refer to unmasking aliases method of Mohammad Gharehyazie [10], but the effect is not very ideal. Finally, we have completed a merge algorithm by ourselves. We use API of GitHub to gain the commits and users information with a key match field named login in order to simplified merger process. We identify all contributors in GitHub and associate identity information associated with Git repository. The number of contributors is 664. The number of identification and association is 663. The correctness is up to 98.43%.

As for merge version, we only consider big version and combine the information of contribution in a big version. The form of tag is transformed into x-y from x-y-z through combining version. The same y is for a version. Finally, the number of tag becomes 31 from 152 with tag time. The processing of dataset as the figure 1 shows.

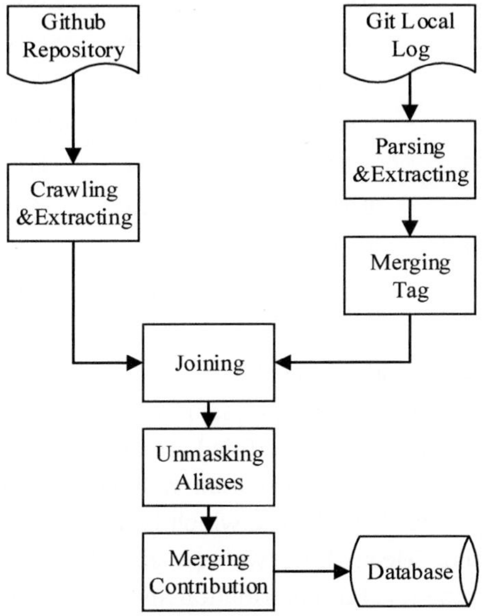

Fig. 1. Processing of dataset

5.2. *Results of contribution influencing factors*

The results are shown in the table 2 after Spearman Rank Correlation analysis, single variable linear regression analysis and variance analysis. Because we choose all contributors to be analyzed including core contributors and non-core contributors. But we can still find some useful information. For example, the largest R-squared whose values is 0.909 is the relationship between bug fixed and contribution. Compared to classic method, which is to use the number of lines of files changed to measure contribution, using the numbers of bug fixed in the project can better reflect the contribution of a developer. The largest Spearman Rank Correlation is pull request, which means there is a strong connection between pull request and contribution. Core developers have permissions accessing to the Git repository, but they still use more pull-request instead of putting commit into repository. The lowest R-squared is observed variables of files. A kind of explanation is that core contributors only maintain a small number of core files instead of involving too many files and many files modified are submitted by the external contributors.

Table 2. Spearman rank correlation and single variable linear regression analysis

Metric	Rho	Coeffs (Estimate)	Std.Error	Sum sq	R-squared
Add	0.64531	0.92378	0.01441	558.90	0.861
Del	0.64778	0.87532	0.01834	503.06	0.774
Files	0.49677	0.58065	0.03176	217.96	0.334
Fixes	0.48661	0.95228	0.01166	590.48	0.909
Closes	0.15215	0.76819	0.02434	390.06	0.600
Pr	0.74323	0.68615	0.02910	296.48	0.456
Issues	0.49598	0.88697	0.01784	512.04	0.788
Comment	0.54722	0.81849	0.02343	430.81	0.663

In order to verify the conclusion above, we use radar chart to visual the first ten developers who contribute to the project most. As figure 2 show, we can find that the files that other developers modified are not many, except the developer who ranks the second on the contribution ranking. Banon Shay, the largest contributor, has only modified 77 files, which is less than 2% of the number of the entire project file. Meanwhile, we can also find that there is a linear relationship between the level of contribution and the number of bug fixed (The greater the contribution is, the more bugs they fix). And core developers may user a lot of pull request, especially Simon Willnauer who ranks the second on the contribution ranking.

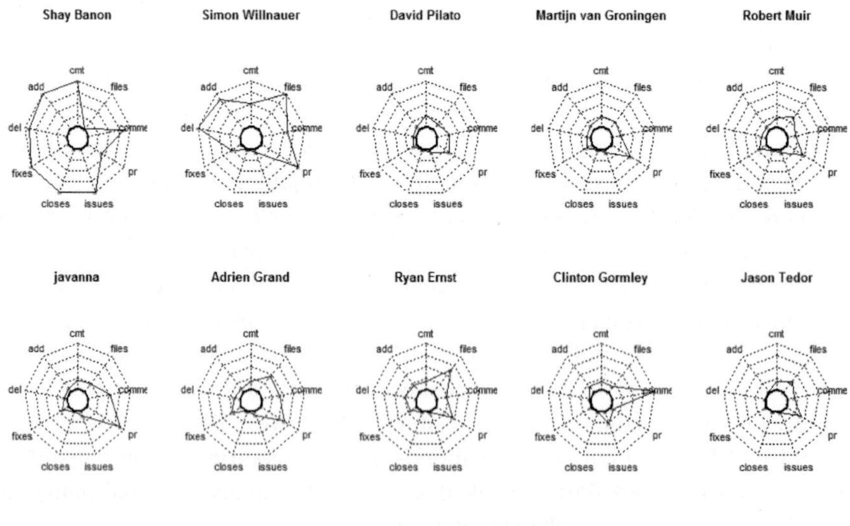

Fig. 2. Top 10 contributors's ability radar chart

5.3. *Results of contribution evolution characteristics*

We firstly get the statistics of the dataset in each metric dimension, and put all the developers' ability metric projected on the radar chart. As you can see figure 3, By using ability radar chart and combining dataset metric in table 2, we find that contribution of the majority of people is very low, which is lower than the average of all contribution and the degree of deviation of the contribution of a very small number of people compared with the average of that is very high. These people are core contributors to the project. When the contribution of a project is enough, it is very difficult to measure the contribution of the majority of people respectively.

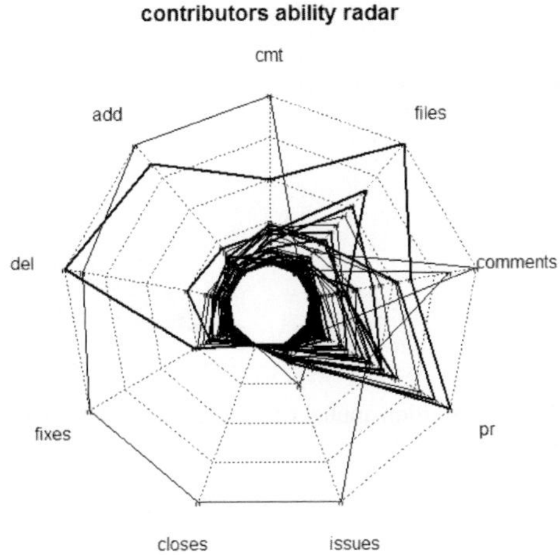

Fig. 3. Ability radar of all contributors

We draw the evolution process of the whole project on each metric through annual ring chart and parallel coordinate linear graph based on the tag time. We can see figure 4.

We visualized the annual ring chart of the evolution of all individual contributions in the project. Because it involves 664 contributors, we chose evolution chart of two developers having high contribution. The charts are as follows figure 5 and figure 6.

We can clearly find a contributor's active period and inertia period from evolution graph. When most metrics gradient of contributors of interval version is zero, developers enter the inertia period, and in this time, other people must dominate the development of the project. For example, Shay Banon entered inertia period after 2014 years, at the same time, the gradient of each measurement metric of Simon Willnauer was very large. And he became the core of project instead of Shay Banon. And at that time, the evolution trend of Simon Willnauer is similar to that of the whole project. The project is still dominated by a small number of elite in the entire development process. That is to say that the rhythm of the evolution of the entire software is driven by the activities of several core developers who contribute to the project continuously.

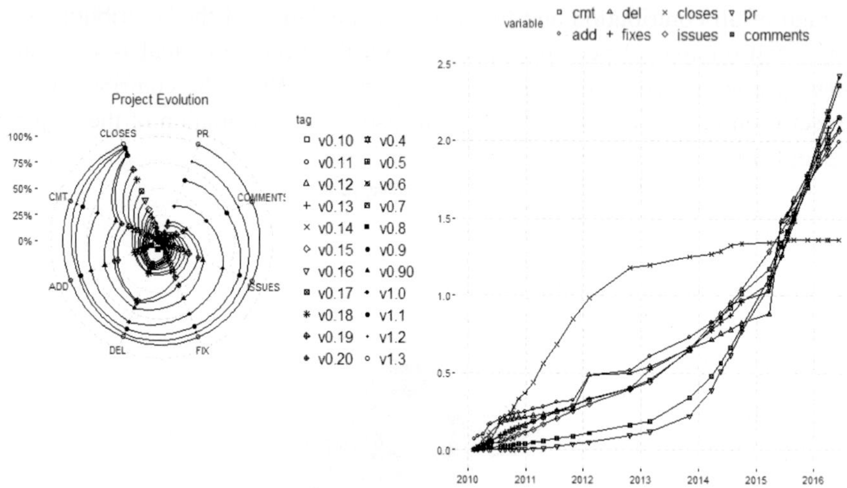

Fig. 4. Project evolution annual ring and parallel coordinate linear graph

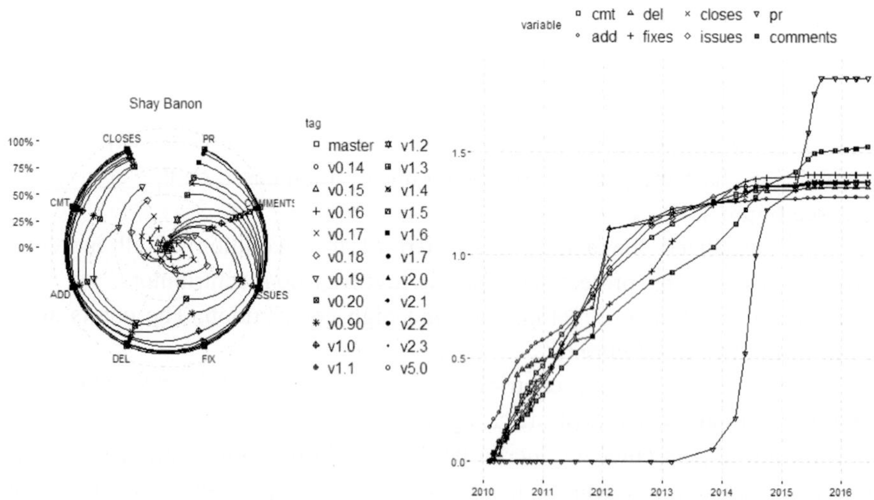

Fig. 5. The contribution evolution of Shay Banon

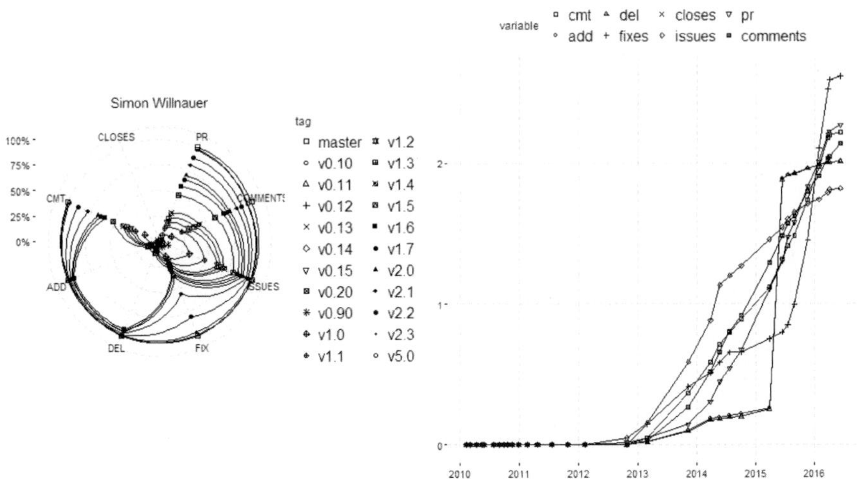

Fig. 6. The contribution evolution of Simon Willnauer

When the project elite leaves from the team, if there are no other people taking over, the project will be in a state of stagnation. In addition to this, we also discovered that the participation of most peripheral developers is random, which may be based on some events. Very few people can develop into long-term contributors. The characteristic of the long-term contributors is that there seldom appear the inertia period from entering the project at the beginning. We can focus on the developers who have contributed to two or more than two versions of the project, in order to guide project owner reasonable configuration of developers.

5.4. ***Results of relation between code and after-code contribution***

In this section, we focus on the relationship between code and after-code. The indexes of after-code are extracted from the interactive activities in GitHub, including establishing issue and comment, contributing to code, which we use the number of commits to represent. In transverse direction, it is the value of contribution ranking from high to low. There are several points representing some contributors. And the three points in the vertical direction is value corresponding to the code and after-code activities. Visualization is as shown in figure 7.

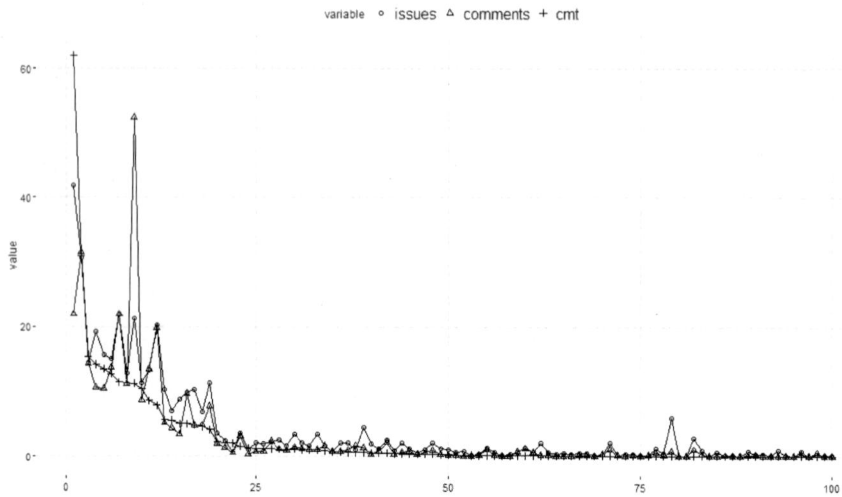

Fig. 7. Relation between commits and after-code activities

We can see that developers who commit highly are significantly more active in after-code activities, which indicates that developers will participate in the activities and communicate with others in the period of activities actively. Table 3 is the result of multiple regression to establish the model for validation.

Table 3. The multiple regression between commits and after-code activities

	Estimate	Std.Error	PR(>|t|)	Sign	Sum sq
(Intercept)	0.00047	0.01545	0.975		
Issues	0.62995	0.02287	<2e-16	***	512.04
Comments	0.34915	0.02301	<2e-16	***	35.40

The value of adjusted R-squared is 0.8431. This indicated that two features (issues and comments) can be used to the commit of contributors. From figure 5 about contribution evolution of Shay Banon we can see, when commit is stagnation, its comments and issues also appear the same stagnation obviously. This indicated that code activity is accompanied by after-code activity.

6. Conclusions

In this paper, we explored contribution characteristics of developers and took elasticsearch project as an example. We studied the relationships between contribution influencing factors by combining correlation analysis and regression technique of single variable and measured developer contribution through the number of bug fixed, the degree of pull request used, the number of file modified. But the effect of social contribution is not obvious. We found out that the contribution of vast number contributors in the project is very small and is very difficult to measure by studying on the evolution characteristics of contribution from annual ring chart and radar chart. We also discover that the rhythm of the entire software evolution is driven by the activities of several core developers who contribute to the project continuously. Finally, the development characteristics that code activity will be accompanied by other communication activities through multiple regression analysis. It is helpful to us to identify the effect of developers on the project and to guide the project owner reasonable configuration of developers through mining contribution characteristics of developers and to identify the development personnel through measuring contribution and ability of developers. That all can improve the productivity of software projects.

In the future, we need to introduce more examples to verify and more detailed metrics to summarize the different types of development model by deeply mining contribution evolution of developers. We hope that our work can support for future research in the area of software evolution and assessing developer contribution.

Acknowledgments

The research is supported by the National Natural Science Foundation of China (Grant No. 61432020, 61472430, 61502512) and National Grand R&D Plan (Grant No. 2016YFB1000805). We would also thank the reviewers for providing us constructive comments and suggestions.

References

1. G. Gousios, E. Kalliamvakou, & D. Spinellis. Measuring developer contribution from software repository data, In Proceedings of the 2008 international working conference on Mining software repositories (pp. 129-132). ACM(2008)
2. G. Yin, T. Wang, H. Wang, Q. Fan, Y. Zhang, Y. Yu, & C. Yang. OSSEAN: Mining Crowd Wisdom in Open Source Communities. In Service-Oriented System Engineering (SOSE), 2015 IEEE Symposium on (pp. 367-371). IEEE(2015)
3. Y. Yu, H. Wang, G. Yin, & T Wang. Reviewer recommendation for pull-requests in GitHub: What can we learn from code review and bug assignment. Information and Software Technology, 74, 204-218(2016).

4. J. Lima, C. Treude, F. Figueira Filho, & U Kulesza,. Assessing developer contribution with repository mining-based metrics. In Software Maintenance and Evolution (ICSME), IEEE International Conference on (pp. 536-540). IEEE (2015).
5. M. Zhou, & A Mockus. What make long term contributors: Willingness and opportunity in OSS community. In Proceedings of the 34th International Conference on Software Engineering (pp. 518-528). IEEE Press(2012).
6. M. Fischer, & H. Gall . Visualizing feature evolution of large scale software based on problem and modification report data. Journal of Software Maintenance and Evolution: Research and Practice, 16(6), 385-403(2004).
7. W. J. Wang, B. Li, & P. He. An analysis of the evolution of developers' role in open-source software community. Complex Systems & Complexity Science, 12(1), 1-7(2015).
8. X. Ben, S. Beijun & Y. Weicheng. Mining developer contribution in open source software using visualization techniques. In Intelligent System Design and Engineering Applications (ISDEA), 2013 Third International Conference on (pp. 934-937). IEEE(2013).
9. A. Sureka, A. Goyal, & A Rastogi. Using social network analysis for mining collaboration data in a defect tracking system for risk and vulnerability analysis. In Proceedings of the 4th India software engineering conference (pp. 195-204). ACM (2011) .
10. M. Gharehyazie, D. Posnett, B. Vasilescu & V. Filkov, developer initiation and social interactions in OSS: A case study of the Apache Software Foundation. Empirical Software Engineering, 20(5), 1318-1353(2015).

Large Mean Margin Distribution Machine and Its Application on Pedestrian Detection

Fan-Yong Cheng[1,2,a], Jing Zhang[1], Hai-Bo Luo[2] and Zuo-Yong Li[2]

[1]*College of electrical and information engineering, Hunan University*
Changsha 410082, China

[2]*Fujian Provincial Key Laboratory of Information Processing and Intelligent Control,*
Department of Computer Science, Minjiang University
Fuzhou 350121, China
E-mail: [a]b12090031@hnu.edu.cn

This paper develops a new pedestrian detector based on margin theory. Support Vector Machine (SVM) with maximized minimum margin is widely applied in pedestrian detection. Recently, margin theory revealed that compared with the minimum margin, margin distribution is more critical to the generalization performance. In view of the imbalanced training data of pedestrian detection and important implication of the sample mean, this paper proposes Large Mean margin Distribution Machine (LMDM) which introduces the mean margin of two classes of sample means to remove the impact of imbalanced training data on the margin mean. LMDM maximizes the mean margin and minimizes the margin variance to regularize the model. Theoretical and experimental results show that LMDM can improve the pedestrian detection rate and have strong generalization performance.

Keywords: LDM; Pedestrian Detection; Sample Mean; Margin distribution.

1. Introduction

Pedestrian detection has a long history and various novel approaches. Dalal et al. [1][2] proposed HOG descriptor for pedestrian detection based on SVM [3][4] and obtained great performance. SVM which has strong generalization performance is very popular in pedestrian detection. SVM maximizes the minimum margin, and handles nonlinearity via the kernel trick. The large minimum margin can help improving generalization performance through decreasing the VC dimension [5][6]. Recent theoretical results revealed that the margin distribution is critical to the generalization performance [7]. Inspired by this, Zhang and Zhou designed LDM which is superior to SVM and many state-of-the-art methods [8][9]. LDM tries to optimize the margin distribution by means of maximizing the margin mean and minimizing the margin variance simultaneously.

Nevertheless, LDM may easily miss pedestrian without considering the influence of imbalanced margin size in the margin mean and it is not consistent with the demand of pedestrian detection. Therefore, we design LMDM via introducing the mean margin of two classes to remove the imbalanced margin size and improve the robustness.

2. Implement of Large Margin

Given a set of instance-label pairs (x_i, y_i) ($i = 1,...,m$, m is the size of training set), $x_i \in R^d$ (d is the dimension of each instance or feature), $y_i \in \{-1, +1\}$, and the final goal is to learn a linear function $f(x) = \omega^T \phi(x)$ to predict unknown instance. $\varphi(x)$ is a feature transform of x induced by a kernel k, for example, $k(x_i, x_j) = \phi(x_i)^T \phi(x_j)$. In the light of [5][10], the margin of instance (x_i, y_i) is expressed as

$$\gamma_i = y_i \omega^T \phi(x_i). \tag{1}$$

Generally, SVM (Soft-margin SVM) is expressed as

$$\begin{aligned} &\min_{\omega,\xi} \frac{1}{2}\omega^T \omega + \sum_{i=1}^{m} \xi_i \\ &s.t.\, y_i \omega^T \phi(x_i) \geq 1 - \xi_i \\ &\quad \xi_i \geq 0, i = 1,...,m \end{aligned}$$

where $\xi = [\xi_1, ...\xi_m]$ are the misclassification penalties of instances, and C is a trade-off parameter [11]. It can be found that SVM considers only a minimum margin and has not considered the whole margin distribution.

LDM proposed by Zhang and Zhou tries to get a strong generalization performance by optimizing the margin distribution [8][9]. The margin distribution is characterized by the first and second-order moments. The margin mean is expressed as

$$\bar{\gamma} = \frac{1}{m}\sum_{i=1}^{m} \gamma_i = \frac{1}{m}\sum_{i=1}^{m} y_i \omega^T \phi(x_i) = \frac{1}{m}(Xy)^T \omega$$

where $X = [\phi(x_1),...,\phi(x_m)]$ represents a matrix ($\phi(x_i)$ is the i-th column of the matrix), and $y = [y_1,...,y_m]^T$ is denoted as a vector. The margin variance is formulated as

$$\begin{aligned}\hat{\gamma} &= \frac{1}{m^2}\sum_{i=1}^{m}\sum_{j=1}^{m}(\gamma_i - \gamma_j)^2 = \frac{1}{m^2}\sum_{i=1}^{m}\sum_{j=1}^{m}(y_i\omega^T\phi(x_i) - y_j\omega^T\phi(x_j))^2 \\ &= \frac{2}{m^2}(m\omega^T XX^T\omega - \omega^T Xyy^T X^T\omega).\end{aligned} \quad (2)$$

LDM maximizes the margin mean and minimizes the margin variance simultaneously. The optimal object function of LDM is formulized as

$$\begin{aligned}&\min_{\omega,\xi} \frac{1}{2}\omega^T\omega + \lambda_1\hat{\gamma} - \lambda_2\bar{\gamma} + C\sum_{i=1}^{m}\xi_i \\ &s.t.\, y_i\omega^T\phi(x_i) \geq 1 - \xi_i \\ &\quad \xi_i \geq 0, i = 1,...,m.\end{aligned}$$

Note that the margin mean is the average of two classes of imbalanced margins on imbalanced data. This easily leads to the misclassification of the minority class instance. Therefore, we propose a new method to remove this influence of imbalanced margin size.

3. Large Mean Margin Distribution Machine

3.1. *Why is sample mean introduced?*

Fig. 1(a) plots the mean of pedestrian HOG descriptors and the mean of non-pedestrian HOG descriptors is shown in Fig. 1(b). Intuitively, Fig. 1(a) is like the skeleton of a person, and Fig. 1(b) is a uniform image. If we want to obtain a pedestrian detector with strong generalization performance, the margin between these two means should be as large as possible. Inspired by this finding, we maximize the mean margin of two means to improve the generalization performance and robustness of pedestrian detection.

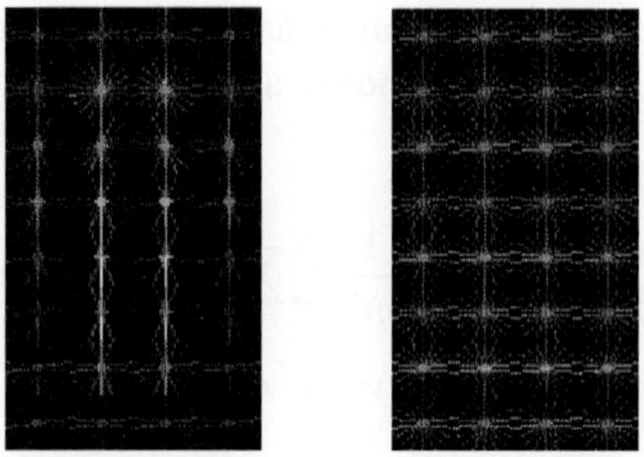

(a) (b)

Fig. 1. HOG descriptors Mean: (a) Pedestrian; (b)non-pedestrian.

3.2. *Formulation*

In this paper, the minority class is defined as the positive class. We define two sets $I_+ \equiv \{i \mid y_i = 1\}$ and $I_- \equiv \{i \mid y_i = -1\}$ as label sets, m_+ as the number of elements in I_+ and m_- as the number of elements in I_+ ($m_+ < m_-$). The positive mean instance is

$$\overline{M_+} = \frac{1}{m}\sum_{i \in m_+} \phi(x_i)$$

and the negative mean instance is

$$\overline{M_-} = \frac{1}{m}\sum_{i \in m_-} \phi(x_i)$$

According to the definition in (1), the positive mean margin is $\overline{\gamma_+} = y_i \omega^T \overline{M_+} (i \in I_+)$ and the negative mean instance is $\overline{\gamma_-} = y_i \omega^T \overline{M_-} (i \in I_-)$. The mean margin is defined as

$$\overline{\overline{\gamma}} = \frac{1}{2}(\overline{\gamma_+} + \overline{\gamma_-}) = \frac{1}{m}\sum_{i=1}^{m} \theta_i y_i \omega^T \phi(x_i) = \frac{1}{m}(XDy)^T \omega \tag{3}$$

where D is a diagonal matrix with diagonal elements $\theta_1, \ldots, \theta_m$, and

$$\theta_i = \begin{cases} m / 2m_+ & i \in I_+ \\ m / 2m_- & i \in I_- \end{cases} \tag{4}$$

The margin variance is adopted to keep the balance between positive and negative mean margin. LMDM with maximized mean margin and minimized margin variance is expressed as

$$\begin{aligned}&\min_{\omega,\xi}\frac{1}{2}\omega^T\omega+\lambda_1\hat{\gamma}-\lambda_2\overline{\overline{\gamma}}+\sum_{i=1}^{m}\xi_i\\&s.t.\,y_i\omega^T\phi(x_i)\geq 1-\xi_i,\\&\quad\xi_i\geq 0,i=1,\ldots,m\end{aligned}\tag{5}$$

where λ_1 , λ_2 and C are trade-off parameters of LMDM. LMDM degenerates into LDM when $m_+ = m_-$, that is $\theta_i = 1$ for all examples. By substituting (2), (3) (4) into (5), LMDM can be solved as LDM [9][12][13]

4. Experiments and Conclusions

We adopt the HOG descriptors of the positive and negative training images, which are drawn from INRIA person data set [1], to train the detector. The trade-off parameters are selected via 5-cross validation. After we have trained the detector, we set scanning step size at x axis to 24, y axis to 48, scanning scale to 4 and scale interval to 1.3. The detector scans all positions and scales of the image. The final location results after non-maximum suppress are shown in Fig.2. As shown in Fig.2, we can find that LMDM detector detects more pedestrians on the image and has low false detection compared with other methods.

(a) (b) (c)

Fig. 2. Location results: (a) SVM; (b)LDM; (c)LMDM.

In the future it will be interesting to study the relationship between sample variance and margin variance, and combine LMDM with cost-sensitive learning method to improve the performance of pedestrian detection.

Acknowledgments

This work is financed by Fund of China National Natural Science Foundation (Approval No. 61573299), the project from Fuzhou science and technology plan(2015-G-52), Program for New Century Excellent Talents in Fujian Province University (NCETFJ), Technology Project of Provincial University of Fujian Province (JK2014040), Fuzhou Science and Technology Planning Project (2016-S-116).

References

1. N. Dalal and T. Bill, Histograms of oriented gradients for human detection. CVPR, pp:886-893 (2005).
2. N. Dalal, Finding People in Images and Videos, Institut National Polytechnique de Grenoble-INPG (2006).
3. C. Cortes and V. Vapnik, Support-vector networks. Machine Learning, 20(3):273-297 (1995).
4. V. Vapnik (eds.), The Nature of Statistical Learning Theory, (Springer-Verlag, 1995).
5. A. J. Smola and P. J. Bartlett, Advances in Large Margin Classifiers. MIT Press, Cambridge, pp 233-251 (2000).
6. R. E. Schapire and Freund, Boosting the margin : A new explanation for the effectiveness of voting methods. Annals of Statistics, 26(5):1651-1686 (1998).
7. W. Gao and Z. H. Zhou, On the doubt about margin explanation of boosting, Artificial Intelligence 203(5):1-18 (2013).
8. Z. H. Zhou, Large Margin Distribution Learning. In Proceedings of the 6th IAPR TC3 International Workshop, ANNPR 2014, pp:1-11 (2014).
9. T. Zhang and Z. H. Zhou, Large margin distribution machine. In Proceedings of the 20th ACM SIGKDD Conference on Knowledge Discovery and Data Mining (KDD). New York, NY, pp:313-322 (2014).
10. S. Theodoridis and K. Koutroumbas (eds.), Pattern Recognition, 4th Ed, (Academic Press, 2008).
11. N. Cristianini and J. Shawe-Taylor (eds.), An introduction to support Vector Machines: and other kernel-based learning methods, (Cambridge University Press, 1999).
12. G. X. Yuan, C. H. Ho, C. J. Lin, Recent Advances of Large-Scale Linear Classification. In Proceedings of the IEEE, 100(9):2584-2603 (2012).
13. C. J. Hsieh, K. W. Chang, C. J. Lin, A Dual Coordinate Descent Method for Large-scale Linear SVM. Icml 9(3):1369-1398 (2008).

The Security Analysis of Strategy on Testing of Public Cloud Applications

Ya-Nan Song[a] and Ping Liu

Army Officer Academy P.L.A,
Hefei, 230031, China
E-mail: [a]Isaiah_nan@126.com

The development of cloud services makes cloud software testing possible, and whether cloud testing in security has become a new focus. This paper combines the characteristics of cloud services and software testing, expounds the problems highlighted during cloud testing and analyses the risk based on the test. According to the security of the network, list the supplier and customer security lists, test encryption, authentication and authorization, formulate the corresponding specification and other aspects, proposes the strategy of the risk aversion in cloud testing and solve the security issues in the procedure of cloud testing to some extent.

Keywords: Cloud Testing; Software Testing; Security Issues; Risk Strategy.

1. Introduction

As cloud computing from the concept to practice on a large scale, just a few of years rapid development has brought many industries to disruptive innovation. For the software industry, the emergence of cloud services not only changed the purchase of software and services, but also greatly shorten the software development life cycle, which means that the test method is also needs to change.

The numerous features of cloud computing along with the different types of deployment models. i.e. public, private, hybrid and community clouds. Using cloud platform in a public cloud environment for software testing can greatly reduce the time. As we already knows, there are three service models in the cloud computing: IaaS (Infrastructure as a Service), PaaS (Platform as a Service), and SaaS(Software as a Service). Therefore, some scholars proposed the fourth kind of service mode outside the context of other three——TaaS

(Testing as a Service) [1]. The cloud testing is discussed in this paper a new method for the load test and general test. This test can effectively leverage cloud computing resources to improve testing capabilities and reduce the cost of test, in order to improve the service and development efficiency of software industry.

Although cloud computing has brought a lot of convenience, we can not ignore the large number of potential security risks caused by the upload data information. Such as unauthorized data access, SQL injection attacks, DNS hijacking, malicious data loss and leak etc. Especially in the process of software testing based on cloud services, not only by measuring software itself maybe have loopholes, but also need consider the safety and potential risks that exist in the testing process, these must be eliminated before the software is put into use. Currently there was no suitable system solutions for testing security based on public cloud [2]. Therefore, its safety and how to avoid the potential risk get more and more attention.

2. Cloud Testing Issues

As a result of the limitation of enterprise infrastructure and computing storage capacity, in a limited budget conditions, the traditional testing model is often not sufficient to test the performance of software including security. This limitation is more obvious in SMEs , cloud testing, on the other hand, is able to better address these problems. Cloud testing services provided by the continuation of the use of the principle of pay-as-cloud services in the past, which gives relatively scarce resources of SMEs to provide a better platform for enhancing their competitiveness to provide more opportunities. Cloud testing process issues that need attention are as follows [3-5]:

(1)Multi-Tenant test

Multi-tenancy refers to software testing is a testing framework to support one instance service multiple users, given different test users the ability to custom the part of system according to their needs. due to the shared development and maintenance costs for SMEs, multi-tenancy provided by cloud testing is a kind of economical solution. During multi-tenant test, the virtual machine is running in "sandbox" environment, so it can be isolation between virtual machines, but the existence of system vulnerability may make a malicious user to escape the "sandbox" environment, complete control of the physical host, which can be completely control other virtual machines, resulting in security risks. Thus, to the multi-tenant testing technology, the implementation is how to improve the test environment among tenants isolation, and isolation of the data, in order to maintain different test users will neither interfere with each other, while retaining the ability of security data.

(2)Test Security

Security testing is one of the main challenges of cloud testing, to identify security risks largely depends on the process level of understanding between the cloud providers and the users. Now about the safety of the public cloud security and service quality assurance is not comprehensive. As a result, users should be aware of the risks posed by public cloud, and shall be established mutual trust mechanism between the cloud service providers, such as signed an SLA agreement in advance.

(3)Data Integrity

In addition to the security testing, the integrity of the data and privacy are clouds test service providers and users need to be considered one of the important issues. Deployed to test applications in the cloud does not always guarantee the integrity and confidentiality of their test data, and there are loopholes in this regard is likely to pose a security risk to the test user.

(4)License Management

To obtain licenses and user access management is an essential step to the user when using test tools. Different types of license models need to be verified during the test. License management is therefore an important parameters in the series of process of cloud testing including regression testing, the maintainability testing, release management and supervision.

3. Security Risks in Cloud Testing

3.1. *Security issues in software testing*

Software exists in the process of testing the following security risks: information by a third party monitoring, tampering or theft, resulting in loss of information leaks, what's more is the virus spread in the software system resulting in huge losses. It would appear that the software security testing is facing very serious challenges, how to ensure that the software testing process information security has become an important issue in software testing needed to solve.

3.2. *Cloud testing and its risk*

According to the basic characteristics of the network cloud testing, it can immediately recognize some of the risks that exist, as shown in Table 1.

Table 1. Risk category and content of cloud testing

Risk categories	Specific content
Authentication model not complete	● Others (possibly a competitor) can gain access ● Unauthorized users can gain access ● Authorized users unable to gain access ● A customer can obtain other customer's data
Authorization model is not perfect	● Users can define the roles and functions too little ● Only a few functions are given a different permissions ● Supplier lack of strict limits on its administrator access customer data
Too many people can access all data (vendor side)	● Access to all data
Data encryption measure is not perfect	● Client-side encryption is not enough ● Not enough encrypted during transmission ● Supplier side encryption is not enough
Loss of data	● Storage device error ● Encryption Error ● Key lost ● Data loss in Capacity expansion process ● Process error ● Software error
Accident supplier side resulting in data inaccessible	● Data inaccessible
Unsafe user behavior lead to unauthorized users to gain access	● Unauthorized users can gain access
Unable to track authorized / unauthorized access operation	● Unable to track access operation
Does not update to in time lead to security risks	● Supplier side ● Client-side interaction system ● User equipment side
Cannot determine whether the user's own equipment safe	● Cannot determine whether the equipment safe
Due to an unexpected cause data to be removed / cannot be deleted	● The data is removed / cannot be deleted
Other causes of (virtual) environment is destroyed	● Environmental destruction
As the investigation or subpoena leading to the third-party obtain access to the data	● Company data ● Log data
Service lack of robustness in the face of the hacker attacks	● Lack of robustness

In order to determine what measures need to be taken to avoid risks, we need to put all the risk map for the test, namely, software security testing. It mainly including the verification application level of security and identification potential security flaws. The main purpose is to find hidden trouble in security programming software itself, and check the application's ability to prevent illegal invasion, according to the different security test index, the test strategy is also different. However, the test does not conclusively proven security applications are secure, but are used to verify the effectiveness of establishment strategies, these strategies are based on the assumptions made in the analysis phase and the threat selected.

Combined with the ISO standards in the field of security, for security risks associated with the above-mentioned about cloud testing, consider the following seven aspects of risk aversion [6].

4. Risk-Averse Strategy

4.1. *Network security*

Cloud testing is the most basic requirement to provide a secure and reliable network environment as much as possible. However, no one can guarantee that the Internet transmission byte stream will be not eavesdropping or interception, so the need for the test environment is encrypted. On the protocol level, it can be encrypted through TLS (Transport Layer Security Protocol Transport Layer Security) or SSL (Secure Sockets Layer Secure Sockets Layer). On the network level, we can use WPA2 encryption or directly using a point-to-point virtual private network (VPN) which has highly security level for security protection.

4.2. *Lists suppliers security list*

There are only two roles in traditional software project——vendors and customers. but in cloud testing, increased the role of suppliers, it not only provides a cloud platform environment, but also can access to the service, so we need to check how the supplier to organize authorization and certification process.

(1) Certification: Authorized users need to access certification through the form of services. Certification process should use encryption methods and mixed use of multiple authentication technologies to enhance the security of authentication.

(2) Authorization: The authorization process is used to verify which roles or individuals can do what kinds of operations, and what kinds of information can be able to have access to.

(3) Log files and audit trail records: Running automated test scripts for daily test. Through the log files with the audit trail records, we can get all the modified data and try to access the data operation record.

4.3. *Lists client security list*

User use the client-side access to the cloud environment software and data, user behavior and unsafe environment is the major problem. Therefore we need to consider the safety of the client side resources:

(1) Whether there is authentication and authorization in the customer network.

(2) Whether mobile devices which the customer used have authentication and authorization.

(3) Whether to use the firewalls and routers or other technical solutions.

(4) Whether to update the middleware and operating systems security patches in time.

4.4. *Testing encryption*

Test encryption include the following aspects:

(1) Check whether the data stream is encrypted.

(2) Check whether the password is stored in encrypted form.

(3) Check if the network equipment set up encryption.

4.5. *Testing certification and authorization*

Using mixed authentication mechanism can provide better protection for the entire service and function testing techniques can easily testing and certification process. For example, the syntax test (legal/illegal registration data), the process cycle test (release certification process), and a data cycle test (certified life cycle).

The functional testing technology could test authorization according to that whether a specific operation could happen to the authorized specific role depends on the authorization chart. Test procedure granted accounts can also use the process cycle testing and data cycle testing techniques.

4.6. *Formulate the corresponding specification*

Develop appropriate regulations and industry standards can enhance the manageability of the test. So it can effectively avoid some potential risk on the system. The content can be specified includes: interface specification, customer resource specification, platform standards, infrastructure standards, documentation standards, incident management processes, protocols, and version control.

4.7. *Others*

Other security measures to avoid the risk are:

(1) Test the safety and stability in the face of the Internet attack.

(2) The test log files and audit trail records.

(3) The timely application of security patches for testing.

(4) Perform audits.

5. Conclusion

This paper analyzes the risk factors that may occur in the cloud testing, and combined with the characteristics of cloud services as well as safety testing of traditional software test method, creatively put forward the strategy to avoid the security risks based on cloud testing environment. On the whole, the author believe that cloud service providers and users should ensure the correct implementation of data security and privacy, running and strive to meet expectations. At the same time, the relevant regulatory agencies should develop more significantly role and ensure that all cloud service providers can satisfy the user's requirements for security and privacy standards, and make the risk in the cloud testing resolved to be able to rely on the safety test.

References

1. Weiss A. Computing in the Clouds[J]. ACM Networker, 2007, 11(4).
2. Subashini S, Kavitha V. A Survey on Security Issues in Service Delivery Models of Cloud Computing[J]. Journal of Network and Computer Applications, 2011, 34(1).
3. Naryanan C. Cloud Testing - Ensuring QOS[EB /OL].[2012-02-10].http://www.iqnite-conferences.com/de/Programm/abstracts/narayanan_ab. pdf.
4. Cochran M, Witman P. Governance and Service Level Agreement Issues in a Cloud Computing Environment [J]. Journal of Information Technology Management, 2011, 22(2).

5. CSA, Cloud Security Alliance. Top Threats to Cloud Computing[EB/OL]. [2012-02-20]. http://www.cloudsecurityalliance.org/topthreats/csathreats.v1. 0. pdf.
6. Wang C, Wang Q, Ren K, et al. Ensuring Data Storage Security in Cloud Computing[C]. In: Proceedings of the 17th International Workshop on Quality of Service, 2009.

Mobile Application of Secure Voice Over Internet

Gui-Fen Zhao[a], Ying Li, Li-Ping Du and Guan-Ning Xu

Beijing Municipal Institute of Science & Technology Information, Beijing, China

E-mail: [a]gfzh@hotmail.com

Communication of voice over internet without encryption is no longer safe, a mobile application solution of secure voice over internet is proposed. The method is on the basis of combined secret key and hardware encryption which guarantees the security of voice communication for mobile phone users. The secure voice over internet protocol is accomplished with the support of smart card. Each secure voice communication over internet owns a different session key and encryption key. The session key is generated randomly, and the encryption key is generated on the basis of key seeds according to random numbers and time-stamp. It is hard to forecast and track the key generation, therefore illegal users cannot encrypt and decrypt the voice data for monitoring the voice communication.

Keywords: Secure Voice Over Internet; Combined Secret Key; SIP; Mobile Voice Over Internet; Smart Card.

1. Introduction

VoIP (Voice over Internet Protocol) firstly performs audio signal digital coding, compression, and then converts to IP packets transmitted over the IP network. VoIP gradually form common application layer control protocols, such as Session Initiation Protocol (SIP) [1].

SIP is a communication protocol for signaling and controlling multimedia communication sessions[2]. SIP works in conjunction with several application layer protocols which identify and carry the session media [3-4]. Media identification and negotiation is achieved with the Session Description Protocol (SDP). SIP typically employs the Real-time Transport Protocol (RTP) or Secure Real-time Transport Protocol (SRTP) for transmission of media streams (voice, video). SIP is independent from the underlying transport protocol. It runs on the

Transmission Control Protocol (TCP), the User Datagram Protocol (UDP) or the Stream Control Transmission Protocol (SCTP). SIP can be used for two-party or multiparty sessions. The protocols are shown in Figure 1.

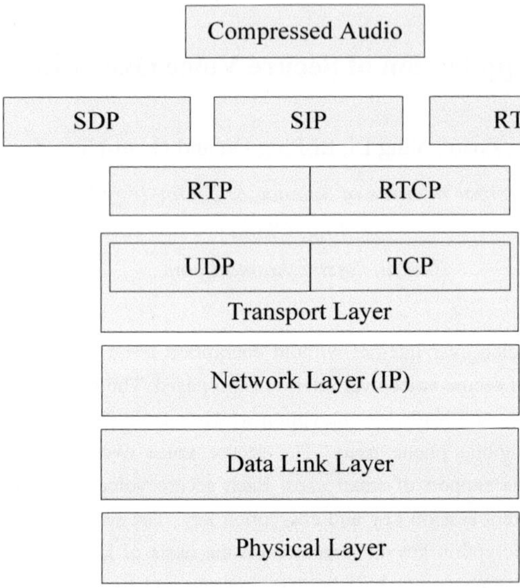

Fig. 1. Protocols of Voice over Internet Protocol (SIP).

How to ensure the security of SIP application has become a hot research topic in recent years. The existing SIP security solutions include http digest authentication, the authentication mechanism based on PKI system, identity authentication and key agreement mechanism based on bilinear on technology, authentication and key agreement mechanism based on password[5-8], encrypted with Transport Layer Security (TLS), etc.

2. Secure Mobile VoIP Scheme

Because the communication over Internet without encryption is no longer safe, the work with the nature of professional confidentiality communicated over Internet should be encrypted.

Set up voice encryption and transmission protocol based on combined secret key and symmetric encryption algorithm. Smart cards and encryption cards are adopted to make up secure voice over internet communication system applied for mobile phone users. The voice data are encrypted while communicating, therefore the security of mobile voice over internet application is enhanced.

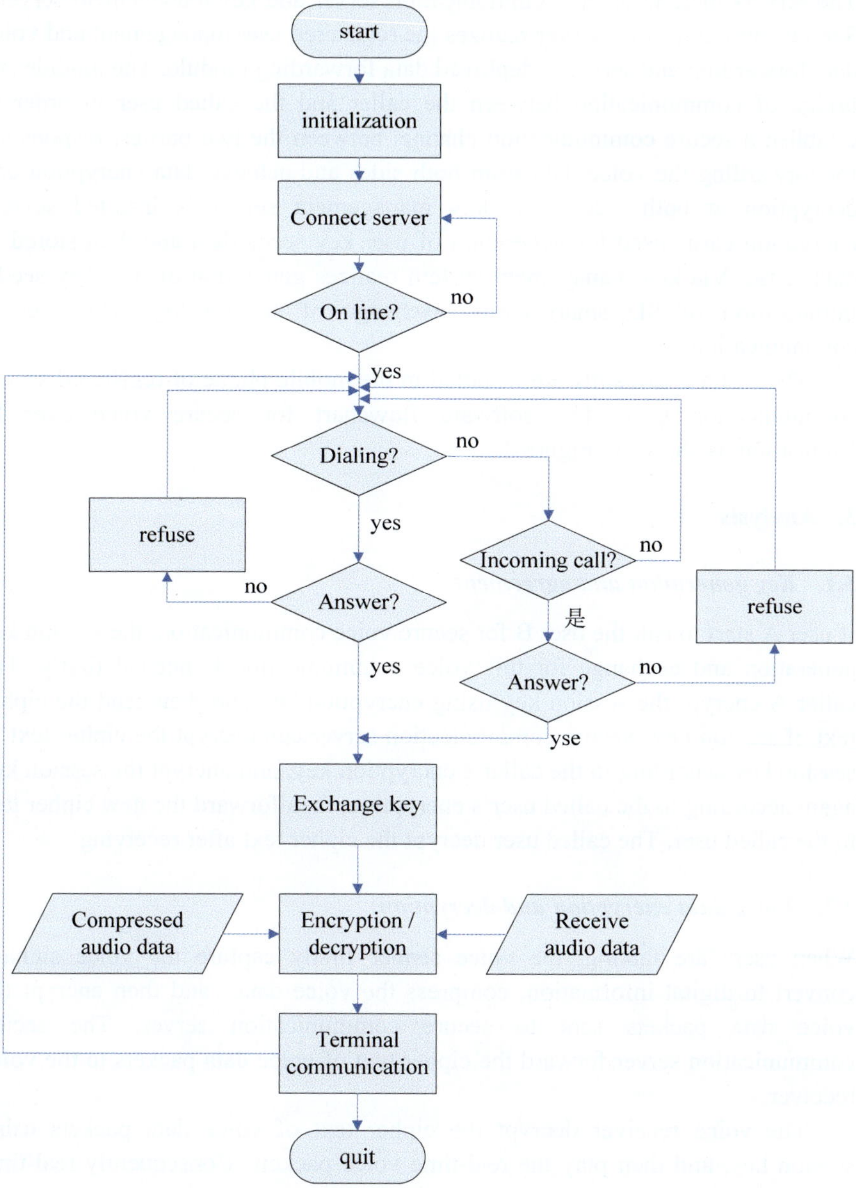

Fig. 2. Software Flowchart for secure voice over IP application.

The secure voice over internet system consists of client and servers. The client refers to mobile phones inserted a smart card with Micro SD interface. The servers include secure communication server and key management servers. Secure communication server realizes the registered user management and voice data forwarding and server is deployed data forwarding module. The module is a bridge of communication between the caller and the called user in order to establish a secure communication channel between the two parties, responsible for forwarding the voice data from both sides and achieve data encryption and decryption at both sides. The key management server is inserted several encryption cards used for generation of user key seeds data and then stored in data base. Via key management system realizes generation of user key seeds, initialization of SD smart cards, exchange of session key while secure communication.

There is a client software installed in the mobile phone of registered secure communication user. The software flowchart for secure voice over IP application is shown in Figure 2.

3. Analysis

3.1. *Key generation and agreement*

If user A start to call the user B for secure voice communication, the session key generation and exchange for this voice communication is needed firstly. The caller A encrypt the session key using encryption key and then send the cipher text of session key. Secure communication server can decrypt the cipher text of session key according to the caller's encryption key, and encrypt the session key again according to the called user's encryption, then forward the new cipher text to the called user. The called user decrypt the cipher text after receiving.

3.2. *Voice data encryption and decryption*

When users are talking, the voice sender firstly capture the voice signals, convert to digital information, compress the voice data, and then encrypt the voice data packets sent to secure communication server. The secure communication server forward the cipher text of voice data packets to the voice receiver.

The voice receiver decrypt the cipher text of voice data packets using session key, and then play the real-time voice packets. Consequently real-time secure voice communication is achieved over internet.

3.3. *Security analysis*

Secure voice over internet system adopts real-time, combined secret key and encryption method to generate encryption key for secure voice communication. Each secure communication owns a different encryption generated on the basis of key seeds according to random numbers and time-stamp. Use encryption key to encrypt the session key in smart card for protection of session key. And the session key is used to encrypt and decrypt the voice data for secure transmission over internet.

Because the combined secret key and session key during secure voice communication is different from other communication keys. It is hard to forecast and track the generation principles, therefore cannot encrypt and decrypt the voice data, i.e. can't tap the voice communication.

4. Conclusions

The mobile application of secure voice over internet based on combined secret key and hardware encryption achieves higher security level, which guarantee voice communication security for mobile phone users.

Secure voice communication system needs a smart card inserted into user's mobile phone to provide symmetric cipher algorithm and combined secret key generation function. Symmetric cipher algorithm and key seeds are written into the smart card. The secure voice over internet protocol is accomplished with support of smart card. Each secure voice communication over internet owns a different session key generated randomly and encryption key generated on the basis of key seeds according to random numbers and time-stamp. It is hard to forecast and track the key generation, therefore cannot encrypt and decrypt the voice data for tapping the voice communication.

Acknowledgments

This work is supported by Beijing Municipal Organization Talents Project (Youth backbone individual project: 2014400685627G274). Giving thanks to the suggestions from researchers in Beijing Key Laboratory of Network Cryptography Authentication during recent years.

References

1. LIU Wei-Ming, XIAN Ji-Qing, CHEN Wei-Ling. VoIP Security-Thorough Analysis and Solution Strategy based on SIP. JOURNAL OF COMPUTER APPLICATIONS. 2006,26(z1). 167-170. (In Chinese)

2. http://www.android-doc.com/guide/topics/connectivity/sip.html
3. CHEN Jing, LI Run-zhi, DONG Xiao-she. Security architecture of mobile P2PSIP based live streaming system. COMPUTER ENGINEERING AND DESIGN. 2009, 30(23). 5332-5336. (In Chinese)
4. https://en.wikipedia.org/wiki/Session_Initiation_Protocol
5. Mohit Kumar Gokhroo and Jaidhar C. D.Two Step Mutual Authentication Scheme for SIP. International Journal of Computer and Communication Engineering, Vol. 2, No. 6, 669-673. 2013.11.
6. Maisam Mohammadian, Naser Mozayani. A New Mechanism For Mutual Authentication In SIP. IJCSI International Journal of Computer Science Issues, Vol. 9, Issue 3, No 1, 505-508. 2012,5.
7. YANG Guang, NIE Min, YANG Wu-Jun. Quantum authentication and key agreement scheme for SIP protocol. Journal of Sichuan University (Natural Science Edition). Vol. 53 No. 1. 2016. 87-92. (In Chinese)
8. ZHANG Zhao-xin, FANG Bin-xing, ZHANG Hong-li, JIANG Chun-xiang. Safe communicated model of SIP network based on improved SIP protocol. Journal on Communications. Vol.28 No.12, 2007. 39-47.

A Model of Resource Service Virtualization in Cloud Manufacturing

H. B. Li[a], M. X. Liang and T. He

College of Computer Science and Technology, Huaqiao University,
Xiamen Enterprise Interoperability & Business Intelligence Engineering Research Center
Xiamen City, Fujian Province 361021, P. R. China
E-mail: [a]lihaibo@hqu.edu.cn

In distributed manufacturing, manufacturing-as-a-service becomes a smart approach to realize cooperation between enterprises. Resource virtualization, which is considered as one of the key technologies, presents a flexible approach for users to use manufacturing resources in collaborative manufacturing systems. By analyzing the characteristics of manufacturing resources, a model of mapping from physical resource services to virtual resource services is proposed first. In the model, three kinds of mapping patterns are introduced to realize the virtualization. Then, the details of the components supporting the mapping are introduced. Finally, a case to show that the model is a practicable approach for resource service virtualization.

Keywords: Cloud Manufacturing; Resource Virtualization; Mapping; Physical Manufacturing Resource; Virtual Manufacturing Resource.

1. Introduction

Nowadays, there is a new trend in global manufacturing industry. That is the transformation and upgrading from a production-oriented manufacturing to service-oriented manufacturing [1]. Collaboration between enterprises has become more and more popular. In this environment, Cloud Manufacturing (CMfg), as a new model of networked manufacturing and service-oriented manufacturing, come into being, that is based on intelligent network. The technologies used by the CMfg includes the Internet of Things (IoT) [2], [3] and cloud service. According to the requirement of users, manufacturing resources are organized and shared online, to provide users with various types of manufacturing services on demand in a mode of service [1], [4]. During this process, resource service virtualization is the most important enabling technologies [5]. By mapping from various of physical resources, including equipment, manpower, fund, etc. into virtual resources, manufacturing resources can be used to achieve on-demand optimally. However, the current methods of resource service virtualization is rudimentary or unpractical. If the resource service virtualization can be tackled well, the efficiency of resource allocation can be improved greatly.

In this paper, a model of resource service virtualization are proposed, in which three mapping rules are included. The mapping can be taken by artificial means or by some mining algorithms. Aggregating physical resources is not a static process, as the uses of resources keep changing all the time. This is not within the scope of the paper.

The rest of the paper is organized as follows. In section 2, the characteristics of manufacturing resource are analyzed. In section 3, a model of resource service virtualization is proposed. A case is presented in section 4. Finally, in section 5, we present a summary and discuss what we intend to do in future work.

2. Characteristics of Manufacturing Resource

Resources are encapsulated as cloud services and deployed to the cloud service platform, where manufacturing resources can be shared and accessed by heterogeneous applications [6]. In manufacturing lifecycle, there are various of manufacturing resources, unlike those computing resource, such as CPU or hard-disk. It is difficult for users to find the massive resources from the global. The types of manufacturing resources are more widely.

From the service level point of view, the physical manufacturing resource is a collection of product manufacturing process required, the virtual manufacturing resources encapsulated into web services support utilization of resources in a high level. Through establishing a physical - virtual mappings, logically aggregating and formatting physical manufacturing resource can decouple the relationship between physical resources and their consumption. This is so call resource service virtualization [5], [6]. Formally, physical manufacturing resource can be defined as follows.

Definition 2.1 Physical Manufacturing Resource (PMR) can be formally described as: PMR = (Pid, PBasicAttri, CustAttri, MngStat), where Pid is a unique identifier of the physical manufacturing resources, PBasicAttri is a set of basic attributes, including resource name, function description, provider, contact information, CustAttri is a set of properties of customized manufacturing resources, different from other physical resources, the part of the property allows enterprise users to customize their own attributes, MngStat is state information of resources, including logistics, performance indicators, service evaluation, service quality of the resource and other information.

3. Model of Resource Service Virtualization

3.1. *Virtual manufacturing resource service*

Different manufacturing enterprises have their different families of resource, and need different resource services. Physical manufacturing resources can be aggregated as a collection to serve enterprise users in the mode of cloud service. So, virtual manufacturing resource can be defined as follows.

Definition 3.1 Virtual Manufacturing Resource (VMR) is a logical description of physical manufacturing resources, and can be formally described as: VMR = (Vid, VBasicAttri, Classification, State, Mapping). Vid is a unique identifier virtual resources, VBasicAttri is basic attributes, including virtual resource name, type, description, unit, rental price, the total number and other information, Classification is their respective resource type, State is VMR usage status information, including the remaining quantity of status and QoS evaluation information, mapping is a mapping from physical to virtual manufacturing resource, determine the logic described virtual resources.

As the platform of CMfg provides enterprise users with resource service in the mode of "centralized resources, dispersed services" [1]-[4], enterprises have the requirement of customizing their own resources classification attributes. To improve the maintainability of virtual resource services, further abstracting the categories of virtual is necessary. So, a template of VR types is introduced, as shown in Fig.1. Before defining virtual resource service, users can fill in the type template and then instantiate the customized properties.

3.2. *Mapping of manufacturing resource services*

The mapping from physical manufacturing resources to virtual manufacturing resources should follow some rules. There are three basic rules listed here: one-to-one, one-to-many and many-to-one. For example, many-to-one mapping means that a set of physical manufacturing resources *PMR* can be mapped into one virtual resource service *VRS*. If users find and use *VRS*, it is equivalent of using *PMR*. The mapping is defined as follows.

Definition 3.2 Mapping from physical manufacturing resource to virtual manufacturing resource can be formally described as Mapping = (Mid, PMRSet,

PMRCompModel), where Mid is mapped identity, PMRSet is involved in mapping physical manufacturing resource set, PMRCompModel is a combination of physical manufacturing resource model, where PMRCompModel = (mMid, PMRCompLogic, PMRCompConstraint), where mMid is a unique identifies, PMRCompLogic is a logical combination of resources description, PMRCompConstraint indicates that the associated resource constraints combined.

The model of resource service virtualization is proposed, as shown in Figure 1. In CMfg system, with the changing of market demand, dynamic mapping is needed, which can produce dynamic aggregation. Resource service virtualization can improve the efficiency of resource allocation and utilization of the physical resources.

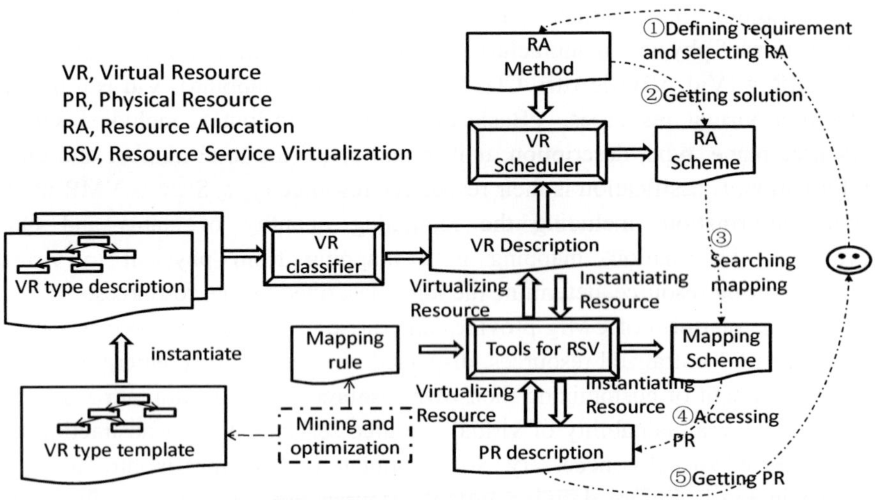

Fig. 1. The model of resource service virtualization

4. A Case Study

Nowadays, the number of medium-sized and small enterprises (SME) is vast in China. Cooperation between enterprises is fairly common. But most of the cooperation are offline, and almost no public service platform provides support. We developed a software system, called "CMfg system for SME". Any enterprise users can shared their remaining or idle manufacturing resources to the system through the virtualization technology. Other enterprise users can rent and use the resources in form of cloud services. There are many workflow models that are deployed in the system to support business processes. This is so called the manufacturing as a service. The architecture for SME can be seen in Figure 2.

RSV, Resource Service Virtualization

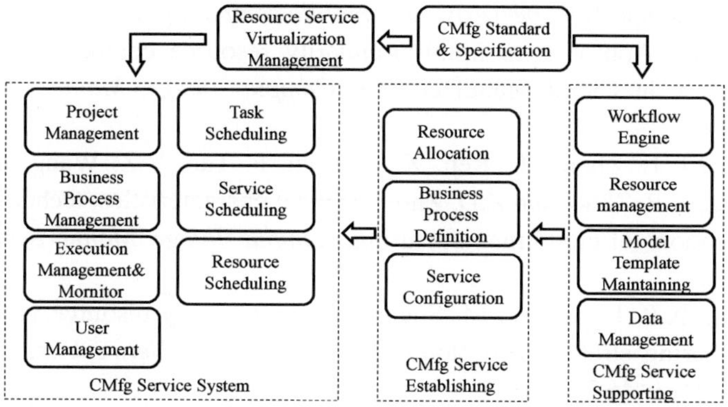

Fig. 2. Cloud manufacturing service system architecture for SME.

5. Conclusions

In this paper, a model of resource service virtualization is proposed to improve the efficiency of resource usage and allocation. The model presents three basic mapping rules to aggregate physical manufacturing resource into virtual resource services. The proposed method has been applied to CMfg system for SME, which is developed by us, and has a good experience. A recommended future work includes a method of resource aggregation mining.

Acknowledgments

This work is supported by grant 71571056 of the Natural Science Foundation of China (NSFC), and by grant 2015Z125 of the Quanzhou Science and Technology Plan Projects.

References

1. H. B. Li, K. Chen, M.X. Liang, X.Y. Luo, Composition of Resource-Service Chain for Cloud Manufacturing, *IEEE Trans. Ind. Informat.***12**, 211 (2016).

2. F. Tao, Y. Zuo, L. D. Xu, and L. Zhang, IoT-Based intelligent perception and access of manufacturing resource toward cloud manufacturing. *IEEE Trans. Ind. Informat.* **10**, 1547 (2014).
3. K. Dar, A. Taherkordi, H. Baraki, F. Eliassen, and K. Geihs, A resource oriented integration architecture for the Internet of Things: a business process perspective, *pervasive and mobile computing*,**20**, 145 (2015).
4. H. B. Li. Approach to multi-granularity resource composition based on workflow in Cloud Manufacturing. *Comput. Integr. Manuf. Syst***19**, 210 (2013).
5. B. H. Li, L. Zhang, L. Ren, X. D. Chai, F. Tao, Y.Z. Wang, C. Yin, P. Huang, X.P. Zhao, and Z.D. Zhou, Typical characteristics, technologies and applications of cloud manufacturing. *Comput. Integr. Manuf. Syst.* **18**, 1345 (2012).
6. N. Liu, X.P. Li and W. M. Shen, Multi-granularity resource virtualization and sharing strategies in cloud manufacturing, *J. Network and Computer Applications***46**,72 (2014).

Energy-Efficient Positioning Approach Based on Multi-Sensors in Smart Phone

Ying Wu[a], Nan-Kai Yu and Jian-Zhong Zhang

College of Computer and Control Engineering, Nankai University
Tianjin, 300071, China
E-mail: [a]wuying@nankai.edu.cn

As smart phone is becoming more powerful, applications providing location-based service have been increasingly popular. Smart phone is commonly equipped with a variety of sensors, such as GPS, accelerometer, orientation sensor, etc. Although GPS can provide adequate location accuracy, it has limitations such as high energy-consumption. This paper presents an approach based on accelerometer, orientation sensor and GPS. It can reduce energy-consumption without compromising on location accuracy. Evaluation shows energy-saving of smart phone and location accuracy in a typical circumstance.

Keywords: Positioning; Smart Phone; GPS; Accelerometer; Orientation Sensor.

1. Introduction

Nowadays, mobile devices such as smart phone are rapidly becoming quite common in our lives, they can provide a robust support to mobile applications based on LBS. With enhancement of processing and sensing capability, although smart phone is capable to accomplish these complicated applications, but they continue to suffer from the limited battery. It is well known that GPS, core enabler of LBS applications, which can provide location accuracy within 10m, is quit energy-hungry. Continuous usage of GPS can cause battery to drain within a few hours [1]. GPS may not function well all the time, especially when user is under the shelter of buildings due to the loss of signal. Above reasons show the necessary to design an energy-efficient and reliable positioning approach.

There are many alternative location sensing technologies, such as Wi-Fi [2] and GSM [3]. For technical reasons, location accuracy of Wi-Fi-based location and GSM-based location are 20-30m and 70-200m respectively. Because increased average error introduced from above technologies, we focus on energy-saving in location process, and assure accuracy is similar to GPS-based location.

In smart phone, energy consumption of GPS is about 135mA, and accelerometer or orientation sensor is relatively low, about 15mA[4]. In order to save energy, this paper presents an location method named GAO, obtains position mainly rely on accelerometer and orientation sensor, and periodically corrects error through GPS. This approach can ensure location accuracy and extend usage time.

2. Related Work

Many low-energy sensors are embedded in smart phone, such as acceleration, gravity, gyroscope, rotation vector, magnetic field and orientation sensor. These sensors can provide some useful information about physical environment, which also can improve the location sensing. Liu [5] presents a seamless and ubiquitous positioning system in indoor and outdoor environment, which based on Wi-Fi, MARG and GPS. Thomas [6] presents a scheme for GPS-free localization and routing estimation based on acceleration and compass. GAC [7] is a hybrid scheme that mainly depends on accelerometer and compass sensor. SensTrack [8] selectively executes a GPS or Wi-Fi sampling. WheelLoc [9] provides a location service for outdoor scenarios, and relies on accelerometer and magnetometer.

3. Approach

3.1. *Position calculation*

During the positioning phase, we need some initial information, such as initial value of position. Then, we require value of position, direction and acceleration, which can be obtained through different sensors.

At time n, current value of position, velocity, direction and acceleration are respectively expressed as p(n), v(n), d(n) and a(n). Here, l(n) is the displacement on direction d(n), which can be calculated through Eq.(1).

$$l(n)=v(n)T+a(n)T^2/2 \tag{1}$$

T is a sampling period, a(n-1) is acceleration at time n-1, and v(n-1) is velocity. Because of smart phone's movement in a sampling period can be uniformly regarded as an accelerated linear motion, v(n) can be calculated through Eq.(2).

$$v(n)=v(n-1)+a(n-1)T \tag{2}$$

Smart phone's movement is on earth's surface, and earth is an ellipsoid, namely the mobile trajectory of is a curve. In order to calculate the curve length between two points on an ellipsoid, we can use Vincent formula which used in geodesy. Position p(n+1) can be calculated through Eq.(3).

$$p(n+1)=f[p(n),l(n),d(n)] \quad (3)$$

Where l(n) is displacement at time n, d(n) is direction, p(n) is position n, and f is function used to return position p(n+1). The value of a position is a coordinate data includes latitude, longitude and azimuth. We will not detail the realization of Vincent formula function.

3.2. *Implementation*

In order to evaluate GAO method, we develop an application on Android, which named GAO_Location. The whole processes are as follows: 1)Open GPS, obtain initial position, then close GPS. 2)If synchronization time reach, correct error through GPS. 3)Read two sensor, obtain direction d(n) and acceleration a(n). 4)Calculate displacement l(n). 5)Calculate position p(n+1). 6)If positioning process not end, loop from step 2 to 5.

We obtain position through GPS in each period. GPS operation are as follows: 1)Declare GPS access permission. 2)Create LocationManager object. 3)Register LocationListener object and obtain position. 4)Replace current value. Because smart phone is fixed on a moving carrier, we need only obtain azimuth and pitching angle. Sensor operation are as follows: 1)Create SensorManager object. 2)Create objects for two sensors. 3)Register and bind two listeners, obtain direction and acceleration.

4. Performance Evaluation

4.1. *Experimental environment*

GAO_Location is compared with GPS_Location in energy consumption and positioning accuracy. GPS_Location only uses GPS. Two applications are running on Samsung i9100. We select two scenarios: campus and urban. In Nankai University, we ride a bike from South Gate to Library, whole path is a typical campus traffic scene. In urban scene, we drive a car from East Gate of Nankai University, along Weijin Road, Anshan Road, Baidi Road and Fukang Road, return to origin. The whole path includes straight roads, curving roads, crossroads and overpasses. In course of driving, we wait for red light at multiple intersections, and make multiple acceleration or deceleration motions.

4.2. *Energy consumption*

In order to evaluate energy consumption, we use PowerTutor, an android application, which can measure the real-time consumption of applications. Figure 1 shows energy consumption of GAO_Location. With increase of synchronization period, energy consumption of GAO_Location decline quickly, from 150mA to 17mA. But energy consumption of GPS_Location basically unchanged. Therefore, GAO_Location can greatly reduce energy consumption.

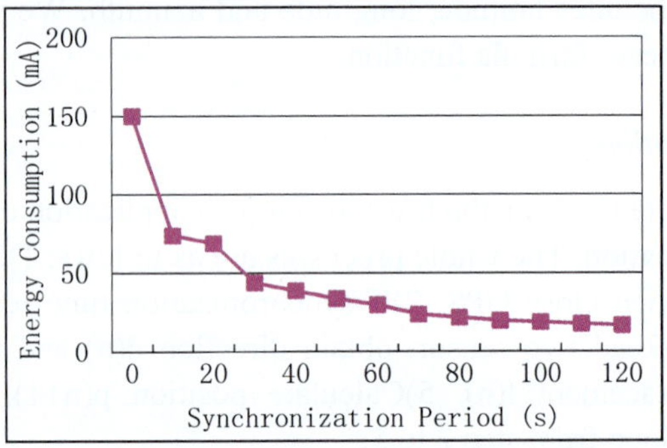

Fig. 1. Energy consumption of GAO_Location

4.3. *Positioning accuracy*

In order to evaluate positioning accuracy, we develop an application named GAO vs GPS, which is based on Google map API. Because we use online map mode, GAO vs GPS need support of Internet. The synchronization period is 10 seconds. In each scene, we get trajectories of GAO_Location and GPS Location. We only want to compare positioning error of two methods, no need to get the actual position in map. Therefore, there is no necessary to correct error.

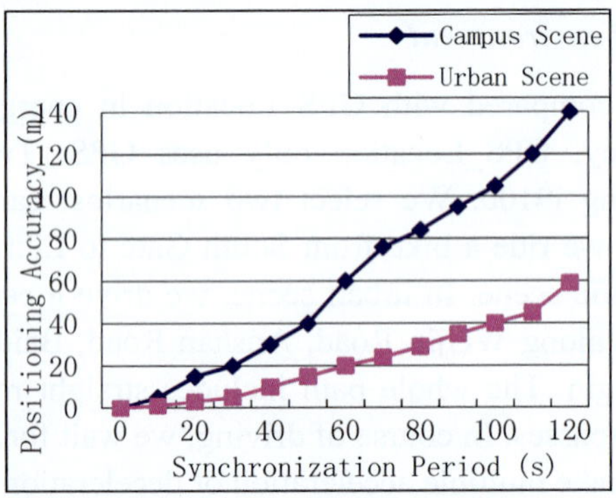

Fig. 2. Positioning accuracy of GAO_Location

Figure 2 shows positioning accuracy of GAO_Location. With increase of synchronization period, positioning accuracy increased quickly. If synchronous period is relatively small, GAO_Location can provide better accuracy, but consume more energy. Therefore, selection of synchronization period is vital.

5. Conclusions

This paper presents an energy-saving positioning method named GAO, mainly uses accelerometer and orientation sensor to obtain position, and supplements by GPS. In premise of ensuing positioning accuracy, this method can minimize the using of GPS, and reduce power consumption of LBS application. GAO method still has some shortcomings. Firstly, GAO is only applicable to outdoor environment. Secondly, we not consider state change of smart phone in acceleration calculation. Finally, In order to reduce the noise of read value from sensor, we use average value of position obtained in one second. In future work, we will use the noise filter to reduce error.

Acknowledgments

This work is supported by the National Natural Science Foundation of China (No.61103214).

References

1. Z. Zhuang, K. Kim, J. Singh, "Improving Energy Efficiency of Location Sensing on Smart phones", Proceedings of 8th International Conference on Mobile Systems, Applications and Services(MobiSys), pp.315-330, 2010
2. I. Bisio, R. L. C. Pan, F. Lavagetto, M. Marchese, A. Sciarrone, C. Fra, M. Valla, "Smart phone-based Automatic Place Recognition with Wi-Fi Signals for Location-aware Services", Proceedings of 2012 IEEE International Conference on Communications(ICC), pp.4943-4938, 2012
3. M. Ibrahim, M. Youssef, "CellSense: An Accurate Energy-Efficient GSM Positioning System", IEEE Transactions on Vehicular Technology, vol. 6, no.1, pp.286-296, 2013
4. G. Aloi, G. Caliciuri, V. Loscri, P. Pace, "Accurate and Energy-Efficient Localization System for Smart phone: A Feasible Implementation", Proceedings of 2013 IEEE International Symposium on Personal Indoor and Mobile Radio Communications(PIMRC), pp.3477-3481, 2013
5. X. Liu, Q. Man, H. Lu, X. Lin, "Wi-Fi/MARG/GPS Integrated System for Seamless Mobile Positioning", Proceedings of 2013 IEEE Wireless

Communications and Networking Conference(WCNC), pp.2323-2328, 2013
6. A. Thomas, J. Geldmacher, J. Gotze, E. Coersmeier, "Azimuth Based Localization for Mobile Phones", Proceedings of 2011 IEEE International Conference on Localization and GNSS(ICL-GNSS), pp.71-76, 2011
7. M. Youssef, M. A. Yosef, M. El-Derini, "GAC: Energy Efficient Hybrid GPS-Accelerometer-Compass GSM Localization", Proceedings of 2010 IEEE Global Communications Conference(GLOBECOM), pp.1-5, 2010
8. L. Zhang, J. Liu, H. Jiang, "SensTrack: Energy-Efficient Location Tracking With Smart phone Sensors", IEEE Sensors Journal, vol.13, no.10, pp.3775-3784, 2013
9. H. Wang, Z. Wang, G. Shen, F. Li, S. Han, F. Zhao, "WheelLoc: Enabling Continuous Location Service on Mobile Phone for Outdoor Scenarios", Proceedings of 2013 IEEE International Conference on Computer Communications(INFOCOM), pp.2733-2741, 2013

A Study on Driving Behavior Analysis Model Based on the Movement Data of the New Energy Bus

Xiao-Ping Du[1,2,a], Xue-Guang Xie[1,b,*], Qing-Hong Yang[1,c] and Wen-Xu Zhou[1,d]

[1]School of Software, Beihang University,
Beijing, 100191, China

[2]Key Laboratory of Advanced Manufacturing Technology for Automobile Parts, Ministry of Education, Chongqing University of Technology, Red Road, Banan District, No. 69 Chongqing, Banan District, China

E-mail: [a]xpdu@buaa.edu.cn, [b]xgxie@buaa.edu.cn, [c]yangqh@buaa.edu.cn, [d]289104379@qq.com

Driving behavior is reflected by the performance of the actual driver's behavior in the driving process. It is an important basis for judging whether the driver is safe. Combining factor analysis, K-means algorithm, naive Bayes algorithm and k-fold cross-Validation algorithm, this paper builds a new driving behavior analysis model based on the movement data of the new energy bus. Then, it uses the real CAN and GPS data of the bus to validate the correctness and effectiveness of the model. The experimental results show that the model can classify the driving behavior excellently. It provides a good basis for standardizing driving behavior in the future.

Keywords: Driving Behavior; Classification; K-Means Clustering; Naive Bayes; GPS.

1. Introduction

Driving behavior is reflected by the performance of the actual driver's behavior in the driving process. Unsafe driving behavior can lead to serious traffic accidents. Therefore, it is very important to analyze and identify the unsafe driving behavior [1]. Nowadays, many scholars have conducted a study on the unsafe driving behavior. The two main research directions are as follows.

(1). Some research gets the data of driver's mental activity through scales and questionnaires. And they analyze the characteristics of driving behavior

*Corresponding author.

[2.3]. The data only are extracted from the drivers who had a traffic accident. Therefore, this method can't cover the situation completely.

(2). Other research measure the vehicle behavior, the drivers' brain activity and eye activity through the sensor to analyze the driving behavior [4]. This method can acquire the data accurately. But in this complex way, we can't analyze and judge every driver.

With the popularity of GPS and vehicle system, a large number of GPS and CAN data are collected. These data record the movement process of vehicles. Besides, they also reflect drivers' driving behavior [5.6]. Hence, this paper proposes a analysis model to study the unsafe driving behavior by data mining technology.

2. Study Design

In this paper, we analyze the unsafe driving behavior to establish our model. The research process is divided into three stages:

1) Establishing our own indicator system [7.8].
2) Driving behavior classification.
3) Establishing the driving behavior prediction model and optimizing it.

3. Driving Behavior Indicator System

In this section, we select four metrics to establishing our indicator system: over speed, sudden braking, sudden acceleration and sharp turn. We define the threshold of every metric in the next discussion. Then we choose three indicators in each aspect. These indicators include the cumulative number of times (CN, times), the cumulative time (CT, seconds) and the cumulative mileage (CM, kilometers) of each behavior. So there are 12 indicators in total. And we use these indicators to quantify the driving behavior. Finally, we reduce the dimensionality of the driving behavior feature matrix using factor analysis algorithm.

In order to establish our model, we get 8549 trains according to 29,735,828 original GPS and CAN data. Then we calculate the driving behavior feature matrix of each train by using our indicator system as discussed above. Table 1 shows a part of feature matrix of driving behavior. This results is a quantization of driving behavior in our model.

Table 1. Driving behavior feature indicators

Trains	Overspeed			Sudden acceleration			Sudden braking			Sharp turn		
	CN (x_1)	CM (x_2)	CT (x_3)	CN (x_4)	CM (x_5)	CT (x_6)	CN (x_7)	CM (x_8)	CT (x_9)	CN (x_{10})	CM (x_{11})	CT (x_{12})
1	6	5044	118	1	24.61	2	0	0	0	2	28.55	4
2	9	1489	36	4	32.42	8	0	0	0	6	83.41	12
3	9	9279	214	1	15.92	2	3	29.50	6	6	83.61	12

3.1. *Dimensionality reduction*

As we said above, we can obtain the feature matrix of driving behavior which has 12 dimensions. Since every three dimensions are from the same aspects, so we guess these features must be existing certain correlation. So we find that these correlation coefficients of the features from each same aspect are almost above 0.8. Then we apply factor analysis method to reduce dimensions. When the dimensions are reduced to 4 factors, the cumulative variance contribution rate reaches 88.6%, which indicates that the new 4 factors are sufficient to characterize our original 12 indicators in the system. We get a new driving behavior feature matrix with 4 dimensions according to these factor expressions. In the section 3, we use these results to cluster.

4. Driver Behavior Classification

In our model, we must classify driving behavior. Current driving behavior classification has many definitions. But these classification pointed at a single variable, or just qualitative classification. How to define the quantitative classification criteria is a problem. To solve this problem, we adopt the K-Means clustering algorithm.

4.1. *Driving behavior clustering*

K-Means clustering algorithm does not require the input distance matrix. And we need to specify the cluster number N in advance. But in some circumstances, we can't know which the right cluster number is. So we need to specify the number by using the following methods. The first method is using heat map or hierarchical clustering to obtain the number. Another method is using $SS_{Between}/ SS_{Total}$ to determine the clustering number. The larger the value is, the better the effect of clustering is.

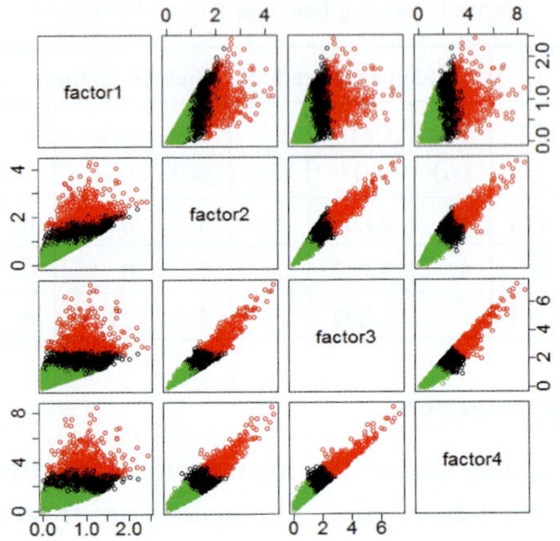

Fig. 1. The result of the K-means clustering

In this paper, we adopt the above two methods to obtain the number of cluster. Synthesizing the analysis results of heatmap clustering and 10 times of K-means clustering, it can be concluded that it is most appropriate to cluster the driving behavior features into three clusters. Figure 1 is the result of the K-means clustering when the cluster number N is three. In the next, we will analyze this result.

4.2. *Analyzing clustering results*

In the above clustering process, the data is divided into 3 clusters, the number of data in each cluster is 3766, 3992, 791. Besides, the value of $SS_{Between}/\ SS_{Total}$ is 71.5%. The following Table 2 shows the each factor average value in each cluster. From this table, there are obvious differences between different clusters. The values of first cluster factors are medium, so this kind of driving behavior is defined as the normal driving behavior. For the second cluster, the values of the factors are on the low side. Therefore the drive behavior is defined as calm driving behavior. The values of third cluster factors are the highest, which should be defined as the aggressive driving behavior. This result is the classification criteria that we established for our analysis model.

Table 2. Each factor average value in each cluster

	Factor1	Factor2	Factor3	Factor4
1	0.9320	1.3702	1.7740	2.2183
2	0.5719	0.7725	0.9369	1.2831
3	1.0335	2.1069	3.1745	3.7500

5. Establishing the Classification and Prediction Model of Driving Behavior

In the above experiments, we obtain the classification criteria using the K-means clustering algorithm. In order to classify other drivers' behavior in the future, it is necessary to establish a classification & prediction model of driving behavior. Furthermore, we evaluate and optimize our model using K-fold cross-Validation algorithm and confusion matrix.

5.1. *The classification and prediction model*

According to the driving behavior features and clustering results, the supervised classification & prediction model is established by using the Naive Bayes algorithm. Then, using 10-fold cross-Validation algorithm, this model can be calibrated step by step so that we can get more accurate classification results. The specific steps are shown in Figure 2.

5.2. *Evaluating the classification model*

In this section, we apply the classification model to the data set. Then, the classification results are obtained. In order to verify the model, we need compare the classification results with the clustering results obtained before. The confusion matrix of this classification is as shown in Table 3. From Table 3, this model predicted some actual second class into the first class and predicted some actual first class into the third class. They are the main errors of classification. Meanwhile, It reflects, overall, the accuracy of the classification results is up to 75%. Therefore, the classification model of driving behavior has a high correctness and effectiveness. It can classify the driving behavior very well.

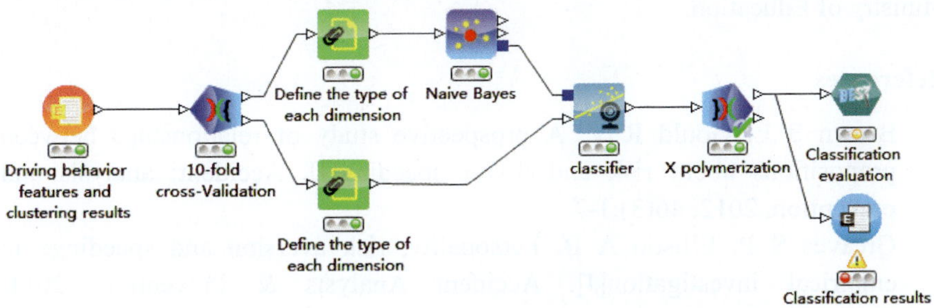

Fig. 2. The process of building classification & prediction model

Table 3. Confusion matrix of classification results

Actual\Predicted	Cluster1	Cluster2	Cluster3
Cluster 1	2962	0	804
Cluster 2	1197	2717	78
Cluster 3	16	0	775

6. Conclusions

This paper establishes the analysis model of driving behavior. Based on the new energy bus movement data including CAN and GPS data, we firstly establish our indicator system and obtain the driving behavior feature matrix with 12 indicators. Through factor analysis, 12 indicators are reduced into 4 new factors. Then the data of driving behavior are clustered into 3 categories by K-Means clustering. So we define the classification criteria of driving behavior. In order to classify other driving behavior using our standard, this paper establishes the classification model of driving behavior by using Naive Bayes algorithm. Meanwhile, this paper combines with the k-fold cross-Validation algorithm to optimize the model. The experimental results show that the classification model can classify the driving behavior and the accuracy is more than 75%. Therefore, the model offers great help for the classification of driving behavior and grading drivers. Further, it provides reference for regulating driving behavior. In our future work, we should focus on optimizing this model using more vehicle information.

Acknowledgments

This research was supported in part by the Opening Foundation of Key Laboratory of Advanced Manufacturing Technology for Automobile Parts, Ministry of Education.

References

1. Brown S L, Gould R V. A prospective study of relationships between propositions about risk and driver speeding[J]. Accident; analysis and prevention, 2012, 46(3):1-7.
2. Greaves S P, Ellison A B. Personality, risk aversion and speeding: an empirical investigation[J]. Accident Analysis & Prevention, 2011, 43(5):1828–1836.
3. Miyaji M, Danno M, Oguri K. Analysis of driver behavior based on traffic incidents for driver monitor systems[C]// IEEE Intelligent Vehicles Symposium. IEEE, 2008:930-935.

4. Newnam S, Vonschuckmann C. Identifying an appropriate driving behaviour scale for the occupational driving context: The DBQ vs. the ODBQ[J]. Safety Science, 2012, 50(5):1268-1274.
5. Zhang L, Zhu H, Chen L, et al. Fractal characteristics analysis on driving behavior time series: Example with speed data as vehicle driving towards an intersection[C]// Transportation Information and Safety (ICTIS), 2015 International Conference on. IEEE, 2015.
6. Wang H, Wu L, Hou C, et al. A GPS-based research on driving range and patterns of private passenger vehicle in Beijing[C]// Electric Vehicle Symposium and Exhibition (EVS27), 2013 World. IEEE, 2013:1-7.
7. Wang Chang. Research on several key problems of vehicle lane change warning[D]. Chang'an University,2012. In Chinese.
8. Zhao H, Zhou H, Chen C, et al. Join driving: A smart phone-based driving behavior evaluation system[C]// GLOBECOM 2013 - 2013 IEEE Global Communications Conference. 2013:48-53.s

Analysis of Six Degrees of Separation in Baidu Encyclopedia Using Breadth-First Search

Yi-Wei Shen

Key Laboratory of Universal Wireless Communications, Ministry of Education, Beijing University of Posts and Telecommunication
Beijing, 100876, China
E-mail: shenyiweiwork@sina.com

The famous theory "Six Degrees of Separation" states that any two people around the world could connect with each other through an average number of six steps. In this paper, an attempt was made to analyze the Six Degrees of Separation in Baidu Encyclopedia which has included more than 1300, 0000 articles as of April 2016. A web crawler is built to get the links of articles in Baidu Encyclopedia and MySQL database is established to store the information in an architecturally sound way to make data analysis easy. The minimum number of links between any two unlikely articles was identified efficiently by using Breadth-First Search. According to the simulation result, even "Five Degrees of Separation" still holds in Baidu Encyclopedia; an article could get to 78% of all other articles within five links.

Keywords: Six Degrees of Separation; Web Crawler; MySQL; Breadth-First Search.

1. Introduction

Six Degrees of Separation [1] is the theory that anyone around the world could be connected to any other people through a chain of acquaintances that no more than six intermediaries. The theory was first proposed in 1929 by the Hungarian writer Frigyes Karinthy in a short story called "Chains" and it was popularized in 1990's by a famous play writer, John Guare.

Years later, a parlor game called" Six Degrees of Kevin Bacon" [2] was developed based on the "Six Degrees of Separation" concept. Movie buffs challenge each other to find the shortest path between an arbitrary actor and prolific character Kevin Bacon. It rests on the assumption that anyone involved in the Hollywood file industry can be linked through their film roles to Bacon within six steps. In this paper, the game would become” Six Degrees of Baidu Encyclopedia”. That is, to find the minimum number of links that take us from start article to target article in Baidu Encyclopedia. The example of Six Degrees of Separation in Wikipedia is showed in Figure 1.

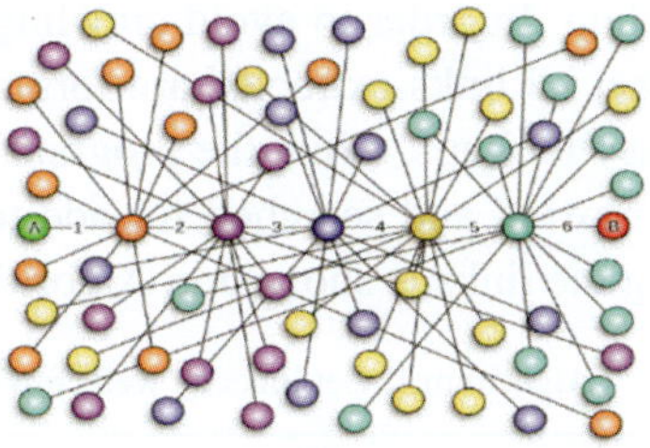

Fig. 1. Example of Six Degrees of Separation in Wikipedia [3]

On the other hand, an algorithm called Breadth-First Search (BFS) [4] was invented by E.F. Moore, who used it to find the shortest path out of a maze, and discovered independently by C.Y. Lee as a wire routing algorithm published in 1961. BFS is an algorithm for traversing or searching trees or graph data structures. It can be quite appropriate when exploring search spaces where there is an expected solution which takes a relatively small number of steps. BFS has been proved useful solving many problems, for example, copying garbage collection, testing a bipartite graph. However, BFS also has the drawback like taking massive space resources.

2. Get Links

To get the links of articles in Baidu Encyclopedia, a web crawler based on Python is built in this paper. Web crawler [5] is an Internet bot which systematically browses the web and gather the data by any means. With the help of the web crawler, any information can be extracted from HTML (or XML) on the web, as long as it has some identifying tag surrounding it. For example, in Baidu Encyclopedia, the link to the article of” England” in the page of “football” is represented by “<a href=” /view/58688”> England</a>” in HTML. The tag name is “a” and its attribute is “href”. What should be gathered is the value of the attribute, like “/view/58688.html” as the link to the article of “England”. In fact, Baidu Encyclopedia is full of different links appear on every page, which could not take us to articles. These links are not needed. To solve these problem,

Regular Expression [6] is used to find the links start with '/view', which take us to different articles.

The number of the links between the start page to the target page is no more than six. To get all these links, the web crawler should take recursion as its core to gather all the information. The web crawler starts with the start article, and search for a list of all links on that page. Every one of those links is then crawled, and additional lists of links are found on each one of them, triggering another round of crawling. In order to avoid crawling the same page twice, it is extremely important that all links extracted are formatted consistently, and kept in a running list for easy lookups, while the program is running. Only links that are "new" should be crawled and searched for additional links. The process of the web crawler getting the links is showed in Algorithm 1.

Algorithm 1. Get links by web crawler

Step 1: **Initialize:** recursionlevel = 0, pageurl='startpage';
Step 2: **if** recursionlevel < 5:
Step 3: **Crawl** pageurl
Step 4: alllinks = startpage.findall("a", href = re.compile("/view"))
 articlelinks = findlinks.attrs['href']
Step 5: **for** link in articlelinks:
 if link **not** in crawledpages: newpage = link crawledpages.add(newpage)
 recursionlevel + 1
 Go back to Step 2

3. Store Information

To find the minimum number of links that take us from start article to target article, the connection between two articles in Baidu Encyclopedia should be identified. In order to solve this problem, it is necessary not only to build web crawler to get links, but to store the information in an architecturally sound way to make data analysis easy. MySQL [7], which has been tested to be a fast, stable and true multi-user, multi-threaded SQL database server, is a popular choice of database for use in web applications. In this paper, to analyze "Six Degrees of Separation" theory using BFS, tables in MySQL database should be created appropriately. In order to identify the connection between two articles, not only the information of the articles but the link between them should be identified. So a two-table database is designed to store pages and links, along with creation dates and unique IDs. Details of the tables is showed in Table 1 and Table 2.

Table 1. Details of Table 'pages'

Field	Type	Null	Key	Extra
PageID	INT	NO	PRI	AUTO_INCREMENT
Url	VARCHAR	NO		
Created	TIMESTAMP	NO		

Table 2. Details of Table 'links'

Field	Type	Null	Key	Extra
LinkID	INT	NO	PRI	AUTO_INCREMENT
FrompageID	INT	YES		
TopageID	INT	YES		
Created	TIMESTAMP	NO		

To store the data of pages and links gathered by web crawler, some SQL commands is added. The whole process of getting and storing links is showed in Algorithm 2.

Algorithm 2. Get and store links

Step 1: **Initialize:** recursionlevel = 0, pageurl

Step 2: **if** recursionlevel < 5;

Step 3: **Crawl** pageurl

Step 4: **Get** alllinks, articlelinks
    Insert (articlelinks) into table 'pages' (url)

Step 5: **for** link in articlelinks:
    if link not in crawledpages: newpage = link crawledpages.add(newpage)
    Insert (pageurl,newpage) into table 'links' (frompageID, topageID)
    recursionlevel + 1 pageurl = newpage
    Go back to Step 2

4. Breadth-First Search

Breadth-First Search [4] is an algorithm for traversing or searching tree or graph data structures. It starts at the tree root (or some arbitrary node of a graph, sometimes referred to as a 'search key') and explores the neighbor nodes first, before moving to the next level neighbors. The order in which the nodes are expanded using BFS is showed in Figure 2.

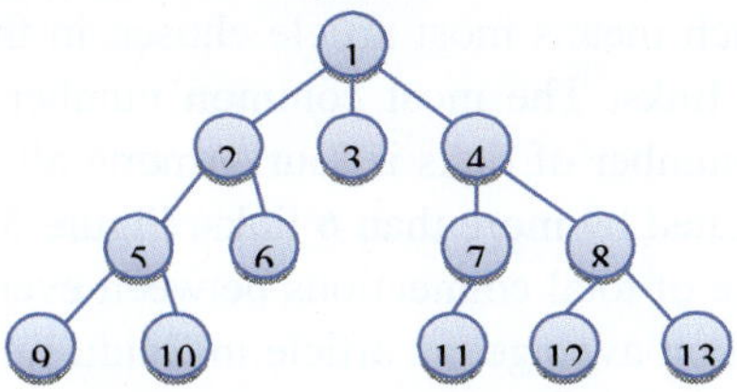

Fig. 2. Order in which the nodes are expanded in BFS

Since every node and every branch will be explored in the worst case, When dealing with trees that are quite large to store explicitly (or infinite), it is practical to describe the complexity as O(B^{M+1}) [8], in which B represents as the maximum number of the braches and M as the maximum path length of the tree.

In this paper, to find the minimum number of links that take us from start article to target article, BFS is performed by first searching all links that link directly to the starting page. If those links do not contain the target page, then a second level of links, pages that a linked by a page that is linked by the starting page, is searched. This process continues until either the depth limit is reached or the target page is found. The whole process of the analysis using BFS is showed in Algorithm 3. The algorithm works recursively to simultaneously construct and search of links, work one level at a time. If the current page contains a link to the page I am searching for, records the pageID of it, resulting in a path leading to the target page.

Algorithm 3. Process of analysis using BFS

Step 1: **Initialize:** depth, startpage, targetpage
Step 2: **if** depth == 0; **Return**
Step 3: **Get** topageID from table 'links'(frompageID = 'startpage')
Step 4: **Construct** path, tree
Step 5: **Search** for targetpage in tree
    if found: **Return** path
    Insert (pageurl,newpage) into table 'links' (frompageID, topageID)
    else frompageID = topageID depth -1
    Go back to Step 2

5. Analysis and Results

In this paper, for the analysis, 500 articles in Baidu Encyclopedia are chosen as the start article or target article. The minimum number of links between every two of these 500 articles will be identified by using BFS. When finding the path from start article to target article, there are many conditions that would influence the performance of BFS like the maximum number of the links contained in one page and the length of the path. The result is showed in Figure 3 and Figure 4.

On average, Baidu encyclopedia has "Five Degrees of Separation" between every two articles, which means most article chosen in this paper could get to each other within five links. The most common number of links is five. The second most common number of links is four. Among all 500 articles, there are still some articles separated by more than 6 links. Figure 5 shows the number of links and the percentage of total connections between every two of 500 articles. According to the result, on average, an article in Baidu Encyclopedia will get to 78% of all other articles within five links.

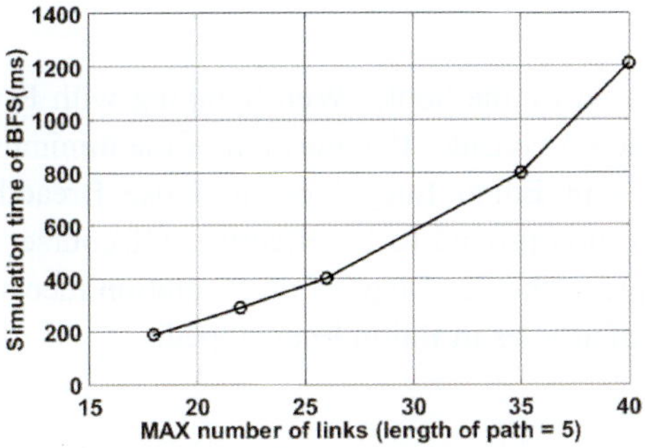

Fig. 3. Simulation time with regard to max number of links contained in one page

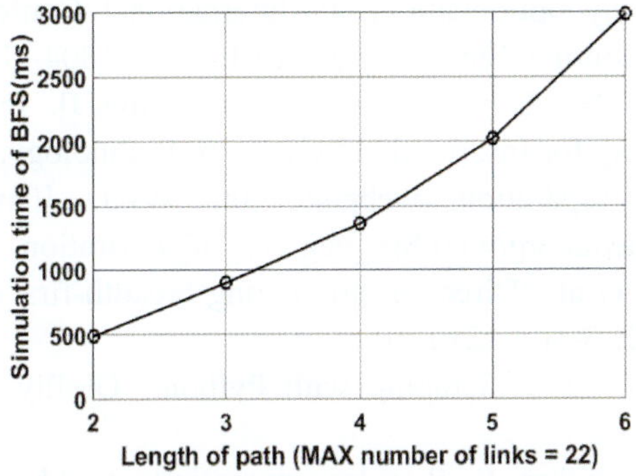

Fig. 4. Simulation time with regard to length of path

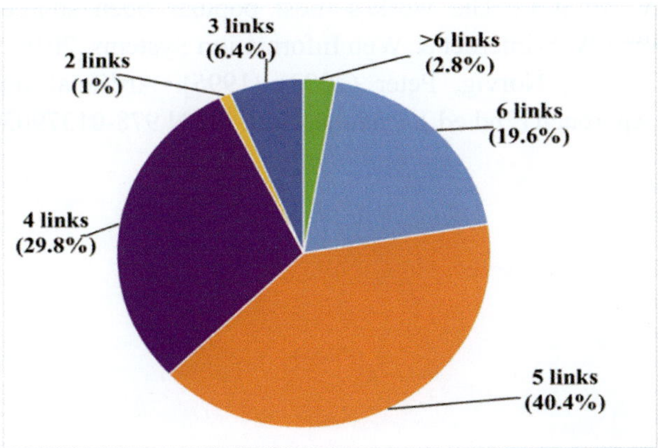

Fig. 5. Number of links between articles in Baidu Encyclopedia

6. Conclusions

This paper is motivated by the book "Web Scraping with Python" authored by Ryan Mitchell and here I consider the question of the minimum number of links between two articles in Baidu Encyclopedia. I use Breadth-First Search for analyzing and the results proved to be effective. Of course, further researches need to be done to prove the Six Degrees of Separation theory as I only tested a quite small number of articles in Baidu Encyclopedia.

References

1. Lawrence E E, Latha R. Analysis of six degrees of separation in Facebook using Ant colony optimization[C]// International Conference on Circuit, Power and Computing Technologies. IEEE, 2015:1804-1808.
2. Buzydlowski J W. Exploring co-citation chains[J]. Proceedings of the American Society for Information Science & Technology, 2006, 43(43):1-8.
3. Six_degrees_of_separation webpage on Wiki. [Online]. Available: https://en.wikipedia.org/wiki/Six_degrees_of_separation
4. Beamer, Scott, et al. "Direction-optimizing breadth-first search." Scientific Programming 21.3-4(2012):1-10.
5. Mitchell, Ryan. "Web Scraping with Python." Oreilly Vlg Gmbh & Co (2015).
6. Goyvaerts J, Levithan S. Regular expressions cookbook Jan Goyvaerts, Steven Levithan[J].
7. Mysql A. MySQL: The world's most popular open source database[J]. World Wide Web-internet & Web Information Systems, 2010.
8. Russell, Stuart; Norvig, Peter (2003) [1995]. Artificial Intelligence: A Modern Approach (2nd ed.). Prentice Hall. ISBN 978-0137903955.

Octopus: A Data Acquisition System for Open Source Communities

Zhi-Xing Li[a], Gang Yin, Tao Wang, Yi-Ang Gan, Yun Zhan[b] and Yang Zhang

National Laboratory for Parallel and Distributed Processing,
National University of Defense Technology,
Changsha, 410073, China
E-mail: [a]starleelzx@163.com, [b]cloud_zhan@163.com

With the rapid development of Open Source Software (OSS), a lot of reusable software resources have been produced in open source communities. This leads to spotty quality and high dispersion of OSS resources so that lots of research works have been conducted for effective location of reliable software resources. To provide convenient data source for such studies, this paper introduces *Octopus*, a data acquisition system for resource of open source software. Octopus is a robust, scalable and efficient system which consists of three main modules that have been well decoupled and can be updated at runtime with flexible configurations. The experiment results show that, *Octopus* can successfully collect two kinds of OSS data sources: software production communities and software consumption communities. The former produce structured software artifacts such as project profiles while the latter contain rich user feedback such as posts and blogs.

Keywords: Open Source Software; Data Acquisition; Web Crawler.

1. Introduction

With the continuous development of open source software, massive reusable software resources are available in open source software communities [1]. Such great many of open source software projects provide rich choices for developers, but it also result in spotty quality and high dispersion [2]. Searching suitable software of high quality for reuse is a tough job with so many candidate resources available. To help user locate reliable software resources effectively and conveniently, more and more researches have been conducted [1.2.7].

An abundant and convenient dataset contributes a lot to such research. With this goal in mind, this paper proposes Octopus, a data acquisition system for resource of open source software. The common way to build a data acquisition system is to take advantage of web spider and crawl target data [8.9]. Commercial search engines are usually built on the base of general web spider, but for studies on a specific topic, focused spider is a better choice [10]. The main functionality of Octopus to crawl data from Internet is achieved by the re-development of Webmagic (webmagic.io), an open source focused web spider.

There are two kinds of communities in open source software domain: software production communities and software consumption communities [1]. Structured software artifacts such as source code, documents and issues are produced in production communities like Openhub (www.openhub.net), SourceForge (sourceforge.net) and Oschina (www.oschina.net) while user feedback such as posts and blogs come from consumption communities like StackOverflow (stackoverflow.com) and CSDN (www.csdn.net). For scalable purpose, we design a uniform interface to process them equally.

Octopus is designed as a staged process and is configured with external file. It is a robust, scalable, and efficient acquisition system for open source communities. For now, Octopus has covered 10 software consumption communities (SCC) and 6 software production communities (SPC).

The rest of paper is organized like this: Section 2 reviews briefly related work and Section 3 explains the architecture of Octopus. Section 4 discusses the result and characteristic of Octopus. Section 5 concludes this paper with future work.

2. Related Work

A lot of research work has been conducted on the problem of data acquisition for open source communities.

Gousios G et al. [3] proposed GHTorrent a scalable off line mirror of GitHub's event streams and persistent data. GHTorrent retrieves raw event contents, store them in MongoDB collections and replay events on top of an initial state. It has provided much service to the research focused on the data of GitHub.

FLOSSmole [4] is originally built by Howison et al. to collect data of open source software projects hosted on SourceForge. The collected data contains numbers of downloads, programming language and other metadata of a project. For now, FLOSSmole has included much more open source software repositories.

S Bajracharya present Sourcerer [5] to gather Java projects from SourceForge and Apache. It employs the structural information like reference in source code, the dependences between libraries and so on to achieve large scale source code indexing and searching.

BlackDuck [6] a massive open source knowledge base is built by Black Duck. It inspects thousands of open source sites and collects millions of open source projects. Upon this they also build a code search engine Koders and an open source software community OpenHub.

Most of these works focus on the software production communities, and some of them even restrict themselves to specific topic. Little work has been paid on the user feedback in consumption communities. This limit the application scope of their dataset. Different from them, Octopus try to include both kinds of communities as many as possible and provide abundant and convenient dataset for crowd wisdom mining in open source communities [1].

3. Architecture of Octopus

3.1. *Overview*

The architecture of Octopus is shown in Figure 1. The main process of Octopus is divided into three modules: *list page crawler*, *URL extractor*, and *detail page crawler*. These three parts are decoupled with database and synchronized with the help of *monitor* so that they can run in parallel. The underlying programming model of crawler is the re-development of WebMagic an open source web spider.

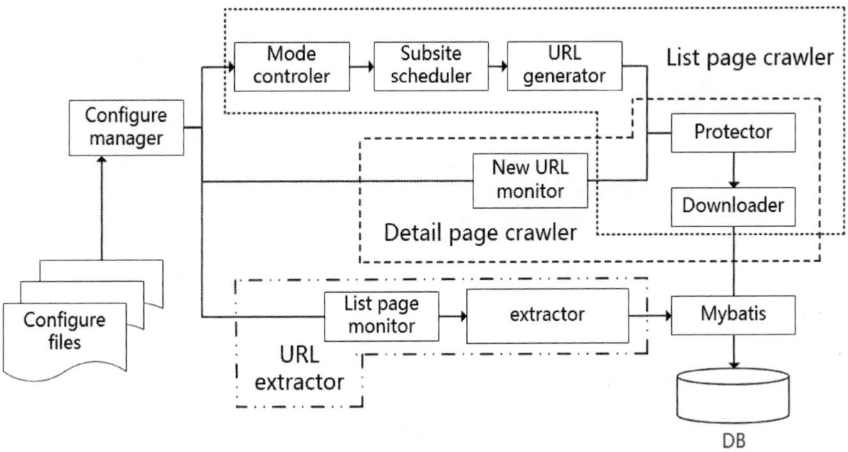

Fig. 1. The architecture of Octopus

The job of *Configure manager* is to load various configure files and influence several behaviors of Octopus. The rule to generate URL of list page, the rate to crawl some specific website, the rule to extract URL of detail page from list page, etc. are all configurable with external xml file. To make Octopus more friendly and tenacious, protector is designed for rate control and alternation of related parameter which will be taken into consideration unless it is absolutely necessary [11]. MyBatis (www.mybatis.org) a first class persistence framework is used to do the data persistence. In the following sections, the implementation of Octopus will be introduced in detail.

3.2. *List page crawler*

As discussed, Octopus is efficient because of its precise location of target resource. Unlike traditional focused web crawler filter valuable information from crawled data[9], Octopus only crawls needed resource. Like Figure 2 shows, most sites relevant to open source software show their content in list pages.

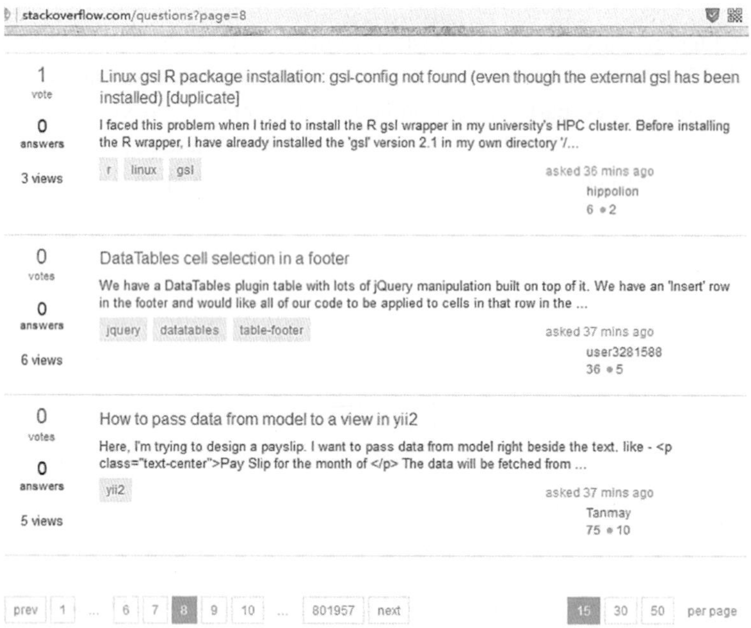

Fig. 2. List page of Stack Over flow

The first step of Octopus is to crawl these list pages. The URLs of list page in a site have the same regular expression: *prefix_url:page_number:postfix_url.* The *prefix_url* and *postfix_url* is invariable for a specific site and *page_number* is an incremental number in the corresponding range. We call this type of regular expression as 3I *(invariable-incremental-invariable)* regular expression. In StackOverflow, these parameters is "stackoverflow.com/questions?page=", a number between (1,801956) for now, and a null string respectively. With this regularization, after start index and end index of *page_number* have been determined, it is convenient to construct all the available URLs of list page automatically by assembling the three parts which is read from external xml file specifying the rule of URLs of list page in a specific site.

To stay updated on new data produced anytime, we give Octopus the ability to be in different mode: mirror mode and increment mode. In the former mode Octopus crawl the history data in one site and in the later mode Octopus crawl the new data produced since last crawl time. For one site, Octopus start to collect data in mirror mode, and change into increment mode after all the history data has been collected. When it is in increment mode, Octopus visit the website periodically according to the update rate which is decided manually with a conservative estimate under actual situation. The general flow chart of *list page crawler* is illustrated in Figure 3. They both call the common modules to assemble URL and download and store pages.

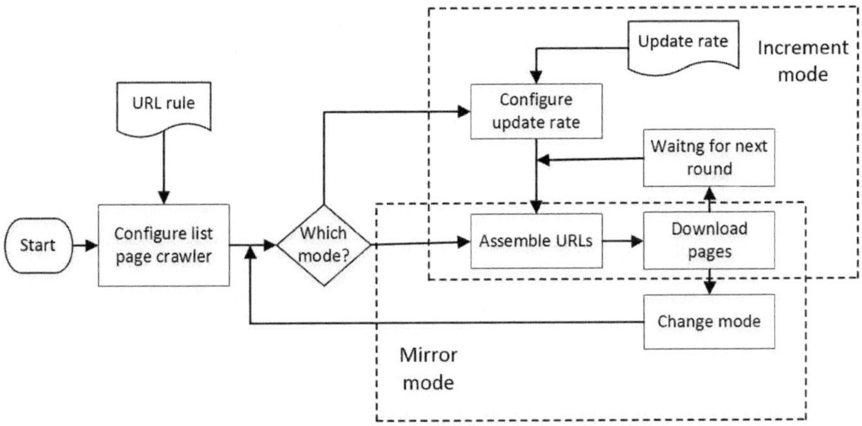

Fig. 3. The flow chart of list page crawler

For forum websites, there is no 3I regular expression of the URL for several subsections. To treat forum websites equally with other sites like StackOverflow, we model a website as a two-depth tree structure where the root node indicates the main site and leaf nodes indicate subsites. For those websites that have 3I regular expression of the URL, like StackOverflow and OpenHub, there is only one leaf node, and for those websites that don't have, the number of leaf nodes is the number of their subsites. List page crawler will process each subsite in a round-robin schedule.

3.3. *Detail page crawler*

Like Figure 4 shows, *URL extractor* listens to the result of *list page crawler* with the help of *monitor*. Once new data has come, *URL extractor* will process the html content of list page and extract the URLs contained in the page. To extract specific URL from a web page, lots of method has been proposed. We apply Jsoup [12] to do this job which is a powerful and easy-to-use HTML parsing tool. With Jsoup, CSSPath can be used to select any specific item in html file. The format of the grammar of CSSPath is like this : "*#postlist>h1>a*". The character "#" before a string indicates the string is an id of some item in a html and character ">" indicates the item before it is the parent of the item behind it. The CSSPath expression of an item in html can be many and varied, but the one that starts with some item specified with id and has a short length is a better one.

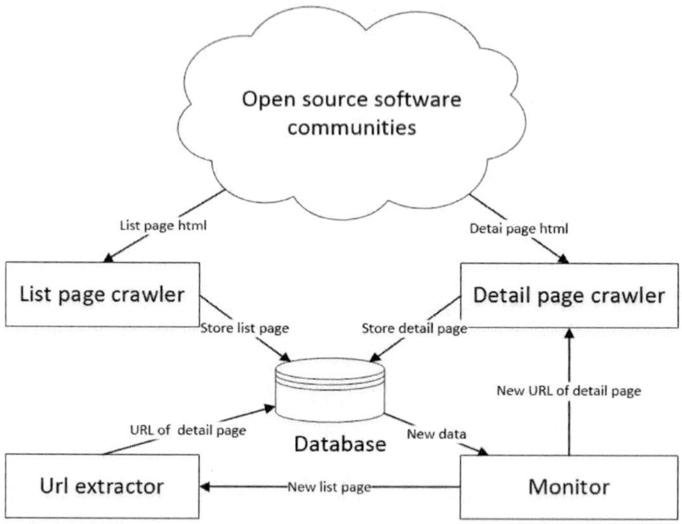

Fig. 4. Interaction among modules

The final step of Octopus is to crawl the detail pages which is our real goal. Like *URL extractor* listens to *list page crawler, detail page crawler* listens to *URL extractor.* Because the URLs of detail page have been extracted to local database, there is no tough job for detail page crawler. What it need to do is just download the detail page according to corresponding URL and persist it.

3.4. *Protector*

Some websites have made a set of criteria to resist web crawler [11]. Sometimes these criteria are so rigorous that crawler can download a very little data against them. There are many ways to make a web crawler smarter to overcome these restricts. Websites usually recognize a web crawler with its User Agent. In HTTP, the User Agent is often used for content negotiation, where the server end response with suitable content [13]. Web crawler need to identify itself in User Agent, such as Baidu's User Agent is "Mozilla/5.0 (compatible; Baiduspider/2.0; +http://www.baidu.com/search/spider.html)". For this reason, many designers build a User Agent pool which containing plenty of available User Agents. When their crawler issues a request it select a User Agent randomly from the pool to act as a famous web crawler or web browser. Another way to decrease the risk of being forbidden is to switch the IP of the server in which the crawler runs in. Websites also analyzes the IP traffic over an interval to decide whether a specific IP is requesting too much and restrict it if so. Dynamic IP switch can be achieved by IP proxy or dial-up connection. But we don't adopt these rude ways to improve the performance of Octopus. Reducing the crawling speed is the most friendly way.

In order to prevent disturbing the performance of target communities, we set Octopus at a friendly state to collect data. First, the crawling speed of Octopus is at a very low level. We set a range of crawl period in advance to constraint it. This range is a conservative estimate which can satisfy our need and don't bother the target communities at the same time. Every time, after Octopus finish downloading a page, it choose a value between that period range and sleep corresponding time to wait for next round. To better keeping Octopus running at an continuous state, we let it work intermittently. After Octopus working for a short interval, it will go into hibernation for a relatively long time. Both work interval and hibernation interval are random value generated in a specific range.

4. Results and Discussion

In this Section, we present the result of the proposed system and the characteristic analysis of Octopus.

4.1. *Results*

Until now, Octopus has covered 10 software consumption communities including StackOverflow, CSDN, 51CTO, etc. and 6 software production communities including SourceForge, OpenHub, Apache, etc.. The data we have collected is shown in Table 1. In software consumption communities, StackOverflow and CSDN, which are the most active software specific website in English and Chinese respectively, are the main data source and we have collected millions of blogs and posts from them. OpenHub and SourceForge contribute most to the quantity of OSS projects in software production communities. Some websites, like Apache and Oschina, provide very few but high quality resources which have been reviewed manually.

For software production communities, data scale means the number of open source software project that one website have hosted, for software consumption communities data scale is the number of posts or blogs that one website has produced. In some communities, like CSDN, there are several individual sub-communities. The data scale is the total number of all the sub-communities.

Table 1. Collecting result of Octopus

Website	Type	Data scale	Website	Type	Data scale
StackOverflow	SCC	3,351,477	CodeProject	SCC	5,296
CSDN	SCC	1,063,453	LinuxTone	SCC	5,552
Cnblogs	SCC	170,086	OpehHub	SPC	660,992
51CTO	SCC	29,429	SourceForge	SPC	465,650
Dewen	SCC	12,311	Oschina	SPC	40,192
PHPChina	SCC	47,505	Freecode	SPC	40,716
ITEye blog	SCC	4,582	Gna	SPC	1,455
Slashdot	SCC	2,172	Apache	SPC	248

As we stated, Octopus collects data from open source communities friendly. It follows the robots exclusion protocol. Robots exclusion protocol, also known as simply robots.txt, is a standard used by websites to communicate with web crawlers to specify which resources of the website should not be processed or scanned. When Octopus crawls, it leaves out the disallowed resources and don’t violate their privacy. Because of friendly strategy, Octopus works in good condition and hasn’t been forbidden by any website.

4.2. *Characteristic analysis*

Octopus is a scalable, robust and efficient data acquisition system. In the following, we will explain these characteristic.

(1)Scalable: Octopus is configured with external xml file. The rules to generate URL of list page, extract URL of detail page form list page, and control of the work rate are all defined in configure file. This provides a plugin-based structure for adding new communities. The only effort to include another community is just to write a new configure file and specify all these rules.

(2)Robust: Open source communities grow at amazing speed and the structure and layout of their web page are often changing. It is difficult to identify whether an error is created in the process of extraction or other valuable information is included in changed pages. To handle this problem, Octopus is designed as a staged process including list page crawling, URL extract, and detail page crawling. These three modules are decoupled with database, and their outputs have all been stored into database. Under this design, we can redo any extraction when error has been found or extract extra valuable information from pages stored in database without network access and crawl them again which is the most time-consuming operation.

(3)Efficient: Unlike traditional focused web crawler filter valuable information from crawled data, Octopus only crawl needed resource. Detail page is downloaded with the URL extracted from list page. There is no irrelevant data for Octopus to collect, so it saves much time on identify and filter.

All these characteristic of Octopus make it a perfect choice for data acquisition of open source communities.

5. Conclusion

In this paper, we proposed Octopus, a data acquisition system for the resource of open source software. With Octopus, we have collected 6 software production communities and 10 software consumption communities. The actual running state shows that Octopus is a robust, scalable, and efficient system. However, there are some limitations needed to be improved. As we have said, there are more and more open source communities, so it is a meaningful work in the future to discover unknown websites automatically that are relevant to open source software.

What's more, to help more empirical software engineering studies and satisfy their need on data acquisition of open source communities, we plan to offer both public dataset and online query interface.

Acknowledgments

The research is supported by the National Natural Science Foundation of China (Grant No.61432020, 61472430, 61502512) and National Grand R&D Plan (Grant No. 2016YFB1000805). We would also thank the reviewers for providing us constructive comments and suggestions.

References

1. Yin G, Wang T, Wang H, et al. OSSEAN: Mining Crowd Wisdom in Open Source Communities[C]//Service-Oriented System Engineering (SOSE), 2015 IEEE Symposium on. IEEE, 2015: 367-371.
2. Fan Q, Wang H, Yin G, et al. Ranking open source software based on crowd wisdom[C]//Software Engineering and Service Science (ICSESS), 2015 6th IEEE International Conference on. IEEE, 2015: 966-972
3. Gousios G, Spinellis D. GHTorrent: GitHub's data from a firehose[C]//Mining software repositories (msr), 2012 9th ieee working conference on. IEEE, 2012: 12-21.
4. Howison J, Conklin M, Crowston K. FLOSSmole: A collaborative repository for FLOSS research data and analyses[J]. International Journal of Information Technology and Web Engineering (IJITWE), 2006, 1(3): 17-26.
5. Linstead E, Bajracharya S, Ngo T, et al. Sourcerer: mining and searching internet-scale software repositories[J]. Data Mining and Knowledge Discovery, 2009, 18(2): 300-336.
6. Bagley C E, Lane D. Black Duck Software. Case Study[J]. Harvard Business School Publishing, 2006.
7. Vasilescu B, Filkov V, Serebrenik A. StackOverflow and GitHub: Associations between software development and crowdsourced knowledge[C]//Social Computing (SocialCom), 2013 International Conference on. IEEE, 2013: 188-195.
8. Heydon A, Najork M. Mercator: A scalable, extensible web crawler[J]. World Wide Web, 1999, 2(4): 219-229.
9. Thelwall M. A web crawler design for data mining[J]. Journal of Information Science, 2001, 27(5): 319-325.
10. S. Chakrabarti, M. van den Berg, and B. Dom. Focused crawling: a new approach to topic-specific Web resource discovery. Computer Networks, 31(11-16):1623–1640, 1999.

11. Fox V, Camp A A, Ibel M, et al. System and method for enabling website owners to manage crawl rate in a website indexing system: U.S. Patent 7,599,920[P]. 2009-10-6.
12. Hedley J. jsoup: Java html parser[J]. 2010.
13. Fielding R, Gettys J, Mogul J, et al. Hypertext transfer protocol--HTTP/1.1[R]. 1999.

A Multi-Dimension Factor Decision-Making Model Framework Using Back-Propagation Neural Networks

Peng Nie

Computer Practice Teaching Center, Jiangxi University of Finance and Economics, Nanchang, 330013, China
E-mail: zeanet@163.com

The cloud-desktop based on Virtual Desktop Infrastructure (VDI) is deployed more often as the advanced mobile office solution. However, it is an assignable challenge to choose a fit VDI product at low cost for too many testing features to be investigated. In this paper, a multi-dimension factor decision-making model framework using back-propagation neural networks (MDMFBP) is proposed for the VDI-based cloud-desktop application evaluation. MDMFBP is highly data adaptive, applies and is able to account for correlation as well as interactions among features. This makes MDMFBP particularly appealing for high-dimensional cloud-desktop testing feature analysis. The experiment results show that our MDMFBP is workable, easy to implement and result in good estimation accuracies.

Keywords: Cloud-Desktop; Software Estimation; Back-Propagation Neural Networks; Machine Learning.

1. Introduction

Nowadays, the cloud-desktop based on Virtual Desktop Infrastructure (VDI) helps the client users simplify provisioning and administration, extending the endpoint hard-ware investments, and making it easier to support employee-chosen endpoint devices. However, it is still an assignable challenge to make a decision which specific VDI software implementation satisfies the given application environment. Lots of evaluation models have been proposed to evaluate the software system on a certain perspective. Jelinski [1] suggested the Markov chain to calculate the software reliability. Goel [2] used a time-dependent error-detection rate model for software performance measures. Sheldon [3] employed the stochastic petri net models to analyze software safety and reliability. Karunanithdi [4], Adnan [5], Kiran [6] et al. applied Neural

Networks in reliability prediction. Afzal, Torkar [7] et al. used the genetic programming for software reliability growth modeling. The works above focused on limited dimensions, mostly only one dimension (such as reliability, safety, availability, survivability, etc) to evaluate a software system. It is quite different from the one dimension evaluation system, the VDI-based cloud-desktop application evaluation is affected by multiple dimensions or a multi-dimension factor matrix, including user experience (UE), tech features (TF), management & control (MC) .

In this paper, we proposed a multi-dimension factor decision-making model framework using back-propagation neural networks (MDMFBP) for the VDI-based cloud-desktop application evaluation.

The rest of this paper is organized as follows. Section 2 presents the proposed MDMFBP model in detail. Section 3 gives the experiments and analysis. Finally, Section 4 concludes this paper.

2. MDMFBP

2.1. *Notations*

D	a multi-dimension feature space
D_i	the i-th sub-class vector of D
$D_{i,j}$	the j-th property of D_i
$R_{i,j}^k$	the estimation of $D_{i,j}$ on the k-th executions
R_i^k	the estimation of D_i on the k-th executions
R^k	the VDI-based cloud-desktop system estimation set on the k-th execution
R_s^k	the VDI-based cloud-desktop system estimation on the k-th execution
S_i^k	the VDI-based cloud-desktop system estimation sensitivity of D_i on the k-th execution
S^k	the software system sensitivity set on the k-th execution
$T_{p,R_i^k}^k$	the relative change of R_i^k to the VDI-based cloud-desktop system estimation R^k
ΔR_i^k	the estimation change of D_i on the k-th execution
$\mathcal{R}_h'^k(t)$	the VDI-based cloud-desktop system estimation output by the h-th neuron of the t-th training iteration on the k-th execution
$\mathcal{F}_h(\cdot)$	the activation function for the h-th neuron
$w_{jh}^q(t)$	the weight of the j-th input estimation for the h-th neuron in the q-th layer of the t-th training iteration
$v_h(t)$	the summing function for the h-th neuron of the t-th training iteration
$\theta_h^q(t)$	the bias for the h-th neuron in the q-th layer of the t-th training iteration

$e_h^q(t)$	the error for the h-th neuron in the q-th layer of the t-th training iteration
R_T , R_E	the observed software system estimation and the evaluated estimation
ε	the error between R_T and R_E

2.2. *MDMFBP neuron*

The key issue for the VDI-based cloud-desktop system estimation is to find the appropriate knowledge between $R_{i,j}^k$ and calculate the accurate $R_{i,j}^k$ of the whole cloud-desktop system.

Our model is implemented based on the back-propagation neural network. The elements in the MDMFBP neuron are introduced in detail as Figure 1.

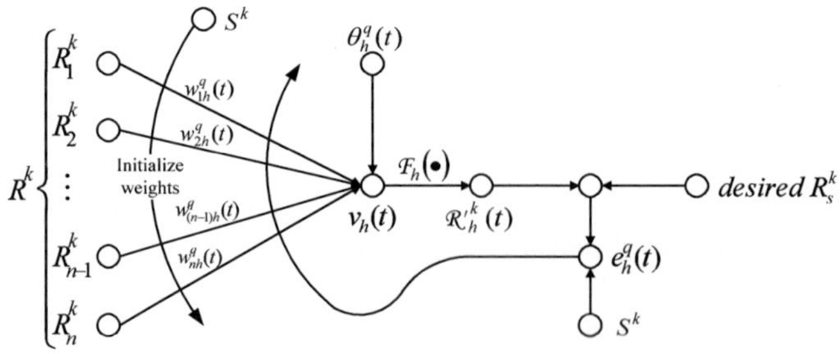

Fig. 1. Signal flow graph of the h-th neuron.

In our proposal, the neuron uses the history factor estimation set R^k after the k-th execution of the software system as its input. S_i^k , the estimation sensitivity of each individual factor is analyzed and assigned to $w_{jh}^q(t)$ as the initial weight. Then $v_h(t)$ sums all of the weighted input estimations altogether and modifies the summation by the bias $\theta_h^q(t)$. Next, the h-th neuron produces an output between 0 and 1 by the activation function $\mathcal{F}_h(\cdot)$ as the software system factor evaluation $\mathcal{R}'^k_h(t)$ in the t-th training iteration. A desired software system estimation R_s^k is compared with $\mathcal{R}'^k_h(t)$ to find the error $e_h^q(t)$. Finally, not only $e_h^q(t)$, but also S^k is propagated back to adjust the weights for a more accurate $\mathcal{R}'^k_h(t)$.

3. Experiments and Analysis

In our testing case, the cloud-desktop system features are divided into 3 dimensions as the tech features, the management & control features, and the user experience features.

The tech features include a five-dimension feature space: Cloud-desktop Sensitivity, CPU Stress, Memo Stress, IO Stress and GPU Stress. The management & control features include three dimensions of User Management, User & Virtual Machine(VM) Mapping, VM Access Strategy. The user experience features includes the dimensions of SQL Workload, Web Visiting Workload, 3D FPS, and High-definition video. All of the features above combines a high dimensional space called the multi-dimension feature space.

3.1. *Testing environment*

Server×1: CPU: Intel Xeon E5-2670 v3, memory: 256G, disk: 2.7T@7200 r/s, no GPU;

PC Client×50: CPU: Intel Core i3-4150, memory: 4G, disk: 1T SATA;

Cloud Desktop VM×50: 2 cores@2 cpus, memory: 4G, disk: 32G.

3.2. *MDMFBP predicting error*

Our cloud desktop system results in 3600 testing reports for the tech & user experience feature testing and estimation reports for the management & control requirement. The top 3000 testing reports and the top 3000 estimation reports are used as the training dataset, and the rest datasets are used to provide the predictive accuracy as the figures from Figure 2 to Figure 5.

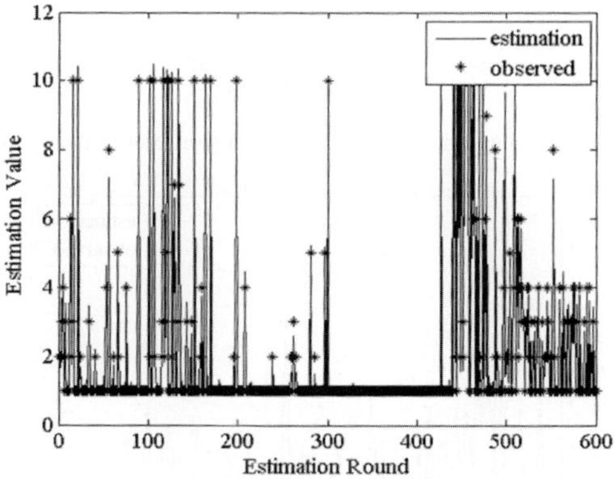

Fig. 2. The tech dimension predictive accuracy.

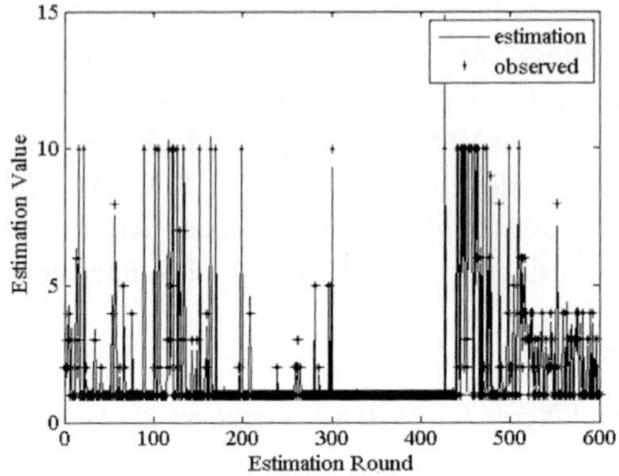

Fig. 3. The user experience dimension predictive accuracy.

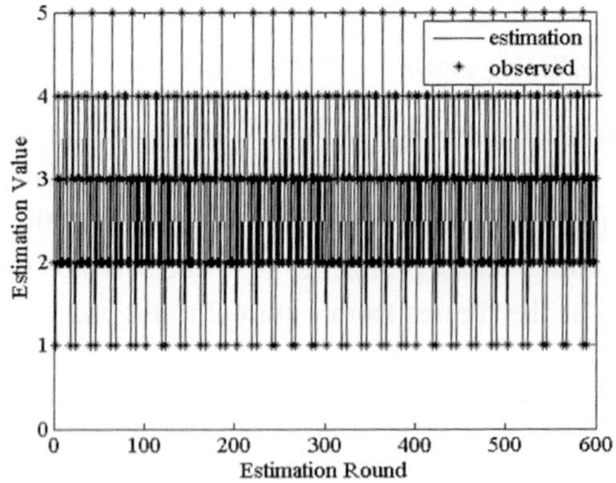

Fig. 4. The management & control dimension predictive accuracy.

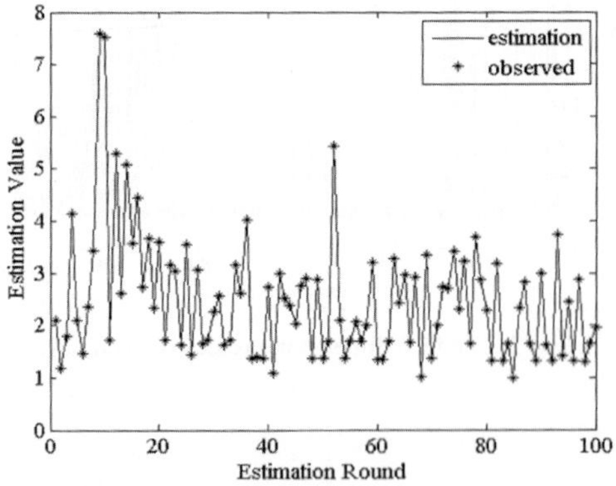

Fig. 5. The entire cloud-desktop predictive accuracy by MDMFBP.

The predictive accuracy is given by Eq. (1).

$$err = \sum_{i=1}^{n} \text{abs}(R_i - Real_i) \Big/ n \tag{1}$$

where $Real_i$ denotes the observed values, $\text{abs}(\cdot)$ is the absolute value of $R_i - Real_i$.

The accuracies of the 3 dimension estimations and the entire system estimation are presented in Table 1.

Table 1. The estimation accuracies of MDMFBP.

	Tech	User experience	Management & control	Cloud desktop system
err	0.018	0.015	0.007	0.012

4. Conclusion

The complexity and high-dimensionality of cloud-desktop system estimation data require flexible and powerful statistical learning tools for an effective estimation process. It has been proven that back-propagation neural networks have high attainable classification accuracy, already having produced numerous successful applications. The experiment results from MDMFBP based on the random forest show that the method is workable, easy to implement and result in good estimation accuracies. Additionally, we demonstrated the usability of our framework on the estimation task of high-dimension feature space for the software system.

References

1. Z. Jelinski and P. B. Moranda, Software Reliability Research, Statistical Computer Performance Evaluation, (1972), pp. 465-484.
2. A. L. Goel and K. Okumoto, Time-Dependent Error-Detection Rate Model for Software Re-liability and Other Performance Measures, IEEE Transactions on Reliability, R-28(3) (1979), pp. 206-211.
3. F. T. Sheldon, S. Greiner, and M. Benzinger, Specification, safety and reliability analysis using stochastic petri net models, In Proc. the 10th International Workshop on Software Specification and Design, (Shelter Island, San Diego, California, USA, 2000), pp. 123-132.
4. N. Karunanithdi, A. Itley and Y. K. Malaiy: Using Neural Networks in Reliability Prediction, IEEE Software, Vol. 9(4) (1992), pp.53-59.

5. W. A. Adnan, M. Yaakob and R. Anas, Artificial neural network for software reliability assessment, In Proc. Tencon 2000, (Kuala Lumpur, Malaysia, 2000), pp. 446-451.
6. N. R. Kiran and V. Ravi, Software reliability prediction using wavelet neural networks, In Proc. International Conference on Computational Intelligence and Multimedia Applications 2007, (Sivakasi, India, 2007),pp. 195-199.
7. W. Afzal, R. Torkar, R. Feldt, Prediction of fault count data using genetic programming. In Proc. IEEE International Multitopic Conference 2008, (Ka-rachi, Pakistan, 2008), pp. 349-356.

The Vehicle License Plate Recognition Using An Improved Le-Net5 Convolutional Neural Network

Yang-Gang Zhou[a], Hong-Mei Xie and Lei Xia

School of Electronic and Information, Northwestern Polytechnical University, Xi'an, Shaanxi, China

E-mail: [a]zhouyanggang@mail.nwpu.edu.cn

To increase the recognition rate of traditional method for license plate character, this paper introduces the Le-Net5 convolutional neural network of deep learning for license plate recognition. Firstly, this paper improves Le-Net5 and make it suitable for the particular task to continue network learning of character samples and optimize the parameters of the network. Finally, this paper tests the character of license plate using the trained network. Test showed that the recognition rate and anti-interference ability are greatly improved using CNN.

Keywords: Improved Le-Net5, Convolutional Neural Network, License Plate Recognition.

1. Introduction

License plate recognition plays an important role in traffic information control and intelligent traffic, such as highway toll management, speeding violation penalties, parking management, traffic data collection and so on. Usually, the license plate recognition system mainly consists of three parts: license plate location, character segmentation [1] and character recognition.

Convolutional neural network can directly identify visual patterns from the original image, which requires very small preprocessing work. Convolutional neural network is better than general neural network in image processing, it has the following advantages: (1) The input image and network topological structure can be excellent agreement; (2) Feature extraction and pattern classification are carried out simultaneously; (3) Weight sharing can reduce the training parameters of the network, and makes the network structure becomes more simple and adaptable.

Convolutional neural network is relatively early in foreign research, but at present the domestic research and application for convolutional neural network is not deep enough. LeNet-5 is a kind of convolutional neural network, used for handwritten numeral recognition originally. This paper will use the LeNet-5 network for Chinese license plate character recognition. Because the type of license plate character recognition is much more than the type of handwritten numeral recognition, so the traditional LeNet-5 cannot be directly applied to the license plate character recognition. Therefore, the structure of traditional LeNet-5 should be improved.

In this paper, we study the character recognition based on the precise license plate location and the ideal character segmentation. Firstly, this paper simply introduces the image preprocessing, license plate location and character segmentation content [1], then introduces the structure of the convolutional neural network and LeNet-5 network [2]. At last we improved the structure of LeNet-5 network, and obtained better character recognition rate.

2. License Plate Recognition Process and Method

2.1. *License plate recognition process*

Usually, the license plate recognition process is divided into five parts: image preprocessing, license plate location, license plate correction, license plate segmentation and license plate recognition.

We take a flow chart to show the basic process of license plate recognition. The fundamental procedure of license plate recognition is shown in Figure 1.

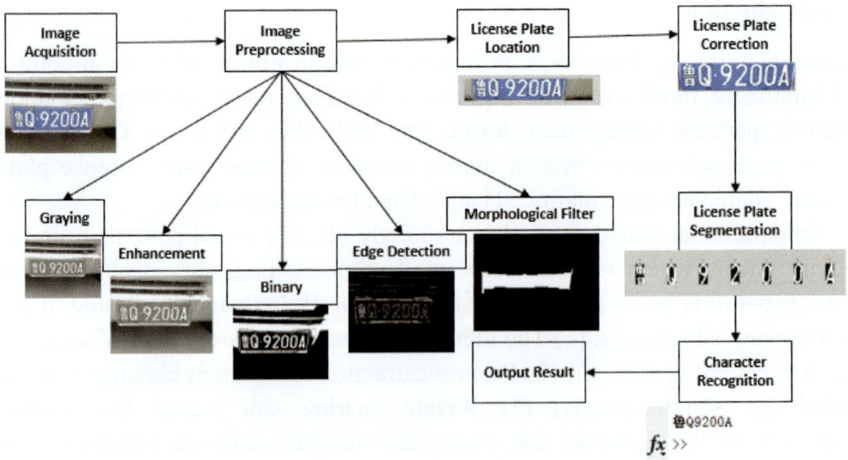

Fig. 1. Flow chart of license plate recognition

2.2. *Character recognition method*

2.2.1. *Convolutional neural network*

Convolutional neural network has been developed in recent years, and it has attracted wide attention. Nowadays, convolutional neural network has become one of the research hotspots in many scientific fields, especially in the field of pattern classification. Due to the network avoids the complex preprocessing of image and directly inputs the original image, so it has been widely used. Convolutional neural networks are implemented by combining three methods to realize the displacement recognition, scaling and distortion invariance: local receptive field, weight sharing and sub sampling. In general, sub sampling layer is used to reduce the computation time and to establish the invariance of space and structure. This method is very simple and effective usually using small sub sampling factor.

(1)Convolution layer: In convolution layer [2], the previous layer feature maps will carry on convolution operation with a learning convolutional kernel. The convolution result will form all the feature maps of this layer after activation function. Each feature map of each layer may be related to the convolution of several feature maps of last layer. In general, the form of the convolution layer is shown in the form of the Eq. (1):

$$x_j^l = f(\sum_{i \in M_j} x_j^{l-1} k_{ij}^l + b_j^l) \tag{1}$$

Among them, l represents the number of layers, k is convolution kernel, M_j represents a choice of the input feature map. Each output map has a bias b.

(2)Sub sampling layer: A sub sampling layer [2] carries out sampling operation for the input. If the input feature maps is n, the number of feature maps after sub sampling is still n, but the output becomes smaller (for example, a half of the original map). The general form of the sub sampling layer is shown in the Eq. (2):

$$x_j^l = f\left(\beta_j^l down\left(x_j^{l-1}\right) + b_j^l\right) \tag{2}$$

Among them, down (•) expresses sub sampling function. The sub sampling function is generally summate a $n \times n$ region of input image in this layer. Therefore, the output image size is 1/n times as much as the input image size. Each output feature map has its own β and b.

(3)Full connection layer: The full connection layer [6] calculates the dot product between the input vector and the weight vector, plus a bias, and then passes it to a status of the generating unit of the sigmoid function.

(4)Output layer: The output layer is composed of Radial Basis Function Euclidean units, one unit per class, each unit has all the input maps of full connection layer. In other words, the Euclidean distance[8] between the input vector and the parameter vector is calculated by each RBF unit. The farther input away from the parameter vector, the greater the RBF output. A RBF output can be understood as a punishment item of measure the input patterns and the matching degree of a model with the RBF associated class.

2.2.2. *Network implementation: structure of LeNet-5*

Convolutional neural network LeNet-5 structure [2] is shown in Figure 2.

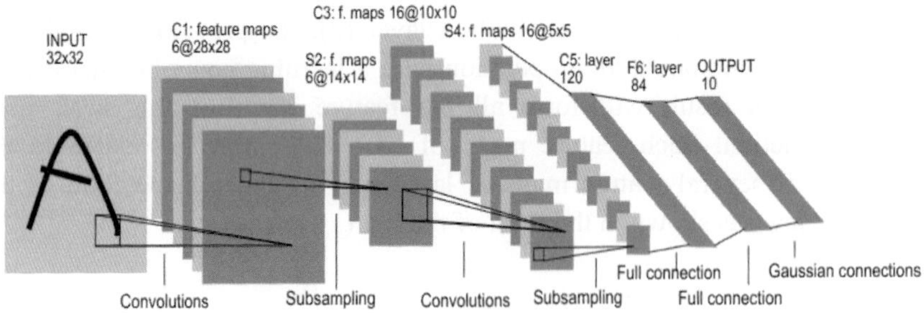

Fig. 2. Le-Net5 convolution neural network structure

Convolutional neural network LeNet-5 does not include the input, consists of 7 layers, each layer includes the training parameters (weights). The input of the network is 32×32 image. The C layer is the network layer consist of the convolution layer neurons, the S layer is the network layer composed of sampling layer neurons.

The network layer C1 is composed of 6 feature maps. Each neuron is connected to a 5×5 neighborhood of the input image, so the size of each feature map is 28×28.

The network layer S2 is a sub sampling layer, which is composed of 6 feature maps with the size of 14×14. Each neuron of feature maps is connected with a 2×2 neighborhood of C1 layer.

The network layer C3 is the convolution layer composed of 16 feature maps with the size of 10×10. Each neuron of the feature maps is connected with several 5×5 neighborhood of the S2 network layer. Table 1 shows that how the S2 layer feature map are combined to form each feature map of C3 layer.

Table 1. The connection method of S2 layer and C3 layer[2].

	0	1	2	3	4	5	6	7	8	9	10	11	12	13	14	15
0	x				x	x	x			x	x	x	x		x	x
1	x	x				x	x	x			x	x	x	x		x
2	x	x	x				x	x	x			x		x	x	x
3		x	x	x			x	x	x	x			x		x	x
4			x	x	x			x	x	x	x		x	x		x
5				x	x	x			x	x	x	x		x	x	x

The network layer S4 is a sub sampling layer composed of 16 feature maps with the size of 5×5. Each neuron in the feature maps is connected to a 2×2 neighborhood of the C3 layer.

The network layer C5 [9] is the convolution layer composed of 120 feature maps. Each neuron is connected to the 5×5 neighborhood of all the feature maps in the S4 network layer. The network layer F6 is full connected with the network layer C5, and includes 84 neurons. Finally, the output layer has 10 neurons, which are composed of the radial basis function unit (RBF). Each neuron in the output layer corresponds to a kind of character. The calculation method of the output y_i of the RBF unit is shown in the Eq. (3):

$$y_i = \sum_j (x_i - w_{ij})^2 \qquad (3)$$

2.2.3. *Improvement of LeNet-5 network*

Convolutional neural network LeNet-5 is originally used for handwritten numeral recognition, the number of output categories is 10. Compare to handwritten numeral recognition, China's license plate recognition needs more categories. In addition to the 10 Arabia figures, there are 24 English letters (not including the letters I and O), the provinces and municipalities, autonomous regions referred to as 31 Chinese characters. In view of the difference between Chinese license plate character recognition and handwritten numeral recognition, the traditional LeNet-5 is improved. Two points are Mainly as follows:

(1) The traditional LeNet-5 output layer is changed from 10 neurons to 65 neurons. The collected license plate character database has 65 types of license plate characters, so the number of output neurons are changed to 65.

(2) The number of traditional Le-Net 5 network C5 layer feature maps is increased from 120 to 480. Because of the number of license plate character recognition categories becomes more, we consider to increase the number of C5

layer feature maps so that progress the recognition performance of the whole network.

3. Experiment Result and Analysis

In order to verify the performance of the improved convolutional neural network LeNet-5, a large number of real license plate data were collected, and the dataset for training and testing was established. License plate image after positioning and character segmentation are fed into the license plate character database, there is no license plate image de-noising process. All the license plate characters are normalized to 32×32.

(1)Experiment data: This experiment established two datasets, in the first dataset, the training set has 400 characters, the test set has 100 characters, in the second dataset, the training set has 1200 characters, the test set has 180 characters.

(2)Relationship between dataset size and recognition rate: Due to limited license plate resources, so we only established two datasets, one has 400 characters, one has 1200 characters. Although the dataset is very small, but it can be seen, with the increase of training set, the recognition rate is increased from 87.6% to 90.76%. The real data is shown in Table 2. Therefore, if there are some larger datasets, the recognition rate will also increase.

Table 2. Relationship between training set size and recognition rate.

Training set	Root-mean-square error	Recognition rate
400	0.22	87.60%
1200	0.05	90.76%

(3)Relationship between iteration times and the recognition rate: In the two training sets, set iteration times as 10,50,100,500,1000. Test results show that with the increase of iteration times, the recognition rate showed the uptrend. But after 500 times, the recognition rate is almost not grow. The main reason is the limit of dataset size, the intensity of training is not enough. The real data is show in Table 3.

Table 3. Relationship between iteration times and the recognition rate.

Training set	Iteration times	Recognition rate
400	10	81.60%
	50	83.28%
	100	84.38%
	500	87.52%
	1000	87.60%
1200	10	85.27%
	50	87.20%
	100	88.58%
	500	90.72%
	1000	90.76%

(4)Recognition result: The license plate characters after segmentation are fed into the convolutional neural network that was trained by 1200 characters, we can get the text-format result.

(5)Comparison with BP neural network: This paper contrasts the recognition rate between the improved Le-Net5 convolution neural network and the traditional BP neural network[3] for license plate character. The comparison result is shown in Table 4.

Table 4. Comparison with BP neural network.

Method of recognition	Accuracy for Chinese	Accuracy for letters	Accuracy for digits	Accuracy for mix characters
BP Network	70%	88%	90%	82.2%
Improved Le-Net5 CNN	77.41%	91.67%	94.56%	90.76%

From Table 4 we can see, for both of Chinese characters, numbers, letters, or mixture of three characters, the recognition rate of the improved Le-Net5 convolutional neural networks for the license plate character is better than BP neural network.

4. Conclusion

In this paper, the traditional Le-Net5 convolutional neural network is improved, so that it can be applied to the recognition of license plate characters. Through image preprocessing, the training and testing of convolutional neural network, we construct a system suitable for license plate recognition. This system has high recognition rate and strong anti-interference, and compares with the traditional BP neural network and reflects the great advantage of the improved Le-Net5 convolutional neural network for the license plate recognition.

Further work prospects: (1) Due to the limitation of the dataset, the convolutional neural network cannot be fully trained, results in the result is affected. We will continue to collect the license plate dataset later, so that the network can be fully trained. (2) We will struggle to search the better convolutional neural network for license plate character recognition other than Le-Net5 network. (3) In this study, we mainly study the static license plate recognition, and then want to try to put license plate recognition in the video for achieving the purpose of application.

Acknowledgments

This work is supported by Key Laboratory of aerospace information and perception of Ministry of Education, School of Electronic and Information, Northwestern Polytechnical University.

References

1. F.Y. Lian, M.X. Fu, Y. Zhang. Research on vehicle license plate recognition based on support vector machine(SVM)[J]. *Computer engineering and design.* 2006,27(21): 4033-4035.
2. Z.H. Zhao, S.P. Yang, Z.Q. Ma. Research on license plate character recognition based on convolutional neural network LeNet-5[J]. *Journal of System Simulation.* 1004-731X (2010) 03-0638-04.
3. X. Han, H.M. Xie, G.Q. Zhang. Novel parallel neural network classifier for automatic vehicle license plate recognition. *WIT Transactions on Information and Communication Technologies.* Vol67, [C] 2014 WIT Press.
4. Z. Wang, M.T. Gao. Design and implementation of image recognition algorithm based on convolution neural network. Journal of graphic image. 1007-1423(2015)20-0061-06.
5. K.Y. Ren, D. Tang, X.D. Yin. Chinese character quick recognition technology of license plate based on character structure knowledge[J]. *Computer measurement and control.* 2005, 13(6): 592-594.
6. Lu G. Recognition of multi-font style characters based on Convolutional neural network [C] *Presented at the Computational Intelligence and Design* (ISCID), HANGZHOU.2011.
7. X.Y. Wang, X.L. Su. Application of digital image processing in license plate recognition. *Process Automation Instrumentation.* Vol.31, No.7, July 2010.

8. Tivive, Fok Hing Chi, Bouzerdoum, Abdesselam. An eye feature detector based on convolutional neural network [C] Proc. 8th Int. Symp. *Signal Process*. Applic. Sydney, New South Wales, Australia. USA: IEEE, 2005: 90-93.
9. Szarvas Mate, Yoshizawa Akira, Yamamoto Munetaka, Ogata Jun. Pedestrian detection with convolutional neural networks [C] IEEE *Intelligent Vehicles Symposium Proceedings.* USA: IEEE, 2005:224-229.

Author Index